Complex-Valued Neural Networks:
Utilizing High-Dimensional Parameters

Tohru Nitta
National Institute of Advanced Industrial Science and Technology, Japan

Information Science REFERENCE
INFORMATION SCIENCE REFERENCE
Hershey · New York

Director of Editorial Content: Kristin Klinger
Assistant Executive Editor: Heather Probst
Director of Production: Jennifer Neidig
Managing Editor: Jamie Snavely
Assistant Managing Editor: Carole Coulson
Typesetter: Carole Coulson
Cover Design: Lisa Tosheff
Printed at: Yurchak Printing Inc.

Published in the United States of America by
Information Science Reference (an imprint of IGI Global)
701 E. Chocolate Avenue, Suite 200
Hershey PA 17033
Tel: 717-533-8845
Fax: 717-533-8661
E-mail: cust@igi-global.com
Web site: http://www.igi-global.com

and in the United Kingdom by
Information Science Reference (an imprint of IGI Global)
3 Henrietta Street
Covent Garden
London WC2E 8LU
Tel: 44 20 7240 0856
Fax: 44 20 7379 0609
Web site: http://www.eurospanbookstore.com

Library of Congress Cataloging-in-Publication Data

Complex-valued neural networks : utilizing high-dimensional parameters / Tohru Nitta, editor.
p. cm.
Includes bibliographical references and index.
Summary: "This book covers the current state-of-the-art theories and applications of neural networks with high-dimensional parameters"--Provided by publisher.
ISBN 978-1-60566-214-5 (hardcover) -- ISBN 978-1-60566-215-2 (ebook) 1. Neural networks (Computer science) 2. Numbers, Complex. I. Nitta, Tohru, 1960-
QA76.87.C6645 2009
006.3'2--dc22

2008043298

British Cataloguing in Publication Data
A Cataloguing in Publication record for this book is available from the British Library.

Editorial Advisory Board

List of Reviewers

Table of Contents

Section II
Applications of Complex-Valued Neural Networks

Section III
Models with High-Dimensional Parameters

Detailed Table of Contents

Foreword xiii

Preface xv

Acknowledgment xxiii

Section I
Complex-Valued Neural Network Models and Their Analysis

Chapter I
Complex-Valued Boltzmann Manifold 1
Masaki Kobayashi, University of Yamanashi, Japan
The author of this chapter constructs the complex-valued Boltzmann machines, and investigates the structure of the complex-valued Boltzmann manifold using information geometry. He also derives an effective learning algorithm, called an *em* algorithm, for complex-valued Boltzmann machines with hidden neurons. Some important notions of information geometry, exponential families, mixture families, Kullback-Leibler divergence, connections, geodesics, Fisher metrics, potential functions and so on, are explained for readers who are unfamiliar with information geometry.

Chapter II
Complex-Valued Neural Network and Inverse Problems 27
Takehiko Ogawa, Takushoku University, Japan

The author of this chapter introduces the complex-valued network inversion method to solve inverse problems with complex numbers. The original network inversion is applied to usual multilayer neural networks with real-valued inputs and outputs, which solves inverse problems to estimate causes from results using a multilayer neural network. Regularization for the complex-valued network inversion is explained, which solves difficulties attributable to the ill-posedness of inverse problems.

Chapter III
Kolmogorov's Spline Complex Network and Adaptive Dynamic Modeling of Data 56
Boris Igelnik, BMI Research, Inc., USA

The author of this chapter attempts to extend the Clustering Ensemble method and the Kolmogorov's Spline Network to complex numbers, in the context of adaptive dynamic modeling of time-variant multidimensional

data. The chapter is intended to provide an introduction to these subjects and to stimulate the participation of both young and experienced researchers in solving challenging and important problems in theory and practice related to this area.

Chapter IV
A Complex-Valued Hopfield Neural Network: Dynamics and Applications 79
V. Srinivasa Chakravarthy, Indian Institute of Technology, Madras, India

This chapter describes a complex-variable version of the Hopfield neural network (CHNN), which can exist in both fixed point and oscillatory modes. In the fixed-point mode, CHNN is similar to a continuous-time Hopfield network. In the oscillatory mode, when multiple patterns are stored, the network wanders chaotically among patterns. It is shown that adaptive connections can be used to control chaos and increase memory capacity. Electronic implementation of the network in oscillatory dynamics, with fixed and adaptive connections, shows an interesting tradeoff between energy expenditure and retrieval performance. Some interesting applications are presented.

Chapter V
Global Stability Analysis for Complex-Valued Recurrent Neural Networks and Its Application to Convex Optimization Problems 104
Mitsuo Yoshida, Kyoto Institute of Technology, Japan
Takehiro Mori, Kyoto Institute of Technology, Japan

This chapter presents global stability conditions for discrete-time and continuous-time complex-valued recurrent neural networks, which are regarded as nonlinear dynamical systems. Global asymptotic stability conditions for these networks are derived by suitably choosing activation functions. According to these stability conditions, there are classes of discrete-time and continuous-time complex-valued recurrent neural networks whose equilibrium point is globally asymptotically stable.

Chapter VI
Models of Complex-Valued Hopfield-Type Neural Networks and Their Dynamics................................ 123
Yasuaki Kuroe, Kyoto Institute of Technology, Japan

This chapter presents models of fully connected complex-valued neural networks which are complex-valued extensions of Hopfield-type neural networks and discusses methods of studying their dynamics. In particular, the author of the chapter investigates existence conditions of energy functions for complex-valued Hopfield-type neural networks. As an application of the energy function, a qualitative analysis of the network by utilizing the energy function is shown and a synthesis method of complex-valued associative memories is discussed.

Section II
Applications of Complex-Valued Neural Networks

Chapter VII
Complex-Valued Symmetric Radial Basis Function Network for Beamforming..................................... 143
Sheng Chen, University of Southampton, UK

The author of this chapter addresses a gray-box approach to complex-valued RBF modeling and develops a complex-valued symmetric RBF (SRBF) network model. The application of this SRBF network is demonstrated using nonlinear beamforming assisted detection for multiple-antenna aided wireless systems that employ complex-valued modulation schemes. Two training algorithms for this complex-valued SRBF network are proposed. The effectiveness of the proposed complex-valued SRBF network and the efficiency of the two training algorithms in a nonlinear beamforming application are demonstrated.

This chapter illustrates the application of various types of complex-valued neural networks such as radial basis function networks (RBFN), multilayer feedforward networks, and recurrent neural networks for training sequence-based as well as blind equalization of communication channels. The structures and algorithms for these equalizers are presented and performances based on simulation studies are analyzed, highlighting their advantages and the important issues involved.

This chapter presents the complex backpropagation (BP) algorithm for complex backpropagation neural networks (BPN) consisting of suitable node activation functions having multi-saturated output regions. The complex BPN is used as a nonlinear adaptive equalizer that can deal with both quadrature amplitude modulation (QAM) and phase shift key (PSK) signals of constellations of any size. In addition, four nonlinear blind equalization schemes using complex BPN for M-ary QAM signals are described and their learning algorithms are presented.

The author of this chapter presents new design methods for the complex-valued multistate Hopfield associative memories (CVHAMs). The stability of the presented CVHAM is analyzed by using the energy function approach which shows that in synchronous update mode a CVHAM is guaranteed to converge to a fixed point from any given initial state. Next, a generalized intraconnected bidirectional associative memory (GIBAM) is introduced, which is a complex generalization of the intraconnected BAM (IBAM).

The author of this chapter proposes a method for automatically estimating nuclear magnetic resonance (NMR) spectra of metabolites in the living body by magnetic resonance spectroscopy (MRS) without human intervention or complicated calculations. In the method, the problem of NMR spectrum estimation is transformed into the estimation of the parameters of a mathematical model of the NMR signal. To estimate these parameters, the author designed a complex-valued Hopfield neural network, noting that NMR signals are essentially complex-valued.

This chapter introduces an Independent Component Analysis (ICA) approach to the separation of linear and nonlinear mixtures in the complex domain. Source separation is performed by an extension of the INFOMAX approach to the complex environment. The neural network approach is based on an adaptive activation function, whose shape is properly modified during learning. A simple adaptation algorithm is derived and several experimental results are shown to demonstrate the effectiveness of the proposed method.

This chapter introduces the authors' qubit neural network, which is a multi-layered neural network composed of quantum bit neurons. In this description, it is indispensable to use the complex-valued representation, which is based on the concept of quantum bits (qubits). The authors clarify that this model outperforms the conventional neural networks via computer simulations such as a bench mark test.

This chapter shows the effectiveness of incorporating quantum dynamics and then proposes a neuromorphic adiabatic quantum computation algorithm based on the adiabatic change of Hamiltonian. The proposed method can be viewed as a complex-valued neural network because a qubit operates like a neuron. Next, the performance of the proposed algorithm is studied by applying it to a combinatorial optimization problem. Finally, the authors discuss learning ability and hardware implementation.

Chapter XV
Attractors and Energy Spectrum of Neural Structures Based on the Model of the Quantum Harmonic Oscillator....................376
G. G. Rigatos, Industrial Systems Institute, Greece
S. G. Tzafestas, National Technical University of Athens, Greece

The authors of this chapter study neural structures with weights that follow the model of the quantum harmonic oscillator. The proposed neural networks have stochastic weights which are calculated from the solution of Schrödinger's equation under the assumption of a parabolic (harmonic) potential. The learning of the stochastic weights is analyzed. In the case of associative memories the proposed neural model results in an exponential increase of pattern storage capacity (number of attractors).

Chapter XVI
Quaternionic Neural Networks: Fundamental Properties and Applications....................411
Teijiro Isokawa, University of Hyogo, Japan
Nobuyuki Matsui, University of Hyogo, Japan
Haruhiko Nishimura, University of Hyogo, Japan

This chapter describes two types of quaternionic neural network model. One type is a multilayer perceptron based on 3D geometrical affine transformations by quaternions. The operations that can be performed in this network are translation, dilatation, and spatial rotation in three-dimensional space. The other type is a Hopfield-type recurrent network whose parameters are directly encoded into quaternions. The fundamental properties of these networks are presented.

Compilation of References....................440

About the Contributors....................470

Index....................476

Foreword

Over the recent years, neural networks in the complex domain have become a very active research field. The first important time in the history of complex-valued neural networks, however, dates back to the early 1990s. That is, to a time that has been characterized by others as the aftermath of the neural network revolution. The two volumes on Parallel Distributed Processing by Rumelhart and McClelland published in 1986 turned neural computation from a niche paradigm into a dominant one for artificial intelligence. The famous chapter on back-propagation paved the way for an uncountable number of applications.

With the success of real-valued neural networks an extension to complex-valued neural networks was on the agenda of that time soon. It turned out that finding suitable activation (or output) functions for complex-valued neurons was more difficult than in the real-valued case. Moreover, the most prominent real-valued feed-forward architectures - multi-layer perceptrons and radial basis function networks - were known to be universal approximators. Meanwhile, complex-valued neural networks have long caught up with the real-valued architectures. What hindered complex-valued networks to break through in the mid 1990s was to great extent the perception of ordinary real-valued networks among researchers. They just seemed to be always good enough.

In many fields, however, real-valued methods are not adequate and complex numbers are more than just handy. We use them naturally to describe waves and related phenomena in physics. We linear combine a signal with its Hilbert transform in order to get the analytic signal. The analytic signal, which consequently lives in the complex domain, is a quite universal tool providing the local amplitude and the local phase for a signal. We make extensive use of the Fourier transform to get a global signal representation in the frequency domain. This established utilization of complex numbers always worked as an impulse to study complex-valued networks. And, it shows how broad and rich the fields of application are for these networks. In this book the reader will find successful applications in image analysis, signal processing, pattern recognition and network communications. All these chapters demonstrate complex-valued neural networks at work. They show unique features of complex-valued architectures and how they lead to effective solutions for real-world problems.

The theory of computation by complex-valued neural networks applies not only to the above-mentioned fields. It is also applicable to the fast growing and important field of quantum computing. This is due to the complex representation of quantum states and operators. The stochastic quantum world, on the other hand, brings us directly to one of the theoretical frontiers of complex-valued neural networks. Consequently, architectures like the Boltzmann machine are covered in the theoretical part of this book. As can be seen from this part, the theory of complex-valued neural computation has developed well and it covers now many architectures and concepts like recurrent networks and associative memory. With its theoretical chapters the book provides a detailed overview on recent research directions on theoretical aspects.

Complex-valued neural networks are the prototype of networks that extend real-valued architectures. Abstractly, their atoms are ordered pairs of real numbers with particular defined operations on them. In that sense, they are the minimal model of multi-dimensional neural computation. The next natural extension of this line is neural networks based on quaternions. Knowledge and understanding of the complex case is crucial for all these further networks.

The thematic and qualitative collection of papers in this book is a sign of excellent editorship. Tohru Nitta is a pioneer of neural networks in the complex domain and he remained faithful to this topic over all the years. This book shows impressive applications of complex-valued neural networks. With the careful chosen emphasis on how to utilize high-dimensional parameters the book shows unique features of complex-valued neural computation in a very original and promising way.

This book really adds momentum to the field.

Sven Buchholz *received his diploma degree in computer science and his PhD degree (summa cum laude) in computer science, both from Christian-Albrechts-Universität Kiel, Germany. His PhD thesis entitled "A Theory of Neural Computation with Clifford Algebras" was awarded as best thesis in the faculty of the academic year 2004/2005. He has authored several publications on the topic of Clifford neural networks. At the moment he is a senior researcher at the Cognitive Systems Group in Kiel. His research interest includes mathematics of neural networks, machine learning, and multidimensional signal theory. Additionally to his academic experience, he also has several years of industrial experience as a statistical consultant.*

Preface

What do you picture when you hear the term neural networks with high-dimensional parameters? Naturally, all neural networks can receive and send two or more signals, process high-dimensional data, and have a large number of parameters. Why are they specified to have high-dimensional parameters? This book describes neural networks with parameters (weights and threshold values) that are high-dimensional, such as complex numbers, quaternions, and *N*-dimensional vectors. The neural network with high-dimensional parameters is high-dimensional in this sense. But what is the significance of creating neural networks with high-dimensional parameters? The answer can be found in (Hirose, 2003, 2006; Nitta, 2008), and in every chapter of this book together with descriptions of possible developments. I had the idea of creating neural networks with high-dimensional parameters in April 1990, when I started to work at the Electrotechnical Laboratory (now National Institute of Advanced Industrial Science and Technology (AIST)) and was looking for a theme to study. During a seminar for newcomers, I learned about a study on a complex autoregressive model by Dr. Otsu (presently an AIST Fellow) (Sekita, Kurita, & Otsu, 1992), mentioning that complex regression coefficients form rotation invariant for two-dimensional figures, and was inspired by his comment that it went well when it was extended to complex numbers. The complex autoregressive models were later extended to quaternionic models, and so forth. (Tanaka, 1996). The section to which I was assigned was working on neural networks, and I started to study complex-valued neural networks under the supervision of Dr. Furuya (presently Professor of Toho University) (Nitta, & Furuya, 1991). At that time in 1990, I assumed I was the first in the world to extend neural networks to complex-valued models but I was wrong, as described below.

Up to the early 1980s, there were many studies on symbolic processing. I was also engaged in R&D of the Expert shell. Along with the development of Von Neumann-type computers, studies started on information processing different from symbolic processing but similar to that in the human brain. The neural network is one of such processes. Neural network is a network composed of artificial neurons and can be trained to find nonlinear relationships in data. Because there are many introductory references (for example, (Rojas, 1996)), only typical examples are outlined in this Preface. The first study on neural networks was reported by MacCulloch and Pitts in 1943. Stimulated by the results of anatomical and physiological studies, they proposed a network model consisting of a small number of very simple neurons and showed that the model could be used for logical calculations, and so forth. The original model of the present neural network was proposed by Rosenblatt in 1958 and was called *Perceptron*. In 1969, Minsky and Perpert showed mathematically that Perceptron cannot solve linearly non-separable problems (Minsky, & Papert, 1969), which requires identifying multi-dimensional data that are mutually interrelated. Perceptron was shown to be applicable only to simple problems. A feedforward neural network is a network in which signals are transmitted only in one direction. Rumelhart, Hinton, and Williams (1986) proposed a learning algorithm called *back-propagation* (BP), which was applicable to multilayer feedforward neural networks (Multilayer Perceptron). Multilayer feedforward neural networks with BP attracted attention as they could solve linearly non-separable problems, which could not be solved by Perceptron. By learning, the multilayer feedforward neural network acquires the ability to generalize. With this helpful ability, the network can output a sort of answer to unlearned patterns. This generalization ability is very useful when using the network in various fields. Hopfield proposed a kind of fully connected recurrent neural network (Hopfield, 1984; Hopfield & Tank, 1985). In fully connected recurrent neural networks, signals are transmitted not only in one direction but also in the opposite direction, and the signals can pass through the same neurons not only once but many times. The operation of the network is very simple. First, an arbitrary neuron is selected, and a simple computation is performed. Then the result of the computation is transmitted to all neurons in the network. Hopfield defined an index for showing the behavior of a fully connected recurrent neural network as a whole and called it *energy function*. He proved mathematically that the energy function decreases monotone with time and showed that combinational optimization problems could be quickly solved by approximation by using the monotone decreasing characteristic of the energy function. Kohonen (1995) showed that concept formation can be achieved using a neural network. Concept formation means automatic classification of a large amount of data. Two two-dimensional planes installed with two or more neurons are used. One plane is for receiving the input pattern (the input layer), and the other outputs the results (the output layer). The neurons on the input and output layers are weighted with weight parameters. The weight value is modified by Hebbian learning, which involves changing the value of the weight parameter according to the activity of the neuron, and a larger change is made at a higher activity.

The usual real-valued neural networks have been applied to various fields such as telecommunications, robotics, bioinformatics, image processing, and speech recognition, in which complex numbers (2 dimensions) are often used with the Fourier transformation. This indicates that complex-valued neural networks, whose parameters (weights and threshold values) are all complex numbers, are useful. In addition, in the human brain, an action potential may have different pulse patterns, and the distance between pulses may be different. This suggests that it is appropriate to introduce complex numbers representing phase and amplitude into neural networks. Furthermore, it is obvious that vectors with more than 2 dimensions are used in the real world to represent a cluster of something, for example, a 4-dimensional vector consisting of height, width, depth and time, and an N-dimensional vector consisting of N particles and so on. Thus, a model neuron that can deal with N signals as a cluster, is useful.

Aizenberg, Ivaskiv, Pospelov, and Hudiakov (1971) (former Soviet Union) proposed a complex-valued neuron model for the first time, and although it was only available in the Russian literature at the time, their work can now be read in English (Aizenberg, Aizenberg & Vandewalle, 2000). Prior to that time, most researchers other than Russians had assumed that the first persons to propose a complex-valued neuron were Widrow, McCool, and Ball (1975). Interest in the field of neural networks started to grow around 1990, and various types of complex-valued neural network models were subsequently proposed. Since then, their characteristics have been researched, making it possible to solve some problems which could not be solved with the real-valued neuron, and to solve many complicated problems more simply and efficiently. From 2001, several special sessions on complex-valued neural networks have been organized in several international conferences (KES, 2001, 2002, 2003; ICONIP, 2002, 2004; ICANN/ICONIP, 2003; IJCNN, 2006, 2008; ICANN, 2007).

There appear to be several approaches for extending the real-valued neural network to higher dimensions. One approach is to extend the number field, that is, from real numbers x (1 dimension), to complex numbers $z = x + iy$ (2 dimensions), to quaternions $q = a + ib + jc + kd$ (4 dimensions; see Chapter XVI), to octonions (8 dimensions), to sedenions (16 dimensions), and so forth (Weyl, 1946; Nitta, 1995; Arena, Fortuna, Muscato, & Xibilia, 1998; Pearson, 2003; Nitta, 2005; Buchholz, & Sommer, 2008). In this approach, the dimension of the input signal fed into the neural network is restricted to the form of $2n$, $n = 1, 2, \ldots$, that is, 1, 2, 4, 8, 16, … Another approach is to extend the dimension of the threshold values and weights from 1 dimension to N dimensions using N-dimensional real-value vectors. In this approach, the dimension of the input signal fed into the neural network takes a natural number, that is, $N = 1, 2, 3, 4, \ldots$ Moreover, there are two types of the latter approach: (a) weights are N-dimensional matrices (Nitta, & Garis, 1992; Nitta, 2006), or (b) weights are N-dimensional vectors (Nitta, 1993, 2007; Kobayashi, 2004). Also, there is an approach using hyperbolic numbers (2 dimensions) (Buchholz, & Sommer, 2000; Nitta, & Buchholz, 2008). Hyperbolic numbers, which are closely related to the popular complex numbers, are numbers of the form $z = x + uy$ where x, y are real numbers and u is called unipotent which has the algebraic property that $u \neq \pm 1$ but $u^2 = 1$ (Sobczyk, 1995). Quantum neural networks can be viewed as one type of complex-valued neural network (see Chapters XIII-XV).

This book describes the latest developments in the theories and applications of neural networks with high-dimensional parameters which have been progressing in recent years. Graduate students and researchers will easily acquire the fundamental knowledge needed to be at the forefront of research, while practitioners will readily absorb the information required for applications. This book also provides a snapshot of current research and thus serves as a workbench for further developments in neural networks with high-dimensional parameters.

The following four books related to neural networks with high-dimensional parameters have been published: (Arena et al., 1998; Aizenberg et al., 2000; Hirose, 2003; Hirose, 2006). (Arena et al., 1998) was the first monograph on neural networks with high-dimensional parameters, and described the results of research on complex-valued neural networks, vectorial neural networks, and quaternary neural networks. The results of research up to 1997 are well organized in the monograph. The detailed descriptions of the function approximation capabilities of complex-valued neural networks with an analytic activation function and networks with a non-analytic activation function are excellent. (Aizenberg et al., 2000) is a comprehensive book on the complex-valued neuron models proposed by the authors, and is well organized from theories to applications. (Hirose, 2003) is an edited book which contains 14 chapters on complex-valued neural networks written by various authors. The chapter on the Clifford neural network written by Pearson is of interest to the complex-valued neural network community. (Hirose, 2006) is a translation of a book in Japanese (Hirose, 2005) that systematically describes complex-valued neural networks in the first half, and application examples obtained by the author's laboratory in the second half.

It took a long time for mathematicians to accept complex numbers (Ebbinghaus, et al., 1988). During the Renaissance, when complex numbers were first discovered, they were called *quantitates impossibiles*. They were carefully calculated but were not recognized in mathematics. In the mid 19th century mathematicians finally recognized the real power of complex numbers. Today, physicists do not hesitate to speak of complex numbers as physical targets. Complex numbers appear in Schrödinger's equation of quantum mechanics and are used in electrical engineering quite naturally. Complex numbers, which were once called *quantitates impossibiles*, are now firmly established in all fields of natural science and engineering, and scientists and engineers do not hesitate to use them in calculations. Unlike complex numbers, complex-valued neural networks were easily accepted in general. In my experience, I received only several negative comments in 1991 when I first proposed a complex-valued neural network. This quick recognition was likely because studies have focused on the engineering usefulness of complex-valued neural networks. Actually, most studies on complex-valued neural networks have been on engineering applications (usefulness) and were independent from those on the brain. It will be interesting to understand the actual relationships with the neural network of the brain. Neural networks are frequently grouped in soft computing together with evolutionary computation and fuzzy computation. Hybridizing neural networks with high-dimensional parameters with evolutionary computation or fuzzy computation looks promising (Chapter XV describes an example) for extending the potential of neural networks with high-dimensional parameters. In practice, there are many more study results and fields of application than are described in this book. Initially, this book was to contain 26 chapters, but the number was reduced to 16 for various reasons. It is a pity that we could not include the study on chaos by Nemoto and Saito (2002) and the studies on fractals by Miura and Aiyoshi (2003). For the special issue on complex-valued neural networks of the *International Journal of Neural Systems* (Rao, Nitta, & Murthy, 2008), for which I served as guest editor, 24 papers were submitted. Special sessions on complex-valued neural networks are also held in many international conferences as described above. We hope that readers all over the world will find this book both useful and enjoyable.

ORGANIZATION OF THE BOOK

The book is divided into three main sections: Complex-Valued Neural Network Models and Their Analysis (Chapters I-VI), Applications of Complex-Valued Neural Networks (Chapters VII-XII), and Models with High-Dimensional Parameters (Chapters XIII-XVI).

A brief description of each of the chapters follows.

Chapter I applies information geometry to complex-valued Boltzmann machines. The author of this chapter constructs the complex-valued Boltzmann machines, and investigates the structure of the complex-valued Boltzmann manifold. The author also derives an effective learning algorithm, called an *em* algorithm, for complex-valued Boltzmann machines with hidden neurons. Some important notions of information geometry, exponential families, mixture families, Kullback-Leibler divergence, connections, geodesics, Fisher metrics, potential functions and so on are explained for readers who are unfamiliar with information geometry.

Chapter II introduces the complex-valued network inversion method to solve inverse problems with complex numbers. The original network inversion is applied to usual multilayer neural networks with real-valued inputs and outputs, which solves inverse problems to estimate causes from results using a multilayer neural network. Regularization for the complex-valued network inversion is explained, which solves difficulties attributable to the ill-posedness of inverse problems.

Chapter III attempts to extend the clustering ensemble method and the Kolmogorov's Spline Network to complex numbers, in the context of adaptive dynamic modeling of time-variant multidimensional data. The chapter is intended to provide an introduction to these subjects and to stimulate the participation of both young and experienced researchers in solving challenging and important problems in theory and practice related to this area.

Chapter IV describes a complex-variable version of the Hopfield neural network (CHNN), which can exist in both fixed point and oscillatory modes. In the fixed-point mode, CHNN is similar to a continuous-time Hopfield network. In the oscillatory mode, when multiple patterns are stored, the network wanders chaotically among patterns. It is shown that adaptive connections can be used to control chaos and increase memory capacity. Electronic implementation of the network in oscillatory dynamics, with fixed and adaptive connections, shows an interesting tradeoff between energy expenditure and retrieval performance. Some interesting applications are presented.

Chapter V presents global stability conditions for discrete-time and continuous-time complex-valued recurrent neural networks, which are regarded as nonlinear dynamical systems. Global asymptotic stability conditions for these networks are derived by suitably choosing activation functions. According to these stability conditions, there are classes of discrete-time and continuous-time complex-valued recurrent neural networks whose equilibrium point is globally asymptotically stable.

Chapter VI presents models of fully connected complex-valued neural networks which are complex-valued extensions of Hopfield-type neural networks and discusses methods of studying their dynamics. In particular, the author investigates existence conditions of energy functions for complex-valued Hopfield-type neural networks. As an application of the energy function, a qualitative analysis of the network by utilizing the energy function is shown and a synthesis method of complex-valued associative memories is discussed.

Chapter VII addresses a grey-box approach to complex-valued RBF modeling and develops a complex-valued symmetric RBF (SRBF) network model. The application of this SRBF network is demonstrated using nonlinear beamforming assisted detection for multiple-antenna aided wireless systems that employ complex-valued modulation schemes. Two training algorithms for this complex-valued SRBF network are proposed. The effectiveness of the proposed complex-valued SRBF network and the efficiency of the two training algorithms in a nonlinear beamforming application are demonstrated.

Chapter VIII illustrates the application of various types of complex-valued neural networks such as radial basis function networks (RBFN), multilayer feedforward networks and recurrent neural networks for training sequence-based as well as blind equalization of communication channels. The structures and algorithms for these equalizers are presented and performances based on simulation studies are analyzed, highlighting their advantages and the important issues involved.

Chapter IX presents the complex backpropagation (BP) algorithm for complex backpropagation neural networks (BPN) consisting of suitable node activation functions having multi-saturated output regions. The complex BPN is used as a nonlinear adaptive equalizer that can deal with both quadrature amplitude modulation (QAM) and phase shift key (PSK) signals of constellations of any size. In addition, four nonlinear blind equalization schemes using complex BPN for M-ary QAM signals are described and their learning algorithms are presented.

Chapter X presents new design methods for the complex-valued multistate Hopfield associative memories (CVHAMs). The stability of the presented CVHAM is analyzed by using the energy function approach which shows that in synchronous update mode a CVHAM is guaranteed to converge to a fixed point from any given initial state. Next, a generalized intraconnected bidirectional associative memory (GIBAM) is introduced, which is a complex generalization of the intraconnected BAM (IBAM).

Chapter XI proposes a method for automatically estimating nuclear magnetic resonance (NMR) spectra of metabolites in the living body by magnetic resonance spectroscopy (MRS) without human intervention or complicated calculations. In the method, the problem of NMR spectrum estimation is transformed into the estimation of the parameters of a mathematical model of the NMR signal. To estimate these parameters, the author designed a complex-valued Hopfield neural network, noting that NMR signals are essentially complex-valued.

Chapter XII introduces an independent component analysis (ICA) approach to the separation of linear and nonlinear mixtures in the complex domain. Source separation is performed by an extension of the INFOMAX approach to the complex environment. The neural network approach is based on an adaptive activation function, whose shape is properly modified during learning. A simple adaptation algorithm is derived and several experimental results are shown to demonstrate the effectiveness of the proposed method.

Chapter XIII introduces the authors' qubit neural network, which is a multilayered neural network composed of quantum bit neurons. In this description, it is indispensable to use the complex-valued representation, which is based on the concept of quantum bits (qubits). The authors clarify that this model outperforms the conventional neural networks via computer simulations such as a bench mark test.

Chapter XIV shows the effectiveness of incorporating quantum dynamics and then proposes a neuromorphic adiabatic quantum computation algorithm based on the adiabatic change of Hamiltonian. The proposed method can be viewed as a complex-valued neural network because a qubit operates like a neuron. Next, the performance of the proposed algorithm is studied by applying it to a combinatorial optimization problem. Finally, the authors discuss learning ability and hardware implementation.

Chapter XV studies neural structures with weights that follow the model of the quantum harmonic oscillator. The proposed neural networks have stochastic weights which are calculated from the solution of Schrödinger's equation under the assumption of a parabolic (harmonic) potential. The learning of the stochastic weights is analyzed. In the case of associative memories the proposed neural model results in an exponential increase of pattern storage capacity (number of attractors).

Chapter XVI describes two types of quaternionic neural network model. One type is a multilayer perceptron based on 3D geometrical affine transformations by quaternions. The operations that can be performed in this network are translation, dilatation, and spatial rotation in three-dimensional space. The other type is a Hopfield-type recurrent network whose parameters are directly encoded into quaternions. The fundamental properties of these networks are presented.

REFERENCES

Aizenberg, N. N., Ivaskiv, Y. L., Pospelov, D. A., & Hudiakov, G. F. (1971). Multiple-valued threshold functions, boolean complex-threshold functions and their generalization. *Kibernetika (Cybernetics), 4,* 44-51 (in Russian).

Aizenberg, I. N., Aizenberg, N. N., & Vandewalle, J. (2000). *Multi-Valued and Universal Binary Neurons*. Boston: Kluwer Academic Publishers.

Arena, P., Fortuna, L., Muscato, G., & Xibilia, M. G. (1998). *Neural Networks in Multidimensional Domains,* (Lecture Notes in Control and Information Sciences, 234). Springer.

Buchholz, S., & Sommer, G. (2000). A hyperbolic multilayer perceptron. *Proc. Int. Joint Conf. on Neural Networks,* Como, Italy, 2, 129-133.

Buchholz, S., & Sommer, G. (2008). On Clifford neurons and Clifford multilayer perceptrons. *Neural Networks, 21*(7), 925-935.

Ebbinghaus, H.-D., Hermes, H., Hirzebruch, F., Koecher, M., Lamotke, K., Mainzer, K., Neukirch, J., Prestel, A., & Remmert, R. (Eds.). (1988). Zahlen, Springer-Verlag Berlin Heidelderg (in German).

Hirose, A. (Ed.) (2003). *Complex-Valued Neural Networks: Theories and Applications.* World Scientific Publishing, Singapore.

Hirose, A. (2005). *Complex-Valued Neural Networks*. SGC Library, 38. Saiensu-sha (in Japanese).

Hirose, A. (2006). Complex-Valued Neural Networks. *Series on Studies in Computational Intelligence, 32.* Springer-Verlag.

Hopfield, J. J. (1984). Neurons with graded response have collective computational properties like those of two-state neurons. Proceedings of the National Academy of Sciences of the United States of America, 81, 3088–3092.

Hopfield, J. J., & Tank, D. W. (1985). Neural computation of decisions in optimization problems. Biological Cybernetics, 81, 141–152.

ICANN. (2007). 6 papers in the special session: Complex-valued neural networks. In de J. M. Sa, L. A. Alexandre, W. Duch, & D. P. Mandic (Eds.), *Artificial neural networks and neural information processing, (*Lecture Notes in Computer Science, 4668) (pp.838-893). Springer-Verlag, Berlin Heidelberg (Proceedings of Int. Conf. on Artificial Neural Networks, ICANN'07-Portugal, Sept.).

ICONIP. (2002). 6 papers in the special session: Complex-valued neural networks. *Proc. Int. Conf. on Neural Information Processing,* Singapore, 3, 1074-1103.

ICONIP/ICANN. (2003). 7 papers in the special session: Complex-valued neural networks. In O. Kaynak, et al. (Eds.), *Artificial neural networks and neural information processing,* (Lecture Notes in Computer Science, 2714). (pp. 943-1002). Springer-Verlag, Berlin Heidelberg. (Proceedings of Int. Conf. on Artificial Neural Networks/Int. Conf. on Neural Information Processing, ICANN/ICONIP'03-Istanbul, June 26-29).

ICONIP. (2004). 5 papers in the special session: Complex-valued neural networks. In N. R. Pal, N. Kasabov, R. K. Mudi, S. Pal, and S. K. Parui (Eds.), *Neural information processing,* (Lecture Notes in Computer Science, 3316) (pp. 104-135). Springer-Verlag, Berlin Heidelberg. (Proceedings of Int. Conf. on Neural Information Processing, ICONIP'04-Calcutta, Nov.).

IJCNN. (2006). 12 papers in the special session: Complex-valued neural networks. *Proc. Int. Joint Conf. on Neural Networks*, Vancouver, BC, Canada, (pp. 595-626, 1186-1224).

IJCNN. (2008, June 1-6). 6 papers in the special session: Complex-valued neural networks. *Proc. Int. Joint Conf. on Neural Networks,* IJCNN'08-HongKong.

KES. (2001). 6 papers in the special session: Complex-valued neural networks and their applications. In N. Baba, L. C. Jain, and R. J. Howlett (Eds.), Knowledge-based intelligent information engineering systems and allied technologies, part I (pp. 550-580). IOS Press, Tokyo.

KES. (2002). 5 papers in the special session: Complex-valued neural networks. In E. Damiani, R. J. Howlett, L. C. Jain, and N. Ichalkaranje (Eds.), *Knowledge-based intelligent information engineering systems and allied technologies, part I* (pp. 623-647). IOS Press, Amsterdam.

KES. (2003). 7 papers in the special session: Complex-valued neural networks. In V. Palade, R. J. Howlett, & L. C. Jain (Eds.), *Knowledge-based intelligent information and engineering systems, part II, (*Lecture Notes in Computer Science 2774), (pp. 304-357). Springer-Verlag.

Kobayashi, M. (2004). Three-dimensional associative memory using exterior product. *IEE Trans. EIS, 124*(1), 150-156 (in Japanese).

Kohonen, T. (1995). *Self-Organizing Maps.* Berlin Heidelberg New York: Springer-Verlag.

Minsky, M. L., & Papert, S. A. (1969). *Perceptrons.* Cambridge: MIT Press.

Miura, M., & Aiyoshi, E. (2003). Approximation and designing of fractal images by complex neural networks. *IEEJ Trans. EIS, 123*(8), 1465-1472 (in Japanese).

Nemoto, I., & Saito, K. (2002). A complex-valued version of Nagumo - Sato model of a single neuron and its behavior. *Neural Networks, 15*(7), 833-853.

Nitta, T., & Furuya, T. (1991). A complex back-propagation learning. *Transactions of Information Processing Society of Japan, 32*(10), 1319-1329 (in Japanese).

Nitta, T., & Garis, H. D. (1992, November 3-6). A 3D vector version of the back-propagation algorithm. *Proceedings of IEEE/INNS International Joint Conference on Neural Networks,* IJCNN'92-Beijing, 2, 511-516.

Nitta, T. (1993, October 25-29). A back-propagation algorithm for neural networks based on 3D vector product. *Proceedings of IEEE/INNS International Joint Conference on Neural Networks*, IJCNN'93-Nagoya,1, 589-592.

Nitta, T. (1995, November 27 - December 1). A quaternary version of the back-propagation algorithm. *Proceedings of IEEE International Conference on Neural Networks,* ICNN'95-Perth, 5, 2753-2756.

Nitta, T. (2005). A solution to the 4-bit parity problem with a single quaternary neuron. *Neural Information Processing - Letters and Reviews, 5*(2), 33-39.

Nitta, T. (2006). Three-dimensional vector valued neural network and its generalization ability. *Neural Information Processing - Letters and Reviews, 10*(10), 237-242.

Nitta, T. (2007, January 6-12). N-dimensional vector neuron, *Proceedings of the IJCAI-2007 Workshop on Complex-Valued Neural Networks and Neuro-Computing: Novel Methods, Applications and Implementations.* (pp.2-7).

Nitta, T. (2008). Complex-valued neural network and complex-valued backpropagation learning algorithm. In P. W. Hawkes (Ed.), *Advances in imaging and electron physics,* 152, 153-220. Elsevier Inc.

Nitta, T., & Buchholz, S. (2008). On the decision boundaries of hyperbolic neurons. *Proceedings of International Joint Conference on Neural Networks,* IJCNN'08-HongKong, June 1-6, 2973-2979.

Pearson, J. (2003). Clifford Networks. In A. Hirose (Ed.), *Complex-valued neural networks – theories and applications* (pp. 81-106). World Scientific Publishing.

Rao, V. S. H., Nitta, T., & Murthy, G. R. (Eds.). (2008). Special issue on complex valued neural networks. *International Journal of Neural Systems, 18*(2), 67-184.

Rojas, R. (1996). *Neural Networks: A Systematic Introduction.* Springer.

Rumelhart, D. E., Hinton, G. E., & Williams, R. J. (1986). *Parallel distributed processing, 1.* MIT Press.

Sekita, I., Kurita, T., & Otsu, N. (1992). Complex autoregressive model for shape recognition. *IEEE Trans. Pattern Anal. & Machine Intelli., PAMI-14*(4).

Sobczyk, G. (1995). The hyperbolic number plane. *The College Mathematics Journal, 26*(4), 268-280.

Tanaka, M. (1996). Three dimensional autoregressive model under rotation. *SPIE VISION GEOMETRY V,* 2826, 172-179.

Weyl, H. (1946). *The classical groups: their invariants and representations*. Princeton University Press.

Widrow, B., McCool, J., & Ball, M. (1975). The complex LMS algorithm. *Proceedings of the IEEE, 63*(4), 719-720.

Acknowledgment

The editor would like to acknowledge the help of all involved in the review process of the book, without whose support the project could not have been satisfactorily completed. Deep appreciation and gratitude is due to Prof. Subhash Kak, Prof. Francisco Ares-Pena, Prof. Paolo Arena, Prof. Charles-Antoine Brunet, Prof. Mika Ala-Korpela, Prof. Jerome R. Busemeyer, Prof. Andrew J. Hanson, Prof. Ton Coolen, Prof. Sudeshna Sinha, and Prof. Ramakrishna Ramaswamy for recommending potential reviewers, and to Prof. Akira Hirose for providing the list of presenters of the special session on complex-valued neural networks at the 2006 International Joint Conference on Neural Networks (IJCNN2006). He would also like to thank Dr. Harumasa Okamoto, former director of Neuroscience Research Institute (NRI), National Institute of Advanced Industrial Science and Technology (AIST), Dr. Takahisa Taguchi, director of NRI, AIST, and Dr. Shotaro Akaho, leader of Mathematical Neuroinformatics Group, NRI, AIST for providing a supportive working environment, allowing him the opportunity to concentrate on the editing.

Most of the authors of chapters included in this book also served as referees for chapters written by other authors. Thanks go to all those who provided constructive and comprehensive reviews.

Special thanks also go to the publishing team at IGI Global, whose contributions throughout the whole process from inception of the initial idea to final publication have been invaluable. In particular to Mr. Deborah Yahnke and Ms. Heather A. Probst, who continuously prodded via e-mail for keeping the project on schedule and to Ms. Lindsay Johnston, Ms. Kristin M. Klinger, and Ms. Corrina Chandler,whose enthusiasm motivated me to initially accept their invitation for taking on this project.

Special thanks go to the members of the Editorial Advisory Board for this book project for their helpful supports. And last but not least, my wife, Eiko, for her unfailing support and encouragement during the months it took to give birth to this book.

In closing, I wish to thank all of the authors for their insights and excellent contributions to this book.

Tohru Nitta
Tsukuba, Japan
September 2008

Section I
Complex-Valued Neural Network Models and Their Analysis

Various types of complex-valued neural network models are presented and their properties are investigated on a theoretical basis or through computer simulations.

Chapter I
Complex-Valued Boltzmann Manifold

Masaki Kobayashi
University of Yamanashi, Japan

ABSTRACT

Information geometry is one of the most effective tools to investigate stochastic learning models. In it, stochastic learning models are regarded as manifolds in the view of differential geometry. Amari applied it to Boltzmann Machines, which is one of the stochastic learning models. The purpose of this chapter is to apply information geometry to complex-valued Boltzmann Machines. First, we construct the complex-valued Boltzmann Machines. Next, the author describes information geometry. The author will know some important notions of information geometry, exponential families, mixture families, Kullback-Leibler divergence, connections, geodesics, Fisher metrics, potential functions and so on. Finally, they apply information geometry to complex-valued Boltzmann Machines. They will investigate the structure of complex-valued Boltzmann manifold and know the notions of the connections and Fisher metric. Moreover we will get an effective learning algorithm, what is called em algorithm, for complex-valued Boltzmann machines with hidden neurons.

INTRODUCTION

These days we can get massive information and it is hard to deal with it without computers. Machine learning is effective for computers to manage massive information. Machine learning uses various learning machine models, for instance, decision trees, Bayesian Networks, Support Vector Machine, Hidden Markov Model, normal mixed distributions, neural networks and so on. Some of them are stochastically constructed.

The neural network is one of the learning machine models. It consists of many units, which are called neurons. We often use binary neurons. Then each neuron takes only two states. The set of neurons, however, takes many states. Various types of neural networks have been proposed. Feed-forward types and symmetric types of neural networks are main models. Feed-forward types of neural networks are often applied to recognize given patterns and are so useful. Symmetric types of neural network are often applied as Associative Memories. The Hopfield Network is one of the most famous models. Boltzmann Machines are stochastic types of Hopfield Networks.

Neurons take only two states in most cases. McEliece, Posner, Rodemich and Venkatech (1987) is a highly recognized critique of the Hopfield memory low capacity. Baldi and Hormik (1989) rigorously showed existence of numerous local minima in objective function for learning a nonlinear perceptron. The presentation capacity of a neuron is too poor. We hope that the neuron models have multi-states. Some researchers have proposed such models. Multi-level neuron is one of them (Zurada, Cloete & Poel, 1996). **Complex-valued neurons** are also multi-states neuron models. Several models of complex-valued neurons have been proposed, for example, phasor neurons (Noest, 1988a), discrete-state phasor neurons (Noest, 1988b), amplitude-phase type of complex-valued neurons (Hirose, 1992; Kuroe, 2003), real part – imaginary part type of complex-valued neurons (Benvenuto & Piazza, 1992; Nitta & Furuta, 1991; Nitta, 1997) and so on (Nemoto & Kubono, 1996; Nemoto, 2003). In this chapter, we deal with the phasor neurons and the discrete phasor neurons. In this chapter, we call phasor neurons continuous phasor neurons to distinguish them clearly from discrete phasor neurons.

Several types of neural networks, feed-forward neural networks, Hopfield Networks and Boltzmann Machines, have been extended to the complex-valued neural networks. Noest proposed complex-valued Hopfield Networks (Noest, 1988a; Noest, 1988b). They are called continuous phasor or discrete phasor neural networks. Hirose proposed back propagation learning algorithms for the amplitude-phase type of complex-valued neural networks (Hirose, 1992). Benvenuto and Piazza (1992) and Nitta and Furuya (1991) independently proposed back propagation learning algorithms for the real part – imaginary part type of complex-valued neural networks. Boltzmann Machines were also extended to the **complex-valued Boltzmann Machines** (Zemel, Williams & Mozer, 1993; Zemel, Williams & Mozer, 1995). The complex-valued Boltzmann Machines proposed by Zemel et al. (1993) are continuous models. Kobayashi and Yamazaki proposed the discrete version of complex-valued Boltzmann Machines (Kobayashi & Yamazaki, 2003).

We have to know learning machines' behaviors to manage them. But the learning machines often behave strangely. For example local minima and plateaus appear. It is called to be caused by the singularities. The learning machines without singularities are called regular models. Regular machines behaviors are so simple, so we can expect it well. For example, AIC (Akaike Information Criterion) is effective for regular models. But we cannot deal with the singular ones by the similar way. The local minima and plateaus in the learning process appear in the feed-forward neural networks with hidden neurons. But they do not appear in a simple perceptron (Fukumizu & Amari, 2000). We need the effective tools to investigate the singularities. **Information geometry** is one of them.

Boltzmann Machines without hidden neurons are regular models. Boltzmann Machines with hidden neurons are singular ones. Complex-valued Boltzmann Machines are also singular. Information geometry is one of the good tools to investigate singularities. In this chapter, we investigate the complex-valued Boltzmann Machines in the view of information geometry. Information geometry provides an efficient learning method, ***em* algorithm** to complex-valued Boltzmann Machines.

BACKGROUND

Information geometry, which is a special type of differential geometry, is mainly constructed by Amari. It is an effective tool to investigate stochastic models. In fact, Amari applied it to the various stochastic models, normal distributions, discrete distributions, stochastic multilayer perceptron, normal mixture with hidden variables, normal multiplication model and Boltzmann Machines (Amari, Kurata & Nagaoka, 1992a; Amari, 1995). In information geometry, a family of probability distributions is considered as a manifold, what is called a stochastic manifold.

Information geometry provides the notions of distance between two given probability distributions to the family of probability distributions. And it also provides the notions of parallel movement on the family of probability distributions.

Identifying of some states causes singularities. Boltzmann Machines with hidden neurons consist of visible neurons and invisible ones. They have identified states, because the states in which the visible neurons are same and the invisible ones are different are identified. Therefore Boltzmann Machines with hidden neurons are singular. On the other hand, Boltzmann Machines without hidden neurons are regular, because they do not have identified states. In information geometry, we can regard the families of Boltzmann Machines with hidden neurons and ones without hidden neurons as singular manifolds and regular manifolds, respectively.

Information geometry provides effective learning algorithms, what is called *em* algorithms, to singular learning machines. It expands the identified states and we get two sub-manifolds, which are called an *e*-autoparallel manifold and an *m*-autoparallel manifold. It repeats projection between two manifolds and gives us the better parameters incrementally.

THE COMPLEX-VALUED HOPFIELD NETWORKS

In this section, we construct the complex-valued Hopfield Networks before the complex-valued Boltzmann Machines. The complex-valued Hopfield Networks behave deterministically and the complex-valued Boltzmann Machines behave stochastically. First, we describe the complex-valued neurons, which are indispensable to constructing the complex-valued Hopfield Networks. Second, we construct the complex-valued Hopfield Networks.

Now we define some notations. We define $\bar{z}$, Re(z) and Im(z) as the complex conjugate, the real part and the imaginary part of complex number z, respectively.

The Complex-Valued Neurons

Complex-valued neurons are the neurons whose input and output signals are complex numbers. Some models of complex-valued neurons have been proposed. The phasor neuron proposed by Noest is one of them (Noest, 1988a; Noest 1988b). It is mainly used for the complex-valued Hopfield Networks. For the complex-valued input signal z, the phasor neuron's output signal is $z/|z|$. It preserves the phases of the input signals. The absolute values of output signals are always one. The output signals are on the unit circle of the complex plane. It is called in a various way. Zemel called them directional units (Zemel et al., 1993; Zemel et al., 1995). Physics researchers call them oscillator neurons. In this chapter, they are called continuous phasor neurons. Next, we define the discrete phasor neurons.

Continuous phasor neurons take all points on the unit circle of the complex plane. Discrete phasor neurons take division points on it. Assume that they take K-division points. K-division points are $\exp(2\pi k\sqrt{-1}/K)$ ($k = 0, 1, 2, \dots, K-1$), where $\sqrt{-1}$ is the imaginary unit. We denote division points $\exp(2\pi k\sqrt{-1}/K)$ as p_k. When a discrete phasor neuron receives a complex-valued input signal z, the output signal is the closest K-division point to z. The discrete phasor neurons don't preserve the phase slightly.

We describe some other complex-valued neuron models. They don't appear from the next section. The model proposed by Nemoto takes a real-valued output signal $\mathrm{sgn}(z-h)$, where h is a real constant number, for a complex-valued input signal z (Nemoto & Kubono, 1996; Nemoto, 2003). It takes ± 1. The model proposed by Nitta and Benvenuto takes

$\mathrm{sigmoid}(\mathrm{Re}(z)) + \mathrm{sigmoid}(\mathrm{Im}(z))\sqrt{-1}$, where $\mathrm{sigmoid}(t) = \frac{1}{1+\exp(-t)}$.

It deals with the real part and the imaginary part of the input signals independently (Nitta & Furuya, 1991; Benvenuto & Piazza, 1992; Nitta, 1997). It does not preserve the phases. Some other models take $\tanh(|z|)\frac{z}{|z|}$ or $\frac{\eta z}{\eta - 1 + |z|}$, where η is a real constant number (Hirose, 1992; Kuroe, 2003). They preserve the phases.

The Complex-Valued Hopfield Networks

In this subsection, we construct the complex-valued Hopfield Networks by using continuous phasor neurons or discrete phasor neurons. We define the connection weight from the neuron i to the neuron j and the bias of neuron i as w_{ji} and w_i, respectively. The parameters w_{ji} and w_i are complex numbers. The real-valued Hopfield Networks require $w_{ij} = w_{ji}$. The complex-valued Hopfield Networks, however, require $w_{ij} = \overline{w}_{ji}$. The real-valued Hopfield Networks with n neurons have $n(n+1)/2$ real-valued weight parameters. The complex-valued Hopfield Networks with n neurons have $n(n+1)/2$ complex-valued weight parameters or $n(n+1)$ real-valued weight parameters. We present the parameters w_{ji} and w_i as follows:

$$w_{ji} = u_{ji} + v_{ji}\sqrt{-1},$$

$$w_i = u_i + v_i\sqrt{-1}.$$

From the equation $w_{ij} = \overline{w}_{ji}$, we obtain

$$u_{ji} = u_{ij},$$

$$v_{ji} = -v_{ij}.$$

We decompose the state z_i of the complex-valued neuron i to $x_i + y_i\sqrt{-1}$. We define the input sum S_i to neuron i as

$$S_i = \sum_{j \neq i} w_{ij} z_j + w_i.$$

We define the connection weights matrix **w** and the states vector **z** of the complex-valued Hopfield Network. The (i,j)th element of the connection weights matrix **w** is w_{ij} and the ith element of the states vector **z** is z_i. We define the energy $H(\mathbf{z};\mathbf{w})$ of the complex-valued Hopfield Network as follows:

$$H(\mathbf{z};\mathbf{w}) = \mathrm{Re}\left(-\frac{1}{2}\sum_{i \neq j} \overline{z}_i w_{ij} z_j - \sum_i \overline{z}_i w_i\right).$$

When the neuron k updates, the state **z** turns to the state **z'**. Suppose that the difference between the states **z** and **z'** is just the neuron k. By calculating the difference ΔH between the energies $H(\mathbf{z};\mathbf{w})$ and $H(\mathbf{z}';\mathbf{w})$, we obtain the following equation:

$$\begin{aligned}
\Delta H &= H(\mathbf{z}';\mathbf{w}) - H(\mathbf{z};\mathbf{w}) \\
&= -\frac{1}{2}\mathrm{Re}\Big(\sum_{j \neq k}(\overline{z}'_k - \overline{z}_k) w_{kj} z_j\Big) - \frac{1}{2}\mathrm{Re}\Big(\sum_{j \neq k} z_j w_{jk}(z'_k - z_k)\Big) - \mathrm{Re}\big((\overline{z}'_k - \overline{z}_k) w_k\big) \\
&= -\frac{1}{2}\mathrm{Re}\Big(\sum_{j \neq k}(\overline{z}'_k - \overline{z}_k) w_{kj} z_j\Big) - \frac{1}{2}\mathrm{Re}\Big(\sum_{j \neq k}(\overline{z}'_k - \overline{z}_k) \overline{w}_{jk} z_j\Big) - \mathrm{Re}\big((\overline{z}'_k - \overline{z}_k) w_k\big) \\
&= \mathrm{Re}\Big(z_k\big(\sum_{j \neq k} w_{kj} z_j + w_k\big)\Big) - \mathrm{Re}\Big(\overline{z}'_k\big(\sum_{j \neq k} w_{kj} z_j + w_k\big)\Big).
\end{aligned}$$

For the third expression, we used the relation $\mathrm{Re}(\overline{z}) = \mathrm{Re}(z)$. For two complex numbers a and b, $\mathrm{Re}(\overline{a}b)$ means the inner product of a and b as 2-dimensional vectors. Since z'_k is selected as to maximize $\mathrm{Re}(z(\sum_{j \neq k} w_{kj} z_j + w_k))$, the energy gap ΔH is always negative or zero. Therefore the energy always decreases and converges.

Let all bias terms w_i vanish. In the real-valued Hopfield Network case, the energy of a state equals the one of the reversed state, that is, it holds $H(\mathbf{z};\mathbf{w}) = H(-\mathbf{z};\mathbf{w})$. In the complex-valued Hopfield Network case, it is well known that the energy of a state equals the one of rotated state, that is, it holds $H(\mathbf{z};\mathbf{w})=H(\rho\mathbf{z};\mathbf{w})$, where ρ is a complex number such as $|\rho|=1$. It is called rotation invariance (Zemel et al., 1993; Zemel et al., 1995).

Learning of the Complex-Valued Hopfield Networks

The complex-valued Hopfield Networks are often applied to associative memories. Associative memories store some given patterns. Some methods to learn given patterns have been proposed.

The complex-valued hebbian rule is often adopted. For given patterns $\mathbf{z}^1, \mathbf{z}^2, \ldots, \mathbf{z}^P$, the complex-valued hebbian rule gives the connection weights as $w_{ij} = \sum_{k=1}^{P} z_i^k \bar{z}_j^k$. When a stored pattern $\mathbf{z}^l$ is given to the complex-valued Hopfield Network with connection weights by the hebbian rule, the input sum S_i to the neuron i is as follows:

$$S_i = \sum_{\substack{j=1\\ j\neq i}}^{n} w_{ij} z_j^l = \sum_{\substack{j=1\\ j\neq i}}^{n} \sum_{k=1}^{P} z_i^k \bar{z}_j^k z_j^l = (n-1) z_i^l + \sum_{\substack{j\neq i\\ k\neq l}} z_i^k \bar{z}_j^k z_j^l .$$

The first term $(n-1)z_i^l$ of the last expression imposes the desirable state $\mathbf{z}^l$ to the complex-valued Hopfield Network. The second term $\sum_{\substack{j\neq i\\ k\neq l}} z_i^k \bar{z}_j^k z_j^l$ is called the crosstalk term or the noisy term and interferes with the correct recall. The storage capacities of the complex-valued hebbian rule have been studied by some researchers. Cook analyzed the storage capacities of the complex-valued Hopfield Networks with continuous phasor neurons by using stochastic physics techniques (Cook, 1989). Jankowski did those with discrete phasor neurons in another way (Jankowski, Lozowski & Zurada, 1996). Both of them showed that the storage capacities by hebbian rule are rather low.

In order to make the storage capacities stronger, some learning methods have been developed. Lee proposed the modified gradient descent rule for complex-valued Hopfield Networks (Lee, 2001; Lee, 2003). The method using the generalized inverse matrix also was proposed (Aoki, 2003). Complex-valued Hopfield Networks with n phasor neurons can surely store $(n-1)$ patterns by the generalized inverse matrix.

Related Models

We can regard phasor neurons as 2-dimensional neurons. Several researchers have attempted to construct higher dimensional neural networks. Rotor neurons are one of them (Gislen, Peterson & Sodeberg, 1992). They are also called spin neurons (Nakamura & Munakata, 1995). The states of the rotor neurons are N-dimensional vectors whose sizes are 1. Of course, the phasor neurons are so. Therefore we can regard the rotor neurons as the generalized phasor neurons. The input and output signals of the rotor neurons are N-dimensional vectors. When a rotor neuron receives an N-dimensional vector $\mathbf{z}$, the output is $\mathbf{z}/|\mathbf{z}|$. The connection weights of the rotor Hopfield Networks are expressed by matrix with real number elements. We denote the state of the neuron i as an N-dimensional row vector $\mathbf{z}_i = (z_{i1}, z_{i2}, \cdots, z_{iN})^T$, where $\mathbf{z}^T$ stands for the transpose of $\mathbf{z}$. The connection weight from the neuron i to the neuron j is expressed as a $N \times N$ matrix $\mathbf{W}_{ji}$. We denote the input sum as S_i and put $\mathbf{S} = (S_1, S_2, \cdots, S_N)^T$. Then the input vector $\mathbf{S}$ is as follows:

$$\mathbf{S} = \sum_{j\neq i} \mathbf{W}_{ij} \mathbf{z}_j .$$

The complex-valued Hopfield Networks require the relations $w_{ij} = \bar{w}_{ji}$ for convergence. The rotor Hopfield Networks require the relations $\mathbf{W}_{ij}^T = \mathbf{W}_{ji}$. It assures that the rotor Hopfield Networks converge. When we express the complex-valued Hopfield Networks, then the matrix $\mathbf{W}_{ij}$ is $\begin{pmatrix} u_{ij} & -v_{ij} \\ v_{ij} & u_{ij} \end{pmatrix}$. So the equation $\mathbf{W}_{ij}^T = \mathbf{W}_{ji}$ holds. The energy $H(\mathbf{z};\mathbf{w})$ of the rotor Hopfield Network is defined as follow:

$$H(\mathbf{z}\,;\mathbf{w}) = -\frac{1}{2}\sum_{i \neq j} \mathbf{z}_i^T \mathbf{W}_{ij} \mathbf{z}_j \,.$$

The energy definitely decreases.

Nakamura and Munakata studied the storage capacities of the rotor Hopfield Networks by using stochastic physics techniques (Nakamura & Munakata, 1995). Parra researched the rotor Boltzmann Machines (Parra & Deco, 1995).

THE COMPLEX_VALUED BOLTZMANN MACHINES

Stochastic Complex-Valued Neurons

Boltzmann Machines are stochastic Hopfield Networks and require stochastic neurons. We construct the stochastic discrete and continuous phasor neurons for the complex-valued Boltzmann Machines. First, we define the stochastic discrete phasor neurons.

The discrete phasor neurons can take K-types of states $p_k = \exp(2\pi k\sqrt{-1}/K)$ ($k = 1, 2, \ldots, K$). We have to define the probability of the states for the input signal z. We define the probabilities $\Pr(p_k \mid z)$ that the discrete phasor neuron turns to the state p_k for the input signal z as follows:

$$\Pr(p_k \mid z) = \frac{\exp(\mathrm{Re}(p_k \bar{z}))}{\sum_{k=1}^{K} \exp(\mathrm{Re}(p_k \bar{z}))} \,.$$

Next, we define the stochastic continuous phasor neurons. The continuous phasor neurons take all points on the unit circle of the complex plane. We define the probability density $\Pr(p \mid z)$ that the continuous phasor neuron turns to the state p for the input signal z as follows:

$$\Pr(p \mid z) = \frac{\exp(\mathrm{Re}(p\bar{z}))}{\int_C \exp(\mathrm{Re}(p\bar{z}))dp} \,.$$

The integral calculus range C is the unit circle of the complex plane. This distribution is called circular normal distribution.

The Complex-Valued Boltzmann Machines

We define the stationary distributions and the transition probabilities from the state $\mathbf{z}$ to the state $\mathbf{z}'$ as $p(\mathbf{z}\,;\,\mathbf{w})$ and $p(\mathbf{z} \to \mathbf{z}'\,;\,\mathbf{w})$, respectively. The state $\mathbf{z}$ and the state $\mathbf{z}'$ are just different in the state of a neuron. Suppose that the different neuron is the neuron k. Then the relation $p(\mathbf{z}\,;\,\mathbf{w})\,p(\mathbf{z} \to \mathbf{z}'\,;\,\mathbf{w}) = p(\mathbf{z}'\,;\,\mathbf{w})\,p(\mathbf{z}' \to \mathbf{z}\,;\,\mathbf{w})$ holds. Therefore we get the following equation:

$$\begin{aligned}
\frac{p(\mathbf{z}' \to \mathbf{z};\mathbf{w})}{p(\mathbf{z} \to \mathbf{z}';\mathbf{w})} &= \frac{p(\mathbf{z}';\mathbf{w})}{p(\mathbf{z};\mathbf{w})} \\
&= \frac{\exp(\mathrm{Re}(\bar{z}_k(\sum_{i \neq k} w_{ki} z_i + w_k)))}{\exp(\mathrm{Re}(\bar{z}_k'(\sum_{i \neq k} w_{ki} z_i + w_k)))} \\
&= \exp(-\Delta H).
\end{aligned}$$

Moreover we obtain

$$p(\mathbf{z};\mathbf{w}) = \frac{\exp(-H(\mathbf{z};\mathbf{w}))}{Z(\mathbf{w})},$$

$$Z(\mathbf{w}) = \begin{cases} \sum \exp(-H(\mathbf{z};\mathbf{w})) & \text{(discrete phasor neurons)} \\ \int_{C^n} \exp(-H(\mathbf{z};\mathbf{w}))d\mathbf{z} & \text{(contiunous phasor neurons).} \end{cases}$$

The term $Z(\mathbf{w})$ is called the partition function. The integral calculus range C^n is n direct product of C.

INFORMATION GEOMETRY

What's Information Geometry

Information geometry is a type of differential geometry on statistical families. It introduces the coordinate systems to the set of probability distributions and each point on the coordinate system corresponds to a probability distribution. There is a notion to measure the difference between two points on the coordinate system, and it is called metric. There are various metrics in the differential geometry. Information geometry uses **Fisher metric**. Fisher metric introduces the difference between two probability distributions. There is also a notion of parallel translation in information geometry. Ordinary differential geometries use one parallel translation, but information geometry mainly uses two types of parallel translations. In this section, information geometry is briefly described. In details, see Amari and Nagaoka (2000).

Introduction to Information Geometry

Let $p(\mathbf{x}\,;\boldsymbol{\theta})$, $\mathbf{x}$ and $\boldsymbol{\theta}$ be a probability density function, the probability variables and the parameters of the probability density function. For example, consider a normal distribution

$p(\mathbf{x}\,;\boldsymbol{\theta}) = \frac{1}{\sqrt{2\pi}\sigma}\exp(-\frac{(x-\mu)^2}{2\sigma^2})$, then we get $\mathbf{x} = x$ and $\boldsymbol{\theta} = (\mu, \sigma)$.

The space of parameters $\boldsymbol{\theta}$ is a coordinate system. That of normal distribution is a 2 dimensional coordinate system. Denote $S = \{p(\mathbf{x}\,;\boldsymbol{\theta})\}$. Information geometry regards S as a set with the coordinate system θ and each point on S as a probability distribution.

Exponential Family

Exponential family is one of the most important families of probability distributions in information geometry. For the probability densities $p(\mathbf{x};\boldsymbol{\theta})$ with the probability variables $\mathbf{x} = (x_1, x_2, \cdots, x_n)$, the function $\mathbf{F}(\mathbf{x}) = (F_1(\mathbf{x}), F_2(\mathbf{x}), \cdots, F_r(\mathbf{x}))$ and the parameters $\boldsymbol{\theta} = (\theta_1, \theta_2, \cdots, \theta_r)$, if there exists a function $\psi(\boldsymbol{\theta})$ of $\boldsymbol{\theta}$ such that

$$p(\mathbf{x}\,;\boldsymbol{\theta}) = \exp(\boldsymbol{\theta}\cdot\mathbf{F}(\mathbf{x}) - \psi(\boldsymbol{\theta})) = \exp(\sum_{i=1}^{r}\theta_i F_i(\mathbf{x}) - \psi(\boldsymbol{\theta})),$$

then it is called an exponential family. The parameter B and the function $\psi(\boldsymbol{\theta})$ are called the natural parameter and the normalizer, respectively. For example, normal distributions

$$p(\mathbf{x}\,;\boldsymbol{\theta}) = \frac{1}{\sqrt{2\pi}\sigma}\exp(-\frac{(x-\mu)^2}{2\sigma^2}) = \exp(-\frac{1}{2\sigma^2}x^2 + \frac{\mu}{\sigma^2}x - \frac{\mu^2}{2\sigma^2} + \log\frac{1}{\sqrt{2\pi}\sigma})$$

form an exponential family, where $\mathbf{F}(\mathbf{x}) = (x, x^2)$, $\boldsymbol{\theta} = (\frac{\mu}{\sigma^2}, -\frac{1}{2\sigma^2})$ and $\psi(\boldsymbol{\theta}) = \frac{\mu^2}{2\sigma^2} - \log\frac{1}{\sqrt{2\pi}\sigma}$.

Since $\int p(\mathbf{x};\boldsymbol{\theta})d\mathbf{x} = 1$, where the integral range is the domain of the probability variable **x**, we can calculate $\psi(\boldsymbol{\theta})$ in the following way:

$$1 = \int p(\mathbf{x};\boldsymbol{\theta})d\mathbf{x} = \exp(-\psi(\boldsymbol{\theta}))\int \exp(\sum_{i=1}^{r}\theta_i F_i(\mathbf{x}))d\mathbf{x},$$
$$\psi(\boldsymbol{\theta}) = \log \int \exp(\sum_{i=1}^{r}\theta_i F_i(\mathbf{x}))d\mathbf{x}.$$

By differentiating the both sides of $\int p(\mathbf{x};\boldsymbol{\theta})d\mathbf{x} = 1$ by θ_i, we get the following equations:

$$\int\left(F_i(\mathbf{x}) - \frac{\partial\psi(\boldsymbol{\theta})}{\partial\theta_i}\right)p(\mathbf{x};\boldsymbol{\theta})d\mathbf{x} = 0,$$

$$\int F_i(\mathbf{x})p(\mathbf{x};\boldsymbol{\theta})d\mathbf{x} = \frac{\partial\psi(\boldsymbol{\theta})}{\partial\theta_i}\int p(\mathbf{x};\boldsymbol{\theta})d\mathbf{x} = \frac{\partial\psi(\boldsymbol{\theta})}{\partial\theta_i}.$$

We denote the expectation $E[F_i(\mathbf{x})] = \int F_i(\mathbf{x})p(\mathbf{x};\boldsymbol{\theta})d\mathbf{x}$ of $F_i(\mathbf{x})$ as η_i. We can use another effective parameter $\boldsymbol{\eta} = (\eta_1, \eta_2, \cdots, \eta_r)$ and it is called the expectation parameter. The transformation $\eta_i = \frac{\partial\psi(\boldsymbol{\theta})}{\partial\theta_i}$ from the natural parameter $\boldsymbol{\theta}$ to the expectation parameter $\boldsymbol{\eta}$ is called Legendre transformation.

We summarize the important results in this subsection.

(1) $p(\mathbf{x};\boldsymbol{\theta}) = \exp(\theta\cdot\mathbf{F}(\mathbf{x}) - \psi(\boldsymbol{\theta})) = \exp(\sum_{i=1}^{r}\theta_i F_i(\mathbf{x}) - \psi(\boldsymbol{\theta}))$ (Definition of exponential family).

(2) $\psi(\boldsymbol{\theta}) = \log \int \exp(\sum_{i=1}^{r}\theta_i F_i(\mathbf{x}))d\mathbf{x}$.

(3) $\eta_i = E[F_i(\mathbf{x})] = \frac{\partial\psi(\boldsymbol{\theta})}{\partial\theta_i}$.

Discrete Distribution

Consider a probability variable x which takes $(n+1)$ values, 0, 1, … , n. Let p_i be the probability that x takes i. Since $\sum_{i=0}^{n} p_i = 1$, the probability density of the probability variable x is determined by the parameters $p_1, p_2, \cdots, p_n$. The set of all probability densities of the probability variable x is parameterized by $(p_1, p_2, \cdots, p_n)$ with $\sum_{i=1}^{n} p_i \le 1$ and $p_i \ge 0$. It is called discrete distribution. Discrete distributions $p(x)$ can be described as $p(x) = \sum_{i=0}^{n} p_i\delta_i(x)$, where when $x = i$ then $\delta_i(x) = 1$, in the other cases, $\delta_i(x) = 0$. Since there exists just a $\delta_i(x)$ which takes 1 and the others take 0, we get

$$\begin{aligned} p(x) &= \exp(\sum_{i=0}^{n}\delta_i(x)\log p_i) = \exp(\delta_0(x)\log p_0 + \sum_{i=1}^{n}\delta_i(x)\log p_i) \\ &= \exp((1-\sum_{i=1}^{n}\delta_i(x))\log p_0 + \sum_{i=1}^{n}\delta_i(x)\log p_i) \\ &= \exp(\log p_0 + \sum_{i=1}^{n}\delta_i(x)\log\frac{p_i}{p_0}). \end{aligned}$$

We put $F_i(\mathbf{x}) = \delta_i(x)$, $\theta_i = \log\frac{p_i}{p_0}$ and $\psi(\theta) = -\log p_0$, then we know that discrete distributions form an exponential family.

Consider the probability density $p(x)$ which is the weighted sum $\sum_{i=0}^{m}\theta_i p_i(x)$ of probability densities $p_i(x)$, where $\sum_{i=0}^{m}\theta_i = 1$. We regard $p(x)$ as the distribution family with the parameter $(\theta_1, \theta_2, \cdots, \theta_m)$. It is called a **mixture family**. Discrete distributions also form a mixture family.

We summarize the important results in this subsection.

(4) Discrete distributions form an exponential family and a mixture family.

Divergence

Divergence is a notion to measure the difference between two given probability distributions. There exist many divergences. **Kullback-Leibler divergence** is the most important divergence. For two given probability densities $p(\mathbf{x})$ and $q(\mathbf{x})$, the Kullback-Leibler divergence $KL(p, q)$ between the probability densities $p(\mathbf{x})$ and $q(\mathbf{x})$ is defined as follows:

$$KL(p, q) = \int p(\mathbf{x}) \log \frac{p(\mathbf{x})}{q(\mathbf{x})} d\mathbf{x}.$$

If the probability variable $\mathbf{x}$ is discrete, we replace the integral to the summation. Kullback-Leibler divergence has the following properties:

$$KL(p, q) \geq 0,$$
$$KL(p, q) = 0 \Leftrightarrow p(\mathbf{x}) \equiv q(\mathbf{x}).$$

We prove them. The inequality $\log x \leq x - 1$ holds. The equality holds if and only if the equation $x = 1$ holds.

$$KL(p,q) = -\int p(\mathbf{x}) \log \frac{q(\mathbf{x})}{p(\mathbf{x})} d\mathbf{x} \geq -\int p(\mathbf{x}) \left(\frac{q(\mathbf{x})}{p(\mathbf{x})} - 1 \right) d\mathbf{x}$$
$$= -\int q(\mathbf{x}) d\mathbf{x} + \int p(\mathbf{x}) d\mathbf{x} = 0$$

The equality holds if and only if the equality $p(\mathbf{x}) \equiv q(\mathbf{x})$ holds. Therefore we complete the proof of the above properties.

Kullback-Leibler divergence is not symmetric, so it is not a distance.

We summarize the important results in this subsection.

(5) $KL(p, q) = \int p(\mathbf{x}) \log \frac{p(\mathbf{x})}{q(\mathbf{x})} d\mathbf{x}$ (Definition of Kullback-Leibler divergence).
(6) $KL(p, q) \geq 0$.
(7) $KL(p, q) = 0 \Leftrightarrow p(\mathbf{x}) \equiv q(\mathbf{x})$.

Connections and Geodesics

Connections are the notions by which straight lines are provided. The straight lines are called **geodesics**. In information geometry, two types of connections are so important. They are called *e*-connection and *m*-connection. The prefixes *e* and *m* of connections stand for exponential and mixture. They are close related and called dual connections. The geodesics of *e*-connections and *m*-connections are called *e*-geodesic and *m*-geodesic, respectively.

Suppose that S is a mixture family. Let the probability densities $p(\mathbf{x})$ and $q(\mathbf{x})$ belong to S. The *m*-geodesic from the probability density $p(\mathbf{x})$ to the one $q(\mathbf{x})$ is defined by the curve $(1 - t)\, p(\mathbf{x}) + t\, q(\mathbf{x})$ $(0 \leq t \leq 1)$. We denote $p(\mathbf{x}) = \sum_i \theta_i r_i(\mathbf{x})$ and $q(\mathbf{x}) = \sum_i \theta'_i r_i(\mathbf{x})$. Then we get the equation $(1 - t)\, p(\mathbf{x}) + t\, q(\mathbf{x}) = \sum_i ((1-t)\theta_i + t\theta'_i) r_i(\mathbf{x})$. Therefore the *m*-geodesic $(1 - t)\, p(\mathbf{x}) + t\, q(\mathbf{x})$ is contained in S again. We describe the *m*-geodesic $\boldsymbol{\eta}(t)$ the expectation parameter.

$$\boldsymbol{\eta}(t) = \mathrm{E}[(1-t)p(\mathbf{x}) + tq(\mathbf{x})] = (1-t)\mathrm{E}[p(\mathbf{x})] + t\,\mathrm{E}[q(\mathbf{x})] = (1-t)\boldsymbol{\eta}(p) + t\boldsymbol{\eta}(q).$$

We can regard the *m*-geodesic as a straight line in the expectation coordinate system. Consider a submanifold M in the manifold S. Let the probability densities $p(\mathbf{x})$ and $q(\mathbf{x})$ be any probability densities belonging to M. If the *m*-geodesic $\boldsymbol{\eta}(t)$ from the probability density $p(\mathbf{x})$ to the one $q(\mathbf{x})$ always belongs to the manifold M again, the manifold M is called an m-autoparallel submanifold. Therefore an m-autopararllel submanifold is equivalent to an affine subset of the mixture family in the expectation coordinate system.

Next, suppose that S is an exponential family. Let the probability densities $p(\mathbf{x})$ and $q(\mathbf{x})$ belong to S again. The e-geodesic $r(t)$ from the probability density $p(\mathbf{x})$ to the one $q(\mathbf{x})$ is defined by the curve $r(t) = p(x)^{1-t} q(x)^t \exp(-\varphi(t))$. We describe the e-geodesic $r(t)$ by the expectation parameter. We denote the probability densities $p(\mathbf{x})$ and $q(\mathbf{x})$ as $p(\mathbf{x}) = \exp(\boldsymbol{\theta}(p) \cdot \mathbf{F}(\mathbf{x}) - \psi(\boldsymbol{\theta}(p)))$ and $q(\mathbf{x}) = \exp(\boldsymbol{\theta}(q) \cdot \mathbf{F}(\mathbf{x}) - \psi(\boldsymbol{\theta}(q)))$. Then the e-geodesic $r(t)$ is as follows:

$$
\begin{aligned}
r(t) &= \exp((1-t)(\boldsymbol{\theta}(p)\cdot\mathbf{F}(\mathbf{x}) - \psi(\boldsymbol{\theta}(p))) + t(\boldsymbol{\theta}(q)\cdot\mathbf{F}(\mathbf{x}) - \psi(\boldsymbol{\theta}(q))) - \phi(t)) \\
&= \exp(((1-t)\boldsymbol{\theta}(p) + t\boldsymbol{\theta}(q))\cdot\mathbf{F}(\mathbf{x}) - (1-t)\psi(\boldsymbol{\theta}(p)) - t\psi(\boldsymbol{\theta}(q)) - \phi(t)).
\end{aligned}
$$

Therefore the probability density $r(t)$ is also included in the exponential family S again. From the equations (1) and (2), the normalizer $(1-t)\psi(\boldsymbol{\theta}(p)) + t\psi(\boldsymbol{\theta}(q)) + \varphi(t)$ is $\log \int \exp(((1-t)\boldsymbol{\theta}(p) + t\boldsymbol{\theta}(q))\cdot\mathbf{F}(\mathbf{x}))d\mathbf{x}$. So we get the equation

$$
\varphi(t) = \log \int \exp(((1-t)\boldsymbol{\theta}(p) + t\boldsymbol{\theta}(q))\cdot\mathbf{F}(\mathbf{x}))d\mathbf{x} - (1-t)\psi(\boldsymbol{\theta}(p)) - t\psi(\boldsymbol{\theta}(q)).
$$

We can describe the e-geodesic $\boldsymbol{\theta}(t) = (1-t)\boldsymbol{\theta}(p) + t\boldsymbol{\theta}(q)$ as a straight line in the natural coordinate system. Consider a submanifold M in the manifold S. Let $p(\mathbf{x})$ and $q(\mathbf{x})$ be any probability densities belonging to M. If the e-geodesic $r(t)$ from the probability density $p(\mathbf{x})$ to the one $q(\mathbf{x})$ always belongs to the manifold M again, the manifold M is called an e-autoparallel submanifold. Therefore an e-autopararllel submanifold is equivalent to an affine subset of the exponential family in the natural coordinate system.

Tangent Spaces

Consider a point on a stochastic manifold. We denote it as the parameter $\boldsymbol{\theta} = (\theta_1, \theta_2, \cdots, \theta_r)$ in the coordinate system. We take r **tangent vectors** $\frac{\partial}{\partial\theta_1}, \frac{\partial}{\partial\theta_2}, \cdots, \frac{\partial}{\partial\theta_r}$, then we can describe the tangent space as vector spaces $\sum_{i=1}^{r} c_i \frac{\partial}{\partial\theta_i}$ by using the local coordinate system $(c_1, c_2, \cdots, c_r)$. We can write tangent spaces in various coordinate systems.

Fisher Metric

Metrics are the notions of length on differential manifolds. Metrics are defined as inner products of two tangent vectors. We introduce the effective metric for information geometry from Kullback-Leibler divergence. From Taylor expansion, we get

$$
\log p(\mathbf{x}; \boldsymbol{\theta} + d\boldsymbol{\theta}) = \log p(\mathbf{x}; \boldsymbol{\theta}) + \frac{1}{p(\mathbf{x};\boldsymbol{\theta})}\left(\frac{\partial p(\mathbf{x};\boldsymbol{\theta})}{\partial\boldsymbol{\theta}}\right)^T d\boldsymbol{\theta} + \frac{1}{2} d\boldsymbol{\theta}^T H(\boldsymbol{\theta}) d\boldsymbol{\theta},
$$

where the matrix $H(\boldsymbol{\theta})$ is as follows:

$$
H(\boldsymbol{\theta}) = \frac{1}{p(\mathbf{x};\boldsymbol{\theta})}\frac{\partial^2 p(\mathbf{x};\boldsymbol{\theta})}{\partial\boldsymbol{\theta}\partial\boldsymbol{\theta}^T} - \frac{1}{p(\mathbf{x};\boldsymbol{\theta})^2}\frac{\partial p(\mathbf{x};\boldsymbol{\theta})}{\partial\boldsymbol{\theta}}\frac{\partial p(\mathbf{x};\boldsymbol{\theta})}{\partial\boldsymbol{\theta}^T}.
$$

We calculate Kullback-Leibler divergence $KL(p(\mathbf{x}; \boldsymbol{\theta}), p(\mathbf{x}; \boldsymbol{\theta} + d\boldsymbol{\theta}))$ from the probability density $p(\mathbf{x}; \boldsymbol{\theta})$ to the one $p(\mathbf{x}; \boldsymbol{\theta} + d\boldsymbol{\theta})$.

$$
\begin{aligned}
KL(p(\mathbf{x};\boldsymbol{\theta}), p(\mathbf{x};\boldsymbol{\theta}+d\boldsymbol{\theta})) &= \int p(\mathbf{x};\boldsymbol{\theta}) \log\frac{p(\mathbf{x};\boldsymbol{\theta})}{p(\mathbf{x};\boldsymbol{\theta}+d\boldsymbol{\theta})} d\mathbf{x} \\
&= \int (p(\mathbf{x};\boldsymbol{\theta})\log p(\mathbf{x};\boldsymbol{\theta}) - p(\mathbf{x};\boldsymbol{\theta})\log p(\mathbf{x};\boldsymbol{\theta}+d\boldsymbol{\theta}))d\mathbf{x} \\
&= -\int \left\{ \left(\frac{\partial p(\mathbf{x};\boldsymbol{\theta})}{\partial\boldsymbol{\theta}}\right)^T d\boldsymbol{\theta} + \frac{1}{2} p(\mathbf{x};\boldsymbol{\theta}) d\boldsymbol{\theta}^T H(\boldsymbol{\theta}) d\boldsymbol{\theta} \right\} d\mathbf{x}.
\end{aligned}
$$

By differentiating the equation $\int p(\mathbf{x})d\mathbf{x} = 1$ by θ_i, we get $\int \frac{\partial p(\mathbf{x};\boldsymbol{\theta})}{\partial \theta_i} d\mathbf{x} = 0$. So the first term vanishes. We obtain the following equation:

$$KL(p(\mathbf{x};\boldsymbol{\theta}), p(\mathbf{x};\boldsymbol{\theta}+d\boldsymbol{\theta}))$$
$$= -\frac{1}{2}\int p(\mathbf{x};\boldsymbol{\theta}) d\boldsymbol{\theta}^T H(\boldsymbol{\theta}) d\boldsymbol{\theta} d\mathbf{x}$$
$$= -\frac{1}{2} d\boldsymbol{\theta}^T \left\{ \int \left(\frac{\partial^2 p(\mathbf{x};\boldsymbol{\theta})}{\partial\boldsymbol{\theta}\partial\boldsymbol{\theta}^T} - \frac{1}{p(\mathbf{x};\boldsymbol{\theta})} \frac{\partial p(\boldsymbol{\theta};\ )}{\partial\,\boldsymbol{\theta}} \frac{\partial p(\mathbf{x};\boldsymbol{\theta})}{\partial\boldsymbol{\theta}^T} \right) d\mathbf{x} \right\} d\boldsymbol{\theta}.$$

By differentiating the equation

$\int \frac{\partial p(\mathbf{x};\boldsymbol{\theta})}{\partial \theta_i} d\mathbf{x} = 0$ by θ_j, we get $\int \frac{\partial^2 p(\mathbf{x};\boldsymbol{\theta})}{\partial \theta_i \partial \theta_j} d\mathbf{x} = 0$.

So the first term vanishes. Therefore we obtain the following equation:

$$KL(p(\mathbf{x};\boldsymbol{\theta}), p(\mathbf{x};\boldsymbol{\theta}+d\boldsymbol{\theta})) = \frac{1}{2} d\boldsymbol{\theta}^T \left\{ \int \frac{1}{p(\mathbf{x};\boldsymbol{\theta})} \frac{\partial p(\boldsymbol{\theta};\ )}{\partial\boldsymbol{\theta}} \frac{\partial p(\mathbf{x};\boldsymbol{\theta})}{\partial\boldsymbol{\theta}^T} d\mathbf{x} \right\} d\boldsymbol{\theta}$$
$$= \frac{1}{2} d\boldsymbol{\theta}^T \left\{ \int p(\mathbf{x};\boldsymbol{\theta}) \frac{\partial \log p(\mathbf{x};\boldsymbol{\theta})}{\partial\boldsymbol{\theta}} \frac{\partial \log p(\mathbf{x};\boldsymbol{\theta})}{\partial\boldsymbol{\theta}^T} d\mathbf{x} \right\} d\boldsymbol{\theta}$$
$$= \frac{1}{2} d\boldsymbol{\theta}^T \left\{ E[\frac{\partial \log p(\mathbf{x};\boldsymbol{\theta})}{\partial\boldsymbol{\theta}} \frac{\partial \log p(\mathbf{x};\boldsymbol{\theta})}{\partial\boldsymbol{\theta}^T}] \right\} d\boldsymbol{\theta}.$$

We denote E[$\frac{\partial \log p(\mathbf{x};\boldsymbol{\theta})}{\partial\boldsymbol{\theta}} \frac{\partial \log p(\mathbf{x},\boldsymbol{\theta})}{\partial\boldsymbol{\theta}^T}$] as $G(\boldsymbol{\theta}) = (g_j(\boldsymbol{\theta}))$. This symmetric matrix is called Fisher metric. Fisher metric is one of the most important notions in information geometry. Consider two tangent vectors $\mathbf{e} = \sum_{i=1}^{r} c_i \frac{\partial}{\partial \theta_i}$ and $\mathbf{e}' = \sum_{i=1}^{r} c_i' \frac{\partial}{\partial \theta_i}$. We define the inner product of two tangent vectors **e** and **e'** as $\langle \mathbf{e}, \mathbf{e}' \rangle = \sum_{i,j} c_i c_j' g_{ij}$ by Fisher metric. If the inner product vanishes, the two tangent vectors are called orthogonal.

Consider $d\boldsymbol{\theta} = \sum_i c_i d\theta_i$, then we get the equation $KL(p(\mathbf{x};\boldsymbol{\theta}), p(\mathbf{x};\boldsymbol{\theta}+d\boldsymbol{\theta})) = \frac{1}{2}\sum_{i,j} c_i c_j g_{ij} d\theta_i d\theta_j$.

We put a tangent vector $\mathbf{e} = \sum_{i=1}^{r} (c_i d\theta_i) \frac{\partial}{\partial \theta_i}$, then we get the equation $\langle \mathbf{e}, \mathbf{e} \rangle = \sum_{i,j} c_i c_j g_{ij} d\theta_i d\theta_j$. Therefore we get the equation $KL(p(\mathbf{x};\boldsymbol{\theta}), p(\mathbf{x};\boldsymbol{\theta}+d\boldsymbol{\theta})) = \frac{1}{2}\langle \mathbf{e}, \mathbf{e} \rangle$. We can regard Kullback-Leibler divergence between two close probability distributions as the square of the length of the tangent vector by Fisher metric.

We summarize the important result in this subsection.

$$\text{Fisher metric } g_{ij}(\boldsymbol{\theta}) = \left\langle \frac{\partial}{\partial \theta_i}, \frac{\partial}{\partial \theta_j} \right\rangle = \text{E}[\frac{\partial \log p(\mathbf{x};\boldsymbol{\theta})}{\partial \theta_i} \frac{\partial \log p(\mathbf{x};\boldsymbol{\theta})}{\partial \theta_j}] \text{ (Definition).} \quad (8)$$

Potential Functions

For an exponential family, we get the equation $\psi(\boldsymbol{\theta}) = \log \int \exp(\sum_{i=1}^{r} \theta_j F_j(\mathbf{x})) d\mathbf{x}$ from the equation (2). The normalizer function $\psi(\boldsymbol{\theta})$ is also called the **potential function** of the exponential family. By differentiating the both sides by θ_i, we get

$$\frac{\partial\psi(\boldsymbol{\theta})}{\partial\theta_i}=\frac{\int F_i(\mathbf{x})\exp(\sum_{j=1}^{r}\theta_j F_j(\mathbf{x}))d\mathbf{x}}{\int \exp(\sum_{j=1}^{r}\theta_j F_j(\mathbf{x}))d\mathbf{x}}=\exp(-\psi(\boldsymbol{\theta}))\int F_i(\mathbf{x})\exp(\sum_{j=1}^{r}\theta_j F_j(\mathbf{x}))d\mathbf{x}$$

$$=\int F_i(\mathbf{x})\exp(\sum_{j=1}^{r}\theta_j F_j(\mathbf{x})-\psi(\boldsymbol{\theta}))d\mathbf{x}$$

And by differentiating the both sides by θ_j again, we get

$$\frac{\partial^2\psi(\boldsymbol{\theta})}{\partial\theta_i\partial\theta_j}=\int F_i(\mathbf{x})(F_j(\mathbf{x})-\frac{\partial\psi(\boldsymbol{\theta})}{\partial\theta_j})\exp(\sum_{j=1}^{r}\theta_j F_j(\mathbf{x})-\psi(\boldsymbol{\theta}))d\mathbf{x}.$$

Since $\eta_j=\frac{\partial\psi(\boldsymbol{\theta})}{\partial\theta_j}$ (3), we get

$$\frac{\partial^2\psi(\boldsymbol{\theta})}{\partial\theta_i\partial\theta_j}=\int F_i(\mathbf{x})(F_j(\mathbf{x})-\eta_j)\exp(\sum_{j=1}^{n}\theta_j F_j(\mathbf{x})-\psi(\boldsymbol{\theta}))d\mathbf{x}.$$

Moreover the following equation holds.

$$\int(F_j(\mathbf{x})-\eta_j)\exp(\sum_{j=1}^{n}\theta_j F_j(\mathbf{x})-\psi(\boldsymbol{\theta}))d\mathbf{x}$$

$$=E[F_j(\mathbf{x})]-\eta_j\int\exp(\sum_{j=1}^{n}\theta_j F_j(\mathbf{x})-\psi(\boldsymbol{\theta}))d\mathbf{x}$$

$$=\eta_j-\eta_j=0.$$

Therefore we obtain

$$E[(F_i(\mathbf{x})-\eta_i)(F_j(\mathbf{x})-\eta_j)]=\int(F_i(\mathbf{x})-\eta_i)(F_j(\mathbf{x})-\eta_j)\exp(\sum_{j=1}^{r}\theta_j F_j(\mathbf{x})-\psi(\boldsymbol{\theta}))d\mathbf{x}$$

$$=\int F_i(\mathbf{x})(F_j(\mathbf{x})-\eta_j)\exp(\sum_{j=1}^{r}\theta_j F_j(\mathbf{x})-\psi(\boldsymbol{\theta}))d\mathbf{x}$$

$$-\eta_i\int(F_j(\mathbf{x})-\eta_j)\exp(\sum_{j=1}^{r}\theta_j F_j(\mathbf{x})-\psi(\boldsymbol{\theta}))d\mathbf{x}$$

$$=\int F_i(\mathbf{x})(F_j(\mathbf{x})-\eta_j)\exp(\sum_{j=1}^{r}\theta_j F_j(\mathbf{x})-\psi(\boldsymbol{\theta}))d\mathbf{x}$$

$$=\frac{\partial^2\psi(\boldsymbol{\theta})}{\partial\theta_i\partial\theta_j}.$$

We calculate $\frac{\partial\log p(\mathbf{x};\boldsymbol{\theta})}{\partial\boldsymbol{\theta}}$.

$$\frac{\partial\log p(\mathbf{x};\boldsymbol{\theta})}{\partial\theta_i}=\frac{\partial(\sum_{j=1}^{r}\theta_j F_j(\mathbf{x})-\psi(\boldsymbol{\theta}))}{\partial\theta_i}=F_i(\mathbf{x})-\frac{\partial\psi(\boldsymbol{\theta})}{\partial\theta_i}=F_i(\mathbf{x})-\eta_i.$$

So we get the equation $g_{ij}(\boldsymbol{\theta})=\frac{\partial^2\psi(\boldsymbol{\theta})}{\partial\theta_i\partial\theta_j}=\frac{\partial\eta_j}{\partial\theta_i}$. From the equation $g_{ij}(\boldsymbol{\theta})=g_{ji}(\boldsymbol{\theta})$, we get the equation $\frac{\partial\eta_j}{\partial\theta_i}=\frac{\partial\eta_i}{\partial\theta_j}$.

From the equation $\boldsymbol{\eta}=\frac{\partial\psi(\boldsymbol{\theta})}{\partial\boldsymbol{\theta}}$ (3), we find that the parameter $\boldsymbol{\eta}$ is a function of the parameter $\boldsymbol{\theta}$. By the inverse function, we find that the parameter $\boldsymbol{\theta}$ is a function of the parameter $\boldsymbol{\eta}$. We define $\varphi(\boldsymbol{\eta})=\sum_i\theta_i\eta_i-\psi(\boldsymbol{\theta})$. We can regard this function as a function of $\boldsymbol{\eta}$. We differentiate it by η_j.

$$\frac{\partial\phi(\boldsymbol{\eta})}{\partial\eta_j}=\sum_i\frac{\partial\theta_i}{\partial\eta_j}\eta_i+\theta_j-\frac{\partial\psi(\boldsymbol{\theta})}{\partial\eta_j}=\sum_i\frac{\partial\theta_i}{\partial\eta_j}\eta_i+\theta_j-\sum_i\frac{\partial\psi(\boldsymbol{\theta})}{\partial\theta_i}\frac{\partial\theta_i}{\partial\eta_j}$$

$$=\sum_i\frac{\partial\theta_i}{\partial\eta_j}\eta_i+\theta_j-\sum_i\eta_i\frac{\partial\theta_i}{\partial\eta_j}=\theta_j.$$

We obtain the equation $\theta_j = \frac{\partial \phi(\boldsymbol{\eta})}{\partial \eta_j}$. The function $\varphi(\boldsymbol{\eta})$ is also called the potential function. We calculate the expectation of $\log p(\mathbf{x};\boldsymbol{\theta})$.

$$E[\log p(\mathbf{x};\boldsymbol{\theta})] = E[\sum_i \theta_i F_i(\mathbf{x}) - \psi(\boldsymbol{\theta})] = \sum_i \theta_i E[F_i(\mathbf{x})] - \psi(\boldsymbol{\theta})$$
$$= \sum_i \theta_i \eta_i - \psi(\boldsymbol{\theta}) = \phi(\boldsymbol{\eta}).$$

Therefore we obtain the equation $\varphi(\boldsymbol{\eta}) = E[\log p(\mathbf{x};\boldsymbol{\theta})]$.

We calculate the expression $\frac{\partial \log p(\mathbf{x};\boldsymbol{\theta})}{\partial \eta_i}$.

$$\frac{\partial \log p(\mathbf{x};\boldsymbol{\theta})}{\partial \eta_i} = \frac{\partial}{\partial \eta_i}\left(\sum_k \theta_k F_k(\mathbf{x}) - \psi(\boldsymbol{\theta})\right) = \sum_k \frac{\partial \theta_k}{\partial \eta_i} F_k(\mathbf{x}) - \sum_k \frac{\partial \theta_k}{\partial \eta_i}\frac{\partial \psi(\boldsymbol{\theta})}{\partial \theta_k}$$
$$= \sum_k \frac{\partial \theta_k}{\partial \eta_i}(F_k(\mathbf{x}) - \eta_k).$$

Let $g^{ij}(\boldsymbol{\eta})$ be Fisher metric for the parameters $\boldsymbol{\eta}$.

$$g^{ij}(\boldsymbol{\eta}) = E[\frac{\partial \log p(\mathbf{x};\boldsymbol{\theta})}{\partial \eta_i}\frac{\partial \log p(\mathbf{x};\boldsymbol{\theta})}{\partial \eta_j}] = E[\sum_{k,l}\frac{\partial \theta_k}{\partial \eta_i}(F_k(\mathbf{x}) - \eta_k)\frac{\partial \theta_l}{\partial \eta_j}(F_l(\mathbf{x}) - \eta_l)]$$
$$= \sum_{k,l}\frac{\partial \theta_k}{\partial \eta_i}\frac{\partial \theta_l}{\partial \eta_j} E[(F_k(\mathbf{x}) - \eta_k)(F_l(\mathbf{x}) - \eta_l)] = \sum_{k,l}\frac{\partial \theta_k}{\partial \eta_i}\frac{\partial \theta_l}{\partial \eta_j} g_{kl}(\boldsymbol{\theta}).$$

Therefore we get the equation $g^{ij}(\boldsymbol{\eta}) = \sum_{k,l}\frac{\partial \theta_k}{\partial \eta_i}\frac{\partial \theta_l}{\partial \eta_j} g_{kl}(\boldsymbol{\theta})$. From the equations $g_{ij}(\boldsymbol{\theta}) = \frac{\partial \eta_j}{\partial \theta_i}$, $\theta_i = \frac{\partial \phi(\boldsymbol{\eta})}{\partial \eta_i}$ and $\frac{\partial \theta_k}{\partial \eta_i} = \frac{\partial \theta_i}{\partial \eta_k}$, we get the following equation.

$$g^{ij}(\boldsymbol{\eta}) = \sum_{k,l}\frac{\partial \theta_k}{\partial \eta_i}\frac{\partial \theta_l}{\partial \eta_j} g_{kl}(\boldsymbol{\theta}) = \sum_{k,l}\frac{\partial \theta_k}{\partial \eta_i}\frac{\partial \theta_l}{\partial \eta_j}\frac{\partial \eta_k}{\partial \theta_l} = \sum_k \frac{\partial \theta_i}{\partial \eta_k}\frac{\partial \eta_k}{\partial \eta_j} = \frac{\partial \theta_i}{\partial \eta_j} = \frac{\partial^2 \phi(\boldsymbol{\eta})}{\partial \eta_i \partial \eta_j}.$$

From the equation $g^{ij}(\boldsymbol{\eta}) = g^{ji}(\boldsymbol{\eta})$, we get the equation $\frac{\partial \theta_j}{\partial \eta_i} = \frac{\partial \theta_i}{\partial \eta_j}$.

We calculate the inner product $\left\langle \frac{\partial}{\partial \eta_i}, \frac{\partial}{\partial \theta_j} \right\rangle$.

$$\left\langle \frac{\partial}{\partial \eta_i}, \frac{\partial}{\partial \theta_j} \right\rangle = \left\langle \frac{\partial}{\partial \eta_i}, \sum_k \frac{\partial \eta_k}{\partial \theta_j}\frac{\partial}{\partial \eta_k} \right\rangle = \sum_k \frac{\partial \eta_k}{\partial \theta_j}\left\langle \frac{\partial}{\partial \eta_i}, \frac{\partial}{\partial \eta_k} \right\rangle$$
$$= \sum_k \frac{\partial \eta_k}{\partial \theta_j} g^{ik}(\boldsymbol{\eta}) = \sum_k \frac{\partial \eta_k}{\partial \theta_j}\frac{\partial \theta_i}{\partial \eta_k} = \frac{\partial \theta_i}{\partial \theta_j} = \delta_{ij}.$$

Therefore if $i \neq j$, then two vectors $\frac{\partial}{\partial \eta_i}$ and $\frac{\partial}{\partial \theta_j}$ are orthogonal.

From the equation $\sum_k g^{ik}(\boldsymbol{\eta}) g_{kj}(\boldsymbol{\theta}) = \sum_k \frac{\partial \theta_k}{\partial \eta_i}\frac{\partial \eta_j}{\partial \theta_k} = \frac{\partial \eta_j}{\partial \eta_i} = \delta_{ij}$, we find that the matrix $(g^{ij}(\boldsymbol{\eta}))$ is the inverse matrix of $(g_{ij}(\boldsymbol{\theta}))$.

We summarize the important results in this subsection.

$$g_{ij}(\boldsymbol{\theta}) = \frac{\partial^2 \psi(\boldsymbol{\theta})}{\partial \theta_i \partial \theta_j} = \frac{\partial \eta_j}{\partial \theta_i} = \frac{\partial \eta_i}{\partial \theta_j} = E[(F_i(\mathbf{x}) - \eta_i)(F_j(\mathbf{x}) - \eta_j)]. \quad (9)$$

$$g^{ij}(\boldsymbol{\eta}) = \frac{\partial^2 \phi(\boldsymbol{\eta})}{\partial \eta_i \partial \eta_j} = \frac{\partial \theta_j}{\partial \eta_i} = \frac{\partial \theta_i}{\partial \eta_j}. \quad (10)$$

$$\varphi(\boldsymbol{\eta}) = \sum_i \theta_i \eta_i - \psi(\boldsymbol{\theta}) = E[\log p(\mathbf{x};\boldsymbol{\theta})]. \quad (11)$$

$$\theta_j = \frac{\partial \phi(\boldsymbol{\eta})}{\partial \eta_j} \text{ (the relation dual to (3)).} \quad (12)$$

$$\left\langle \frac{\partial}{\partial \eta_i}, \frac{\partial}{\partial \theta_j} \right\rangle = \delta_{ij}. \quad (13)$$

The matrix $(g^{ij}(\boldsymbol{\eta}))$ is the inverse matrix of $(g_{ij}(\boldsymbol{\theta}))$. (14)

Pythagorean Theorem

For two probability densities $p(\mathbf{x})$ and $q(\mathbf{x})$ included in the discrete distribution S, we calculate Kullback-Leibler divergence $KL(p, q)$ by the natural and expectation parameters.

$$\int p(\mathbf{x}) \log p(\mathbf{x}) d\mathbf{x} = \int p(\mathbf{x})(\boldsymbol{\theta}(p) \cdot \mathbf{F}(\mathbf{x}) - \psi(\boldsymbol{\theta}(p))) d\mathbf{x} = \boldsymbol{\theta}(p) \cdot \boldsymbol{\eta}(p) - \psi(\boldsymbol{\theta}(p)),$$

$$\int p(\mathbf{x}) \log q(\mathbf{x}) d\mathbf{x} = \int p(\mathbf{x})(\boldsymbol{\theta}(q) \cdot \mathbf{F}(\mathbf{x}) - \psi(\boldsymbol{\theta}(q))) d\mathbf{x} = \boldsymbol{\theta}(q) \cdot \boldsymbol{\eta}(p) - \psi(\boldsymbol{\theta}(q)),$$

$$\begin{aligned} KL(p,q) &= \int p(\mathbf{x}) \log p(\mathbf{x}) d\mathbf{x} - \int p(\mathbf{x}) \log q(\mathbf{x}) d\mathbf{x} \\ &= \psi(\boldsymbol{\theta}(q)) + \boldsymbol{\theta}(p) \cdot \boldsymbol{\eta}(p) - \psi(\boldsymbol{\theta}(p)) - \boldsymbol{\theta}(q) \cdot \boldsymbol{\eta}(p) \\ &= \psi(\boldsymbol{\theta}(q)) + \phi(\boldsymbol{\eta}(p)) - \boldsymbol{\theta}(q) \cdot \boldsymbol{\eta}(p). \end{aligned}$$

We get the formula $KL(p, q) = \psi(\boldsymbol{\theta}(q)) + \varphi(\boldsymbol{\eta}(p)) - \boldsymbol{\theta}(q) \cdot \boldsymbol{\eta}(p)$.

Consider three points p, q and r in S. Moreover consider two geodesics, the m-geodesic from probability density p to the one q and the e-geodesic from the probability density r to the one q. We know that the m-geodesic is the curve $(1-t)\,\boldsymbol{\eta}(p) + t\,\boldsymbol{\eta}(q)$ with expectation parameters and the e-geodesic is the one $(1-t)\,\boldsymbol{\theta}(r) + t\,\boldsymbol{\theta}(q)$ with natural parameters. Since S is the family of discrete distributions, they are included in S again. The tangent vector of the m-geodesic on q is $\sum_i (\eta_i(q) - \eta_i(p)) \frac{\partial}{\partial \eta_i}$. That of the e-geodesic on q is $\sum_i (\theta_i(q) - \theta_i(r)) \frac{\partial}{\partial \theta_i}$.

If the two vectors are orthogonal, then we get the following equation.

$$\begin{aligned} &\left\langle \sum_i (\eta_i(q) - \eta_i(p)) \frac{\partial}{\partial \eta_i}, \sum_i (\theta_i(q) - \theta_i(r)) \frac{\partial}{\partial \theta_i} \right\rangle \\ &= \sum_{i,j} (\eta_i(q) - \eta_i(p))(\theta_j(q) - \theta_j(r)) \left\langle \frac{\partial}{\partial \eta_i}, \frac{\partial}{\partial \theta_j} \right\rangle \\ &= \sum_i (\eta_i(q) - \eta_i(p))(\theta_i(q) - \theta_i(r)) \\ &= (\boldsymbol{\eta}(q) - \boldsymbol{\eta}(p))(\boldsymbol{\theta}(q) - \boldsymbol{\theta}(r)) = 0. \end{aligned}$$

Here we used the relation $\left\langle \frac{\partial}{\partial \eta_i}, \frac{\partial}{\partial \theta_j} \right\rangle = \delta_{ij}$ (13). We calculate the expression $KL(p, q) + KL(p, r)$.

$$\begin{aligned} &KL(p,q) + KL(q,r) \\ &= \psi(\boldsymbol{\theta}(q)) + \phi(\boldsymbol{\eta}(p)) - \boldsymbol{\theta}(q) \cdot \boldsymbol{\eta}(p) + \psi(\boldsymbol{\theta}(r)) + \phi(\boldsymbol{\eta}(q)) - \boldsymbol{\theta}(r) \cdot \boldsymbol{\eta}(q) \\ &= \psi(\boldsymbol{\theta}(r)) + \phi(\boldsymbol{\eta}(p)) + \psi(\boldsymbol{\theta}(q)) + \phi(\boldsymbol{\eta}(q)) - \boldsymbol{\theta}(q) \cdot \boldsymbol{\eta}(p) - \boldsymbol{\theta}(r) \cdot \boldsymbol{\eta}(q) \\ &= KL(p,r) + \boldsymbol{\theta}(r) \cdot \boldsymbol{\eta}(p) + \boldsymbol{\theta}(q) \cdot \boldsymbol{\eta}(q) - \boldsymbol{\theta}(q) \cdot \boldsymbol{\eta}(p) - \boldsymbol{\theta}(r) \cdot \boldsymbol{\eta}(q) \\ &= KL(p,r) + (\boldsymbol{\theta}(r) - \boldsymbol{\theta}(q)) \cdot (\boldsymbol{\eta}(p) - \boldsymbol{\eta}(q)) = KL(p,r). \end{aligned}$$

We obtain **Pythagorean Theorem**.

Pythagorean Theorem.
Let three points p, q and r be in given discrete distribution. If the m-geodesic from the probability density p to the one q and the e-geodesic from the probability density q to the one r are orthogonal, then the equation $KL(p, r) = KL(p, q) + KL(q, r)$ holds (Figure 1).

Let S and M be discrete distribution and an e-autoparallel submanifold in S, respectively. And let p be a point in S. Consider the closest point q in M to the point p. From Pythagorean Theorem, we easily know that the m-geodesic from the probability density p to the one q and the submanifold M are orthogonal. The point q is called the m-projection from the probability density p to the submanifold M. Next, let M be an m-autoparallel submanifold in S. Consider the closest point q in M to the point p again. By the same way, we know that the e-geodesic from the probability density p to the one q and M are orthogonal. The point q is called the e-projection from the probability density p to the submanifold M. They are called Projection Theorem.

Projection Theorem.
Let S be the family of discrete distributions. Then the following theorems hold.

1. Let M be an e-autoparallel submanifold in S. For any $p \in S$, the point $q \in M$ such that minimizes $KL(p,q)$ is given by the m-projection from the probability density p to the submanifold M (Figure 2 (1)).
2. Let M be an m-autoparallel submanifold in S. For any $p \in S$, the point $q \in M$ such that minimizes $KL(q, p)$ is given by the e-projection from the probability density p to the submanifold M (Figure 2 (2)).

Mixed Coordinate Systems

Consider an exponential family S. Let I be the subset of $\{1,2,...,r\}$. For simplicity, we assume $I = \{1, 2, ..., k\}$, then $I^c = \{k+1, k+2, \ldots, r\}$. We consider the new coordinate system in S, which takes the natural parameter θ_i for $i \in I$ and the expectation parameter η_i for the others. It is called a **mixed coordinate system**. Take a point in S and fix it. We denote it as $(c_1, \cdots, c_{k,} d_{k+1}, \cdots, d_r)$ by the mixed coordinate system. From the relation

$$\left\langle \frac{\partial}{\partial \eta_i}, \frac{\partial}{\partial \theta_j} \right\rangle = \delta_{ij} \quad (13),$$

we know that the spaces $(\theta_1, \cdots, \theta_{k,} d_{k+1}, \cdots, d_r)$ and $(c_1, \cdots, c_{k,} \eta_{k+1}, \cdots, \eta_r)$ are orthogonal on the point $(c_1, \cdots, c_{k,} d_{k+1}, \cdots, d_r)$ (Figure 3).

Figure 1. If the m-geodesic from the probability density p to the one q and the e-geodesic from the one q to the one r are orthogonal, then the equation KL(p, r) = KL(p, q) + KL(q, r) holds.

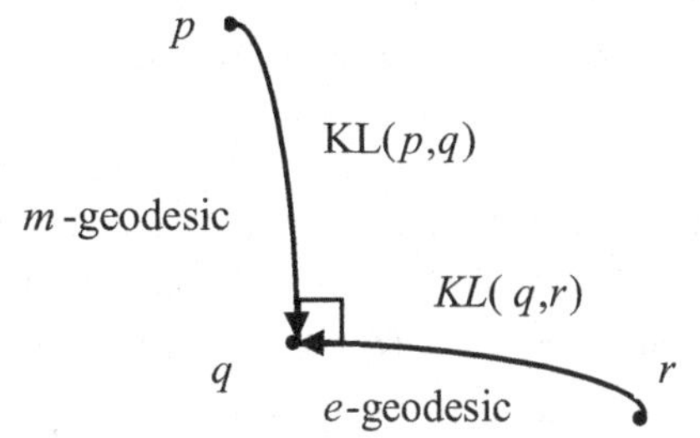

Figure 2. (1) The manifold M is an e-autoparallel submanifold in S. The point q is in the submanifold M. If and only if the m-geodesic from the point p to the point q is orthogonal, then the point q minimizes KL(p, q). (2) The manifold M is an m-autoparallel submanifold in S. The point q is in the submanifold M. If and only if the e-geodesic from the point p to the point q is orthogonal, then the point q minimizes KL(q, p).

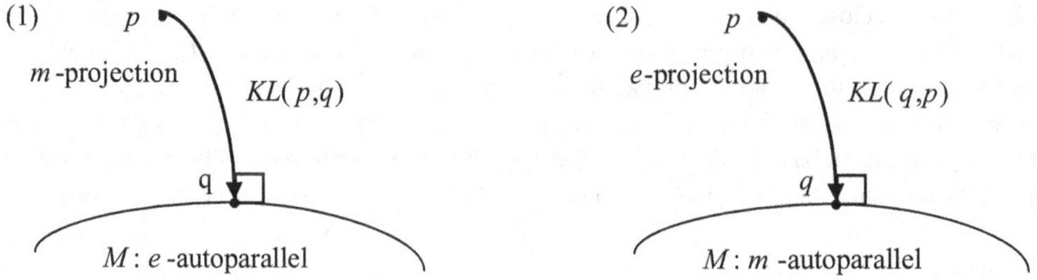

Figure 3. The coordinate systems $(\theta_1,\cdots,\theta_k, d_{k+1},\cdots,d_r)$ *and* $(c_1,\cdots,c_k,\eta_{k+1},\cdots,\eta_r)$ *are orthogonal at the point* $(c_1,\cdots,c_k, d_{k+1},\cdots,d_r)$

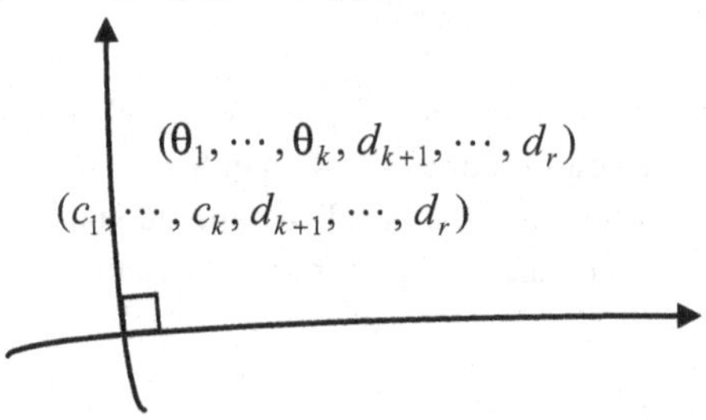

INFORMATION GEOMETRY OF THE COMPLEX_VALUED BOLTZMANN MACHINES

Fisher Metric of the Complex-Valued Boltzmann Machines

The complex-valued Boltzmann Machine with n complex-valued neurons has $n\ (n + 1)$ real-valued parameters $\{ u_{ji}, v_{ji}, u_i, v_i \}_{i<j}$. We can naturally regard all probabilities $p(\mathbf{z};\, \mathbf{w})$ of the complex-valued Boltzmann Machine as the $n\ (n + 1)$ dimensional statistic manifold. We denote the suffices i, ij and so on, which stand for the connection parameters, as α or β. We can describe the connection parameters of the complex-valued Boltzmann Machine as $(\mathbf{u}, \mathbf{v}) = (u_\alpha, v_\alpha)_\alpha$. In this subsection, we calculate Fisher metric of the complex-valued Boltzmann manifold.

We define the logarithmic likelihood of the probability density $p(\mathbf{z};\, \mathbf{w})$ as $l(\mathbf{z};\, \mathbf{w}) = \log p(\mathbf{z};\, \mathbf{w})$. From $p(\mathbf{z};\, \mathbf{w}) = \frac{\exp(-H(\mathbf{z};\mathbf{w}))}{Z(\mathbf{z};\mathbf{w})}$, then we get the equation $l(\mathbf{z};\, \mathbf{w}) = - H(\mathbf{z};\, \mathbf{w}) - \log Z(\mathbf{z};\, \mathbf{w})$. For a function $f(\mathbf{z})$, we denote the expectation $f(\mathbf{z})$ by the probability density $p(\mathbf{z};\, \mathbf{w})$ as $E_W\,[f(\mathbf{z})]$. Fisher metric g of the complex-valued Boltzmann Machine is

$$g\left(\frac{\partial}{\partial s},\frac{\partial}{\partial t}\right) = \mathrm{E}_{\mathrm{W}}\left[\frac{\partial l(\mathbf{z};\mathbf{w})}{\partial s}\frac{\partial l(\mathbf{z};\mathbf{w})}{\partial t}\right],$$

where s and t stand for the connection parameters. From now on, we denote Fisher metric as $g^{uv}_{jk,l} = \frac{\partial l(\mathbf{z};\mathbf{w})}{\partial s}\frac{\partial l(\mathbf{z};\mathbf{w})}{\partial t}$ and so on. Moreover we define as follows:

$$R_{jk} \equiv \mathrm{Re}(z_j\bar{z}_k), R_j \equiv \mathrm{Re}(z_j),$$
$$I_{jk} \equiv \mathrm{Im}(z_j\bar{z}_k), I_j \equiv \mathrm{Im}(z_j).$$

First we prove two following lemmas.

Lemma 1.

$$H(\mathbf{z};\mathbf{w}) = -\sum_{\alpha}(R_\alpha u_\alpha + I_\alpha v_\alpha).$$

Proof.

$$\begin{aligned} H(\mathbf{z};\mathbf{w}) &= -\frac{1}{2}\mathrm{Re}(\sum_{i<j}(x_i - y_i\sqrt{-1})(u_{ij}+v_{ij}\sqrt{-1})(x_j+y_j\sqrt{-1})) \\ &\quad -\frac{1}{2}\mathrm{Re}(\sum_{i<j}(x_j - y_j\sqrt{-1})(u_{ij}-v_{ij}\sqrt{-1})(x_i+y_i\sqrt{-1})) \\ &\quad -\mathrm{Re}(\sum_{i}(x_i - y_i\sqrt{-1})(u_i+v_i\sqrt{-1})) \\ &= -\sum_{i<j}\left((x_ix_j+y_iy_j)u_{ij}+(x_jy_i-x_iy_j)v_{ij}\right)-\sum_i(x_iu_i+y_iv_i) \\ &= -\sum_{i<j}(R_{ij}u_{ij}+I_{ij}v_{ij})-\sum_i(R_iu_i+I_iv_i) \\ &= -\sum_{\alpha}(R_\alpha u_\alpha + I_\alpha v_\alpha). \end{aligned}$$

Lemma 2.

$$\frac{1}{Z(\mathbf{w})}\frac{\partial Z(\mathbf{w})}{\partial u_\alpha} = \mathrm{E}_{\mathrm{W}}[R_\alpha],$$
$$\frac{1}{Z(\mathbf{w})}\frac{\partial Z(\mathbf{w})}{\partial v_\alpha} = \mathrm{E}_{\mathrm{W}}[I_\alpha].$$

Proof.

We only prove the first equation of the continuous complex-valued Boltzmann Machine. We can prove the other cases by the same way. First we calculate the expression $\frac{\partial Z(\mathbf{w})}{\partial u_\alpha}$.

$$\frac{\partial Z(\mathbf{w})}{\partial u_\alpha} = \frac{\partial}{\partial u_\alpha}\int \exp(-H(\mathbf{z};\mathbf{w}))d\mathbf{z} = \int R_\alpha \exp(-H(\mathbf{z};\mathbf{w}))d\mathbf{z}.$$

Next we calculate the expression $\frac{1}{Z(\mathbf{w})}\frac{\partial Z(\mathbf{w})}{\partial u_\alpha}$.

$$\frac{1}{Z(\mathbf{w})}\frac{\partial Z(\mathbf{w})}{\partial u_\alpha} = \int R_\alpha \frac{\exp(-H(\mathbf{z};\mathbf{w}))}{Z(\mathbf{w})}d\mathbf{z} = \int R_\alpha p(\mathbf{z};\mathbf{w})d\mathbf{z} = \mathrm{E}_{\mathrm{W}}[R_\alpha].$$

We complete the proof of Lemma 2.

At last we calculate Fisher metric of the complex-valued Boltzmann Machine.

Theorem 1.

$$g^{uu}_{\alpha,\beta} = \mathrm{E}_{\mathrm{W}}[R_\alpha R_\beta] - \mathrm{E}_{\mathrm{W}}[R_\alpha]\,\mathrm{E}_{\mathrm{W}}[R_\beta],$$

$$g^{uv}_{\alpha,\beta} = \mathrm{E}_{\mathrm{W}}[R_\alpha I_\beta] - \mathrm{E}_{\mathrm{W}}[R_\alpha]\,\mathrm{E}_{\mathrm{W}}[I_\beta],$$

$$g^{vu}_{\alpha,\beta} = \mathrm{E}_{\mathrm{W}}[I_\alpha R_\beta] - \mathrm{E}_{\mathrm{W}}[I_\alpha]\,\mathrm{E}_{\mathrm{W}}[R_\beta],$$

$$g^{vv}_{\alpha,\beta} = \mathrm{E}_{\mathrm{W}}[I_\alpha I_\beta] - \mathrm{E}_{\mathrm{W}}[I_\alpha]\,\mathrm{E}_{\mathrm{W}}[I_\beta].$$

Proof.

We only prove the second equation. We can prove the other equations by the same way. From Lemma 1, Lemma 2 and the equation $l(\mathbf{z};\mathbf{w}) = -H(\mathbf{z};\mathbf{w}) - \log Z(\mathbf{z};\mathbf{w})$, we get the following equations.

$$\frac{\partial l(\mathbf{z};\mathbf{w})}{\partial u_\alpha} = R_\alpha - \frac{1}{Z(\mathbf{z};\mathbf{w})}\frac{\partial Z(\mathbf{z};\mathbf{w})}{\partial u_\alpha} = R_\alpha - \mathrm{E}_{\mathrm{W}}[R_\alpha],$$

$$\frac{\partial l(\mathbf{z};\mathbf{w})}{\partial v_\beta} = I_\beta - \frac{1}{Z(\mathbf{z};\mathbf{w})}\frac{\partial Z(\mathbf{z};\mathbf{w})}{\partial v_\beta} = I_\beta - \mathrm{E}_{\mathrm{W}}[I_\beta].$$

We calculate Fisher metric $g^{uu}_{\alpha,\beta}$.

$$g^{uu}_{\alpha,\beta} = \mathrm{E}_{\mathrm{w}}\left[\frac{\partial l(\mathbf{z};\mathbf{w})}{\partial u_\alpha}\frac{\partial l(\mathbf{z};\mathbf{w})}{\partial v_\beta}\right] = \mathrm{E}_{\mathrm{w}}[(R_\alpha - \mathrm{E}_{\mathrm{w}}[R_\alpha])(I_\beta - \mathrm{E}_{\mathrm{w}}[I_\beta])]$$
$$= \mathrm{E}_{\mathrm{w}}[R_\alpha I_\beta] - \mathrm{E}_{\mathrm{w}}[R_\alpha]\mathrm{E}_{\mathrm{w}}[I_\beta].$$

We complete the proof of the second equation.

Consider the discrete complex-valued Boltzmann Machine with $K = 2$. It is equivalent to the real-valued Boltzmann Machine and the parameter **v** is in vain. In Theorem 1, we get the equations $g^{uv}_{\alpha,\beta} = g^{vu}_{\alpha,\beta} = g^{vv}_{\alpha,\beta} = 0$ and $g^{uu}_{ijkl} = \mathrm{E}_{\mathrm{W}}[x_i x_j x_k x_l] - \mathrm{E}_{\mathrm{W}}[x_i x_j]\,\mathrm{E}_{\mathrm{W}}[x_k x_l]$. It equals the result for the real-valued Boltzmann Machine by Amari (1992a).

Potential Functions and Parameters of the Complex-Valued Boltzmann Machine

We can describe the probability density of the complex-valued Boltzmann Machine as

$$p(\mathbf{z};\mathbf{w}) = \exp\Big(\sum_\alpha (R_\alpha u_\alpha + I_\alpha v_\alpha) - \log Z(\mathbf{w})\Big).$$

We can regard the parameter $(\mathbf{u}, \mathbf{v})$ as the natural parameter of the complex-valued Boltzmann manifold M. So we find that the complex-valued Boltzmann manifold is an exponential family.

We denote the expectation parameter as $(\mathbf{u}^*, \mathbf{v}^*)$; $u^*_\alpha = \mathrm{E}_{\mathrm{W}}[R_\alpha]$ and $v^*_\alpha = \mathrm{E}_{\mathrm{W}}[I_\alpha]$. And we write $\mathbf{w}^* = \mathbf{u}^* + \mathbf{v}^*\sqrt{-1}$. From the definition (1) of the exponential family, we know the equation $\psi(\mathbf{w}) = \log Z(\mathbf{w})$. From the definition (11) of the potential function φ and Lemma 1, we calculate the potential function $\varphi(\mathbf{w})$, where we can regard φ as the function of the natural parameter $\mathbf{w}$, not the expectation parameter $\mathbf{w}^*$.

$$\varphi(\mathbf{w}) = \mathrm{E}_{\mathrm{W}}[\log p(\mathbf{z};\mathbf{w})] = -\mathrm{E}_{\mathrm{W}}[H(\mathbf{z};\mathbf{w})] - \log Z(\mathbf{w}).$$

From the relations between the natural parameter and the expectation parameter, we know the equations

$$\frac{\partial s^*_\alpha}{\partial t_\beta} = g^{st}_{\alpha,\beta} \text{ and } \frac{\partial s_\alpha}{\partial t^*_\beta} = g^{\alpha,\beta}_{st},$$

where the parameters s and t stand for u or v. And from the relations (3) and (12) between the potential functions and the parameters, we know

$$s^*_\alpha = \frac{\partial \psi(\mathbf{w})}{\partial s_\alpha} \text{ and } s_\alpha = \frac{\partial \phi(\mathbf{w})}{\partial s^*_\alpha},$$

where the parameter s stands for u or v.

We denote Fisher metric of the expectation parameters $\frac{\partial}{\partial s^*_\alpha}$ and $\frac{\partial}{\partial t^*_\beta}$ of the complex-valued Boltzmann Machine as $g^{\alpha,\beta}_{st}$. From (14), we know that the matrix $(g^{\alpha,\beta}_{st})$ is the inverse matrix of $(g^{st}_{\alpha,\beta})$.

Information Geometric Structure of the Complex-Valued Boltzmann Manifold

In this subsection, we only deal with Boltzmann Machines with discrete complex-valued neurons. If we hope to manage those with continuous ones, we need the infinite version of information geometry (Piston & Sempi, 1995; Piston & Rogantin, 1999).

Let V be the set of all states of the complex-valued Boltzmann Machine. And let S be the stochastic manifold of all probability distributions on V. Since V is a finite set, S is the family of discrete distributions.

Amari et al. (1992a) proved the following theorem in the real-valued Boltzmann manifold.

Theorem 2.
The connection parameters of higher order Boltzmann Machine are the natural parameters of S. And some of them are the natural parameters of Boltzmann manifold.

Theorem 2 implies that the real-valued Boltzmann manifold is an e-autoparallel submanifold in S. But in the complex-valued Boltzmann manifold, it is hard to take the explicit natural parameters of S, because we hardly define higher order Boltzmann Machines. So it is more difficult to prove the complex-valued version of Theorem 2.

The following theorem is effective for proving the complex-valued version of Theorem 2 (Amari & Nagaoka, 2000).

Theorem 3.
The submanifold in an exponential family is e-autoparallel if and only if it is an exponential family.

From Theorem 3, we know the following theorem.

Theorem 4.
The complex-valued Boltzmann manifold is an exponential family and an e-autoparallel submanifold in S.

We prove the following theorem, which is the complex-valued version of Theorem 2.

Theorem 5.
There exists $K^n - n(n+1) - 1$ dimensional parameter $\tilde{\mathbf{w}}$ satisfying the following conditions (Figure 4).

1. The parameter $(\mathbf{w}, \tilde{\mathbf{w}})$ is a natural parameter and for any $p(\mathbf{z}; \mathbf{w}, \tilde{\mathbf{w}}) \in S$ there exist F_j and $\tilde{\psi}$ such that $p(\mathbf{z}; \mathbf{w}, \tilde{\mathbf{w}}) = \exp\left(\sum_\alpha (R_\alpha u_\alpha + I_\alpha v_\alpha) + \sum F_j(\mathbf{z})\tilde{w}_j - \tilde{\psi}(\mathbf{w}, \tilde{\mathbf{w}})\right)$.
2. The probability density $p(\mathbf{z}; \mathbf{w}, \mathbf{0})$ is the complex-valued Boltzmann manifold M.
3. $\tilde{\psi}(\mathbf{w}, \mathbf{0}) = \log Z(\mathbf{w})$.

Proof.
Since the complex-valued Boltzmann machine has K^n states, we know that the manifold S is a $K^n - 1$ dimensional manifold.

We know that the statistical manifolds S and M are exponential families. From Theorem 3, M is an e-autoparallel submanifold in S and an affine subspace of S in the natural coordinate system. We take the affine subspace $\tilde{M}$ of S satisfying the following conditions.

1. The affine subspace $\tilde{M}$ includes the origin of M in the natural coordinate system.
2. The intersection of M and $\tilde{M}$ is just a point.

So the intersection is the origin of M. We give $\tilde{M}$ an affine coordinate system whose origin is that of M. We denote the affine coordinate system of $\tilde{M}$ as $\tilde{\mathbf{w}}$. Then the parameter $(\mathbf{w}, \tilde{\mathbf{w}})$ is a natural parameter of S. Therefore for any $p(\mathbf{z}; \mathbf{w}, \tilde{\mathbf{w}}) \in S$, there exist F_j, C and $\tilde{\psi}$ such that

$$p(\mathbf{z}; \mathbf{w}, \tilde{\mathbf{w}}) = \exp\left(\sum_{\alpha}(R_\alpha u_\alpha + I_\alpha v_\alpha) + \sum_j F_j(\mathbf{z})\tilde{w}_j + C(\mathbf{z}) - \tilde{\psi}(\mathbf{w}, \tilde{\mathbf{w}})\right).$$

From the way to take the coordinate system, we know that the probability density $p(\mathbf{z}; \mathbf{w}, \mathbf{0})$ is the complex-valued manifold M. We set $\tilde{\mathbf{w}} = \mathbf{0}$, then we get $p(\mathbf{z}; \mathbf{w}, \mathbf{0}) = \exp\left(\sum_{\alpha}(R_\alpha u_\alpha + I_\alpha v_\alpha) + C(\mathbf{z}) - \tilde{\psi}(\mathbf{w}, \mathbf{0})\right)$. Since this must equal to the equation $p(\mathbf{z}; \mathbf{w}) = \exp\left(\sum_{\alpha}(R_\alpha u_\alpha + I_\alpha v_\alpha) - \log Z(\mathbf{w})\right)$, we obtain the equations $C(\mathbf{z}) \equiv 0$ and $\tilde{\psi}(\mathbf{w}, \mathbf{0}) = \log Z(\mathbf{w})$. We complete the proof.

Complex-Valued Boltzmann Learning

Consider the problem to find the complex-valued Boltzmann Machine $p(\mathbf{z}; \mathbf{w}) \in M$ closest to a given probability density $q(\mathbf{z})$. Ackley, Hinton and Sejnowski (1985) solved the real-valued version of that. It is called Boltzmann learning. We can regard the problem as finding $\mathbf{w}$ minimizing $KL(q(\mathbf{z}), p(\mathbf{z}; \mathbf{w}))$. In the other word, the required probability density $p(\mathbf{z})$ is the m-projection from the probability density $q(\mathbf{z})$ to the submanifold M.

We derive the learning rule, which we call the complex-valued Boltzmann learning, by steepest gradient descent.

$$\Delta u_\alpha = -\varepsilon \frac{\partial KL(q(\mathbf{z}), p(\mathbf{z}; \mathbf{w}))}{\partial u_\alpha},$$

$$\Delta v_\alpha = -\varepsilon \frac{\partial KL(q(\mathbf{z}), p(\mathbf{z}; \mathbf{w}))}{\partial v_\alpha}.$$

Figure 4. There exists an coordinate system $(\mathbf{w}, \tilde{\mathbf{w}})$ of S such that $(\mathbf{w}, \mathbf{0})$ express the submanifold M and the axes $\mathbf{w}$ and $\tilde{\mathbf{w}}$ are orthogonal

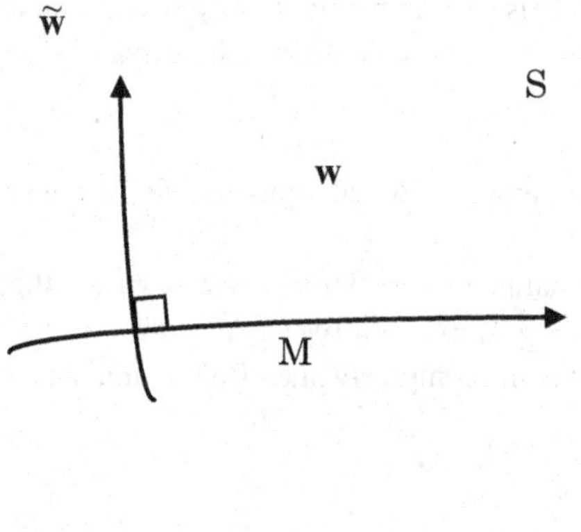

We calculate the expression Δu_α.

$$\Delta u_\alpha = -\varepsilon \frac{\partial}{\partial u_\alpha} \sum_{\mathbf{z}\in V} q(\mathbf{z}) \log \frac{q(\mathbf{z})}{p(\mathbf{z};\mathbf{w})} = \varepsilon \sum_{\mathbf{z}\in V} q(\mathbf{z}) \frac{\partial l(\mathbf{z};\mathbf{w})}{\partial u_\alpha}$$
$$= \varepsilon \sum_{\mathbf{z}\in V} q(\mathbf{z})(R_\alpha - E_{\mathbf{w}}[R_\alpha]) = \varepsilon\,(E_q[R_\alpha] - E_{\mathbf{w}}[R_\alpha]).$$

where $E_q[\bullet]$ stands for the expectation by $q(\mathbf{z})$. By the same way, we get the equation

$$\Delta v_\alpha = \varepsilon\,(E_q[I_\alpha] - E_{\mathbf{w}}[I_\alpha]).$$

Boltzmann learning depends on the coordinate system. Amari (1998) proposed the learning method not depending on the coordinate systems. It is called natural gradient descent. It is also effective for the complex-valued Boltzmann Machines. The complex-valued version of the natural gradient descent is as follows:

$$\Delta u_\alpha = -\varepsilon \sum_\beta (g_{uu}^{\alpha,\beta}(E_q[R_\beta] - E_{\mathbf{w}}[R_\beta]) + g_{uv}^{\alpha,\beta}(E_q[I_\beta] - E_{\mathbf{w}}[I_\beta])),$$

$$\Delta v_\alpha = -\varepsilon \sum_\beta (g_{vu}^{\alpha,\beta}(E_q[R_\beta] - E_{\mathbf{w}}[R_\beta]) + g_{vv}^{\alpha,\beta}(E_q[I_\beta] - E_{\mathbf{w}}[I_\beta])).$$

Amari proved that natural gradient descent does not depend on the coordinate systems by using Theorem 2 and the mixed coordinate system. We can also prove that the complex-valued version of natural gradient descent does not depend on the coordinate systems by using Theorem 5 and the mixed coordinate system.

The em Algorithm for the Complex-Valued Boltzmann Machine with Hidden Neurons

When then complex-valued Boltzmann Machines have hidden neurons, the *em* algorithm is effective (Amari et al., 1992a). When the complex-valued Boltzmann Machine has the complex-valued discrete neurons, the number of states of the complex-valued Boltzmann Machine is finite. Therefore the dimension of the manifold S is finite. But when the complex-valued Boltzmann Machine has the continuous complex-valued neurons, the number of states of the complex-valued Boltzmann Machine is infinite and the dimension of the manifold S is infinite. Therefore we need the infinite-version of information geometry for S. So we just deal with the discrete type of complex-valued Boltzmann Machines. We divide the state $\mathbf{z}$ of the complex-valued Boltzmann Machine into two states $(\mathbf{Z}^V, \mathbf{Z}^H)$, which consist of the state $\mathbf{Z}^V$ of the visible neurons and the state $\mathbf{Z}^H$ of the invisible neurons. We want to find the parameter $\mathbf{w}$ such that $p(\mathbf{Z}^V; \mathbf{w})$ is closest to a given probability density $q(\mathbf{Z}^V)$ for the visible states. In the other words, we want to find the parameter $\mathbf{w}$ minimizing $KL(q(\mathbf{Z}^V), p(\mathbf{Z}^V; \mathbf{w}))$.

We define the data manifold D as

$$D = \left\{ r(\mathbf{z}); \sum_{\mathbf{z}^H} r(\mathbf{z}) = q(\mathbf{z}^V) \right\}.$$

For any probability densities $r(\mathbf{z})$ and $r'(\mathbf{z})$ pertaining to D, the following equation holds.

$$\sum_{\mathbf{z}^H} (1-t) r(\mathbf{z}) + t\, r'(\mathbf{z}) = (1-t) \sum_{\mathbf{z}^H} r(\mathbf{z}) + t \sum_{\mathbf{z}^H} r'(\mathbf{z})$$
$$= (1-t) q(\mathbf{z}^V) + t\, q(\mathbf{z}^V) = q(\mathbf{z}^V).$$

So the m-geodesic $(1-t)\, r(\mathbf{z}) + t\, r'(\mathbf{z})$ from the probability density $r(\mathbf{z})$ to the one $r'(\mathbf{z})$ belongs to D again. Therefore the stochastic manifold D is the m-autoparallel submanifold in S. The *em* algorithm starts from any initial parameter $\mathbf{w}$ and repeats two steps, which are called e-step and m-step, until the convergence (Figure 5).

Figure 5. e-step is the e-projection from the point of M to D. The e-projection from the point p to D is the point r of M such that the e-geodesic from p to r and D are orthogonal. m-step is the m-projection from the point of D to M. The m-projection from the point p to M is the point r of D such that the m-geodesic from p to r and M are orthogonal.

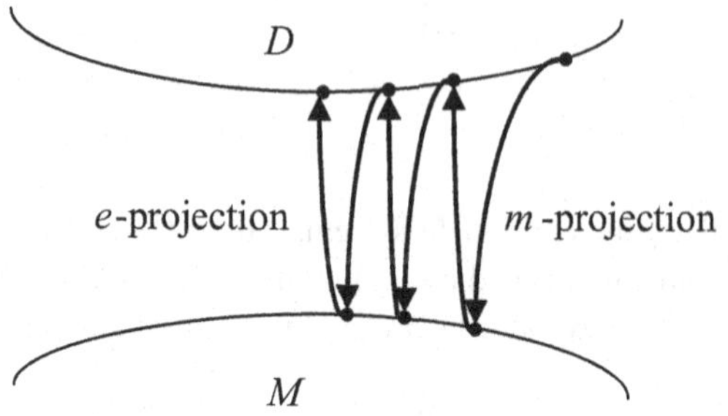

- ***e*-step:** We find the *e*-projection $r(\mathbf{z})$ from the probability density $p(\mathbf{z};\ \mathbf{w})$ to the data manifold D. We can obtain $r(\mathbf{z})$ by $r(\mathbf{z}) = q(\mathbf{Z}^V)\, p(\mathbf{Z}^H \mid \mathbf{Z}^V;\ \mathbf{w})$.
- ***m*-step:** We find the *m*-projection from the probability density $r(\mathbf{z})$ to the complex-valued Boltzmann manifold M and denote it as $p(\mathbf{z};\ \mathbf{w})$. The algorithm of *m*-step is equivalent to the complex-valued Boltzmann learning.

CONCLUSION

In this chapter, we investigated the complex-valued Boltzmann Machine in the view of information geometry. We revealed the following results.

1. Fisher metric of the complex-valued Boltzmann manifold.
2. The complex-valued Boltzmann manifold is an exponential family.

Moreover we found the following results about the discrete complex-valued Boltzmann manifold.

1. There exist natural parameters of S including the natural parameter of M.
2. The complex-valued Boltzmann manifold is an *e*-autoparallel submanifold in S.
3. Natural gradient descent learning of the complex-valued Boltzmann Machine does not depend on the coordinate systems.
4. The *em* algorithm for the complex-valued Boltzmann Machine

They are rather similar to the real-valued Boltzmann Machine. There are some essential different points.

1. S is not higher order Boltzmann Machine in the complex-valued Boltzmann Machine.
2. In the continuous complex-valued Boltzmann manifold, S is an infinite dimension stochastic manifold.

FUTURE RESEARCH DIRECTIONS

The *em* algorithm of complex-valued Boltzmann Machines with continuous phasor neurons has not been settled yet. It will require the infinite-dimensional version of information geometries. For infinite-dimensional information geometries, see Piston and Sempi (1995) or Piston and Rogantin(1999). Information geometries of rotor neural networks also are future works.

Moreover Amari applied information geometry for feed-forward neural networks (Amari, 1992b). It should be applied for the following feed-forward complex-valued or higher-dimensional neural networks:

1. Real-Imaginary type of Complex-valued Neural Networks (Benvenuto & Piazza, 1992; Nitta & Furuya, 1991; Nitta, 1997)
2. Amplitude-Phase type Complex-valued Neural Networks (Hirose, 1992)
3. Three-dimensional Neural Networks by Quaternion Numbers (Arena, Fortuna, Muscato & Xibilia, 1998)
4. Three-dimensional Rotation Neural Networks (Nitta & Garis, 1992; Nitta, 1993a; Nitta, 1994; Nitta, 2006)
5. Three-dimensional Neural Networks by Vector Product (Nitta, 1993b; Nitta, 1993c; Nitta, 1993d)
6. Quaternion Neural Networks (Nitta, 1995; Nitta, 1996)
7. High-dimensional Neural Networks by Linear Connections of Matrices (Kobayashi, Muramatsu & Yamazaki, 2003)
8. Clifford Networks (Pearson, 2003)

The quantum version of information geometry has also been proposed (Amari et al., 1992a). It may be applied to the quantum version of neural networks.

REFERENCES

Ackley, D. H., Hinton, G. E., & Sejnowski, T., J. (1985). A learning algorithm for boltzmann machines. *Cognitive Science, 9*, 147-169.

Amari, S. (1991). Dualistic geometry of the manifold of higher-order neurons. *Neural Networks, 4*(4), 443-451.

Amari, S., Kurata, K., & Nagaoka, H. (1992a). Information geometry of boltzmann machines. *IEEE Transactions on Neural Networks, 3*(2), 260-271.

Amari, S. (1992b). Information geometry of neural networks. *IEICE Transactions on Fundamentals, E75-A*(5), 531-536.

Amari, S. (1995). Information geometry of the EM and em algorithms for neural networks. *Neural Networks, 8*(9), 1379-1408.

Amari, S. (1998). Natural gradient works efficiently in learning. *Neural Computation, 10*(2), 251-276.

Amari, S., & Nagaoka, H. (2000). *Methods of information geometry.* AMS & Oxford University Press.

Aoki, H. (2003). Applications of complex-valued neural networks for image processing. In A. Hirose (Ed.), *Complex-Valued Neural Networks: Theories and Applications,* (pp. 181-204). USA, World Scientific Pub Co Inc.

Arena, P., Fortuna, L., Muscato, C., & Xibilia M. G. (1998). *Neural networks in multidimensional domains: fundamentals and new trends in modelling and control* (Lecture notes in control and information sciences), Springer-Verlag.

Aoki, H. (2003). Applications of complex-valued neural networks for image processing. In A. Hirose (Ed.), *Complex-Valued Neural Networks: Theories and Applications,* (pp. 181-204). USA, World Scientific Pub Co Inc.

Baldi, P., & Hormik, K. (1989). Neural networks and principal component analysis, learning from examples without local minima. *Neural Networks, 2*(1), 53-58.

Benvenuto, N., & Piazza, F. (1992). On the complex backpropagation algorithm. *IEEE Transactions on Signal Processing, 40*(4), 967-969.

Cook, J. (1989). The mean-field theory of a Q-state neural networks. *Journal of Physics A: Mathematical and General, 22*(12), 2057-2067.

Fukumizu, K., & Amari, S. (2000). Local minima and plateaus in hierarchical structures of multilayer perceptrons. *Neural Networks, 13*(3), 317-327.

Gislen, L., Peterson, C., & Sodeberg, B. (1992). Rotor Neurons: Basic Formalism and Dynamics. *Neural Computation, 4*, 737-745.

Hirose, A. (1992). Continuous complex-valued back-propagation learning. *Electronics Letters, 28*(20), 1854-1855.

Jankowski, S., Lozowski, A., & Zurada, J. M. (1996). Complex-valued multistate neural associative memory. *IEEE Transactions on Neural Networks, 7*(6), 1491-1496.

Kobayashi, M., Muramatsu, J., & Yamazaki, H. (2003). Construction of high-dimensional neural networks by linear connections of matrices. *Electronics and Communications in Japan, Part 3, 86*(11), 38-45.

Kobayashi, M., & Yamazaki, H. (2003). Information geometry of complex-valued boltzmann machines. (in Japanese) *IEICE Transactions on Fundamentals of Electronics, Communications and Computer Sciences, J87-A*(8), 1093-1101.

Kuroe, Y. (2003). A model of complex-valued associative memories and its dynamics. In A. Hirose (Ed.), *Complex-Valued Neural Networks: Theories and Applications,* (pp. 57-80). USA, World Scientific Pub Co Inc.

Lee, D. L. (2001). Improving the capacity of complex-valued neural networks with a modified gradient descent learning rule. *IEEE Transactions on Neural Networks, 12*(2), 439-443.

Lee, D. L. (2003). Complex-valued neural associative memories: Network stability and learning algorithm. In A. Hirose (Ed.), *Complex-Valued Neural Networks: Theories and Applications,* (pp. 29-55). USA, World Scientific Pub Co Inc.

McEliece, R. J., Posner, E. C., Rodemich, E. R., & Venkatech, E. R. (1987). The capacity of the Hopfield associative memory. *IEEE Transactions on Information Theory, 33*(4), 461-482.

Nakamura, Y., & Munakata, T. (1995). Neural network model composed of multidirectional spin neurons. *Physical Review E, 51*(2), 1538-1546.

Nemoto, I., & Kubono, M. (1996). Complex associative memory. *Neural Networks, 9*(2), 253-261.

Nemoto, I. (2003). Complex associative memory and complex single neuron models. In A. Hirose (Ed.), *Complex-Valued Neural Networks: Theories and Applications,* (pp. 107-130). USA, World Scientific Pub Co Inc.

Nitta, T., & Furuya, T. (1991). A complex back-propagation learning (in Japanese). *Transactions of Information Processing Society in Japan, 132*(10), 1319-1329.

Nitta, T., & Garis, H. D. (1992). A 3D vector version of the back-propagation algorithm. *Proceedings of IEEE/INNS International Joint Conference on Neural Networks, 2*, 511-516.

Nitta, T. (1993a). A three-dimensional back-propagation. *Proceedings of INNS World Congress on Neural Networks, 3*, 572-575.

Nitta, T. (1993b). A back-propagation algorithm for neural networks based on 3D vector product. *Proceedings of IEEE/INNS International Joint Conference on Neural Networks, 1*, 589-592.

Nitta, T. (1993c). Proposal of neural networks based on vector product. *Proceedings of CIE/IEEE International Conference on Neural Networks and Signal Processing,* (pp. 397-402).

Nitta, T. (1993d). An extension of the back-propagation algorithm to three dimensions by vector product. *Proceedings of the 5th IEEE International Conference on Tools with Artificial Intelligence,* (pp. 460-461).

Nitta, T. (1994). Generalization ability of the three-dimensional back-propagation network. *Proceedings of IEEE International Conference on Neural Networks, 5*, 2895-2900.

Nitta, T. (1995). A quaternion version of the back-propagation algorithm. *Proceedings of IEEE International Conference on Neural Networks, 5*, 2753-2756.

Nitta, T. (1996). An extension of the back-propagation algorithm to quaternion. *Proceedings of International Conference on Neural Information Processing, 1*, 247-250.

Nitta, T. (1997). An extension of the back-propagation algorithm to complex numbers. *Neural Networks, 10*(8), 1391-1415.

Nitta, T. (2006). Three-dimensional vector valued neural network and its generalization abilities. *Neural Information Processing – Letters and Reviews, 10*(10), 237-242.

Noest, A. J. (1988a). Phasor neural networks. In D. Z. Anderson (Ed.), *Neural Information Processing Systems,* (pp. 584-591). New York, AIP.

Noest, A. J. (1988b). Discrete-state phasor neural networks. *Physical Review A, 38*(4), 2196-2199.

Parra, L., & Deco, G. (1995). Continuous boltzmann machine with rotor neurons. *Neural Networks, 8*(3), 375-385.

Pearson, J. (2003). Clifford Networks. In A. Hirose (Ed.), *Complex-Valued Neural Networks: Theories and Applications,* (pp. 81-106). USA, World Scientific Pub Co Inc.

Pistone, G., & Sempi, C. (1995). An infinite-dimensional geometric structure on the space of all the probability measures equivalent to a given one. *The Annals of Statistics, 23*(5), 1543-1561.

Pistone, G., & Rogantin, M. P. (1999). The exponential statistical manifold: mean parameters, orthogonality and space transformations. *Bernoulli, 5*(4), 721-760.

Zemel, R. S., Williams, C. K. I., & Mozer, M. C. (1993). Directional unit boltzmann machines. *Advances in Neural Information Processing Systems 5,* 172-179. San Francisco, CA. USA: Morgan Kaufmann Publishers Inc.

Zemel, R. S., Williams, C. K. I., & Mozer, M. C. (1995). Lending direction to neural networks. *Neural Networks, 8*(4), 503-5Zurada, J. M., Cloete, J., & Poel, E. (1996). Generalized hopfield networks for associative memories with multi-valued stable states. *Neurocomputing, 13*, 135-149.

ADDITIONAL READING

Some advanced books and articles about information geometry or complex-valued neural networks are introduced.

Amari, S. (1987). Differential geometry of a parametric family of invertible learner systems – Riemannian metric, dual affine connections and divergence. *Mathematical Systems Theory, 20*, 53-82.

Amari, S. (1991). Dualistic geometry of the Manifold of higher-order neurons. *Neural Networks, 4*(4), 443-451.

Amari, S., Kurata, K., & Nagaoka, H. (1992). Information geometry of boltzmann machines. *IEEE Transactions on Neural Networks, 3*(2), 260-271.

Amari, S.(1992). Information geometry of neural networks. *IEICE Transactions on Fundamentals, E75-A*(5), 531-536.

Amari, S. (1994). Information geometry and manifolds of neural network. In Grossberger, P., & Nadal, J., P., *Statistical Physics to Statistical Inference and Back,* (pp. 113-138). Kluwer Academic Publishers.

Amari, S. (1995). Information geometry of the EM and em algorithms for neural networks. *Neural Networks, 8*(9), 1379-1408.

Amari, S. (1995). The EM algorithm and Information geometry in neural network learnings. *Neural Computation, 7*(1), 13-18.

Amari, S. (1998). Natural gradient works efficiently in learning. *Neural Computation, 10*(2), 251-276.

Amari, S., & Nagaoka, H. (2000). *Methods of information geometry.* AMS & Oxford University Press.

Amari, S. -I., Barndorff-Nielsen, O. E., Kass, R. E., Lauritzen, S. L., & Rao, C. R. (1987). Differential Geometry in Statistical Inference. In Gupta, S. S. (Ed.), *Institute of Mathematical Statistics, Lecture Notes-Monograph Series.* Hayward, California.

Arena, P., Fortuna, L., Muscato, C., & Xibilia M. G. (1998). Neural networks in multidimensional domains: Fundamentals and new trends in modelling and control (Lecture notes in control and information sciences). Springer-Verlag.

Hirose, A. (Ed.), (2004). Complex-Valued Neural Networks: Theories and Applications. *Series on Innovative Intelligence, 5.* World Scientific Pub Co Inc.

Hirose, A., (2006). *Complex-valued Neural Networks, Studies in Computational Intelligence.* Springer-Verlag New York Inc.

Murray, M. K., & Rice, J. W., (1993). Differential Geometry and Statistics. *Monographs on Statistics and Applied Probability 48.* Chapman & Hall.

Chapter II
Complex-Valued Neural Network and Inverse Problems

Takehiko Ogawa
Takushoku University, Japan

ABSTRACT

Network inversion solves inverse problems to estimate cause from result using a multilayer neural network. The original network inversion has been applied to usual multilayer neural networks with real-valued inputs and outputs. The solution by a neural network with complex-valued inputs and outputs is necessary for general inverse problems with complex numbers. In this chapter, we introduce the complex-valued network inversion method to solve inverse problems with complex numbers. In general, difficulties attributable to the ill-posedness of inverse problems appear. Regularization is used to solve this ill-posedness by adding some conditions to the solution. In this chapter, we also explain regularization for complex-valued network inversion.

INTRODUCTION

It is necessary to solve inverse problems for estimating causes from observed results in various engineering fields. In particular, inverse problems have been studied in the field of mathematical science (Groetsch, 1993). The inverse problem determines the inner mechanisms or causes of an observed phenomenon. The cause is estimated from the fixed model and the given result in the inverse problem, while the result is determined from the given cause by using a certain fixed mathematical model in the forward problem. As a solution of inverse problems, the neural network based method has been proposed while other method such as the statistical method (Kaipio & Somersalo, 2005) and parametric method (Aster, Borchers, & Thurber, 2005) have also been studied.

The idea of inverting network mapping was proposed by Williams (1986). Then, Linden and Kindermann proposed a method of network inversion (Linden & Kindermann, 1989). Also, the algorithms and applications of network inversion are summarized by Jansen et al. (1999). In this method, inverse problems are solved by the inverse use of the input-output relation of trained multilayer neural networks. In other words, the corresponding input is estimated from the provided output via fixed weights, after finding the forward relation by network training. The direction of the input-output relation between the training and the inverse estimation is important in this method. The estimation process in multilayer neural networks is considered from the viewpoint of forward and inverse problems. The usual estimation process of multilayer neural networks provides a solution for forward problems because the network estimates the output from the input provided by the forward relation obtained in the training. On the other hand, we can solve inverse problems using multilayer neural networks that learn the forward relation by estimating the input from the given output inversely. Network inversion has been applied to actual problems; e.g., medical image processing (Valova, Kameyama, & Kosugi, 1995), robot control (Lu & Ito, 1995; Ogawa, Matsuura, & Kanada, 2005), optimization problems, and so on (Murray, Heg, & Pohlhammer, 1993; Ogawa, Jitsukawa, Kanada, Mori, & Sakata, 2002; Takeuchi & Kosugi, 1994). Moreover, the answer-in-weights scheme has been proposed to solve the difficulty of ill-posed inverse problems, as a related model of network inversion (Kosugi & Kameyama, 1993).

The original network inversion method proposed by Linden and Kindermann solves an inverse problem by using a usual multilayer neural network that handles the relation between real-valued input and output. However, a network method for complex-valued input and output is required to solve the general inverse problem whose cause and result extend to the complex domain. On the other hand, there exists an extension of the multilayer neural network to the complex domain (Benvenuto & Piazza, 1992; Hirose, 2005; Nitta, 1997). The complex-valued neural network learns the relations between complex-valued input and output in the form of complex-valued weights. This complex-valued network inversion was considered to solve inverse problems that extended to complex-valued input and output. In this method, the complex-valued input is inversely estimated from the provided complex-valued output by extending the input correction of the original network inversion method to the complex domain. Actually, the complex-valued input is estimated from the complex-valued output by giving a random input to the trained network, back-propagating the output error to the input, and correcting the input (Ogawa & Kanada, 2005a).

In the forward problem, the existence, uniqueness, and stability of solution are guaranteed. When all these three conditions are satisfied, the problem is called a well-posed problem. In the inverse problem, it is often difficult to obtain a solution because of ill-posedness (Petrov & Sizikov, 2005; Tikhonov & Arsenin, 1977). Regularization imposes specific conditions on an ill-posed inverse problem to convert it into a well-posed problem. We consider introducing regularization to complex-valued network inversion. Tikhonov regularization, which is a conventional regularization method, uses a constant coefficient for the regularization term. On the other hand, dynamic regularization (Kosugi, Uemoto, & Ogawa, 1998) was proposed for changing the effect of regularization in each stage of the process.

The first objective of this chapter is to demonstrate the procedure of the complex-valued network inversion method to solve complex-valued inverse problems. The other objective is to show the effect of the regularization method. To achieve these two objectives, the following problems are examined: inverse estimation of complex-valued mapping, inverse Fourier transform problem, and inverse estimation of complex-valued mapping with ill-posedness.

BACKGROUND

Inverse Problems

An inverse problem determines the inner mechanism or cause of an observed phenomenon. For the relation $Kx = y$, where K is some mathematical model, we consider the forward problem, which determines the result y from the cause x. In this forward problem, generally, the definition of the operator K is fixed and its mapping is supposed to be continuous. For this forward problem, we can define an inverse problem that determines the cause x from the operator K and result y or one that estimates the operator K from the cause x and the result y. The relation between the forward and inverse problems is shown in Figure 1.

The relation of the given cause x and the result y is continuous in the forward problem. In the inverse problem, the existence or uniqueness of cause x is not guaranteed for a given or observed result y. Even if the cause

Figure 1. Forward and inverse problems

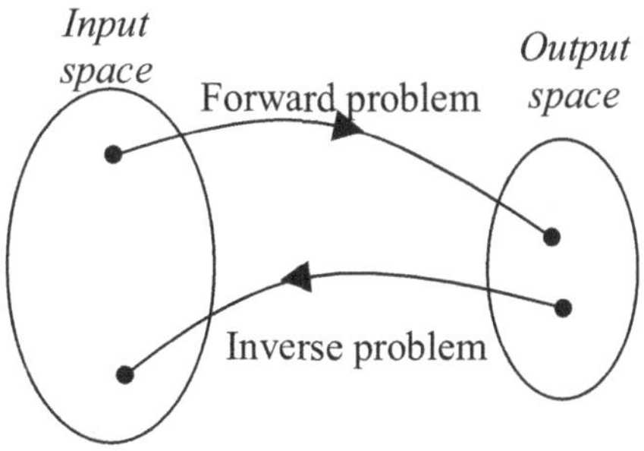

Figure 2. Ill-posedness of inverse problems

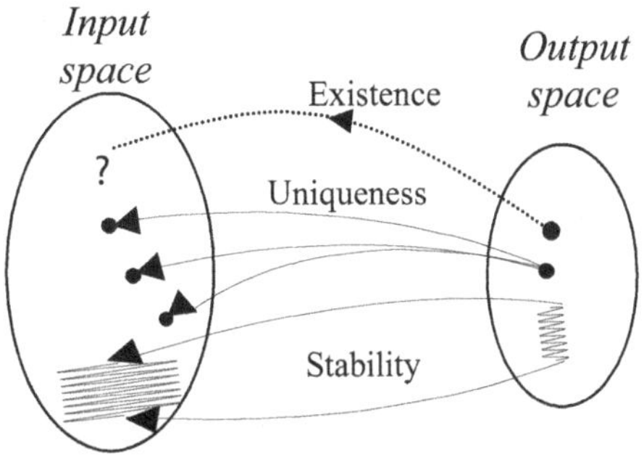

x is determined or estimated uniquely, it sometimes becomes unstable to minute perturbations of the result y. Existence, uniqueness, and stability are necessary conditions to ensure the well-posedness of a problem. In the inverse problem, it might be difficult to obtain a solution because the well-posedness of the problem is not always guaranteed. The difficulty is often referred as an ill-posedness. The concept of ill-posedness with regard to existence, uniqueness, and stability is shown in Figure 2.

In general, locating a source from observed data is known as an inverse problem. Two examples of such problems are the localization of active nerves from their evoked potential waveforms and the localization of objects from their echoes using an active sonar system.

Example: Nerve Bundle Localization with Evoked Potentials.
During neurosurgical operations, in addition to approaching and correcting malfunctioning parts, the localization of healthy nerves that must not be injured is an important and difficult task. Estimating the location of active nerves by observing evoked potentials during surgery has been proposed as a method to simplify this task. Experience with the standard approach of using electrodes on the surface of the scalp indicates that the determination of nerve location during surgery should satisfy two conditions: it should be performed in real time and the observation device (probe) should be introduced intracranially (Watanabe & Kosugi, 1991).

A percutaneous stimulus of the nerves generates evoked potentials that are synchronized with the stimulus. Since the nerve bundles consist of many axons with different transmission velocities, the pulse transmission in the nerve bundle $\boldsymbol{P}$ is approximated as the sum of dipole moment P_i. For example, the potential V at point A in Figure 3 can be approximated by

$$V = \sum_i \frac{P_i}{4\pi\varepsilon_0 r_i^2} \cos\theta_i \,,\; P_i = \delta_i Q_i \tag{1}$$

Figure 3. The physical principle of evoked potential generation. (a) The transmission of the pulse in the nerve bundle. (b) The dipole moment used to approximate the pulse.

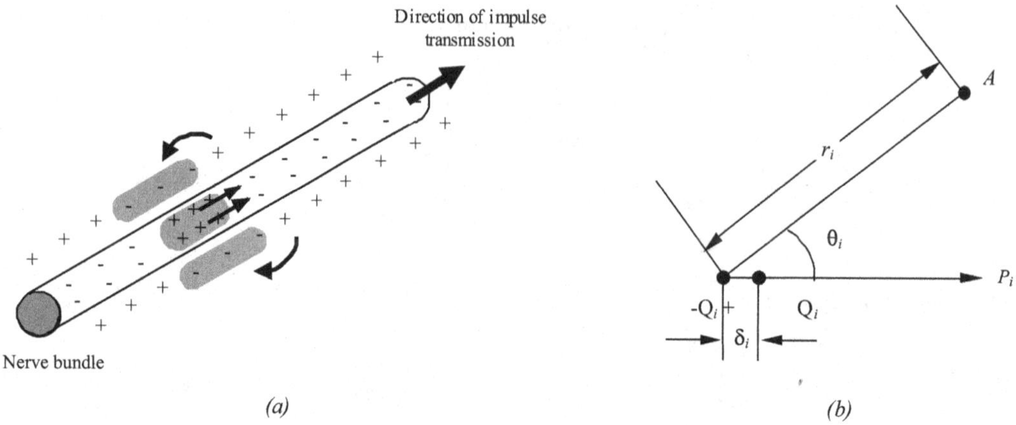

Figure 4. The probe with four pairs of electrodes to detect each directional component of the evoked potential

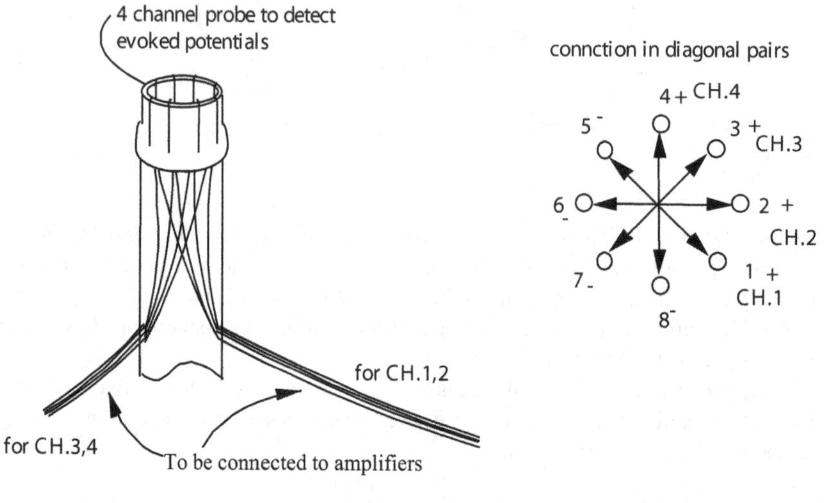

where Q_i is an electrical charge; ε_0, the permittivity of free space; and δ_i, the separation between charges. The detecting probe, shown in Figure 4, consists of four pairs of electrodes that are connected in diagonal pairs to detect each directional component of the evoked potential. When the probe direction is changed relative to the nerves, each electrode pair detects the charge in the evoked potential. An example of evoked potential waveform of the median nerve is shown in Figure 5. The changes in the detected waveforms facilitate the observation of the location of the nerves with respect to the probe. The localization of the median nerve within the arm was attempted as a preliminary experiment to locate nerves within the brain for neurosurgical operations. There are some differences in the pulse width of the evoked potential, as well as the transmission characteristics in the surrounding tissues, between those in the brain and in the arm, but the principles of generation and transmission of the evoked potentials is essentially the same. Therefore, the experiment gives important insights prior to the location of nerves within the brain.

It is assumed that the detected evoked potential waveform is determined by the relation between the location of nerves (source location) and the probe position (sensor position). Thus, we can form an inverse problem

Figure 5. The evoked potential waveform of the median nerve

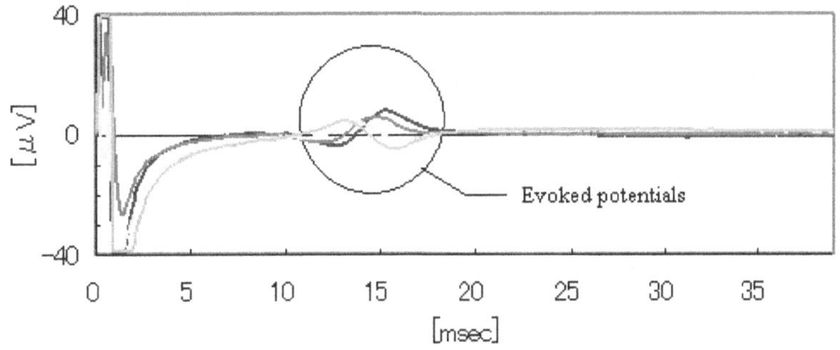

Figure 6. The Bat-Like Sonar system

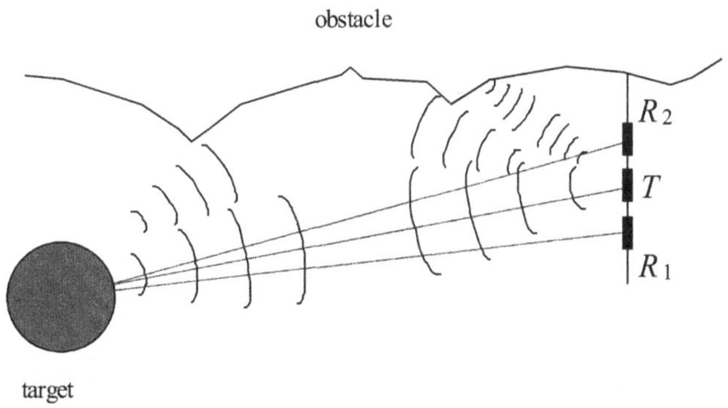

to estimate the source location from the detected waveform, with the aid of the relations among the detected waveform, source location, and sensor position (Ogawa, Kameyama, Kuc, & Kosugi, 1996).

Example: Source Localization with Bat-Like Sonar

Sonar systems using ultrasonic waves have been employed for navigation, registration, obstacle avoidance, and sonar map building, since they can determine the object location easily and inexpensively. Among these object recognition systems, the bat-like sonar system (Barshan & Kuc, 1992; Kuc & Barshan, 1991), shown in Figure 6 was implemented to simulate a biological system. In this system, the middle transducer T transmits an ultrasonic pulse, and two transducers R_1 and R_2 receive the echoes reflected by the objects. A typical received echo is shown in Figure 7. The pressure amplitude of the propagating pulse is given by

$$p(r,\theta) \cong \frac{P_0 r_0}{r} e^{-\frac{\theta^2}{2\sigma_T^2}}, \; r > r_0, \qquad (2)$$

where r is the radial distance from the transducer; θ, the azimuth; and P_0, the propagating pressure amplitude at range r_0 along the line-of-sight ($\theta = 0$ degree). For our sensor, $r_0 \cong 100mm$ and the beam-width parameter σ_t equals 30°.

In the ideal environment, we assume that no object other than the target object reflects waves. However, in the actual environment, there may be many objects that produce echoes. As a result, we may not be able to tell which

Figure 7. The typical received echo waveforms detected by bat-like sonar system

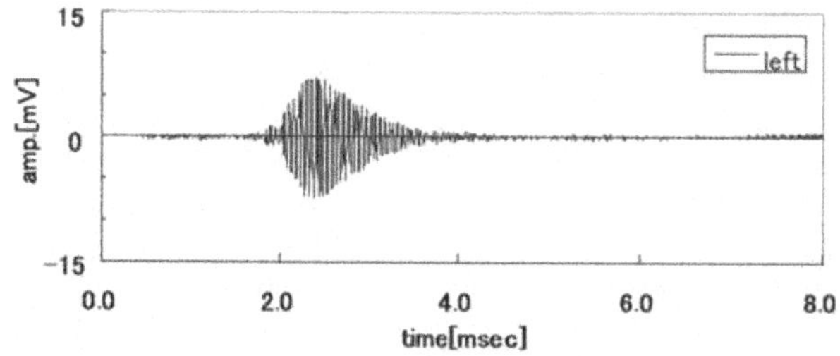

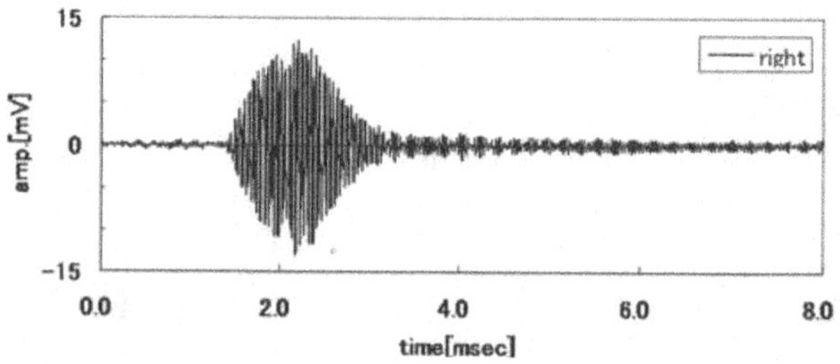

echoes belong to the desired object whose location we wish to determine. Bats living in a narrow cave receive many echoes, but they still manage to determine the location of a desired object, like a perch. In the bat-like sonar problem, the relation between the waveforms and the object location is determined by the relation between the object location (source location) and the detector position at which the sensors detect the waves reflected by the object (sensor position). In other words, we want to estimate the object location from a pair of physical quantities describing the detector position and the detected waveforms. Thus, we can form an inverse problem to estimate the target location to compose the environmental map from the detected waveforms (Ogawa et al., 1996).

Network Inversion

A conventional multilayer neural network is used to solve the forward problem by the learned forward relation. In a usual multilayer network whose training has completed, the input-output relation is given by

$$y = f(w, x) \tag{3}$$

where x, y, and f are the input vector, the output vector, and the function defined by the interlayer weights w of the network, respectively. For a given input vector x, the network calculates the output vector y.

Linden and Kindermann proposed the method of network inversion. In this method, we can apply the observed output data y with f fixed, after finding forward relation f by training. Then, the input x can be updated according to the calculated input correction signal, based on the duality of the weights and input in eqn. (3). Actually, the input is estimated from the output by an iterative update of the input based on the output error. By this method, the inverse problem for estimating the input x from the output y is solved by the multilayer neural network by using the forward relation inversely.

The network is used in the two phases: the forward training and the inverse estimation to solve the inverse problem by network inversion. The two-step procedure is shown in Figure 8. In the training phase, we provide the training input x and the training output y and calculate the output error E. Then, the weight w is updated by

$$w(t+1) = w(t) - \varepsilon_t \frac{\partial E}{\partial w} \tag{4}$$

where ε_t represents the training gain, because the output error is due to the misadjustments of weights. By repeating this update procedure shown in Figure 9 (a), the forward relation is obtained by the distribution of weights. This is the procedure based on the usual back-propagation method. In the inverse estimation phase, we fix the relation obtained in the training, provide the random input x and the test output y, and calculate the output error E. Then, the input x is updated by

$$x(t+1) = x(t) - \varepsilon_e \frac{\partial E}{\partial x} \tag{5}$$

where ε_e represents the input update gain, because the output error is due to the error of the input. By repeating this update procedure shown in Figure 9 (b), the input is estimated from the output.

Linden and Kindermann mentioned in their paper (Linden & Kindermann, 1989) that the inversion method was presented as a tool for understanding network behavior. The purpose of the original network inversion was not to serves as a solution of an inverse problem. However, in their paper, they posed the question of which input should be fed into the net to produce an output that approximates a given target vector. This is an inverse problem in itself. Network inversion has been applied to a number of inverse problems: impedance tomography, segmentation of brain MR images, inverse kinematics, and so on (Lu & Ito, 1995; Takeuchi & Kosugi, 1994; Valova et al., 1995).

Since network inversion solves inverse problems by a two-stage procedure of forward training and inverse estimation, this method needs an iterative procedure not only in forward training but also in inverse estimation. The iterative update of inputs in inverse estimation is done only to one provided an output pattern while the iterative update of weights in the forward training is performed on all the given training patterns. Therefore, the calculation time is much shorter than that by iteration in training, even though the calculation time for iteration in inverse estimation is definitely required.

However, the computing time is obviously long as compared to that in the case where there is no repetition. For instance, we can perform estimation without iteration by using the "inverse solver" network, which studies the inverse relation between inputs and outputs. However, we can use the inverse solver network only when the relation of a simple one-to-one correspondence is guaranteed between the input and output.

Therefore, the use of the network inversion method is significant in the case where it is used to solve an inverse problem with the possibility of many-to-one correspondence between the input and output. To solve an inverse problem with the many-to-one correspondence of the input-output relation by the usual feed-forward network, the network must learn the one-to-many correspondence of the input-output relation. Because it is difficult for a network to do this, network training does not converge, even if we attempt to make the network actually learn the relation. In the case of network inversion, it is possible to learn the many-to-one correspondence of the input-output relation by training. In other words, this relation signifies the ill-posed inverse problem. It is not necessary for well-posed inverse problems to be solved by network inversion methods. However, there are merits to using the network inversion method to solve inverse problems, because a one-to-one relation is often not guaranteed.

Consequently, it is significant to apply network inversion methods to solve ill-posed inverse problems. Therefore, the solution of ill-posedness is inevitably required. Generally, an ill-posed inverse problem can be converted into a well-posed one by adding an *a priori* given condition. Techniques such as the regularization method and the answer-in-weights scheme have been examined to provide a condition for network inversion.

Regularization

In general, inverse problems include difficulties with regard to ill-posedness. The ill-posedness problem is important in network inversion as well. Regularization, which has been studied in the field of mathematical science, is a solution to the problem of ill-posedness. The use of regularization has been studied for network inversion.

Figure 8. Two-step procedure to solve an inverse problem by network inversion

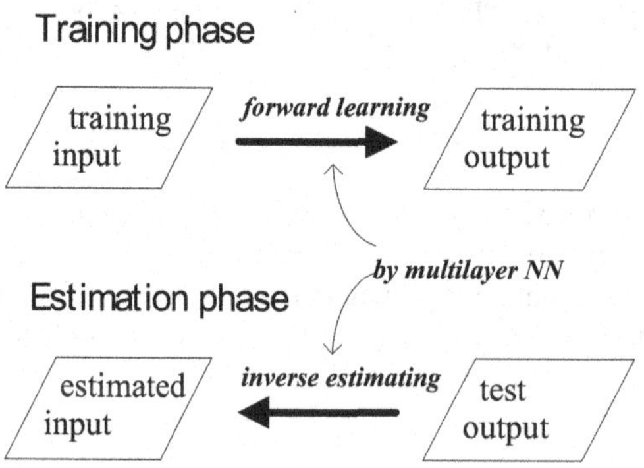

Figure 9. Weights and input update procedure. (a) Weight update based on error back-propagation learning, and (b) input update in inverse estimation based on network inversion

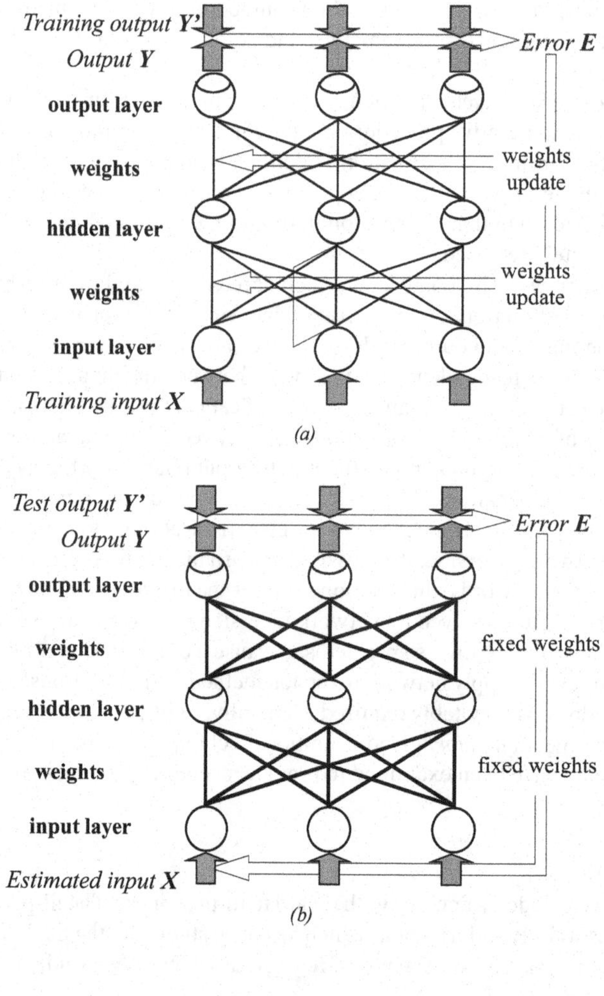

We consider regularization for network inversion. The method is based on Tikhonov regularization, which provides the constraint condition to the solution. To estimate the input from a given output, network inversion minimizes the output error, as expressed in eqn. (5). To provide the constraint condition, we use the regularization functional to be minimized in accordance with the output error in the inverse estimation phase. The energy function $E(x)$ with the regularization functional $\Omega(x)$ is defined as

$$E = \|\tilde{y} - Kx\|^2 + \lambda\Omega(x) \tag{6}$$

where $\tilde{y}$, K, and x are the network output, translation, and input, respectively. The first and second terms represent the output error of the network and the regularization functional. The parameter λ is the regularization coefficient. It is possible to consider a number of regularization functionals: maximum norm, minimum norm, maximum inclination, minimum inclination, and so on.

For example, we consider the case of regularization of the minimum squared norm solution. In this case, this regularization method solves the ill-posed inverse problem by finding the minimum squared norm solution. The functional to minimize the squared norm is added to the output error function of network inversion. The functional and the output error function are minimized at the same time in the inverse estimation phase of network inversion. The output error E of the network inversion is defined as

$$E = \sum_{i=1}^{M}(y_i - \tilde{y}_i)^2 - \lambda\|X\|^2 \tag{7}$$

where $\tilde{Y} = \{\tilde{y}_i\}$, $Y = \{y_i\}$, $(i = 1, \cdots, M)$ and $X = \{x_j\}$, $(j = 1, \cdots, N)$ are the network output, the given output, and the input to be estimated, respectively. The regularization functional is defined as the product of the squared norm $\|X\|^2$ and regularization parameter λ. The network input is updated by minimizing the squared norm $\|X\|^2$. The input is corrected by

$$x_j(t+1) = \lambda x_j(t) + \eta\delta_j \tag{8}$$

where δ_j represents the error signal for the j-th input neuron that is generated by the output error and is propagated from the output layer. The parameter η is the coefficient for the iterative update of the input.

The coefficient λ is usually fixed and determined empirically or by trial and error. However, the balance between output error minimization and regularization is often uncertain. Actually, the regularization coefficient might be reduced with a decrease in the output error. We refer to this as dynamic regularization. For example, the regularization coefficient $\lambda(t)$ is reduced for each correction of input as

$$\lambda(t) = \lambda(0)\exp(-mt) \tag{9}$$

where $\lambda(0)$, t, and m, are the initial value of λ, the current epoch number, and a decay coefficient, respectively. The parameter $\lambda(t)$ decays from $\lambda(0)$ to zero with the epoch number t.

Another approach for solving ill-posedness is the answer-in-weights scheme (Kosugi & Kameyama, 1993). In the original network inversion approach, only one port is used as the input port because the input is used as the output port, corresponding to the answer-in-input scheme. However, it is difficult to efficiently embed the relation between two different data types such as the signal waveform and the sensor location into the network architecture. Therefore, the method that seeks an answer from neither the input nor the output but from the weights in between the layers of the network is considered. In this approach, we assign different data types to the input and output, and obtain an answer satisfying their relationship in weights. This strategy is referred to as the answer-in-weights scheme. In this method, the physical conditions that the solution of the inverse problem has to satisfy can be easily built into the network architecture using the relation between the input and output. We can reduce the difficulty due to the ill-posedness of inverse problems, since more comprehensive constraints, i.e., relations among three physical or mathematical quantities, can be applied to the answer-in-weights network than those in the conventional feed-forward network. The concept of the answer-in-weights scheme is shown in Figure 10.

Figure 10. The general structure of the answer-in-weights scheme network

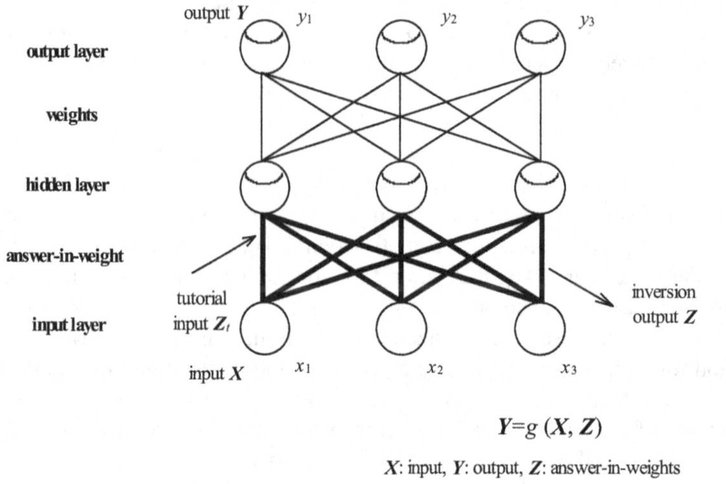

Example: Inverse Kinematics of Robot Arm

The network inversion has been applied to the inverse kinematics problem to estimate joint angles from the given end effector's coordinate. The inverse kinematics problem of multi degree-of-freedom (DOF) is an ill-posed inverse problem. For example, we consider the inverse kinematics of the three DOF robot arm. The joint angles to realize for the given end effector's coordinate is not unique in the inverse kinematics, while an end effector's coordinate is uniquely decided from the given joint angles in the forward kinematics, as shown in Figure 11.

To show the procedure of the network inversion, we examine the inverse kinematics of the three DOF robot arm. We attempt to estimate the joint angles to realize the given end effector's coordinate. The network architecture used in the simulation is shown in Figure 12. The joint angles $(\theta_1,\theta_2,\theta_3)$ and the end effector's coordinate (x, y) are provided as the input and output, respectively. The parameters of the network and the robot arm are shown in Table 1. In the learning phase, the network learns the forward relation between input and output. The error for forward epoch is shown in Figure 13(a).The joint angles and end effector's coordinate are provided as the training input and output, respectively. In the inverse estimation phase, the joint angles $(\theta_1',\theta_2',\theta_3')$ are estimated from the given end effector's coordinate (x',y'). The initial joint angles are set to random values. The regularization functional and its parameter used here is the same as the equations (7) and (9). We prepared the five test output data of the end effector's coordinate arranged on the arc. By repeating this input update procedure, the input is estimated from the output.

The error for inverse epoch is shown in Figure 13(b). From the decrease in the error, we confirm that the inputs are updated correctly. The obtained pose of robot arm and end effector's coordinates are shown in Figure 14(a). The estimated coordinates are almost corresponding to the target. Also, we tried the inverse estimation five times. The results are shown in Figure 18(b). The estimated five trajectories of the end effector's coordinates are almost corresponding to the target. From the above results, the estimated joint angles with the regularization functional are almost similar to the target angles. This means the network inversion is able to solve the ill-posed inverse problems with regularization functional. As a result, we confirm the correct solution of inverse kinematics by the network inversion with regularization.

Figure 11. An example of three DOF robot arm, (a) joint angles and end effector's coordinate, (b) combination of joint angles for an end effector's coordinate

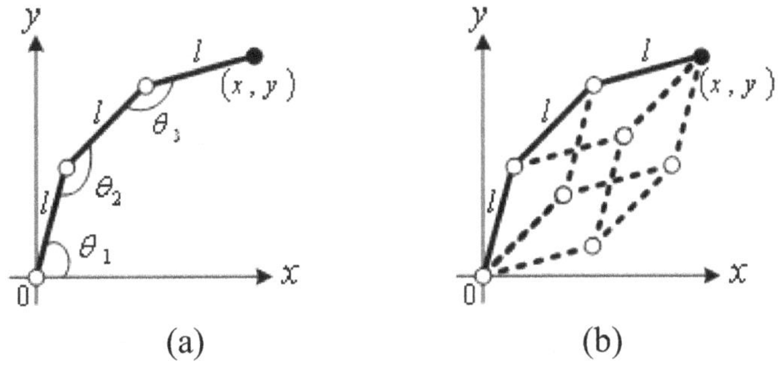

Figure 12. Network architecture for inverse kinematics of three DOF robot arm

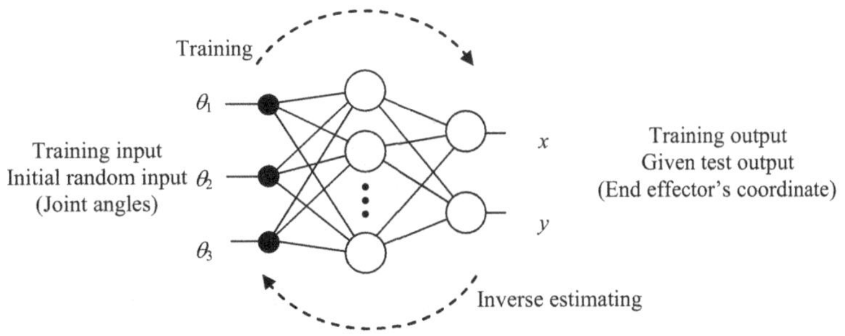

Table 1. Network and robot arm parameters

Number of input neurons		3
Number of hidden neurons		60
Number of output neurons		2
Training gain ε_t		0.001
Estimation gain ε_e		0.001
Maximum number of training epochs		10000
Maximum number of estimation epochs		10000
Joint angles for learning data (degree)	θ_1	0, 10, …, 90
	θ_2	0, 15, …, 345
	θ_3	0, 30, …, 330
Length of arms (cm)		30

Figure 13. Error curves for (a) learning epoch and (b) inverse epoch

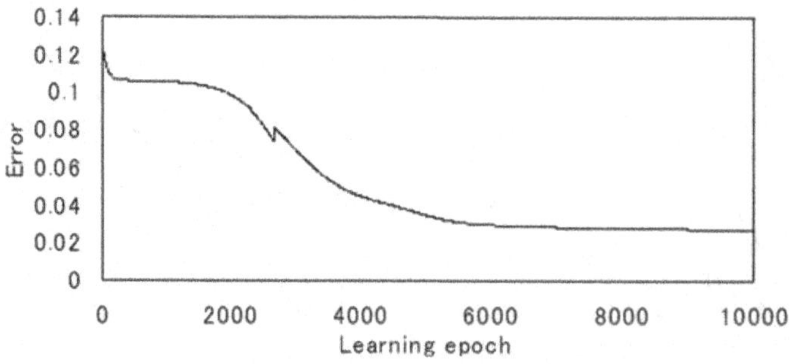

(a)

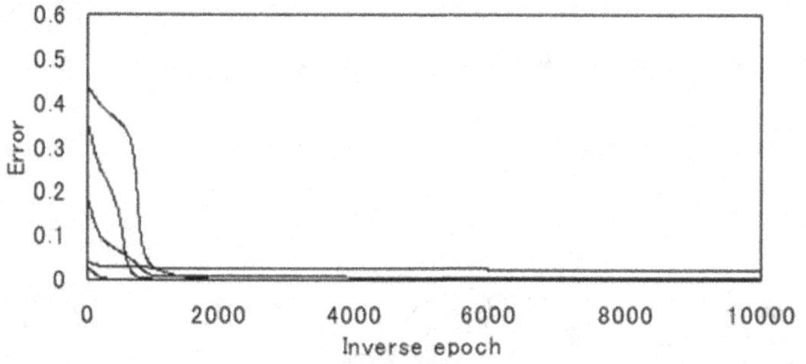

(b)

Figure 14. Estimated results (a) pose of robot arm(b) five trajectories of end effector's coordinate figured by estimated joint angles

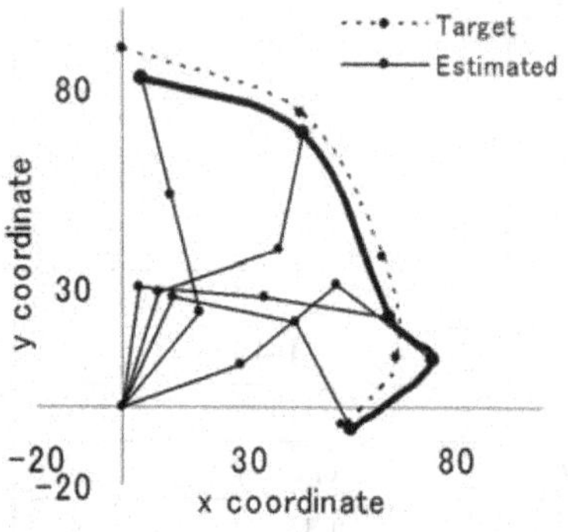

(a)

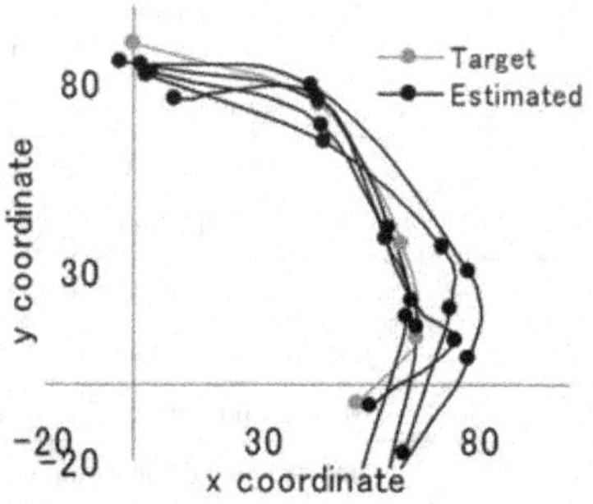

(b)

COMPLEX-VALUED NETWORK INVERSION

The network inversion method proposed by Linden and Kindermann solves an inverse problem by a usual multilayer neural network that handles the relation between a real-valued input and output. However, a network method for complex-valued input and output is required to solve the general inverse problem whose cause and result expand into the complex domain. On the other hand, the extension of the multilayer neural network to the complex domain has already been proposed.

In this section, a complex-valued network inversion that handles complex input and output is explained. The method uses a multilayer neural network that has complex weights and complex neurons. In this method, the complex-valued neural network estimates the complex input from the complex output using the trained network. It is an extension of the input correction principle of usual network inversion to the complex domain. Actually, the complex input is estimated from the complex output by providing a random input to the trained network, back-propagating the output error to the input, and repeating the input.

We consider the effectiveness of the complex-valued neural network and complex-valued network inversion. If only complex-valued input and output need to be handles, it can be done by a real-valued neural network whose input and output are allocated to two neurons. It is considered that complex-valued network inversion can be substituted by real-valued network inversion through a similar allocation. One of the most significant features of the complex-valued neural network is the restriction of flexibility based on the fundamental arithmetic rule of multiplication of complex numbers (Hirose, 2005). A neural network has to construct this relation from the data provided by learning when a complex-valued neural network is substituted with a real-valued one. On the other hand, we consider that there is merit in using this relation as a restraint condition in learning in the complex-valued neural network.

Similar to real-valued network inversion, the network is used in two phases: forward training and inverse estimation to solve the inverse problem in complex-valued network inversion. In the training phase, we provide the training input $x = x_R + ix_I$ and training output $y = y_R + iy_I$, and calculate the output error $E = E_R + iE_I$, where i is the imaginary unit. Then, the weight $w = w_R + iw_I$ is updated by

$$w_R(t+1) = w_R(t) - \varepsilon_t\left(\frac{\partial E_R}{\partial w_R} + \frac{\partial E_I}{\partial w_R}\right),\ w_I(t+1) = w_I(t) - \varepsilon_t\left(\frac{\partial E_I}{\partial w_I} - \frac{\partial E_R}{\partial w_I}\right) \tag{10}$$

where ε_t represents the training gain, because the output error is due to the misadjustment of weights. By repeating this update procedure, the forward relation is obtained in the distribution of weights. This is a procedure based on the usual back-propagation method. In the inverse estimation phase, we fix the relation obtained in the training, provide the random input $x = x_R + ix_I$ and the test output $y = y_R + iy_I$, and calculate the output error $E = E_R + iE_I$. Then, the input $x = x_R + ix_I$ is updated by

$$x_R(t+1) = x_R(t) - \varepsilon_e\left(\frac{\partial E_R}{\partial x_R} + \frac{\partial E_I}{\partial x_R}\right),\ x_I(t+1) = x_I(t) - \varepsilon_e\left(\frac{\partial E_I}{\partial x_I} - \frac{\partial E_R}{\partial x_I}\right) \tag{11}$$

where ε_e represents the input update gain, because the output error is due to the error of the input. By repeating this update procedure, the input is estimated from the output.

As an actual example, we consider the training and inverse estimation procedures of a three-layer complex-valued neural network shown in Figure 15. In this network, a complex-valued neuron is used for the hidden layer and the output layer. The complex input becomes a complex output through complex weights between each layer. The neuron uses a complex sigmoid function that applies the sigmoid function to the real and imaginary parts independently; this function is defined as follows:

$$f_C(s) = f(s_R) + if(s_I),\quad f(u) = \frac{1-e^{-u}}{1+e^{-u}} \tag{12}$$

where $s = s_R + is_I$ represents the weighted sum of the neuron input. This complex-valued neuron model, which is shown in Figure 16, is referred to as a real-imaginary-type activation function (Benvenuto & Piazza, 1992; Hirose,

Figure 15. Three-layered network and its parameters

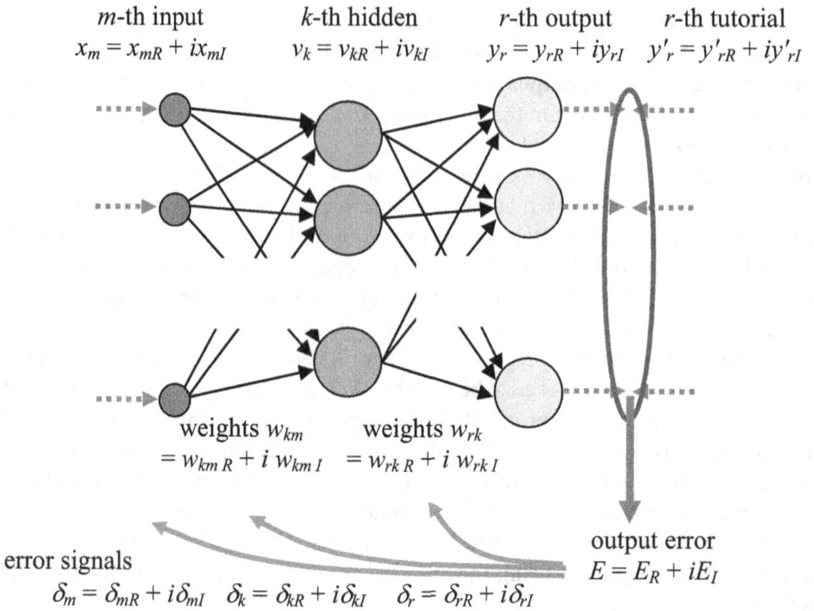

Figure 16. Complex-valued neuron with real-imaginary-type activation function

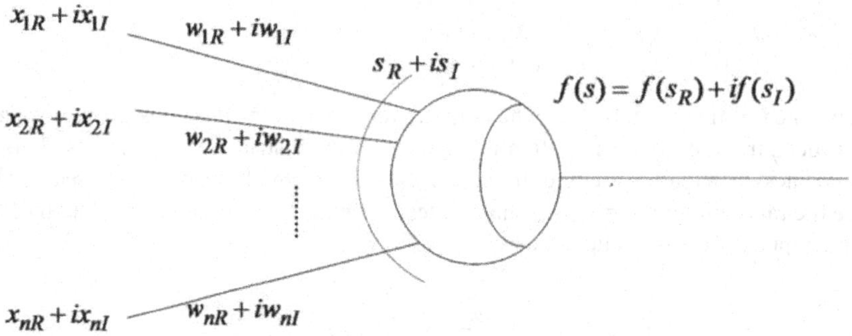

2005; Nitta, 1997). Here, we consider the activation function of the hyperbolic tangent type $f(u) = (1 - e^{-u})/(1 + e^{-u})$ for the real and imaginary parts. But other activation functions, e.g., $f(u) = 1/(1 + e^{-u})$, are also available for complex-valued network inversion (Ogawa & Kanada, 2005a; 2005b).

Training Phase

The training of the network is done in the same way employed for a usual complex-valued network. The output error $E = E_R + iE_I$ is defined by the squared error

$$E_R = \frac{1}{2}\sum_r (y'_{rR} - y_{rR})^2, \quad E_I = \frac{1}{2}\sum_r (y'_{rI} - y_{rI})^2, \tag{13}$$

where $y'_r = y'_{rR} + y'_{rI}$ and $y_r = y_{rR} + y_{rI}$ are r-th tutorial output and network output. First, the weight update procedure between the hidden and output layers is formulated. The error signal from the output layer is calculated by

$$\delta_{rR} = (y'_{rR} - y_{rR})(1 - y_{rR})(1 + y_{rR}), \quad \delta_{rI} = (y'_{rI} - y_{rI})(1 - y_{rI})(1 + y_{rI}). \tag{14}$$

which represents the gradient of the output error for the weight $w_{rk} = w_{rkR} + iw_{rkI}$ between the hidden and output layer. Therefore, the weights are updated by

$$w_{rkR}(t+1) = w_{rkR}(t) - \varepsilon_t(\delta_{rR} v_{kR} + \delta_{rI} v_{kI}), \quad w_{rkI}(t+1) = w_{rkI}(t) - \varepsilon_t(\delta_{rI} v_{kR} - \delta_{rR} v_{kI}) \tag{15}$$

where $v_k = v_{kR} + iv_{kI}$ and ε_t mean the input from k-th hidden neuron and a training gain, respectively.

Next, the weight's update procedure between input and hidden layer is formulated. The error signal from the hidden layer is calculated by

$$\delta_{kR} = (1 - v_{kR})(1 + v_{rR})\sum_r (\delta_{rR} w_{rkR} + \delta_{rI} w_{rkI}), \quad \delta_{kI} = (1 - v_{kI})(1 + v_{rI})\sum_r (\delta_{rI} w_{rkR} - \delta_{rR} w_{rkI}), \tag{16}$$

which represents the gradient of the output error for the weights $w_{km} = w_{kmR} + iw_{kmI}$ between the input and hidden layer. Therefore, the weights are updated by

$$w_{kmR}(t+1) = w_{kmR}(t) - \varepsilon_t(\delta_{kR} x_{mR} + \delta_{kI} x_{mI}), \quad w_{kmI}(t+1) = w_{kmI}(t) - \varepsilon_t(\delta_{kI} x_{mR} - \delta_{kR} x_{mI}) \tag{17}$$

where ε_t is a training gain. The input-output relation is learned by correcting each complex weight according to the above equations.

Inverse Estimation Phase

In the inverse estimation phase, the input is estimated from the provided output. In other words, the provided initial random input is repeatedly updated by the output error that is back-propagated to the input via the fixed weights. This procedure is similar to error back-propagation training.

The output error for the input is defined similar to eqn. (13). In addition, the error signals from the output layer to hidden layer are formulated similar to eqns. (14) and (16). The error signal to the input layer is calculated by

$$\delta_{mR} = (1 - x_{mR})(1 + x_{mR})\sum_k (\delta_{kR} w_{kmR} + \delta_{kI} w_{kmI}), \quad \delta_{mI} = (1 - x_{mI})(1 + x_{mI})\sum_k (\delta_{kI} w_{kmR} - \delta_{kR} w_{kmI}) \tag{18}$$

Then, the input can be updated by the error signal, which is expressed by eqn. (18), instead of the weight update, which is described by

$$x_{mR}(t+1) = x_{mR}(t) - \varepsilon_e \delta_{mR}, \quad x_{mI}(t+1) = x_{mI}(t) - \varepsilon_e \delta_{mI} \tag{19}$$

where ε_e is the inverse estimation gain. Thus, the input is corrected iteratively. When the error reaches the target, the input correction is terminated and the obtained complex input becomes a solution.

As a result, a complex input can be inversely estimated from a complex output by using the complex weight distribution obtained by training. This is similar to correcting the weights or the input iteratively, during training and inverse estimation. However, inverse estimation is iterative correction for a provided pattern, and it differs from training by repeated correction for plural patterns.

Regularization

In this section, we explain the introduction of regularization to complex-valued network inversion for solving ill-posed inverse problems. We examine static and dynamic regularization.

The error function of a complex-valued network inversion with static regularization is expressed by

$$E_R = \frac{1}{2}\sum_r (y'_{rR} - y_{rR})^2 + \lambda \|Kf_R\|^2, \quad E_I = \frac{1}{2}\sum_r (y'_{rI} - y_{rI})^2 + \lambda \|Kf_I\|^2, \tag{20}$$

where the first and second terms in each equation represent the usual error term and the regularization term. In this study, we use the regularization term defined as

$$\|Kf_R\|^2 = \frac{1}{2}\sum_m x_{mR}^2, \ \|Kf_I\|^2 = \frac{1}{2}\sum_m x_{mI}^2. \tag{21}$$

This regularization serves to minimize the input value. The input of complex-valued network inversion with regularization is also updated based on eqn. (19). In contrast to real-valued network inversion, the input must be updated in both real and imaginary parts during complex-valued network inversion, which is expressed by

$$x_{mR}(t+1) = x_{mR}(t) - \varepsilon_e \cdot \delta_{mR} - \lambda x_{mR}(t), \ x_{mI}(t+1) = x_{mI}(t) - \varepsilon_e \cdot \delta_{mI} - \lambda x_{mI}(t). \tag{22}$$

Ill-posedness in the complex domain can be reduced by the iterative correction of the input by eqn. (22). While the regularization parameter is constant in static regularization, it changes as a function of the epoch number t in dynamic regularization. The regularization parameter is defined as

$$\lambda(t) = \lambda(0) \exp(-mt) \tag{23}$$

where m is the decay coefficient. The parameter $\lambda(t)$ decays from $\lambda(0)$ to zero with the epoch number t.

SAMPLE PROBLEMS FOR COMPLEX-VALUED NETWORK INVERSION

The first objective of this section is to demonstrate the complex-valued network inversion method to solve complex-valued inverse problems. To attain this objective, two problems—inverse estimation of complex-valued mapping and inverse Fourier transform— are examined. The second objective is to show the effect of the regularization method. To attain this objective, inverse estimation of complex-valued mapping with ill-posedness is examined.

Example: Inverse Estimation of Complex-Valued Mapping

The inverse complex-valued mapping problem is examined as a simple example of the inverse problem. In this problem, the mapping between the points on the complex plane is learned by a complex-valued neural network. Then, the point before mapping is estimated from the given point after mapping by using learned mapping inversely. In other words, the inverse mapping of an arbitrary point on the complex plane is estimated by inversely using the forward mapping obtained in the training. The network is assumed to have an input and an output.

First, we examine the inverse use of enlargement mapping. In the training phase, tutorial input and output patterns are provided to the network. The tutorial patterns are 11 points that satisfy the conditions $y_n = 3x_n/2$, $x_{nR} = x_{nI} = \{-0.5, -0.4, \ldots, 0.4, 0.5\}$ for the input $x_n = x_{nR} + ix_{nI}$ and output $y_n = y_{nR} + iy_{nI}$. In other words, the network learns the relation mapped to 3/2 times coordinates, which implies enlargement mapping in the direction of the real and imaginary axes. In the inverse estimation phase, the weights obtained in the training phase are fixed to estimate the complex input from a complex test output. The complex test output patterns are 36 points that satisfy the condition $y_{nR}^2 + y_{nI}^2 = 0.75^2$. To provide the test output patterns, the corresponding input patterns are inversely estimated by the network. Because the inverse relation of the tutorial patterns results in reduction mapping, the input patterns to be estimated are expected to satisfy the condition $y_{nR}^2 + y_{nI}^2 = 0.5^2$.

In addition, we examine the inverse use of rotation mapping. The tutorial patterns are 11 points that satisfy the conditions $y_{nI} = x_{nI}/2$, $x_{nR} = y_{nR} = \{-1.0, -0.8, \ldots, 0.8, 1.0\}$ for the input $x_n = x_{nR} + ix_{nI}$ and output $y_n = y_{nR} + iy_{nI}$. In other words, the network learns the relation mapped to 1/2 times in imaginary coordinates, which implies rotation mapping. In the inverse estimation phase, the complex test output patterns are 36 points that satisfy the

Figure 17. Network architecture for the inverse estimation problem of complex-valued mapping

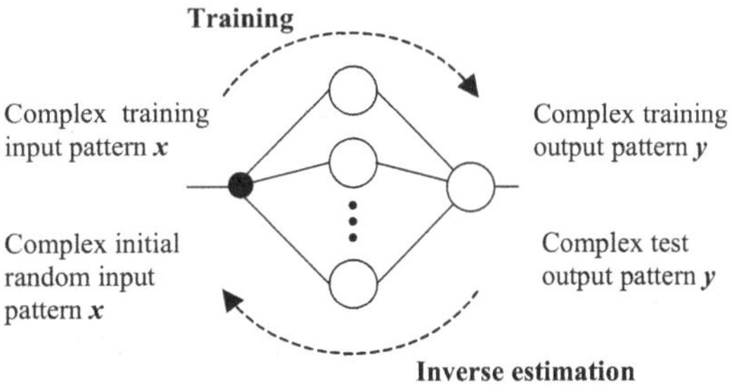

Table 2. Network parameters for the inverse estimation problem of complex mapping

Number of input neurons	1
Number of hidden neurons	5
Number of output neurons	1
Training gain ε_t	0.01
Estimation gain ε_e	0.01
Final training error level	0.0001
Final estimation error level	0.001
Maximum number of training epochs	20000
Maximum number of estimation epochs	10000
Number of training sets	11
Number of test sets	36

condition $y_{nR}^2 + 4y_{nI}^2 = 0.5^2$. To provide the test output patterns, the estimated input points are expected to lies on an inversely rotated ellipse, because the inverse relation of the tutorial patterns results in rotation mapping.

The network architecture and the allocation of the input and output patterns for training and inverse estimation are shown in Figure 17. The parameters of the network are shown in Table 2.

First, we show the simulation result of the inverse use of enlargement mapping. The plots of the tutorial and test input and outputs are shown in Figure 18 as the simulation result. The inverse estimated inputs are distributed as points on a circle of radius 0.5, and the test outputs are distributed as points on a circle of radius 0.75, according to the inverse estimated result of the input. This indicates that the input was correctly estimated from the test output by using the relation between the training input and output inversely. In other words, the reduction mapping of 2/3 is achieved by using an enlargement mapping of 3/2 inversely. Next, we show the simulation result of the inverse use of rotation mapping. The plots of the tutorial and test input and output are shown in Figure 19. The inverse estimated inputs are distributed as points on a rotated ellipse. Inverse rotation mapping is realized by using learned rotation mapping. To show the convergence of learning and inverse estimation, the learning and inverse estimation errors of the enlargement mapping are shown in Figure 20.

The fundamental inverse estimation operation of complex-valued network inversion was confirmed from these simulation results. In this method, a complex-valued input is estimated from the provided complex-valued output by using the trained forward complex-valued relation.

Figure 18. Result of inverse estimation of complex-valued mapping (enlargement)

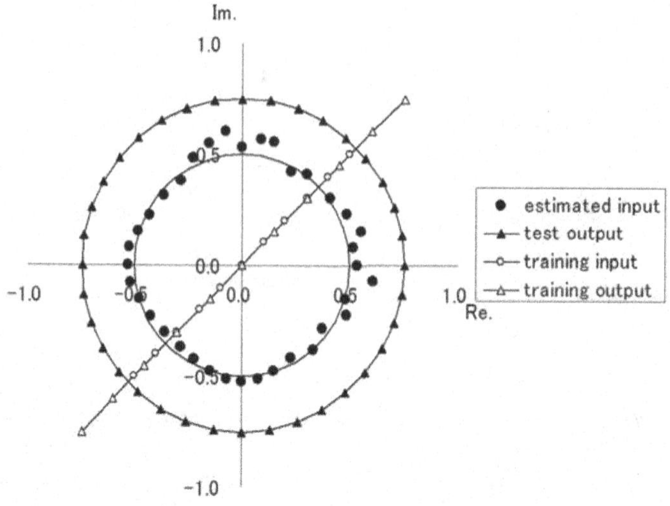

Figure 19. Result of inverse estimation of complex-valued mapping (rotation)

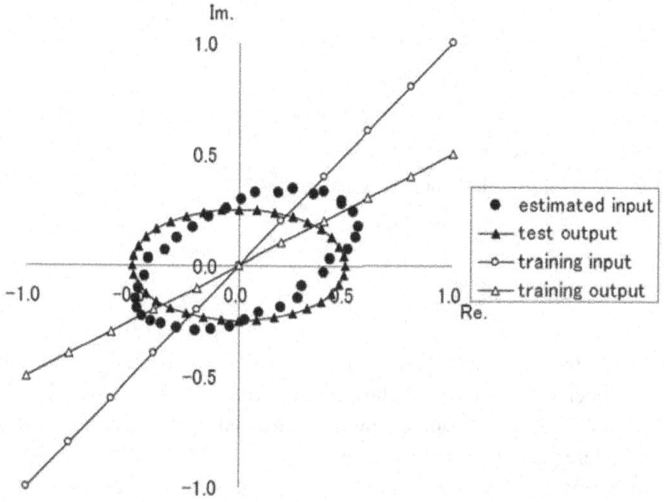

Example: Inverse Fourier Transform Problem

The inverse Fourier transform is solved by complex-valued network inversion by considering it as an inverse problem. Fourier transform and its inversion are considered to be a mapping between a signal and a complex-valued spectrum. The mapping from the signal to spectrum is learned by a complex-valued neural network. Then, the signal is estimated from the given spectrum by using the learned mapping inversely. In fact, we consider the discrete Fourier transform (DFT) and its inversion. The signal and the spectrum in DFT are assumed to be input and output, respectively, and the relation is learned by the network. Using the network learned by complex-valued network inversion, the signal is inversely estimated from the given spectrum. In learning phase, the network is studied by nine kinds of sinusoidal signal input and their corresponding spectrum outputs. While the weights obtained in learning are fixed for inverse estimation, the input is estimated from the test output pattern of the complex-valued spectrum.

Figure 20. Error curves of enlargement mapping for (a) learning epoch and (b) inverse epoch

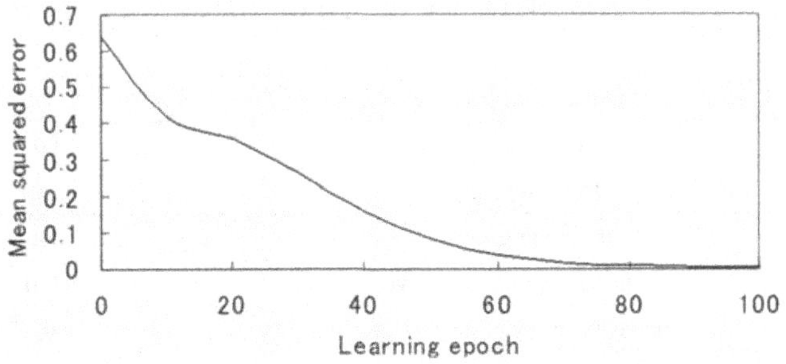

(a)

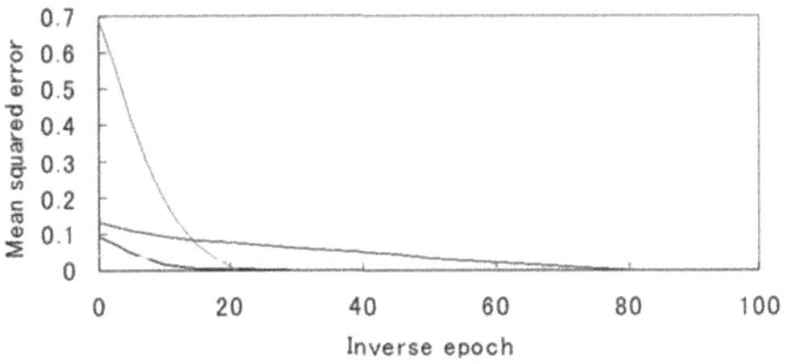

(b)

The inverse Fourier transform problem is examined to show the procedure of the complex-valued network inversion. Though the significance as a practical problem are not so large, the inverse Fourier transform problem is more concrete than the complex mapping problem as an example with the complex-valued input and output. It is possible to enhance the solution of the inverse Fourier transform problem to nonlinear mappings between the complex-valued input and output.

In the simulation, we use the complex-valued network with eight inputs and eight outputs. The input and output are the waveform and its spectrum, respectively. Both waveform and spectrum are sampled at eight points to be provided to the network. After several-time trials, we decided the number of hidden layer neurons. Because the number of training sets is small, we used the smaller number of hidden layer neurons. The tutorial inputs for the network training are the sinusoidal waveforms expressed by

$$x_n = a\cos\left(2\pi\frac{n}{N}b - \frac{\pi}{4}c\right), \quad (b = 1,2,3,\ c = 0,1,2) \tag{24}$$

where a and N are the amplitude and number of sampling points, respectively. The input waveforms are magnified and translated versions of the sinusoidal waveform $x_n = a\cos(2\pi n/N)$, ($a = 0.8$, $N = 8$, $n = 0, 1,\ldots, 7$). The tutorial outputs are the complex-valued spectrum $y_n = F(n, \omega)$, ($n = 0, \ldots, 7$) of the input waveforms. In the inverse estimation phase, a random input pattern is given to the input layer while fixing the weights obtained in the training phase, and the input is iteratively corrected from the given test output pattern (complex-valued spectrum). The network parameters are summarized in Table 3. The network architecture is shown in Figure 21.

The three estimated input patterns—$x_n = a\cos(2\pi n/N)$, $x_n = a\cos(4\pi n/N - \pi/2)$, and $x_n = a\cos(6\pi n/N - \pi/2)$—are shown in Figure 22. These are three of nine training patterns shown in eqn. (24). According to the results, the original shape of the waves is almost estimated for a given test output of the complex-valued spectrum. In the

Table 3. Network parameters for the inverse estimation problem of Fourier transform

Number of input neurons	8
Number of hidden neurons	4
Number of output neurons	8
Training gain ε_t	0.001
Estimation gain ε_e	0.01
Final training error level	0.0005
Final estimation error level	0.001
Maximum number of training epochs	10000
Maximum number of estimation epochs	10000
Number of training sets	9
Number of test sets	9

Figure 21. Network architecture for the inverse estimation problem of Fourier transform

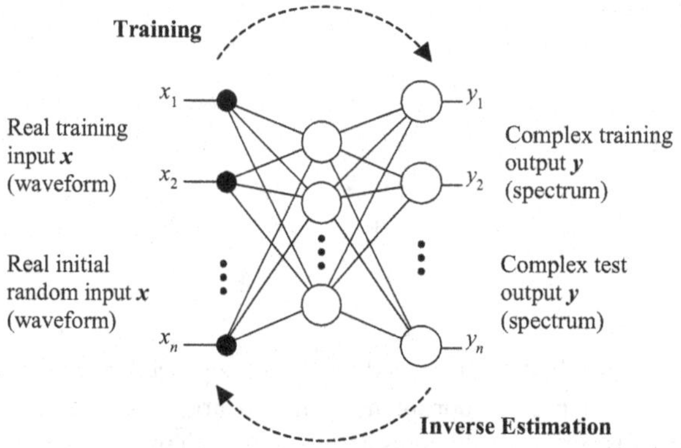

signal with different phases and same cycle, the ratio of the imaginary part to the real part of the spectrum is different. The signals with different phases can be estimated by complex-valued network inversion. The reason for this result is that the crossover among the input and the weights was correctly realized by the complex-valued neural network. Consequently, the inverse estimation of the input from a given output by complex-valued network inversion can be confirmed by the inverse Fourier transform of the signals corresponding to the given complex-valued spectrum.

In general, the estimated result is not guaranteed for untrained data in network inversion. However, inverse estimation is performed on test data that are distributed on a complex plane for training data distributed within a limited range in the above-mentioned result. In other words, it seems that inverse estimation is carried out from untrained data. This feature is explained with relation to the identity theorem in complex analysis. However, it is necessary that training data are distributed over the entire area in the real and imaginary parts. The inverse estimation of the input by complex network inversion was confirmed from these results. In this section, two kinds of conversion were examined for testing complex-valued network inversion. It is necessary to confirm various conversion abilities to verify the feature of complex-valued network inversion.

In the training phase, the network learns the relation between the input and output from the provided tutorial input and output patterns. The relations to be learned are enlargement, reduction in real and imaginary axis, and rotation at the origin. In the inverse estimation phase, the complex-valued input is estimated from the provided complex-valued output while fixing the complex-valued weights obtained in the training phase. After the network

Figure 22. Simulation results of inverse Fourier transform. (a) $x_n = a\cos(2\pi n/N)$, (b) $x_n = a\cos(4\pi n/N - \pi/2)$, (c) $x_n = a\cos(6\pi n/N - \pi/2)$

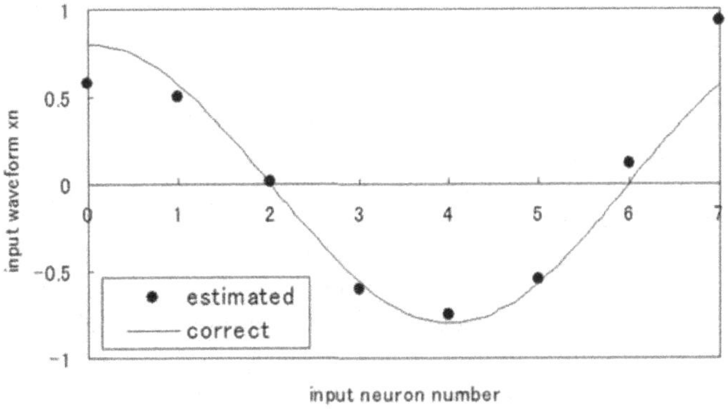

(a)

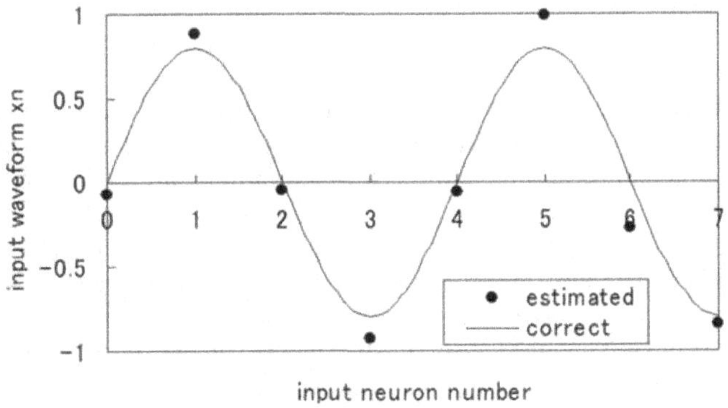

(b)

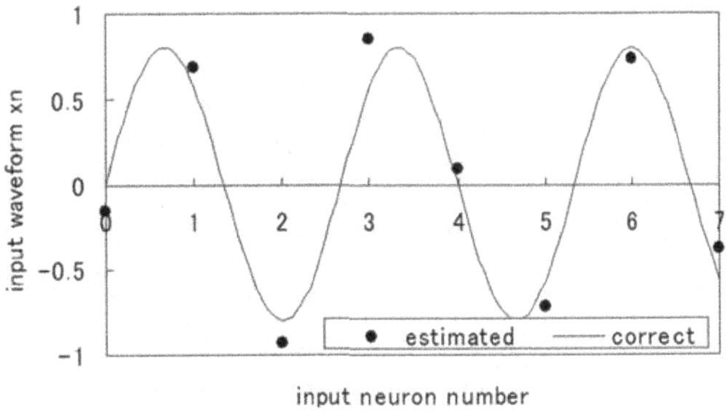

(c)

learns the forward relation from the input to the output, it estimates the corresponding input from the given test output by using the relation inversely. According to the result of inverse estimation, we obtained an almost correct input value. This means that the input was correctly estimated from the given test output by using the forward relation between the training input and output inversely. Inverse estimation of the input by complex-valued network inversion was confirmed by these simulations.

Example: Inverse estimation of Complex-Valued Mapping with Ill-Posedness

We examined complex-valued network inversion with regularization to solve the ill-posed inverse complex mapping problem. In this problem, the mapping between the points on the complex plane is learned by the complex-valued neural network. The complex-valued mapping concerning the absolute value is inversely estimated as an ill-posed inverse problem. To demonstrate the effect of regularization, three inverse estimations by complex-valued network inversion were examined. These estimations were (i) without regularization, (ii) with regularization directed to the maximum value, and (iii) with regularization directed to the minimum value. Here, we use the dynamic regularization method, which dynamically changes the coefficient, because it provides an advantage in that parameter setting of regularization is easier in dynamic regularization than in static regularization. Consequently, the solution that satisfies a specific condition is estimated almost correctly by this regularization.

In the training phase, the tutorial input and output patterns are provided to the network. The tutorial patterns are 31 points that satisfy the conditions $x_{nR} = x_{nI}$, $y_{nR} = x_{nR}$, and $y_{nI} = |x_{nI}|$ for the input $x_n = x_{nR} + ix_{nI}$ and output $y_n = y_{nR} + iy_{nI}$. In the inverse estimation phase, the weights obtained in the training phase are fixed to estimate the complex input from the complex test output. Both the real and imaginary parts of the initial input are set to random values from –1.0 to 1.0. The complex test output patterns are the same as those for the tutorial input. The input and output patterns for training are shown in Figure 23. The output patterns are also used for inverse estimation. In inverse estimation, there are two possible answers for data in the second and third quadrants, because the input is estimated as an inversion of the absolute value. Therefore, this problem contains the non-uniqueness of ill-posedness. The network architecture is the same as that shown in Figure 17. The parameters of the network are shown in Table 4.

The plot of the estimated input is shown in Figure 24 as the simulation result. The input estimated without regularization is shown in Figure 24 (a). Two correct solutions exist in the area of $y_R < 0$ while the solution is decided uniquely in the area of $y_R > 0$, where y_R is the value of the real part. The estimated inputs divide in the solutions of $y_I > 0$ and $y_I < 0$ and settle in the area of $y_R < 0$. It is considered that this division of solutions depends on the value of random numbers given as input initial values in complex-valued network inversion. On the other

Figure 23. The input and output patterns for training

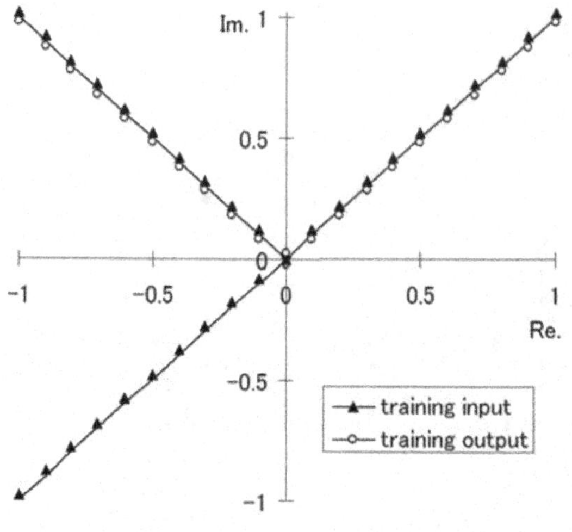

Table 4. Network parameters

	Without regularization	Dynamic regularization
Number of input neurons	1	
Number of hidden neurons	10	
Number of output neurons	1	
Training gain ε_t	0.01	
Estimation gain ε_e	0.01	
Final training error level	0.0001	
Final estimation error level	0.001	
Maximum number of training epochs	10000	
Maximum number of estimation epochs	10000	
Number of training sets	31	
Number of test sets	31	
Regularization coefficient λ	0	0.25
Decay coefficient m	0	0.001

hand, the input estimated by adding the regularization is shown in Figure 24 (b) and (c). The former is regularization directed at the maximum value, and it is expressed by

$$x_{mR}(t+1) = x_{mR}(t) - \varepsilon_e \cdot \delta_{mR} - \lambda x_{mR}(t),\ x_{mI}(t+1) = x_{mI}(t) - \varepsilon_e \cdot \delta_{mI} - \lambda x_{mI}(t). \tag{25}$$

The latter is regularization directed at the minimum value,

$$x_{mR}(t+1) = x_{mR}(t) - \varepsilon_e \cdot \delta_{mR} + \lambda x_{mR}(t),\ x_{mI}(t+1) = x_{mI}(t) - \varepsilon_e \cdot \delta_{mI} + \lambda x_{mI}(t), \tag{26}$$

where ε_e and λ represent the input correction coefficient and regularization coefficient, respectively.

According to these results, we can estimate the directed solution from the possible solutions by complex-valued network inversion with regularization. In other words, regularization solves ill-posed inverse problems with regard to uniqueness. The effectiveness of the regularization method in the complex-valued network inversion was depicted from this result. The effect on ill-posedness concerning existence and stability is currently under research. We expect that the problem of existence is solved by the generalization ability of the neural network. Moreover, we consider that the problem of stability is reduced by regularization that minimizes the fluctuations of the solution.

As described previously, the practical significance of network inversion is in the solution of ill-posed inverse problems. In the case of a well-posed problem with one-to-one correspondence between the input and output, we can estimate the inputs by the inverse solver network that reverses the input and the output. In other words, we can solve a well-posed inverse problem by forward learning and forward estimation. However, the inverse solver network does not solve ill-posed problems with many-to-one correspondence by forward learning and forward estimation, because the learning itself is unsuccessful.

To depict this feature, we consider three training data sets with one-to-one, many-to-one, and one-to-many correspondences of the complex-valued mapping problem. The network is assumed to have one input and one output, and the parameters are shown in Table 5. The first data set indicates a well-posed problem, which can be solved by the inverse solver network with reversed input and output. The second one indicates a problem that

Figure 24. Estimated results of complex-valued mapping with ill-posedness. (a) Without regularization, (b) with regularization for positive direction, (c) with regularization for negative direction.

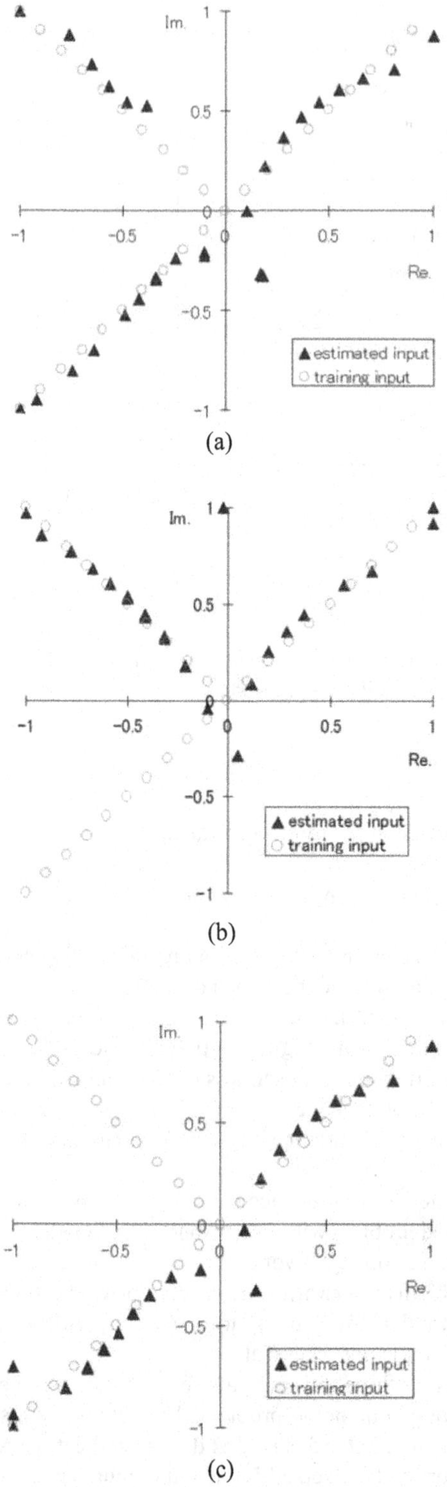

Table 5. Network parameters

Number of input neurons	1
Number of hidden neurons	10
Number of output neurons	1
Training rate ε_t	0.01
Maximum training epoch	10000
Number of training data	10

Table 6. Training data set

One-to-one correspondence		Many-to-one (2:1) correspondence		One-to-many (1:2) correspondence	
Input	Output	Input	Output	Input	Output
$-1.0-1.0i$	$-1.0-1.0i$	$-1.0-1.0i$	$1.0+1.0i$	$1.0+1.0i$	$-1.0-1.0i$
$-0.8-0.8i$	$-0.8-0.8i$	$1.0+1.0i$			$1.0+1.0i$
$-0.6-0.6i$	$-0.6-0.6i$	$-0.8-0.8i$	$0.8+0.8i$	$0.8+0.8i$	$-0.8-0.8i$
$-0.4-0.4i$	$-0.4-0.4i$	$0.8+0.8i$			$0.8+0.8i$
$-0.2-0.2i$	$-0.2-0.2i$	$-0.6-0.6i$	$0.6+0.6i$	$0.6+0.6i$	$-0.6-0.6i$
$0.2+0.2i$	$0.2+0.2i$	$0.6+0.6i$			$0.6+0.6i$
$0.4+0.4i$	$0.4+0.4i$	$-0.4-0.4i$	$0.4+0.4i$	$0.4+0.4i$	$-0.4-0.4i$
$0.6+0.6i$	$0.6+0.6i$	$0.4+0.4i$			$0.4+0.4i$
$0.8+0.8i$	$0.8+0.8i$	$-0.2-0.2i$	$0.2+0.2i$	$0.2+0.2i$	$-0.2-0.2i$
$1.0+1.0i$	$1.0+1.0i$	$0.2+0.2i$			$0.2+0.2i$

becomes ill-posed in inverse estimation. The forward training of this problem is to be confirmed. The third one indicates forward training for solving the ill-posed problem by the inverse solver network. These three data sets used in the simulation are shown in Table 6.

The error curve obtained when these data are learned is shown in Figure 25. The input-output relation is learned sufficiently in the first and second data sets because the error decreases. From the result of the first data set, this implies that the forward relation of the well-posed problem is correctly learned. In addition, the forward relation of the ill-posed problem is correctly learned from the result of the second data set. On the other hand, the inverse input-output relation cannot be learned because the error does not decrease in the third data sets. This result indicates that the inverse solver network cannot handle the ill-posed inverse problem. Consequently, the inverse solver network in which the input-output relation was reversed cannot solve the ill-posed inverse problem because the learning does not succeed; however, the problem can be solved by network inversion with appropriate regularization.

Because the inverse problem can be solved by the inverse solver network if data without ill-posedness are prepared, the practical significance of network inversion is reduced. However, it is difficult to exclude ill-posedness completely in the general problem. Therefore, it is considered that there is practical significance of network inversion as well as complex-valued network inversion.

CONCLUSION

In this chapter, we introduced a method involving a complex-valued neural network to solve inverse problems that extend to the complex domain. This method extends the network inversion method to the complex domain by solving inverse problems on a multilayer neural network. In this method, the complex-valued input is estimated from the provided complex-valued output by using a trained complex-valued multilayer neural network. Actually,

Figure 25. The error curve for the data: One-to-one, many-to-one, and one-to-many correspondence are learned

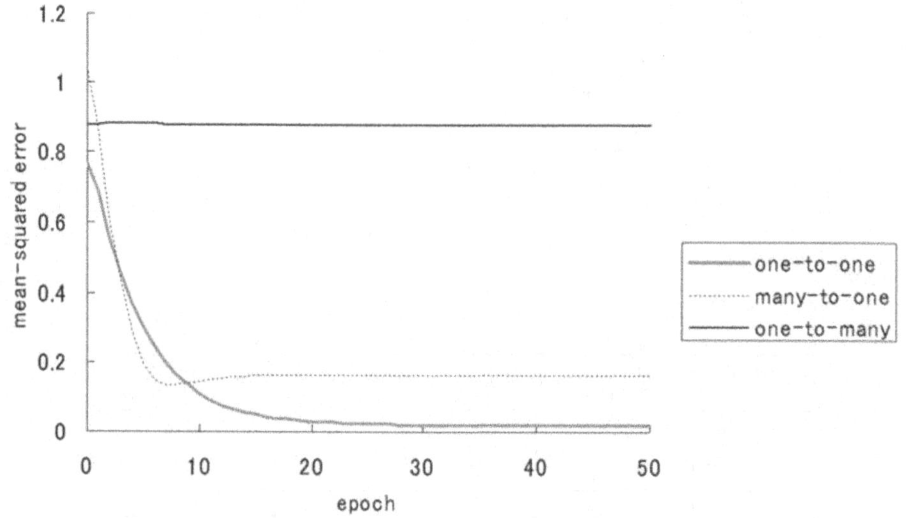

this method estimates the complex-valued input by propagating the complex-valued output error inversely and by correcting the complex-valued input value repeatedly.

An inverse problem, which is one by which the cause is estimated from the given result, is an important problem in field of science and engineering field. In this chapter, we explained the inverse problems as a background and introduced two examples: nerve bundle localization by evoked potentials and source localization using a bat-like sonar system. Next, we explained the principles of network inversion and regularization. The main focus of this chapter is on the introduction of the complex-valued network inversion method and the explanation of the regularization method for reducing ill-posedness. To confirm the procedure of complex-valued network inversion, we carried out two simulations: inverse estimation of complex-valued mapping and inverse Fourier transform. In both simulations, inverse estimated results with almost correct complex-valued inputs obtained from complex-valued outputs were observed, and the operation of complex-valued network inversion was confirmed according to the results of each simulation.

Moreover, complex-valued network inversion with regularization was applied to the ill-posed inverse problem of complex-valued mapping. The solution was confirmed to converge to a directed solution by the regularization method. Therefore, the effectiveness of the complex-valued network inversion method was confirmed. As future problems, we will consider applying complex-valued network inversion with regularization to actual engineering problems such as medical signal analysis and image recognition. Moreover, we will examine the effects of reducing ill-posedness by various regularizations.

FUTURE RESEARCH DIRECTIONS

In this chapter, the solution of inverse problems by complex-valued network inversion was clarified. In addition, the effect of the addition of regularization to solve ill-posedness, which poses a difficulty in actual inverse problems, was examined and illustrated by simulation.

We are considering three directions of future research. The first one involves studying the characteristics of the complex-valued network inversion thoroughly and researching its feature to solve inverse problems theoretically. The purpose of this would be to examine possible conversion and mapping by complex-valued network inversion, and to examine the characteristics experimentally and theoretically. As a result, it is necessary to clarify theoretical and methodological features of complex-valued network inversion. The second study involves applying complex-valued network inversion to actual problems. For example, we believe that this inversion can be applied to actual problems such as image processing and sonar signal analysis. In this case, because the problem of ill-posedness often arises in the actual problem, it is necessary to develop a method of regularization that corresponds to an actual case and examine this method. We consider that enhancement of the answer-in-weights scheme to the complex domain is a solution to the problem. The third study involves examining various methods of regularization. It is necessary to examine the regularization functional, including theoretical effects, because various situations of a problem are possible. Moreover, we consider that the method of providing the restraint condition is effective according to a method such as the answer-in-weights scheme. We think that this line of research will help make the complex-valued network inversion method a step in the development of complex-valued neural networks.

REFERENCES

Aster, R. C., Borchers, B., & Thurber, C. H. (2005). *Parameter estimation and inverse problems.* Elsevier.

Barshan, B., & Kuc, R. (1992). A bat-like sonar system for obstacle localization. *IEEE Transaction on Systems, Man, and Cybernetics, 22*, 636–646.

Benvenuto, N., & Piazza, F. (1992). On the complex backpropagation algorithm. *IEEE Transaction on Signal Processing, 40*(4), 967–969.

Groetsch, C. W. (1993). *Inverse problems in the mathematical sciences.* Wiesbaden, Germany: Informatica International.

Hirose, A. (2005). *Complex-valued neural networks.* Springer.

Jensen, C. A., Reed, R. D., Marks, R. J., El-Sharkawi, M. A., Jung, J. B., Miyamoto, R. T., Anderson, G. M., & Eggen, C. J. (1999). Inversion of feedforward neural networks: algorithms and applications. *Proceedings of the IEEE, 87*, 9, 1536–1549.

Kaipio, J., & Somersalo, E. (2005). *Statistical and computational inverse problems.* Springer.

Kosugi, Y., & Kameyama, K. (1993). Inverse use of BP net in answer-in-weights scheme for arithmetic calculations. *Proceeding of the World Congress on Neural Networks, III*, 462–465.

Kosugi, Y., Uemoto, N., & Ogawa, T. (1998). Dynamic regularization in the network inversion, *IEICE Transaction on Information and Systems, J81-D-II*(7), 1639–1646 (in Japanese).

Kuc, R., & Barshan, B. (1991). Bat-like sonar for guiding mobile robots. *IEEE Control Systems*, (pp. 4–12).

Linden, A., & Kindermann, J. (1989). Inversion of multilayer nets. *Proceedings of International Joint Conference on Neural Networks*, (pp. 425–430).

Lu, B. L., & Ito, K. (1995). Regularization of inverse kinematics for redundant manipulators using neural network inversions. *Proceedings of the IEEE International Conference on Neural Networks, 5*, 2726-2731.

Murray, W. R., Heg, C. T., & Pohlhammer, C. M. (1993). Iterative inversion of a neural network for estimating the location of a planar object. *Proceedings of World Congress on Neural Networks, 3*, 188-193.

Nitta, T. (1997). An extension of the backpropagation algorithm to complex numbers. *Neural Networks, 10*(8), 1392-1415.

Ogawa, T., Jitsukawa, N., Kanada, H., Mori, K., & Sakata, M. (2002). Neural network estimation of elastic moduli of composites by impact sound. *Japanese Journal of Applied Physics, 41*(5B), 3333-3338.

Ogawa, T., Kameyama, K., Kuc, R., & Kosugi Y. (1996). Source localization with network inversion using an answer-in-weights scheme. *IEICE Transaction on Information and Systems, E79-D*(5), 608-619.

Ogawa, T., & Kanada, H. (2005a). Complex-valued network inversion for solving complex-valued inverse problems, *IEICE Transaction on Information and System, J88-D-II*(9), 1954-1962 (in Japanese).

Ogawa, T., & Kanada, H. (2005b). Network inversion for complex-valued neural networks. In *Proceedings of the 2005 IEEE International Symposium on Signal Processing and Information Technology*, (pp. 850-855).

Ogawa, T., Matsuura, H., & Kanada, H. (2005). A solution of inverse kinematics of robot arm by network inversion. *Proceeding of the International Conference on Computational Intelligence for Modeling*, 1, 858-862.

Petrov, Y. P., & Sizikov, V. S. (2005). *Well-posed, ill-posed, and intermediate problems with application*. Koninklijke Brill NV.

Takeuchi, J., & Kosugi, Y. (1994). Neural network representation of finite element method. *Neural Networks, 7*(2), 389-395.

Tikhonov, A. N., & Arsenin, V. Y. (1977). Solutions *of ill-posed problems*. Winstion and Sons.

Valova, I., Kameyama, K., & Kosugi, Y. (1995). Image decomposition by answer-in-weights neural network, *IEICE Transaction on Information and Systems, E78-D-9*, 1221–1224.

Watanabe, E., & Kosugi, Y. (1991). New technique for intraoperative localization and monitoring of cranial nerves - preliminary study. In J. Schramm et al. (*Eds.*), *Intraoperative neurophysiologic monitoring in neurosurgery* (pp. 53–59), Berlin: Springer-Verlag.

Williams, R. J. (1986). Inverting a connectionist network mapping by backpropagation of error. *Proceedings of 8th Annual Conference on Cognitive Science Society* (pp. 859–865). Hillsdale, NJ: Lawrence Erlbaum.

ADDITIONAL READING

Baker, C. T. H. (1977). *Numerical treatment of integral equations* (p. 665). Oxford: Clarendon Press.

Baker, C. T. H., Fox, L., Mayers, D., & Wright, K. (1964). Numerical solution of Fredholm integral equations of the first kind. *The Computer Journal, 7*, 141–147.

Benson, J., Chapman, N. R., & Antoniou, A. (2000). Geoacoustic model inversion using artificial neural networks. *Inverse Problems, 16*(6), 1627–1639.

Calvetti, D., & Somersalo, E. (2007). Microlocal sequential regularization in imaging. Inverse *Problems and Imaging, 1*(1), 1–11.

Craig, I. J. D., & Brown, J. C. (1986). *Inverse problems in astronomy*. Adam Hilger.

Groetsch, C. W. (1984). *The theory of Tiknonov regularization for Fredholm equations of the first kind*. Pitman.

Kimura, J., Mitsudome, A., Yamada, T., & Dickins, S. (1984). Stationary peaks from a moving source in far-field recording. *Electro-encephalography and clinical Neurophysiology, 58*, 351–361.

Kindermann, J., & Linden, A. (1990). Inversion of neural networks by gradient descent. *Parallel Computing, 14*(3), 277–286.

Korovkin, N. V., Chechurin, V. L., & Hayakawa, M. (2007) *Inverse problems in electric circuits and electromagnetics*. Springer.

Kosugi, Y., Sase, M., Suganami, Y., Momose, T., & Nishikawa, J. (1996). Dissolution of partial volume effect in PET by an inversion technique with the MR-embedded neural network model. In R. Mayers, et al. (Eds.), *Quantification of brain function*. Academic Press.

Kosugi, Y., Sase, M., Suganami, Y., & Uemoto, N. (1996). Neural network based PET image reconstruction. *Proceedings of 2nd International Workshop on Biomedical Interpretation*, (pp. 163–166).

Kubo, S. (1988). Inverse problems related to the mechanics and fracture of solids and structures. *JSME International Journal*, Series I, (pp. 31-2, 157–166).

Lu, B. L., Kita, H., & Nishikawa, Y. (1999). Inverting feedforward neural networks using linear and nonlinear programming. *IEEE Transactions on Neural Networks*, *10*(6), 1271–1290.

Phillips, D. L. (1962). A technique for the numerical solution of certain integral equations of the first kind. *Journal of the Association for Computing Machinery*, *9*, 84–97.

Poggio, T., & Girosi, F. (1990). Regularization algorithms for learning that are equivalent to multilayer networks. *Science*, *247*, 978–982.

Sase, M., Kinoshita, N., & Kosugi, Y. (1994). A neural network for fusing the MR information into PET images to improve spatial resolution. *Proceedings of IEEE International Conference on Image Processing*, (pp. 908–911).

Thrun, S., & Linden, A. (1990) Inversion in time. *Proceedings of EURASIP Workshop*, (pp. 130–140).

Tosaka, N., Onishi, K., & Yamamoto, M, (1999). *Mathematical approach and solution methods for inverse problems*. University of Tokyo Press (in Japanese).

Witwer, J. G., Trezek, G. J., & Jewett, D. L. (1972). The effect of media inhomogeneities upon intracranial electrical fields. *IEEE Transaction on Biomedical Engineering*, *BME-19*, 352–362.

Yamamoto, M. (1995). Stability, reconstruction formula and regularization for an inverse source hyperbolic problem by a control method. *Inverse Problems*, *11*, 481–496.

Chapter III
Kolmogorov's Spline Complex Network and Adaptive Dynamic Modeling of Data

Boris Igelnik
BMI Research Inc., USA

ABSTRACT

This chapter describes the clustering ensemble method and the Kolmogorov's Spline Complex Network, in the context of adaptive dynamic modeling of time-variant multidimensional data. The purpose of the chapter is to give an introduction in these subjects and to stimulate a participation of both young and experienced researchers in a solution of challenging and important for theory and practice problems related to this area.

INTRODUCTION

This chapter describes specific neural network architecture with complex weights and potentially complex inputs in the context of adaptive dynamic modeling of *time-varying* multidimensional data. The technological and scientific developments in many areas of human activity have reached a level, requiring adequate changes in traditional methods of data modeling. Consider just two examples. One is related to coal-operating power stations. Coal might provide a fuel for world power industry for hundreds of years, making a good alternative to rapidly decreasing oil. But coal combustion produces harmful pollutions. Mitigation of this problem by controlling combustion requires modeling of power data, which are time-variant, highly multidimensional, nonlinear, non-stationary, and influenced by complicated, interacting chemical, electro-magnetic, and mechanical processes. There is no way to do such modeling by traditional methods of control theory (Ljung, 2000; Astrom & Wittenmark, 1995). The second example is related to defense, in particular to problems of detection, identification, and tracking targets in the clutter environment, utilizing sensors, such as radar, sonar, infrared (Hovanessian, 1984; Scolnik, 1990), and others. A possibility of having multiple moving and interacting targets, clutters, and sensors makes these problems extremely difficult for solution in real applications. The methods for solution of these problems, basically Bayesian ones (Antony, 1995; Congdon, 2006; Stone, Barlow, & Corvin, 1999), are founded on the theory developed 30-50 years ago, and inadequate to currently existing reality.

There is a long history of signal and noise representation, utilizing complex numbers in signal processing (Oppenheim & Schafer, 1975; Rihaczek & Hershkowitz, 1996; Haykin, 2001). Relatively recently it was recognized that complex representation of inputs and adaptively adjusted weights may be helpful in *neural network* (*net*) modeling, especially for pattern recognition (Kim & Guest, 1990; Leung & Haykin, 1991; Georgiu & Koutsougeras, 1992; Nitta, 1997, 2003; Arena, Fortuna, Muscato, & Xibilia, 1998; Aizenberg, Aizenberg, & Vandewalle, 2000; Igelnik, Tabib-Azar, & Leclair, 2001a; Hirose, 2003, 2006).

This chapter has the following objectives: 1) introducing basic principles, ideas, and algorithms of adaptive neural net modeling of *time-varying*, highly multidimensional data; 2) introducing a specific complex-valued neural network, the *Kolmogorov's Spline Complex Network* (KSCN), which might be advantageous especially in various tasks of pattern recognition.

BACKGROUND

There are several approaches to modeling, divided into two intersecting groups of methods, Artificial Intelligence (AI) (Nilsson, 1998; Jackson, 1986) and Computational Intelligence (CI) (Bezdek, 1992, 1994; Zurada, Marks, & Robinson, 1994; Pedrycz, 1998) groups. It is believed that the AI group is more appropriate for symbol processing, while the CI group fits more data processing. The CI group contains different methods: neural nets (Haykin, 1994, 2001; Bishop, 1995; Luo & Unbehauen, 1997), statistical pattern recognition (Fukunaga, 1990), fuzzy sets methods (Bezdek, Keller, Krishnapuram, & Pal, 1999), wavelets (Goswami & Chen, 1999), genetic (Mitchell, 1996) and evolutionary algorithms (Bäck, 1996), support vector machines (Cristianini & Shawe-Taylor, 2000), classification and regression trees (Breiman, Friedman, Olsen, & Stone, 1984) and so on.

This chapter considers only *neural nets* methods. Several reasons stand behind the preference given to *neural nets*. These are: 1) one-hidden layer feed-forward *neural nets* have a firm theoretical basis provided by the Kolmogorov's Superposition Theorem (KST) (Kolmogorov, 1957); 2) one-hidden layer Nonlinear Perceptron (NP) can learn a nonlinear mapping more efficiently than any linear network (Barron, 1993, 1994); 3) applied in combination with *clustering* (Duda, Hart, & Stork, 2001; Breiman, 1999), *neural nets* can efficiently learn time-varying, highly multidimensional, nonlinear, and non-stationary data; 4) in spite of common opinion that *neural nets* require utilization of large learning sets and large size of networks (Adeli & Hung, 1995; Adeli & Samant, 2000), there exist several practical ways to significantly mitigate these problems; 5) *neural nets* allow for solving efficiently such important tasks related to modeling (and data mining), as feature selection and visualization.

Consider the advantages of *neural nets* more in detail. There is an old problem of approximation of a continuous real-valued function f of d variables (input dimension) defined on the closed bounded set E (assumed here as a unit hypercube) with a given error ε based on information about P values of the function. For the class of continuous functions the lower bound for P grows exponentially with growth of d. This fact (known under name the "curse of dimensionality") makes reliable approximation of an arbitrary continuous multidimensional function practically impossible for relatively high dimensions. But there exist examples of reliable approximation of functions with high values of d. How may it occur? Modeling a function, one discerns a function from a noise. Actually all methods of modeling explicitly or implicitly assume, that a function has a bounded rate of variability, while the noise may have variability rate higher than that bound. Designers of complex systems often make preliminary statistical system modeling, imitating noise as a statistical distribution with some probability density function (*pdf*). In practice, realizations of a noise with some *pdf* are obtained as continuous functions of a noise with some elementary *pdf*, so-called uniform distribution in the unit interval [0, 1] (Fishman, 1995). The realizations of the uniform distribution are implemented as subsequent values of a continuous piece-wise linear function with very high absolute values of the derivative. Thus, actually a noise is a continuous function with very high rate of variability. In order to discern a function and a noise one has to consider functions from a subclass of the class of continuous functions. Additionally, distribution of a noise is unknown in applications, forcing a designer to choose among several known distributions, such as Gaussian, Weibull (Li & Yu, 1988), and so on, verifying type of distribution using statistical criteria.

Any approximation of a continuous real-valued multidimensional function f can be derived from the Kolmogorov's representation of such a function given by the KST. The KST states that any continuous function of d variables can be represented exactly as a finite sum of superpositions of univariate functions, where the number of terms in the sum depends only on value of d and does not depend on the function to be approximated. But that representation looks almost like a *neural net* approximation of a continuous function. One but extremely important difference is that the number of terms N in the sum (number of *basis functions*) for a neural net depends on the function f to be approximated and on required approximation error ε. Generally N tends to infinity, if ε tends to zero. Thus, it seems, that the KST gives an ideal *neural net* representation of a continuous multidimensional function with error $\varepsilon = 0$ and with seemingly finite complexity N, if the number of basis functions measures complexity. The KST considers neither the complexity of univariate functions, implementing Kolmogorov's representation, nor inevitable influence of noise on measured values of a function f, as was pointed out in Girosi, 1989. That only says (Kurková, 1991), that only approximate models make sense for real applications. The KST still can serve as an ideal model, showing ways of improving currently existing models in terms of efficiency. Indeed, traditional currently used adaptive models (for example, NP or RBF nets) are implemented as weighted sums of fixed shape *basis functions* with adaptively adjusted on the data internal parameters. The proof of KST utilizes basis functions with a shape adjustable on the data. Therefore, a necessary condition for improving efficiency appears to be an increasing degree of adaptivity of the basis functions.

Barron 1993, 1994 has introduced a broad family of functions with limited variability, which is a subclass of the class of multidimensional continuous functions. He also introduces two measures efficiency for the class of models, approximating functions from this subclass. One of these measures is the mean squared approximating error (approximating MSE), which measures the maximal approximating MSE for a function in the subclass, obtained by a best model from the class of models. Another measure, closer to the reality, measures maximal estimating MSE for a function in subclass, obtained by a model trained on a dataset with a finite size P. Since these measures are impossible to derive, Barron concentrated on the lower asymptotic bounds for approximating and estimating MSE for the subclass of continuous functions, and compared these bounds for two classes of models, linear one and Nonlinear Perceptron (NP), when both N and P tend to infinity. Because of noise for each class of models there exists least achievable approximation MSE error ε. Let N_l, N_p be the numbers of basis functions needed to achieve ε for linear models and for nonlinear perceptrons respectively. Then the bounds in (Barron, 1993) imply, that $N_l = O\left[1/\left(d\varepsilon^{2d}\right)\right]$, $N_p = O\left(1/\varepsilon^2\right)$. Obviously inequality $N_l \gg N_p$ holds for sufficiently small ε and $d > 1$. Therefore, the class of linear models need much more complexity than the class of nonlinear perceptrons, and is less efficient. Similar for this subclass of continuous functions results were obtained for some other classes of neural nets, for example, RBF nets (Mhaskar & Michelli, 1992) and hinging hyperplanes (Breiman, 1993).

Thus, the general scheme for developing a new class of *neural net* architectures should include the following steps: 1) define a subclass of the class of continuous multidimensional functions, broad enough to include current applications and having a well defined measure of variability; 2) derive a bound on (at least) the achievable approximation error ε as a function of class complexity N; 3) derive an estimate of required class complexity $N_e = F(\varepsilon)$; 4) compare N_e with the best known estimate of complexity N_b, when $\varepsilon \to 0$; 5) if $N_e < N_b$ for sufficiently small values of ε, then suggested class of *neural net* architectures outperforms existing classes of *neural net* architectures (on the suggested subclass of continuous functions) and deserves to be included in the set of recognized neural net architectures. The Kolmogorov's *Spline* Network (KSN) (Igelnik & Parikh, 2003a) has complexity (measured as the total number of parameters, which can be adjustable from the data) $N_{ks}(\varepsilon) = O\left(1/\varepsilon^{3/2}\right)$, which is obviously less than $N_p = O\left(1/\varepsilon^2\right)$ for sufficiently small values of ε. That proves an advantage of the KSN over NP in modeling the subclass of multidimensional continuous functions with bounded absolute value of the gradient (Igelnik & Parikh, 2003a). It is worth note that the criterion formulated above measures an average efficiency in the subclass of modeling, it is based on asymptotic bounds, and it does not take into account distribution of data. That means, that classes of *neural nets*, which already have proved their efficiency in many applications (such as RBF and NP nets), have to be included among good modeling tools. In any particular application their representatives may outperform (or may not) a representative of the class with better average modeling efficiency. Therefore, several classes of *neural nets* should be tested off-line.

The approach to modeling, presented in this chapter is significantly based on the modern understanding of the nature of human intellect. According to (Hawkins, 2004), the cortex is the primary area in the humans responsible for the intellect. The intellectual activity in the cortex is a combination of memory and prediction, used for updating the memory. This chapter considers only the specific implementation of the prediction module, because work on neural net implementation of memory is still in progress, and available only in some pending proposals. The suggested implementation of the prediction module is through the *Clustering Ensemble Approach (CEA)* described in (Igelnik et al.,1995-2003). The *CEA* is a combination of clustering and *neural net* modeling, featuring many steps for mitigating the problems of the "curse of dimensionality", a large size of the net, a large size of the data set for learning, the stability of training and testing, and allowing for dynamic modeling of *time-varying* data, feature selection and visualizations. These unique steps of *CEA* are described in detail in the next section.

There exist a number of important problems in which one has to discriminate two very similar patterns, for example, discriminating a target in clutter from the clutter or law-abiding from criminal patterns in making bank transactions. In these cases the problem reduces to the problem of efficient construction of decision boundaries between regions for acceptance of two mutually exclusive hypotheses. Use of complex inputs and weights may significantly amplify the problem solution in these cases (Nitta, 2003; Rihaczek & Hershkowitz, 1996; Igelnik et al., 2001a). The *KSCN*, suggested in this chapter, might be the most efficient complex-valued model for pattern recognition.

THE CEA METHOD

Basics of the CEA. The *CEA* method starts by dividing the whole data set available for learning in two sets, for learning and for validation, leaving 97% of the whole data for learning and 3% for validation. The training set uses 75% of learning data, while the testing set utilizes remaining 25%. The features of the objects of the data set are divided in the inputs and the outputs. The training set is used for optimization of the training mean squared error (MSE), while the testing set is used for optimizing the testing (generalization) MSE. Both optimizations are used to select the final learned model, which is validated on the validation set. The whole procedure of training consists of the following steps: 1) clustering; 2) building a set of *local neural nets*, using the *CEA* on each cluster; 3) building one *global net* from the set of local nets; 4) utilizing the global net for predictions; 5) short-term and long-term *updating* of relevant local nets and the *global net* on the basis of learning data. Short-term updating includes *updating* of one *local net* and *updating* of the *global net* and some cluster parameters. It is performed after each new pattern arrival. Long-term *updating* includes additionally updating of all *local nets* and complete re-clustering.

The *CEA* currently includes the following neural net architectures: NP net, RBF net, Complex Weights Net (CWN) (Igelnik et al., 2001a), and the KSN. It is planned to include the *KSCN* in the *CEA* in the near future. Availability of a variety of modeling architectures, including currently the most efficient ones, favorably distinguishes the *CEA* from other existing modeling tools. But the *CEA* has several other distinguished features related to: (1) mitigating the "curse of dimensionality", avoiding a large size of a net and a large size of the learning set; (2) neural net training and testing stability; (3) dealing with *time-varying* data; and (4) treating data with different sets of inputs (data fusion). These features are considered in detail in the following subsections.

Clustering. *Clustering* can significantly reduce the size of the search space. Another advantage of clustering is that the training, testing and validation of a number of small local nets, trained separately on each cluster, could be made significantly faster than the training of one big net, built on the whole set. Thus, *clustering* is helpful in both coping with problems of the "curse of dimensionality" and increasing the speed of the algorithm by using smaller nets trained on smaller sets. The *clustering* algorithm makes patterns inside one cluster more similar to each other than the patterns belonging to different clusters, trying to minimize the following objective function

$$J_e = \sum_{i=1}^{c} \sum_{x \in C_i} \left\| x - m_i \right\|^2 \underset{C_i, m_i, n_i}{\to} \min,$$

where c is the number of clusters, m_i is the center of the cluster C_i, n_i is the number of patterns in the cluster C_i. In order to control the size of clusters, another objective function has been added

$$J_u = \sum_{i=1}^{c} \left(n_i - P / c \right)^2 \underset{n_i}{\to} \min,$$

where P is the total number of patterns. The final goal of *clustering* is to minimize the following objective

$$J = \lambda J_e + \mu J_u \underset{C_i, m_i, n_i}{\to} \min,$$

where λ and μ are nonnegative scaling coefficients satisfying the condition $\lambda + \mu = 1$.

The algorithm was developed and tested in (Igelnik, 2003b), and is based on dynamical version of the K-means clustering (Duda et al., 2001, pp. 548-550), with an advanced initialization step (Bradley & Fayyad, 1998; Duda et al., 2001, p.550), mitigating the deficiencies of the K-means algorithm. As to unknown number of clusters we follow a general leader-follow *clustering* strategy (Duda et al, 2001, pp. 562-563). This strategy suggests that initial number of clusters is found off-line by experimentation, while only a center of a cluster, closest to a new pattern being presented, is changed on-line. This is a part of short-term *updating* procedure in the *CEA* described below in this section. Clustering is related to (1) - (3) of *CEA* distinguished features, described above.

Building the Set of Local Nets and the Ensembles of the Local Nets. The general form of a *local net*, built by the CEA method, the following:

$$\tilde{f}_N(x, W) = w_0^{ext} + \sum_{n=1}^{N} w_n^{ext} \psi_n(x, w_n^{\text{int}}), \tag{1a}$$

where $\tilde{f}_N(x, W) \triangleq y_N = (y_1, ..., y_D)$ is the multidimensional output, $x = (x_1, ..., x_d)$ is the multi-dimensional input, $\{w_n^{ext}, n = 0, 1, ..., N\}$ is the set of external parameters, $\{w_n^{\text{int}}, n = 1, ..., N\}$ is the set of internal parameters, W is the set of net parameters, which include both the external and internal parameters, $\{\psi_n, n = 1, ..., N\}$ is the set of *basis functions* (nodes), and $N_{\max}$ is the maximal number of nodes ($1 \le N \le N_{\max}$), dependent on the class of application, time and memory constraints. The *basis functions* ψ_n are calculated in general for a net with real weights through superposition and summation of univariate functions as follows

$$\psi_n(x, w_n^{\text{int}}) = g_n\left[\sum_{i=1}^{d} \varphi_{ni}(x_i, w_{ni}^{\text{int}})\right], \tag{1b}$$

where g_n and φ_{ni} are the univariate functions. In standard architectures, such as NP or RBF nets, the functions φ_{ni} are linear in x_i and in w_{ni}^{int} for NP nets and they are quadratic in the same arguments for RBF nets. The functions g_n, called the activation functions, are nonlinear univariate functions. They are chosen from a finite set of fixed form functions, such as the logistic function, the hyperbolic tangent, the Gaussian function, and so on, for standard architectures. For nonstandard architectures, using complex weights or/and *splines*, the *basis functions* (nodes) ψ_n will be defined in the appropriate places of this chapter.

The process of building a learned net by the *CEA* has the following characteristics[1]. The *CEA* builds a set of $(N+1)$ learned nets defined by equation (1) with the number of nodes N, $0 \le N \le N_{\max}$, starting from the net with $N = 0$, that is, building a net $\tilde{f}_0(x, W) = w_0^{ext}$. Nets for $N > 0$ are obtained from the learned net with $(N - 1)$ nodes by a recursive step, going from a net with $(N - 1)$ to a net with N nodes. For some integer K the *ensemble* of K candidate learned nets $\tilde{f}_{N,k}, k = 1, ..., K$ with N nodes is obtained as follows. Keeping the internal parameters of learned net with $(N - 1)$ nodes as a part of internal parameters of each member of the ensemble, an adaptive random number generator (ARG) generates the *ensemble* of internal parameters for N-th node. Therefore, all the internal parameters are defined for each member of the ensemble of nets with N nodes, and each member of the *ensemble* becomes a linear net. The optimal values of external parameters for each net $\tilde{f}_{N,k}$ from the ensemble $\{\tilde{f}_{N,k}, k = 1, ..., K\}$ are obtained using the formulas of recursive linear regression (RLR) (Albert, 1972, p. 44). The RLR starts with $N = 0$. For this case the net output is a constant, which optimal value can be calculated directly as

$$\tilde{f}_0(x, W) = \frac{1}{P_t} \sum_{p=1}^{P_t} y_p, \tag{2}$$

where $y_p, p = 1, ..., P_t$ are the vector-values of the outputs in the training set, P_t is the number of patterns in the training set. For the purpose of further discussion of the *CEA* one has to introduce a design matrix P_N and its pseudo-inverse matrix P_{N+} (the pseudo-inverse matrix is a generalization of the inverse matrix for non-squared rectangular matrices) for a net with N nonlinear nodes

$$P_N = \begin{bmatrix} 1 & \psi_1(x_1, w_1) & \dots & \psi_N(x_1, w_N) \\ 1 & \psi_1(x_2, w_1) & \dots & \psi_N(x_2, w_N) \\ \dots & \dots & \dots & \dots \\ 1 & \psi_1(x_P, w_1) & \dots & \psi_N(x_P, w_N) \end{bmatrix}. \tag{3}$$

If the matrix P_{N-1} is known then the matrix P_N can be obtained by a recurrent equation

$$P_N = \begin{bmatrix} P_{N-1} & \begin{matrix} \psi_N(x_1, w_N^{\text{int}}) \\ \psi_N(x_2, w_N^{\text{int}}) \\ \dots \\ \psi_N(x_P, w_N^{\text{int}}) \end{matrix} \end{bmatrix}. \tag{4}$$

The matrix P_{N+} can be calculated by the following recurrent equations

$$P_{N+} = \begin{bmatrix} P_{N-1,+} - P_{N-1,+} p_N k_N^T \\ k_N^T \end{bmatrix}, \tag{5a}$$

$$p_N = \left[\psi_N(x_1, w_N^{\text{int}}), \dots, \psi_N(x_{P_t}, w_N^{\text{int}})\right]^T, \tag{5b}$$

$$k_N = \frac{p_N - P_{N-1} P_{N-1,+} p_N}{\left\| p_N - P_{N-1} P_{N-1,+} p_N \right\|^2} \text{ if } p_N - P_{N-1} P_{N-1,+} p_N \neq 0 \cdot \tag{5c}$$

In order to start using formulas (4) and (5) for recurrent calculation of the matrices P_N and P_{N+} through the matrices P_{N-1} and $P_{N-1,+}$, and the vector-column P_N, the initial conditions are defined as

$$P_0 = \Big[\underbrace{1, 1, \dots, 1}_{P_t \text{ times}}\Big]^T, \; P_{0+} = \Big[\underbrace{1/P_t, 1/P_t, \dots, 1/P_t}_{P_t \text{ times}}\Big]. \tag{6}$$

Then formulas (4), (5) are applied in the following order for $N = 1$. First the one-column matrix p_1 is computed by (5b). Then the matrix P_0 and the matrix p_1 are used to compute the matrix P_1 in formula (4). After that the one-column matrix k_1 is computed by formula (5c), using P_0, P_{0+} and p_1. Finally, the matrix P_{1+} is computed by formula (5a). That completes computation of P_1 and P_{1+} using P_0 and P_{0+}. The external parameters and the values of the model output for the training set are determined as

$$w^{ext} = P_{N+} y, \quad \tilde{y} = P_N w^{ext}, \tag{7}$$

where $w^{ext} = \left[w_0^{ext}, w_1^{ext}, \dots, w_N^{ext}\right]^T$ is the $(N+1) \times D$ matrix of the values of external parameters for a net with N nodes,

$$\tilde{y} = \left[\tilde{f}_N\left(x_1^t, W\right), ..., \tilde{f}_N\left(x_{P_t}^t, W\right)\right]^T$$

is the $P_t \times D$ matrix of the values of the net training outputs for a net with N nodes. After training of all linear nets with N nodes included in the ensemble is completed, the *CEA* computes the training MSEs for these nets. At the end of this recursive step, the unique net $\tilde{f}_N(x, W)$ with the minimal training MSE in the ensemble is selected, and the testing MSE is determined for this net. Calculation of the testing/validation MSE for this optimal net uses formulas (7) with the only difference: the matrix P_N is calculated by the formula (3) where the values of the net training inputs $x_p, p = 1, ..., P_t$ are replaced by the values of generalization/validation inputs and the number of training inputs P_t is replaced by the number of generalization/validation ones.

The process of building *local nets* through *ensemble* of nets was first considered in (Igelnik & Pao, 1995), where a close connection between training and testing of a *neural net* and approximate calculation of multiple integrals was shown. The idea of utilizing the *ensemble* of randomly selected nets was considered in (Igelnik & Pao, 1995), since it was known, that the most efficient way of calculating multiple integrals is through stochastic, or quasi-stochastic methods (Stroud, 1971; Niederreiter, 1978).

Adaptive Random Generator (ARG). The ARG generates random values of each one-dimensional component of the vector of internal parameters for each member of the *ensemble*. Consider the generation of some component of the internal parameter for the first member of the ensemble ($k = 1$) by the ARG. Since no information on the performance of the net (in terms of the value of training MSE) is available at this moment the plot of *pdf*, $y = p(w)$, is chosen flat as shown in Fig. 1.

Consider the generation of the same component of the internal parameter for k-th member of the *ensemble* ($k > 1$) by the ARG. By that moment the information about training MSE for ($k - 1$) previously chosen members of the ensemble is known, as well as the *pdfs* for these members of the *ensemble*. The plot of *pdf* for $k > 1$ looks like shown in Figure 2a (Phase 1) or in Figure 2b (Phase 2).

The plot of the *pdf* has the form of a triangle with a base equal to1 and parallel to the axis w, if the triangle does not intersect line $y = 1/L$ and $k < K_1$, where L is a positive integer number, K_1 is the maximal number of iterations in Phase 1. Suppose the ARG samples the value of the internal parameter component for the k-th member of *ensemble*, $k > 1$. The vertex of the triangle has the abscissa c, equal to a value of the parameter-component, which brings minimum to the training MSE for previously chosen members of ensemble (a record). The ordinate of the vertex is defined by the condition that the area, bounded by the plot of *pdf* (two thick lines) and lines $w = 1, w = 0, y = 0$, equals to 1. It is easy to see, that if the number of cases for breaking the record tends to infinity,

Figure 1. Plot of pdf as a function of value of the internal component-parameter for k = 1

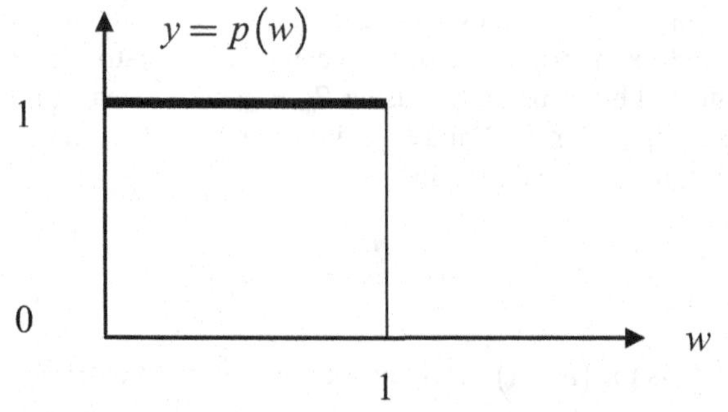

Figure 2. Plots of the pdf for k > 1

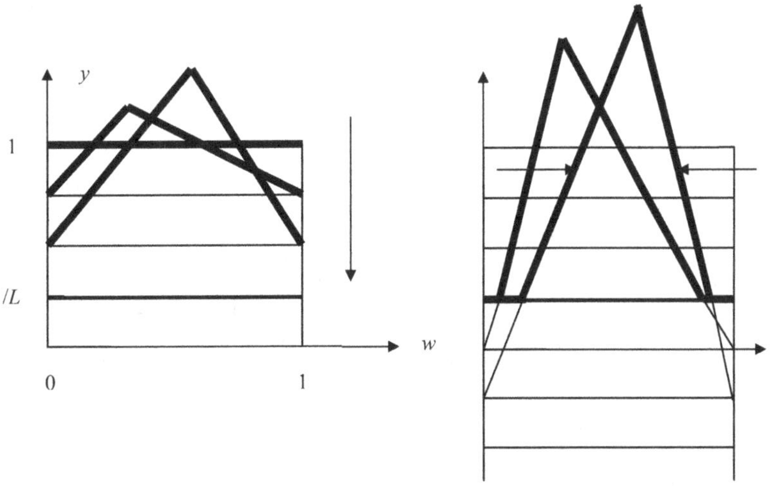

(a) *pdf* plot does not intersect line $y = 1/L$ (b) *pdf* plot intersects line $y = 1/L$

then the height of triangle also tends to infinity, while the base of triangle tends to zero. Thus, in this case, as was shown in (Igelnik, Pao, & LeClair, 1996), the *CEA* will find the global minimum of training MSE. This argument neither takes into account that the *ensemble* has a finite size *K*, nor that the whole algorithm has a random nature. When the area at the *w*-axis, where pdf > 0, is shrinking to zero, the probability that global minimum of the training MSE is out of the search area is increasing to a dangerous level. To avoid this the ARG acts as shown in Fig. 2b, when a triangle intersects line $y = 1/L$. In this case the ARG retains only a part of the triangle above this line, and adds to the plot of *pdf* the parts of line $y = 1/L$ defined on the rest of the interval [0, 1]. The base *b* of the part of the triangle and the height *h* of the whole triangle are determined uniquely, where formulas for their computing are found from a simple geometrical argument (similarity of triangles) and from a condition that area, bounded by the plot of *pdf* and lines $w = 1$, $w = 0$, $y = 0$, equals to 1. These formulas are given in the listing of subroutine *RGPhase*2() below. Moreover, a correctness of these formulas was proved experimentally. The data were simulated, using formulas described in listings of subroutines *RGPhase*1() and *RGPhase*2(), and the forms of histograms of the data were compared with the forms of *pdf* plots in Figure 2a and Figure 2b. The perfect fit among compared plots was observed. The *pdf* satisfies inequality $pdf \geq 1/L > 0$, and, therefore, each value of the parameter *w* in the interval [0, 1] is possible in the random sampling. In the limit, when a number of cases for breaking the record tend to infinity, the *pdf* tends to the function defined as

$$y = p(w) = \begin{cases} 1/L, \text{ if } w \neq w_* \\ (1 - 1/L)\delta(w), \text{ if } w = w_*, \end{cases}$$

where δ is the Dirac delta-function.

The ARG is described by a subroutine *RGPhase1*(float *c*, int *k*, float *x*), $1 \leq k \leq (K_1 - 1)$ for the members of ensemble, generated according to Figure 2a. Before starting the *ensemble*, one sets $k = 0$ and generate $y = random(32767)/32767.0$ (a sample from the uniform distribution in C++) for each component of the internal parameter w_n. After receiving a value of the training error for first member of the *ensemble*, one replaces *k* by $(k + 1)$ for each component of w_n, generates a random number $x = random(32767)/32767.0$ and calls *RGPhase1*(float *c*, int *k*, float *x*) with $c = y$ to get the second member of the *ensemble*. The choice of parameters $K, L,$ and K_1 is discussed in this subsection after describing the subroutines *RGPhase*1 and *RGPhase*2. These subroutines can be derived, using inverse transform method (Kalos & Witlock, 1986, pp. 45-48; Fishman, 1995, pp. 145-155), after simple calculations.

RGPhase1(float c, int k, float x)
{
float y;

$$y=\begin{cases} \dfrac{-c(L-k)+\sqrt{[c(L-k)]^2+4kLxc}}{2k}, & \text{if } 0\le x\le c, \\ c+\dfrac{(1-c)(L+k)-\sqrt{[(1-c)(L+k)]^2-4kL(x-c)(1-c)}}{2k}, & \text{if } c\le x\le\ ; \end{cases}$$

return y;
}

The ARG is described by the subroutine *RGPhase2*(float c, int k, float x), $K_1 \le k < K - K_1$ for the members of *ensemble*, generated according to Figure 2b.

RGPhase2(float c, int k, float x)
{

float y, h, b, b_1, b_2;

$$h=(1-1/L)+\sqrt{(1-1/L)^2+2(1-1/L)\frac{k}{L}};$$

$$b=\frac{h}{h+k/L};\ b_1=bc;\ b_2=b(1-c);$$

$$y=\begin{cases} Lx, \ \text{if } 0\le x\le (c-b_1)/L, \\ c+\dfrac{-[2c(L-1)+b_1]+\sqrt{[2c(L-1)+b_1]^2-4c^2(L-1)^2+4c(L-1)(Lx-c)}}{Lh}, \\ \quad \text{if } (c-b_1)/L\le x\le c, \\ c+\dfrac{b_2+2(L-1)(1-c)-\sqrt{[b_2+2(L-1)(1-c)]^2-4(1-c)(L-1)L(x-c)}}{Lh}, \\ \quad \text{if } c\le x\le\ -(1-c-b_2)/L, \\ Lx-L+1, \ \text{if } 1-(1-c-b_2)/L\le x\le 1. \end{cases}$$

return y;
}

Clustering allows for sampling relatively good *basis functions*, and the RLR procedure, following the ARG sampling, automatically leads to the optimal training MSE. These circumstances justify choice of a relatively small size of the ensemble. In particular, the author of this chapter has found, that the choice of $K = 100$ worked close to optimum for data from many different power plants. The value of K_1 was derived from K as $K_1 \approx K/4$ and inequality $K_1 < K/2$. The value of $K_1 = 25$ worked as well as $K = 100$ in all mentioned above applications. Obviously, the value of L should satisfy inequality $L \ll K_1$ but should not be too small. The experiments have shown, that values of L, satisfying inequality $4 \leq L \leq 6$, covered satisfactory all mentioned above power applications. Some work done in other areas (for example, satellite data) also demonstrated that values of $K = 100, K_1 = 25,$ and L between 4 and 6 are a good starting point for choosing these parameters.

It is important that a relatively small size of ensemble, *clustering*, and use of efficient *neural net* architectures allows for making short-term *updating* of a *local net* and the *global net* in real time.

Optimizing the Number of Nodes. A special procedure uses the set of testing errors for determining the optimal number of nodes. This procedure finds the global minimum of the testing MSE $e_{N,g}$ ($testMSE_N$) and selects the learned net with the number of nodes $N_{opt} = \arg \min_{0 \leq N \leq N_{\max}} \left(e_{N,g}\right)$.

Using smallest possible nets is the way of increasing stability of training and testing, and at the same time decreasing running time of modeling algorithms.

Filters for New Basis Functions and New Data. The RLR is a recursive process, when having a net with N *basis functions* defined by equation (1a), one adds a new basis function ψ_{N+1} from the ensemble in order to obtain a net with $N + 1$ *basis functions*. The adding of a new *basis function*, as a rule, increases the instability of learning, which has to be compensated by an increase of information about data provided by the new *basis function*. However, this increase will be insignificant, if the vector

$$p_{N+1} = \left(\psi\left(x_1, w_{N+1}^{\text{int}}\right), ..., \psi\left(x_P, w_{N+1}^{\text{int}}\right)\right),$$

where $x_1, ..., x_P$ are input parts of the patterns from the training set, is too close to the linear space $L\left(p_0, p_1, ..., p_N\right)$ spanned by the vectors-columns $p_0, p_1, ..., p_N$, forming the design matrix

$$P_N = \left[p_0, p_1, ..., p_N\right].$$

To avoid such a situation, the RLR computes absolute value of the sine of the angle between the vector p_{N+1} and space $L\left(p_0, p_1, ..., p_N\right)$, and rejects p_{N+1}, if this value is less than some small number $\eta > 0$. If value of η is not small enough, then the rejections will occur too often, leading to a significant increase of running time. From the other hand, too small values of η may result in a situation when rejections never occur. For power applications the value $\eta = 10^{-7}$ worked well. This value may be a reasonable starting point for other applications.

The filter of *basis functions* described above increases computational stability of training and testing in RLR.

The space $L\left(p_0, p_1, ..., p_N\right)$ can be considered as spanned by vector-rows

$$q_p = \left(1, \psi\left(x_p, w_1^{\text{int}}\right), ..., \psi\left(x_p, w_N^{\text{int}}\right)\right), p = 1, ..., P.$$

There exist formulas in RLR (Albert, 1972, pp.126, 127), allowing for recursive computing of a net with N basis functions trained on the set $\left\{x_1, ..., x_P, x_{P+1}\right\}$ from a net with same N basis functions trained on the set $\left\{x_1, ..., x_P\right\}$. It seems plausible, that patterns x_{P+1} too close to $L\left(p_0, p_1, ..., p_N\right)$ will add relatively small information to the training set $\left\{x_1, ..., x_P\right\}$ and can be filtered out by a procedure similar to procedure of filtering out unacceptable basis functions.

The work on justification of such a filter is in progress. If successful such a filter can be applied for choosing a pattern to remove in the short-term *updating*, and, therefore, keeping size of a training set bounded without significant loss of information for learning.

Training with Noise. One additional measure for validation, mitigating to some degree the effect of choosing the validation set from the same total set of data used for learning, is training (testing, validation) with noise (Breiman, 1996, 1999). That means, that every output value y is replaced by the sum $y + n$, where n is a simulated Gaissian noise with the zero mean and standard deviation equal to the standard deviation of the data used for training, or testing, or validation. The training with noise reduces time of learning compared to traditional cross-validation method (Stone, 1974) at least by an order of magnitude, without making worse the performance.

Global Net. For each cluster $c = 1,...,C$ a learned net $\mathcal{N}_c(x_c)$ has been built. The following equation gives a simple model of a *global net*

$$\mathcal{N}(x,w) = w_0 + \sum_{c=1}^{C} w_c \mathcal{N}_c(x_c)\exp(-\|x - \tilde{m}_c\|^2 / 2\sigma_c^2), \tag{8}$$

where $\mathcal{N}$ is the global net, $\mathcal{N}_c$ is a *local net* related to cluster *c*, *C* is the number of clusters, x_c is a vector of inputs to $\mathcal{N}_c$, x is the union of all x_c, $\tilde{m}_c$ is the input part of the cluster-center of *c*, $\|x - \tilde{m}_c\|$ is the distance between points x and $\tilde{m}_c$, σ_c is the in tra-distance for a cluster *c*, $c = 1,...,C$ (the intra-distance is defined as the shortest distance of a pattern, not belonging to cluster *c*, to the cluster-center $\tilde{m}_c$). The vectors x_c can be replaced by the vector x, if equation (8) is used before feature selection and ranking. Then the chosen features in different clusters can be different, that is why notation x_c for different clusters is utilized in equation (8). Another reason for choosing the notation x_c is a possible use of a *global net* for data fusion. In this case the different sets of cluster inputs are related to the different input sensors, while the *global* net combines them for common outputs. Cluster-centers and intra-distances are updated before *updating* the global net. Thus, the only unknown parameters with numerical values established during the learning are the parameters $w_0, w_1,..., w_C$. Therefore, the *global net* is a linear net. The training of the *global net* can be performed by the RLR on the total training set and can be done fast (usually value of *C* is significantly less than the value of $N_{\max}$, and there is no need for generating *ensembles*).

The *global net* plays important role in the CEA by: 1) expanding areas of reliable prediction around the clusters; 2) allowing for treating not perfect clustering, with intersecting clusters; 3) eliminating possible discontinuity of a model on the borders of clusters; 4) treating the local nets with different sets of inputs.

Updating the Model by the CEA. When a new pattern of data arrives the model is subjected to a short-term *updating* that include: determining the cluster-center $\tilde{m}_{\tilde{c}}$ closest to the new pattern; temporarily including new pattern in the training part of the cluster $\tilde{c}$; excluding one of the old patterns from the cluster training set (at random or by other strategy); *updating* the parameters $\tilde{m}_c$, σ_c; retraining the local net $\mathcal{N}_{\tilde{c}}(x_{\tilde{c}})$; retraining the global net $\mathcal{N}(x, w^{ext})$. Long-term updating includes additionally re-clustering and retraining of all local nets.

General Comment on Choosing Global Parameters. The global parameters of the *CEA* (those having default values) sometimes are chosen using: the constraints by memory and running time considerations (examples are the parameters $N_{\max}$, η); the general strategy and experience of recognized experts (example is a number of clusters *C*); a personal experience of the inventor of the *CEA* (choice of parameters *L*, *K*, and K_1). Where possible, choice of parameters is automatic (an optimal number of nodes in the net N_{opt}). The recommended values of these parameters defined above can be used as a good starting point for off-line experimentation in a specific area of applications, if necessary. Additionally, a variety of possible neural net architectures give a broad set of choices. The author of this chapter does not think that one could achieve higher level of performance by choosing large number of default values for global parameters. He believes, that the software producers, using such a strategy (with a number of default values typically hidden from a user) may only slightly polish the software performance, which depends mainly on the methods and the architectures built-in in software design.

The CEA Implementation. The previous subsections described numerous features of the *CEA* and could make an impression of its excessive complexity. But the only complexity (not excessive at all for moderately experienced programmer) of *CEA* is in programming. The following example illustrates a *CEA* application in power industry. In this example dynamic updating of the set of training data was applied, using as a validation a source of new on-line data. The learning set was extracted from the set of historical data, which played the role of the total set. The results of updating are presented in Table 1. They demonstrate that the updating was successful. In this example, the total number of patterns and numbers of patterns for training, testing, and validation equal to 3450, 2504, 843, and 103, respectively, the dimension of input equals to 34, the dimension of output (content of nitrogen oxides in the atmosphere due to power generation) equals to 1, the number of clusters equals to 10. The *CEA* program was running on PC with Pentium-4 processor, 2.66 GHZ and was written in C/C++. Following

Table 1.

Error	Training	Testing	Validation
MSE	8.35E-05	8.65E-05	8.9E-05
MAE	0.0064	0.0066	0.0069
RMAE	2.216%	2.25%	2.33%
STD RAE	2.12%	2.06%	1.67%
Running time for:	Long-term retraining = 20 sec		Short-term retraining = 2 sec.

notations are used in the Table 1: MSE-mean squared error, MAE -mean absolute error, RMAE-relative MAE, STD- standard deviation.

It should be mentioned that in this example performance of the *CEA*, measured in RMAE was 2 times better, and running time was 5 times better than for a traditional method of modeling time-variant data based on the Kalman filtering. It can be claimed in general that advantages of the *CEA* in performance, running time, and stability of training and testing, far outweigh some difficulties in its programming.

CEA Application in Feature Selection and Ranking. Feature selection is the process of finding the minimal set of inputs to a system, which determine its output. The suggested approach is an alternative to an approach popular in engineering (Zapranis, 1999, pp. 79-85), utilizing estimates of partial derivatives of the system output over its inputs. However, the estimates of partial derivatives as the ratio of two small quantities are sensitive to both, noise and computational errors. Alternatively, in the first stage of the suggested approach one is attempting to get rid of features correlated to other features. Some approaches to the first stage, using visualization and expert knowledge, are considered in (Igelnik, 2003b, 2003c) and will not be considered in this chapter. A sketch of the ranking procedure (second stage of approach) is given below.

Suppose that the system output y is related to the set of its inputs $x_1,...,x_d$ by the equation $y = f(x_1,...,x_d)$, and a local neural net has learned from data the approximate model $y \approx \tilde{f}(x_1,...,x_d)$. Assume that all variables are independent and normalized to the interval $[0,1]$. Fix all the inputs $x_1,...,x_d$ except one $x_i, i = 1,...,d$. The average value of the approximation over the variable x_i, given constant values of all other variables, can be expressed as

$$E_i(x_{-i}) = \int_0^1 \tilde{f}(x_1,...,x_d)dx_i.$$

The deviation of the approximation from its average value is measured by the quantity

$$\mathrm{var}_i(x_{-i}) = \int_0^1 \left[\tilde{f}(x_1,...,x_{\tilde{d}}) - E_i(x_{-i})\right]^2 dx_i.$$

The total effect on the output by the variable x_i (rank) is measured by the quantity

$$J_i = \int_0^1 \ldots \int_0^1 \mathrm{var}_i(x_{i-})dx_{-i}, i = 1,...,d,$$

where $dx_{\tilde{d}i} = dx_1...dx_{i-1}dx_{i+1}...dx_{\tilde{d}}$. To make ranks sum to 1, they should be replaced by the normalized quantities $j_i = J_i / \sum_{k=1} J_k$. Suppose normalized ranks j_i are arranged in the ascending order $j_1 \leq j_2 \leq ... \leq j_d$ and let α be a small positive number, compared to 1, say $\alpha = 0.05$. Then one can discard the k features having sum of ranks total not more than $100\alpha\%$. The important thing is that all integrals necessary to compute ranks can be obtained either explicitly, or approximately with any desired accuracy.

The novelty of this approach is in the use of the approximate model. While traditional ranking uses partial derivatives for measuring sensitivity of the output, which increase the noise contained in the data, this approach uses integrals over the model. The latter approach decreases noise.

NEURAL NETS BASED ON THE KOLMOGOROV'S SUPERPOSITION THEOREM

The Kolmogorov's Superposition Theorem (KST). The KST gives a general and very parsimonious representation of a multivariate continuous function through superposition and addition of univariate functions. According to (Lorentz, von Golitschek, & Makovoz, 1996), the KST states that any function *f* continuous in standard unit hypercube of dimension *d* has the following representation

$$f(x) = \sum_{n=1}^{2d+1} g\left[\sum_{i=1}^{d} \lambda_i \psi_n(x_i)\right] \tag{9}$$

with some continuous univariate function *g* depending on *f*, while univariate functions, ψ_n, and constants λ_i are independent of *f*.

Hecht-Nielsen (1987) was the first who recognized that the KST could be utilized in *neural network* computing. He proved that the Kolmogorov's superpositions could be interpreted as a four-layer feed-forward neural network, using Sprecher's enhancement of the KST (Sprecher, 1965). Girosi & Poggia (1989) pointed out, that the KST is irrelevant to *neural network* computing, because of very high complexity of computation of the functions *g* and ψ_n from the finite set of data. However, Kurkova (1991) noticed, that in the Kolmogorov's proof of the KST the fixed number of basis functions, $2d+1$, can be replaced by a variable *N*, and, the task of function representation by the task of function approximation. She also demonstrated (Kurkova, 1992), how to approximate Hecht-Nielsen's network by the traditional neural network. Numerical implementation of the Kolmogorov's superpositions was analyzed in Sprecher (1996, 1997). All these works were the attempts to preserve the efficiency of the Kolmogorov's theorem in representation of a multivariate continuous function in its practical implementation. If implemented with reasonable complexity this feature can make a breakthrough in building efficient approximations. However, since the estimates of the complexity of the suggested algorithms of the KST implementation were not available so far, the arguments against those efforts (Girosi & Poggio, 1989) were not yet refuted until 2003.

The Kolmogorov's Spline Network. The approach adopted in (Igelnik & Parikh, 2003a) is different. The starting point is a function approximation, from the finite set of data, by a neural net of the type given by equation (1). The function *f* to be approximated belongs to the class Φ of continuously differentiable functions with bounded gradient, which is wide enough for applications. A qualitative improvement of the approximation $f \approx f_N$, f and $f_N \in \Phi$, using some of the ideas of the KST proof, was sought. The KST proof was utilized to derive, that the *neural networks* with the shape of *basis functions,* varying dependent on data, may achieve better performance with the same net complexity (or the same performance with smaller complexity) than traditional *neural networks* with fixed-shape *basis functions.*

Here the Kolmogorov's Spline Network, (KSN) is introduced. The distinctive features of this architecture are: it is obtained from (9) by replacing the fixed number of *basis functions*, $2d+1$, by the variable *N*, and by replacing both external function *g* and the internal functions ψ_n by cubic *spline* functions (Prenter, 1975, pp. 77-93), $s_n(.,w_n^{\text{int}})$ and $s_{ni}(,w_{ni}^{\text{int}})$ respectively. Use of cubic *splines* allows for varying the shape of basis functions in the KSN by adjusting the spline parameters w_n^{int} and w_{ni}^{int}. Thus, the KSN, f_N, is defined as follows

$$f_N(x,W) = w_0^{ext} + \sum_{n=1}^{N} w_n^{ext} s_n\left[\sum_{i=1}^{d} \lambda_i s_{ni}\left(x_i, w_n^{\text{int}}\right), w_{ni}^{\text{int}}\right], \tag{10}$$

where $\lambda_1,\ldots,\lambda_d$, like in KST, are rationally independent numbers (Shidlovskii, 1989, pp. 69-74), satisfying the conditions $\lambda_1 > 0,\ldots,\lambda_d > 0$, $\sum_{i=1}^{d} \lambda_i \leq 1$. These numbers are not adjustable on the data and can be chosen independent of an application. The following theorem formulates the main result in (Igelnik & Parikh, 2003a), that the rate of convergence of approximation error to zero with $N \to \infty$ is significantly higher for KSN than the corresponding rate for existing currently *neural networks*. Define the complexity P^{2} of the approximation of the function f by a network (10) as the number of adjustable parameters needed to achieve a given approximation error. Then the theorem states

Theorem (Estimate of the Rate of Convergence of the KSN to the Target Function): For any function $f \in \Phi$ and any natural number N there exists a KSN defined by equation (10) with the cubic *spline* univariate functions s_n^s, s_{ni}^s, defined on [0,1], and rationally independent numbers $\lambda_1 > 0, \ldots, \lambda_d > 0, \sum_{i=1}^{d} \lambda_i \le 1$, such that

$$\|f - f_N\| = O\left(\frac{1}{N}\right). \tag{11}$$

The complexity of a net expressed in terms of its number of parameters P satisfies the equation

$$P = O\left(N^{3/2}\right). \tag{12}$$

This statement favorably compares the KSN with other networks currently in use. Most of the existing *neural networks*, f_W, provide the estimate of approximation error by the following equation

$$\|f - f_N\| = O\left(1/\sqrt{N}\right).$$

Suppose N is the number of *basis functions* for KSN needed to achieve an approximation error equal to $\varepsilon > 0$. Comparison of the last equation and (11) shows that the number of *basis functions* for existing networks N_* is $N_* = O\left(N^2\right)$, where N refers to the case of KSN. Therefore, the number of their parameters, P_*, is $P_* = O\left(N^2\right)$. It is obvious, that $P_* >> P$ for large values of N.

Kolmogorov's Spline Complex Network (KSCN). The motivation for work on the *KSCN* came as a result of analyzing papers Igelnik et al. (2001a), Igelnik & Parikh (2003a). The CWN net was obtained by a generalization of the RBF net, using complex weight parameters. It was shown, that the CWN outperforms the RBF net in a number of difficult classification tasks, while in the regression problems performance of the both nets has not demonstrated significant difference. The universal approximation capability of the CWN net was proved, although no results on the rate of convergence of the training MSE to zero were received. From the other hand the KSN has estimates of the rate of convergence of the training MSE to zero, and its advantage over existing neural networks in performance was demonstrated in the previous subsection. Then it was natural to combine ideas of the CWN and KSN in a net with complex weights, and to explore if this combination can be advantageous in case of classification tasks. This argument led to the following definition of the *KSCN* given by the equation

$$f_N(x, W) = w_0^{ext} + \sum_{n=1}^{N} w_n^{ext} s_n\left[\left|\sum_{i=1}^{d} \lambda_i s_{ni}\left(x_i, w_{ni}^{\text{int}}\right)\right|, w_n^{\text{int}}\right], \tag{13}$$

where $W = \left\{w_0^{ext}, w_n^{ext}, w_n^{\text{int}}, w_{ni}^{\text{int}}, n = 1, \ldots, N, i = 1, \ldots, d\right\}$ is the set of all adjustable net parameters, w_{ni}^{int} are complex weights (parameters). We show that the *KSCN* is at least as good in classification and regression tasks as the CWN, and it is likely that this advantage is significant. It should be noticed in advance that the estimate of the rate of convergence of training MSE to zero is evaluated for the best possible net in the class. Indeed, the *splines* s_n can be chosen so, that they will approximate any activation function used for the CWN (for example, Gaussians) with any desired accuracy. From the other hand, *splines* s_{ni} can be chosen so that that they will be represented by the piecewise linear functions on the almost all interval [0,1], with cubic *spline* connections, occupying arbitrary small part of this interval. In particular this representation can be chosen even linear for almost all interval [0,1]. Thus, the *KSCN* will be reduced to the arbitrary CWN net in this last case. Therefore, the best *KSCN* is at least as best as the best CWN. It looks quite plausible that the advantage of the best *KSCN* over the best CWN will be significant because 1) piecewise linear functions have much better approximation capability than linear ones; 2) more than that, piecewise qubic polynomials have much better approximation capability than piecewise linear functions.

Implementation of the KSN and the KSCN. The *CEA* allows for treating neural nets having basis functions with adjustable shape (such as KSN and *KSCN*) exactly in the same manner as basis functions with fixed shape. The main scheme of the *CEA* consists of generating *ensemble* of internal parameters inside basis functions, and then determining the external parameters of a net by the RLR for each member of the *ensemble*. The only additional module for the KSN and the *KSCN* is the module for construction the splines, described in Igelnik & Parikh (2003a). We consider here only implementation of *splines* s_{ni}. The *splines* s_n are implemented in a similar manner. The splines $s_{ni}\left(x_i, w_{ni}^{\text{int}}\right)$ can be expanded as a unique linear combination of the elementary *splines* $B_m(x_i)$ (Prenter, 1975, pp.79-81) as follows

$$s_{ni}\left(x_i, w_{ni}^{\text{int}}\right) = \sum_{m=-1}^{M+1} y_{nim} B_m(x_i), \tag{14}$$

where $M+1$ is the number of equally spaced knots $t_0 = 0, t_1, \ldots, t_{M-1}, t_M = 1$ for a spline $s_{ni}\left(x_i, w_{ni}^{\text{int}}\right)$,

$$B_m(x_i) = \left(1/h^3\right)\begin{cases} (x_i - t_{m-2})^3, \text{ if } x_i \in [t_{m-2}, t_{m-1}] \\ (x_i - t_{m-1} + h)^3 - 4(x_i - t_{m-1})^3, \text{ if } x_i \in [t_{m-1}, t_m] \\ (t_m - x_i + h)^3 - 4(t_m - x_i)^3, \text{ if } x_i \in [t_m, t_{m+1}] \\ (t_{m+2} - x_i)^3, \text{ if } x_i \in [t_{m+1}, t_{m+2}] \\ 0, \text{ otherwise} \end{cases} \quad . \tag{15}$$

Graph of a function $y = B_m(x)$ is shown in Figure 3. This graph is symmetric with respect to the line $x = t_m$. The maximal value of the function, equal to 4, is achieved when $x = t_m$.

An important note is that the values of the *splines* $B_m(x_i)$ at the x_i, belonging to training, testing, and validation sets, can be calculated before the *CEA* starts, because these values does not depend on the values of adjustable parameters w_{ni}^{int}. The coefficients y_{nim} satisfy the set of $M+3$ linear equations

$$Ay_{ni} = w_{ni}^{\text{int}}, \tag{16}$$

Figure 3. Graph of $y = B_m(x)$, $m = 2, h = 0.2, t_{m-2} = 0, t_{m-1} = 0.2, t_m = 0.4, t_{m+1} = 0.6, t_{m+2} = 0.8$

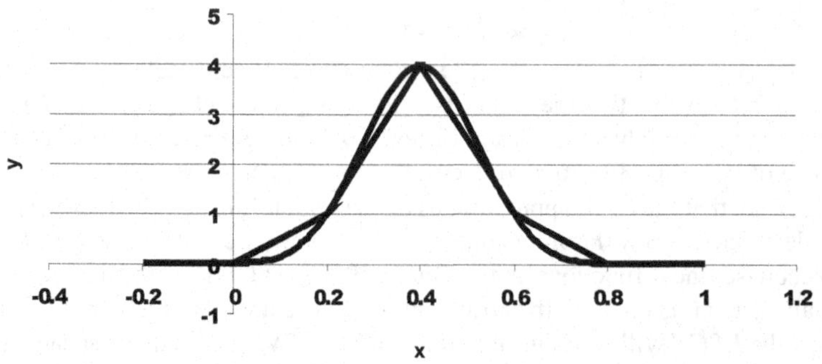

where

$$A=\begin{bmatrix} -3/h & 0 & 3/h & 0 & & 0 & 0 & \ldots \\ 1 & 4 & 1 & 0 & & 0 & 0 & \ldots \\ 0 & 1 & 4 & 1 & & 0 & 0 & \ldots \\ 0 & 0 & 1 & 4 & & 1 & 0 & \ldots \\ \ldots \\ 0 & 0 & 0 & \ldots & 0 & 1 & 4 & 1 \\ 0 & 0 & 0 & \ldots & 0 & -3/h & 0 & 3/h \end{bmatrix}, \tag{17a}$$

$$y_{ni}=\left(y_{ni,-1},y_{ni0},\ldots,y_{ni,M+1}\right)^T, w_{ni}^{\text{int}}=(s'_{ni}(t_0),s_{ni}(t_0),\ldots,s_{ni}(t_M),s'_{ni}(t_M))^T, \tag{17b}$$

$$t_m=mh, m=-2,-1,0,\ldots,M,M+1,M+2, h=1/M. \tag{17c}$$

Thus, the components of the internal parameter w_{ni}^{int} are values of the *spline* s_{ni} at the knots $t_0,\ldots,t_M$, as well as values of the derivative s'_{ni} at the knots $t_0,\ldots,t_M$, adjusted on the data. The system of equations (16) can be transformed to the following system of triangle form (Igelnik & Parikh, 2003a)

$$\begin{aligned} y_{-1}+4y_0+y_1 &= \sigma_0 \\ y_0+4y_1+y_2 &= \sigma_1 \\ &\ldots\ldots\ldots \\ y_{M-1}+4y_M+y_{M+1} &= \sigma_M \\ l_M y_M + r_M y_{M+1} &= c_M \\ (4\nu r_M-2\nu l_M)y_{M+1} &= 4\nu c_M - l_M(\sigma_{M+1}+\nu\sigma_M). \end{aligned} \tag{18}$$

The system (18) has the following unique solution

$$\begin{aligned} y_{M+1} &= \left[4\nu c_M - l_M(\sigma_{M+1}+\nu\sigma_M)\right]/\left[2\nu^2\sqrt{3}\left(\zeta_1^l-\zeta_2^l\right)\right], \\ y_M &= (c_M-r_M y_{M+1})/l_M, \\ y_m &= \sigma_{m+1}-4y_{m+1}-y_{m+2}, m=M-1,M-2,\ldots,0,-1. \end{aligned} \tag{19}$$

where

$$l_m=-\nu\left(\zeta_1^{m+1}+\zeta_2^{m+1}\right), r_m=\nu\left(\zeta_1^m+\zeta_2^m\right) \text{ for } m=0,1,2,\ldots \tag{20a}$$

$$c_m=\sigma_{-1}+\nu\left[\sigma_0+\sum_{k=1}^{m}\left(\zeta_1^k+\zeta_2^k\right)\sigma_k\right], \tag{20b}$$

$$\sigma_{-1}=s'_{ni}(t_0), \sigma_m=s_{ni}(t_m), m=0,1,\ldots,M, \sigma_{M+1}=s'_{ni}(t_M), \tag{20c}$$

$$\zeta_1=-2+\sqrt{3} \text{ and } \zeta_2=-2-\sqrt{3}, \nu=3/h. \tag{20d}$$

The total algorithm of training, testing, and validation. We give an informal description of this algorithm below.

The total algorithm.

1. **Divide** the total set of data in the subsets for training, testing, and validation.
2. **Combine** the training and the testing sets in the learning set.
3. **Divide** the learning set in a number of clusters *c*, using the *clustering* algorithm.
4. **Divide** the learning sets for each cluster in the cluster training and testing sets.
5. **Build** the *local nets* on each cluster using the *CEA*. **For** each *local net* **do**

    5.1 **Select** a type of the *neural net* architecture;

    5.2 **Let** $N = 0$ and **calculate** P_0 and P_{0+} by equation (6);

    5.3 **For** $N = 1,\ldots,N_{\max}$ **do**

    5.3.1 **For** $k = 1,\ldots,K$ **do**

    5.3.1.1 **For** $i = 1,\ldots,d$ and for all x from the cluster training set **do**

    Generate w_{ni}^{int};
    Calculate $\varphi_{ni}\left(x_i, w_{ni}^{\text{int}}\right)$;

    End.

    5.3.1.2 **Calculate** $\psi_N\left(x, w_N^{\text{int}}\right), P_N, P_{N+}, w_0^{ext},\ldots, w_N^{ext}, \tilde{f}_N(x)$;
    5.3.1.3 **Calculate** the training MSE, **compare** this MSE with the currently minimal MSE;
    4.4.4.4 **If** (training MSE) < minimal training MSE)
    Replace the parameters P_{N*}, P_{N+*}, corresponding minimal MSE, by P_N, P_{N+}.
    End.

    5.3.2 **Select** a net with the minimal training MSE from the ensemble, **keep** P_N, P_{N+}, and the training MSE for this net;

    5.3.3 **Calculate** and **keep** the testing MSE for this net.
    End.

    5.4 **Calculate** a net with N_{opt} *basis functions* with the minimal testing MSE, keep P_N, P_{N+}, the training and testing MSEs for this net.

6. **Train** a *global net* on the total learning set, using RLR procedure.
7. **Calculate** the training, the testing, and the validation MSE for the *global net.*
8. **If** ((weighted sum of the testing and the validation MSE exceeds prescribed threshold)&&(running time does not exceed prescribed threshold))

Return to 5.
Else

End.

Comments.

1. **To** 5.1. The types of neural net architecture affect only calculations of $\varphi_{ni}\left(x_i, w_{ni}^{\text{int}}\right)$ and $\psi_N\left(x, w_N^{\text{int}}\right)$, see equations (1b, 9, 10, 13).
2. **To** 5.3.1.1. Initialization of the net with minimal testing error is made when $k = 1$. The testing error, and values of P_N, P_{N+} for this net are assigned to initial value of minimal testing MSE and values of P_{N*}, P_{N+*} respectively.
3. **To** 8. The total algorithm ends either if there exist a *neural net* architecture satisfying prescribed constraints on performance, or it does not. The latter case means that uncontrolled factors (like low signal/noise ratio) do not allow for achieving prescribed level of performance.

CONCLUSION

This chapter has discussed the *CEA* method and the *Kolmogorov's Spline Complex Network*, neural network architecture with complex weights and potentially complex inputs, in the context of adaptive dynamic modeling of time-variant multidimensional data. There exist a number of important problems, mentioned in the previous sections and left for future work. These problems are summarized in the next section.

FUTURE RESEARCH DIRECTIONS

The primary area in the humans responsible for the intellect is the cortex. The intellectual activity in the cortex related to pattern recognition is a combination of memory and prediction (Hawkins, 2004, pp. 65-84, 85-105). The main properties of the human memory are: 1) the cortex stores sequences of patterns; 2) the cortex recalls patterns auto-associatively; 3) the cortex stores patterns in invariant forms; 4) the cortex stores patterns in a hierarchy. Storing patterns in sequences means that sequences contain patterns connected in space and time. Recalling patterns auto-associatively assumes that incomplete and partially corrupted sequences can be correctly recalled. Storing patterns in invariant form and in hierarchy means storing sequences of patterns in the hierarchically structured systems of layers, where the lowest layer contains the most detailed features, while the highest layer contains the least detailed features, invariant to some group of data transformations. This layer can be called as a layer of invariant forms. The prediction module takes a new input, uses the invariant forms for pattern detection and identification, and uses the prediction step to find the output.

Complex-valued nets can be helpful in storing sequences of patterns and, probably in auto-associative recall. In this more general setting we expect progress in solving the following problems:

1. Search for new net architectures more efficient than the KSN and *KSCN*;
2. Building a net implementation of a combination of memory and prediction;
3. Search for efficient net implementation of dynamic knowledge modeling;
4. Search for efficient methods of dynamic visualization and feature selection;
5. Further amplification of methods for reducing a large size of the training set and a large size of a net;
6. Applications of results obtained in 1)-5) to areas of biotechnology, medicine, defense, space exploration, finance, environmental problems, homeland security, and so on.

REFERENCES

Adeli, H., & Hung, S-L. (1995). *Machine learning. Neural networks, genetic algorithms, and fuzzy systems.* New York, NY: John Wiley & Sons.

Adeli, H., & Samant, A. (2000). Wavelets to enhance computational intelligence. In P. Sincak (Ed). *Quo vadis computational intelligence? New trends and approaches in computational intelligence* (pp. 399-407). Heidelberg; New York: Physica-Verlag.

Aizenberg, I., N., Aizenberg, N. N., & Vandewalle, J. (2000). *Multi-valued and universal binary neurons- Theory, learning, and applications.* Boston, MA: Kluwer Academic Publishers.

Albert, A. (1972). *Regression and the Moore-Penrose pseudoinverse.* New York, NY: Academic Press.

Antony, R. T. (1995). *Principles of data fusion automation.* Norwood, MA: Artech House.

Arena P., Fortuna, L., Muscato, G., & Xibilia, M. G. (1998). *Neural networks in multidimensional domains. Fundamentals and new trends in modeling and control.* New York: Springer.

Astrom, K., & Wittenmark, B. (1995). *Adaptive control.* Reading, MA: Addison-Wesley.

Bäck, T. (1996). *Evolutionary algorithms in theory and practice.* New York, NY: Oxford University Press.

Barron, A. R. (1993). Universal approximation bounds for superpositions of a sigmoidal function. *IEEE Transactions on Information Theory, 39*(4), 930-945.

Barron, A. R. (1994). Approximation and estimation bounds for artificial neural networks. *Machine Learning, 14*(1), 115-133.

Bezdek, J. (1992). On the relationship between neural networks, pattern recognition and intelligence. *International Journal on Approximating Reasoning, 6*(2), 85-107.

Bezdek, J. C., Keller, J., Krishnapuram, R., & Pal, N. R. (1999). *Fuzzy models and algorithms for pattern recognition and image processing.* Norwell, MA: Kluwer Academic Publishers.

Bishop, C. M. (1995). *Neural networks for pattern recognition.* New York, NY: Oxford University Press.

Bradley, P. S., & Fayyad, U. M. (1998). Refining initial points for K-means clustering. In *15th International Conference on Machine Learning* (pp. 91-99). Los Altos, CA: Morgan Kaufmann.

Breiman, L., Friedman, J. H., Olshen, R. A, & Stone, C. J. (1984). *Classification and regression trees.* Boca Raton, FL: Chapman & Hall/CRC.

Breiman, L. (1993). Hinging hyperplanes for regression, classification, and function approximation. *IEEE Transactions on Information Theory, 39*(4), 999-1013.

Breiman, L. (1996). Bagging predictors. *Machine Learning, 24*(1), 123-140.

Breiman, L. (1999). Combining predictors. In A. Sharkey (Ed.), *Combining artificial neural nets: Ensemble and modular multi-net systems* (pp. 31-50). London: Springer.

Congdon, P. (2006). *Bayesian statistical modeling.* Chichester, West Sussex: John Wiley & Sons, Ltd.

Cristianini, N., & Shawe-Taylor, J. (2000). *An introduction to support vector machines.* Cambridge, UK: Cambridge University Press.

Duda, R. O., Hart, P. E., & Stork, D. G. (2001). *Pattern classification.* New York, NY: JohnWiley & Sons, Inc.

Fishman, G. S. (1995). *Monte Carlo. Concepts, algorithms, and applications.* New York, NY: Springer.

Fukunaga, K. (1990). *Introduction to statistical pattern recognition.* New York, NY: Academic Press.

Georgiou, G, & Koutsougeras, C. (1992). Complex domain back-propagation. *IEEE Transactions on Circuits and Systems-II: Analog and Digital Signal Processing, 39*(5), 330-334.

Girosi, F., & Poggio, T. (1989). Representation properties of networks: Kolmogorov's theorem is irrelevant. *Neural Computation, 1*(4), 465-469.

Goswami, J. C., & Chan, A. K. (1999). *Fundamentals of wavelets. Theory, algorithms, and applications.* New York, NY: John Wiley & Sons, Inc.

Hawkins, J, & Blakeslee, S. (2004). *On intelligence.* New York: Henry Holt and Company.

Haykin, S. (2002). *Adaptive filter theory. Fourth edition.* Upper Saddle River, NJ: Prentice Hall.

Haykin, S. (1994). *Neural networks, a comprehensive foundation.* New York, NY: IEEE Press.

Haykin, S. (Ed.) (2001). *Kalman filtering and neural networks.* New York, NY: John Wiley & Sons.

Hecht-Nielsen, R. (1987). Kolmogorov's mapping neural network existence theorem. In *IEEE International Conference on Neural Networks, 3*, 11-13. New York, NY: IEEE Press.

Hirose, A. (Ed.) (2003). *Complex-valued neural networks.* Singapore: World Scientific Publishers.

Hirose, A. (2006). *Complex-valued neural networks.* Berlin: Springer.

Hovanessian, S. A. (1984). *Introduction to sensor systems.* Norwood, MA: Artech House.

Igelnik, B., & Pao, Y-H. (1995). Stochastic choice of basis functions in adaptive function approximation and the functional-link net. *IEEE Transactions on Neural Networks, 6*(6), 1320-1329.

Igelnik, B., Pao, Y-H., & LeClair, S. R. (1996). An approach for optimization of a continuous function with many local minima. In 30th *Annual Conference on Information Sciences and Systems, 2*, 912-917. Department of Electrical Engineering, Princeton University, Princeton, NJ.

Igelnik, B., Pao, Y-H., LeClair, S. R., & Shen, C. Y. (1999). The ensemble approach to neural network learning and generalization. *IEEE Transactions on Neural Networks, 10*(1), 19-30.

Igelnik, B. (2000). Some new adaptive architectures for learning, generalization, and visualization of multivariate data. In P. Sincak & J. Vascak (Eds.), *Quo Vadis Computational Intelligence? New Trends and Approaches in Computational Intelligence* (pp. 63-78). Heidelberg; New York, NY: Physica-Verlag.

Igelnik, B., Tabib-Azar, M., & LeClair, S. (2001a). A net with complex weights. *IEEE Transactions on Neural Networks, 12*(2), 236-249.

Igelnik, B. (2001b). Method for visualization of multivariate data in a lower dimension. In *SPIE Visual Data Exploration and Analysis VIII, 4302*, 168-179, San Jose, CA.

Igelnik, B., & Parikh, N. (2003a). Kolmogorov's spline network. *IEEE Transactions on Neural Networks, 14*(3), 725-733.

Igelnik, B. P.I. (2003b). *Visualization of large multidimensional datasets in a lower dimension.* SBIR Phase I Final Report, #0232775, NSF.

Igelnik, B. P.I. (2003c). *Visualization of large multidimensional datasets in a lower dimension.* SBIR Phase II Proposal, #0349713, NSF.

Jackson, P. (1986). *Introduction to expert systems.* Reading, MA: Addison-Wesley.

Kalos, M., & Witlock, P. A. (1986). *Monte Carlo methods.* New York, NY: John Wiley & Sons.

Kim, M. S., & Guest, C. C. (1990). Modification of back-propagation for complex-valued signal processing in frequency domain. In *International Joint Conference on Neural Networks* 1990 San Diego (pp. 27-31). New York: IEEE.

Kurková, V. (1991). Kolmogorov's theorem is relevant. *Neural Computation, 3*(4), 617-622.

Kurková, V. (1992). Kolmogorov's theorem and multilayer neural networks. *Neural Networks, 5*(3), 501-506.

Kolmogorov, A. N. (1957). On the representation of continuous functions of many variables by superposition of continuous functions of one variable and addition. *Doklady Akademii Nauk SSSR, 114*(5), 953-956. (1963). *Translations American Mathematical Society, 2*(28), 55-59.

Leung, H., & Haykin, S. (1991). The complex backpropagation algorithm. *IEEE Transactions on Signal Processing, 39*(9), 2101-2104.

Li, G., &Yu, K. B. (1988). Modeling and simulation of coherent Weibull clutter. *IEE Proceedings, Part. F, 136*(1), 1-9.

Ljung, L. (2000). *System identification theory for the user.* Englewood Cliffs, NJ: Prentice Hall.

Lorentz, G. G., von Golitschek, M., & Makovoz, Y. (1996). *Constructive approximation. Advanced problems.* New York: Springer.

Luo, F-L., & Unbehauen, R. (1997). *Applied neural networks for signal processing.* NY: Cambridge University Press.

Mhascar, H., & Miccheli, C. (1992). Approximation by superposition of sigmoidal and radial basis functions. *Advances in Applied Mathematics, 13*(3), 350-373.

Mitchell, M. (1996). *An introduction to genetic algorithms.* Cambridge, MA: The MIT Press.

Niederreiter, H. (1978). Quasi-Monte Carlo methods and pseudorandom numbers. *Bulletin of American Mathematical Society, 84*, 957-1041.

Nilsson, N., J. (1998). *Artificial intelligence. A new synthesis.* SanFrancisco, CA: Morgan Kaufmann Publishers.

Nitta, T. (1997). An extension of the backpropagation algorithm to complex numbers. *Neural Networks, 10*(8), 1391-1415.

Nitta, T. (2003). On the inherent property of the decision boundary in complex-valued neural networks. *Neurocomputing, 50*(1), 291-303.

Oppenheim, A. V., & Schafer, R. W. (1975). *Digital signal processing.* Englewood Cliffs, NJ: Prentice Hall.

Pedricz, W. (1998). *Computational intelligence. An introduction.* Boca Raton, FL: CRC Press.

Prenter, P. M. (1975). Splines and variational methods. New York, NY: John Wiley & Sons.

Rihaczek, A. W., & Hershkowitz, S. J. (1996). *Radar resolution and complex-image analysis.* Norwood, MA: Artech House.

Scolnik, M. I. (Ed.) (1990). *Radar handbook. Second edition.* New York, NY: McGraw-Hill.

Shidlovskii, A. B. (1989). *Transcendental numbers.* Berlin: Walter de Gruyter.

Sprecher, D. A. (1965). On the structure of continuous functions of several variables. *Transactions of American Mathematical Society, 115*(3), 340-355.

Sprecher, D. A. (1996). A numerical implementation of Kolmogorov's superpositions. *Neural Networks, 9*(5), 765-772.

Sprecher, D. A. (1997). A numerical implementation of Kolmogorov's superpositions II. *Neural Networks, 10*(3), 447-457.

Stone, M. (1974). Cross-validatory choice and assessment of statistical predictions. *Journal of the Royal Statistical Society, B 36*(1), 11-147.

Stone, L. D., Barlow, C. A., & Corwin, T. L. (1999). *Bayesian multiple target tracking.* Boston, MA: Artech House.

Stroud, A. H. (1971). *Approximate calculation of multiple integrals.* Englewood Cliffs, NJ: Prentice-Hall.

Zapranis, A. D., & Refenes, A-P. (1999). *Principles of neural model identification, selection and adequacy.* London: Springer.

Zurada, J., Marks, R., & Robinson, C. (Eds.) (1994). *Introduction to computational intelligence: Imitating life.* Piscataway, NJ: IEEE Press.

ADDITIONAL READINGS

Baccheschi, N. L., Brown, S., Kerekes, J., & Schott, J. (2005). Generation of a combined dataset of simulated radar and EO/IR imagery. *Proc. of* SPIE, *5806*, 88-99.

Bar-Shalom, Y., Kirubarajan, T., & Lin, X. (2005). Probabilistic data association techniques for target tracking with applications to sonar, radar and EO sensors. *IEEE Aerospace and Electronic Systems Magazine*, *20*(8), Part 2, 37-56.

Birx, D. L., & Pipenberg. (1993). A complex mapping network for phase sensitive classification. *IEEE Transactions on Neural Networks*, *4*(1), 127-135.

Chakravarthy, S. V., & Ghosh, J. (1996). A complex-valued associative memory for storing patterns as oscillatory states. *Biological Cybernetics*, *75*(3), 229-238.

Guarnieri, S., Piazza, F., & Uncini, A. (1995). Multilayer neural networks with adaptive spline-based activation functions. In *International Neural Network Society, Annual Meeting WCNN* (pp. 1695-1699). Washington, DC.

Guarnieri, S., Piazza, F., & Uncini, A. (1999). Multilayer feedforward networks with adaptive spline activation function. *IEEE Transactions on Neural Networks*, *10*(3), 672-683.

Hara, T., & Hirose, A. (2004). Plastic mine detecting radar system using complex-valued self-organizing map that deals with multi-frequency interferometric images. *Neural Networks*, *17*(8-9), 1201-1210.

Hirose, A., & Eckmiller, R. (1996). Coherent optical neural networks that have optical-frequency-controlled behavior and generalization ability in the frequency domain. *Applied Optics*, *35*(5), 836-843.

Hopfield, J. J. (1982). Neural networks and physical systems with emergent collective computational abilities. *Proceedings National Academy of Sciences USA*, *79*(8), 2554-2558.

Jankowski, S., Lozowski, A., & Zurada, J. M. (1996). Complex-valued multistate neural associative memory. *IEEE Transactions on Neural Networks*, *7*(6), 1491-1496.

Kadtke, J., & Kremliovsky, M. (1996). Signal classification using global dynamical models, part I, theory. In Katz, R. A. (Ed). *Chaotic, Fractal, and Nonlinear Signal Processing* (pp. 189-201). Woodbury, NY: AIP Press.

Kadtke, J., & Kremliovsky, M. (1996). Signal classification using global dynamical models, part II, sonar data analysis. In Katz, R. A. (Ed.), *Chaotic, Fractal, and Nonlinear Signal Processing* (pp. 205-216). Woodbury, NY: AIP Press.

Kuroe, Y., Hashimoto, N., & Mori, T. (2001). Qualitative analysis of a self-correlation type complex-valued associative memories. *Nonlinear Analysis- Theory and Applications*, *47*(9), 5795-5806.

Lee, D. L. (2001). Relaxation of the stability condition of the complex-valued neural networks. *IEEE Transactions on Neural Networks*, *12*(5), 1260-1262.

McEliece, R., Posner, E., Rodemich, E., & Venkatesh, S. (1987). The capacity of the Hopfield associative memory. *IEEE Transactions on Information Theory*, *33*(4), 461-482.

Mitchell, R. L. (1976). *Radar signal simulation.* Dedham, MA: Artech House: Dedham.

Muezzinoglu, M. K., Guzelics, C., & Zurada, J. M. (2003). A new design method for the complex-valued multistate Hopfield associative memory. *IEEE Transactions on Neural Networks*, *14*(4), 891-899.

Narendra, K. S., Balakrishnan, J., & Giliz, M. K. (1995). Adaptation and learning using multiple models, switching, and tuning. *IEEE Control Systems Magazine*, *15*(3), 37-51.

Nemoto, I., & Kubano, M. (1996). Complex associative memory. *Neural Networks*, *9*(2), 253-261.

Nitta, T. (2000). An analysis of the fundamental structure of complex-valued neurons. *Neural Processing Letters, 12*(3), 239-246.

Omori, T., Mochizuki, A., & Mizutani, K. (1999). Emergence of symbolic behavior from brain like memory with dynamic attention. *Neural Networks, 12*(7-8), 1157-1172.

Suksmono, A. B., & Hirose, A. (2002). Interferometric SAR image restoration using Monte-Carlo Metropolis method. *IEEE Transactions on Signal Processing, 50*(2), 290-298.

Uncini, A., Vecci, L., Campolucci, P., & Piazza, F. (1999). Complex-valued neural networks with adaptive spline activation function for digital radio links nonlinear equalization. *IEEE Transactions on Signal Processing, 47*(2), 505-514.

Vecci, L., Piazza, F., & Uncini, A. (1998). Learning and approximation capabilities of adaptive spline activation function neural networks. *Neural Networks, 11*(2), 259-270.

Wolpert, D. M., Miall, C. M., & Kawato, M. (1998). Internal models in the cerebellum. *Trends in Cognitive Sciences, 2*(9), 79-87.

ENDNOTES

1 Possible dependency of a characteristic of a particular local net from a number of local nets is omitted in notations.

2 Notation P is used for complexity, not for the number of patterns in the training set, only in this subsection.

Chapter IV
A Complex-Valued Hopfield Neural Network: Dynamics and Applications

V. Srinivasa Chakravarthy
Indian Institute of Technology, Madras, India

ABSTRACT

This chapter describes Complex Hopfield Neural Network (CHNN), a complex-variable version of the Hopfield neural network, which can exist in both fixed point and oscillatory modes. Memories can be stored by a complex version of Hebb's rule. In the fixed-point mode, CHNN is similar to a continuous-time Hopfield network. In the oscillatory mode, when multiple patterns are stored, the network wanders chaotically among patterns. Presence of chaos in this mode is verified by appropriate time series analysis. It is shown that adaptive connections can be used to control chaos and increase memory capacity. Electronic realization of the network in oscillatory dynamics, with fixed and adaptive connections shows an interesting tradeoff between energy expenditure and retrieval performance. It is shown how the intrinsic chaos in CHNN can be used as a mechanism for "annealing" when the network is used for solving quadratic optimization problems. The network's applicability to chaotic synchronization is described.

INTRODUCTION

Drawing important ideas from several sources, - the idea of associative memory from psychology (Kohonen, 1977), the idea of Hebbian adaptation from neurophysiology (Hebb, 1949), the idea of neuron as a thresholding device from prior modeling work (McCulloch & Pitts, 1943) etc., - Hopfield presented an elegant model of associative memory storage and retrieval in the brain (Hopfield, 1982; Hopfield, 1984). Most importantly, an original contribution of the Hopfield model is the suggestion that memories correspond to attractors of neural network dynamics. This essential insight has helped to create a whole class of "neural memories."

Since memories, by their very nature, must have certain stability, and there must be mechanisms for storage and retrieval of the same, it is reasonable to think of memories as attractors of brain dynamics. There is also some experimental evidence towards that end. But where experimental data differs from Hopfield's model memories is that brain memories are not fixed point attractors, the way Hopfield's memories are. For example, work done by Freeman and his group with mammalian olfactory cortex revealed that odors are stored as oscillatory states (Skarda & Freeman, 1987). Synchronization, an important phenomenon related to oscillations plays a significant role in information processing in the brain. It has been suggested that oscillations in visual cortex may provide an explanation for the binding problem (Gray & Singer, 1989). This result has come as experimental support to Malsburg's labeling hypothesis (von der Malsburg, 1988), which postulates that neural information processing is intimately related to the temporal relationships between the phase- and/or frequency-based "labels" of oscillating cell assemblies. All these phenomena cannot be captured by neural models that exhibit only fixed-point behavior.

Neural models in which memories can be stored as oscillations have been proposed before. Abbot (1990) studied a network of oscillating neurons in which binary patterns can be stored as phase relationships between individual oscillators. The Hopfield model too can exhibit limit cycles and chaos but only when the symmetry condition on weights is relaxed (Sompolinsky, Crisanti & Sommers, 1988; Albers, Sprott, & Dechert, 1998). When the symmetry condition is violated, the Hebb's rule for storing patterns is no more valid in general, except in special cases like storing short sequences.

BACKGROUND

It has been shown that by extending Hopfield's real-valued model to complex –variable domain, it is possible to preserve the symmetric Hebbian synapses, while permitting the network to have oscillatory states (Chakravarthy & Ghosh, 1996). Pioneering work on complex-valued versions of Hopfield network was done by Hirose (1992). Other studies in the area of complex neural networks include complex backpropagation algorithm for training complex feedforward networks (Leung & Haykin, 1991; Nitta, 1997) and a similar extension for complex-valued recurrent neural networks (Mandic & Goh, 2004). For a comprehensive review of complex neural models the reader may consult (Hirose, 2003).

In the present chapter, we discuss the properties and applications of a particular complex neural network model viz., the complex Hopfield neural network (CHNN). The chapter is organized as follows. We begin with a brief review of the original real-valued Hopfield network, which is followed by a plausible biological interpretation of the complex state of a neuron in the next Section. The model equations of CHNN are presented in the subsequent Section, which is followed by a Section that presents learning mechanisms. Learning can be a one-shot affair where the weights are pre-calculated by a complex Hebb's rule. Or learning can occur continuously, with weight update described by differential equations. The following section describes the two modes in which the proposed network operates: 1) fixed point mode and 2) oscillatory mode. In the subsequent two sections, associative memory function of CHNN in the two modes is described. It will be shown that memory capacity of the network in oscillatory mode is very poor. However, it will be also shown, in the subsequent Section, that by allowing the weights to adapt dynamically, *even during retrieval*, memory capacity can be enhanced significantly even in the oscillatory mode. The next Section presents an electronic realization of the model. The following Section describes application of CHNN for quadratic optimization. The chaotic dynamics of the network in oscillatory mode is exploited as a mechanism for avoiding getting stuck in a local minimum. An application of CHNN for chaotic synchronization useful for secure communications is discussed in the following Section. An overview of the work and challenges for future are discussed in the final Section.

THE REAL-VALUED HOPFIELD NETWORK

In a landmark paper, Hopfield (1982) proposed a neural network implementation of an associative memory in which binary patterns can be stored and retrieved. The McCulloch-Pitts (McCulloch & Pitts, 1943) binary neuron is used in this network. In the Hopfield's neural network each neuron is connected to every other neuron through weights $T = \{ T_{jk} \}$, where T_{jk} is the weight connecting j'th and k'th neuron. Each neuron receives inputs from all other neurons, performs a weighted sum of the inputs, passes the sum through an activation function and updates its own output as follows:

$$V_j(t+1) = g(\sum_k T_{jk} V_k(t)) \tag{1}$$

$V_j(t)$ is the output of j'th neuron at time t; T_{jk} is the weight connecting j'th and k'th neurons; $g(\bullet)$ is the activation function which is usually the sign() function. An important result about the Hopfield network is that if the weights are symmetric, there exists a Lyapunov function, E, which governs the network dynamics (Hopfield, 1982).

$$E = -\frac{1}{2}\sum_j \sum_k T_{jk} V_j V_k \tag{2}$$

The existence of a Lyapunov function and nonlinearity of dynamics opens the possibility of existence of multiple attractors, which is exploited ingeniously to implement an associative memory. The attractors of the network dynamics are interpreted as memories, and the basins of the attractors as corrupt or noisy forms of memories, which serve as cues to retrieve memories. Hopfield's (1982) original model addresses an important question and provides a solution *viz.*, how does one store patterns in the network? In other words, how can the patterns to be stored be encoded as the weights of the network? To answer this question, Hopfield invoked a concept from psychology known as Hebbian learning (Hebb, 1949), which describes a possible cellular level mechanism for imprinting memories in the nervous system. In Hebb's own words this mechanism may be stated as follows (Hebb, 1949):

When an axon of cell A is near enough to excite a cell B and repeatedly or persistently takes part in firing it, some growth process or metabolic change takes place in one or both cells such that A's efficiency, as one of the cells firing B, is increased.

In other words, correlated or simultaneous activation of a pair of connected neurons must strengthen that connection; uncorrelated activation must attenuate the same. For this reason, this class of learning mechanisms are called "correlational learning" mechanisms. A mathematical formulation of Hebbian mechanism is used in the Hopfield network to compute the weights as follows. If S is a binary (± 1) pattern to be stored in the network, and S_j and S_k are j'th and k'th components of S respectively, the weight T_{jk} connecting j'th and k'th neurons is given by the formula:

$$T_{jk} = \frac{1}{N} S_j S_k$$

where N is the number of neurons in the network. Note that T_{jk} is positive if both S_j and S_k have the same sign, and negative if S_j and S_k have the opposite signs. When multiple patterns (P) are stored, the above rule is extended as follows:

$$T_{jk} = \frac{1}{N}\sum_{p=1}^{P} S_j^p S_k^p \tag{3}$$

However, as more and more patterns are stored, spurious states (states that are stable but not one of the stored patterns) emerge interfering with stored patterns. As a result performance of the network as a memory deteriorates. Error analysis of memory retrieval performance reveals that as P passes the critical value of 0.138*N, there is a sharp rise in retrieval errors. Therefore, the capacity of a N-neuron network equals $P = 0.138 * N$ (Amit, Gutfreund, and Sompolinsky, 1987). Note that this capacity is extremely poor compared to indexed memories in which 2^N slots can be indexed with an N-bit address. However, this loss of capacity is exchanged with a capability to store and retrieve memories solely by association, without needing a separate address.

Thus in the '80s which saw a sudden emergence of some of the fundamental models of neural networks, Hopfield network emerged as an elegant model that synthesized four key ideas – (1) the idea of an associative memory (which is more akin to human memory, in contrast to indexed memory used in computers), (2) the idea of Hebbian learning from psychology, (3) the idea of memories as attracting states, (4) a network structure comprising of McCulloch-Pitts neurons – into a single neural network model. A variety of extensions of Hopfield's network have been proposed since then. The present chapter describes one such an extension to the complex-variable domain.

INTERPRETATION OF THE COMPLEX STATE

In real-valued neuron models, the real-valued output of the neuron typically represents the firing rate of the neurons, a practice known as *rate coding.* Rate codes are rather coarse models of neural code, since it is known that significant information is encoded in precise spike times (Maass & Bishop, 1998). As a first step to go beyond rate code, it has been suggested that temporal derivative of firing rate can be included explicitly in a two-variable neuron state = {firing rate, temporal derivative of firing rate}. These temporal derivatives, sometimes known as *signal velocities*, appear in associative memory models (Kosko, 1987). Signal velocities have an elegant significance, considering the pulse-coded nature of neural signal. The firing rate of a neuron can be calculated by adding the number of spikes in neuron output that occurred over a finite time window. Alternatively the counting can be done by integrating the neuron output, x(t), along with an exponentially decaying weighting function, which gives more preference to recent spikes. Using an exponential weighting function, short-time firing rate of a neuron can be calculated as follows:

$$S(t) = \int_{-\infty}^{t} x(\tau)\exp(\tau - t)d\tau \tag{4}$$

where $x(t)$ equals 1 if there is a spike at time t, and 0 if there is no spike. There exists an elegant relation between dS/dt and $x(t)$ which is presented here without proof:

$$\dot{S}(t) = x(t) - S(t) \tag{5}$$

Thus, signal velocity can be expressed in terms of pulse-coded signal and its short-term frequency. This so-called velocity-difference property of pulse-coded signal functions suggests that neurons can easily compute time-derivatives of incoming signals without using sophisticated differencing techniques. Following these considerations, several models that incorporate signal velocities explicitly in dynamics have been suggested. In one such model, the Differential Hebbian Adaptive Bidirectional Associative Memory (Kosko, 1987), the signal velocity of input signal also contributes to neuron output. Thus neuron output can be represented as an ordered pair = $\{S, dS/dt\}$. It may be shown that such a formalism paves way naturally to a complex-valued neuron state (Chakravarthy & Ghosh, 1993).

COMPLEX-VALUED HOPFIELD NEURAL NETWORK

In CHNN, the neuron state is represented by a complex variable, z, whose temporal dynamics are expressed as (Chakravarthy & Ghosh, 1996),

$$\tau_a \frac{dz_j}{dt} = \sum_k T_{jk}V_k - \beta z_j + I_j \tag{6}$$

$$V_j = g(\alpha z_j^*) \tag{7}$$

where α and β are complex coefficients, '*' denotes complex conjugate, τ_a is the time constant for the above activation dynamics and I_j is the sum of the external currents entering the neuron, *j*. T_{jk}, a complex quantity, is the weight or strength of the synapse connecting *j*'th and *k*'th neurons. The activation function, *g(.)* is chosen to be the *tanh(.)* function because of its sigmoidal nature.

LEARNING: ONE-SHOT AND ADAPTIVE

Learning can be performed in a one-shot manner by which weights are calculated from stored patterns by applying a formula. In this case, a Hebb-like *complex outer product rule* for determining the weight matrix required to store the desired patterns, S^p, is given as:

$$T_{jk} = \frac{1}{2N}\sum_p S_j^p S_k^{p*} \tag{8}$$

where N is the number of neurons in the network. The summation is carried over all the patterns to be stored. The above rule ensures Hermiticity of T (Chakravarthy & Ghosh, 1994).

Alternatively, weights can be adapted continuously as a function neuron outputs as follows:

$$\tau_w \dot{T}_{jk} = -T_{jk} + V_j V_k^* \tag{9}$$

where V_j and V_k are the outputs of *j*'th and *k*'th neurons; τ_w is the time-constant associated with weight dynamics (Chakravarthy & Ghosh, 1996).

NETWORK DYNAMICS: THE TWO NETWORK MODES

The model exists in two distinct modes: (i) the fixed point mode, and (ii) the oscillatory mode. Mode switching can be done by varying a *mode parameter*, v ($\nu \in [0,1]$). In eqns. (6,7), let $\beta = v + i(1-v)$, $\tau_a = 1$ and $\alpha = \lambda\beta$, where λ is a positive number, known as *steepness factor*. The above equations can be rewritten as

$$\frac{dz_j}{dt} = \sum_k T_{jk}V_k - (\nu + i(1-\nu))z_j + I_j \tag{10}$$

$$V_j = g(\lambda(\nu + i(1-\nu))z_j^*) \tag{11}$$

We now take a closer look at the network behavior in the two modes.

The Fixed Point Mode: The network exhibits fixed-point dynamics when the mode parameter, v, equals 1 (Chakravarthy & Ghosh 1994). The network dynamics reduce to:

$$\frac{dz_j}{dt} = \sum_k T_{jk}V_k - z_j + I_j \tag{12}$$

$$V_j = g(\lambda z_j^*) \tag{13}$$

If the weight matrix, T, is a Hermitian, the dynamics are stable since a Lyapunov function, E, can be associated with the above system:

$$E = -\frac{1}{2}\sum_j\sum_k T_{jk}V_j^*V_k + \mathrm{Re}[\sum_j \int_0^{V_j^*} g^{-1}(V)dV - \sum_j I_j V_j^*]$$

$$E = -\frac{1}{2}\sum_j\sum_k T_{jk}V_j^*V_k + \mathrm{Re}[\sum_j \int_0^{V_j^*} g^{-1}(V)dV - \sum_j I_j V_j^*]$$

$$E = -\frac{1}{2}\sum_j \sum_k T_{jk} V_j^* V_k + \text{Re}[\sum_j \int_0^{V_j^*} g^{-1}(V)dV - \sum_j I_j V_j^*] \quad (14)$$

The existence of Lyapunov function implies that the system is of dissipative nature. $V_j(t)$, usually settles in a fixed point approaching $\pm$ 1. The complex tanh(.) is chosen as the sigmoidal nonlinearity since it has certain necessary properties for stability of the system. For the necessary conditions on complex tanh() function and for proof that the expression in eqn. (14) is the Lyapunov function of dynamics of eqns. (10-11), the reader may refer to (Appendix – Theorem 1). As in the original Hopfield network, patterns can be stored in CHNN also using a complex version of Hebb's rule (see Section titled "Learning: one-shot and adaptive").

Example 1: Consider a 2-neuron network with a weight matrix, T given as:

$$T = \begin{bmatrix} 1 & -1 \\ -1 & 1 \end{bmatrix}$$

The above T corresponds to loading the pattern $S = [1, -1]^T$. The mode parameter v is set to 1. $Re[V_1]$ and $Re[V_2]$ are plotted in Figure 1. Real parts of the states of individual neurons smoothly approach ± 1 in a manner similar to Hopfield's continuous model. Imaginary parts ($Im[V_1]$ and $Im[V_2]$) simply tend to zero and hence not shown in the figure. Since the two neurons in the network have mutually inhibitory connections, their corresponding outputs have opposite sign.

For all practical purposes CHNN in fixed-point mode ($v = 1$) is nearly the same as the continuous-time Hopfield network (Hopfield, 1984). Novel effects start manifesting when CHNN is operated in the oscillatory mode.

The Oscillatory Mode: The network exhibits oscillatory behavior when the parameter v is set to zero (Chakravarthy & Ghosh, 1996). In this case, the output of each neuron does not smoothly tend to $\pm$ 1 as in the fixed point case, but flips between +1 and –1 at regular intervals, producing an output resembling a square wave. The equations of dynamics can now be written as:

Figure 1. Dynamics of CHNN state in a 2-neuron network in fixed-point mode (v = 1). Each neuron state approaches ± 1 and settles there. Only a single (P=1) two-dimensional pattern, S (=[1,-1]), is stored in the network.

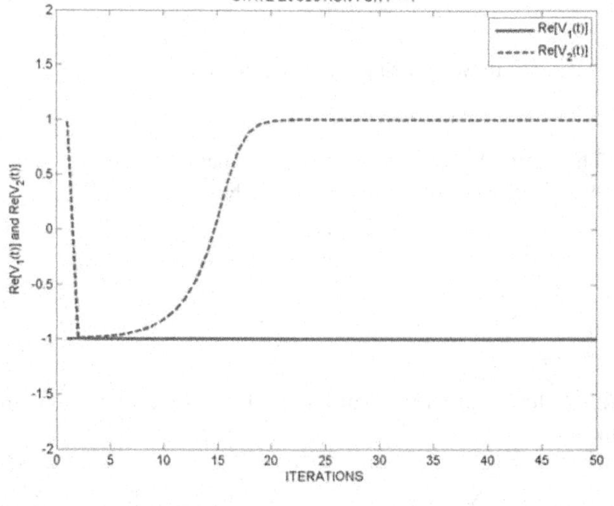

$$\frac{dz_j}{dt} = \sum_k T_{jk} V_k - iz_j + I_j \tag{15}$$

$$V_j = g(i\lambda z_j^*) \tag{16}$$

The properties in this mode are fundamentally different from the fixed point mode, as these equations describe a *conservative system* (see Appendix – Theorem 2 for proof). In this mode also patterns stored using the complex version of Hebb's rule (see Section titled "Learning: one-shot and adaptive"), and can be retrieved as oscillatory outputs where the individual components of the pattern vector are stored as phase differences among neuron outputs. For instance, if the jth and k^{th} components of a stored pattern are +1 and –1 respectively, the output of the kth neuron ($Re\,[V_k]$) lags that of the jth ($Re\,[V_j]$) by 180 degrees.

Example 2: Consider again the 2-neuron network of example 1, but this time in the oscillatory mode (v=0). $Re[V_1]$ and $Re[V_2]$ are plotted in Figure 3. Individual neurons oscillate between -1 and 1 producing an output similar to a square-wave. Since the two neurons in the network have mutually inhibitory connections, their corresponding outputs have a phase difference of 180 degrees. In other words, in the oscillatory mode (with a single stored pattern, S_1) the network oscillates between S_1 and $-S_1$ (Figure 2(a), (b)).

The previous example shows that a single pattern can be stored in a small network and retrieved successfully in the oscillatory mode. Even when a small number of patterns are stored, patterns can be retrieved if the initial state of the network is sufficiently close to the pattern to be retrieved. But the next example shows that as the number of stored patterns is increased, the network no more settles down in the vicinity of the nearest pattern, but wanders chaotically from one stored pattern to another (Figure 3(b)).

Example 3: Consider a network of N=100 neurons in which random binary patterns S_p (p=1 to P) are stored. Figure 3(a) shows the variation of network state, $V(t) = [V_1(t), \ldots, V_N(t)]^t$, relative to the stored patterns when P =

Figure 2. (a) When a single pattern, S_1, is stored the state of CHNN in oscillatory mode shuttles between S_1 and $-S_1$. (b) Dynamics of network state ($Re[V_1(t)]$ and $Re[V_2(t)]$) in a 2-neuron network in oscillatory mode (v = 0). Each neuron state switches between +1 and –1. Phase difference between the two oscillatory waveforms depends on coupling weights, T_{12} (=T_{21}). Only a single (P=1) two-dimensional pattern, S (=[1,-1]), is stored in the network.

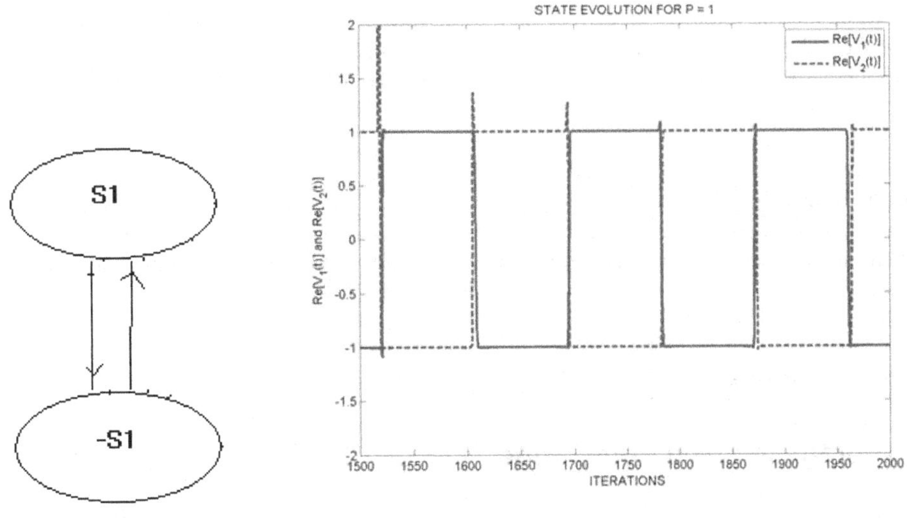

(a) (b)

Figure 3. Evolution of network state ($N = 100$, $v = 0.0$) as the number of stored patterns (P) is increased. (a) When $P = 2$, the network still switches periodically between S_1 and $-S_1$. (b) When $P = 5$, the network displays chaotic wandering. Solid line represents $g_1(t) = |V(t) \bullet S_1| / N$, and dashed line represents $g_2(t) = |V(t) \bullet S_2| / N$. Note that the network wanders chaotically from one stored pattern (S_1) to the other (S_2).

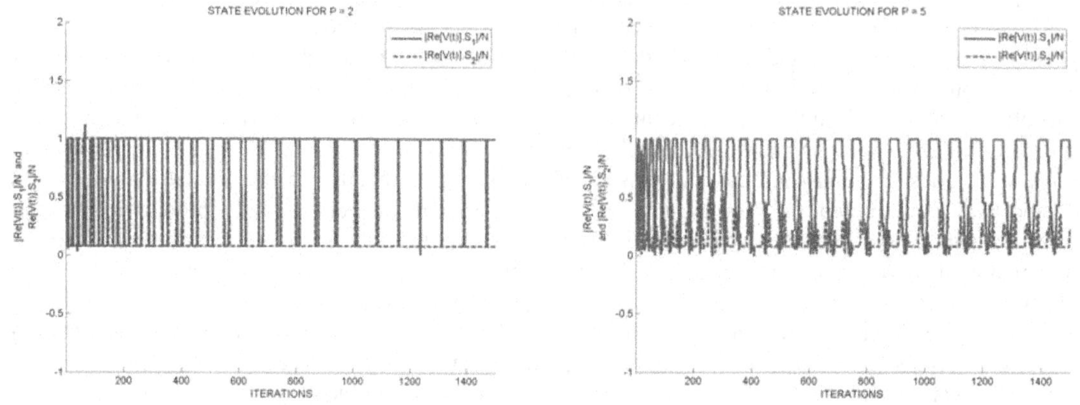

(a) *(b)*

2. The graphs of $g_1(t) = |\text{Re}[V(t)] \bullet S_1| / N$, and $g_2(t) = |\text{Re}[V(t)] \bullet S_2| / N$ are superimposed in Figure 3(a), where '•'refers to inner product. Note that the system still switches between S_1 and $-S_1$ periodically. That is, the network spends most of the time near (S_1 or $-S_1$) but briefly visits $\pm S_2$ at the time of transition of individual neural states between 1 and –1. Now consider a network in which 5 (S_1 to S_5) patterns are stored. Figure 3(b) shows evolution of $g_1(t) = |\text{Re}[V(t)] \bullet S_1| / N$, and $g_2(t) = |\text{Re}[V(t)] \bullet S_2| / N$ as before. Note that the system exhibits chaotic wandering.

The Complete Scenario

So far the network modes have been described at two extreme values of v. The fixed point and oscillatory modes actually correspond to two distinct ranges of v. As v is varied from 0 to 1, at a critical value of v, say, v_{crit}, a sudden transition from the oscillatory to fixed point mode is observed. The value of v at which this transition takes place depends on network parameters like weights, λ etc. Finally, the network dynamics can be summarized as follows:

i. The dynamics are conservative *only* at $v = 0$;
ii. Lyapunov function exists *only* at $v = 1$;
iii. For $v = (0,1]$ dynamics are dissipative.
iv. For $v \in [0, v_{crit})$, dynamics are oscillatory; for $v \in [v_{crit}, 1]$ the system has fixed-point dynamics (Figure 4).

NETWORK APPLICATIONS

Memory Storage in Fixed Point Mode

In the fixed point mode, first let us consider the situation when the stored patterns are real binary patterns, and the steepness factor, λ, is a large positive number. In this condition, the CHNN behaves very much like a continuous-time Hopfield network. Any imaginary components in initial state of the network are suppressed. This

Figure 4. Frequency of a single neural oscillator as a function of v. Zero frequency denotes that the neuron is in fixed-point mode.

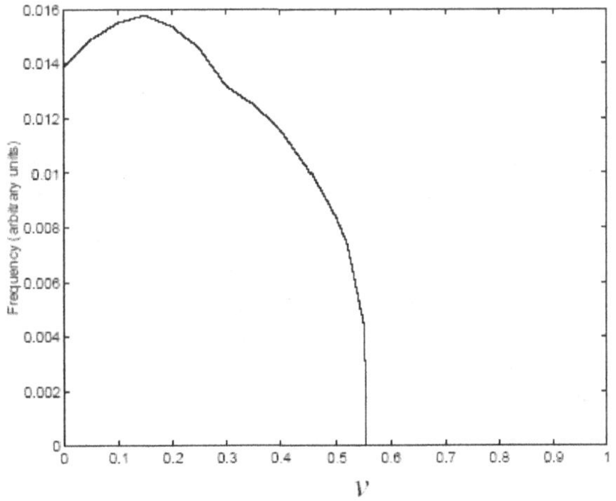

suppression of imaginary component is due to a property of the specific form of complex sigmoid function used, viz., tanh(). Therefore, when tanh() function is used as the sigmoid nonlinearity in the neuron, only real-valued patterns can be stored in the CHNN operating in fixed-point mode. (For storing complex binary patterns (± 1 $\pm i$), the function that must be used is: *tanh(λu) - i tan(λu)* (Chakravarthy & Ghosh, 1994)).

However, when a small imaginary component is added to the steepness factor, λ, network performance depends on imaginary components in interesting ways (Chakravarthy & Ghosh, 1993). In this case, when the real part of the initial state is set to zero, the network settles in the final state closest to the imaginary part of the initial state. For example, if the initial state, $u = iS_1 + noise$, where S_1 is the first stored pattern (real-valued), and 'noise' is imaginary noise with small amplitude (|noise| < 1), the final state will be S_1. This phenomenon can be explained by considering the argument of tanh(.) function. If $\lambda = \lambda_x + i\lambda_y$ ($\lambda_y > 0$) and $u = u_x + iu_y$ then $\mathrm{Re}[\lambda u^*] = u_x\lambda_x + \lambda_y u_y$. Since the real part of the initial state is zero (u_x=0, in all its components), $\mathrm{Re}[\lambda u^*] = \lambda_y u_y$. Thus the imaginary part is amplified and the network state is driven towards the stable state closest to the imaginary part of the initial state.

Memory Storage in Oscillatory Mode

The Hebbian formula of eqn. (8) is used in oscillatory mode also. Let us contrast the operation of the network in oscillatory mode with that in fixed-point mode. When a single real pattern is stored in CHNN, with the network operating in fixed-point mode, the network settles near the state, *S*, in steady state conditions. Contrarily, when a single real pattern, *S*, is stored in a network operating in oscillatory mode, the network state shuttles between *S* and $-S$ (Figure 2). Further, this is true only when a single pattern is stored. When multiple patterns are stored, the network no longer settles down in the vicinity of the nearest pattern, but wanders chaotically from one stored pattern to another (Figure 3). The situation gets worse as more and more patterns are stored in the network.

We have simulated a 100 neuron CHNN with multiple stored patterns. Figure 6 shows percentage error in retrieved pattern as a function of number of stored patterns with the network in oscillatory mode. It is a known result from Hopfield network theory that retrieval error increases with the number of stored patterns. The same general trend is seen even in the CHNN. To evaluate error, the pattern-to-be-retrieved is defined as follows. The initial condition is defined as, $V(0) = S_i + noise$, where '*noise*' is typically 5%. Therefore, the final desired pattern is S_i. Network simulation is continued for '*niter*' iterations at the end of which the state *V(niter)* is compared to S_i and - S_i. Error between V(niter) and the closer of S_i or - S_i is taken as retrieval error. By this measure, error is found to increase rapidly with increasing P. Error shoots up sharply (to more than 40%, implying near total failure) even when 2 patterns are stored (Figure 6).

This dramatic degradation in performance when multiple patterns are stored can be related to presence of chaos in the network operating in oscillatory mode. To demonstrate presence of chaos in the network, the following analysis is performed. The evolution of the state vector, $V(t)$, for a 100 neuron network, with 20 stored patterns, is used for analysis. The stored patterns are random binary vectors. The network state is initialized randomly. Other parameters are: $v = 0$, $\lambda = 7.5$. Network evolution is simulated for 20,000 time steps, i.e., $V(t)$, for $t = 1$ to 20,000. The points, $V(t)$, are translated to $V_z(t)$ such that the new set of points have zero mean over time. Let, X, be the matrix (of size 20,000 × 100) of the data, $V_z(t)$. The autocorrelation matrix, $R = X^T X$ is computed. Eigenvectors, e_1, e_2, etc., of R are found and the projections of $V_z(t)$ onto the eigenvectors are investigated. Lower projections (corresponding to largest eigenvalues) are nearly periodic but the projections become more and more noisy for higher components. We have chosen the 3rd projection $z_3(t) = V_z(t) \bullet e_3$. Standard tests of chaos are applied on the time series, $z_3(t)$, t=1 to 20,000, and following quantities are estimated: time delay =4 from the first minimum of the mutual information, embedding dimension = 4, correlation dimension = 1.4, and Lyapunov exponent = 0.4 (from Poincare map with average time sampling of 26 points – Figure 5) (Hegger & Kantz, 1999). These measurements provide strong ground to believe presence of low-dimensional chaos in CHNN.

We will now describe a method by which this chaotic activity of CHNN in oscillatory mode can be controlled and the network can be used reliably as an associative memory.

Enhanced Memory Capacity by Dynamic Connections

We have just seen that retrieval performance in the oscillatory mode drops dramatically when 2 or more patterns are stored. Instead of oscillating between a specific pattern and its negative, the network wanders chaotically from one stored pattern to another. The situation gets worse as more and more patterns are stored in the network. In Hopfield network retrieval performance drops radically when about 0.14N patterns are stored (N = #neurons). However, in CHNN in oscillatory mode, retrieval performance drops to about 50% even when only two patterns are stored. There is a need to search for techniques to control the chaos (Ott, Grebogi & James, 1990) and improve the network's storage capacity.

Adaptive control methods have been applied to maintain stable behavior (Huberman & Lumer, 1990) and to control chaos in dynamical systems (Sinha & Gupte, 1998). In the class of adaptive control algorithms presented

Figure 5. Determination of Lyapunov Exponent for a CHNN with 100 neurons and 20 stored patterns (see text for details).

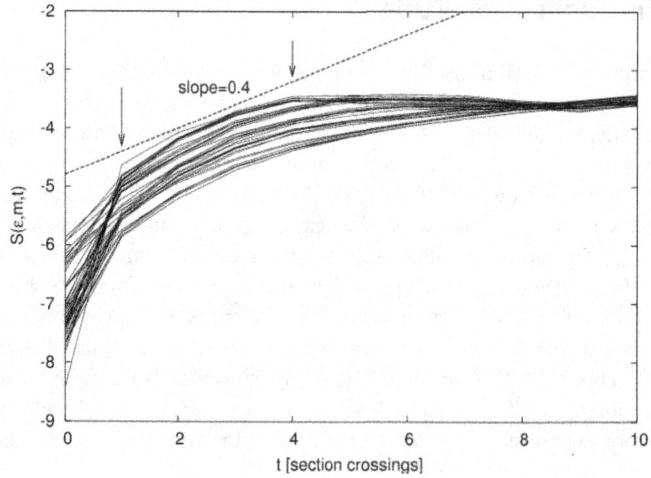

in (Sinha & Gupte, 1998), a chaotic dynamic system is driven towards a desirable state by allowing the "error" between the desired and actual state control appropriate parameters of the chaotic dynamical system. There has also been extensive work on application of neural networks to control chaos (Alsing, Gavrielides, & Kovanis, 1994). In the present case, we show how chaos in a neural network can be controlled by adapting the connections.

It can be shown that this problem can be solved by adapting weights during retrieval (Udayshankar, Chakravarthy, Prabhakar & Gupte 2003a). Usually weights are adapted during training (storage) and frozen during retrieval. However, we now adapt the weights during retrieval following the adaptive Hebbian mechanism of eqn. (8), which is assumed to take place at a slower time scale than activation dynamics of eqns. (10) and (11). The retrieval process in case of adaptive weights progresses as follows.

Initially, the weight matrix has all the stored patterns encoded in itself. That is, the initial weight matrix is calculated using eqn. (8). The network state starts within the neighborhood of a stored pattern, say, S_p. As the network state evolves, the weights are also simultaneously adapted according to eqn. (9) at a slower time scale. Finally, once the network state settles on the nearest stored pattern, S_p, it turns out that the weight matrix sheds all the components other than those that correspond to S_p. In such a state, the network has only one stored pattern; information regarding all other stored patterns is destroyed in the process of retrieving one particular pattern. Therefore, to retrieve a different pattern in a subsequent session the weight matrix must be reloaded (using the eqn. (8) again) so that all the patterns are encoded. It can be shown that performance with adaptive weights is far superior to that with non-adaptive weights (Figure 6). Unlike the case of fixed weights, growth of error with number of stored patterns is more gradual.

Physical Realization of CHNN

Two op-amp based electronic realizations of CHNN corresponding to fixed-point and oscillatory modes respectively are presented in this section. In the fixed point mode the single neuron model has only an op-amp, a capacitor and a resistor (Figure 7(a)); in the oscillatory mode, particularly at $v = 0$, the single neuron model has an inductor, a capacitor and an op-amp (Figure 7(b)). It can be shown that the energy spent by the former neuron model is higher than that of the latter.

Figure 6. Graph showing comparison of Performance (Percentage error) Vs. no of stored patterns P (Memory Capacity) between Nonadaptive (solid line) CHNN and Adaptive (dashed) CHNN. Percentage error refers to the percentage of wrong bits in the retrieved pattern.

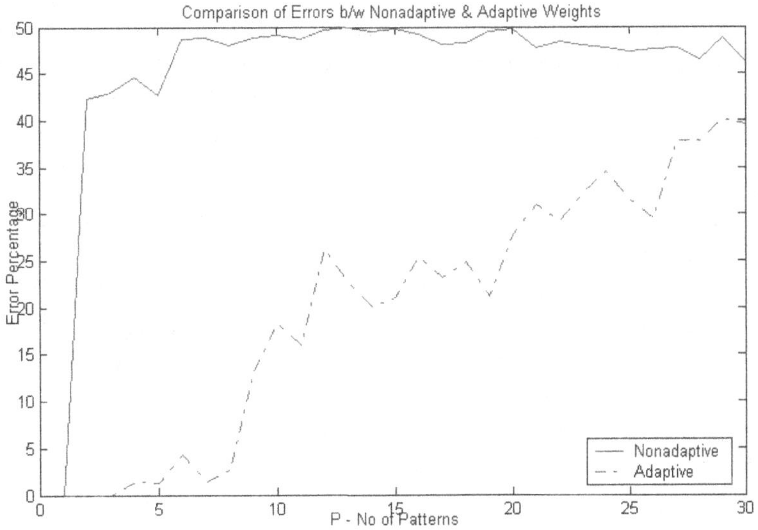

This throws up an interesting question regarding the energetics of neural information processing. Since the same information is encoded in the network in either of the modes, it makes more sense, in terms of energy expenditure, to use the network in oscillatory mode since energy-wise it is the more efficient of the two. However, we can easily see that (since there is no "free lunch"), this lesser energy efficiency in fixed-point mode is compensated by greater retrieval performance. The storage capacity of the CHNN in fixed-point mode is the same as the storage capacity of real-valued Hopfield network viz, $0.14N$, where N is the number of neurons in the network. However, we have seen above that the storage capacity of CHNN in oscillatory mode is practically 1, irrespective of the value of N. These results bring up the general question of the possible link between informational performance and energy expenditure in electronic realizations of neural networks (Kumar, Manmohan, Udayshankar, Vishwanathan, & Chakravarthy, 2002; Udayshankar, Viswanathan & Chakravarthy, 2003b). A related issue is the question of energetic cost of information processing in the brain. Investigation along these lines might yield important insights into brain's energy utilization strategies.

Even though we have seen that CHNN in oscillatory mode with fixed weights has low storage capacity, we have also seen that in the same mode, storage capacity can be enhanced significantly by using dynamic connections (see Section "Enhancing memory capacity by dynamic connections"). What happens to the "no free lunch" intuition in that situation? We show now that in an electronic implementation of the CHNN with and without dynamic connections, energy expenditure with dynamic connections is considerably high.

Figure 8 shows an electronic realization of a neuron in CHNN in oscillatory mode. The neuron model of Figure 7(b) and that of Figure 8 differ in several respects. In the model of Figure 7(b), the negative terminal of the op-amp is grounded, whereas in Figure 8, in all op-amps the positive terminals are grounded. Furthermore, there is no inductor in the model of Figure 8, while the model of Figure 7(b) has an inductor. Now, in Figure 8 above, the coupling connections represented by the resistors R_{ij}, are replaced by dynamic resistances implemented by a Field Effect Transistor (FET). This resistor obeys Hebbian dynamics and depends on the product of voltages of the neurons connected by it (Figure 9).

Energy utilization of the electronic version of CHNN is calculated as the number of stored patterns, P is varied for a network of size $N = 100$ (see Figure 10). Note that energy consumed is far greater with dynamic connections than with fixed connections. This result restores the common intuition of "no free lunch" when in comes to energy expenditure. The increased storage capacity obtained with dynamic connections (Figure 6) is obtained at a cost in terms of energy expenditure (Figure 10). The above results suggest that increased computation in a computing device – here a neural network with a physical implementation - is obtained only at an increased cost in energy expenditure.

Figure 7,a,b. (a) Electronic realization of the complex neuron in fixed point mode. Since the imaginary part is suppressed in this mode, the model in this mode is the same as the electrical analog of the real Hopfield neuron. (b) Electronic realization of the complex neuron model in the oscillatory mode (near v = 0). For v > 0 resistors are present in the circuit and there is dissipation of energy. For v = 0, the resistors disappear and the (idealized) circuit conserves energy.

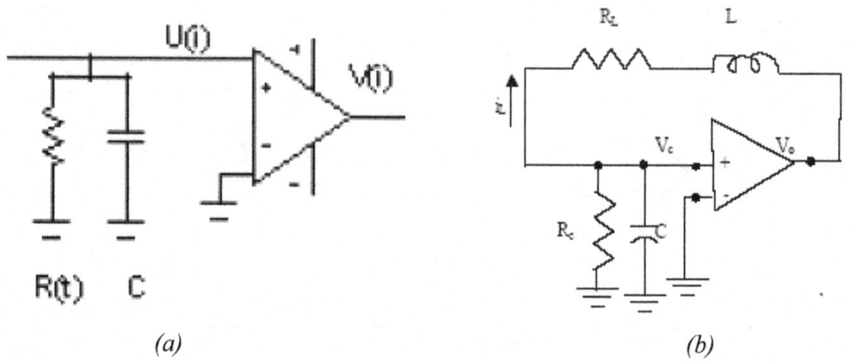

(a) (b)

Figure 8. Equivalent circuit of a single neuron of CHNN in oscillatory mode with fixed connections represented by the resistors R_{ij}

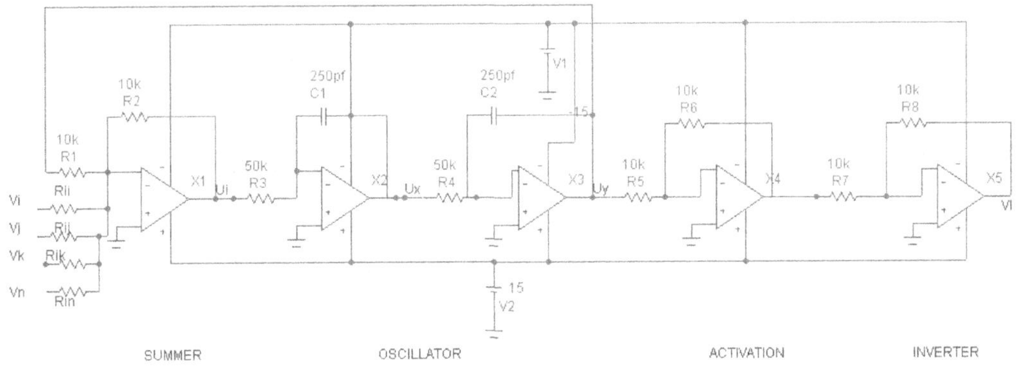

Figure 9. Equivalent circuit of weight adaptation dynamics (eqn. (9)). The FET (inside the dashed box) replaces the fixed weights, R_{ij}, of Figure 8

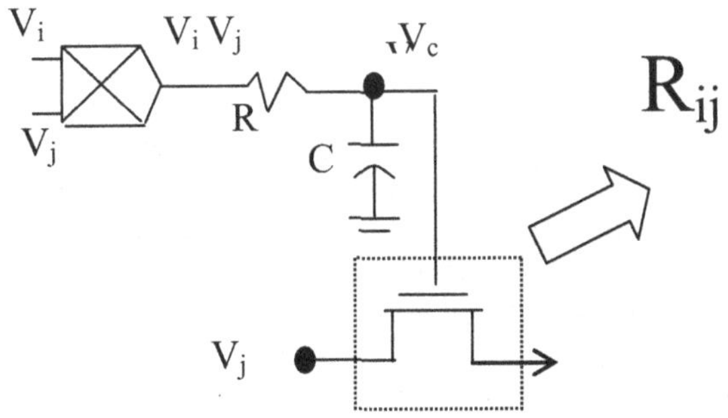

Is the above relation between energy expenditure and computation merely a coincidence, or is it based on a deep principle governing the physics of computation? In any machine that expends energy to perform useful work, there is a more or less well-defined relationship between the amount of work done and energy spent. The only apparent exception to this is a computing device where the work performed is "informational work" which is an abstract quantity. But in a seminal paper Landauer (1961) raised the question of "thermodynamic cost" of computation; this work led to the important area of *reversible computing* (Fredkin & Toffoli, 1980). The possibility of a close relationship between energy and computation becomes more relevant in case of neural networks, which may be considered as a specific class of computing models, since there is a close link between "computation" (viz. neural activity) and energy consumption (viz., glucose metabolism, cerebral blood flow etc) in the brain (Sokoloff 1984; Raichle 1986). A systematic investigation along these lines might reveal important insights into brain's energy utilization strategies.

CHNN for Quadratic Optimization

Hopfield network has been used for quadratic optimization since the network performs gradient descent on a Lyapunov function, which is a quadratic function (Hopfield & Tank, 1985). The quadratic cost function that needs to be optimized is coded as the Lyapunov function i.e., the coefficients of the cost function are encoded as the network connections. However, since the original Hopfield network performs "greedy" descent, it has the prob-

Figure 10. Graph showing comparison of Average Energy Dissipated (mJ) vs. no of stored patterns (P) between Non- adaptive CHNN (solid) and Adaptive CHNN (dashed)

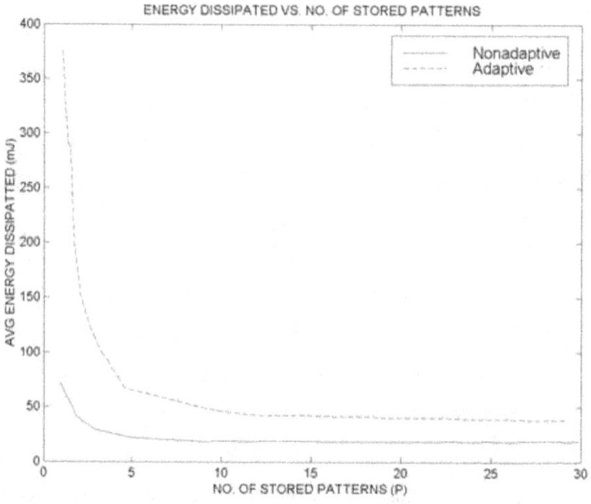

lem of getting stuck in local minima. The same exercise can be repeated with a CHNN operating in fixed-point mode. It will be interesting to see, however, what happens when a quadratic optimization problem is mapped onto the weights of a CHNN operated in oscillatory mode. Since the network exhibits chaotic wandering behavior in oscillatory mode without settling anywhere, such chaotic dynamics might resemble the stochastic "annealing" mechanisms used to prevent confinement to local minima (Kirkpatrick , Gelatt, & Vecchi, 1983).

With the above considerations, our approach to use CHNN for optimization is as follows. We apply CHNN to graph bisection problem, which can be formulated as a quadratic optimization problem. Consider a general graph, a set of N points or vertices and a set of edges, which connect pairs of the vertices. (N is assumed to be even). The task is to divide the vertices into two sets of equal size in such a way as to minimize the number of edges going between the sets.

Let $C_{ij} = 1$ if vertices i and j are connected and $C_{ij} = 0$ if they are not. At each vertex define a variable V_i which is +1 if the site is in one set and -1 if it is in the other. Then the function to be minimized is:

$$E = -\frac{1}{2}\sum_i \sum_j C_{ij} V_i V_j \tag{17}$$

subject to the constraint,

$$\sum_i V_i = 0 \tag{18}$$

which ensures the division into equal number of vertices

A way to enforce the constraint softly is to add to the effective energy a term that penalizes the violation of the constraint. Thus we use the composite cost function:

$$E = -\frac{1}{2}\sum_i \sum_j C_{ij} V_i V_j + \gamma (\sum_i V_i)^2 \tag{19}$$

where γ is the parameter which makes sure that the constraints are satisfied.

Algebraically expanding the expression, we get,

$$E = N\gamma - \frac{1}{2}\sum_i \sum_j W_{ij} V_i V_j \tag{20}$$

where,

$$W_{ij} = C_{ij} - 2\gamma \tag{21}$$

Since the cost function C is a symmetric matrix, weight matrix is also symmetric (from the above equation).

Start the CHNN in oscillatory mode (ν=0) (eqns. (15) & (16)) and gradually increase ν to 1. Preliminary work along these lines with graph bisection problem involving graphs with high symmetry yielded interesting results. Since the problem has multiple (degenerate) solutions (due to symmetry), the network is found to hop from one degenerate solution to another, following a complex temporal pattern of evolution. This approach seems to be suitable for searching a high-dimensional space for multiple equivalent solutions.

To test this idea, the CHNN is used to partition graphs with high level of symmetry so that the problem would have degenerate solutions. A simple example of such a graph is a 2D square grid with even number of nodes per side. Such graphs have 2 identical solutions – the vertical bisection and the horizontal bisection. Note that each of these solutions can be coded in two ways (+/-1 or –/+1). Network performance on a 10 × 10 network is described below.

Figure 11(a) is a plot of variation of cost or energy, E, of the network with time or the iteration number. It can be clearly seen that the energy function (which is the cost function of our problem) oscillates between select values after a certain initial settling time. It visits both the minimum energy solutions several times in the process. Figure 11(b) is the history of the outputs 'V_i' (real parts only) vs. time. The two different colors indicate +1 and -1. These observations and the calculations suggest that the two bisection solutions (which correspond to four network solutions) are actually repeated cyclically. In this case, the four solutions which the network sees occur in this order: A, B, C, D, where (A, C) and (B, D) are the pairs which represent the same solution in reality. Figure 11(c) depicts the variation of ν with time. The graph is a straight line since ν is kept constant in the trial. Figure 11(d) is the histogram of energy or cost. This shows that the network spends most of its time in the low energy states. Studies with regular grids of 3, 4 and 5 dimensions also yielded similar results.

These studies represent a novel approach regarding use of CHNN in oscillatory mode to solve quadratic optimization problem. The proposed approach has two advantages: 1) the network does not get stuck in local minima, 2) it seeks not just a single minimum, but ideally all the minima comparable to the global optimum. Hence it is particularly suitable to large real world problems in which there might be a large number of local minima with cost values comparable to that of the global minimum. However, while the current preliminary results are encouraging, it is only an empirical study of a specific class of optimization problems. There is a need for a thorough investigation to evaluate the scope of the present approach to solve general degenerate quadratic optimization problems.

CHNN FOR CHAOTIC SYNCHRONIZATION

Synchronization of chaotic low-dimensional systems has been a topic of much recent research (Boccaletti, Kurths, Osipov, Valladres & Zhou, 2002). Such systems have found applications for secure communications. Since chaotic systems are sensitive to initial conditions, even the synchronization of two identical chaotic systems is a non-trivial task as a very small difference in the initial conditions of the two systems can lead to drastically different chaotic trajectories for the two systems. Pecora and Caroll (1990) devised an ingenious method by which two chaotic systems were made to follow the same trajectory by passing one or more variable (the drive variables) from the first system to the other. The remaining variables (called the response variables) are allowed to evolve freely (Figure 12). If the subsystem Lyapunov exponents of the response system are less than one, the response variables are enslaved by the drive variables and start reproducing the trajectory followed by the corresponding variables of the first system. The two systems thus start following identical trajectories.

Figure 11. Variation of cost with time for bipartition of a 2-D grid of size 10 × 10. (a) Variation of cost, E, with iterations. (b) Variation of the real part of the state, Re[V(t)], of the 100 (= 10 × 10) neuron network with iterations. Each column represents the instantaneous state, V(t), at a given iteration. (c) Variation of v with iterations. In this case v is constant at 0.4. (d) Histogram of the values taken by the cost function, E, throughout the simulation. See text for explanation.

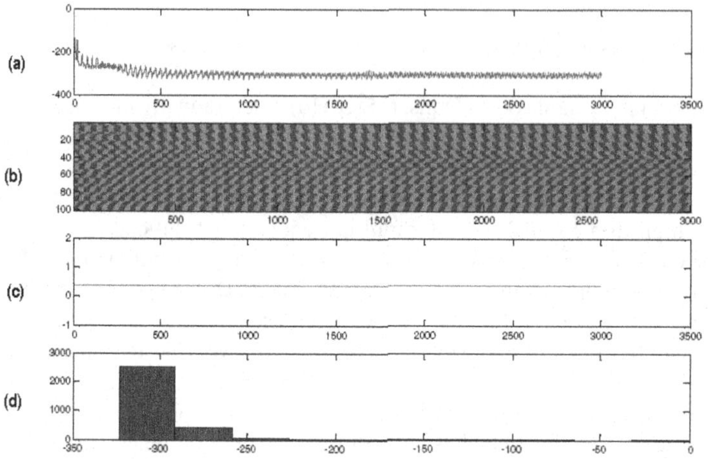

Early work on synchronizing low-dimensional chaotic systems like the one studied in (Pecora & Carroll, 1990) was subsequently extended to high dimensional systems (Kocarev, 1995) and neural networks. Milanovic and Zaghloul (1996) achieved synchronization in a small network of chaotic neurons using an enhanced chaotic masking technique. Lu and Chen (2004) studied synchronization in chaotic neural networks with delays. Wang and Lu (2005) investigated phase synchronization in a network of chaotic neural network with a small world structure. Li, Sun & Kurths (2007) studied synchronization in a pair of complex networks, with identical topologies, connected in a unidirectional fashion. Theoretical conditions for synchronization were also derived.

In order to synchronize a pair of CHNNs we adopt a procedure analogous to the one followed by Peccorra and Carroll (1990). We consider a large CHNN in oscillatory mode, since the network exhibits chaotic behavior only in the oscillatory mode (Chakravarthy, Gupte, Yogesh & Salhotra 2008). For a network of N neurons, the state vector $V \in C^N$, where $V = \{V_i\}$, V_i is the output of i'th neuron, of a N-neuron network. The components of the state vector are divided into a 'drive (V^d)' and 'response (V^r)' subsystems, i.e. $V = [V^d, V^r]$. Accordingly, the state of the transmitting network is denoted by, $V^t = [V^{td}, V^{tr}]$, and that of the receiving network by, $V^r = [V^{rd}, V^{rr}]$ Simulation, following eqns. (15) and (16), of the transmitting and receiver CHNNs, is started simultaneously, but from different initial conditions. It need not be repeated that the CHNNs are identical in size and weight values. On the transmitter side, the dynamics of all the N-neurons are simulated. However, on the receiver side, at every time step, the drive subsystem of the transmitter (V^{td}), is copied onto the corresponding components of the receiver (V^{rd}), i.e., $V^{rd} = V^{td}$. Only the response subsystem (V^{rr}) of the receiver is allowed to evolve following eqns. (15) and (16). Under such circumstances, we study the degree of synchronization that develops between the states of the two networks.

Two identical 100 neuron CHNNs operating in the oscillating mode are used in our simulations. The complex Hebb-rule eqn. (8) is used to calculate the weight matrices of the network by storing random binary (±1) patterns. The effect of key network parameters like the number of stored patterns (P), the mode parameter (v),

Figure 12. Synchronization of chaotic systems using the same driving signal for both the original and duplicated synchronizing subsystems

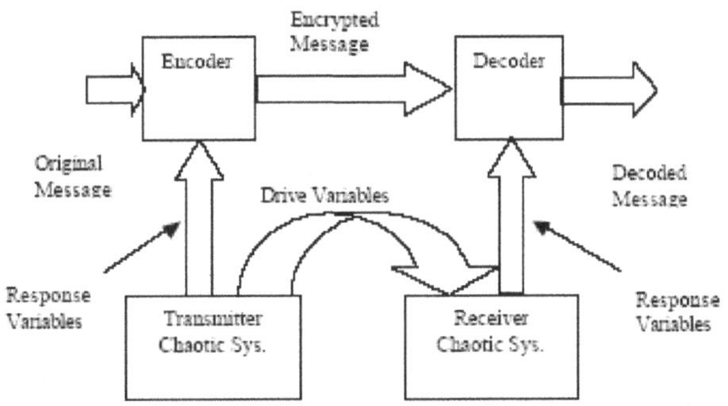

and the size of the drive subsystem, 'm_d', on the degree of synchronization is investigated. Synchronization is quantified by 'correlation' between the two network states defined as follows. Let $V_i(k) = V_i(t_0 + k\Delta t)$, be the discrete-time representation of the i'th component of a network state, where Δt is the time-step. Correlation is calculated for each component (C_i) separately and then averaged over all the N-components. Thus, correlation of the i'th component is,

$$C_i = \frac{\sum_{k=n_0}^{n_1} \mathrm{Re}[(V_i^t(k) - \bar{V}_i^t)]\mathrm{Re}[(V_i^r(k) - \bar{V}_i^r)]}{(\sum_{k=n_0}^{n_1} \mathrm{Re}[(V_i^t(k) - \bar{V}_i^t)]^2)^{1/2}(\sum_{k=n_0}^{n_1} \mathrm{Re}[(V_i^r(k) - \bar{V}_i^r)]^2)^{1/2}}, \quad (22)$$

where n_0 and n_1 are limits of the interval over which correlation is computed. The overall correlation is,

$$C = (\sum_i^N C_i) / N. \quad (23)$$

The parameter values used in the simulations are:

$N = 100$	- Number of neurons
$\Delta t = 0.08$	- Discrete time-step
$\lambda = 7.5$	- Steepness of the tanh() nonlinearity
n_0	- 1
n_1	- 2000 (number of iterations)

We now study the effect of network parameters like the size of the drive subsystem, 'm_d', the number of stored patterns (P), and the mode parameter (ν), on the synchronization represented by overall correlation, C.

Effect of drive subsystem size (m_d): It is intuitively expected that a larger drive subsystem improves synchronization because there is a greater exchange of information between the transmitting and the receiver networks. The same is observed in the simulations. Fixing the number of stored patterns (P=10) correlation is calculated for various values of m_d, with a fixed value of mode parameter (ν = 0.1) (see Figure 13). The plot is obtained by averaging over several trials (=20) since there is considerable variation from trial to trial. The initial state of the

Figure 13. Dependence of correlation on the number of common components, m_d ($N = 100$, $P = 10$, $v=0.1$). Results are averaged over 20 trials.

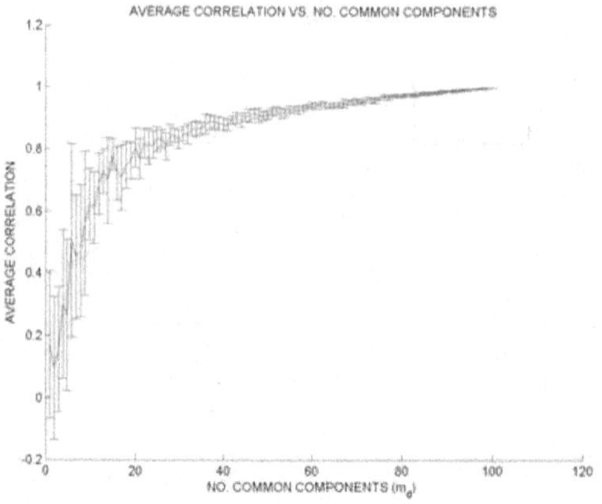

network is varied from trial to trial. Error bars reveal variation over trials. Note that variation is more for smaller values of m_d; synchronization is more robust for larger values.

Effect of Mode parameter (v): From Theorem 2 (Appendix), we have seen that v controls the dissipativity of CHNN. Since dissipativity increases stability one may expect v to have a positive effect on synchronization, which is supported by simulations. Figure 14 shows a plot of correlation, C, against v, keeping the other two parameters in question fixed ($P = 10$, $m_d = 30$). The error bar summarizes the result obtained over 20 trials. Note that inter-trial variation is higher for smaller values of v, which is understandable since higher values of v increase stability of dynamics.

Effect of number of Stored Patterns (P): It was noted in Section titled "The two network modes" that in the oscillatory mode the CHNN wanders chaotically from one stored pattern to another when multiple patterns are stored. Thus it appears that it might be more difficult to synchronize two CHNNs with a large number of stored patterns. Fixing m_d at 30, and v at 0.1, correlation is plotted against P (Figure 15). The plots are obtained by averaging over 20 trials. As expected synchronization deteriorates with increasing P, but roughly plateaus between $P = 10$ and $P = 15$.

Thus we show how a pair of identical high-dimensional CHNNs can be synchronized by communicating only a subset of state vector components. The synchronizability of such a system is characterized through simulations.

CONCLUSION

The real value of the neuron state is usually interpreted as short-time firing rate of the neuron. The complex-valued neuron state acquires a natural interpretation as an ordered pair consisting of firing rate and its temporal derivative. The proposed complex network, the CHNN, operates in two modes: 1) fixed-point mode and 2) oscillatory mode. The CHNN is identical to Hopfield network under limiting conditions (mode parameter, $v = 1$). Patterns can be stored using a complex-valued variation of Hebb's or outer product rule. Performance of CHNN in fixed-point mode is identical to that of Hopfield network. However, in the oscillatory mode, performance deteriorates drastically even when two patterns are stored. This problem is circumvented by the use of dynamic synapses.

Figure 14. Dependence of correlation on the dissipation parameter, v. ($N = 100$, $P = 10$, $m_d = 30$). Results are averaged over 20 trials

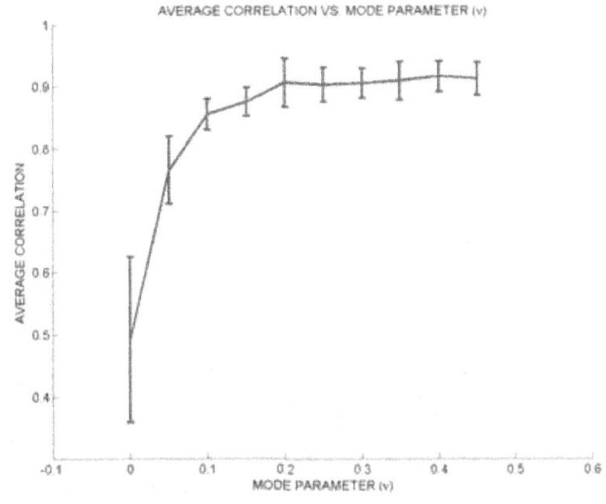

Figure 15. Dependence of synchronization on the number of stored patterns, P. ($N = 100$, $m_d = 30$, $v=0.1$). Results are averaged over 20 trials

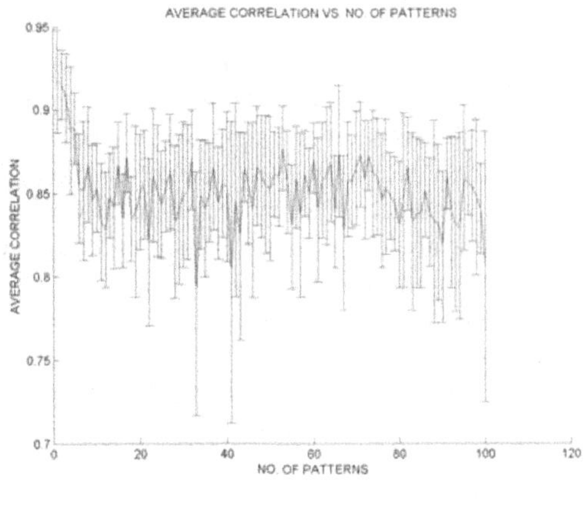

Electronic realizations of CHNN in the two modes of operation are given and relative advantages discussed. Such a discussion brings up a more intriguing question of energetic costs of informational performance in neural network models and ultimately in the brain.

CHNN is also applied to quadratic optimization problem. It is shown how chaotic wandering behavior inherent in CHNN can be exploited as an "annealing" mechanism, which reduces the probability of the network getting stuck in a local minimum. Results with graph bisection problems are discussed.

The network is also applied to the problem of chaotic synchronization, a technique with applications in secure communications. Chaotic synchronization is usually demonstrated with low-dimensional chaotic systems. Here we use a high-dimensional CHNN to the same problem. The effect of various network parameters on the synchronization performance of the CHNN is characterized.

Stability is obviously a desirable property of memories and therefore of memory models, which justifies existence of neural memory models with fixed-point dynamics. What is found regularly in our subjective experience of memory recall is not absolute stability but metastability. Memories recalled emerge transiently and fade away from our mind; attentional effort is needed to hold the recalled memory longer. This is reasonable since a recalled memory that persists for all eternity is no memory but a nightmarish fixation; brain has to then invoke auxiliary mechanisms to get out of such fixations every time it gets stuck in one. Oscillatory memories, like CHNN, that are transiently stable, are therefore more natural candidates as memory models. Hence stability of memories but over a finite time-scale is not only desirable but indispensable for continual adaptation of an organism in a changing environment. Chaotic wandering of network state in CHNN in oscillatory model readily provides such a mechanism.

FUTURE RESEARCH DIRECTIONS

An exciting direction of future development for complex neural networks is perhaps in the area of quantum neurodynamics (Kak, 1995; Menneer, 1998). The problem of consciousness is the holy grail of all brain research. There is a whole body of literature that generated quantum mechanical models, in the "dualist" tradition, of mind-brain interaction (Jibu & Yasue, 1995). Since the primary equation of quantum mechanics – the Schrodinger equation – is a complex equation, and since most quantum quantities are complex, a theory of quantum neural dynamics will necessarily involve complex quantities.

Quantum neural models of associative memory have been proposed (Ventura & Martinez 1998; Perus, 1996; Jibu, Pribram & Yasue, 1996). In one such model (Perus, 1996), an interesting parallel between quantum wavefunction collapse and retrieval from associative memories is observed. According to this interpretation quantum wave function collapse "is very similar to neuronal-pattern- reconstruction from memory. In memory, there is a superposition of many stored patterns. One of them is selectively 'brought forward from the background' if an external stimulus triggers such a reconstruction" (Perus, 1996). Interestingly the framework of CHNN also permits such an interpretation of memory retrieval. The chaotic wandering of CHNN among multiple stored patterns in oscillatory mode, is analogous to evolution of a superposition of many quantum states in a quantum mechanical system. When CHNN is switched suddenly from oscillatory mode to fixed point mode, by rapidly varying v from 0 to 1, the network stops its wandering behavior and quickly settles on a fixed-point state, which is probably a stored pattern. Thus, something analogous to wavefunction collapse can be simulated in the CHNN by switching between oscillatory and fixed-point modes.

Thus the study of complex neural networks seems to lead us on directly towards the mind-brain problem via quantum neural modeling route. Combined with physical theories of brain function with quantum mechanical underpinnings (Beck & Eccles, 1992; Hameroff, 2007), this line of research may turn out to be one of the highest crests in the advancing wavefront of contemporary brain research.

ACKNOWLEDGMENT

The author would like to thank Neelima Gupte for her contributions to the work on adaptive weights and chaotic synchronization. The author is grateful to Anil Prabhakar for his help with chaotic time series analysis. The author would like to thank Shiva Kesavan for reviewing the final document.

REFERENCES

Abbot, L. F. (1990). A network of oscillators. *J. Phys. A, 23*, 3835-3859.

Albers, D. J., Sprott, J. C., & Dechert, W. D. (1998). Routes to chaos in neural networks with random weights. *Int. J. of Bifurcation and Chaos*, *8*(7), 1463-1478.

Alsing, P. M., Gavrielides, A., & Kovanis, V. (1994). Using neural networks for controlling chaos. *Phys. Rev. E*, *49*, 1225-1231.

Amit, D., Gutfreund, H., & Sompolinsky, H. (1987). Information storage in Neural Networks with low levels of activity. *Physical Review Letters, 55*, 1530-1533.

Beck, F., & Eccles, J. C. (1992). Quantum Aspects of Brain Activity and the Role of Consciousness. *Proceedings of the National Academy of Sciences, 89*, 11357-11361.

Boccaletti, S., Kurths, J., Osipov, G., Valladres, D. L., & Zhou, C. S. (2002). The synchronization of chaotic systems. *Phys. Rep., 366*(1).

Chakravarthy, S. V., & Ghosh, J. (1993). Studies on a network of complex neurons. *In Proc. of SPIE vol. 1965 Applications of Artificial Neural Networks IV,* (pp. 31 -43), April, 1993. (invited paper).

Chakravarthy S. V., & Ghosh, J. (1994). A neural network-based associative memory for storing complex-valued patterns. In *Proc IEEE Int Conf Syst Man Cybern*, (pp. 2213-2218).

Chakravarthy S. V., & Ghosh, J. (1996). A complex-valued associative memory for storing patterns as oscillatory states. *Biological Cybernetics, 75*, 229-238.

Chakravarthy, V. S., Gupte, N., Yogesh, S., & Salhotra, A. (2008). Chaotic Synchronization using a Network of Neural Oscillators. *International Journal of Neural Systems, 18*(2), 1-8.

Fredkin, E., & Toffoli, T. (1980). *Reversible Computing.* MIT Report MIT/LCS/TM-151.

Gray, C., & Singer, W. (1989). Stimulus-specific neuronal oscillations in orientation columns of cat visual cortex. *Proc Natl Acad Sci, 86*, 1698–1702.

Hameroff, S. R. (2007). The Brain is both Neurocomputer and Quantum Computer. *Cognitive Science, 31*, 1035–1045.

Hebb, D. O. (1949). *The organization of behavior.* New York, NY: John Wiley.

Hegger, R., & Kantz, H. (1999). Practical implementation of nonlinear time series methods: The TISEAN package. *Chaos*, *9*(2), 413-435.

Hirose, A. (1992). Proposal of fully complex-valued neural networks. In *Proceedings of Intl' Jnt' Conf. On Neural Networks*, *4*, 152-157.

Hopfield, J. J. (1982). Neural networks and physical systems with emergent collective computational abilities. *Proceedings of the National Academy of Sciences USA*, *9*(2554).

Hopfield, J. J. (1984). Neurons with graded response have collective computational properties like those of two state neurons. *Proceedings of the National Academy of Sciences, 79*, 2554-2558.

Hopfield, J. J., & Tank, D. W. (1985). "Neural" computation of decisions in optimization problems. *Biological Cybernetics, 55*, 141-146.

Huberman, B. A., & Lumer, E. (1990). Dynamics of adaptive systems. *IEEE Transactions on Circuits and. Systems, 37*(4), 547-550.

Jibu, M., Pribram, K. H., Yasue, K. (1996). From conscious experience to memory storage and retrieval: The role of quantum brain dynamics and Boson condensation of evanescent photons. *Int J Modern Physics, B 10*(13 & 14), 1735-1754.

Jibu, M., & Yasue, K. (1995). *Quantum brain dynamics: An introduction.* Amsterdam: John Benjamins.

Kak, S. (1995). Quantum Neural Computing, *Advances in Imaging and Electron Physics, 94*, 259-313.

Kirkpatrick, S., Gerlatt, C. D., & Vecchi, M. P. (1983). Optimization by simulated annealing. *Science, 220*, 671–680.

Kocarev, L. J. (1995). Chaos synchronization of high-dimensional dynamical systems. *Proc. of IEEE Int'l Symp. on Circ. Sys.*, Seattle, WA, April 29 - May 3, (pp. 1009-1012).

Kohonen, T. (1977). *Associative Memory: A system theoretic approach*. Berlin: Springer-Verlag.

Kosko, B. (1987, December). Adaptive Bidirectional Associative Memories. *Applied Optics*, *26*(23), 4947-4960.

Kumar, A., Manmohan V., Udayshankar, M., Vishwanathan, M., & Chakravarthy, V. S. (2002). Link between Energy and Computation in a Physical Model of Hopfield Network. *Proc. of the 9th International Conference on Neural Information Processing* (pp. 267-270). Singapore.

Landauer, R. (1961, July). Irreversibility and Heat Generation in the Computing Process. *IBM Journal of Research and Development*, *3*, 183-191.

Leung, H., & Haykin, S. (1991, September). The complex backpropagation algorithm. *IEEE Transactions on Signal Processing*, *39*(9), 2101-2104.

Li, C., Sun, W., & Kurths, J. (2007). Synchronization between two coupled complex networks, *Phys Rev E Stat Nonlin Softmatter Phys*, October, 76(4-2).

Lu, W., & Chen, T. (2004). Synchronization of coupled connected neural networks with delays. *IEEE Trans Circ Syst I*, ***51***, 2491–2503.

Maass, W., & Bishop, C. (1999). *Pulsed Neural Networks*. Cambridge, MA: MIT Press.

Mandic P. D., & Goh, S. L. (2004, December). A complex-valued RTRL Algorithm for recurrent Neural networks. *Neural Computation*, *16*(12), 2699–2713.

McCulloch, W. S., & Pitts, W. (1943). A logical calculus of the ideas immanent in nervous activity. *Bull. of Mathematical Biophysics*, *5*, 115-133.

Menneer, T. (1998, May). Quantum Artificial Neural Networks. Ph.D. thesis of The University of Exeter, UK.

Milanovic, V., & Zaghloul, M. E. (1996). Synchronization of chaotic neural networks and applications to comminications. *Int'l J. of Bifur. Chaos*, *6*, 2571-2585.

Nitta, T. (1997). An Extension of the Back-Propagation Algorithm to Complex Numbers. *Neural Networks*, *10*(8), 1391-1415.

Ott, E., Grebogi, C., James, A. Y. (1990, March). Controlling chaos. *Physical Review letters*, *64*(11), 1196-1199.

Pecora, L. M., & Carroll T. L. (1990). Synchronization in Chaotic Systems. *Physical Review Letters*, *64*(8), 821-824.

Perus, M. (1996). Neuro-Quantum Parallelism in Brain-Mind and Computers. *Informatica*, *20*, 173-83.

Raichle, M. E. (1986). Neuroimaging. *Trends in Neuroscience*, *9*, 525-529.

Skarda, C. A., & Freeman, W. (1987). How brains make chaos in order to make sense of the world, *Behavioral and Brain Sciences*, *10*, 161-195.

Sinha, S., & Gupte, N. (1998). Adaptive control of spatially extended systems: Targeting spatiotemporal patterns and chaos. *Physical Review E*, *58*(5), R5221-R5224.

Sokoloff, L. (1984). *Metabolic Probes of Central Nervous System Activity in Experimental Animals*. Sunderland, MA: Sinauer Associates.

Sompolinsky, H., Crisanti, A., & Sommers, H. J. (1988). Chaos in neural networks, *Phys. Rev. Lett.*, *61*, 259-262.

Udayshankar, M., Chakravarthy, V. S., Prabhakar, A., & Gupte, N. (2003a, December). Controlling chaos using adaptive weights in an oscillatory neural network. *National Conference on Nonlinear Systems and Dynamics*, IIT, Kharagpur.

Udayshankar, M., Viswanathan, M., & Chakravarthy, V. S (2003b, December). Inevitable Energy Cost of Storage Capacity Enhancement in an Oscillatory Neural Network. *46th IEEE International Midwest Symposium on Circuits and Systems*, Cairo, Egypt.

Ventura, D., & Martinez, T. (1998, May). Quantum Associative Memory with Exponential Capacity. *Proc. of the International Joint Conference on Neural Networks*, (pp. 509-13).

von der Malsburg, C. (1988). Pattern recognition by labeled graph matching. *Neural Networks, 1*, 141–148.

Wang, Q. Y., & Lu, Q. S. (2005). Phase Synchronization in Small World Chaotic Neural Networks. *Chinese Physics Letters*, *22*(6), 1329-1332.

ADDITIONAL READING

Hirose, A., (Ed.) (2003, November). *Complex-Valued Neural Networks (Theories and Applications).* World Scientific Publishing. Company.

MATHEMATICAL APPENDIX

Lemma 1: If $\lambda\,|\,\mathrm{Re}[z]\,|>>1$ and $g(\lambda z)\equiv\tanh(\lambda z)$, then $g(\lambda z)\approx\tanh(\lambda(\mathrm{Re}[z]))$.

Proof: Expanding $\tanh(\lambda z)$ into real and imaginary parts,

$$\tanh(\lambda z)=g_x(\lambda x,\lambda y)+ig_y(\lambda x,\lambda y)$$

$$=\frac{\sinh(2\lambda x)}{\cosh(2\lambda x)+\cos(2\lambda y)}+i\frac{\sin(2\lambda y)}{\cosh(2\lambda x)+\cos(2\lambda y)}$$

Now, for $\lambda|x|>>1$,

$\cosh(2\lambda x)>>1\geq|\cos(2\lambda y)|$, i.e.,
$\cosh(2\lambda x)+\cos(2\lambda y)\approx\cosh(2\lambda x)$,

in the given conditions. Substituting this in the expansion for $\tanh(\lambda z)$, we get,

$\tanh(\lambda z)=\tanh(\lambda x)+i(a\ \ small\ \ number)$.

Therefore, the above approximation is valid everywhere in the complex plane except within a thin strip, whose width decreases with increasing λ, about the imaginary axis. The approximation fails at the singularities of $\tanh(\lambda z)$, an infinite set of points located at $z=(2n+1)i\pi/2$, where n is an integer.

Theorem 1: If the weight matrix, T, is Hermitian, i.e., $T_{jk}=T_{kj}^*,\ \forall\ j,k,$ then the energy function, E in eqn. (14) is a Lyapunov function of the dynamical system (eqns. (12) and (13)), defined over a region in which $g()$ is analytic and $\partial g_x/\partial x>0$. ($z=x+iy;\ g=g_x+i\,g_y$)

Proof: Consider the energy term E defined in eqn. (14). We compute dE/dt to show monotonic decrease of E with time. Differentiating the first term in the expression for E gives rise to pairs of terms of the form:

$$\frac{1}{2}\frac{dV_k^*}{dt}T_{kj}V_j+\frac{1}{2}\frac{dV_j}{dt}T_{kj}V_k^*,\ and,\ \frac{1}{2}\frac{dV_j^*}{dt}T_{kj}V_k+\frac{1}{2}\frac{dV_k}{dt}T_{jk}V_j^*.$$

Using the Hermitian property of the T matrix, these pairs can be grouped as,

$$\frac{1}{2}\mathrm{Re}[\frac{dV_k^*}{dt}T_{kj}V_j],\ and,\ \frac{1}{2}\mathrm{Re}[\frac{dV_j^*}{dt}T_{kj}V_k].$$

Therefore,

$$\frac{dE}{dt}=-\mathrm{Re}[\sum_j\frac{dV_k^*}{dt}(\sum_k T_{jk}V_k-z_j+I_j)]=-\mathrm{Re}[\sum_j\frac{dV_j^*}{dt}\frac{dz_j}{dt}].$$

Let,

$$V^*=g(z)=g_x(x,y)+i\,g_y(x,y)$$

where the subscript j has been dropped for convenience. Then,

continued on following page

MATHEMATICAL APPENDIX. CONTINUED

$$\mathrm{Re}[\frac{dV^*}{dt}\frac{dz}{dt}] = \frac{dg_x}{dt}\frac{dx}{dt} + \frac{dg_y}{dt}\frac{dy}{dt}$$
$$= \frac{\partial g_x}{\partial x}(\frac{dx}{dt})^2 + \frac{\partial g_y}{\partial y}(\frac{dy}{dt})^2 + (\frac{\partial g_x}{\partial y} + \frac{\partial g_y}{\partial x})\frac{dx}{dt}\frac{dy}{dt}$$

Since *g(.)* is analytic, from Cauchy-Riemann equations,

$$\frac{\partial g_x}{\partial x} = \frac{\partial g_y}{\partial y}; \qquad (\frac{\partial g_x}{\partial y} + \frac{\partial g_y}{\partial x}) = 0 \tag{A1}$$

we obtain,

$$\frac{dg_x}{dt}\frac{dx}{dt} + \frac{dg_y}{dt}\frac{dy}{dt} = \frac{\partial g_x}{\partial x}[(\frac{dx}{dt})^2 + (\frac{dy}{dt})^2] \tag{A2}$$

The right hand side of eqn. (A2) is positive when $\partial g_x / \partial x$ is positive, which is true for $-\pi / 4 \le \mathrm{Im}[z] \le \pi / 4$. Therefore, when the conditions of the theorem are satisfied it can be seen that E decreases monotonically and, since it is bounded from below within an analytic domain of *g(.)*, must reach a minimum. Hence the theorem.

Theorem 2: The dynamics described by eqns. (15) and (16) are: (i) conservative for $v = 0$, and (ii) dissipative for $\nu \in (0,1]$.

Proof: This can be proved very elegantly if we adopt complex notation. Consider,

$$\frac{\partial \dot{x}_j}{x_j} + \frac{\partial \dot{y}_j}{y_j} \equiv \mathrm{Re}[\frac{\partial \dot{z}_j}{\partial z_j}] = \mathrm{Re}[T_{jj}\frac{\partial g(\alpha z_j^*)}{\partial z_j} - \beta] = \mathrm{Re}[0 - (\nu + i(1-\nu))] = -\nu,$$

where $\alpha = \beta\lambda$, and $\beta = (v + i(1- v))$.

Hence,

$$\frac{\partial \dot{x}_j}{x_j} + \frac{\partial \dot{y}_j}{y_j} < 0, \quad for\ \nu \in (0,1],$$

i.e., the phase volume contracts with time. Hence, the dynamics are dissipative and,

$$\frac{\partial \dot{x}_j}{x_j} + \frac{\partial \dot{y}_j}{y_j} = 0, \quad for\ \nu = 0,$$

implying a conserved phase volume, hence conservative dynamics.

Chapter V
Global Stability Analysis for Complex-Valued Recurrent Neural Networks and Its Application to Convex Optimization Problems

Mitsuo Yoshida
Kyoto Institute of Technology, Japan

Takehiro Mori
Kyoto Institute of Technology, Japan

ABSTRACT

Global stability analysis for complex-valued artificial recurrent neural networks seems to be one of yet-unchallenged topics in information science. This chapter presents global stability conditions for discrete-time and continuous-time complex-valued recurrent neural networks, which are regarded as nonlinear dynamical systems. Global asymptotic stability conditions for these networks are derived by way of suitable choices of activation functions. According to these stability conditions, there are classes of discrete-time and continuous-time complex-valued recurrent neural networks whose equilibrium point is globally asymptotically stable. Furthermore, the conditions are shown to be successfully applicable to solving convex programming problems, for which real field solution methods are generally tedious.

INTRODUCTION

Recurrent neural networks whose neurons are fully interconnected have been utilized to implement associative memories and solve optimization problems. These networks are regarded as nonlinear dynamical feedback systems. Stability properties of this class of dynamical networks are an important issue from applications point of view.

On the other hand, several models of neural networks that can deal with complex numbers, the complex-valued neural networks, have come to forth in recent years. These networks have states, connection weights, and activation functions, which are all complex-valued. Such networks have been studied in terms of their abilities of information processing, because they possess attractive features which do not exist in their real-valued counterparts (Hirose, 2003; Kuroe, Hashimoto & Mori, 2001, 2002; Kuroe, Yoshida & Mori, 2003; Nitta, 2000; Takeda & Kishigami, 1992; Yoshida, Mori & Kuroe, 2004; Yoshida & Mori, 2007). Generally, activation functions of neural networks crucially determine their dynamic behavior. In complex-valued neural networks, there is a greater choice of activation functions compared to real-valued networks. However, the question of appropriate activation functions has been paid insufficient attention to in the past.

Local asymptotic stability conditions for complex-valued recurrent neural networks with an energy function defined on the complex domain have been studied earlier and synthesis of complex-valued associative memories has been realized (Kuroe et al., 2001, 2002). However, studies on their application to *global* optimization problems and theoretical analysis for *global* asymptotic stability conditions remain yet-unchallenged topics.

The purpose of this chapter is to analyze global asymptotic stability for complex-valued recurrent neural networks. Two types of complex-valued recurrent neural networks are considered: discrete-time model and continuous-time model. We present global asymptotic stability conditions for both models of the complex-valued recurrent neural networks. To ensure global stability, classes of complex-valued functions are defined as the activation functions, and therewith several stability conditions are obtained. According to these conditions, there are classes of discrete-time and continuous-time complex-valued recurrent neural networks whose common equilibrium point is globally asymptotically stable. Furthermore, the obtained conditions are shown to be successfully applicable to solving convex programming problems.

The chapter is organized as follows. In Background, a brief summary of applications to associative memories and optimization problems in real-valued recurrent neural networks is presented. Moreover, results on stability analysis and applications of these real-valued neural networks are introduced. Next, models of discrete-time and continuous-time complex-valued neural networks are described. For activation functions of these networks, two classes of complex-valued function are defined. In the next section, global asymptotic stability conditions for the discrete-time and continuous-time complex-valued neural networks are proved, respectively. Some discussions thereof are also given. Furthermore, applications of complex-valued neural networks to convex programming problems with numerical examples are shown in the subsequent section. Finally, concluding remarks and future research directions are given.

Before going into the body of the chapter, we first list the glossary of symbols. In the following, the sets of $n \times m$ real and complex matrices are defined by $\mathbf{R}^{n\times m}$, $\mathbf{C}^{n\times m}$, respectively. $\mathbf{I}_n$ denotes the identity matrix in $\mathbf{R}^{n\times n}$. $\mathbf{R}_+$ means the nonnegative space in $\mathbf{R}$ defined by $\mathbf{R}_+ = \{x \mid x \in \mathbf{R}, x \geq 0\}$. For a complex number $x \in \mathbf{C}$, $|x|$ stands for the absolute value, and $\bar{x}$ is the complex conjugate number. Re(x) denotes the real part of $x \in \mathbf{C}$, and Im(x) denotes the imaginary part of $x \in \mathbf{C}$. For any pair of complex numbers $x, y \in \mathbf{C}$, $\langle x, y\rangle$ denotes the inner product defined by $\langle x, y\rangle = \bar{x}y$. For a vector $\mathbf{x} \in \mathbf{C}^n$, $\|\mathbf{x}\|$ means the Euclidean norm defined by $\|\mathbf{x}\|^2 = \mathbf{x}^*\mathbf{x}$. For a complex matrix $\mathbf{X} \in \mathbf{C}^{n\times m}$ represented by $\mathbf{X} = \{x_{ij}\}$, $\mathbf{X}^t$ and $\mathbf{X}^*$ denotes the transpose and conjugate transpose, respectively. If $\mathbf{X} \in \mathbf{C}^{n\times n}$ is a Hermitian matrix ($\mathbf{X} = \mathbf{X}^*$), $\mathbf{X} > 0$ denotes that $\mathbf{X}$ is positive definite. $\lambda_{\min}(\mathbf{X})$ and $\lambda_{\max}(\mathbf{X})$ represent the minimum and the maximum eigenvalue of a Hermitian matrix $\mathbf{X}$, respectively. $|\mathbf{X}|$ represents the element-wise absolute-value matrix defined by $|\mathbf{X}| = \{|x_{ij}|\}$, and $\|\mathbf{X}\|_2$ is the induced matrix 2-norm defined by $\|\mathbf{X}\|_2 = \sqrt{\lambda_{\max}(\mathbf{X}^*\mathbf{X})}$. Suppose that $\mathbf{X}$ is an $n \times n$ real matrix with nonnegative off-diagonal elements, then $\mathbf{X}$ is a nonsingular M-matrix if and only if all principal minors of $\mathbf{X}$ are positive.

BACKGROUND

Proposals of models for neural networks and its applications by Hopfield et al. have triggered the research interests of neural networks in the last two decades (Hopfield, 1984; Hopfield & Tank, 1985; Tank & Hopfield, 1986). They introduced the idea of an energy function to formulate a way of understanding the computational ability that performed by fully connected recurrent neural networks. The energy functions have been applied to various problems such as qualitative analysis of neural networks, synthesis of associative memories, combination optimization problems, and linear programming problems.

When used as associative memories, neural networks are designed so that memory pattern vectors correspond to locally stable equilibrium points of the networks. To realize that an imperfect input pattern matches a correct stored pattern, local stability and attracting region of the equilibrium points become important issues. Such stability analysis and synthesis of associative memories using neural networks have been studied actively in the past (see, for example, Li, Michel & Porod, 1988).

In case of optimization problems, the neural networks are constructed in such a way that locally or globally optimal solutions correspond to equilibrium points of the networks. To obtain optimal solutions, it is desired that the state evolution of the networks converges to the equilibrium points independent of the initial conditions. Especially, global asymptotic stability guarantees to find the global optimal solution, which corresponds to the sole equilibrium. This prompted global asymptotic stability analysis for the networks, which has been intensively carried out in recent years. In the following, some major results on global stability analysis for discrete-time and continuous-time real-valued neural networks are introduced.

For the discrete-time recurrent neural networks with the activation functions which are belong to the class of *sigmoid* functions, functions that are bounded, continuously differentiable and strictly monotone increasing, global asymptotic stability conditions are derived as Lyapunov matrix inequality form (Jin & Gupta, 1996). For larger class of activation functions that are globally Lipschitz continuous and monotone non-decreasing, global asymptotic and exponential stability conditions are shown (Hu & Wang, 2002).

On the other hand, for the continuous-time recurrent neural networks, when it is assumed that the activation functions belong to the class of *sigmoid* functions, and the connection weight matrix is symmetric, a necessary and sufficient condition for global asymptotic stability of the networks is formulated as negative semi-definiteness of the connection weight matrix (Forti, Manetti & Marini, 1994). If activation functions are unbounded, monotone non-decreasing and globally Lipchitz continuous, a sufficient condition for global asymptotic stability is derived as the form of Lyapunov matrix inequality for the connection weight matrix and the Lipschitz numbers (Forti & Tesi, 1995). Furthermore, with the same class of activation functions, a sufficient condition of global exponential stability is presented (Liang & Si, 2001). For general class of activation functions, that is, unbound and monotone non-decreasing functions, Lyapunov matrix inequality and row or column dominance conditions for connection weight matrix are presented (Arik & Tavsanoglu, 2000; Forti & Tesi, 1995).

For applications of the real-valued recurrent neural networks, Hopfield applied to linear programming problems (Tank & Hopfield, 1986). Moreover, for extension of this application, applications to upper and lower bounded constrained quadratic programming problems (Bouzerdoum & Pattison, 1993), linearly constrained quadratic programming problems (Maa & Shanblatt, 1992) and nonlinear optimization problems (Kennedy & Chua, 1988) are presented. Furthermore, applications to general class of optimization problems, that is, variational inequality problems including convex programming problems and complementarity problems are investigated with global asymptotic or exponential stability conditions (Liang & Si, 2001; Xia, & Wang, 2000, 2001, 2004, 2005).

In this chapter, we explore the line of the above-mentioned investigations, global stability analysis and applications, for complex-valued recurrent neural networks.

COMPLEX-VALUED NEURAL NETWORKS

This section presents models of discrete-time and continuous-time recurrent neural networks whose states, input and output variables, and connection weight coefficients are all complex-valued. The discrete-time complex-valued recurrent neural network is described by difference equations of the form:

$$\begin{cases} \mathbf{u}[k+1] = \mathbf{A}\mathbf{u}[k] + \mathbf{W}\mathbf{v}[k] + \mathbf{b} \\ \mathbf{v}[k] = \mathbf{f}(\mathbf{u}[k]) \end{cases} \quad . \tag{1}$$

While, the continuous-time complex-valued recurrent neural network is given by differential equations of the form:

$$\begin{cases} \dfrac{d\mathbf{u}(t)}{dt} = -\mathbf{D}\mathbf{u}(t) + \mathbf{W}\mathbf{v}(t) + \mathbf{b} \\ \mathbf{v}(t) = \mathbf{f}(\mathbf{u}(t)) \end{cases} \quad . \tag{2}$$

In these models, n is a number of neuron units, $\mathbf{u} = [u_1, u_2, \cdots, u_n]^t \in \mathbf{C}^n$ and $\mathbf{v} = [v_1, v_2, \cdots, v_n]^t \in \mathbf{C}^n$ are the state and output vector respectively, $\mathbf{b} = [b_1, b_2, \cdots, b_n]^t \in \mathbf{C}^n$ is the external input vector, and $\mathbf{W} = \{w_{ij}\} \in \mathbf{C}^{n \times n}$ is the connection weight matrix.

$\mathbf{A} = \mathbf{diag}\{a_1, a_2, \cdots, a_n\} \in \mathbf{R}^{n \times n}$ with $|a_i| < 1$ $(i = 1, 2, \cdots, n)$ and $\mathbf{D} = \mathbf{diag}\{d_1, d_2, \cdots, d_n\} \in \mathbf{R}^{n \times n}$ with $d_i > 0$ $(i = 1, 2, \cdots, n)$

specify the local feedbacks around each neuron. $|a_i| < 1$ and $d_i > 0$ indicate self-inhibitions. $\mathbf{f}(\mathbf{u}) = [f_1(u_1), f_2(u_2), \cdots, f_n(u_n)]^t : \mathbf{C}^n \to \mathbf{C}^n$ is the vector-valued activation function whose elements consist of complex-valued nonlinear functions .

The activation functions $f_i(\cdot) : \mathbf{C} \to \mathbf{C}$ will be assumed to belong to the following classes of complex-valued functions.

Definition 1. A set of complex-valued functions f_i $(i = 1, 2, \cdots, n)$ satisfying the following conditions is said to be class F^{lm}.

1. $f_i(0) = 0$,
2. f_i is bounded,
3. there exists a positive real value $l_i > 0$ such that, $|f_i(x_i) - f_i(y_i)| \le l_i |x_i - y_i|$ $(\forall x_i, y_i \in \mathbf{C})$
4. $\mathrm{Re}\{\langle x_i - y_i, f_i(x_i) - f_i(y_i)\rangle\} \ge 0$ $(\forall x_i, \forall y_i \in \mathbf{C})$.

Definition 2. A set of complex-valued functions f_i $(i = 1, 2, \cdots, n)$ is said to be class S if its member functions are represented by:

$$f_i(u_i) = \varphi_i(|u_i|) \frac{u_i}{|u_i|} \tag{3}$$

with nonnegative real-valued function $\varphi_i(r_i) : \mathbf{R}_+ \to \mathbf{R}_+$ which satisfies the following conditions.

1. $\varphi_i(0) = 0$,
2. φ_i is bounded,
3. there exists a continuous derivative function $\dfrac{d\varphi_i}{dr_i}$ in $\mathbf{R}_+$,
4. there exists a positive real value $l_i > 0$ such that $0 < \dfrac{d\varphi_i}{dr_i}(\xi) \le l_i < +\infty$ $(\forall \xi \in \mathbf{R}_+)$.

Note that, in Definition 2, because $u_i / |u_i|$ is bounded, $f_i(0) = 0$. The following properties about the class S will be utilized for proving stability theorem in the next section.

Property 1. Let us define a complex-valued function as $h_i(u_i) := f_i(u_i + u_i^e) - f_i(u_i^e) : \mathbf{C} \to \mathbf{C}$ with an arbitrary fixed complex number $u_i^e \in \mathbf{C}$.

If $h_i(u_i) \in S$, then $\dfrac{\partial \mathrm{Re}(h_i)}{\partial \mathrm{Im}(u_i)} = \dfrac{\partial \mathrm{Im}(h_i)}{\partial \mathrm{Re}(u_i)}$.

Property 2. If $f_i(\cdot) \in S$, then

$$\mathrm{Re}\{\langle x_i - y_i, f_i(x_i) - f_i(y_i)\rangle\} \ge l_i^{-1} |f_i(x_i) - f_i(y_i)|^2 \quad (\forall x_i, \forall y_i \in \mathbf{C}). \tag{4}$$

Property 1 can be immediately derived by calculating the partial derivatives as follows:

$$\frac{\partial \operatorname{Re}(h_i)}{\partial \operatorname{Im}(u_i)} = \frac{\partial \operatorname{Im}(h_i)}{\partial \operatorname{Re}(u_i)} = \left(\frac{d\varphi_i}{dr_i}(|u_i|) - \frac{\varphi_i(|u_i|)}{|u_i|} \right) \frac{\operatorname{Re}(u_i)\operatorname{Im}(u_i)}{|u_i|^2} .$$

The proof of Property 2 is given in Appendix. Regarding a complex-valued function as 2-dimentional vector-valued map, Property 1 means that f_i is a kind of symmetric map, and Property 2 means a globally Lipschitz continuous and monotone non-decreasing map.

According to the Liouville's theorem (Churhill & Brown, 1984, p. 119), every bounded holomorphic function must be constant. It is therefore assumed that $f_i \in F^{lm}$ or $f_i \in S$ is not a holomorphic function throughout this chapter to avoid triviality. When a complex-valued function is regarded as a 2-dimentional real vector-valued function, the condition 4 in Definition 1 and Definition 2 imply that the mappings $f_i \in F^{lm}$ and $f_i \in S$ are monotone. We note that the monotonic function is in general suitable for formulation of global optimization problems.

As a specific example of the functions which belong to the class F^{lm},

$$\psi_{K_i}(u_i) = \arg\min_{z_i} \left\{ |u_i - z_i| \;\; | \; z_i \in K_i \right\} \tag{5}$$

will be considered with $K_i \subset \mathbf{C}$ being any bounded, closed and convex set including the origin. This function is said to be *Convex projection* in optimization theory (Fukushima, 2001), and has been often used when real-valued neural networks are applied to solve convex programming problems (Xia & Wang, 2004). In addition, the following functions are typical to the class $f_i \in F^{lm}$ or $f_i \in S$ and are often used in the analysis and design with the complex-valued neural networks (Hirose, 2003; Kuroe et al., 2001, 2002; Kuroe et al., 2003; Takeda & Kishigami, 1992; Yoshida et al., 2004),

$$f_i(u_i) = \tanh\left(|u_i|\right)\frac{u_i}{|u_i|}, \tag{6}$$

$$f_i(u_i) = \frac{u_i}{1+|u_i|}. \tag{7}$$

If all the activation functions of complex-valued recurrent neural networks satisfy that $f_i \in F^{lm}$ or $f_i \in S$ ($i = 1, 2, \cdots, n$), there exists a positive diagonal matrix $\mathbf{L} = \mathbf{diag}\{l_1, l_2, \cdots, l_n\} \in \mathbf{R}^{n\times n}$ from the condition 3 of Definition 1 and the condition 4 of Definition 2. Particularly, if f_i is selected as the form of Eq. (5), then $\mathbf{L} = \mathbf{I}_n$. This property will be used in later section: Application to convex programming problems. The matrix $\mathbf{L}$ will be used to derive stability conditions in the next section.

GLOBAL ASYMPTOTIC STABILITY CONDITIONS

This section provides global asymptotic stability conditions for the discrete-time and continuous-time complex-valued neural networks with the activation functions $f_i \in F^{lm}$ or $f_i \in S$.

Discrete-Time Neural Networks

For the discrete-time neural network (Eq. (1)), the following theorem ensures global asymptotic stability of the network under the condition expressed in terms of the connection weight matrix.

Theorem 1. Suppose that all the activation functions satisfy $f_i \in F^{lm}$ for the discrete-time complex-valued neural network (Eq. (1)). The network (Eq. (1)) has a unique globally asymptotically stable equilibrium point, if there exists a positive definite diagonal matrix $\mathbf{P} = \mathbf{diag}\{p_1, p_2, \cdots, p_n\} \in \mathbf{R}^{n\times n}$ such that

$$\left(\frac{\gamma}{1+\gamma}\mathbf{P} - \gamma\mathbf{A}^*\mathbf{P}\mathbf{A}\right)\mathbf{L}^{-2} - |\mathbf{W}|^t\mathbf{P}|\mathbf{W}| > 0 \tag{8}$$

with the diagonal matrix given by $\mathbf{L} = \mathbf{diag}\{l_1, l_2, \cdots, l_n\} \in \mathbf{R}^{n\times n}$ and the real positive number γ.

Proof: The equilibrium points are nothing but the fixed points of the continuous map $\boldsymbol{\chi}(\mathbf{u}) := (\mathbf{I}_n - \mathbf{A})^{-1}(\mathbf{Wf}(\mathbf{u}) + \mathbf{b})$. According to Brower's fixed-point theorem (Luenberger, 1969, p. 272; Nakaoka, 1977, pp. 7-14), if the continuous map $\boldsymbol{\chi}(\mathbf{u})$ is bounded, then $\boldsymbol{\chi}(\mathbf{u})$ has at least one fixed point. Since all the activation functions of the network (Eq. (1)) are bounded, the network has at least one equilibrium point.

Let us represent one of the equilibrium points by $\mathbf{u}^e \in \mathbf{C}^n$. By means of the coordinate shift $\mathbf{z} = \mathbf{u} - \mathbf{u}^e$, Eq. (1) can be put into the form:

$$\begin{cases} \mathbf{z}[k+1] = \mathbf{A}\mathbf{z}[k] + \mathbf{W}\mathbf{h}(\mathbf{z}[k]) \\ \mathbf{h}(\mathbf{z}[k]) = \mathbf{f}(\mathbf{z}[k] + \mathbf{u}^e) - \mathbf{f}(\mathbf{u}^e). \end{cases} \tag{9}$$

Thus, Eq. (9) has an equilibrium point at the origin, i.e. $\mathbf{z} = \mathbf{0}$ and we therefore focus on the stability property of the origin. To prove that $\mathbf{z} = \mathbf{0}$ is globally asymptotically stable, consider a candidate Lyapunov function of the quadratic form:

$$V_1(\mathbf{z}[k]) = \mathbf{z}[k]^*\mathbf{P}\mathbf{z}[k] \tag{10}$$

where $\mathbf{P}$ is a positive definite diagonal matrix which satisfies the condition of Theorem 1. In the following, we simply write $\mathbf{z} = \mathbf{z}[k]$ for the sake of convenience. The forward difference ΔV_1 of V_1 along the trajectory of Eq. (9) is calculated as follows:

$$\begin{aligned}\Delta V_1(\mathbf{z})|_{(9)} &= \mathbf{z}[k+1]^*\mathbf{P}\mathbf{z}[k+1] - \mathbf{z}[k]^*\mathbf{P}\mathbf{z}[k] \\ &= -\mathbf{z}^*(\mathbf{P} - \mathbf{A}^*\mathbf{P}\mathbf{A})\mathbf{z} + 2\,\mathrm{Re}\{\mathbf{z}^*\mathbf{A}^*\mathbf{P}\mathbf{W}\mathbf{h}(\mathbf{z})\} + \mathbf{h}^*(\mathbf{z})\mathbf{W}^*\mathbf{P}\mathbf{W}\mathbf{h}(\mathbf{z})\end{aligned} \tag{11}$$

where $\Delta V_1(\mathbf{z})|_{(9)}$ denote the difference along the trajectories of Eq. (9). Here we introduce free parameter γ satisfying the condition of Theorem 1. By expanding the obvious inequality,

$$\left\|\mathbf{P}^{1/2}\{\gamma^{1/2}\mathbf{A}\mathbf{z} - \gamma^{-1/2}\mathbf{W}\mathbf{h}(\mathbf{z})\}\right\|^2 \geq 0,$$

we have

$$2\,\mathrm{Re}\{\mathbf{z}^*\mathbf{A}^*\mathbf{P}\mathbf{W}\mathbf{h}(\mathbf{z})\} \leq \gamma\mathbf{z}^*\mathbf{A}^*\mathbf{P}\mathbf{A}\mathbf{z} + \gamma^{-1}\mathbf{h}^*(\mathbf{z})\mathbf{W}^*\mathbf{P}\mathbf{W}\mathbf{h}(\mathbf{z})$$

with $\mathbf{P}^{1/2} = \mathrm{diag}\{p_1^{1/2}, p_2^{1/2}, \cdots, p_n^{1/2}\}$. Hence,

$$\begin{aligned}\Delta V_1(\mathbf{z})|_{(9)} &\leq -\mathbf{z}^*\{\mathbf{P} - (1+\gamma)\mathbf{A}^*\mathbf{P}\mathbf{A}\}\mathbf{z} + (1+\gamma^{-1})\mathbf{h}^*(\mathbf{z})\mathbf{W}^*\mathbf{P}\mathbf{W}\mathbf{h}(\mathbf{z}) \\ &\leq -|\mathbf{z}|^t\{\mathbf{P} - (1+\gamma)\mathbf{A}^*\mathbf{P}\mathbf{A}\}|\mathbf{z}| + (1+\gamma^{-1})|\mathbf{h}(\mathbf{z})|^t|\mathbf{W}|^t\mathbf{P}|\mathbf{W}||\mathbf{h}(\mathbf{z})|.\end{aligned}$$

From the condition 3 of Definition 1, it follows that

$$\Delta V_1(\mathbf{z})|_{(9)} \leq -|\mathbf{z}|^t\{\mathbf{P} - (1+\gamma)\mathbf{A}^*\mathbf{P}\mathbf{A}\}|\mathbf{z}| + (1+\gamma^{-1})|\mathbf{z}|^t\mathbf{L}|\mathbf{W}|^t\mathbf{P}|\mathbf{W}|\mathbf{L}|\mathbf{z}|$$

$$= -(1+\gamma^{-1})|\mathbf{z}|^t \mathbf{LRL}|\mathbf{z}| \tag{12}$$

where

$$\mathbf{R} = \left(\frac{\gamma}{1+\gamma}\mathbf{P} - \gamma \mathbf{A}^* \mathbf{PA}\right)\mathbf{L}^{-2} - |\mathbf{W}|^t \mathbf{P}|\mathbf{W}|.$$

Since the matrix **R** is positive definite due to Eq. (8), $\Delta V_1(\mathbf{z})|_{(9)} < 0$, $\mathbf{z} \neq \mathbf{0}$, and if $\mathbf{z} = \mathbf{0}$, then $\Delta V_1(\mathbf{z})|_{(9)} = 0$. Hence $\mathbf{z} = \mathbf{0}$ that is, the equilibrium point $\mathbf{u}^e$, is unique and asymptotically stable. Now, it is easy to see that the positive definite Lyapunov function (Eq. (10)) is radially unbounded, i.e. $|V_1(\mathbf{z})| \to \infty$ as $\|\mathbf{z}\| \to \infty$. Therefore, the equilibrium point $\mathbf{u}^e$ is globally asymptotically stable. (Q. E. D.)

In particular case, if $\mathbf{A} = \mathbf{0}$, then the following corollary immediately follows by letting $\mathbf{A} = \mathbf{0}$ and $\gamma \to \infty$ in the proof of Theorem 1.

Corollary 1. Suppose that all the activation functions satisfy $f_i \in F^{lm}$ and $\mathbf{A} = \mathbf{0}$ for the discrete-time complex-valued neural network (Eq. (1)). The equilibrium point of the network (Eq. (1)) is unique and globally asymptotically stable, if there exists a positive definite diagonal matrix $\mathbf{P} = \mathbf{diag}\{p_1, p_2, \cdots, p_n\} \in \mathbf{R}^{n \times n}$ such that

$$\mathbf{L}^{-1}\mathbf{PL}^{-1} - |\mathbf{W}|^t \mathbf{P}|\mathbf{W}| > 0 \tag{13}$$

with the diagonal matrix given by $\mathbf{L} = \mathbf{diag}\{l_1, l_2, \cdots, l_n\} \in \mathbf{R}^{n \times n}$.

This corollary will be utilized in applications to convex programming problems in the next section.

Continuous-Time Neural Networks

For the continuous-time complex-valued recurrent neural network (Eq. (2)) with the activation functions which belong to the class F^{lm}, the global asymptotic stability condition is derived as in the following theorem.

Theorem 2. Suppose that $f_i \in F^{lm}$ for the continuous-time complex-valued neural network (Eq. (2)). The network (Eq. (2)) has a unique and globally asymptotically stable equilibrium point, if there exists a positive definite diagonal matrix $\mathbf{P} = \mathbf{diag}\{p_1, p_2, \cdots, p_n\} \in \mathbf{R}^{n \times n}$ such that

$$\mathbf{P}\left(\mathbf{DL}^{-1} - |\mathbf{W}|\right) + \left(\mathbf{DL}^{-1} - |\mathbf{W}|\right)^t \mathbf{P} > 0 \tag{14}$$

with the diagonal matrix given by $\mathbf{L} = \mathbf{diag}\{l_1, l_2, \cdots, l_n\} \in \mathbf{R}^{n \times n}$.

Proof: The equilibrium points correspond to the fixed points of the continuous map $\boldsymbol{\chi}(\mathbf{u}) := \mathbf{D}^{-1}(\mathbf{Wf}(\mathbf{u}) + \mathbf{b})$. Similar to the proof of Theorem 1, the network has at least one equilibrium point.

Let us represent one of the existing equilibrium points by $\mathbf{u}^e \in \mathbf{C}^n$. By the coordinate translation $\mathbf{z} = \mathbf{u} - \mathbf{u}^e$, Eq. (2) can be put into the form:

$$\begin{cases} \dfrac{d\mathbf{z}}{dt} = -\mathbf{Dz} + \mathbf{Wh}(\mathbf{z}) \\ \mathbf{h}(\mathbf{z}) = \mathbf{f}(\mathbf{z} + \mathbf{u}^e) - \mathbf{f}(\mathbf{u}^e). \end{cases} \tag{15}$$

The network (Eq. (15)) has an equilibrium point $\mathbf{z} = \mathbf{0}$. To prove that $\mathbf{z} = \mathbf{0}$ is unique and globally asymptotically stable, consider a candidate Lyapunov function of the quadratic form:

$$V_2(\mathbf{z}(t)) = \mathbf{z}(t)^* \mathbf{Qz}(t) \tag{16}$$

where **Q** has the form of **Q=LP** with **P** and **L** being positive definite diagonal matrices which satisfy the condition of Theorem 2 and the condition 3 of Definition 1, respectively. By regarding $V_2(\mathbf{z}(t))$ as the real-valued function $V_2\left(\text{Re}\{\mathbf{z}(t)\}, \text{Im}\{\mathbf{z}(t)\}\right): \mathbf{R} \to \mathbf{R}^{2n} \to \mathbf{R}$, the time derivative of V_2 along the trajectory of Eq. (15) is calculated as follows:

$$\begin{aligned}\left.\frac{dV_2(\mathbf{z})}{dt}\right|_{(15)} &= -2\mathbf{z}^*\mathbf{QDz} + 2\,\text{Re}\left\{\mathbf{z}^*\mathbf{QWh}(\mathbf{z})\right\} \\ &= -2\,|\mathbf{z}|^t\,\mathbf{QD}\,|\mathbf{z}| + 2\,\text{Re}\left\{\mathbf{z}^*\mathbf{QWh}(\mathbf{z})\right\} \\ &\le -2\,|\mathbf{z}|^t\,\mathbf{QD}\,|\mathbf{z}| + 2\,|\mathbf{z}|^t\,\mathbf{Q}\,|\mathbf{W}|\,|\mathbf{h}(\mathbf{z})|.\end{aligned} \tag{17}$$

Here we simply omit the argument of $\mathbf{z}(t)$. From the condition 3 of Definition 1, it follows that

$$\begin{aligned}\left.\frac{dV_2(\mathbf{z})}{dt}\right|_{(15)} &\le -2\,|\mathbf{z}|^t\,\mathbf{QD}\,|\mathbf{z}| + 2\,|\mathbf{z}|^t\,\mathbf{Q}\,|\mathbf{W}|\,\mathbf{L}\,|\mathbf{z}| \\ &= -2\,|\mathbf{z}|^t\,\mathbf{Q}(\mathbf{D} - |\mathbf{W}|\,\mathbf{L})\,|\mathbf{z}| \\ &= -2\,|\mathbf{z}|^t\,\mathbf{LP}(\mathbf{DL}^{-1} - |\mathbf{W}|)\mathbf{L}\,|\mathbf{z}| \\ &= -2\,|\mathbf{z}|^t\,\mathbf{L}\left\{\mathbf{P}\left(\mathbf{DL}^{-1} - |\mathbf{W}|\right) + \left(\mathbf{DL}^{-1} - |\mathbf{W}|\right)^t\mathbf{P}\right\}\mathbf{L}\,|\mathbf{z}|\end{aligned} \tag{18}$$

Since the matrix $\mathbf{P}\left(\mathbf{DL}^{-1} - |\mathbf{W}|\right) + \left(\mathbf{DL}^{-1} - |\mathbf{W}|\right)^t\mathbf{P}$ is positive definite because of Eq. (14), $dV_2(\mathbf{z})/dt\,|_{(15)} < 0$, $\mathbf{z} \neq \mathbf{0}$, and if $\mathbf{z} = \mathbf{0}$, then $dV_2(\mathbf{z})/dt\,|_{(15)} = 0$. Hence $\mathbf{z} = \mathbf{0}$, that is, the equilibrium point $\mathbf{u}^e$ of the network (Eq. (2)), is unique and asymptotically stable. Now, it is easy to see that the positive definite Lyapunov function (Eq. (16)) is radially unbounded, that is, $|V_2(\mathbf{z})| \to \infty$ as $\|\mathbf{z}\| \to \infty$. This shows that the unique equilibrium point $\mathbf{u}^e$ is globally asymptotically stable. (Q. E. D.)

When the activation functions belong to the class S, the global asymptotic stability condition for the network (Eq. (2)) is derived as in the following theorem.

Theorem 3. Suppose that $f_i \in S$ for the continuous-time complex-valued neural network (Eq. (2)). The network (Eq. (2)) has a unique and globally asymptotically stable equilibrium point, if there exists a positive definite diagonal matrix $\mathbf{P} = \mathbf{diag}\{p_1, p_2, \cdots, p_n\} \in \mathbf{R}^{n\times n}$ such that

$$\mathbf{P}\left(\mathbf{DL}^{-1} - \mathbf{W}\right) + \left(\mathbf{DL}^{-1} - \mathbf{W}\right)^*\mathbf{P} > 0 \tag{19}$$

with the diagonal matrix given by $\mathbf{L} = \mathbf{diag}\{l_1, l_2, \cdots, l_n\} \in \mathbf{R}^{n\times n}$.

Proof: The equilibrium points are equivalent to the fixed points of the continuous map $\boldsymbol{\chi}(\mathbf{u}) := \mathbf{D}^{-1}(\mathbf{Wf}(\mathbf{u}) + \mathbf{b})$. Similar to the proofs of Theorem 1 and Theorem 2, the network has at least one equilibrium point.

Let us represent one of the existing equilibrium points by $\mathbf{u}^e \in \mathbf{C}^n$. By the coordinate shifting $\mathbf{z} = \mathbf{u} - \mathbf{u}^e$, Eq. (2) can be put into the form of Eq. (15). This has an equilibrium point $\mathbf{z} = \mathbf{0}$. To prove that $\mathbf{z} = \mathbf{0}$ is unique and globally asymptotically stable, consider a candidate Lyapunov function of the following form:

$$V_3(\mathbf{z}(t)) = \frac{1}{2}\mathbf{z}(t)^*\mathbf{D}^{-1}\mathbf{z}(t) + \frac{k}{\varepsilon}\sum_{i=1}^{n} p_i G_i\left(\text{Re}(z_i), \text{Im}(z_i)\right) \tag{20}$$

where $\mathbf{P} = \text{diag}\{p_1, p_2, \cdots, p_n\}$ is the positive definite diagonal matrix which satisfies Eq. (19), ε and k are constant parameters given by

$$\begin{cases} \varepsilon \in (0,1), \\ k = \dfrac{\left\|\mathbf{D}^{-1}\mathbf{W}\right\|_2^2}{4\lambda_{\min}(\mathbf{Q})} > 0, \\ 2\mathbf{Q} = \mathbf{P}\left(\mathbf{D}\mathbf{L}^{-1} - \mathbf{W}\right) + \left(\mathbf{D}\mathbf{L}^{-1} - \mathbf{W}\right)^* \mathbf{P}, \end{cases} \tag{21}$$

and $G_i(\cdot,\cdot)\,(i = 1,\ 2,\ \cdots,\ n)$ are defined by

$$G_i\left(\mathrm{Re}(z_i),\ \mathrm{Im}(z_i)\right) = \int_0^{\mathrm{Re}(z_i)} \mathrm{Re}\left\{h_i(\rho + j0)\right\} d\rho + \int_0^{\mathrm{Im}(z_i)} \mathrm{Im}\left\{h_i(\mathrm{Re}(z_i) + j\rho)\right\} d\rho \tag{22}$$

where j is the imaginary unit. From Property 1 for the class S, Eq. (22) can be transformed into the following form:

$$G_i\left(\mathrm{Re}(z_i), \mathrm{Im}(z_i)\right) = \int_0^1 \mathrm{Re}\left\{\bar{z}_i h_i(\eta z_i)\right\} d\eta \tag{23}$$

According to Property 2, Eq. (23) is nonnegative. Hence, $V_3(\mathbf{z})$ is also nonnegative and $V_3(\mathbf{z}) \geq \left(\tfrac{1}{2}\right)\mathbf{z}^*\mathbf{D}^{-1}\mathbf{z}$. Here again we simply omit the argument of $\mathbf{z}(t)$.

By regarding $V_3(\mathbf{z}(t))$ as the real-valued function $V_3\left(\mathrm{Re}\{\mathbf{z}(t)\},\ \mathrm{Im}\{\mathbf{z}(t)\}\right) : \mathbf{R} \to \mathbf{R}^{2n} \to \mathbf{R}$, the time derivative of V_3 along the trajectory of Eq. (15) is calculated as follows:

$$\begin{aligned} \left.\frac{dV_3(\mathbf{z})}{dt}\right|_{(15)} &= \sum_{i=1}^{n} \frac{\partial V_3}{\partial \mathrm{Re}(z_i)}\frac{d\,\mathrm{Re}(z_i)}{dt} + \frac{\partial V_3}{\partial \mathrm{Im}(z_i)}\frac{d\,\mathrm{Im}(z_i)}{dt} \\ &= \mathrm{Re}\left\{\left[\mathbf{D}^{-1}\mathbf{z} + \frac{k}{\varepsilon}\mathbf{P}\mathbf{h}(\mathbf{z})\right]^* \frac{d\mathbf{z}}{dt}\right\} \\ &= -\|\mathbf{z}\|^2 + \mathrm{Re}\left\{\mathbf{z}^*\mathbf{D}^{-1}\mathbf{W}\mathbf{h}(\mathbf{z})\right\} - \frac{k}{\varepsilon}\mathrm{Re}\left\{\mathbf{z}^*\mathbf{P}\mathbf{D}\mathbf{h}(\mathbf{z}) - \mathbf{h}(\mathbf{z})^*\mathbf{P}\mathbf{W}\mathbf{h}(\mathbf{z})\right\} \end{aligned}$$

where in the first equality, the following fact is used:

$$\begin{aligned} \left.\frac{dG_i}{dt}\right|_{(15)} &= \frac{\partial G_i}{\partial \mathrm{Re}(z_i)}\frac{d\,\mathrm{Re}(z_i)}{dt} + \frac{\partial G_i}{\partial \mathrm{Im}(z_i)}\frac{d\,\mathrm{Im}(z_i)}{dt} \\ &= \mathrm{Re}\left\{h_i(z_i)\right\}\frac{d\,\mathrm{Re}(z_i)}{dt} + \mathrm{Im}\left\{h_i(z_i)\right\}\frac{d\,\mathrm{Im}(z_i)}{dt} \\ &= \mathrm{Re}\left\{\overline{h_i(z_i)}\frac{dz_i}{dt}\right\}. \end{aligned}$$

We furthermore use the inequality $\mathrm{Re}\left\{\mathbf{z}^*\mathbf{P}\mathbf{D}\mathbf{h}(\mathbf{z})\right\} \geq \mathbf{h}(\mathbf{z})^*\mathbf{P}\mathbf{D}\mathbf{L}^{-1}\mathbf{h}(\mathbf{z})$, which comes from Eq. (4) in Property 2. By substituting this inequality, we have

$$\left.\frac{dV_3(\mathbf{z})}{dt}\right|_{(15)} \le -\|\mathbf{z}\|^2 + \mathrm{Re}\{\mathbf{z}^*\mathbf{D}^{-1}\mathbf{W}\mathbf{h}(\mathbf{z})\} - \frac{k}{\varepsilon}\mathrm{Re}\{\mathbf{h}(\mathbf{z})^*\mathbf{P}\mathbf{D}\mathbf{L}^{-1}\mathbf{h}(\mathbf{z}) - \mathbf{h}(\mathbf{z})^*\mathbf{P}\mathbf{W}\mathbf{h}(\mathbf{z})\}$$

$$= -\|\mathbf{z}\|^2 + \mathrm{Re}\{\mathbf{z}^*\mathbf{D}^{-1}\mathbf{W}\mathbf{h}(\mathbf{z})\} - \frac{k}{\varepsilon}\mathbf{h}(\mathbf{z})^*\mathbf{Q}\mathbf{h}(\mathbf{z}).$$

Since $\varepsilon \in (0,1)$, by expanding $\left\|\sqrt{\varepsilon}\,\mathbf{z} + \frac{\mathbf{D}^{-1}\mathbf{W}\mathbf{h}(\mathbf{z})}{2\sqrt{\varepsilon}}\right\|^2 \ge 0$, we obtain

$$\mathrm{Re}\{\mathbf{z}^*\mathbf{D}^{-1}\mathbf{W}\mathbf{h}(\mathbf{z})\} \le \varepsilon\|\mathbf{z}\|^2 + \frac{\|\mathbf{D}^{-1}\mathbf{W}\mathbf{h}(\mathbf{z})\|^2}{4\varepsilon}.$$

Hence, it follows that

$$\left.\frac{dV_3(\mathbf{z})}{dt}\right|_{(15)} \le -(1-\varepsilon)\|\mathbf{z}\|^2 + \left(\frac{\|\mathbf{D}^{-1}\mathbf{W}\|_2^2}{4\varepsilon} - \frac{k\lambda_{\min}(\mathbf{Q})}{\varepsilon}\right)\|\mathbf{h}(\mathbf{z})\|^2$$

$$= -(1-\varepsilon)\|\mathbf{z}\|^2.$$

We now have $dV_3(\mathbf{z})/dt\,|_{(15)} < 0$, $\mathbf{z} \ne \mathbf{0}$, and if $\mathbf{z} = \mathbf{0}$, then $dV_3(\mathbf{z})/dt\,|_{(15)} = 0$. Thus $\mathbf{z} = \mathbf{0}$, that is, the equilibrium point $\mathbf{u}^e$ of the network (Eq. (2)), is unique and asymptotically stable. Because $\mathbf{D}$ is positive definite diagonal matrix and $G_i(\cdot,\cdot)$ $(i = 1, 2, \cdots, n)$ are positive, it is easy to see that the positive definite Lyapunov function (Eq. (20)) is radially unbounded, that is, $|V_3(\mathbf{z})| \to \infty$ as $\|\mathbf{z}\| \to \infty$. This shows that the unique equilibrium point $\mathbf{u}^e$ is globally asymptotically stable. (Q. E. D.)

Discussions

Now, we compare Theorem 1 and Theorem 2 with some results of previous stability investigations for the real-valued recurrent neural networks (Forti & Tesi, 1995; Jin & Gupta, 1996), by regarding **C** as $\mathbf{R}^2$. Leaving minor details aside, we find that our class of activation functions is more general than theirs, but the conditions for the connection weight matrix are stricter.

For the condition of Theorem 1, it is necessary to choose suitable **P** and γ. As to γ, since Eq. (8) is the matrix inequality involving this single variable, it is rather easy to choose γ by the trial and error. Once γ is fixed, Eq. (8) is just the Lyapunov equation with respect to the positive definite diagonal matrix **P**, and solutions of this equation can be easily obtained. We note that, for the condition (Eq. (14)), the above discussion similarly holds.

According to Theorem 1 and Theorem 2, it follows that there are classes of discrete-time and continuous-time complex-valued recurrent neural networks whose equilibrium point is identical and globally asymptotically stable. This fact is summarized in the following theorem.

Theorem 4. Suppose that $f_i \in F^{lm}$. If the connection weight matrix **W** satisfies the condition that $\mathbf{L}^{-1} - |\mathbf{W}|$ is a nonsingular M-matrix, then there exist a discrete-time and a continuous-time complex-valued recurrent neural networks whose unique equilibrium points coincide with each other and are globally asymptotically stable.

Proof: It is easy to see that the networks (Eqs. (1) and (2)) can share the same equilibrium point. Suppose that the matrix $\mathbf{X} = \mathbf{L}^{-1} - |\mathbf{W}|$ is a nonsingular M-matrix. The matrix $\mathbf{DX} = \mathbf{DL}^{-1} - |\mathbf{DW}|$ is also a nonsingular M-matrix. Furthermore, there exists a positive definite diagonal matrix **P** such that $\mathbf{L}^{-1}\mathbf{P}\mathbf{L}^{-1} - |\mathbf{W}|^t\,\mathbf{P}\,|\mathbf{W}| > 0$ and $\mathbf{PDX} + (\mathbf{DX})^t\mathbf{P} > 0$ (Araki, 1974; 1977). Hence, from Corollary 1 and Theorem 2, the networks (Eqs. (1) and (2)) have a common equilibrium point and it is globally asymptotically stable. (Q. E. D.)

Under the condition of Theorem 4, the networks given by

$$\mathbf{u}[k+1] = \mathbf{W}\mathbf{f}(\mathbf{u}[k]) + \mathbf{b}, \tag{24}$$

$$\frac{d\mathbf{u}(t)}{dt} = -\mathbf{D}\mathbf{u}(t) + \mathbf{D}\mathbf{W}\mathbf{f}(\mathbf{u}(t)) + \mathbf{D}\mathbf{b} \tag{25}$$

where $\mathbf{D} \in \mathbf{R}^{n \times n}$ is an arbitrary positive definite diagonal matrix, are those mentioned in the theorem. The advantage of Theorem 4 lies in the point that both the discrete-time and continuous-time neural networks can be made simultaneously available depending on the applications of various optimization problems.

APPLICATION TO CONVEX PROGRAMMING PROBLEMS

For the complex-valued recurrent neural networks (Eqs. (24), (25) and (2)), an application of the global asymptotical stability conditions to a convex programming problem is presented in this section. Consider the following convex programming problem whose variables are constrained by an arbitrary bounded, closed, and convex region in complex space.

$$\begin{aligned} &\min_{\mathbf{v}} J(\mathbf{v}) = \frac{1}{2}\mathbf{v}^*\mathbf{M}\mathbf{v} + \mathrm{Re}(\mathbf{q}^*\mathbf{v}) \\ &\text{s. t.} \quad v_i \in K_i, \ (i = 1, 2, \cdots, n) \end{aligned} \tag{26}$$

where $\mathbf{M} \in \mathbf{C}^{n \times n}$ is a positive definite Hermitian matrix, $K_i \subset \mathbf{C}$ is a bounded, closed, and convex set including the origin of $\mathbf{C}$, $\mathbf{q} = [q_1, q_2, \cdots, q_n]^t \in \mathbf{C}^n$, and $\mathbf{v} = [v_1, v_2, \cdots, v_n]^t \in \mathbf{C}^n$.

In general, for a point $\mathbf{v}^e \in \mathbf{C}^n$ to be an optimal solution of Eq. (26) it is necessary and sufficient that $\mathbf{v}^e$ is a fixed point of the map $\mathbf{H}(\mathbf{v}) : \mathbf{C}^n \to \mathbf{C}^n$:

$$\mathbf{H}(\mathbf{v}) = \mathbf{\Psi}(\mathbf{v} - \alpha\mathbf{M}\mathbf{v} - \alpha\mathbf{q}) \ (\forall\ \alpha > 0) \tag{27}$$

where $\mathbf{\Psi} = \left[\psi_{K_1}(u_1), \psi_{K_2}(u_2), \cdots, \psi_{K_n}(u_n)\right]^t$ with $\psi_{K_i}(u_i)$ being the *Convex projection* to K_i as given in Eq. (5). This can be understood in the following way. Because a complex plane can be regarded as two-dimensional real space, the problem (Eq. (26)) can be represented as the problem on $\mathbf{R}^{2n}$. From the literature (Fukushima, 2001, pp. 203-241), this problem on $\mathbf{R}^{2n}$ is further reduced to a fixed-point problem on $\mathbf{R}^{2n}$ which is equivalent to the fixed-point problem for Eq. (27). Hence, the fixed point of Eq. (27) corresponds to the optimal solution of Eq. (26).

For the networks (Eqs. (24) and (25)), when specified as $\mathbf{W} = \mathbf{I}_n - \alpha\mathbf{M}$, $\mathbf{b} = -\alpha\mathbf{q}$, $\mathbf{f} = \mathbf{\Psi}$, and $\mathbf{D}$ is an arbitrary positive definite diagonal matrix, their equilibrium points are the fixed points of Eq. (27). Therefore, if these networks are globally asymptotically stable, the trajectories of the networks converge to the global optimal solution. For that property, Theorem 4 gives the condition that there exists an $\alpha > 0$ such that $\mathbf{I}_n - |\mathbf{I}_n - \alpha\mathbf{M}|$ is a nonsingular M-matrix. One of the sufficient conditions for the above stability condition is provided as follows.

Lemma 1. If a Hermitian matrix $\mathbf{M} = \{m_{ij}\} \in \mathbf{C}^{n \times n}$ satisfies that

$$|m_{ii}| > \sum_{\substack{j=1 \\ i \neq j}}^{n} |m_{ij}| \quad (i = 1, 2, \cdots, n), \tag{28}$$

and $0 < \alpha < 1/\max|m_{ij}|$, then the real matrix $\mathbf{I}_n - |\mathbf{I}_n - \alpha\mathbf{M}|$ is a nonsingular M-matrix.

Proof: Suppose that **M** and α satisfy the condition of Lemma 1. Since $1-\alpha\,|m_{ii}|>0$, it holds that

$$1-\left|1-\alpha\,|m_{ii}|\right|=\alpha\,|m_{ii}|>\alpha\sum_{\substack{j=1\\ i\neq j}}^{n}|m_{ij}|\;.$$

Hence, $\mathbf{I}_n-|\mathbf{I}_n-\alpha\mathbf{M}|$ is a nonsingular M-matrix from the property of M-matrix (Araki, 1974; 1976). (Q. E. D.)

In a special case, where the constraint conditions of problem (Eq. (26)) are such that

$$v_i\in K_i=\{v_i\mid v_i\in C,\,\kappa_i>0,\,|v_i|\le\kappa_i\}\quad(i=1,2,\cdots,n)\,, \tag{29}$$

then relying on the following continuous-time complex-valued neural network, Theorem 3 gives the global optimal solution of the problem (Eqs. (26) and (29)),

$$\begin{cases}\dfrac{d\mathbf{u}(t)}{dt}=-\mathbf{D}\mathbf{u}(t)+(-\mathbf{M})\mathbf{f}(\mathbf{u}(t))+(-\mathbf{q})\\[2ex] f_i(u_i)=\varphi_i(|u_i|)\dfrac{u_i}{|u_i|}\in S,\ \varphi_i(\cdot)\le\kappa_i,\ (i=1,\,2,\,\cdots,\,n)\;.\end{cases} \tag{30}$$

This can be shown in the following way similar to the case of real-valued neural networks. Consider the following energy function of the network (Eq. (30)),

$$E(\mathbf{v})=\frac{1}{2}\mathbf{v}^{*}\mathbf{M}\mathbf{v}+\mathrm{Re}(\mathbf{q}^{*}\mathbf{v})+\sum_{i=1}^{n}d_i\int_0^{|v_i|}\varphi_i^{-1}(\rho)d\rho \tag{31}$$

where $\varphi_i^{-1}(\cdot)$ is the inverse function of real-valued function $\varphi_i(\cdot)$. Since $\varphi_i(0)=0$ and $\varphi_i(\cdot)$ is a monotone increasing function, the integral term of Eq. (31) is positive. Hence, the energy function (Eq. (31)) is lower bounded. With the polar-coordinate expression, define $r_i=|u_i|$ and $\theta_i=\arg(u_i)$, then the time derivative of Eq. (31) along the trajectory of Eq. (30) is calculated as follows:

$$\left.\frac{dE}{dt}\right|_{(30)}=-\sum_{i=1}^{n}d_i\left[\frac{d\varphi_i}{dr_i}\left(\frac{dr_i}{dt}\right)^2+r_i\varphi_i(r_i)\left(\frac{d\theta_i}{dt}\right)^2\right]\le 0.$$

Furthermore, $dE/dt|_{(30)}=0$ if and only if $dr_i/dt=0$, $d\theta_i/dt=0$, Hence the network (Eq. (30)) behaves so as to decrease the value of Eq. (31). Now because **M** is a positive definite Hermitian matrix, the connection weight matrix of Eq. (30) satisfies the condition (Eq. (19)) of Theorem 3. Therefore, the trajectories of Eq. (30) converge to the unique and globally asymptotically stable equilibrium point independently of initial conditions. Moreover, this equilibrium point is also the minimum point of the energy function (Eq. (31)). The energy function (Eq. (31)) is the objective function of the problem, which is translated from the convex programming problem (Eqs. (26) and (29)) to the unconstrained minimization problem with the nonlinear function term $\int_0^{|v_i|}\varphi_i^{-1}(\rho)d\rho$. This third term of Eq. (31) and $d_i>0$ $(i=1,2,\cdots,n)$ are the penalty term and the penalty parameters, respectively. By suitably adjusting $d_i>0$ $(i=1,\,2,\cdots,\,n)$, the global optimal solution of problem (Eqs. (26) and (29)) can be approximated by the minimum of energy function (Eq. (31)). In this way, the complex-valued neural network (Eq. (30)) yields the approximate solution of the convex programming problem (Eqs. (26) and (29)).

Generally, real-valued recurrent neural networks can also solve this problem (Xia & Wang 2004). In this case, however, problem formulations may become much more complex depending on constraints. On the other hand, with the complex-valued recurrent neural networks, it is sometimes possible to design and solve the problems much easier than the case of real-valued counterparts. Such a case can be shown in the next section.

NUMERICAL EXAMPLE

To demonstrate applications of the complex-valued neural networks (Eqs. (24), (25), and (30)) to solve convex programming problems, numerical examples are shown in this section.

Example 1

Consider the problem (Eq. (26)) whose parameters and constraints are set as follows:

$$\mathbf{M} = \begin{pmatrix} 6.0 & -4.0 + j2.0 \\ -4.0 - j2.0 & 7.0 \end{pmatrix},$$

$$\mathbf{q} = (6.0 + j9.0 \quad j10.0)^t,$$

$$K_1 = \{v_1 \in \mathbf{C} \mid |v_1| \le 1, |\arg v_1| \le \pi/6\},$$

$$K_2 = \{v_2 \in \mathbf{C} \mid |v_2| \le 1, |\arg v_2| \le \pi/6\}$$

where $\arg v_i$ denotes the argument of $v_i \in \mathbf{C}$, and j is the imaginary unit. In this example, the convex set K_i is a bounded sector region on the complex plane, and the following projection function is available for the activation functions.

$$\psi_{K_i}(u_i) = g_2(g_1(u_i)) \tag{32}$$

where $\mu = \tan(\pi/6)$, $\sigma_1 = \mu^{-1}\,\mathrm{Re}(u_i) + |\mathrm{Im}(u_i)|$, $\sigma_2 = \mu^{-1}\,\mathrm{Re}(u_i) - |\mathrm{Im}(u_i)|$, and

$$g_1(u_i) = \frac{1}{1+\mu^2}\Big[\mu\big(\max\{0,\sigma_1\} + \max\{0,\sigma_2\}\big) + j\,\mathrm{sgn}(\mathrm{Im}(u_i))\cdot\big(\max\{0,\sigma_1\} - \mu^2\max\{0,\sigma_2\}\big)\Big],$$

$$g_2(u_i) = \min(1, |u_i|)\frac{u_i}{|u_i|}.$$

It can be shown that the matrix $\mathbf{M}$ satisfies the condition of Lemma 1. Parameter values and the activation functions of the complex-valued recurrent neural networks (Eqs. (24) and (25)) can be set as $\alpha = 0.125$, $\mathbf{D} = \mathrm{diag}\{2.0, 5.0\}$ $\mathbf{W} = (\mathbf{I}_n - \alpha\mathbf{M})$, $\mathbf{b} = -\alpha\mathbf{q}$, and f_1 and f_2 are given by Eq. (32). Note that the global optimal solution of this example is known as $(v_1^{opt}, v_2^{opt}) = (0.48 - j0.28, 0.87 - j0.50)$. As a result of simulations, both the networks (Eqs. (24) and (25)) converge towards the point $(v_1^{opt}, v_2^{opt}) = (0.477 - j0.275, 0.866 - j0.500)$, showing that the global optimal solution has been obtained. The output trajectories of neural networks (Eqs. (24) and (25)) converging to the global optimum point from an arbitrary taken initial conditions are shown in Figure 1.

Example 2

Next, we demonstrate an application of the network (Eq. (30)) to the problem (Eq. (26)) with constraint condition (Eq. (29)). Consider the problem (Eqs. (26) and (29)) whose parameters and constraints are set as follows:

$$\mathbf{M} = \begin{pmatrix} 3.0 & 1.0 - j1.0 \\ 1.0 + j1.0 & 4.0 \end{pmatrix}$$

$$\mathbf{q} = (15 + j5.0 \quad 20 + j20)^t$$

$$\kappa_1 = 1.0, \kappa_2 = 1.0$$

In this example, the convex set K_i is a unit circle region on the complex plane. Parameter values and the activation functions of the complex-valued recurrent neural network (Eq. (30)) can be set as, $\mathbf{D} = \mathrm{diag}\{0.01, 0.01\}$, $\mathbf{W} = -\mathbf{M}$, $\mathbf{b} = -\mathbf{q}$, and f_1 and f_2 are given by Eq. (7). Because $\mathbf{W}$ is a Hermitian matrix and its eigenvalues are -2.0 and -5.0, this network satisfies the condition of Theorem 3. Therefore, it has unique and globally asymptotically stable equilibrium point. Note that the global optimal solution of this example is known as $\left(v_1^{opt}, v_2^{opt}\right) = (0.94 + j0.35, 0.72 + j0.69)$. As a result of simulations, the network (Eq. (30)) converges towards the point, $\left(v_1^{opt},\ v_2^{opt}\right) = (0.938 + j0.347,\ 0.720 + j0.694)$ showing that the global optimal solution has been obtained. The output trajectories of the variable v_1 of neural network (Eq. (30)) converging to the global optimum point with some arbitrary initial conditions are shown in Figure 2.

CONCLUSION

In this chapter, the global asymptotic stability conditions for discrete-time and continuous-time complex-valued recurrent neural networks are presented. To derive the stability conditions, classes of complex-valued functions suitable for the activation functions are defined, and Lyapunov function method is used. According to the derived stability conditions, there are classes of discrete-time and continuous-time complex-valued networks whose equilibrium points coincide and are globally asymptotically stable. Furthermore, these networks are shown to be successfully applicable to solving convex programming problems with nonlinear, bounded, closed, and convex constraints.

Figure 1. Output trajectories of neural networks (Eqs. (24) and (25)) converging to the optimum point in complex plane. (a) Output trajectories of v_1. (b) Output trajectories of v_2.

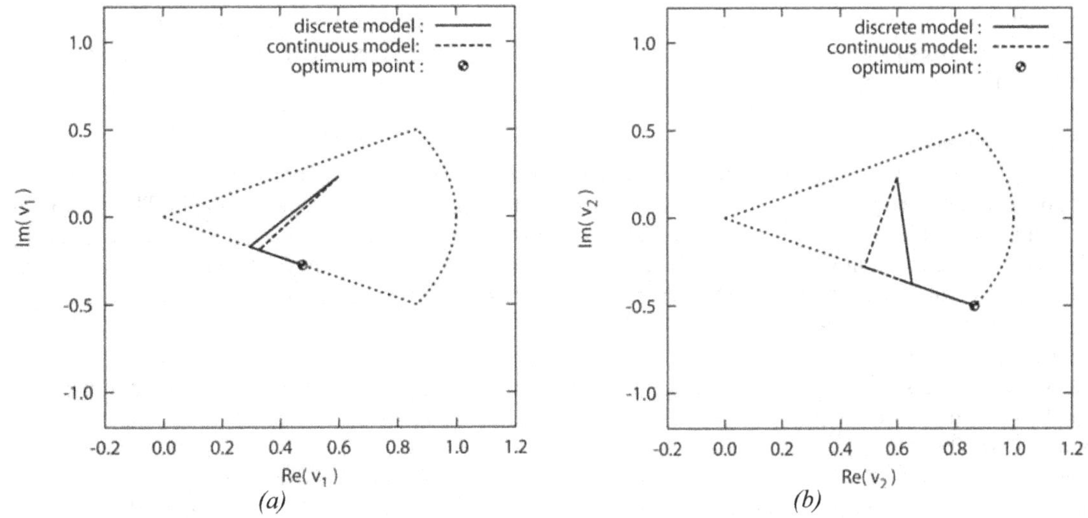

Figure 2. Output trajectories of the variable v_1 of neural network (Eq. (30)) converging to the optimum point in complex plane

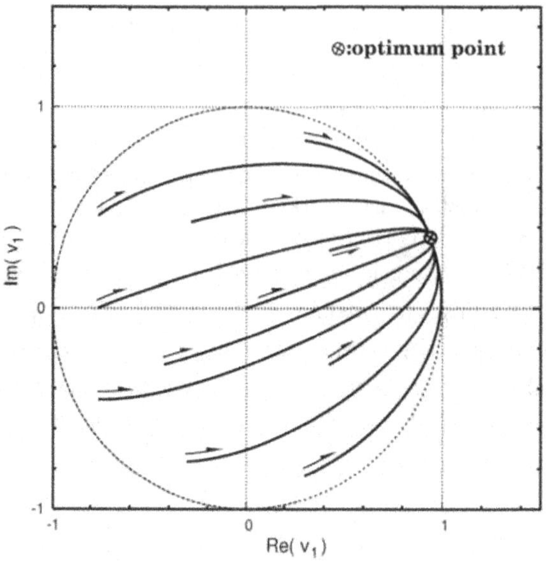

Compared with real-valued recurrent neural networks, complex-valued neural networks possess deep potential for a wide variety of applications in mathematical optimization field. This is because of the added freedom in choosing activation functions other than the connection weight matrix.

FUTURE RESEARCH DIRECTIONS

In technological world, there are many occasions where one is often required to deal with complex-valued variables, especially in analysis and design of physical systems such as optical or electronic networks and appliances. Handling them optimally according to a given criterion or cost function so that it yields sole extreme value leads to an attempt explored in this chapter: solving global optimization problems with complex-valued recurrent neural networks. The attempt is still at a primary stage and much work is to be done. Here are some directions towards completion as a comprehensive optimization tool.

1. *Problem Formulations*
It is first noted that in general what can be done by complex-valued recurrent neural networks can also be essentially done by real-valued recurrent neural networks or any other problem solvers in real number field. There comes the importance of problem formulations. Once a task of optimization with regard to some physical systems is given, it is recommended to examine first if one could take advantage of using complex-valued networks, compared to real-valued counterparts. Studying such problem formulations is an elaborate but challenging theme.

2. *Choice of Activation Functions*
One of the strengths of complex-valued recurrent neural networks lies in the fact that their activation functions, complex-valued functions with complex-valued arguments, have much more freedom of choice than real-valued counterparts whose tuning ability hinges solely on the weight matrices. As demonstrated in the example of this chapter, a certain activation function may fit in a given optimization problem. This gives rise to matching between optimization problems and suitable activation functions with suitable parameters. The task appears to be little tricky,

but accumulated case-studies would help to consolidate a comprehensive way towards finding the fittest.

3. *Digital Implementation*
Recurrent Neural networks are usually realized in computers, while given global optimization problem is used to be formulated in continuous-time framework, and the fit neural network as its solver is at first designed in the same framework. This entails digital implementation of designed neural network in such a way that the global equilibrium and its stability are preserved under discretizations. In the presented chapter, a possible approach to making this happen is suggested, but more works are anticipated about digital implementation.

REFERENCES

Araki, M. (1974). *M-Matrices.* Publication 74/19, London: Imperial College of Science and Technology.

Araki, M. (1976). M-Matrices and their applications I. *Journal of the Institute of Systems, Control and Information Engineers: Systems and Control, 20(12)*, 675-680 (in Japanese).

Araki, M. (1977). M-Matrices and their applications II. *Journal of the Institute of Systems, Control and Information Engineers: Systems and Control, 21(2)*, 114-121 (in Japanese).

Arik, S., & Tavsanoglu, V. (2000). A sufficient condition for absolute stability of a larger class of dynamical neural networks. *IEEE Transactions on Circuits and Systems I, 47(5)*, 758-760.

Bouzerdoum, A., & Pattison, T. R. (1993). Neural network for quadratic optimization with bound constraints. *IEEE Transactions on Neural Networks, 4(2)*, 293-304.

Churhill, R. V., & Brown, J. W. (1984). *Complex variables and applications* (4th ed.). NY: McGraw-Hill Book Company.

Forti, M., Manetti, S., & Marini, M. (1994). Necessary and sufficient condition for absolute stability of neural networks. *IEEE Transactions on Circuits and Systems I, 41(7)*, 491-494.

Forti, M., & Tesi, A. (1995). New conditions for global stability of neural networks with application to linear and quadratic programming problems. *IEEE Transactions on Circuits and Systems I, 42(7)*, 354-366.

Fukushima, M. (2001). *Fundamentals of nonlinear optimization.* Tokyo: Asakura Pub. Co., Ltd. (in Japanese).

Hirose, A. (Ed.) (2003). *Complex-valued neural networks: theories and applications* (Series on Innovative Intelligence 5). Singapore: World Scientific Publishing.

Hopfield, J. J. (1984). Neurons with graded response have collective computational properties like those of two-state neurons. *Proceedings of the National Academy of Sciences of the United States of America, 81*, 3088-3092.

Hopfield, J. J., & Tank, D. W. (1985). "Neural" computation of decisions in optimization problems. *Biological Cybernetics, 52*, 141-152.

Hu, S., & Wang, J. (2002). Global stability of a class of discrete-time recurrent neural networks. *IEEE Transactions on Circuits and Systems I, 49(8)*, 1104-1117.

Jin, L., & Gupta, M. M. (1996). Globally asymptotical stability of discrete-time analog neural networks. *IEEE Transactions on Neural Networks, 7(4)*, 1024-1031.

Kennedy, M. P., & Chua, L. O. (1988). Neural networks for nonlinear programming. *IEEE Transactions on Circuits and Systems, 35(5)*, 554-562.

Kuroe, Y., Hashimoto, N., & Mori, T. (2001). Qualitative analysis of continuous complex-valued associative memories. In G. Dorffner, H. Bischof, and K. Hornik (Eds.), *Lecture Notes in Computer Science, 2130. Artificial Neural Networks - ICANN 2001* (pp. 843-850). Berlin: Springer-Verlag.

Kuroe, Y., Hashimoto, N., & Mori, T. (2002). On energy function for complex-valued neural networks and its applications. *Proceedings of the 9th International Conference on Neural Information Processing* [CD-ROM], Singapore.

Kuroe, Y., Yoshida, M., & Mori, T. (2003). On activation functions for complex-valued neural networks: existence of energy functions. In O. Kaynak et al. (Eds.), *Lecture Notes in Computer Science, 2714. Artificial Neural Networks and Neural Information Processing - ICANN/ICONIP 2003* (pp. 985-992). Berlin: Springer-Verlag.

Li, J. H., Michel, A. N., & Porod, W. (1988). Qualitative analysis and synthesis of a class of neural networks. *IEEE Transactions on Circuits and Systems, 35(8)*, 976-986.

Liang, X. -B., & Si, J. (2001). Global exponential stability of neural networks with globally Lipschitz continuous activations and its application to linear variational inequality problem. *IEEE Transactions on Neural Networks, 12(2)*, 349-359.

Luenberger, D. G. (1969). *Optimization by vector space methods.* NY: John Wiley.

Maa, C. -Y., & Shanblatt, M. A. (1992). Linear and quadratic programming neural network analysis. *IEEE Transactions on Neural Networks, 3(4)*, 580-594.

Nakaoka, M. (1977). *Fixed point theorem and its circumference.* Tokyo: Iwanami Pub. Co., Ltd., (in Japanese).

Nitta, T. (2000). Complex-valued neural networks. *The Journal of the Institute of Electronics, Information, and Communication Engineers, 83(8)*, 612-615 (in Japanese).

Takeda, M., & Kishigami, T. (1992). Complex neural fields with a Hopfield-like energy function and an analogy to optical fields generated in phase-conjugate resonators. *Journal of the Optical Society of America A, 9(12)*, 2182-2191.

Tank, D. W., & Hopfield, J. J. (1986). Simple "neural" optimization networks: an A/D converter, signal decision circuit, and a linear programming circuit. *IEEE Transactions on Circuits and Systems, CAS-33*(5), 533-541.

Xia, Y., & Wang, J. (2000). Global exponential stability of recurrent neural networks for solving optimization and related problems. *IEEE Transactions on Neural Networks, 11*(4), 1017-1022.

Xia, Y., & Wang, J. (2001). Global asymptotic and exponential stability of a dynamic neural system with asymmetric connection weights. *IEEE Transactions on Automatic Control, 46*(4), 635-638.

Xia, Y., & Wang, J. (2004). A recurrent neural network for nonlinear convex optimization subject to nonlinear inequality constraints. *IEEE Transactions on Circuits and Systems I, 51*(7), 1385-1394.

Xia, Y., & Wang, J. (2005). A recurrent neural network for solving nonlinear convex programs subject to linear constraints. *IEEE Transactions on Neural Networks, 16*(2), 379-386.

Yoshida, M., Mori, T., & Kuroe, Y. (2004). Global asymptotic stability condition for complex-valued recurrent neural networks and its application. *Transactions of the Institute of Electrical Engineers of Japan. C, 124-C*(9), 1847-1852 (in Japanese).

Yoshida, M., & Mori, T. (2007). Global stability analysis for complex-valued recurrent neural networks and its application to convex optimization problems. *The Transactions of the Institute of Electronics, Information and Communication Engineers. A, J90-A*(5), 415-422 (in Japanese).

ADDITIONAL READINGS

Fukushima, M., Luo, Z. Q., & TSENG, P. (2001). Smoothing functions for second-order-cone complementarity problems. *SIAM Journal on Optimization*, *12*(2), 436-460.

Hayashi, S., Yamashita, N., & Fukushima, M. (2005). A combined smoothing and regularization method for monotone second-order cone complementarity problems. *SIAM Journal on Optimization*, *15*(2), 593-615.

Kinderlehrer, D., & Stampacchia, G. (1980). *An introduction to variational inequalities and their applications*. NY: Academic Press.

Xia, Y., & Feng, G. (2006). A neural network for robust LCMP beamforming. *Signal Processing*, *86*(10), 2901-2912.

Xia, Y., Leung, H., & Wang, J. (2002). A projection neural network and its application to constrained optimization problems. *IEEE Transactions on Circuits and Systems I*, *49*(4), 447-458.

Xia, Y. S. (2004). Further results on global convergence and stability of globally projected dynamical systems. *Journal of Optimization Theory and Applications*, *122*(3), 627-649.

APPENDIX: PROOF OF PROPERTY 2

Because the relation is obvious in case of $x_i = y_i$, consider the case of $x_i \neq y_i$. With representing complex numbers as $x_i = r_1 e^{j\theta_1}$, $y_i = r_2 e^{j\theta_2}$, Property 2 can be proved as follows.

(i) If $r_1 \neq r_2$, it is satisfied that

$$0 < \frac{\varphi(r_1) - \varphi(r_2)}{r_1 - r_2} \leq l_i < +\infty.$$

By multiplying the inverse of this both side by $[\varphi(r_1) - \varphi(r_2)]^2$, we have

$$l_i^{-1}[\varphi(r_1) - \varphi(r_2)]^2 \leq [\varphi(r_1) - \varphi(r_2)](r_1 - r_2). \tag{33}$$

Notice that $\varphi(0) = 0$ and hence $l_i^{-1}\varphi(r_k) \leq r_k$, $(k = 1, 2)$. The left hand side(LHS) of the inequality of Property 2 is calculated as follows.

$$\begin{aligned}\mathrm{Re}\{\langle x_i - y_i,\ f_i(x_i) - f_i(y_i)\rangle\} &= r_1\varphi(r_1) + r_2\varphi(r_2) - \{r_1\varphi(r_2) + r_2\varphi(r_1)\}\cos(\theta_1 - \theta_2) \\ &= \{\varphi(r_1) - \varphi(r_2)\}(r_1 - r_2) + \{r_1\varphi(r_2) + r_2\varphi(r_1)\}\{1 - \cos(\theta_1 - \theta_2)\}.\end{aligned}$$

From Eq. (33), and $1 - \cos(\theta_1 - \theta_2) > 0$,

$$\begin{aligned}&\mathrm{Re}\{\langle x_i - y_i,\ f_i(x_i) - f_i(y_i)\rangle\} \geq l_i^{-1}[\varphi(r_1) - \varphi(r_2)]^2 + \{r_1\varphi(r_2) + r_2\varphi(r_1)\}\{1 - \cos(\theta_1 - \theta_2)\} \\ &= l_i^{-1}\left|\varphi(r_1)e^{j\theta_1} - \varphi(r_2)e^{j\theta_2}\right|^2 + \left[\{r_1 - l_i^{-1}\varphi(r_1)\}\varphi(r_2) + \{r_2 - l_i^{-1}\varphi(r_2)\}\varphi(r_1)\right]\{1 - \cos(\theta_1 - \theta_2)\} \\ &\geq l_i^{-1}\left|f_i(x_i) - f_i(y_i)\right|^2.\end{aligned}$$

(ii) If $r_1 = r_2$ and $\theta_1 \neq \theta_2$, from $l_i^{-1}\varphi(r_k) \leq r_k$, $(k = 1, 2)$, the LHS of the inequality is evaluated as follows.

$$\begin{aligned}\mathrm{Re}\{\langle x_i - y_i,\ f_i(x_i) - f_i(y_i)\rangle\} &= r_1\varphi(r_1)\left|e^{j\theta_1} - e^{j\theta_2}\right|^2 \\ &\geq l_i^{-1}\varphi(r_1)^2\left|e^{j\theta_1} - e^{j\theta_2}\right|^2 \\ &= l_i^{-1}\left|\varphi(r_1)e^{j\theta_1} - \varphi(r_1)e^{j\theta_2}\right|^2.\end{aligned}$$

Since, $r_1 = r_2$, we have

$$\begin{aligned}\mathrm{Re}\{\langle x_i - y_i,\ f_i(x_i) - f_i(y_i)\rangle\} &\geq l_i^{-1}\left|\varphi(r_1)e^{j\theta_1} - \varphi(r_2)e^{j\theta_2}\right|^2 \\ &= l_i^{-1}\left|f_i(x_i) - f_i(y_i)\right|^2.\end{aligned}$$

Hence, Property 2 is proved. (Q. E. D.)

Chapter VI
Models of Complex-Valued Hopfield-Type Neural Networks and Their Dynamics

Yasuaki Kuroe
Kyoto Institute of Technology, Japan

ABSTRACT

This chapter presents models of fully connected complex-valued neural networks which are complex-valued extension of Hopfield-type neural networks and discusses methods to study their dynamics. In particular the authors investigate existence conditions of energy functions for complex-valued Hopfield-type neural networks. Emphasized are the properties of the activation functions which assure the existence of an energy function for the networks. As an application of the energy function, qualitative analysis of the network by utilizing the energy function is shown and a synthesis method of complex-valued associative memories is discussed.

INTRODUCTION

In recent years, there have been increasing research interests of artificial neural networks and many efforts have been made on applications of neural networks to various fields. As applications of the neural networks spread more widely, developing neural network models which can directly deal with complex numbers is desired in various fields. Several models of complex-valued neural networks have been proposed and their abilities of information processing have been investigated.

The purpose of this chapter is to present models of fully connected complex-valued neural networks which are complex-valued extension of Hopfield-type neural networks and to discuss methods to investigate their dynamics. In particular, we investigate existence conditions of energy functions and propose a function as an energy function for the complex-valued neural networks. In the complex region there are several possibilities in choosing an activation function because of a variety of complex functions. Based on the existence condition we investigate the properties of the complex functions which assure the existence of an energy function and discuss about how to find them. Several classes of complex functions which are widely used as activation functions in the models of complex-valued neural networks proposed so far are considered.

Once energy functions are constructed for neural networks, they are expected to be applied to various problems of various fields such as qualitative analysis of the neural networks, synthesis of associative memories and several optimization problems, similar to the real-valued ones. As applications, this chapter presents qualitative analysis of dynamics of the complex-valued neural networks by using the energy function. Furthermore a synthesis method of complex-valued associative memories by utilizing the analysis results is discussed.

In the following, the imaginary unit is denoted by i ($i^1 = -1$). The set of complex (real) numbers is denoted by $\mathbb{C}$ ($\mathbb{R}$). The n-dimensional complex (real) space is denoted by $\mathbb{C}^n$ ($\mathbb{R}^n$) and the set of $n \times m$ complex (real) matrices is denoted by $\mathbb{C}^{n\times m}$ ($\mathbb{R}^{n\times m}$). For $\boldsymbol{A} \in \mathbb{C}^{n\times m}$ ($\boldsymbol{a} \in \mathbb{C}^n$), its real and imaginary parts are denoted by $\boldsymbol{A}^R$ ($\boldsymbol{a}^R$) and $\boldsymbol{A}^I$ ($\boldsymbol{a}^I$), respectively.

BACKGROUND

It is well known that one of the pioneering works that triggered the research interests of neural networks in the last two decades is the proposal of models for neural networks by J. J. Hopfield (Hopfield, 1984; Hopfield & Tank, 1985), which are fully connected recurrent neural networks. He introduced the idea of an energy function to formulate a way of understanding the computation performed by dynamics of fully connected neural networks and showed that a combinatorial optimization problem can be solved by the neural networks. The neural network models proposed by Hopfield are called Hopfield type neural networks and by using concept of energy functions they have been applied to various problems such as qualitative analysis of neural networks, synthesis of associative memories, optimization problems etc. ever since. It is, therefore, of great interest to develop models of complex-valued neural network of Hopfield type and to investigate their dynamics.

In extending the discussions on real-valued neural networks to the complex plane it is important to note the following. One of the important factors to characterize behavior of a complex-valued neural network is its activation function which is a nonlinear complex function. In the real-valued neural networks, the activation is usually chosen to be a smooth and bounded function such as a sigmoidal function. In the complex region, however, there are several possibilities in choosing an activation function because of a variety of complex functions. It is expected, therefore, that complex-valued neural networks exhibit wide variety of dynamics depending on which type of complex functions is used as activation functions and their applications spread widely by using their wide variety of dynamics.

HOPFIELD TYPE NEURAL NETWORKS

J. J. Hopfield proposed discrete- and continuous-time models of fully connected recurrent neural networks and introduced the idea of an energy function to formulate a way of understanding the computation performed by their dynamics, which triggered the research interests of neural networks. In this chapter we consider the continuous-time Hopfield type neural network, which is implemented by an electric circuit shown in Fig. 1 (Hopfield, 1984; Hopfield & Tank, 1985).

The circuit consists of n nonlinear amplifiers interconnected by an RC (resistor-capacitor) network, and conductances and ideal current sources. Each amplifier provide an output voltage x_j given by $f(u_j)$, where u_j is the input voltage and f is a nonlinear activation function. For each amplifier, it contains an inverting amplifier whose output is $-x_j$ which permits a choice of the sign of the amplifier. The outputs x_j and $-x_j$ are usually provided by two output terminals of the same operational amplifier circuit. The pare of nonlinear amplifiers with an RC network is refereed to as a "neuron" and the RC network partially defines the time constant of the neuron and provides for integrative analog summation of the synaptic input currents from other neurons in the network. A synapse between two neurons is defined by a conductance T_{jk} which connects one of the two outputs (x_k or $-x_k$) of amplifier k to the input of amplifier j and this connection is made with a resistor of value $R_{jk} = 1/ \mid T_{jk} \mid$. As shown in Fig. 1, the circuit included an externally supplied input current I_j for each neuron, which represents an external input signal (or bias) to neuron j.

Figure 1. Hopfield type neural network

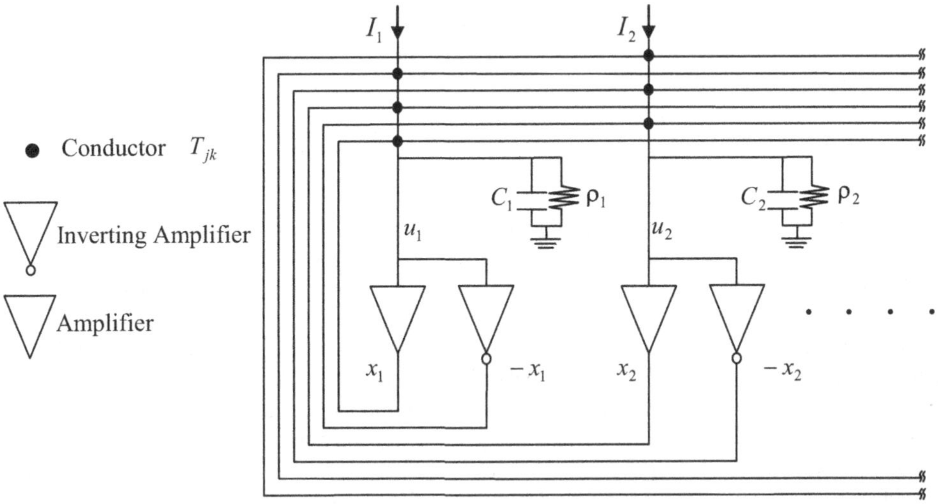

Writing the Kirchhoff's current law at the input node of amplifier j, we obtain

$$\begin{cases} C_j \dfrac{d}{dt} u_j = -\dfrac{1}{R_j} u_j + \sum_{k=1}^{n} T_{jk} x_j + I_j \\ x_j = f(u_j) \end{cases} \qquad j = 1, 2, \cdots, n \tag{1}$$

where

$$\frac{1}{R_j} = \frac{1}{\rho_j} + \sum_{k=1}^{n} \frac{1}{R_{jk}}.$$

In order to analyze dynamics of the neural network, the following function was defined as an energy function of the network (Hopfield, 1984).

$$E(\boldsymbol{x}) = -\frac{1}{2} \sum_{j=1}^{n} \sum_{k=1}^{n} T_{jk} x_j x_k - \sum_{j=1}^{n} I_j x_j + \sum_{j=1}^{n} \frac{1}{R_j} \int_0^{x_j} f^{-1}(\sigma) d\sigma \tag{2}$$

where $f^{-1}(\cdot)$ is the inverse function of $f(\cdot)$. By using the energy function J. J. Hopfield showed that if the activation function is bounded, continuously differentiable and monotonically increasing, and $T_{jk} = T_{kj}$, then the time evolution of the network is a motion in state space that seeks out the minima of E and comes to a stop such points, and E is a Liapunov function of the network. Moreover any optimization problem that is mapped to the energy function Eq. (2) can be solved by this neural network.

Letting $\tau_j := R_j C_j$, $w_{jk} := R_j T_{jk}$ and $\theta_j := R_j I_j$, we can rewrite Eq.(1) as

$$\begin{cases} \tau_j \dfrac{du_j}{dt} = -u_j + \sum_{k=1}^{n} w_{jk} x_k + \theta_j \\ x_j = f(u_j) \end{cases} \qquad j = 1, 2, \cdots, n \tag{3}$$

MODEL OF COMPLEX-VALUED NEURAL NETWORKS OF HOPFIELD TYPE

Consider a class of complex-valued neural networks described by differential equations of the form:

$$\begin{cases} \tau_j \dfrac{du_j}{dt} = -u_j + \sum_{k=1}^{n} w_{jk} x_k + \theta_j & j = 1, 2, \cdots, n \\ x_j = f(u_j) \end{cases} \quad (4)$$

where n is the number of neurons comprising the neural network, $x_j \in \mathbb{C}$, $u_j \in \mathbb{C}$ and $\theta_j \in \mathbb{C}$ are the output, the membrane potential and the threshold value of the jth neuron, respectively, $\tau_j \in \mathbb{R}$ is the time constant ($\tau_j > 0$), and $w_{jk} \in \mathbb{C}$ is the connection weight from the kth neuron to the jth neuron, and $f(\cdot)$ is an activation function which is a nonlinear complex function ($f : \mathbb{C} \to \mathbb{C}$).

Note that the neural network described by Eq. (4) is a direct complex-valued extension of the real-valued neural network of Hopfield type (Eq. (3)). In the real-valued neural networks, the function $f(\cdot)$ is usually chosen to be a smooth (continuously differentiable) and bounded function such as sigmoidal functions. In the complex region, however, we should recall the Liouville's theorem, which says that 'if $f(u)$ is analytic (differentiable) at all $u \in \mathbb{C}$ and bounded, then $f(u)$ is a constant function'. Since a suitable $f(u)$ should be bounded, it follows from the theorem that if we choose an analytic function for $f(u)$, it is constant, which is clearly not suitable, as is discussed in Georgiou and Koutsougeras, (1992). In place of an analytic function we choose a function which satisfies the followings as an activation function of the neural network Eq. (4). Let us express $f(u)$ by separating into its real and imaginary parts as:

$$f(u) = f^R(u^R, u^I) + i f^I(u^R, u^I) \quad (5)$$

where $f^R : \mathbb{R}^2 \to \mathbb{R}$ and $f^I : \mathbb{R}^2 \to \mathbb{R}$. We assume the following on the activation function $f(\cdot)$.

Assumption *The activation function $f(\cdot)$ satisfies the following two conditions.*

i. *$f^R(u^R, u^I)$ and $f^I(u^R, u^I)$ are continuously differentiable with respect to u^R and u^I, that is , the partial derivatives $\partial f^R / \partial u^R$, $\partial f^R / \partial u^I$, $\partial f^I / \partial u^R$ and $\partial f^I / \partial u^I$ exist and they are continuous, and*

ii. *$f(\cdot)$ is bounded, that is, there exists some $M > 0$ such that $|f(\cdot)| \le M$.*

In order to write Eq. (4) in an abbreviated form, we define vectors $\boldsymbol{u} \in \mathbb{C}^n$, $\boldsymbol{x} \in \mathbb{C}^n$, $\boldsymbol{\theta} \in \mathbb{C}^n$ and $\boldsymbol{f}(\boldsymbol{u}) \in \mathbb{C}^n$ by $\boldsymbol{u} := (u_1, u_2, \cdots, u_n)^t$, $\boldsymbol{x} := (x_1, x_2, \cdots, x_n)^t$, $\boldsymbol{\theta} := (\theta_1, \theta_2, \cdots, \theta_n)^t$ and $\boldsymbol{f}(\boldsymbol{u}) := (f(u_1), f(u_2), \cdots, f(u_n))^t$, respectively, and matrices $\boldsymbol{T} \in \mathbb{R}^{n \times n}$ and $\boldsymbol{W} \in \mathbb{C}^{n \times n}$ by $\boldsymbol{T} = \mathrm{diag}(\tau_1, \tau_2, \cdots, \tau_n)$ and

$$\boldsymbol{W} := \begin{bmatrix} w_{11} & w_{12} & \cdots & w_{1n} \\ w_{21} & w_{22} & & w_{2n} \\ \vdots & & \ddots & \vdots \\ w_{n1} & w_{n2} & \cdots & w_{nn} \end{bmatrix}.$$

With this notation, the model of complex-valued neural networks Eq. (4) is rewritten as

$$\begin{cases} \boldsymbol{T}\dfrac{d\boldsymbol{u}}{dt} = -\boldsymbol{u} + \boldsymbol{W}\boldsymbol{x} + \boldsymbol{\theta} \\ \boldsymbol{x} = \boldsymbol{f}(\boldsymbol{u}). \end{cases} \tag{6}$$

ENERGY FUNCTION FOR COMPLEX-VALUED NEURAL NETWORKS

Definition of Energy Function

If the neural network Eq. (6) is real, that is, $\boldsymbol{u}$, $\boldsymbol{x}$, $\boldsymbol{\theta}$, $\boldsymbol{W}$, and $\boldsymbol{T}$ are all real and $f(\cdot)$ is a real nonlinear function ($f:\mathbb{R}\to\mathbb{R}$) in Eq. (6), the following function has been proposed as an energy function for it, which is corresponding to the energy function given by Eq.(2) for the network Eq. (1).

$$E(\boldsymbol{x}) = -\frac{1}{2}\boldsymbol{x}^t\boldsymbol{W}\boldsymbol{x} - \boldsymbol{\theta}^t\boldsymbol{x} + \sum_{j=1}^{n}\int_0^{x_j} f^{-1}(\sigma)\,d\sigma \tag{7}$$

where $f^{-1}(\cdot)$ is the inverse function of $f(\cdot)$. The function $E(\boldsymbol{x})$ is a mapping $E:\mathbb{R}^n\to\mathbb{R}$ and has the following property.

Let

$$\left.\frac{dE(\mathbf{x})}{dt}\right|_{Eq.(6)^R}$$

be the time derivative of $E(\boldsymbol{x})$ along the trajectories of Eq. (6) when $\boldsymbol{u}$, $\boldsymbol{x}$, $\boldsymbol{\theta}$, $\boldsymbol{W}$, and $\boldsymbol{T}$ are all real and $f(\cdot)$ is a real nonlinear function in Eq. (6). If the connection weight matrix is symmetric ($\boldsymbol{W}^t = \boldsymbol{W}$) and the nonlinear function $f(\cdot)$ is continuously differentiable, bounded and monotonically increasing, then $\left.\dfrac{dE(\boldsymbol{x})}{dt}\right|_{Eq.(6)^R} \le 0$, and furthermore $\left.\dfrac{dE(\boldsymbol{x})}{dt}\right|_{Eq.(6)^R} = 0$ if and only if $\dfrac{d\boldsymbol{x}}{dt} = 0$.

This fact is proved as follows. The time derivative of $E(\boldsymbol{x})$ along the trajectories of Eq. (6) when $\boldsymbol{u}$, $\boldsymbol{x}$, $\boldsymbol{\theta}$, $\boldsymbol{W}$, and $\boldsymbol{T}$ are all real and $f(\cdot)$ is a real nonlinear function in Eq. (6) can be calculated as follows.

$$\left.\frac{dE(\boldsymbol{x})}{dt}\right|_{Eq.(6)^R} = \nabla E(\boldsymbol{x})^t\frac{d\boldsymbol{x}}{dt}$$

$$= \left\{-\frac{1}{2}(\boldsymbol{x}^t\boldsymbol{W}^t + \boldsymbol{x}^t\boldsymbol{W}) - \theta^t + \boldsymbol{u}^t\right\}\frac{d\boldsymbol{x}}{dt}.$$

Using the fact that the connection weight matrix $\boldsymbol{W}$ is symmetric gives

$$\left.\frac{dE(\boldsymbol{x})}{dt}\right|_{Eq.(6)^R} = (-\boldsymbol{x}^t\boldsymbol{W}^t - \boldsymbol{\theta}^t + \boldsymbol{u}^t)\frac{d\boldsymbol{x}}{dt}$$

$$= -\left(T\frac{du}{dt}\right)^t \frac{dx}{dt}$$

$$= -\sum_{j=1}^{n} \tau_j \left[f^{-1}(x_j)\right]' \left[\frac{dx_j}{dt}\right]^2.$$

Since $f^{-1}(x_j)$ is a monotonically increasing function and τ_j is positive, each term on the right-hand side is nonnegative. Therefore

$$\left.\frac{dE(x)}{dt}\right|_{Eq.(6)} \le 0, \quad \left.\frac{dE(x)}{dt}\right|_{Eq.(6)} = 0 \leftrightarrow \frac{dx}{dt} = 0.$$

It is a question in controversy what is an energy function for complex-valued neural networks and how to define and construct one. At the first step to the problem, we define an energy function for the complex-valued neural network Eq. (6) as follows, by the analogy to that for real-valued neural networks.

Definition 1. *$E(\boldsymbol{x})$ is an energy function of the complex valued neural network Eq. (6) if $E(\boldsymbol{x})$ is a mapping $E:\mathbb{C}^n \to \mathbb{R}$ and the derivative of E along the trajectories of the network Eq. (6), denoted by*

$$\left.\frac{dE(\boldsymbol{x})}{dt}\right|_{Eq.(6)},$$ *satisfies*

$$\left.\frac{dE(\boldsymbol{x})}{dt}\right|_{Eq.(6)} \le 0.$$

Furthermore $\left.\frac{dE(\boldsymbol{x})}{dt}\right|_{Eq.(6)} = 0$ *if and only if* $\frac{dx}{dt} = 0$.

Energy Function and Its Existence Conditions

In this subsection we discuss about existence conditions of an energy function for the complex-valued neural network Eq. (6) and propose an energy function. Let us define a class of functions denoted by F^{ε} as follows.

Definition 2. *A complex function $f:\mathbb{C}\to\mathbb{C}$ satisfying Assumption is said to belong to F^{ε} ($f(\cdot)\in\mathcal{F}^{\varepsilon}$), if f is one to one, and satisfies the following three conditions.*

$$\text{(i)}\ \frac{\partial f^R}{\partial u^R} \ne 0, \quad \text{(ii)}\ \frac{\partial f^R}{\partial u^I} = \frac{\partial f^I}{\partial u^R}, \quad \text{(iii)}\ \frac{\partial f^R}{\partial u^R}\frac{\partial f^I}{\partial u^I} - \frac{\partial f^R}{\partial u^I}\frac{\partial f^I}{\partial u^R} > 0 \qquad (8)$$

for all $u \in \mathbb{C}$.

The following lemma is obtained.

Lemma 1. *Let* $g = f^{-1}$ *be the inverse function of f. If the activation function* $f(\cdot) \in \mathcal{F}^{\varepsilon}$*, then there exists a function* $G(x^R, x^I) : \mathbb{R} \times \mathbb{R} \to \mathbb{R}$ *such that the following relations hold.*

$$\frac{\partial G}{\partial x^R} = g^R(x^R, x^I), \qquad \frac{\partial G}{\partial x^I} = g^I(x^R, x^I) \tag{9}$$

where $g(x) = g^R(x^R, x^I) + ig^I(x^R, x^I)$.

Proof. $\partial g^R / \partial x^I$ and $\partial g^I / \partial x^R$ are derived as follows.

$$\frac{\partial g^R}{\partial x^I} = \frac{\partial f^R}{\partial u^I} \Big/ \left(\frac{\partial f^R}{\partial u^I}\frac{\partial f^I}{\partial u^R} - \frac{\partial f^R}{\partial u^R}\frac{\partial f^I}{\partial u^I}\right),$$
$$\frac{\partial g^I}{\partial x^R} = \frac{\partial f^I}{\partial u^R} \Big/ \left(\frac{\partial f^R}{\partial u^I}\frac{\partial f^I}{\partial u^R} - \frac{\partial f^R}{\partial u^R}\frac{\partial f^I}{\partial u^I}\right).$$

From the condition $\partial f^R / \partial u^I = \partial f^I / \partial u^R$ in Definition 2, we have

$$\frac{\partial g^R}{\partial x^I} = \frac{\partial g^I}{\partial x^R}.$$

Define G by

$$G(x^R, x^I) := \int_0^{x^R} g^R(x, 0)dx + \int_0^{x^I} g^I(x^R, y)dy. \tag{10}$$

It is easy to check that G satisfies Eq. (9).

We now propose a candidate of the energy function for the complex-valued neural network Eq. (6) as follows.

$$E(\boldsymbol{x}) := -\frac{1}{2}(\boldsymbol{x}^*\boldsymbol{W}\boldsymbol{x} + \boldsymbol{\theta}^*\boldsymbol{x} + \boldsymbol{x}^*\boldsymbol{\theta}) + \sum_{j=1}^{n} G(x_j^R, x_j^I) \tag{11}$$

A sufficient condition for the existence of an energy function is obtained as follows

Theorem 1. *The complex-valued neural network Eq. (6) has an energy function if the connection weight matrix W is a Hermitian matrix,* $\boldsymbol{W}^* = \boldsymbol{W}$*, and the activation function* $f(\cdot) \in \mathcal{F}^{\varepsilon}$.

Proof. We will show the complex-valued neural network Eq. (6) has the energy function given by Eq. (11). Without loss of generality, we can assume $\partial f^R / \partial u^R > 0$ in Definition 2. The function *E*(***x***) defined by Eq. (11) is rewritten as

$$E(\boldsymbol{x}) = -\frac{1}{2}\boldsymbol{y}'\boldsymbol{\Pi}\boldsymbol{y} - \boldsymbol{\Theta}'\boldsymbol{y} + \sum_{j=1}^{n} G(x_j^R, x_j^I)$$

where $\boldsymbol{y} := (x_1^R, x_2^R, \cdots, x_n^R, x_1^I, x_2^I, \cdots, x_n^I)^t \in \mathbb{R}^{2n}$, $\boldsymbol{\Theta} := (\theta_1^R, \theta_2^R, \cdots, \theta_n^R, \theta_1^I, \theta_2^I, \cdots \theta_n^I)^t \in \mathbb{R}^{2n}$ and

$$\boldsymbol{\Pi} := \begin{bmatrix} \boldsymbol{W}^R & -\boldsymbol{W}^I \\ \boldsymbol{W}^I & \boldsymbol{W}^R \end{bmatrix} \in \mathbb{R}^{2n \times 2n}.$$

Let $g_j^R := g^R(x_j^R, x_j^I)$ and $g_j^I := g^I(x_j^R, x_j^I)$. From the assumption that $\boldsymbol{W}$ is a Hermitian matrix and Lemma 1, the derivative of $E(\boldsymbol{x})$ along the trajectories of Eq. (6) is calculated as follows.

$$\left.\frac{dE(\boldsymbol{x})}{dt}\right|_{Eq.(6)} = \nabla_{\boldsymbol{y}} E(\boldsymbol{x})^t \left.\frac{d\boldsymbol{y}}{dt}\right|_{Eq.(6)}$$

$$= \left\{ \boldsymbol{\Pi y} - \boldsymbol{\Theta} + \left(g_1^R, g_2^R, \cdots, g_n^R, g_1^I, g_2^I, \cdots, g_n^I\right)^t \right\} \left.\frac{d\boldsymbol{y}}{dt}\right|_{Eq.(6)}$$

$$= -\sum_{j=1}^{n} \mathrm{t}_j \left\{ \frac{du_j^R}{dt} \frac{dx_j^R}{dt} + \frac{du_j^I}{dt} \frac{dx_j^I}{dt} \right\}$$

$$= -\sum_{j=1}^{n} \mathrm{t}_j \left[\frac{\partial g_j^I}{\partial x_j^I} \left\{ \left(\frac{dx_j^I}{dt} \right) + \left(\frac{\partial g_j^I}{\partial x_j^R} \Big/ \frac{\partial g_j^I}{\partial x_j^I} \right) \frac{dx_j^R}{dt} \right\}^2 + \frac{\dfrac{\partial g_j^R}{\partial x_j^R} \dfrac{\partial g_j^I}{\partial x_j^I} - \left(\dfrac{\partial g_j^I}{\partial x_j^R} \right)^2}{\dfrac{\partial g_j^I}{\partial x_j^I}} \left(\frac{dx_j^R}{dt} \right)^2 \right]$$

Noting that

$$\frac{\partial g^I}{\partial x^I} = \frac{\partial f^R}{\partial u^R} \Big/ \left(\frac{\partial f^R}{\partial u^R} \frac{\partial f^I}{\partial u^I} - \frac{\partial f^R}{\partial u^I} \frac{\partial f^I}{\partial u^R} \right)$$

and

$$\frac{\partial g^R}{\partial x^R} \frac{\partial g^I}{\partial x^I} - \left(\frac{\partial g^I}{\partial x^R} \right)^2 = 1 \Big/ \left(\frac{\partial f^R}{\partial u^R} \frac{\partial f^I}{\partial u^I} - \frac{\partial f^I}{\partial u^R} \frac{\partial f^R}{\partial u^I} \right),$$

we have $\partial g^I / \partial x^I > 0$ and $(\partial g^R / \partial x^R) \times (\partial g^I / \partial x^I) - (\partial g^I / \partial x^R)^2 > 0$ from the assumption $f(\cdot) \in \mathcal{F}^{\varepsilon}$. Therefore $dE(x)/dt \leq 0$, and $\left.\dfrac{dE(\boldsymbol{x})}{dt}\right|_{Eq.(6)} = 0$ if and only if $\dfrac{d\boldsymbol{x}}{dt} = 0$.

Remark 1. *In the proof we assume* $\partial f^R / \partial u^R > 0$ *in Definition 2. Consider here the case* $\partial f^R / \partial u^R < 0$. *Assume that f satisfies* $\partial f^R / \partial u^R < 0$, *and define* $h := -f$. *The model of the complex-valued neural network Eq. (6) can be rewritten as*

$$\begin{cases} \boldsymbol{T} \dfrac{d\boldsymbol{u}}{dt} = -\boldsymbol{u} + \hat{\boldsymbol{W}} \hat{\boldsymbol{x}} + \boldsymbol{\theta} \\ \hat{\boldsymbol{x}} = \boldsymbol{h}(\boldsymbol{u}) \end{cases} \tag{12}$$

where we let $\hat{\boldsymbol{x}} := -\boldsymbol{x}$, $\hat{\boldsymbol{W}} := -\boldsymbol{W}$ *and* $\boldsymbol{h}(\boldsymbol{u}) := (h(u_1), h(u_2), \cdots, h(u_n))^t$. *Clearly,* $\hat{\boldsymbol{W}}$ *is a Hermitian matrix,* $\hat{\boldsymbol{W}}^* = \hat{\boldsymbol{W}}$ *and the function h belongs to the class* F^{ε} *(*$f(\cdot) \in \mathcal{F}^{\varepsilon}$*) and* $\partial h^R / \partial u^R > 0$. *Therefore we can apply Theorem 1 to the network Eq. (12) and conclude that the network Eq. (12) has the energy function.*

Remark 2. *If we let imaginary parts of all the variables and parameters of the energy function Eq. (11) be zero, that is,* $\boldsymbol{u}^I = \boldsymbol{0}$, $\boldsymbol{x}^I = \boldsymbol{0}$, $\boldsymbol{\theta}^I = \boldsymbol{0}$ *and* $\boldsymbol{W}^I = \boldsymbol{0}$, *then the energy function Eq. (11) is reduced to*

$$E(x) = -\frac{1}{2}\left(\boldsymbol{x}^R\right)^t \boldsymbol{W}^R \boldsymbol{x}^R - \left(\theta^R\right)^t \boldsymbol{x}^R + \sum_{j=1}^{n} \int_0^{x_j^R} g^R(\sigma, 0) d\sigma$$

Clearly, the above equation is equivalent to the energy function Eq. (7), which implies that the energy function Eq. (11) includes Eq. (7) as a special case (a real-valued version).

EXISIENSE CONDITION OF ENERGY FUNCTION ON ACTIVATION FUNCTIONS

Function Classes and Existence Conditions

In the complex region there are several possibilities in choosing an activation function because of a variety of complex functions. In this section we investigate what kinds of complex functions satisfy the existence conditions of an energy function and discuss how to find them. We consider the following two classes of complex functions $f(\cdot)$ which are used in most of the models of complex-valued neural networks proposed so far. Let us express u in the polar representation as $u = re^{i\theta}$.

- Type A: $f(u) = f^R(u^R) + if^I(u^I)$ (13)

- Type B: $f(u) = \psi(r) e^{j\phi(\theta)}$ (14)

In Type A, $f^R(\cdot)$ and $f^I(\cdot)$ are nonlinear real functions, $f^R : \mathbb{R} \to \mathbb{R}$ and $f^I : \mathbb{R} \to \mathbb{R}$. In Type B, $\psi(\cdot)$ and $\phi(\cdot)$ are nonlinear real functions, $\psi : \mathbb{R}_{0+} \to \mathbb{R}_{0+}$, $\phi : \mathbb{R} \to \mathbb{R}$, where $\mathbb{R}_{+_0} = \{x \mid x \geq 0 x \in \mathbb{R}\}$. Note that in Type A the real and imaginary parts of an input go through nonlinear functions separately, and in Type B the magnitude and the phase of an input go through nonlinear functions separately. Most of the activation functions yet proposed for the models of complex-valued neural networks belong to either of Type A or Type B.

For the activation functions of Type A, the following theorem is obtained immediately from Theorem 1.

Theorem 2. *Consider the activation function f of Type A:* $f(u) = f^R(u^R) + if^I(u^I)$. *Suppose that* f^R *and* f^I *are continuously differentiable with respect to* u^R *and* u^I, *respectively, and are bounded.* $f \in F^{\varepsilon}$ *if and only if*

$$\text{(i)}\ \frac{\partial f^R}{\partial u^R} > 0,\ \frac{\partial f^I}{\partial u^I} > 0 \quad or \quad \text{(ii)}\ \frac{\partial f^R}{\partial u^R} < 0,\ \frac{\partial f^I}{\partial u^I} < 0 \tag{15}$$

for all $u \in \mathbb{C}$.

In the above theorem, there are two cases, (i) and (ii), in which an activation function satisfies the existence conditions Eq. (8) of energy functions (belongs to F^{ε}). However, it is sufficient to consider only one of them because of the fact discussed in Remark 1.

The following theorem can be obtained for the activation functions of Type B.

Theorem 3. *Consider the activation function f of Type B:* $f(u) = \psi(r)e^{i\phi(\theta)}$ *where* $u = re^{i\theta}$*. Suppose that* ψ *is continuously differentiable with respect to r for* $r \geq 0$ *and bounded, and* $\phi(\theta)$ *is continuously differentiable with respect to* θ*.* $f \in F^{\varepsilon}$ *if and only if*

$$\frac{d\psi(r)}{dr} > 0 \quad \textit{for all} \quad r \geq 0, \quad \lim_{r \to 0} \frac{\psi(r)}{r} > 0 \quad \textit{and} \tag{16}$$

$$\phi(\theta) = \theta + n\pi \tag{17}$$

where n is an integer.

Proof. Suppose that the activation function f is of Type B. From Eq. (14), $\frac{\partial f^R}{\partial u^R}$, $\frac{\partial f^R}{\partial u^I}$, $\frac{\partial f^I}{\partial u^R}$ and $\frac{\partial f^I}{\partial u^I}$ are obtained in the polar representation as follows.

$$\begin{cases} \dfrac{\partial f^R}{\partial u^R} = \dfrac{\partial \psi}{\partial r} \cdot \cos\phi(\theta) \cdot \cos\theta + \dfrac{\psi(r)}{r} \cdot \dfrac{\partial \phi}{\partial \theta} \cdot \sin\phi(\theta) \cdot \sin\theta \\ \dfrac{\partial f^R}{\partial u^I} = \dfrac{\partial \psi}{\partial r} \cdot \cos\phi(\theta) \cdot \sin\theta - \dfrac{\psi(r)}{r} \cdot \dfrac{\partial \phi}{\partial \theta} \cdot \sin\phi(\theta) \cdot \cos\theta \\ \dfrac{\partial f^I}{\partial u^R} = \dfrac{\partial \psi}{\partial r} \cdot \sin\phi(\theta) \cdot \cos\theta - \dfrac{\psi(r)}{r} \cdot \dfrac{\partial \phi}{\partial \theta} \cdot \cos\phi(\theta) \cdot \sin\theta \\ \dfrac{\partial f^I}{\partial u^I} = \dfrac{\partial \psi}{\partial r} \cdot \sin\phi(\theta) \cdot \sin\theta + \dfrac{\psi(r)}{r} \cdot \dfrac{\partial \phi}{\partial \theta} \cdot \cos\phi(\theta) \cdot \cos\theta \end{cases} \tag{18}$$

By using the above relations, the conditions (ii) and (iii) in Definition 2 are rewritten as the following conditions, Eq. (19) and Eq. (20), respectively.

$$\frac{\partial f^R}{\partial u^I} - \frac{\partial f^I}{\partial u^R} = \left(\frac{\partial \psi}{\partial r} + \frac{\psi(r)}{r} \frac{\partial \phi}{\partial \theta} \right) \sin(\phi(\theta) - \theta) = 0 \tag{19}$$

$$\frac{\partial f^R}{\partial u^R} \frac{\partial f^I}{\partial u^I} - \frac{\partial f^R}{\partial u^I} \frac{\partial f^I}{\partial u^R} = \frac{\psi(r)}{r} \cdot \frac{\partial \psi}{\partial r} \cdot \frac{\partial \phi}{\partial \theta} > 0 \tag{20}$$

It can be seen that the conditions, Eq. (19) and Eq. (20), are equivalent to the following conditions.

$$\frac{d\psi(r)}{dr} > 0 \text{ for all } r \geq 0, \quad \lim_{r \to 0} \frac{\psi(r)}{r} > 0 \tag{21}$$

$$\phi(\theta) = \theta + n\pi \tag{22}$$

Thus the condition (ii) and (iii) in Definition 2 are equivalent to the conditions Eq. (16) and Eq. (17) in Theorem 3. By using Eq. (17), $\frac{\partial f^R}{\partial u^R}$ is calculated as follows.

$$\begin{aligned} \frac{\partial f^R}{\partial u^R} &= \frac{\partial \psi}{\partial r} \cos^2\theta \cos(n\pi) + \frac{\psi(r)}{r} \sin^2\theta \cos(n\pi) \\ &= \begin{cases} \dfrac{\partial \psi}{\partial r} \cos^2\theta + \dfrac{\psi(r)}{r} \cdot \sin^2\theta & (\mathrm{n : even}) \\ -\dfrac{\partial \psi}{\partial r} \cos^2\theta - \dfrac{\psi(r)}{r} \cdot \sin^2\theta & (\mathrm{n : odd}) \end{cases} \end{aligned} \tag{23}$$

From Eq. (16) and Eq. (23), we can obtain the condition (i) in Definition 2; $\frac{\partial f^R}{\partial u^R} \neq 0$. This completes the proof.

Remark 3. *It is seen from the theorem that the activation of Type B must take the form:*

$$f(u) = \psi(r)e^{i\theta} \quad or \quad f(u) = -\psi(r)e^{i\theta}$$

for belonging to F^{ε} because $\phi(\theta) = \theta + n\pi$. Note also that the latter form is reduced to the former one by rewriting the model of the complex-valued neural network Eq. (6) as Eq. (12).

Discussions

As stated in before, in the case that the neural network Eq. (6) is real-valued, that is, ***u**, **x**, **θ**, **W**,* and ***T*** are all real numbers and $f(\cdot)$ is a real nonlinear function ($f: \mathbb{R} \to \mathbb{R}$) in Eq. (6), an existence condition of energy function on the activation function is that $f(\cdot)$ is continuously differentiable, bounded and monotonically increasing (the condition on the connection weight matrix is $\boldsymbol{W}^t = \boldsymbol{W}$). It is seen from Theorem 2 that, for the case that the activation function is of Type A in the complex-valued neural network Eq. (6), the existence condition is a direct extension of that of the real-valued Hopfield type neural networks. On the other hand, for the case that the activation function is of Type B, only the condition on its magnitude function is similar to that of the real-valued networks (Theorem 3). Note that, the activation function of Type B satisfying the existence condition (belonging to F^{ε}) does not vary the phase of an input signal.

There have been several activation functions proposed for complex-valued neural networks. Typical examples are as follows.

$$f(u) = \frac{1}{1+e^{-u^R}} + i\frac{1}{1+e^{-u^I}} \tag{24}$$

(Birx & Pipenberg, 1992; Benvenuto & Piazza, 1992).

$$f(u) = \tanh(u^R) + i\tanh(u^I) \tag{25}$$

(Kechriotis & Manolakos, 1994; Kinouchi & Hagiwara, 1995).

$$f(u) = \frac{u^R}{c + \frac{1}{\gamma}|u^R|} + i\frac{u^I}{c + \frac{1}{\gamma}|u^I|} \tag{26}$$

where c and γ are real positive constants (Kuroe & Taniguchi, 2005).

$$f(u) = \frac{u}{|u|} \tag{27}$$

(Noest, 1988a; Noest, 1988b).

$$f(u) = \tanh(|u|)\exp(i\arg u) \tag{28}$$

(Hirose, 1994).

$$f(u) = \frac{u}{c + \frac{1}{\gamma} |u|} \tag{29}$$

(Georgiou & Koutsougeras, 1992; Kuroe, Hashimoto & Mori, 2001a; Kuroe, Hashimoto, & Mori, 2001b).

$$f(u) = \frac{|u|}{c + \frac{1}{\gamma}|u|} \exp\left[i\{\arg u - \frac{1}{2^n} \sin(2^n \arg u)\} \right] \tag{30}$$

where $-\pi \leq \arg u < \pi$ (Kuroe & Taniguchi, 2005).

$$f(u) = \frac{1}{1 + e^{-u}} \tag{31}$$

(Leung & Haykin, 1991).

The functions Eq. (24), Eq. (25) and Eq. (26) are of Type A and satisfy the conditions of Theorem 2. The functions Eq. (27), Eq. (28), Eq. (29) and Eq. (30) are of Type B. Among them Eq. (28) and Eq. (29) satisfy the conditions of Theorem 3, but Eq. (27) and Eq. (30) do not. The function Eq. (27) is not defined at $u = 0$. The function Eq. (30) is obtained by modifying the discrete complex-valued activation function based on the complex-signam function used in (Jankowski, Lozowski, & Zurada, 1996) so as that it becomes a smooth function. In this function the magnitude and the phase of an input go through the nonlinear function separately. The function Eq. (31) is neither of Type A nor Type B and does not belong to F^{ε}, but is analytic except the points $u = (2k+1)\pi i \quad (k = 0, 1, 2, \cdots)$. It is concluded, therefore, that the complex-valued neural network with the activation function Eq. (24), Eq. (25), Eq. (26), Eq. (28) or Eq. (29) and a Hermitian weight matrix $\boldsymbol{W}$ has an energy function Eq. (11).

Georgiou and Koutsougeras (1992) discuss about properties that a suitable activation should possess for complex-valued backpropagation of complex-valued feedforward neural networks. Their suggested properties are:

1. $f(\cdot)$ is nonlinear and bounded,
2. $f(\cdot)$ is not entirely analytic and the partial derivatives $\frac{\partial f^R}{\partial u^R}$, $\frac{\partial f^R}{\partial u^I}$, $\frac{\partial f^I}{\partial u^R}$ and $\frac{\partial f^I}{\partial u^R}$ exist and are bounded, and
3. $\frac{\partial f^R}{\partial u^R}\frac{\partial f^I}{\partial u^I} - \frac{\partial f^R}{\partial u^I}\frac{\partial f^I}{\partial u^R} \neq 0$ for all $u \in \mathbb{C}$.

They propose the function Eq. (29) as an activation function which satisfies these properties and give its hardware implementation. They show that if the property 3 is violated, no learning takes place in complex domain backpropagation. Note that, in addition to the property 3, the positive definiteness and symmetry conditions ((ii) and (iii) of Definition 2) are required for existence of an energy function.

By utilizing Theorems 2 and 3 other functions which satisfy the existence conditions can be easily found out because there are a large choice of real functions $f^R(u^R)$, $f^I(u^I)$ in Type A and $\psi(r)$ in Type B, which are continuously differentiable and monotonically increasing. It seems to be challenging to find out complex functions belonging to F^{ε} which are neither of Type A nor Type B, but are of the general form Eq. (5) or

$$f(u) = \psi(r, \theta) e^{j\phi(r, \theta)}. \tag{32}$$

This problem remains for future study. Note also that the discussions here are based on the condition $f(\cdot) \in F^{\varepsilon}$ which is a sufficient condition for existence of an energy function. To derive another existence condition is also a subject for future study.

APPLICATION OF ENERGY FUNCTION

Qualitative Analysis of Complex-Valued Neural Networks

In the real valued neural networks energy functions have been applied to various problems such as qualitative analysis of neural networks, synthesis of associative memories, optimization problems and etc.. It is expected that the energy function Eq. (11) is able to be applied to various problems as is the real-valued neural networks. The energy function Eq. (11) enable us to analyze qualitative behavior of the complex-valued neural networks Eq. (6). In this section we present some results obtained by qualitative analysis using the energy function Eq. (11). These results will be utilized to obtain a synthesis procedure of complex-valued associative memories in the next subsection.

It is easy to see that $\tilde{x} \in \mathbb{C}$ is an equilibrium point of the neural network Eq. (6) if only if $\nabla y E(\tilde{x}) = 0$. Let $\boldsymbol{H}(\boldsymbol{x})$ be the Hessian matrix of the energy function E, defined by

$$\boldsymbol{H}(\boldsymbol{x}) := \nabla \boldsymbol{y}(\nabla \boldsymbol{y} E(\boldsymbol{x}))'$$

$$= \begin{bmatrix} \dfrac{\partial^2 E}{\partial y_1 \partial y_1} & \cdots & \dfrac{\partial^2 E}{\partial y_1 \partial y_{2n}} \\ \vdots & \ddots & \vdots \\ \dfrac{\partial^2 E}{\partial y_{2n} \partial y_1} & \cdots & \dfrac{\partial^2 E}{\partial y_{2n} \partial y_{2n}} \end{bmatrix}.$$

From Eq. (11), $\boldsymbol{H}(\boldsymbol{x})$ is computed as

$$\boldsymbol{H}(\boldsymbol{x}) = - \quad + \Gamma \tag{33}$$

where $\Gamma \in \mathbb{R}^{2n \times 2n}$ is given by

$$\Gamma := \begin{bmatrix} \operatorname{diag}\left(\dfrac{\partial g_1^R}{\partial x^R}, \dfrac{\partial g_2^R}{\partial x^R}, \cdots, \dfrac{\partial g_n^R}{\partial x^R} \right) & \operatorname{diag}\left(\dfrac{\partial g_1^R}{\partial x^I}, \dfrac{\partial g_2^R}{\partial x^I}, \cdots, \dfrac{\partial g_n^R}{\partial x^I} \right) \\ \operatorname{diag}\left(\dfrac{\partial g_1^I}{\partial x^R}, \dfrac{\partial g_2^I}{\partial x^R}, \cdots, \dfrac{\partial g_n^I}{\partial x^R} \right) & \operatorname{diag}\left(\dfrac{\partial g_1^I}{\partial x^I}, \dfrac{\partial g_2^I}{\partial x^I}, \cdots, \dfrac{\partial g_n^I}{\partial x^I} \right) \end{bmatrix}.$$

From the Inverse Function theorem, if an equilibrium point $\tilde{\boldsymbol{x}}$ satisfies the condition $\det(\boldsymbol{H}(\tilde{\boldsymbol{x}})) \neq 0$, then it is an isolated equilibrium point of the network Eq. (6). The following theorems are obtained.

Theorem 4. *Consider the complex-valued neural network Eq. (6) and assume that the connection weight matrix* $\boldsymbol{W}$ *is a Hermitian matrix,* $\boldsymbol{W}^* = \boldsymbol{W}$*, and the activation function* $f(\cdot) \in F^{\varepsilon}$*. If there is no* $\boldsymbol{x}$ *satisfying the equations* $\nabla_{\boldsymbol{y}} E(\boldsymbol{x}) = 0$ *and* $\det(H(\boldsymbol{x})) = 0$ *simultaneously, then no nontrivial periodic solutions exist and each non-equilibrium solution converges to an equilibrium point of Eq. (6) as* $t \to \infty$.

Theorem 5. *Consider the complex-valued neural network Eq. (6) and assume that the connection weight matrix* $\boldsymbol{W}$ *is a Hermitian matrix,* $\boldsymbol{W}^* = \boldsymbol{W}$*, and the activation function* $f(\cdot) \in F^{\varepsilon}$*.* $\tilde{\boldsymbol{x}}$ *is an asymptotically stable equilibrium point if and only if*

$$\nabla y E(\tilde{x}) = 0, \quad \boldsymbol{H}(\tilde{x}) > 0 \tag{34}$$

These theorems can be proved in the similar manner as the corresponding results of real-valued neural networks (Li & Michel, 1988).

Synthesis of Complex-Valued Associative Memories

One of typical examples of applications of energy functions is a synthesis problem of associative memories. For real-valued neural networks several studies on synthesis of associative memories by using energy functions have been done (Li & Michel, 1988; Das, 1991). In this subsection we show a synthesis method of complex-valued associative memories by using the energy function Eq. (11).

Synthesis Procedure

Associative memories are realized by utilizing the nonlinear dynamics of a neural network, specifically, the multiplicity of asymptotically stable equilibria. We formulate a problem of synthesizing associative memories in such a way that, for a given set of desired memory vectors, the weights of the synaptic connections and the threshold values of the network are determined so that each desired memory vector becomes an asymptotically stable equilibrium point of the neural network. Let m be the number of memory patterns to be stored, and each memory pattern is an n dimensional complex vector, denoted by $\boldsymbol{a}^{(r)}=\left[a_1^{(r)}, a_2^{(r)}, \cdots, a_n^{(r)}\right]^t \in \mathbb{C}^n, r = 1, 2, \cdots, m$.

In order to make all the memory vectors $\boldsymbol{a}^{(1)}, \boldsymbol{a}^{(2)}, \cdots, \boldsymbol{a}^{(m)}$ equilibrium points of the complex-valued neural network Eq. (6), the following conditions must be satisfied for all $r = 1, 2, \cdots, m$.

$$\boldsymbol{0} = -\boldsymbol{b}^{(r)} + \boldsymbol{W}\boldsymbol{a}^{(r)} + \boldsymbol{\theta} \tag{35}$$

$$\boldsymbol{a}^{(r)} = \boldsymbol{f}(\boldsymbol{b}^{(r)}) \tag{36}$$

where $\boldsymbol{b}^{(r)}=\left[b_1^{(r)}, b_2^{(r)}, \cdots, b_n^{(r)}\right]^t \in \mathbb{C}^n$ and $b_j^{(r)} := f^{-1}(a_j^{(r)})$. These conditions are equivalent to

$$\boldsymbol{B} = \boldsymbol{W}\boldsymbol{A} \tag{37}$$

$$\boldsymbol{\theta} = \boldsymbol{b}^{(m)} - \boldsymbol{W}\boldsymbol{a}^{(m)} \tag{38}$$

where

$$\boldsymbol{A} = [\boldsymbol{a}^{(1)} - \boldsymbol{a}^{(2)}, \boldsymbol{a}^{(2)} - \boldsymbol{a}^{(3)}, \cdots, \boldsymbol{a}^{(m-1)} - \boldsymbol{a}^{(m)}] \in \mathbb{C}^{n\times(m-1)},$$
$$\boldsymbol{B} = [\boldsymbol{b}^{(1)} - \boldsymbol{b}^{(2)}, \boldsymbol{b}^{(2)} - \boldsymbol{b}^{(3)}, \cdots, \boldsymbol{b}^{(m-1)} - \boldsymbol{b}^{(m)}] \in \mathbb{C}^{n\times(m-1)}.$$

From the existence condition of a solution of simultaneous linear algebraic equations[1] and the assumption that $\boldsymbol{W}$ is a Hermitian matrix, there exists $\boldsymbol{W}$ which satisfies Eq. (37) if and only if the following conditions hold:

$$\boldsymbol{A}^*\boldsymbol{B} = \boldsymbol{B}^*\boldsymbol{A} \tag{39}$$

$$\operatorname{rank}(\boldsymbol{A}^t) = \operatorname{rank}(\boldsymbol{A}^t, \boldsymbol{B}_j^t), \quad j = 1, 2, \cdots, n \tag{40}$$

where $\boldsymbol{B}_j$ is the jth row of $\boldsymbol{B}$.

The synthesis procedure is summarized as follows.

Step 1: Check whether the conditions Eq. (39) and Eq. (40) hold for a given set of $\boldsymbol{a}^{(r)}(r=1,2,\cdots,m)$.

Step 2: Obtain the connection weight matrix $\boldsymbol{W}$ which satisfies Eq. (37). Compute threshold vector θ according to Eq. (38).

Step 3: Compute $H(\boldsymbol{a}^{(r)})$ by using Eq. (33) and check if the condition Eq. (34) in Theorem 5 holds for each $\boldsymbol{a}^{(r)},(r=1,2,\cdots,m)$. If this is true for all $\boldsymbol{a}^{(r)}, r=1,2,\cdots,m$, stop. Otherwise go to Step 2.

Numerical Experiment

Consider the complex neural network Eq. (6) where $n=3$. As an activation function we use $f(u)=u/(1+|u|)$, which belongs to the function class F^{ε}. The following two vectors $\boldsymbol{a}^{(1)}$ and $\boldsymbol{a}^{(2)}$ are specified to be stored in the network Eq. (6).

$$\boldsymbol{a}^{(1)}=\begin{pmatrix} 0.692820323+i0.400000000 \\ -0.636396103+i0.636396103 \\ 0.000000000+i0.700000000 \end{pmatrix}$$

$$\boldsymbol{a}^{(2)}=\begin{pmatrix} -0.800000000+i0.000000000 \\ 0.450000000-i0.779422863 \\ -0.494974746-i0.494974746 \end{pmatrix}. \tag{41}$$

We compute $\boldsymbol{A}$, $\boldsymbol{B}$, $\boldsymbol{A}^*\boldsymbol{B}$ and $\boldsymbol{B}^*\boldsymbol{A}$ as

$$\boldsymbol{A}=\begin{bmatrix} 1.4928203230+i0.4000000000 \\ -1.0863961030+i1.4158189660 \\ 0.4949747460+i1.1949747460 \end{bmatrix}$$

$$\boldsymbol{B}=\begin{bmatrix} 7.4641016146+i1.9999999998 \\ -10.863961008+i14.158189626 \\ 1.6499158135+i3.9832491469 \end{bmatrix}$$

$$\boldsymbol{A}^*\boldsymbol{B}=\boldsymbol{B}^*\boldsymbol{A}=[49.367109681].$$

Note that the condition Eq. (39) holds. We compute $\text{rank}(\boldsymbol{A}^t)$ and $\text{rank}(\boldsymbol{A}^t,\boldsymbol{B}_j^t)$ as

$$\begin{aligned}&\text{rank}(\boldsymbol{A}^t)=1\\ &\text{rank}(\boldsymbol{A}^t,\boldsymbol{B}_j^t)=1,\quad j=1,2,3.\end{aligned} \tag{42}$$

This implies that there exists a connection weight matrix $\boldsymbol{W}$ such that $\boldsymbol{a}^{(1)}$ and $\boldsymbol{a}^{(2)}$ become equilibrium points of the network (Step 1). In Step 2, we use a gradient descent search in order to obtain $\boldsymbol{W}$ which satisfies Eq. (37). As a result, $\boldsymbol{W}$ and $\boldsymbol{\theta}$ are obtained as follows.

$$W = \begin{bmatrix} -0.09+i0.00 & -1.97-i3.57 & 0.80-i0.01 \\ -1.97+i3.57 & 4.86+i0.00 & 1.59+i1.67 \\ 0.80+i0.01 & 1.59-i1.67 & -0.36+i0.00 \end{bmatrix}$$

$$\boldsymbol{\theta} = \begin{pmatrix} -0.0043436+i0.4600908 \\ 0.6954562+i0.4687374 \\ -0.6005583+i0.1770916 \end{pmatrix}$$

In Step 3, with the obtained W and $\boldsymbol{\theta}$ we compute $H(\boldsymbol{a}^{(1)})$ and $H(\boldsymbol{a}^{(2)})$ by using Eq. (33). They are both found to be positive definite, which completes the synthesis procedure. Thus the vectors $\boldsymbol{a}^{(1)}$ and $\boldsymbol{a}^{(2)}$ become asymptotically stable equilibrium points of the network and the desired complex-valued associative memory is obtained. To verify this, we simulate the network Eq. (6) with the various initial conditions in the neighborhood of $\boldsymbol{a}^{(1)}$ and $\boldsymbol{a}^{(2)}$. It is confirmed through the simulation that $\boldsymbol{a}^{(1)}$ and $\boldsymbol{a}^{(2)}$ are correctly recalled. Figures 2 and 3 show the examples of the trajectories of x_2 starting from four different initial conditions in the neighborhood of $\boldsymbol{a}^{(1)}$ and $\boldsymbol{a}^{(2)}$, respectively.

CONCLUSION

This chapter presented models of fully connected complex-valued neural networks which are complex-valued extension of Hopfield-type neural networks and discussed methods to study their dynamics. In particular we investigated existence conditions of energy functions for complex-valued Hopfield-type neural networks. Emphasized were the properties of the activation functions which assure the existence of an energy function for the networks. Several classes of activation functions which are used in most of the models of complex-valued neural networks were considered. Furthermore we investigated the properties of activation functions which assure existence of energy functions and discussed about how to find out complex functions which satisfy the properties.

As an application of the energy function some results on qualitative analysis of the network by utilizing the energy function was shown. A synthesis method of complex-valued associative memories by utilizing the analysis results was also discussed.

The author believes that the energy function can be applied to several engineering problems such as synthesis of associative memories, optimization problems and so on as is the case of real valued ones. There have been done some studies on applications to real world problems. One example is the application to a traffic signal control problem, which is studied in the literatures (Nishikawa & Kuroe, 2004; Nishikawa, Iritani, Sakakibara, & Kuroe, 2005; Nishikawa, Sakakibara, Iritani, & Kuroe, 2005). In the literatures they use different activations and compare the control performance, and show that the energy function plays an important role.

FUTURE RESEARCH DIRECTIONS

There considered several research directions on the topic of this chapter. One important research direction is to develop applications of the neural network models discussed in this chapter, that is, complex-valued neural networks of Hopfield type. In developing an engineering application it might become keys which type of nonlinear complex function is chosen as activation functions and how to construct energy functions to solve the problem.

In the chapter we introduce a definition of energy functions which are direct extension of energy function of the real-valued neural networks. Developing another definition of energy functions is also a future research direction, which could bring new paradigm of theory and applications of the neural networks. One approach to

Figure 2. Trajectories of x_2 in the neighborhood of $\boldsymbol{a}^{(1)}$

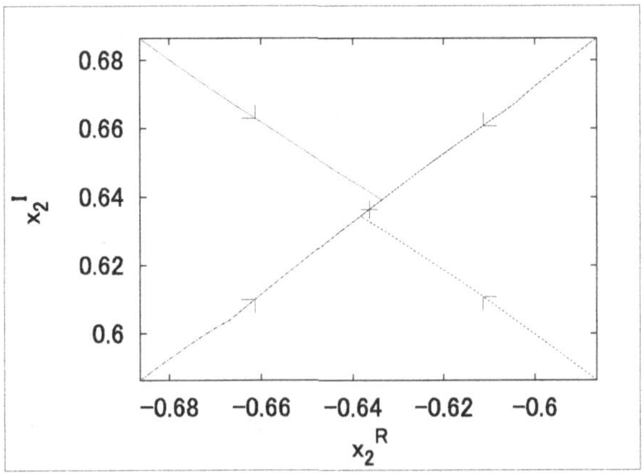

Figure 3. Trajectories of x_2 in the neighborhood of $\boldsymbol{a}^{(2)}$

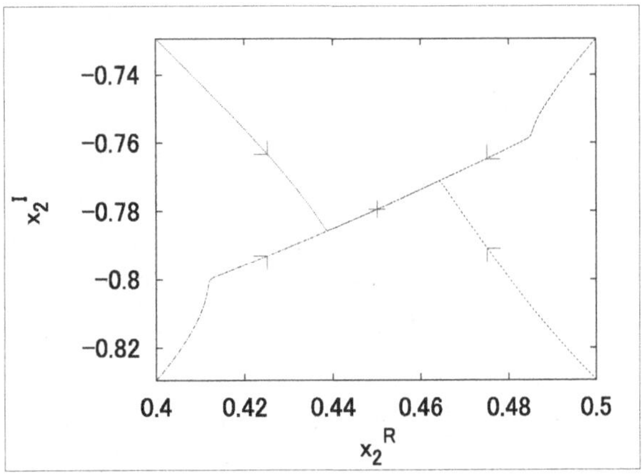

this problem could be to receive the aid of recent development of quantum computing. The other future direction is to extend the studies in this chapter in neural networks with higher dimensional parameters such as quaternion neural networks and Clifford neural networks. A study has been done for quaternion neural networks and some results have been already obtained. See Yoshida, Kuroe, and Mori, (2005).

ACKNOWLEDGMENT

The contribution of this chapter is based on the studies (Kuroe, Hashimoto, & Mori, 2002; Kuroe, Yoshida, & Mori, 2003). The author would like to express his gratitude to Prof. T. Mori, Dr. N. Hashimoto and Dr. M. Yoshida for their valuable and continuous discussions.

REFERENCES

Benvenuto, N., & Piazza, F. (1992). On the Complex Backpropagation Algorithm. *IEEE Transactions on Signal Processing, 40*, 967–969.

Birx, D. L., & Pipenberg, S. J. (1992). Chaotic Oscillators and Complex Mapping Feed Forward Networks (CMFFNS) for Signal Detection in Noisy Environments. *Proceedings of IEEE International Joint Conference on Neural Networks, II*, 881–888.

Das, S. R. (1991). On the Synthesis of Nonlinear Continuous Neural Networks. *IEEE Transactions on Systems, Man, and Cybernetics, 21*(2), 413–418.

Georgiou, G. M., & Koutsougeras, C. (1992). Complex Domain Backpropagation. *IEEE Transactions on Circuits and Systems-II, 39*(5), 330–334.

Hirose, A. (1994). Applications of Complex-Valued Neural Networks to Coherent Optical Computing Using Phase-Sensitive Detection Scheme. *Information Sciences - Applications*, 2(2), 103–117.

Hopfield, J. J. (1984). Neurons with graded response have collective computational properties like those of two-state neurons. *Proceedings of the National Academy of Sciences of the United States of America, 81*, 3088–3092.

Hopfield, J. J., & Tank, D. W. (1985). "Neural" Computation of Decisions in Optimization Problems. *Biological Cybernetics, 81*, 141–152.

Jankowski, S., Lozowski, A., & Zurada, J. M. (1996). Complex-valued multistate neural associative memory. *IEEE Transactions on Neural Networks, 7*(4), 1491–1496.

Kechriotis, G., & Manolakos, E. S. (1994). Training Fully Recurrent Neural Networks with Complex Weights. *IEEE Transactions on Circuits and Systems-II, 41*(2), 235–238.

Kinouchi, M., & Hagiwara, M. (1995). Learning Temporal Sequences by Complex Neurons with Local Feedback. *Proceedings of IEEE International Conference on Neural Networks, VI*, 3165–3169.

Kuroe, Y., Hashimoto, N., & Mori, T. (2001a). Qualitative analysis of a self-correlation type complex-valued associative memories. *Nonlinear Analysis, 47*, 5795-5806.

Kuroe, Y., Hashimoto, N., & Mori, T. (2001b). Qualitative Analysis of Continuous Complex-Valued Associative Memories. *Artificial Neural Networks - ICANN 2001*, George Dorffner et. al. (Eds.), Lecture Notes in Computer Science, *2130*, 843-850, Springer.

Kuroe, Y., Hashimoto, N., & Mori, T. (2002). On energy function for complex-valued neural networks and its applications. *CD-ROM Proceedings of International Conference on Neural Information Processing*, Singapore.

Kuroe, Y., & Taniguchi, T. (2005). Models of Self-Correlation Type Complex-Valued Associative Memories and Their Dynamics. In W. Duch et. al.(Eds.), *Artificial Neural Networks: Biological Inspirations - ICANN 2005*, Lecture Notes in Computer Science, *3696*, 185-192. Springer-Verlag.

Kuroe, Y., Yoshida, M., & Mori, T. (2003). On activation functions for complex-valued neural networks - existence of energy functions -. In Kaynak, O., Alpaydin, E., Oja, E., & Xu, L. (Eds.), *Artificial Neural Networks and Neural Information Processing ICANN/ICONIP 2003*, Lecture Notes in Computer Science, *2714*, 985–992.

Leung, H., & Haykin, S. (1991). The Complex Backpropagation Algorithm. *IEEE Transactions on Signal Processing, 39*, 2101–2104.

Li, J. H., & Michel, A. N. (1988). Qualitative Analysis and Synthesis of a Class of Neural Networks. *IEEE Transactions on Circuits and Systems, 35*(8), 976–986.

Nishikawa, I., Iritani, T., Sakakibara, K., & Kuroe, Y. (2005) Phase Dynamics of Complex-valued Neural Networks and Its Application to Traffic Signal Control. *International Journal of Neural Systems, 15*(1 & 2), 111-120.

Nishikawa, I., & Kuroe, Y. (2004). Dynamics of Complex-Valued Neural Networks and Its Relation to a Phase Oscillator System. In N. R. Pal, N. Kasabov, R. K. Mudi, S. Pal, & S. K. Parui (Eds.), *Neural Information Processing ICONIP 2004*, Lecture Notes in Computer Science, *3316*, 122-129. Springer-Verlag.

Nishikawa, I., Sakakibara, K., Iritani, T., & Kuroe, Y. (2005). 2 Types of Complex-Valued Hopfield Networks and the Application to a Traffic Signal Control. *Proceedings of International Joint Conference on Neural Networks*, 782-787.

Noest, A. J. (1988a). Phaser Neural Network. In D. Z.Anderson, (Ed.), *Neural Information Processing Systems*, (pp. 584–591). New York: AIP.

Noest, A. J. (1988b). Associative Memory in Sparse Phasor Neural Networks. *Europhysics Letters*, *6*(4), 469–474.

Yoshida, M., Kuroe, Y., & Mori, T. (2005). Models of Hopfield-Type Quaternion Neural Networks and Their Energy Functions. *International Journal of Neural Systems, 15*(1 & 2), 129-135.

ADDITIONAL READING

Hassoun, H. M. (1995). *Fundamentals of Artificial Neural Networks.* Cambrige, MA: The MIT Press.

Khalil, H. K. (1992). *Nonlinear Systems.* New York: Macmillan Publishing Company.

Kuroe, Y. (2003). A Models of Complex-Valued Associative Memories and Its Dynamics. In A. Hirose (Ed.), *Complex-Valued Neural Networks Theories and Applications* (pp. 57–79). World Scientific.

Luo, F., & Unbehauen, R. (1997). *Applied Neural Networks for Signal Processing.* Cambridge University Press.

ENDNOTE

1 Consider a linear algebraic equation $\boldsymbol{Ax} = \boldsymbol{b}$ where $\boldsymbol{A} \in \mathbb{C}^{m \times n}$, $\boldsymbol{x} \in \mathbb{C}^n$ and $\boldsymbol{b} \in \mathbb{C}^m$. It is known that the equation has a solution if and only if rank($\boldsymbol{A}$) = rank($\boldsymbol{A}$, $\boldsymbol{b}$).

Section II
Applications of Complex-Valued Neural Networks

Six applications of complex-valued neural networks are given, which include nonlinear beamforming, digital communication, associative memory, nuclear magnetic resonance (NMR) spectrum estimation, and independent component analysis (ICA) in the complex domain.

Chapter VII
Complex-Valued Symmetric Radial Basis Function Network for Beamforming

Sheng Chen
University of Southampton, UK

ABSTRACT

The complex-valued radial basis function (RBF) network proposed by Chen et al. (1994) has found many applications for processing complex-valued signals, in particular, for communication channel equalization and signal detection. This complex-valued RBF network, like many other existing RBF modeling methods, constitutes a black-box approach that seeks typically a sparse model representation extracted from the training data. Adopting black-box modeling is appropriate, if no a priori information exists regarding the underlying data generating mechanism. However, a fundamental principle in practical data modelling is that if there exists a priori information concerning the system to be modeled it should be incorporated in the modeling process. Many complex-valued signal processing problems, particularly those encountered in communication signal detection, have some inherent symmetric properties. This contribution adopts a grey-box approach to complex-valued RBF modeling and develops a complex-valued symmetric RBF (SRBF) network model. The application of this SRBF network is demonstrated using nonlinear beamforming assisted detection for multiple-antenna aided wireless systems that employ complex-valued modulation schemes. Two training algorithms for this complex-valued SRBF network are proposed. The first method is based on a modified version of the cluster-variation enhanced clustering algorithm, while the second method is derived by modifying the orthogonal-forward-selection procedure based on Fisher ratio of class separability measure. The effectiveness of the proposed complex-valued SRBF network and the efficiency of the two training algorithms are demonstrated in nonlinear beamforming application.

INTRODUCION

The radial basis function (RBF) network is a popular artificial neural network (ANN) architecture that has found wide-ranging applications in many diverse fields of engineering, see for example, (Chen *et al.*, 1990; Leonard & Kramer, 1991; Chen *et al.*, 1993; Caiti & Parisini, 1994; Gorinevsky *et al.*, 1996; Cha & Kassam, 1996; Rosenblum & Davis, 1996; Refaee *et al.*, 1999; Muraki *et al.*, 2001; Mukai, *et al.*, 2002; Su *et al.*, 2002; Li *et al.*, 2004; Lee & Choi, 2004; Ng *et al.*, 2004; Oyang *et al.*, 2005; Acir *et al.*, 2005; Tan *et al.*, 2005). The RBF method is a classical numerical technique for nonlinear functional interpolation with real-valued data (Powell, 1987). A renewed interest in the RBF method coincided with a recent resurgence in the field of ANNs. Connections between the RBF method and the ANN was made and the RBF model was re-interpreted as a one-hidden-layer feedforward network (Broomhead & Lowe, 1988; Poggio & Girosi, 1990). Specifically, by adopting the ANN interpretation, a RBF model can be considered as a processing structure consisting of a hidden layer and an output layer. Each node in the hidden layer has a radially symmetric response around a node parameter vector called a centre, with the hidden node's response shape determined by the chosen basis function as well as a node width parameter, while the output layer is a set of linear combiners with linear connection weights.

The parameters of the RBF network include its centre vectors and variances or covariance matrices of the basis functions as well as the weights that connect the RBF nodes to the network output. All the parameters of a RBF network can be learned together via nonlinear optimisation using the gradient based algorithms (Chen *et al.*, 1990a; An *et al.*, 1993; McLoone *et al.*, 1998; Karayiannis *et al.*, 2003; Peng *et al.*, 2003), the evolutionary algorithms (Whitehead & Choate, 1994; Whitehead, 1996; Gonzalez *et al.*, 2003) or the expectation-maximisation algorithm (Yang & Chen, 1998; Mak & Kung, 2000). Generally, learning based on such a nonlinear approach is computationally expensive and may encounter the problem of local minima. Additionally, the network structure or the number of RBF nodes has to be determined via other means, typically based on cross validation. Alternatively, clustering algorithms can be applied to find the RBF centre vectors as well as the associated basis function variances (Moody & Darken, 1989; Chen *et al.*, 1992; Chen, 1995; Uykan, 2003). This leaves the RBF weights to be determined by the usual linear least squares solution. Again, the number of the clusters has to be determined via other means, such as cross validation. One of the most popular approaches for constructing RBF networks however is to formulate the problem as a linear learning one by considering the training input data points as candidate RBF centres and employing a common variance for every RBF node. A parsimonious RBF network is then identified using the orthogonal least squares (OLS) algorithm (Chen *et al.*, 1989; Chen *et al.*, 1991; Chen *et al.*, 1999; Chen *et al.*, 2003; Chen *et al.*, 2004a).

Many practical signal processing applications deal with complex-valued signals and data. This motivates the research in complex-valued ANNs, which have found wide-ranging applications in complex-valued signal processing problems (Uncini *et al.*, 1999; Kim & Adali, 2003; Li *et al.*, 2005; Yang & Bose, 2005; Hirose, 2006). A particular complex-valued ANN architecture proposed by Chen *et al.* (1994) is the complex-valued RBF network, which takes the following form

$$y(k) = \sum_{i=1}^{N_c} w_i \varphi(\mathbf{x}(k); \mathbf{c}_i, \rho^2), \tag{1}$$

where $y(k) \in C$ (C being the field of complex-valued numbers) and $\mathbf{x}(k) \in C^L$ denote the complex-valued RBF network output and input vector, respectively, N_c denotes the number of RBF units, w_i are the complex-valued RBF weights, $\mathbf{c}_i \in C^L$ are the complex-valued RBF centres, ρ^2 is the positive RBF variance, and $\varphi(\bullet)$ is the real-valued radial basis function. When $y(k)$ and w_i are real-valued, this complex-valued RBF network reduces to the special case of the usual real-valued RBF network (Moody & Darken, 1989; Chen *et al.*, 1991). Each RBF unit in the complex-valued RBF network (1) can be interpreted as some underlying probability density function (Chen *et al.*, 1994). Such a physical interpretation makes this complex-valued RBF network a powerful tool in processing complex-valued signals, particularly, in applications to communication channel equalisation and signal detection (Chen *et al.*, 1994a; Cha & Kassam, 1995; Gan *et al.*, 1999; Deng *et al.*, 2002; Botoca & Budura, 2006).

Like many existing neural network models, this complex-valued RBF network, however, constitutes a black-box approach that seeks a sparse model representation extracted from the training data. Adopting black-box modelling is appropriate, if no *a priori* information exists regarding the underlying data generating mechanism. However, if there exists *a priori* information concerning the system to be modelled, it should be incorporated in the modelling process. The use of available prior knowledge in data modelling often leads to an improved performance. For real-valued signal processing applications, it has been recognised that many real-life phenomena exhibit inherent symmetry and these properties are hard to infer accurately from noisy data with the aid of black-box real-valued neural network models. However, by imposing appropriate symmetry on the model's structure, exploiting the symmetry properties becomes easier and this leads to substantial improvements in the achievable modelling performance. For example, in regression-type applications, how to exploit odd or even symmetry of the underlying system explicitly in both the real-valued RBF network and least squares support vector machine has been demonstrated (Aguirre *et al.*, 2004; Espinoza *et al.*, 2005), while in two-class classification-type applications, a novel real-valued symmetric RBF (SRBF) network has been proposed for communication signal detection (Chen *et al.*, 2004; Chen *et al.*, 2007; Chen *et al.*, 2007a; Chen *et al.*, 2007b), which explicitly utilises odd symmetry of the underlying optimal Bayesian detection solution.

This contribution continues this theme and extends the grey-box approach to complex-valued RBF modelling. Instead of simple odd or even symmetry typically found in real-valued signal processing problems, symmetry properties inherented in many complex-valued signal processing problems are more complicated, and this is demonstrated using the application to nonlinear beamforming assisted detection for multiple-antenna aided wireless systems that employ complex-valued quadrature phase shift keying (QPSK) modulation scheme. This naturally leads to our proposed complex-valued SRBF network. Two training algorithms for this complex-valued SRBF network are proposed. The first method is based on a modified version of the cluster-variation enhanced clustering algorithm (Chinrungrueng & Séquin, 1995; Chen, 1995; Chen *et al.*, 2007a). The second method is derived by modifying the orthogonal-forward-selection (OFS) procedure based on the Fisher ratio of class separability measure (FRCSM) (Mao, 2002; Chen *et al.*, 2004; Chen *et al.*, 2007b) through changing the two-class FRCSM into the multi-class (four-class) one. The effectiveness of the proposed complex-valued SRBF network and the efficiency of the two training algorithms are demonstrated in nonlinear beamforming application. Although the proposed complex-valued SRBF network is derived in the context of nonlinear beamforming for QPSK wireless systems, it is applicable to the generic complex-valued signal processing problem that exhibits a similar symmetric behaviour.

The remainder of this contribution is organised as follows. We first present the complex-valued signal model for the multiple-antenna aided wireless system that employs the QPSK signalling as well as the optimal Bayesian nonlinear beamforming or detection solution. The inherent symmetric structure of this Bayesian nonlinear beamforming solution is then highlighted. This naturally leads to the proposed complex-valued SRBF network, which can easily be constructed using a cluster-variation enhanced clustering algorithm. While the clustering-based SRBF network developed is a direct "carbon-copy" of the symmetric Bayesian beamformer, a more generic complex-valued SRBF is also proposed and a multi-class FRCSM-based OFS algorithm is derived to construct a parsimonious SRBF network model. Finally, some concluding remarks are offerred.

BACKGROUND

A coherent wireless communication system supports M users, where each user transmits on the same angular carrier frequency ω with a single transmit antenna while the receiver is equipped with a linear antenna array consisting of L uniformly spaced elements in order to achieve user separation in the angular domain (Paulraj *et al.*, 2003; Tse &Viswanath, 2005). Assume furthermore that the channel is non-dispersive and hence it does not induce intersymbol interference.

Beamforming Signal Model

The symbol-rate complex-valued received signal vector $\mathbf{x}(k) = [x_1(k)\, x_2(k) \cdots x_L(k)]^T$ can be expressed as (Litva & Lo, 1996; Blogh & Hanzo, 2002)

$$\mathbf{x}(k) = \mathbf{P}\mathbf{b}(k) + \mathbf{n}(k) = \bar{\mathbf{x}}(k) + \mathbf{n}(k), \tag{2}$$

where $\bar{\mathbf{x}}(k)$ denotes the noise-free part of the received signal vector, $\mathbf{n}(k) = [n_1(k)\, n_2(k) \cdots n_L(k)]^T$ and $n_l(k)$ denotes the complex-valued white Gaussian noise associated with the l-th channel having $E[|n_l(k)|^2] = 2\sigma_n^2$, while $\mathbf{P}$ is the $L \times M$ complex-valued system's channel matrix and $\mathbf{b}(k) = [b_1(k)\, b_2(k) \cdots b_M(k)]^T$ with $b_i(k)$ denoting the k-th transmitted symbol of user i. The system's channel matrix $\mathbf{P}$ is defined by

$$\mathbf{P} = [A_1\mathbf{s}_1 \; A_2\mathbf{s}_2 \cdots A_M\mathbf{s}_M], \tag{3}$$

where A_i denotes the i-th complex-valued non-dispersive channel tap and the steering vector of user i is given by

$$\mathbf{s}_i = \left[e^{j\omega t_1(\theta_i)} \; e^{j\omega t_2(\theta_i)} \cdots e^{j\omega t_L(\theta_i)} \right]^T \tag{4}$$

with θ_i and $t_i\theta_i$ denoting the angle of arrival and the relative time delay at array element l for user i, respectively. The modulation scheme is assumed to be the QPSK and, therefore, $b_i(k)$ takes values from the QPSK symbol set

$$B_{\text{QPSK}} \triangleq \left\{ b^{[1]} = +1+j, b^{[2]} = -1+j, b^{[3]} = -1-j, b^{[4]} = +1-j \right\}. \tag{5}$$

Let source i be the desired user and the rest of the sources be the interfering users. The average signal-to-noise ratio (SNR) of the system is given by

$$\text{SNR} = \left(\frac{1}{M} \sum_{i=1}^{M} |A_i|^2 \right) \sigma_b^2 / 2\sigma_n^2, \tag{6}$$

where σ_b^2 is the QPSK symbol energy, and the desired signal-to-interferer q ratio (SIR) is defined by

$\text{SIR}_{i,q} = |A_i|^2 / |A_q|^2$, for $q \neq i$.

Traditionally, a linear beamformer is adopted to detect the desired user's signal (Litva & Lo, 1996; Blogh & Hanzo, 2002). The linear beamformer for user i is defined by $y_{\text{Lin}}(k) = \alpha_i^H \mathbf{x}(k)$, where $\alpha_i = [\alpha_{1,i} \; \alpha_{2,i} \cdots \alpha_{L,i}]^T$ is the complex-valued i-th linear beamformer's weight vector. The decision regarding the transmitted symbol $b_i(k)$ is given by $\hat{b}_i(k) = \text{sgn}(y_{\text{Lin}}(k))$ with

$$\text{sgn}(y) = \begin{cases} b^{[1]} = +1+j, & y_R \geq 0 \text{ and } y_I \geq 0, \\ b^{[2]} = -1+j, & y_R < 0 \text{ and } y_I \geq 0, \\ b^{[3]} = -1-j, & y_R < 0 \text{ and } y_I < 0, \\ b^{[4]} = +1-j, & y_R \geq 0 \text{ and } y_I < 0, \end{cases} \tag{7}$$

where $y_R = \Re[y]$ and $y_I = \Im[y]$ denote the real and imaginary parts of y, respectively. The optimal weight vector designed for the linear beamformer is known to be the minimum bit error rate (L-MBER) solution (Chen *et al.*, 2005), which directly minimises the bit error rate (BER) of the linear beamformer. However, if one is willing to extend the concept of beamforming from linear to nonlinear, significant performance improvement can be achieved, at the cost of considerably increased complexity (Chen *et al.*, 2008).

Optimal Bayesian Beamforming Solution

Denote the $N_b = 4^M$ legitimate combinations of $\mathbf{b}(k)$ as $\mathbf{b}_q$, $1 \leq q \leq N_b$. The noiseless channel output $\bar{\mathbf{x}}(k)$ takes values from the vector state set

$$\bar{\mathbf{x}}(k) \in X \triangleq \{ \bar{\mathbf{x}}_q = \mathbf{P}\mathbf{b}_q, 1 \leq q \leq N_b \}. \tag{8}$$

The signal state set X can be divided into the four subsets conditioned on the value of $b_i(k)$ as follows

$$X^{[m]} \triangleq \{\bar{\mathbf{x}}_q^{[m]} \in X, 1 \le q \le N_{sb} : b_i(k) = b^{[m]}\}, \quad (9)$$

for $1 \le m \le 4$, where the size of $X^{[m]}$ is $N_{sb} = 4^{M-1}$. Denote the conditional probabilities of receiving $\mathbf{x}(k)$ given $b_i(k) = b^{[m]}$ as $p^{[m]}(\mathbf{x}(k)) = p(\mathbf{x}(k) \mid b_i(k) = b^{[m]})$. According to Bayes' decision theory (Duda & Hart, 1973), the optimal detection strategy is

$$\hat{b}_i(k) = b^{[m^*]} \quad (10)$$

where

$$m^* = \arg \max_{1 \le m \le 4} p^{[m]}(\mathbf{x}(k)). \quad (11)$$

If we introduce the following complex-valued Bayesian decision variable (Chen *et al.*, 1994a),

$$y_{\text{Bay}}(k) \triangleq \sum_{m=1}^{4} b^{[m]} \cdot p^{[m]}(\mathbf{x}(k)), \quad (12)$$

the optimal Bayesian detection rule (10) and (11) is equivalent to $\hat{b}_i(k) = \text{sgn}(y_{\text{Bay}}(k))$.

The conditional probability $p^{[m]}(\mathbf{x}(k))$, $1 \le m \le 4$, can be expressed as

$$p^{[m]}(\mathbf{x}(k)) = \sum_{q=1}^{N_{sb}} \beta_q e^{\frac{\|\mathbf{x}(k) - \bar{\mathbf{x}}_q^{[m]}\|^2}{2\sigma_n^2}}, \quad (13)$$

where $\bar{\mathbf{x}}_q^{[m]} \in X^{[m]}$, and β_q is proportional to the *a priori* probability of $\bar{\mathbf{x}}_q^{[m]}$. Since all the $\bar{\mathbf{x}}_q^{[m]}$ are equiprobable, $\beta_q = \beta = \frac{1}{N_{sb}(2\pi\sigma_n^2)^L}$.

It can be seen from (13) that the optimal Bayesian decision variable (12) takes the structure of a complex-valued RBF network (Chen *et al.*, 1994a) with a Gaussian RBF function. In fact, substituting (13) into (12) provides a physical motivation for Chen *et al.* (1994) to derive the complex-valued RBF network (1).

The state subsets $X^{[m]}$, $1 \le m \le 4$, are distributed symmetrically with respect to each other as summarised in the following lemma.

Lemma 1. The four subsets $X^{[m]}$, $1 \le m \le 4$, satisfy

$$X^{[2]} = +j \cdot X^{[1]}, X^{[3]} = -1 \cdot X^{[1]}, X^{[4]} = -j \cdot X^{[1]}. \quad (14)$$

Proof: Consider any $\bar{\mathbf{x}}_q^{[1]} = \mathbf{P}\mathbf{b}_q^{[1]} \in X^{[1]}$, where the i-th element of $\mathbf{b}_q^{[1]}$ is $b^{[1]} = +1 + j$. Noting $+j \cdot b^{[1]} = b^{[2]}$,

$$+j \cdot \bar{\mathbf{x}}_q^{[1]} = \mathbf{P}\left(+j \cdot \mathbf{b}_q^{[1]}\right) \in X^{[2]}. \quad (15)$$

This proves the first relationship in (14). The proofs of the other two relationships are similar. Given this symmetry, the optimal Bayesian solution (12) can alternatively be expressed as

$$y_{\text{Bay}}(k) = \sum_{q=1}^{N_{sb}} \left\{ b^{[1]}\beta \cdot e^{-\frac{\|\mathbf{x}(k)-\bar{\mathbf{x}}_q^{[1]}\|^2}{2\sigma_n^2}} + b^{[2]}\beta \cdot e^{-\frac{\|\mathbf{x}(k)-j\cdot\bar{\mathbf{x}}_q^{[1]}\|^2}{2\sigma_n^2}} + b^{[3]}\beta \cdot e^{-\frac{\|\mathbf{x}(k)+\bar{\mathbf{x}}_q^{[1]}\|^2}{2\sigma_n^2}} + b^{[4]}\beta \cdot e^{-\frac{\|\mathbf{x}(k)+j\cdot\bar{\mathbf{x}}_q^{[1]}\|^2}{2\sigma_n^2}} \right\}, \tag{16}$$

where $\bar{\mathbf{x}}_q^{[1]} \in X^{[1]}$. Note that the symmetric property of the Bayesian detection solution for the QPSK communication system is more complex than the simple odd symmetry of the Bayesian detection solution for the binary communication system derived in (Chen *et al.*, 2006; Chen *et al.*, 2007; Chen *et al.*, 2007a; Chen *et al.*, 2007b). Even more complicated symmetric property exists for the generic higher-order quadrature amplitude modulation (QAM) case (Chen *et al.*, 2006a). Extension to the higher-order QAM case is beyond the scope of this contribution.

CLUSTERING-BASED SYMMETRIC RBF BEAMFORMING

Consider the problem of realising the optimal Bayesian beamforming solution using a complex-valued RBF network. The symmetry of the Bayesian solution (16) should be explicitly exploited, and one way to guarantee this desired symmetry is to employ the following SRBF network for the detection of user *i* data

$$y_{\text{SRBF}}(k) = \sum_{q=1}^{N_c} \beta_q \phi(\mathbf{x}(k);\mathbf{c}_q,\rho^2), \tag{17}$$

with the decision $\hat{b}_i(k) = \text{sgn}(y_{\text{SRBF}}(k))$. Unlike the complex-valued RBF network (1), here the RBF weights β_q are real-valued and the RBF nodes' response $\phi(\mathbf{x}(k);\mathbf{c}_q,\rho^2)$ are complex-valued, defined as

$$\phi(\mathbf{x};\mathbf{c},\rho^2) = b^{[1]}\varphi(\mathbf{x};\mathbf{c},\rho^2) + b^{[2]}\varphi(\mathbf{x};j\mathbf{c},\rho^2) + b^{[3]}\varphi(\mathbf{x};-\mathbf{c},\rho^2) + b^{[4]}\varphi(\mathbf{x};-j\mathbf{c},\rho^2), \tag{18}$$

where $\varphi(\bullet;\bullet)$ is the usual real-valued radial basis function. In this study, the Gaussian function of the form

$$\varphi(\mathbf{x};\mathbf{c},\rho^2) = e^{-\frac{\|\mathbf{x}-\mathbf{c}\|^2}{2\rho^2}}. \tag{19}$$

is used. Note that the standard complex-valued RBF network (1) does not guarantee to posses the same symmetry property of the optimal Bayesian solution (16), particularly when the RBF centres $\mathbf{c}_q$ are obtained directly from the channel-impaired observation data. By contrast, the SRBF network (17) with the symmetric node structure (18) guarantees to have the same symmetry property of the optimal Bayesian solution (16).

Clustering-Based Training Algorithm

Given a set of the K training data $D_K = \{\mathbf{x}(k), d(k)\}_{k=1}^{K}$, where $d(k) = b_i(k) \in B_{\text{QPSK}}$, the task is to construct this SRBF network from the training data set D_K. Since the number of users is usually known, the number of RBF centres can be set to $N_c = N_{sb}$. To further exploit the structure of the optimal Bayesian solution (16), all the real-valued RBF weights can be set to a positive constant $\beta_q = \beta > 0$. Specific value of $\boldsymbol{\beta}$ has no influence to the detection performance. Furthermore, set the RBF variance to $\rho^2 = \hat{\sigma}_n^2$, where $\hat{\sigma}_n^2$ is an estimate of the noise variance. It is worth emphasising that the performance of the SRBF network is not sensitive to the value of $\boldsymbol{\rho}^2$ used and there exist a wide-range values of $\boldsymbol{\rho}^2$ which enable the SRBF network to approach the optimal Bayesian performance. This will further be demonstrated in the following simulation study. The insensitiveness of the SRBF network to the value of ρ^2 used is a direct consequence of the insensitiveness of the Bayesian detection solution to the value of the noise variance used. Thus, adaptation of the SRBF network (17) with the node structure (18) becomes the task of finding appropriately the RBF centre vectors c_q.

To use the channel-impaired training data D_K to directly obtain the RBF centre vectors for the SRBF network (17) and hence to approximate the optimal Bayesian solution, we propose to use a modified version of the cluster-variation assisted clustering algorithm (Chinrungrueng & Séquin, 1995; Chen, 1995). Specifically, during training, the RBF centres are adjusted according to

$$\mathbf{c}_l(k) = \mathbf{c}_l(k-1) + \mu_c M_l(\breve{\mathbf{x}}(k))(\breve{\mathbf{x}}(k) - \mathbf{c}_l(k-1)), \tag{20}$$

where

$$\breve{\mathbf{x}}(k) = \begin{cases} +1 \cdot \breve{\mathbf{x}}(k), & b_i(k) = b^{[1]}, \\ -j \cdot \breve{\mathbf{x}}(k), & b_i(k) = b^{[2]}, \\ -1 \cdot \breve{\mathbf{x}}(k), & b_i(k) = b^{[3]}, \\ +j \cdot \breve{\mathbf{x}}(k), & b_i(k) = b^{[4]}, \end{cases} \tag{21}$$

μ_c is the step size and the membership function $M_l(\mathbf{x})$ is defined as

$$M_l(\mathbf{x}) = \begin{cases} 1, & \text{if } \overline{v}_l \left\| \mathbf{x} - \mathbf{c}_l \right\|^2 \le \overline{v}_q \left\| \mathbf{x} - \mathbf{c}_q \right\|^2, \forall q \ne l, \\ 0, & \text{otherwise}, \end{cases} \tag{22}$$

with $\overline{v}_l$ being the variation of the l-th cluster. In order to estimate the associated variation $\overline{v}_l$, the following updating rule (Chinrungrueng & Séquin, 1995; Chen, 1995) is used

$$\overline{v}_l(k) = \mu_v \overline{v}_l(k-1) + (1-\mu_v) M_l(\breve{\mathbf{x}}(k)) \| \breve{\mathbf{x}}(k) - \mathbf{c}_l(k-1) \|^2, \tag{23}$$

where μ_v is a constant slightly less than 1.0 . The initial variations $\overline{v}_l(0)$, $\forall l$, are set to the same small positive number.

It is known that this cluster-variation enhanced clustering algorithm is capable of obtaining the optimal cluster partitioning structure and all the cluster variations converge to the same value (Chinrungrueng & Séquin, 1995). Specifically, in our particular application, the RBF centre vectors $\mathbf{c}_q$ converge to the noise-free signal states $\overline{\mathbf{x}}_q^{[1]}$ and all the cluster variations converge to the noise variance $2\sigma_n^2$.

Simulation Study

A simulation study was carried out to investigate performance of the proposed clustering-based SRBF network in nonlinear beamforming application.

Example One. The system employed a two-element antenna array to support three QPSK users. Figure 1 depicts the angular positions of the three users with respect to the antenna array. The simulated narrowband channels were $A_i = 1 + j0, 1 \le i \le 3$, and all the three users had an equal power. Thus all the SIRs were 0 dB. First, we demonstrated the performance improvement achievable by the optimal nonlinear beamforming over the optimal linear one, when the system's channel matrix **P** and the noise statistics σ_n^2 were known. Figure 2 compares the BER performance of the Bayesian beamforming and the L-MBER beamforming. As expected, the Bayesian beamforming achieved much better BER performance over the optimal linear beamforming. This performance gain was of course obtained at the cost of an increased complexity. From Figure 2, it can be seen that the performance of the individual linear beamformer depended on the particular user's angular position as well as the other users' locations. For user 3, the underlying system was not linearly separable and hence the L-MBER beamformer exhibits a high error floor. By contrast, all the three Bayesian beamformers had the similar performance, as a nonlinear beamformer can operate successfully even in the linearly nonseparable senario. Because of this remarkable robustness property, we only concentrated on the user one when investigating the SRBF beamforming.

The clustering-based SRBF beamforming for user one was then studied. For this example, the number of the subset channel states was $N_{sb} = 16$, and we used the first 16 data points $\mathbf{x}(k)$, $1 \le k \le 16$, as the initial RBF centres. The initial cluster variations were set to $\overline{v}_l(0) = 0.02$ for $1 \le l \le N_{sb}$, and the adaptive constant for updating the cluster variations was chosen to be $\mu_v = 0.995$. Note that the general rule is that all the initial cluster variations $\overline{v}_l(0)$ should be set to the same small positive number and μ_v should be set to a constant slightly less than 1.0. Convergence performance of the cluster-variation enhanced clustering algorithm was assessed in the simulation based on the Euclidean distance between the set of the RBF centres $\{\mathbf{c}_l\}_{l=1}^{N_{sb}}$ and the set of the true subset channel states $\{\overline{\mathbf{x}}_l^{[1]}\}_{l=1}^{N_{sb}}$ defined as

$$\mathrm{ED}(k) = \frac{1}{N_{sb}} \sum_{l=1}^{N_{sb}} \| \mathbf{c}_l(k) - \overline{\mathbf{x}}_l^{[1]} \|^2 . \tag{24}$$

Given SNR = 20 dB, Figure 3 plots the learning curves of the clustering algorithm in terms of the Euclidean distance (24) averaged over 10 different random runs for the three values of the adaptive gain μ_c. It is seen from Figure 3 that for this example the best convergence performance was achieved with $\mu_c = 0.2$. The robustness of the clustering-based adaptive SRBF beamforming with respect to the value of the RBF variance ρ^2 used is demonstrated in Figure 4, where it can be seen that there exist a wide-ranging values of the RBF variance ρ^2 for the clustering-based SRBF network to achieve the Bayesian beamforming performance. Figure 5 compares the BER performance of the clustering-based adaptive SRBF beamformer for user one after convergence with that of the Bayesian beamformer, given the RBF variance $\rho^2 = \sigma_n^2$.

Example Two. A three-element antenna array was designed to support four QPSK users. Figure 6 shows the angular positions of the four users with respect to the antenna array. The simulated narrowband channels were $A_i = 1 + j0$ for $1 \le i \le 4$, and all the four users had the same power. Figure 7 demonstrates the BER performance improvement achievable by the Bayesian beamforming over the L-MBER beamforming. Again, the robustness of the Bayesian beamforming is clearly shown in Figure 7, where it can be seen that all the four Byesian beamformers had the similar performance.

Figure 1. Angular locations of the three QPSK users with respect to the two-element linear antenna array having $\lambda/2$ spacing, where λ is the wavelength

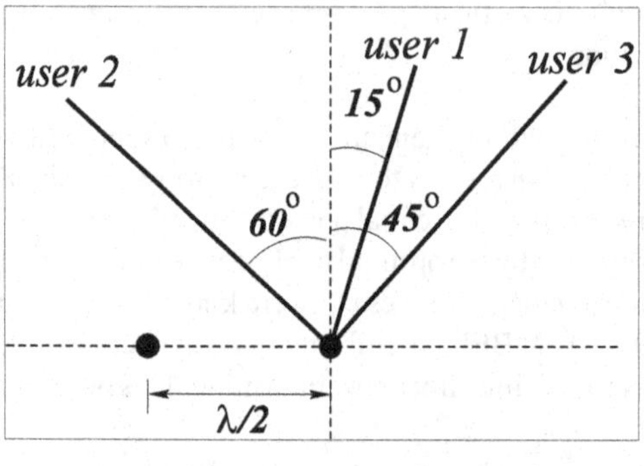

Figure 2. BER performance comparison of the optimal nonlinear beamforming with the optimal linear beamforming, for the two-element array system supporting three QPSK users

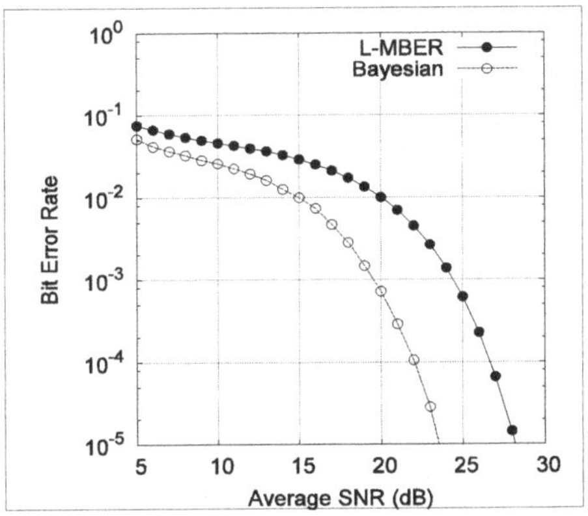

(a) user 1

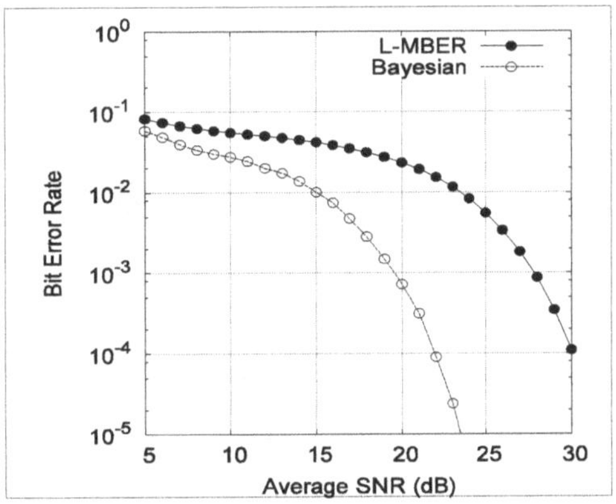

(b) user 2

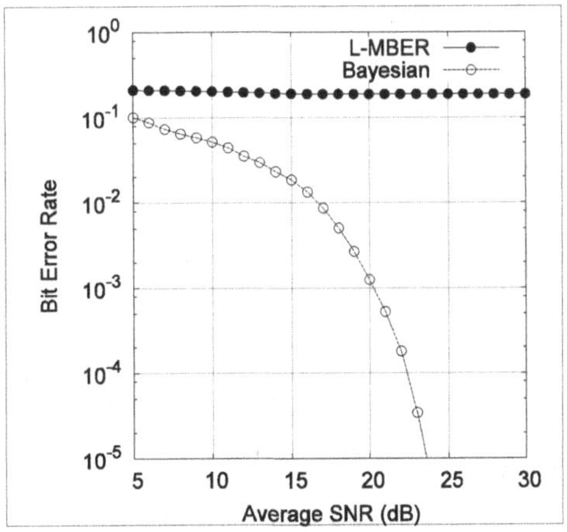

(c) user 3

The clustering-based SRBF beamforming for user one was investigated. Note that the number of the subset channel states in this case was $N_{sb} = 64$ and, therefore, the first 64 data points $\mathbf{x}(k)$, $1 \le k \le 64$, were used as the initial RBF centres. The initial cluster variations were all set to $\overline{v}_l(0) = 0.1$ for $1 \le l \le N_{sb}$, and the adaptive constant for updating the cluster variations was set to $\mu_v = 0.995$. Figure 8 depicts the learning curves of the clustering algorithm in terms of the Euclidean distance (24) averaged over 10 different random runs for the three values of the adaptive gain μ_c, given SNR=7 dB. It is seen that for this example the best convergence performance was achieved with $\mu_c = 0.4$. Given SNR=7 dB, Figure 9 illustrates the influence of the RBF variance ρ^2 to the BER performance of the clustering-based SRBF network, where it was demonstrated again that there existed a wide-ranging values of ρ^2 which enabled the clustering-based SRBF network to approach the Bayesian performance. Finally, Figure 10 depicts the BER performance of the clustering-based SRBF beamformer for user one after convergence, given the RBF variance $\rho^2 = \sigma_n^2$, in comparison with the Bayesian benchmark.

Figure 3. Learning curves of the cluster algorithm for user one of the two-element array system supporting three QPSK users, in terms of Euclidean distance between the RBF centres and true channel states averaged over ten runs, given SNR =20 dB.

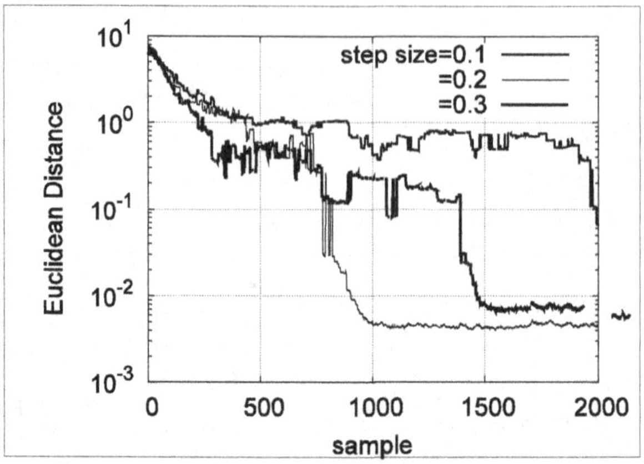

Figure 4. Influence of the RBF variance on the BER performance of the clustering-based SRBF beamformer for user one of the two-element array system supporting three QPSK users, given SNR =20 dB

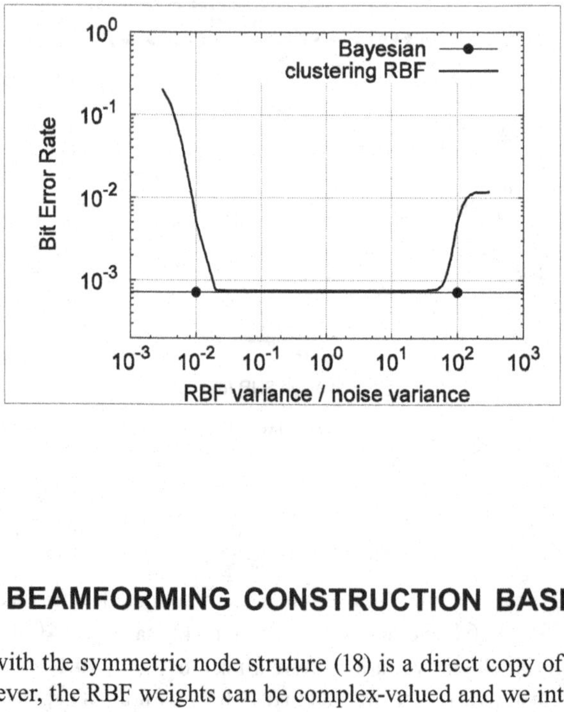

SYMMETRIC RBF BEAMFORMING CONSTRUCTION BASED ON OFS

The SRBF network (17) with the symmetric node struture (18) is a direct copy of the Bayesian detection solution (16). In general, however, the RBF weights can be complex-valued and we introduce the following generic complex-valued SRBF network

$$y_{\mathrm{SRBF}}(k) = \sum_{q=1}^{N_c} w_q \phi(\mathbf{x}(k); \mathbf{c}_q, \rho^2), \tag{25}$$

where w_q are complex-valued RBF weights and the complex-valued RBF nodes' response $\phi(\mathbf{x}(k); \mathbf{c}_q, \rho^2)$ are defined by (18). Thus, this more general complex-valued RBF network also guarantees to process the desired

Figure 5. User-one BER performance of the clustering-based SRBF beamformer for the two-element array system supporting three QPSK users, given $\rho^2 = \sigma_n^2$, in comparison with the Bayesian beamforming performance.

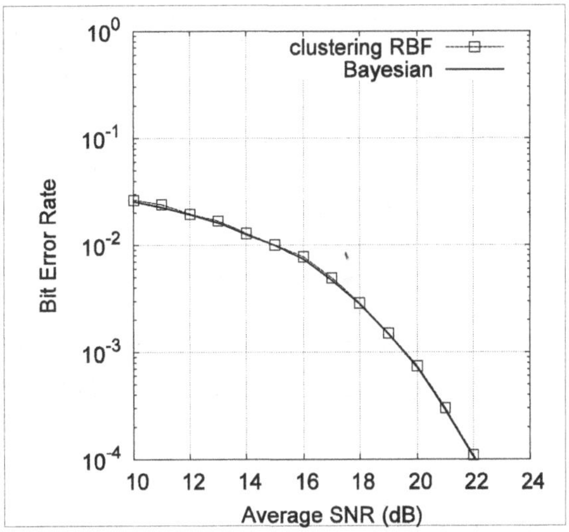

Figure 6. Angular locations of the four QPSK users with respect to the three-element linear antenna array having $\lambda/2$ spacing, where λ is the wavelength

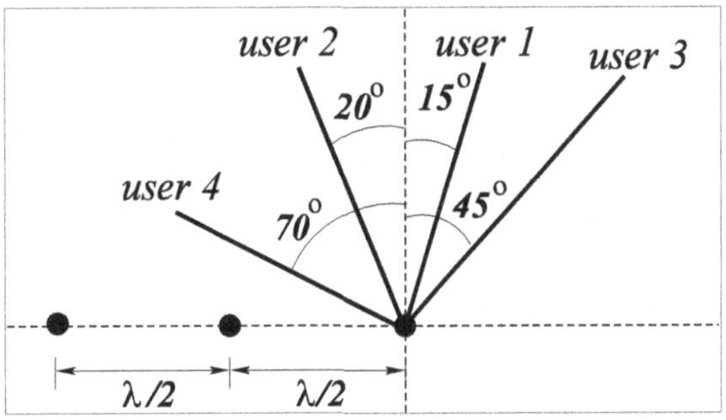

symmetric property. Given the training data set $D_K = \{\mathbf{x}(k), d(k)\}_{k=1}^{K}$, where $d(k) = b_i(k) \in B_{\text{QPSK}}$, we now present an efficient algorithm for constructing this complex-valued SRBF network.

OFS Based on Fisher Ratio of Class Separability Measure

Consider using every data points as candidate RBF centres, namely, setting $N_c = K$ and $\mathbf{c}_q = \mathbf{x}(q)$ for $1 \le q \le K$. Further assume that the value of the RBF variance ρ^2 is specified. Let us define the modelling residual for $\mathbf{x}(k) \in D_K$ as $e(k) = d(k) - y_{\text{SRBF}}(k)$ and introduce the notation $\phi_{k,q} = \phi(\mathbf{x}(k); \mathbf{c}_q, \rho^2)$. Then the regression model over the data set D_K is expressed as

$$\mathbf{d} = \boldsymbol{\Phi}\,\mathbf{w} + \mathbf{e}, \qquad (26)$$

Figure 7. BER performance comparison of the optimal nonlinear beamforming with the optimal linear beamforming, for the three-element array system supporting four QPSK users.

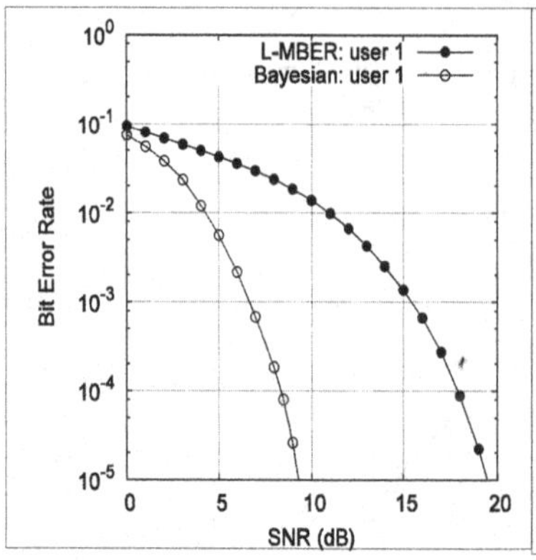

(a) user 1

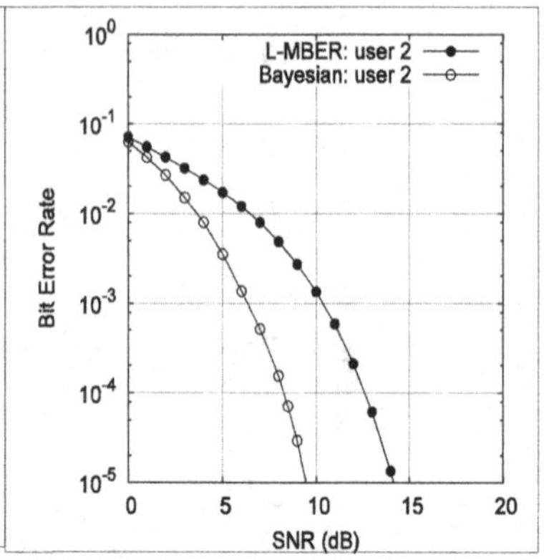

(b) user 2

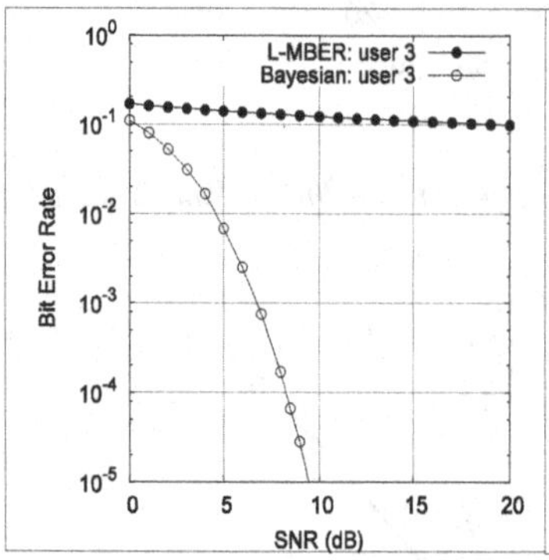

(c) user 3

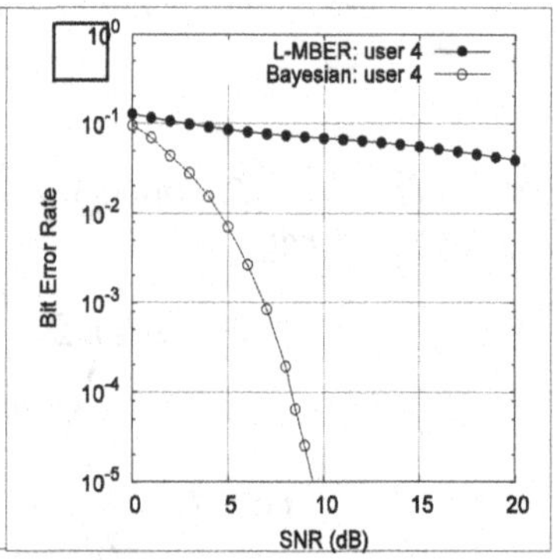

(d) user 4

Figure 8. Learning curves of the cluster algorithm for user one of the three-element array system supporting four QPSK users, in terms of Euclidean distance between the RBF centres and true channel states averaged over ten runs, given SNR=7 dB.

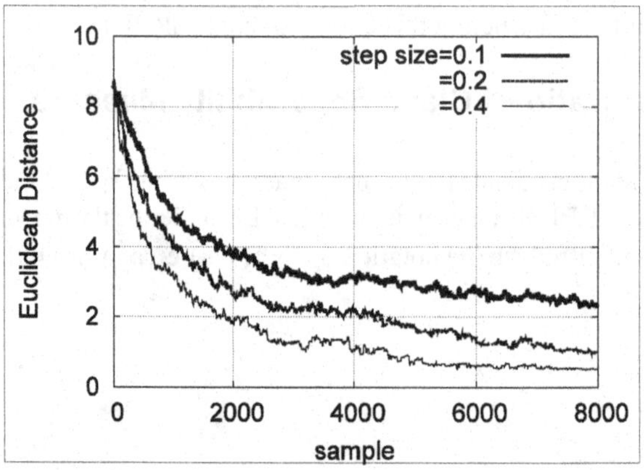

Figure 9. Influence of the RBF variance on the BER performance of the clustering-based SRBF beamformer for user one of the three-element array system supporting four QPSK users, given SNR=7 dB

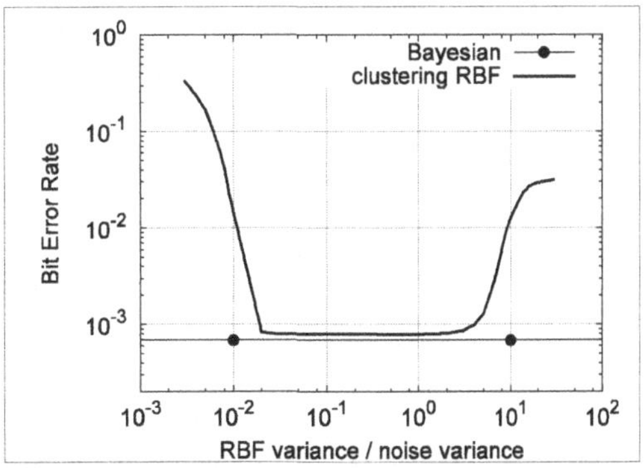

Figure 10. User-one BER performance of the clustering-based SRBF beamformer for the three-element array system supporting four QPSK users, given $\rho^2 = \sigma_n^2$, in comparison with the Bayesian beamforming performance.

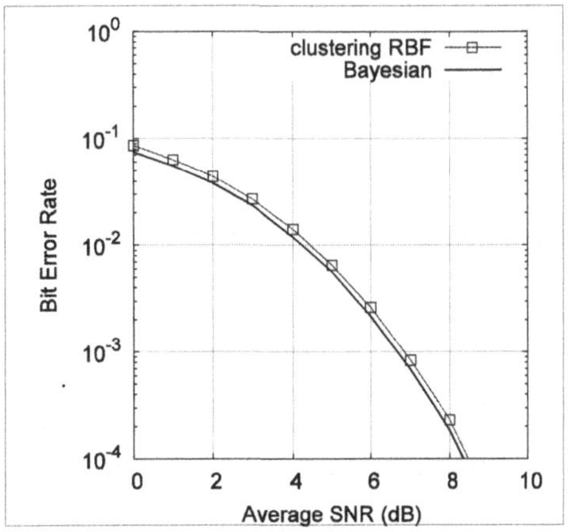

where $\mathbf{d} = [d(1)\ d(2) \cdots d(K)]^T$, $\mathbf{w} = [w_1\ w_2 \cdots w_K]^T$, $\mathbf{e} = [e(1)\ e(2) \cdots e(K)]^T$, and the complex-valued regression matrix

$$\Phi = [\phi_1\ \phi_2 \cdots \phi_K] \tag{27}$$

with columns $\phi_q = [\phi_{1,q}\ \phi_{2,q} \cdots \phi_{K,q}]^T$. Let an orthogonal decomposition of Φ be $\Phi = \mathbf{UA}$, where

$$\mathbf{A} = \begin{bmatrix} 1 & a_{1,2} & \cdots & a_{1,K} \\ 0 & 1 & \ddots & \vdots \\ \vdots & \ddots & \ddots & \alpha_{K-1,K} \\ 0 & \cdots & 0 & 1 \end{bmatrix} \tag{28}$$

with complex-valued $\alpha_{q,l}$, $1 \le q < l \le K$, and the complex-valued orthogonal matrix

$$\mathbf{U} = [\mathbf{u}_1\ \mathbf{u}_2 \cdots \mathbf{u}_K] = \begin{bmatrix} u_{1,1} & u_{1,2} & \cdots & u_{1,K} \\ u_{2,1} & u_{2,2} & \cdots & u_{2,K} \\ \vdots & \vdots & \cdots & \vdots \\ u_{K,1} & w_{K,2} & \cdots & w_{K,K} \end{bmatrix} \tag{29}$$

with columns satisfying $\mathbf{u}_q^H \mathbf{u}_l = 0$, if $q \ne l$. The regression model (26) can alternatively be expressed as

$$\mathbf{d} = \mathbf{U}\,\mathbf{g} + \mathbf{e}, \tag{30}$$

where the weight vector $\mathbf{g} = [g_1\ g_2 \cdots g_K]^T$ defined in the orthogonal model space satisfies the following triangular system $\mathbf{Aw} = \mathbf{g}$.

Recall that the output of the complex-valued SRBF network is used to provide an estimate for $d(k)$ according to the decision rule $\hat{d}(k) = \mathrm{sgn}(y_{\mathrm{SRBF}}(k))$. Since $d(k) \in B_{\mathrm{QPSK}}$, this is a four-class classification problem. Let us first divide the training feature vectors $\mathbf{X} = \{\mathbf{x}(k)\}_{k=1}^{K}$ into the four classes

$$\mathbf{X}^{[i]} \triangleq \{\mathbf{x}(k) \in \mathbf{X} : d(k) = b^{[i]}\}, 1 \le i \le 4. \tag{31}$$

Assume that the number of samples in $\mathbf{X}^{[i]}$ is $K^{[i]}$. Obviously

$$\sum_{i=1}^{4} K^{[i]} = K. \tag{32}$$

Define furthermore the mean and variance of samples belonging to class $\mathbf{X}^{[i]}$ in the direction of basis $\mathbf{u}_l$ as $m_{i,l}$ and $\sigma_{i,l}^2$, respectively, which are calculated according to

$$m_{i,l} = \frac{1}{K^{[i]}} \sum_{k=1}^{K} \delta\left(d(k) - b^{[i]}\right) u_{k,l} \tag{33}$$

and

$$\sigma_{i,l}^2 = \frac{1}{K^{[i]}} \sum_{k=1}^{K} \delta\left(d(k) - b^{[i]}\right)\left(u_{k,l} - m_{i,l}\right)^2, \tag{34}$$

where the indicator function

$$\delta(x) = \begin{cases} 1, & x = 0 + j0, \\ 0, & x \ne 0 + j0. \end{cases} \tag{35}$$

Denote the Fisher ratio of the class separation between classes $\mathbf{X}^{[i]}$ and $\mathbf{X}^{[q]}$ in the direction of basis $\mathbf{u}_l$ as $F_{i,q,l}$ Fisher ratio is defined as the ratio of the interclass difference to the intraclass spread (Duda & Hart, 1973)

$$F_{i,q,l} = \frac{\left(m_{i,l} - m_{q,l}\right)^2}{\left(\sigma_{i,l}^2 + \sigma_{q,l}^2\right)}. \quad (36)$$

Fisher ratio provides a good class separability measure because its maximisation leads to the interclass difference being maximised and the intraclass spread being minimised.

Because the problem is a four-class classification one, we define the average Fisher ratio of the class separation in the direction of basis $\mathbf{u}_l$ as

$$F_l = \frac{1}{6}\sum_{i=1}^{3}\sum_{q=i+1}^{4} F_{i,q,l}. \quad (37)$$

Based on this average Fisher ratio, significant RBF nodes or regressors can be selected in an OFS procedure, just as in the case of two-class problems (Mao, 2002; Chen et al., 2004). Specifically, at the l-th stage of the OFS procedure, a regressor is chosen as the l-th term in the selected complex-valued SRBF network if it produces the largest F_l among the candidates terms, $\mathbf{u}_q$, $l \le q \le K$. The procedure is terminated with a sparse n_c-node network when

$$\frac{F_{n_c}}{\sum_{l=1}^{n_c} F_l} \le \xi, \quad (38)$$

where the threshold ξ determines the sparsity of the selected network model. The detailed OFS procedure based on the four-class FRCSM is summarised in Appendix. The least squares (LS) solution for the corresponding sparse model weight vector $\mathbf{w}_{n_c} = [w_1\ w_2 \cdots w_{n_c}]^T$ is readily available from $\mathbf{A}_{n_c}\mathbf{w}_{n_c} = \mathbf{g}_{n_c}$, given the LS solution of $\mathbf{g}_{n_c}$. In general, a desired value for the threshold ξ has to be determined via cross validation. However, in our particular application to nonlinear beamforming for multiple-antenna aided communication systems, we can simply set $n_c = N_{sb}$. Thus, in this particular application, we do not need to employ costly cross validation to determine the model size.

Simulation Study

A simulation study involving the two same examples used in the previous section was performed to investigate the multi-class FRCSM-based OFS algorithm for constructing the complex-valued SRBF network (25).

Example One. This was the same two-element array system supporting three QPSK users with the users' angular positions shown in Figure 1. Constructing the complex-valued SRBF network (25) for user one was first considered using the multi-class FRCSM-based OFS algorithm. Given each SNR value, a training set of $K = 200$ samples was generated. For this example, $N_{sb} = 16$ and, therefore, we stopped the selection procedure after choosing $n_c = 16$ nodes. Unlike the clustering-based SRBF network, the RBF variance ρ^2 has important influence on the BER performance. The value of the RBF variance ρ^2, therefore, was determined using cross validation, and appropriate values were found in the range of $[0.2, 2.0]$ depending on the SNR value and noise realisation in the training data. The BER performance of the 16-term complex-valued SRBF beamformer obtained by the multi-class FRCSM-based OFS algorithm is plotted in Figure 11, in comparison with the Bayesian and theoretic L-MBER benchmarks. It is surprising to see that the 16-term complex-valued SRBF network outperformed the Bayesian detector. A possible explanation is as follows. The Bayesian solution is derived under the assumption of white noise $\mathbf{n}(k)$. In the simulation, the noise was slightly colourred. Note that the weights of the SRBF network (25) are complex-valued. Therefor, a 16-term complex-valued SRBF network has a larger model size than the Bayesian solution (whose weights are real-valued). This doubled model size might have allowed the complex-valued

SRBF network to exploit the noise statistics in the training data better. The influence of the RBF variance ρ^2 to the performance of the OFS-based SRBF network is demonstrated in Figure 12, given SNR=16 dB.

The beamforming for detecting the user-three data was also considered. For each SNR value, a training data set consisting of $K = 200$ samples was used to construct a 16-term complex-valued SRBF network using the multi-class FRCSM-based OFS, and the BER performance of the resulting SRBF beamformer is depicted in Figure 13, together with the Bayesian and theoretic L-MBER bermforming benchmarks. Again the value of the RBF variance was determined via cross validation, and appropriate values were found in the range of $[1.6, 2.0]$, depending on the SNR value. Detection of user-three data was a more difficult task than detection of user-one data as the former was a nonlinearly separable problem. It can be seen from Figure 13 that the performance of the 16-term complex-valued SRBF network was indistinguishable from that of the Bayesian beamformer.

Example Two. The same three-element array system was used to support the same four QPSK users which had the users' angular positions as shown in Figure 6. Detection of users one and four was considered. For user one, the underlying system was linearly separable, while for user four it was a more difficult nonlinearly separable problem. Given each SNR value, a training set of $K = 600$ samples was generated to construct the complex-val-

Figure 11. User-one BER performance of the OFS-based SRBF beamformer for the two-element array system supporting three QPSK users, in comparison with the Bayesian and theoretic L-MBER beamforming performance.

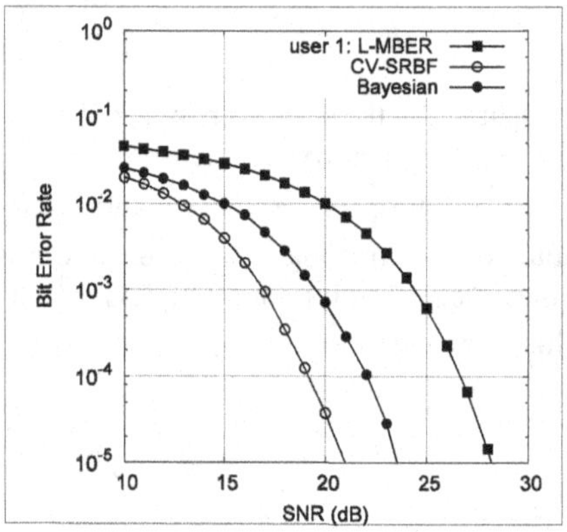

Figure 12. Influence of the RBF variance on the BER performance of the OFS-based SRBF beamformer for user one of the two-element array system supporting three QPSK users, given SNR=16 dB.

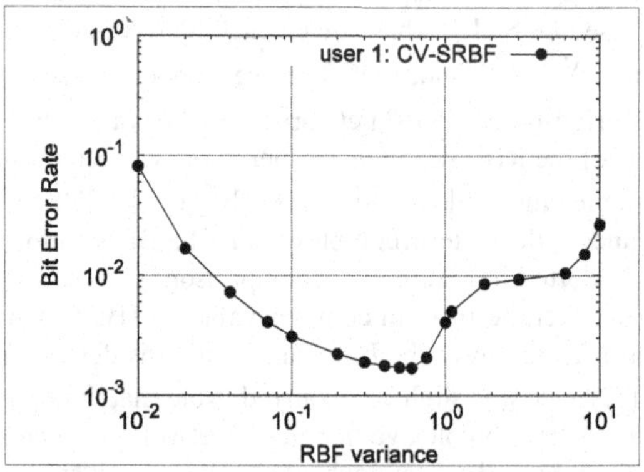

Figure 13. User-three BER performance of the OFS-based SRBF beamformer for the two-element array system supporting three QPSK users, in comparison with the Bayesian and theoretic L-MBER beamforming performance.

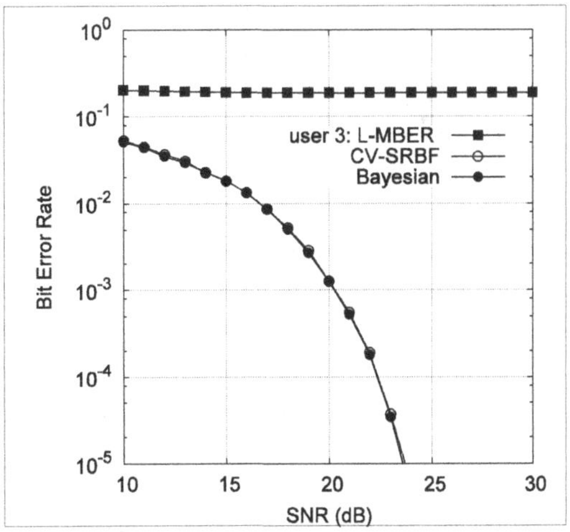

ued SRBF network (25) using the multi-class FRCSM-based OFS algorithm. Because $N_{sb} = 64$, we terminated the selection procedure after choosing $n_c = 64$ nodes. The value of the RBF variance ρ^2 was determined using cross validation.

For user one, appropriate values of ρ^2 were found in the range of $[0.6, 2.0]$, depending on the SNR value, and the BER performance of the resulting 64-term complex-valued SRBF beamformer is depicted in Figure 14, in comparison with the two benchmarks. The influence of the RBF variance ρ^2 to the performance of the 64-term complex-valued SRBF network for user one is illustrated in Figure 15, given SNR=6 dB. The beamforming for detecting the user-4 data was demonstrated in Figure 16, where the BER performance of the 64-term complex-valued SRBF network constructed by the multi-class FRCSM-based OFS was compared with the two benchmarks.

CONCLUSION

A grey-box approach has been adopted to complex-valued RBF modelling in this constribution. By exploiting the inherent symmetry of the Bayesian beamforming solution for multiple-antenna aided QPSK wireless systems, a complex-valued SRBF network has been proposed for adaptive nonlinear beamforming. Two SRBF network structures have been proposed. The first SRBF network architecture has real-valued RBF weights and the desired complex-valued symmetric nodes' response, just as the Bayesian detection solution, and therefore it is a direct carbon-copy of the Bayesian solution. A modified version of the cluster-variation enhanced clustering algorithm has been derived to implement this SRBF network. The second SRBF network architecture is more general. Unlike the first SRBF network structure, it has complex-valued RBF weights, while maintaining the desired complex-valued symmetric nodes' response. A multi-class FRCSM-based OFS algorithm has been proposed to construct the sparse model for this complex-valued SRBF network.

Although the proposed complex-valued SRBF network is presented in the context of nonlinear detection in QPSK communication systems, it is generically applicable to other classification problems having similar symmetric properties. An important message from this study is that one should always incorporate available a priori information in data modelling applications.

Figure 14. User-one BER performance of the OFS-based SRBF beamformer for the three-element array system supporting four QPSK users, in comparison with the Bayesian and theoretic L-MBER beamforming performance

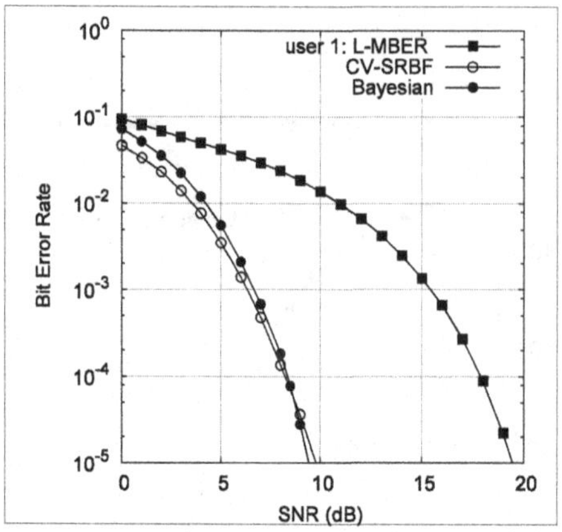

Figure 15. Influence of the RBF variance on the BER performance of the OFS-based SRBF beamformer for user one of the three-element array system supporting four QPSK users, given SNR=6 dB

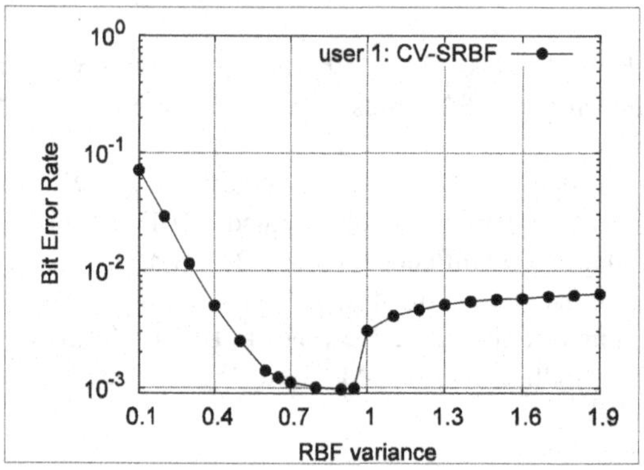

Figure 16. User-four BER performance of the OFS-based SRBF beamformer for the three-element array system supporting four QPSK users, in comparison with the Bayesian and theoretic L-MBER beamforming performance.

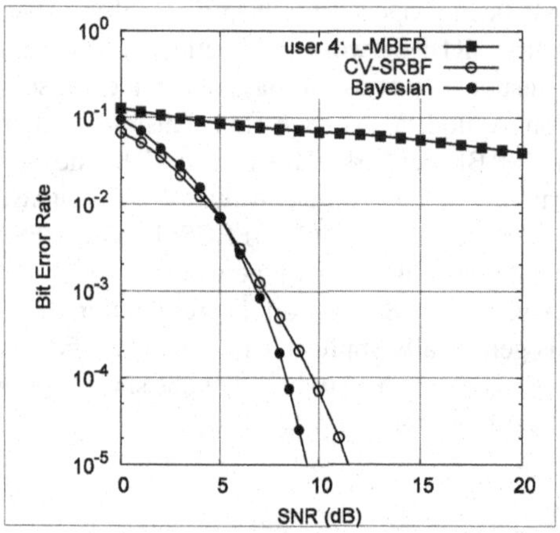

FUTURE RESEARCH DIRECTIONS

Like other complex-valued neural network models, the standard complex-valued RBF network is a black-box model that does not exploit any *a priori* information exists regarding the underlying data generating mechanism. Grey-box approach that explicitly incorporates known knowledge of the system to be modelled is much desired, as it is capable of substantially improving modelling performance. How to adopt *a priori* information into the structure or architecture of complex-valued RBF network, however, is highly problem dependent. In this contribution, we have demonstrated how to modify the architecture of complex-valued RBF network so that the data modelling process guarantees capturing the known symmetric properties of the underlying data generating mechanism. Although we have developed this novel symmetric complex-valued RBF structure in the context of classification applications, the same idea is equally applicable to regression application. Consider for example modelling a system or function from noisy observation data. Let us assume that the function is known to have some symmetric property. A black-box neural network modelled from data may not capture this symmetric property well, while a grey-box model that explicitly incorporates this symmetric property in its topology will guarantee to capture this symmetric property, despite of the presence of noise in data. Another common *a priori* information existed in many data modelling problems is manifested as boundary value constraints. Standard neural network models have difficulties in this type of data modelling problems. For real-valued data modelling problems, Hong and Chen (2008) have recently developed a novel topology of RBF network, which is able to automatically satisfy a set of boundary value constraints and yet maintains the efficiency of the original RBF modelling procedure. It is of great practical interests to extend this novel RBF topology to the complex-valued domain. Another interesting extension of the present work is to investigate how to adopting *a priori* information in other complex-valued neural network architectures.

REFERENCES

Acir, N., Oztura, I., Kuntalp, M., Baklan, B., & Guzelis, C. (2005). Automatic detection of epileptiform events in EEG by a three-stage procedure based on artificial neural networks. *IEEE Trans. Biomedical Engineering,* (1), 30–40.

Aguirre, L. A., Lopes, R. A. M., Amaral, G. F. V., & Letellier, C. (2004). Constraining the topology of neural networks to ensure dynamics with symmetry properties. *Physical Review E*, 026701-1–026701-11.

An, P. E., Brown, M., Chen, S., & Harris, C. J. (1993). Comparative aspects of neural network algorithms for on-line modelling of dynamic processes. *Proc. I. MECH. E., Pt.I, J. Systems and Control Eng.*, 223–241.

Blogh, J. S., & Hanzo, L. (2002). *Third Generation Systems and Intelligent Wireless Networking – Smart Antennas and Adaptive Modulation.* Chichester, UK: Wiley.

Botoca, C., & Budura, G. (2006, June 12-14). Symbol decision equalizer using a radial basis functions neural network. In *Proc. 7th WSEAS Int. Conf. Neural Networks* (Cavtat, Croatia), (pp.79–84).

Broomhead, D. S., & Lowe, D. (1988). Multivariable functional interpolation and adaptive networks. *Complex Systems*, (2), 321–355.

Caiti, A., & Parisini, T. (1994). Mapping ocean sediments by RBF networks. *IEEE J. Oceanic Engineering*, (4), 577–582.

Cha, I., & Kassam, S. A. (1995). Channel equalization using adaptive complex radial basis function networks. *IEEE J. Selected Areas in Communications*, (1), 122–131.

Cha, I., & Kassam, S. A. (1996). RBFN restoration of nonlinearly degraded images. *IEEE Trans. Image Processing*, (6), 964–975.

Chen, S., Billings, S. A., & Luo, W. (1989). Orthogonal least squares methods and their application to non-linear system identification. *Int. J. Control*, (5), 1873–1896.

Chen, S., Billings, S. A., Cowan, C. F. N., & Grant, P. M. (1990). Non-linear systems identification using radial basis functions. *Int. J. Systems Sci.*, (12), 2513–2539.

Chen, S., Cowan, C. F. N., Billings, S. A., & Grant, P. M. (1990a). Parallel recursive prediction error algorithm for training layered neural networks. *Int. J. Control*, (6), 1215–1228.

Chen, S., Cowan, C. F. N., & Grant, P. M. (1991). Orthogonal least squares learning algorithm for radial basis function networks. *IEEE Trans. Neural Networks*, (2), 302–309.

Chen, S., Billings, S. A., & Grant, P. M. (1992). Recursive hybrid algorithm for non-linear system identification using radial basis function networks. *Int. J. Control*, (5), 1051–1070.

Chen, S., Mulgrew, B., & Grant, P. M. (1993). A clustering technique for digital communications channel equalization using radial basis function networks. *IEEE Trans. Neural Networks*, (4), 570–579.

Chen, S., McLaughlin, S., & Mulgrew, B. (1994). Complex-valued radial basis function network, Part I: network architecture and learning algorithms. *Signal Processing*, (1), 19–31.

Chen, S., McLaughlin, S., & Mulgrew, B. (1994a). Complex-valued radial basis function network, Part II: application to digital communications channel equalisation. *Signal Processing*, (2), 175–188.

Chen, S. (1995). Nonlinear time series modelling and prediction using Gaussian RBF networks with enhanced clustering and RLS learning. *Electronics Letters*, (2), 117–118.

Chen, S., Wu, Y., & Luk, B. L. (1999). Combined genetic algorithm optimisation and regularised orthogonal least squares learning for radial basis function networks. *IEEE Trans. Neural Networks*, (5), 1239–1243.

Chen, S., Hong, X., & Harris, C. J. (2003). Sparse kernel regression modelling using combined locally regularized orthogonal least squares and D-optimality experimental design. *IEEE Trans. Automatic Control*, (6), 1029–1036.

Chen, S., Hanzo, L., & Wolfgang, A. (2004). Kernel-based nonlinear beamforming construction using orthogonal forward selection with Fisher ratio class separability measure. *IEEE Signal Processing Letters*, (5), 478–481.

Chen, S., Hong, X., Harris, C. J., & Sharkey, P. M. (2004a). Sparse modelling using orthogonal forward regression with PRESS statistic and regularization. *IEEE Trans. Systems, Man and Cybernetics, Part B*, (2), 898–911.

Chen, S., Hanzo, L., Ahmad, N. N., & Wolfgang, A. (2005). Adaptive minimum bit error rate beamforming assisted receiver for QPSK wireless communication. *Digital Signal Processing*, (6), 545–567.

Chen, S., Wolfgang, A., Benedetto, S., Dubamet, P., & Hanzo, L. (2006, Sept. 20-22). Symmetric radial basis function network equaliser. In *Proc. NEWCOM-ACoRN Joint Workshop* (Vienna, Austria),.

Chen, S., Du, H.-Q., & Hanzo, L. (2006a). Adaptive minimum symbol error rate beamforming assisted receiver for quadrature amplitude modulation systems. In *Proc. VTC2006-Spring* (Melbourne, Australia), May 7-10, 2006, (pp. 2236-2240).

Chen, S., Labib, K., Kang, R., & Hanzo, L. (2007, June 24-28). Adaptive radial basis function detector for beamforming. In *Proc. ICC 2007* (Glasgow, Scotland), (pp. 2967-2972).

Chen, S., Labib, K., & Hanzo, L. (2007a). Clustering-based symmetric radial basis function beamforming. *IEEE Signal Processing Letters*, (9), 589-592.

Chen, S., Wolfgang, A., Harris, C. J., & Hanzo, L. (2007b, August 12-17). Symmetric kernel detector for multiple-antenna aided beamforming systems. In *Proc. IJCNN 2007* (Orlando, USA), (pp. 2486–2491).

Chen, S., Hanzo, L., & Tan, S. (2008, May 19-23). Nonlinear beamforming for multiple-antenna assisted QPSK wireless systems. In *Proc. ICC 2008* (Beijing, China).

Chinrungrueng, C., & Séquin, C. H. (1995). Optimal adaptive k-means algorithm with dynamic adjustment of learning rate. *IEEE Trans. Neural Networks*, (1), 1873–1896.

Deng, J., Sundararajan, N., & Saratchandran, P. (2002). Communication channel equalization using complex-valued minimal radial basis function neural networks. *IEEE Trans. Neural Networks*, (3), 687–696.

Duda, R. O., & Hart, P. E. (1973). *Pattern Classification and Scene Analysis*. New York: Wiley.

Espinoza, M., Suykens, J. A. K., & De Moor, B. (2005, Dec.12-15). Imposing symmetry in least squares support vector machines regression. In *Proc. Joint 44th IEEE Conf. Decision and Control, and European Control Conf. 2005* (Seville, Spain), (pp. 5716–5721).

Gan, Q., Saratchandran, P., Sundararajan, N., & Subramanian, K. R. (1999). A complex valued radial basis function network for equalization of fast time varying channels. *IEEE Trans. Neural Networks*, (4), 958–960.

Gonzalez, J., Rojas, I., Ortega, J., Pomares, H., Fernandez, F. J., & Diaz, A. F. (2003). Multiobjective evolutionary optimization of the size, shape, and position parameters of radial basis function networks for function approximation. *IEEE Trans. Neural Networks*, (6), 1478–1495.

Gorinevsky, D., Kapitanovsky, A., & Goldenberg, A. (1996). Radial basis function network architecture for nonholonomic motion planning and control of free-flying manipulators. *IEEE Trans. Robotics and Automation*, (3), 491–496.

Hirose, A. (2006). *Complex-Valued Neural Networks*. Berlin: Springer.

Karayiannis, N. B., & Randolph-Gips, M. M. (2003). On the construction and training of reformulated radial basis function neural networks. *IEEE Trans. Neural Networks*, (4), 835–846.

Kim, T., & Adali, T. (2003). Approximation by fully complex multilayer perceptrons. *Neural Computation*, (7), 1641–1666.

Lee, M.-J., & Choi, Y.-K. (2004). An adaptive neurocontroller using RBFN for robot manipulators. *IEEE Trans. Industrial Electronics*, (3), 711–717.

Leonard, J. A., & Kramer, M. A. (1991). Radial basis function networks for classifying process faults. *IEEE Control Systems Magazine*, (3), 31–38.

Li, M.-B., Huang, G.-B., Saratchandran, P., & Sundararajan, N. (2005). Fully complex extreme learning machine. *Neurocomputing*, (68), 306–314.

Li, Y., Sundararajan, N., Saratchandran, P., & Wang, Z. (2004). Robust neuro-H_∞ controller design for aircraft auto-landing. *IEEE Trans. Aerospace and Electronic Systems*, (1), 158–167.

Litva, J., & Lo, T. K. Y. (1996). *Digital Beamforming in Wireless Communications*. London: Artech House.

Mak, M.-W., & Kung, S.-Y. (2000). Estimation of elliptical basis function parameters by the EM algorithm with application to speaker verification. *IEEE Trans. Neural Networks*, (4), 961–969.

Mao, K. Z. (2002). RBF neural network center selection based on Fisher ratio class separability measure. *IEEE Trans. Neural Networks*, (5), 1211–1217.

McLoone, S., Brown, M. D., Irwin, G., & Lightbody, A. (1998). A hybrid linear/nonlinear training algorithm for feedforward neural networks. *IEEE Trans. Neural Networks*, (4), 669–684.

Moody, J., & Darken, C. J. (1989). Fast-learning in networks of locally-tuned processing units. *Neural Computation*, (2), 281–294.

Mukai, R., Vilnrotter, V. A., Arabshahi, P., & Jamnejad, V. (2002). Adaptive acquisition and tracking for deep space array feed antennas. *IEEE Trans. Neural Networks*, (5), 1149–1162.

Muraki, S., Nakai, T., Kita, Y., & Tsuda, K. (2001). An attempt for coloring multichannel MR imaging data. *IEEE Trans. Visualization and Computer Graphics*, (3), 265–274.

Ng, S. X., Yee, M.-S., & Hanzo, L. (2004). Coded modulation assisted radial basis function aided turbo equalization for dispersive Rayleigh-fading channels. *IEEE Trans. Wireless Communications*, (6), 2198–2206.

Oyang, Y.-J., Hwang, S.-C., Ou, Y.-Y., Chen, C.-Y., & Chen, Z. W. (2005). Data classification with radial basis function networks based on a novel kernel density estimation algorithm. *IEEE Trans. Neural Networks*, (1), 225–236.

Paulraj, A., Nabar, R., & Gore, D. (2003). *Introduction to Space-Time Wireless Communications*. Cambridge, U.K.: Cambridge University Press.

Peng, H., Ozaki, T., Haggan-Ozaki, V., & Toyoda, Y. (2003). A parameter optimization method for radial basis function type models. *IEEE Trans. Neural Networks*, (2), 432–438.

Poggio, T., & Girosi, F. (1990). Networks for approximation and learning. *Proc. IEEE*, (9), 1481–1497.

Powell, M. J. D. (1987). Radial basis functions for multivariable interpolation: a review. In J. C. Mason & M. G. Cox (Eds.), *Algorithms for Approximations* (pp. 143–167). Oxford.

Refaee, J. A., Mohandes, M., & Maghrabi, H. (1999). Radial basis function networks for contingency analysis of bulk power systems. *IEEE Trans. Power Systems*, (2), 772–778.

Rosenblum, M., & Davis, L. S. (1996). An improved radial basis function network for visual autonomous road following. *IEEE Trans. Neural Networks*, (5), 1111–1120.

Su, C.-T., Yang, T., & Ke, C.-M. (2002). A neural-network approach for semiconductor wafer post-sawing inspection. *IEEE Trans. Semiconductor Manufacturing*, (2), 260–266.

Tan, K. K., Zhao, S., & Huang, S. (2005). Iterative reference adjustment for high-precision and repetitive motion control applications. *IEEE Trans. Control Systems Technology*, (1), 85–97.

Tse, D., & Viswanath, P. (2005). *Fundamentals of Wireless Communication*. Cambridge, UK: Cambridge University Press.

Uncini, A., Vecci, L., Campolucci, P., & Piazza, F. (1999). Complex-valued neural networks with adaptive spline activation function for digital ratio links nonlinear equalization. *IEEE Trans. Signal Processing*, (2), 505–514.

Uykan, Z. (2003). Clustering-based algorithms for single-hidden-layer sigmoid perceptron. *IEEE Trans. Neural Networks*, (3), 708–715.

Whitehead, B. A., & Choate, T. D. (1994). Evolving space-filling curves to distribute radial basis functions over an input space. *IEEE Trans. Neural Networks*, (1), 15–23.

Whitehead, B. A. (1996). Genetic evolution of radial basis function coverage using orthogonal niches. *IEEE Trans. Neural Networks*, (6), 1525–1528.

Yang, C.-C., & Bose, N. K. (2005). Landmine detection and classification with complex-valued hybrid neural network using scattering parameters dataset. *IEEE Trans. Neural Networks*, (3), 743–753.

Yang, Z. R., & Chen, S. (1998). Robust maximum likelihood training of heteroscedastic probabilistic neural networks. *Neural Networks*, (4), 739–747.

ADDITIONAL READING

Chen, S., Livingstone, A., Du, H.-Q., & Hanzo, L. (2008). Adaptive minimum symbol error rate beamforming assisted detection for quadrature amplitude modulation. *IEEE Trans. Wireless Communications*, (7), 1140-1145.

Hong, X., & Chen, S. (2008). A new RBF neural network with boundary value constraints. to be published in *IEEE Trans. Systems, Man. and Cybernetics, Part B.*

Nitta, T. (1997). An extension of the back-propagation algorithm to complex numbers. *Neural Networks,* (10), 1391-1415.

Nitta, T. (2004). Orthogonality of decision boundaries in complex-valued neural networks. *Neural Computation*, (16), 73-97.

Pande, A., Thakur, A.K., & Roy, S. (2008). Complex-valued neural network in signal processing: A study on the effectiveness of complex valued generalized mean neuron model. *Proc. World Academy of Science, Engineering and Technology*, (27), 240-245.

APPENDIX

Like the real-valued modified Gram-Schmidt orthogonalisation procedure (Chen *et al.*, 1989), the complex-valued version of the modified Gram-Schmidt orthogonalisation procedure calculates the complex-valued $\mathbf{A}$ matrix row by row and orthogonalises the complex-valued regression matrix Φ as follows: at the l-th stage make the columns ϕ_i, $l+1 \le i \le K$, orthogonal to the l-th column and repeat the operation for $1 \le l \le K-1$. Specifically, denoting $\phi_i^{(0)} = \phi_i$, $1 \le i \le K$, then for $l = 1, 2, \cdots, K-1$

$$\left.\begin{aligned} \mathbf{u}_l &= \phi_l^{(l-1)}, \\ a_{l,i} &= \mathbf{u}_l^H \phi_i^{(l-1)} / \mathbf{u}_l^H \mathbf{u}_l, l+1 \le i \le K, \\ \phi_i^{(l)} &= \phi_i^{(l-1)} - a_{l,i}\mathbf{u}_l, l+1 \le i \le K. \end{aligned}\right\} \tag{39}$$

The last stage of the procedure is simply $\mathbf{u}_K = \phi_K^{(K-1)}$. The elements of $\mathbf{g}$ are computed by transforming $\mathbf{d}^{(0)} = \mathbf{d}$ in a similar way

$$\left.\begin{aligned} g_l &= \mathbf{u}_l^H \mathbf{d}^{(l-1)} / \mathbf{u}_l^H \mathbf{u}_l, \\ \mathbf{d}^{(l)} &= \mathbf{d}^{(l-1)} - g_l \mathbf{u}_l, \end{aligned}\right\} 1 \le l \le K. \tag{40}$$

This orthogonalisation scheme can be used to derive a simple and efficient algorithm for selecting subset models in a forward-regression manner, just as in the real-valued case. First define

$$\Phi^{(l-1)} = \left[\mathbf{u}_1 \cdots \mathbf{u}_{l-1}\, \phi_l^{(l-1)} \cdots \phi_K^{(l-1)}\right]. \tag{41}$$

If some of the columns $\phi_l^{(l-1)}, \cdots, \phi_K^{(l-1)}$ in $\Phi^{(l-1)}$ have been interchanged, this will still be referred to as $\Phi^{(l-1)}$ for notational convenience. Recall the notation $\phi_q^{(l-1)} = [\phi_{1,q}^{(l-1)}\, \phi_{2,q}^{(l-1)} \cdots \phi_{K,q}^{(l-1)}]^T$. Given a very small positive number T_z, which specifies the zero threshold, the l-th stage of the OFS procedure is given as follows.

Step 1. For $l \le q \le K$:

Test–Conditioning number check. If $\left(\phi_q^{(l-1)}\right)^H \phi_q^{(l-1)} < T_z$, the q-th candidate is not considered.

Compute for $1 \le i \le 4$

$$m_{i,l}^{(q)} = \frac{1}{K^{[i]}} \sum_{k=1}^{K} \delta\left(d(k) - b^{[i]}\right) \phi_{k,q}^{(l-1)}$$

and

$$\left(\sigma_{i,l}^{(q)}\right)^2 = \frac{1}{K^{[i]}} \sum_{k=1}^{K} \delta\left(d(k) - b^{[i]}\right)\left(\phi_{k,q}^{(l-1)} - m_{i,l}^{(q)}\right)^2.$$

Then calculate

$$F_{i,p,l}^{(q)} = \frac{\left(m_{i,l}^{(q)} - m_{p,l}^{(q)}\right)^2}{\left(\left(\sigma_{i,l}^{(q)}\right)^2 + \left(\sigma_{p,l}^{(q)}\right)^2\right)}, 1 \le i < p \le 4,$$

and

$$F_l^{(q)} = \frac{1}{6}\sum_{i=1}^{3}\sum_{p=i+1}^{4} F_{i,p,l}^{(q)}.$$

Let the index set J_q be

$$J_q = \{l \le q \le K \text{ and } q \text{ passes Test}\}.$$

Step 2. Find:

$$F_l = F_l^{(q_l)} = \max\{F_l^{(q)}, q \in J_q\}.$$

Then the q_l-th column of $\Phi^{(l-1)}$ is interchanged with the l-th column of $\Phi^{(l-1)}$, and the q_l-th column of $\mathbf{A}$ is interchanged with the l-th column of $\mathbf{A}$ up to the $(l-1)$-th row. This selects the q_l-th candidate as the l-th term in the subset model.

Step 3. Perform the orthogonalisation as indicated in (39) to derive the l-th row of $\mathbf{A}$ and to transform $\Phi^{(l-1)}$ into $\Phi^{(l)}$. Calculate g_l and update $\mathbf{d}^{(l-1)}$ into $\mathbf{d}^{(l)}$ in the way shown in (40).

Chapter VIII
Complex-Valued Neural Networks for Equalization of Communication Channels

Rajoo Pandey
National Institute of Technology, Kurukshetra, India

ABSTRACT

The equalization of digital communication channel is an important task in high speed data transmission techniques. The multipath channels cause the transmitted symbols to spread and overlap over successive time intervals. The distortion caused by this problem is called inter-symbol interference (ISI) and is required to be removed for reliable communication of data over communication channels. In this task of ISI removal, the signals are complex-valued and processing has to be done in a complex multidimensional space. The growing interest in complex-valued neural networks has spurred the development of many new algorithms for equalization of communication channels in the recent past. This chapter illustrates the application of various types of complex-valued neural networks such as radial basis function networks (RBFN), multilayer feedforward networks and recurrent neural networks for training sequence-based as well as blind equalization of communication channels. The structures and algorithms for these equalizers are presented and performances based on simulation studies are analyzed highlighting their advantages and the important issues involved.

INTRODUCTION

The complex-valued neural networks have attracted a great deal of interest in recent years. The growing interest could be attributed to superior learning ability of complex-valued neural networks in comparison with the real valued counterparts. A number of new low complexity and fast learning algorithms have also been proposed by the researchers for complex-valued neural networks, facilitating their use in various applications (Nitta, 1997; Leung & Haykin, 1991). The applications of complex-valued neural networks have emerged in the areas of seismic, sonar and radar signal processing, speech and image processing, environmental science and wireless communications where signals are typically complex valued (Haykin, 1994a; Mandic & Chambers, 2001).

Digital communication through multipath channels is subject to intersymbol interference and its cancellation using adaptive equalizers has been studied for several years by the signal processing community. Also, in order to maximize efficiency of digital radio links, the transmitter high-power amplifiers are often required to operate near saturation, introducing nonlinearities which in turn cause degradation of the received signal. The nonlinearity may affect both amplitude and phase of the signal. It is well known that the signals like QAM are very sensitive to nonlinear distortion which causes spectral spreading, inter-symbol interference (ISI) and constellation warping. The classical approaches to equalization rely on the existence of a training sequence in the transmitted signal to identify the channel (Proakis, 1995).

In adaptive equalization, when the channel is varying, even slowly, the training sequence has to be sent periodically to update the equalizer. Since the inclusion of reference training signals in conventional equalizers sacrifices valuable channel capacity, adaptation without using the training signals i.e. blind equalization is preferred (Godard, 1980; Haykin, 1994b).

With the development of complex-valued versions of training algorithms, the nonlinear adaptive filters can be realized as neural networks for both conventional as well as blind equalization as they are well suited to deal with the complex-valued communication signals. Although, the real valued and complex-valued networks have been both extensively studied for equalization of communication channels, the advantages of using complex-valued neural networks instead of a real valued counterpart fed with a pair of real values is well established. Among neural network equalizers, the application of radial basis function networks (RBFN) has been extensively covered in the literature. The studies of Chen, Mulgrew and, Grant (1993), Cha and Kassam (1995), Jianping, Sundarrajan, and, Saratchandran (2002) and Li, Huang, Saratchandran and, Sundarrajan (2006) are some of the examples. The technique proposed by Chen et al. (1993) is based on the clustering of data and uses a real valued network. Cha and Kassam (1995) have proposed an adaptive complex-valued RBFN for equalization. In their approach, the inputs and outputs of the network are both complex-valued while the radial basis functions are real valued. Jianping et al. (2002) and Li et al. (2006) have considered RBFN- based equalization of channels, where growing and pruning strategy is used for selection of nodes. All these approaches show a remarkable improvement in the performance of the equalizers in comparison with conventional equalizers.

Uncini, Vecci, Campolucci, and Piazza (1999) have presented a study on the use of complex-valued neural networks with adaptive activation functions. An intelligent use of activation function has been shown to reduce the number of synaptic interconnections while preserving the universal approximation and regularization properties of the network, resulting in efficient implementation of nonlinear filters.

For blind equalization of communication channels, the neural network approaches are, generally, based on higher order statistics (HOS) where the minimization of a cost function is required. You and Hong (1998) have argued that these cost functions are non-convex and nonlinear functions of tap weights, when implemented using linear FIR filter structures. A linear FIR filter, however, has a convex decision region, and hence, is not adequate to optimize such cost functions. Therefore, a blind equalization scheme with a nonlinear structure that can form nonconvex decision regions, is desirable. Some blind equalization schemes based on complex-valued neural networks with higher level complex-valued signal constellations such as M-ary phase shift keying (PSK) and quadrature amplitude modulation (QAM) are proposed in (Pandey, 2001).

Most of the communication channels are non-stationary and the performance of the equalizers in nonstationary environment is governed by its training algorithm. Therefore, the development of suitable models and algorithms for equalization in nonstationary environment is important. Gan, Saratchandran, Sundararajan, and Subramanian (1999) and Wolfgang, Chen, and Hanzo (2004) have studied the use of RBFNs for equalization of time-varying channels. For blind equalization, a scheme with adaptive activation function is considered by Pandey (2004) to improve the performance of blind equalizers.

The feedforward neural equalizers usually require a large amount of storage and computation. Therefore, to reduce the burden of the feedforward neural equalizers, recurrent neural networks (RNN) for the equalization have been used. Parisi, Elio Claudio, Orlandi, and Rao (1997) consider a least squares approach with RNN for equalization with higher convergence rate, whereas Kechriotis, Zervas, and Manolakos (1994) have applied RNN for linear and nonlinear equalization with 4-PAM and 4-QAM symbol constellations. Another study on RNN as infinite impulse response (IIR) filter can be found in (Ong, You, Choi, & Hong, 1997). The application of complex-valued RNN for blind equalization with higher order constellations is shown in (Pandey, 2005a).

As there are several ways in which neural networks have been applied for equalization, the chapter presents, in subsequent sections, an RBFN based equalizer for symbol assisted equalization, MLP-based blind equalizers for M-ary QAM and M-ary PSK signal constellations and their extensions to recurrent structures for better performance. Then a modified model is presented for blind equalization in nonstationary environment. The discussion includes the structural details, choice of activation functions and the learning algorithms for implementation of various equalizers. A comparison of the performance of complex-valued neural network-based equalizers is shown with some other traditional equalizers. The performance of various equalizers is judged on the basis of resulting symbol error rate (SER) and the rate of convergence. The models presented in this chapter directly obtain the transmitted symbols and are not based on the estimation of communication channels for their equalization. The equalizers based on neural networks, generally, have higher computational complexity but the performance is significantly better than the conventional equalizers.

BACKGROUND

The application of complex-valued neural networks for equalization of communication channels has been widely studied by the research community. Neural networks have been applied in several different ways for both symbol assisted as well as blind equalization of channels. These models have their own merits and limitations. In most of the studies, the signal constellations considered are low-order. Higher order signal constellations are known for their bandwidth efficiency. With the emergence of multimedia applications, there is an increased demand for higher bandwidth in recent times. The bandwidth efficient transmission methods are thus preferred. The development of suitable equalization methods with higher order signal constellations has also received a lot of attentions. An example of equalization of communication channels with higher order constellation is available in (You & Hong, 1998), where the activation functions are specially designed for M-ary QAM signals. Another important signal constellation is M-ary-PSK for which the suitable activation functions and algorithms are presented in (Pandey, 2005b). These HOS-based blind equalization methods try to minimize a cost function and have been implemented by complex-valued multilayer feedforward neural networks.

RBF networks are important for their close relation with Bayesian estimators and give better performance in symbol assisted equalization methods. The emphasis is on developing complex-valued RBF networks with compact size for equalization of communication channels. Recurrent neural networks, on the other hand, have the advantage of compact size and also the presence of feedback which helps in better cancellation of inter-symbol interference as observed in decision feedback equalizers (DFE), specially, in channels with distant echoes.

Thus, it is observed that any single neural network structure cannot be ideal for every situation. Based on these observations, some of the important equalization models based on complex-valued neural networks studied recently, are presented here. Since, each equalization model has its own limitations, the challenges and the important issues involved are also identified.

SYSTEM MODEL FOR EQUALIZATION PROBLEM

The basic equalization model for a communication system is described in Figure 1. A signal sequence of independent and identically distributed (iid) data is transmitted through a communication channel with an impulse response *h(t)*.

The task of the equalizer is to recover the transmitted symbols based on the channel observations. The output of the channel is represented by

$$x(t) = \sum_{k=-\infty}^{\infty} s_k h(t - kT) + \nu(t) \tag{1}$$

Figure 1. Blind equalization structure in digital communication

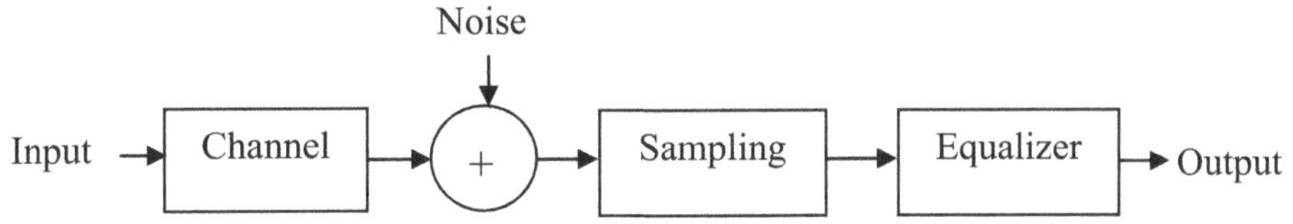

where $\{s_k\}$ represents the data sequence of complex-valued symbols, which is sent over the channel with symbols spaced time T apart and $v(t)$ is additive white Gaussian noise.

The received signal is sampled by substituting $t = nT$ in equation (1)

$$x(nT) = \sum_{k=-\infty}^{\infty} s_k h[(n-k)T] + \mathrm{v}(nT). \quad (2)$$

In simplified form, sampled signal of equation (2) is described as

$$x(n) = \sum_{k=0}^{L} s_k h_{n-k} + \mathrm{v}(n) \quad (3)$$

where the channel is modeled as an FIR filter of length L. $x(n)$ and $v(n)$ represent the sampled channel output and the sampled noise, respectively.

The input to the equalizer is formed by N samples of channel output as

$$\mathbf{x}(n) = [x(n), x(n-1), \ldots..x(n-N+1)]^T. \quad (4)$$

The output of a conventional linear FIR equalizer is expressed as

$$y(n) = \mathbf{W}^H \mathbf{x}(n) \quad (5)$$

where $\mathbf{W}$ is an $N\times1$ vector representing the weights of the equalizer and $y(n)$ is the output, which is obtained as a delayed version of the transmitted signal. A training sequence is periodically transmitted for updating the tap weights of the adaptive equalizer filter by using some training algorithm. Generally, an equalizer is operated in two different modes: (i) training mode and (ii) decision directed mode. In case of decision directed mode, the output decisions are used in place of desired symbol values when the training symbols are not available. The equalizer can also track slow variations of communication channel in decision directed mode. In equalization using neural networks, the linear FIR structure is replaced by a complex-valued neural network.

RBFN EQUALIZER

Since radial basis function networks are known to approximate the Baysian equalizer, RBFN-based equalizers yield better performance than other commonly used equalizers. A training set of input-output pairs is presented to the RBFN-based equalizer for its training to learn the nonlinear mapping from the input to the output. The optimum decision boundaries for the partition of equalizer inputs are nonlinear hyper surfaces in the complex observation space. This equalizer essentially carries out an approximation for the nonlinear mapping from the input to the output. There are several algorithms based on growing and pruning RBFNs such as generalized growing and pruning RBF (GGAP-RBF) of Huang, Saratchandran, and Sundarrajan (2005), complex-valued growing and pruning RBF of Li et al. (2006) and complex minimal resource allocation network (CMRAN) equalizer of Jianping et al (2002). The model discussed here is based on the RBFN equalizer of Cha and Kassam (1995) and Jianping et al (2002) for the equalization of communication channels based on training symbols.

Model

The schematic diagram of the equalizer shown in Figure 2 has three layers with the hidden layer consisting of Gaussian functions. The input to the network is the noisy vector $\mathbf{x}(n)$ of channel output. If an M-ary input sequence is passed through a noiseless channel of order L and the equalizer takes the input vector of length N, then there are M^{L+N-1} different input states. The noisy observations of the channel form Gaussian clusters centered at the desired states. The equalizer attempts to partition the set of M^{L+N-1} equalizer input states into M subsets corresponding to each symbol. Therefore, it can be viewed as a classification problem. The learning algorithm uses the output and the desired response for training.

The response of hidden neurons to the input vector is expressed as follows:

$$\phi_k(\mathbf{x}) = \exp\left(-\frac{1}{\sigma_k^{2}}(\mathbf{x}-\boldsymbol{\mu}_k)^H(\boldsymbol{\mu}-\mathbf{x}_k)\right); \quad k = 1, 2, ..., h \tag{6}$$

where $\boldsymbol{\mu}_k$ denotes the N-dimensional complex center vector for the kth hidden neuron, σ_k is the width of the Gaussian function and h indicates the total number of hidden neurons in the network. The output layer of the RBFN is a linear combiner. The weight of the link connecting the kth hidden neuron to output neuron is denoted by w_k which can be separated in to w_{Rk} and w_{Ik} as the real and imaginary parts, respectively.

The network output can be expressed as

$$\begin{aligned} y &= \left(w_{R0} + \sum_{k=1}^{h} w_{Rk}\phi_k(\mathbf{x})\right) + j\left(w_{I0} + \sum_{k=1}^{h} w_{Ik}\phi_k(\mathbf{x})\right) \\ &= w_0 + \sum_{k=1}^{h} w_k\phi_k(\mathbf{x}). \end{aligned} \tag{7}$$

Figure 2. A Complex-Valued RBFN Equalizer (© IEEE 1995, used with permission)

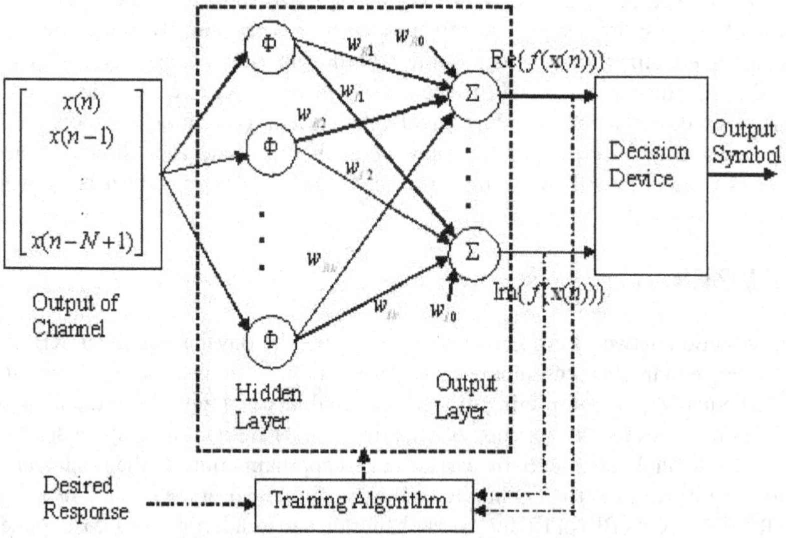

Learning Rules

For the selection of centers of Gaussian nodes, k-means clustering algorithm can be used, as it can effectively filter out the noise and ensure that the RBF centers converge to the desired states (Chen et al., 1993). For nonstationary channels, an adaptive procedure based on LMS algorithm is preferred. The weight parameters of the RBFN equalizer may be adapted by any adaptive algorithm. Cha and Kassam (1995) have used stochastic gradient (SG) algorithm. For example, a parameter w_j may be adapted as:

$$w_j(n+1) = w_j(n) + \mu_w e_n \phi_j(\mathbf{x}(n)) \tag{8}$$

and

$$e_n = f(\mathbf{x}(n)) - d(n) \tag{9}$$

where $d(n)$ is the desired value of the output, $f(\mathbf{x}(n))$ denotes the output of the network and μ_w is the learning rate parameter.

Alternatively, some other algorithm such as extended Kalman filter (EKF), as used in (Jianping et al., 2002), may be used. The learning process of this algorithm, based on growing and pruning, involves allocation of new hidden neurons as well as adjusting network parameters, according to the data received. Initially, the network begins with no hidden neurons. The error is computed as each input-output training pair ($y(n)$, $s(n-\tau)$), where τ denotes the delay, is received and the following growth criteria are used for building up the network.

$$(\mathbf{x}(n) - \boldsymbol{\mu}_{nr})^H (\mathbf{x}(n) - \boldsymbol{\mu}_{nr}) > \varepsilon_n \tag{10}$$

$$(s(n-\tau) - y(n))^H (s(n-\tau) - y(n)) > e_{\min} \tag{11}$$

where $\boldsymbol{\mu}_{nr}$ denotes the center of the hidden neuron closest to the received data $\mathbf{x}(n)$. The thresholds ε_n and $e_{\min}$ are appropriately selected. The criterion stated in equation (10) ensures that the new neuron to be added is sufficiently far from all the existing neurons, whereas equation (11) helps in deciding if the existing neurons are insufficient to meet the error specification. The algorithm begins with ε_n equal to the size of entire input space $\varepsilon_{\max}$, and then it is decayed exponentially as $\varepsilon_n = \max\{\varepsilon_{\max}\gamma^n \varepsilon_{\min}\}$, where $0<\gamma<1$ is a decay constant. In order to reduce the effect of the noise in the growth of the network and to make the transition of the number of the hidden neurons smooth, a third criterion is used which is based on the rms value of the output at nth observation as follows:

$$e_{rmsn} = \sqrt{\sum_{i=n-(M-1)}^{n} \frac{e_i^* e_i}{M}}. \tag{12}$$

The criterion used is, $e_{rmsn} > e_{\min 1}$, where $e_{\min 1}$ is a threshold value.

A new hidden neuron is added only when all three criteria are met. When a new hidden neuron is added, it has the following parameters associated with it

$$\begin{aligned} w_{h+1} &= e_n, \quad \boldsymbol{\mu}_{h+1} = \mathbf{x}(n) \\ \sigma_{h+1}^2 &= \kappa(\mathbf{x}(n) - \boldsymbol{\mu}_{nr})^H (\mathbf{x}(n) - \boldsymbol{\mu}_{nr}) \end{aligned} \tag{13}$$

where the parameter κ determines the overlap of the responses of the hidden neurons in the input space. When there are no hidden neurons to be added, the parameters are adapted using EKF algorithm as given below.

First of all, the parameters to be updated are combined into a vector $\mathbf{v}$ as

$$\begin{aligned} \mathbf{v} = [&\mathrm{Re}(w_0), \mathrm{Im}(w_0), \mathrm{Re}(w_1), \mathrm{Im}(w_1), \mathrm{Re}(\boldsymbol{\mu}_1^T), \mathrm{Im}(\boldsymbol{\mu}_1^T), \sigma_1, \ldots \\ &\ldots, \mathrm{Re}(w_h), \mathrm{Im}(w_h), \mathrm{Re}(\boldsymbol{\mu}_h^T), \mathrm{Im}(\boldsymbol{\mu}_h^T), \sigma_h]^T \end{aligned} \tag{14}$$

where Re(.) and Im(.) represent the real and imaginary parts. Now the vector **v** is adapted as follows:

$$\mathbf{v}_n = \mathbf{v}_{n-1} + \mathbf{k}_n \times [\mathrm{Re}(e_n), \mathrm{Im}(e_n)]^T. \tag{15}$$

The Kalman gain vector $\mathbf{k}_n$ is given by

$$\mathbf{k}_n = \mathbf{P}_{n-1}\mathbf{a}_n[\mathbf{R}_n + \mathbf{a}_n^T \mathbf{P}_{n-1}\mathbf{a}_n]^{-1} \tag{16}$$

where the gradient vector $\mathbf{a}_n$ has the following form:

$$\begin{aligned}\mathbf{a}_n = {} & [I_{2\times2}, \phi_1(\mathbf{x}(n))I_{2\times2}, \phi_1(\mathbf{x}(n))(2\beta_1/\sigma_1^2).[\mathrm{Re}(\mathbf{x}(n)) - \boldsymbol{\mu}_1)^T, \mathrm{Im}(\mathbf{x}(n)) - \boldsymbol{\mu}_1)^T] \\ & .\phi_1(\mathbf{x}(n))(2\beta_1/\sigma_1^3)(\mathbf{x}(n) - \boldsymbol{\mu}_1)^H(\mathbf{x}(n) - \boldsymbol{\mu}_1), \ldots .\phi_h(\mathbf{x}(n))I_{2\times2}, \phi_h(\mathbf{x}(n))(2\beta_h/\sigma_h^2) \\ & .[\mathrm{Re}(\mathbf{x}(n)) - \boldsymbol{\mu}_h)^T, \mathrm{Im}(\mathbf{x}(n)) - \boldsymbol{\mu}_h)^T].\phi_h(\mathbf{x}(n))(2\beta_h/\sigma_h^3)(\mathbf{x}(n) - \boldsymbol{\mu}_h)^H(\mathbf{x}(n) - \boldsymbol{\mu}_h)]^T.\end{aligned} \tag{17}$$

Here $\beta_1 = [w_{R1}, w_{I1}]^T, \ldots\ldots, \beta_h = [w_{Rh}, w_{Ih}]^T$, $\mathbf{R}_n$ is the covariance matrix of the measurement noise and $\mathbf{P}_n$ is the error covariance matrix which is updated as

$$\mathbf{P}_n = [\mathbf{I} - \mathbf{k}_n \mathbf{a}_n^T]\mathbf{P}_{n-1} + Q\mathbf{I} \tag{18}$$

where Q is a scalar that determines the allowed random step in the direction of the gradient vector, **I** is the identity matrix, and $\mathbf{P}_n$ is an $K \times K$ positive definite symmetric matrix when there are K parameters to be adjusted. When a new hidden neuron is added, the dimensionality of $\mathbf{P}_n$ changes as

$$\mathbf{P}_n = \begin{pmatrix} \mathbf{P}_{n-1} & 0 \\ 0 & p_0\mathbf{I}_0 \end{pmatrix} \tag{19}$$

where p_0 initializes the new row and columns and is an estimate of the uncertainty in the initial values assigned to the parameters. The dimensions of the identity matrix $\mathbf{I}_0$ is equal to the number of new parameters introduced by the new hidden neuron.

For pruning of a node, the output is observed for a predefined period and if the neuron does not contribute significantly, it can be removed from the network. The normalized output of the node is compared with a threshold and if found smaller then the node is removed and the parameters are readjusted using EKF. This is based on the observation that if the response of a hidden neuron or the value of the weight associated with it is small, the output of this node becomes small. This means that the input is far away from the center of this hidden neuron. When the output of a node is small, its real and imaginary parts are both small. The real and imaginary values of output are normalized with their respective maximum values among all the hidden neurons so that the inconsistency caused by using the absolute values is reduced. The threshold values are obtained by trial and error to get the best results for the training data. The selected values are then used for the testing purposes.

During data transmission, supervised learning no longer applies and adaptation has to rely on unsupervised or decision-directed learning.

Simulation Results

To show the performance of the complex-valued RBFN equalizer, one of the simulation examples of (Jianping et al., 2002) is considered in this section. The nonlinear channel used in the simulation is described below.

$$x(n) = o_n + 0.1o_n^2 + 0.05o_n^3 + \nu_n \quad (20)$$

where ν_n is the Gaussian noise with variance equal to 0.01 and

$$o_n = (0.34 - j0.27)s_n + (0.87 + j0.43)s_{n-1} + (0.34 - j0.21)s_{n-2}. \quad (21)$$

The signal constellation has four symbols with real and imaginary points taken from the set {±0.7}. The equalizer order is 3 and the delay τ is equal to 1. The parameters for the training algorithm are set as:

$$e_{\min} = 0.01, e_{\min 1} = 0.5, \varepsilon_{\max} = 0.16, \gamma = 1,$$

the sliding window parameters M is10 and the threshold for pruning is taken as 0.01. The performance is compared with another equalizer of (Cha & Kassam, 1995). The plot of probability of error is shown in Figure 3 for the equalizers of (Jianping et al., 2002), (Cha & Kassam, 1995) and the Bayesian equalizer. It is reported that with 18 hidden neurons, the performance of the equalizer of (Jianping et al., 2002) is better than that of (Cha & Kassam, 1995) with 30 hidden neurons.

Although the Bayesian equalizer has the best performance, however, it has 1024 states, which implies that there will be 1024 hidden neurons in the RBF network.

Similar results are reported in (Jianping et al., 2002) for other channel models. In general, the input dimension and the number of hidden nodes both have to be increased in order to maintain good performance when the channel order increases. The main advantage of growing and pruning-based equalizer is the compact structure in comparison with other RBFN-based equalizers. The main limitation of this algorithm is the choice of various thresholds. The values of threshold parameters generally, depend upon the application. Therefore, they must be selected trough exhaustive trial and error studies.

Figure 3. Plots of probability of Error for various Equalizers (© IEEE 2002, used with permission)

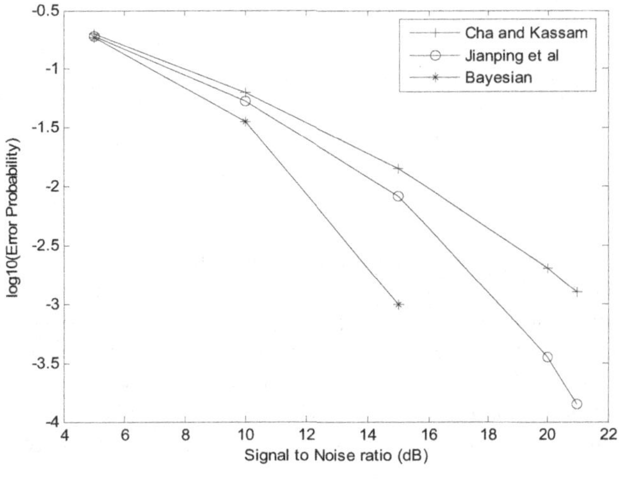

COMPLEX-VALUED NEURAL NETWORKS FOR BLIND EQUALIZATION

Model

A three-layer complex valued feedforward neural network for blind equalization is shown in Figure 4. The network has N input nodes, H hidden layer nodes and one output node. The complex valued weight $w_{kl}^{(1)}$ denotes the synaptic weight, connecting the output of node l of input layer to the input of neuron k in the hidden layer. $w_k^{(2)}$ refers to the synaptic weight connected between neuron k of hidden layer and the output neuron.

The input of the equalizer is formed by N samples of the received signal as given below.

$$\mathbf{x}(n) = [x(n)\ x(n-1),....x(n-N+1)]^{T} \tag{22}$$

and represented as

$$\mathbf{x}(n) = [x_1(n), x_2(n), ...x_N(n)]^T. \tag{23}$$

The activation sum $net_k^{(1)}(n)$ and the output $u_k(n)$ of neuron k in the hidden layer are:

$$net_k^{(1)}(n) = net_{k,R}^{(1)}(n) + j net_{k,I}^{(1)}(n) = \sum_{l=1}^{N} w_{kl}^{(1)}(n) x_l(n) + \theta_k^{(1)}(n) \tag{24}$$

and

$$u_k(n) = \phi^{(1)}(net_k^{(1)}(n))\ ; k = 1, 2, ...H \tag{25}$$

where $net_{k,R}^{(1)}(n)$ and $net_{k,I}^{(1)}(n)$ are, respectively, the real and imaginary parts of the activation sum $net_k^{(1)}(n)$, at time n, $\phi^{(1)}(.)$ represents the nonlinear activation function of neurons in hidden layer and $\theta_k^{(1)}(n)$ denotes the threshold of neuron k of the hidden layer.

For the neuron of the output layer, the activation sum and the output are expressed as

$$net^{(2)}(n) = net_R^{(2)}(n) + j net_I^{(2)}(n) = \sum_{k=1}^{H} w_k^{(2)}(n) u_k(n) + \theta^{(2)}(n) \tag{26}$$

and

$$y(n) = \phi^{(2)}(net^{(2)}(n)) \tag{27}$$

where $y(n)$ denotes the output of the equalizer, $net_R^{(2)}(n)$ and $net_I^{(2)}(n)$ are, respectively, the real and imaginary parts of the activation sum $net^{(2)}(n)$, at time n, and $\phi^{(2)}(.)$ is the activation function of the neuron in output layer.

Activation Functions

In the present model of complex-valued neural blind equalizer, the activation functions are chosen according to the M-ary signal constellation. The choice of activation function plays an important role in the performance of the blind equalizers. Georgiou and Koutsougeras (1992) have identified some desirable properties of a complex activation function. Recently, Kim and Adali (2002) have presented a study of some complex activation functions for realizing fully complex multi-layer perceptron network for nonlinear signal processing. The main difficulty in finding a nonlinear complex activation function for an MLP is the conflict between the boundedness and the differentiability of complex functions in the whole complex plane $\mathbb{C}$. This problem is generally avoided by split-

Figure 4. Complex-valued multilayer feedforward neural network equalizer (© ENFORMATIKA 2004, used with permission)

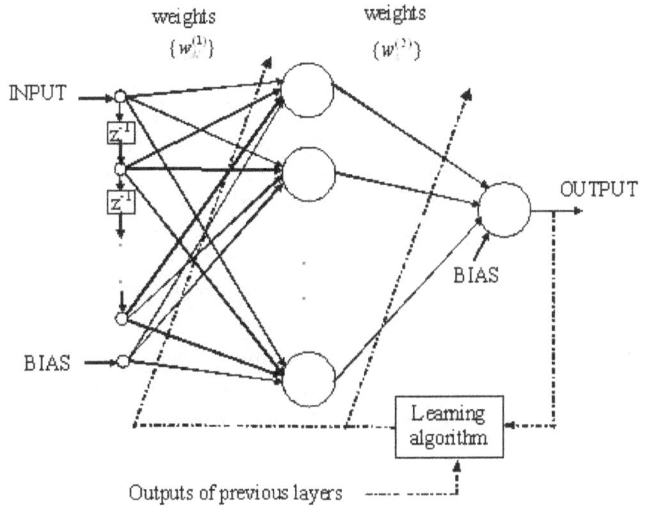

ting the activation function into a pair of real functions for the real and imaginary components. The elementary transcendental functions considered in (Kim & Adali, 2002), which provide adequate nonlinear discriminant as an activation function and have some of the desirable conditions, include circular functions like $\tan z$; inverse circular functions such as $\arctan z$ and $\arccos z$; hyperbolic function, $\tanh z$ and inverse hyperbolic functions arctanh z and arcsinh z. These elementary transcendental functions are shown to perform better than the conventional activation functions when the domain is bounded. The functions having decreasing rates of amplitude growth as we move away from the origin, require application of scaling coefficient in the activation function when data shows large dynamic range. Among the elementary transcendental functions studied in (Kim & Adali, 2002), inverse hyperbolic functions are reported to perform better than other functions in the simulations of nonlinear channel equalization. The complex activation functions based on the elementary transcendental functions and the approximation capabilities of fully complex MLPs with these activation functions are also studied in (Kim & Adali, 2003).

In the present model following activation functions are considered for QAM signal.

(1) For the neurons of hidden layer, the activation function $\varphi^{(1)}$ is described as

$$\varphi^{(1)}(z) = \varphi^{(1)}(z_R) + j\,\varphi^{(1)}(z_I) \tag{28}$$

where z_R and z_I are the real and imaginary parts of the complex quantity z, and $\phi^{(1)}(.)$ is a function defined by

$$\varphi^{(1)}(x) = \alpha\tanh(\beta x) \tag{29}$$

while α and β are two real constants.

(2) For the neuron of output layer, the activation function is described as

$$\varphi^{(2)}(z) = \varphi^{(2)}(z_R) + j\,\varphi^{(2)}(z_I) \tag{30}$$

where $\phi^{(2)}(.)$ is a real valued function defined by

$$\phi^{(2)}(x) = x + c\sin(\pi x) \tag{31}$$

and c is a positive constant.

The activation function of the neuron of output layer given by equation (31) is same as that used in (You & Hong, 1998). However, in that model, identical functions have been used in both hidden and output layers. The nonlinear activation function of equation (31) is shown in Figure 5 (a) for 16-QAM signal where the real and imaginary values are taken from the set {±1, ±3}. Here, it can be noted that the same activation functions can be used for any higher order QAM signal constellation. From this Figure, it can be seen that the nonlinear activation function has saturation regions around the symbol values of the QAM signal constellation signifying the amplitudes of in-phase and quadrature-phase carriers in the transmitted waveforms.

For PSK signals the activation functions used in neural network equalizers are as given in (Pandey, 2004; 2005b).

(1) For hidden layer, the activation functions are same as defined for QAM signals in equations (28) and (29).

(2) For the output layer node, the activation functions are similar to continuous linear functions introduced in (Hirose, 1992a) for error back-propagation learning applied to realize fully complex-valued neural networks. In this work, a gradient descent method in complex space is used for realizing smooth convergence of the weighting factors. The activation functions of (Hirose, 1992a) are as follows.

$$f(z) = \tanh\frac{|z|}{m}\exp(j\angle z) \tag{32}$$

where $|z|$ and $\angle z$ are the modulus and the argument of the complex quantity z denoting the summation of the input vectors fed from the hidden layer i.e. $z = net^{(2)}(n)$.The constant m is inversely related to the gradient of the absolute function value $|f|$ along the radius direction around the origin of the complex coordinate.

For equalization of PSK signals, the activation functions used in the present multilayer neural network also treat the norm and argument parts separately. However, these activation functions involve nonlinear functions for both modulus and argument parts of complex quantity z (Pandey 2004; 2005b). The nonlinear function used for $|z|$ is same as that in equation (32). However, the nonlinear function for $\angle z$ part is designed to generate saturation regions around the phase angles of symbol points in a given PSK constellation. Thus, in the present model, the activation function for the output layer node is given by

$$\begin{aligned}\phi^{(2)}(z) &= f_1(|z|).\exp(jf_2(\angle z))\\ &= f_1(|z|).\cos(f_2(\angle z)) + jf_1(|z|).\sin(f_2(\angle z))\end{aligned} \tag{33}$$

where $|z|$ and $\angle z$ denote the modulus and the angle of a complex quantity z. The function $f_1(.)$ and $f_2(.)$ are defined as

$$f_1(|z|) = a\tanh(b.|z|) \tag{34}$$

and

$$f_2(\angle z) = \angle z - b\sin(m\angle z) \tag{35}$$

where b is a constant, $\angle z$ is expressed in radians and m is the order of PSK signals.

Figure 5(b) shows the plot of nonlinear function $f_2(.)$ for m=8 i.e. 8-PSK signal. In this Figure, the saturation regions of the function correspond to the phase angles of the symbols in the PSK constellation plotted in the range from $-\pi$ to π. The phase angles of symbols signify the phase value of the PSK modulated carrier. The multisaturation characteristics of the activation functions make the networks robust to noise.

The complex valued processing elements of output layers of the equalizers, defined by equations (31) and (33)-(35) are illustrated in Figure 6 (Pandey, 2001).

You and Hong (1998) have considered some properties of a suitable complex activation function for their equalizer. It has been noted that it is sufficient to optimize the filter design if the gradient of the cost function exists. The gradient is defined as

$$\nabla_k J = \frac{\partial J}{\partial w_{k,R}} + j\frac{\partial J}{\partial w_{k,I}}; \qquad k = 0, 1, 2.... \tag{36}$$

where $w_{k,R}$ and $w_{k,I}$ denote the real and imaginary parts of k'th element w_k of the vector **w**. This gradient will exist if the activation functions of both hidden and output layers have the following first order derivatives

$$\frac{\partial \phi_R(z_R)}{\partial z_R}, \frac{\partial \phi_R(z_R)}{\partial z_I}, \frac{\partial \phi_I(z_I)}{\partial z_R} \text{ and } \frac{\partial \phi(z_I)}{\partial z_I}, \text{ for } \phi = \phi^{(1)} \text{ and } \phi^{(2)}.$$

The activation functions defined by equations (29) and (31) satisfy the following requirements (You & Hong, 1998).

Figure 5. Activation Functions for (a) 16-QAM and (b) 8-PSK symbol constellations

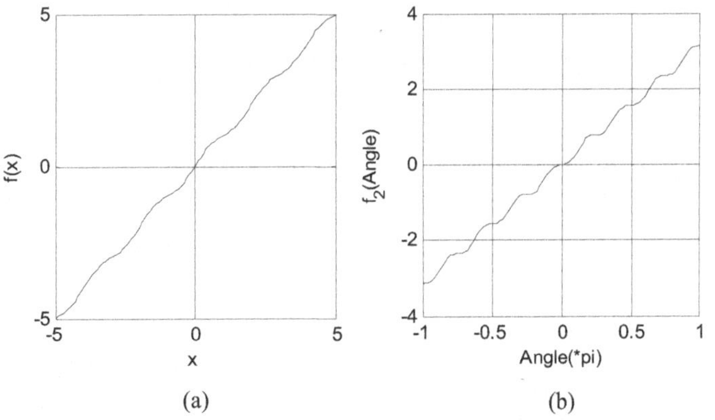

Figure 6. A complex valued processing element for (a) M-QAM and (b) M-PSK signals

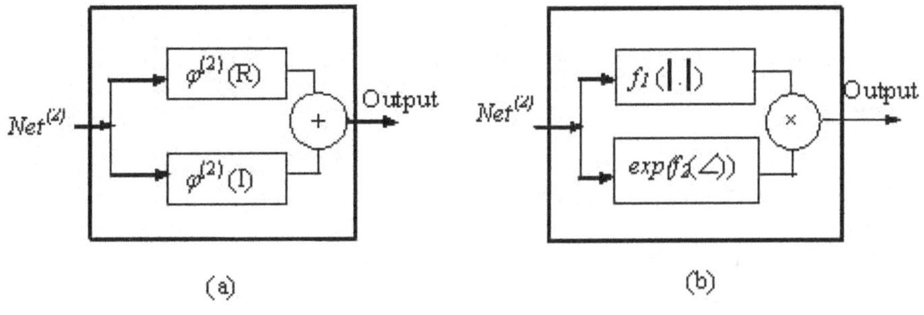

1. $\varphi(z)$ should be nonlinear in both z_R and z_I.
2. For the stability of the system, $\varphi(z)$ should have no singularities and be bounded for all z in a bounded set S. If $\varphi(z)$ is not analytic, it must be continuous at all z in S.
3. The first order partial derivatives mentioned above should be continuous and bounded.

In case of the activation function of equation (33), used for M-ary PSK signal, the gradient of the constant modulus algorithm (CMA) cost function, which is explained later, is obtainable, as the required partial derivative can be easily computed w.r.t. $|z|$. In general, the nonlinear functions defined in this section have the following useful properties.

1. Real and imaginary parts of the complex activation functions have same dynamic range.
2. Real and imaginary parts are symmetric with respect to the real and imaginary axes.
3. Real and imaginary parts of the complex activation functions of the output layer are saturated according to the signal constellation.

Learning Rules

The update rules for the weights of neural networks are obtained by using the gradient descent approach to minimize the CMA cost function. The CMA cost function (Johnson et al., 1998), expressed in terms of the output, is given below.

$$J = \tfrac{1}{4}E[(|y(n)|^2 - R_2)^2] \tag{37}$$

where $R_2 = E[|s(n)|^4]/E[|s(n)|^2]$, and E[] denotes the expectation operator. The updating rules are described as follows.

(i) For the weights, connected between hidden layer and output layer:

$$w_k^{(2)}(n+1) = w_k^{(2)}(n) + \eta\delta^{(2)}(n)u_k^*(n) \tag{38}$$

where, for M-ary QAM and PSK signal, respectively, $\delta^{(2)}(n)$ is given as

$$\delta^{(2)}(n) = \{\phi^{(2)}(net_R^{(2)}(n))\phi^{(2)'}(net_R^{(2)}(n)) + j\phi^{(2)}(net_I^{(2)}(n))\phi^{(2)'}(net_I^{(2)}(n))\}(R_2 - |y(n)|^2) \tag{39}$$

and $\delta^{(2)}(n) = (|y(n)|^2 - R_2)|y(n)|(ab - \frac{b}{a}|y(n)|^2)(net^{(2)}(n)/|net^{(2)}(n)|)$. (40)

(ii) For the weights connected between input and hidden layer:

$$w_{kl}^{(1)}(n+1) = w_{kl}^{(1)}(n) + \eta\delta_k^{(1)}(n)x_l^*(n) \tag{41}$$

where $\delta_k^{(1)}(n)$ is given, for M-ary QAM signal, by

$$\delta_k^{(1)}(n) = \phi^{(1)'}(net_{k,R}^{(1)}(n))\,\mathrm{Re}(\delta^{(2)}(n)w_k^{(2)*}(n)) + j\phi^{(1)'}(net_{k,I}^{(1)}(n))\,\mathrm{Im}(\delta^{(2)}(n)w_k^{(2)*}(n)) \tag{42}$$

and for M-ary PSK signal, by

$$\delta_k^{(1)}(n) = \frac{\delta^{(2)}(n)}{net^{(2)}(n)}\{\phi^{(1)'}(net_{k,R}^{(1)}(n))\,\mathrm{Re}(w_k^{(2)}(n)net^{(2)*}(n)) -$$
$$\varphi^{(1)'}(net_{k,I}^{(1)}(n))\,\mathrm{Im}(w_k^{(2)}(n)net^{(2)*}(n))\}. \tag{43}$$

Here $u_k^*(n)$ and $x_l^*(n)$ denote the complex conjugate of kth and lth elements of **u**(n) and **x**(n) respectively. η is the learning rate parameter while $\varphi^{(1)}(.)$ and $\varphi^{(2)}(.)$ represent the derivatives of $\varphi^{(1)}(.)$ and $\varphi^{(2)}(.)$. The derivations of the update rules of equations (38) – (43) can be found in (Pandey, 2001).

Simulation Results

To compare the performances of different blind equalizers, the example of a complex-valued channel of (You et al., 1998) given below, is used.

$$H(z) = (0.0410 + j0.0109) + (0.0495 + j0.0123)z^{-1} + (0.0672 + j0.0170)z^{-2}$$
$$+ (0.0919 + 0.0235)\, z^{-3} + (0.7920 + j0.1281)\, z^{-4} + (0.3960 + j0.0871)\, z^{-5}$$
$$+ (0.2715 + j0.0498)\, z^{-6} + (0.2291 + j0.0414)\, z^{-7} + (0.1287 + j0.0154)\, z^{-8}$$
$$+ (0.1032 + j0.0119)\, z^{-9}. \qquad (44)$$

In the simulation, two different symbol constellations, namely, 16-QAM and 8-PSK are used. Details of various equalizers are given in Table1.

The performance of the neural equalizers is compared with conventional FIR equalizers.

The parameters of the activation functions of hidden layer neurons are chosen according to the channel output. In this simulation $\eta = 0.00001$ and the parameter c of the activation function of equation (31) is taken as 0.15. Figure 7(a-b) shows the plot of output of the channel for 16-QAM and 8-PSK signals, whereas the outputs of the complex valued feedforward equalizers for these constellations are depicted in Figure 7(c-d) at 20 dB SNR. For the satisfactory convergence of CMA based equalizers, the central tap of linear FIR equalizer is initialized as 1 and other taps are set to zero. For the neural network equalizer, the weights $w_{ij}^{(1)}$ and $w^{i(2)}$ are initialized by small random values, except for the real parts of the central elements of the weights i.e. $w_{58,R}^{(1)}$ and $w_{5,R}^{(2)}$. The weight $w_{58,R}^{(1)} = 1$ while $w_{5,R}^{(2)}$ is chosen according to the channel output and is 1.5.

The MSE curves for the two equalizers are shown in Figure 8 (a) and (c). MSE curves are obtained by averaging 50 independent runs. The symbol error rate performance of these blind equalizers is illustrated in Figure 8 (b) and (d). It can be observed that in comparison with linear FIR equalizer, the NN equalizers achieve lower MSE and symbol error rate. MSE of NN equalizer is less than the MSE of linear FIR equalizer by about 4 dB for PSK signal and about 3 dB for QAM signal as shown by Figure 8 (a) and Figure 8 (c), respectively. The study in (Pandey, 2001) has shown that the convergence of the neural equalizer with sigmoidal nonlinearities in the hidden layer is faster than the equalizer of (You & Hong, 1998).

The improvement in performance is due to multisaturation characteristics of the activation functions which also provide decorrelation of the input data, helping in the equalization process. Another advantage of these activation functions is the automatic phase correction provided by them. In linear blind equalizers, the output

Table 1. Structural details of various blind equalizers used in simulation ($a = 2$, $b = 0.5$, $\alpha = 4$, $\beta = 0.4$ for PSK signal and $\alpha = 20$, $\beta = 1/20$ for QAM signal)

Type of blind equalizer	Number of nodes in the input layer	Number of nodes in hidden layer	Number of taps
NN Equalizer for 16-QAM signal	15 $w_{58,R}^{(1)} = 1$	9 $w_{5,R}^{(2)} = 1.5$	-
NN Equalizer for 8-PSK signal	17 $w_{59,R}^{(1)} = 1$	9 $w_{5,R}^{(2)} = 2.5$	-
Linear FIR equalizer	-	-	23 for QAM signal 25 for PSK signal

Figure 7. (a) Output of the channel for 16-QAM signal (b) Output of the channel for 8-PSK signal (c) Output of the feedforward Equalizer for 16-QAM signal (d) Output of the feedforward Equalizer for 8-PSK signal

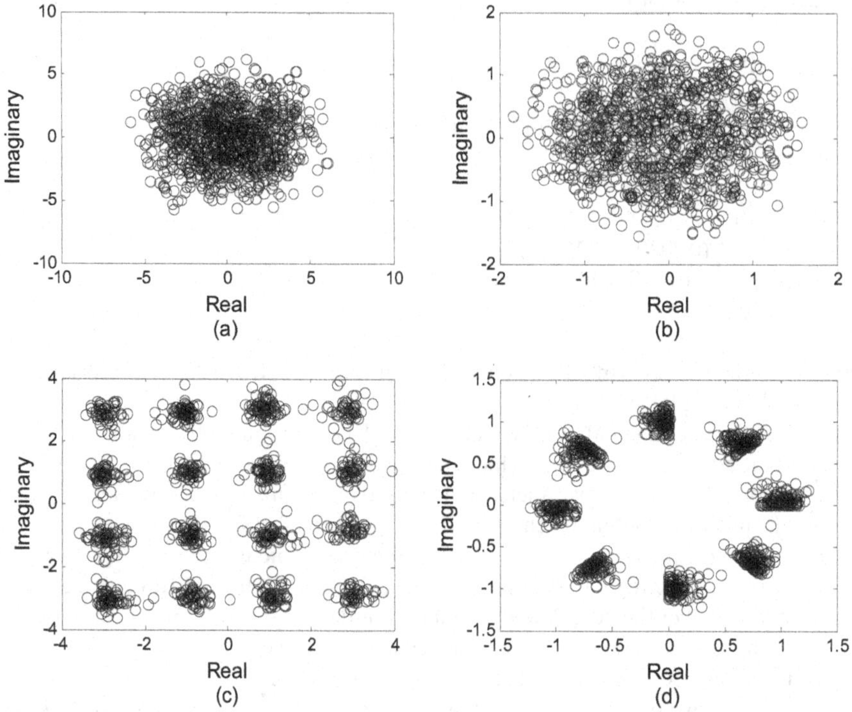

symbols are rotated by an arbitrary phase angle (You & Hong, 1998). However, the main limitations are their convergence speed and the higher computational complexity of neural network blind equalizers.

COMPLEX VALUED RECURRENT EQUALIZER

The equalizers using feedforward neural networks yield a significant improvement in performance relative to the equalizers with linear FIR structures. However, these feedforward neural equalizers usually require a large amount of storage and computation. To reduce the burden of the feedforward neural equalizers, recurrent neural networks for the equalization are used (Kechriotis et al., 1994; Ong et al., 1997; Parisi et al., 1997). In this chapter, a complex valued recurrent neural structure based on CMA cost function (Pandey, 2005a), is used for blind equalization, and its learning rules are derived. This model is suitable for higher order signal constellations. Finally, the comparison of performances is presented.

A blind equalizer using recurrent neural network is depicted in Figure 9. The recurrent network consists of M neurons and has N external input connections. Let $\mathbf{x}(n)$ denote the N-by-1 input vector, consisting of (N-1) samples of received signal and a fixed bias term, at discrete time n. Let $\mathbf{y}(n+1)$ denote the corresponding M-by-1 vector of individual neuron outputs produced one step later at time n+1. The input vector $\mathbf{x}(n)$ and one-step delayed output vector $\mathbf{y}(n)$ are concatenated to form the (N+M)-by-1 vector $\mathbf{u}(n)$.

The kth element $u_k(n)$ of the vector $\mathbf{u}(n)$ is expressed as

Figure 8. (a) MSE plot for 16-QAM signal (b) SER performance for 16-QAM signal (c) MSE plot for 8-PSK signal (d) SER performance for 8-PSK signal

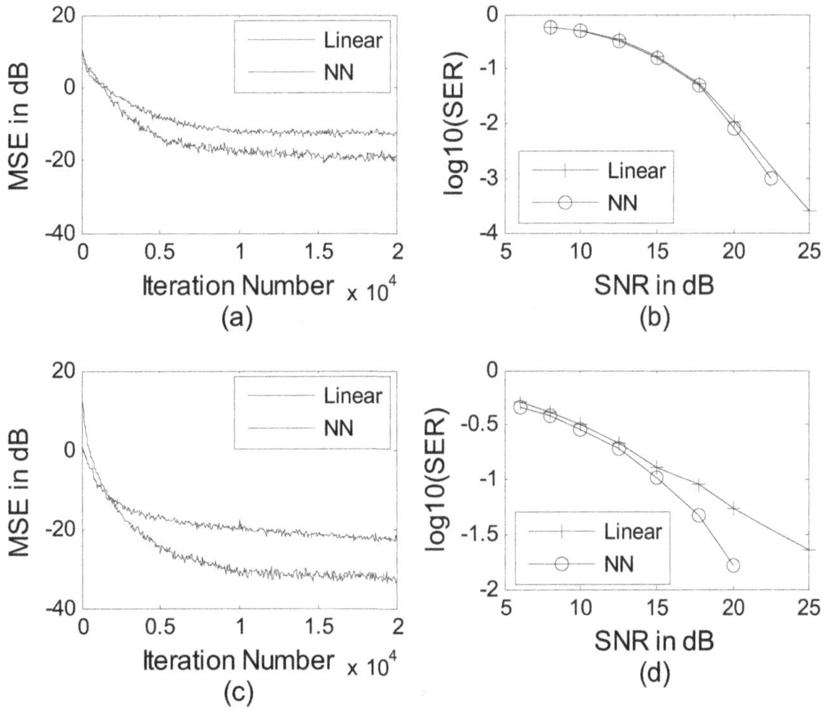

$$u_k(n) = \begin{cases} x_k(n) & \text{if } k \in A \\ y_k(n) & \text{if } k \in B \end{cases} \tag{45}$$

where A and B denote the sets of indices k for which $u_k(n)$ is an external input and an output of a neuron, respectively. Let **W** denote the M-by-(N+M) recurrent weight matrix of the network, and let the element $y_{out}(n)$ of the output vector **y**(n) denote the externally reachable output. The remaining neurons of the processing layer are hidden.

The net activity of neuron l, at time n, for $l \in B$ is given as

$$net_l(n) = \sum_{k \in A \cup B} w_{lk}(n) u_k(n) \tag{46}$$

where $A \cup B$ represents the union of sets A and B. The output of neuron l, at next time step n+1, is then expressed as

$$y_l(n+1) = \phi(net_l(n)) \tag{47}$$

Figure 9. Recurrent neural network as a blind equalizer (© ACTA Press 2005, used with permission)

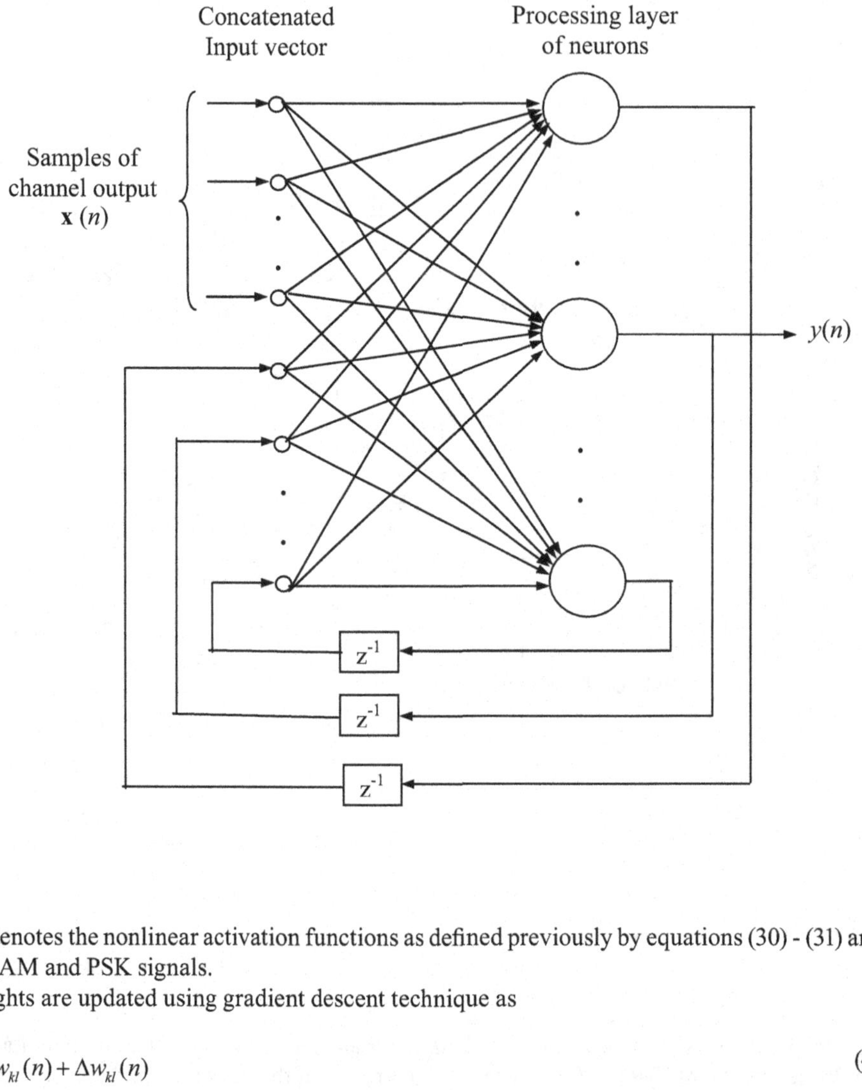

where $\phi(.)$ denotes the nonlinear activation functions as defined previously by equations (30) - (31) and (33) – (35) for M-ary QAM and PSK signals.

The weights are updated using gradient descent technique as

$$w_{kl}(n+1) = w_{kl}(n) + \Delta w_{kl}(n) \tag{48}$$

where the adjustment applied to the weight $w_{k}(n)$ at iteration n is defined as

$$\begin{aligned}\Delta w_{kl}(n) &= -\eta \nabla_{w_{kl}} J(n)\\ &= -\eta\left(|y_{out}(n)|^2 - R_2\right)\left[y_{out,R}(n)\left(\frac{\partial y_{out,R}(n)}{\partial w_{kl}(n)}\right) + y_{out,I}(n)\left(\frac{\partial y_{out,I}(n)}{\partial w_{kl}(n)}\right)\right]\end{aligned} \tag{49}$$

where the updates of derivatives of outputs are obtained as (Pandey, 2005a):

$$\frac{\partial y_{j,R}(n+1)}{\partial w_{kl}(n)} = \varphi'(net_{j,R}(n))\left[\sum_{i\in B}\left(w_{ji,R}(n)\frac{\partial y_{i,R}(n)}{\partial w_{kl}(n)} - w_{ji,I}(n)\frac{\partial y_{i,I}(n)}{\partial w_{kl}(n)}\right) + \delta_{kj}u_l^*(n)\right] \tag{50}$$

$$\frac{\partial y_{j,I}(n+1)}{\partial w_{kl}(n)} = \varphi'(net_{j,I}(n))\left[\sum_{i\in B}\left(w_{ji,R}(n)\frac{\partial y_{i,I}(n)}{\partial w_{kl}(n)} + w_{ji,I}(n)\frac{\partial y_{i,R}(n)}{\partial w_{kl}(n)}\right) + j\,\delta_{kj}u_l^*(n)\right]. \tag{51}$$

Here δ_{kj} is the kronecker delta, η represents the learning rate, $j \in B$, $k \in B$, and $l \in A \cup B$. The derivative terms of equations (50) - (51) are initialized by zeros. Out of all updates of equations (50) – (51), those corresponding to the accessible node, i.e. $j = out$, are used in equation (49) for updating the weights.

Simulation Results

Feedback equalizers, generally, exhibit improved performance in comparison with feedforward equalizers when there are strong distant echoes in the channel. In this simulation example, a channel with some distant echoes is used. The discrete time impulse response $h(n)$ of this channel is plotted against sample number n in Figure 10. Four different equalizers, namely, a linear FIR equalizer, a decision feedback equalizer (DFE), a feedforward neural network equalizer, and an RNN equalizer are used in the study. The details of their structures are summarized in Table 2. In the recurrent neural network blind equalizer, fifth node is used as the accessible output (i.e. $out = 5$). Learning rate parameter for all the blind equalizers is $\eta = 5\times10^{-6}$.

The MSE plots of complex valued feedforward neural network and complex-valued RNN equalizers used in the simulation, at 20 dB SNR with 16 – QAM signal are illustrated in Figure 11(a). After 8000 iterations the MSE obtained with RNN equalizer is less than the MSE of feedforward NN equalizer. Figure 11(b) shows the symbol error rate plots of these blind equalizers. In terms of SER also, the performance of the recurrent blind equalizer is better than the other blind equalizers. Similar observations are made when simulations are performed with 8 – PSK signal.

Another recurrent structure for blind equalization is presented in (Pandey, 2005a) which uses a complex valued MPL for feedforward section of a DFE whereas the feedback filter is a linear filter. This model gives a better performance for channels with distant echoes, when compared with RNN model. The limitation of this RNN equalizer is the convergence speed as this is also based on the minimization of a cost function like other higher order statistics-based blind equalizers. However, the performance of this RNN equalizer is better than that of (Kechriotis et al., 1994), as it is based on CMA cost function. Further, the model of (Kechriotis et al., 1994) is not used for higher order signal constellations (Pandey, 2001).

EQUALIZATION OF TIME VARYING CHANNELS

For the equalization of time varying channels, training symbols are periodically sent through the channel and equalization is accomplished with the help of these symbols. However, in blind equalization, training symbols are not used. In general, the performance of an adaptive system in nonstationary environment depends upon the tracking ability of the training algorithm employed. The feedforward neural network-based equalizer models described in the previous sections are trained by using stochastic gradient descent technique. Therefore, the performance of these neural networks in nonstationary environment will be governed by this training algorithm. However, in order to compare the performances of linear and neural blind equalizers, both trained by the same stochastic

Table 2. Structural details of various blind equalizers used in simulation (Copyright ACTA Press 2005)

Equalizer Type	Feedforward part	Feedback part
Linear FIR Filter	35 taps	----
Decision Feedback Equalizer	19 taps	16 taps
Multilayer feedforward Neural Network	19 Input nodes 15 Hidden nodes	----
Recurrent Neural Network	26 Input nodes (including feedback)	9 Hidden nodes

Figure 10. A Channel with distant Echoes (© ACTA Press 2005, used with permission)

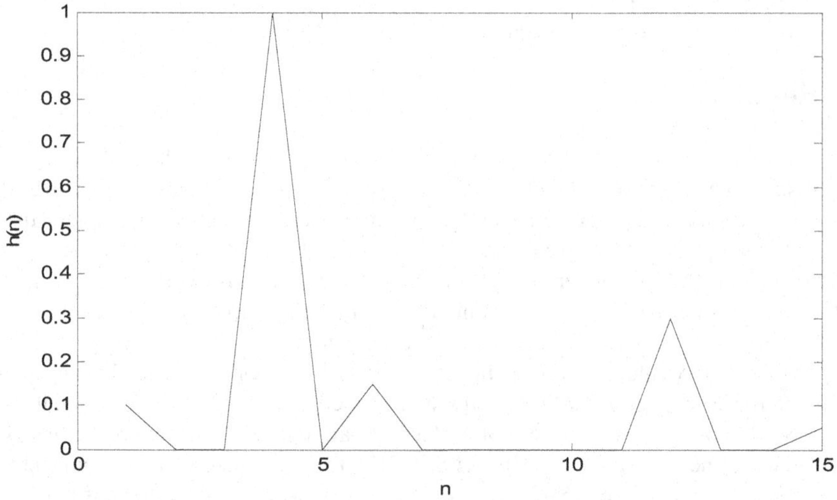

Figure 11. (a) MSE plot for 16-QAM signal (b) SER performance for 16-QAM signal (© ACTA Press 2005, used with permission)

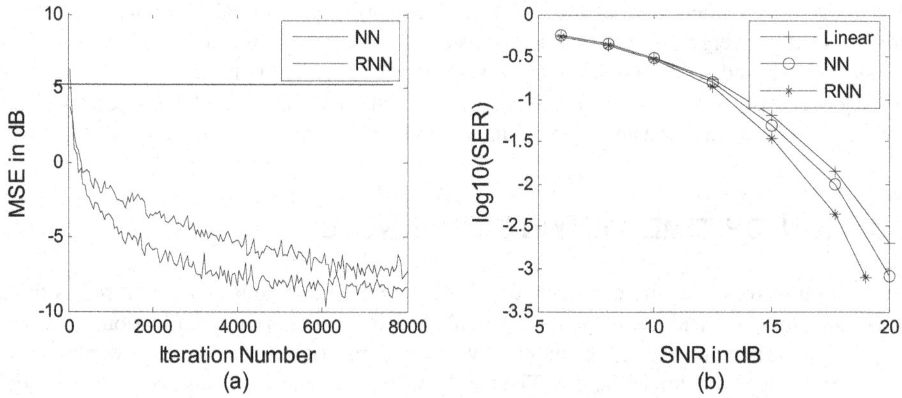

gradient method in nonstationary environment, the simulation of a nonstationary channel is presented in this section. In (You & Hong, 1998), the study is limited to a stationary channel. This equalizer has been extended for nonstationary environment by introducing a modified activation function (Pandey, 2004).

The nonstationary channel used for the simulation incorporates both, a sudden change and a gradual change in the environment. There is a fixed zero at $z_1 = 0.5$. After 3000 iterations another zero which is a mobile zero, appears as given below.

$$z_2(n) = 1.6\exp(j2\pi/3) + 0.2\exp(j\pi.(n-3000).10^{-4}). \tag{52}$$

The channel suddenly changes after $n = 3000$ and becomes a continuously varying medium. For 16-QAM signal, Figure 12 (a) shows the plots of 1000 output symbols of neural blind equalizer, after 10000 iterations.

Figure 12. (a) Output of Equalizer NN1 (b) Output of Equalizer NN2 (© ENFORMATIKA 2004, used with permission)

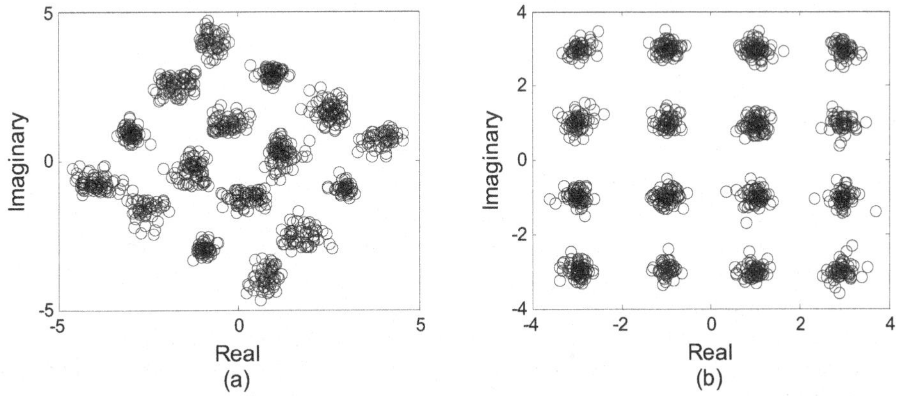

It can be seen that the neural blind equalizer described in the previous section, denoted as NN1, could not correct the arbitrary phase shift of the output symbols automatically, in case of the time varying channel used in the present simulation. Therefore, some external phase correction algorithm that can continually correct the arbitrary phase shift of output symbols is required. An algorithm for this arbitrary phase estimation is mentioned in (Labat, Macchi, & Laot, 1998). Here, an alternative algorithm, inspired by the CMA cost function, to correct the arbitrary phase shift as given in (Pandey, 2004) is used.

The phase angle $\theta(n)$ in the phase shift term $e^{-j\theta(n)}$ is recursively updated as

$$\theta(n+1) = \theta(n) + \mu \, \mathrm{Im}[y(n)].\mathrm{Re}[y(n)].\{(\mathrm{Re}[y(n)])^2 - \bar{R}_2\} \quad (53)$$

where $$\bar{R}_2 = E\left[(\mathrm{Re}[y(n)])^4\right] / E\left[(\mathrm{Re}[y(n)])^2\right]. \quad (54)$$

The constant $\bar{R}_2 = 8.2$ for 16 – QAM signal.

To take the full advantage of multi-saturated activation function of the neural network, the phase correction should be applied to the signal in the network, before it passes through the nonlinearity of the output node. For example, the arbitrary phase shift can be corrected at the output of the hidden layer nodes. This can also be achieved by modifying the activation function of the output layer neuron as described below.

$$\phi^{(2)}(z) = f(z_R \cos\theta - z_I \sin\theta) + jf(z_R \sin\theta + z_I \cos\theta) \quad (55)$$

where $z = z_R + jz_I$ is a complex quantity, the function *f*(.) is defined as $f(x) = x + c\sin(\pi x)$, and c is a positive real number. The parameter θ is adapted by the following update equation.

$$\theta(n+1) = \theta(n) + \mu \, \mathrm{Im}[net^{(2)}(n)].\mathrm{Re}[net^{(2)}(n)].\left((\mathrm{Re}[net^{(2)}(n)])^2 - \bar{R}_2\right) \quad (56)$$

Figure 12 (b) shows the output of neural network equalizer with phase correcting node of equation (55), denoted as NN2.

The weights connected between hidden and output layer are updated by

$$w_k^{(2)}(n+1) = w_k^{(2)}(n) + \eta\delta^{(2)}(n)u_k^*(n)e^{-j\theta(n)} \quad (57)$$

where $\delta^{(2)}(n)$ is same as defined by equation (39).

By using the stochastic gradient algorithm, the update rule for weights $\{w_{kl}^{(1)}\}$, connected between input and hidden layer, is given by equations (41), where for the present case, $\delta_k^{(1)}(n)$ is defined by

$$\delta_k^{(1)}(n) = \Big[\phi^{(1)'}(net_{k,R}^{(1)}(n).\mathrm{Re}\big[\delta^{(2)}(n).w_k^{(2)*}(n).e^{-j\theta(n)}\big] + j\varphi^{(1)'}(net_{k,I}^{(1)}(n)).\mathrm{Im}\big[\delta^{(2)}(n).w_k^{(2)*}(n).e^{-j\theta(n)}\big]\Big]. \tag{58}$$

Simulation Results

The MSE plots obtained with and without phase correction node are shown in Figure 13 (a) and 13(c) for 16-QAM and 8-PSK signals, respectively. The symbol error rate curves obtained with neural network NN2 for these two constellations and those for NN1 with external phase correction are shown in Figure 13(b) and 13(d). From these figures it can be observed that the use of activation function of equation (55) gives lower MSE and SER than those obtained when the arbitrary phase shift is corrected at the output.

The present equalizer is faster than that discussed in previous section in tracking the time varying channels. However, its tracking ability is not as good as obtained by second order statistics-based equalizers. In order to improve the performance its use with a channel estimator needs further investigation.

CONCLUSION

The chapter has provided an overview of some equalization techniques using complex-valued neural networks for removing ISI in digital communication. A model based on complex-valued RBFN is discussed and the algorithm for its training is described. The performance is compared with some other neural networks based equalizers on the basis of resulting bit error rate. For blind equalization, complex-valued MLP-based models are discussed with two different symbol constellations viz M-QAM and M-PSK. Then a recurrent equalizer is discussed for equalization of channels with distant echoes. Its performance is also compared with equalizers based on feedforward structures. The extension of feedforward models for equalization of time-varying channel is described. Finally, some observations are made regarding the advantages and limitations of various equalizers.

FUTURE RESEARCH DIRECTIONS

According to study of Cha and Kassam (1995), the performance obtained by complex- valued RBFN equalizers is better than that of complex - valued MLP equalizers. However, it is also pointed out that this does not necessarily mean that other neural network structures or their complex extensions are generally inferior to the CRBFN equalizers. More rigorous analysis is required before any meaningful comparison between these structures is made. Also, the performance needs to be evaluated with different basis functions. Further investigations would be required to judge the performance of RBFN's performance in blind equalization.

Recently, Kim and Adali (2000; 2001a; 2001b; 2002; 2003) have studied a fully complex MLP equalizer in which the activation functions of the neural networks are all complex functions and better performance has been reported. The application of fully complex activation functions with various feedforward and recurrent neural networks is required to be studied for their better understanding. The convergence speed and resulting symbol error rate need to be investigated for applications of equalization of nonlinear and time-varying communication channels. A similar approach for complex RBFN equalizer would be interesting.

As a general observation, in order to obtain good performance, the order of the equalizer must be high. This implies that there is an exponential increase in the number of nodes of RBFN equalizers. The application of equalizer in conjunction with a channel estimator can be a viable solution to keep the complexity of the equalizer under practicable limits, as suggested in (Gan et al., 1999). In MLP-based equalizers also the computational complexity is higher than the conventional linear equalizers. Some new ingenuous methods are needed for reducing the complexity of neural equalizers.

Figure 13. (a) MSE curves for NN1 and NN2 with 16-QAM signal (b) SER performance for NN1 and NN2 with 16-QAM signal (c) MSE curves for NN1 and NN2 with 8-PSK signal (d) SER performance for NN1 and NN2 with 8-PSK signal (© ENFORMATIKA 2004, used with permission)

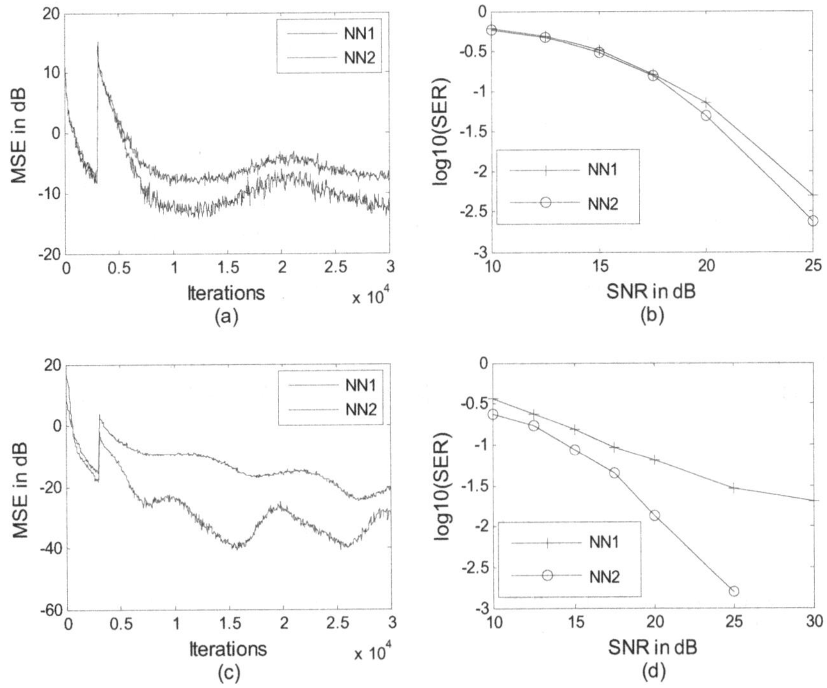

The convergence time of training algorithm is another important aspect in equalization. For the equalization of fast time varying channels, the convergence time must be small. The frequent transmission of long training sequences restricts the use of these equalizers in fast fading environments. Therefore, development of new models and faster algorithms is another challenge in this research area.

The next important issue is the choice of adaptable activation functions for equalizers, based on neural networks. The application of multi-saturated activation functions plays an important role in improving the performance of MLP-based blind equalizers. The use of adaptable activation function can also lead to further improvement in the performance of equalizers as indicated by the study of Uncini et al. (1999). This is another area which needs further investigations.

The second order statistics (SOS) based equalization methods are generally, faster than higher order statistics (HOS) based equalization. Most of the recently studied equalization methods, with linear filters, are based on SOS. In (Fang & Chow, 1999), the application of neural network for equalization of communication channels is based on SOS. The extension of SOS-based neural equalizers to complex valued structures could be a new direction in the research related to channel equalization.

Finally, theoretical analysis of the fundamental properties and convergence analysis of various models for equalization is required for better understanding of the behavior of equalizers which is crucial for further development of the filed.

REFERENCES

Benvenuto, N., Marchesi, M., Piazza, F., & Uncini A. (1991). A comparison between real and complex valued neural networks in communication applications. *Proc. Int. Conf. Neural Networks ICANN*, Espoo, Finland.

Cha, I., & Kassam, S. A. (1995). Channel equalization using adaptive complex radial basis function networks. *IEEE J. Sel. Areas Commn.*, *13*(1), 122-131.

Chen, S., Maclaughlin, S., & Mulgrew, B. (1994). Complex-valued radial basis function networks, Part II: Application to digital communication channel equalization. *Signal Processing*, *36*, 175-188.

Chen, S., Mulgrew, B., & Grant, P. M. (1993). A clustering technique for digital communications channel equalization using radial basis function networks. *IEEE Trans. Neural Networks*, *4*(4), 570-579.

Fang, Y., & Chow, T. W. S. (1999). Blind equalization of a noisy channel by linear neural network. *IEEE Trans. Neural Networks*, *10*(4), 925 – 929.

Gan, Q., Saratchandran, P., Sundararajan, N., & Subramanian, K. R. (1999). A complex valued radial basis function network for equalization of fast time varying channels. *IEEE Trans. Neural Networks*, *10*(4), 958 – 960.

Georgiou, G., & Koutsougeras C. (1992). Complex Backpropagation. *IEEE Trans. Circuits and Systems II*, *39*(5), 330-334.

Godard, D. N. (1980). Self-recovering equalization and carrier tracking in two dimensional data communication systems. *IEEE Trans. Communications*, *28*, 1867– 875.

Gomes, J., & Barroso, V. (1997). Using an RBF network for blind equalization: Design and performance evaluation. *Proc. ICASSP*, 4, 3285–3288, Munich, Germany.

Haykin, S. (Ed.). (1994a) *Neural Networks: A Comprehensive Foundation.* Upper Saddle River, New Jersey: Prentice –Hall.

Haykin, S. (Ed.). (1994b). *Blind Deconvolution.* Englewood Cliffs, New Jersey: Prentice-Hall.

Hirose, A. (1992a). Continuous complex-valued back-propagation learning. *Electronics Letters*, *28*(20), 1854-1855.

Huang, G. B., Saratchandran, P., & Sundarrajan N. (2005). A generalized growing and pruning RBF (GGAP-RBF) neural network for function approximation. *IEEE Trans. Neural Networks*, *16*(1), 57-67.

Jianping, D., Sundarrajan, N., & Saratchandran, P. (2002). Communication channel equalization using complex-valued minimal radial basis function neural networks. *IEEE Trans. Neural networks*, *13*(3), 687-697.

Johnson, R., Jr., Schniter, P., Endres, T. J., Behm, J. D., Brown, D. R., & Casas, R. A. (1998). Blind equalization using the constant modulus criterion: A review. *Proc. IEEE*, *86*(10), 1927–1950.

Katz, G., & Sadot, D. (2007). Radial basis function network equalizer for optical communication OOK system. *Journal of Light Wave Technology*, *25*(9), 2631-2637.

Kechriotis, G., Zervas, E., & Manolakos, E. S. (1994). Using recurrent neural networks for adaptive communication channel equalization. *IEEE Trans. Neural Networks*, *5*(2), 267–278.

Kim, T., & Adali, T. (2000). Fully complex backpropagation for constant envelope signal Processing. *Proc. IEEE Workshop on Neural Networks for Signal Processing (NNSP)*, *1*, 231-240, Sydney Australia.

Kim, T., & Adali, T. (2001a). Complex backpropagation neural network using elementary transcendental activation function. *Proc. IEEE Int. Conf. on Acoustics, Speech, Signal Processing (ICASSP)*, Salt Lake city UT, *2*, 1281-1284.

Kim, T., & Adali, T. (2001b). Nonlinear satellite channel equalization using fully complex feed-forward neural networks. *Poc. of IEEE Workshop on Nonlinear Signal and Image Processing*. Baltimore.

Kim, T., & Adali, T. (2002). Fully complex multilayer perceptron network for nonlinear signal processing. *Journal of VLSI Signal Processing Systems for Signal, Image and Video Technology, Special Issue: Neural Networks for Signal Processing, 32*, 29-43.

Kim, T., & Adali, T. (2003). Approximation by fully- complex multilayer perceptrons. *Neural Computation, 15*(7), 1641-1666.

Labat, J., Macchi, O., & Laot, C. (1998). Adaptive decision feedback equalization: Can you skip the training period. *IEEE Trans. Communications, 46*(7), 921–930.

Leung, H., & Haykin, S. (1991). The complex backpropagation algorithm. *IEEE Trans. Accoust., Speech, Signal Processing, 39*, 2101-2104.

Li, M. B., Huang, G. B., Saratchandran, P., & Sundarrajan, N. (2006). Complex-valued growing and pruning RBF neural networks for communication channel equalization. *IEE Proc. Vision, Image and Signal Processing, 153*(4), 411-418.

Mandic, D. P., & Chambers, J. A. (2001). *Recurrent neural networks for prediction: Learning algorithms Architectures and stability*. John Wiley and Sons.

Nitta, T. (1997). An extension of the back-propagation to complex numbers. *Neural Networks, 10*(8), 1391-1415.

Ong, S., You, C., Choi, S., & Hong D. (1997). A decision feedback recurrent neural equalizer as an infinite impulse response filter. *IEEE Trans. Signal Processing, 45*(11), 2851–2858.

Pandey, R. (2001). *Blind equalization and source separation using neural networks*. Doctoral dissertation, I.I.T. Roorkee, India.

Pandey, R. (2004). Complex Valued Neural Networks for Blind Equalization of Time- Varying Channels. *International Journal of Signal Processing, 1*(1), 1-8.

Pandey, R. (2005a). Complex Valued Recurrent Neural Networks for Blind Equalization. *International Journal of Modelling and Simulation, 25*(3), 182-189.

Pandey, R. (2005b). A Feedforward Neural Network for Blind Equalization with PSK Signal. *Neural Computing & Applications, 14*(4), 290-298.

Parisi, R., Elio Claudio D. D., Orlandi G., & Rao B. D.(1997). Fast adaptive digital equalization by recurrent neural network. *IEEE Trans. Signal Processing, 45*(11), 2731 – 2739.

Proakis, J. G. (1995). *Digital Communications*. Singapore: McGraw Hill.

Uncini, A., Vecci, L., Campolucci, P., & Piazza, F. (1999). Complex-valued neural networks with adaptive spline activation function for digital radio links nonlinear equalization. *IEEE Trans. Signal Processing, 47*(2), 505-514.

Wolfgang, A., Chen, S., & Hanzo, S. (2004). Radial basis function assisted space time equalization for dispersive fading environment. *Electronics Letters, 40*(16).

You, C., & Hong, D. (1998). Nonlinear blind equalization schemes using complex valued multilayer feedforward neural networks. *IEEE Trans., Neural Networks, 9*(6), 1442 -1455.

ADDITIONAL READING

Amari, S. I., & Cichocki A.(1998). Adaptive blind signal processing – Neural network approaches. *Proc. IEEE, 86*(10), 2026 - 2048.

Choi, S., Cichocki, A., & Amari, S. I. (1998). Blind equalization of SIMO channels via spatio – temporal anti Hebbian learning rule. *Proc. Neural Networks for Signal Processing, VIII- IEEE Signal Processing Society Workshop*. Cambridge, UK.

Cichocki, A., & Unbehauen, R. (1994). *Neural Networks for Optimization and Signal Processing.* Chichester: John Wiley & Sons.

Cirpan, H. A., & Tsatsanis, M. K. (1999). Maximum likelihood blind channel estimation in the presence of Doppler shifts. *IEEE Trans. Signal Processing, 47*(6), 1559-1569.

Destro Filho, J. B., Favier, G., & Travassos Romano, J. M.(1996). Neural networks for blind equalization. *Proc. IEEE Globcom., 1*, 96-200.

Eweda, E. (1997). Tracking analysis of the sign-sign algorithm for nonstationary adaptive filtering with Gaussian data. *IEEE Trans. Signal Processing, 45*(5), 1375-1378.

Ghosh, M. (1998). Blind decision feedback equalization for terrestrial television receivers. *Proc. IEEE, 86*(10), 2070-2081.

Gomes, J., & Barroso, V. (1997). Using an RBF network for blind equalization: Design and performance evaluation. *Proc. ICASSP, 4*, Munich Germany, 3285-3288.

Hanna, A., & Mendic, D. (2002). A data-reusing nonlinear gradient descent algorithm for a class of complex-valued neural adaptive filters. *Neural Processing Letters, 17*, 1-7.

Hirose, A. (1992b). Dynamics of fully complex-valued neural networks. *Electronics Letters, 28*(18), 1492-1494.

Lee, D. D. (2001). Improving the capacity of complex-valued neural networks with a modified gradient descent learning rule. *IEEE Trans. Neural Networks,* 12(2), 439-443.

Li, X., & Fan, H. (2000). QR factorization based blind channel identification and equalization with second order statistics. *IEEE Trans. Signal Processing, 48*(1), 60-69.

Liavas, A. P., Regalia, P. A., & Delmas J. P. (1999). Blind channel approximation: Effective channel order determination. *IEEE Trans. Signal Processing, 47*(12), 3336 – 3344.

Medsker, L. R., & Jain, L. (2000). *Recurrent Neural Networks: Design and Applications.* CRC Press.

Mandic, D. (2002). Data reusing recurrent neural adaptive filters. *Neural Computation, 14*(11), 2693-2707.

Meraim, K. A., Hua, Y., Loubaton, P., & Mouline, E. (1997). Subspace method for blind identification of multichannel FIR systems in noise field with unknown spatial covariance. *IEEE Signal Processing Letters, 4*(5), 135 – 137.

Nitta, T. (1994). An analysis on decision boundaries in the complex back-propagation network. *IEEE Int. Conf. on Neural Networks*, (pp. 934-939).

Nitta, T. (2002). On the critical points of the complex-valued neural networks. *Proc. of 9th Int. Conf. on Neural Information Processing (ICONIP02), 3*, 1099-1103.

Pandey, R. (2005). Fast Blind Equalization Using Complex-Valued MLP. *Neural Processing Letters, 21*(3), 215-225.

Pandey, R., & Gautam, J. K. (2001). RBF Based Nonlinear Estimator for Blind Equalization of Communication Channels. *National Conf. On Electronics*, ELCTRO- 2001, BHU Varanasi, India.

Pandey, R., & Gautam, J. K. (2002). Blind Equalization of Nonlinear Communication Channels Using Modified FLANN. *IETE Journal of Research*, *48*(2), 12-132.

Patra, J. C., Pal, R. N., Baliarsingh, R., & Panda, G. (1999). Nonlinear channel equalization for QAM signal constellation using Artificial Neural Network. *IEEE Trans. Syst. Man Cybern. – Part B*, *29*(2), 262-271.

Shen, J., & Ding Z. (2000). Direct blind MMSE channel equalization based on second order statistics. *IEEE Trans. Signal Processing*, *48*(4), 1015-1022.

Chapter IX
Learning Algorithms for Complex-Valued Neural Networks in Communication Signal Processing and Adaptive Equalization as its Application

Cheolwoo You
Myongji University, South Korea

Daesik Hong
Yonsei University, South Korea

ABSTRACT

In this chapter, the complex Backpropagation (BP) algorithm for the complex backpropagation neural networks (BPN) consisting of the suitable node activation functions having multi-saturated output regions is presented and analyzed by the benchmark testing. And then the complex BPN is utilized as nonlinear adaptive equalizers that can deal with both quadrature amplitude modulation (QAM) and phase shift key (PSK) signals of any constellation sizes. In addition, four nonlinear blind equalization schemes using complex BPN for M-ary QAM signals are described and their learning algorithms are presented. The presented complex BP equalizer (CBPE) gives, compared with conventional linear complex equalizers, an outstanding improvement with respect to bit error rate (BER) when channel distortions are nonlinear.

INTRODUCTION

Intersymbol interference (ISI) of the digital communication channel becomes a main drawback to efficient use of frequency bandwidth efficiency and performance improvement. So, it is necessary to use adaptive equalizers to restore the digital signal distorted by ISI. For equalization, many powerful adaptive algorithms have been developed such as the least mean squares (LMS) algorithm, the recursive least squares (RLS) algorithm and so on. But, the linear adaptive algorithms were not successful occasionally when channel distortion is nonlinear because of the assumption that the equalizer output is a linear function of the inputs. On this account, nonlinear adaptive equalization techniques have been required and developed. Among these nonlinear adaptive equalization algorithms, the backpropagation (BP) algorithm has occupied an important position because of its ease of implementation and nontrivial mapping capabilities (Arai, 1989, June).

On the other hand, in conventional equalizers, we assume that the receiver has knowledge of the transmitted information sequence in forming of the error signal between the desired symbol and its estimate for initially adjusting the equalizer weights. However, there are some applications, such as multipoint communication networks involving a control unit connected to several data terminal equipments (DTEs) and wireless communication systems using digital technology, where it is desirable for the receiver to adjust the equalizer weights without a known training sequence available. Equalization techniques based on initial adjustment of the weights without a training sequence are said to be *self-recovering* or *blind* (Proakis, 1989; Godard, 1980; Haykin, 1989). Among the useful blind equalization algorithms, stochastic-gradient iterative equalization schemes are based on minimizing a nonconvex and nonlinear cost function. However, as they use a linear FIR filter with a convex decision region, their residual estimation error is high.

In this chapter, the complex BP algorithm is described where the node activation function is composed of two real activation functions for the real and the imaginary net value of the node output. Also, the general characteristics of the required activation function are introduced and some examples are presented. In an example, each real activation function has multi-saturated output region in order to deal with signals of any constellation sizes. Also, a nonlinear adaptive equalizer scheme using the complex BP algorithm is presented. To see whether the complex BP algorithm works or not, the benchmark tests are introduced. In addition, four nonlinear blind equalization schemes employing a complex-valued multilayer perceptron instead of the linear filter are presented and their learning algorithms are derived. After the important properties that a suitable complex-valued activation function must possess are discussed, the suitable complex-valued activation function is introduced to deal with QAM signals of any constellation sizes. It has been proven that by the nonlinear transformation of the activation function, the correlation coefficient between the real and imaginary parts of input data decreases when they are jointly Gaussian random variables. Lastly, the effectiveness of the presented schemes is verified in terms of initial convergence speed and MSE in the steady state.

BACKGROUND

Many authors have studied to solve equalization problems by using BP algorithm (Gibson, Siu, & Cowan, 1989, May) and have acquired the good results. Their applications, however, have been limited to binary {0, 1} or bipolar {-1, 1} valued signals, due to the sigmoid function or the $\tanh(ax/2)$ taken as the nonlinear activation function. The used channels are also the real-valued models. But, as applications of the BP algorithm have progressed in various fields, the BP algorithm for complex-valued channel models and complex-valued signals with bigger signal constellation, which have been used widely in many applications of the digital communications or signal processing, has been requisite. For instance, the modulation techniques such as M-ary QAM (Quadrature Amplitude Modulation) or MPSK (M-ary phase shift key) in digital communications use the signal that has two components, i.e., amplitude and phase. Therefore, algorithms for the complex BP and activation functions for signals with multi-level constellation communication are very important in related fields.

Beginning with the paper by Sato (Sato, 1975) that is focused on PAM signal constellations, several blind equalization algorithms using a stochastic gradient approach have been developed. Sato's original work was generalized to two-dimensional and multidimensional signal constellations in the algorithms devised by Godard (Godard, 1980), Benveniste and Goursat (Benveniste, & Goursat, 1984), and Picchi and Prati (Picchi, & Prati, 1987). Such stochastic-gradient iterative equalization schemes are based on LMS adaptation, and apply a memoryless nonlinearity in the output of a linear finite-duration impulse response (FIR) equalization filter for the purpose of generating the "desired response", as shown in Fig. 1. Thus, the cost functions of these LMS-type blind algorithms are nonconvex and nonlinear functions of the tap weights. However, a linear FIR filter structure

Figure 1. Block diagram of stochastic-gradient iterative blind equalization schemes

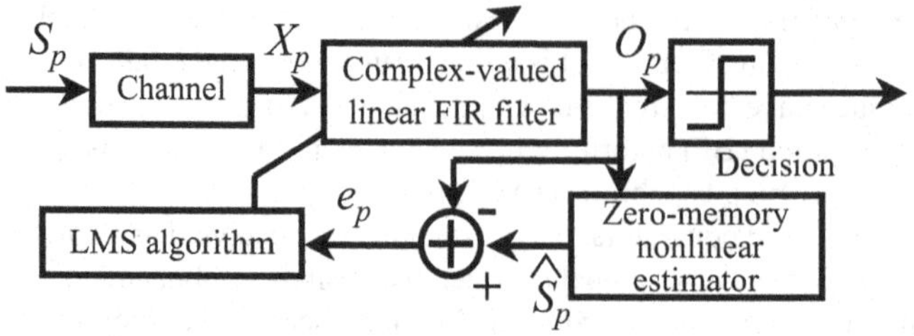

Figure 2. The characteristic of (a) the real part and (b) the imaginary part of the activation function in Eq. (1)

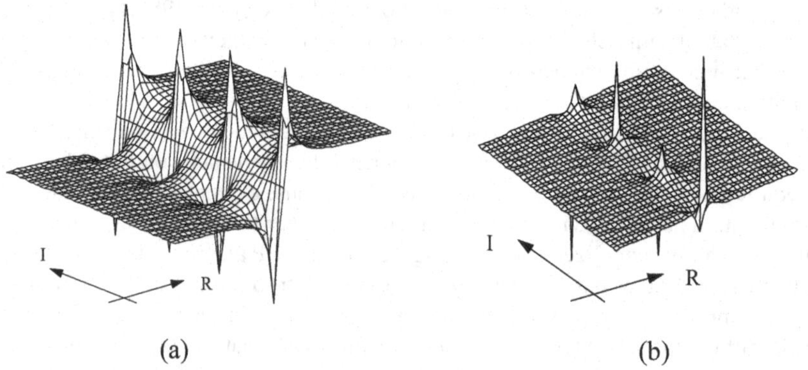

is not adequate to optimize such functions because its decision region is convex (Duda, & Hart, 1973). Therefore, a blind equalization scheme with a nonlinear structure that can form nonconvex decision regions is necessary.

Multilayer feedforward neural networks provide a powerful device for approximating a nonlinear input-output mapping of a general nature. Many studies have shown that multilayer feedforward neural networks can form convex and nonconvex decision regions because of their nontrivial mapping capability (Arai, 1989; Freemann, & Skapura, 1991; Hecht-Nielson, 1988; Irie, & Miyake, 1988; Funahasi, 1989; Nilsson, 1965). Some authors have effectively utilized neural networks as adaptive equalizers for a simplistic FIR channel model, a nonlinear satellite channel, and so on (Gibson, Siu, & Cowan, 1989, May; Balay, & Palicot, 1994; Al-Mashouq, & Reed, 1994; You, & Hong, 1995, June; Cho, You, & Hong, 1996, June). Nevertheless, their applications have been limited to equalization problems with a training sequence for bipolar {-1, 1} and ternary {-1, 0, 1} signals transmitted through real-valued baseband channel models. Thus, whether a training sequence is used or not, there is a great need to develop a neural network equalizer that can deal with not only complex-valued channel models, but also higher level signal constellations such as *M*-ary QAM which is a very effective technique to achieve a high bit-rate transmission without increasing the bandwidth.

Some authors have already recognized the usefulness of a complex-valued neural network. The complex backpropagation (CBP) algorithm was developed independently by several researchers (Leung, & Haykin, 1991; Georgiou, & Koutsougeras, 1992; Benvenuto, & Piazza, 1992; You, & Hong, 1996, June). Also, the training algorithm for complex-valued recurrent neural networks is presented in (Kechriototic, Zervas, & Manolakos, 1994). But, in their papers, a complex-valued activation function that could deal with signals of any constellation size is not mentioned. In (Chang, Yeh, & Chang, 1994), Chang *et al.* proposed a neural equalizer with a training sequence for QAM signals. However, they used two real-valued feedforward networks, not one complex-valued neural network. In addition, they used a bipolar representation for QAM signals. Thus, as the signal constellation becomes larger the network complexity must also increase accordingly. The case of a blind equalizer using a complex-valued multilayer feedforward neural network (CFNN) is found in (Benvenuto, Marchesi, Piazza, & Uncini, 1991, May). However, their applications were limited to bipolar signals.

THE LEARNING ALGORITHM OF THE COMPLEX-VALUED NEURAL NETWORKS

Node Activation Function

Complex Processing Element

Properties

The BP algorithm is probably the most widely used supervised learning algorithm in neural networks (NNs) applications. The activation function differentiates the BP algorithm from the conventional LMS algorithm. Various dynamic functions can be used as the activation function if continuously differentiable. Usually, the choice of the activation function depends on how we choose to represent the output signal. For example, if we want the output units to be binary {0, 1}, the sigmoid function is used as the node activation function and then the binary threshold function can be finally used, and when the signal value is bipolar {-1, 1}, a tanh($\alpha x/2$) is used since this function is output-limiting and quasi-bistable but is also differentiable (Freemann, & Skapura, 1991). Of course, we can use the linear activation function. However, because the relationship we want to map is likely to be compound, a nonlinear function is very often used as the activation function.

For the sake of the complex BP algorithm, the activation function must be used in its complex version. In (Leung, & Haykin, 1991), the sigmoid function 1/{1+exp($-\alpha x$)} was taken as the nonlinear node activation function. The bipolar version of this sigmoid is

$$\begin{aligned} f_\alpha(x) &= \frac{2}{1+e^{-\alpha x}} - 1 \\ &= \frac{1-e^{-\alpha x_R} - \cos(\alpha x_I) + j\sin(\alpha x_I)}{1+e^{-\alpha x_R} + \cos(\alpha x_I) - j\sin(\alpha x_I)} \end{aligned} \tag{1}$$

where x is a complex number defined by $x=x_R+jx_I$ and α is a real number. Fig. 2 shows the characteristics of the real part and the imaginary part of $f_\alpha(x)$ in Eq. (1). As shown in this figure, the unnecessary periodicity occurs and the shapes of the saturation regions are not adequate to the signal, i.e., -1 and 1. The major causing such results is the characteristic of the exponential function, exp($-x$), that gives rise to phase distortion. Because of these effects, it is very difficult to train the system with this activation function. In addition, the development of various activation functions such as the activation function with multi-saturated output region becomes an arduous job.

Because of the problems mentioned above, the complex BP algorithm requires the new activation function that has the appropriate saturation regions and no additional phase-distortion caused by its input-output characteristic. Moreover, because the real part and the imaginary part of the complex signal usually have correlation, the two parts of the complex signal after the activation function must be able to affect each other as it used to be.

Now, we introduce the complex processing element (PE) with the nonlinear complex activation function that has no additional phase-distortion caused by its input-output characteristic. Fig. 3 shows a single complex PE. This PE has two real activation functions for the real and the imaginary net value of the node output, where these real activation functions are the same kinds of dynamic equations used in real signal processing. And, the real and the imaginary part of the node input signal can affect each other after the activation function. The complex activation function F for the complex BP algorithm is

Figure 3. A single complex processing element (PE) with the nonlinear activation functions

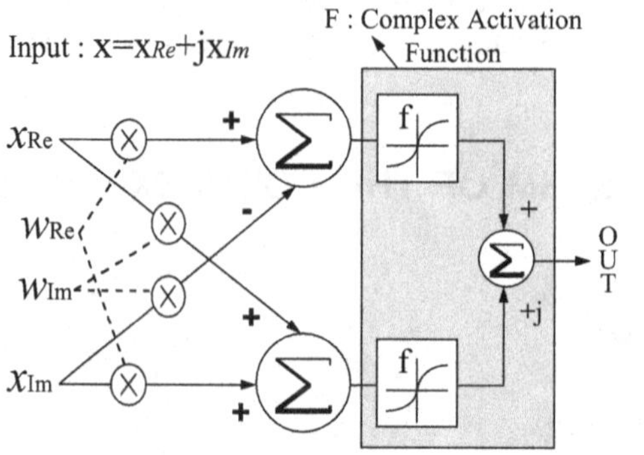

Figure 4. The characteristic of the real part of the activation function in Eq. (3)

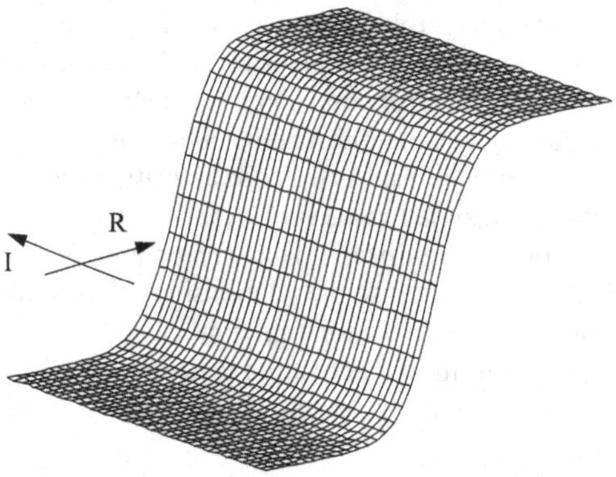

$$F(x) = f(x_R) + jf(x_I), \quad (2)$$

where f is a real activation function (Benvenuto, & Piazza, 1992; Nitta, & Furuya, 1991; Nitta, 1997). In this case, the design of activation functions for many kinds of complex signal processing becomes easy. Fig. 4 shows the characteristics of the real part and the imaginary part of the complex activation function F when $f(x_{R \text{ or } I})$ is $\tanh(\alpha x_{R \text{ or } I}/2)$, as defined by

$$F(x) = \tanh(\frac{\alpha}{2} x_R) + j \tanh(\frac{\alpha}{2} x_I). \quad (3)$$

Node Activation Function for Signal of Any Constellation Size in Communication Systems

Now, in order to deal with signals of any constellation size, we introduce the generalized activation function f that has multi-output values and multi-saturation regions

$$f(x) = Ax + B\sin(A\pi x) \quad (4)$$

and its differential is

$$f'(x) = A + AB\pi \cos(A\pi x), \quad (5)$$

where A and B are constant values. These values decide the step size and the nonlinearity in the activation function f.

Fig. 5 and Fig. 6 show the activation function f when A is 0.5 and B is 0.3. As shown in Fig. 5, Eq. (4) can form arbitrary output levels and saturation regions even if signals have any constellation size.

The Complex Backpropagation Algorithm

The Generalized Complex BP Algorithm

In this section, we shall present a detailed derivation of the generalized complex BP algorithm for the complex BPN consisting of many PEs shown in Fig. 3. Fig. 7 serves as the reference for most of the discussion.

To begin with, let's consider the equations for information processing in the three-layer network shown in Fig. 7. A complex input vector, $Xp = (x_{p1}, x_{p2}, \dots, x_{pN})^t$, is applied to the input layer of the network. The input units (or PEs) distribute the values to the hidden-layer units. The net input to the jth hidden units is

Figure 5. The activation function ***f*** *of Eq. (4) (**A** = 0.5, **B** = 0.3)*

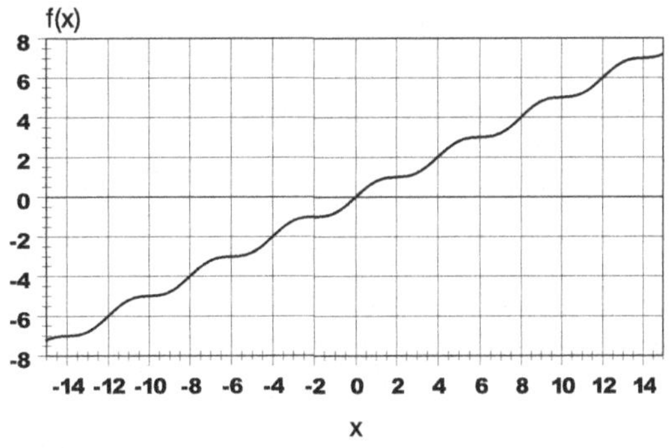

Figure 6. The differential of the activation function in Fig. 5

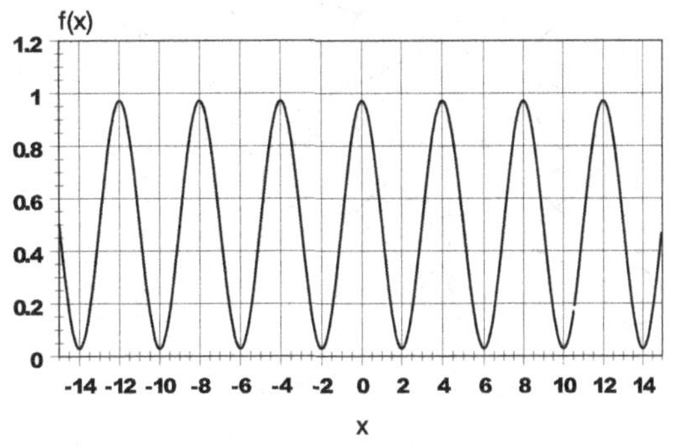

$$net^h_{pj} = net^h_{pj,R} + j net^h_{pj,I} = \sum_{i=1}^{N} w^h_{ji} x_{pi} + \theta^h_j$$
$$= \sum_{i=1}^{N} (w^h_{ji,R} x_{pi,R} - w^h_{ji,I} x_{pi,I}) + \theta^h_{j,R} + j[\sum_{i=1}^{N} (w^h_{ji,R} x_{pi,I} + w^h_{ji,I} x_{pi,R}) + \theta^h_{j,I}], \quad (6)$$

where w^h_{ji} is the complex weight on the connection from the ith input unit, and θ^h_j is the bias terms. The "h" superscript refers to quantities on the hidden layer. The output of this hidden node is

$$i_{pj} = i_{pj,R} + j i_{pj,I} = F^h_j(net^h_{pj}) = f^h_j(net^h_{pj,R}) + j f^h_j(net^h_{pj,I}), \quad (7)$$

where the "R" subscript and the "I" subscript refer to quantities on the real part and the imaginary part of the values these subscripts are written, respectively. The complex activation function F is identical with Eq. (2).

The equations for output nodes are

$$net^o_{pk} = net^o_{pk,R} + j net^o_{pk,I} = \sum_{j=1}^{L} w^o_{kj} i_{pj} + q^o_k$$
$$= \sum_{j=1}^{L} (w^o_{kj,R} i_{pj,R} - w^o_{kj,I} i_{pj,I}) + q^o_{k,R} + j[\sum_{j=1}^{L} (w^o_{kj,R} i_{pj,I} + w^o_{kj,I} i_{pj,R}) + q^o_{k,I}], \quad (8)$$

$$O_{pk} = O_{pk,R} + j O_{pk,I} = F^o_k(net^o_{pk}) = f^o_k(net^o_{pk,R}) + j f^o_k(net^o_{pk,I}) \quad (9)$$

where the "o" superscript refers to quantities on the output layer.

Figure 7. The three-layer BPN architecture (The bias terms are optional)

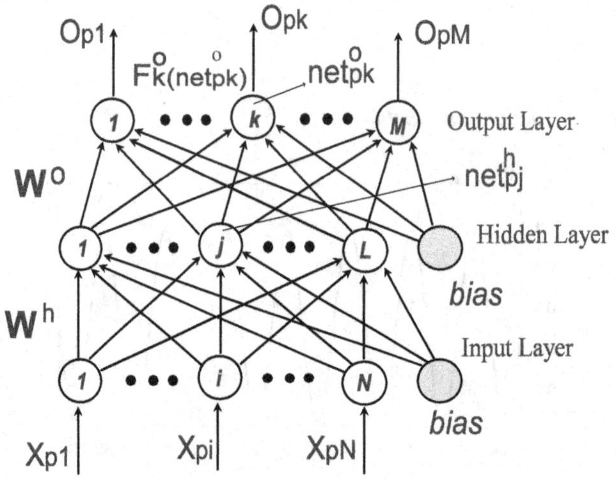

Update of Output-Layer Weights

We shall define the error at a single output unit to be $\delta_{pk} = (D_{pk} - O_{pk})$, where the subscript "$p$" refers to the pth training vector, and "k" refers to the kth output unit. And, D_{pk} is the desired output value, and O_{pk} is the actual output from the kth unit. The error that is minimized by the complex algorithm is the sum of the squares of the errors for all output units:

$$\begin{aligned} E_p &= \frac{1}{2}\sum_{k=1}^{M} \delta_{pk}\delta_{pk}^* \\ &= \frac{1}{2}\sum_{k=1}^{M} \left\langle D_{pk} - f_k^o(net_{pk,R}^o) - j f_k^o(net_{pk,I}^o)\right\rangle \left\langle D_{pk}^* - f_k^o(net_{pk,R}^o) + j f_k^o(net_{pk,I}^o)\right\rangle, \end{aligned} \tag{10}$$

where the asterisk denotes complex conjugation and M is the node number of the output layer. The factor of 1/2 in Eq. (10) is there for convenience in calculating derivatives later. To determine the direction in which to change the weights, the negative of the gradient of E_p with respect to the real and imaginary part of the coefficients is calculated. Writing the weights, w_{kj}, as

$$w_{kj}^o(t) = w_{kj,R}^o(t) + j w_{kj,I}^o(t). \tag{11}$$

First, let us consider the adaptation rule of the output layer. Using the steepest descent rule, the weights can be updated as

$$w_{kj,R}^o(t+1) = w_{kj,R}^o(t) - \eta \frac{\partial E_p}{\partial w_{kj,R}^o(t)}, \tag{12}$$

$$w_{kj,I}^o(t+1) = w_{kj,I}^o(t) - \eta \frac{\partial E_p}{\partial w_{kj,I}^o(t)}, \tag{13}$$

where η is a positive constant.

Combining (12) and (13), we have

$$w_{kj}^o(t+1) = w_{kj}^o(t) - \eta \left(\frac{\partial E_p}{\partial w_{kj,R}^o(t)} + j \frac{\partial E_p}{\partial w_{kj,I}^o(t)} \right). \tag{14}$$

Now, we find some expressions for the partial derivative:

$$\begin{aligned} \frac{\partial E_p}{\partial w_{kj,R}^o(t)} =& -\frac{1}{2}(D_{pk}^* - O_{pk}^*)\left[\frac{\partial f_k^o(net_{pk,R}^o)}{\partial net_{pk,R}^o}\frac{\partial net_{pk,R}^o}{\partial w_{pk,R}^o(t)} + j\frac{\partial f_k^o(net_{pk,I}^o)}{\partial net_{pk,I}^o}\frac{\partial net_{pk,I}^o}{\partial w_{pk,R}^o(t)} \right] \\ & -\frac{1}{2}(D_{pk} - O_{pk})\left[\frac{\partial f_k^o(net_{pk,R}^o)}{\partial net_{pk,R}^o}\frac{\partial net_{pk,R}^o}{\partial w_{pk,R}^o(t)} - j\frac{\partial f_k^o(net_{pk,I}^o)}{\partial net_{pk,I}^o}\frac{\partial net_{pk,I}^o}{\partial w_{pk,R}^o(t)} \right], \end{aligned} \tag{15}$$

where we have used Eq. (9) for the output value, O_{pk}, and the chain rule for partial derivatives. Evaluating all the partial derivatives in Eq. (15) by using Eq. (10) and Eq. (11), we get

$$\frac{\partial E_p}{\partial w^o_{kj,R}(t)} = -\frac{1}{2}(D^*_{pk} - O^*_{pk})\left[f'^o_k(net^o_{pk,R}) i_{pj,R} + j f'^o_k(net^o_{pk,I}) i_{pj,I} \right]$$
$$-\frac{1}{2}(D_{pk} - O_{pk})\left[f'^o_k(net^o_{pk,R}) i_{pj,R} - j f'^o_k(net^o_{pk,I}) i_{pj,I} \right]. \tag{16}$$

Similarly

$$\frac{\partial E_p}{\partial w^o_{kj,I}(t)} = -\frac{1}{2}(D^*_{pk} - O^*_{pk})\left[f'^o_k(net^o_{pk,R})(-i_{pj,I}) + j f'^o_k(net^o_{pk,I}) i_{pj,R} \right]$$
$$-\frac{1}{2}(D_{pk} - O_{pk})\left[f'^o_k(net^o_{pk,R})(-i_{pj,I}) - j f'^o_k(net^o_{pk,I}) i_{pj,R} \right]. \tag{17}$$

Combining (16) and (17), we get

$$\frac{\partial E_p}{\partial w^o_{kj,R}(t)} + j\frac{\partial E_p}{\partial w^o_{kj,I}(t)} = -\frac{1}{2}\left[(D_{pk,R} - O_{pk,R}) f'^o_k(net^o_{pk,R}) + j(D_{pk,I} - O_{pk,I}) f'^o_k(net^o_{pk,IR}) \right] i^*_{pj}. \tag{18}$$

The weight-update equations are summarized by defining a quantity

$$\delta^o_{pk} = f'^o_k(net^o_{pk,R}) \mathrm{Re}(D_{pk} - O_{pk}) + j f'^o_k(net^o_{pk,I}) \mathrm{Im}(D_{pk} - O_{pk}). \tag{19}$$

The weight-update equation can be written as

$$w^o_{kj}(t+1) = w^o_{kj}(t) + \eta\, \delta^o_{pk} i^*_{pj} \tag{20}$$

or

$$w^o_{kj,R}(t+1) = w^o_{kj,R}(t) + \eta \left(\delta^o_{pk,R} i_{pj,R} + \delta^o_{pk,I} i_{pj,I} \right) \tag{21-1}$$

$$w^o_{kj,I}(t+1) = w^o_{kj,I}(t) + \eta \left(\delta^o_{pk,I} i_{pj,R} - \delta^o_{pk,R} i_{pj,I} \right) \tag{21-2}$$

regardless of the function form of the output activation function, f_k^o.

Update of Hidden-Layer Weights

The adaptation rule for the hidden-layer weights is

$$w_{ji}^h(t+1) = w_{ji}^h(t) - \eta \left(\frac{\partial E_p}{\partial w_{ji,R}^h(t)} + j \frac{\partial E_p}{\partial w_{ji,I}^h(t)} \right). \tag{22}$$

The gradient of E_p with respect to the hidden-layer weights is

$$\begin{aligned} \frac{\partial E_p}{\partial w_{ji,R}^h(t)} + j \frac{\partial E_p}{\partial w_{ji,I}^h(t)} = &- \sum_{k=1}^{M} (D_{pk,R} - O_{pk,R}) f_k'^{\,o}(net_{pk,R}^o) w_{kj,R}^o f_j'^{\,h}(net_{pj,R}^h) x_{pi}^* \\ &+ j \sum_{k=1}^{M} (D_{pk,R} - O_{pk,R}) f_k'^{\,o}(net_{pk,R}^o) w_{kj,I}^o f_j'^{\,h}(net_{pj,I}^h) x_{pi}^* \\ &- j \sum_{k=1}^{M} (D_{pk,I} - O_{pk,I}) f_k'^{\,o}(net_{pk,I}^o) w_{kj,R}^o f_j'^{\,h}(net_{pj,I}^h) x_{pi}^* \\ &- \sum_{k=1}^{M} (D_{pk,I} - O_{pk,I}) f_k'^{\,o}(net_{pk,I}^o) w_{kj,I}^o f_j'^{\,h}(net_{pj,R}^h) x_{pi}^*. \end{aligned} \tag{23}$$

We can use the definition given in the previous section to write

$$\begin{aligned} \frac{\partial E_p}{\partial w_{ji,R}^h(t)} + j \frac{\partial E_p}{\partial w_{ji,I}^h(t)} &= - \sum_{k=1}^{M} \Big[(\delta_{pk,R}^o w_{kj,R}^o + \delta_{pk,I}^o w_{kj,I}^o) f_j'^{\,h}(net_{pj,R}^h) \\ &\quad + j(\delta_{pk,I}^o w_{kj,R}^o - \delta_{pk,R}^o w_{kj,I}^o) f_j'^{\,h}(net_{pj,I}^h) \Big] x_{pj}^* \\ &= -\left[f_j'^{\,h}(net_{pj,R}^h) \operatorname{Re}\left(\sum_{k=1}^{M} \delta_{pk}^o w_{kj}^{o*} \right) + f_j'^{\,h}(net_{pj,I}^h) \operatorname{Im}\left(\sum_{k=1}^{M} \delta_{pk}^o w_{kj}^{o*} \right) \right] x_{pj}^*. \end{aligned} \tag{24}$$

By defining a hidden-layer error term

$$\delta_{pj}^h = f_j'^{\,h}(net_{pj,R}^h) \operatorname{Re}\left(\sum_{k=1}^{M} \delta_{pk}^o w_{kj}^{o*}\right) + j f_j'^{\,h}(net_{pj,I}^h) \operatorname{Im}\left(\sum_{k=1}^{M} \delta_{pk}^o w_{kj}^{o*}\right). \tag{25}$$

We cause the weight update equations to become analogous to those for the output layer:

$$w_{ji}^h(t+1) = w_{ji}^h(t) + \eta \, \delta_{pj}^h x_{pi}^* \tag{26}$$

Table 1. The complex backpropagation training algorithm

1. Initialize the weights with small complex random numbers.
2. Present the input vector, *Xp*, and the desired output vector.
3. Calculate the net-input values, net_{pj}^{h}, to the hidden layer units and the outputs, i_{pj}, from the hidden layer.
4. Calculate the net-input values, net_{pk}^{o}, to each output layer unit and the outputs, O_{pk}.
5. Calculate the error terms for the output units

$$\delta_{pk}^{o} = f_k'^{o}(net_{pk,R}^{o})\,\mathrm{Re}(D_{pk} - O_{pk}) + j\, f_k'^{o}(net_{pk,I}^{o})\,\mathrm{Im}(D_{pk} - O_{pk})$$

and the error terms for the hidden units

$$\delta_{pj}^{h} = f_j'^{h}(net_{pj,R}^{h})\,\mathrm{Re}(\sum_{k=1}^{M} \delta_{pk}^{o} w_{kj}^{o*}) + j\, f_j'^{h}(net_{pj,I}^{h})\,\mathrm{Im}(\sum_{k=1}^{M} \delta_{pk}^{o} w_{kj}^{o*}).$$

6. Update weights on the output layer according to

$$w_{kj}^{o}(t+1) = w_{kj}^{o}(t) + \eta\, \delta_{pk}^{o}\, i_{pj}^{*}$$

or

$$w_{kj,R}^{o}(t+1) = w_{kj,R}^{o}(t) + \eta < \delta_{pk,R}^{o} i_{pj,R} + \delta_{pk,I}^{o} i_{pj,I} >,$$

$$w_{kj,I}^{o}(t+1) = w_{kj,I}^{o}(t) + \eta < \delta_{pk,I}^{o} i_{pj,R} - \delta_{pk,R}^{o} i_{pj,I} >,$$

and update weights on the hidden layer according to

$$w_{ji}^{h}(t+1) = w_{ji}^{h}(t) + \eta\, \delta_{pj}^{h}\, x_{pi}^{*}$$

or

$$w_{ji,R}^{h}(t+1) = w_{ji,R}^{h}(t) + \eta < \delta_{pj,R}^{h} x_{pi,R} + \delta_{pj,I}^{h} x_{pi,I} >,$$

$$w_{ji,I}^{h}(t+1) = w_{ji,I}^{h}(t) + \eta < \delta_{pj,I}^{h} x_{pi,R} - \delta_{pj,R}^{h} x_{pi,I} >,$$

regardless of the function form of the output activation function, *f*.

Note that the momentum term can also be added to the above formula.

or

$$w_{ji,R}^{h}(t+1) = w_{ji,R}^{h}(t) + \eta \left(\delta_{pj,R}^{h} x_{pi,R} + \delta_{pj,I}^{h} x_{pi,I}\right) \quad (27\text{-}1)$$

$$w_{ji,I}^{h}(t+1) = w_{ji,I}^{h}(t) + \eta \left(\delta_{pj,I}^{h} x_{pi,R} - \delta_{pj,R}^{h} x_{pi,I}\right) \quad (27\text{-}2)$$

Table 1 shows all of the relevant equations for the complex BP algorithm.

Benchmark Testing

To investigate whether the CBP algorithm works or not, two benchmarking tests, the 4-2-4 encoder and the *XOR* problem, have been performed. For the *XOR* problem, the neural network consists of one input unit, two hidden units, and one output unit. The *XOR* problem is to train the weights in this network so that the output unit will turn on if one or the other of the inputs is on, but not both. And, when we speak of a "the 4-2-4 encoder." we mean that a neural network is composed of four input units, two hidden units, and four output units. This is relatively "tight" encoder problem (Fahlman, 1988). The complex activation function used in testing is defined by Eq. (3), and the real activation function of this complex activation function has the dynamic range of [-1, 1].

Simulation results are shown in Tables 2 and 3, where "Noise-scale" is the standard deviation of random Gaussian noise added to the input patterns, the "η" is the learning parameter and (x, y) denotes the complex value $z=x+jy$. The described complex BP algorithm works very well in all benchmark testings. Especially, the complex BPN can learn complex signals in spite of using the input patterns corrupted by additive Gaussian random noise. The convergence of its mean square error (MSE) is also stable, as shown Fig. 8.

APPLICATIONS IN COMMUNICATION SIGNAL PROCESSING

Basic Application: Nonlinear Adaptive Equalization

In this section, the complex BPN using the complex BP algorithm is shown as a nonlinear adaptive equalizer that can deal with signals of any constellation sizes. The used complex node activation function F takes the real

Table 2. The XOR-testing results by the complex BP algorithm

Input	Output		
	Target Values	Simulation I [2000 trainings, η=0.05, Noise-scale=0.0]	Simulation II [2000 trainings, η=0.05, Noise-scale=0.1]
(+1, -1)	(+1, -1)	(0.959918, -0.930750)	(0.967129, -0.933158)
(+1, +1)	(-1, +1)	(-0.941673, 0.942162)	(-0.942102, 0.943796)
(-1, -1)	(-1, +1)	(-0.939690, 0.954705)	(-0.941356, 0.957203)
(-1, +1)	(+1, -1)	(0.962169, -0.936485)	(0.968435, -0.938358)

Table 3. The "4-2-4 encoder" results by the complex BP algorithm

Input	Output	
	Target Values	Simulation III [1000 trainings, η=0.1, Noise-scale=0.1]
(1,1) (-1,-1) (-1,-1) (-1,-1)	(1,1) (-1,-1) (-1,-1) (-1,-1)	(0.983,0.921) (-0.951,-0.956) (-0.994,-0.999) (-0.972,-0.962)
(-1,-1) (1,1) (-1,-1) (-1,-1)	(-1,-1) (1,1) (-1,-1) (-1,-1)	(-0.954,-0.942) (0.958,0.933) (-0.941,-0.942) (-0.972,-0.962)
(-1,-1) (-1,-1) (1,1) (-1,-1)	(-1,-1) (-1,-1) (1,1) (-1,-1)	(-0.999,-0.996) (-0.946,-0.949) (0.943,0.939) (-0.933,-0.935)
(-1,-1) (-1,-1) (-1,-1) (1,1)	(-1,-1) (-1,-1) (-1,-1) (1,1)	(-0.952,-0.945) (-0.999,-0.999) (-0.950,-0.951) (0.957,0.924)

Figure 8. MSE versus number of iterations for the ***XOR*** *problem*

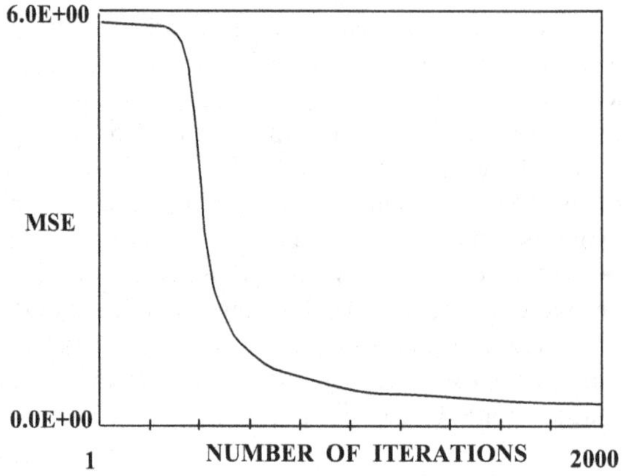

function defined by Eq. (4) as the real node activation function f. This real activation function has the multi-saturated output region.

The block diagram for simulation is described in Fig. 9. The performance of the complex BP equalizer (CBPE) is evaluated by calculating the mean square error (MSE) and the bit error rate (BER) of the output of the equalizer. Signal-energy-per-bit to noise-energy ratio (Eb/No) is calculated at the input of the equalizer. The constant value A of the activation function used in simulations is 0.5 for the output layer and 1 for the hidden layer. The value B is 0.3 for the output layer and 0.1 for the hidden layer. These values can be adjusted according to the degree of the nonlinearity the CBPE must have.

The z-transform notation of the linear channel (Biglieri, Divsalar, McLane, & Simon, 1991) used in simulations is

$$\begin{aligned} H(z)=&(0.0485+j0.0194) + (0.0573+j0.0253)z^{-1} + (0.0786+j0.0282)\, z^{-2} + (0.0874+j0.0447)\, z^{-3} \\ &+ (0.9222+j0.3031)\, z^{-4} + (0.1427+j0.0349)\, z^{-5} + (0.0835+j0.0157)\, z^{-6} \\ &+ (0.0621+j0.0078)\, z^{-7} + (0.0359+j0.0049)\, z^{-8} + (0.0214+j0.0019)\, z^{-9}. \end{aligned} \quad (28)$$

The MSE comparison between the CBPE and the complex LMS equalizer on above linear channel is shown in Fig. 10. In this figure, the line labeled **CBPE(15, 15, 1), η=0.0003** is the performance of the CBPE when the complex BPN consisting of 15 input nodes, 15 hidden nodes and one output node is used and the learning parameter η is 0.0003. And, the line labeled **CLMSE(15), μ=0.0001** is the performance of the complex LMS equalizer when the complex equalizer with 15 input units is used and the learning parameter μ is 0.0001. As known in this figure, the MSE of the CBPE is lower than that of the CLMSE in the steady state.

Fig. 11 and Fig. 12 are the constellations of the 64-QAM signals equalized by the complex LMS equalizer and the CBPE, respectively. We can see that the CBPE equalizes the corrupted signals better than the complex LMS equalizer. These results show that the CBPE can perform as well as the complex LMS equalizer and is better in terms of the MSE.

To see real improvements in performance with the CBPE, we give nonlinear channel distortion

$$\tilde{r}_k = 0.5 r_k + 0.3 r_k^2 + 0.1 r_k^3, \quad (29)$$

which was used in (Gibson, Siu, & Cowan, 1989, May), where r_k is the output of the channel given in Eq. (28). As shown in Fig. 13, the MSE difference between the CBPE and the complex LMS equalizer is larger than the MSE difference (see Fig. 10) that is obtained when nonlinear distortion is not present. The curves of the Fig. 14 show

Figure 9. The block diagram for simulation

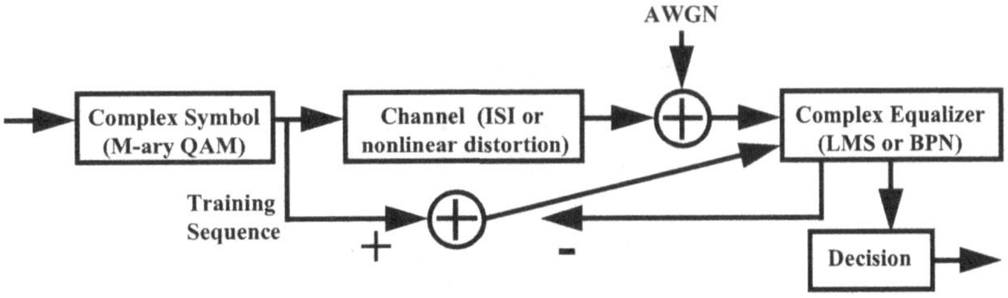

Figure 10. MSE comparison between the complex LMS equalizer and the CBPE

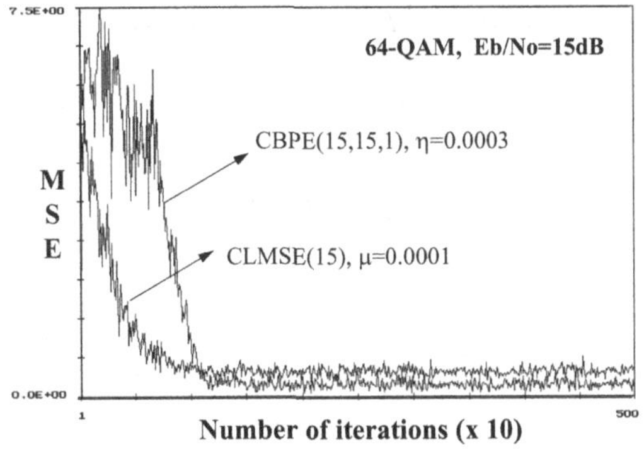

Figure 11. The constellation of the 64-QAM after the complex LMS equalizer

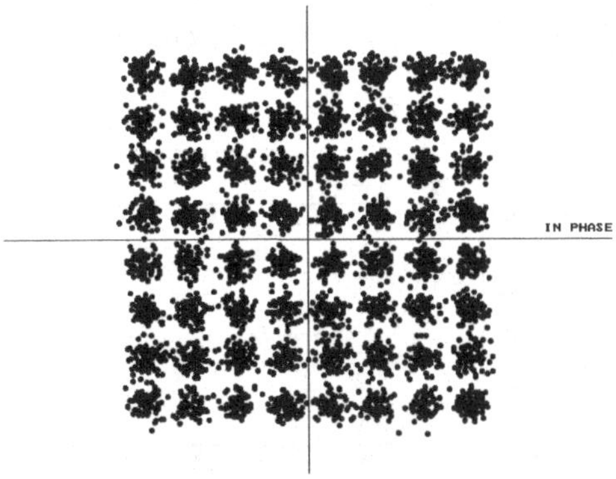

the performances of the CBPE and the complex LMS equalizer when nonlinear distortion exists. We can observe the better results obtained with the complex BPE compared to the complex LMS equalizer. For a BER of 10^{-4} the improvement is about 3.5 dB. This result is not surprising because the complex LMS equalizer can reduce only linear channel distortions, on the other hand the CBPE can handle nonlinear channel distortions as well.

Figure 12. The constellation of the 64-QAM after the CBPE

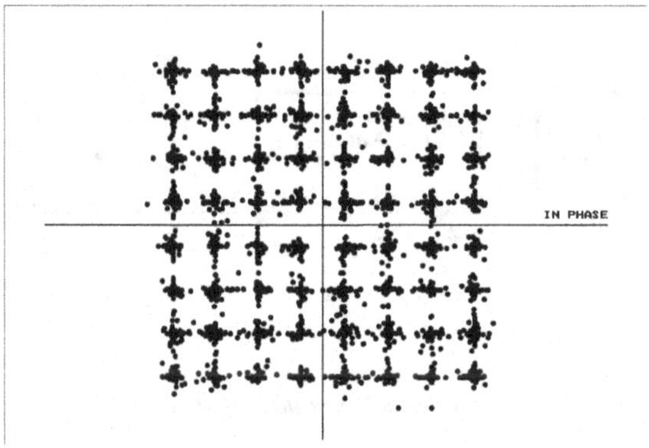

Figure 13. MSE comparison between the complex LMS equalizer and the CBPE

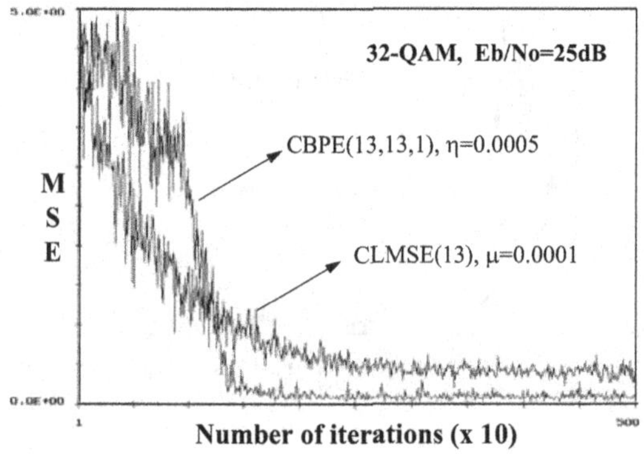

Figure 14. Bit error rate versus Eb/No when the nonlinear distortion exists (32-QAM).

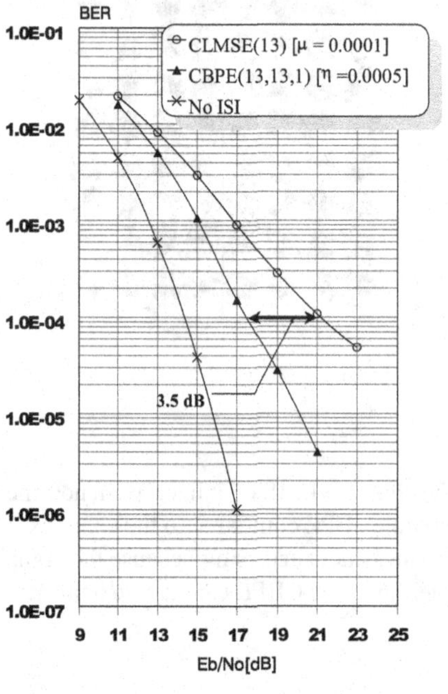

Nonlinear Blind Equalization

A complex-valued multilayer perceptron (CMLP) has one or more layers of identical complex-valued processing elements (CPE). A CPE is an adaptive linear combiner with a nonlinear activation function for complex signals as shown in Fig. 15, where $\boldsymbol{X}$ and $\boldsymbol{W}$ are complex vectors defined as

$$\begin{aligned}\boldsymbol{X} &= [X_1, X_2, \cdots, X_N]^T \\ &= [x_{1,R}, \cdots, x_{N,R}]^T + j[x_{1,I}, \cdots, x_{N,I}]^T, \\ \boldsymbol{W} &= [W_1, W_2, \cdots, W_N]^T \\ &= [w_{1,R}, \cdots, w_{N,R}]^T + j[w_{1,I}, \cdots, w_{N,I}]^T,\end{aligned}$$

respectively, and O is the complex-valued output defined by $O = F(\boldsymbol{X}^T\boldsymbol{W})$ where the subscripts R and I refer to the real and imaginary parts, respectively, and $F(\cdot)$ is a complex-valued activation function. In Fig. 15, $f_R(\cdot)$ and $f_I(\cdot)$ are some real-valued functions.

Complex-Valued Activation Function

In this section, some properties that a useful complex-valued activation function must satisfy are mentioned (You, & Hong, 1998). Subsequently, a complex activation function adequate in dealing with *M*-ary QAM is presented. Moreover, to understand the nonlinear effects of the presented activation function, the change in the correlation between its input and output is investigated.

Properties

When the real domain is extended to the complex domain, there exist many difficulties involving the appropriate choice of activation function due to a set of properties that a suitable complex-valued activation function F(Z) must possess. Let a complex-valued function be

$F(Z) = f_R(z_R, z_I) + jf_I(z_R, z_I)$.

Georgiou and Koutsougeras have proposed the properties satisfied by a suitable complex activation function (Georgiou, & Koutsougeras, 1992). For convenience we will call these properties **P1-P5**.

P1 (i.e., a suitable activation function *F(Z)* must be nonlinear in z_R and z_I) is reasonable because if *F(Z)* is linear there is no advantage in using a CMLP.

By *Liouville's theorem* (Trim, 1996), if **P2** (i.e., *F(Z)* must be bounded) is requisite, **P3** (i.e., *F(Z)* must not be entire) is also true because a constant activation function is not suitable. However, **P2** and **P3** are the properties satisfied by a suitable complex activation function *F(Z)* on condition that *F(Z)*is analytic in an open set *S*, i.e.,

Figure 15. A complex-valued processing element (CPE)

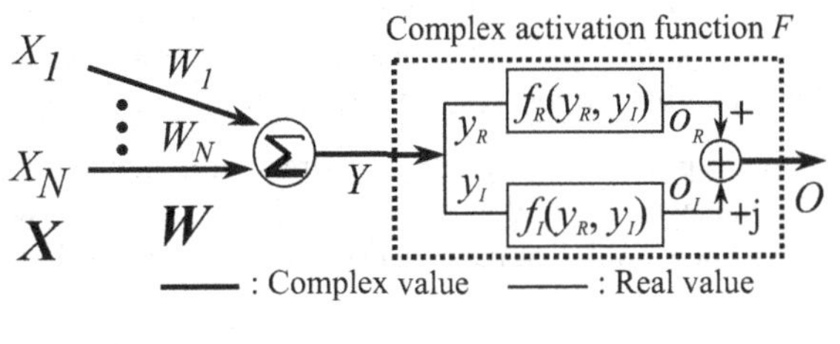

it has a derivative at every points of S (Trim, 1996). However, most functions encountered in physical sciences and engineering are not analytic. It is, therefore, difficult to find a suitable complex activation function that is analytic. Moreover, a complex activation function does not need necessarily be analytic because what we want to find to optimize the filter design is not the derivatives, but the *gradient* of the cost function. Therefore, the following proposition can be suggested:

Proposition 1: If the cost function is a real-valued scalar function, a suitable complex activation function $F(Z)$ must have the following first-order partial derivatives:

$$\frac{\partial f_R(z_R, z_I)}{\partial z_R}, \frac{\partial f_R(z_R, z_I)}{\partial z_I}, \frac{\partial f_I(z_R, z_I)}{\partial z_R}, \text{ and } \frac{\partial f_I(z_R, z_I)}{\partial z_I}. \qquad (30)$$

The proof of Proposition 1 follows directly from the following Definition 1, Theorem 1, and the chain rule.

Definition 1 (Widrow, McCool, & Ball, 1995): For the *real* cost function J that defines the error-performance surface of a linear transversal filter whose tap-weight vector is $\boldsymbol{W}$, the kth element of ∇J is

$$\nabla_k J = \frac{\partial J}{\partial w_{k,R}} + j\frac{\partial J}{\partial w_{k,I}}, \quad \mathrm{k} = 0, 1, 2, \cdots \qquad (31)$$

where $w_{k,R}$ and $w_{k,I}$ denote the real and imaginary parts of the kth element W_k of the vector $\boldsymbol{W}$.

Theorem 1 *(Gradient)* (Trim, 1996): Let $f(P)=f(x, y, z)$ be a *scalar* function having continuous first partial derivatives. Then ∇f exists and its length and direction are independent of the particular choice of Cartesian coordinates in space. If at a point P the *gradient of* f is not the zero vector, it has the direction of maximum increasing of f at P.

Note that for the definition given in (31) to be valid, it is essential that J be *real.*

***Corollary**:* For the cost function J that is a function of the absolute values of complex numbers, but not analytic, the gradient of J can be found once a complex activation function $F(Z)$ has the continuous first partial derivatives defined in (30).

By the above corollary, we can see that if a cost function J is defined from the absolute value of the estimation error and a complex activation function of a CMLP has the continuous first partial derivatives of (30), the gradient of J can be found.

On the other hand, the partial derivatives of (30) must be bounded because the weights are updated by amounts proportional to the partial derivatives. Thus, **P4** (i.e., the partial derivatives exist and they are bounded) is also true. However, **P2** may be the tight condition because it is very difficult to make a bounded complex activation function holding the following characteristics that may be useful in particular applications such as channel equalization:

C1. $f_R(\cdot)$ and $f_I(\cdot)$ have the same dynamic ranges; in communication systems, at large uncorrupted complex-valued signals are equally spaced with respect to the real and imaginary axes.

C2. $f_R(\cdot)$ and $f_I(\cdot)$ are symmetric with respect to the real and imaginary axes, respectively; in communication systems, mostly the real and imaginary parts of undistorted complex signals are symmetrically distributed with respect to the real and imaginary axes, respectively.

C3. It is desirable that the output regions of $f_R(\cdot)$ and $f_I(\cdot)$ are saturated according to the signal values used in applications; in an analogous way, the real hyperbolic tangent that shows the saturation characteristic of S-shape is most widely used when bipolar signals are used. The saturation characteristic makes the network robust to noise.

If the output characteristics of $f_R(\cdot)$ and $f_I(\cdot)$ are not identical, the weights of the network can show favoritism either of the real and imaginary parts of signals. For a practical implementation of the activation function, as singular points must be avoided, the loose proposition of **P2** is suggested as follows:

Proposition 2: For all *Z* in a *bounded* set *S*, a suitable complex activation function *F*(*Z*) must have no singularities (especially poles) and be bounded.

The above proposition indicates that the system using *F*(*Z*) is stable in the bounded-input bounded-output (BIBO) sense. Note that *F*(*Z*) that is not analytic in an open set *S* has no singularities, because every neighborhood of a singularity must contain a point at which the function is analytic; thus, first of all, the function *F*(*Z*) must be continuous at all *Z* in *S* in order to be a suitable activation function.

P5 (i.e., $(\partial f_R/\partial z_R)(\partial f_I/\partial z_I) \neq (\partial f_I/\partial z_R)(\partial f_R/\partial z_I)$) is also the tight condition because there are the exceptions that are mentioned in the following proposition:

Proposition 3: If not **P5**, then *F*(*Z*) is not a suitable complex activation function except the following cases:

$$\frac{\partial f_R}{\partial z_R} = \frac{\partial f_I}{\partial z_R} = 0 and \frac{\partial f_R}{\partial z_I} \neq 0, \frac{\partial f_I}{\partial z_I} \neq 0, \tag{32}$$

$$\frac{\partial f_R}{\partial z_I} = \frac{\partial f_I}{\partial z_I} = 0 and \frac{\partial f_R}{\partial z_R} \neq 0, \frac{\partial f_I}{\partial z_R} \neq 0. \tag{33}$$

Proof: Suppose that $X_i \neq (0, 0)$ and the estimation error $\delta_{pk} \neq (0, 0)$. From proof done in the original paper (Georgiou, & Koutsougeras, 1992), the weight updating does not occur when the following equations are true at the same time:

$$\frac{\partial f_R}{\partial z_R}\delta_{pk,R} + \frac{\partial f_I}{\partial z_R}\delta_{pk,I} = 0, \tag{34}$$

$$\frac{\partial f_R}{\partial z_I}\delta_{pk,R} + \frac{\partial f_I}{\partial z_I}\delta_{pk,I} = 0. \tag{35}$$

If either of (34) and (35) is not true, the weight updating occurs with respect to the real or imaginary parts of δ_{pk} even though not **P5**. Thus, in the cases of (32) and (33) the weight updating occurs. Besides these cases, a nontrivial solution of (34) and (35) can be found if and only if not **P5.**

By the above discussion, a suitable complex activation function *F*(*Z*) should satisfy the following properties:

F1. *F*(*Z*) should be nonlinear in both z_R and z_I.
F2. For the stability of a system, *F*(*Z*) should have no singularities and be bounded for all *Z* in a bounded set *S*. If *F*(*Z*) is not analytic, above all *F*(*Z*) must be continuous at all *Z* in *S*.
F3. *F*(*Z*) should have the continuous first partial derivatives of (30) that are bounded.
F4. **P5** should be satisfied. Otherwise, either of (32) and (33) must be satisfied at least.

Figure 16. M-ary QAM signal constellations

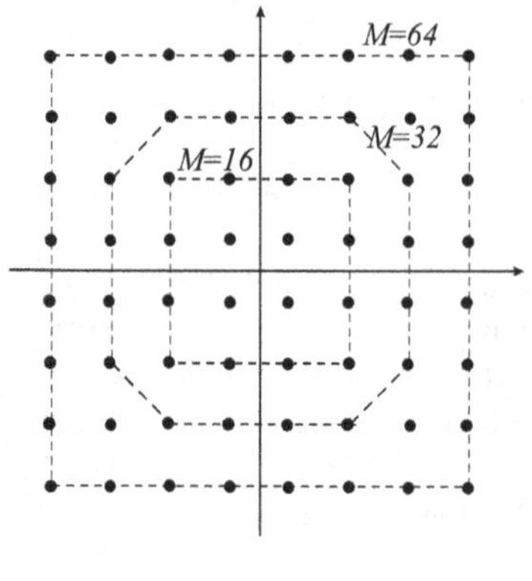

Some Suitable Complex-Valued Activation Functions

In general, the activation function is very important because its nonlinearity differentiates neural networks from conventional linear systems (Freemann, & Skapura, 1991). The choice of these functions depends on how we want to represent the output values.

A QAM signal with amplitude and phase is two-dimensional. For two-dimensional bipolar signals, the complex-valued activation functions have been developed by several researchers (Leung, & Haykin, 1991; Georgiou, & Koutsougeras, 1992; Benvenuto, & Piazza, 1992; Benvenuto, Marchesi, Piazza, & Uncini, 1991, May). However, their functions are not pertinent to *M*-ary QAM signals with various amplitudes and phases as shown in Fig. 16.

Now, a complex activation function is described as follows:

$$F(Z) = f(z_R) + jf(z_I) \tag{36}$$

where $f(\cdot)$ is a real function defined by

$$f(x) = x + \alpha \sin(\pi x) \tag{37}$$

where the *slope parameter* α that determines the degree of nonlinearity is a positive real constant [Note that Eq. (37) is an example of Eq. (4)]. Even if not analytic, the function $F(Z)$ meets all the useful characteristics **C1-C3** as well as all the suitable properties **F1-F4**. In addition, the function can deal with *M*-ary QAM signals of any constellation sizes. Fig. 17 shows the nonlinearity of $f(\cdot)$ for varying α. After both ends of the function that are unnecessary are removed, the region that is of concern to us may be realized as in the case of a linear filter. The multi-saturation characteristic of *S*-shape that the output of this function shows is pertinent to *M*-ary QAM signals with discrete amplitudes, and makes the network robust to noise because Δy is small for large Δx. The derivative of $f(\cdot)$ is given by $f'(x) = 1 + \alpha\pi\cos(\pi x)$. As shown in Fig. 18, $f(\cdot)$ is differentiable at all points, and its derivative is bounded in the interval $1 - \pi\alpha < f'(x) < 1 + \pi\alpha$. Therefore, $F(Z)$ satisfies **F1**, **F2**, and **F3**. In order to satisfy **F4**, $f'(x)$ must be non-zero for all x, or equivalently, satisfy the following inequality:

$$f'(x) = 1 + \alpha\pi\cos(\pi x) > 0, \qquad \text{for all } x,$$

that is, $0 < a < 1/p \cong 0.318$. Under the above condition, if the estimation error is not zero, the weight updating is guaranteed.

The aforementioned activation function $F(\cdot)$ has a nonlinearity caused by $\sin(\cdot)$. In order to understand the nonlinear effects of the function, we investigate with emphasis on the change in the correlation between the input and output of the activation function.

In this case, we consider the CPE shown in Fig. 15. The CPE has N input nodes, and employs the activation function $F(\cdot)$ defined in (36) and (37). According to the *central limit theorem*, the weighted sums y_R and y_I are asymptotically jointly Gaussian when the inputs or the weights are perturbed randomly (Papoulis, 1991), where $y_R = (\boldsymbol{X}^T\boldsymbol{W})_R$ and $y_I = (\boldsymbol{X}^T\boldsymbol{W})_I$. Two jointly Gaussian random variables (r. v.) y_R and y_I with means m_R and m_I are nonlinearly transformed into o_R and o_I as follows:

$$o_R = y_R + \alpha \sin(\pi y_R), \tag{38}$$

$$o_I = y_I + \alpha \sin(\pi y_I) \tag{39}$$

where the joint probability density function (pdf) of y_R and y_I is given by

$$f(y_R, y_I) = \frac{\exp\left\{-\frac{1}{2(1-r^2)}\left[\frac{(y_R - m_R)^2}{\sigma_{y_R}^2} - 2r\frac{(y_R - m_R)(y_I - m_I)}{\sigma_{y_R}\sigma_{y_I}} + \frac{(y_I - m_I)^2}{\sigma_{y_I}^2}\right]\right\}}{2\pi\sigma_{y_R}\cdot\sigma_{y_I}\sqrt{1-r^2}} \tag{40}$$

where $r = \mathrm{Cor}(y_R, y_I)$ that denotes the correlation coefficient between y_R and y_I.

Assuming without loss of generality that m_R and m_I are zero such as the case of M-ary QAM signal. Then we have

$$Cor(o_R, o_I) = \frac{M + N}{\sigma_{o_R}\cdot\sigma_{o_I}} \tag{41}$$

where

$$\sigma_{o_R} = \sqrt{\sigma_{y_R}^2\left(1 + 2\pi\alpha\cdot\exp[-\pi^2\sigma_{y_R}^2/2]\right) + \frac{\alpha^2}{2}\left(1 - \exp[-2\pi^2\sigma_{y_R}^2]\right)}, \tag{42}$$

$$\sigma_{o_I} = \sqrt{\sigma_{y_I}^2\left(1 + 2\pi\alpha\cdot\exp[-\pi^2\sigma_{y_I}^2/2]\right) + \frac{\alpha^2}{2}\left(1 - \exp[-2\pi^2\sigma_{y_I}^2]\right)}, \tag{43}$$

$$M = \sigma_{o_R}\sigma_{o_I} r\left[1 + \pi\alpha\left(\exp[-\pi^2\sigma_{y_R}^2/2] + \exp[-\pi^2\sigma_{y_I}^2/2]\right)\right], \tag{44}$$

$$N = \frac{\alpha^2}{2}\exp\left[-\frac{\pi^2(\sigma_{y_R}^2 + \sigma_{y_I}^2)}{2}\right]\left(\exp[\pi^2\sigma_{y_R}\sigma_{y_I} r] - \exp[-\pi^2\sigma_{y_R}\sigma_{y_I} r]\right). \tag{45}$$

From the above (42) to (45), we see that the obtained $Cor(o_R, o_I)$ is independent of the mean values of the inputs, m_R and m_I. Detailed derivations are presented in Appendix.

The examination of the correlation coefficient given in (41) is as follows:

Case 1 (r=0): When r=0, y_R and y_I are uncorrelated (i.e., independent). Thus, o_R and o_I also become independent, and $Cor(o_R, o_I)$=0. This result is well consistent with (41).

Case 2 (r≠0, α=0): When α=0, $f(\cdot)$ becomes a linear function. Thus, the transformation does not change the correlation coefficient. That is, $Cor(o_R, o_I) = Cor(y_R, y_I)$ As might be expected, this result also agrees with (41).

Case 3 (r≠0, α≠0): In this case, the correlation between y_R and y_I exists, and y_R and y_I are nonlinearly transformed by $f(\cdot)$. By some approximations [see Appendix], (41) can be written as

$$Cor(o_R, o_I) \cong \frac{\sigma_{y_R}\sigma_{y_I} \cdot r}{\sqrt{\sigma_{y_R}^2 + \alpha^2/2}\sqrt{\sigma_{y_I}^2 + \alpha^2/2}}, \quad (41\text{-}1)$$

and we get $|r| - |Cor(o_R, o_I)| > 0$ for an arbitrary positive real number α. (i.e., $|Cor(o_R, o_I)|$ has a smaller value than $|r|$).

Remark: Based on all the cases discussed, it is clear that $|Cor(o_R, o_I)|$ has the maximum value $|r|$ when $f(\cdot)$ is linear, while it is less than $|r|$ when $f(\cdot)$ is nonlinear (i.e., α is a non-zero positive value). Therefore, we can say that by the nonlinear transformation of the activation function, the real and imaginary parts of the output of the activation function become more independent of each other, and thus the information redundancy among hidden neurons of a CMLP using the function may be reduced. In fact, similar results were acquired for real-valued MLPs. In (Oh. & Lee, 1994), authors considered a real-valued MLP using sigmoidal transformation as a special type of nonlinear whitening filter.

Examples of Blind Equalization Algorithms Using Complex-Valued Neural Networks

In this section, the following four blind equalization schemes are invested and their learning algorithms are presented.

NNS&G

Among the useful LMS-type blind algorithms, the "stop-and-go" decision-directed algorithm (S&G) devised by Picchi and Prati (Picchi, & Prati, 1987) uses a simple flag telling both the equalizer and the synchronizer whether

Figure 17. Input-output characteristic of $f(x) = x + \alpha \sin(\pi x)$

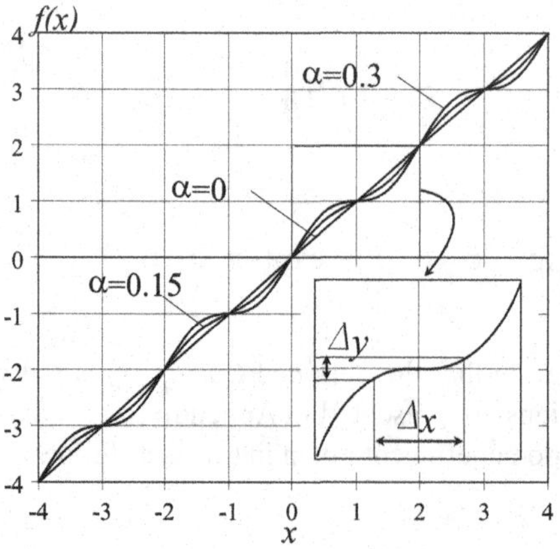

Figure 18. The derivative of $f(x) = x + \alpha\sin(\pi x)$

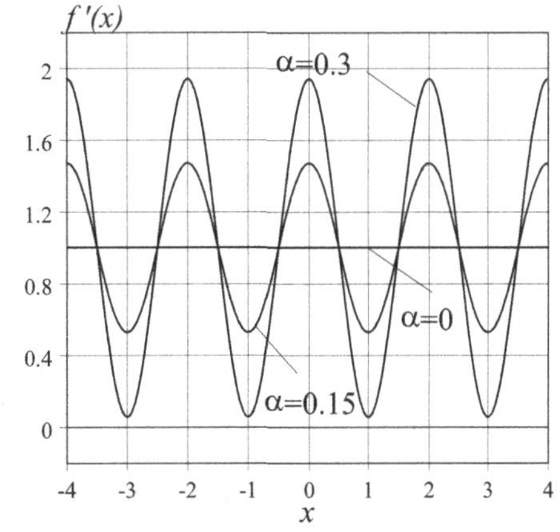

Figure 19. The block diagram of a blind equalizer using the CMLP

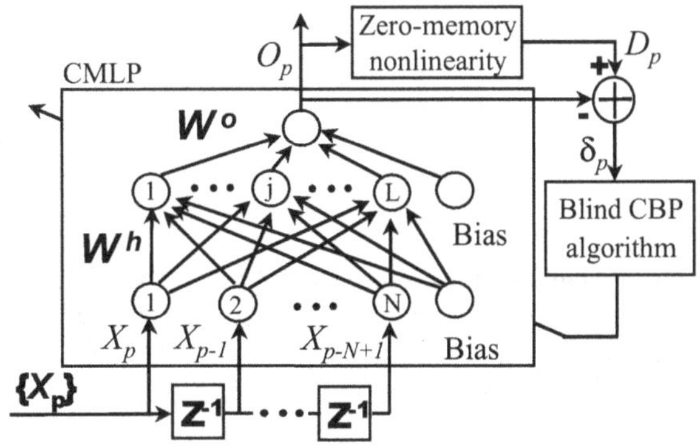

the current output error with respect to the decided symbol is sufficiently reliable to be used. If not, adaptation is stopped for the current iteration. As a result, this algorithm provides effective blind convergence in the MSE sense. If a CMLP is used instead of the linear FIR filter in the above algorithm, an improved performance will be acquired.

To begin with, let's consider the CMLP with one hidden layer and one output neuron [see Fig. 19]. Let $\boldsymbol{X}_p$ be the complex input vector and O_p the output of the CMLP. The estimated error is

$$\begin{aligned}\delta_p &= \delta_{p,R} + j\delta_{p,I} \\ &= \hat{O}_p - O_p\end{aligned}$$

where $O_p = F^o(NET_p^o)$, and $\hat{O}_p$ is the decided complex symbol that functions as the desired output value D_p. The net-input value to a hidden layer neuron of the CMLP is

Exhibit 1.

Type	Name	Description
Scheme 1	NNS&G	The "stop-and-go" decision-directed (DD) algorithm based on neural networks
Scheme 2	NNGA	The Godard algorithm based on neural networks
	NNCMA	The constant modulus algorithm based on neural networks (NNGA's special case choosing n=2)
Scheme 3	NNDD- MMA	The decision-directed multiple modulus algorithm based on neural networks
Scheme 4	S&G-DDMMA	The "stop-and-go" decision-directed multiple modulus algorithm for a linear FIR filter
	NNS&G-DDMMA	The neural version of S&G-DDMMA

$$\begin{aligned} NET_{pj}^h &= \sum_{i=1}^{N} W_{ji}^h X_i + \Theta_j^h \\ &= net_{pj,R}^h + j net_{pj,I}^h \end{aligned}$$

where W_{ji}^h is the complex-valued weight on the connection from the ith input node to the jth hidden neuron, Θ_j^h is the bias term, and the superscript h refers to quantities on the hidden layer.

The net-input value to the output layer neuron is

$$NET_p^o = \sum_{j=1}^{L} W_j^o I_{pj} + \Theta^o$$

where W_j^o is the weight on the connection from the jth hidden neuron to the output neuron, the superscript o refers to quantities on the output layer, and $I_{pj} = F_j^h(NET_{pj}^h)$. In this case, the error terms of the conventional CBP algorithm can be written as

$$\delta_p^o = f'^o(net_{p,R}^o)\delta_{p,R} + jf'^o(net_{p,I}^o)\delta_{p,I},$$

$$\delta_{pj}^h = f'^h(net_{pj,R}^h)\mathrm{Re}\left[\delta_p^o W_j^{o*}\right] + jf'^h(net_{pj,I}^h)\mathrm{Im}\left[\delta_p^o W_j^{o*}\right]$$

where the asterisk denotes complex conjugation (You, & Hong, 1996, June).

When flags are newly defined for weights of the CMLP after splitting the CBP algorithm into real and imaginary parts, the S&G can be naturally extended to a blind equalization algorithm using the CMLP. NNS&G is as follows:

$$\begin{cases} w_{j,R}^o(p+1) = w_{j,R}^o(p) + \eta\left(\zeta_{p,R}\delta_{p,R}^o i_{pj,R} + \zeta_{p,I}\delta_{p,I}^o i_{pj,I}\right) \\ w_{j,I}^o(p+1) = w_{j,I}^o(p) - \eta\left(\zeta_{p,R}\delta_{p,R}^o i_{pj,I} - \zeta_{p,I}\delta_{p,I}^o i_{pj,R}\right) \end{cases},$$

$$\begin{cases} w^o_{j,R}(p+1) = w^o_{j,R}(p) + \eta\left(\zeta_{p,R}\delta^o_{p,R} i_{pj,R} + \zeta_{p,I}\delta^o_{p,I} i_{pj,I}\right) \\ w^o_{j,I}(p+1) = w^o_{j,I}(p) - \eta\left(\zeta_{p,R}\delta^o_{p,R} i_{pj,I} - \zeta_{p,I}\delta^o_{p,I} i_{pj,R}\right) \end{cases}.$$

The above algorithm uses the following flags, respectively:

$$\zeta_{p,R} = \begin{cases} 1 & if \operatorname{sgn}\delta_{p,R} = \operatorname{sgn}\tilde{\delta}_{p,R} \\ 0 & if \operatorname{sgn}\delta_{p,R} \neq \operatorname{sgn}\tilde{\delta}_{p,R}, \end{cases}$$

$$\zeta_{p,I} = \begin{cases} 1 & if \operatorname{sgn}\delta_{p,I} = \operatorname{sgn}\tilde{\delta}_{p,I} \\ 0 & if \operatorname{sgn}\delta_{p,I} \neq \operatorname{sgn}\tilde{\delta}_{p,I} \end{cases}$$

where two Sato-like errors

$$\tilde{\delta}_{P,R} = \operatorname{sgn}(o_{P,R})\beta_P - o_{P,R},$$
$$\tilde{\delta}_{P,I} = \operatorname{sgn}(o_{P,I})\beta_P - o_{P,I}$$

are used, with β_P being a suitable real value possibly changing with p. The Signum function sgn(·) is equal to +1 if the argument is positive, and -1 if it is negative.

S&G-DDMMA and NNS&G-DDMMA

The decision-directed multiple modulus algorithm (DDMMA) (Sethares, Rey, & Johnson, 1989, April) is a hybrid of the constant modulus algorithm (CMA) (Godard, 1980) and the DD approach, and thus has some profitable characteristics that can be observed in them (Macchi, & Eweda, 1984). The DDMMA using the CMLP (NNDDMMA) can also be acquired by combining the CMA using the CMLP (NNCMA) and the DD approach (NNCMA and NNDDMMA are derived in Appendix). However, when the DD strategy is used parallel with the multiple constant modulus, there is a problem in stability. That is, as the number of points increases, finer

Figure 20. Regions of the 16-QAM constellation plane where (a) the event $\{\operatorname{sgn}\varepsilon_p = \operatorname{sgn}\varepsilon_{true,p} \mid |S_p|^2 = M_i\}$ *occurs and (b) the event* $\{\operatorname{sgn}\varepsilon_p = \operatorname{sgn}\tilde{\varepsilon}_p\}$ *occurs with* $R_2 = 13.2$

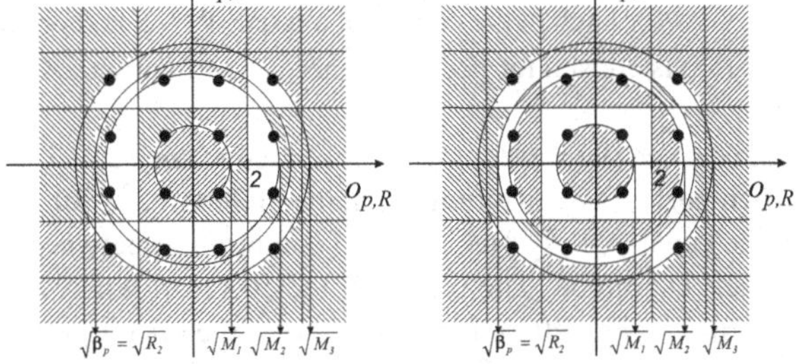

distinctions must be made by the DDMMA, and thus the probability of erroneous decisions increases. Based on the above considerations, it is worth exploring the possibility of retaining the advantages of the DDMMA while attempting to substantially improve its blind convergence capabilities. This can be achieved by stopping adaptation when the reliability (in a probabilistic sense) of the self-decided estimation error is not high enough; that is, a flag can be used.

The "stop-and-go" decision-directed multiple modulus algorithm (S&G-DDMMA) is now described. The basic concept of the S&G-DDMMA is identical to that of the "stop-and-go" DD algorithm. However, there are some different points in the use of flags.

Assume that the transmitted symbol is known to lie on k circles of known radius, and let $M_1, M_2, \ldots, M_k$ designate the squares of the moduli; that is,

$$M_i = |dec(O_p)|^2, \tag{46}$$

where $dec(\cdot)$ represents a decision device. Given O_p, the decision device makes a decision in favor of a particular value in the known alphabet of the transmitted data sequence that is closest to O_p. Note that M_i of (46) is different from that of the original DDMMA proposed in (Sethares, Rey, & Johnson, 1989, April) where M_i is one of the n known radii which minimizes $J = (M_i - |O_p|^2)^2$. The signal $\varepsilon_p = O_p(M_i - |O_p|^2)$ replaces the estimated error in the LMS algorithm, and the true error can be written as $\varepsilon_{true,p} = O_p\left(|S_p|^2 - |O_p|^2\right)$.

S&G-DDMMA is as follows:

$$\boldsymbol{W}(p+1) = \boldsymbol{W}(p) + \mu\vartheta_p \boldsymbol{X}_p^* O_p (M_i - |O_p|^2),$$

where the following flag is used:

$$\vartheta_p = \begin{cases} 1 & \textit{if } \operatorname{sgn}\varepsilon_p = \operatorname{sgn}\tilde{\varepsilon}_p \\ 0 & \textit{if } \operatorname{sgn}\varepsilon_p \neq \operatorname{sgn}\tilde{\varepsilon}_p \end{cases}, \tag{47}$$

where a Sato-like error

$$\tilde{\varepsilon}_P = O_P\left(\operatorname{sgn}(M_i)\beta_P - |O_P|^2\right) \tag{48}$$

is used, with β_P being a suitable real value possibly changing with *p*. As with the case of the S&G, when $\operatorname{sgn}\varepsilon_p = \operatorname{sgn}\tilde{\varepsilon}_p$ and the choice of β_P is proper, the conditional probability

$$\begin{aligned} P_{n|go} &= P\{no \text{ error}|\text{go}\} \\ &= P\left\{\operatorname{sgn}\varepsilon_p = \operatorname{sgn}\varepsilon_{true,p} \,|\, \operatorname{sgn}\varepsilon_p = \operatorname{sgn}\tilde{\varepsilon}_p\right\} \end{aligned}$$

is high enough. Thus, it is apparent that the choice of β_P is crucial for a stable and fast convergence.

Though an optimum value of β_P exists for each p, the choice of a fixed $\beta_P = \beta$ is more convenient (Sethares, Rey, & Johnson, 1989, April). If R_2 of (57) is chosen for β, $\tilde{\varepsilon}_p$ becomes the estimation error of the CMA because sgn(M_i) is always *+1*. That is, $\tilde{\varepsilon}_p = O_p(R_2 - |O_p|^2)$.

Choosing $\beta_P = R_2$ is very reasonable since the constant R_2 was chosen in such a way that the gradient of the cost function of the CMA is zero when perfect equalization is attained (Godard, 1980). As might be expected, it has been found by simulation that the value $\beta_P = R_2$ yields a good compromise between speed of convergence and smooth steady state for all channels examined. The region of the 16-QAM where the conditional event $\{\operatorname{sgn}\varepsilon_p = \operatorname{sgn}\varepsilon_{true,p} \,|\, |S_p|^2 = M_1\}$ occurs is shown in Fig. 20(a). Fig. 20(b) shows the operation intervals when $\beta_P = R_2$. The intersection of the shaded regions of Fig. 20(a) and (b) indicates where S&G-DDMMA operates correctly.

The S&G-DDMMA can also be extended to a neural version of its own. By applying a flag to the NNDD-MMA, we can also get NNS&G-DDMMA

$$\begin{cases} W_j^o(p+1) = W_j^o(p) + \eta\, \vartheta_p\, \delta_p^o I_{pj}^* \\ \delta_p^o = \left[f^o(net_{p,R}^o) f'^o(net_{p,R}^o) + j f^o(net_{p,I}^o) f'^o(net_{p,I}^o) \right] (\varepsilon_p / O_p) \end{cases}$$

$$\begin{cases} W_{ji}^h(p+1) = W_{ji}^h(p) + \eta \vartheta_p \delta_{pj}^h X_{pi}^* \\ \delta_{pj}^h = f'^h(net_{pj,R}^h) \operatorname{Re}\left[\delta_p^o W_j^{o*}\right] + j f'^h(net_{pj,I}^h) \operatorname{Im}\left[\delta_p^o W_j^{o*}\right] \end{cases}$$

where $\beta_P = R_2$ and ϑ_P is defined by (47) and (48).

In fact, the necessity for the use of a flag is greater for NNDDMMA than for the DDMMA. When large amounts of data are incorrectly decided as in the case of the DDMMA, the CMLP repeatedly comes to learn these incorrect data. As a result, either convergence will not take place or, even if convergence occurs, the CMLP will be easily trapped in local minima that are unacceptable. The adverse effects of the incorrect data in the case of the CMLP are more severe than in the case of the linear FIR filter because of the CMLP's powerful mapping capability. Therefore, it is necessary to develop a method for reducing the probabilities of erroneous decisions and the possibility of converging to a local minimum that is unacceptable. One of the methods for confronting with such an ordeal may be the use of a flag.

Performance

The initial coefficients of the conventional equalizers are set to *zero* except for the reference tap w_r that is used as a reference to update weights and usually fixed in the center (Baek, Park, & Seo, 2006). However, if the initial weights of the CMLP are set to *zero*, the weight updating does not occur because the error can not be backpropagated. Thus, the weights of the CMLP have been initialized to small random values satisfying $\left|w_{R\,\mathrm{or}\,I}^{h\,\mathrm{or}\,o}\right| < 10^{-5}$ except for $w_{[L+1/2][N+1/2]R}^h$ and $w_{[L+1/2]R}^o$ where $[x]$ is the largest integer less than or equal to x. $w_{[L+1/2][N+1/2]R}^h$ is the reference tap of the CMLP that plays the same role as w_r, and $w_{[L+1/2]R}^o$ is always set to *one*. The reference taps w_r and $w_{[L+1/2][N+1/2]R}^h$ have been set according to channel characteristics, the QAM signals, and the algorithm.

The channel used in simulations is one of typical digital radio channels. Its z-transform notation is

$$\begin{aligned} H(z) = {} & (0.0410+j0.0109)+(0.0495+j0.0123)z^{-1}+(0.0672+j0.0170)z^{-2}+(0.0919+j0.0235)z^{-3} \\ & +(0.7920+j0.1281)z^{-4}+(0.3960+j0.0871)z^{-5}+(0.2715+j0.0498)z^{-6} \\ & +(0.2291+j0.0414)z^{-7}+(0.1287+j0.0154)z^{-8}+(0.1032+j0.0119)z^{-9}. \end{aligned}$$

The above channel has a relatively flat frequency response. However, its binary eye is closed and the DD attempt to achieve equalizer training was failed. For the reference channel, the three data symbol constellations given in Fig. 16 have been tested, corresponding to bit rates of 7.2, 9.6, and 12 kbits/s. To analyze the performance of the described schemes, evaluations of the symbol error rate (SER) and the corresponding convergence curves are calculated. Each convergence curve is obtained by averaging fifty computer runs with different initializations of noise and data sources. No phase offset is assumed in this example.

In the sequel, we use the following notations: (k) refers to the linear FIR equalization filter with k tap weights. (N, L) refers to the CMLP with N input nodes, L hidden neurons, and one output neuron. μ and η are the step-size parameters of the linear FIR equalization filter and the CMLP, respectively. Finally, [α_1, α_2] indicates the slope parameters of the activation functions for the neurons of the hidden layer and the output neuron, respectively.

In the simulations, α_1 and α_2 can have different values according to the degree of nonlinearity of the network and the ease of training. The values of μ and η are set to optimum values by many tests in terms of stability and speed in convergence. The resulting values are dependent on the used algorithm, signal constellation, the number of taps, and so on. Note that hardware implementation can be made easier for larger values of μ and η if stable convergence is guaranteed. The values of k, N, and L are also decided from experience based on numerous simulations. (N, L) is more complex than (k) in terms of hardware complexity by a factor of $L(N+1)/k$.

NNS&G

We first tested the performance of NNS&G. It has been found by simulations that the values β_p=6 and β_p=5 yield the best compromise for the 64-QAM signal and the 32-QAM signal, respectively, between speed of convergence and smooth steady state for several examined channels of practical interest. These values are identical with those obtained for S&G by simulation.

As shown in Fig. 21, as α_1 and α_2 increase the convergence speed becomes low but the MSE in the steady state decreases. This is due to the fact that the increased nonlinearity of the activation function accomplishes more powerful mapping capability, but causes the learning process to be difficult. For varying the number of input nodes, both NNS&G and S&G have shown similar trend; that is, as the number of tap-weights increases, the convergence speed becomes low but the MSE in the steady state decreases. The performance comparison between NNS&G and S&G is shown in Fig. 22. By adjusting α_1 and α_2, NNS&G achieves a lower MSE in the steady state and a higher convergence speed than S&G. Such results are also observed for the 32-QAM signal, as shown in Fig. 23.

These results are due to the fact that the CMLP can approximate the inverse of the FIR channel more accurately than the linear FIR filter because of its mapping capability that can learn and approximate an arbitrary nonlinear function. The powerful mapping capability of NNS&G is more easily observed when the constellation of the QAM signals after convergence is plotted. As we can see from Fig. 24, the symbols are more clearly distinguishable at the output of the NNS&G equalizer. We have also observed that the increased nonlinearity of the activation function makes the QAM symbols aggregate more densely. Of course, we can see intuitively that such a powerful mapping capability is predominantly generated by the saturation characteristics of the activation function [see Fig. 17].

Figure 21. Convergence of MSE versus number of transmitted symbols for NNS&G (15, 9) with the 64-QAM signal (β_p=6, $w^h_{58,R}$ =1.0)

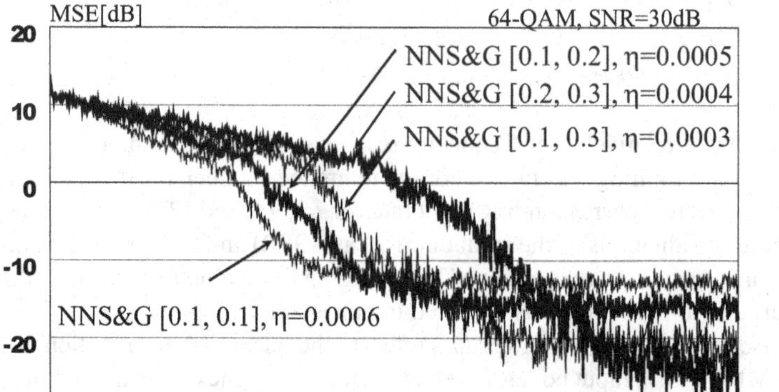

NNCMA and NNDDMMA

The performance comparison between CMA and NNCMA has been done for the 16- and 32-QAM signals. For higher constellations, both the algorithms did not succeed in opening the eye. As shown in Fig. 25, although CMA shows conspicuous convergence speed, the performance after the initial convergence is poor. This is due to the facts that the error signal of CMA used in the tap adaptation is generated based only on the single constant modulus according to the signal constellation, and on that account the accuracy in locating the tap settings for minimum MSE is poor. On the other hand, NNCMA has a low convergence speed compared with CMA, but a very low MSE in the steady state. Of course, large values of the learning parameter make NNCMA achieve a higher convergence speed. However, it might cause instability because the multi-saturated output characteristic of the activation function is not suitable for generating the error signal based only on a single constant modulus.

On the other hand, in the case of 16-QAM signal NNDDMMA has shown a high convergence speed and its MSE in the steady state is prominently lower than that of DDMMA because the output characteristic of the activation function is fit to generate the error signal based on the multiple constant modulus [see Fig. 26]. However, in the case of the 32-QAM signal the convergence speed of NNDDMMA is very low compared with DDMMA even though the performance after the initial convergence is fully satisfactory. As the number of points increases a large amount of data will be decided erroneously. Because of its powerful mapping capability, the CMLP is

Figure 22. (a) Convergence of MSE and (b) measured symbol error rate versus number of transmitted 64-QAM symbols (β_p=6, $w^h_{58,R}$=1.0, w_r =1.0)

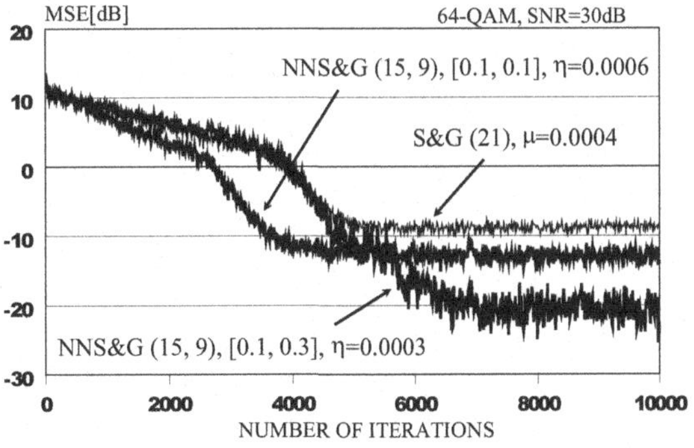

(a)

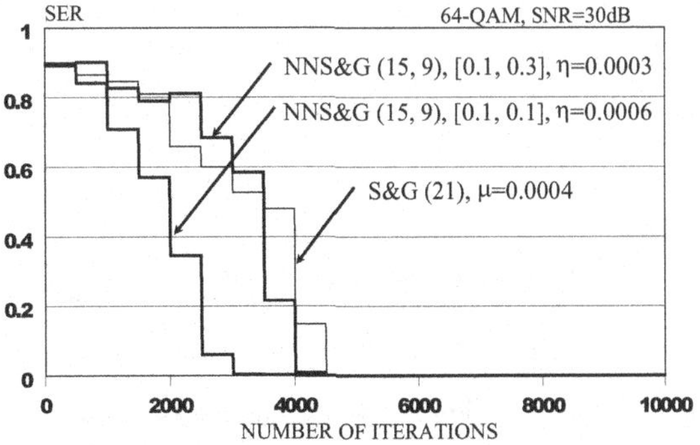

(b)

Figure 23. Convergence of MSE versus number of transmitted symbols for NNS&G [0.1, 0.3] and S&G with the 32-QAM signal (β_p =5, $w^h_{58,R}$=1.0, w_r =1.0)

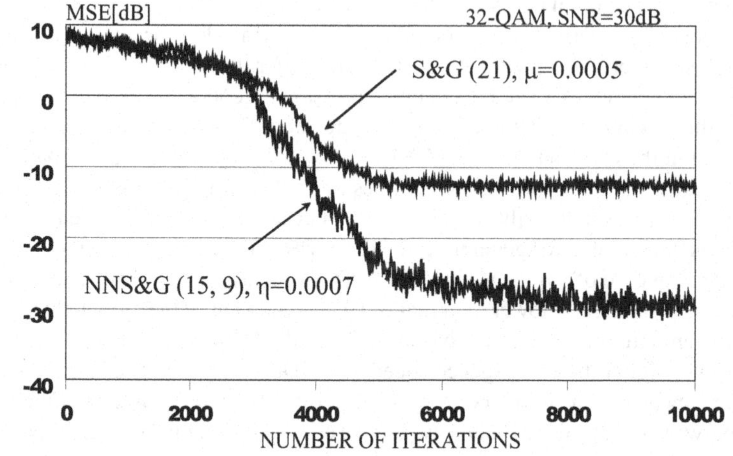

Figure 24. Constellation of QAM symbols equalized by (a), (b) S&G, (c), and (d) NNS&G

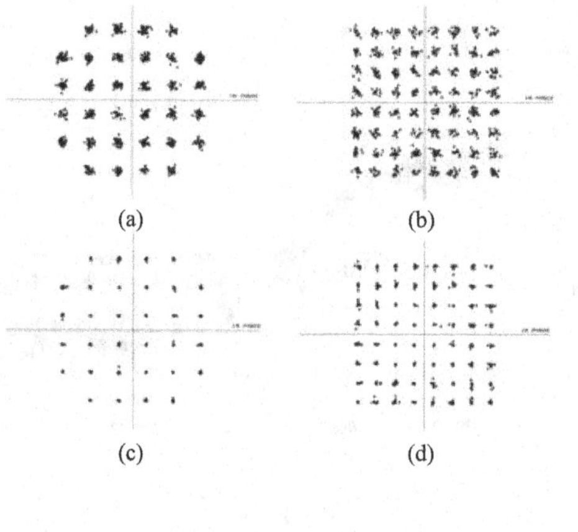

Figure 25. Convergence of MSE versus number of transmitted 32-QAM symbols ($w^h_{58,R}$=1.5, w_r =2.5)

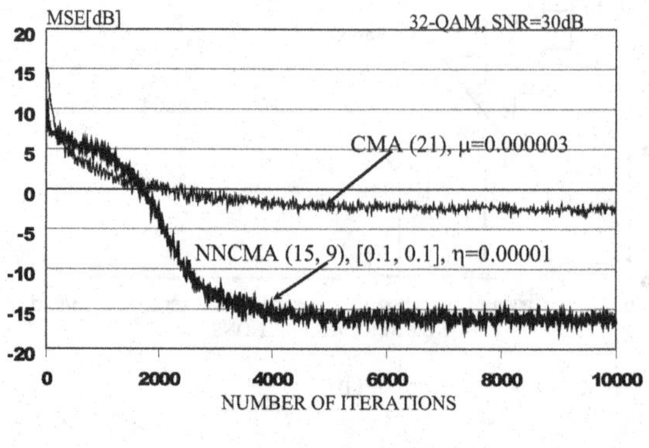

Figure 26. Convergence of MSE versus number of transmitted 16-QAM symbols ($w^h_{58,R}$=1.5, w_r =2.5)

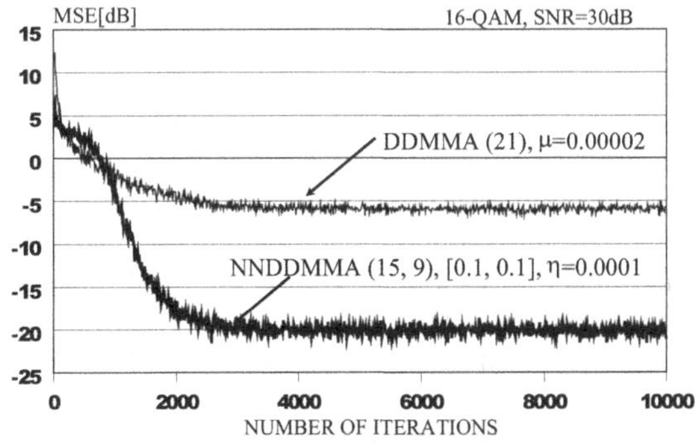

more sensitive to incorrectly decided data than linear FIR filters. That is, the learning using incorrect data exerts a more critical effect on the system stability of the CMLP. However, this problem may be overcome by using a flag for reducing the probabilities of erroneous decisions.

As shown in Fig. 27, the constellation of the 32-QAM signals equalized by CMA and DDMMA shows an arbitrary phase rotation φ_o introduced by the reference channel, which can not be corrected by these algorithms. This result rests on the fact that since their cost functions are based only on the equalizer output modulus, the equalizers are converged independently of a phase error. On the contrary, NNCMA and NNDDMMA correct φ_o . This is because the real and imaginary parts of the activation function have an output region saturated according to the discrete values taken by the QAM signals; hence, the CMLP approximates the real and imaginary parts of the equalizer output to the desired discrete values as if each part is equalized independently by using the saturated region of the activation function. Therefore, even though NNCMA and NNDDMMA do not have an additional carrier phase tracking procedure, the phase rotation φ_o can be corrected.

S&G-DDMMA and NNS&G-DDMMA

Figs. 28 and 29 illustrate the speed of convergence of S&G-DDMMA and NNS&G-DDMMA when using the 16-QAM signal with R_2=13.2 and the 32-QAM signal with R_2=26.2, respectively. Two algorithms exhibit equally fast convergence speed compared to CMA and DDMMA. Such results are achieved by virtue of a flag telling both S&G-DDMMA and NNS&G-DDMMA whether the current output error with respect to the decided symbol is sufficiently reliable to be used.

As indicated in the previous section, the strategy of a flag is more effective on NNS&G-DDMMA than on S&G-DDMMA. In the case of the 32-QAM signal, NNS&G-DDMMA shows a very high convergence speed unlike the case of NNDDMMA, and the performance of NNS&G-DDMMA after the initial convergence is very excellent as compared with S&G-DDMMA.

Considering the case of the 64-QAM signal, we can see more clearly that the above judgment is true. As shown in Fig. 30, S&G-DDMMA exhibits a very low convergence speed, and at the same time the performance after the initial convergence is very poor. On the contrary, NNS&G-DDMMA achieves a very low MSE in the steady state and a fairly high convergence speed. Besides, NNS&G-DDMMA corrects the phase rotation φ_o . However, S&G-DDMMA fails to correct as shown in Fig. 31.

Lastly, Fig. 32 shows the performance comparison of NNS&G-DDMMA, S&G, CMA, and NNS&G. Based on Fig. 32, we can conclude that NNS&G-DDMMA provides an excellent trade-off between the initial convergence speed and the MSE in the steady state.

Comparison

First, NNS&G achieves a much lower MSE in the steady state and a higher convergence speed than S&G for the 32- and 64-QAM. However, as in the case of S&G, NNS&G's weak point is the initial convergence speed that is relatively low compared with the other schemes; nevertheless, the robustness of convergence makes NNS&G attractive in contrast to the other schemes.

NNCMA also achieves a much lower MSE in the steady state than CMA, but its initial convergence speed is somewhat low compared with CMA. Moreover, the MSE of the NNCMA in the steady state is higher than NNS&G. NNDDMMA shows a very high convergence speed and its MSE in the steady state is prominently lower than those of DDMMA and NNCMA when using the 16-QAM signal. However, in the case of the 32-QAM signal the convergence speed of NNDDMMA is very low compared with that of DDMMA even though the performance after the initial convergence is fully satisfactory.

Lastly, NNS&G-DDMMA shows an outstanding convergence speed compared with the other schemes. Also, its performance after the initial convergence is very excellent. However, due to a flag employed for performance improvement, hardware-complexity increases.

Figure 27. Constellation of 32-QAM symbols equalized by (a) CMA, (b) DDMMA, (c) NNCMA, and (d) NND-DMMA

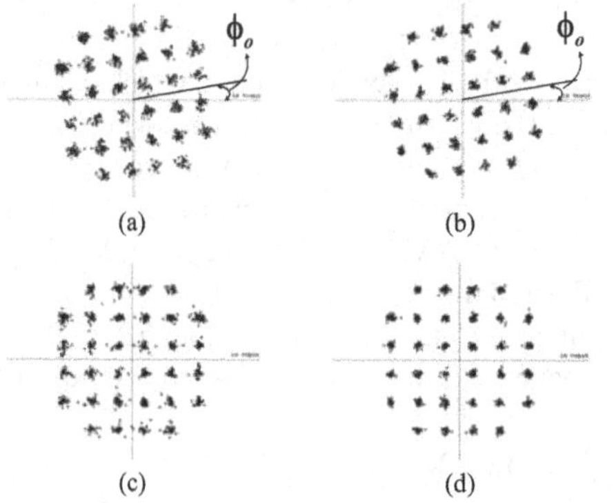

Figure 28. Convergence of MSE versus number of transmitted 16-QAM symbols ($w^{h}_{58,R}$ =1.5, w_r =1.5)

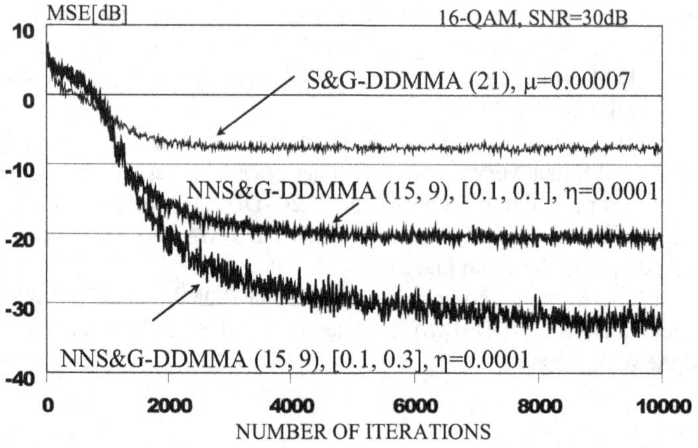

Figure 29. Convergence of MSE versus number of transmitted 32-QAM symbols ($w^h_{58,R}$=1.5, w_r =1.5)

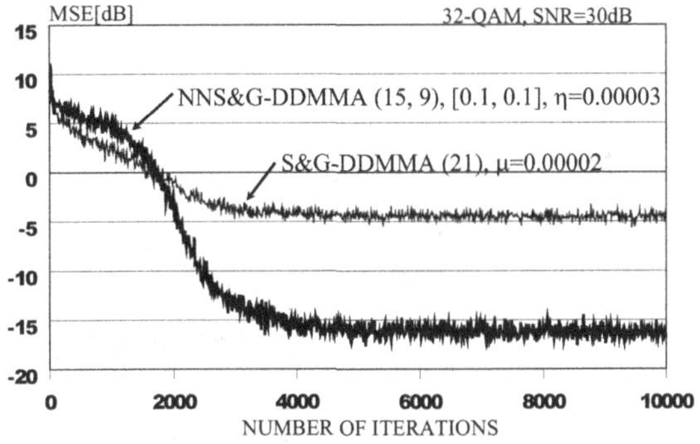

Figure 30. Convergence of MSE versus number of transmitted 64-QAM symbols ($w^h_{58,R}$=1.5, w_r =1.5)

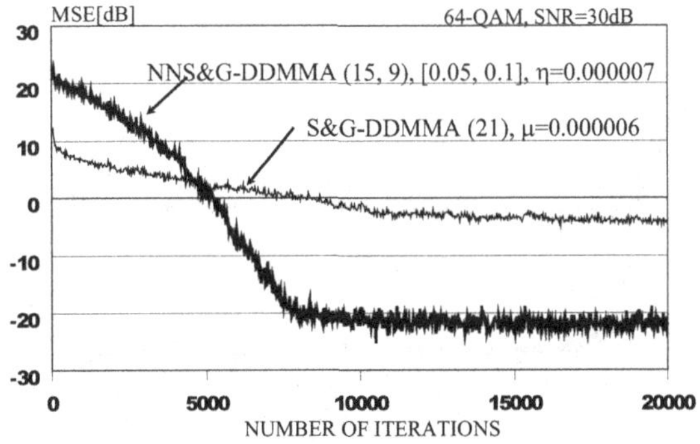

Figure 31. Constellation of M-ary QAM symbols equalized by (a), (b), (c) S&G-DDMMA, (d), (e), and (f) NNS&G-DDMMA

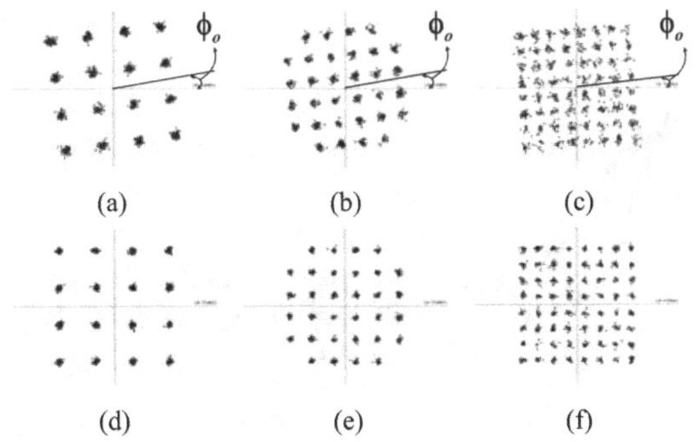

Figure 32. Convergence of MSE versus number of transmitted symbols for NNS&G-DDMMA, NNS&G, S&G, and CMA with the 32-QAM signal

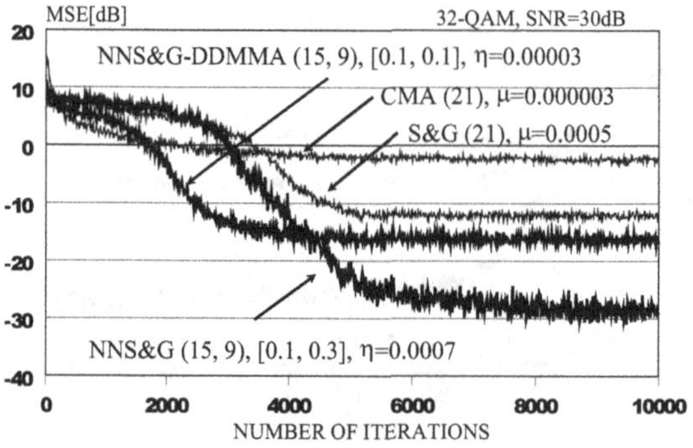

Figure 33. Convergence of MSE versus number of transmitted symbols for NNS&G-DDMMA, NNS&G, S&G, and CMA for the channel given in (Irie, & Miyake, 1988) ($w^h_{58,R}$=1.0, w_r=3.0)

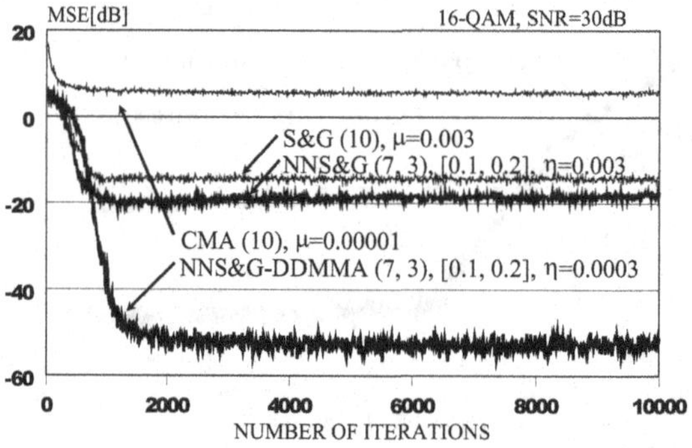

Figure 34. Convergence of MSE versus number of transmitted symbols for NNS&G and S&G for the channel given in (Irie, & Miyake, 1988)

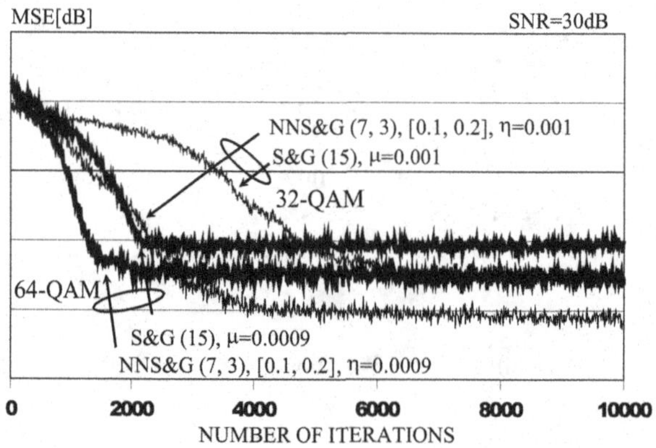

On the other hand, even if there is no carrier phase tracking procedure, all the schemes using the CMLP correct the arbitrary phase rotation introduced by the channel distortion. Therefore, their MSE values are very low compared with those of CMA, DDMMA, and S&G-DDMMA, which fail to correct the arbitrary phase rotation. Such a result would be caused from the saturation characteristics of the activation function as well as the CMLP's powerful mapping capability.

Additional Example

Among the schemes, NNS&G-DDMMA and NNS&G which showed good performance in the previous example have also been simulated for the digital radio channel given in (Picchi, & Prati, 1987), where S&G has been successfully implemented and tested. Fig. 33 shows the performance comparison of NNS&G-DDMMA, S&G, CMA, and NNS&G for the 16-QAM signal. Both NNS&G-DDMMA and NNS&G achieve lower MSEs in the steady state than S&G. In addition, they exhibit equally fast convergence speed compared to S&G. Note that CMA failed in opening the eye. Fig. 34 illustrates the convergence speed of NNS&G and S&G for higher constellations (i.e., 32- and 64-QAM signal). NNS&G achieves lower MSEs and higher convergence speeds than S&G. On the contrary, NNS&G-DDMMA failed to show satisfactory performance. This may be due to the fact that CMA is not competent for the above channel, and NNS&G-DDMMA is derived from CMA even though its performance is improved.

CONCLUSION

The complex BP algorithm for the complex BPN composed of complex processing elements (PEs) is described. The PE has two real activation functions for the real and the imaginary net value of the node output. By dividing the complex node activation function into two real node activation functions for the complex net value of the node output, the complex BP algorithm has many attractive properties. Its unique property is the flexibility in designing the activation function adequate to complex signals that we will use in various applications. On the benchmarking problems, we can conclude that the complex BP algorithm can deal with complex signals very well.

Also, the CBPE is shown as the nonlinear equalizer for complex signals of any constellation sizes. On the simulation results, the CBPE can remarkably deal with the distortion due to band-limited channels. In terms of the MSE, the complex BPE performs better than the complex LMS equalizer. In addition to, the complex BPE outperforms the complex LMS equalizer when the channel introduces major nonlinear distortion. These results are caused by the nonlinearity of the CBPE that is decided by the constant values of the activation function, i.e., A and B. But, these values must be carefully adjusted because the increased nonlinearity can generate problems of training.

On the other hand, in this chapter, four types of blind adaptive equalization schemes have been presented for M-ary QAM signal of any constellation size. For the presented schemes, the complex-valued activation function that can deal with M-ary QAM signals of any constellation sizes is shown. It has been proven by the investigation on the correlation between the input and output of the function that the activation function can reduce the information redundancy among hidden neurons of a CMLP.

Simulation results have shown that all the presented schemes employing the CMLP work well with QAM signals as nonlinear blind equalizers, and that they can correct an arbitrary phase rotation introduced by the channel distortion even if there is no carrier phase tracking procedure.

Finally, even though we employ the CMLP for equalization, we can not say that the CMLP is a best solution for equalization application. Other neural networks may be a better solution under some environments with trade-off of performance and complexity. For example, complex-valued symmetric radial basis function network (Chen, McLaughlin, & Mulgrew, 1994) can be used as a good alternative.

FUTURE RESEARCH DIRECTION

It is possible for the complex BP algorithm to be applied to many other applications such as the complex decision feedback BPE for the channels with deep spectral nulls in their bands. Also, we need to develop the complex-valued activation function whose real and imaginary parts co-operate each other.

Finally, it is important to design new complex-valued activation function with good characteristics for various applications.

REFERENCES

Al-Mashouq, K. A., & Reed, I. S. (1994). The use of neural nets to combine equalization with decoding for severe intersymbol interference channels. *IEEE Trans. on Neural Networks*, *5*(6), 982-988.

Arai, M. (1989, June). Mapping abilities of tree-layer neural networks. *Proc. Int'l Joint Conf. on Neural Networks:* (pp. 419-423). Washington D. C., USA.

Baek, J. S., Park, S. W., & Seo, J. S. (2006). Novel techniques to minimize the error propagation of decision feedback equalizer in 8VSB DTV system. *Proc., IEEE VTC Spring, 5*, 2329–2333.

Balay, P., & Palicot, J. (1994). Equalization of nonlinear perturbations by a multilayer perceptron in satellite channel transmission. *Proc. IEEE GROBECOM* (pp. 1183-1186). San Francisco, CA.

Benveniste, A., & Goursat, M. (1984). Blind equalizers. *IEEE Trans. on Comm.*, *32*, 871-883.

Benvenuto, N., Marchesi, M. Piazza, F. & Uncini, A. (1991, May). Nonlinear satellite radio links equalized using blind neural networks. *Proc. IEEE ICASSP* (pp. 1521-1524). Toronto, USA.

Benvenuto, N., & Piazza, F. (1992). On the complex backpropagation algorithm. *IEEE Trans. on Signal Processing*, *40*(4), 967-969.

Biglieri, E., Divsalar, D., McLane, P. J., & Simon, M. K. (1991). *Introduction to trellis-coded modulation with applications.* Macmillan.

Chang, P. R., Yeh, B. F., & Chang, C. C. (1994). Adaptive packet equalization for indoor radio channel using multilayer neural networks. *IEEE Trans. on Vehicular Tech.*, *43*(3), 773-780.

Chen, S., McLaughlin, S., & Mulgrew, B. (1994). Complex-valued radial basis function network, Part I: network architecture and learning algorithms. *Signal Processing*, *35*(1), 19–31.

Cho, J. H., You, C., & Hong, D. (1996, June). The neural decision feedback equalizer for the nonlinear digital magnetic recording channel. *Proc. IEEE ICC* (pp. 573-576). Dallas, TX.

Duda, R. O., & Hart, P. E. (1973). *Pattern Classification and Scene Analysis.* John Wiley & Sons.

Fahlman, S. E. (1988, June). Faster-learning variation on backpropagation: An empirical study. *Proc. of the Connectionist Model Summer School* (pp. 17-26).

Freemann, J. A., & Skapura, D. M. (1991). *Neural Networks: Algorithm and Programming Techniques.* Addition Wesley.

Funahasi, K. (1989). On the approximate realization of continuous mapping by neural networks. *Neural Networks*, *2*, 183-192.

Georgiou, G. M., & Koutsougeras, C. (1992). Complex domain backpropagation. *IEEE Trans. on Circuits and Systems-II*, *39*(5), 330-334.

Gibson, G. J., Siu, S., & Cowan, C. F. N. (1989, May). Application of multilayer perceptrons as adaptive channel equalizers. *Proc. IEEE ICASSP* (pp. 1183-1186). Glasgow, Scotland.

Godard, N. (1980). Self recovering equalization and carrier tracking in two-dimensional data communication system. *IEEE Trans. on Comm., 28*, 1867-1875.

Haykin, S. (1989). *Adaptive Filter Theory*. Prentice-Hall.

Hecht-Nielson, R. (1988). Kolmogorov's mapping neural network existence theorem. *Proc. IEEE ICNN* (pp. III 11-13).

Irie, B., & Miyake, S. (1988). Capabilities of three-layered perceptrons. *Proc. IEEE ICNN* (pp. I 641-648).

Kechriototic, G., Zervas, E., & Manolakos, E. S. (1994). Using recurrent neural networks for adaptive communication channel equalization. *IEEE Trans. on Neural Networks, 5*(2), 267-278.

Leung, H., & Haykin, S. (1991). The complex backpropagation algorithm. *IEEE Trans. Signal Processing, 39*(9), 2101-2104.

Macchi, O., & Eweda, E. (1984). Convergence analysis of self-adaptive equalizers. *IEEE Trans. on Inform. Theory, 30*, 161-176.

Nilsson, N. J. (1965). *Learning Machines*. McGraw-Hill.

Nitta, T. (1997). An extension of the back-propagation algorithm to complex numbers. *Neural Networks, 10*(8), 1391-1415.

Nitta, T., & Furuya, T. (1991). A complex back-propagation learning. *Transactions of Information Processing Society of Japan, 32*(10), 1319-1329.

Oh. S. H., & Lee, Y. (1994). Effect of nonlinear transformation on correlation between weighted sums in multilayer perceptron. *IEEE Trans. on Neural Networks, 5*(3), 508-510.

Papoulis, A. (1991). *Probability, random variables, and stochastic processes.* Third Edition, New York, McGraw-Hill.

Picchi, G., & Prati, G. (1987). Blind equalization and carrier recovery using a 'stop & go' decision-directed algorithm. *IEEE Trans. on Comm., 35*, 877-887.

Proakis, J. G. (1989). *Digital Communications*. McGraw-Hill.

Sato, Y. (1975). A method of self-recovering equalization for multilevel amplitude-modulation systems. *IEEE Trans. on Comm., 23*, 679-682.

Sethares, W. A., Rey, G. A., & Johnson, C. R. (1989, April). Approach to blind equalization of signal with multiple modulus. *Proc. IEEE ICASSP* (pp. 972-975).

Trim, D. W. (1996). *Introduction to complex analysis and its applications.* PWS Publishing Company.

Widrow, B., McCool, J., & Ball, M. (1995). The complex LMS algorithm. *Proc. IEEE, 63*, 710-720.

You, C., & Hong, D. (1995, June). Neural convolutional decoders in the satellite channel. *Proc. IEEE ICNN:* (pp. 443-448). Perth, Australia.

You, C., & Hong, D. (1996, June). Adaptive equalization using the complex backpropagation algorithm. *Proc. IEEE ICNN:* (pp. IV 2136-2141). Washington D. C., USA.

You, C., & Hong, D. (1998). Nonlinear blind equalization schemes using complex valued multilayer feedforward neural networks. *IEEE Trans., Neural Networks, 9*(6), 1442–1455.

ADDITIONAL READING

Benedetto, S., & Biglieri, E. (1983). Nonlinear equalization of digital satellite channel. *IEEE Journal on Selected Areas in Comm., 1*, 57-62.

Benedetto, S., Biglieri, E., & Daffara, R. (1979). Modeling and performance evaluation of non-linear satellite links-a Volterra series approach. *IEEE Trans. on Aerospace, 15*, 494-507.

Benvenuto, N., Marchesi, M. Piazza, F., & Uncini, A. (1991, June). A comparison between real and complex-valued neural networks in communication applications. *Proc. Int. Conf. Artificial Neural Networks* (pp. 1177-1180). Espoo, Finland.

Biglieri, E., Gersho, A., Gitlin, R.D., & Lim, T. L. (1984). Adaptive cancellation of nonlinear intersymbol interference for voiceband data transmission. *IEEE Journal on Selected Areas in Comm., 2*, 765-777.

Ding, Z., & Kennedy, R. A. (1992). On the whereabouts of local minima for blind adaptive equalizers. *IEEE Trans. on Circuits and Systems, 39*, 119-123.

Ersoy, O. K., & Hong, D. S. (1993). Parallel, self-organizing, hierarchical neural networks-II. *IEEE Trans. on Industrial Electronics, 2*(2), 218-227.

Gutierrez, A., & Ryan, W. E. (1995, June). Performance of adaptive Volterra equalizers on nonlinear satellite channels. *Proc. IEEE ICC* (pp. 488-492). Seattle, USA.

Horowitz, L. L., & Senne, K. D. (1981). Performance advantages of complex LMS for controlling narrow-band adaptive arrays. *IEEE Trans. on Acoust. Speech Signal Process., 29*, 722-736.

Lapeda, A., & Farber, R. (1988). *How neural nets work?* (Preprint la-ur-88-418). Los Alamos, NM, Los Alamos Nat. Lab.

Lee, D. L. (2001). Improving the capacity of complex-valued neural networks with a modified gradient descent learning rule. *IEEE Transactions on Neural Networks, 12*(2), 439-443.

Mohler, R. R. (1991). *Nonlinear Systems: vol. II.* Prentice-Hall.

Wiener, N. (1958). *Nonlinear Problems in Random Theory.* New York, Wiley.

Yang, C. C., & Bose, N. K. (2005). Landmine detection and classification with complex-valued hybrid neural network using scattering parameters dataset. *IEEE Transactions on Neural Networks, 16*(3), 743-753.

APPENDIX

Correlation

By definition, we get

$$Cor(o_R, o_I) = \frac{E[o_R \cdot o_I] - E[o_R] \cdot E[o_I]}{\sigma_{o_R} \cdot \sigma_{o_I}}. \tag{49}$$

The following improper integral is easily calculated by residues:

$$\int_0^\infty \cos(bx) e^{-ax^2} dx = \frac{1}{2}\sqrt{\frac{\pi}{a}} \exp[-b^2/(4a)]. \tag{50}$$

Using (50), we get

$$E[o_R] = m_R + \alpha \sin(\pi m_R) \exp(-\pi^2 \sigma_{y_R}^2 / 2), \tag{51}$$

$$E[o_I] = m_I + \alpha \sin(\pi m_I) \exp(-\pi^2 \sigma_{y_I}^2 / 2). \tag{52}$$

In order to obtain the variance of r. v. o_R, we must calculate $E[o_R^2]$. Using (50) and the facts that if $h(x)$ is an odd function, then

$$\int_{-T/2}^{T/2} h(x) dx = 0 \tag{53}$$

and that

$$\int_0^\infty \sin(A\sqrt{t}) e^{-t} dt = \frac{A\sqrt{\pi}}{2} \exp(-A^2/4), \tag{54}$$

$E[o_R^2]$ can be readily found as follows:

$$E[o_R^2] = \sigma_{y_R}^2 + m_R^2 + \frac{\alpha^2}{2}\left[1 - \cos(2\pi m_R) \exp(-2\pi^2 \sigma_{y_R}^2)\right]$$
$$+ 2\alpha\left[\pi\sigma_{y_R}^2 \cos(\pi m_R) + m_R \sin(\pi m_R)\right] \exp(-\pi^2 \sigma_{y_R}^2 / 2).$$

Similarly,

$$E[o_I^2] = \sigma_{y_I}^2 + m_I^2 + \frac{\alpha^2}{2}\left[1 - \cos(2\pi m_I) \exp(-2\pi^2 \sigma_{y_I}^2)\right]$$
$$+ 2\alpha\left[\pi\sigma_{y_I}^2 \cos(\pi m_I) + m_I \sin(\pi m_I)\right] \exp(-\pi^2 \sigma_{y_I}^2 / 2).$$

Next, we need to find $E[o_R \cdot o_I]$. If let $y_R - m_R = w$ and $y_I - m_I = z$, we may get

continued on following page

APPENDIX CONTINUED

$$
\begin{aligned}
E[o_R \cdot o_I] &= E[w \cdot z] + m_I E[w] + m_R E[z] + m_R m_I \\
&+ \alpha E[w \cdot \sin\{\pi(z + m_I)\}] + \alpha E[z \cdot \sin\{\pi(w + m_R)\}] \\
&+ \alpha m_R E[\sin\{\pi(z + m_I)\}] + \alpha m_I E[\sin\{\pi(w + m_R)\}] \\
&+ \alpha^2 E[\sin\{\pi(w + m_R)\} \cdot \sin\{\pi(z + m_I)\}]
\end{aligned} \tag{55}
$$

and the joint PDF of $\boldsymbol{w}$ and $\boldsymbol{z}$ is

$$
f(w,z) = \frac{1}{2\pi\sigma_{y_R} \cdot \sigma_{y_I}\sqrt{1-r^2}} \exp\left\{-\frac{1}{2(1-r^2)}\left[\frac{w^2}{\sigma_{y_R}^2} - 2r\frac{w \cdot z}{\sigma_{y_R}\sigma_{y_I}} + \frac{z^2}{\sigma_{y_I}^2}\right]\right\}
$$

where $E[w] = E[z] = 0$ and $E[w \cdot z] = \sigma_{y_R}\sigma_{y_I} r$.

Using (50), (53), and (54), we obtain

$$
\begin{aligned}
E[o_R \cdot o_I] &= \sigma_{y_R}\sigma_{y_I} r + m_R m_I + \pi\alpha \cos(\pi m_R)\sigma_{y_R}\sigma_{y_I} r \cdot \exp[-\pi^2\sigma_{y_R}^2/2] \\
&+ \pi\alpha \cos(\pi m_I)\sigma_{y_R}\sigma_{y_I} r \cdot \exp[-\pi^2\sigma_{y_I}^2/2] + m_R\alpha \sin(\pi m_I) \cdot \exp[-\pi^2\sigma_{y_I}^2/2] \\
&+ m_I\alpha \sin(\pi m_R) \cdot \exp[-\pi^2\sigma_{y_R}^2/2] + \frac{\alpha^2}{2} \cdot \exp[-\pi^2(\sigma_{y_R}^2 + \sigma_{y_I}^2)/2] \\
&\times \{\cos[(m_R - m_I)\pi]\exp(\pi^2\sigma_{y_R}\sigma_{y_I} r) - \cos[(m_R + m_I)\pi]\exp(-\pi^2\sigma_{y_R}\sigma_{y_I} r)\}.
\end{aligned} \tag{56}
$$

Assuming without loss of generality that m_R and m_I are zero such as the case of M-ary QAM signal and substituting (51), (52), (56) into (49), then we have $Cor(o_R, o_I)$ defined by (41) to (45).

For a comparison between r and $Cor(\boldsymbol{o}_R, \boldsymbol{o}_I)$, some approximations are needed because a rigorous analysis of $Cor(\boldsymbol{o}_R, \boldsymbol{o}_I)$ is difficult. Based on the facts that exp[-x]→0 as x→∞, and that $\sigma_{y_R}^2 + \sigma_{y_I}^2 \pm 2\sigma_{y_R}\sigma_{y_I} r \geq 0$ because $|r| \leq 1$, we have the following approximations of (41) to (45): $M \approx \sigma_{y_R}\sigma_{y_I} r$, $N \approx 0$, $\sigma_{o_R}^2 \approx \sigma_{y_R}^2 + \alpha^2/2$, and $\sigma_{o_I}^2 \approx \sigma_{y_I}^2 + \alpha^2/2$. In this case, we have assumed without loss of generality that $\sigma_{y_R}^2, \sigma_{y_I}^2$ >>0.1 because signals transmitted through channels are subject to noise. Thus, $Cor(\boldsymbol{o}_R, \boldsymbol{o}_I)$ can be approximated as (41-1).

NNGA

The Godard algorithm (Godard, 1980) minimizes a nonconvex cost function, called the *dispersion of order n*, defined as $G_p^{(n)} = E[(|O_p|^n - R_n)^2]$, where n is a positive integer, and R_n is a positive real constant defined by

$$
R_n = E(|S_p|^{2n}) / E(|S_p|^n) \tag{57}
$$

continued on following page

APPENDIX CONTINUED

where O_p is the pth estimated output of the equalizer and $\{S_p\}$ represents the information sequence.

For the Godard algorithm to be extended to blind equalization algorithm for the CMLP, we redefine the cost function of the CBP algorithm as follows:

$$E_p^{(n)} = \frac{1}{2}\left(|O_p|^n - R_n\right)^2. \quad (58)$$

The gradient of (58) can be found [see Proposition 1 and Corollary 1]. First, let us consider the adaptation rule of the output layer. Using the steepest descent rule, the weights can be updated as

$$W_j^o(p+1) = W_j^o(p) - \mu \cdot \nabla E_p^{(n)}\Big|_{W_j^o}$$

where μ is a positive real number and

$$\nabla E_p^{(n)}\Big|_{W_j^o} = \left(|O_p|^n - R_n\right)\cdot n \cdot \left|O_p\right|^{(n-1)} \cdot \left(\frac{\partial\left|O_p\right|}{\partial w_{j,R}^o(t)} + j\frac{\partial\left|O_p\right|}{\partial w_{j,I}^o(t)}\right). \quad (59)$$

Using the chain rule, we find some expressions for the partial derivative:

$$\frac{\partial\left|O_p\right|}{\partial w_{j,R}^o(t)} = \frac{1}{|O_p|}\left[f^o(n_R^o)f'^o(n_R^o)i_{pj,R} + jf^o(n_I^o)f'^o(n_I^o)i_{pj,I}\right],$$

$$\frac{\partial\left|O_p\right|}{\partial w_{j,I}^o(t)} = \frac{1}{|O_p|}\left[f^o(n_R^o)f'^o(n_R^o)(-i_{pj,I}) + jf^o(n_I^o)f'^o(n_I^o)i_{pj,R}\right].$$

where $n_R^o = net_{p,R}^o$ and $n_I^o = net_{p,I}^o$. By defining a quantity

$$\delta_p^o = \left(f^o(n_R^o)f'^o(n_R^o) + jf^o(n_I^o)f'^o(n_I^o)\right)\left|O_p\right|^{(n-2)} \cdot \left(R_n - |O_p|^n\right), \quad (60)$$

the weights of the output layer are updated as

$$W_j^o(p+1) = W_j^o(p) + \eta\,\delta_p^o I_{pj}^*$$

where η is a real-valued learning-rate parameter.

To show the process for updating the hidden layer, we must first find the gradient of the cost function with respect to the complex weights in the hidden layer. Using the chain rule, we may write

continued on following page

APPENDIX CONTINUED

$$\frac{\partial |O_p|}{\partial w^h_{ji,R}(t)} = \frac{1}{|O_p|}\left[f^o(n^o_R)\frac{\partial f^o}{\partial n^o_R}\frac{\partial n^o_R}{\partial w^h_{ji,R}(t)} + jf^o(n^o_I)\frac{\partial f^o}{\partial n^o_I}\frac{\partial n^o_I}{\partial w^h_{ji,R}(t)} \right], \tag{61}$$

$$\frac{\partial |O_p|}{\partial w^h_{ji,I}(t)} = \frac{1}{|O_p|}\left[f^o(n^o_R)\frac{\partial f^o}{\partial n^o_R}\frac{\partial n^o_R}{\partial w^h_{ji,I}(t)} + jf^o(n^o_I)\frac{\partial f^o}{\partial n^o_I}\frac{\partial n^o_I}{\partial w^h_{ji,I}(t)} \right] \tag{62}$$

where

$$\frac{\partial n^o_R}{\partial w^h_{ji,R}(t)} = w^o_{j,R}(t) f'^h_j(n^h_R) x_{pi,R} - w^o_{j,I}(t) f'^h_j(n^h_I) x_{pi,I},$$

$$\frac{\partial n^o_I}{\partial w^h_{ji,R}(t)} = w^o_{j,R}(t) f'^h_j(n^h_I) x_{pi,I} + w^o_{j,I}(t) f'^h_j(n^h_R) x_{pi,R},$$

$$\frac{\partial n^o_R}{\partial w^h_{ji,I}(t)} = -w^o_{j,R}(t) f'^h_j(n^h_R) x_{pi,I} - w^o_{j,I}(t) f'^h_j(n^h_I) x_{pi,R},$$

$$\frac{\partial n^o_I}{\partial w^h_{ji,I}(t)} = w^o_{j,R}(t) f'^h_j(n^h_I) x_{pi,R} - w^o_{j,I}(t) f'^h_j(n^h_R) x_{pi,I}.$$

where $n^h_R = net^h_{p,R}$ and $n^h_I = net^h_{p,I}$. Using (61), (62), and the definition given in (60), we may express the gradient of interest as

$$\nabla E^{(n)}_p \Big|_{W^h_{ji}} = -n \cdot X^*_{pi} \delta^h_{pj},$$

where

$$\delta^h_{pj} = f'^h_j(n^h_R)\,\mathrm{Re}\left(\delta^o_p W^{o*}_j\right) + jf'^h_j(n^h_I)\,\mathrm{Im}\left(\delta^o_p W^{o*}_j\right). \tag{63}$$

Finally, we cause the weight update equations to become analogous to that for the output layer:

$$W^h_{ji}(p+1) = W^h_{ji}(p) + \eta\, \delta^h_{pj} X^*_{pi}.$$

When the network has more than two hidden layers, the same type of calculation we did for the CMLP with a single hidden layer is repeated, and similar equations result. As shown in (63), therefore, the known error on the output layer (or output neuron) may be backpropagated to the input layer in a layer-by-layer manner.

Like the Godard algorithm, two cases are of specific interest. For n=1, NNGA may be viewed as a modification of the Sato algorithm. And, choosing n=2 leads to NNCMA.

continued on following page

APPENDIX CONTINUED

NNDDMMA

To derive NNDDMMA, after converting R_n of the cost function of (58) into M_i defined in (46), the same type of calculation we did for deriving NNGA is repeated. Eventually, NNDDMMA can be defined as follows:

$$\begin{cases} W_j^o(p+1) = W_j^o(p) + \eta\, \delta_p^o I_{pj}^*, \\ \delta_p^o = \left[f^o(n_R^o) f'^o(n_R^o) + j f^o(n_I^o) f'^o(n_I^o) \right] \left(M_i - |O_p|^2 \right), \end{cases}$$

$$\begin{cases} W_j^o(p+1) = W_j^o(p) + \eta\, \delta_p^o I_{pj}^*, \\ \delta_p^o = \left[f^o(n_R^o) f'^o(n_R^o) + j f^o(n_I^o) f'^o(n_I^o) \right] \left(M_i - |O_p|^2 \right), \end{cases}$$

Chapter X
Image Reconstruction by the Complex-Valued Neural Networks:
Design by Using Generalized Projection Rule

Donq-Liang Lee
Ming-Chuan University, Taiwan

ABSTRACT

New design methods for the complex-valued multistate Hopfield associative memories (CVHAMs) are presented. The author of this chapter shows that the well-known projection rule can be generalized to complex domain such that the weight matrix of the CVHAM can be designed by using the generalized inverse technique. The stability of the presented CVHAM is analyzed by using energy function approach which shows that in synchronous update mode a CVHAM is guaranteed to converge to a fixed point from any given initial state. Moreover, the projection geometry of the generalized projection rule is discussed. In order to enhance the recall capability, a strategy of eliminating the spurious memories is reported. Next, a generalized intraconnected bidirectional associative memory (GIBAM) is introduced. A GIBAM is a complex generalization of the intraconnected BAM (IBAM). Lee shows that the design of the GIBAM can also be accomplished by using the generalized inverse technique. Finally, the validity and the performance of the introduced methods are investigated by computer simulation.

INTRODUCTION

Storing gray-scale images with neural networks is a challenging problem and has received much attention in the past two decades. There are four main approaches for storing images with n pixels and K gray levels. The first approach is to encode the gray level of each pixel by R ($R = \log_2 K$) *binary* neurons (Taketa & Goodman, 1986; Cernuschi-Frias, 1989; Lee, 1999). However, this method needs great numbers of neurons (nR) and interconnection weights (n^2R^2). The second approach is based on neural networks with multivalued stable states (Si & Michel, 1991; Zurada, Cloete, & van der Poel, 1996). The activation function is a quantized nonlinearity with *K plateaus* corresponding to the K gray levels. The required number of neurons is n and the number of interconnections is n^2. The third approach is to decompose the K gray-level image into R gray-coded images (Costantini, Casali, & Pefetti, 2003). These images are then stored by using R independent *binary* neural networks. The required number of interconnections is $n^2 R$. The fourth approach is based on complex-valued neural networks (Jankowski, Lozowski, & Zurada, 1996; Lee, 2001a, 2001b, 2003). The neuron state can assume one of K complex values, equally spaced on the unit circle. Each phase angle corresponds to a gray level. The number of neurons is n; the number of interconnections is n^2.

The objective of this chapter is to review and discuss some recent developments of the complex-valued neural networks (CVNNs). Here we present two types of CVNNs: *auto-associative* network and *hetero-associative* network. Network structures, evolution equations, stability, and design methods are discussed in detail. For simplicity, the CVNNs considered here have no threshold (bias) vectors though the including of them adds substantial degree of freedom to the design

The complex-valued Hopfield associative memory (CVHAM) proposed by Jankowski, Lozowski, and Zurada (1996) is a kind of *auto-associative* network. It can be referred to as a modified Hopfield network (Hopfield, 1984) having complex-signum activation functions and complex weighting connections. The learning algorithms of conventional CVHAMs include: generalized Hebb rule (Jankowski, Lozowski, & Zurada, 1996), gradient descent learning rule (Lee, 2001a, 2003), energy design method (Müezzinoğlu, Güzeliş, & Zurada, 2003), etc. However, the recall capability of the CVHAMs is limited because these methods do not consider the attraction of the fixed point seriously. In this chapter, the generalized projection rule for the CVHAM is introduced.

In 1991, Jeng and Yeh introduced a modified *intraconnected* bidirectional associative memory (MIBAM). It is a two-layer *hetero–associative* memory in which the *intralayer* feedback processes run in *parallel*, instead of *sequentially* as in the IBAM (Simpson, 1990), with the *interlayer* processes. Compared with IBAM, the MIBAM yields both improved storage capacity and error correcting capability. However, the improvements are minor because the design of the MIBAM does not seriously consider the safe storage of all training pairs. With the help of the generalized inverse technique, a generalized model of the IBAM (GIBAM) is proposed in this chapter. Computer simulation demonstrates that the GIBAM has better recall performances than does the MIBAM.

This chapter is organized as follows. The background of the CVHAMs is introduced first. The structure and some conventional learning methods of the CVHAM are briefly reviewed. Next, the energy design method proposed by Müezzinoğlu, Güzeliş, and Zurada (2003) are discussed. Then, the generalized projection rule (GPR) and the modified projection rule (MPR) are presented to improve the recall performance of the CVHAM. Extension of the auto-associative CVHAM to the hetero-associative GIBAM is also discussed. The validity and the effectiveness of the presented methods are demonstrated by a lot of simulation results. Finally, a concluding remark is given in the final section.

BACKGROUND

The CVHAM (Jankowski, Lozowski, & Zurada, 1996) is an *auto-associative* memory that stores complex-valued prototype vectors X^k, $k = 1,\ldots,m$ where m is the number of the prototype vectors and $X^k = (x_1^k\ x_2^k \cdots x_N^k)^T$. The components $x_i^k s$ are all quantization values that are defined by

$$x_i^k \in \{\exp[j2\pi v / K]\}_{v=0}^{K-1} \quad i = 1,\ldots,N. \tag{1}$$

The resolution factor K divides the complex unit circle into K quantization values so that $|x_i^k| = 1;\ \forall i, k$. Let $X \in C^N$ and $S \in C^{N\times N}$ denote the state vector and the connection weight matrix of the CVHAM, respectively. The output of each neuron is determined by the following equation:

$$x_i' = \varphi\left\{\sum_{j=1}^{N} s_{ij} x_j\right\} \tag{2}$$

in which x_i is the ith component of X; x_i' denotes the next state of x_i. Moreover, $\varphi(\cdot)$ is a complex-signum function,

$$\varphi(Z) = \begin{cases} \exp(j0) & 0 \le \arg\left[Ze^{j(\theta_0/2)}\right] < \theta_0 \\ \exp\left(j\dfrac{2\pi}{K}\right) & \theta_0 \le \arg\left[Ze^{j(\theta_0/2)}\right] < 2\theta_0 \\ \vdots & \\ \exp\left[j\dfrac{2\pi(K-1)}{K}\right] & (K-1)\theta_0 \le \arg\left[Ze^{j(\theta_0/2)}\right] < K\theta_0 \end{cases} \tag{3}$$

where $\arg[\alpha]$ is the phase angle of α, θ_0 is a phase quantum which is delimited by $K: \theta_0 = 2\pi / K$. From equation (3) we know that $\varphi(Z)$ is the quantization value whose phase is closest to the phase of Z. The resolution factor K divides the complex plane unit circle into K separate sectors and each of them has an angle of θ_0 (see Figure 1). Note that if K=2, the CVHAM will be functionally equivalent to the Hopfield network (Hopfield, 1984) in which all neuron states are bipolar real values (i.e., 1 or -1). The only difference is that the former permits complex-valued weighting connections but the latter does not.

The recall process (2) is a stochastic process that starts with an initial vector X presented to the network. Then, neuron states are updated *one at a time* by following (2) with equal probabilities. In 1996, Jankowski Lozowski, and Zurada proved that the *asynchronous* process (2) converges to one of the fixed points X_f in a finite number of iterations if $S = [s_{ij}]$ is a Hermitian matrix with nonnegative diagonal elements (the stability property for CVHAM with non-Hermitian weight matrix has also been discussed (Lee, 2001b)).
A fixed point $X_f = [x_{f1}\ x_{f2} \cdots x_{fN}]$ has the following properties,

Figure 1. Location of the elements of the state vector

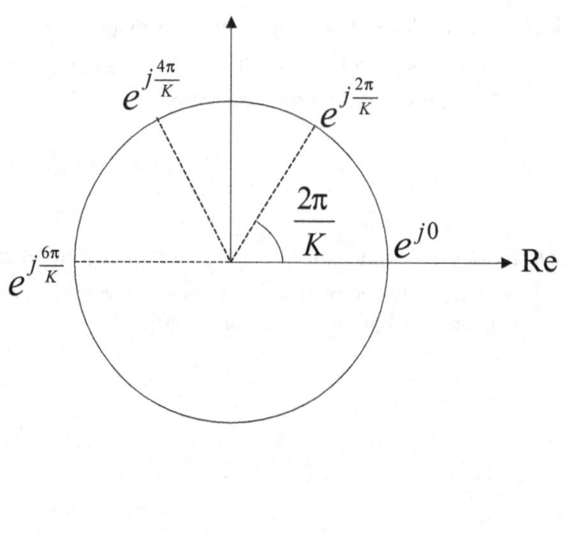

$$x_{fi} = \varphi\left\{\sum_{j=1}^{N} s_{ij} x_{fj}\right\}, \quad i = 1, ..., N. \tag{4}$$

Obviously, a prototype vector can be recalled only if it is a fixed point. In the original model (Jankowski, Lozowski, & Zurada, 1996) the m prototype vectors are stored in the connection weights according to the *generalized Hebb rule*,

$$s_{ij} = \frac{1}{N}\sum_{k=1}^{m} x_i^k \bar{x}_j^k \quad i, j = 1, ..., N \tag{5}$$

where $\bar{x}_j^k$ denotes the complex conjugate of x_j^k. Unfortunately, as the case of bipolar networks (Hopfield, 1984), the encoding rule (5) does not ensure that all the prototype vectors are fixed points defined in equation (4). In other words, the capacity of the conventional CVHAM is limited. Based on the Hermitian weight matrix, a gradient descend learning rule (Lee, 2001a) has been introduced to improve the capacity of the CVHAM. However, the problem of improving the recall capability of the CVHAMs has not been solved until 2003.

NEW LEARNING ALGORITHMS FOR THE CVHAMS

Energy Design Method (EDM)

In 2003, Müezzinoğlu, Güzeliş, and Zurada proposed an energy design method (EDM for short hereafter) which employs a set of inequalities to render each prototype vector as a strict local minimum of a quadratic energy landscape. The EDM is briefly summarized in the following.

Consider the following energy function proposed in by Müezzinoğlu, Güzeliş, and Zurada (2003),

$$E(X) = -\frac{1}{2} X^* S X \tag{6}$$

The recipe for EDM consists in performing a search for the connection weight matrix S, such that the real-valued energy (6) attains a local minimum at each training vector. Let Z be a vector in N-dimensional complex vector space, $Z \in C^N$. Let $B_1^K(Z)$ be the 1-neighborhood of Z defined as

$$B_1^K(Z) := \bigcup_{i=1}^{n} \{V : v_i = z_i e^{j2\pi/K} \vee v_i = z_i e^{-j2\pi/K}, v_j = z_j, j \neq i\} \cup \{Z\} \tag{7}$$

Note that $B_1^K(Z)$ consists of vectors each has only one entry being different from Z and their (phase) difference is only $\theta_0 (= 2\pi / K)$. Müezzinoğlu, Güzeliş, and Zurada (2003) impose a set of strict inequalities

$$E(X) < E(Y), \forall Y \in B_1^K(X) - \{X\} \tag{8}$$

to be satisfied for each training vector $X \in \{X^k\}_{k=1}^{m}$. The main result proposed by them is summarized in the following theorem:

Theorem 1 (Müezzinoğlu, Güzeliş, & Zurada, 2003): Given a CVHAM defined by equation (4), the quadratic form (6) possesses a strict local minimum at each training vector $X \in \{X^k\}_{k=1}^{m}$ if and only if the homogeneous inequality

$$\sum_{1\le i\le j\le N} \left\{\mathrm{Re}\{s_{ij}\}\left[\cos(x_j - x_i) - \cos(y_j - y_i)\right] + \mathrm{Im}\{s_{ij}\}\left[\sin(y_j - y_i) - \sin(x_j - x_i)\right]\right\} > 0 \quad (9)$$

is satisfied by the weight matrix S for all $X \in \left\{X^k\right\}_{k=1}^m$ and for all $Y \in B_1^K(X) - \{X\}$.

Proof: (see Müezzinoğlu, Güzeliş, & Zurada, 2003)

Remark 1: If (9) is a feasible inequality system for a given training set $\left\{X^k\right\}_{k=1}^m$, any linear programming procedure, e.g., the primal-dual method (Luenberger, 1973), or the perceptron learning algorithm (Rosenblatt, 1962), would provide a solution. However, since there are a total of $2mN$ inequalities, as the dimension N increases, the EDM becomes time and memory consuming when compared to the generalized Hebb rule (Jankowski, Lozowski, & Zurada, 1996).

Remark 2: Since

$$x_i^k \in \exp\{[j2\pi v / K]\}_{v=0}^{K-1} \quad i = 1, \ldots, N,$$

from equation (9) we can observe that only the differences between the phases of the entries of the training vectors, not their actual values, are used in the construction of the design inequalities. In other words, a weight matrix calculated from the solution of equation (9) will introduce at least $(K\text{-}1)m$ additional vectors as spurious memories to the network. A way of eliminating such trivial spurious memories can be found (Müezzinoğlu, Güzeliş, & Zurada, 2003).

Remark 3: In simulation (see later) we find that the recall capability of CVHAM by using the above EDM is effective only when the resolution factor K is small. If K is large, then the recall capability will fall sharply (Lee, 2006).

In the following section we generalize the projection rule proposed by Personnaz, Guyon, and Dreyfus (1986) and show that the generalized projection rule (GPR) can be used to improve the recall capability of the CVHAM.

GENERALIZED PROJECTION RULES FOR CVHAMS

If we can find a matrix S such that

$$SX^k = X^k, \quad k = 1, \ldots, m \quad (10)$$

then each of the prototype vectors will be a fixed point defined in equation (4). Hereinafter let $\varphi\{V\}$ be a pointwise function that operates on each component of V as in (3). The condition (10) is more conservative than

$$X^k = \varphi\left\{SX^k\right\}, \quad k = 1, \ldots, m \quad (11)$$

since the transformation between prototype vectors is strictly linear in the former case. Let $\Sigma = (X^1\ X^2 \cdots X^m)$, then equation (10) yields the matrix equation

$$S\Sigma = \Sigma. \quad (12)$$

One solution of this set of *Nm* linear equations is given by

$$S = \Sigma^{I}, \tag{13}$$

where Σ^I denotes the *generalized inverse* (Albert, 1972; Lancaster & Tismenetsky, 1985) of Σ. Let us assume that $X^1\ X^2 \cdots X^m$ are linearly independent so that Σ has full column rank, i.e., ($\Sigma^*\Sigma$) is invertible (Σ^* denotes the conjugate transposition of Σ). Then, Σ^I can be computed by using a simple matrix equation:

$$\Sigma^I = (\Sigma^*\Sigma)^{-1}\Sigma^*. \tag{14}$$

In this case,

$$S = \Sigma(\Sigma^*\Sigma)^{-1}\Sigma^* \tag{15}$$

will be a *Hermitian* and *nonnegative definite* matrix. Note that *S* in equation (15) is constructed by using simple *generalized inverse* technique. The matrix *S* can be computed by using an iterative algorithm with *m* iteration steps (Albert, 1972). A CVHAM designed by this technique has the ability of *learning* and *forgetting* (Personnaz, Guyon, Dreyfus, & Toulouse, 1986). That is, once a weight matrix has been computed according to a given set of prototype vectors, the addition of one extra prototype vector or the deletion of an existing prototype vector only needs one more step of the iterative algorithm instead of recomputing the *entire* weight matrix.

In the following we show that the proposed CVHAM is stable under *synchronous* mode. A CVHAM is said to be operated in the synchronous mode if all neurons are updated simultaneously instead of one at a time as in equation (2). Its recall process can be described by

$$X' = \varphi\{SX\}. \tag{16}$$

Next, we introduce the following theorems.

Theorem 2 (Lee, 2006): Given a CVHAM with a weight matrix defined in equation (15). If it is operating in the *synchronous* mode defined by equation (16), then the CVHAM will converge to a fixed point from any given initial state.

Proof: Consider the following energy function (same as equation (6))

$$E(X) = -\frac{1}{2}X^*SX \tag{17}$$

Since *S* in equation (15) is Hermitian, the energy change from the current state X to the next state X' is

$$\begin{aligned}\Delta E &= E(X') - E(X)\\ &= -\frac{1}{2}(X'-X)^*S(X'-X) - X^*S(X'-X)\\ &\le -X^*S(X'-X)\end{aligned}$$

The last inequality follows from the fact that *S* is also nonnegative definite. Now let $\sum s_{ij}x_j = r_i\exp(j\varphi_i)$, $\bar{x}_i = \exp(-j\phi_i)$, and $\bar{x}'_i = \exp(-j\phi'_i)$ where r_i and φ_i denotes the modulus and phase angle of $\sum s_{ij}x_j$, respectively; ϕ_i and ϕ'_i denote the phase angle of x_i and x'_i, respectively. We find that

$$
\begin{aligned}
& -X^{*}S(X'-X) \\
= \; & -(X'-X)^{*}SX \\
= \; & -\sum_{i=1}^{N}(\overline{x}_i'-\overline{x}_i)\left\{\sum_{j=1}^{N}s_{ij}x_j\right\} \\
= \; & \sum_{i=1}^{N} r_i \operatorname{Re}\{\exp[j(\varphi_i-\phi)-\exp[j(\varphi_i-\phi_i')]\} \\
= \; & \sum_{i=1}^{N} r_i \{\cos(\varphi_i-\phi)-\cos(\varphi_i-\phi_i')\} \\
\leq \; & 0
\end{aligned}
$$

The last inequality follows because ϕ_i' is the quantization value which is closest to φ_i. Finally, we conclude that $\Delta E \leq 0$ and $\Delta E = 0$ if and only if $\phi_i' = \phi_i \; \forall i$, i.e., $X' = X$. Note that E is bounded from below as long as $|s_{ij}|$ is bounded for all i and j. Therefore, in synchronous mode and starting with any initial vector, the CVHAM always converges to a fixed point. The proof is thus complete.

Theorem 3 (Lee, 2006): Under the standing assumptions of the projection learning rule (i.e., linear independence of prototypes), *global* energy minima are formed at the prototype states for the GPR.

Proof: The energy of a prototype vector X^k and its negative $-X^k$ is given by

$$E(X^k) = E(-X^k) = -\frac{1}{2}(X^k)^{*}SX^k = -\frac{N}{2}. \qquad (18)$$

Let Ψ^N be the set of vectors whose components $x_i s$ satisfy

$$x_i \in \exp\{[j2\pi v/K]\}_{v=0}^{K-1} \qquad (19)$$

Each vector in Ψ^N is located on a complex discrete hyper-sphere surface since its Euclidean distance to the origin is $\sqrt{N}$. Moreover, let L_S be the subspace spanned by the prototype vectors $X^1, X^2, \cdots, X^m$. Since S is an orthogonal projection matrix that projects any vector onto L_S, $SX = V \in L_S$. For any $X \in \Psi^N$, we can represent it in the form $X = V + X_0$ where X_0 is a vector in the subspace orthogonal to L_S. Then its energy is given by

$$
\begin{aligned}
E(X) &= -\frac{1}{2}X^{*}(SX) \\
&= -\frac{1}{2}(V+X_0)^{*}V \\
&= -\frac{1}{2}\|V\|^2 \\
&\geq -\frac{1}{2}\|X\|^2 \\
&= -\frac{N}{2}
\end{aligned}
$$

Above inequality follows from the Pythagorean theorem (Lancaster & Tismenetsky, 1985) that

$$\|X\|^2 = \|V\|^2 + \|X_0\|^2. \qquad (20)$$

The proof is thus complete.

In our simulation the GPR shows better performance than the EDM not only in the computation efficiency but also in the recall capability. Figs. 2 and 3 give a comparison of recall capability by training CVHAMs of fixed size N=30. For a fixed K, the components of the prototype vectors are generated from random complex values chosen from the K quantization values in equation (19) with equal probabilities. The sizes of the training set being studied are m=5 and 10, respectively. After training was carried out for a set of training vectors, the CVHAM is tested with a test set which contains 10m noisy versions of the prototype vectors (ten for each prototype vector). Each noisy version of a specific prototype vector is generated by replacing n components of the original prototype vector by some random complex values chosen from the other K-1 quantization values. For each combination (m, n, K), 10 independent sets are tested and the average of successful recall is recorded. As seen in Figure 2 and Figure 3, for both learning methods the recall capability degenerates as K increases. In most cases, the GPR yields a better result than the EDM does. For example, when m=5 and K=8 the EDM has over 98% of success if the number of corrupted components $n \leq 4$. It can be improved to $n \leq 6$ by using the GPR under the same conditions. The EDM yields better results only when K is small. A reasonable explanation of this result is that in EDM the weight matrix is designed such that the energy of each prototype vector is lower than the energy of all of its *1-neighborhood.* The 1-neighborhood of a prototype vector X^k is defined as those states that differ from X^k at most one entry and their difference is only $\theta_0(=2\pi / K)$ (Müezzinoğlu, Güzeliş, & Zurada, 2003). Even if a distorted version $\tilde{X}^k$ being generated by corrupting one component of X^k, the larger the value of K, the lower the probability that $\tilde{X}^k$ be the 1-neighborhood of X^k. In other words, the attraction basin around each prototype vector is limited. In the following section projection geometry of the GPR is analyzed in detail. We show that although the GPR is better than the EDM when K is large, the recall capability of the CVHAMs can be further improved.

A STRATEGY TO FURTHER IMPROVE THE RECALL CAPABILITY OF THE CVHAMS

Geometry of the Generalized Projection Rule

Since for any $X \in \Psi^N$, $SX = V \in L_S$, S can be referred to as an orthogonal projection matrix from Ψ^N into the subspace spanned by prototype vectors. The projection dynamic can be described as follows. Given any initial state X, the projection vector V=SX is evaluated. Next, $X' = \varphi\{V\}$ will be the discrete hyper-sphere surface point which is closest to V. The procedure in equation (16) is repeated until a fixed point X_f is reached. However, the final state is sometimes a spurious memory instead of one of the prototype vectors. Here a spurious memory is defined as any X_f such that $X_f = \varphi\{SX_f\}$ and $X_f \notin \{X^k\}_{k=1}^m$. From the geometry of the projection dynamic, spurious memories are of the following two types, i.e.,

i. If $X_f \in (L_S \cap \Psi^N)$ but $X_f \notin \{X^k\}_{k=1}^m$ then X_f is a spurious memory.
ii. If $X_f \notin L_S$ but $X_f = \varphi\{SX_f\}$ then X_f is also a spurious memory (see Figure 4).

A Modified Projection Rule

Although it is difficult to distinguish between the spurious memory of type (i) and the prototype vectors, spurious memory of type (ii) can be detected easily. The reason is that, under the case of type (ii), $\|V_f\| < \sqrt{N}$ and $V_f \notin \Psi^N$, where $V_f = SX_f$ (see Figure 4). In fact, the recall capability can be improved by the following two-phase projection rule as follows. In phase I, projection dynamic (16) is performed until a fixed state X_f is reached. In phase II, $V_f(=SX_f)$ is checked. If $V_f \notin \Psi^N$, then a new initial state $\hat{X}$ is picked. Here $\hat{X} \in \Psi^N$ is a point (on the hyper-sphere surface) very close to V_f. Above two phases iterate alternatively until $V_f \in \Psi^N$.

Figure 2. Recall capability test when the number of training patterns is 5

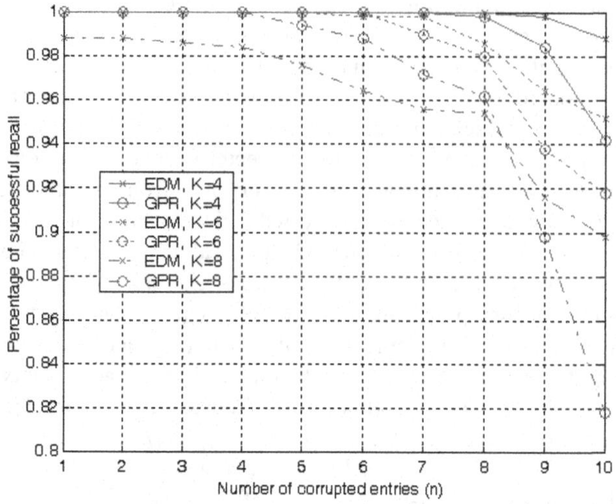

Figure 3. Recall capability test when the number of training patterns is 10

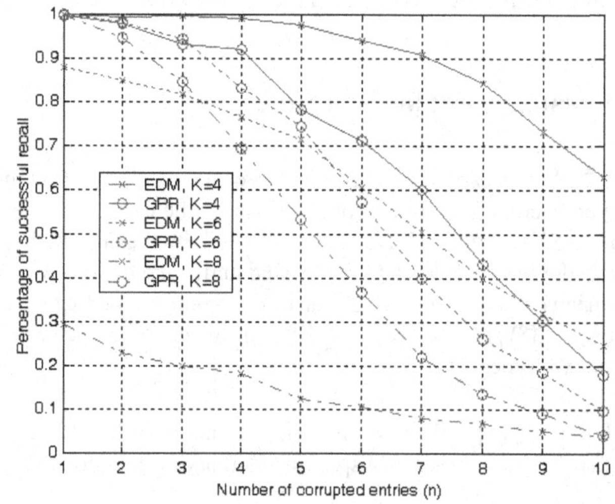

The main idea in phase II involves moving a spurious memory X_f to a nearby state $\hat{X}$. This remedy provides a trapped spurious memory another chance to project into L_S. In other words, it is desirable that all final states satisfy $X_f = V_f \in (L_S \bigcap \Psi^N)$. Moreover, the displacement (from X_f to $\hat{X}$) should be kept minimal so that a correct recall will not be disturbed. In the absence of available analytical methods to find the best $\hat{X}$, we propose choosing $\hat{X}$ from the *1-neighborhood* (Müezzinoğlu, Güzeliş, & Zurada, 2003) of X_f. That is, $\hat{X}$ can be obtained by randomly choosing one component of X_f, then increasing or decreasing its phase angle by $2\pi / K$.

Figure 4. Geometrical representation of the spurious memory of type (ii)

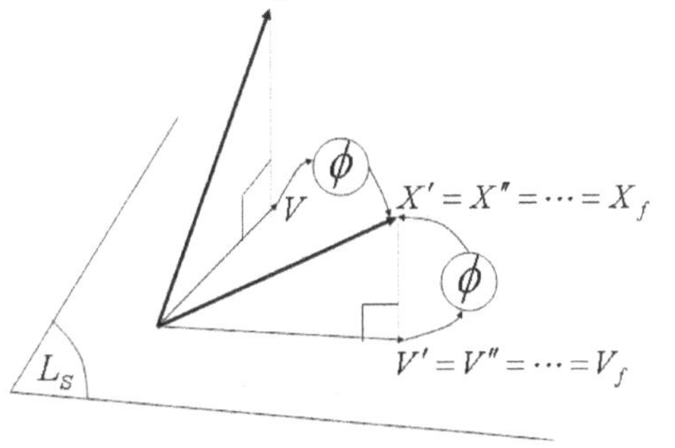

The modified projection rule (MPR) is summarized as follows:

Step 1: Given an initial state X.
Step 2: Perform the projection dynamic (16) until the fixed state $X_f = \varphi\{V_f\}$ is reached.
Step 3: If $V_f \in \Psi^N$, then stop. Otherwise, obtain a new initial state $\hat{X}$ by randomly choosing one component of X_f, increasing or decreasing its phase angle by $2\pi / K$. Then, assign the new initial state $X = \hat{X}$ and go to Step 2.

GENERALIZED INVERSE TECHNIQUE FOR IBAMS

This section describes how to apply the generalized inverse technique to the intraconnected bidirectional associative memory (IBAM).

Structure of the MIBAM

Assume that there are m training pairs $\{X^k, Y^k\}_{k=1}^m$, where $X^k \in \{-1,1\}^n$ and $Y^k \in \{-1,1\}^p$. The evolution equations of the MIBAM (Jeng & Yeh, 1991) are

$$Y' = \text{sgn}\{XM + YB\} \tag{21a}$$

$$X' = \text{sgn}\{Y'M^T + XA\} \tag{21b}$$

Here we assume X^k and Y^k are row vectors as they first appeared in the original BAM model (Kosko, 1988). The *interlayer* connections M and *intralayer* connections A, B, ($M \in R^{n \times p}$; $A \in R^n$; $B \in R^p$) are constructed by using the Hebbian type correlation rule (Jeng & Yeh, 1991), respectively:

$$M = \sum_{k=1}^{m} (X^k)^T Y^k \quad A = \sum_{k=1}^{m} (X^k)^T X^k \quad B = \sum_{k=1}^{m} (Y^k)^T Y^k$$

$\mathrm{sgn}\{\cdot\}$ is a point-wise function that operates on each component α of a vector.

$$\mathrm{sgn}\{\alpha\} = \begin{cases} 1 & \text{for } \alpha \geq 0 \\ -1 & \text{otherwise} \end{cases} \tag{22}$$

As mentioned by Jeng and Yeh (1991), the MIBAM yields better recall performances than those of the intraconnected BAM (IBAM) proposed by Simpson (1990). However, the improvements are minor, because the authors use the Hebbian type correlation rule to construct the weight matrices, *M*, ***A***, and *B*. In some cases (e.g. when the continuity assumption (Kosko, 1988)

$$H(X^i, X^j)/n \approx H(Y^i, Y^j)/p \quad \forall\, i, j \tag{23}$$

does not hold, where *H(.,.)* denotes the Hamming distance) this method does not guarantee perfect storage of all training pairs as stable states of the MIBAM. For example, assume

$$X^1 = (+1 \ \ +1 \ \ -1 \ \ -1) \quad Y^1 = (+1 \ \ -1 \ \ +1 \ \ -1)$$
$$X^2 = (+1 \ \ +1 \ \ -1 \ \ +1) \quad Y^2 = (+1 \ \ +1 \ \ +1 \ \ -1)$$
$$X^3 = (-1 \ \ +1 \ \ -1 \ \ -1) \quad Y^3 = (+1 \ \ +1 \ \ +1 \ \ -1)$$

where $n = p = 4$ and $m = 3$. The continuity assumption does not hold in this example because $H(X^2, X^3)/n = 1/2 \neq H(Y^2, Y^3)/p = 0$. With X^k, $k = 1, 2, 3$ as input patterns presented to the MIBAM, the only two stable points are (X^1, Y^2) and (X^2, Y^2). In other words, it is impossible to recall (X^1, Y^1) and (X^3, Y^3) by the MIBAM.

Generalized IBAM (GIBAM)

Let the components in X^k and Y^k to be complex values in a quantized complex unit circle, i.e.

$$x_i^k, y_j^k \in \{\exp[j2\pi v/K]\}_{v=0}^{K-1} \quad \forall\, i, j \tag{24}$$

Now, $\{(X^k, Y^k)\}_{k=1}^{m}$ becomes a set of *m* complex-valued training pairs. The following evolution equations are defined for the GIBAM:

$$Y' = \varphi\{XM + YB\} \tag{25a}$$

$$X' = \varphi\{Y'M^* + XA\} \tag{25b}$$

where $A \in C^{n \times n}$, $B \in C^{p \times p}$, $M \in C^{n \times p}$ and M^* denotes the conjugate transposition of *M*. The function $\varphi\{\cdot\}$ operates on each component α of a vector as in equation (3). Recall from the preceding sections that $\varphi(Z)$ is the quantization value whose phase is closest to the phase of *Z*. Instead of using the Hebbian type correlation rule, weight matrices *M*, *A* and *B* can be constructed by a different method. Let

$$V^k = \left[X^k \,\middle|\, Y^k \right] \tag{26}$$

be an augmentation vector that is obtained by concatenating row vectors X^k and Y^k. Moreover, let

$$U^T = \left[(V^1)^T \middle| (V^2)^T \middle| \cdots \middle| (V^m)^T \right]. \tag{27}$$

Then all the training pairs can be stored as stable states of a GIBAM if the augmentation matrix

$$W = \begin{bmatrix} A & M \\ M^* & B \end{bmatrix} \tag{28}$$

satisfies $UW = U$. The solution of W will be

$$W = U^I U \tag{29}$$

where U^I is the generalized inverse of U. It is assumed that Rank(U) = m, so

$$U^I = U^*(UU^*)^{-1} \tag{30}$$

and thus W, A and B are all nonnegative definite. The GIBAM can be used to store and recall multivalued training pairs, since there are K quantized phase angles. Also note that if K=2, the GIBAM will be functionally equivalent to the MIBAM. However, the GIBAM can improve on the performance of the MIBAM because of the use of equation (29). In fact, if we test the same training pairs as were used in the preceding example for the GIBAM, it is found that all of them are stable states. Next, we introduce the following theorem.

Theorem 4 (Lee, 1998a): Given a GIBAM with a weight matrix defined in (29). If its state (X, Y) is updated according to the evolution equations defined in equation (25), then the GIBAM will converge to a fixed point from any given initial state.

Proof: The following energy function is defined for the GIBAM:

$$E(X,Y) = -\frac{1}{2}\mathrm{Re}\left\{XAX^* + 2XMY^* + YBY^*\right\} \tag{31}$$

First, we assume that the current state is (X, Y); the next state will be (X, Y'). Let $\Delta E_y = E(X,Y') - E(X,Y)$, we obtain

$$\begin{aligned} \Delta E_y &= -\mathrm{Re}\left\{(XM + YB)(Y' - Y)^* + \frac{1}{2}(Y' - Y)B(Y' - Y)^*\right\} \\ &\leq -\mathrm{Re}\left\{\sum_{j=1}^{p}(\bar{y}_j' - \bar{y}_j)\left\{\sum_{i=1}^{n} m_{ij}x_i + \sum_{k=1}^{p} b_{jk}y_k\right\}\right\} \end{aligned}$$

where we use the fact that B is a Hermitian and non-negative definite matrix. Now let

$$\begin{aligned} net_j &= \sum_{i=1}^{n} m_{ij}x_i + \sum_{k=1}^{p} b_{jk}y_k = r_j \exp(j\varphi_j), \\ \bar{y}_j &= \exp(-j\psi_j), \\ \bar{y}_j' &= \exp(-j\psi_j'), \end{aligned}$$

where r_j and φ_j denote the modulus magnitude and phase angle of net_j, respectively. Moreover, $\psi_j = \arg(y_j)$, and $\psi_j' = \arg(y_j')$. From equation (25), there holds

$$\begin{aligned}\Delta E_y &\le -\mathrm{Re}\left\{\sum_{j=1}^{p} r_j \left\{\exp[j(\varphi_j - \psi_j')] - \exp[j(\varphi_j - \psi_j)]\right\}\right\} \\ &= -\sum_{j=1}^{p} r_j \left\{\cos(\varphi_j - \psi_j') - \cos(\varphi_j - \psi_j)\right\} \\ &\le 0\end{aligned}$$

The last inequality follows from the fact that $\cos(\varphi_j - \psi_j') \ge \cos(\varphi_j - \psi_j), \forall j$. Similarly, one can prove that $\Delta E_x \le 0$ for any state change in X. Because $E(X,Y)$ is bounded ,

$$|E(X,Y)| \le \frac{1}{2}\sum_i\sum_k |a_{ik}| + \sum_i\sum_j |m_{ij}| + \frac{1}{2}\sum_j\sum_k |b_{jk}| \quad \text{for all } X \text{ and } Y, \tag{32}$$

the stability of the GIBAM is guaranteed. This completes the proof.

EXPERIMENTAL RESULTS

Recall Capability Test for CVHAMs

Recall capabilities of CVHAMs with the GPR and the MPR are both investigated. The network size is fixed at N=50. For a fixed K, the components of the prototype vectors are assigned to complex random values from the K quantization values in equation (19) with equal probabilities. The sizes of the training set being studied are m=15, 21, and 25, respectively. Each point in Figs. 5~7 is obtained by using the same procedure as in the preceding section. As seen from Figs. 5~7, the recall capability degenerates as K increases. However, the MPR yields improvements over the GPR. For example, when m=15 and K=4 the GPR has over 98% of success if the number of corrupted components $n \le 7$. It can be improved to $n \le 9$ by using the MPR with the same conditions. Moreover, when m=21 and n=3 the GPR has nearly 82% of success if K=4. Under the same conditions, the percent of success can be preserved by using the MPR even when K=8.

Comparison of the Transition of CVHAM Using GPR and the MPR

This simulation shows how the vector length changes with time when the initial state X is randomly chosen from the noisy versions of the prototype vectors. The number of different components is fixed at 10. Figs. 8 and 9 show the variations of the vector lengths of V from 15 distinct initial states by using the GPR and the MPR, respectively. The vector lengths are measured here according to the square of the Euclidean norm. As shown in Figure 8, a final state X_f is a spurious memory if $\|V_f\|^2 < 50$ and 3 vector length trajectories converge to spurious memories of type (ii). On the other hand, Figure 9 shows that the number of undesired trajectories in Figure 8 has been markedly reduced from 3 to 0.

A CVBAM Image Reconstruction Example

Gray-scale image reconstruction using neural networks has been widely explored (Müezzinoğlu, Güzeliş, & Zurada, 2003; Costantini, Casali, & Pefetti, 2003; Si & Michel, 1991; Taketa & Goodman, 1986). These methods require either a larger number of connection weights or a more complicated learning procedure. For example, the method proposed by Costantini, Casali, and Pefetti (2003) consists in the decomposition of the K gray-scale

Figure 5. Recall capability when the resolution factor is 4 (K=4) (+: GPR, o: MPR)

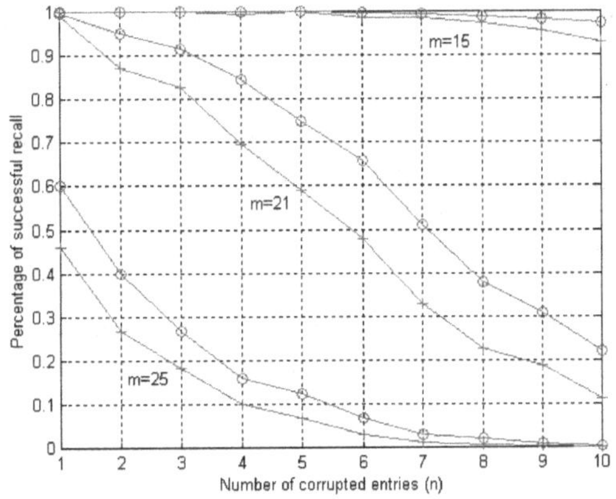

Figure 6. Recall capability when the resolution factor is 8 (K=8) (+: GPR, o: MPR)

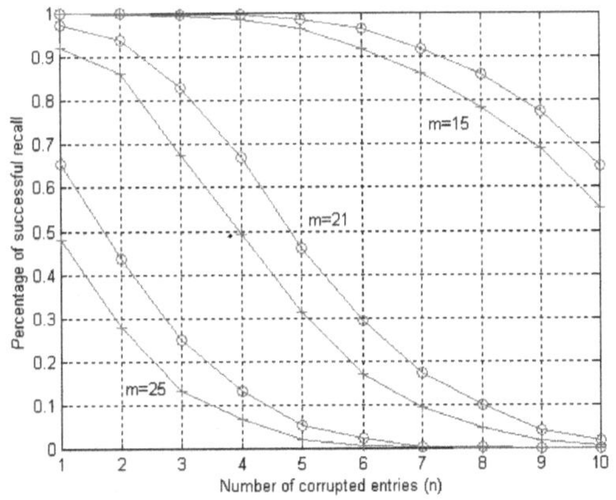

Figure 7. Recall capability when the resolution factor is 12 (K=12) (+:GPR, o:MPR)

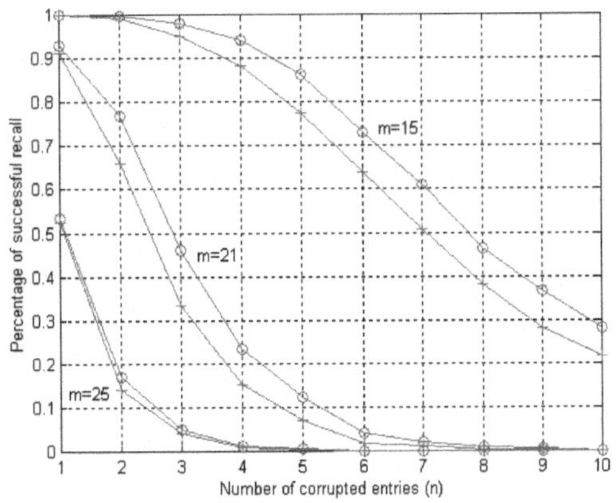

image into R ($= \log_2 K$) gray-coded images, stored using R independent *binary* brain-state-in-a-box (BSB) networks. Here we use the same images for simulation. Figure10 shows two images *lenna* and *stefan* with 200 × 200 pixels and K=256 gray levels. As in the example of Costantini, Casali, and Pefetti (2003), each image is partitioned into 16 parts, each of size 50 × 50. In this way we obtain a total of 32 images that can be stored using only *one* CVHAM with 2500 neurons. Unlike the constraint satisfaction learning proposed by Costantini, Casali, and Pefetti (2003), the GPR (13) is very fast. It takes about 2 minutes to obtain the weight matrix S. Most of the computation is spent on obtaining the generalized inverse of Σ. After learning, we use the CVHAM to recall the stored images starting from a noisy initial state. Gaussian noise is simulated first. Noisy initial states are generated by adding a Gaussian noise with zero mean and standard deviation σ to each pixel of the stored images. The recall results after network converges are summarized in Table I. In general, the CVHAM can correctly recall all 32 images if $\sigma \leq 5$. By recombining them we can obtain the two full-size images in Figure 10. When $\sigma = 80$, only 1 out of 32 images is correctly recalled. However, from Table I we can see that the *peak signal to noise ratio*

Figure 8. Vector length trajectories of the GPR

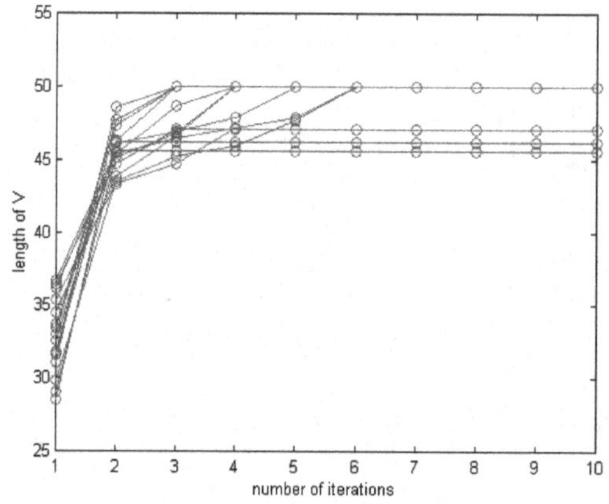

Figure 9. Vector length trajectories of the MPR

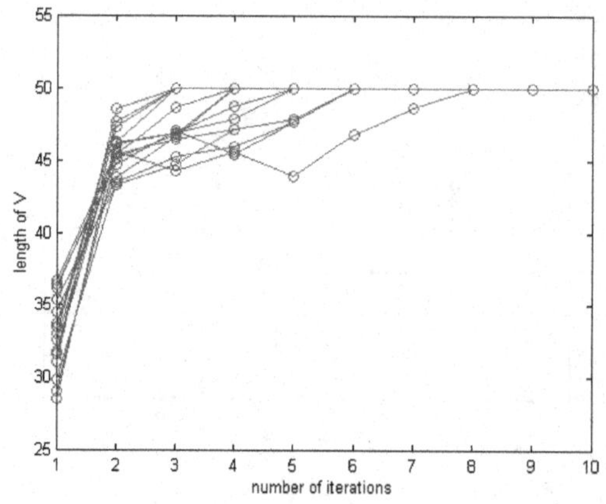

Table 1. Results of the image reconstruction example (Gaussian noise)

σ	1	5	10	20	40	80
# of correctly recalled images	32	32	23	13	7	1
PSNR1 original / recalled (dB)	42.15 / –	28.17 / –	22.13 / 55.11	16.22 / 46.77	10.59 / 41.30	5.57 / 23.21
PSNR2 original / recalled (dB)	42.13 / –	28.15 / –	22.13 / 54.86	8.86 / 47.81	10.24 /34.61	5.29 / 18.92

Figure 10. Images stored in the CVHAM for reconstruction

Figure 11. Images corrupted by Gaussian noise with σ =80 (top) and their reconstructions obtained by the network (bottom)

Table 2. Results of the image reconstruction example (salt and pepper noise)

% of noise	1	2	4	10	20	30
# of correctly recalled images	30	16	5	1	0	0
PSNR1 original / recalled (dB)	19.23 / 294.85	15.97 / 47.12	13.35 / 43.57	9.06 / 35.65	6.15 / 28.61	4.30 / 23.19
PSNR2 original / recalled (dB)	19.84 / 66.09	16.66 / 49.51	13.64 / 44.05	9.72 / 31.14	6.63 / 26.57	4.81 / 20.60

Figure 12. Images corrupted by 30% salt and pepper noise (top) and their reconstructions obtained by the network (bottom)

(PSNR1 and PSNR2 for images *lenna* and *stefan*, respectively) has improved more than 12 dB for both images. Figure 11 shows the two reconstructed images (bottom) by using two noisy images (top) as the initial states of the CVHAM. From Table I it is found that the performance of the proposed method is comparable to the method proposed by Costantini, Casali, and Pefetti (2003).

Next, the CVHAMs are tested by images corrupted by salt and pepper noise. From Table II one can see that the performance is as good as in the case of Gaussian noise. Figure 12 shows the two reconstructed images (bottom) by using two noisy images (top) as the initial states of the CVHAM.

Comparison of Storage Capacities and Error Correction Capabilities of GIBAM and MIBAM

In Figure 13, the storage capacities of the GIBAM and the MIBAM are measured by the number of successful recalls among m randomly generated training pairs. At the same time, the error correcting capabilities are tested.

*Figure 13. Comparison of storage capacities and error correction capabilities of GIBAM and MIBAM. Recall probabilities for GIBAM (K = 2, 8) are 100% at top line of figure frame (+: r=0, o: r=2, *: r=4, -.-.: MIBAM, ---: GIBAM for K=2, -: GIBAM for K=8)*

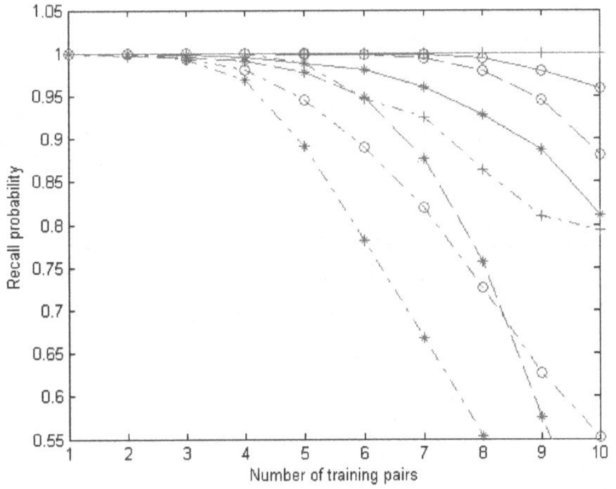

Table 3. Number of required connection weights for different design methods (n pixels, K gray levels, $R = log_2(K)$)

method	Binary coding	Multilevel function.	Gray coding	Energy design method	Generalized projection rule
# of weights	n^2R^2	n^2	n^2R	n^2	n^2

Each pattern of the stored pairs was degraded by r bits and presented as inputs to the MIBAM and the GIBAM, respectively. All the pattern dimensions are fixed ($n = p = 16$). The recall probabilities, the percentage of successful recalls of the tested patterns, are calculated by averaging over 100 independent trials. As shown in Figure 13, even if $K = 8$, the GIBAM has a much higher storage capacity and much better error correcting capability than the MIBAM.

CONCLUDING REMARKS

The generalized projection rule for the complex-valued multistate Hopfield associative memory (CVHAM) has been introduced. We have shown that the well- known projection rule can be generalized to complex domain such that the weight matrix of the CVHAM can be designed by using the generalized inverse technique. The stability property of the CVHAM under synchronous mode is discussed by using the energy function approach and it shows that the CVHAM is guaranteed to converge to a fixed point from any initial state. We also analyzed the projection geometry of the GPR. Since the projection dynamic sometimes converges to a spurious memory that does not belong to the subspace spanned by the prototype vectors, a strategy (MPR) to eliminate such spurious memories is also discussed. Computer simulation shows that the recall capability of the CVHAM is improved markedly by using the introduced methods. Comparing with other methods (Zurada, Cloete, & van der Poel, 1996; Jankowski, Lozowski, & Zurada, 1996; Müezzinoğlu, Güzeliş, & Zurada, 2003; Taketa & Goodman, 1986; Costantini, Casali, & Pefetti, 2003; Si & Michel, 1991) for storing and recalling gray-scale images, the introduced methods have the following features:

- Learning is simple and fast
- No complicated transformation or extra coding process is required
- Number of required connection weights is small

Table III summarizes the number of required connections for different methods. It is obvious that the proposed method needs a less number of connection weights. Therefore, the GPR and MPR are good methods for storing gray-scale images by neural networks.

The generalized inverse technique can be applied to not only the auto-associative CVHAMs but also the hetero-associative GIBAMs. Simulation results also show that the storage capacity and the error correction capability of the GIBAM are both better than those of the MIBAM.

FUTURE RESEARCH DIRECTIONS

Further research includes the application of the CVNNs to multistep pattern recognition (Lee, 1998b) and digital image compression. How to design CVNNs with optimal recall capability is also an open problem deserving further study.

REFERENCES

Albert, A. (1972). *Regression and the Moore-Penrose Pseudoinverse.* Academic Press, New York.

Cernuschi-Frias, B. (1989). Partial simultaneous updating in Hopfield memories. *IEEE Trans. Syst. Man Cybern,. 19*, 887-888.

Costantini, G., Casali, D., & Pefetti, R. (2003). Neural associative memory storing gray-coded gray-scale images. *IEEE Trans. Neural Networks, 14*(3), 703-707.

Hopfield, J. J. (1984). Neurons with graded response have collective computational properties like those of two-state neurons. *Proc. Nat. Acad. Sci. USA, 81*, 3088-3092.

Jankowski, S., Lozowski, A., & Zurada, J. M. (1996). Complex-valued multistate neural associative memory. *IEEE Trans. Neural Networks, 7*(6), 1491-1496.

Jeng, Y. J., & Yeh, C. C. (1991). Modified intraconnected bidirectional associative memory. *Electron. Lett., 27*, 1818-1819.

Kosko, B. (1987). Adaptive bidirectional associative memories. *Appl. Opt., 26*(23), 4947-4960.

Kosko, B. (1988). Bidirectional associative memories. *IEEE Trans. Syst. Man Cybern., 18*, 49-60.

Lancaster P., & Tismenetsky, M. (1985). *The Theory of Matrices: With Applications*, 2nd ed. Academic Press, New York.

Lee, D.-L. (1998a). Generalised Intraconnected Bidirectional Associative Memories. *Electronics Letters, 34*(8), 736-738.

Lee, D. L. (1998b). A discrete sequential bidirectional associative memory for multistep pattern recognition. *Pattern Recognit. Lett., 19*, 1087–1102.

Lee, D.-L. (1999). New stability conditions for Hopfield networks in partial simultaneous update mode. *IEEE Trans. Neural Networks.*, *10*(4), 975-978.

Lee, D.-L. (2001a). Improving the capacity of complex-valued neural networks with a modified gradient descent learning rule. *IEEE Trans. Neural Networks*, *12*(2), 439-443.

Lee, D.-L. (2001b). Relaxation of the stability condition of the complex-valued neural networks. *IEEE Trans. Neural Networks*, *12*(5), 1260-1262.

Lee, D.-L. (2003). Complex-valued Neural Associative Memories: Network Stability and Learning Algorithms. In A. Hirose (Ed.), *Complex-valued Neural Networks: Theories and Applications* (pp. 29-55). World Scientific.

Lee, D.-L. (2006). Improvement of Complex-valued Hopfield Associative Memory by using Generalized Projection Rules. *IEEE Trans. on Neural Networks*, *17*(5), 1341-1347.

Luenberger, D. G. (1973). *Introduction to Linear and Nonlinear Programming.* Reading, MA: Addison-Wesley.

Müezzinoğlu, M. K., Güzeliş, C., & Zurada, J. M. (2003). A new design method for the complex-valued multistate Hopfield associative memory. *IEEE Trans. Neural Networks*, *14*(4) 891-899.

Personnaz, L., Guyon, I, & Dreyfus, G (1986). Collective computational properties of neural networks: new learning mechanisms. *Phys. Rev.*, *A34*, 4217-4228.

Personnaz, L., Guyon, I., Dreyfus, G.., & Toulouse, G. (1986). A biologically constrained learning mechanism in networks of formal neurons. *J. Statistical Phys.*, *43*, 411-422.

Rosenblatt, F. (1962). *Principles of Neurodynamics*. New York: Spartan.

Si, J., & Michel, A. N. (1991). Analysis and syntehsis of discrete-time neural networks with multilevel threshold functions. *Proc. ISCAS*, (pp. 1461–1464).

Simpson, P. K. (1990). Higher-ordered and intraconnected bidirectional associative memories. *IEEE Trans. Syst. Man Cybern. 2*, 637-653.

Taketa, M., & Goodman, J. W. (1986). Neural networks for computation: number representations and programming complexity. *Applied Optics*, *25,* 3033–3046.

Zurada, J. M., Cloete, I., & van der Poel, E. (1996). Generalized Hopfield networks with multiple stable states. *Neurocomput.*, *13*, 135-149.

ADDITIONAL READING

Aoki, H., Azinmi-Sadajadi, M., R., & Kosugi, Y. (2000). Image association using a complex-valued associative memory model. *IEICE Transactions on Fundamentals of Electronics, Communication and Computer Sciences*, *E83A*, 1824-1832.

Chartier S., & Boukadoum, M. (2006) A bidirectional heteroassociative memory for binary and grey-level patterns. *IEEE Trans. Neural Networks*, *17*(2), 385-396.

Chen, S., Chen, L., &Zhou, Z.-H. (2005). A unified SWSI-KAMs framework and performance evaluation on face recognition. *Neurocomputing*, *68*, 54-69.

Costantini, G., Casali, D., & Perfetti, R. (2006). Associative memory design for 256 gray-level images using a multilayer neural network. *IEEE Trans. Neural Networks*, *17*(2), 519–522.

Rama M. & Praveen, D. (2004). Complex-valued neural associative memory on the complex hypercube. *Proc. IEEE Conf. on Cybernetics and Intelligent Systems, 1*, 649-653.

Chapter XI
A Method of Estimation for Magnetic Resonance Spectroscopy Using Complex-Valued Neural Networks

Naoyuki Morita
Kochi Gakuen College, Japan

ABSTRACT

The author proposes an automatic estimation method for nuclear magnetic resonance (NMR) spectra of the metabolites in the living body by magnetic resonance spectroscopy (MRS) without human intervention or complicated calculations. In the method, the problem of NMR spectrum estimation is transformed into the estimation of the parameters of a mathematical model of the NMR signal. To estimate these parameters, Morita designed a complex-valued Hopfield neural network, noting that NMR signals are essentially complex-valued. In addition, we devised a technique called "sequential extension of section (SES)" that takes into account the decay state of the NMR signal. Morita evaluated the performance of his method using simulations and shows that the estimation precision on the spectrum improves when SES is used in combination the neural network, and that SES has an ability to avoid the local minimum solution on Hopfield neural networks.

INTRODUCTION

Magnetic resonance spectroscopy (MRS) is used to determine the quantity of metabolites, such as creatine phosphate (PCr) and adenocine triphosphate (ATP), in the living body by collecting their nuclear magnetic resonance (NMR) spectra. In the field of MRS, the frequency spectrum of metabolites is usually obtained by applying the fast Fourier transform (FFT) (Cooley & Tukey, 1965) to the NMR signal collected from the living body. Then, quantification of the metabolites is carried out by estimating the area under each spectral peak using a curve fitting procedure (Maddams, 1980; Mierisová & Ala-Korpel, 2001; Sijens et al., 1998), as described in the **BACKGROUND** section. However, this method is not suitable for processing large quantities of data because human intervention is necessary. In this chapter, an automatic spectral estimation method, which we developed in order to process large quantities of data without human intervention, is presented.

This chapter is organized as follows: **BACKGROUND** reviews MRS and some conventional estimation methods of NMR spectra, and briefly outlines our method. **MATHEMATICAL MODEL OF THE NMR SIGNAL AND ESTIMATION OF SPECTRA** first, gives an overview of NMR phenomenon and NMR signal, next, presents a mathematical model of the NMR signal; and finally, describes our approach to spectral estimation. **DESIGN OF A COMPLEX-VALUED HOPFIELD NEURAL NETWORK AS A SPECTRAL ESTIMATIOR** describes the design of our complex-valued Hopfield neural network. **SEQUENTIAL EXTENSION OF SECTION (SES)** explains the concept of SES. For performance evaluation of our method, simulations were carried out using sample signals that imitate an actual NMR signal, and the results of those simulations are given in **SIMULATIONS**. The results are evaluated and discussed in **DISCUSSION**. Finally, we give some conclusions and future research directions.

BACKGROUND

Magnetic resonance imaging (MRI) systems, which produce medical images using the nuclear magnetic resonance (NMR) phenomenon, have recently become popular. Additional technological innovations, such as high-speed imaging technologies (Feinberg & Oshio, 1991; Henning, Nauerth, & Fnedburg, 1986; Mansfield, 1977; Melki, Mulkern, Panych, & Joles, 1991; Meyer, Hu, Nishimura, & Macovski, 1992) and imaging of brain function using functional MRI (Belliveau et al., 1991; Kwong et al., 1992; Ogawa, Lee, Nayak, & Glynn, 1990), are also rapidly progressing. Currently, the above-mentioned imaging technologies mainly take advantage of the NMR phenomena of protons. The atomic nuclei used for analyzing metabolism in the living body include proton, phosphorus-31, carbon-13, fluorine-19 and sodium-22. Phosphorus-31 NMR spectroscopy has been widely used for measurement of the living body, because it is able to track the metabolism of energy.

NMR was originally developed and used in the field of analytical chemistry. In that field, NMR spectra are used to analyze the chemical structure of various materials. This is called NMR spectroscopy. In medical imaging, it is also possible to obtain NMR spectra. In this case, the technique is called magnetic resonance spectroscopy (MRS), and it can be used to collect the spectra of metabolites in organs such as the brain, heart, liver and muscle. The difference between NMR spectroscopy and MRS is that in MRS, we collect spectra from the living body in a relatively low magnetic field (usually, about 1.5 Tesla); in NMR spectroscopy, small chemical samples are measured in a high magnetic field.

In MRI systems, the Fourier transform is widely used as a standard tool to produce an image from the measured data and to obtain NMR spectra. In NMR spectroscopy, we can obtain a frequency spectrum by applying the fast Fourier transform (FFT) to the free induction decay (FID) that is observed as a result of the magnetic relaxation phenomenon (Derome, 1987). Here the FID is an NMR signal in the time domain and it is a time series, that is, it can be modeled as a set of sinusoids exponentially damping with time. When the FFT is applied to such a signal, the spectral peaks obtained are of the form called a Lorentz curve (Derome, 1987). If the signal is damped rapidly, the height of the spectral peaks will be decreased and the width of the peaks will increase. This is an inevitable result of applying FFT to FIDs. In addition, the resolution of the spectrum collected in a low magnetic field is much lower than a typical spectrum obtained by NMR spectroscopy. Thus, the spectra by MRS are quite different from those by NMR spectroscopy. That is, the spectral peaks obtained by MRS are spread out and the spectral distribution obtained is very different from the original distribution as shown in Figure 1. Thus, we cannot use a peak height to quantify a metabolite. Instead, we estimate the area under each peak using curve-fitting procedures (Figure 1(d): non-linear least square methods) (Maddams, 1980; Mierisová & Ala-Korpela, 2001; Sijens et al., 1998). However, existing curve-fitting procedures are inadequate for processing large quantities of data because they require human intervention. The aim of us is to devise a method that does not require such a human intervention.

Figure 1. The effect of the Fourier transform for the spectral estimation in MRS: (a) The spectrum corresponding to the FID shown in Figure 1(b), (c) The spectrum obtained by applying the Fourier transform to Figure 1(b), (d) The curve-fitting procedure using the Lorentz function. The area of each Lorentz curve approximates the area of each spectral peak

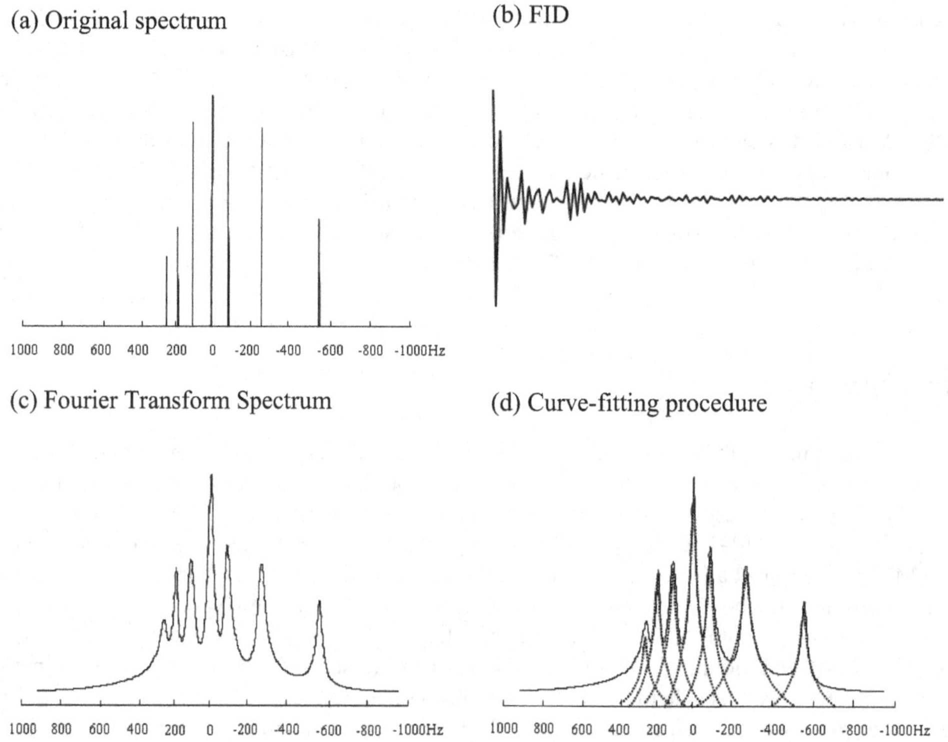

We can consider two approaches to this problem: (1) automating the description of spectral peaks and the determination of the peak areas, and (2) using methods of estimation and quantification other than the Fourier transform. In the first approach, attempts at automatic quantification of NMR spectra using hierarchical neural networks have been reported (Ala-Korpela et al., 1997; Kaartinen et al., 1998). In this research, a three-layered network based on back propagation (Rumelhart, Hinton, & Williams, 1986) was employed to estimate spectra in the frequency domain. The fully-trained network had the ability to quantify unknown spectra automatically, and curve fitting procedures were not necessary. However, large amounts of training data were necessary to increase the precision of quantification. These methods quantify the spectra instead of performing the curve fitting procedures. In the second approach, the maximum entropy method (MEM), derived from the autoregressive (AR) model and the linear prediction (LP) method, and other similar methods have been studied widely (Haselgrove, Subramanian, Christen, & Leigh, 1988; van Huffel, Chen, Decanniere, & Hecke, 1994). These are parametric methods, that is, in these methods, a mathematical model of the signal is assumed and the parameters of that model are estimated from observed data. The spectrum can then be estimated from the model parameters. However, methods based on AR modeling require large amounts of calculation.

Our objective is to develop a method to estimate NMR spectra without human intervention or complicated calculations. For this, we took a parametric approach in which a neural network is used (Han & Biswas, 1997), and used Hopfield neural network (Hopfield, 1982, 1984), which does not have a learning process. It is possible to estimate the parameters using the ability of the neural network to find a local minimum solution or a minimum solution. In addition, we noted that NMR signals are essentially complex-valued and developed a method to estimate the spectrum using complex-valued Hopfield networks (Hirose, 1992a, 1992b; Zhou & Liu, 1993), in which the weights and thresholds for conventional networks are expanded to accommodate complex numbers. Both a hierarchical type (Benvenuto & Piazza, 1992; Georgiou & Koutsougeras, 1992; Nitta, 1991, 1997) and a recurrent type (Jankowski, Lozowski, & Zurada,1996; Nemoto & Kono, 1991) have been proposed as complex-valued neural networks. Furthermore, we have devised a technique that takes into account the decay state of the NMR signal, which we call "sequential extension of section" (SES), and have used it with the above-mentioned method.

MATHEMATICAL MODEL OF THE NMR SIGNAL AND ESTIMATION OF SPECTRA

NMR Background

If the number of neutrons plus the number of protons is odd, or if the number of neutrons and the number of the protons are both odd, nuclei possess a property called spin. In quantum mechanics, spin is represented by a spin magnetic quantum number. Spin can be visualized as a rotating motion of the nucleus. Since a nucleus is a charged particle, the spinning motion causes a magnetic moment in the direction of the spin axis as shown in Figure 2. Quantum mechanics tells us that a nucleus of spin I will have $2I$+1 possible orientations. Considering a nucleus of spin ½, it will have two possible orientations.

We now consider a nucleus of spin ½ (such as proton, carbon-13 and phosphorus-31). In the absence of an externally applied magnetic field, the magnetic moments are randomly oriented, but when a field B_0 is applied, they are constrained to adopt one of two orientations, denoted parallel and anti-parallel with respect to B_0 (Figure 3). These two orientations correspond to the two energy levels: the lower and the higher, respectively. Nuclei with higher spin magnetic quantum number will adopt more than two orientations. The spin axes cannot be oriented exactly parallel (or anti-parallel) with the direction of B_0, hence, they precess around B_0 with a characteristic frequency as shown in Figure 4. The Larmor equation expresses the relationship between the strength of a magnetic field B_0 and the precessional frequency (Larmor frequency) ω_0 of an individual spin:

$$\omega_0 = \gamma B_0 \quad (\gamma \text{ : the gyromagnetic ratio of the nucleus}). \tag{1}$$

When the nucleus is in a static magnetic field B_0, the initial populations of the energy levels are determined by thermodynamics, as described by the Boltzmann distribution. It means that the lower energy level will contain slightly more nuclei than the higher level. That is, let the numbers of spins adopting the parallel and anti-parallel be P_1 and P_2 respectively, we have $P_1 > P_2$.

At any given instant, the magnetic moments of nuclei can be represented as vectors, as shown in Figure 5(b). Every vector can be described by its components perpendicular to and parallel to B_0. For a large enough number

Figure 2. A charged, spinning nucleus creates a magnetic moment which acts like a bar magnet (dipole)

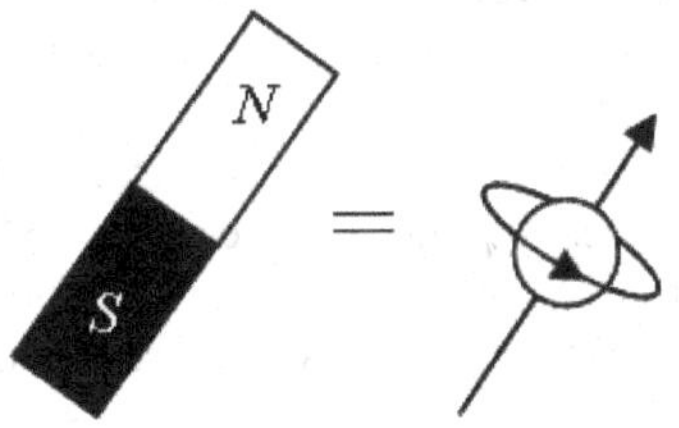

Figure 3. (a) Nuclei in the absence of an externally applied magnetic field. (b) An external magnetic field B_0 is applied which cause the nuclei to align themselves in one of two orientations with respect to B_0 (denoted parallel and anti-parallel)

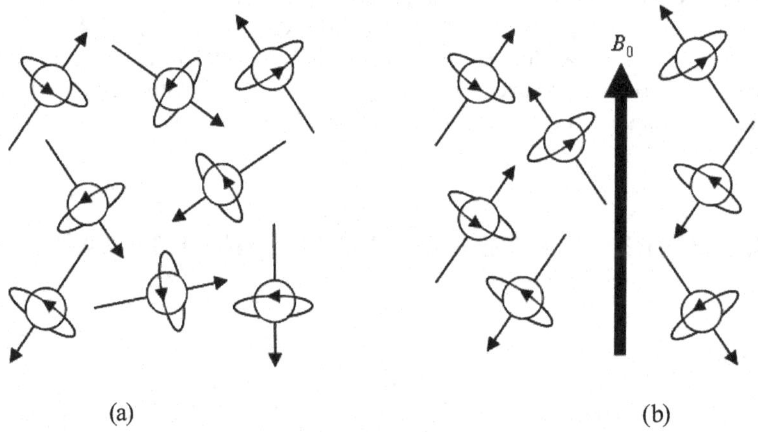

Figure 4. (a) In the presence of an externally applied magnetic field B_0, nuclei are constrained to adopt one of two orientations with respect to B_0. Since the nuclei possess spin, these orientations are not exactly at 0 and 180 degrees to B_0. θ is the angle between of the applied field and the axis of nuclear rotation. (b) A magnetic moment precessing around B_0

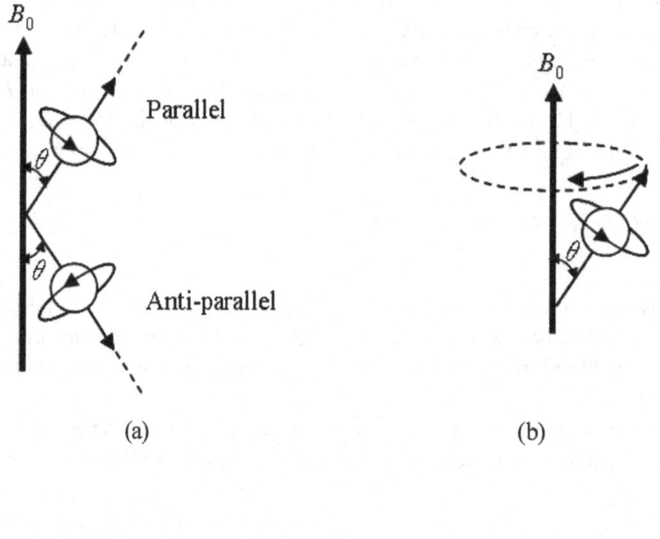

of spins, all the opposing components will cancel each other out. That is, individual components perpendicular to B_0 will cancel, and a bulk magnetization vector (called the net magnetization M) will create in the direction of the B_0 field, because of $P_1 > P_2$ (Figure 5(c)).

Suppose the direction of B_0 is aligned with the z-axis of three-dimensional Euclidean space. The plane perpendicular to B_0 contains the x and y-axes. In order to observe an NMR signal from nuclei, we must apply a radio frequency (RF) pulse at the Larmor frequency (the resonance frequency) of the nuclei. When the RF pulse is irradiated along the x-axis as shown in Figure 6(a), this pulse causes nuclear spins to swap between parallel

Figure 5. (a) A processing nucleus. (b) Vector representations of the magnetic moments at any given instant. (c) A small net magnetization M is detectable in the direction of the B_0

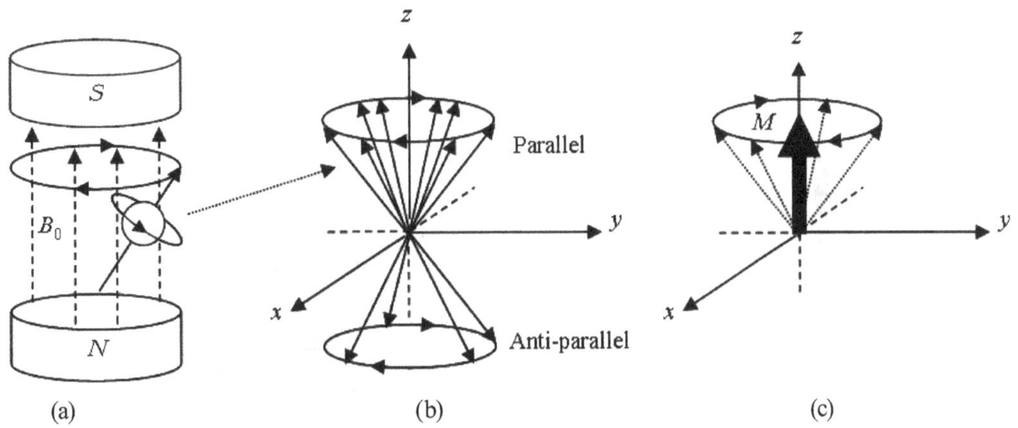

an anti-parallel states, and every phase of spins becomes in-phase along the direction of y-axis. As a result, the population of spins will change, and the net magnetization M will rotate clockwise about the x-axis (Figure 6(b)). Especially, the RF pulse that rotates M into the x-y plane is called "90-degree pulse" (Figure 7(a)(b)).

Following termination of an RF pulse, the restoration of M to its equilibrium state (the direction of the z-axis) known as relaxation begins. Figure 7(a-e) describes the relaxation following a 90-degree pulse.

Let M_0 be the amount of magnetization of equilibrium state before an RF pulse is irradiated. Let M_z be the z component of M at time t, following a 90-degree pulse at time $t = 0$. It can be shown that the process of equilibrium restoration is described by the equation:

$$M_z = M_0(1 - e^{-t/T_1}). \quad (2)$$

Where T_1 is the longitudinal relaxation time. Let M_{0xy} be the amount of transverse magnetization immediately following a 90-degree pulse.

Let M_{xy} be the amount of transverse magnetization at time t, following a 90-degree pulse at time $t = 0$. Following the RF pulse, the magnetic moments interact with each other causing a decrease in the transverse magnetization. It can be shown that

$$M_{xy} = M_{0xy} \cdot e^{-t/T_2^*}. \quad (3)$$

Where T_2^* characterizes the dephasing due to both B_0 inhomogeneity and true transverse relaxation, and it is called the apparent transverse relaxation time. In order to obtain a true transverse relaxation time T_2, we must use a pulse sequence such as the spin-echo method (Denome, 1987).

Every magnetization vector is precessing about the applied magnetic field B_0. Therefore, the component in the x-y plane is inevitably precessing about the B_0 axis. In addition, as described above, the magnetization in the x-y plane decays with time. Accordingly, the magnetization in the x-y plane rotates about the z-axis, and decays over time. If we place a receiver coil in the x-y plane, this rotating magnetization will induce an electromotive force in it. The signal induced in the receiver coil is termed a free induction decay (FID). An FID is an NMR signal. Figure 8 shows the phenomenon described here.

Figure 6. (a) A radio frequency (RF) pulse at the Larmor frequency is applied along the x-axis. (b) The RF pulse causes the net magnetization M to rotate clockwise about the x-axis

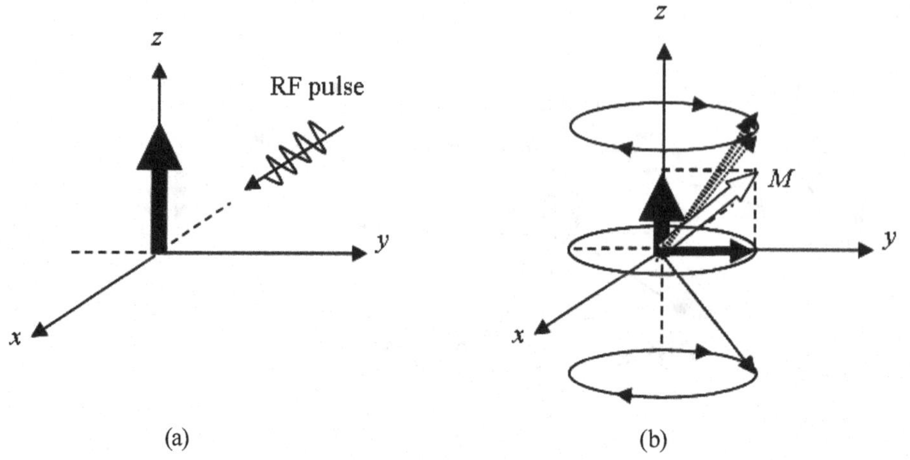

Figure 7. The restoration of the net magnetization M to its equilibrium state, following a 90-degree pulse. Relaxation progresses from (a) to (e) in turn. (b) M lies in the x-y plane immediately following a 90-degree pulse, and the component of the z-axis is zero. (c) - (e) Over time, the longitudinal magnetization gradually increases whereas the transverse decreases, and M recovers to its equilibrium state

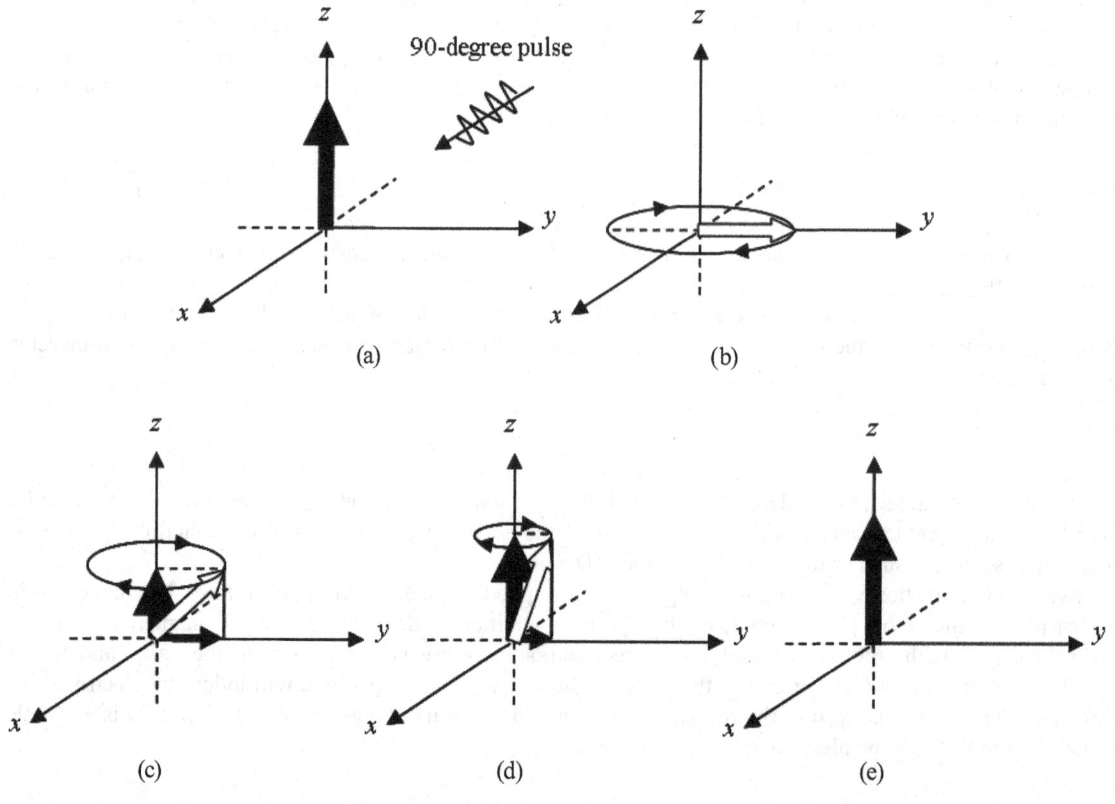

Figure 8. (a) The transverse magnetization in the x-y plane rotates about the z-axis. The measurement of the component of the transverse magnetization in the x-y plane decays over time. An alternating signal shown in Figure (b) is induced in the receiver coil

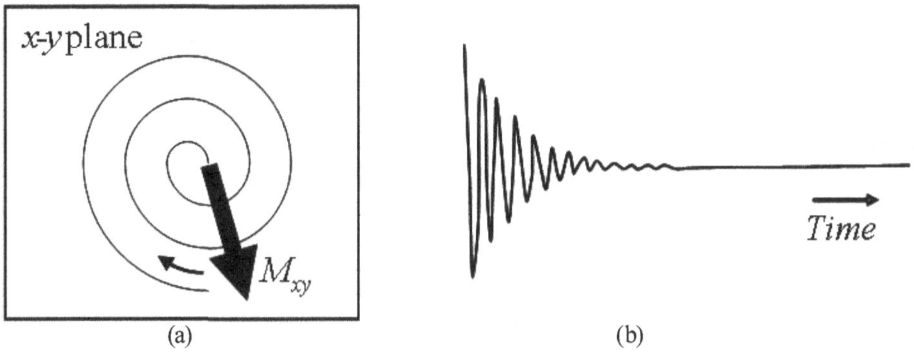

Mathematical Model of the NMR Signal

An NMR signal (FID) with m components is modeled as follows:

$$\hat{x}_n = \sum_{k=1}^{m} A_k \exp(-b_k n)\exp[j(2\pi f_k n + \varphi_k)], \quad n = 0, 1, \cdots, N-1, \tag{4}$$

where $\hat{x}_n$ $(n=0,1,\cdots,N-1)$ denotes the observed signal, which is complex-valued, n denotes the sample point on the time axis and the sample period T is taken for T=1 to simplify the expression of Eq. (4). A_k, b_k, f_k, and φ_k are real number and denote the spectral composition, damping factor, rotation frequency and phase in the rotation, respectively, of each metabolite. m is the number of the metabolites composing a spectrum, and $j = \sqrt{-1}$.

NMR Spectra

The position of each peak appearing in a NMR spectrum depends on its offset frequencies (chemical shifts) from the resonance frequency of a target nucleus under a specified static magnetic field (Derome, 1987). These offset frequencies are f_k (k=1,...,m).

In a common pulse method, each peak possesses the offset phase expressed by a linear function of its offset frequencies f, as follows (Derome, 1987):

$$\theta(f) = \alpha + \beta \cdot f. \tag{5}$$

Where, α is called the zero-dimensional term of phase correction, and is a common phase error influencing every peak. β is called the one-dimensional term of phase correction, and is a phase error that is dependent on the offset frequencies, or more specifically, the positions of each peak.

Thus, in NMR spectra, the position of each peak and the scale of their offset phase are determined by the measurement condition used. Because of this fact, it is possible to make a rough prediction of the position of each peak of a NMR spectrum under specified measurement conditions. This positional can be used as a constrained condition when estimating unknown parameters using our neural network. In addition, because the relationship between a specified static magnetic field and the apparent transverse relaxation time T_2^* of a target nucleus are known in MRS (Haselgrove, Subramanian, Christen, & Leigh, 1988), it is possible to determine the rough scale of T_2^* for a target nucleus when the strength of the static magnetic field is known. This information regarding T_2^* can also be used as a constraint condition. That is, it can be used for the estimation of b_k.

Estimation of NMR Spectra

The following approach is used in our method of parametric spectral estimation.

1. A mathematical model of the NMR signal is given, as described above.
2. Adequate values are supplied as initial values of the parameters A_k, b_k, f_k, and φ_k, and an NMR signal is simulated.
3. The sum of the squares of the difference, at each sample point, between the simulated signal and the actual observed signal is calculated.
4. The parameters are varied to give optimum estimates for the observed signal by minimizing the error sum of squares.

DESIGN OF A COMPLEX-VALUED HOPFIELD NEURAL NETWORK AS A SPECTRAL ESTIMATOR

Energy Function on the Complex-Valued Neural Network

For the estimation of NMR spectra, the error sum of squares of the parameter estimation problem is defined as the energy function of a Hopfield network. This means that the parameter estimation problem is converted to an optimization problem for the Hopfield network. The energy function is defined as

$$E = -\frac{1}{2}\sum_{n=0}^{N-1}\left|\hat{x}_n - \sum_{k=1}^{m} A_k \exp(-b_k n)\exp\{j(2\pi f_k n + \varphi_k)\}\right|^2, \tag{6}$$

where, as in Eq.(4), n denotes the sample point on the time axis and $\hat{x}_n$ denotes the complex-valued observed signal at n.

The energy function E of complex-valued neural networks should have the following properties (Hashimoto, Kuroe, & Mori, 1999; Kuroe, Hashimoto, & Mori, 2002):

1. A function that relates the state $\hat{x}_n$ denoted by a complex number to a real-valued number.
2. To converge on the optimum solution, it is always necessary to satisfy the following condition in the dynamic updating of the Hopfield network:

$$\frac{dE(\cdot)}{dt} \le 0, \tag{7}$$

where t means the time on updating the network.

The energy function defined by Eq.(6) satisfies property 1. In Eq.(6), if

$$\hat{d}_n = \hat{x}_n - \sum_{k=1}^{m} A_k \exp(-b_k n)\exp\{j(2\pi f_k n + \varphi_k)\}, \tag{8}$$

then the energy function can be expressed as

$$E = -\frac{1}{2}\sum_{n=0}^{N-1}\left|\hat{d}_n\right|^2 = -\frac{1}{2}\sum_{n=0}^{N-1}\hat{d}_n\hat{d}_n^* \tag{9}$$

(*: denotes the complex conjugate).

From Eq.(6), when the parameters A_k, b_k, f_k, and φ_k in Eq.(4) are replaced by P_k, the time variation of the above energy function can be expressed as

$$\frac{dE}{dt} = \sum_{k=1}^{m}\sum_{P_k}\frac{\partial E}{\partial P_k}\frac{dP_k}{dt}, \qquad (P_k:\ A_k, b_k, f_k, \varphi_k,\ k=1,\cdots,m). \tag{10}$$

Here, suppose that

$$\frac{dP_k}{dt} = -\frac{\partial E}{\partial P_k}. \tag{11}$$

Then,

$$\frac{dE}{dt} = -\sum_{k=1}^{m}\sum_{P_k}\left(\frac{\partial E}{\partial P_k}\right)^2 \le 0 \tag{12}$$

will hold, and property 2 is satisfied. Hence, the convergence in the dynamic updating of the complex-valued neural network is guaranteed.

Design of the Network

From Eq.(9), the variation of the energy function with respect to the variation of the parameters is as follows:

$$\frac{\partial E}{\partial P_k} = -\frac{1}{2}\sum_{n=0}^{N-1}\left(\frac{\partial \hat{d}_n}{\partial P_k}\hat{d}_n^* + \frac{\partial \hat{d}_n^*}{\partial P_k}\hat{d}_n\right). \tag{13}$$

Then, by Eq.(11), we have

$$\begin{aligned}\frac{dP_k}{dt} &= -\frac{\partial E}{\partial P_k}\\ &= \frac{1}{2}\sum_{n=0}^{N-1}\left(\frac{\partial \hat{d}_n}{\partial P_k}\hat{d}_n^* + \frac{\partial \hat{d}_n^*}{\partial P_k}\hat{d}_n\right).\end{aligned} \tag{14}$$

Eq. (14) expresses the time variation of the parameters P_k, that is, the updating of the parameters. If we suppose that $\hat{d}_n^*$ and $\hat{d}_n$ on the right-hand side of the equation are the inputs to the complex-valued Hopfield neural network and $\partial\hat{d}_n/\partial P_k$ and $\partial\hat{d}_n^*/\partial P_k$ are the input weights in the network, a complex-valued network can be designed. The inputs and the input weights are then calculated by Eq.(8). In this network, two complex-valued input systems conjugated to each other are input to the network. The updating of the parameters is then carried out by complex calculation. However, because the two terms on the right-hand side of Eq.(14) are complex conjugates to each other, the left-hand side is a real number. The structure of the complex-valued network is depicted in Figure 9, where the coefficient 1/2 in Eq.(14) is omitted. Two complex-valued input systems conjugated to each other are input to one unit, and the updating of the parameters is carried out by complex-valued calculation.

Here, Eq. (8) can be decomposed into a real part $d_{re}(n)$ and an imaginary part $d_{im}(n)$:

$$\hat{d}_n = d_{re}(n) + jd_{im}(n). \tag{15}$$

Suppose that the real and imaginary parts of $\hat{x}_n$ are denoted as $x_{re}(n)$ and $x_{im}(n)$, respectively. We then have

$$d_{re}(n) = x_{re}(n) - \sum_{k=1}^{m} A_k \exp(-b_k n)\cos(2\pi f_k n + \varphi_k), \tag{16}$$

$$d_{im}(n) = x_{im}(n) - \sum_{k=1}^{m} A_k \exp(-b_k n)\sin(2\pi f_k n + \varphi_k). \tag{17}$$

From these,

$$\begin{aligned} |\hat{d}_n|^2 &= \hat{d}_n \hat{d}_n^* \qquad (*: \text{complex conjugate}) \\ &= \{d_{re}(n) + jd_{im}(n)\}\{d_{re}(n) - jd_{im}(n)\} \\ &= \{d_{re}(n)\}^2 + \{d_{im}(n)\}^2. \end{aligned} \tag{18}$$

Then, Eq.(9) can be developed as follows:

$$E = -\frac{1}{2}\sum_{n=0}^{N-1}|\hat{d}_n|^2 = E_{re} + E_{im}, \tag{19}$$

$$E_{re} = -\frac{1}{2}\sum_{n=0}^{N-1}\{d_{re}(n)\}^2, \tag{20}$$

$$E_{im} = -\frac{1}{2}\sum_{n=0}^{N-1}\{d_{im}(n)\}^2. \tag{21}$$

Figure 9. Structure of the complex-valued Hopfield network

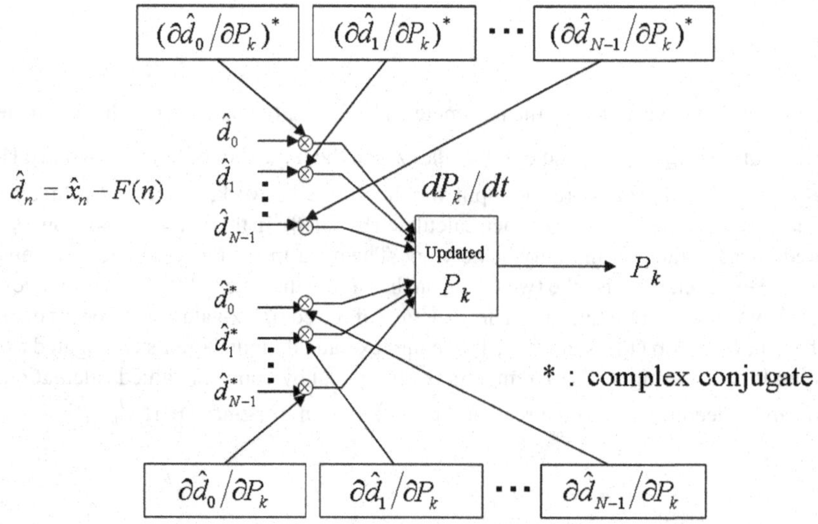

From Eqs.(10) and (19), we obtain

$$\begin{aligned}\frac{dE}{dt} &= \sum_{k=1}^{m}\sum_{P_k}\frac{\partial E}{\partial P_k}\frac{dP_k}{dt}\\ &= \frac{dE_{re}}{dt}+\frac{dE_{im}}{dt}\\ &= \sum_{k=1}^{m}\sum_{P_k}\left(\frac{\partial E_{re}}{\partial P_k}+\frac{\partial E_{im}}{\partial P_k}\right)\frac{dP_k}{dt},\end{aligned} \tag{22}$$

where,

$$\frac{dE_{re}}{dt} = \sum_{k=1}^{m}\frac{\partial E_{re}}{\partial P_k}\frac{dP_k}{dt}, \tag{23}$$

$$\frac{dE_{im}}{dt} = \sum_{k=1}^{m}\frac{\partial E_{im}}{\partial P_k}\frac{dP_k}{dt} \tag{24}$$

$$(P_k : A_k, b_k, f_k, \varphi_k).$$

Here, if we assume that

$$\frac{dP_k}{dt} = -\left(\frac{\partial E_{re}}{\partial P_k}+\frac{\partial E_{im}}{\partial P_k}\right) \tag{25}$$

$$(P_k : A_k, b_k, f_k, \varphi_k, \quad k=1,\cdots,m),$$

we obtain the following:

$$\frac{dE}{dt} = -\sum_{k=1}^{m}\sum_{P_k}\left(\frac{\partial E_{re}}{\partial P_k}+\frac{\partial E_{im}}{\partial P_k}\right)^2 \le 0. \tag{26}$$

From Eqs.(20) and (21), we obtain

$$\frac{\partial E_{re}}{\partial P_k} = -\sum_{n=0}^{N-1}\frac{\partial d_{re}(n)}{\partial P_k}d_{re}(n), \tag{27}$$

$$\frac{\partial E_{im}}{\partial P_k} = -\sum_{n=0}^{N-1}\frac{\partial d_{im}(n)}{\partial P_k}d_{im}(n). \tag{28}$$

Hence, Eq.(25) can be expressed as follows:

$$\begin{aligned}\frac{dP_k}{dt} &= -\left(\frac{\partial E_{re}}{\partial P_k} + \frac{\partial E_{im}}{\partial P_k}\right) \\ &= \sum_{n=0}^{N-1}\left(\frac{\partial d_{re}(n)}{\partial P_k} d_{re}(n) + \frac{\partial d_{im}(n)}{\partial P_k} d_{im}(n)\right) \\ &(P_k:\ A_k,\ b_k,\ f_k,\ \varphi_k,\quad k = 1,\cdots,m).\end{aligned} \tag{29}$$

From Eqs.(14) and (29), the complex-valued network can be expressed as an equivalent real-valued network which has two real-valued input systems. That is, let the parameters change with time as shown in Eq.(29). Then, the energy function E satisfies property 2, above. Thus, the convergence in the updating of the complex-valued network can be guaranteed. The equivalent network is depicted in Figure 10. In addition, the parameters are updated by the steepest descent method as follows:

$$P_k^{new} = P_k^{old} + \varepsilon \frac{dP_k^{old}}{dt}, \qquad (\varepsilon > 0) \qquad (P_k:\ A_k,\ b_k,\ f_k,\ \varphi_k,\quad k = 1,\cdots,m). \tag{30}$$

For every parameter P_k, this equivalent network forms a unit which has two input systems, corresponding to the real and imaginary parts of the NMR signal. Each input system has inputs d and input weights $\partial \hat{d}_n / \partial P_k$ corresponding to the number of sample points, and d is calculated by Eqs.(16) and (17). These mean that the inputs and input weights are calculated using the previous values of the parameters and the observed signal. By means of these inputs, the state of the unit is changed and every parameter is updated. The inputs and the input weights are recalculated with the updated parameters. We implemented this equivalent network for estimating NMR spectra.

Incidentally, k in Eqs.(29) and (30) represents one of the components of an NMR signal. Because Eq.(29) is applied to each k, the updating of parameters A_k, b_k, f_k, and φ_k is simultaneously carried out on k. As described, in

Figure 10. Structure of the real-valued network equivalent to the complex-valued network of Figure 9

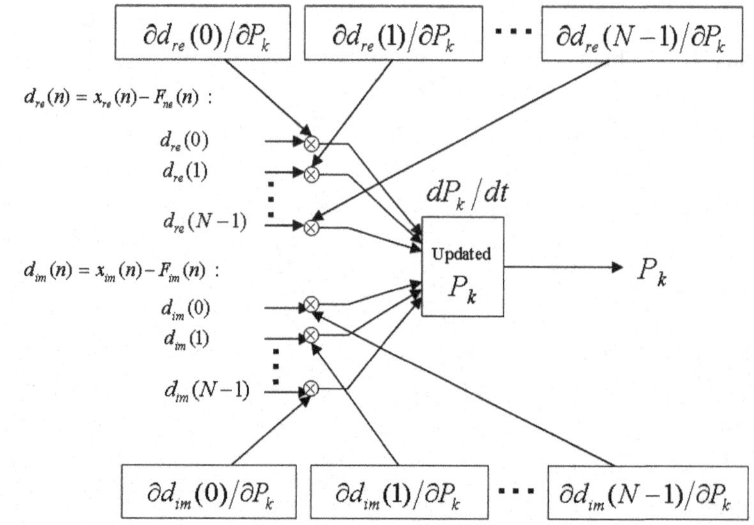

the network used in this chapter, the sequential updating of each unit, which is a feature of the Hopfield network, is transformed to sequential updating of every unit group A_k, b_k, f_k, and φ_k on k.

SEQUENTIAL EXTENSION OF SECTION (SES)

As expressed in Eq. (4), the NMR signal is a set of sinusoidal waves in which the spectral components A_k are exponentially damped with time n. We introduced the operation shown in Figure 11 so that our network would recognize the decay state more accurately. In the figure, the horizontal axis shows the sample points at time n, and the vertical axis shows the NMR signal. In this operation, first, appropriate values are assigned as initial values for each of the parameters. Then, our network operates on section A from time 0 ($n = 0$) to an adequate time k_1 ($n = k_1$). The parameter estimates are obtained when the network has equilibrated. Next, the network operates on section B from time 0 to an adequate time k_2 ($k_1 < k_2$), and the equilibrium values in section A are used as the initial values in section B. Thereafter, we extend the section in the same way, and finally, the network operates on the entire time interval corresponding to all sample points. This operation is equivalent to recognizing the shape of the signal by gradually extending the observation section while taking into account the detailed aspects of the signal during its rapid variation.

For operating the SES, the length and number of above-mentioned sections naturally depend on the decay state of a target signal, and those values should be properly determined in objective and quantitative ways. However, because we did not find such a way, we applied the other one, as mentioned in "**Sections Used for Sequential Extension of Section (SES) Method**" of "**SIMULATIONS**".

SIMULATIONS

Sample Signals

We simulated sample signals equivalent to NMR signals that consisted of 1024 data points on a spectrum with a bandwidth of 2000 Hz, which is equivalent to the range of about 58ppm on chemical shift, in order to deal with

Figure 11. Illustration of the sequential extension of section (SES) method

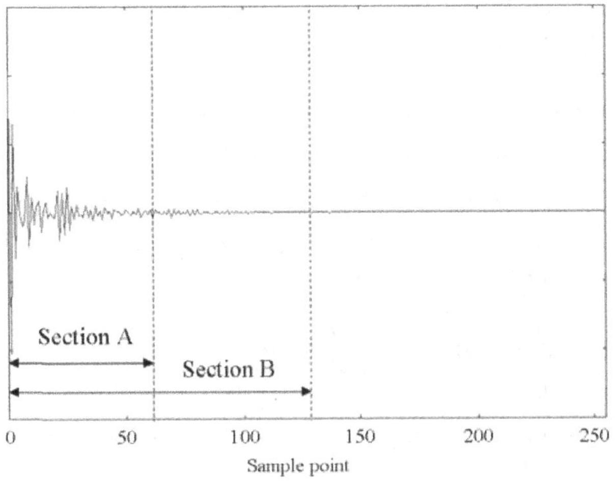

every spectral peak of the atomic nucleus of phosphorus-31 in a static magnetic field of 2 Tesla. The three signals shown in Table 1 and Figs. 12-14 were used.

In Table 1, peaks 1 through 7 represent phosphomonoester (PME), inorganic phosphate (Pi), phosphodiester (PDE), creatine phosphate (PCr), γ-adenocine triphosphate (γ-ATP), α-ATP, and β-ATP, respectively.

Signals 1 and 3 are equivalent to the spectra of healthy cells with a normal energy metabolism. Pi is one of relatively-small spectral components in their signals. Signal 2 is equivalent to the spectrum of a cell that is approaching necrosis. In such cells, the metabolism of energy is decreased and Pi is large in comparison with other components, as shown in Table 1. This signal is analogous to a single-component spectral signal (a monotonic damped signal) compared with signal 1 and 3. Among these signals, only the spectral component A_k is different.

Implementation of the Network

We introduced some auxiliary operations that are necessary for stable implementation of our network.

Initial Values of the Parameters

The settings of the initial values of the parameters are shown in Table 2. For the amplitude A_k, the amplitudes of the real part and the imaginary part were compared; the larger was divided by 7, the number of signal components; and the result was used as the initial value for all seven components. For the initial values of the frequency f_k and the damping coefficient b_k of each metabolite, rough values are known for f_k and b_k under observation conditions, as described in "**NMR Spectra**" above. Therefore, the initial values were set close to their rough values. In addition, all of the initial phases were set to zero.

Updating of Units

In the steepest descent method in Eq.(30), two values, 10^{-5} and 10^{-6} were used as learning rate ε. By setting the upper limit of the number of the parameter updates to 50,000, we ensure that the units continue to be renewed until the energy function decreases. Then, the parameters can be updated while the energy function is decreasing and the number of renewals does not exceed the upper limit. By using these procedures, it is possible to operate the network in a stable condition. In addition, the following two conditions for stopping the network are set.

1. The updates of all parameters are terminated
2. The energy function reaches an equilibrium point

Table 1. Parameters of sample signals

Peak	Metabolite	f_k*	b_k	φ_k**	A_k		
					(1)	(2)	(3)
1	Phosphomonoester (PME)	0.368	0.05395	0.4774	0.726	0.7	0.996
2	Inorganic phosphate (Pi)	0.397	0.03379	0.3699	1.02	6.246	0.5
3	Phosphodiester (PDE)	0.435	0.05918	0.2296	2.1	1.8	2.1
4	Creatine phosphate (PCr)	0.485	0.03785	0.051	2.37	1.2	3.6
5	γ-adenocine triphosphate (γ-ATP)	0.526	0.04858	-0.1002	1.89	0.5	1.15
6	α-adenocine triphosphate (α-ATP)	0.616	0.05744	-0.4264	2.04	0.5	2.2
7	β-adenocine triphosphate (β-ATP)	0.763	0.04035	-0.9657	1.1	0.3	0.7

** : Relative values corresponding to the range from 1000 Hz to –1000 Hz around the resonance frequency. 0.0 is 1000 Hz, and 1.0 is –1000 Hz. ** : Values normalized to π.*

Figure 12. Signal 1

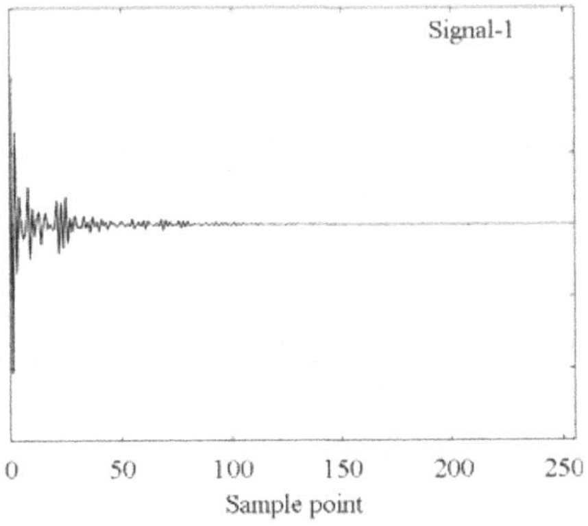

Figure 13. Signal 2

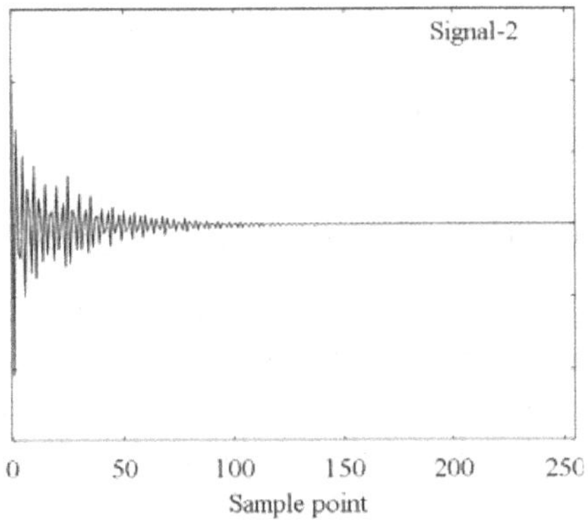

Figure 14. Signal 3

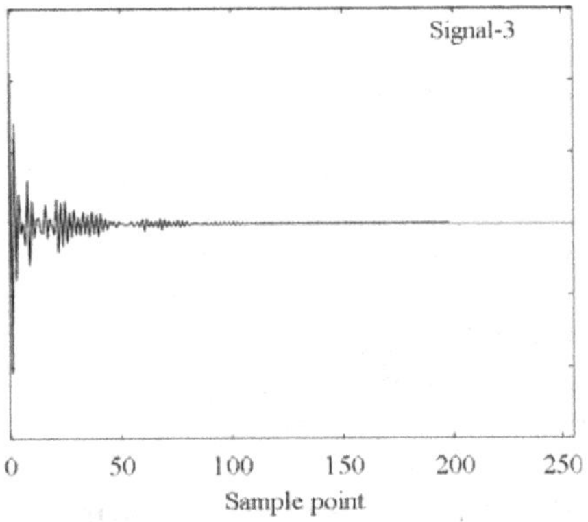

Table 2. Initial values of parameters

Peak	Metabolite	f_k	b_k	φ_k	A_k		
					(1)	(2)	(3)
1	Phosphomonoester (PME)	0.35	0.1	0.0	1.481595	1.502836	1.505209
2	Inorganic phosphate (Pi)	0.4	0.1	0.0	1.481595	1.502836	1.505209
3	Phosphodiester (PDE)	0.45	0.1	0.0	1.481595	1.502836	1.505209
4	Creatine phosphate (PCr)	0.5	0.1	0.0	1.481595	1.502836	1.505209
5	γ-adenocine triphosphate(γ-ATP)	0.55	0.1	0.0	1.481595	1.502836	1.505209
6	α-adenocine triphosphate(α-ATP)	0.6	0.1	0.0	1.481595	1.502836	1.505209
7	β-adenocine triphosphate (β-ATP)	0.75	0.1	0.0	1.481595	1.502836	1.505209

The criterion for condition 1 is a limit on the time variation of the parameter P_k: if $dP_k/dt \leq 0.01$, we set $dP_k/dt = 0$ and terminate the updating of the parameter.

Regarding condition 2, we judge that the energy function has reached an equilibrium point when the energy function increases, or when the number of the updates exceeds the upper limit mentioned above. Theoretically, the network stops and an optimum solution is obtained when the above two conditions are satisfied simultaneously. However, because a monotonic decrease of the energy function is produced by the above-described operations, in practice, we forced the network to stop when either of the two conditions occurs.

In each renewal of the unit, we also adjusted the network so that the updated values do not depart greatly from the actual values by using the prior knowledge of the spectrum outlined in **"Initial Values of the Parameters"** above. For the frequency f_k, we adopted only values within a range of 0.05 around the values indicated in Table 1. A similar procedure was also carried out for the phase φ_k : the range is ±1.0. For the damping coefficient b_k, we adopted only values below 0.1.

Sections Used for Sequential Extension of Section (SES) Method

As shown in Figs. 12-14, the sample signals have decayed to near-zero amplitude after 255 points on the time axis (each full data set has 1024 points). Therefore, only the section of [0-1023] was adopted, as one of exceeding [0-255]. In addition, because those signals seem to be oscillating before 125 points, we mechanically performed the following processes in the section before 255 point: the section of [0-255] was divided into halves, which resulted in the section of [0-127]. The [0-127] was also divided into halves, as resulting in the section of [0-63]. In the same way, the sections of [0-31] and [0-15] was set. When performing the SES, those sections are incorporated sequentially for more accurately recognizing the decay state of the target signal. We performed the SES method for the following three sets of sections:

a. **Four sections:** [0-63], [0-127], [0-255], [0-1023]
b. **Five sections:** [0-31], [0-63], [0-127], [0-255], [0-1023]
c. **Six sections:** [0-15], [0-31], [0-63], [0-127], [0-255], [0-1023]

Estimation with the Complex-Valued Hopfield Neural Network

We first performed parameter estimations of the sample signals using the complex-valued Hopfield neural network without the SES technique. The results are shown in Table 3(a-f). For signal 1, the result of the estimation using $\varepsilon = 10^{-6}$ was better than for $\varepsilon = 10^{-5}$. In the case using $\varepsilon = 10^{-6}$, the spectral composition A_k and the frequency f_k were more accurately estimated than the damping coefficient b_k and the phase φ_k. Except for peaks 1 and 2, the errors in A_k were less than 20% in relative terms, and all of the errors in f_k were less than 10%. For signals 2 and 3, the same tendency was also shown, although the effects of the difference of ε became quite small for signal 2. However, even using $\varepsilon = 10^{-6}$, the estimations of signals 2 and 3 were not as good as the estimation of signal 1. In these results, all of the errors in f_k are less than 10%, but the only peaks with errors of less than 20% of A_k were peak 3 (about 11%) in signal 2 (Table 3d), and peaks 3 (19.7%) and 6 (4.38%) in signal 3 (Table 3f).

In summary, the estimation of signal 1 using $\varepsilon = 10^{-6}$ was the best result.

Estimation with the Network in Combining Sequential Extension of Section (SES)

The effects of the SES are shown in Table 4(a-d). For signal 1, when we applied four- and five-section extension method using $\varepsilon = 10^{-6}$, the accuracies of estimations of the damping coefficient b_k and the phase φ_k were improved overall compared to Table 3b. The accuracy of estimation of the frequency f_k, however, was only slightly improved overall. Compared to Table 3b, the accuracy of the spectral composition A_k for the four-section was improved at peaks 2 and 4, but degraded at peaks 1 and 3, whereas that for the five-section was degraded overall. Eventually, for signal 1, it appears that when the four-section extension method is applied using $\varepsilon = 10^{-6}$, we can obtain the best result (Table 4a).

For signal 2, when we applied the six-section extension method using $\varepsilon = 10^{-5}$, the errors were improved overall compared to the complex-valued network alone, but we were not able to obtain an estimation at the same level as signal 1 (Table 4d). For signal 3, we were not able to improve the accuracies of estimations of the parameters effectively, especially for the spectral composition A_k, in any combination on the choices for ε and the number of sections.

Table 3a. Estimation error (%) of signal 1 with the complex-valued neural network ($\varepsilon = 10^{-5}$)

Peak	f_k	b_k	φ_k	A_k
1	8.69	-2.25	-110.1	86.3
2	9.21	195.9	55.9	46.5
3	-0.41	58.6	158.3	-24.2
4	0.11	-6.12	-100.4	-25.1
5	0.32	-20.3	-100.2	-29.6
6	0.24	24.6	68.8	19.3
7	-0.10	11.4	-10.1	5.86
	f_k	b_k	φ_k	A_k
SAEP	19.1	319.2	603.9	236.7
TAE		1178.9		

Table 3b. Estimation error (%) of signal 1 with the complex-valued neural network (($\varepsilon = 10^{-6}$)

Peak	f_k	b_k	φ_k	A_k
1	7.82	-20.9	-83.4	58.9
2	9.65	195.9	-25.4	37.5
3	0.16	57.5	22.9	-14.6
4	0.47	-32.9	-100.4	-19.9
5	0.08	-29.3	-213.1	-2.1
6	-0.28	-2.92	-49.3	-3.97
7	0.05	0.77	-0.58	0.45
	f_k	b_k	φ_k	A_k
SAEP	18.5	340.3	495.1	137.4
TAE		991.3		

SAEP: Sum of the absolute error (%) of each parameter. TAE: Total absolute error (%) of parameters.

Table 3c. Estimation error (%) of signal 2 with the complex-valued neural network ($\varepsilon = 10^{-5}$)

Peak	f_k	b_k	φ_k	A_k
1	6.23	0.95	109.5	658.2
2	2.32	23.1	-348.9	-48.8
3	0.64	33.0	-195.9	48.6
4	0.83	164.2	-343.6	28.4
5	-4.94	105.8	64.1	85.0
6	-1.49	74.1	-154.2	117.3
7	-2.20	147.8	-138.2	-74.8
	f_k	b_k	φ_k	A_k
SAEP	18.7	549.0	1354.3	1061.1
TAE		2983.1		

Table 3d. Estimation error (%) of signal 2 with the complex-valued neural network (($\varepsilon = 10^{-6}$)

Peak	f_k	b_k	φ_k	A_k
1	7.80	-61.4	-109.5	258.4
2	0.29	3.04	47.0	-66.7
3	-8.05	-53.2	-421.0	11.1
4	-0.78	164.2	-625.1	38.0
5	-4.94	105.8	180.5	206.4
6	-0.75	74.0	-55.9	97.4
7	-1.68	147.8	-111.1	98.2
	f_k	b_k	φ_k	A_k
SAEP	24.3	609.6	1550.0	776.2
TAE		2960.1		

Table 3e. Estimation error (%) of signal 3 with the complex-valued neural network (ε = 10^{-5})

Peak	f_k	b_k	φ_k	A_k
1	1.11	85.4	-11.1	70.0
2	9.02	195.9	77.4	190.6
3	-0.50	69.0	186.1	-30.9
4	0.51	15.5	-788.7	-48.6
5	-4.94	104.5	-98.9	66.2
6	0.99	-8.51	-0.83	-12.2
7	-0.23	147.8	-17.0	60.9
	f_k	b_k	φ_k	A_k
SAEP	17.3	626.6	1180.2	479.6
TAE		2303.7		

Table 3f. Estimation error (%) of signal 3 with the complex-valued neural network ((ε = 10^{-6})

Peak	f_k	b_k	φ_k	A_k
1	1.41	85.4	-30.3	35.2
2	8.86	195.9	38.4	185.2
3	-0.63	69.0	137.0	-19.7
4	0.34	-46.5	-46.6	-45.5
5	-4.94	105.8	-98.1	55.7
6	0.30	-2.53	44.4	-4.38
7	-0.26	147.8	-23.4	62.2
	f_k	b_k	φ_k	A_k
SAEP	16.7	653.0	418.1	407.8
TAE		1495.7		

Estimation for the Signal with Noise

Real NMR signals always include noise. Therefore, we need to verify the ability of our method, that is, the complex-valued Hopfield neural network combined with SES, to estimate parameters for NMR signals that include noise. For that purpose, we used sample signals in which three levels of white Gaussian noise with signal to noise ratios (*SNR*s) of 10, 5, or 2 were added to signal 1, which was well-estimated compared to other two signals. The *SNR* was defined as follows:

$$SNR = \sum_{k=0}^{n-1} |F(t_k)|^2 \Big/ n\sigma^2 . \tag{31}$$

Where, $F(t_k)$ is the signal composition at sampling time t_k, σ^2 is the variance of the noise, and n is the total number of sample points (in this case, 1024). The sample signal with $SNR = 2$ is shown in Figure 15, and the results of the estimation of signals with each *SNR* are shown in Tables 5(a-c). For these results, we used ε= 10^{-6} and the SES method with four sections.

Comparing these results to those obtained from the sample data with no noise indicated in Table 4a, there was almost no change in estimation error for the frequency f_k, and the estimation error exceeds 10% only at peak 2 (11.9%) for $SNR = 2$. For the spectral composition A_k, peaks 4, 5, 6, and 7 that had less than 10% error in Table 4a maintained the same error level for SNR=10 and 5. In the case of $SNR = 2$, peaks 4 and 6 were estimated with better than 10% error, but -16.3% was obtained at peak 5 and -21.9% was obtained at peak 7. For the damping coefficient b_k, the peaks with small estimation errors in Table 4a maintained relatively-small error levels in the presence of noise. Thus, we conclude that the estimates of f_k, A_k and b_k were not so much influenced by the degradation of *SNR*, whereas the estimate of phase φ_k was more influenced.

DISCUSSION

The results of the simulations indicated that our complex-valued neural network has the ability to estimate four different parameters of the NMR signal. It was also shown that in our method, the frequency composition f_k and the spectral composition A_k can be estimated with less error than the damping coefficient b_k and the phase φ_k.

Table 4a. Estimation error (%) of signal 1, case of four-section (ε = 10^{-6})

Peak	f_k	b_k	φ_k	A_k
1	8.67	-20.8	-163.2	78.9
2	5.26	195.9	6.84	28.4
3	-0.11	-15.1	123.4	-18.8
4	0.04	-3.9	55.9	-4.3
5	0.08	-0.5	3.4	-1.2
6	0.02	-1.83	-2.1	-1.96
7	0.09	-2.03	-0.99	-2.1
	f_k	b_k	φ_k	A_k
SAEP	14.3	240.0	355.9	135.6
TAE		745.8		

Table 4b. Estimation error (%) of signal 1, case of five-section (ε = 10^{-6})

Peak	f_k	b_k	φ_k	A_k
1	8.55	-7.63	-115.4	100.8
2	8.70	195.90	68.6	17.9
3	0.27	-6.67	-48.6	-30.6
4	0.04	-1.39	64.4	-1.19
5	0.03	0.44	-32.0	0.15
6	0.0	-3.25	-5.45	-3.32
7	0.10	-2.31	0.98	-2.35
	f_k	b_k	φ_k	A_k
SAEP	17.7	217.6	335.4	156.3
TAE		727.0		

SAEP: Sum of the absolute error (%) of each parameter. TAE: Total absolute error (%) of parameters.

Table 4c. Estimation error (%) of signal 1, case of six-section (ε = 10^{-6})

Peak	f_k	b_k	φ_k	A_k
1	8.49	-6.32	-103.8	98.9
2	9.70	80.9	-43.8	123.8
3	11.5	-50.0	-44.1	-31.6
4	-0.28	115.2	114.8	-39.3
5	-0.06	-8.07	-120.2	-8.61
6	0.01	-5.76	-5.34	-6.05
7	0.11	-4.01	2.48	-4.06
	f_k	b_k	φ_k	A_k
SAEP	30.2	270.3	434.5	312.2
TAE		1047.1		

Table 4d. Estimation error (%) of signal 2, case of six-section (ε = 10^{-5})

Peak	f_k	b_k	φ_k	A_k
1	-0.33	85.4	-220.8	205.7
2	-2.14	96.2	170.3	29.1
3	3.59	68.8	-535.5	26.7
4	0.39	43.7	55.2	38.2
5	0.87	39.9	365.1	50.2
6	-0.10	15.7	-21.3	19.3
7	-0.30	5.84	-45.5	2.40
	f_k	b_k	φ_k	A_k
SAEP	7.7	355.5	1413.7	371.7
TAE		2148.6		

When SES was applied to this neural network method, it was found that the estimation precisions of b_k and φ_k were improved. In addition, it was shown that this combined method experiences no rapid decline in accuracy when applied to noisy signals. However, the estimation error levels were very different among parameters.

In our estimation method, preliminary knowledge about the targeted spectrum is indispensable when determining the initial value of the parameters and updating them during the estimation process. If there is no preliminary knowledge, the network must search for the solution in an unlimited solution space, and the probability of reaching an optimum solution in a reasonable time period becomes very small. In addition, because the steepest descent method is used to update the parameters, it is difficult for the network to reach the optimum solution if it begins to operate from inappropriate initial values.

Figure 15. Noisy NMR signal with SNR = 2

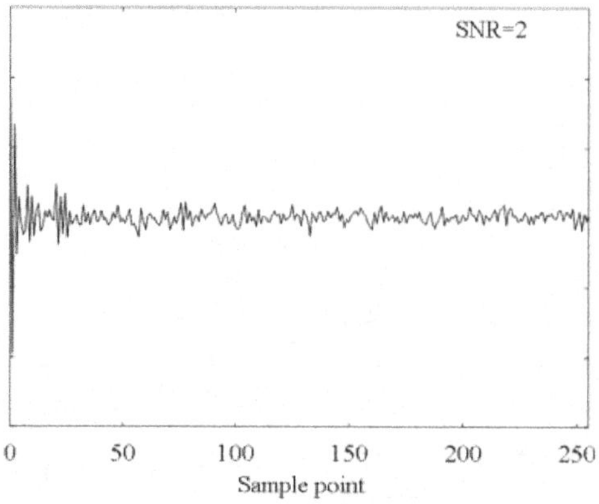

Table 5a. Estimation error (%) of signal 1 with noise, case of SNR = 10

Peak	f_k	b_k	φ_k	A_k
1	8.69	-13.7	-135.6	91.7
2	6.78	195.9	-0.53	15.3
3	0.14	-26.7	82.7	-31.4
4	-0.04	2.01	144.7	0.97
5	0.13	-1.59	-24.1	0.26
6	0.03	4.14	4.92	-0.34
7	0.16	-4.83	-3.54	-5.45
	f_k	b_k	φ_k	A_k
SAEP	16.0	248.9	396.1	145.4
TAE		806.4		

Table 5b. Estimation error (%) of signal 1 with noise, case of SNR = 5

Peak	f_k	b_k	φ_k	A_k
1	8.67	-31.5	-111.1	81.8
2	7.68	195.9	-16.40	15.9
3	0.16	-31.2	49.2	-34.6
4	0.04	-11.0	38.2	-8.31
5	0.27	-1.34	-115.5	0.11
6	-0.16	1.83	18.6	4.75
7	0.08	11.4	-3.55	5.0
	f_k	b_k	φ_k	A_k
SAEP	17.1	284.2	352.6	150.5
TAE		804.3		

Table 5c Estimation error (%) of signal 1 with noise, case of SNR = 2

Peak	f_k	b_k	φ_k	A_k
1	8.39	-60.4	-121.8	26.7
2	11.9	195.9	-60.4	72.6
3	0.29	-18.9	-216.4	-24.8
4	-0.29	9.33	420.4	7.97
5	0.17	-22.2	-53.7	-16.30
6	-0.52	-1.49	49.4	-5.54
7	0.07	-3.84	-1.44	-21.9
	f_k	b_k	φ_k	A_k
SAEP	21.6	312.1	923.5	175.8
TAE		1433.0		

SAEP: Sum of the absolute error (%) of each parameter. TAE: Total absolute error (%) of parameters.

SES uses the equilibrium values of the parameters calculated in one section as the initial values for the following section in a sequence. In other words, every time a section is extended, the neural network operates to minimize a new energy function with new initial values and with a new group of data. Thus, when calculation on the new section begins, the direction in which a minimum solution has previously been sought is reset, and the network is free to search in another direction. Such a behavior probably reduces the danger of falling into a local minimum solution.

As the results of simulations, the optimal section on which to apply SES and the optimal step size of ε were different for every simulated NMR signal, and it was verified that those have a direct effect to the estimation accuracy. In addition, when the damping of the target signal is monotonic like signal 2 in "**SIMULATIONS**", it appears the search direction may no longer be effectively reset and that the network cannot escape from a local minimum solution.

The signal in Figure15, which contains noise, maintains the characteristics of the initial damping for the noise-free version of the same signal in Figure12. It seems that this fact was advantageous in SES. Also, it is reasonable to conclude that relatively-stable estimation accuracy in the presence of noise results from using the preliminary knowledge of the parameters, and the SES method.

Usually, a Hopfield network cannot reach the optimum solution from a local solution without restarting from different initial values (Dayhoff, 1989). SES carries out this operation automatically. A Boltzmann machine (David, Hinton, & Sejnowski, 1985; Geman & Geman, 1984; Hinton & Sejnowski, 1986) can be used to avoid local solutions and approach the optimum solution. However, in that method, the state of the network is updated, not determinately but stochastically. Thus, stability of the decrease in energy with state transitions is not guaranteed. Compared to the avoidance of the local solution by the Boltzmann machine, SES seems to be more elegant because it is free of the uncertainty associated with the stochastic operation. However, the reliable operation of SES to the optimal solution is influenced by the decay state of the targeted signal, and we must overcome this problem.

In the avoidance of local solutions, consideration of the use of a natural gradient approach (Amari, 1998) is also necessary instead of the steepest descent method. Does the natural gradient approach provide a more stable estimation when applying it? Does SES become unnecessary when applying the natural gradient approach? Verifications of these questions must be necessary. Also, comparison of the estimation ability between our method and existing approaches for noisy signals must be necessary.

CONCLUSION

As an application of the complex-valued neural networks, this chapter described the development of an automatic estimation method for NMR spectra in which human intervention or complicated matrix calculations are not necessary. For that purpose, we devised an NMR spectrum estimation method using a complex-valued Hopfield neural network, which does not required a learning process, unlike the conventional quantitative methods of NMR spectrum estimation using hierarchical neural networks. In addition, the SES method that takes into account the decay state of the NMR signal was devised, and was used in combination with above-mentioned neural network. For performance evaluation of our estimation method, simulations were carried out using sample signals composed of seven different metabolites to simulate in vivo Phosphorus-31 NMR spectra, with and without added noise.

The results of the simulations indicated that our complex-valued neural network has the ability to estimate the modeling parameters of the NMR signal. However, the estimation error levels were very different among parameters, and we found that its ability is affected to the decay state of the signals.

Our investigation has indicated that SES probably reduces the danger of falling into a local minimum in the search for the optimum solution using a Hopfield neural network. Although we can employ a Boltzmann machine to avoid local solutions, it is stochastic and requires much futile searching before it reaches the optimum solution. Compared to the avoidance of the local solution by the Boltzmann machine, SES seems to be more elegant because it is free of the uncertainty associated with the stochastic operation. However, for the reliable operation of it, we found that it is indispensable to find the optimal sections and learning rate ε for the target signal.

Since NMR signals are essentially complex signals, we believe that those can be a candidate for the application of the complex-valued neural networks. The approach presented in this chapter is an example of applying the complex-valued networks to NMR signals. It is still inadequate for a practical application at present, because there are some problems to be solved. Solving them and/or finding the more adequate approaches are our future work.

FUTURE RESEARCH DIRECTIONS

Applications of magnetic resonance imaging were started in MRI which is a technique imaging the human anatomy, and they include various specialized technique such as diffusion-weighted imaging (DWI), perfusion-weighted imaging (PWI), magnetic resonance angiography (MRA) and magnetic resonance cholangio-pancreatography (MRCP). Functional MRI (fMRI) that is an innovative tool for functional measurement of human brain and that is a technique imaging brain functions, also became practical and has been widely using in recent years. In contrast with MRI and fMRI, magnetic resonance spectroscopy (MRS) is a technique that measures the spectra of the metabolites in a single region, and magnetic resonance spectroscopic imaging (MRSI), which obtains the spectra from many regions by applying imaging techniques to MRS, has also been developed. Although ^{31}P-MRS was widely performed in MRS before, recently, proton MRS is mostly performed. ^{13}C-MRS using heteronuclear single-quantum coherence (HSQC) method has also been developed (Watanabe et al., 2000). However, MRS and MRSI compared to MRI have remained underutilized together due to their technical complexities.

At present, MRS is technically evolved and its operability has remarkably improved. Also the measurement of MRS has started to be automatically analyzed and be indicated.

In addition, MRSI has the big feature that is not in MRI and fMRI, that is, it can detect internal metabolite non-invasively, track the metabolic process and perform the imaging. Thus, the importance of it is huge. MRSI is also expected as an imaging technique realizing the molecular imaging.

For commonly performing the MRSI, quantifying NMR spectra automatically is an indispensable technique, and progressing the techniques for the automatic analysis of them is also important. At present, there are some representative analysis software introduced in the Internet, LCModel: an automatic software packages for in-vivo proton NMR spectra including the curve-fitting procedure (Provencher, 2001), and MRUI: Magnetic Resonance User Interface including the time-domain analysis of in-vivo MR data (Naressi, Couturier, Castang, de. Beer, & Graveron-Demilly, 2001; van den Boogaart et al., 1996).

As described in the conclusion, our method is still inadequate for a practical application at present. Since MRUI includes algorithms executing in the time-domain, they may be useful to improve our proposed technique. Finding the more adequate approaches is our future work.

It is necessary to develop a novel method introducing neural network techniques including our proposing approach, as well as existing analysis software, and it is important to proceed with the investigation of this territory.

REFERENCES

Ala-Korpela, M., Changani, K. K., Hiltunen, Y., Bell, J. D., Fuller, B.J., Bryant, D.J., Taylor-Robinson, S. D., & Davidson, B. R. (1997). Assessment of quantitative artificial neural network analysis in a metabolically dynamic ex vivo 31P NMR pig liver study. *Magnetic Resonace in Medicine*, *38*, 840-844.

Amari, S. (1998). Natural Gradient Works Efficiently in Learning. *Neural Computation*, 10, 251-276.

Belliveau, J. W., Kennedy Jr, D. N., McKinstry, R. C., Buchbinder, B. R., Weisskoff, R. M., Cohen, M. S., Vevea, J. M., Brandy, T. J., & Rosen, B. R. (1991). Functional mapping of the human visual cortex by magnetic resonance imaging. *Science*, *254* (5032), 716-719.

Benvenuto, N., & Piazza, F. (1992). On the complex backpropagation algorithm. *Institute of Electrical and Electronic Engineers (IEEE) Transaction on Signal Processing*, *40*(4), 967-969.

Cooley, J. W., & Tukey, J. W. (1965). An algorithm for machine calculation of complex Fourier series. *Mathematics and Computation, 19*(90), 297-301.

David, H. A., Hinton, G. E., & Sejnowski, T. J. (1985). A Learning Algorithm for Boltzmann Machines. *Cognitive Science: A Multidisciplinary Journal, 9*(1), 149-169.

Dayhoff, J. E. (1989). *Neural Network Architectures: An Introduction.* New York: Van Nostrand Reinhold.

Derome, A. E. (1987). *Modern NMR Techniques for Chemistry Research (Organic Chemistry Series, Vol 6).* Oxford, United Kingdom: Pergamon Press.

Feinberg, D. A., & Oshio, K. (1991). GRASE (gradient and spin echo) MR imaging: A new fast clinical imaging technique. *Radiology, 181,* 597-602.

Geman, S., & Geman, D. (1984). Stochastic Relaxation, Gibbs Distribution and the Bayesian Restoration of Images. *Institute of Electrical and Electronic Engineers (IEEE) Transactions on Pattern Analysis and Machine Intelligence, 6,* 721-741.

Georgiou, G. M., & Koutsougeras, C. (1992). Complex domain backpropagation. *Institute of Electrical and Electronic Engineers (IEEE) Transactions on Circuits and System: Analog and Digital Signal Processing, 39*(5), 330-334.

Han, L., & Biswas, S. K. (1997). Neural networks for sinusoidal frequency estimation. *Journal of The Franklin Institute, 334B*(1), 1-18.

Haselgrove, J. C., Subramanian, V. H., Christen, R., & Leigh, J. S. (1988). Analysis of in-vivo NMR spectra. *Reviews of Magnetic Resonance in Medicine, 2,* 167-222.

Hashimoto, N., Kuroe, Y., & Mori, T. (1999). On Energy Function for Complex-valued Neural Networks. The Institute of Electronics, *Information and Communication Engineers (IEICE) Technical report Neurocomputing, 98*(673), 121-128 (in Japanese).

Henning, J., Nauerth, A., & Fnedburg, H. (1986). RARE imaging: A first imaging method for clinical MR. *Magnetic Resonance in Medicine, 3*(6), 823-833.

Hinton, G. E., & Sejnowski, T. J. (1986). *Learning and Relearning in Boltzmann Machines. Parallel distributed processing: explorations in the microstructure of cognition*, *vol. 1*: *foundations* (pp. 282-317). Cambridge, MA: MIT press.

Hirose, A. (1992a). Dynamics of fully complex-valued neural networks. *Electrronics Letters, 28*(16), 1492-1494.

Hirose, A. (1992b). Proposal of fully complex-valued neural networks. *Proceedings of International Joint Conference on Neural Networks, 4,* 152-157. Baltimore, MD.

Hopfield, J. J. (1982). Neural networks and physical systems with emergent collective computational abilities. *Proceeding of National Academic of Science in USA, 79,* 2554-2558.

Hopfield, J. J. (1984). Neurons with graded response have collective computational properties like those of two-state neurons. *Proceeding of National Academic of Science in USA, 81,* 3088-3092.

Jankowski, S., Lozowski, A. & Zurada, J. M. (1996). Complex-valued multistate neural associative memory. *Proceedings of the Institute of Electrical and Electronic Engineers (IEEE) Transactions on Neural Networks, 7*(6), 1491-1496.

Kaartinen, J., Mierisova, S., Oja, J. M. E., Usenius, J. P., Kauppinen, R. A., & Hiltunen, Y. (1998). Automated quantification of human brain metabolites by artificial neural network analysis from in vivo single-voxel 1H NMR spectra. *Journal of Magnetic Resonance, 134,* 176-179.

Kuroe, Y., Hashimoto, N., & Mori, T. (2002). On energy function for complex-valued neural networks and its applications. Neural information proceeding. *Proceedings of the 9th International Conference on Neural Information Processing. Computational Intelligence for the E-Age, 3*, 1079-1083.

Kwong, K., Belliveau, J. W., Chesler, D. A., Goldberg, I. E., Weisskoff, R. M., Poncelet, B. P., Kennedy, D. N., Hoppel, B. E., Cohen, M. S., Turner, R., Cheng, H., Brady, T. J., & Rosen, B. R. (1992). Dynamic magnetic resonance imaging of human brain activity during primary sensory stimulation. *Proceedings of the National Academy of Sciences, 89(12)*, 5675-5679.

Maddams, W. F. (1980). The scope and Limitations of Curve Fitting. *Applied Spectroscopy, 34*(3), 245-267.

Mansfield, P. (1977). Multi-planar image formation using NMR spin echoes. *Journal of Physical C: Solid State Physics, 10*, L55-L58.

Melki, P. S., Mulkern, R. V., Panych, L. S., & Jolesz, F. A. (1991). Comparing the FAISE method with conventional dual-echo sequences. *Journal of Magnetic Resonance Imaging, 1*, 319-326.

Meyer, C. H., Hu, B. S., Nishimura, D. G., & Macovski, A. (1992). Fast Spiral Coronary Artery Imaging. *Magnetic Resonance in Medicine, 28*(2), 202-213.

Mierisová, S., & Ala-Korpela, M. (2001). MR spectroscopy quantification: a review of frequency domain methods. *NMR in Biomedicine, 14*, 247-259.

Naressi, A., Couturier, C., Castang, I., de. Beer, R., & Graveron-Demilly, D. (2001). Java-based graphical user interface for MRUI, a software package for quantitation of in vivo medical magnetic resonance spectroscopy signals. *Computers in Biology and Medicine, 31*, 269-286.

Nemoto, I., & Kono, T. (1991). Complex-Valued Neural Networks. *The Institute of Electronics, Information and Communication Engineers (IEICE) Transaction on Information and Systems, 74-D-*(9), 1282-1288 (in Japanese).

Nitta, T. (1991). A Complex Back-propagation Learning, *Transactions of Information Processing Society of Japan, 32*(10), 1319-1329 (in Japanese).

Nitta, T. (1997). An Extention of the Back-Propagation Algorithm to Complex Numbers. *Neural Networks, 10*(8), 1392-1415.

Ogawa, S., Lee, T. M., Nayak, A. S., & Glynn, P. (1990). Oxygenation-sensitive contrast in magnetic resonance image of rodent brain at high magnetic fields. *Magnetic Resonance in Medicine, 14*(1), 68-78.

Provencher, S. W. (2001). Automatic quantification of localized in vivo ^{1}H spectra with LCModel. *NMR in Biomedicine, 14*(4), 260-264.

Rumelhart, D. E, Hinton, G. E., & Williams, R. J. (1986). Learning internal representations by error propagation. In D. E. Rumelhart & J. L. McClelland (Eds.), *Parallel Distributed Processing: Volume 1: Foundations* (pp.318-362). Cambridge, MA, USA: MIT press.

Sijens, P. E., Dagnelie, P. C., Halfwrk, S., van Dijk, P., Wicklow, K., & Oudkerk, M. (1998). Understanding the discrepancies between 31P MR spectroscopy assessed liver metabolite concentrations from different institutions. *Magnetic Resonance Imaging, 16*(2), 205-211.

van den Boogaart, A., Van Hecke, P., Van Hulfel, S., Graveron-Dermilly, D., van Ormondt, D., & de Beer, R. (1996). MRUI: a graphical user interface for accurate routine MRS data analysis. *Proceeding of the European Society for Magnetic Resonance in Medicine and Biology 13th Annual Meeting* (p. 318). Prague.

van Huffel, S., Chen, H., Decanniere, C., & Hecke, P. V. (1994). Algorithm for time-domain NMR data fitting based on total least squares. *Journal of Magnetic Resonance A, 110*, 228-237.

Watanabe, H., Ishihara, Y., Okamoto, K., Oshio, K., Kanamatsu, T., & Tsukada, Y. (2000). 3D localized ^{1}H-^{13}C heteronuclear single-qunantum coherence correlation spectroscopy in vivo. *Magnetic Resonance in Medicine, 43*(2), 200-210.

Zhou, C., & Liu, L. (1993). Complex Hopfield model. *Optics Communications, 103*(1-2), 29-32.

ADDITIONAL READING

NMR and MRS

Brandao, L. A., & Domingues, R. C. (2003). *MR Spectroscopy of the Brain.* Philadelphia, USA: Lippincott Williams & Wilkins.

Damon, B. M., & Price, T. B. *Frequency Asked Questions about Magnetic Resonance Spectroscopy (MRS)*, from http://vuiis.vanderbilt.edu/~nins/MRS_FAQ.htm

De Graaf, R. A. (1999). *In Vivo NMR Spectroscopy: Principles and Techniques.* New York, USA: John Wiley & Sons.

De Graaf, R. A. (2007). *In Vivo NMR Spectroscopy: Principles and Techniques, 2nd Edition.* New York, USA: John Wiley & Sons.

Gadian, D. G. (1995). *NMR and its applications to living systems, second edition* (Oxford Science Publications). New York: Oxford University Press.

Hoch, J. C., & Stern, A. S. (1996). *NMR Data Processing.* New York: Wiley-Liss.

Mukherji, S. K. (Ed.) (1998). *Clinical Applications of MR Spectroscopy.* New York: Wiley-Liss.

Rudin, M. (Ed.) (1992). *In Vivo Magnetic Resonance Spectroscopy I: Probeheads and Radiofrequency Pulses Spectrum Analysis.* Berlin Heidelberg, Germany: Springer-Verlag.

Rudin, M. (Ed.) (1992). *In Vivo Magnetic Resonance Spectroscopy II: Localization and Spectral.* Berlin Heidelberg, Germany: Springer-Verlag.

Rudin, M. (Ed.) (1992). *In Vivo Magnetic Resonance Spectroscopy III: In-Vivo MR Spectroscopy: Potential and Limitations.* Berlin Heidelberg, Germany: Springer-Verlag.

Salibi, N. M., & Brown, M. A. (1997). *Clinical MR Spectroscopy: First Principles.* New York, USA: Wiley-Liss.

Young, I. R., & Charles, H. C. (Ed.) (1996). *MR Spectroscopy: Clinical Application and Techniques.* London: Taylor & Francis Group.

Complex-Valued Neural Networks

Aizenber, I., Myasnikova, E. & Samsonova, M. (2001). Classification of the Images of Gene Expression Patterns Using Neural Networks Based on Multi-valued Neurons. *Bio-Inspired Applications of Connectionism: 6th International Work-Conference on Artificial and Natural Neural Networks, IWANN 2001 Granada, Spain, June 13-15, 2001, Proceedings, Part II, Vol.2085.* (pp. 219-226).

Aizenber, I., Myasnikova, E., Samsonova, M. & Reinitz, J. (2001). Application of the Neural Networks Based on Multi-valued Neurons to Classification of the Images of Gene Expression Patterns. Computational Intelligence. Theory and Applications : *International Conference, 7th Fuzzy Days Dortmund, Germany, October 1-3, 2001, Proceedings, Vol. 2206.* (pp.291-304).

Aoki, H., Azimi-Sadjadi, M.R. & Kosugi, Y. (2000). Image Association Using a Complex-Valued Associative Memory Model. *The Institute of Electronics, Information and Communication Engineers (IEICE) Transaction on Fundamentals of Electronics, Communications and Computer Sciences, E83-A*(9), 1824-1832.

Ceylan, M., Özbay, Y. & Pektatlý, R. (2003). Complex-valued neural network for pattern classification, *Proceedings of the International Journal of Computational Intelligence (IJCI) Proceedings of the International XII, Turkish Symposium on Artificial Intelligence and Neural Networks, vol. 1*, (pp. 344-347).

Ceylan, M., Ceylan, R., Dirgenali, F., Kara, S. & Özbay, Y. (2007). Classification of carotid artery Doppler signals in the early phase of atherosclerosis using complex-valued artificial neural network. *Computers in Biology and Medicine*, 37 (1), 28-36.

De Castro, M.C.F., De Castro, F.C.C., Amaral, J.N. & Franco, F.R.G. (1998). A complex valued Hebbian learning algorithm. *Institute of Electrical and Electronic Engineers (IEEE) International Joint Conference On Neural Networks Processing, Vol.2*, (pp. 1235-1238).

Hirose, A. (Ed.). (2003). *Complex-Valued Neural Networks: Theories and Applications.* Singapore: World Scientific Publishing Co. Pre. Ltd..

Hirose, A. (Ed.). (2006). *Complex-Valued Neural Networks (Studies Computational Intelligence 32).* New York, USA: Springer-Verlag.

Hui, Y. & Smith, M.R. (1995). MRI reconstruction from truncated data using a complex domainbackpropagation neural network. *Proceedings of the Institute of Electrical and Electronic Engineers (IEEE) Pacific Rim Conference on Communications, Computers, and Signal Processing.* (pp.513-516).

Kataoka, M., Kinouchi, M. & Hagiwara, M. (1998). Music information retrieval system using complex-valued recurrentneural networks. *Proceedings of the Institute of Electrical and Electronic Engineers (IEEE) International Conference on Systems, Man, and Cybernetics. Vol.5.* (pp.4290-4295).

Kinouchi, M. & Hagiwara, M. (1996). Memorization of melodies by complex-valued recurrent network. *Proceedings of the Institute of Electrical and Electronic Engineers (IEEE) International Conference on Neural Networks. Vol. 2.* (pp. 1324-1328).

Kondo, K., Iguchi, M., Ishigaki, H., Konishi, Y. & Mabuchi, K. (2001). Design of complex-valued CNN filters for medical image enhancement. *Proceedings of the Joint 9th International Fuzzy Systems Association (IFSA) World Congress and 20th North American Fuzzy Information Processing Society (NAFIPS) International Conference. Vol.3.* (pp.1642-1646).

Morita, N. & Konishi, O. (2004). A Method of Estimation of Magnetic Resonance Spectroscopy Using Complex-Valued Neural Networks, *Transactions of the Institute of Electronics, Information and Comunication engineering D-2*, 86(10), 1460-1467 (in Japanese).

Nitta, T. (2000). An Analysis of the Fundamental Structure of Complex-Valued Neurons. *Neural Processing Letters*, 12 (3), 239-246.

Nitta, T. (2002). Redundancy of the Parameters of the Complex-valued Neural Networks. *Neurocomputing*, 49(1-4), 423-428.

Nitta, T. (2003). On the Inherent Property of the Decision Boundary in Complex-valued Neural Networks, *Neurocomputing*, 50(c), 291-303.

Nitta, T. (2003). Solving the XOR Problem and the Detection of Symmetry Using a Single Complex-valued Neuron, *Neural Networks*, 16,(8), 1101-1105.

Nitta, T. (2003). The Uniqueness Theorem for Complex-valued Neural Networks and the Redundancy of the Parameters, *Systems and Computers in Japan*, 34(14), 54-62.

Nitta, T. (2004). Orthogonality of Decision Boundaries in Complex-Valued Neural Networks, *Neural Computation*, 16(1), 73-97.

Nitta, T. (2004). Reducibility of the Complex-valued Neural Network, *Neural Information Processing - Letters and Reviews*, 2(3), 53-56.

Chapter XII
Flexible Blind Signal Separation in the Complex Domain

Michele Scarpiniti
University of Rome "La Sapienza", Italy

Daniele Vigliano
University of Rome "La Sapienza", Italy

Raffaele Parisi
University of Rome "La Sapienza", Italy

Aurelio Uncini
University of Rome "La Sapienza", Italy

ABSTRACT

This chapter aims at introducing an Independent Component Analysis (ICA) approach to the separation of linear and nonlinear mixtures in complex domain. Source separation is performed by an extension of the INFOMAX approach to the complex environment. The neural network approach is based on an adaptive activation function, whose shape is properly modified during learning. Different models have been used to realize complex nonlinear functions for the linear and the nonlinear environment. In nonlinear environment the nonlinear functions involved during the learning are implemented by the so-called "splitting functions", working on the real and the imaginary part of the signal. In linear environment instead, the "generalized splitting function" which performs a more complete representation of complex function is used. Moreover a simple adaptation algorithm is derived and several experimental results are shown to demonstrate the effectiveness of the proposed method.

INTRODUCTION

In the last years *Blind Source Separation (BSS)* realized through *Independent Component Analysis (ICA)* have raised great interest in the signal processing community (Cichocki & Amari, 2002; Haykin, 2000; Roberts & Everson, 2001). In this context the neural network approach (Haykin, 1999) (usually based on a single layer perceptron (SLP) or a multilayer perceptron (MLP)) seems to be one of the preferred methodologies (Jutten & Herault, 1991; Bell & Sejnowski, 1995); this interest is justified by the large number of different approaches and applications. As a matter of fact, in several fields, from multimedia to telecommunication and to biomedicine, ICA is currently employed to effectively recover the original sources from their mixtures or to remove interfering signals from the signal of interest. Initial studies on ICA aimed at solving the well-known *cocktail party problem*, in a instantaneous or slightly reverberant environment. Pioneering works in ICA appeared at the beginning of the 90's, when Jutten and Herault (1991) presented their "*neurometric architecture*" and Comon (1994) published his often referenced work.

Recently the problem of source separation has been extended to the complex domain (Cardoso & Laheld, 1996; Fiori, Uncini & Piazza, 1999; Bingham & Hyvärinen, 2000), due to the need of frequency domain signal processing which is quite common in telecommunication (Benvenuto, Marchesi, Piazza & Uncini, 1991) and biomedical applications (Calhoun, Adali, Pearlson & Pekar, 2002b; Calhoun, Adali, Pearlson, Van Zijl & Pekar, 2002c). One of the most critical issues in ICA is the matching between the *probability density function (or pdf)* of sources (usually unknown) and the algorithm's parameters (Yang & Amari, 1997). In this way one of the most important issues in designing complex neural networks consists in the definition of the complex activation function (Clarke, 1990; Benvenuto & Piazza, 1992; Kim & Adali, 2001a). In order to improve the pdf matching for the learning algorithm, the so called *Flexible ICA* was recently introduced in (Choi, Cichocki & Amari, 2000; Fiori, 2000; Solazzi, Piazza & Uncini, 2000a; Vigliano & Uncini, 2003; Vigliano, Parisi & Uncini, 2005). Flexible ICA is the approach in which the *activation function (AF)* of the neural network is adaptively modified during the learning. This approach provides faster and more accurate learning by estimating the parameters related to the pdf of signals. In literature it is possible to find several methods based on polynomials (Amari, Cichocki & Yang, 1996) and on parametric function approaches (Pham, Garrat & Jutten, 1992; Solazzi, Piazza & Uncini, 2001).

Moreover the main properties that the complex activation function should satisfy (Kim & Adali, 2002a; Vitagliano, Parisi & Uncini, 2003) are that it should be non linear and bounded and its partial derivatives should exist and be bounded. Unfortunately the analytic and boundedness characteristics are in contrast with the Liouville theorem (Clarke, 1990; Kim & Adali, 2001a). In other words, according to this theorem, an activation function should be bounded almost everywhere in the complex domain (Clarke, 1990; Leung & Haykin, 1991; Georgiou & Koutsougeras, 1992; Kim & Adali, 2000, 2001a, 2002b; Adali, Kim & Calhoun, 2004).

In this context, spline-based nonlinear functions seem to be particularly appealing as activation functions. In fact splines can model a very large number of nonlinear functions and can be easily adapted by suitably varying their control points, with low computational burden.

Unfortunately linear instantaneous mixing models are too unrealistic and unsatisfactory in many applications. Recent studies on ICA in the real domain showed that source separation can be effectively performed also in the case of convolutive nonlinear mixing environments, (Jutten & Karhunen, 2003; Vigliano et al., 2005). In the case of the complex domain only linear instantaneous mixtures have been considered so far (Uncini, Vecci, Campolucci & Piazza, 1999; Bingham & Hyvärinen, 2000; Calhoun et al., 2002b, 2002c; Adali et al., 2004).

A more realistic mixing system inevitably introduces a nonlinear distortion in the signals. In this way the possibility of taking into account these distortions can give better results in signal separation. The problem is that in the nonlinear case the uniqueness of the solution is not guaranteed.

The solution becomes easier in a particular case, called *Post Nonlinear (PNL) mixture*, well-known in literature in the case of the real domain (Taleb & Jutten, 1999; Taleb, 2002). In this context the solution is unique too.

The work here exploited extends the linear and PNL mixture to the complex domain (complex-PNL). This extension requires proper modelling of the nonlinear distorting functions and of the activation functions of a feed-forward network. In this work this modelling has been performed by use of the *splitting functions* described in (Uncini & Piazza, 2003). Another important issue is the definition of the theoretical conditions that grant the uniqueness of the solution.

The chapter is organized as follows: the "Background" describes the most important issues on ICA both in linear and nonlinear case. Next section ("The complex environment") defines the problem of separation in the complex domain. "The flexible activation function" section introduces the solution to the problem of flexibility used in this chapter, while "The de-mixing algorithm and separation architecture" defines in detail the networks used to solve the ICA problems introduced in previous sections. Finally the section "Results" describes experimental tests that demonstrate the effectiveness of the proposed approach.

BACKGROUND

Let us consider M observed signals $x_1[n],\ldots,x_M[n]$ at time n, which are assumed to be the mixtures of N independent source signals $s_1[n],\ldots,s_N[n]$ at time n. The vectors $\mathbf{s}[n]=\left[s_1[n],\ldots,s_N[n]\right]^T$ and $\mathbf{x}[n]=\left[x_1[n],\ldots,x_M[n]\right]^T$ are called the *source vector* and the *observation vector* respectively, T is the transpose operator. The observation vector is obtained by an unknown mixing system $\mathcal{F}\{\bullet\}$: $\mathbf{x}[n]=\mathrm{F}\{\mathbf{s}[n]\}$. In the general form, $\mathcal{F}\{\bullet\}$ may be nonlinear or may be convolutive. The goal of *Blind Signal Separation (BSS)* realized by conventional ICA is to construct a separating system $\mathcal{G}\{\bullet\}$ in order to obtain from the *output vector* $\mathbf{u}[n]=\mathcal{G}\{\mathbf{x}[n]\}$ the estimate of the original source vector (see Figure 1) (Hyvärinen & Oja, 2000; Hyvärinen, Karhunen & Oja, 2001; Roberts & Everson, 2001).

In BSS only one a priori assumption is requested: sources must be statistically independent. However, the *probability density functions (pdf)* of the sources are usually unknown.

The separating system $\mathcal{G}\{\bullet\}$ is constructed in such a way to obtain independent components, since the unique information about the sources is their statistical independence. This fact justifies the use of the Independent Component Analysis (ICA) approach in BSS.

The issue is to understand if the independence of the components of $\mathbf{u}$ implies necessarily the separation of the sources $\mathbf{s}$. Usually the approach to the problem is completely blind and no other knowledge is available on the mixing environment, it is possible only to make some hypotheses and provide the solution for this particular problem. In other words, considering the space of all possible mixing environments, it is possible to grant that output independence produces the separation of signals only making some particular a priori assumption on the mixing environment.

The Case of Linear Mixing Model

First of all the linear and instantaneous mixing model is introduced.

In linear environment both the mixing and the de-mixing models are linear. Under this condition the independence of the output insures the separation of the sources. In other words, linear instantaneous mixtures are separable. The separability and identifiability of the linear mixing model is presented in (Comon, 1994; Eriksson & Koivunen, 2004; Theis, 2004a) as an application of the Darmois-Skitovich's theorem. A consequence of this result is that the vector $\mathbf{s}$ must have at most one Gaussian component.

By a linear instantaneous mixture we mean a mixture of the form

$$\mathbf{x}[n]=\mathbf{A}\mathbf{s}[n] \tag{1}$$

where $\mathbf{A}$ is called the *mixing matrix*. Then a *separating* or *de-mixing matrix* $\mathbf{W}$ must be estimated to generate independent component outputs

$$\mathbf{u}[n]=\mathbf{W}\mathbf{x}[n] \tag{2}$$

Figure 1. Model of the mixing/de-mixing system

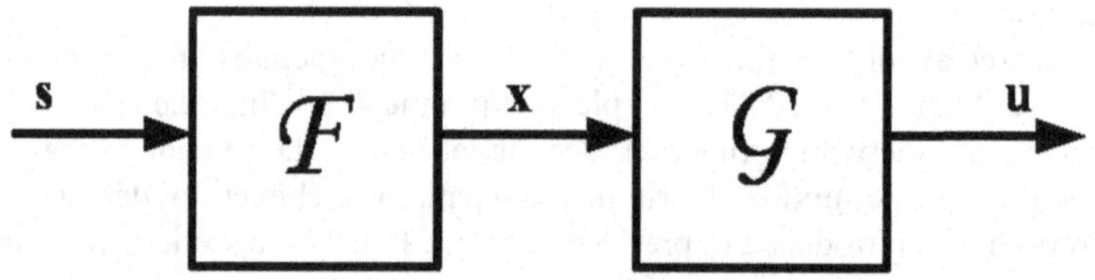

Figure 2. Mixing (left side) and de-mixing (rigth side) models

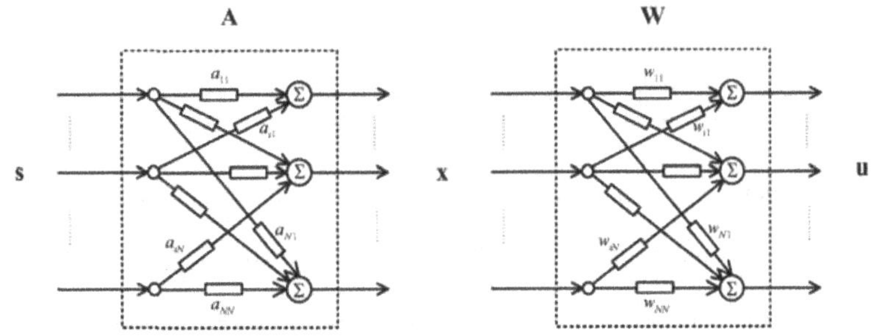

where $\mathbf{u}[n]$ is an estimate of the source vector $\mathbf{s}[n]$ and its components are as independent as possible.

For simplicity we assume that the unknown mixing matrix is square ($M = N$). The linear mixing/de-mixing model is shown in Figure 2.

Although the solution is unique, it suffers for two kinds of ambiguities (Hyvärinen & Oja, 2000; Hyvärinen et al., 2001): it is not possible to determine the variances (energies) of the independent components, so we have a *scaling ambiguity* (in the complex case we have a rotation ambiguity due to the phase); it is not possible to determine the order of the independent components, so we have a *permutation ambiguity*. Formally these two ambiguities can be represented as a permutation $\mathbf{P}$ and a scaling $\mathbf{D}$ (diagonal) matrix:

$$\mathbf{WA} = \mathbf{PD} \tag{3}$$

The Case of Nonlinear Mixing Model

Since the linear mixing model is too poor and unrealistic in many applications, the complexity of the mixing model has been improved considering non linear models.

If the mixing-separating system is nonlinear and no other assumption is given for the mixing operator $\mathcal{F}\{\bullet\}$, a generic de-mixing model $\mathcal{G}\{\bullet\}$ does not assure the existence and uniqueness of the solution, so the separation is not guaranteed. Hence, in general, non-linear mixing models with no particular a priori assumptions are affected by a strong non-uniqueness (Jutten & Herault, 1991; Eriksson & Koivunen, 2002; Theis & Gruber, 2005).

In order to better illustrate this aspect, consider two independent random variables s_1 with uniform distribution in $[0,\ 2\pi)$ and s_2 with Rayleigh distribution, so that its pdf is $p_{s_2}(s_2) = \frac{s_2}{\sigma_2^2} e^{-s_2^2/2}$, with variance $\sigma_2^2 = 1$ (Papoulis, 1991). Given the two nonlinear transformations $y_1 = s_2 \cos s_1$ and $y_2 = s_2 \sin s_1$, the random variables y_1 and y_2 are still independent but are Gaussian distributed, so they cannot be separated as a consequence of the Darmois-Skitovich's theorem (Jutten & Karhunen, 2003). In fact the Jacobian $\mathbf{J}$ of this transformation is:

$$\det(\mathbf{J}) = \det\begin{pmatrix} \dfrac{\partial y_1}{\partial s_1} & \dfrac{\partial y_1}{\partial s_2} \\ \dfrac{\partial y_2}{\partial s_1} & \dfrac{\partial y_2}{\partial s_2} \end{pmatrix} = \det\begin{pmatrix} -s_2 \sin s_1 & \cos s_1 \\ s_2 \cos s_1 & \sin s_1 \end{pmatrix} = -s_2$$

so the joint pdf of $\mathbf{y} = [y_1,\ y_2]$ can be expressed as

$$p_{y_1,y_2}(y_1,y_2)=\frac{p_{s_1,s_2}(s_1,s_2)}{|\det(\mathbf{J})|}=\frac{1}{2\pi}\exp\left(-\frac{y_1^2+y_2^2}{2}\right)=$$
$$=\left(\frac{1}{\sqrt{2\pi}}\exp\left(-\frac{y_1^2}{2}\right)\right)\left(\frac{1}{\sqrt{2\pi}}\exp\left(-\frac{y_2^2}{2}\right)\right)\equiv p_{y_1}(y_1)\cdot p_{y_2}(y_2).$$

This simple example shows that in many cases the independence constraint is not strong enough to recover the original sources, unless additional assumptions about the transformation $\mathcal{F}\{\bullet\}$ or the mixing and de-mixing model are taken.

In practice the main issue is to find the theoretical conditions in terms of sources, mixing environment and recovering architecture capable of guaranteeing the existence of the solution (Theis & Gruber, 2005).

In (Taleb & Jutten, 1999) it has been presented an important result in nonlinear real valued environments: the solution to the BSS problem exists and is unique if we consider a particular mixing model called *Post Non-Linear (PNL) Mixtures*. This model consists in a cascade of a linear mixing stage and a set of nonlinear functions. Hence the mixing system $\mathcal{F}\{\bullet\}$ is (see left side of Figure 3):

$$\mathbf{x}[n]=\mathcal{F}\{\mathbf{s}[n]\}=\mathbf{F}(\mathbf{A}\mathbf{s}[n])=\mathbf{F}(\mathbf{v}[n]) \tag{4}$$

where $\mathbf{v}[n]=\mathbf{A}\mathbf{s}[n]$, the nonlinear function $\mathbf{F}(\mathbf{v}[n])=\left[f_1(v_1[n]),\ldots,f_N(v_N[n])\right]^T$ is the model of the nonlinear distortion and $\mathbf{A}$ is an $N\times N$ matrix ($a_{ij}\in\mathbb{R}$).

The de-mixing model $\mathcal{G}\{\bullet\}$ is constructed by the well-known *mirror model*: the de-mixing system is the mirror image of the mixing one (see right side of Figure 3):

$$\mathbf{u}[n]=\mathcal{G}\{\mathbf{x}[n]\}=\mathbf{W}\cdot\mathbf{G}(\mathbf{x}[n]) \tag{5}$$

where the nonlinear function $\mathbf{G}(\mathbf{x}[n])=\left[g_1(x_1[n]),\ldots,g_N(x_N[n])\right]^T$ is the model of the nonlinear compensating functions and $\mathbf{W}$ is the de-mixing matrix.

Taleb and Jutten (1999) have demonstrated that if $\mathbf{A}$ and $\mathbf{W}$ are regular matrices, $f_i(v_i)$ ($\forall i=1,2,\ldots,N$) are differentiable invertible functions and $h_i=g_i\circ f_i$ satisfy the property that $h_i'(\vartheta)\neq 0$ ($\forall\vartheta\in\mathbb{R}$ and $\forall i=1,2,\ldots,N$) then the PNL mixtures are separable. However the proof in Taleb and Jutten (1999) contains an inaccuracy which was solved by Theis and Gruber (2005).

THE COMPLEX ENVIRONMENT

The aim of this section is to extend the BSS problem introduced above to the complex domain. Let us consider a vector $\mathbf{s}[n]=\left[s_1[n],\ldots,s_N[n]\right]^T$ of N complex sources at time n ($\mathbf{s}[n]\in\mathbb{C}^N$). The k-th source can be expressed as $s_k[n]=s_{Rk}[n]+js_{Ik}[n]$, where s_{Rk} and s_{Ik} are the real and imaginary parts of the k-th complex-valued source signal and $j=\sqrt{-1}$ is the imaginary unit. The goal of BSS is to recover the complex signal $\mathbf{s}[n]$ from observations of the complex mixture $\mathbf{x}[n]=\left[x_1[n],\ldots,x_N[n]\right]^T$, where the k-th mixture can be expressed as $x_k[n]=x_{Rk}[n]+jx_{Ik}[n]$, x_{Rk} and x_{Ik} are its real and imaginary part. In this way the model in eqs. (1) and (2) are still valid but the mixing matrix $\mathbf{A}$ and the de-mixing matrix $\mathbf{W}$ are complex matrices ($a_{ij}\in\mathbb{C}$ and $w_{ij}\in\mathbb{C}$):

Figure 3. The PNL model: mixing model (on left side) and de-mixing mirror model (on rigth side)

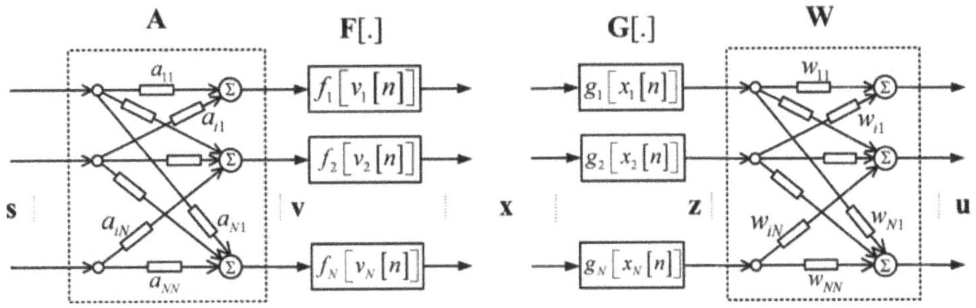

$$\mathbf{x}[n] = \mathbf{A}\mathbf{s}[n] \tag{6}$$

for the mixing model and

$$\mathbf{u}[n] = \mathbf{W}\mathbf{x}[n] \tag{7}$$

for the de-mixing model (see Figure 2).

In similar way we can describe the case of PNL mixtures where the nonlinear function involved in the models are complex functions too:

$$\mathbf{x}[n] = \mathbf{x}_R[n] + j\mathbf{x}_I[n] = \mathbf{F}(\mathbf{v}[n]) \tag{8}$$

where $\mathbf{v}[n] = \mathbf{A}\mathbf{s}[n]$, the nonlinear function $\mathbf{F}(\mathbf{v}[n])$ is the model of the nonlinear distortion in the complex domain and $\mathbf{F}(\mathbf{v}[n]) = \left[f_1(v_1[n]), \cdots, f_N(v_N[n])\right]^T$, where $f_k(v_k[n])$ is the *k*-th complex nonlinear distorting function. For the mirror de-mixing model:

$$\mathbf{u}[n] = \mathbf{u}_R[n] + j\mathbf{u}_I[n] = \mathbf{W}\mathbf{r}[n] = \mathbf{W} \cdot \mathbf{G}(\mathbf{x}[n]) \tag{9}$$

where $\mathbf{r}[n] = \mathbf{G}(\mathbf{x}[n])$, the nonlinear function $\mathbf{G}(\mathbf{x})$ is the model of nonlinear compensating function in the complex domain and $\mathbf{G}(\mathbf{x}[n]) = \left[g_1(x_1[n]), \cdots, g_N(x_N[n])\right]^T$, where $g_k(x_k[n])$ is the *k*-th complex nonlinear compensating function.

The separability, identifiability and uniqueness of the solution are demonstrated in Theis (2004b) and Eriksson and Koivunen (2006) in the linear and instantaneous case, while the PNL mixtures are not treated yet in literature. It is intention of this chapter to extend these results in the nonlinear environment.

The Complex Nonlinear Activation Function

One of the main issues in designing complex neural networks is the presence of complex nonlinear functions involved in the learning processing (Pham et al., 1992; Calhoun et al., 2002c), i.e. complex activation functions or distorting functions (for the nonlinear mixing environment).

Let *h*(*z*) be a complex nonlinear activation function (AF), where $z = z_R + jz_I \in \mathbb{C}$, z_R and z_I are the real and imaginary parts of the complex variable *z*.

The main challenge is the dichotomy between boundedness and analyticity in the complex domain (Kim & Adali, 2002a), as stated by the *Liouville's theorem: complex functions, bounded on the whole complex plane, are either constant or not analytic.* Thus this kind of complex nonlinear functions are not suitable as activation functions of neural networks.

Georgiou and Koutsougeras (1992) defined five properties which should be satisfied by complex nonlinear functions in neural network applications:

1. $h(z)=h(z_R,z_I)=h^R(z_R,z_I)+jh^I(z_R,z_I)$ is nonlinear in z_R and z_I;
2. $h(z)$ is bounded: $|h(z)|\le c<\infty$
3. $h^R_{z_R},h^R_{z_I},h^I_{z_R},h^I_{z_I}$ exist and are bounded (10)
4. $h(z)$ is not entire[1]
5. $h^R_{z_R}h^I_{z_I}\neq h^R_{z_I}h^I_{z_R}$

where $h^R(z_R,z_I)$ and $h^I(z_R,z_I)$ are known as the real part function and imaginary part function of the complex function $h(z)$ respectively, while $h^R_{z_R}=\frac{\partial h^R}{\partial z_R}$, $h^R_{z_I}=\frac{\partial h^R}{\partial z_I}$, $h^I_{z_R}=\frac{\partial h^I}{\partial z_R}$, $h^I_{z_I}=\frac{\partial h^I}{\partial z_I}$.

It should be noted that the properties in eq. (10) require the boundedness of the nonlinear function and its derivatives even when the function is defined in a local domain (Calhoun & Adali, 2002a). By the Liouville's theorem the cost for this restriction is that the function is not analytic.

The boundedness of the AF is essential to prove the universal approximation of a complex feed-forward neural network (Kim & Adali, 2001b, 2002b, 2003). These works have shown that, for the multilayer perceptron (MLP), a complex counterpart of the universal approximation theorem can be realized with activation functions that are entire (analytic for all values of z) but bounded only almost everywhere. This is an extension of the real-valued result in Cybenko (1989) to the complex case.

In this context Kim and Adali (2001a, 2002a, 2003) proposed the use of the so-called *elementary transcendental functions (ETF)*. They classified the ETFs into two categories of unbounded functions, depending on which kind of singularities[2] they possess. The following functions are noted to provide the nonlinear decorrelation required for ICA when used for the nonlinear activation function $h(z)$:

- Circular functions: $tan(z)$, $sin(z)$ and $cot(z)$;
- Inverse circular functions: $tan^{-1}(z)$, $sin^{-1}(z)$ and $cos^{-1}(z)$;
- Hyperbolic functions: $tanh(z)$, $sinh(z)$ and $coth(z)$;
- Inverse hyperbolic functions: $tanh^{-1}(z)$, $sinh^{-1}(z)$ and $cosh^{-1}(z)$.

As expected the trigonometric and the corresponding hyperbolic functions behave very similarly.

Recently Adali et al. (2004) have used these above ETFs as complex activation functions in BSS problems. In particular, the functions: $tan^{-1}(z)$, $sin^{-1}(z)$, $cos^{-1}(z)$ and $tan(z)$, and their hyperbolic counterparts performed consistently well over a wide range of input and mixtures, while the functions: $sin(z)$, $cos(z)$, $cot^{-1}(z)$, $sinh(z)$, $cosh(z)$ and $coth^{-1}(z)$ exhibited unstable behaviour when used for ICA with the algorithm proposed by Bell and Sejnowski (1995) and described later.

According to the properties in eq. (10) listed above, in order to overcome the dichotomy between boundedness and analyticity, complex nonlinear *splitting functions* have been introduced. In this approach real and imaginary parts are processed separately by real-valued nonlinear functions (Benvenuto et al., 1991; Smaragdis, 1998; Uncini & Piazza, 2003). The splitting function

$$h(z) = h(z_R, z_I) = h^R(z_R) + jh^I(z_I) \tag{11}$$

avoids the problem of unboundedness of complex nonlinearities, as stated above, but it cannot be analytic (see Figure 4).

The splitting model of a nonlinear complex valued function is not realistic because usually the real and imaginary part are correlated. According to this issue it is useful to perform a more realistic model of the nonlinear functions. In this way, Vitagliano et al. (2003) proposed a complex neural network based on a couple of bi-dimensional functions (Figure 5) called *generalized splitting function*:

$$h(z) = h(z_R, z_I) = h^R(z_R, z_I) + jh^I(z_R, z_I). \tag{12}$$

In this way $h(z)$ is bounded but it is not analytic. The *Cauchy-Riemann conditions* ($h^R_{z_R} = h^I_{Z_I}$, $h^I_{z_R} = -h^R_{Z_I}$) are not satisfied by the complex function in eq. (12) itself, but can be imposed by an algorithm constraint during the learning process: $h^R_{z_R} = h^I_{z_I} = \left(h^R_{z_R} + h^I_{z_I}\right)/2$ and $h^R_{z_I} = -h^I_{z_R} = \left(h^I_{z_R} + h^R_{z_I}\right)/2$. Note that the Cauchy-Riemann conditions are equivalent to the fifth property in eq. (10).

Another approach for adapting the nonlinearity to the source distribution is introduced in Adali and Li, (2007). It is based on the idea that the simple substitutions $z_R = \left(z + z^*\right)/2$ and $z_I = \left(z - z^*\right)/2j$ (where $(\bullet)^*$ denotes the complex conjugate) allow us to write a given pdf that is $\mathbb{R} \times \mathbb{R} \to \mathbb{R}$ in terms of a function $\mathbb{C} \times \mathbb{C} \to \mathbb{R}$.

The Choice of the De-Mixing Model in the Nonlinear Case

In designing the de-mixing model in the nonlinear environment, it is important to find the theoretical conditions in terms of sources, mixing environment and recovering architecture capable of guaranteeing the existence of the solution (Taleb, 2002).

The model of nonlinear complex compensating functions $\mathbf{G}(\mathbf{x}[n])$ and the activation functions (AF) considered in this chapter are realized by *splitting function* according to eq. (11) (technical details on the implementation of splitting functions will be given in the following sections).

Let $\mathcal{U}$ be the set of all complex vectors $\mathbf{u}$ with joint pdf $p_{\mathbf{u}}(\mathbf{u})$ (see Figure 3) having independent components u_i with marginal pdf $p_{u_i}(u_i)$

$$\mathcal{U} = \left\{ \mathbf{u} \middle| p_{\mathbf{u}}(\mathbf{u}) = \prod_i p_{u_i}(u_i);\ \mathbf{u} = \mathcal{G}\{\mathbf{x}\} = \mathcal{G} \circ \mathcal{F}\{\mathbf{s}\} = \mathcal{H}\{\mathbf{s}\} \right\} \tag{13}$$

Figure 4. Splitting function realization of a complex activation function (AF)

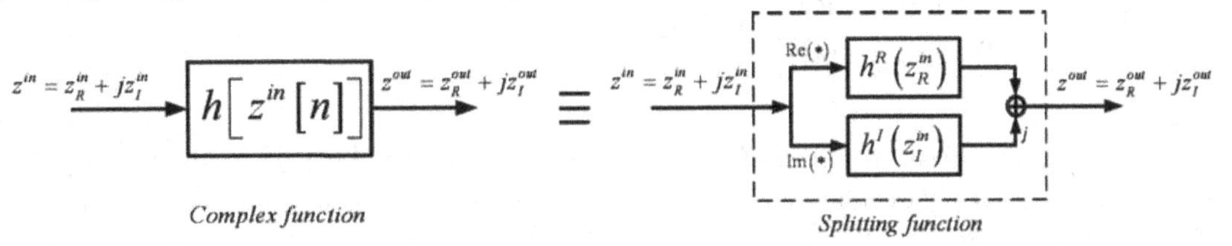

Figure 5. Generalized splitting function realization of a complex activation function (AF)

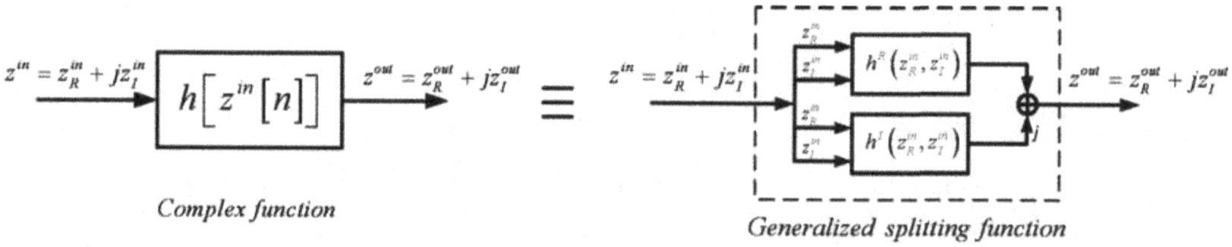

where $\mathcal{H}\{\bullet\}$ is an unspecified application with a non-diagonal Jacobian matrix in general. As a matter of fact, it is possible to find an infinite number of models $\mathcal{G}\{\bullet\}$ such that $\mathbf{u} = \mathcal{G}\{\mathbf{x}\} \in \mathcal{U}$, but not all of them have a diagonal Jacobian matrix. So most of the solutions in $\mathcal{U}$ are not of interest, meaning that output independence by itself is a weak approach to the BSS problem in a general nonlinear environment.

Considering the splitting realization of the complex nonlinear distorting function

$$\mathbf{F}(\mathbf{v}[n]) = \mathbf{F}_R(\mathbf{v}_R[n]) + j\mathbf{F}_I(\mathbf{v}_I[n]), \mathbf{F}_R(\mathbf{v}_R[n]) = \left[f_{R1}(v_{R1}[n]), \ldots, f_{RN}(v_{RN}[n])\right]^T \text{ and}$$
$$\mathbf{F}_I(\mathbf{v}_I[n]) = \left[f_{I1}(v_{I1}[n]), \ldots, f_{IN}(v_{IN}[n])\right]^T,$$

the complex domain mixing environment in eq. (8), represented in Vigliano, Scarpiniti, Parisi and Uncini (2006a, 2008), can be rewritten in the following way:

$$\tilde{\mathbf{x}}[n] = \begin{bmatrix} \mathbf{x}_R[n] \\ \mathbf{x}_I[n] \end{bmatrix} = \begin{bmatrix} \mathbf{F}_R(\mathbf{v}_R[n]) \\ \mathbf{F}_I(\mathbf{v}_I[n]) \end{bmatrix},$$
$$\tilde{\mathbf{v}}[n] = \begin{bmatrix} \mathbf{v}_R[n] \\ \mathbf{v}_I[n] \end{bmatrix} = \begin{bmatrix} \mathbf{A}_R & -\mathbf{A}_I \\ \mathbf{A}_I & \mathbf{A}_R \end{bmatrix} \begin{bmatrix} \mathbf{s}_R[n] \\ \mathbf{s}_I[n] \end{bmatrix} = \tilde{\mathbf{A}}\tilde{\mathbf{s}} \tag{14}$$

where $\mathbf{A}_R$ and $\mathbf{A}_I$ are the real and imaginary parts of the complex mixing matrix $\mathbf{A} = \mathbf{A}_R + j\mathbf{A}_I$.

Equations (14) have the very attractive property of involving only real quantities, thus making it possible to convert complex mixing models into real models of increased size.

It is now possible to define the de-mixing models and to design the network performing the source separation. In particular, a priori knowledge about the mixing model is exploited to design the recovering network. So the *mirror model* in eq. (9) has been introduced to grant the existence and the uniqueness of the solution (up to the trivial indeterminacy of the ICA approach to BSS) as described in (Vigliano et al., 2005, 2008).

The nonlinear complex compensating functions $\mathbf{G}(\bullet)$ have been realized as splitting functions according to eq. (11):

$$\mathbf{G}(\mathbf{x}_R[n] + j\mathbf{x}_I[n]) = \mathbf{G}_R(\mathbf{x}_R[n]) + j\mathbf{G}_I(\mathbf{x}_I[n]).$$

Similarly to eq. (14) it is possible to express the complex de-mixing model in eq. (9) by using real expressions only:

$$\tilde{\mathbf{u}} = \begin{bmatrix} \mathbf{u}_R[n] \\ \mathbf{u}_I[n] \end{bmatrix} = \begin{bmatrix} \mathbf{W}_R & -\mathbf{W}_I \\ \mathbf{W}_I & \mathbf{W}_R \end{bmatrix} \begin{bmatrix} \mathbf{G}_R(\mathbf{x}_R[n]) \\ \mathbf{G}_I(\mathbf{x}_I[n]) \end{bmatrix} = \tilde{\mathbf{W}} \cdot \tilde{\mathbf{G}}[\tilde{\mathbf{x}}] \tag{15}$$

in which $\mathbf{G}_R(\mathbf{x}_R[n]) = \left[g_{R1}(x_{R1}[n]), \cdots, g_{RN}(x_{RN}[n])\right]^T$ and $\mathbf{G}_I(\mathbf{x}_I[n]) = \left[g_{I1}(x_{I1}[n]), \cdots, g_{IN}(x_{IN}[n])\right]^T$ are the real and imaginary parts of the nonlinear compensating functions while $\mathbf{W}_R$ and $\mathbf{W}_I$ are the real and imaginary parts of the complex mixing matrix $\mathbf{W} = \mathbf{W}_R + j\mathbf{W}_I$. Equation (15) represents a real-valued PNL model and preserves all the properties of PNL BSS in the real domain. In particular it is possible to extend to the complex domain the results of (Taleb & Jutten, 1999) for the real PNL case (already applied in Vigliano et al., 2005 for the real convolutive PNL mixture, also known as C-PNL), specifically the proof of existence and uniqueness of the solution.

For the problem herein considered, elements of set $\mathcal{U}$, under proper constraints, differ only for a trivial ambiguity if the mixing model is eq. (8) and the de-mixing model is eq. (9). This is shown in the following proposition.

Proposition 1 *Given the nonlinear complex mixing model* $\mathcal{F}\{\mathbf{A},\mathbf{F}\}$ *in eq. (8) and the recovery model* $\mathcal{G}\{\mathbf{G},\mathbf{W}\}$ *in eq. (9), let us assume that:*

a. $\mathbf{A}$ is a non-singular matrix of non zero entries (both for real and imaginary part);
b. $f_{Ri}(\bullet)$, $f_{Ii}(\bullet)$, $g_{Ri}(\bullet)$, $g_{Ii}(\bullet)$ $(i=1,\ldots,N)$ are differentiable, invertible and zero preserving monotonic functions;
c. $\mathbf{s}[n]=\mathbf{s}_R[n]+j\mathbf{s}_I[n]$ is a complex random vector in which $\mathbf{s}_R[n],\mathbf{s}_I[n]\in\mathbb{R}$. The components of $\mathbf{s}[n]$ are statistically independent and have finite support;
d. the pdf of $s_i[n]$ $(i=1,\ldots,N)$ vanishes for at least one complex component, i.e. $i = 1$.

Then the components of the output vector $\mathbf{u}[n]=\mathbf{u}_R[n]+j\mathbf{u}_I[n]$ are independent if and only if:

$$\mathbf{u}[n]=\mathbf{P\Lambda}\,\mathbf{s}[n]=\mathbf{P}\begin{bmatrix}\lambda_1 & & 0\\ & \ddots & \\ 0 & & \lambda_N\end{bmatrix}\mathbf{s}[n] \tag{16}$$

In eq. (16) $\mathbf{P}$ *is a real permutation matrix and* $\ddot{\mathbf{E}}$ *is a complex diagonal matrix such that each element can be only purely real or imaginary.*

Proof. See Appendix.

Proposition 1 ensures the existence and uniqueness of the solution at the expense of strong constraints on the real and the imaginary parts of the signals.

THE FLEXIBLE ACTIVATION FUNCTION

A second problem in choosing complex AF is the matching between the shape of the AF and the cumulative density function (cdf) of the unknown sources (Yang & Amari, 1997). In fact the separation can be well performed in the case that the AF coincides with the source cdf, as explained hereinafter (see eq. (31)). The idea is to adopt a flexible solution (Choi et al., 2000): the shape of the AF is adaptively changed from data by the use of flexible functions, performing the so-called *Flexible ICA*[3]. This solution allows the separation of signal with a no predefined cumulative density function (cdf) and moreover increases the quality of the separation.

In the last years an increasingly interest in adaptive activation functions has arisen. The simplest solution consists in involving a parametric gain and slope of a sigmoid AF in the learning process. A different approach is based on the use of polynomial functions which allows reducing the size of the network and the connection complexity (Uncini et al., 1999). The digital implementation of this kind of activation function through a look-up-table (LUT) keeps the complexity under control (Piazza, Uncini & Zenobi, 1993) and is easy to realize. The LUT values can be seen as the curve sample points and one can think to iteratively adapt them in order to change the function shape. Only after a certain number of adaptation steps the shape of the activation function can reflect the information represented by data.

However the direct use of a LUT activation function can lead to a huge number of free parameters, so it is more desirable using a suitable interpolation or approximation scheme. The choice of these schemes is not an obvious one: a wrong choice of the interpolation scheme can lead to problems in the development of the learning algorithm (Benvenuto et al., 1991; Guarnieri, Piazza & Uncini, 1999; Uncini et al., 1999; Solazzi et al., 2000a; Solazzi & Uncini, 2000b).

A good interpolation scheme should guarantee a continuous first derivate and the capability to locally adapt the curve: such properties are exhibited by the so-called *piecewise polynomial spline interpolation scheme*. For BSS we prefer an interpolation scheme, due to its local characteristics, which avoids the oscillatory behaviour of the global adaptation of the approximation scheme. There are few splines that interpolate their control points. One that also has a very low computational overhead is the so-called *Catmull-Rom cubic spline* (CR) (Catmull & Rom, 1974; Vecci, Piazza & Uncini, 1998; Uncini et al., 1999; Uncini & Piazza, 2003). There is a regularization property common to most of the polynomial spline basis sets called variation diminishing property (Cottin, Gavrea, Gonska, Kacsò & Zhou, 1999; Schoenberg, 1959; Marsden & Schoenberg, 1998), which ensures the absence of unwanted oscillations of the curve between two consecutive control points. So we can have an exact representation of linear segments.

It is possible to represent the abscissa of each point of the activation function using two parameters: the span index i and the local parameter υ. The i index is used to address the local control points, while the fractional part υ is passed as normalized input to cubic spline function.

A spline approximating its control points is the so-called *B-Spline* (De Boor, 2001; Pierani, Piazza, Solazzi & Uncini, 2000b; Unser, Aldroubi & Eden, 1993). A comparison between these two schemes is shown in left side of Figure 6 which shows graphically the difference between Catmull-Rom Spline and B-Spline for the mono-dimensional spline function; these expressions differ only in the entries of the matrix **M** in eq. (18).

A common expression of these spline activation functions, is the following matrix notation:

$$y = \hat{h}(i,\mathrm{v}) = \mathbf{T}_{\mathrm{v}} \cdot \mathbf{M} \cdot \mathbf{Q}_i \tag{17}$$

which makes explicit the actual parameter vector, a basis matrix and a control points vector, combined using row by column multiplications, where

$$\mathbf{T}_{\mathrm{v}} = \begin{bmatrix} \mathrm{v}^3 & \mathrm{v}^2 & \mathrm{v} & 1 \end{bmatrix}, \mathbf{M} = \frac{1}{2}\begin{bmatrix} -1 & 3 & -3 & 1 \\ 2 & -5 & 4 & -1 \\ -1 & 0 & 1 & 0 \\ 0 & 2 & 0 & 0 \end{bmatrix} \text{ and } \mathbf{Q}_i = \begin{bmatrix} Q_i \\ Q_{i+1} \\ Q_{i+2} \\ Q_{i+3} \end{bmatrix} \tag{18}$$

where $Q_i = \begin{bmatrix} q_{u,i} & q_{y,i} \end{bmatrix}^T$, $q_{u,i}$ and $q_{y,i}$ are the coordinates of the i-th control point Q_i (contained in the two-dimensional vector y) and $0 \le \mathrm{v} < 1$ is the local abscissa. If the abscissas along the u-axis are uniformly sampled,

Figure 6. Mono and Bi-dimensional cubic spline functions

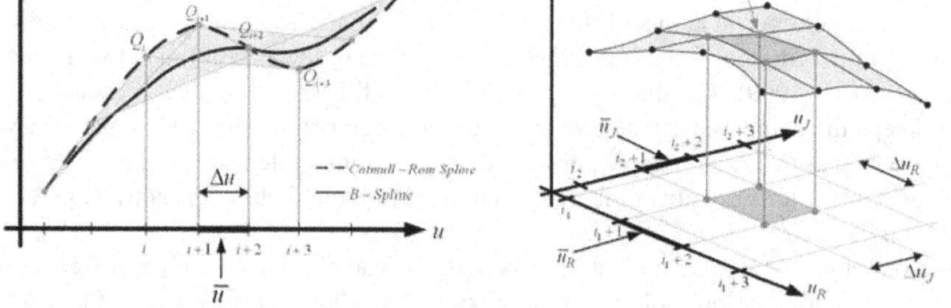

$\Delta u = q_{u,i+1} - q_{u,i} = const$ for every i, then the cubic polynomial becomes a first degree polynomial and the vector y becomes a one-dimensional vector containing only the y-axis of the curve.

The entire approximation is represented through the concatenation of local cubic spline functions each controlled by 4 control points defined by the two local parameters: i and υ. Given an input value $\overline{u}$ we can calculate these parameters using two internal dummy variables ζ and $\overline{\zeta}$ as follows:

$$\begin{aligned}
\overline{\zeta} &= \frac{\overline{u}}{\Delta u} + \frac{N-2}{2} \\
\zeta &= \begin{cases} 1 & \overline{\zeta} < 1 \\ \overline{\zeta} & 1 \leq \overline{\zeta} \leq N-3 \\ N-3 & \overline{\zeta} > N-3 \end{cases} \\
i &= \lfloor \zeta \rfloor \\
\nu &= \zeta - i
\end{aligned} \tag{19}$$

where $\lfloor \bullet \rfloor$ is the floor operator that returns the highest integer less than or equal to its input and N is the number of spline control points.

An additional and important constraint is to force the activation function to be a limiting function, imposing to be constant for $u \to \pm\infty$, while maintaining the ability to modify its shape inside these constant values. We can fix the first two and the last two control points. So for each input $\overline{u}$, we can adapt two points on the left and two on the right, while all the other control points are fixed.

We can generalize the theory discussed above to realize these functions as hyper-surface interpolation of some control points using higher order interpolants (Solazzi et al., 2000a; Solazzi & Uncini, 2000b, 2004). In particular piecewise of cubic spline are here employed in order to render the hyper-surface continuous in its partial derivatives. The entire approximation is represented through the concatenation of local functions each centered and controlled by $4^2 = 16$ control points, which lie on a regular 2D grid in $\mathbb{R}^2$, defined over the region $0 \leq \nu_R, \nu_I < 1$, and in matrix formulation it is expressed as follows:

$$y = \hat{h}(i_R, i_I; \nu_R, \nu_I) = \mathbf{T}_{\nu I} \cdot \mathbf{M} \cdot (\mathbf{T}_{\nu R} \cdot \mathbf{M} \cdot \mathbf{Q}_{[2]}^{(i_R, i_I)})^T \tag{20}$$

where $\mathbf{T}_{\nu R} = \begin{bmatrix} \nu_R^3 & \nu_R^2 & \nu_R & 1 \end{bmatrix}$, $\mathbf{T}_{\nu I} = \begin{bmatrix} \nu_I^3 & \nu_I^2 & \nu_I & 1 \end{bmatrix}$, $\mathbf{M}$ is the same defined in (18) and $\mathbf{Q}_{[2]}^{(i_R, i_I)}$ is a structure collecting the local control points:

$$\mathbf{Q}_{[2]}^{(i_R, i_I)} = \begin{bmatrix} Q^{(i_R-1, i_I-1)} & Q^{(i_R-1, i_I)} & Q^{(i_R-1, i_I+1)} & Q^{(i_R-1, i_I+2)} \\ Q^{(i_R, i_I-1)} & Q^{(i_R, i_I)} & Q^{(i_R, i_I+1)} & Q^{(i_R, i_I+2)} \\ Q^{(i_R+1, i_I-1)} & Q^{(i_R+1, i_I)} & Q^{(i_R+1, i_I+1)} & Q^{(i_R+1, i_I+2)} \\ Q^{(i_R+2, i_I-1)} & Q^{(i_R+2, i_I)} & Q^{(i_R+2, i_I+1)} & Q^{(i_R+2, i_I+2)} \end{bmatrix}$$

where $Q^{(i_R, i_I)} = \begin{bmatrix} q_{u_R,i} & q_{u_I,i} & q_{y,i} \end{bmatrix}^T$, $q_{u_R,i}$, $q_{u_I,i}$ are the abscissas along the u_R-axis and the u_I-axis and $q_{y,i}$ is the ordinate of the control point $Q^{(i_R, i_I)}$. If the abscissas along the u_R-axis and the u_I-axis are uniformly sampled, the structure $\mathbf{Q}_{[2]}^{(i_R, i_I)}$ becomes a simple 4×4 matrix. An example of cubic 2D spline is showed in the right side of Figure 6.

The new idea is to use spline-based functions for $h^R(\bullet)$ and $h^I(\bullet)$ in eq. (11). Thus, remembering the spline matrix formulation in eq. (17) we can use two mono-dimensional spline functions. First we calculate the indexes span i_R and i_I, and the local parameters ν_R and ν_J, as stated by equations (19), then the AF in eq. (11) can be written as follows using eq. (17):

$$y_k = h_k^R(u_{Rk}) + jh_k^I(u_{Ik}) = \mathbf{T}(u_{Rk})\cdot\mathbf{M}\cdot\mathbf{Q}_{i_R}^R + j\mathbf{T}(u_{Ik})\cdot\mathbf{M}\cdot\mathbf{Q}_{i_I}^I \tag{21}$$

where $y_k = y_{Rk} + jy_{Ik}$ is the k-th complex output corresponding to the k-th input $u_k = u_{Rk} + ju_{Ik}$ of the k-th activation function, $\mathbf{Q}_{i_R}^R$ and $\mathbf{Q}_{i_I}^I$ collect the control points of the real and imaginary curve, respectively. The data path is reported in Figure 7.

The corresponding neural network is called *Complex valued Adaptive Spline Neural Network (CASNN).*

Unfortunately the real and imaginary parts of a complex signal are usually correlated, not split in separate channels. In this way we need a better model of the complex AF. In this way, Vitagliano et al. (2003) proposed a complex neural network based on bi-dimensional spline AF.

If we consider the expression (12) of a complex function in relation to the real and imaginary part, we can render each of the two bi-dimensional real functions $h^R(u_R, u_I)$ and $h^I(u_R, u_I)$ with bi-dimensional splines: one plays the role of the real part and one the imaginary part of the complex activation function. This AF is known as *generalized splitting activation function (GSAF)* (Vitagliano et al, 2003; Scarpiniti, Vigliano, Parisi & Uncini, 2007).

Using the compact matrix formulation in eq. (20) we have for the k-th AF:

$$\begin{aligned} y_{Rk} &= h_k^R(u_{Rk}, u_{Ik}) = \mathbf{T}_{\nu I}(u_{Ik})\cdot\mathbf{M}\cdot(\mathbf{T}_{\nu R}(u_{Rk})\cdot\mathbf{M}\cdot\mathbf{Q}_{[2]R}^{(i_R,i_I)})^T, \\ y_{Ik} &= h_k^I(u_{Rk}, u_{Ik}) = \mathbf{T}_{\nu I}(u_{Ik})\cdot\mathbf{M}\cdot(\mathbf{T}_{\nu R}(u_{Rk})\cdot\mathbf{M}\cdot\mathbf{Q}_{[2]I}^{(i_R,i_I)})^T, \\ y_k &= y_{Rk} + jy_{Ik}. \end{aligned} \tag{22}$$

Both the real and imaginary part of the k-th input signal u_k are evaluated by two flexible and bi-dimensional functions. The output of each function is real-valued; we impose these two outputs to be the real and the imaginary part of the output of the complex activation function respectively. The data path is reported in Figure 8.

THE DE-MIXING ALGORITHM AND SEPARATION ARCHITECTURE

Efficient design of the de-mixing strategy requires the choice of a proper de-mixing model, a cost function able to measure the independence of the outputs and an effective optimization method. In this section a feed-forward neural network will be proposed and investigated as effective de-mixing model. Network parameters will be iteratively adapted (i.e. learned) on the basis of a measure of the output independence.

As said in the Introduction section several approaches to blind separation of sources exist, but in this chapter we focus the attention on a set of algorithms which are based on the *INFOMAX principle* introduced by Bell and Sejnowski (1995). This learning algorithm maximizes information transferred by the nonlinear network shown in Figure 9, assuming no knowledge on input vector distribution.

INFOMAX addresses the problem of maximizing the mutual information $I(\mathbf{y}, \mathbf{x})$ (Cover & Tomas, 2006), between the input vector $\mathbf{x}$ and an invertible nonlinear transform of it, $\mathbf{y}$ obtained as

$$\mathbf{y} = \mathbf{h}(\mathbf{u}) = \mathbf{h}(\mathbf{W}\mathbf{x}) \tag{23}$$

where $\mathbf{W}$ is an $N \times N$ matrix and $\mathbf{h}(\mathbf{u}) = \left[h_1(u_1), \ldots, h_N(u_N)\right]^T$ is the nonlinear function vector (see the sixth chapter in Haykin, 2000). Because the mapping in eq. (23) is deterministic, maximizing $I(\mathbf{y}, \mathbf{x})$ is the same that maximizing the joint entropy $H(\mathbf{y})$. In fact the following relation holds:

Figure 7. Mono-dimensional spline data path of a complex activation function (AF)

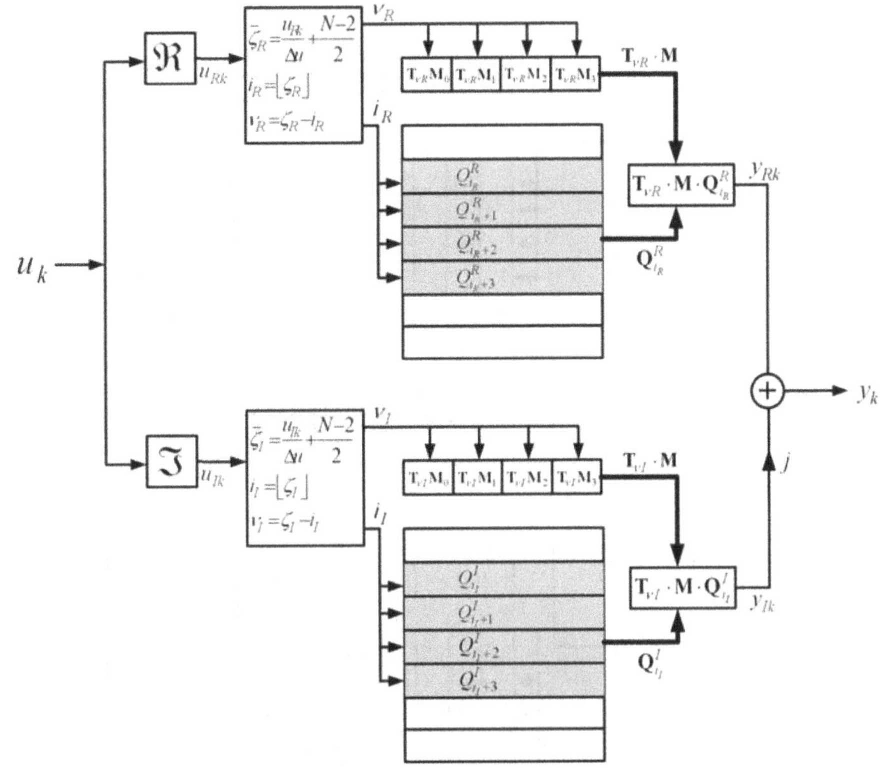

$$I(\mathbf{y},\mathbf{x}) = H(\mathbf{y}) - H(\mathbf{y}|\mathbf{x}) \tag{24}$$

In this way INFOMAX is equivalent to the entropy maximization.

The aim of INFOMAX algorithm is to adapt the entries of the matrix $\mathbf{W}$ maximizing the joint entropy $H(\mathbf{y})$ in eq. (24). In order to derive the learning algorithm let we pose $p_{\mathbf{x}}(\mathbf{x})$ and $p_{\mathbf{y}}(\mathbf{y})$ the probability density functions (pdf) of the network input and output respectively which have to satisfy the relation (Papoulis, 1991):

$$p_{\mathbf{y}}(\mathbf{y}) = \frac{p_{\mathbf{x}}(\mathbf{x})}{|\det \mathbf{J}|} \tag{25}$$

where $|\bullet|$ denotes the absolute value and $\mathbf{J}$ the Jacobian matrix of the transformation: $\mathbf{J} = \left[\partial y_i / \partial x_j\right]_{ij}$.

Since the joint entropy of network output is defined as $H(\mathbf{y}) = -E\{\ln p_{\mathbf{y}}(\mathbf{y})\}$ (Cover & Tomas, 2006), where $E\{\bullet\}$ is the expected value operator, substituting into it the eq. (25) we obtain:

$$H(\mathbf{y}) = E\{\ln|\det \mathbf{J}|\} + H(\mathbf{x}). \tag{26}$$

Now we can note that $\frac{\partial y_i}{\partial x_j} = \frac{\partial y_i}{\partial u_i}\frac{\partial u_i}{\partial x_j} = h_i'(u_i)\cdot w_{ij}$, so we obtain

Figure 8. Bi-dimensional spline data path of a complex activation function (AF)

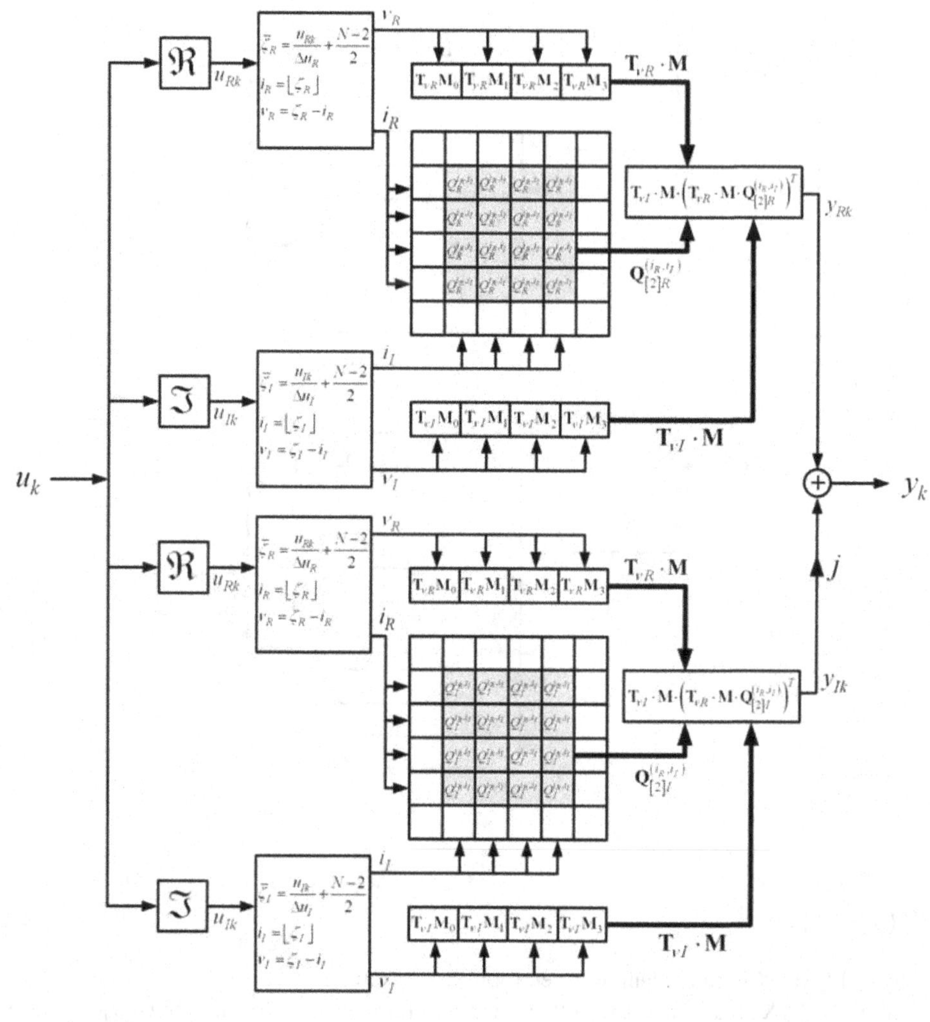

$$\ln|\det \mathbf{J}| = \ln \det \mathbf{W} + \sum_{i=1}^{N} \ln|h_i'|. \tag{27}$$

Hence, the expression of the joint entropy $H(\mathbf{y})$ (ignoring the expected value operator $E\{\bullet\}$, replacing by instantaneous values) is:

$$H(\mathbf{y}) = H(\mathbf{x}) + \ln \det \mathbf{W} + \sum_{i=1}^{N} \ln|h_i'|. \tag{28}$$

The maximization (or minimization) of a generic cost function $\mathcal{L}\{\mathbf{\Phi}\}$ with respect a parameter Φ can be obtained by the application of the stochastic gradient method at ($l+1$)-th iteration

$$\mathbf{\Phi}(l+1)=\mathbf{\Phi}(l)+\eta_{\mathbf{\Phi}}\frac{\partial\mathcal{L}\{\mathbf{\Phi}(l)\}}{\partial\mathbf{\Phi}}=\mathbf{\Phi}(l)+\eta_{\mathbf{\Phi}}\Delta\mathbf{\Phi}(l) \tag{29}$$

where η_{Φ} is the learning rate.

Remembering that $H(\mathbf{x})$ is not affected by the parameters that we are learning, it is possible to write the learning rule for $\mathbf{W}$ using the stochastic gradient method in eq. (29) as follows:

$$\Delta\mathbf{W}=\frac{\partial H(\mathbf{y})}{\partial\mathbf{W}}=\mathbf{W}^{-T}+\mathbf{\Psi}\mathbf{x}^{T} \tag{30}$$

where $\mathbf{W}^{-T}=\left(\mathbf{W}^{-1}\right)^{T}$, $\mathbf{\Psi}=\left[\Psi_{1},\ldots,\Psi_{N}\right]^{T}$ and $\Psi_{k}=h_{k}''(u_{k})\big/h_{k}'(u_{k})$.

Moreover we can introduce the mutual information of the linear outputs $\mathbf{u}$ as the Kullback-Leibler distance (Cover & Tomas, 2006) of the output distribution $I(\mathbf{u})=E\left\{\ln\left(p_{\mathbf{u}}(\mathbf{u})\big/\prod_{i=1}^{N}p_{u_i}(u_i)\right)\right\}$, where $p_{\mathbf{u}}(\mathbf{u})$ is the joint pdf of the output vector $\mathbf{u}$ and $p_{u_i}(u_i)$ are the marginal pdfs. Using this relation and the eq. (27) in the definition of entropy, after some easy passes, we obtain:

$$H(\mathbf{y})=-I(\mathbf{u})+E\left\{\sum_{i=1}^{N}\ln\frac{|h_i'|}{p_{u_i}(u_i)}\right\}. \tag{31}$$

Thus if $|h_i'|=p_{u_i}(u_i)$ $(\forall i)$ then maximizing the joint entropy $H(\mathbf{y})$ can solve the ICA problem. In this way $h_i(u_i)$ should be the cumulative density function (cdf) of the *i*-th estimated source. The use of an adaptive AF can successfully fulfils the matching of $h_i(u_i)$ to the cdf of the *i*-th source.

From eq. (31) the INFOMAX algorithm can be performed by two equivalent approach: maximizing the joint entropy of the network output (*ME approach*) or minimizing the mutual information (*MMI approach*) (Yang & Amari, 1997; Theis, Bauer & Lang, 2002).

Our approach performs separation by maximization of the joint entropy of the network outputs $\mathbf{y}$, extending the conventional real-domain *INFOMAX algorithm* to the complex domain (Calhoun & Adali, 2002a). The choice of the ME approach is supported by the fact that the joint entropy is an intuitively meaningful contrast function (an objective function for source separation, which measures the statistical independence), it usually allows simple learning rules and it is closely related to several other approaches (Lee, Girolami, Bell & Sejnowsky, 2000).

The Case of Linear Environment

The architecture used to realize the model $\mathbf{W}$ in eq. (7) is represented in Figure 10a.

Let we consider first the case of using the splitting activation function in eq. (11) realized through the mono-dimensional spline activation function in eq. (21), assuming

$$\begin{aligned}\mathbf{y}&=\mathbf{h}(\mathbf{u})=\mathbf{h}_R(\mathbf{u}_R)+j\mathbf{h}_I(\mathbf{u}_I)\\ y_k&=y_{Rk}+jy_{Ik}=h_{Rk}(u_{Rk})+jh_{Ik}(u_{Ik})\end{aligned} \tag{32}$$

where $\mathbf{h}$ is the activation function vector and y_k is the *k*-th element in $\mathbf{y}$, the expression of the complex output vector $\mathbf{y}$ can be rewritten (see eqs. (14) and (15)) by using only real terms:

Figure 9. The nonlinear network used to introduce the INFOMAX principle

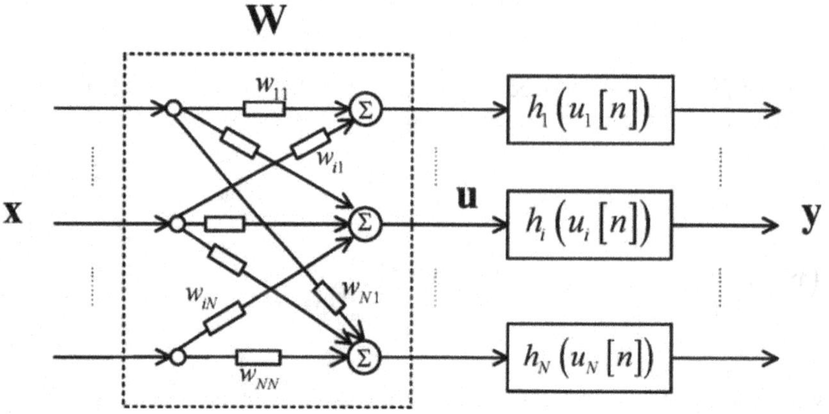

$$\tilde{\mathbf{y}} = \begin{bmatrix} \mathbf{y}_R[n] \\ \mathbf{y}_I[n] \end{bmatrix} = \begin{bmatrix} \mathbf{h}_R(\mathbf{u}_R[n]) \\ \mathbf{h}_I(\mathbf{u}_I[n]) \end{bmatrix}. \tag{33}$$

In this way $\tilde{\mathbf{y}}$ is a real vector of 2N elements. Considering a de-mixing model with parameters $\mathbf{\Phi} = \{w_{ij}, \mathbf{\Phi}_h | \forall i, j\}$, where w_{ij} are the entries in matrix **W** and $\mathbf{\Phi}_h = \{Q_R^h, Q_I^h\}$ are the spline control points for the real and imaginary part of the AF, the cost function to be maximized is the joint entropy of the signals after the activation functions, similarly to the eq. (26):

$$\mathcal{L}\{\mathbf{y}[n], \mathbf{\Phi}\} = H(\tilde{\mathbf{y}}) = -E\{\ln(p_{\tilde{\mathbf{y}}}(\tilde{\mathbf{y}}))\} = H(\tilde{\mathbf{x}}) + E\{\ln(\tilde{\mathbf{J}})\} \tag{34}$$

In eq. (34) the output pdf $p_{\tilde{\mathbf{y}}}(\tilde{\mathbf{y}})$ can be expressed using eq. (25) as a function of the model's parameters and of $H(\tilde{\mathbf{x}})$which does not depend on the model's parameter. In this case the Jacobian of the transformation between $\tilde{\mathbf{x}}$ and $\tilde{\mathbf{y}}$ can be expressed as follows:

$$\det(\tilde{\mathbf{J}}) = \prod_{k=1}^{N} \dot{y}_k \det(\tilde{\mathbf{W}}). \tag{35}$$

In eq. (35) $\dot{y}_k$ is the derivative of the *k*-th elements of $\tilde{\mathbf{y}}$.

Having explored the mixing model, the associated cost function and the recovering network, the next step is to derive the learning rules. Substituting eq. (35) in eq. (34) we obtain the cost function whose derivation with respect the elements of Φ leads to

$$\frac{\partial}{\partial \mathbf{\Phi}} \mathcal{L}\{\mathbf{y}, \mathbf{\Phi}\} = \frac{\partial}{\partial \mathbf{\Phi}} \left[\ln\left(\det(\tilde{\mathbf{W}})\right) + \sum_{k=1}^{N} \ln \dot{y}_{Rk} + \sum_{k=1}^{N} \ln \dot{y}_{Ik} \right] \tag{36}$$

where $\dot{y}_{Rk}$ and $\dot{y}_{Ik}$ denote the derivative of the *k*-th real and imaginary parts of the network output **y**. In eq. (36) expected values have been replaced by instantaneous values.

Maximization of eq. (36) by the stochastic gradient method in eq. (29) yields three learning rules (see Uncini and Piazza (2003) for major details). The learning rule for the network's weights is:

$$\Delta\mathbf{W} = \Delta\mathbf{W}_R + j\Delta\mathbf{W}_I = \mathbf{W}^{-H} + \mathbf{\Psi}\mathbf{x}^H \tag{37}$$

where H is the Hermitian operator,

$$\mathbf{W}^{-H} = \left(\mathbf{W}^{-1}\right)^{H}, \boldsymbol{\Psi} = \boldsymbol{\Psi}_R + j\boldsymbol{\Psi}_I, \psi_R = \left[\Psi_{R1},\ldots,\Psi_{RN}\right]^T, \psi_I = \left[\Psi_{I1},\ldots,\Psi_{IN}\right]^T, \Psi_{Rk} = \ddot{y}_{Rk} / \dot{y}_{Rk}, \Psi_{Ik} = \ddot{y}_{Ik} / \dot{y}_{Ik},$$

$\dot{y}_{Rk}$ is the derivative of the k-th real part element of $\mathbf{y}$ while $\ddot{y}_{Rk}$ is the second order derivative and similarly for the imaginary counterpart $\dot{y}_{Ik}$ and $\ddot{y}_{Ik}$. Using the matrix notation in eq. (17) the terms Ψ_{Rk} and Ψ_{Ik} can be expressed as follows:

$$\Psi_{Rk} = \frac{1}{\Delta u_R} \frac{\ddot{\mathbf{T}}_{\nu R}\mathbf{M}\mathbf{Q}_R^h}{\dot{\mathbf{T}}_{\nu R}\mathbf{M}\mathbf{Q}_R^h},$$
$$\Psi_{Ik} = \frac{1}{\Delta u_I} \frac{\ddot{\mathbf{T}}_{\nu I}\mathbf{M}\mathbf{Q}_I^h}{\dot{\mathbf{T}}_{\nu I}\mathbf{M}\mathbf{Q}_I^h} \qquad (38)$$

where $\dot{\mathbf{T}}_{\nu R} = \begin{bmatrix} 3\nu_R^2 & 2\nu_R & 1 & 0 \end{bmatrix}$, $\ddot{\mathbf{T}}_{\nu R} = \begin{bmatrix} 6\nu_R & 2 & 0 & 0 \end{bmatrix}$ and similar for the imaginary counterpart $\dot{\mathbf{T}}_{\nu I}$ and $\ddot{\mathbf{T}}_{\nu I}$.

The learning rules for the spline activation functions are:

$$\Delta\mathbf{Q}^h_{\mathrm{R},k,i+m} = \frac{\dot{\mathbf{T}}_{\nu R}(u_{\mathrm{R}k})(\mathbf{M})_m}{\dot{\mathbf{T}}_{\nu R}(u_{\mathrm{R}k})\mathbf{M}\mathbf{Q}^h_{\mathrm{R},k,i+m}},$$
$$\Delta\mathbf{Q}^h_{\mathrm{I},k,i+m} = \frac{\dot{\mathbf{T}}_{\nu I}(u_{\mathrm{I}k})(\mathbf{M})_m}{\dot{\mathbf{T}}_{\nu I}(u_{\mathrm{I}k})\mathbf{M}\mathbf{Q}^h_{\mathrm{I},k,i+m}} \qquad (39)$$

where $(\mathbf{M})_m$ is the m-th column of the $\mathbf{M}$ matrix.

We can generalize this algorithm using the generalized splitting function in eq. (12) realizing the complex AFs with the *bi-dimensional spline function* in eq. (22) (Scarpiniti et al., 2007, 2008) shown in Figure 10b. In this case the algorithm is formally very similar to the previous case: the learning rule for the matrix weights w_{ij} is formally identical to eq. (37), but the generic k-th terms Ψ_{Rk} and Ψ_{Ik} of the vector $\boldsymbol{\Psi}$ contain the partial and cross derivatives of network outputs y_{Rk} and y_{Ik} (outputs of bi-dimensional functions) with respect the two variables u_{Rk} and u_{Ik}.

The learning rule for the real activation function becomes

$$\Delta\mathbf{Q}^h_{\mathrm{R},k,i_R+m_R,i_I+m_I} = 2\left(\frac{\left(\mathbf{T}_{\nu I}\cdot\mathbf{M}\cdot\left(\dot{\mathbf{T}}_{\nu R}\cdot\mathbf{M}\cdot\mathbf{Q}^{(i_R,i_I)}_{[2]R}\right)^T\right)\left(\mathbf{T}_{\nu I}\cdot\mathbf{M}_{m_J}\cdot\left(\dot{\mathbf{T}}_{\nu R}\cdot\mathbf{M}_{m_R}\right)^T\right)}{\left(\mathbf{T}_{\nu I}\cdot\mathbf{M}\cdot\left(\dot{\mathbf{T}}_{\nu R}\cdot\mathbf{M}\cdot\mathbf{Q}^{(i_R,i_I)}_{[2]R}\right)^T\right)^2+\left(\dot{\mathbf{T}}_{\nu I}\cdot\mathbf{M}\cdot\left(\mathbf{T}_{\nu R}\cdot\mathbf{M}\cdot\mathbf{Q}^{(i_R,i_I)}_{[2]R}\right)^T\right)^2} + \right.$$
$$\left. + \frac{\left(\dot{\mathbf{T}}_{\nu I}\cdot\mathbf{M}\cdot\left(\mathbf{T}_{\nu R}\cdot\mathbf{M}\cdot\mathbf{Q}^{(i_R,i_I)}_{[2]R}\right)^T\right)\left(\dot{\mathbf{T}}_{\nu I}\cdot\mathbf{M}_{m_J}\cdot\left(\mathbf{T}_{\nu R}\cdot\mathbf{M}_{m_R}\right)^T\right)}{\left(\mathbf{T}_{\nu I}\cdot\mathbf{M}\cdot\left(\dot{\mathbf{T}}_{\nu R}\cdot\mathbf{M}\cdot\mathbf{Q}^{(i_R,i_I)}_{[2]R}\right)^T\right)^2+\left(\dot{\mathbf{T}}_{\nu I}\cdot\mathbf{M}\cdot\left(\mathbf{T}_{\nu R}\cdot\mathbf{M}\cdot\mathbf{Q}^{(i_R,i_I)}_{[2]R}\right)^T\right)^2} \right) \qquad (40)$$

where $\mathbf{M}_k$ is a matrix in which all the elements are zero, except the k-th column, which is equal to the k-th column of $\mathbf{M}$. A similar equation can be resulted for the imaginary surface $\Delta\mathbf{Q}^h_{\mathrm{I},k,i_R+m_R,i_I+m_I}$. For a complete derivation of the learning rules see (Scarpiniti et al., 2008).

The Case of Nonlinear Environment

The architecture used to realize the model $\mathcal{G}\{\mathbf{G},\mathbf{W}\}$ in eq. (9) is shown in Figure 11.

In the same way as the case of linear environment the de-mixing algorithm is based on an extension of the *INFOMAX algorithm* (Bell & Sejnowski, 1995), performing the ME approach.

The network output $\mathbf{y}$ is similar to eq. (32). The network parameters are $\mathbf{\Phi} = \{w_{ij}, \mathbf{\Phi}_h, \mathbf{\Phi}_G \,|\, \forall i,j\}$, where w_{ij} are the entries in matrix $\mathbf{W}$, $\mathbf{\Phi}_h = \{Q_R^h, Q_I^h\}$ are the spline control points for the real and imaginary part of the AF and $\mathbf{\Phi}_G = \{Q_R^G, Q_I^G\}$ are the spline control points for the real and imaginary part of the nonlinear compensating functions $\mathbf{G}(\bullet)$. So using eq. (33) the cost function $\mathcal{L}\{\mathbf{y}[n],\mathbf{\Phi}\}$ to be maximized is the joint entropy in eq. (34).

In this case the Jacobian of the transformation between $\tilde{\mathbf{x}}$ and $\tilde{\mathbf{y}}$ can be expressed as follows:

$$\det(\tilde{\mathbf{J}}) = \prod_{k=1}^{N} \dot{\tilde{y}}_k \dot{\tilde{r}}_k \det(\tilde{\mathbf{W}}). \tag{41}$$

In eq. (41) $\dot{\tilde{y}}_k$ and $\dot{\tilde{r}}_k$ are the derivative of the k-th element of $\tilde{\mathbf{y}}$ and $\tilde{\mathbf{r}}$ respectively.

Inserting eq. (41) in the derivation of the cost function eq. (34) with respect to the elements of parameters $\mathbf{\Phi}$ we obtain

$$\frac{\partial}{\partial \mathbf{\Phi}} \mathcal{L}\{\mathbf{y},\mathbf{\Phi}\} = \frac{\partial}{\partial \mathbf{\Phi}} \left[\ln\left(\det(\tilde{\mathbf{W}})\right) + \sum_{k=1}^{N} \ln \dot{y}_{Rk} + \sum_{k=1}^{N} \ln \dot{y}_{Ik} + \sum_{k=1}^{N} \ln \dot{r}_{Rk} + \sum_{k=1}^{N} \ln \dot{r}_{Ik} \right]. \tag{42}$$

In eq. (42) expected values have been replaced by instantaneous values.

Maximization of eq. (42) by the stochastic gradient method eq. (29) yields to five learning rules (see Vigliano et al. (2008) for major details). The learning rule for the network's weights is:

$$\Delta\mathbf{W} = \Delta\mathbf{W}_R + j\Delta\mathbf{W}_I = \mathbf{W}^{-H} + \mathbf{\Psi}\,\mathbf{r}^H \tag{43}$$

Figure 10. De-mixing model in linear environment. The activation functions are realized with splitting functions a) and generalized splitting functions b)

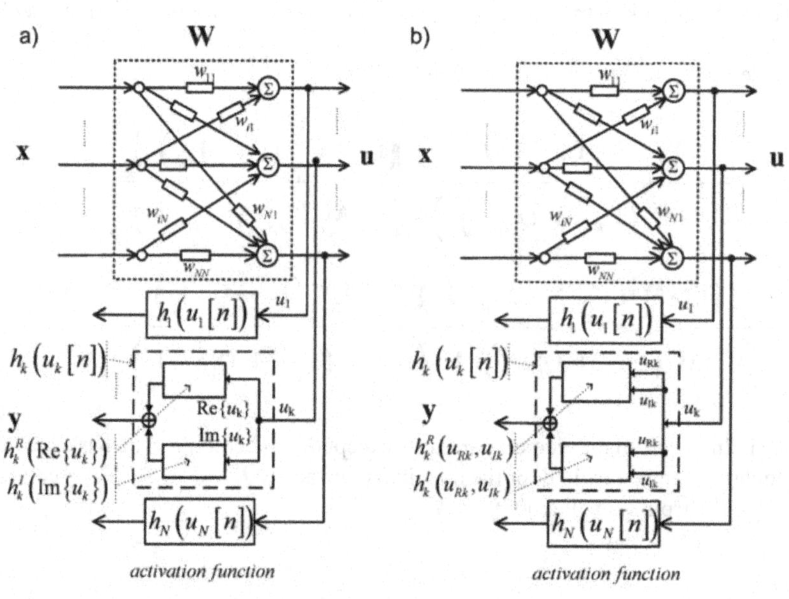

that is formally identical to eq. (37) and $\boldsymbol{\Phi}$ is defined analogously. The learning rules for the spline activation functions are:

$$\Delta \mathbf{Q}^{h}_{\mathrm{R},k,i+m} = \frac{\dot{\mathbf{T}}_{\mathrm{v}}(u_{\mathrm{R}})(\mathbf{M})_{m}}{\mathbf{T}_{\mathrm{v}}(u_{\mathrm{R}})\mathbf{M}\mathbf{Q}^{h}_{\mathrm{R},k,i+m}},$$

$$\Delta \mathbf{Q}^{h}_{\mathrm{I},k,i+m} = \frac{\dot{\mathbf{T}}_{\mathrm{v}}(u_{\mathrm{I}})(\mathbf{M})_{m}}{\mathbf{T}_{\mathrm{v}}(u_{\mathrm{I}})\mathbf{M}\mathbf{Q}^{h}_{\mathrm{I},k,i+m}} \tag{44}$$

where $(\mathbf{M})_m$ is a vector composed by the m-th column of the matrix $\mathbf{M}$. The learning rules for the spline compensating functions are:

$$\Delta \mathbf{Q}^{G}_{\mathrm{R},k,i+m} = \frac{\dot{\mathbf{T}}_{\mathrm{v}}(u_{\mathrm{R}})(\mathbf{M})_{m}}{\mathbf{T}_{\mathrm{v}}(u_{\mathrm{R}})\mathbf{M}\mathbf{Q}^{G}_{\mathrm{R},k,i+m}} + \mathrm{Re}\left\{\boldsymbol{\Psi}\left(\mathbf{W}^{H}\right)_{k}\right\}\frac{1}{2}\mathbf{T}_{\mathrm{v}}(u_{\mathrm{R}})(\mathbf{M})_{m},$$

$$\Delta \mathbf{Q}^{G}_{\mathrm{I},k,i+m} = \frac{\dot{\mathbf{T}}_{\mathrm{v}}(u_{\mathrm{I}})(\mathbf{M})_{m}}{\mathbf{T}_{\mathrm{v}}(u_{\mathrm{I}})\mathbf{M}\mathbf{Q}^{G}_{\mathrm{I},k,i+m}} + \mathrm{Im}\left\{\boldsymbol{\Psi}\left(\mathbf{W}^{H}\right)_{k}\right\}\frac{1}{2}\mathbf{T}_{\mathrm{v}}(u_{\mathrm{I}})(\mathbf{M})_{m} \tag{45}$$

where $(\mathbf{W})_k$ is a vector composed by the k-th column of the matrix $\mathbf{W}$, $\mathrm{Re}\{\bullet\}$ and $\mathrm{Im}\{\bullet\}$ are the operators that return the real and imaginary parts of their inputs, respectively. For a complete derivation of the learning rules see Vigliano et al. (2008).

An alternative algorithm can be obtained using the MMI approach deducing similar learning rules. This approach is presented in Vigliano, Scarpiniti, Parisi and Uncini (2006b).

Other Approaches

Before showing experimental results we want to summarize briefly other approaches to the problem of BSS in complex domain. The aim of this section is not to describe each approach (see references for this scope) but only to have an overview of the most meaningful results showing the progress of the research in this field. The existent approaches perform separation only in linear and instantaneous environment.

In 2000 a complex-valued version of the well-known Fast ICA algorithm was proposed (Bingham & Hyvärinen, 2000). This algorithm is based on a non-Gaussianity maximization derived from the Negentropy (Cover & Tomas, 2006) but it works well only for circular sources.

Recently in Li and Adali (2006) a class of complex-valued ICA algorithms by maximizing the kurtosis cost function is derived.

Moreover Cardoso and Adali (2006) proposed an approach based on the maximization of the log-likelihood function extended in Li and Adali (2008). This approach is strongly linked with the INFOMAX principle (Lee et al., 2000). A maximum likelihood (ML) solution to BSS problem was first derived in Pham et al. (1992).

Lately Novey and Adali (2008) solved the limit on circularity in the complex Fast ICA algorithm using complex analytic functions by introducing the complex maximization of non-Gaussianity (CMN) algorithm. The authors also showed the connection among ICA methods through maximization of non-Gaussianity, mutual information and maximum likelihood (ML) for the complex case.

RESULTS

This section collects some experimental results in order to demonstrate the effectiveness of our complex domain approach both in linear and nonlinear environment.

There are no standardized method to realize performance analysis but there exist several indexes and algorithms less or more diffused in literature; the best choice is to select the index adequate to the problem and to the mixing/de-mixing environment.

Figure 11. De-mixing model in nonlinear environment

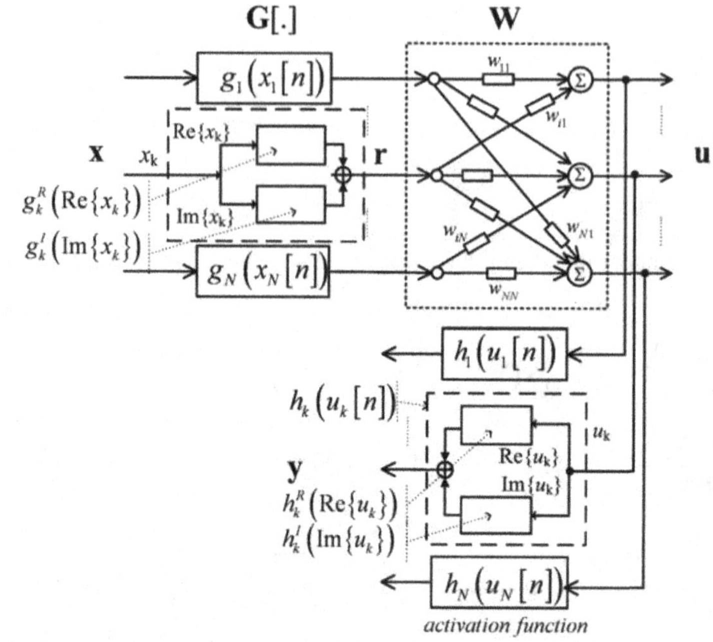

In order to compare performances we adopt the index introduced in Schobben, Torkkola and Smaragdis (1999), which evaluates the presence of the desired signal for each channel. In this way the quality of separation of the k-th separated output can be defined by the *Signal to Interference Ratio (SIR)* as

$$SIR(k) = 10\log\left[E\left\{\left(u|_{\sigma(k),k}\right)^2\right\} \Big/ E\left\{\sum_{i\neq k}\left(u|_{\sigma(k),i}\right)^2\right\}\right]. \tag{46}$$

In eq. (46) $u_{i,k}$ is the i-th output signal when only the k-th input signal is present, while $\sigma(k)$ is the output channel corresponding to the k-th input. This index is able to provide the evaluation of separation results without considering the particular mixing/de-mixing structure but only the original sources and the recovered signals. This is a very attractive characteristic which leads this index to be used to compare the performance of separation also in case of different mixing/de-mixing models.

Another way to evaluate the performance of an algorithm in linear case only is to analyze the matrix product $\mathbf{WA}$ which has to be close to the product of a diagonal matrix and a permutation matrix. Thus according to the desired solution to BSS problem, only one element in each row and column can be substantially a non zero element. Let us assume q_{ij} the generic element of the matrix $\mathbf{Q} = \mathbf{WA}$, we can define the following performance index (Amari et al., 1996)

$$S = \sum_{i=1}^{N}\left(\frac{\sum_{k=1}^{N}|q_{ik}|^2}{\max_p\left[|q_{ip}|^2\right]} - 1\right) + \sum_{k=1}^{N}\left(\frac{\sum_{i=1}^{N}|q_{ik}|^2}{\max_p\left[|q_{pk}|^2\right]} - 1\right). \tag{47}$$

The index in eq. (47) is a non-negative number and it is equal to zero only for perfect separation.

Performance Test in Linear Mixing Environment

The subsection is dedicated to the evaluation of algorithm proposed to solve the BSS problem in linear environment. The free parameters of algorithm are the following ones: the number N_h of spline control points used in eq. (19), the learning rate η_W involved in the adaptation of the entries in the de-mixing matrix, the learning rate η_W involved in the adaptation of the spline control points and the number of runs (or epochs) of the algorithm n_R.

In the first experiment we adopt the algorithm with the bi-dimensional AF in eq. (22), using the following four complex sources: s_1 is a 8-PSK (*Phase Shift Keying*) modulation, s_2 is a 16-QAM (*Quadrature Amplitude Modulation*) modulation, s_3 is a 4-QAM modulation and s_4 is a uniform random noise (Proakis, 1995).

The mixing environment (eq. (6)) is:

$$\mathbf{A} = \begin{bmatrix} 1.5 - j0.5 & -0.4 + j0.6 & 0.5 + j0.1 & 0.1 \\ 0.5 + j & 0.4 + j0.2 & -0.1 + j0.3 & 0.2 + j0.5 \\ 0.2 - j0.4 & -0.6 + j & 1.3 + j0.6 & 0.4 + j \\ 0.2 + j & -0.7 + j0.1 & -0.1 - j0.1 & 0.8 - j0.7 \end{bmatrix}$$

while the free parameters are summarized in Table 1.

In Figure 12 we present the joint pdf of the original signals (the first row), of the mixtures (the second row) and of the separated signals (the third row). In Figure 13 we report the performance of the algorithm. Comparing the two performance graphics we can note that the algorithm converge in about 50 epochs and the SIR index for the separated signals is between 26 dB and 37 dB. We can compare this result with respect the same test done with a fully-complex $tanh(z)$ AF as described in Adali et al. (2004) (see Figure 14); in this case the training was stopped after 1000 epochs. We do not report the scatter plot of signals because these are very similar to the first ones. We can note that in the case of the fully-complex $tanh(z)$ AF the convergence is slower (about 200 epochs), while the performance is between 25 dB and 39 dB.

While the quality of separation is very similar, the flexible approach is faster.

In the second experiment we adopt the algorithm with the bi-dimensional AF in eq. (22) using the following three complex sources: s_1 is a 8-PSK modulation, s_2 is a 4-QAM modulation and s_3 is a uniform random noise. Then we modified these signals in order to correlate the real and imaginary part. The correlation between the real and imaginary part is obtained by varying the length $\boldsymbol{M}$ of a moving average FIR filter (FIRMA). In this way each sample of the imaginary part of the k-th signal s_{Ik} is obtained as the mean over $\boldsymbol{M}$ past samples of its real part s_{Rk}:

$$s_{Ik}(n) = \frac{1}{M}\sum_{p=0}^{M-1} s_{Rk}(n-p). \tag{48}$$

The mixing environment (eq. (6)) is:

$$\mathbf{A} = \begin{bmatrix} 1.5 - j0.5 & -0.4 + j0.6 & 0.5 + j0.1 \\ 0.5 + j & 0.4 + j0.2 & -0.1 + j0.3 \\ 0.2 - j0.4 & -0.6 + j & 1.3 + j0.6 \end{bmatrix}$$

while the free parameters are summarized in Table 2.

In Figure 15 we report the performance index in eq. (47) of the algorithm versus the $\boldsymbol{M}$ parameter in eq. (48) comparing this result with respect the same test done with the algorithm described in Adali et al. (2004) using the $tanh(z)$ AF; in this case the training was stopped after 1000 epochs.

Table 1. Free parameters in test 1

N_h	η_W	η_h	n_R
21	$2{,}3 \cdot 10^{-3}$	$5 \cdot 10^{-4}$	100

Figure 12. Scatter plot of original signals (first row), mixtures (second row) and separated signals (third row)

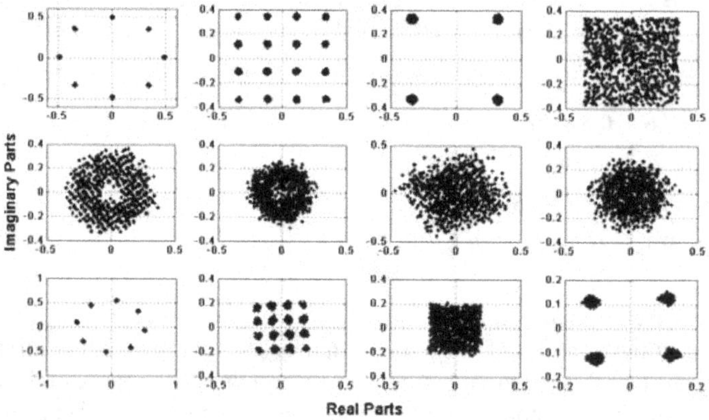

Comparing the two performance graphics we can note that the convergence is more accurate and stable even the parameter $\boldsymbol{M}$ is varied.

A third test is performed adopting the three signals involved in the previous example but varying the number N_h of spline control points in the following set of values: **{13, 16, 21, 31, 61}**. The other parameters are the same that in Table 2.

Figure 16 shows the separation index in eq. (47) for the five different values of N_h. The index profile shows that $N_{h=21}$ points the best choice. If the number of control points is large the quality of separation is bad while if it is too small the index has an oscillatory behaviour.

Performance Test in PNL Mixing Environment

This subsection is dedicated to the evaluation of the algorithm proposed to solve the BSS problem in nonlinear environment. The free parameters of algorithm are the following ones: the number N_h and N_G of spline control points used for the complex activation functions and the nonlinear compensating functions, the learning rate η_W involved in the adaptation of the entries in the de-mixing matrix, the learning rate η_h involved in the adaptation of the activation functions, the learning rate η_G involved in the adaptation of the nonlinear compensating functions and the number of runs (or epochs) of the algorithm n_R.

For the first test we adopt the algorithm with the mono-dimensional AF in eq. (20) using a 4-QAM signal, a uniform random signal and a PSK signal.

The mixing environment (eq. (8)) is:

$$\mathbf{A} = \begin{bmatrix} 0.90 - j0.30 & -0.24 + j0.36 & 0.30 + j0.06 \\ 0.30 + j0.60 & 0.24 + j0.12 & -0.06 + j0.18 \\ 0.12 - j0.24 & -0.36 + j0.60 & 0.78 + j0.36 \end{bmatrix},$$

Figure 13. Performance indexes for the first experiment

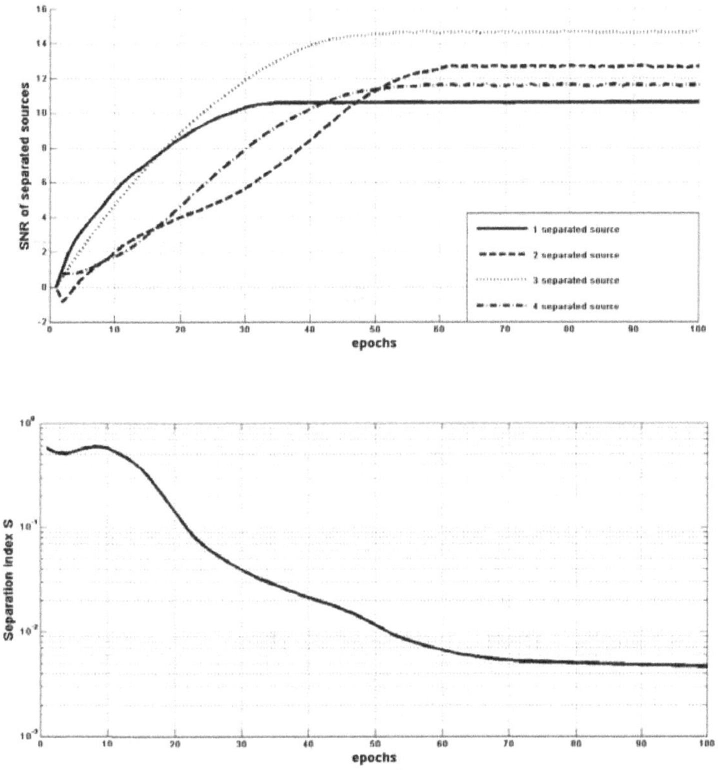

*Figure 14. Performance indexes in the case of **tanh(z)** activation function*

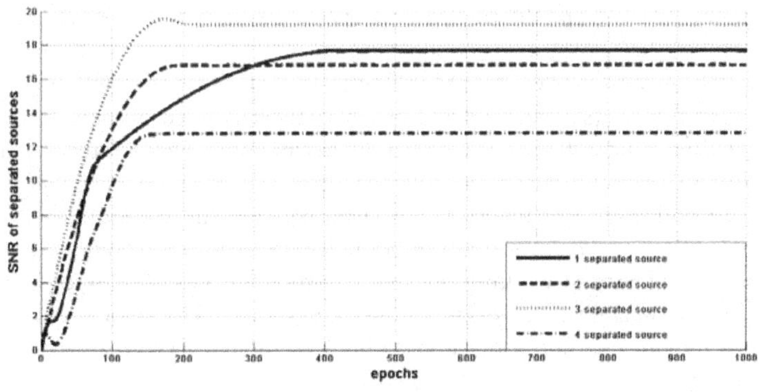

continued on following page

Figure 14. continued

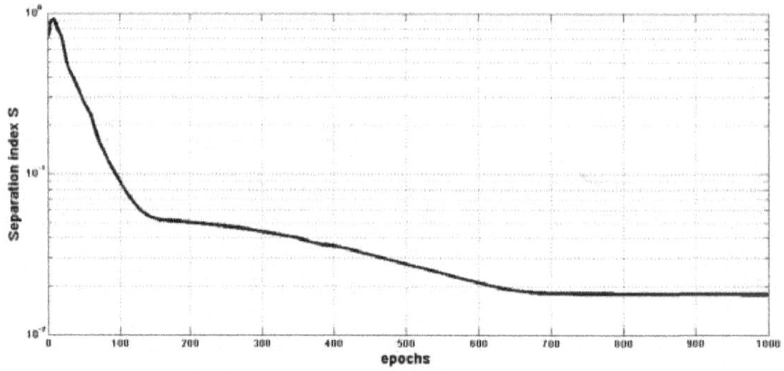

Table 2. Free parameters in test 2

N_h	η_W	η_h	n_R
21	$2{,}3 \cdot 10^{-3}$	$5 \cdot 10^{-4}$	100

$$\mathbf{F}[\mathbf{v}] = \begin{bmatrix} f_1[v_1] = \left(v_{R1} + 0.7v_{R1}^3\right) + j\left(v_{I1} + 0.7v_{I1}^3\right) \\ f_2[v_2] = \left(v_{R2} + 0.7\tanh\left(3v_{R2}^3\right)\right) + j\left(v_{R2} + 0.7\tanh\left(3v_{R2}^3\right)\right) \\ f_3[v_3] = \left(v_{R3} + 0.7v_{R3}^3\right) + j\left(v_{R2} + 0.7\tanh\left(3v_{R2}^3\right)\right) \end{bmatrix}$$

while the free parameters are summarized in Table 3.

The effectiveness of the separation is evidenced in Figure 17 that shows the joint pdf of the original sources (first row), of the nonlinear mixture (second row) and finally of the separated signals (third row).

Figure 18 shows that after about 200 epochs the training became stable and more accurate. So the profiles of the separation index $SIR(k)$ for each channel assures the effectiveness of the learning.

A second test is done with 16-QAM signal, a 8-PSK signal and an artificial Bernoulli's lemniscate signal. The choice of this particular and strange signal is due to the fact that we are interested in test our algorithm in signal with a real and imaginary part strongly correlated.

The mixing environment (eq. (8)) and the free parameters are the same values of the previous test, see Table 3.

The effectiveness of the separation is evidenced in Figure 19 that shows the joint pdf of the original sources (first row), of the nonlinear mixture (second row) and finally of the separated signals (third row).

Figure 20 shows that after about 200 epochs the training became stable and more accurate. So the profiles of the separation index $SIR(k)$ for each channel assures the effectiveness of the learning.

Last experimental test collects the results of comparison between the algorithm here introduced for PNL mixtures (named *Flexible Complex Post Non-Liner ICA* or *FC-PNLICA*) and another algorithm. Unfortunately in literature there is not any algorithm working on PNL mixtures in the complex case. In this sense we can compare the results only with an algorithm working on linear mixtures. The algorithm chosen for the comparison is that described in a previous section and proposed by Adali et al. (2004) that uses the ETFs (here named *Complex Linear ICA* or *C-LICA*). The comparison has been performed both in linear mixing environment and in the nonlinear one. Here, the Separation Index has been evaluated for both algorithms modifying the shape of the nonlinear distorting functions. Just to simplify the exposition of the results, parametric non linear function have been used for this test:

*Figure 15. Performance index vs. the length **M** of the MA filter: the flexible generalized splitting activation function (top) and a **tanh(z)** activation function (bottom)*

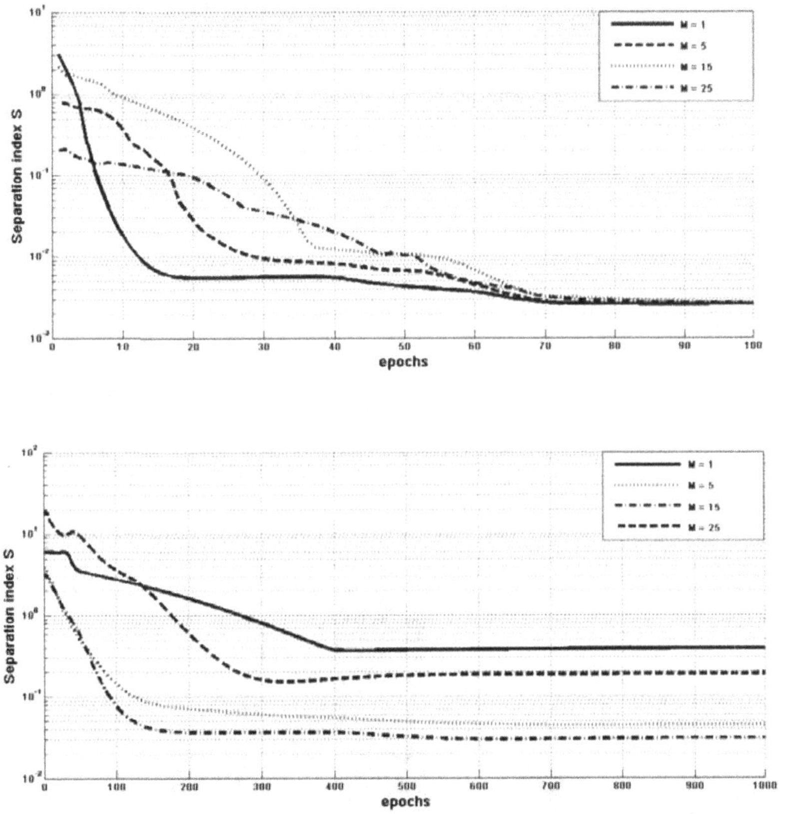

Figure 16. Performance index vs. the number of spline control points

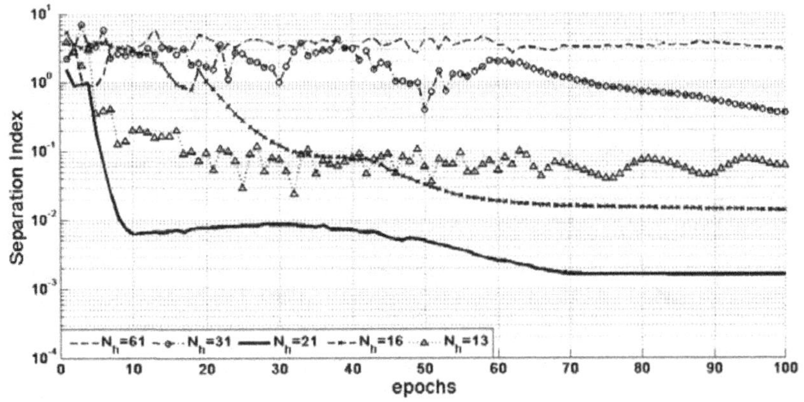

$$\mathbf{F}\left[\mathbf{v},\alpha,\beta,\gamma\right]=\begin{bmatrix} f_1\left[v_1,\alpha\right]=\left(v_{R1}+\alpha v_{R1}^3\right)+j\left(v_{I1}+\alpha v_{I1}^3\right) \\ f_2\left[v_2,\beta\right]=\left(v_{R2}+\beta\tanh\left(3v_{R2}^3\right)\right)+j\left(v_{R2}+\beta\tanh\left(3v_{R2}^3\right)\right) \\ f_3\left[v_3,\gamma\right]=\left(v_{R3}+\gamma\, v_{R3}^3\right)+j\left(v_{R2}+\gamma\tanh\left(3v_{R2}^3\right)\right) \end{bmatrix}. \quad (49)$$

The following table collects the Separation Index in eq. (46) after 600 epochs with the same learning rate of test 1 but random starting conditions with different value of $\left[\alpha,\beta,\gamma\right]$ in eq. (49) such that $\left[\alpha,\beta,\gamma\right]=\left\{\left[0,0,0\right]\ \left[0.4,0.4,0.4\right]\ \left[0.7,0.7,0.7\right]\ \left[1,1,1\right]\right\}$.

Table 3. Free parameters in test 1

N_h	N_G	η_W	η_h	η_G	η_R
31	31	$5\cdot 10^{-5}$	$5\cdot 10^{-6}$	$5\cdot 10^{-6}$	400

Figure 17. Scatter plot of original sources (first row), mixtures (second row) and separated sources (third row)

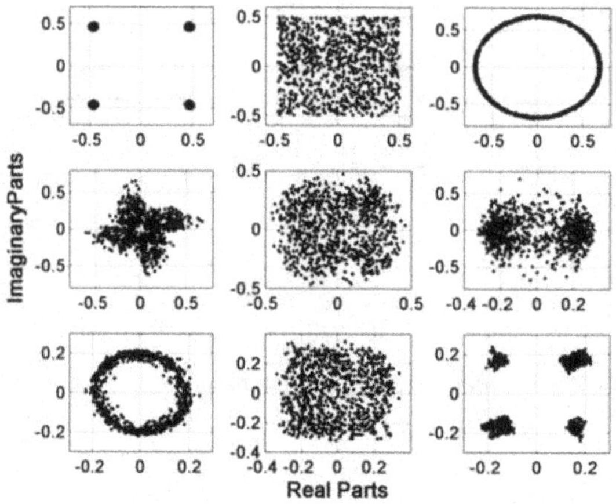

Figure 18. Separation index during training for the first experiment in PNL mixing environment

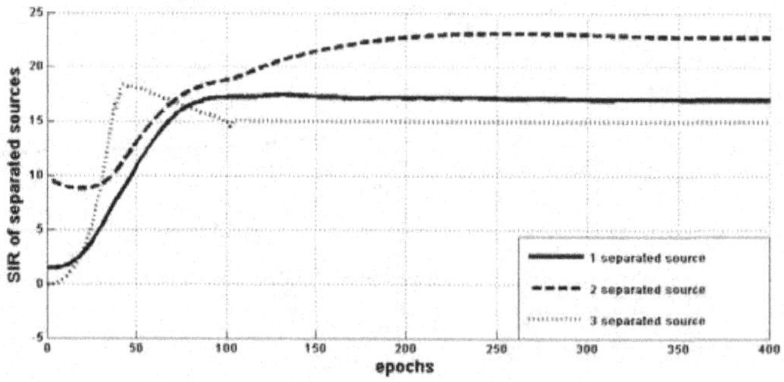

Figure 19. Scatter plot of original sources (first row), mixtures (second row) and separated sources (third row)

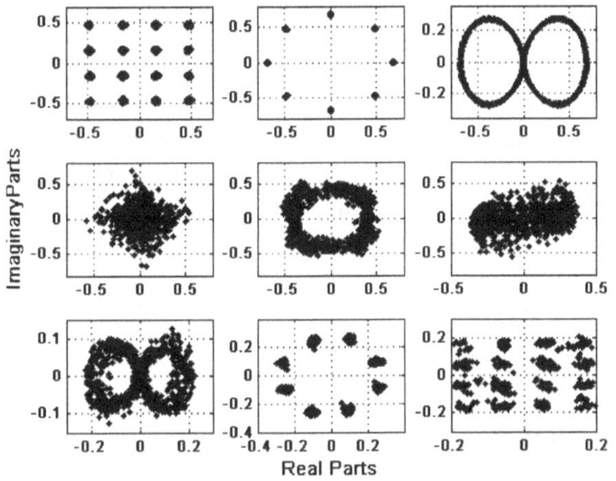

Figure 20. Separation index during training for the second experiment in PNL mixing environment

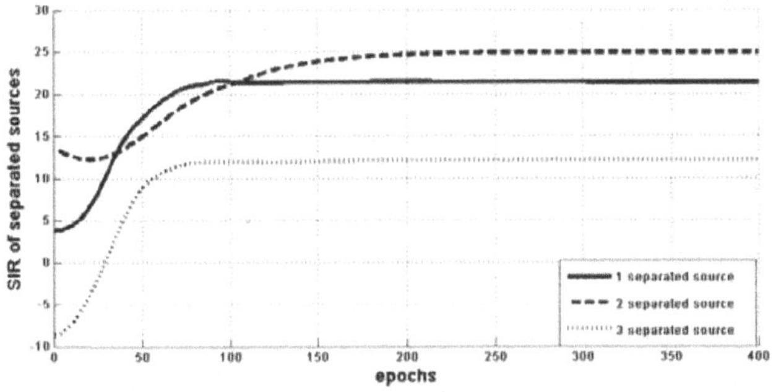

Table 4. Comparison of SIR values for two algorithms

SIR(k)	$\alpha = \beta = \gamma = 0$	$\alpha = \beta = \gamma = 0.4$	$\alpha = \beta = \gamma = 0.7$	$\alpha = \beta = \gamma = 1$
FC-PNLICA	[77.70, 49.84, 101.10]	[20.14, 40.15, 26.70]	[30.94, 14.53, 8.94]	[26.65, 12.09, 6.59]
C-LICA	[80.16, 39.84, 120.38]	[6.02, 24.55, 36.91]	[25.02, 1.4, -7.72]	[-6.37, -6.58, -9.52]

The results collected in Table 4 show how the separation performance of the algorithm FC-PNLICA and the C-LICA are comparable if the parameter of non-linear distortion are $\alpha = \beta = \gamma \leq 0.4$. With higher level of distortion the C-LICA is no more able to reach the separation but the FC-PNLICA is able to guarantee still good results.

CONCLUSION

Considering the evolution of ICA algorithms in solving BSS problems it is important to underline that, although several studies exist in the real domain, in the case of the complex domain the state of art is not so advanced. This chapter collects a first trial to enhance the state of art of mixing environment for which ICA algorithms can provide a solution.

In this chapter a novel complex model of mixing environment has been introduced and described even in linear that in nonlinear mixing model. The BSS problem in this new environment is solved by exploiting an ICA-based algorithm. The proposed approach extends the well-known INFOMAX algorithm to the complex domain and is based on the use of flexible spline networks to perform local on-line estimation of the activation functions and nonlinear compensating functions.

Quality of the separation has been evaluated in terms of separation index in a number of experimental tests.

FUTURE RESEARCH DIRECTION

This is an initial work on efficient and flexible neural architectures for Blind Signal Separation in complex environment. Necessary extensions of the research in BSS to complex domain environments via ICA approach must be addressed to improvements of the mixing models. A first necessary extension is the employment of the generalized splitting function in the nonlinear case, even if the learning rules could seem to be very hard. Secondly it could be interesting to extend the flexible methods to other approaches, i.e. the complex maximization of non-Gaussianity (CMN) algorithm.

Another fundamental extension is an approach based on a complex and convolutive environment in order to better model real world application, as telecommunication applications.

REFERENCES

Adali, T., & Li, H. (2007). A practical formulation for computation of complex gradients and its application to maximum likelihood ICA. *In Proc. of IEEE Int. Conf. on Acoustic, Speech and Signal Processing (ICASSP)*, (pp. 633-636).

Adali, T., Kim, T., & Calhoun, V. D. (2004). Independent Component Analysis by Complex Nonlinearities. *In Proc. ICASSP 2004*, (pp. 525-528).

Amari, S., Cichocki, A., & Yang, H. H. (1996). A New Learning Algorithm for Blind Signal Separation. *Advances in Neural Information Processing Systems, 8*, 757-763.

Bell, A. J., & Sejnowski, T. J. (1995). An information-maximization approach to blind separation and blind deconvolution. *Neural Computation, 7*, 1129-1159.

Benvenuto, N., Marchesi, M., Piazza, F., & Uncini, A. (1991). Nonlinear satellite radio links equalized using Blind Neural Network. *In Proc. of ICASSP*, (pp. 1521-1524).

Benvenuto, N., & Piazza, F. (1992). On the complex backpropagation algorithm. *IEEE Transactions on Signal Processing, 40*(4), 967-969.

Bingham, E., & Hyvärinen, A. (2000). A fast fixed-point algorithm for independent component analysis of complex valued signals. *International Journal of Neural Systems 10*(1), 1-8.

Calhoun, V. D., & Adali, T. (2002a). Complex Infomax: Convergence and Approximation of Infomax With Complex Nonlinearities. *In Proc. NNSP*, (pp. 307-316).

Calhoun, V. D., Adali, T., Pearlson, G. D., & Pekar, J. J. (2002b). On Complex Infomax Applied to Complex FMRI Data. *In Proc. ICASSP, I*, 1009-1012.

Calhoun, V. D., Adali, T., Pearlson, G. D., Van Zijl, P. C., & Pekar, J. J. (2002c). Independent Component Analysis of FMRI Data in the Complex Domain. *Magn. Reson. Med., 48*, 180-192.

Cardoso, J., & Laheld, B. H. (1996). Equivariant Adaptive Source Separation. *IEEE Trans. on Signal Processing, 45*(2), 3014-3030.

Cardoso, J., & Adali, T. (2006). The Maximum Likelihood Approach to Complex ICA. *In Proc. of Int. Conf. on Acoustic, Speech and Signal Processing*, (pp. 673-676).

Catmull, E., & Rom, R. (1974). A class of local interpolating splines. In R. E. Barnhill, & R.F. Riesenfeld (Eds.), *Computer-Aided Geometric Design*, (pp. 317-326). New York: Accademic.

Choi, S., Cichocki, A., & Amari, S. (2000). Flexible Independent Component Analysis. *Journal of VLSI Signal Processing - Systems for, Image and video Technology, X*(1).

Cichocki, A., & Amari, S. (2002). *Adaptive Blind Signal and Image Processing.* John Wiley.

Clarke, T. L. (1990). Generalization of Neural Networks to the Complex Plane. *In Proc. of IJCNN*, (pp. 435-440).

Comon, P. (1994). Independent Component Analysis, A new Concept? *Signal Processing, 36*, 287-314.

Cottin, C., Gavrea, I., Gonska, H. H., Kacsò, D. P., & Zhou, D. (1999). Global Smoothness Preservation and the Variation-Diminishing Property. *Journal of Inequality & Applications, 4*, 91-114.

Cover, T. M., & Thomas, J. A. (2006). *Elements of Information Theory.* 2nd edition.John WIley & Sons, Inc.

Cybenko, G. (1989). Approximation by superpositions of a sigmoidal function. *Mathematics of Control, Signals and Systems, 2*, 303-314.

De Boor, C. (2001). *A practical guide to spline.* Springer.

Eriksson, J., & Koivunen, V. (2002). Blind Identifiability of Class of Nonlinear Instantaneous ICA Models. *In XI European Signal Processing Conference EUSIPCO2002*, (pp. 7-10).

Eriksson, J., & Koivunen, V. (2004). Identifiability, separability and uniqueness of linear ICA models. *Signal Processing Letters, IEEE, 11*(7), 601-604.

Eriksson, J., & Koivunen, V. (2006). Complex random vectors and ICA models: identifiability, uniqueness, and separability. *Information Theory, IEEE Transactions on 52*(3), 1017-1029.

Fiori, S., Uncini, A., & Piazza, F. (1999). Neural Blind Separation of Complex Sources by Extended APEX Algorithm (EAPEX). *In Proc. of IEEE ISCAS'99*, (pp. 627-630).

Fiori, S. (2000). Blind Signal Processing by the Adaptive Activation function Neuron. *Neural Networks, 13*(6), 597-611.

Georgiou, G. M., & Koutsougeras, C. (1992). Complex Domain Backpropagation. *IEEE Trans. On Circuit and System II, 39*(5), 330-334.

Guarnieri, S., Piazza, F., & Uncini, A. (1999). Multilayer Feedforward Networks with Adaptive Spline Activation Function. *IEEE Trans. on Neural Network, 10*(3), 672-683.

Haykin, S. (1999). *Neural Networks, a comprehensive foundation.* Prentice-Hall.

Haykin, S. (Ed.) (2000). *Unsupervised Adaptive Filtering, Volume1: Blind Source Separation.* John Wiley & Sons, Inc.

Hyvarinen, A., & Oja, E. (2000). Independent component analysis: algorithms and applications. *Neural Networks, 13*, 411-430.

Hyvärinen, A., Karhunen, J., & Oja, E. (2001). *Independent Component Analysis*. John Wiley & Sons, Inc.

Jutten, C., & Herault, J. (1991). Blind Separation of Sources, Part I: An Adaptive Algorithm Based on Neuromimetic Architecture. *Signal Processing, 24*, 1-10.

Jutten, C., & Karhunen, J. (2003). Advances in Nonlinear Blind Sources Separation. *In 4th International Symposium on Independent Component Analisys and Blind Signal Separation (ICA2003),* (pp. 245-256).

Kim, T., & Adali, T. (2000). Fully complex backpropagation for constant envelope signal processing, *in Neural Networks for Signal Processing X, 2000. Proceedings of the 2000 IEEE Signal Processing Society Workshop, 1*, 231-240.

Kim, T., & Adali, T. (2001a). Complex backpropagation neural network using elementary trascende ntal activation functions. *In Proc. of IEEE ICASSP*, (pp. 1281-1284).

Kim, T.. & Adali, T. (2001b)/ Approximation by fully complex MLP using elementary transcendental activation functions. *In Proceedings of Neural Networks for Signal Processing XI*, (pp. 203-212).

Kim, T., & Adali, T. (2002a). Fully complex multilayer perceptron for nonlinear signal processing. *Journal of VLSI Signal Processing Systems for Signal, Image, and Video Technology, 32*, 29-43.

Kim, T., & Adali, T. (2002b). Universal approximation of fully complex feed-foreward neural network. *In Proc. Of IEEE ICASSP'02*, (pp. 973-976).

Kim, T., & Adali, T. (2003). Approximation by Fully-complex Multilayer Perceptrons. *Neural Computation, 15*(7), 1641-1666.

Lee, T. W., Girolami, M., Bell, A. J., & Sejnowsky, T. J. (2000). A Unifying Information-Theoretic framework for independent Component Analysis. *In Computer & Mathematics with applications, 39*(11), 11-21.

Leung, H., & Haykin, S. (1991). The complex backpropagation algorithm. *IEEE Transactions on Signal Processing, 39*(9), 2101-2104.

Li, H., & Adali, T. (2006). Gradient and Fixed-Point Complex ICA Algorithms Based on Kurtosis Maximization. *In Proceedings of the 16th Workshop on Machine Learning for Signal Processing*, (pp. 85-90).

Li, H., & Adali, T. (2008). Stability analysis of complex maximum likelihood ICA using Wirtinger calculus. *In Proc. of IEEE Int. Conf. on Acoustic, Speech and Signal Processing*, (pp. 1801-1804).

Marsden, M., & Schoenberg, I. J. (1998). On Variation Diminishing Spline Approximation Methods, Technical report, Defense Technical Information Center OAI-PMH Repository (United States).

Novey, M., & Adali, T. (2008). Complex ICA by Negentropy Maximization. *IEEE Transaction on Neural Networks, 19*(4), 596-609.

Papoulis, A. (1991). *Probability, Random Variables and Stochastic Process*. McGraw-Hill.

Pham, D. T., Garrat, D., & Jutten, C. (1992). Separation of mixture of independent sources through maximum likelihood approach. *In Proc. EUSIPCO*, (pp. 771-774).

Piazza, F., Uncini, A., & Zenobi, M. (1993). Neural Networks with Digital LUT Activation Function. *In Proceedings of IJCNN*, (pp. 1401-1404).

Pierani, A., Piazza, F., Solazzi, M., & Uncini, A. (2000). Low Complexity Adaptive Non-Linear Function for Blind Signal Separation. *In Proc. of IEEE IJCNN2000*, (pp. 333-338).

Proakis, J. G. (1995). *Digital Communications*. McGraw-Hill.

Roberts, S. & Everson, R., (Ed.) (2001). *Independent Component Analysis: Principles and Practice*. Cambridge University Press.

Scarpiniti, M., Vigliano, D., Parisi, R., & Uncini, A. (2007). Generalized Flexible Splitting Function Outperforms Classical Approaches in Blind Signal Separation of Complex Environment. *In Proc. of DSP2007*, (pp. 215-218).

Scarpiniti, M., Vigliano, D., Parisi, R., & Uncini, A. (2008). Generalized Splitting Functions for Blind Separation of Complex Signals. *Neurocomputing, 71*(10-12), 2245-2270.

Schobben, D., Torkkola, K., & Smaragdis, P. (1999). Evaluation of blind signal separation methods. *In Proc. of ICA and BSS*, (pp. 239-244).

Schoenberg, I. J. (1959). On variation diminishing approximation methods. *Journal of Inequality & Applications, 12*, 249-274.

Smaragdis, P. (1998). Blind separation of convolved mixtures in the frequency domain. *In Proc. International workshop on Independence and Artificial Neural Networks.*

Solazzi, M., Piazza, F., & Uncini, A. (2000a). An adaptive Spline Nonlinear Function for Blind Signal Processing. *In Proc. of IEEE Whorkshop on neural networks for signal Processing*, (pp. 396-404).

Solazzi, M., & Uncini, A. (2000b). Artificial neural networks with adaptive multidimensional spline activation functions. *In Proceedings of the IEEE-INNS-ENNS International Joint Conference on Neural Networks (IJCNN 2000), 3*, 471-476.

Solazzi, M., Piazza, F., & Uncini, A. (2001). Nonlinear Blind Source Separation by Spline neural Network, *in Proc.of ICASSP 2001*, (pp. 2781-2784).

Solazzi, M., & Uncini, A. (2004). Regularizing Neural Networks using Flexible Multivariate Activation Function. *Neural Networks, 17*, 247-260.

Taleb, A., & Jutten, C. (1999). Source Separation in post nonlinear mixtures. *IEEE Trans. on Signal Processing, 47*(10), 2807-2820.

Taleb, A. (2002). A Generic Framework for Blind Source Separation in Structured Nonlinear Models. *IEEE Trans. on signal processing, 50*(8), 1819-1830.

Theis, F. J., Bauer, C., & Lang, E. (2002). Comparison of maximum entropy and minimal mutual information in a nonlinear setting. *Signal Processing, 82*, 971-980.

Theis, F. J. (2004a). A New Concept for Separability Problems in Blind Source Separation. *Neural Computation, 16*, 1827-1850.

Theis, F. J. (2004b). Uniqueness of complex and multidimensional independent component analysis. *Signal Processing, 84*, 951-956.

Theis, F. J., & Gruber, P. (2005). On model identifiability in analytic postnonlinear ICA. *Neurocomputing, 64*, 223-234.

Uncini, A., Vecci, L., Campolucci, P., & Piazza, F. (1999). Complex-valued Neural Networks with Adaptive Spline Activation Function for Digital Radio Links Nonlinear Equalization. *IEEE Trans. on Signal Processing, 47*(2), 505-514.

Uncini, A., & Piazza, F. (2003). Blind Signal Processing by Complex domain Adaptive Spline Neural Network. *IEEE Trans. on Neural Networks, 14*(2), 399-412.

Unser, M., Aldroubi, A., & Eden, M. (1993). B-spline signal processing. I. Theory. *IEEE Transactions on Signal Processing, 41*(2), 821-833.

Vecci, L., Piazza, F., & Uncini, A. (1998). Learning and Approximation Capabilities of Adaptive Spline Activation Function Neural Networks. *Neural Networks, 11*(2), 259-270.

Vigliano, D., & Uncini, A. (2003). Flexible ICA solution for a novel nonlinear blind source separation problem. *Electronics Letters, 39*(22), 1616-1617.

Vigliano, D., Parisi, R., & Uncini, A. (2005). An Information Theoretic Approach to a Novel Nonlinear Independent Component Analysis Paradigm. *Elsevier Information Theoretic Signal Processing, 85*, 997-1028.

Vigliano, D., Scarpiniti, M., Parisi, R., & Uncini, A. (2006a). A flexible Blind source recovery in complex nonlinear environment. *In IEEE International Symposium on Intelligent Control,* (pp. 3059-3063).

Vigliano, D., Scarpiniti, M., Parisi, R., & Uncini, A. (2006b). Flexible ICA in Complex and Nonlinear Environment by Mutual Information Minimization. *In Proc. IEEE Workshop on Machine Learning for Signal Processing*, (pp. 59-63).

Vigliano, D., Scarpiniti, M., Parisi, R., & Uncini, A. (2008). Flexible Nonlinear Blind Signal Separation in the Complex Domain. *International Journal of Neural System, 18*(2), 105-122.

Vitagliano, F., Parisi, R., & Uncini, A. (2003). Generalized Splitting 2D Flexible Activation Function. *In Lecture Notes in Computer Science, 2859/2003*, 85-95.

Yang, H. H., & Amari, S. (1997). Adaptive Online Learning Algorithms for Blind Separation: Maximum Entropy and Minimum Mutual Information. *Neural Computation, 9*, 1457-1482.

ADDITIONAL READING

Adali, T., & Calhoun, V. (2007). Complex ICA of Brain Imaging Data. *IEEE Signal Processing Magazine, 24*(5), 136-139.

Amari, S., & Cichocki, A. (1998). Adaptive Blind Signal Processing - Neural Network Approaches. *In Proceedings of IEEE*, (pp. 2026-2048).

Benesty, J., & Huang, (Ed.) (2003). *Adaptive Signal Processing.* Springer.

Benesty, J., Makino, S., & Chen, (Ed.) (2005). *Speech Enhancement.* Springer.

Cardoso, J. (1997). Infomax and maximum likelihood for blind source separation. *Signal Processing Letters, IEEE, 4*(4), 112-114.

Cardoso, J., & Comon, P. (1996). Independent component analysis, a survey of some algebraic methods. *In IEEE International Symposium on Circuits and Systems ISCAS '96, 2*, 93-96.

Cardoso, J. (1998). Blind signal separation: statistical principles. *Proceedings of the IEEE, 86*(10), 2009-2025.

Cichocki, A., & Amari, S. (2002). *Adaptive Blind Signal and Image Processing.* John Wiley.

Eriksson, J., Seppola, A., & Koivunen, V. (2005). Complex ICA for circular and non-circular sources. *In 13th European Signal Processing Conference EUSIPCO 2005.*

Girolami, M. (Ed.) (1999). *Self-organising Neural Networks: Independent Component Analysis and Blind Source Separation.* Springer.

Girolami, M. (2000). *Advances in Independent Component Analysis (Perspectives in Neural Computing).* Springer.

Hyvärinen, A., Karhunen, J., & Oja, E. (2001). *Independent Component Analysis.* John WIley & Sons, Inc.

Hyvarinen, A. (1999). Beyond independent components. *In Artificial Neural Networks, 1999. ICANN 99. Ninth International Conference on (Conf. Publ. No. 470), 2*, 809-814.

Huang, Y., Benesty, J., & Chen, J. (2006). *Acoustic MIMO Signal Processing.* Springer.

Jutten, C., & Taleb, A. (2000). Source separation: from dusk till dawn. *In Proceeding of 2nd Int. Workshop on Independent Component Analysis and Blind Source Separation (ICA'2000)* (pp. 15-26).

Lee, T. W. (1998). *Independent Component Analysis - Theory and Applications.* Springer.

Makino, S., Lee, T., & Sawada, H. (Ed.) (2007). *Blind Speech Separation.* Springer.

Mandic, D., Javidi, S., Souretis, G., & Goh, V. (2007). Why a Complex Valued Solution for a Real Domain Problem. *In Proc. IEEE Workshop on Machine Learning for Signal Processing,* (pp. 384-389).

Novey, M., & Adali, T. (2007). Complex Fixed-Point ICA Algorithm for Separation of QAM Sources using Gaussian Mixture Model. *In IEEE International Conference on Acoustics, Speech and Signal Processing (ICASSP),* (pp. II 445-448).

Picinbono, B., & Bondon, P. (1997). Second-order statistics of complex signals. *IEEE Transactions on Signal Processing, 45*(2), 411-420.

Remmert, R. (1991). *Theory of Complex Functions.* Springer.

Schoenberg, I. J. (1967). On spline functions. *Journal of Inequality & Applications, 18*, 255-291.

Schumaker, L. L. (2007). *Spline Functions: Basic Theory.* Cambridge Mathematical Library, 3-rd edition.

Stone, J. V. (2004). *Independent Component Analysis: A Tutorial Introduction.* Bradford Books.

Unser, M., Aldroubi, A., & Eden, M. (1993). B-spline signal processing. II. Efficiency design and applications. *IEEE Transactions on Signal Processing, 41*(2), 834-848.

Unser, M., & Blu, T. (2007). Self-Similarity: Part I - Splines and Operators. *IEEE Transactions on Signal Processing, 55*(4), 1352-1363.

Unser, M. (1999). Splines: a perfect fit for signal and image processing. *IEEE Signal Processing Magazine, 16*(6), 22-38.

Wahba, G. (1990). *Spline models for observational data.* Society for Industrial Mathematics.

ENDNOTES

1 A function $h(z)$ is said *analytic* in z_0 if its derivative exists throughout some neighbourhoods of z_0. If is analytic in all points $z \in \mathbb{C}$, it is called *entire*.

2 A *singularity* is a point in which a function is not analytic and thus not differentiable: if $\lim_{z \to z_0} h(z) \to \infty$ but the function is analytic in a deleted neighbourhood of z_0 (that is a *pole*), the singularity is said to be *isolated*; if $\lim_{z \to z_0} h(z)$ exists it is isolated but *removable*; if none of these cases are met, the function has an isolated *essential* singularity.

3 *Flexible ICA* defines an ICA algorithm having flexible activation functions which are able to match adaptively the cumulative density function (cdf) of the original signals.

APPENDIX

We report the proof of proposition 1.

Sufficient condition: existence of the solution.

Given the channel model in eq. (8), it is easy to verify that if $\mathbf{s}[n]$ is a statistically independent complex random vector, under the given assumptions, $\mathbf{u}[n]$ will be statistically independent too because the channel does not produce any mixing. Given the mixing model $\mathcal{F}\{\mathbf{A},\mathbf{F}\}$, assumptions a), b), and c) guarantee that there exists a matrix $\mathbf{W}$ and N functions $g_i(\bullet)$ such that:

$$\begin{aligned} &\mathbf{G}(\mathbf{F}(\mathbf{A}\mathbf{s}[n])) = \mathbf{A}\mathbf{s}[n], \\ &\mathbf{W}\mathbf{A}\mathbf{s}[n] = \mathbf{P}\boldsymbol{\Lambda}\mathbf{s}[n]. \end{aligned} \tag{50}$$

Based on eq. , the input-output transformation can be written as $\mathbf{W}\mathbf{G}\left[\mathbf{F}(\mathbf{A}\mathbf{s}[n])\right] = \mathbf{P}\boldsymbol{\Lambda}\,\mathbf{s}[n]$.

Necessary condition: uniqueness of the solution.

This condition proves that if $\mathbf{u}[n]$ is a statistically independent random vector, the channel model must be eq. (8).

The complex transformation which maps $\mathbf{s}[n]$ into $\mathbf{u}[n]$ is:

$$\mathbf{u}[n] = \mathbf{W}\mathbf{G}\left[\mathbf{F}(\mathbf{A}\mathbf{s}[n])\right] = \\ = \mathbf{W}\begin{bmatrix} g_{R1}\left(f_{R1}\left(\sum_{i=1}^{N} a_{1i}s_i[n]\right)\right) + jg_{I1}\left(f_{I1}\left(\sum_{i=1}^{N} a_{1i}s_i[n]\right)\right) \\ \vdots \\ g_{RN}\left(f_{RN}\left(\sum_{i=1}^{N} a_{Ni}s_i[n]\right)\right) + jg_{IN}\left(f_{IN}\left(\sum_{i=1}^{N} a_{Ni}s_i[n]\right)\right) \end{bmatrix}. \tag{51}$$

It is possible to rewrite the complex map in eq. in a real form as follows:

$$\begin{aligned} &\tilde{\mathbf{u}} = \begin{bmatrix} \mathbf{u}_R[n] \\ \mathbf{u}_I[n] \end{bmatrix} = \begin{bmatrix} \mathbf{W}_R & -\mathbf{W}_I \\ \mathbf{W}_I & \mathbf{W}_R \end{bmatrix} \begin{bmatrix} \mathbf{G}_R(\mathbf{x}_R[n]) \\ \mathbf{G}_I(\mathbf{x}_I[n]) \end{bmatrix} = \tilde{\mathbf{W}}\tilde{\mathbf{r}}, \\ &\begin{bmatrix} \mathbf{x}_R[n] \\ \mathbf{x}_I[n] \end{bmatrix} = \begin{bmatrix} \mathbf{F}_R(\mathbf{v}_R[n]) \\ \mathbf{F}_I(\mathbf{v}_I[n]) \end{bmatrix}, \\ &\tilde{\mathbf{v}}[n] = \begin{bmatrix} \mathbf{v}_R[n] \\ \mathbf{v}_I[n] \end{bmatrix} = \begin{bmatrix} \mathbf{A}_R & -\mathbf{A}_I \\ \mathbf{A}_I & \mathbf{A}_R \end{bmatrix} \begin{bmatrix} \mathbf{s}_R[n] \\ \mathbf{s}_I[n] \end{bmatrix} = \tilde{\mathbf{A}}\tilde{\mathbf{s}} \end{aligned} \tag{52}$$

in which $\tilde{\mathbf{A}} = \begin{bmatrix} \mathbf{A}_R & -\mathbf{A}_I \\ \mathbf{A}_I & \mathbf{A}_R \end{bmatrix}$ and $\tilde{\mathbf{W}} = \begin{bmatrix} \mathbf{W}_R & -\mathbf{W}_I \\ \mathbf{W}_I & \mathbf{W}_R \end{bmatrix}$ are $2N$ x $2N$ matrices. It is important to underline that in eq. there are only real elements. For assumption (a) matrix $\mathbf{A}$ is non-singular, then due to its structure it is evident that $\tilde{\mathbf{A}}$ has to be non-singular too.

The pdf of $\tilde{\mathbf{s}}$ can be written as a function of the pdf of $\tilde{\mathbf{u}}$:

continued on following page

APPENDIX CONTINUED

$$p_{\tilde{\mathbf{s}}}(\tilde{\mathbf{s}})=\prod_{i=1}^{N} p_{s_{Ri}}(s_{Ri})p_{s_{Ii}}(s_{Ii})=$$

$$=\prod_{i=1}^{N} p_{u_{Ri}}\left(\begin{array}{l}\sum_{j=1}^{N} w_{Rij}g_{Rj}\left[f_{Rj}\left(\sum_{m=1}^{N} a_{Rjm}s_{Rm}-\sum_{m=1}^{N} a_{Ijm}s_{Im}\right)\right]+\\ -\sum_{j=1}^{N} w_{Iij}g_{Ij}\left[f_{Ij}\left(\sum_{m=1}^{N} a_{Ijm}s_{Rm}+\sum_{m=1}^{N} a_{Rjm}s_{Im}\right)\right]\end{array}\right) p_{u_{Ii}}(u_{Ii})\left|\tilde{\mathbf{J}}\right| \qquad \forall \tilde{\mathbf{s}}\in\mathbb{R}^{2N} \tag{53}$$

in which $\tilde{\mathbf{J}}$ is the Jacobian matrix of the application which maps $\tilde{\mathbf{s}}$ into $\tilde{\mathbf{u}}$.

From assumption (d) $\exists\overline{\mathbf{s}}\in\mathbb{C}^{N}$ such that $p_{\mathbf{s}}(\overline{\mathbf{s}})\equiv 0$. Then considering $\tilde{\mathbf{s}}[n]=\left[\mathbf{s}_R[n],\mathbf{s}_I[n]\right]^T$ in which $\mathbf{s}_R[n],\mathbf{s}_I[n]\in\mathbb{R}$ the assumption (d) can be reformulated as follows: $\exists\overline{\tilde{\mathbf{s}}}\in\mathbb{R}^{2N}\ \left|p_{\tilde{\mathbf{s}}}(\overline{\tilde{s}})=0\right.$.

From eq. , for a non null Jacobian $\tilde{\mathbf{J}}$, there exists some $\tilde{\mathbf{u}}^0=\left[u_{R1}^0,\cdots,u_{RN}^0,u_{I1}^0,\cdots,u_{IN}^0\right]\in\mathbb{R}^{2N}$ such that $\prod_{i=1}^{N} p_{u_{Ri}}(u_{Ri}^0)p_{u_{Ii}}(u_{Ii}^0)=0$. Consequently there exists at least one integer *i* such that $p_{u_{Ri}}(u_{Ri}^0)=0$ or $p_{u_{Ii}}(u_{Ii}^0)=0$. This leads to the following equation:

$$\tilde{u}_i^0=\sum_{j=1}^{N} w_{Rij}g_{Rj}\left[f_{Rj}\left(\sum_{m=1}^{N} a_{Rjm}s_{Rm}-\sum_{m=1}^{N} a_{Ijm}s_{Im}\right)\right]+$$
$$-\sum_{j=1}^{N} w_{Iij}g_{Ij}\left[f_{Ij}\left(\sum_{m=1}^{N} a_{Rjm}s_{Im}+\sum_{m=1}^{N} a_{Ijm}s_{Rm}\right)\right] \tag{54}$$

in which $\tilde{u}_i^0$ is the *i*-th element of the vector $\tilde{\mathbf{u}}^0$.

Solutions of eq. lie on $\mathcal{H}_i(\tilde{\mathbf{s}})$, which is a hypersurface in $\mathbb{R}^{2N}$. It is evident that $\forall\tilde{\mathbf{s}}\in\mathcal{H}_i(\tilde{\mathbf{s}})\Rightarrow p_{\tilde{\mathbf{s}}}(\tilde{\mathbf{s}})=0$. For a given *i*, $\mathcal{H}_i(\tilde{\mathbf{s}})$ is parallel to the hyperplane orthogonal to the axis $\tilde{s}_i$ (considering as $\tilde{s}_i$ the *i*-th element of the vector $\tilde{\mathbf{s}}$).

Suppose that $\mathcal{H}_i(\tilde{\mathbf{s}})$ is not parallel to any $\tilde{s}_i=0$ plane. The projection of $\mathcal{H}_i(\tilde{\mathbf{s}})$ onto $\tilde{s}_i$ should be $\mathbb{R}$:

$$\forall\tilde{s}_i\in\mathbb{R}\ \ \exists\tilde{s}_1,\ldots,\tilde{s}_{i-1},\tilde{s}_{i+1},\ldots,\tilde{s}_N,\ldots,\tilde{s}_{2N}:\tilde{\mathbf{s}}\in\mathcal{H}_i\Rightarrow p_{\tilde{\mathbf{s}}}(\tilde{\mathbf{s}})\equiv 0.$$

This cannot be true since $\int_S p_{\tilde{s}}(\tilde{\mathbf{s}})d\tilde{s}=1$. Without loss of generality, it can be noted that:

$$\sum_{j=1}^{N} w_{Rij}g_{Rj}\left[f_{Rj}\left(\sum_{m=1}^{N} a_{Rjm}s_{Rm}-\sum_{m=1}^{N} a_{Ijm}s_{Im}\right)\right]+$$
$$-\sum_{j=1}^{N} w_{Iij}g_{Ij}\left[f_{Ij}\left(\sum_{m=1}^{N} a_{Ijm}s_{Rm}+\sum_{m=1}^{N} a_{Rjm}s_{Im}\right)\right]=b_{\sigma(i)}\left(\tilde{s}_{\sigma(i)}\right)\quad i=1,\ldots,N,$$
$$\sum_{j=1}^{N} w_{Iij}g_{Rj}\left[f_{Rj}\left(\sum_{m=1}^{N} a_{Rjm}s_{Rm}-\sum_{m=1}^{N} a_{Ijm}s_{Im}\right)\right]+$$
$$+\sum_{j=1}^{N} w_{Rij}g_{Ij}\left[f_{Ij}\left(\sum_{m=1}^{N} a_{Ijm}s_{Rm}+\sum_{m=1}^{N} a_{Rjm}s_{Im}\right)\right]=b_{\sigma(i)}\left(\tilde{s}_{\sigma(i)}\right)\quad i=N+1,\ldots,2N \tag{55}$$

continued on following page

APPENDIX CONTINUED

where $b_{\sigma(i)}\left(\tilde{s}_{\sigma(i)}\right)$ is a generic function depending only on $\tilde{s}_{\sigma(i)}$ (that is the source for the i-th output). Then without any loss of generality taking $\sigma(i) = i$

$$\begin{aligned}
&\sum_{j=1}^{N} w_{Rij} g_{Rj}\left[f_{Rj}\left(\sum_{m=1}^{N} a_{Rjm} s_{Rm} - \sum_{m=1}^{N} a_{Ijm} s_{Im}\right)\right] + \\
&-\sum_{j=1}^{N} w_{Iij} g_{Ij}\left[f_{Ij}\left(\sum_{m=1}^{N} a_{Ijm} s_{Rm} - \sum_{m=1}^{N} a_{Rjm} s_{Im}\right)\right] = b_i(\tilde{s}_i) \quad i = 1 \ldots N, \\
&\sum_{j=1}^{N} w_{Iij} g_{Rj}\left[f_{Rj}\left(\sum_{m=1}^{N} a_{Rjm} s_{Rm} - \sum_{m=1}^{N} a_{Ijm} s_{Im}\right)\right] + \\
&+\sum_{j=1}^{N} w_{Rij} g_{Ij}\left[f_{Ij}\left(\sum_{m=1}^{N} a_{Ijm} s_{Rm} - \sum_{m=1}^{N} a_{Rjm} s_{Im}\right)\right] = b_i(\tilde{s}_i) \quad i = N+1 \ldots 2N.
\end{aligned} \tag{56}$$

Derivation with respect to **s** yields

$$\begin{bmatrix} \dot{b}_1(s_1) & 0 \\ 0 & \dot{b}_{2N}(\tilde{s}_{2N}) \end{bmatrix} = \tilde{\mathbf{W}} \begin{bmatrix} \dot{g}_{R1}\left[f_{R1}\left(\mathbf{v}_R(\tilde{\mathbf{s}})\right)\right] & 0 \\ 0 & \dot{g}_{IN}\left[\left(\mathbf{x}_I(\tilde{\mathbf{s}})\right)\right] \end{bmatrix} \cdot \begin{bmatrix} \dot{f}_{R1}\left(\mathbf{v}_R(\tilde{\mathbf{s}})\right) & 0 \\ 0 & \dot{f}_{IN}\left(\mathbf{v}_I(\tilde{\mathbf{s}})\right) \end{bmatrix} \tilde{\mathbf{A}}\,. \tag{57}$$

Considering $\tilde{\mathbf{s}}_1$ and $\tilde{\mathbf{s}}_2$ as coordinates of the hypersurface $\mathcal{H}(\tilde{\mathbf{s}})$, eq. can be evaluated in $\tilde{\mathbf{s}}_1$ and in $\tilde{\mathbf{s}}_2$ as follows:

$$\begin{cases} \mathbf{D}(\tilde{\mathbf{s}}_1) = \tilde{\mathbf{W}}\mathbf{\Lambda}_{\dot{\mathbf{G}}}(\tilde{\mathbf{s}}_1)\mathbf{\Lambda}_{\dot{\mathbf{F}}}(\tilde{\mathbf{s}}_1)\tilde{\mathbf{A}} = \\ \mathbf{D}(\tilde{\mathbf{s}}_2) = \tilde{\mathbf{W}}\mathbf{\Lambda}_{\dot{\mathbf{G}}}(\tilde{\mathbf{s}}_2)\mathbf{\Lambda}_{\dot{\mathbf{F}}}(\tilde{\mathbf{s}}_2)\tilde{\mathbf{A}} = \end{cases} \rightarrow \begin{cases} \mathbf{D}(\mathbf{s}_1) & \tilde{\mathbf{W}}\mathbf{\Lambda}_{\dot{\mathbf{G}}\dot{\mathbf{F}}}(\tilde{\mathbf{s}}_1)\tilde{\mathbf{A}} \\ \mathbf{D}(\mathbf{s}_2) & \tilde{\mathbf{W}}\mathbf{\Lambda}_{\dot{\mathbf{G}}\dot{\mathbf{F}}}(\tilde{\mathbf{s}}_2)\tilde{\mathbf{A}} \end{cases}. \tag{58}$$

Then eliminating $\tilde{\mathbf{W}}$ from eq. (58):

$$\tilde{\mathbf{A}} \underbrace{\mathbf{D}^{-1}(\tilde{\mathbf{s}}_2)\mathbf{D}(\tilde{\mathbf{s}}_1)}_{\begin{bmatrix} d_{11}(\tilde{\mathbf{s}}_2,\tilde{\mathbf{s}}_1) & & 0 \\ & \ddots & \\ 0 & & d_{2N2N}(\tilde{\mathbf{s}}_2,\tilde{\mathbf{s}}_1) \end{bmatrix}} = \underbrace{\mathbf{\Lambda}_{\dot{\mathbf{G}}\dot{\mathbf{F}}}^{-1}(\tilde{\mathbf{s}}_2)\mathbf{\Lambda}_{\dot{\mathbf{G}}\dot{\mathbf{F}}}(\tilde{\mathbf{s}}_1)}_{\begin{bmatrix} \lambda_{11}(\tilde{\mathbf{s}}_2,\tilde{\mathbf{s}}_1) & & 0 \\ & \ddots & \\ 0 & & \lambda_{2N2N}(\tilde{\mathbf{s}}_2,\tilde{\mathbf{s}}_1) \end{bmatrix}} \tilde{\mathbf{A}}\,. \tag{59}$$

As $\tilde{\mathbf{A}} = \begin{bmatrix} \mathbf{A}_R & -\mathbf{A}_I \\ \mathbf{A}_I & \mathbf{A}_R \end{bmatrix}$ is regular and non-singular, from eq. (59) for each pair of non zero elements of $\tilde{\mathbf{A}}$ it is possible to write:

$$\begin{cases} \tilde{a}_{ij}\left[d_{jj}(\tilde{\mathbf{s}}_2,\tilde{\mathbf{s}}_1) - \lambda_{ii}(\tilde{\mathbf{s}}_2,\tilde{\mathbf{s}}_1)\right] = 0 \\ \tilde{a}_{hj}\left[d_{jj}(\tilde{\mathbf{s}}_2,\tilde{\mathbf{s}}_1) - \lambda_{hh}(\tilde{\mathbf{s}}_2,\tilde{\mathbf{s}}_1)\right] = 0 \end{cases} \Rightarrow \lambda_{ii}(\tilde{\mathbf{s}}_2,\tilde{\mathbf{s}}_1) = \lambda_{hh}(\tilde{\mathbf{s}}_2,\tilde{\mathbf{s}}_1) \quad \forall \tilde{\mathbf{s}}_2,\tilde{\mathbf{s}}_1 \in \mathrm{H} \tag{60}$$

continued on following page

APPENDIX CONTINUED

in which $\tilde{a}_{ij}$ for $i, j = 1, \ldots, 2N$ is an element of $\tilde{\mathbf{A}}$. From eq. it follows:

$$\frac{\dot{\tilde{g}}_i\left[\hat{\tilde{f}}_i\left(\left(\tilde{\mathbf{A}}\right)_{\sigma(i)}\tilde{\mathbf{s}}_1\right)\right]\dot{\hat{\tilde{f}}}_i\left(\left(\tilde{\mathbf{A}}\right)_i\tilde{\mathbf{s}}_1\right)}{\dot{\tilde{g}}_h\left[\hat{\tilde{f}}_h\left(\left(\tilde{\mathbf{A}}\right)_h\tilde{\mathbf{s}}_2\right)\right]\dot{\hat{\tilde{f}}}_h\left(\left(\tilde{\mathbf{A}}\right)_h\tilde{\mathbf{s}}_2\right)} = C \quad i = 1, \ldots, 2N \quad \forall \tilde{\mathbf{s}}_2, \tilde{\mathbf{s}}_1 \tag{61}$$

where $\tilde{f}_i$ is the i-th element of the vector $\left[\mathbf{F}_R, \mathbf{F}_I\right]^T$, $\hat{\tilde{f}}_i\left(\left(\tilde{\mathbf{A}}\right)_i\tilde{\mathbf{s}}_1\right) = \alpha\tilde{f}_i\left(\left(\tilde{\mathbf{A}}\right)_i\tilde{\mathbf{s}}_1\right)$ and C is a constant. For the two linear forms in eq. (61) $\left(\tilde{\mathbf{A}}\right)_i\mathbf{s}_1$, $\left(\tilde{\mathbf{A}}\right)_h\mathbf{s}_2$ are independent as assumed in (a), it is possible to express the eq. (61) in the following way: $\dot{\tilde{g}}_i\left[\hat{\tilde{f}}_i(\vartheta)\right]\dot{\hat{\tilde{f}}}_i(\vartheta) = C\dot{\tilde{g}}_h\left[\hat{\tilde{f}}_h(\zeta)\right]\dot{\hat{\tilde{f}}}_h(\zeta)\ \forall\ \vartheta \in \mathbb{R}$. This can be true if and only if $\tilde{g}_i(\cdot)$ is the inverse of $\tilde{f}_i(\cdot)$, up to a scaling factor.

From eq. , by previous results it follows:

$$\tilde{\mathbf{u}}[n] = \tilde{\mathbf{W}}\begin{bmatrix}\xi_1 & & \\ & \ddots & \\ & & \xi_{2N}\end{bmatrix}\tilde{\mathbf{A}}\tilde{\mathbf{s}}[n] \tag{62}$$

where $\xi_1, \ldots, \xi_{2N}$ are scaling coefficients.

This method reduces the mixing/de-mixing nonlinear channel in eq. to the simpler linear model in eq. . By considering:

$$\tilde{\mathbf{W}}' = \tilde{\mathbf{W}}\begin{bmatrix}\xi_1 & & \\ & \ddots & \\ & & \xi_N\end{bmatrix},$$

$$\tilde{\mathbf{u}}[n] = \tilde{\mathbf{W}}\begin{bmatrix}\xi_1 & & \\ & \ddots & \\ & & \xi_{2N}\end{bmatrix}\tilde{\mathbf{A}}\tilde{\mathbf{s}}[n] \tag{63}$$

eq. can be transformed into $\tilde{\mathbf{u}} = \tilde{\mathbf{W}}'\tilde{\mathbf{A}}\tilde{\mathbf{s}}$. For this formulation independent outputs can be obtained if and only if

$$\tilde{\mathbf{W}}'\tilde{\mathbf{A}} = \tilde{\mathbf{P}}\begin{bmatrix}\varepsilon_1 & & \\ & \ddots & \\ & & \varepsilon_{2N}\end{bmatrix} \tag{64}$$

where $\tilde{\mathbf{P}}$ is a $2N \times 2N$ permutation matrix.

Considering the structure of $\tilde{\mathbf{A}} = \begin{bmatrix}\mathbf{A}_R & -\mathbf{A}_I \\ \mathbf{A}_I & \mathbf{A}_R\end{bmatrix}$ and $\tilde{\mathbf{W}}' = \begin{bmatrix}\mathbf{W}_R\mathbf{D}_1 & -\mathbf{W}_I\mathbf{D}_1 \\ \mathbf{W}_I\mathbf{D}_2 & \mathbf{W}_R\mathbf{D}_2\end{bmatrix}$ in which $\mathbf{D}_1 = \begin{bmatrix}\xi_1 & 0 \\ 0 & \xi_N\end{bmatrix}$ and $\mathbf{D}_2 = \begin{bmatrix}\xi_{N+1} & 0 \\ 0 & \xi_{2N}\end{bmatrix}$ are $N \times N$ matrices, it is possible to rewrite eq. in the following way:

continued on following page

APPENDIX CONTINUED

$$\begin{bmatrix} \mathbf{W}_R\mathbf{D}_1 & -\mathbf{W}_I\mathbf{D}_1 \\ \mathbf{W}_I\mathbf{D}_2 & \mathbf{W}_R\mathbf{D}_2 \end{bmatrix} \begin{bmatrix} \mathbf{A}_R & -\mathbf{A}_I \\ \mathbf{A}_I & \mathbf{A}_R \end{bmatrix} = \begin{bmatrix} \mathbf{P}_R & -\mathbf{P}_I \\ \mathbf{P}_I & \mathbf{P}_R \end{bmatrix} \begin{bmatrix} \varepsilon_1 & & \\ & \ddots & \\ & & \varepsilon_{2N} \end{bmatrix} \tag{65}$$

in which the permutation matrix $\tilde{\mathbf{P}}$ has four blocks, $\mathbf{P}_R$ and $\mathbf{P}_I$ are themselves permutation matrix of dimension $N \times N$. For the independence of output signals the generic element p_{ij} of the matrix $\tilde{\mathbf{P}}$ is such that

$$\begin{cases} p_{i,j} \neq 0 \Leftrightarrow p_{i+N,j+N} \neq 0 \\ p_{i,j+N} \neq 0 \Leftrightarrow p_{i+N,j} \neq 0 \end{cases} \quad i, j \in 1,..,N .$$

Section III
Models with High-Dimensional Parameters

Neural network models with high-dimensional parameters based on quantum computation and quaternions are presented. Their remarkable properties are elucidated.

Chapter XIII
Qubit Neural Network:
Its Performance and Applications

Nobuyuki Matsui
University of Hyogo, Japan

Haruhiko Nishimura
University of Hyogo, Japan

Teijiro Isokawa
University of Hyogo, Japan

ABSTRACT

Recently, quantum neural networks have been explored as one of the candidates for improving the computational efficiency of neural networks. In this chapter, after giving a brief review of quantum computing, the authors introduce our qubit neural network, which is a multi-layered neural network composed of quantum bit neurons. In this description, it is indispensable to use the complex-valued representation, which is based on the concept of quantum bit (qubit). By means of the simulations in solving the parity check problems as a bench mark examination, we show that the computational power of the qubit neural network is superior to that of the conventional complex-valued and real-valued neural networks. Furthermore, the authors explore its applications such as image processing and pattern recognition. Thus they clarify that this model outperforms the conventional neural networks.

INTRODUCTION

Since Shor (1994) proposed a way of factorizing large integers in polynomial time by using a quantum computing algorithm, the study of quantum information science, including quantum communication, quantum cryptography, quantum computer and so on, has been intensified (Nielsen & Chuang,2000). Shor's proposal has not only proved itself to be a milestone in quantum computing, but also created a novel research paradigm of neural computing, i.e., quantum neural computing (Kak, 1995). Since then, various quantum neural computing models have been proposed for the improvement of the computational ability of neural networks so as to expand their applications

(Peruš, 1996, 2004; Behrman, Nash, Steck, Chandrashekar, & Skinner, 2000; Narayanan, & Menneer, 2000; Ezhov, Nifanova, & Ventura, 2000; Matsui, Takai, & Nishimura, 1998, 2000; Kouda, Matsui, & Nishimura, 2002, 2004; Kouda, Matsui, Nishimura, & Peper, 2005a, 2005b; Mori, Isokawa, Kouda, Matsui, & Nishimura, 2006; Rigui, Nan, & Qiulin, 2006). In this chapter, we introduce a qubit neural network model that is a complex-valued multi-layered neural network composed of quantum bit neurons. We also clarify its learning performance numerically through the benchmark simulations by comparing it to that of the conventional neural networks. The quantum bit (hereafter qubit) neuron model was one that we proposed for the first time, inspired by quantum computation and quantum circuit (see the reference, Matsui, Takai, & Nisimura,1998 in Japanese, 2000 in English) and we also proved that our qubit neural network model (hereafter Qubit NN) is more excellent in learning ability than the conventional real-valued neural network model through solving the image compression problem (Kouda, Matsui, & Nishimura, 2002) and the control problem of inverted pendulum (Kouda, Matsui, Nishimura, & Peper, 2005b). We indicated that these results could be ascribed to the effects of quantum superposition and probabilistic interpretation in the way of applying quantum computing to neural network, in addition to the complex number representation. In the formulation of our model, complex numbers play an essential role, as a qubit is based on the concept of quantum mechanics. Here, to clarify these quantum effects, we show the characteristic features of Qubit NN are superior to those of the old-fashioned conventional complex-valued and/or real-valued neural networks by means of the simulations in solving the parity check problems and the function identification problem as a bench mark examination (see, Kouda, Matsui, Nishimura, & Peper, 2005a). Lastly, we add to the results of the new application examples: the well-known iris data classification and the night vision image processing. Thus we conclude that Qubit NN model outperforms Classical NNs. Here, we call the conventional neural networks Classical NNs according to the traditional comparison: Classical physics versus Quantum physics.

BACKGROUND

Before entering into the discussion of Qubit NN, we introduce its study background. Neural computing and quantum computing, both considered as promising innovative computation models, have attracted much interest from researchers. Neural computing is based on the intellectual and soft information processing of the brain that fuses and harmonizes the analog computation with the digital computation. It has been studied not only in modeling brain functions but also in solving various practical problems in industry such as data classification, pattern recognition, motion control, image processing and so on. Recently, in order to make it a reliable technology of information processing, as well as to expand its applications, Complex-valued, Quaternion-valued and Clifford-algebra neural networks have been explored (Hirose, 2003). We hypothesize that their computational ability can become higher than Real-valued one. This is not a clear problem, but Siegelmann (1999) shows that the computational ability of a neural network depends on the type of numbers utilized as its weight parameters: Integer-valued, Rational-valued and Real-valued type networks are computationally equivalent to finite automata, Turing machine and non-uniform computational models, respectively. Then, we speculate that hyper complex-valued NNs are beyond the computational ability that Turing model has achieved. It is also widely known that the computation based on quantum mechanics has higher computational ability than the Turing model. As for quantum computing, Feynman (1982) raised a question about the feasibility of the computing architectures based on quantum mechanics, and Deutsch (1985) started the study of quantum computing by proposing a computer model that operates according to principles of quantum mechanics—namely, the universal quantum Turing machine was proposed. Deutsch and Jozsa (1992) put forward a prototypical quantum algorithm for the first time, and proved their algorithm was able to speed up the computational processing ability by means of the quantum parallelism. Consequently, the study of quantum computer began to be more accelerated aiming at making clear its computational properties. Bernstein and Vazirani (1993, 1997) showed the existence of universal quantum Turing machines capable of simulating other quantum Turing machines in polynomial time, and Yao (1993) proved that quantum Turing machines are computationally equivalent to quantum circuits. Then, Shor (1994) showed how a solution of a large integer factorization problem in polynomial time is possible in principle by utilizing an algorithm operating on a quantum computer. His algorithm has attracted widespread interest because of the security of modern cryptography. Next, Grover (1996, 1997) discovered a fast quantum algorithm for database search. His algorithm was a significant breakthrough for wide applications. At the present, no quantum algorithms have been discovered beyond the capacity of these three quantum algorithms. On the other hand, neural computing, though successful in modeling information processing in the brain above mentioned, has faced problems in practice, since the massively parallel characteristics of most models in this framework are not suitable for the simulation in a reasonable time on classical computers. It is indeed a problem that today's computer algorithms based on classical physics fail to fully describe the basic nature of neural networks, which encompasses the unification of distributed neuron operation and integrated coherent behavior. To accomplish such characteristics in a computing system, therefore, we need a new computational principle.

Kak (1995) and Peruš (1996) drew attention to the similarity between the description of neuron states and that of quantum mechanical states and discussed a notion of quantum neural computing that is in accordance with quantum theory. Similar early works have been explored by Menneer et.al. (1995), Behrman et.al. (1996), and Ventura et.al. (1997). In these approaches, they discussed the possibilities of a quantum neural network inspired by the many-worlds interpretation (Menneer et.al.), a quantum dot neural network (Behrman et.al.) and a neuron model with its weight vectors as the quantum wave functions (Ventura et.al.). These models were theoretically interesting and stimulating. However, to make progress with regard to practical enhancement of neural networks' computational power, we have to construct a neural network capable of industrial applications. We, therefore, have attempted to establish a correspondence between neural networks and quantum circuits by proposing a qubit neuron model (Matsui et.al., 1998). In our neuron model, called Qubit neuron model, the states of neurons and their interactions with other neurons are based on the laws of quantum physics.

Now we aim to develop practical quantum neural networks and expect to establish these schemes as a step for a novel quantum algorithm.

QUANTUM COMPUTING AND NEURON MODEL

Qubit neuron and its neural network are neural models based on the concept of 'quantum bit' called *qubit* as the counterpart of the classical concept of 'bit'. We start this section with a brief review of quantum computing to explain the neural network inspired by the quantum concept.

Qubit and Its Representation

The qubit is a two-state quantum system. It is typically realized by an atom with its ground state and one of its excited states, an electronic spin with its up state and down one, or a photon with its two polarization states. These two states of a qubit are represented by the computational basis vectors $|0\rangle$ and $|1\rangle$ in a two-dimensional Hilbert space. An arbitrary qubit state $|\varphi\rangle$ maintains a coherent superposition of the basis states $|0\rangle$ and $|1\rangle$ according to the expression:

$$|\varphi\rangle = c_0|0\rangle + c_1|1\rangle; \quad |c_0|^2 + |c_1|^2 = 1, \tag{1}$$

where c_0 and c_1 are complex numbers called the probability amplitudes. When one observes the $|\varphi\rangle$, this qubit state $|\varphi\rangle$ collapses into either the $|0\rangle$ state with the probability $|c_0|^2$, or the $|1\rangle$ state with the probability $|c_1|^2$. These complex-valued probability amplitudes have four real numbers; one of these is fixed by the normalization condition. Then, the qubit state (1) can be written by

$$|\varphi\rangle = e^{i\lambda}(\cos\theta|0\rangle + e^{i\chi}\cdot\sin\theta|1\rangle), \tag{2}$$

where λ, χ, and θ are real-valued parameters. The global phase parameter λ usually lacks its importance and consequently the state of a qubit can be determined by the two phase parameters χ and θ without loss of generality.

That is

$$|\varphi\rangle = \cos\theta|0\rangle + e^{i\chi}\cdot\sin\theta|1\rangle \tag{3}$$

Thus, the qubit can store the value 0 and 1 in parallel so that it carries much richer information than the classical bit.

Quantum Gates

To create a novel neuron model inspired by the concept of qubit, we need to incorporate the concept of quantum logical gates into our neuron model. In quantum computing, the logical operations are realized by reversible, unitary transformations on qubit states (Nielsen & Chuang, 2000). Here, in order to explain the idea of our qubit neuron model, we introduce the symbols for the logical universal operations, i.e., the single-qubit rotation gate U_θ shown in Figure 1 and the two-qubit controlled NOT gate U_{CNOT} shown in Figure 2.

First we sketch the single-qubit rotation gate U_θ. We can represent the computational basis vectors $|0\rangle$ and $|1\rangle$ as vectors in a two- dimensional Hilbert space as follows:

$$|0\rangle = \begin{pmatrix}1\\0\end{pmatrix}, |1\rangle = \begin{pmatrix}0\\1\end{pmatrix}. \tag{4}$$

In such a case we have the representation of $|\varphi\rangle = \cos\theta_i|0\rangle + \sin\theta_i|1\rangle$:

$$|\phi\rangle = \begin{pmatrix}\cos\theta_i\\ \sin\theta_i\end{pmatrix},$$

and the matrix representation of U_θ operation can be described by Eq.(5).

$$U_\theta = \begin{pmatrix}\cos\theta & -\sin\theta\\ \sin\theta & \cos\theta\end{pmatrix}. \tag{5}$$

This gate varies the phase of the probability amplitudes from θ_i into $\theta_i + \theta$ as follows:

$$|\varphi'\rangle = U_\theta|\varphi\rangle = \begin{pmatrix}\cos\theta & -\sin\theta\\ \sin\theta & \cos\theta\end{pmatrix}\begin{pmatrix}\cos\theta_i\\ \sin\theta_i\end{pmatrix} = \begin{pmatrix}\cos\theta\cdot\cos\theta_i - \sin\theta\cdot\sin\theta_i\\ \sin\theta\cdot\cos\theta_i + \cos\theta\cdot\sin\theta_i\end{pmatrix}$$

$$= \begin{pmatrix}\cos(\theta_i + \theta)\\ \sin(\theta_i + \theta)\end{pmatrix}. \tag{6}$$

Next we outline the two-qubit controlled NOT gate U_{CNOT}. From Figure 2 we see the U_{CNOT} gate operates on two-qubit states. These are states of the form $|a\rangle\otimes|b\rangle$, which can be written more simply as $|ab\rangle$, as a tensor product of two vectors $|a\rangle$ and $|b\rangle$. It is usual to represent these states as follows:

$$|00\rangle = \begin{pmatrix}1\\0\\0\\0\end{pmatrix}, |01\rangle = \begin{pmatrix}0\\1\\0\\0\end{pmatrix}, |10\rangle = \begin{pmatrix}0\\0\\1\\0\end{pmatrix}, |11\rangle = \begin{pmatrix}0\\0\\0\\1\end{pmatrix}. \tag{7}$$

Figure 1. Single-qubit rotation gate

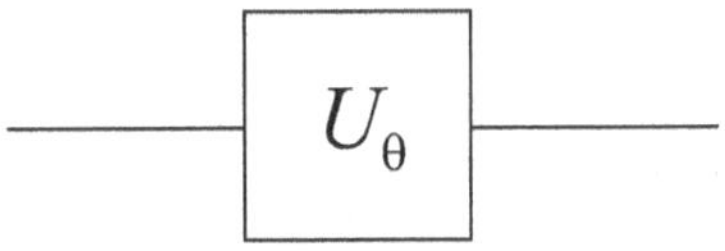

Figure 2. Two-qubit controlled NOT gate ($\oplus$: XOR operation)

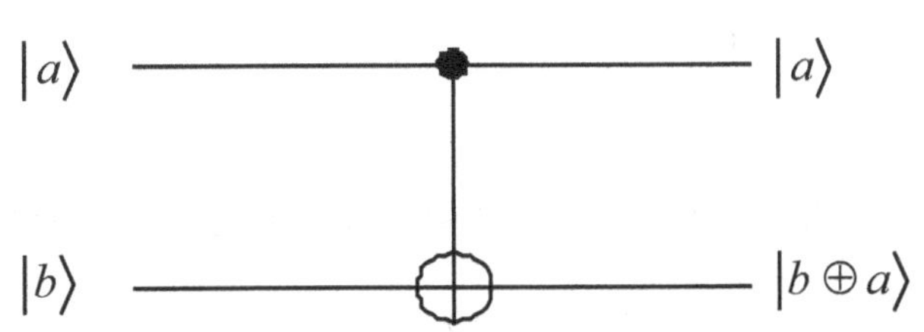

This standard representation is one of several important bases in quantum computing. When the U_{CNOT} gate works on these two-qubit states as vectors (7) in a four-dimensional Hilbert space, the matrix representation of the U_{CNOT} operation can be described by

$$U_{\mathrm{CNOT}} = \begin{pmatrix} 1 & 0 & 0 & 0 \\ 0 & 1 & 0 & 0 \\ 0 & 0 & 0 & 1 \\ 0 & 0 & 1 & 0 \end{pmatrix}. \tag{8}$$

This controlled NOT gate has a resemblance to a XOR logic gate that has $|a\rangle$ and $|b\rangle$ inputs. As shown in Figure 2, this gate operation regards the $|a\rangle$ as the control and the $|b\rangle$ as the target. If the control qubit is $|0\rangle$, then nothing happens to the target one. If the control qubit is $|1\rangle$, then the NOT matrix is applied to the target one. That is, $|a,b\rangle \rightarrow |a,b \oplus a\rangle$. The symbol $\oplus$ indicates the XOR operation.

An arbitrary quantum logical gate or quantum circuit is able to be constructed by these universal gates. For example, the three-bit quantum circuit, which is a minimum logical operation circuit constructed by four rotation gates and three controlled NOT gates, is shown in Figure 3. Its operator matrix U_c is as follows:

$$U_c = \begin{pmatrix} U_1 & & & \mathbf{0} \\ & U_2 & & \\ & & U_3 & \\ \mathbf{0} & & & U_4 \end{pmatrix}, \tag{9}$$

$$U_i = \begin{pmatrix} \cos\Theta_i & -\sin\Theta_i \\ \sin\Theta_i & \cos\Theta_i \end{pmatrix}, \quad \begin{matrix} \Theta_1 = \theta_1 + \theta_2 + \theta_3 + \theta_4, & \Theta_3 = \theta_1 - \theta_2 - \theta_3 + \theta_4, \\ \Theta_2 = \dfrac{\pi}{2} - (\theta_1 + \theta_2 - \theta_3 - \theta_4), & \Theta_4 = \dfrac{\pi}{2} - (\theta_1 - \theta_2 + \theta_3 - \theta_4), \end{matrix}$$

$i \in \{1,2,3,4\}$.

Figure 3. Three-bit quantum circuit

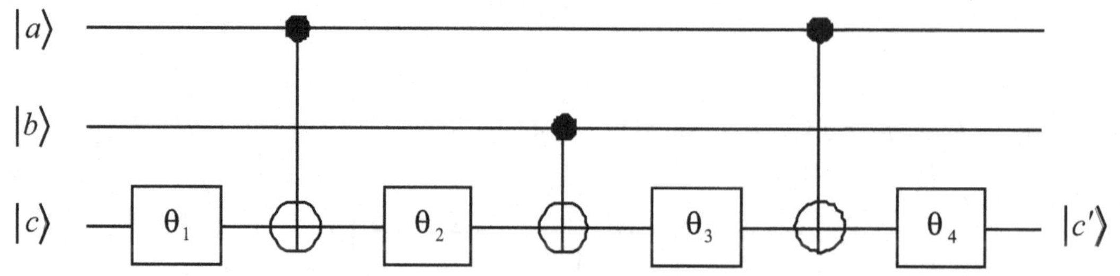

This quantum circuit can realize several two-input logic functions by setting the $\theta_1 \sim \theta_4$ into the appropriate values. In the case of $\theta_1 = \theta_2 = \pi/8, \theta_3 = \theta_4 = -\pi/8$ for example, it becomes AND or NAND logic gate depending on the state of $|c\rangle$. When the $|c\rangle$ is $|0\rangle$, the output $|c'\rangle$ in this quantum circuit results in the output for AND gate with two inputs $|a\rangle$ and $|b\rangle$. The circuit works as the NAND gate when the $|c\rangle$ is $|1\rangle$. The NAND gate can construct any logical functions by itself on conventional classical computing. Thus, this quantum circuit can construct any logical functions.

Complex-Valued Description of Qubit Neuron State

Now we proceed to describe our qubit neuron model. Our qubit neuron model is a neuron model inspired by the quantum logic gate functions: its neuron states are connected to qubit states, and its transitions between neuron states are based on the operations derived from the two quantum logic gates. To make the connection between the neuron states and the qubit states, we assume that the state of a firing neuron is defined as a qubit basis state $|1\rangle$, the state of a non-firing neuron is defined as a qubit basis state $|0\rangle$, and the state of an arbitrary qubit neuron is the coherent superposition of the two:

$$\text{neuron state}\rangle = \alpha \cdot |0\rangle + \beta \cdot |1\rangle;\ |\alpha|^2 + |\beta|^2 = 1 \tag{10}$$

corresponding to Eq.(1). In this qubit-like description, the ratio of firing and non-firing states is represented by the probability amplitudes α and β. These amplitudes are generally complex-valued. We, however, consider the following state as shown in Figure 4, which is a special case of Eq. (3) with $\chi = 0$:

$$\text{neuron state}\rangle = \cos\theta \cdot |0\rangle + \sin\theta \cdot |1\rangle \tag{11}$$

as a qubit neuron state in order to give the complex-valued representation of the functions of the single-qubit rotation gate U_θ and the two-qubit controlled NOT gate U_{CNOT}. To this end, in addtion, we introduce the following expression instead of Eq.(11):

$$f(\theta) = \cos\theta + i \cdot \sin\theta = e^{i\theta}, \tag{12}$$

where i is the imaginary unit $\sqrt{-1}$ and θ is defined as the quantum phase. The complex-valued description (12) can express the corresponding functions to the operations of the rotation gate and the controlled NOT gate.

a) Phase rotation operation as a counterpart of U_θ

As shown in Figure 5, the rotation gate is a phase shifting gate that transforms the phase of qubit neuron state. Since the qubit neuron state is represented by Eq. (12), the following relation holds:

Figure 4. Qubit-like description of neuron state

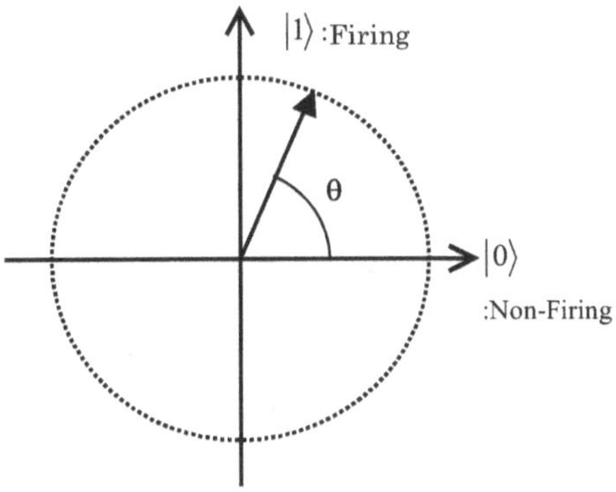

Figure 5. Phase rotation operation in a qubit neuron state as a counterpart of U_θ

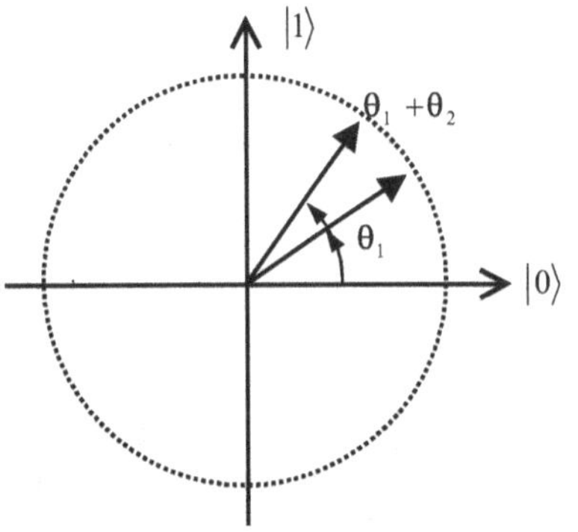

$$f(\theta_1 + \theta_2) = f(\theta_1) \cdot f(\theta_2). \qquad (13)$$

b) Phase reverse operation as a counterpart of U_{CNOT}
This operation is defined with respect to the controlled input parameter γ corresponding to the control qubit as follows:

$$f\left(\frac{\pi}{2}\gamma - \theta\right) = \begin{cases} \cos\theta - i \cdot \sin\theta & (\gamma = 0) \\ \sin\theta + i \cdot \cos\theta & (\gamma = 1) \end{cases}, \qquad (14)$$

where γ=1 corresponds to the control qubit=$|1\rangle$, i.e., the role reversal-rotation of basic states, and γ=0 corresponds to the control qubit=$|0\rangle$, i.e., the role conservable-rotation of basic states. In the case of γ =0, the phase of the probability amplitude of quantum state $|1\rangle$ is reversed as shown in Figure 6. However, its observed probability is invariant so that we are able to regard this case as the role conservable-rotation of basic states.

Qubit Neuron Model vs. Classical Neuron Model

Now we are ready to formulate the qubit neuron model by using the above complex-valued description of qubit neuron state. Before we discuss our qubit neuron model, we summarize the well-known classical neuron models to clarify the differences between the qubit and the classical ones.

Figure 6. Phase reverse operation in a qubit neuron state as a counterpart of U_{CNOT}

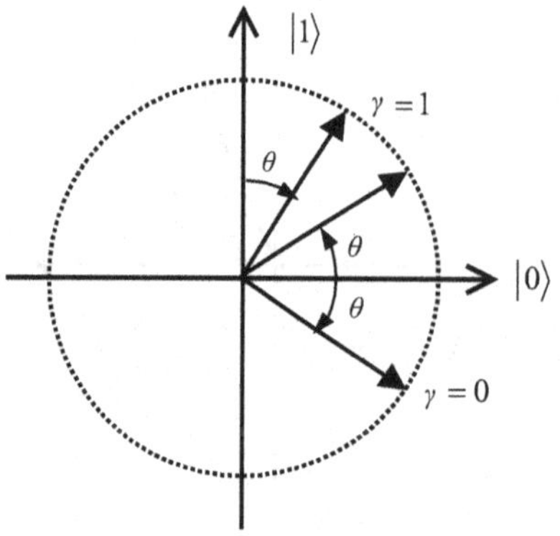

Classical Neuron Models

The well known real-valued conventional neuron model is expressed by the equations:

$$u = \sum_{m=1}^{M} w_m \cdot x_m - v, \tag{15}$$

$$y = (1 + e^{-u})^{-1}. \tag{16}$$

Here, u is the internal state of a neuron y. x_m is the neuron state of the m-th neuron as one of M inputs to y. w_m and v are the weight connection between x_m to y and the threshold value, respectively. These neuron parameters are real numbers.

The complex-valued neuron model is like a real-valued one except that the neuron parameters are extended to the complex numbers W_l as the weight, X_l and Y as the neuron state, V as the threshold and so on(Nitta, 1997) giving rise to the following equations that correspond to Eqs. (15) and (16), respectively:

$$U = \sum_{l}^{L} W_l \cdot X_l - V, \tag{17}$$

$$Y = (1 + e^{-\mathrm{Re}(U)})^{-1} + i \cdot (1 + e^{-\mathrm{Im}(U)})^{-1}. \tag{18}$$

Qubit Neuron Model

We have to observe the transition of the state of the qubit neuron in terms of the unitary transformation as the qubit concept is used for the description of the neuron state. A certain unitary transformation can be realized by the combination of the single-qubit rotation gate U_θ and the two-qubit controlled NOT gate U_{CNOT}. It is natural, therefore, to construct a computing model whose transition of the neuron state is performed according to these two quantum logic gates. We try to incorporate their concept to the framework of the above- mentioned classical neuron model Eqs. (15) and (16) (or Eqs. (17) and (18)) using the descriptions of Eqs. (13) and (14) that correspond to U_θ and U_{CNOT} operations respectively. In this case, the output state of qubit neuron has to be also described by Eq.(12). To implement this scheme, we assume the following: we replace the classical neuron weight parameter w_l (or W_l) with the phase rotation operation $f(\theta_l)$ as a counterpart of U_θ and install the phase reverse operation as a counterpart of U_{CNOT} instead of using the non-linear function in Eq.(16) (or Eq.(18)), and then we consider the following equations:

$$u = \sum_{l}^{L} f(\theta_l) \cdot x_l - f(\lambda) = \sum_{l}^{L} f(\theta_l) \cdot f(y_l) - f(\lambda), \tag{19}$$

$$y = \frac{\pi}{2} g(\delta) - \arg(u), \tag{20}$$

$$z = f(y). \tag{21}$$

Here, u is the internal state of a qubit neuron z. x_l is the qubit neuron state of the l-th neuron as one of inputs from L other qubit neurons to z. θ_l and λ are the phases regarded as the weight connecting x_l to z and the threshold value, respectively. y and y_l are the quantum phases of z and x_l, respectively. f is the same function as defined in Eq.(12) and g is the sigmoid function with the range (0,1) given by

$$g(\delta) = \frac{1}{1+e^{-\delta}}. \tag{22}$$

Two kinds of parameters exist in this neuron model: phase parameters in the form of weight connection θ_l and threshold λ, and the reversal parameter δ in Eq.(22). The phase parameters correspond to the phase of the rotation gate, and the reversal parameter to the controlled NOT gate. By substituting $\gamma = g(\delta)$ in Eq.(14), we obtain a generalized approximate reversal representation operating as the controlled NOT gate, the basic logic gate in quantum computing. We assume that Eq.(19) expresses the state u of a neuron in the usual way, i.e., as the weighted sum of the states of the inputs minus a threshold. Eq.(20) adjusts the output quantum phase y more roughly than Eq.(19). In Eq.(20), arg(u) means the argument of complex number u, and is implemented by arctan(Im(u)/Re(u)). By doing so, we can calculate the transition of these phases. We, thus, describe the transition of the qubit neuron state according to the phase transition, while a typical classical model does not use these phases for describing the state transition. That is, the multiplication of weights $f(\theta_l)$ to the inputs $x_l = f(y_l)$ results in the rotation of the neuron state based on the rotation gate. This we call is Qubit neuron model. A theoretical ground for adopting the classical model has not been sought for; we just adopt its formalism capable of applying to our model. Therefore the qubit neuron is not a reversible model on precise bases of quantum computing; this is an analogical model of quantum state.

Figs.7 and 8 give the qubit neuron model and its quantum gate diagram respectively. These diagrams may be useful for readers to understand our qubit neuron model.

Figure 7. Qubit neuron model

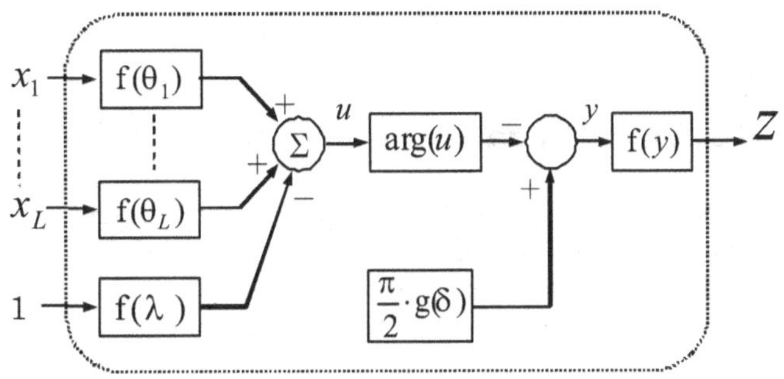

Figure 8. Quantum gate diagram of Qubit neuron

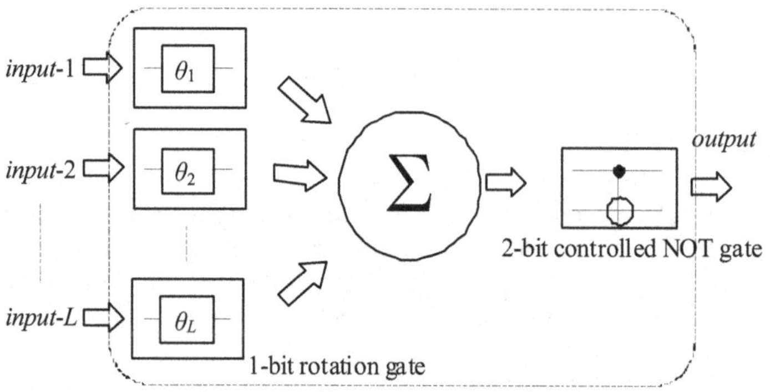

QUBIT NEURAL NETWORK

Now we proceed to construct the three-layered neural network employing qubit neurons called "qubit neural network: Qubit NN".

Network Structure

As shown in Figure 9, Qubit NN has the three sets of neuron elements: $\{ I_l \}$(l=1,2,...,L), $\{ H_m \}$ (m=1,2,...,M) and $\{ O_n \}$ (n=1,2,...,N), whereby the variables I, H, and O indicate the Input, Hidden, and Output layers, and L, M and N are the numbers of neurons in the input, hidden and output layers, respectively. We denote this structure of the three-layered NN by the numbers of L-M-N.

When input data (denoted by $input_l$) is fed into the network, the input layer consisting of the neurons in $\{ I_l \}$ converts input values in the range [0, 1] into quantum states with phase values in the range [0,π/2]. The output z_n^I of input neuron I_l becomes the input to the hidden layer:

$$z_l^I = f(\frac{\pi}{2} \cdot input_l). \quad (23)$$

The hidden and output layers with neurons from the sets $\{ H_m \}$ and $\{ O_n \}$, respectively, obey Eqs.(19), (20) and (21). We obtain the output to the network, denoted by $output_n$, by calculating the probability for the basic state $|1\rangle$ in the n-th neuron state z_n^O in the output layer:

$$output_n = |\mathrm{Im}(z_n^o)|^2 \quad (24)$$

This *output* definition is based on the probabilistic interpretation in the way of applying quantum computing to neural network.

Quantum Modified Back Propagation Learning

Next, we define a quantum version of the well-known Back Propagation algorithm (BP algorithm) in order to incorporate learning process in Qubit NN. The gradient-descent method, often used in the BP algorithm, is employed as the learning rule. This rule is expressed by the following equations:

Figure 9. Three layered neural network

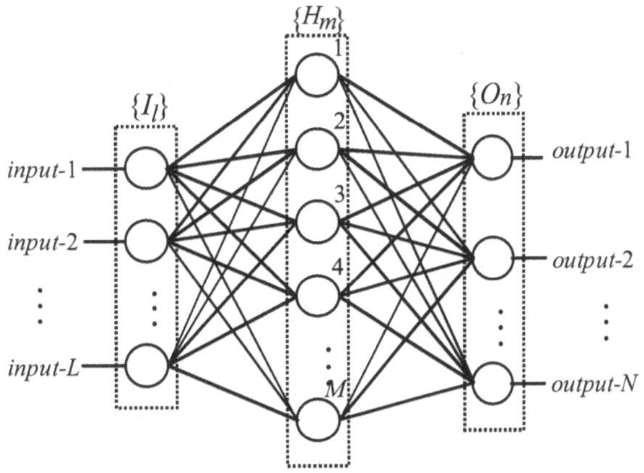

$$\theta_l^{new} = \theta_l^{old} - \eta \frac{\partial E_{total}}{\partial \theta_l} \tag{25}$$

$$\lambda^{new} = \lambda^{old} - \eta \frac{\partial E_{total}}{\partial \lambda} \tag{26}$$

$$\delta^{new} = \delta^{old} - \eta \frac{\partial E_{total}}{\partial \delta} \tag{27}$$

where η is a leaning rate. E_{total} is the squared error function defined by

$$E_{total} = \frac{1}{2} \cdot \sum_p^P \sum_n^N (t_{p,n} - output_{p,n})^2. \tag{28}$$

This quantity is the cost function to be minimized as part of the learning process. Here, P is the number of learning patterns, $t_{p,n}$ is the target signal for the n-th neuron and $output_{p,n}$ means $output_n$ of the network when it learns the p-th pattern.

LEARNING PERFORMANCES: QUBIT NN VS. CLASSICAL NNS

We now investigate the information processing ability of Qubit NN using benchmark learning problems for training our network and compare its performance with that of classical neural networks, i.e., Real-valued NN and Complex-valued NN. Here, Real-valued NN is a network constructed with the well known real-valued conventional neuron model as shown in the above-mentioned Eqs.(15) and (16). Similarly, Complex-valued NN is a network with the complex-valued neuron model described by Eqs. (17) and (18).

Both the classical NNs use the BP learning algorithm. The neuron parameters w_m, θ of Real-valued NN and W_l, V of Complex-valued NN are updated in the same way as in Eqs.(25), (26) and (27). As a footnote, in Complex-valued NN, the real parts, Re(W_l), Re(V) and the imaginary parts, Im(W_l), Im(V) are updated independently.

Learning Conditions

In all simulations, the sizes of the above NNs are chosen such that all networks have almost the same number of neural parameters, thus ensuring that all networks have nearly the same degrees of freedom, which is an important factor determining the learning ability. The numbers of neural parameters NUM of Qubit NN and classical NNs can be determined as follows.

$$\text{Qubit NN}: \; NUM_{qubit} = LM + MN + 2M + 2N \tag{29}$$

$$\text{Real-valued NN}: \; NUM_{real} = LM + MN + M + N \tag{30}$$

$$\text{Complex-valued NN}: \; NUM_{complex} = 2(LM + MN + M + N) \tag{31}$$

The subscripts, *qubit, real* and *complex* mean Qubit NN, Real-valued NN and Complex-valued NN, respectively. In these simulations, we consider that a network succeeds in training when the value of the squared error function E_{total} decreases to less than a certain bound 'E_{lower}' and it fails in training when it does not converge within a certain number of learning iterations, denoted by 'L_{upper}'. In both cases the network finishes the training. Here, one learning iteration encompasses the process of updating the learning parameters as the result of feeding all input patterns into the network exactly once.

The simulations are conducted in a number of epochs and the results are averaged, resulting in the average number of learning iterations required for a NN to learn a certain training set. We define the success rate as the percentage of simulation sessions in which the NN succeeded in its training, i.e., in which the NN required less than L_{upper} iterations. The success rates and the average numbers of learning iterations are indicators of the processing efficiencies, by which the performances of the different models can be compared.

The simulations in accordance to the above conditions are carried out on the so-called *4, 6-bit parity check problems* and the *general function identification problem*, described in the following sections.

Parity Check Problems

First, we investigate the performances of Qubit NN and Classical NNs in learning the 4 bit parity check problem in detail. For this simulation, we use a 4-6-1 Qubit NN, i.e., a three layered Qubit NN that has 4 neurons in the input layer, 6 neurons in the hidden layer and 1 neuron in the output layer mentioned previously. According to Eq.(29), the 4-6-1 Qubit NN has 44 neural parameters to be trained. A 4-8-1 Real-valued NN with 49 neural parameters and a 2-6-1 Complex-valued NN with 50 neural parameters are used for comparing the efficiencies.

These simulation results show in Figs.10 a), b) and c). In these figures, we denote the network structure and neural parameters by *L-M-N*: *NUM.*

As in the case of the 4-bit parity check problem, for the simulations with Real-valued NN and Qubit NN we use 16 input patterns, i.e., all the 4-tuple patterns in the range {0,0,0,0} ~{1,1,1,1}, and we use as target signals the scalars 0 and 1 obtained from XORing all elements of the 4-tuples inputs. In case of Complex-valued NN, the input patterns are the 2-tuple patterns in the range {0+i0, 0+i0}~{1+i1, 1+ i1} and the target signals are again the scalars 0 and 1 obtained from XORing all elements of the inputs. It is important for the performance comparisons to determine the optimal learning rate of each NN, but this is a difficult problem when doing simulations on NN. To cope with this we define a finite set of possible learning rates and try all values in the simulations. This procedure is followed for the learning rates η_q, η_r, η_c of Qubit NN, Real-valued NN and Complex-valued NN, respectively.

The number of simulation sessions is set to 100 epochs for each learning rate value tested. In each epoch the values of the network parameters are initialized to random values. For each learning rate value the simulation results are averaged, giving rise to one data point, plotted in a figure that shows the learning abilities of the neural networks in terms of the average numbers of required learning iterations on the vertical axis with respect to the success rate on the horizontal axis. From this axis definition, the nearer a dot in the figure is to the corner right below, the more efficient the corresponding network is. The initial values of the parameters are in the ranges [-π,

Figure 10. Learning performance in the 4-bit parity check problem

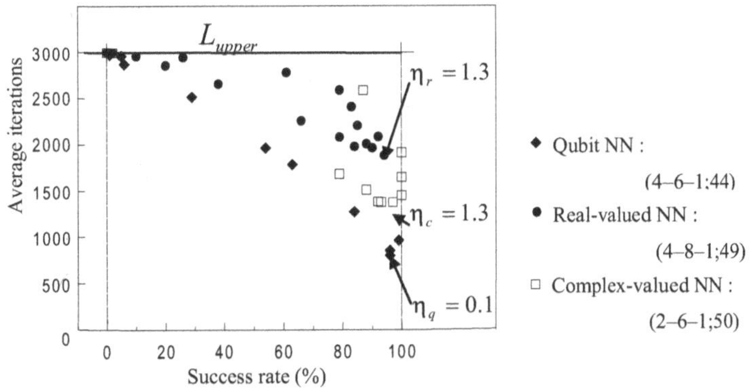

(a)

Average number of learning iterations vs. success rate (Condition for success: E_{lower} = 0.005, L_{upper} = 3000)

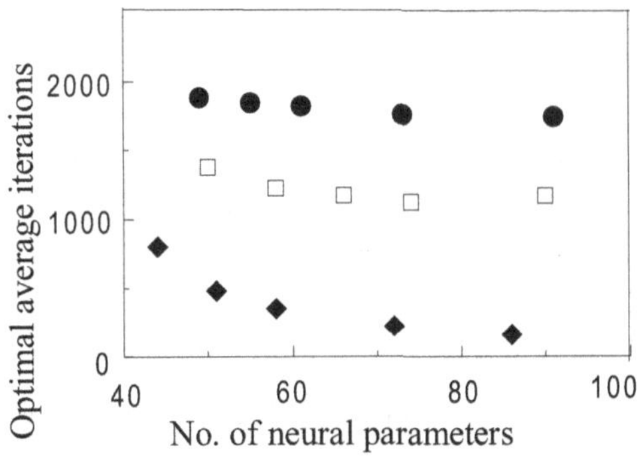

(b)

Dependence of optimal average number of learning iterations on the number of neural parameters in network

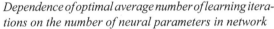

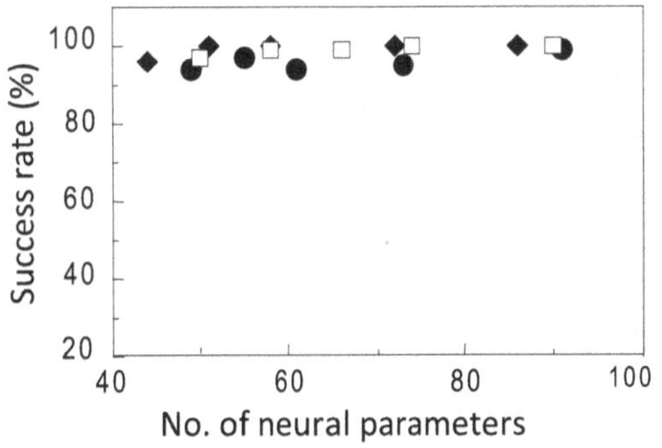

(c)

Dependence of success rate, by which learning is accomplished within the optimal average number of iterations, on the number of neural parameters in network.

π] for Qubit NN, [-1, 1] for Real-valued NN and [-1-*i*1, 1+*i*1] for Complex-valued NN. L_{upper} is set to 3000 and E_{lower} is set to 0.005 in the 4-bit parity check problem. We observe from Figure 10(a) that the optimal average numbers of required iterations of the respective models are about 800 iterations at η_q = 0.1, about 1900 iterations at η_r = 1.3 and about 1380 iterations at η_c = 1.3. Of all the models, the dot of Qubit NN is the nearest to the corner right below. Figs.10 b) and c) show the influence of the number of hidden layer neurons (or neural parameters) on the optimal average number of learning iterations and on the success rate, respectively. Learning is considered successful if E_{lower} =0.005, L_{upper} =3000. From these figures, we observe only Qubit NN accomplishes training with an average number of iterations lower than 500. We also see that Qubit NN excels over Classical NNs in all cases with respect to the average number of required iterations. Furthermore, when the number of hidden layer neurons increases, the average number of required iterations of Qubit NN decreases more than that of Classical models.

Next, in Figure 11, we show the result for the 6-bit parity check problem, which is a more complicated problem. The input patterns for the 6-bit problem are established by following the same principles as in the 4-bit parity check problem. L_{upper} is set to 10000 and E_{lower} is set to 0.006. The results for Qubit NN are the nearest to the corner

Figure 11. Learning performance in the 6-bit parity check problem

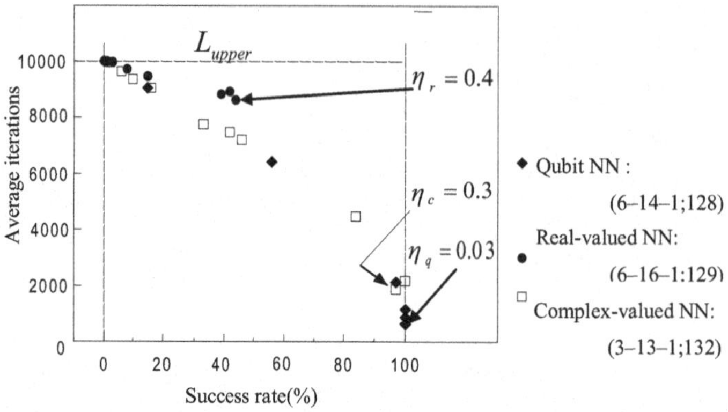

(a)

Average number of learning iterations vs. success rate (Condition for success : E_{lower} = 0.006, L_{upper} = 10000)

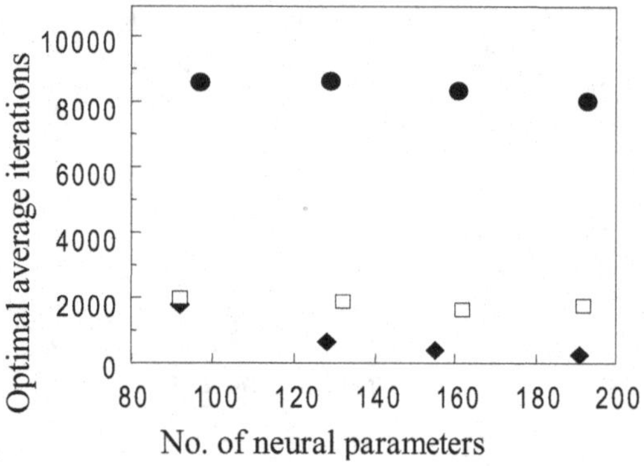

(b)

Dependence of optimal average number of learning iterations on the number of neural parameters in network

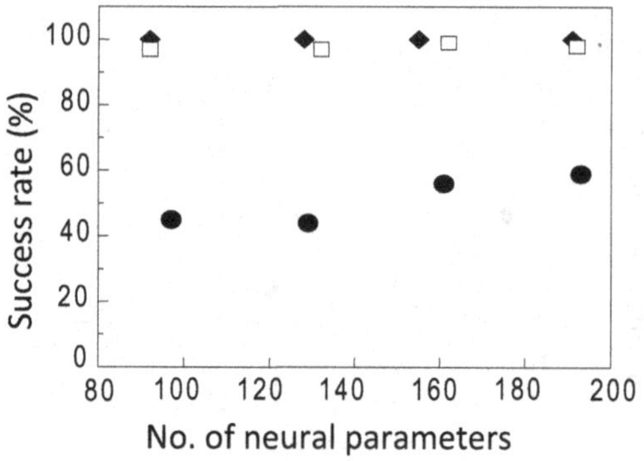

(c)

Dependence of success rate, by which learning is accomplished within the optimal average number of iterations, on the number of neural parameters in network.

right below, similar to the 4-bit parity check. We see Qubit NN finishes the training within 1000 iterations. From Figs.10 and 11 we conclude that Qubit NN shows better efficiency than Classical NNs for the 6-bit parity check problem and the 4-bit parity check problem.

General Function Identification Problem

In this simulation, we test the abilities of the neural networks to learn the function defined by

$$P(x) = \frac{\sin \pi x + \sin 2\pi x + 2.0}{4.0} \qquad (0 \le x < 2)\,. \tag{32}$$

We use a 2-14-1 Qubit NN which has 72 neural parameters, a 2-18-1 Real-valued NN with 73 parameters and a 1-12-1 Complex-valued NN with 74 parameters. Similar to the previous parity check problem section, the networks have almost the same degrees of freedom. The input is set to $\{input_1, input_2\}=\{x, 0.0\}$ in the range $0.0 \leq x \leq 1.0$ and $\{input_1, input_2\}=\{0.0, x\text{-}1.0\}$ in the range $1.0 < x \leq 2.0$ and the training target is $P(x)$. In this simulation we adopt a step size of 0.1, giving rise to 21 data points. So the input patterns become $\{0.0, 0.0\}\sim\{1.0, 0.0\}$ in $0.0 \leq x \leq 1.0$ and $\{0.0, 0.1\}\sim\{0.0, 0.9\}$ in $1.0 < x < 2.0$.

The initial values of the neural parameters and the learning rates are in the same respective ranges as in the previous section. The value of E_{lower} is 0.01, and the value of L_{upper} is 10000.

The learning abilities of the respective networks are shown in Figure 12. From the figure it can be seen that the Qubit NN requires 2000 iterations to achieve a 100% success rate, while the Classical NN takes 4500 iterations and the complex NN takes 3100 iterations to achieve this.

Finally we check how well Qubit NN can make approximations on data that have not been used for training. The output of the network is plotted against the actual graph of $P(x)$ in Figure 13. The squared mean error is 0.011, which is close to E_{lower}, even though the data points were not part of the training data.

Quantum Effects in Learning Performances

In this section, we explore the reason why the proposed Qubit NN is more efficient than Classical NNs, by analyzing the results of the simulations on the 4-bit and 6-bit parity check problems. We clarify the following three points:

a. Does the superiority of Qubit NN consist in its being complex valued?
b. Does the superiority of Qubit NN consist in its state of quantum superposition?
c. Does the superiority of Qubit NN consist in its probabilistic interpretation?

First of all, we consider the point (a).

Figure 12. Learning performance in the identification of an arbitrary function

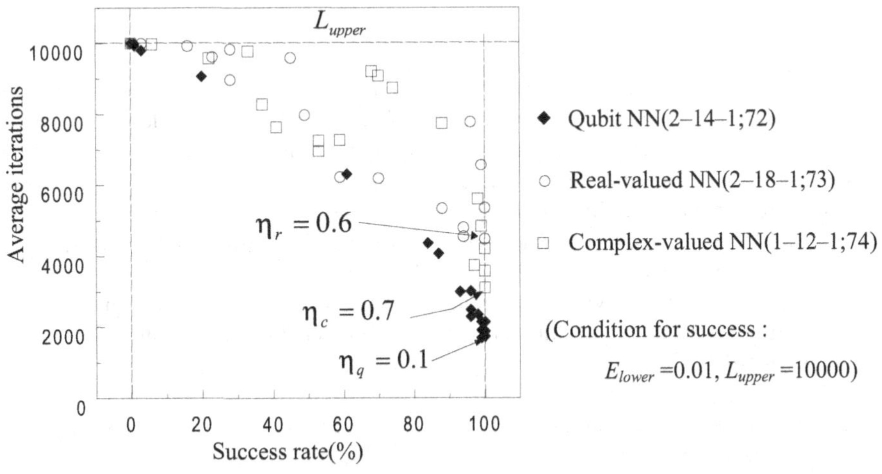

Figure 13. Ability of the network to approximate function P(x)

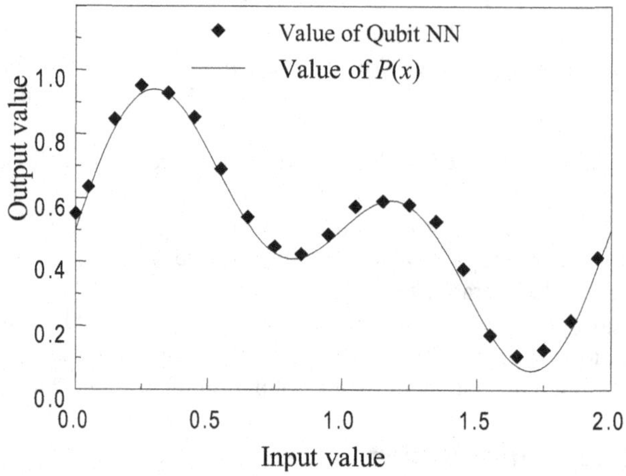

Figure 14. Learning performance in the 4-bit parity check problem by a radius-restricted complex-valued NN, and Qubit NN (Point (a))

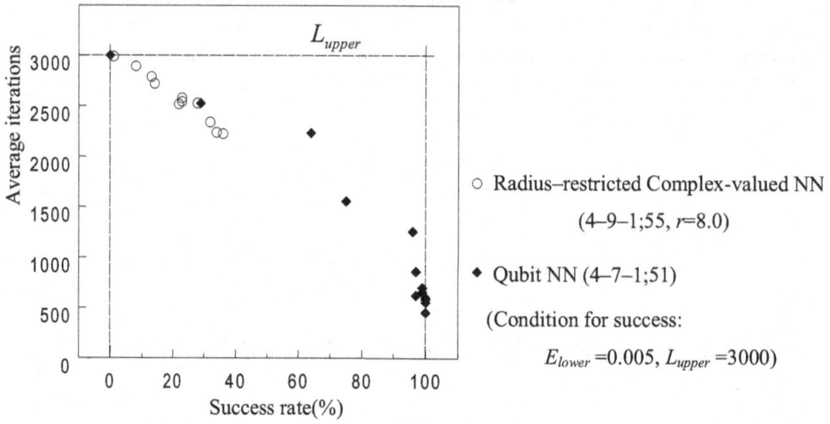

Qubit NN restricts its use of complex numbers in its states to those with polar radius "1" due to the state descriptions based on quantum superposition, whereas Complex-valued NN uses complex numbers in its states without this restriction. To check whether the better performance of Qubit NN was not due to its states being restricted to polar radius 1, we carried out simulations on Complex-valued NN whose neuron parameters also had restrictions with regard to the polar radius: in this case we used polar radii of the values 1, 5, 8, and 10. The best results of these simulations were obtained when the radius was 8 (see Figure 14). The number of neurons in the hidden layers of the radius-restricted complex-valued NN is more than twice that of the free-radius Complex-valued NN, to compensate for the halving of the number of free parameters in the former as compared to the latter. Even in the optimal radius 8, the results for the radius-restricted Complex-valued NN are inferior to the results obtained for Qubit NN.

Next, we proceed to investigate the point (b).

To clarify the advantages of the quantum description, i.e. the quantum superposition in Eq.(11), we evaluate Qubit NN from which the quantum superposition is removed. Figure 15 shows the results of simulations on

Figure 15. Quantum superposition effect in Learning performance (♦ : Qubit NN, □ : Qubit NN without quantum superposition)

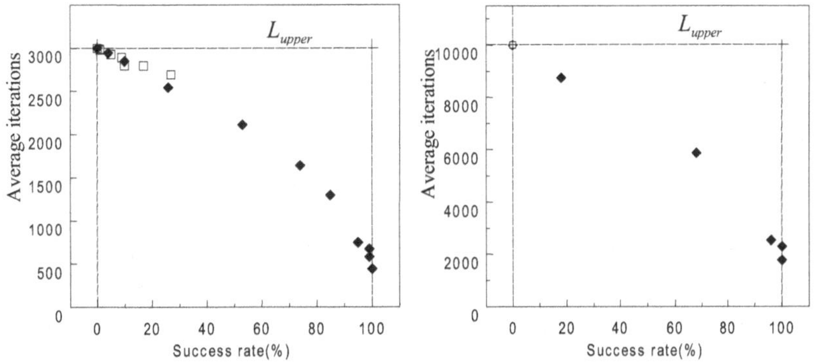

(a) The case of 4-bit parity check problem *(b) The case of 6-bit parity check problem*

the models with and without quantum superposition: in this case, the concrete values of the phase of the qubit state on the hidden layer is $n\pi/2$ (n=0,1,2, ···). From Figure 15, we see the removal of superposition substantially downgraded the performance of the model in both the 4-bit and 6-bit cases. In the removal case of 6-bit parity check, we cannot complete the training successfully. The simulation conditions for the 4-bit parity check and 6-bit parity check problems are the same as in Figure 10 and Figure 11, respectively.

Lastly, we discuss the point (c).

By changing the $output_n = \left|\mathrm{Im}(z_n^o)\right|^2$ into $\left|\mathrm{Im}(z_n^o)\right|$ in Eq.(15), we realized a model without a probability interpretation in the quantum description. The results in the 4-bit and 6-bit cases are shown in Figure 16. We find, in the removal case of the 6-bit parity check, the success rate stays below 10 %, even in the optimal case. From these figures, we see that the removal of the partial description or features from Qubit NN resulted in a decrease of its performance.

The above results thus indicate that the high learning efficiency of Qubit NN is due not to the restriction of the polar radius but to the description in terms of the quantum superposition and the probability interpretation inspired by quantum computation.

PRACTICAL APPLICATIONS

We have discussed the basic computational power of Qubit NN by solving bench mark problems in the previous section. In this section we investigate the solvable performance of Qubit NN in practical and knotty engineering problems. We have already found that this model outperforms to Real-valued NN in solving the image compression problem (Kouda, Matsui, & Nishimura, 2002) and the control problem of inverted pendulum (Kouda, Matsui, Nishimura, & Peper, 2005b) and confirmed its efficiency. Here, in order to confirm its solvable ability and expand its industrial applications we examine its information processing power in the well-known Iris data classification problem and the night vision processing.

Figure 16. Probabilistic interpretation effect in Learning performance (♦ : Qubit NN, ○ : Qubit NN without probabilistic interpretation)

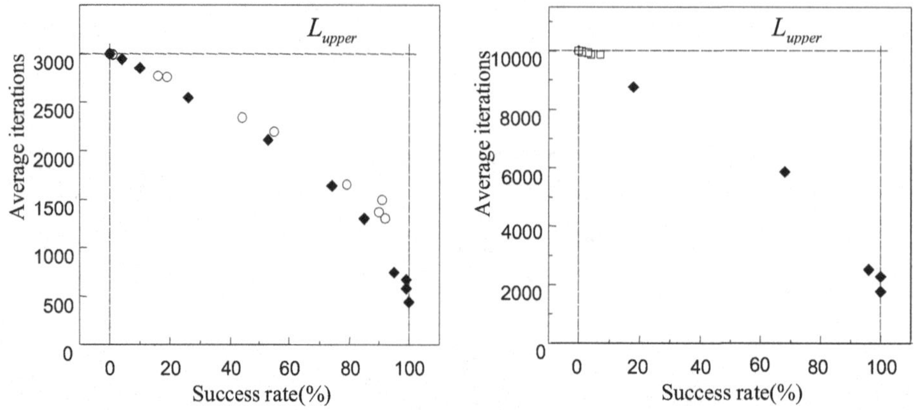

(a) The case of 4-bit parity check problem *(b)The case of 6-bit parity check problem*

Iris Data Classification Problem

Let's start our simulations with solving the Iris data classification problem. This problem is to classify the iris data set into three species. The iris data set consists of 4 measurements from 150 random iris flower samples (Blake, & Merz, 1998): 50 setosa (class1), 50 versicolor (class2), and 50 virginica (class3). As an example of the Iris data distribution shown in Figure 17, we see this distribution is uneven and very difficult to classify between the class2 and the class3.

First, we determine the optimal learning rates $\eta_q = 0.1$ and $\eta_r = 0.5$ at which performances of Qubit NN and Real-valued NN are best. The performances in this case are evaluated by the averaged *NCE*s for 30 trials with L_{upper} =1500. Here, *NCE* is a normalized cumulative error defined by

$$NCE = \frac{1}{L_{upper}} \sum_{l=1}^{L_{upper}} E(l), \quad E(l) = \sum_{p=1}^{P} E_p(l). \tag{33}$$

Where *E(l)* is the total squared error at *l*-th learning iteration. In each learning iteration, the network accepts *P* training samples and modifies its network parameters. The networks undergo L_{upper} learning iterations, i.e., $l \le L_{upper}$.

In order to evaluate the network performances in this Iris problem, we introduce the following normalized cumulative right answer *NCR*:

$$NCR = \frac{1}{L_{upper}} \sum_{l=1}^{L_{upper}} R_A(l), \quad R_A(l) = \frac{\text{the number of correct classification data}}{\text{the number of all test data}}, \tag{34}$$

where $R_A(l)$ is the rate of success to the correct classification in the *l*-th learning iteration.

Figure 18 shows the transitions of the total squared error *E(l)* and the correct classification rate $R_A(l)$. This

Figure 17. Example of Iris data distribution

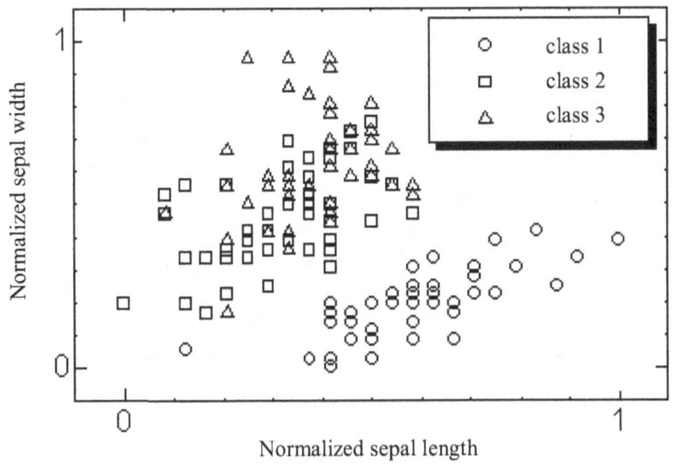

Figure 18. Qubit NN vs. Real-valued NN in performances on $R_A(l)$ and $E(l)$

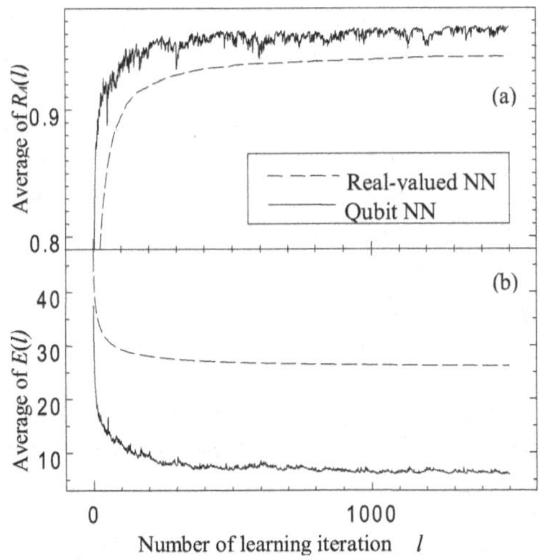

value becomes 1.0 when all the input data are correctly classified. From this figure, we see that Qubit NN has better classification ability than Real-valued NN, and Qubit NN can avoid the standstill states in learning while the learning in Real-valued NN may get stuck at one of local minima. We furthermore investigate the performances for Qubit NN and Real-valued NN from the viewpoint of generalization ability. It is conducted by applying 5-hold cross validation to the learning and evaluating processes. First we investigate the performances for evenly divided data set. In evenly divided condition, the data set for evaluating consists of 10 data for the setosa class (classl), 10 data for the versicolor class (class2) and 10 data for virginica (class3), and remaining 120 data (40 data for each class) are used for training. In other words, under this condition, the number of data for each class is set to be same. For 100 trials, we obtain *NCR*=92.7% for Qubit NN and *NCR* =91.7% for Real-valued NN. Next we conduct the performance evaluations under biased conditions. In these conditions, the data set is divided into two subsets for training and evaluating, but the number of data for one class may be different from others. We prepare three cases for dividing data set, as shown in Table 1. For example in the training data set in case 1, the number of data for class 1 is less than those for other classes and there are only class 1 data set for evaluation. For 500 trials for each case, we obtain *NCR*=72.5% for Qubit NN and 46.5% for Real-valued NN. Under biased conditions, the networks have difficulty for acquiring the characteristics from the training data set. But in these conditions, the performance of Qubit NN tops that of Real-valued NN, so we can conclude that our Qubit NN has better ability at acquiring the feature even from less data set, than Real-valued NN.

Night Vision Processing

The night vision processing is an image processing in which finer pixel values are estimated from gloomy ones as shown in Figure 19. In this work, we follow the scheme of the night vision processing with neural network that has been proposed in (Kusamichi et.al., 2004). The night vision processing has aimed to extract information from night scenes, in other words, to estimate the value of pixel in image taken in enough illumination from the value of pixel in image taken in night or twilight. Therefore, to train the network, the images from one scene taken in different illumination are necessary. For example, the image for input to the network is shown as Dark image in Figure 19 and the image for correspond to target is shown as Output image in Figure 19. These images has resolution of 160×120 (=19,200 pixels) and its intensity value is normalized from 0.0 to 1.0.

The network structure for this task is 9-*n*-1. The input data to the network consist of the value of the pixel located at (x, y) and its eight direct neighboring pixels located at $(x+i, y+i)$ of the input image, where $(i,j)=\{(-1,-1),(0,-1),(1,-1),(-1,0),(1,0),(-1,1),(0,1),(1,1)\}$.The corresponding output is the pixel value located at (x, y) of the target image. For the image with the resolution of 160×120, the number of the training pattern is 18,644 (=158×118) due to the incompleteness of input on the edge pixels. An outline of training the network is shown in Figure 20, where the pixels corresponding to each location are applied to the network in training.

The network structures of Qubit NN and Real-valued NN used in the following simulations are 9-5-1 and 9-6-1, and the neural parameters are 62 and 67, respectively. For the evaluation of images output from the networks, we introduce the *PSNR* (peak-signal to noise ratio) of these images with respect to the target image. The *PSNR* between two images, named Φ and Φ' consist of $X \times Y$ pixels is defined as

$$PSNR = 10\log_{10}\left(\frac{1}{MSE}\right), \quad MSE = \frac{1}{X \times Y}\sum_{x}^{X}\sum_{y}^{Y}\left(I(x,y) - I'(x,y)\right)^2, \tag{35}$$

where $I(x, y)$ and $I'(x, y)$ represent the intensities of the pixels at the location (x, y) in the images Φ and Φ' respectively. First, as well as the iris data classification, we investigate the optimal learning rate. By calculating the averages of *NCE* on 30 trials under L_{upper}=500, we find the optimal values in this application η_q=0.01 for Qubit NN and η_r =1.0 for Real-valued NN. In Figure 21, we show the averages of $E(l)$ at each optimal parameter.

By using these optimal values, we compare the output images of Qubit NN with those of Real-valued NN. In Figure 22, for example, we show typical images obtained at l=500 together with $E(500)$ values and their *PSNR* values. From Figs.21 and 22 we see that Qubit NN outperforms to Real-valued one.

Figure 19. Night vision system based on neural network

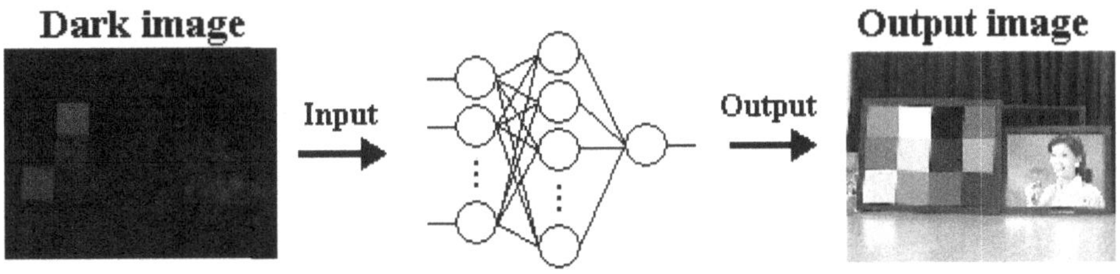

Figure 20. Training procedure in Night Vision Processing

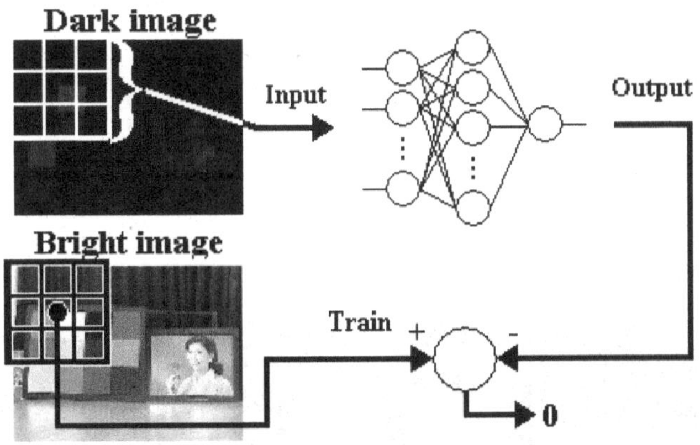

Table 1. Classification experiments data

experiments	the number of training data			the number of test data		
	class 1	class 2	class 3	class 1	class 2	class 3
case 1	20	50	50	30	0	0
case 2	50	20	50	0	30	0
case 3	50	50	20	0	0	30

Next, we consider the output images as shown in Figure 23. In this case, the output image from Qubit NN seems to be better than that from Real-valued NN, although we compare the best error value image for Real-valued NN with the average error one for Qubit NN. Figure 24 shows the distribution of pixel values for images after training and the relations between input and output images. We observe from Figs24 (a), (b) that values of pixels in output image for Qubit NN present linear behavior, but ones for Real-valued NN seem to reach saturation. This behavior of Real-valued NN is one of causes lowering the quality of image. In other words, it is insufficient in only error as the evaluation of the images. To explain this point, we import "*margin*" as follows:

$$margin(x,y) = |V(x,y) - V(x+1,y)| + |V(x,y) - V(x,y+1)|, \quad (36)$$

where, $margin(x,y)$ and $V(x,y)$ are the "*margin*" and the value of pixel located at (x, y) in the image. Now, we create the histogram of this "*margin*" as shown in Figure 25. In Figure 25, the histogram for Qubit NN is

Figure 21. Averages of total squared error E(l)

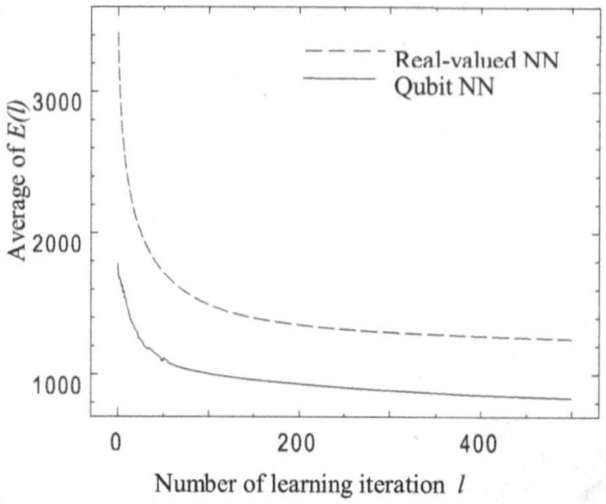

Figure 22. Original image and output images from networks

(a) Target(Original) image *(b) Image from Real-valued NN [E(500) =1212, PSNR=14.28]* *(c) Image from Qubit NN [E(500) =833, PSNR=15.91]*

Figure 23. The image output from neural networks

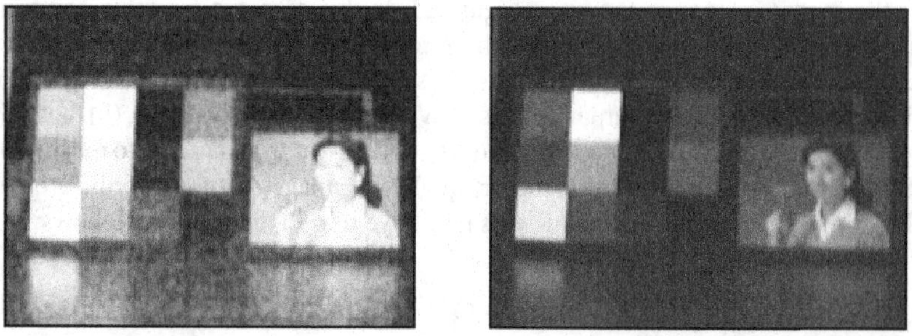

(a) The image from Real-valued NN [E(500) =297, PSNR=17.98] *(b) The image from Qubit NN [E(500) =919, PSNR=13.07]*

Figure 24. Distribution of pixel values for images after training

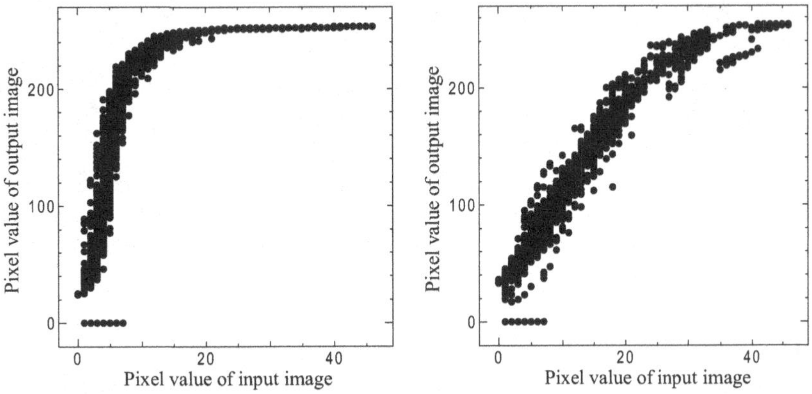

(a) Real-valued NN *(b) Qubit NN*

Figure 25. Histogram of "margin" for images shown in Figure 23

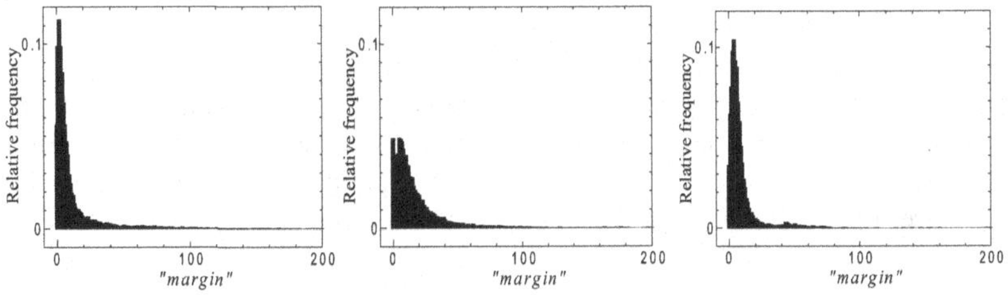

(a) Target *(b) Real-valued NN* *(c) Qubit NN*

more similar to one for target than one for Real-valued NN. In order to evaluate quantitatively, we calculate the Kullback-Leibler distance (K-L distance) D_{KL} by the thought that histogram is probability density function. The K-L distance is a natural distance measure from a "true" probability distribution P to an arbitrary probability distribution Q, and widely used in information theory. For probability distributions P and Q, the K-L distance of Q from P is defined as

$$D_{KL}(P,Q) = \sum_i P(i)\log\frac{P(i)}{Q(i)}. \tag{37}$$

As the result, K-L distance for Real-valued NN $D_{KL,R}$ is 0.2457 and one for Qubit NN $D_{KL,Q}$ is 0.0904. We confirm the similar results by using the test image: Paper bag (provided from Seiko Instruments Inc.) in Figure 26. In this case, the error of image is E=467 for Real-valued NN, and E=1009 for Qubit NN and the higher quality of image and linear behavior are shown in only Qubit NN solution. In addition, K-L distance $D_{KL,R}$ and $D_{KL,Q}$ are 0.1156 and 0.0960 for the paper bag image respectively. That is, even if the error and the *PSNR* of Real-valued are both better than those of Qubit one, we can obtain that Qubit NN has better image quality than Real-valued. This result is confirmed by using another image such as anime character. This is one of the advantageous features of Qubit NN.

Figure 26. The image output from Real-valued NN and Qubit NN by using test image

(a) *Target(Original) image* | (b) *Image from Real-valued NN [E(500) =467, PSNR=16.01]* | (c) *Image from Qubit NN [E(500) =1009, PSNR=12.67]*

CONCLUSION

In this chapter, we have introduced a scheme of quantum neural computing, namely, Qubit NN inspired by quantum computing. We compared its information processing performances with those of Classical NNs by means of solving the 4 and 6-bit parity check problems and the general function identification problem as a benchmark. In all simulations for the benchmark problems, we have observed that Qubit NN has more efficient processing abilities than Classical NNs and also revealed that the excellent computational ability of Qubit NN is not simply due to the complex-valued neural parameters or the introduction of the restricted polar radius, but to the characteristics inspired by quantum superposition and probabilistic interpretation. Furthermore, we have shown that Qubit NN outperforms Real-valued NN in the two practical applications. In the iris data classification by using non-uniformly data, there is a difference between Qubit NN and Real-valued NN in the classification performance. In the night vision processing, Qubit NN has a linear-like behavior between input and output images, which, we have observed, in turn contributes to enhancing the quality of output images. Thus we have made clear the advantage features of our Qubit NN in these numerical experiments.

FUTURE RESEARCH DIRECTIONS

From simulation experiments examined in our works, we conclude the efficiency of Qubit NN as probable. Of course, it is an open question that whether our Qubit NN outperforms Classical NNs in all information-processing problems or not, and that whether it is confirmed, without any mathematical proof, quantum computing descriptions enhance the computational power in neural information processing. At the present, to finalize this proof seems to be impossible. It is left for future studies. However, in order to validate the advantages of Qubit NN, it is worth investigating its computational ability in learning chaos systems and then improving its learning method. In addition, we will try to apply our qubit neuron model not only to multi-layered networks but also to the other networks such as a Hopfield-type and a cellular one, considering the other schemes of learning. We will challenge the integer prime-factorization problem using Qubit NN. At present, Classical NN method seems to be not sufficient for such a trial (Jansen, & Nakayama, 2005). This may be interesting and give a breakthrough for creating the scheme of neural quantum computing to establish these schemes as a step for a novel quantum algorithm provided that the comparison with Shor's algorithm is possible. It is also attractive to incorporate Grover's algorithm into the learning method of Qubit NN. By trying these, we expect to establish Qubit NN as a step for a novel quantum algorithm.

Other future work will focus on the use of Qubit NN in practical applications with more neural parameters to establish this method concretely. We, furthermore, will compare Qubit NN with Hypercomplex-valued NNs including Complex-valued NN in detail. It is true that Qubit NN method is an interesting method as a new complex-valued NN, and has a great potential for enlarging applications of complex-valued NN.

ACKNOWLEDGMENT

The contribution for this chapter is based on the studies in (Kouda, Matsui, Nishimura, & Peper,2005a) (Mori, Isokawa, Kouda, Matsui, & Nishimura,2006). Part of this research is supported by Grant-in-Aid for Scientific Research(C-16500135) Japan Society for the Promotion of Science.

REFERENCES

Behrman, E.C., Niemel, J., Steck, J.E., & Skinner, S.R. (1996). A quantum dot neural network. *Proceedings of the 4th Workshop on Physics of Computation*, 22-24.

Behrman, E. C., Nash, L. R., Steck, J. E., Chandrashekar, V. G., & Skinner, S. R. (2000). Simulations of quantum neural networks. *Information Sciences, 128*, 257-269.

Bernstein, E., & Vazirani, U.(1993). Quantum complexity theory. *Proceedings of the 25th Annual ACM Symposium on the Theory of Computing*, (pp. 11-20).

Bernstein, E., & Vazirani, U. (1997). Quantum complexity theory. *SIAM Journal of Computing, 26*(5), 1411-1473.

Blake, C. L., & Merz, C. J. (1998). *UCI repository of machine learning databases.* Retrieved 1998, from http://www.ics.uci.edu/~mlearn/MLRepository.html

Deutsch, D. (1985). Quantum theory, the Church-Turing principle, and the universal quantum computer. *Proceedings of the Royal Society London A, 400*, 97-117.

Deutsch, D., & Jozsa, R.(1992). Rapid solution of problems by quantum computation. *Proceedings of the Royal Society London A, 439*, 553-558.

Ezhov, A. A., Nifanova, A. V., & Ventura, D. (2000). Quantum associative memory with distributed queries. *Information Sciences, 128*, 271-293.

Feynman, R. P. (1982). Quantum mechanical computers. *Optics News, 11*, 11-20.

Grover, L. V. (1996). A fast quantum mechanical algorithm for database search. *In Proceedings of the ACM Symposium on the Theory of Computing* (pp.212-219). New York: ACM Press.

Grover, L. V. (1997). Quantum mechanics helps in searching for a needle in a haystack. *Physical Review Letters, 78*, 325-328.

Hirose, A. (Ed.) (2003). *Complex-Valued Neural Networks: Theories and Applications.* Singapore: World Scientific.

Jansen, B., & Nakayama, K. (2005). Neural networks following a binary approach to the integer prime-factorization problem. *Proceedings of the International Joint Conference on Neural Networks, 4*, 2577-2582.

Kak, S. C. (1995). On quantum neural computing. *Information Sciences, 83*, 143-163.

Kouda, N., Matsui, N., & Nishimura, H. (2002, 2004). A multi-layered feed-forward network based on qubit neuron model. (2002 in Japanese) *IEICE, J85-DII(4)*, 641-648. (2004 in English) *Systems and Computers in Japan, 35(13)*, 43-51.

Kouda, N., Matsui, N., & Nishimura, H. (2002). Image Compression by Layered Quantum Neural Networks. *Neural Processing Letters, 16(1)*, 67-80.

Kouda, N., Matsui, N., Nishimura, H., & Peper, F. (2005a). Qubit Neural Network and Its Learning Efficiency, *Neural Computing and Applications, 14(2)*, 114-121.

Kouda, N., Matsui, N., Nishimura, H., & Peper, F. (2005b). An Examination of Qubit Neural Network in Controlling an Inverted Pendulum. *Neural Processing Letters, 22(3)*, 277-290.

Kusamichi, H., Isokawa, T., Matsui, N., Ogawa, Y., & Maeda, K. (2004). A New Scheme for Color Night Vision by Quaternion Neural Network. In *Proceedings of the 2nd International Conference on Autonomous Robots and Agents* (pp.101–106).

Matsui, N., Takai, M., & Nishimura, H. (1998, 2000). A network model based on qubit-like neuron corresponding to quantum circuit. (1998 in Japanese) *IEICE, J81-A(12)*, 1687-1692. (2000 in English) *Electronics and Communications in Japan, part III, 83(10)*, 67-73.

Menneer, T., & Narayanan, A. (1995). *Quantum-inspired neural networks* (Tech. Rep. R329). Exeter, United Kingdom: University of Exeter, Department of Computer Science.

Mori, K., Isokawa, T., Kouda, N., Matsui, N., & Nishimura, H. (2006). Qubit Inspired Neural Network towards Its Practical Applications. In *Proceedings of 2006 International Joint Conference on Neural Networks* (pp. 616-621).

Narayanan, A., & Menneer, T. (2000). Quantum artificial neural network architectures and components. *Information Sciences, 128*, 231-255.

Nielsen, M. A., & Chuang, I. L. (2000). *Quantum Computation and Quantum Information.* Cambridge: Cambridge University Press.

Nitta, T. (1997). An Extension of the Back-Propagation Algorithm to Complex Numbers. *Neural Networks, 10(8)*, 1391-1415.

Shor, P. W. (1994). Algorithm for quantum computation: discrete logarithms and factoring. *Proccedings of the 35th Annual IEEE Symposium on Foundations of Computer Science*, (pp. 124-134).

Siegelmann, H. T. (1999). Neural Networks and Analog Computation: Beyond the Turing Limit. Boston: Birkhäuser.

Peruš, M. (1996). Neuro-Quantum Parallelism in Brain-Mind and Computers. *Informatica, 20*, 173-183.

Peruš, M., Bischof, H., Caulfield, H. J., & Loo, C. K. (2004). Quantum-Implementable Selective Reconstruction of High-Resolution Images. *Applied Optics, 43(Issue 33)*, 6134-6138.

Rigui, Z., Nan, J., & Qiulin, D. (2006). Model and training of QNN with weight. *Neural Processing Letters, 24*, 261-269.

Ventura, D., Martinez, T. (1997). An artificial neuron with quantum mechanical properties. In *Proceedings of the International Conference on Artificial Neural Networks and Genetic Algorithms* (pp. 482-485).

Yao, A. (1993). Quantum circuit complexity. *Proceedings of the 34th IEEE Symposium on Foundations of Computer Science* (pp. 352-360). Los Alamitos, CA: IEEE Society Press.

ADDITIONAL READING

Arena, P., Fortuna, L., Muscato, G., & Xibilia, M. G. (1998). *Neural Networks in Multidimensional Domains.* Lecture Notes in Computer Sciences, *234*. Springer-Verlag.

Bouwmeester, D., Ekert, A., & Zeilinger, A. (Ed.) (2000). *The physics of quantum information.* Berlin Heidelberg: Springer.

Iwasaki, I., Nakajima, H., & Shimizu, T. (1998). Interacting Brownian particles as a model of neural network. *International Journal of Bifurcation and Chaos, 8(4)*, 791-797.

Ekert, A.K., & Jozsa, R. (1996). Quantum computation and Shor's quantum factoring algorithm. *Review of Modern Physics, 68*, 733-753.

Ezhov, A. A., & Ventura, D. (2000). Quantum neural networks. In N. Kasabov (Ed.), *Future Directions for Intelligent Systems and Information Science* (pp. 213-235). Physica-Verlag.

Gruska, J. (1999). *Quantum computing.* London, UK: McGraw-Hill.

Gupta, S., & Zia, R. K. P. (2001). Quantum neural networks. *Journal of Computer and System Sciences, 63*(3), 355-383.

Kasabov, N. (2007). Brain-, gene-, and quantum inspired computational intelligence: Challenges and opportunities. *Studies in Computational Intelligence, 63*, 193-219.

Kullback, S., & Leibler, R. A. (1951). On Information and Sufficiency. *The annals of Mathematical Statistics, 22(1)*, 79-86.

Stenholm, S., & Suominen, K-A. (2005). *Quantum approach to informatics.* Hoboken, NJ: Wiley.

Williams, C. P., & Clearwater, S. H. (1998). *Explorations in quantum computing.* New York: Springer.

Zhou, R., Qin, L., & Jiang, N.(2006). Quantum perceptron network. *Lecture Notes in Computer Science, 4131, LNCS(I)*, 651-657.

Chapter XIV
Neuromorphic Adiabatic Quantum Computation

Shigeo Sato
Tohuku University, Japan

Mitsunaga Kinjo
University of the Ryukus, Japan

ABSTRACT

The advantage of quantum mechanical dynamics in information processing has attracted much interest, and dedicated studies on quantum computation algorithms indicate that a quantum computer has remarkable computational power in certain tasks. Quantum properties such as quantum superposition and quantum tunneling are worth studying because they may overcome the weakness of gradient descent method in classical neural networks. Also, the technique established for neural networks can be useful for developing a quantum algorithm. In this chapter, first the authors show the effectiveness of incorporating quantum dynamics and then propose neuromorphic adiabatic quantum computation algorithm based on the adiabatic change of Hamiltonian. The proposed method can be viewed as one of complex-valued neural networks because a qubit operates like a neuron. Next, the performance of the proposed algorithm is studied by applying it to a combinatorial optimization problem. Finally, they discuss the learning ability and hardware implementation.

INTRODUCTION

Real parallel computing is possible with a quantum computer which makes use of quantum states (Nielsen & Chuang, 2000). It is well known that a quantum computation algorithm for factorization discovered by Shor (1994) is faster than any classical algorithm. Also a quantum algorithm for database search in $O\left(\sqrt{N}\right)$ quantum computation steps instead of $O(N)$ classical steps has been proposed by Grover (1996). These algorithms are often referred to as representative quantum algorithms utilizing features of quantum dynamics. A quantum algorithm not limited to a specific problem is needed for the development of a quantum computer from the practical viewpoint. Farhi et al. have proposed an adiabatic quantum computation (AQC) for solving the three-satisfiability (3-SAT) problem (Farhi, Goldstone, Gutmann, & Sipser, 2000). AQC can be applied to various problems including non-deterministic polynomial time problems (NP Problems) if one can obtain proper Hamiltonians. A few methods have been proposed such as the original AQC by Farhi et al. (Farhi & Gutmann, 1996; Farhi et al., 2000; Farhi et al., 2001), AQCs utilizing analogy to quantum circuits (Aharonov et al., 2004; Siu, 2005), and neuromorphic AQC(Sato, Kinjo, & Nakajima 2003; Kinjo, Sato, Nakamiya, & Nakajima, 2005).

Neural networks can be applied to such combinatorial optimization problems. The most popular approach is to utilize a Hopfield neural network (HNN) (Hopfield, 1982). However, it has been known that an HNN is often trapped in local minima, and an optimal solution is not obtained in this case. This is because the dynamics of the network is determined by the local features of the energy potential. On the other hand, if we can incorporate quantum dynamics into a neural network, such undesired behavior could be avoided.

Many studies inspired by quantum computation or quantum mechanics have been reported in order to improve the performance of neural networks related to associative memories, learning ability, and so on (Ventura & Martinez, 2000; Ezhov & Ventura, 2000; Matsui, Takai, & Nishimura 1998, 2000; Peruš, Bischof, Caulfield, & Loo, 2004; Mori, Isokawa, Kouda, Matsui, & Nishimura, 2006). Neural networks having quantum properties can be viewed as one of complex-valued neural networks since its neuron state is expressed in complex numbers. Good introductions on quantum neural networks (QNN) are found in some chapters of this book. Also the study described in this chapter is related to QNN, and the research purpose is to introduce methods used in conventional neural networks to quantum computation. We focus on AQC inspired from an HNN. First the advantages of quantum dynamics and quantum computation are described together with simple examples. Next, neuromorphic adiabatic quantum computation (NAQC) is proposed by relating AQC with HNN in order to incorporate neuromorphic techniques to quantum computation. The performance of NAQC is evaluated when it is applied to the N-queen problem, which is one of the NP problems. The effect of energy dissipation is studied for favorable state transitions to lower energy states resulting in performance enhancement. Then, a learning method in NAQC is studied for practical use. Finally, hardware implementation of the proposed method is discussed.

BACKGROUND

Quantum Computation

Recent development in nanotechnology makes it possible to fabricate nano-scale devices. It is known that we can confirm the wave nature of an electron when it is confined in a nano-scale region, and the energy of an electron is quantized depending on potential barrier. The behavior of a particle in such a very tiny region is explained not by classical mechanics but by quantum mechanics. Quantum mechanics says that a quantum state can be expressed as a superposition of certain states. For example, let us consider a spin-1/2 particle and suppose that its state $|\psi\rangle$ is given as

$$|\psi\rangle = \frac{1}{\sqrt{2}}\left(|\uparrow\rangle + |\downarrow\rangle\right), \tag{1}$$

where $|\uparrow\rangle$ and $|\downarrow\rangle$ denote the spin-up and down states, respectively. If we measure the spin state in Eq.(1), $|\uparrow\rangle$ and $|\downarrow\rangle$ are found with the same probability 1/2. This superposition is the most important characteristic for quantum computation. Next, we execute the NOT operation with this particle. Usually, we use $|\uparrow\rangle = |0\rangle = (1\ 0)'$, $|\downarrow\rangle = |1\rangle = (0\ 1)'$, and a quantum NOT operator is given as

$$\mathcal{N} = \begin{pmatrix} 0 & 1 \\ 1 & 0 \end{pmatrix}, \tag{2}$$

The time evolution of a quantum system is given as

$$i\frac{\partial|\psi(t)\rangle}{\partial t} = H|\psi(t)\rangle, \tag{3}$$

$$|\psi(t)\rangle = U(t)|\psi(0)\rangle, \quad (4)$$

$$U(t) = \exp(-iHt), \quad (5)$$

where H and $U(t)$ are Hamiltonian and its Unitary operators, respectively. Note that we use $\hbar = 1$ for simplicity. When $\mathcal{N}$ is chosen as the Hamiltonian H and t is equal to π, $U(t)$ is identical with $\mathcal{N}$. Thus the NOT operation can be done, in which two independent state changes $|0\rangle \rightarrow |1\rangle$, $|1\rangle \rightarrow |0\rangle$ occur simultaneously. Note that the initial state is recovered at $t = 2\pi$. This is the simplest example of quantum logic operations, where $|\psi(t)\rangle$ denotes a single qubit state and is given as a superposition of $|0\rangle$ and $|1\rangle$. The term "qubit" is used for clarifying the difference with a classical digital bit. To be exact, the single qubit state is given as

$$|\psi\rangle = C_0|0\rangle + C_1|1\rangle, \quad (6)$$

where C_0 and C_1 are complex numbers. By considering the normalized condition $|C_0|^2 + |C_1|^2 = 1$, $|\psi\rangle$ is rewritten as

$$|\psi\rangle = e^{i\gamma}\left\{\cos\frac{\theta}{2}|0\rangle + e^{i\varphi}\sin\frac{\theta}{2}|1\rangle\right\} \quad (7)$$

Furthermore, since the phase factor $e^{i\gamma}$ does not affect observable physical states, it is convenient to use the following representation in Bloch sphere as shown in Fig.1.

$$|\psi\rangle = \cos\frac{\theta}{2}|0\rangle + e^{i\varphi}\sin\frac{\theta}{2}|1\rangle, \quad (8)$$

where $0 \leq \theta \leq \pi$ and $0 \leq \varphi \leq 2\pi$.

Figure 1. Bloch vector of a qubit

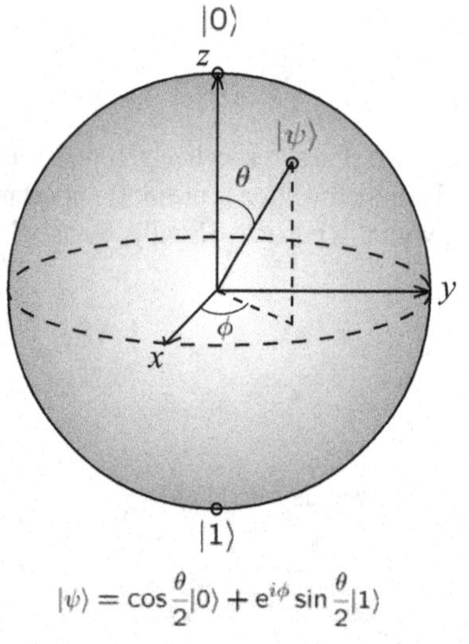

In general, quantum computation is done by executing a set of quantum logic operations. For example, a single qubit rotation gate changes $|\psi(\theta,\varphi)\rangle$ to $|\psi(\theta',\varphi')\rangle$ in Bloch sphere. Also, a two-qubit controlled-NOT (CNOT) gate inverts a target bit if the other control qubit is $|1\rangle$, namely the state changes as $|00\rangle \rightarrow |00\rangle$, $|01\rangle \rightarrow |01\rangle$, $|10\rangle \rightarrow |11\rangle$, $|11\rangle \rightarrow |10\rangle$. Note that $|x_2 x_1\rangle$ is the binary notation of the two-qubit state. Any quantum logic is realized with the pair of a single qubit rotation gate and a two-qubit CNOT gate, and thus this pair is one of the quantum universal gates (Nielsen & Chuang, 2000).

To utilize quantum parallelism fully, dedicated quantum algorithms have been proposed. One of the most famous quantum computation algorithms is Shor's factorization algorithm (Shor, 1994). We do not explain the algorithm entirely, but describe the algorithm for finding the period of a given function, which is the most important computational step in Shor's factorization algorithm. Two quantum registers are required for finding the period of a function $f(x)$. X and Y registers store x and $f(x)$ values, respectively, and they must be coupled in a quantum manner. At the beginning of the calculation, all possible values for the argument x and corresponding $f(x)$ are set to these registers as a superpositional state

$$|\psi\rangle = \frac{1}{\sqrt{2^n}} \sum_{x=0}^{2^n-1} |x, f(x)\rangle, \tag{9}$$

where n denotes the number of qubits in the X register. By applying the following discrete Fourier transform acting on the X register,

$$|x\rangle \Rightarrow \frac{1}{\sqrt{2^n}} \sum_{k=0}^{2^n-1} e^{2\pi ikx/2^n} |k\rangle, \tag{10}$$

the whole state $|\psi\rangle$ in Eq.(9) changes to the state given as

$$|\psi'\rangle = \frac{1}{2^n} \sum_{x=0}^{2^n-1} \sum_{k=0}^{2^n-1} e^{2\pi ikx/2^n} |k, f(k)\rangle. \tag{11}$$

To view how this calculation works, let us consider a simple case in which we choose $n = 3$ and $T = 2$, where T denotes the period of the function $f(x)$. Now, we obtain the following result.

$$|\psi'\rangle = \frac{1}{2}\left\{|0, f(0)\rangle + |0, f(1)\rangle + |4, f(0)\rangle + e^{i\pi}|4, f(1)\rangle\right\}, \tag{12}$$

where the relations $f(0) = f(2) = f(4) = f(6)$, $f(1) = f(3) = f(5) = f(7)$ are considered. It can be seen that many terms are canceled out due to the periodicity of $f(x)$. By measuring the X register, we find 0 or 4 with the same probability 1/2. According to Shor's algorithm, the measured value takes one of the following values,

$$0, \frac{2^n}{T}, \frac{2\times 2^n}{T}, \frac{3\times 2^n}{T}, \ldots, \frac{(T-1)\times 2^n}{T}. \tag{13}$$

Therefore, we find the period T is equal to 2. The advantage of this calculation is that all possible values of the argument x are embedded in a single superpositional state and processed simultaneously. The detail of Shor's algorithm is found in references (Shor, 1994; Nielsen & Chuang, 2000).

Adiabatic Quantum Computation

In order to apply quantum computation to practical problems, the development of an algorithm for general purpose computation is crucially important. One of such algorithms is the adiabatic quantum computation (AQC) proposed by Farhi et al. (2000). Unlike Shor's algorithm, AQC is not based on quantum logic operations. Instead, the computation is executed by the continuous change of a Hamiltonian. The Hamiltonian change is given as

$$H(t)=\left(1-\frac{t}{T}\right)H_I+\frac{t}{T}H_F, \tag{14}$$

where H_I and H_F are the initial and final Hamiltonians, and T denotes the period of the Hamiltonian change. The initial state $|\psi(0)\rangle$ is set to the ground state of H_I, which is composed of all possible states. The final Hamiltonian H_F should be chosen according to a desired operation or a target problem. If T is large enough, the quantum state change becomes adiabatic, and the quantum system stays in a ground state during the evolution. Initially all possible states can be found in $|\psi\rangle$, and non-desired states vanish gradually as time goes on, as shown in Fig.2. Finally desired states can be found by the measurement of $|\psi\rangle$. Because H_F can be chosen arbitrary, the scope in which AQC is applied to has not been limited to a specific problem. Farhi et al. demonstrated that the NP-complete problem exact cover (3-SAT) is solved efficiently by AQC (Farhi et al., 2000; Farhi et al., 2001). The exact cover is a problem for determining whether there is some assignment of the n-bit values that satisfies all of the given clauses. The clause means the requirement imposed to a 3-bit group in which one of three bits must have the value 1 and the other two must have the value 0. The final Hamiltonian H_F for exact cover is given as

$$H_F=\sum_{x=0}^{2^n-1}h(x)|x\rangle\langle x|=\sum_{x=0}^{2^n-1}\sum_{c}h_c(x_{i_c},x_{j_c},x_{k_c})|x\rangle\langle x|, \tag{15}$$

$$h_c(x_{i_c},x_{j_c},x_{k_c})=\begin{cases}0, & \text{if clause } C \text{ satisfied}\\ 1, & \text{if clause } C \text{ violated}\end{cases}, \tag{16}$$

where the suffixes i_c, j_c, k_c denote the bit indices defined by the clause C, and $x_{i_c}, x_{j_c}, x_{k_c}$ are binary variables, whereas x denotes an assignment given in decimal notation of an n-bit integer. The value of $h(x)$ gives the number of clauses violated, and it equals zero if and only if x satisfies all the clauses. Note that non-zero matrix elements appear only as diagonal elements of the final Hamiltonian H_F as seen in Eq.(15).

Grover's database search is another quantum algorithm that can be applied to general problems (Grover, 1996, 1997). This algorithm consists of repeated application of a quantum subroutine called Grover iteration. The

Figure 2. Probability change of each quantum state in adiabatic quantum computation

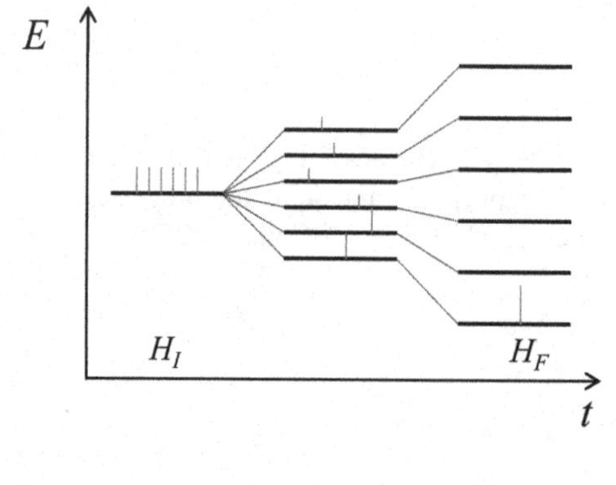

most important operator called "oracle" in Grover iteration can be chosen arbitrary as in the AQC, so that it can be applied to various problems. Though Grover's algorithm is based on discrete quantum logic operations, the analogy with AQC has been studied (Farhi & Gutmann, 1996; Aharonov et al., 2004). Roland and Cerf (2002) reported that the required computation time T for database search by AQC with optimized Hamiltonian change, is reduced to $\sqrt{N}$, where N is the number of data. This means that AQC and Grover's algorithm have the same computational power.

Let us describe some theoretical background related to AQC. The basic requirement in executing AQC is that a quantum system must stay always in each ground state during the Hamiltonian evolution. This is why the period T of the Hamiltonian evolution must be long enough. The adiabatic theorem says that the quantum state remains close to each ground state as long as the following relation is kept (Messiah, 1958).

$$\frac{D_{\max}}{g_{\min}^2} \le \varepsilon << 1. \tag{17}$$

$g_{\min}$ denotes the minimum energy gap between the first excited state and the ground state, and is given as

$$g_{\min} = \min_{0 \le t \le T} \left[E_1(t) - E_0(t) \right]. \tag{18}$$

$D_{\max}$ is defined as

$$D_{\max} = \max_{0 \le t \le T} \left| \left\langle \frac{dH}{dt} \right\rangle_{1,0} \right|. \tag{19}$$

where $\langle dH/dt \rangle_{1,0} = \langle E_1(t) | dH/dt | E_0(t) \rangle$. The relation in Eq.(17) indicates that the speed of Hamiltonian change must be adjusted properly according to the magnitude of the minimum gap $g_{\min}$. A bigger gap requires shorter computation time. However, even if the period T is long enough, successful operation is not guaranteed in the case that there exists any degeneracy in energy levels or any energy crossing during the evolution. This may be the most severe requirement for real applications.

NEUROMORPHIC ADIABATIC QUANTUM COMPUTATION

Hamiltonian and Qubit Interaction

In the previous section, we introduce that AQC has a possibility to be applied to various problems for utilizing computational power of quantum systems. But a guideline to design a final Hamiltonian H_F has not been provided yet. For the application to the NP-complete problem exact cover (3-SAT), Farhi et al. (2000) use a Hamiltonian composed only of diagonal elements. AQC works well if we can obtain a similar Hamiltonian for a certain problem. But when we consider a general case, we have to calculate all diagonal elements in the worst case. Since it costs calculation of $O(2^n)$ as huge as a heuristic search, where n is the number of qubits, an efficient method for designing a final Hamiltonian is worth studying. It has been known that the function of a neural network is determined by its synaptic weights. If we know the relation between the function of a quantum system composed of qubits and its interactions, the method to design a final Hamiltonian H_F could be obtained in consideration of the analogy with a neural network.

Let us consider a quantum system of two qubits to view the effect of qubit-qubit interaction. Suppose we have three Hamiltonians given as

$$H_1 = \begin{pmatrix} E & 0 & 0 & 0 \\ 0 & E & 0 & 0 \\ 0 & 0 & E & 0 \\ 0 & 0 & 0 & E \end{pmatrix}, H_2 = \begin{pmatrix} E & 0 & 0 & 0 \\ 0 & E & A & 0 \\ 0 & A & E & 0 \\ 0 & 0 & 0 & E \end{pmatrix}, H_3 = \begin{pmatrix} E & 0 & 0 & A \\ 0 & E & 0 & 0 \\ 0 & 0 & E & 0 \\ A & 0 & 0 & E \end{pmatrix} \quad (20)$$

Simple algebra gives eigenvectors and eigenvalues. For H_1, the two qubits have no interaction and eigenvectors $|00\rangle$, $|01\rangle$, $|10\rangle$, $|11\rangle$ have the same eigenvalue *E*. Note that, for example, $|00\rangle$ is given as the tensor product $|0\rangle \otimes |0\rangle = (1\ 0)^t \otimes (1\ 0)^t = (1\ 0\ 0\ 0)^t$. On the other hand, the interactions denoted by *A* are added in H_2 and H_3. The eigenvectors $1/\sqrt{2}\left(|01\rangle - |10\rangle\right)$ and $1/\sqrt{2}\left(|00\rangle - |11\rangle\right)$ have the minimum eigenvalue $E - |A|$ for H_2 and H_3, respectively. If we measure the two qubit system in the ground state of the Hamiltonian H_2, $|01\rangle$ and $|10\rangle$ are found with the same probability 1/2. In these two ground states, the qubits take the opposite states each other. In other words, inhibitory interaction is realized in H_2. In the same manner, we can find excitatory interaction in H_3. Thus we find a method for relating synaptic weights with qubit interactions (Sato et al., 2003). A negative synaptic weight corresponds to H_2 and a positive synaptic weight corresponds to H_3. Note that three Hamiltonians are rewritten in a rather simple form as

$$H_1 = E(I \otimes I), \quad H_2 = H_1 + A\left(a^\dagger \otimes a + a \otimes a^\dagger\right), \quad H_3 = H_1 + A\left(a^\dagger \otimes a^\dagger + a \otimes a\right), \quad (21)$$

$$I = \begin{pmatrix} 1 & 0 \\ 0 & 1 \end{pmatrix}, \quad a^\dagger = \begin{pmatrix} 0 & 0 \\ 1 & 0 \end{pmatrix}, \quad a = \begin{pmatrix} 0 & 1 \\ 0 & 0 \end{pmatrix}, \quad (22)$$

where *I*, $a^\dagger$ and *a* denote the 2x2 identity matrix, a creation operator and an annihilation operator, respectively. Of course, H_2 or H_3 is not real Hamiltonian based on some physical device and is chosen for our convenience. They can be replaced properly by other Hamiltonians in consideration of the characteristic of each qubit.

Relation Between Hopfield Neural Network and Neuromorphic Adiabatic Quantum Computation

A Hopfield neural network (HNN) is an artificial neural network model which can be applied to combinatorial optimization problems (Hopfiled & Tank, 1985; Tank & Hopfield, 1986). An HNN has symmetrical synaptic weights, and the energy function is defined as

$$E_{HN} = -\frac{1}{2}\sum_{i,j} w_{ij} o_i o_j, \quad (23)$$

where o_i is the output of the neuron *i* and takes a value between -1 and 1, and w_{ij} is the synaptic weight from the neuron *j* to the neuron *i*. Now we relate neurons, synaptic interaction, and an energy function to qubits, qubit-qubit interaction, and a Hamiltonian, respectively. Fig.3 shows the relation between an HNN and a quantum system composed of spin-1/2 particles.

Here, we consider a simple example where the synaptic matrix of the HNN in Fig.3 is given as

$$W = \begin{pmatrix} 0 & -1 & 1 \\ -1 & 0 & -1 \\ 1 & -1 & 0 \end{pmatrix} \quad (24)$$

Let us apply the relationship in Table 1. Since the absolute values of nonzero components of *W* are the same, we focus only on the sign of the synaptic weights, so that the final Hamiltonian is obtained as

Figure 3. Neural network and quantum system composed of spin-1/2 particles

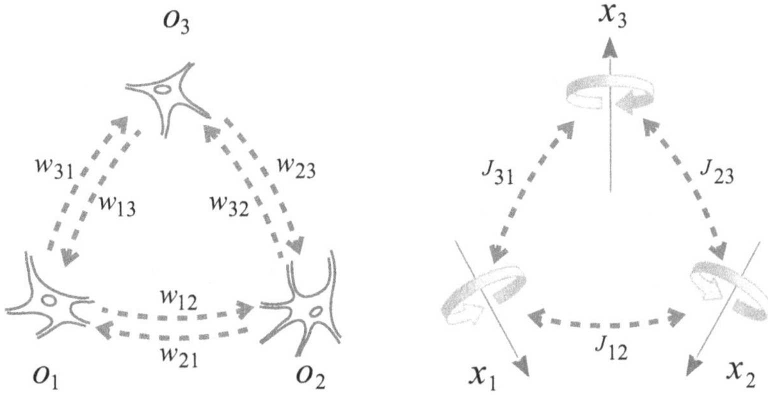

$$
\begin{aligned}
H_F &= EI' + A\left(H^{(w_{21}<0)} + H^{(w_{31}>0)} + H^{(w_{32}<0)}\right) \\
&= E(I\otimes I\otimes I) + A\left(I\otimes a^{\dagger}\otimes a + I\otimes a\otimes a^{\dagger}\right) + A\left(a^{\dagger}\otimes I\otimes a^{\dagger} + a\otimes I\otimes a\right) + A\left(a^{\dagger}\otimes a\otimes I + a\otimes a^{\dagger}\otimes I\right) \\
&= E\begin{pmatrix} 1&0&0&0&0&0&0&0\\ 0&1&0&0&0&0&0&0\\ 0&0&1&0&0&0&0&0\\ 0&0&0&1&0&0&0&0\\ 0&0&0&0&1&0&0&0\\ 0&0&0&0&0&1&0&0\\ 0&0&0&0&0&0&1&0\\ 0&0&0&0&0&0&0&1 \end{pmatrix} + A\begin{pmatrix} 0&0&0&0&0&0&0&0\\ 0&0&1&0&0&0&0&0\\ 0&1&0&0&0&0&0&0\\ 0&0&0&0&0&0&0&0\\ 0&0&0&0&0&0&0&0\\ 0&0&0&0&0&0&1&0\\ 0&0&0&0&0&1&0&0\\ 0&0&0&0&0&0&0&0 \end{pmatrix} + A\begin{pmatrix} 0&0&0&0&0&1&0&0\\ 0&0&0&0&0&0&0&0\\ 0&0&0&0&0&0&0&1\\ 0&0&0&0&0&0&0&0\\ 0&0&0&0&0&0&0&0\\ 1&0&0&0&0&0&0&0\\ 0&0&0&0&0&0&0&0\\ 0&0&1&0&0&0&0&0 \end{pmatrix} \\
&+ A\begin{pmatrix} 0&0&0&0&0&0&0&0\\ 0&0&0&0&0&0&0&0\\ 0&0&0&0&1&0&0&0\\ 0&0&0&0&0&1&0&0\\ 0&0&1&0&0&0&0&0\\ 0&0&0&1&0&0&0&0\\ 0&0&0&0&0&0&0&0\\ 0&0&0&0&0&0&0&0 \end{pmatrix} = \begin{pmatrix} E&0&0&0&0&A&0&0\\ 0&E&A&0&0&0&0&0\\ 0&A&E&0&A&0&0&A\\ 0&0&0&E&0&A&0&0\\ 0&0&A&0&E&0&0&0\\ A&0&0&A&0&E&A&0\\ 0&0&0&0&0&A&E&0\\ 0&0&A&0&0&0&0&E \end{pmatrix},
\end{aligned}
\tag{25}
$$

where I' denotes the 8x8 identity matrix. The initial Hamiltonian is given as

Table 1. Relationship between Hamiltonians and neural interactions

Hamiltonian	$\begin{pmatrix} E & 0 & 0 & 0 \\ 0 & E & 0 & 0 \\ 0 & 0 & E & 0 \\ 0 & 0 & 0 & E \end{pmatrix}$	$\begin{pmatrix} E & 0 & 0 & 0 \\ 0 & E & A & 0 \\ 0 & A & E & 0 \\ 0 & 0 & 0 & E \end{pmatrix}$	$\begin{pmatrix} E & 0 & 0 & A \\ 0 & E & 0 & 0 \\ 0 & 0 & E & 0 \\ A & 0 & 0 & E \end{pmatrix}$
Ground States	$\|00\rangle, \|01\rangle, \|10\rangle, \|11\rangle$	$\|01\rangle - \|10\rangle$	$\|00\rangle - \|11\rangle$
Measured States	$\|00\rangle, \|01\rangle, \|10\rangle, \|11\rangle$	$\|01\rangle, \|10\rangle$	$\|00\rangle, \|11\rangle$
Interaction	None	Inhibitory	Excitatory

$$H_I = \sigma_0^x + \sigma_1^x + \sigma_2^x = I \otimes I \otimes \sigma^x + I \otimes \sigma^x \otimes I + \sigma^x \otimes I \otimes I = \begin{pmatrix} 0 & 0 & 0 & 0 & 0 & 0 & 0 & 1 \\ 0 & 0 & 0 & 0 & 0 & 0 & 1 & 0 \\ 0 & 0 & 0 & 0 & 0 & 1 & 0 & 0 \\ 0 & 0 & 0 & 0 & 1 & 0 & 0 & 0 \\ 0 & 0 & 0 & 1 & 0 & 0 & 0 & 0 \\ 0 & 0 & 1 & 0 & 0 & 0 & 0 & 0 \\ 0 & 1 & 0 & 0 & 0 & 0 & 0 & 0 \\ 1 & 0 & 0 & 0 & 0 & 0 & 0 & 0 \end{pmatrix} \quad (26)$$

where σ_i^x denotes the x-component of the Pauli's spin matrix, and is identical with $\mathcal{N}$ in Eq.(2). The initial state of the quantum system is set to the ground state of H_I as

$$|\psi(0)\rangle = \frac{1}{\sqrt{8}} \sum_{i=0}^{7} |i\rangle = \frac{1}{\sqrt{8}} \left(|000\rangle + |001\rangle + |010\rangle + |011\rangle + |100\rangle + |101\rangle + |110\rangle + |111\rangle \right) \quad (27)$$

The state change of the quantum system can be simulated according to Eq.(3) for each instantaneous Hamiltonian given by Eq. (14). In actual numerical simulations, we calculate the state change for each time step by Eq.(4) instead of Eq.(3) as,

$$|\psi(t+1)\rangle = U(1)|\psi(t)\rangle = \exp\left(-iH(t)\Delta_t\right)|\psi(t)\rangle \quad (28)$$

where Δ_t denotes the period for the quantum system to evolve under a given instantaneous Hamiltonian $H(t)$, and $U(1)$ is obtained by Padé approximation (Golub & van Loan, 1996). The simulation results are shown in Fig.4, where $T = 2 \times 10^3$ and $\Delta_t = 10^4$ are chosen for adiabatic change. The parameter E works as bias and is set to 0 in this study. The sign of A in H_F changes the quantum dynamics significantly in the relation to H_I, and we use a negative A in order to avoid energy level crossing of the ground state. Therefore, A is set to -1. It can be seen from the figures that the adiabatic change is done successfully. The most probable states $|010\rangle$ and $|101\rangle$ for the given synaptic matrix W have the largest probability 25%, also undesired states have nonzero probability. Because our final Hamiltonian is composed of off-diagonal elements, inclusion of such undesired states is inevitable. But the probability of finding a state should be inversely proportional to an exponential function of its energy value, then we can find a desired state by repeating this AQC certain times. We refer this computation method as Neuromorphic Adiabatic Quantum Computation (NAQC), in which H_F is obtained after consideration of the analogy between qubit interaction and neural interaction.

Figure 4. Changes of energy levels and probabilities during the Hamiltonian evolution from H_I in Eq.(26) to H_F in Eq.(25)

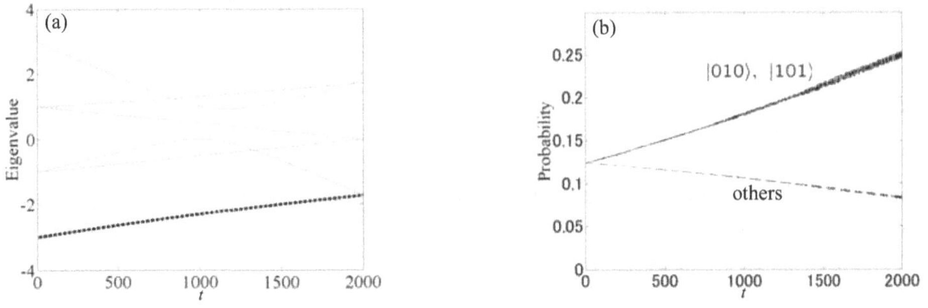

APPLICATION TO COMBINATORIAL OPTIMIZATION PROBLEMS

Classical Method with Hopfield Neural Network

The energy function E_{HN} of an HNN (Hopfield, 1982) decreases with time,

$$\frac{dE_{HN}}{dt} = -\sum_i \frac{do_i}{du_i}\left(\frac{du_i}{dt}\right)^2 \leq 0, \tag{29}$$

$$o_i = f(u_i), \tag{30}$$

where u_i is the membrane potential of the neuron i, and $f(u_i)$ is a monotonic sigmoid function. The network state changes accompanying with the decrease of E_{HN}. When the network reaches a state satisfying $dE / dt = 0$, such a state corresponds to an equilibrium point and no further state change occurs. In other words, the network can search an energy minimum. Thus, E_{HN} is a function of w_{ij} s and regulates the network behavior. If we know any cost function for a target problem in a quadratic form, its solutions can be given by the gradient descent method with synaptic weights obtained by comparing the cost function with the energy function in Eq.(23). For example, the traveling-salesman problem is implemented on an HNN as demonstrated by Hopfield and Tank (1985). It is well known that an HNN is often trapped at local minima and outputs error. Note that the calculation realized on a neural network accompanies with energy dissipation. On the other hand, energy is conserved in a quantum system. Instead a Hamiltonian evolves dynamically in quantum computation.

Various combinatorial optimization problems can be solved efficiently with specific synaptic weights obtained by comparing E_{HN} and cost functions. Let us see the detailed procedure by taking the N-queen problem as an example. The N-queen problem is a placement problem of N queen figures of chess on an NxN chess board, so that no two queens attack each other according to the rules of the game. We choose $N = 4$ to be a suitable size for the problem. The cost function of the four-queen problem is given as

$$E_{\text{cost}} = a\sum_i^4\left(\sum_j^4 o'_{ij} - 1\right)^2 + b\sum_j^4\left(\sum_i^4 o'_{ij} - 1\right)^2 + c\sum_{q=3}^{7}\sum_{i+j=q}\sum_{k+l=q}\sum_{k\neq i}\sum_{l\neq j} o'_{ij}o'_{kl} + d\sum_{q=-2}^{2}\sum_{i-j=q}\sum_{k-l=q}\sum_{k\neq i}\sum_{l\neq j} o'_{ij}o'_{kl}, \tag{31}$$

where $o'_{ij} = (o_{ij} + 1)/2$ takes a value between 0 and 1, the two suffixes *i* and *j* indicate the position of the neuron on the 4x4 chess board, and *a,b,c,d* are arbitrary positive constants. The first and second terms correspond to the vertical and horizontal movement of a queen. Also, the third and forth terms correspond to the diagonal movement. The synaptic weights w_{ijkl} s are given by comparing E_{cost} in Eq.(31) and the following energy E_{HN} of a Hopfield network,

$$E_{HN} = -\frac{1}{2}\sum_{i,j}\sum_{k,l} w_{ij\,kl}\, o_{ij} o_{kl}. \tag{32}$$

This is another representation of Eq.(23) reflecting 2D placement of neurons. As a result, the synaptic weights are obtained as

$$w_{ij\,kl} = -2a\,\delta_{j,l}(1-\delta_{i,k}) - 2b\delta_{i,k}(1-\delta_{j,l}) - 2c\delta_{i+j,k+l}(1-\delta_{i,k}) - 2d\delta_{i-j,k-l}(1-\delta_{i,k}) \tag{33}$$

where $\delta_{i,j}$ is the Kronecker delta. The synaptic weights for the four queen problem are either 0 or -1 with parameters $a = b = c = d = 1/2$. Note that we neglect bias terms in the energy function for simplicity because they are not essential in the following discussions and do affect quantum dynamics in a rather complicated way (Kinjo, Sato, & Nakajima, 2003).

Quantum Mechanical Method with Spin Qubits

In the previous section, we did not use real Hamiltonians for simplicity. But, in this section, we try to use a real Hamiltonian. It is known that transformations of variables in the energy function relate an HNN to a magnetic Ising system, with w_{ij} equivalent to the exchange J_{ij} between Ising spins *i* and *j*. In consideration of the facts that both Ising and Heisenberg models describe the dynamics of magnetic, and the energy of a spin-1/2 network is given by a Heisenberg Hamiltonian, it is plausible for us to relate a neuron to a spin-1/2 particle. For two spin-1/2 particles, the Heisenberg Hamiltonian is given in a matrix form as

$$H_{12} = J_{12}\sigma_1 \cdot \sigma_2 = J_{12}\left(\sigma^x \otimes \sigma^x + \sigma^y \otimes \sigma^y + \sigma^z \otimes \sigma^z\right) = J_{12}\begin{pmatrix} 1 & 0 & 0 & 0 \\ 0 & -1 & 2 & 0 \\ 0 & 2 & -1 & 0 \\ 0 & 0 & 0 & 1 \end{pmatrix} \tag{34}$$

where $\sigma_i = (\sigma_i^x, \sigma_i^y, \sigma_i^z)$ is the Pauli's spin matrix acting on the *i*-th spin-1/2 particle. Inhibitory interaction can be realized by H_{12} because $1/\sqrt{2}\left(|01\rangle - |10\rangle\right)$ is obtained as its ground state for positive J_{12}. The final Hamiltonian of NAQC is obtained by converting the synaptic weights in Eq. (33) to spin-1/2 interactions as

$$H_F = \sum_{i=0}^{15}\sum_{j>i}^{15} J_{ij}\sigma_i \cdot \sigma_j \tag{35}$$

where J_{ij} takes a value 0 or 1 according to the synaptic weights w_{ij}. Note that the calculation cost of the Hamiltonian is $O(16^{12})$ in this case. Unfortunately, energy level crossings have been found in the Hamiltonian evolution when we employ spin-1/2 interactions. Such undesired characteristic of a Hamiltonian violates the requirement of the adiabatic theorem and a successful operation of AQC cannot be obtained (Sato, Kinjo, Takahashi, Nakamiya, & Nakajima, 2004).

Effect of Energy Dissipation

In actual situation a quantum device is always affected by external noise, and quantum coherence disappears gradually as time goes on. It is a basic requirement that quantum coherence must be kept during operation for a conventional quantum computation algorithm. Though it has been reported that AQC can be intrinsically robust against environmental noise if decoherence occurs in the instantaneous eigenstate basis (Childs, Farhi, & Preskill, 2001; Sarandy & Linder, 2005; Åberg, Kult, & Sjöqvist, 2005), quantum coherence must also be kept for AQC. However, some decoherence is worthwhile for AQC eventually. This is because the successful execution of AQC is not guaranteed for a quantum system with energy level crossing or degenerated states during the Hamiltonian evolution, and then decoherence can be helpful for the state transition from a degenerated state to a lower energy state. Thus we evaluate performance enhancement of AQC after introducing energy dissipation which is one of the factors that cause decoherence (Kinjo et al., 2005). We suppose a quantum system obeying Boltzmann distribution as the simplest case and use the Monte Carlo method in numerical simulations. This assumption is valid for the case that the energy levels of environment are quasicontinuous and a quantum system interacts with environment in thermal equilibrium (Feynman, 1972). The energy dissipation is incorporated as fluctuation of a Hamiltonian. Therefore the magnitude λ of fluctuation as the result of thermal fluctuation is set to $\beta^{-1} = k_B\tau$, where k_B and τ are the Boltzmann constant and the temperature, respectively. Table 2 shows the proposed algorithm for adiabatic evolution with energy dissipation. At first, the quantum state $|\psi(0)\rangle$ is set to the ground state of the initial Hamiltonian $H(0) = H_I$. Next, let the quantum system change from $|\psi(t)\rangle$ to $|\psi(t+1)\rangle$ adiabatically, and we calculate the energy $E(t+1)$. Then, ΔH_k, which is introduced in order to simulate energy dissipation, is generated at random. Namely the value of the random component $(\Delta h_{ij})_k$ of the perturbed Hamiltonian ΔH_k has the range from $-\lambda$ to λ. After letting the quantum system evolve from $|\psi(t)\rangle$ to $|\psi_k(t+1)\rangle$ according to $H(t)+\Delta H_k$, we calculate the probability $P(k)$ for the state $|\psi_k(t+1)\rangle$ to be observed according to the Boltzmann distribution, and pick a state $|\psi_j(t+1)\rangle$ from among $k_{\max}(=10)$ states according to $P(k)$s. Thus $|\psi(t+1)\rangle = |\psi_j(t+1)\rangle$ is obtained. Repeating the procedure T times results in $|\psi(T)\rangle$. Finally we get a result for a target problem by observing the final state.

Table 2. Algorithm for adiabatic evolution with energy dissipation

1. Generate the initial state $|\psi(0)\rangle$ and $H(0)$
2. for $0 \le t \le T$
3. $\quad |\psi(t+1)\rangle = \exp\{-i\Delta_t H(t)\}|\psi(t)\rangle$
4. $\quad E(t+1) = \langle\psi(t+1)|H(t)|\psi(t+1)\rangle$
5. $\quad$ for $1 \le k \le k_{\max}$
6. $\qquad$ Generate ΔH_k at random
7. $\qquad |\psi_k(t+1)\rangle = \exp\{-i\Delta_t[H(t)+\Delta H_k]\}|\psi(t)\rangle$
8. $\qquad E_k(t+1) = \langle\psi_k(t+1)|H(t)|\psi_k(t+1)\rangle$
9. $\quad$ Calculate Boltzmann distribution,
   $$Z = \sum_k \exp\{-\beta[E_k(t+1) - E(t+1)]\},$$
   $$P(k) = \frac{1}{Z}\exp\{-\beta[E_k(t+1) - E(t+1)]\}$$
10. $\quad$ Pick a state $|\psi_j(t+1)\rangle$ from among $k_{\max}$ states according to $P(k)$
11. $\quad |\psi(t+1)\rangle = |\psi_j(t+1)\rangle$
12. $\quad H(t+1) = \left(1 - \frac{t+1}{T}\right)H_I + \frac{t+1}{T}H_F$
13. Measure the final state $|\psi(T)\rangle$

Although 16 qubits are required to solve the 4-queen problem, in actual numerical simulations half the qubits are fixed to 0 and other half can change as,

$$\left|0x_8x_70\ \ x_600x_5\ \ x_400x_3\ \ 0x_2x_10\right\rangle \equiv \left|m\right\rangle \qquad (36)$$

where $\left|m\right\rangle$ is the decimal notation of the quantum state $\left|\psi\right\rangle$, and $m = \sum_{i=1}^{8} 2^{i-1}x$. This irregular representation is used for keeping the required memory size reasonable, so that the numerical calculation can be executed on an ordinary PC. Both two states $\left|0010\ \ 1000\ \ 0001\ \ 0100\right\rangle = \left|102\right\rangle$ and $\left|0100\ \ 0001\ \ 1000\ \ 0010\right\rangle = \left|153\right\rangle$ are the optimal solutions in this case and are included in the ground state of H_F which is recalculated for eight qubits according to Eq. (35).

In Fig.5, the thin gray lines denote energy changes in which some degenerated points and level crossings are found. The thick solid line represents the actual energy change of the system without decoherence. The quantum system does not stay in the ground state and finally reaches the highest energy state. Three other energy changes with energy dissipation for different λs are shown as the other thick dotted lines. The energies are kept near the lowest energy before $t \cong 220$. Then the system meets the first degenerated point and its energy change differs

Figure 5. Energy changes of the 1/2-spin qubit network by NAQC with energy dissipation

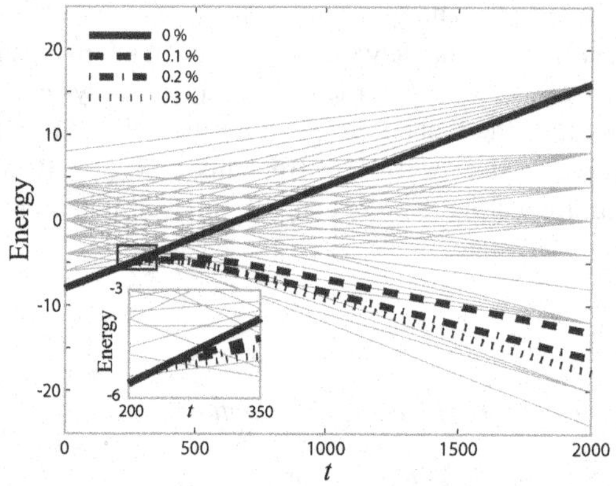

Figure 6. Averaged final energy and successful probability as a function of the energy dissipation rate; o, the average of the final energy; x, the average of the successful probability. Solid line is for the ground energy; dashed line is for the theoretical probability of the solutions. Each point is the average of 20 trials

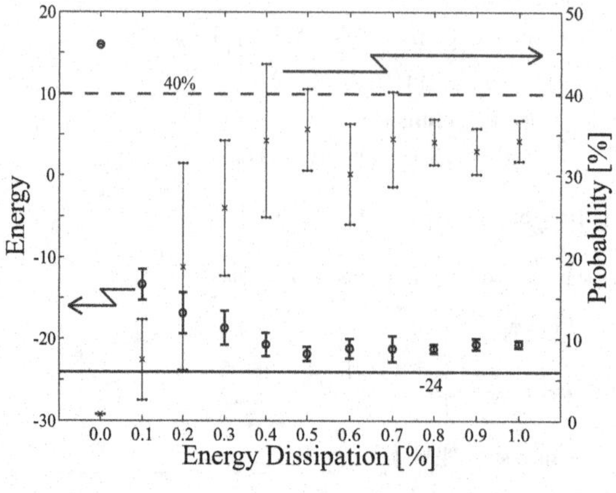

thereafter depending on the magnitude of dissipation. The energy of the final state decreases with increasing λ. We calculate the averages both of the final energy and successful probability of a solution as a function of λ, as shown in Fig. 6. The ground state of H_F is given as the superposition of two solution states and others, and the theoretical and ideal probability for observing solutions is 40%. As λ increases, the final energy reaches close to the ground energy −24 and the successful probability increases toward 40%. Note that the final energy does not reach the ground energy exactly with any λ since the finite error rises from the fluctuation of a Hamiltonian in this numerical simulation. This also means that there exists an upper limit for λ. However, the successful probability is vastly improved as compared with the case without energy dissipation.

Quantum Annealing and Neuromorphic Quantum Computation

So far a large number of studies to overcome the difficulty related to local minima have been carried out. An efficient method for avoiding such local minima is simulated annealing (SA) with a Boltzmann machine (Ackley, Hinton, & Sejnowski, 1985), which is a well-known classical neural network model with symmetrical synaptic weights as same as an HNN. The dynamics of the Boltzmann machine is not deterministic but stochastic, and the state transition probability is given according to Boltzmann distribution, namely the network behavior is affected by thermal noise. Therefore, it can be viewed as a stochastic version of an HNN. When the temperature is high, the network can move entire region, so that global and rough search is possible. On the contrary, local and fine search is realized at lower temperature. In SA, the temperature τ is set to certain high value at the beginning, then by decreasing the temperature gradually according to a proper schedule

$$\tau \geq \frac{N}{\log t}, \tag{37}$$

where N and t are the system size and time, respectively, the network state converges to a global minimum in the limit $t \to \infty$ (Kirkpatrick, Gelatt, &Vecchi, 1983; Geman & Geman, 1984). It is expected that such global search is also possible by introducing quantum dynamics. In particular, quantum tunneling can be efficient for this purpose. Actually, a quantum version of the simulated annealing called quantum annealing (QA) has been proposed (Kadowaki & Nishimori, 1998; Brooke, Bitko, Rosenbaum, & Aeppli, 1999; Santoro, Martoňák, Tosatti, & Car, 2002). QA is realized by employing adjustable quantum fluctuations, namely a quantum tunneling term is introduced in a Hamiltonian as

$$H(t) = \Gamma(t) H_t + H_C, \tag{38}$$

where H_C and $\Gamma(t)$ denote the classical Hamiltonian representing a given cost function and the parameter controlling quantum fluctuation, respectively. The quantum fluctuation in QA plays the same role of thermal noise in SA, and the tunneling term H_t provides paths to a global minimum. If we adopt the Hamiltonian change like in AQC, Eq.(14) is rewritten as

$$H(t) = \left(1 - \frac{t}{T}\right) H_t + \frac{t}{T} H_C. \tag{39}$$

It can be seen that QA and AQC are closely related, but in QA the quantum term disappears finally at $t = T$. Since the classical term H_C can be replaced by E_{HN} given in Eq.(32), Eq.(39) can be written in spin notation as

$$H(t) = \left(1 - \frac{t}{T}\right) \sum_i \sigma_i^x + \frac{t}{T} \sum_{i,j} J_{ij} \sigma_i^z \sigma_j^z, \tag{40}$$

where $J_{ij} = -w_{ij}$, and the classical neuron output o_i is replaced by the z-component of the Pauli's spin matrix σ_i^z. In order to evaluate the performance of these annealing methods, it is common to evaluate the residual energy ΔE as a function of the annealing time T. ΔE is defined as the difference between the actual energy of the quantum system after annealing and the minimum energy calculated from a cost function or a final Hamiltonian. For SA, the following relation has been known (Huse & Fisher, 1986; Shinomoto & Kabashima, 1991),

$$\Delta E \sim \frac{1}{(\ln T)^{\zeta}}, \quad 1 \leq \zeta \leq 2. \tag{41}$$

On the other hand, Suzuki and Okada (2005) reported that

$$\Delta E \sim \frac{1}{T^{\zeta}}, \quad \zeta = 2 \quad , \tag{42}$$

holds when QA is applied to a random Ising spin model. Their result indicates that great enhancement can be achieved by quantum dynamics. Though AQC is not identical with QA, we expect similar results for AQC and NAQC. Actually, we have confirmed that the relation in Eq.(42) holds for NAQC with H_I and H_F in Eqs.(25) and (26), respectively. Fig.7 shows the change of the residual energy $\Delta E = \langle \psi(T) | H_F | \psi(T) \rangle - E_{\min}$ as a function of T. Note that in this case there is no crossing or degeneracy on the ground state during the Hamiltonian evolution from H_I to H_F.

The main difference between AQC and NAQC is that the ground state of the final Hamiltonian in AQC proposed by Farhi et al. represents purely the solution of a given problem (Farhi et al., 2000; Farhi et al. 2001), whereas that of NAQC includes both solution and non-solution states. The same difference holds between QA and NAQC. When ΔP denotes the difference between the actual and ideal solution probabilities in the same manner, its scaling law

$$\Delta P \sim \frac{1}{T^{\zeta}}, \quad \zeta = 2 \tag{43}$$

Figure 7. Residual energy as a function of the computation time T. Hamiltonians H_I in Eq.(26) and H_F in Eq.(25) are used

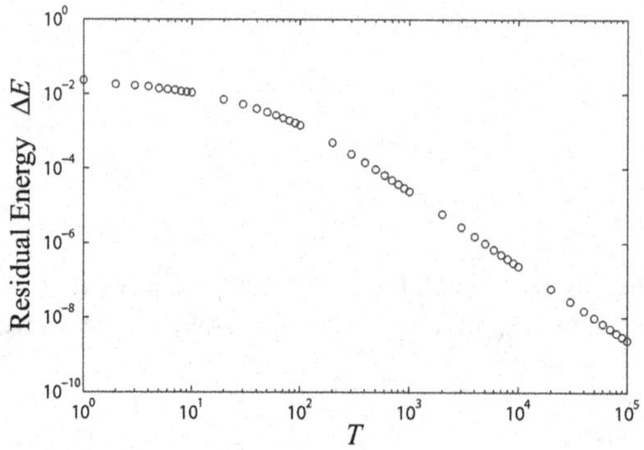

is obtained for AQC and QA. However, in NAQC, the scaling law is not known. Though the study on this issue remains as a future subject, our preliminary result using the same H_I and H_F in the above indicates the relation (Ono, Sato, Kinjo, & Nakajima, 2008),

$$\Delta P \sim \frac{1}{T^{\zeta}}, \quad 1 \le \zeta \le 2 \tag{44}$$

where ζ changes according to the details of the Hamiltonian change from H_I to H_F.

There is no guarantee for keeping out any energy level crossing or degeneracy in NAQC. The scaling property of NAQC must be affected by such undesired properties. However, decoherence effects discussed in the previous subsection is inevitable when one executes NAQC with real devices. Therefore, the scaling property of NAQC should be discussed together with these non-ideal effects. They may result in significant enhancement or degradation according to Hamiltonians used.

QUANTUM HEBB LEARNING

An interesting subject related to NAQC is learning. Learning is the most attractive feature for implementing an adaptive system with a classical neural network. This must also be true for NAQC. Especially, difficulties for implementing real quantum computers are not comparable to neural networks, so that learning ability shall be quite important for adjusting device fluctuations and achieving reliable computation. We focus on Hebb learning in NAQC as a first step for a devising quantum learning function.

First, in order to introduce learning to NAQC, let us consider an HNN which behaves as an auto-associative memory. The synaptic weights used here are given as,

$$W = \frac{1}{4} p^T p = \begin{pmatrix} 0 & -1 & 1 & -1 \\ -1 & 0 & -1 & 1 \\ 1 & -1 & 0 & -1 \\ -1 & 1 & -1 & 0 \end{pmatrix} \tag{45}$$

where $p = (-1\ 1\ -1\ 1)$ is a memorized pattern. Please note that the inverted pattern $\overline{p} = (1\ -1\ 1\ -1)$ is also embedded automatically in W. By using the relationship shown in Table 1 again, the final Hamiltonian H_F is obtained. Fig.8 shows the probability changes of all states. It can be seen that the probability of two memorized patterns $|5\rangle = |0101\rangle$ and $|10\rangle = |1010\rangle$ grow as time goes on and have the same largest probability after the evolution.

As is well known, the synaptic weights shown in Eq.(45) are obtained easily by Hebb learning. Also, it is employed in the learning with a Boltzmann Machine (Ackley et al., 1985). Therefore, again from the analogy between HNN and NAQC, we propose a quantum learning method similar to Hebb learning (Kinjo, Sato, & Nakajima, 2006). The learning sequence is as follows,

1. Initialize the final Hamiltonian randomly
2. Simulate adiabatic evolution
3. Measure the final state and find a corresponding neuron state
4. Update the synaptic weights according to Hebb rule
5. Update the final Hamiltonian
6. Repeat 2-5

Figure 8. Probability changes of memorized patterns when NAQC is applied to an auto-associative memory

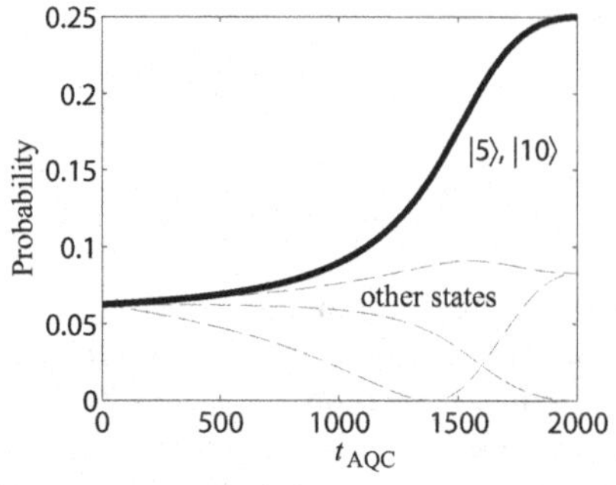

Figure 9. Probability changes by the proposed learning method for three different initial H_F s. Thick solid lines denote the probabilities of memorized patterns. Random Hamiltonians are used as the initial H_Fs in (a) and (b), whereas the H_F obtained from the synaptic weights in Eq.(45) is used as the initial H_F in (c)

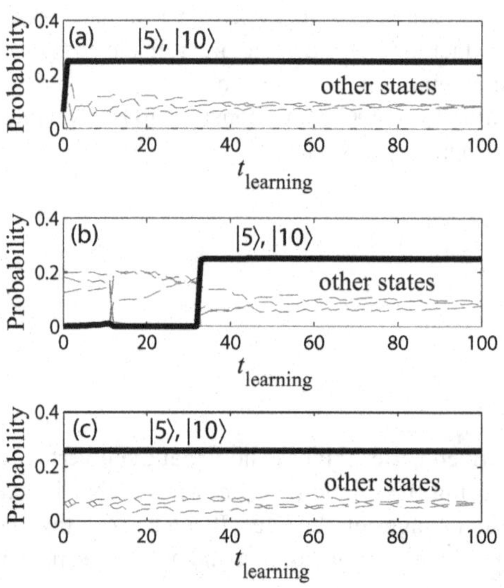

According to this sequence the probability changes through the learning is obtained as shown in Figs. 9(a) and (b). It can be seen that successful learning is realized for two different initial H_Fs. Both probabilities of memorized patterns $|5\rangle$ and $|10\rangle$ converge to 25%. This is the same probability shown in Fig.8. These results indicate two important facts. The Hamiltonian synthesizing method is a proper one for constructing a NAQC similar to an HNN. Furthermore, learning is possible in NAQC by simulating Hebb learning. One of the problems is that the final state is a superpositional state of solution states and error states. Therefore, it is important to study a method to decrease the probability of error states. Let us consider the case in which the initial H_F is chosen as the same one in Fig.8. Fig.9(c) shows the probability change of all states for this case. It can be seen that the probabilities both of the solution states and error states do not change in average. Small perturbations found in the figure are caused by stochastic effect originated from quantum mechanical principle, i.e. the measured states are chosen stochastically and thus H_F is changed slightly in short time. The result suggests that H_F in Fig.8 could be optimal.

The learning function inspired by Hebb rule has been confirmed in the above. The basic leaning behavior is the same as an HNN, but some quantitative difference has been found. This is because NAQC is based on quantum mechanical principle, and finite error probability exists. For further study, the learning ability should be evaluated together with its retrieval property as an associative memory. As discussed in the above, the final state obtained by NAQC is given as a superpositional state of memorized states and others with different probabilities. Quantitative discussion on the memory capacity also seems possible for a quantum associative memory realized by NAQC. But for this purpose, the size of the network should be much larger, namely at least 10^2 qubits are required for studying its statistical property. Unfortunately an ordinary commercial PC can simulate at most ~10 qubits due to the limited memory size. Some approximation techniques should work well for this purpose.

HARDWARE IMPLEMENTATION

Recently, in order to realize a quantum computer, many researchers study very important subjects, such as fabricating, controlling, and measuring qubits. Among them, the nuclear spin qubit in Si proposed by Kane (1998) is one of the most likely candidates for implementing the proposed algorithm. Let us briefly introduce it in this section, and show the relation between qubit and neuron. ^{31}P donors (nuclear spin 1/2) in isotopically pure silicon ^{28}Si (spin 0) are employed as qubits as shown in Fig.10. The donor electron wavefunction extends over large distance through the crystal lattice, and two nuclear spins can consequently interact with the same electron, leading indirect nuclear spin coupling. A-gate above the nucleus controls the strength of the interaction between the nuclear spin and the electron spin. J-gate between the nuclei controls the strength of the interaction between the electron spins. The decoherence time, which is an important factor for realizing a qubit, is very long since a nuclear spin is well isolated from the environment. Therefore a nuclear spin qubit is expected as one of the promising candidates.

The Hamiltonian of this system is given as,

$$H = \sum_{i<j} J_{ij}\sigma_{ie} \cdot \sigma_{je} + \sum_{i,j} A_{ij}\sigma_{in} \cdot \sigma_{je} \qquad (46)$$

Figure 10. Nuclear spin qubit proposed by Kane. Both interactions between electrons and between an electron and a ^{31}P nucleus are controlled by J-gate and A-gate, respectively. J_{ij} (>0) corresponds to the synaptic weight w_{ij} (<0). The strength of their interactions is controlled by external voltages

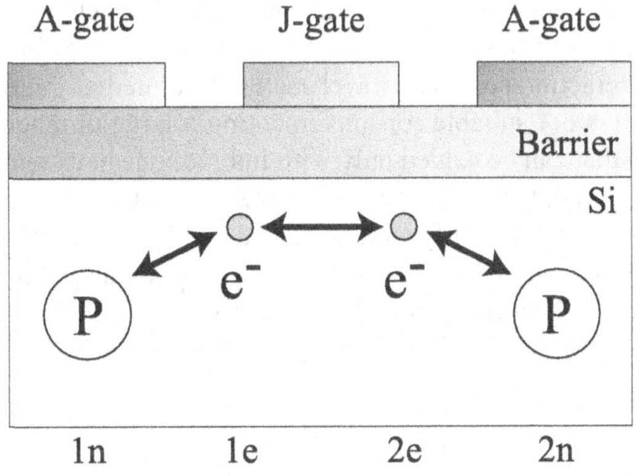

Figure 11. Probability changes of 5 Kane's qubits placed in one dimension

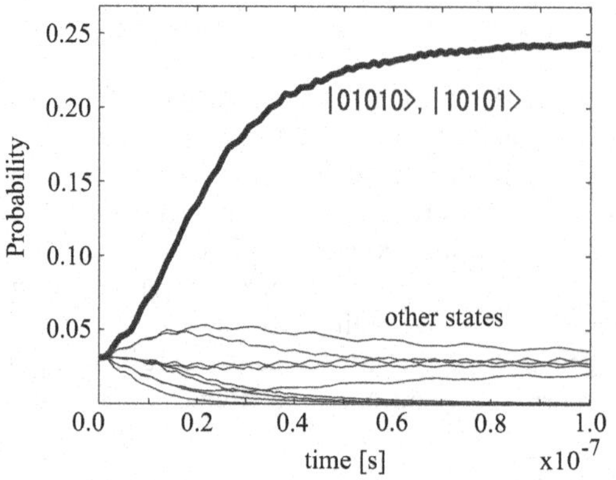

where J_{ij} and A_{ij} are the strength of the interactions between i-th and j-th electron spins, and between i-th nuclear and j-th electron spins, respectively. They are positive parameters and changed by external voltages applied to J- and A-gates. Both bias voltages of J- and A-gates are adjusted to obtain a suitable Hamiltonian for the required quantum operators. σ_{ie} and σ_{in} are the Pauli's spin matrices related to the i-th electron spin and the i-th nuclear spin, respectively. If we focus on two nuclei, the system behaves as well as two neurons coupled with inhibitory interaction (Nakamiya, Kinjo, Takahashi, Sato, & Nakajima, 2006). For example, if the first nuclear spin is $|0_n\rangle$, the first electron spin is $|1_e\rangle$ affected by the second term in the Hamiltonian Eq.(46). Then the second electron spin is $|0_e\rangle$ affected by the first term. Finally the second nuclear spin is $|1_n\rangle$, and we find the state of two nuclei is $|1_n0_n\rangle$ Inhibitory interaction between nuclei is realized with the Hamiltonian in Eq.(46), where the electron-electron interaction $J_{ij}(>0)$ corresponds to the neuron-neuron interaction $w_{ij}(<0)$. In order to confirm this property by numerical simulations, let us consider a one dimensional array of spin qubits with the above Hamiltonian, and suppose only the nuclear spins correspond to the qubits. When we increase the qubit-qubit interaction J_{ij} from zero to a certain value, AQC can be simulated as the simplest case. At the initial state, each pair of nuclear and electron spins does not interact with other pairs, so that all possible states are embedded in $|\psi(0)\rangle$. According to the increase of J_{ij}, the nuclear spin qubits interact inhibitorily with neighboring qubits via mediator electrons. It can be seen in Fig.11 that the expected two states, in which inhibitory interactions are confirmed, have the largest probability. The parameters used in numerical simulations are, $J_{ij}: 0 \rightarrow 1.50\times10^{-25}$ [J] only if $j = i =+ 1$, $A_{ij} = 1.92\times10^{-26}$ [J] only if $j = i$, and $T = 1.00\times10^{-7}$ [sec].

The advantage of Kane's qubit when one executes NAQC is that the interaction between nuclear spin qubits can be controlled by externally applied voltage, so that it is not difficult to change the Hamiltonian adiabatically. It means also that an adjustable H_F is obtained according to a given problem. On the contrary, the disadvantage is the limited range of qubit interaction since the wavefunction of a mediator electron is centered to a nucleus. Therefore its physical structure is not suitable for implementing a large number of qubits. The system can be applied to a particular problem that can be solved only with interactions between neighbors as well as a cellular neural network (Chua & Yang, 1988). On the other hand, superconducting qubits (Nakamura, Pashkin, & Tsai, 1999; You & Nori, 2005) can interact coherently with displaced qubits via superconductive wires in a rather easy way. Superconducting is one of the macroscopic quantum phenomena and it can be thought as robust to noise. Though the adjustable change of the Hamiltonian with superconducting is not so easy in comparison with Kane's qubit, but of course it is also a candidate for implementing the proposed method.

CONCLUSION

In this chapter, neuromorphic quantum adiabatic computation as an application of a complex valued neural network has been proposed in order to incorporate quantum dynamics to a classical neural network. The proposed computation method can be applied to optimization problems if a cost function can be expressed in a quadratic form. This is because the final Hamiltonian of NAQC is given as the sum of Hamiltonians which correspond to two qubit interactions, and is obtained from the synaptic interactions of an HNN. Successful operations of NAQC have been confirmed by numerical simulations.

Energy dissipation is introduced in order to keep a quantum state in each ground state because original AQC fails if a quantum system has energy degeneration or level crossing during the Hamiltonian evolution. Because energy dissipation always affects a quantum system and fluctuation of quantum devices is inevitable, the proposed method is preferable from the practical view point. Moreover, a learning method in NAQC has been proposed in analogy with Hebb learning, where a quantum system operating as an associative memory has been considered. Note that quantum dynamics is more suitable for optimization problems than associative memories because the purpose of associative memories is to retrieve a memorized pattern according to a given initial state , while quantum dynamics is very useful for finding a global minimum independently of an initial state. Finally, the hardware implementation of the proposed method has been discussed by taking a nuclear spin qubit as an example.

The disadvantage of the proposed method is the fact that the final state is composed both of desired and undesired states. This is inevitable because its Hamiltonian is obtained only from qubit interactions. But when we try to solve the N-queen problem, such undesired states having small probability do not degrade the performance significantly because a measured result from the qubits can be instantaneously confirmed as a valid or invalid solution.

FUTURE RESEARCH DIRECTIONS

There are two purposes for the study on NAQC because it can be viewed as a method for incorporating quantum dynamics into a classical neural network, and also a method for applying AQC to various problems. In both cases, NAQC can play an important role for further improvements. Quantum dynamics is superior to classical dynamics for searching a global minimum in a given potential. On the other hand, amplification of the probability for finding such a minimum is not possible by a quantum system due to energy conservation law. Solution probability decreases with increasing the number of qubits, in contrast with the increase of quantum computational power. A possible answer for this difficulty is to employ a device which can operate both as a qubit and a classical neuron. Besides the physical implementation of such a device, fusion of quantum and classical dynamics is interesting for practical quantum computation.

Hardware implementation of NAQC is an important subject in order to utilize computational power fully. The fact that the number of qubits shown in this chapter is small reflects that numerical simulations of quantum systems are resource hungry tasks for a conventional computer. To look this from the opposite point of view, a quantum computer has remarkable computational power. For further study on NAQC, its performance evaluation with a larger network is required and a dedicated quantum simulator could be useful. For practical use of quantum computers, the nature of quantum devices should be considered carefully and restrictions related to each device characteristic should be eliminated in an effective way by employing a neuromorphic technique. Furthermore, undesired effects against quantum computation such as energy dissipation, phase relaxation, fluctuation of devices should be incorporated in studies on quantum computation algorithms. In this sense, learning function on real qubits will be much important in future. Because the development of a quantum computer is not an easy subject, research subjects easing any requirement for qubit implementation could be quite important.

REFERENCES

Ackley, D. H., Hinton, G. E., & Sejnowski, T. J. (1985). A Learning Algorithm for Boltzmann Machines. *Cognitive Science, 9*(1), 147-169.

Aharonov, D., van Dam, W., Kempe, J., Landau, Z., Lloyd, S., & Regev, O. (2004). Adiabatic Quantum Computation is Equivalent to Standard Quantum Computation. *Proceedings of the 45th Annual IEEE Symposium on Foundations of Computer Science*, (pp. 42-51).

Brooke, J., Bitko, D., Rosenbaum, T. F., & Aeppli, G. (1999). Quantum Annealing of a Disordered Magnet. *Science, 284*(5415), 779-781.

Childs, A. M., Farhi, E., & Preskill, J. (2001). Robustness of adiabatic quantum computation. Phys. Rev. A, *65*(1), 012322.

Chua, L. O., & Yang, L. (1988). Cellular neural networks: Theory. *IEEE Trans. Circuits and Systems, 35*(10), 1257-1272.

Ezhov, A., & Ventura, D. (2000). Quantum Neural Networks. In N. Kasabov (Ed.), *Future Directions for Intelligent Systems and Information Science*. Heidelberg: Physica-Verlag.

Farhi, E., Goldstone, J., Gutmann, S., Lapan, J., Lundgren, A., & Preda, D. (2001). A Quantum Adiabatic Evolution Algorithm Applied to Random Instances of an NP-Complete Problem. *Science, 292*(5516), 472-475.

Farhi, E., Goldstone, J., Gutmann, & Sipser, M. (2000). Quantum Computation by Adiabatic Evolution. *quant-ph,* 0001106.

Farhi, E., & Gutmann, S. (1996). An Analog Analogue of a Digital Quantum Computation. *quant-ph*, 9612026.

Feynman, R. P. (1972). *Statistical Mechanics.* Reading: W.A. Benjamin.

Geman, D., & Geman, S. (1984). Stochastic Relaxation, Gibbs Distribution, and the Bayesian Restoration of Images. *IEEE Trans. Pattern Analysis and Machine Intelligence, 6*(6), 721-741.

Golub, G. H., & van Loan, C. F. (1996). *Matrix Computations 3rd Ed.* Baltimore: Johns Hopkins University Press.

Grover, L. K. (1996). A fast quantum mechanical algorithm for database search. *Twenty-Eighth Annual ACM Symp. on the Theory of Computing*, (pp. 212-219).

Grover, L. K. (1997). Quantum Mechanics Helps in Searching for a Needle in a Haystack. *Phys. Rev. Lett., 79*(2), 325-328.

Hopfield, J. J. (1982). Neural networks and physical systems with emergent collective computational abilities. *Proceedings of the National Academy of Sciences of the USA, 79*(8), 2554-2558.

Hopfield, J. J., & Tank, D. W. (1985). Neural computation of decisions in optimization problems. *Biological Cybernetics, 52*, 141-152.

Huse, D. A., & Fisher, D. S. (1986). Residual Energies after Slow Cooling of Disordered Systems. *Phys. Rev. Lett., 57*(17), 2203-2206.

Kadowaki, T., & Nishimori, H. (1998). Quantum annealing in the transverse Ising model. *Phys. Rev. E, 58*(5), 5355-5363.

Kane, B. E. (1998). A silicon-based nuclear spin quantum computer. *Nature, 393*(6681), 133-137.

Kinjo, M., Sato, S., & Nakajima, K. (2003). Quantum Adiabatic Evolution Algorithm for a Quantum Neural Network. In Kaynak, Alpaydin, Oja, & Xu (Eds.), *Artificial Neural Networks and Neural Information Processing* (pp. 951-958). Berlin: Springer.

Kinjo, M., Sato, S., Nakamiya, Y., & Nakajima, K. (2005). Neuromorphic quantum computation with energy dissipation. *Physical Review A*, *72*(5), 052328.

Kinjo, M., Sato, S., & Nakajima, K. (2006). A Study on Learning with a Quantum Neural Network. *Proceedings of IEEE World Congress on Computational Intelligence, 1618.*

Kirkpatrick, S., Gelatt, C. D., & Vecchi, M. P. (1983). Optimization by Simulated Annealing. *Science*, *220*(4598), 671-680.

Matsui, N., Takai, M., & Nishimura, H. (1998, 2000). A network model based on qubit-like neuron corresponding to quantum circuit. (1998 in Japanese) *IEICE, J81-A*(12), 1687-1692. (2000 in English) *Electronics and Communications in Japan, part III, 83*(10), 67-73.

Messiah, A. (1958). *Quantum Mechanics.* New York: John Wiley & Sons.

Mori, K., Isokawa, T., Kouda, N., Matsui, N., & Nishimura, H. (2006). Qubit Inspired Neural Network towards Its Practical Applications. *Proceedings of IEEE World Congress on Computational Intelligence, 1873.*

Nakamiya, Y., Kinjo, M., Takahashi, O., Sato, S., & Nakajima, K. (2006). Quantum neural network composed of Kane's qubits. *Jpn. J. Appl. Phys.*, *45*(10A), 8030-8034.

Nakamura, Y., Pashkin, Y., & Tsai, J. S. (1999). Coherent control of macroscopic quantum states in a single-Cooper-pair box. *Nature*, *398*(6730), 786-788.

Nielsen, M. A., & Chuang, I. L. (Eds.). (2000). *Quantum Computation and Quantum Information.* Cambridge, UK: Cambridge University Press.

Ono, A., Sato, S., Kinjo, M., & Nakajima, K. (2008). Study on the Performance of Neuromorphic Adiabatic Quantum Computation Algorithms. *Proceedings of the 2008 IEEE World Congress on Computational Intelligence*, (pp. 2508-2512).

Peruš, M., Bischof, H., Caulfield, J., & Loo, C.K. (2004). Quantum implementable selective reconstruction of high resolution images. *Applied Optics*, *43*(33), 6134-6138.

Roland, J., & Cerf, N. J. (2002). Quantum Search by Local Adiabatic Evolution. *Physical Review A*, *65*(4), 042308.

Santoro, G. E., Martoňák, R., Tosatti, E., & Car, R. (2002). Theory of Quantum Annealing of an Ising Spin Glass. *Science*, *295*(5564), 2427-2430.

Sarandy, M. S., & Linder, D. A. (2005). Adiabatic approximation in open quantum systems. *Phys. Rev. A*, *71*(1), 012331.

Sato, S., Kinjo, M., & Nakajima, K. (2003). An Approach for Quantum Computing using Adiabatic Evolution Algorithm. *Jpn. J. Appl. Phys.*, *42*(11), 7169-7173.

Sato, S., Kinjo, M., Takahashi, O., Nakamiya, Y., & Nakajima, K. (2004). A Study on Neuromorphic Quantum Computation. *Proceedings of the 2004 Int. Joint Conf. on Neural Networks*, (pp. 3253-3256).

Shinomoto, S., & Kabashima, Y. (1991). Finite time scaling of energy in simulated annealing. *J. Phys. A: Math. Gen.*, *24*(3), L141-L144.

Shor, P. W. (1994). Polynomial-time algorithm for prime factorization and discrete logarithms on a quantum computer. *Proceedings of the 35th Annual Symposium on Foundations of Computer Science*, (pp. 116-123).

Siu, M. S. (2005). From quantum circuits to adiabatic algorithms. *Phys. Rev. A*, *71*(6), 062314.

Suzuki, S., & Okada, M. (2005). Residual Energies after Slow Quantum Annealing. *Journal of the Physical Society of Japan*, *74*(6), 1649-1652.

Tank, D. W., & Hopfield, J. J. (1986). Simple 'neural' optimization networks: An A/D converter, signal decision circuit, and a linear programming circuit. *IEEE Trans. Circuits Syst.*, *33*(5), 533-541.

You, J. Q., & Nori, F. (2005). Superconducting circuits and quantum information. *Physics Today*, *58*(11), 42-47.

Ventura, D., & Martinez, T. (2000). Quantum associative memory. *Information Sciences*, *124*(1-4), 273-296.

Åberg, J., Kult, D., & Sjöqvist, E. (2005). Robustness of the adiabatic quantum search. *Phys. Rev. A*, *71*(6), 060312.

ADDITIONAL READING

Aaronson, S. (2008). The Limits of Quantum Computers, *Scientific American*, *298*(3), 62-69.

Amit, D. J. (1989). *Modeling Brain Function: The World of Attractor Neural Networks*. New York: Cambridge University Press.

Averin, D. V. (1998). Adiabatic Quantum Computation with Cooper Pair. *Solid State Communication*, *105*(10), 659-664.

Barenco, A., Deutsch, D., Ekert, A., & Jozsa R. (1995). Conditional Quantum Dynamics and Logic Gates. *Physical Review Letters*, *74*(20), 4083-4086.

Benioff, P. (1982). Quantum Mechanical Models of Turing Machines That Dissipate No Energy. *Physical Review Letters*, *48*(23), 1581-1585.

Berman, G. P., Doolen, G. D., Mainieri, R., & Tsifrinovich, V. I. (1998). *Introduction To Quantam Computers*. Los Alamos: World Scientific Publishing Co.

Cirac, J. I., & Zoller, P. (1995). Quantum Computations with Cold Trapped Ions. *Physical Review Letters*, *74*(20), 4091-4094.

Cirac, J. I., & Zoller, P. (2000). A scalable quantum computer with ions in an array of microtraps. *Nature*, *404*(6778), 579-581.

Das, A. & Chakrabarti, B. K. (2008). Quantum Annealing and Analog Quantum Computation. *quant-ph*, 0801.2193.

Deutsch, D., & Jozsa, R. (1992). Rapid solutions of problems by quantum computation. *Proc. the Royal Society of London*, *A439*, 553-558.

Farhi, E., Goldstone, J., & Gutmann, S. (2000). A Numerical Study of the Performance of a Quantum Adiabatic Evolution Algorithm for Satisfiability. *quant-ph*, 0007071.

Farhi, E., Goldstone, J., & Gutmann, S. (2002). Quantum Adiabatic Evolution Algorithms versus Simulated Annealing. *quant-ph*, 0201031

Feynman, R. P. (1985). Quantum Mechanical Computers. *Optics News*, *11*(2), 11-20.

Feynman, R. P., Leighton, R. B., & Sands, M. L. (1965). *THE FEYNMAN LECTURES ON PHYSICS Vol. III*. Reading, MA: Addison-Wesley.

Galindo, A., & Martin-Delgado, M. A. (2002). Information and computation: Classical and quantum aspects. *Reviews of Modern Physics*, *74*(2), 347-423.

Garey, M. R., & Johnson, D. S. (1979). *Computers and Intractability A Guide to the Theory of NP-Completeness*. New York: W. H. FREEMAN AND COMPANY.

Gershenfeld, N. A., & Chuang, I. L. (1997). Bulk Spin-Resonance Quantum Computation. *Science*, *275*(5298), 350-356.

Hallgren, S. (2002). Polynomial-time quantum algorithms for Pell's equation and the principal ideal problem. *Journal of the ACM*, *54*(1), 1.

Hertz, J., Krogh, A., & Palmer, R. G. (1991). *Introduction to the Theory of Neural Computation*, Redwood City, CA: Addison-Wesley

Makhlin, Y., Schön, G., & Shnirman, A. (2001). Quantum-state engineering with Josephson-junction devices. *Reviews of Modern Physics*, *73*(2), 357-400.

Rabi, I. I. (1937). Space Quantization in a Gyrating Magnetic Field. *Physical Review*, *51*(8), 652-654.

Ronald, J., & Cerf, N. J. (2004). Noise resistance of adiabatic quantum computation using random matrix theory. *quant-ph*, 0409127.

Rumelhart, D. E., & McClelland, J. L. (Eds.) (1986). *Parallel Distributed Processing: Explorations in the Microstructure of Cognition*. Cambridge, MA: MIT Press.

Sakurai, J. J. (1985). *Modern Quantum Mechanics*. Redwood City, CA: Benjamin/Cummings Publishing Company.

Sipser, M. (1996). *Introduction to the Theory of Computation*. Boston: PWS Publishing Co.

Vandersypen, L. M. K., Steffen, M., Breyta, G., Yannoni, C. S., Sherwood, M. H., & Chuang, I. L. (2001). Experimental realization of Shor's quantum factoring algorithm using nuclear magnetic resonance. *Nature*, *414*(6866), 883-887.

Williams, C. P., & Clearwater, S. H. (1997). *Explorations in Quantum Computation*, New York: Springer-Verlag.

Yamamoto, T., Pashkin, Yu. A., Astafiev, O., Nakamura, Y., & Tsai, J. S. (2003). Demonstration of conditional gate operation using superconducting charge qubits. *Nature*, *425*(6961), 941-944.

Chapter XV
Attractors and Energy Spectrum of Neural Structures Based on the Model of the Quantum Harmonic Oscillator

G.G. Rigatos
Industrial Systems Institute, Greece

S.G. Tzafestas
National Technical University of Athens, Greece

ABSTRACT

Neural computation based on principles of quantum mechanics can provide improved models of memory processes and brain functioning and is of primary importance for the realization of quantum computing machines. To this end, this chapter studies neural structures with weights that follow the model of the quantum harmonic oscillator. The proposed neural networks have stochastic weights which are calculated from the solution of Schrödinger's equation under the assumption of a parabolic (harmonic) potential. These weights correspond to diffusing particles, which interact with each other as the theory of Brownian motion (Wiener process) predicts. The learning of the stochastic weights (convergence of the diffusing particles to an equilibrium) is analyzed. In the case of associative memories the proposed neural model results in an exponential increase of patterns storage capacity (number of attractors). It is also shown that conventional neural networks and learning algorithms based on error gradient can be conceived as a subset of the proposed quantum neural structures. Thus, the complementarity between classical and quantum physics is also validated in the field of neural computation.

INTRODUCTION

In this chapter, neural structures with weights that follow the model of the quantum harmonic oscillator will be studied. Connectionist structures which are compatible with the theory of quantum mechanics and demonstrate the particle-wave nature of information, have been analyzed in (Hagan et. al., 2002), (Perus et. al., 2004), (Rigatos & Tzafestas, 2007a). This chapter extends results on the compatibility of neural structures with quantum mechanics principles, presented in (Rigatos &. Tzafestas, 2002), (Rigatos & Tzafestas, 2006a).

It is assumed that the neural weights are stochastic variables which correspond to diffusing particles, and interact to each other as the theory of Brownian motion predicts. Brownian motion is the analogous of the quantum harmonic oscillator (Q.H.O.), i.e. of Schrödinger's equation under harmonic (parabolic) potential. It will be shown that the update of the stochastic weights is described by Langevin's stochastic differential equation which is a generalization of conventional gradient algorithms. It will also be shown that weights following the Q.H.O. model give to associate memories significant properties: (i) the learning of the weights is a Wiener process, and (ii) the number of attractors increases exponentially comparing to conventional associative memories.

The structure of the chapter is as follows: In Section "*Equivalence between Schrödinger's equation and a diffusion process*", an analysis of the diffusive motion of particles (stochastic weights) is given and the background that relates Schrödinger's equation with diffusive motion is analyzed. It is shown that Schrödinger's equation with harmonic potential is equivalent to a stationary diffusion, and that the motion of the diffusing particles is described by Langevin's equation. In section "*Interacting diffusing particles as a model of neural networks*", a neural model based on interacting diffusing particles, is proposed. In Section "*Compatibility with principles of quantum mechanics*", it is shown that using directly Schrödinger's equation in place of the previously analyzed stochastic processes, the stochastic weights of the neural network can be described by a probability density function which stems again from the model of the quantum harmonic oscillator. In section "*Attractors in Associative Memories based on the Q.H.O. model*", it is shown that the Q.H.O. model in associative memories results in exponential increase of the number of attractors while the the update of the weights stands for a Wiener process. In section "*Spectral analysis of associative memories that follow the QHO model*", spectral analysis shows that the stochastic weights satisfy a relation analogous to the principle of uncertainty. In section "*Simulation tests*", simulation results are presented about the convergence of Brownian weights to attractors and about the exponential increase of the number of attractors in associative memories with Brownian weights. Finally, in Section "*Conclusions*", concluding remarks are stated.

BACKGROUND

A detailed analysis of the current status of research on neural networks and cognitive models based on the principles of quantum mechanics will be given. As it can be observed from the relevant bibliography the field is wide and with enormous potential. Without excluding other approaches on neural structures with quantum mechanical features, in this chapter three main research directions are distinguished: (1) Neural structures which use as activation functions the eigenstates of the quantum harmonic oscillator, (2) Neural structures with stochastic weights. Sub-topics in this area are (a) neural structures with stochastic weights which stem from the solution of Schrödinger's linear equation for constant or zero potential (b) stochastic neural networks which can be modelled as gene networks (3). Neural structures with stochastic weights which stem from the model of the quantum harmonic oscillator

1. Results on neural structures which use as activation functions the eigenstates of the quantum harmonic oscillator: Feed-forward neural networks (FNN) are the most popular neural architectures due to their structural flexibility, good representational capabilities, and availability of a large number of training algorithms. The hidden units in a FNN usually have the same activation functions and are usually selected as sigmoidal functions or gaussians. Feed-forward neural networks that use the eigenstates of the quantum harmonic oscillator (QHO) as basis functions have some interesting properties: (i) the basis functions are invariant under the Fourier transform, subject only to a change of scale (ii) the basis functions are the eigenstates of the QHO, and are derived from the solution of Schrödinger's harmonic equation. The proposed neural networks belong to the general category of nonparametric estimators and are suitable for function approximation, system modelling and image processing. Two-dimensional QHO-based neural networks can be also constructed by taking products of the one-dimensional basis functions.

Feed-forward neural networks that use the eigenstates of the quantum harmonic oscillator demonstrate the particle-wave nature of information as described by Schrödinger's diffusion equation (Cohen-Tannoudji et al, 1998),(Strauss, 1992). Attempts to enhance the connectionist neural models with quantum mechanics properties can be also found in (Kosko, 1992), (Ventura & Martinez 2000), (Resconi et al, 2002), (Perus 2001). An analysis of NNs which use as activation functions the QHO eigenstates is given in (Rigatos & Tzafestas, 2006b), (Rigatos, 2006c). It is considered that the input variable x of the neural network can be described not only by crisp values (particle equivalent) but also by the normal modes of a wave function (wave equivalent). Since the basis functions of the proposed FNN are the eigenstates of the quantum harmonic oscillator, the FNN's output will be the weighted sum of these eigenfunctions, while the the square of the output will be the probability that the input of the neural network (quantum particle equivalent) is found in the uncertainty interval $[x, x+\Delta x]$. Thus, in these NNs the weights provide a measure of the probability to find the input on the neural network in the region associated with the eigenfunction $\psi_k(x)$.

Furthermore, issues related to the uncertainty principle have been examined in case of the QHO-based neural network. The uncertainty principle can be expressed first through the Balian-Low theorem for the case of Gabor frames. Next an expression of the uncertainty principle for basis functions that follow the model of the quantum harmonic oscillator can be given. The uncertainty principle is a measure of the time-frequency localization of the activation functions in the QHO-based neural network and evaluates the degradation of localization when successive elements of these orthonormal basis functions are considered. It is shown that the Hermite basis functions as well as their Fourier transforms cannot be uniformly concentrated in the time-frequency plane (Jamming et al, 2007), (Powell 2005).

2. Results on neural structures with stochastic weights

2a. Neural structures with stochastic weights which stem from the solution of Schrödinger's linear equation for zero or constant potential. Modelling of brain processes has emerged as a promising research topic, which can help in the understanding of the human cognition (Hopfield,1982), (Pribram,1991), (Kosko,1992), (Petritis 1996), (Resconi, 2002). Investigations in this field have delivered successful implementations of learning and memory along with lines inspired by neural architectures. These findings have promoted optimism that a sufficiently complex artificial neural network would reproduce the full spectrum and extent of the relevant brain processes involved in human cognition and consciousness. However, physical effects in the functioning of the nervous system, which lie outside classical physics suggest that conventional neural networks may ultimately prove insufficient for this task. One finds ample support for this in an analysis of the sensory organs, the operation of which is quantized at levels varying from the reception of individual photons by the retina, to thousands of phonon quanta in the auditory system. Of further interest is the argument that synaptic signal transmission has a quantum character, although the debate on this issue has not been conclusive. In any case it is known that quantum modes exist in peptides, DNA and proteins. For instance, in (Hagan et al, 2002) it is argued that superposition of quantum states for a significant time interval takes place in the microtubules of the brain and that memory recall is the result of quantum measurement. Moreover, it has been argued that human cognition must involve an element inaccessible to simulation on classical neural networks and this might be realized through a biological instantiation of quantum computation. In the same direction, in (Petritis 2008), the statistics of the genomic sequences are studied (which are usually confronted with stochastic or quantum models of computing) and it is established that certain aspects of these statistics are not in contradiction with quantum mechanical Turing computation, corroborating thus the thesis of quantum nature of cognitive processes (at least not invalidating this thesis).

Quantum computation gives a new perspective in computer science and can help in the modelling of cognitive processes (Perus, 2001), (Rigatos & Tzafestas, 2006a). The association of neural structures with quantum information processing results in an exponential increase of patterns storage capacity and can explain the extensive memorization and inferencing capabilities of humans (Kak,1999), (Ventura,1999). Several models of quantum neural networks containing stochastic parameters have been proposed: in (Ventura, 1997) the weight vector which is associated with a quantum neuron is a linear superposition (wave function) of crisp weight vectors, while in (Purosathaman et al, 1997) the quantum neuron has a multilevel transfer function, which is the result of the linear superposition of sigmoid functions. In (Ventura et al, 2000) quantum associative memories with exponential storage capacity are presented. The stored patterns are considered to be basis states of a quantum wave function. Rotation operators increase the probability to recall the basis state associated with the input pattern. This work is extended in (Ezhov et al, 2000) where fuzzy queries to a quantum memory end up at the retrieval of valid stored patterns. In (Resconi et al, 2002) it is stated that the property of linear superposition indicates an equivalence between neural and quantum computation. The proposed quantum neural structures are non-diagonal recurrent neural networks where the output of each neuron corresponds to a quantum state. The evolution of the states in time is realized through unitary operators. In (Behrman et al, 2000) quantum dot molecules which are spatially distributed on a suitable substrate and which affect each other through phononic and Coulombic interactions are viewed as a quantum Hopfield net. Several other papers have been published outlining similar ideas (De Garis, 2003). Finally, the use of quantum diodes in the realization of nanocircuits with neural computing attributes is shown in (Banyopadhyay et al, 2002).

In (Rigatos & Tzafestas, 2006a), (Rigatos, 2006d) neural connectionist structures with stochastic weights that stem from Schrödinger's linear equation for zero or constant potential have been studied and a model of quantum associative memories has been introduced. The main features of this memory model are summarized in the following:

a. The proposed quantum associative memories result from neural associative memories if the elements of the weight matrix are taken to be stochastic (fuzzy) variables. The probability density function of each weight is given by the solution of Schrödinger's diffusion equation. The correspondence of quantum mechanics to fuzzy logic has been demonstrated.
b. The weights of the proposed associative memories are updated with the use of a learning algorithm that satisfies quantum mechanics postulates. Instead of Hebbian learning, it is assumed that the incremental changes of the weights are performed with the use of fuzzy inference. This fuzzy learning rule is proved to satisfy two basic postulates of quantum mechanics: (i) existence in superimposing states, (ii) evolution between the superimposing states with the use of unitary operators. Therefore it can be considered as a quantum learning algorithm.
c. Taking the elements of the weight matrix of the associative memory to be stochastic (fuzzy) variables means that the initial weight matrix can be decomposed into a superposition of associative memories. This is equivalent to mapping the fundamental memories (attractors) of the associative memory into the vector spaces which are spanned by the eigenvectors of the superimposing matrices and which are related to each other via unitary rotations. In this way, it can be shown that the storage capacity of the associative memories with stochastic weights increases exponentially with respect to the storage capacity of conventional associative memories.

2b. Stochastic neural networks which can be modelled as gene networks . Although the term *quantum* is not used explicitly in their description there are stochastic neural networks with features that are reminiscent of quantum mechanical principles and which are worth to be presented in this background overview. The pattern formation ability of some genetic circuits has been studied and the behaviour of such networks under stochastic disturbances has been examined (Vakulenko & Grigoriev, 2006). Fundamental learning theory for pattern recognition problems was proposed by L. Valiant and developped by many authors. After, evolutionary algorithms for machine learning (for example, for boolean formula recognition) are proposed by L. Valiant in (Valiant, 2007). In the boolean case, many algorithms need an exponentially large running time. The following ideas have been proposed: To recognize real patterns one can use results (Grigoriev et al, 1991a), (Grigoriev et al., 1990), (Grigoriev et al. 1994), (Grigoriev et al. 1991b) that allow to construct fast algorithms of adaptive learning. These ideas are applicable to patterns which are sparse sums of polynomial, rational functions, or, in general, functions which are eigenfunctions of some linear operators (Grigoriev et al, 1991a), (Grigoriev et al., 1990), (Grigoriev et al. 1994), (Grigoriev et al. 1991b). Such algorithms can be realized physically by networks consisting of quantum or optical devices.

To extend these algorithms to a large class of patterns, a new idea has been proposed (Valiant, 2007), (Grigoriev et al, 1991a), (Grigoriev et al., 1990), (Grigoriev et al. 1994), (Grigoriev et al. 1991b): a technique based on pffaffian functions (Khovanskii, 1991) together with evolutionary algorithms from (Valiant 2007). Earlier this pfaffian approach has been applied to some important genetic and neural network problems (Vakulenko et al 2003a), (Vakulenko et al 2005a), (Vakulenko et al 2003b), (Vakulenko et al. 2003c), (Vakulenko et al 2005b), (Vakulenko et al 2006), (Vakulenko et al, 2002). The main idea is that one can recognize a complicated pattern step by step, using previous patterns and trying to present a given pattern as a sparse sum of functions of previous patterns and space variables.

The goal of the above mentioned stochastic neural networks is to construct a physical model of networks which can realize new algorithms. Such a network can be based on quantum or optical physical mechanisms. Quantum systems to resolve complicated problems are proposed in (Grigoriev et al, 2007). Non-quantum physical realizations of neural networks have been proposed in (Vakulenko 2000). In (Vakulenko 2000), (Vakulenko 2002) it was also shown that Hopfield networks generate any structurally stable dynamics and control algorithms have been proposed.

3. Results on neural structures with stochastic weights which stem from the model of the quantum harmonic oscillator. Conventional neural networks may prove insufficient for modelling memory and cognition, as indicated by physical effects in the functioning of the nervous system which can be better interpreted with the use of quantum mechanics instead of classical physics (Hagan,2002), (Behrman et. al., 2000), (Deutch, 1989), (Feynman, 1986) and (Perus, 2001). To evaluate the validity of the aforementioned arguments, in this chapter elements of stochastic calculus will be used (Klebaner, 2005). It will be assumed that the neural weights are stochastic variables that follow the model of the quantum harmonic oscillator. Stochastic variables that are associated with quantum mechanics equations and which demonstrate the particle-wave nature of information, have been analyzed in (Mahler & Weberuss, 1998), (Muller, 1998), (Cohen-Tannoudji et al., 1998), and (Nielsen et al., 2000). The use of neural networks compatible with quantum mechanics principles in image processing, function approximation and system modelling can be found in (Perus,2000), (Perus et al., 2004) and (Resconi et al, 2002), while the relation between random oscillations and diffusion equations has been studied in (Soong et al, 1992) and (Gitterman, 2005). Other studies on neural models with quantum mechanical properties can be found in (Refregier, 2003), (Rigatos et al., 2006b), (Rigatos, 2007b) and (Ventura et al, 2000). In (Rigatos, 2008b) it has been assumed that the weights of neural networks are stochastic variables. These weights correspond to diffusing particles which interact with each other as the theory of Brownian motion (Wiener process) predicts. This assumption has been also used in (Iwasaki et. al., 1998).

Brownian motion is the analogous of the quantum harmonic oscillator (Q.H.O.), i.e. of Schrödinger's equation under harmonic (parabolic) potential (Comets et al., 2006). Instead of trying to solve Schrödinger's equation for various types of the potential $V(x)$ one can study the time evolution of the particle through an equivalent diffusion equation, assuming probability density function depending on Q.H.O's ground state, (Faris, 2006). This is the model of the Ornstein-Uhlenbeck diffusion which has previously been analyzed in (Basseville et al, 1993). It is shown that the diffusive motion of the stochastic particles (weights' update) can be described by Langevin's equation which is a stochastic linear differential equation (Gitterman, 2005) and (Faris, 2006). Using the theoretical analysis of gradient algorithms given in (Duflo,1996) and (Benveniste et al., 1990), it is proved that Langevin's equation is a generalization of conventional gradient algorithms, (Rigatos, 2007c), (Rigatos, 2008c). Therefore neural structures with crisp numerical weights can be considered as a subset of NN with stochastic weights based on the Q.H.O model. Additionally, more practical issues have been taken into account and a neural associative memory with stochastic weights following the Q.H.O. model is studied. From the results given in (Levine et al, 2000) it is known that the convergence of multi-particle systems to an attractor can be studied with the use of Lyapunov stability theory. Lyapunov stability analysis has been performed in (Rigatos 2008a) and following this methodology one can provide sufficient conditions for the weights (Brownian particles) to converge to stability points (attractors). It has been shown that: (i) the learning of the weights stands for a Wiener process, (ii) in

Q.H.O-based associative memories the number of attractors increases exponentially, comparing to conventional associative memories. This in turn gives an explanation for the advanced memorization and inference capabilities of the human brain. Furthermore, the energy spectrum of the stochastic weights that follow the Q.H.O model is studied. To this end, previous results on wavelets' energy spectrum are used (Addison, 2002), (Debauchies, 1990), (Mallat, 1998), and (Torresani, 1995). Spectral analysis of the stochastic weights has shown that: (i) the Gaussian membership functions of the weights express the distribution of energy with respect to the weights' value. The smaller the spread of the basis functions is, the larger becomes the spectral (energy) content that can be captured therein, (ii) the stochastic weights satisfy a relation analogous to the principle of uncertainty.

4. Modelling of diffusion processes with the use of density estimators. Another important issue for research on quantum neural networks is the modelling of diffusion processes. It has been assumed that the diffusing particles interact to each other as the theory of Brownian motion predicts (Rigatos, 2007c), (Rigatos, 2008c). Brownian motion is the analogous of the quantum harmonic oscillator (Q.H.O.), i.e. of Schrödinger's equation under harmonic (parabolic) potential. However, the analytical or numerical solution of Schrödinger's equation, is computationally intensive, since for different values of the potential $V(x)$ it is required to calculate the modes $\psi_k(x)$ in which the particle's wave-function $\psi(x)$ is decomposed (Chung 2002), (Chuong et al., 2007). Moreover, the solution of Schrödinger's equation contains non-easily interpretable terms such as the complex number probability amplitudes which are associated with the modes $\psi(x)$, or the path integrals that constitute the particle's trajectory. On the other hand, instead of trying to solve Schrödinger's equation for various types of $V(x)$ one can study the time evolution of the particles through an equivalent diffusion equation, assuming probability density function depending on Q.H.O's ground state, i.e. (Faris, 2006), (Rigatos, 2008c).

An outline of the research work contained in this chapter is given in Table 1.

EQUIVALENCE OF SCHRÖDINGER'S EQUATION TO A DIFFUSION PROCESS

1. Wiener Walk And Wiener Process

First, the Wiener walk will be analyzed and the Wiener process will be derived as a limit case of the walk. The Wiener walk describes a simple symmetric random walk. Assume $\xi_1, \xi_2, \ldots, \xi_n$ a finite sequence of independent random variables, each one of which takes the values ± 1 with the same probability. The random walk is the sequence

$$s_k = \xi_1 + \xi_2 + \ldots + \xi_k, \quad 0 \le k \le n \qquad (1)$$

Table 1. Associative memories based on the QHO model

1. The weighs of the quantum associative memory correspond to interacting Brownian particles.
2. The dynamic behaviour of the weights can be described by a stochastic process (Ornstein-Uhlenbeck diffusion) which is shown to be analogous to the model of the quantum harmonic oscillator.
3. The dynamic behaviour of the weights is also described by the probability density function. which is calculated from the solution of Schrödinger's harmonic equation.
4. For a large number of weights (high-dimensional neural network) the dynamics of the associative memory can be studied with the use of statistical methods, such as the Central Limit Theorem (C.L.T.)
5. The probability distribution of the stochastic weights can be substituted by a fuzzy possibility function. This enables to show the decomposition of the weight matrix into a superposition of individual matrices and the existence of stochastic attractors
6. Comparing to conventional associative memories, the number of attractors of the proposed quantum associative memories increases exponentially.
7. Spectral analysis shows that the stochastic weights satisfy a relation which is equivalent to the principle of uncertainty.

Figure 1.

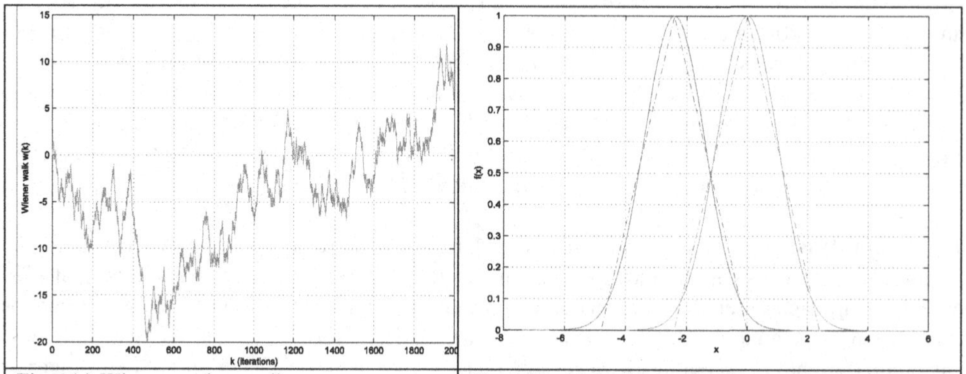

Fig. 1(a) Wiener random walk

Fig. 1(b) p.d.f. of the ground state of the solution of Schrodinger's equation for harmonic potential.

The n-step Wiener walk is considered in the time interval $[0,T]$, where the time step Δt is associated with particle's displacement Δx. Thus the following random variable $w(t_k)$ can be defined:

$$w(t_k)=\xi_1\Delta x+...+\xi_k\Delta x \Rightarrow w(t_k)=w(t_{k-1})+\xi_k\Delta x \tag{2}$$

The random function that is described by Eq. (2) is the Wiener walk (Faris, 2006). A sample of the Wiener walk in depicted in Fig. 1(a). The Wiener walk (also known as Brownian motion) is an important topic in the theory of stochastic processes since it provides a model for the motion of a particle under the effect of a potential (Comets & Meyre, 2006). The Wiener process is the limit of the Wiener walk for $n\rightarrow\infty$, and using the central limit theorem (C.L.T.) it can be shown that the distribution of the Wiener process is Gaussian (Rigatos & Tzafestas, 2006a), (Faris, 2006). Indeed, since the random variable $w(t_k)$ of Eq. (2) is the sum of an infinitely large number of increments, then according to the C.L.T. it must follow a Gaussian distribution. Thus one obtains (Faris, 2006):

$$E\{w(t)\}=0, \text{ while } E[w(t)-E\{w(t)\}]^2=\sigma^2\cdot t \tag{3}$$

2. The Wiener Process Corresponds To A Diffusion Partial Differential Equation

It has been shown that the limit of the Wiener walk for $n\rightarrow\infty$ is the Wiener process, which corresponds to the partial differential equation (p.d.e) of a diffusion (Faris, 2006). For $t>0$, function $\rho(x,t)$ is defined as the probability density function (p.d.f) of the Wiener process $f(w(t)$, i.e.

$$E[f(w(t))]=\int_{-\infty}^{+\infty}f(x)\rho(x,t)dx \tag{4}$$

The p.d.f. $\rho(x,t)$ is a Gaussian variable with mean value equal to 0 and variance equal to σ^2 and satisfies a diffusion p.d.e of the form

$$\frac{\partial\rho}{\partial t}=\frac{1}{2}\sigma^2\frac{\partial^2\rho}{\partial t^2} \tag{5}$$

which is the simplest diffusion equation (heat equation). The generalization of the Wiener process in an infinite dimensional space is the *Ornstein-Uhlenbeck* process, where the joint probability density function is also Gaussian

(Faris, 2006), (Basseville & Nikiforov, 1993). In that case there are *n* Brownian particles, and each one performs a Wiener walk, given by $w^i(t_k)$, i=1,..., n of Eq. (2).

3. Schrödinger's Equation With Nonzero Potential Stands For A Diffusion with Drift

The equivalence between Wiener process and the diffusion process was demonstrated. Next, the direct relation between diffusion and quantum mechanics will be shown (Faris,2006). The basic equation of quantum mechanics is Schrödinger's equation, i.e.

$$i\frac{\partial\psi}{\partial t} = H\psi(x,t) \quad (6)$$

where $\psi(x,t)$ is the probability density function of finding the particle at position x at time instant t, and H is the system's Hamiltonian, i.e. the sum of its kinetic and potential energy, which is given by $H = \frac{p^2}{2m} + V$, with p being the momentum of the particle, m the mass and V an external potential. It holds that $\frac{p^2}{2m} = -\frac{1}{2}\frac{\hbar}{m}\frac{\partial^2}{\partial x^2}$ thus the Hamiltonian can be also written as $H = -\frac{1}{2}\frac{\hbar}{m}\frac{\partial^2}{\partial x^2}$. The solution of Eq. (6) is given by (Cohen-Tannoudji et. al, 1998)

$$\psi(x,t) = e^{-iHt}\psi(x,0) \quad (7)$$

A simple way to transform Schrödinger's equation into a diffusion equation is to substitute variable *it* with *t*. This passage from imaginary time to real time is convenient but artificial. However, in the domain of non-relativistic quantum mechanics there is a closer connection between diffusion theory and quantum theory. In stochastic mechanics, the real time of quantum mechanics is also the real time of diffusion and in fact quantum mechanics is formulated as conservative diffusion (Faris, 2006). This change of variable results in the *Fokker-Planck* partial differential equation (Gitterman, 2005), (Faris,2006).

$$\frac{\partial\rho}{\partial t} = [\frac{1}{2}\sigma^2\frac{\partial^2}{\partial x^2} - V(x)]\,\rho \quad (8)$$

Eq. (8) can be also written as

$$\frac{\partial\rho}{\partial t} = -H\rho \quad (9)$$

where H is the associated Hamiltonian and the solution is of the form $\rho(x,t) = e^{-tH}\rho(x)$, and variable σ^2 is a diffusion constant.

The Fokker-Planck equation can be used for the calculation of the mean position of the diffused particle, as well as for the calculation of its variance (Gitterman, 2005). An equivalent model of the motion of the diffused particle is based on Langevin's equation, and will be analyzed in the sequel.

Now, as known from quantum mechanics, particle's probability density function $\rho(x)$ is a wave-function for which holds $\rho(x) = |\psi(x)|^2$, with $\psi(x) = \sum_{k=0}^{N} c_k\psi_k(x)$, where $\psi_k(x)$ are the associated eigenfunctions (Müller, 1998)), (Cohen-Tannoudji, 1998). It can be assumed that $|\rho_0(x) = \psi_0^2(x)|$, i.e. the p.d.f includes only the basic mode, while higher order modes are truncated. Thus, it is considered that the initial probability density function is $\rho(x) = \rho_0(x)$, which is independent of time. Consequently, from Eq. (9) one has $H\rho_0 = 0$, which means that the p.d.f. remains independent of time and the examined diffusion process is a stationary one, i.e. $\rho(x,t) = \rho_0(x)\ \forall t$. A form of the probability density function for the stationary diffusion is that of shifted, partially overlapping Gaussians, which is depicted in Fig. 1(b). In place of Gaussian p.d.f, symmetric triangular possibility distributions have been also proposed (Rigatos & Tzafestas, 2002), (Dubois et. al., 2004). The equation that describes the shifted Gaussians is (Faris, 2006)

$$\rho_0(x) = \frac{1}{2}C^2 e^{-\frac{\omega}{\sigma^2}(x-\alpha)^2} + \frac{1}{2}C^2 e^{-\frac{\omega}{\sigma^2}(x+\alpha)^2} \qquad (10)$$

4. Study Of The Q.H.O Model Through The Ornstein-Uhlenbeck Diffusion

The Ornstein-Uhlenbeck diffusion is a model of the Brownian motion (Basseville & Nikiforov, 1993). The particle tries to return to the equilibrium $x = 0$ under the influence of a linear force, i.e. there is a spring force applied to the particle as a result of the potential $V(x)$. The corresponding phenomenon in quantum mechanics is that of the quantum harmonic oscillator (Q.H.O.) (Cohen-Tannoudji, 1998) and (Gitterman, 2005). In the Q.H.O. model the motion of the particle is affected by the parabolic (harmonic) potential

$$V(x) = \frac{1}{2}\frac{\omega^2}{\sigma^2}x^2 \qquad (11)$$

It is known that the ground mode of the quantum harmonic oscillator of Eq. (6) is a Gaussian function (Rigatos & Tzafestas, 2006b), (Faris, 2006) i.e.

$$\psi_0(x) = Ce^{-\frac{\omega x^2}{2\sigma^2}} \qquad (12)$$

while it can be proved easily that the associated eigenvalue is $\lambda_0 = \frac{1}{2}\omega$. A diagram of $V(x) - \lambda_0$ is given in Fig. 2(a).

For the diffusion constant σ holds $\sigma^2 = \hbar / m$ where $\hbar$ is Planck's constant and this finally gives $V(x) = \frac{1}{2}m\omega^2 x^2$.

Figure 2.

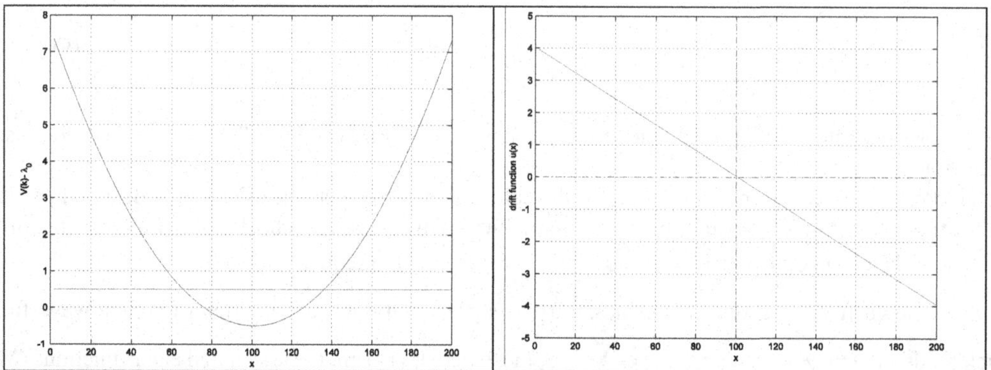

Fig. 2(a) Diagram of $V(x) - \lambda_0$ where $V(x)$ is the harmonic potential of the Q.H.O. and λ_0 is the associated eigenvalue	Fig. 2 (b) Linear drift force applied to the diffused particle as a result of the harmonic potential $V(x)$

Assuming the stationary p.d.f. of Eq. (10), i.e. $\rho(x)=\psi_0(x)^2=C^2e^{-\frac{\omega x^2}{2\sigma^2}}$, the force applied to the particle due to the harmonic potential $V(x)$ is given by Eq. (12), and is of the form

$$u(x)=-kx \tag{13}$$

which means that the drift is a spring force applied to the particle and which aims at leading it to an equilibrium position. The drift force is depicted in Fig. 2(b).

5. The Motion Of The Q.H.O. Particle Is A Generalization Of Gradient Algorithms

As mentioned above the Q.H.O. model describes the motion of a particle. Here, a kinematic model for particle's motion will be derived, using Langevin's equation. The stochastic differential equation for the position of the particle is (Faris, 2006):

$$dx(t)=u(x(t))dt+dw(t) \tag{14}$$

where $u(x)=-kx$ is the drift function of Eq. (13), i.e. a spring force generated by the harmonic potential $V(x)$, which tries to bring the particle to the equilibrium $x=0$. The term $w(t)$ denotes a random force (due to interaction with other particles) and results in a Wiener walk. For each continuous random path $w(t)$, a continuous random path $x(t)$ is also generated, which can be written in the form

$$x(t)=x(0)+\int_0^t u(x(s))ds+w(t) \tag{15}$$

The integration of Langevin's equation and certain assumptions about the noise $w(t)$, for instance white noise, dichotomic noise (also known as Ornstein-Uhlenbeck noise) etc., enable the calculation of the mean position of the particle $E(x)$ and of its variance $E(x-E(x))^2$ (Gitterman, 2005).

Langevin's equation gives a model of an harmonic oscillator, driven by noise. Apart from the spring force, a friction force that depends on the friction coefficient γ and on the velocity of the particle can be considered. Thus, the model of motion of the particle can then be also written as (Gitterman, 2005), (Astrom, 2006):

$$\frac{d^2x}{dt^2}+\gamma\frac{dx}{dt}+kx=\xi(t) \tag{16}$$

Knowing that the Q.H.O. model imposes to the particle a spring force Eq. (16), can be formulated as

$$dx(t)=-kxdt+w(t). \tag{17}$$

Equation (16) is close to robotics and control models (Tzafestas & Rigatos, 2000), (Rigatos, 2002). Eq. (17) can be also written as.

$$dx(t)=h(x(t))dt+w(t) \tag{18}$$

where $h(x(t))=\alpha\frac{\partial V(x)}{\partial t}$, with a being a learning gain, $V(x)$ being the harmonic potential and $w(t)$ being a noise function. Eq. (18) is a generalization of gradient algorithms based on the ordinary differential equation (O.D.E) concept, where the gradient algorithms are described as trajectories towards the equilibrium of an ordinary differential equation (Duflo, 1996), (Benveniste et. al., 1990). Indeed, conventional gradient algorithms with diminishing step are written as

$$dx(t) = h(x(t))dt \quad (19)$$

The comparison of Eq. (18) and Eq. (19) verifies the previous argument. The update of the neural weights that follow the model of the quantum harmonic oscillator is given by Eq. (18), which is a description of Schrödinger's equation for parabolic potential. The force that drives $x(t)$ to the equilibrium is the derivative of the harmonic potential, and there is also an external noisy force $w(t)$ which is the result of collisions or repulsive forces due to interaction with neighbouring particles. Similarly, in the update of neural weights with a conventional gradient algorithm, the weight is driven towards an equilibrium under the effect of a potential's gradient, and the potential is usually taken to be a quadratic error cost function. Feedback from neighbouring neurons can affect the weight's update.

INTERACTING DIFFUSING PARTICLES AS A MODEL OF NEURAL NETWORKS

The concept of a neural network with weights defined by the position x^i of interacting Brownian particles can be also found in (Iwasaki et al. 1998). The interaction g between the stochastic weights (Brownian particles) contains attractive forces (spring-mass forces) and repulsive forces (defined by a Gaussian term). In this neural network the update of the weights is finally the kinematic model of the Q.H.O. particles and can be approximated by:

$$x^i(t+1) = x^i(t) + \gamma^i(t)[-\nabla_{x^i} V^i(x^i) + e^i(t+1)] + \sum_{j=1, j\neq i}^{M} g(x^i - x^j) \quad (20)$$

with $i = 1, 2, ..., M$ to be the weight's (particle's) index, $\gamma^i(t) = 1$ and $e^i(t+1)$ to be a noise term.

The term $g(x^i - x^j)$ is defined as

$$g(x^i - x^j) = -(x^i - x^j)(\alpha - b e^{-\frac{(x^i - x^j)^2}{\sigma^2}}) \quad (21)$$

and denotes the interaction between particle i and particle j. Coefficient α defines an attractive (spring-type) force between the particles, while coefficient b defines a repulsive force between the particles.

Eq. (20) is in accordance with Eq. (18) and shows that weights' update is finally described by interacting gradient algorithms. The stability of the learning algorithm, i.e. the convergence of the Brownian weights to the

Figure 3.(a) A neural associative memory: there are N neurons and each neuron i receives feedback from the rest N-1 neurons (b) The stochastic weights are described by a fuzzy possibility distribution

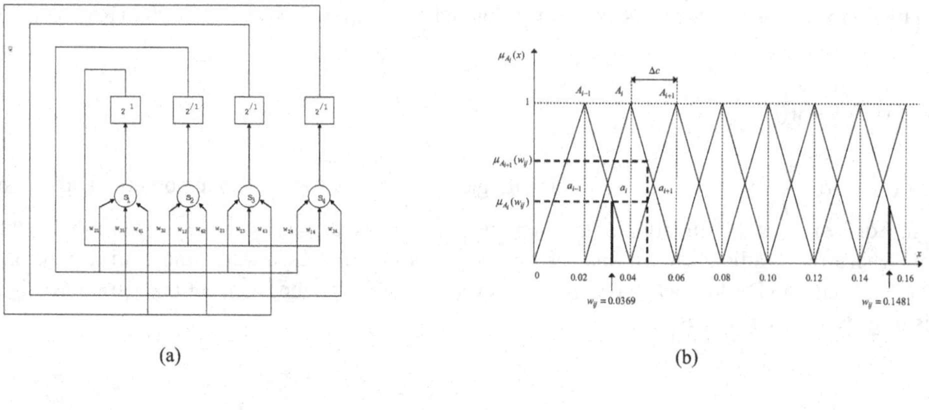

(a) (b)

desirable values is equivalent to the convergence of the interacting particles to an attractor and can be studied using Lyapunov stability analysis and LaSalle's theorem (Gazi &Passino 2004), (Rigatos, 2008a).

COMPATIBILITY WITH PRINCIPLES OF QUANTUM MECHANICS

The neural network which is based on the motion interacting diffusing particles was shown to stem from a stochastic process (Ornstein-Uhlenbeck diffusion) which is analogous to the model of the quantum harmonic oscillator. It was shown that the particle's diffusive motion is characterised by a probability density function (p.d.f.) which is represented by a mixture of Gaussians (see Eq. (8) and Fig. 1(b)). The same result can be reached if theory of quantum mechanics is used.

1. Free Schrödinger's Equation and Wave-Packets

It is assumed that each weight of the neural network is a stochastic variable with probability density function which is calculated from the solution of Schrödinger's equation. The case in which the external potential V is zero or constant at every point of the space is considered. Then, a solution of Schrödinger's equation is the plane wave $\psi(x,t) = Ae^{i(kx-\omega t)}$, where k, ω satisfy the L. de Broglie relations $k = p\hbar$ and $\omega = E\hbar$. According to the principle of superposition any linear combination of these plane waves (wavepacket) is a solution of Schrödinger's equation, $\psi(x,t) = A_l \int g(k)e^{i(kx-\omega t)}dk$. The wave-packet can be interpreted from the point of view of spectral decomposition. Assume that a particle at time instant $t=0$ is described by the wave function $\psi(x,0) = Ae^{ikx}$ and has a well defined momentum, which means that a measurement of the momentum at this time instant will certainly give $p = \hbar k$. Thus one can deduce that e^{ikx} characterizes the eigenstate which corresponds to $p = \hbar k$. Since, on the other hand, there is a plane wave for each real value of k, the eigenvalues that one can expect in a certain measurement of the momentum are all real values (in this case there is no quantification of the possible results: as in classical mechanics all values of the momentum are permitted).

At $t=0$ variables $\psi(x,0)$ and $g(k)$ are connected through a Fourier transform pair (Cohen-Tannoudji et al., 1998), which is $\psi(x,0) = \frac{1}{\sqrt{2\pi}}\int g(k)e^{ikx}dx$ and $g(k) = \frac{1}{\sqrt{2\pi}}\int \psi(x,0)e^{-ikx}dx$. Setting $g(k) = |g(k)|e^{i\alpha k}$ and taking the Taylor expansion of $a(k)$round k_0, permits to rewrite the wave-packet at $t=0$ as

$$\psi(x,0) \approx \frac{e^{i[k_0x+a(k_0)]}}{\sqrt{2\pi}}\int_{-\infty}^{+\infty} |g(k)|e^{i(k-k_0)(x-x_0)}dk \tag{22}$$

with $x_0 = -\frac{da(k)}{dk}|_{k=k_0}$. When $x-x_0$ is large Eq.(22) represents a function of k which performs very fast oscillations in the interval Δk. In case that $|g(k)|$ is a Gaussian, and $|x-x_0| > \frac{1}{\Delta k}$, the real part of function $|g(k)|e^{i(k-k_0)(x-x_0)}$ is depicted in Fig. 4(a), while for $|x-x_0| < \frac{1}{\Delta k}$, the real part of function $|g(k)|e^{i(k-k_0)(x-x_0)}$ is depicted in Fig. 4(b).

When x moves far from x_0, $\psi(x,0)$ decreases. This decrease becomes significant when $e^{i(k-k_0)(x-x_0)}$ completes one oscillation while k covers the domain Δk, i.e. when $\Delta k(x-x_0) \approx 1$. If Δx is the approximative width of the wave packet one obtains $\Delta k \Delta x \geq 1$, which is the classical relation between the width of two functions, related to each other through a Fourier transform. One can write the above relation as

$$\Delta x \Delta p \geq \hbar \tag{23}$$

where $\Delta p = \hbar \Delta k$ is the spread of the curve representing $g(k)$. The interpretation of Eq. (23) is as follows: it is impossible to define at a certain time instant both the position and the momentum of the particle with arbitrary precision. When the limit imposed by Eq. (23) is approached, the increase of the accuracy of the position measurement (decrease of Δx) implies a decrease in the accuracy of the momentum measurement (increase of Δp) and vice-versa. This relation is Heisenberg's principle of uncertainty.

Figure 4.

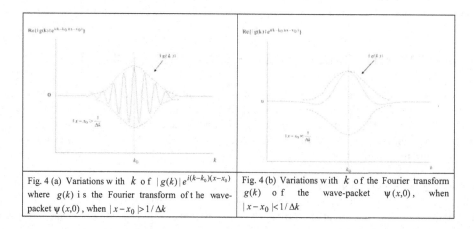

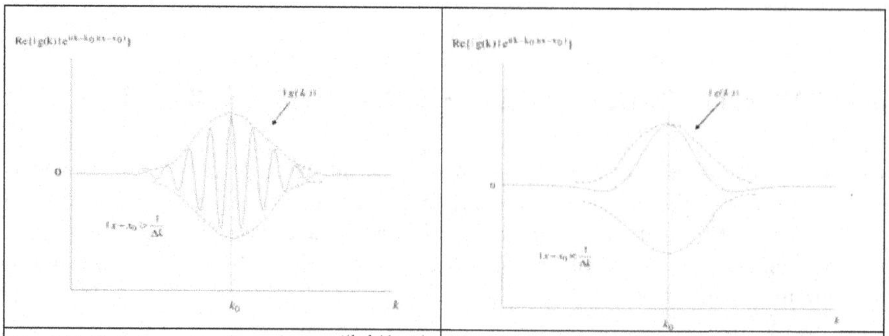

Fig. 4 (a) Variations with k of $\lvert g(k) \rvert e^{i(k-k_0)(x-x_0)}$ where $g(k)$ is the Fourier transform of the wave-packet $\psi(x,0)$, when $\lvert x-x_0 \rvert > 1/\Delta k$	Fig. 4 (b) Variations with k of the Fourier transform $g(k)$ of the wave-packet $\psi(x,0)$, when $\lvert x-x_0 \rvert < 1/\Delta k$

2. The Gaussian Wave-Packet

The wave packet associated with the free quantum particle ($V(x)=0$) is considered and function $g(k)$ is taken to be Gaussian. In that case $\psi(x,0)$ is found to be $\psi(x,0)=\sqrt{C}e^{ik_0x}e^{-x^2/a^2}$, where C is a normalization coefficient. The probability to find the particle (stochastic weight), at time instant $t=0$, in the interval $[x, x+\Delta x]$ is given by $|\psi(x,0)|^2 = Ce^{-2x^2/a^2}$.

Therefore, the probability density function of the particle is given by the well known bell-shaped curve, centered at $x=0$ (see Fig. 5(a)). Similarly, the probability to find the quantum particle in the intervals $[x_i, x_i+\Delta x]$, $i=1,2,...,n$ is given by Gaussian functions, centered at x_i (Fig. 5(b)). The constraint that the total probability equals 1 should be satisfied.

3. Eigenstates of the Quantum Harmonic Oscillator

In case that a potential $V(x)$ exists, Schrödinger's equation (Eq. (6)) becomes

$$i\frac{\partial\psi(x,t)}{\partial t} = -\frac{\hbar^2}{2m}\nabla^2\psi(x,t) + V(x)\psi(x,t) \Rightarrow i\frac{\partial\psi(x,t)}{\partial t} = H\,\psi(x,t) \tag{24}$$

where H is the Hamiltonian, i.e. the sum of the potential $V(x)=\frac{p^2}{2m}+E$ and of the Laplacian $-\frac{\hbar}{2m}\nabla^2\psi(x,t) = -\frac{\hbar}{2m}\frac{\partial^2}{\partial x^2}\psi(x,t)$. The solution of Eq. (24) can be found using the separation of variables method, i.e. $\psi(x,t)=X(x)T(t)$. It has been proved that $T(t)$ is given by (Strauss,1992)

$$\frac{\partial T}{\partial t}(t) = \lambda T(t) \Rightarrow T(t) = e^{i\lambda t} \tag{25}$$

while $X(x)$ corresponds to an undamped oscillation, with boundary condition $\lim_{x\to\infty} X(x) = 0$. In case of Eq. (24), i.e. when Schrödinger's equation contains a potential term, the following solution of the harmonic quantum oscillator is considered

$$X_k(x) = H_k(x)e^{-x^2/2} \quad k = 0,1,2,... \tag{26}$$

Figure 5.

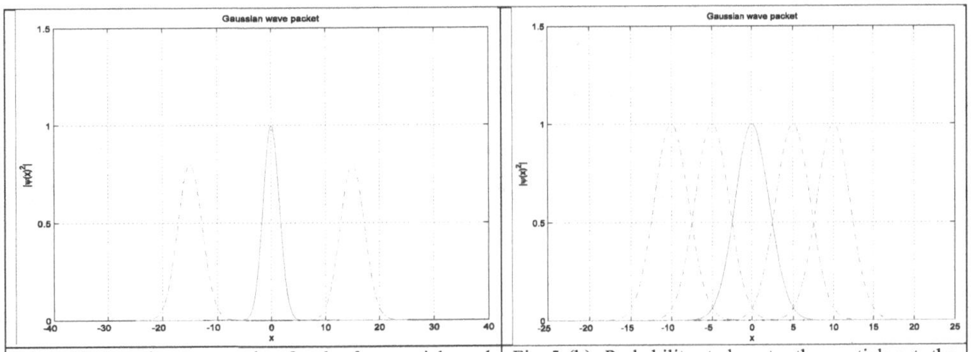

Fig. 5 (a) Gaussian wavepacket for the free particle and its evolution in time	Fig. 5 (b) Probability to locate the particle at the interval $[x_i x_i + \Delta x], i = 1,2,...,n$ at $t = 0$

Figure 6.

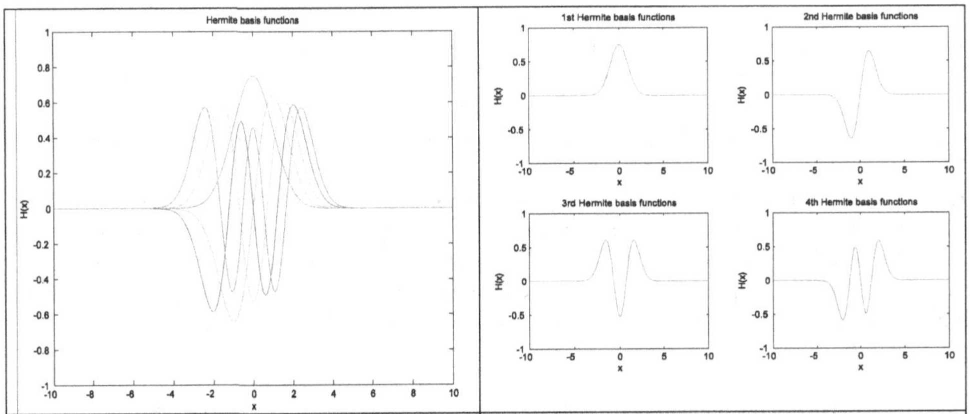

Fig. 6 (a) Hermite basis functions in the one-dimensional data space	Fig. 6 (b) The first four modes of the Hermite series expansion

where $H_k(x)$ are the Hermite orthogonal functions. The Hermite functions $H_k(x)$are the eigenstates of the quantum harmonic oscillator (Fig. 6(a) and Fig. 6(b)). The general relation for the Hermite polynomials is

$$H_k(x) = (-1)^k e^{x^2} \frac{d^k}{dx^{(k)}} e^{-x^2} \tag{27}$$

According to Eq. (27) the first five Hermite polynomials are $H_0(x) = 1$, $H_1(x) = 2x$, $H_2(x) = 4x^2 - 2$, $H_3(x) = 8x^3 - 12x$, $H_4(x) = 16x^4 - 48x^2 + 12$, and are depicted in Fig. 6(b). The general solution of the Schrödinger' equation both in time and space is written as:

$$\psi_k(x,t) = H_k(x) e^{-x^2/2} e^{-i(2k+1)t} \quad k = 0,1,2,... \tag{28}$$

Eq. (28) satisfies the boundary condition $\lim_{x \to \infty} X(x) = 0$. It can be observed that if only the basic mode of the Q.H.O. is maintained then again the position of the particle (stochastic weight) is described by the p.d.f. depicted in Fig. 1(b).

ATTRACTORS IN ASSOCIATIVE MEMORIES BASED ON THE Q.H.O. MODEL

1. Weights Learning In Associative Memories is a Wiener Process

The patterns to be stored in an associative memory are denoted by x_k, $k=1,2,..,p$ and their elements are given by x_k^j, $j=1,2,...,N$ (see Fig. 3(a)). The weights of the associative memory, are selected using Hebb's postulate of learning, i.e. $w_{ji}=\frac{1}{N}\sum_{k=1}^{p}x_k^j x_k^i$, $j\neq i$ and $w_{ji}=0$, $j=i$, where $i,j=1,2,...N$. The above can be summarized in the network's correlation weight matrix which is given by $W=\frac{1}{N}\sum_{k=1}^{p}x_k^T x_k$. In the case of binary fundamental memories the weights learning is given by Hebb's rule

$$w_{ji}(n+1)=w_{ji}(n)+\text{sgn}(x_{k+1}^j x_{k+1}^i) \tag{29}$$

where k denotes the k-th fundamental memory. The increment $\text{sgn}(x_{k+1}^j x_{k+1}^i)$ may have the values +1 or -1. Thus, the weight w_{ji} is increased or decreased by 1 each time a new fundamental memory is presented to the network. The maximum number of fundamental memories that can be retrieved successfully from an associative memory of N neurons (error probability <1% is given by $p_{\max}=\frac{N}{2\ln N}$ (Ayier et al., 1990), (Haykin, 1994). Thus, for $N=16$ the number of fundamental memories should not be much larger than 2.

The equivalence between Eq. (2) and Eq. (29) is obvious and becomes more clear if in place of $\text{sgn}(x_{k+1}^j x_{k+1}^i)$, the variable $\xi_{k+1}=\pm 1$ is used, and if ξ_{k+1} is also multiplied with the increment Δx. Thus the learning of the weights of an associative memory is a Wiener process. Consequently, the weights can be considered as Brownian particles and for large N their mean value and variance can be calculated using the Central Limit Theorem.

2. Attractors in High Dimensional Spaces Coincide with Eigenvectors Of Weight Matrix *W*

It can be shown that the memory vectors of an associative memory become collinear to the eigenvectors of matrix *W*, thus constituting an orthogonal basis if the following two conditions are satisfied: (i) the number of neurons *N*, is large (high dimensional spaces), and (ii) the memory vectors are chosen randomly. The following lemmas give sufficient conditions for the fundamental memory vectors (attractors) to coincide with the eigenvectors of the weight matrix *W*.

Lemma 1: If the fundamental memory vectors (attractors) of the associative memory are chosen to be orthogonal, then they are collinear to the eigenvectors of matrix *W* (Rigatos & Tzafestas, 2006a).

Proof: The fundamental memory vectors $\bar{x}$ are taken to be orthogonal to each other, i.e. $\bar{x}_i\bar{x}_j=\delta(i-j)$, where $i,j=1,2,...,N$. The weight matrix *W* is given by Eq. $W=\frac{1}{N}\sum_{k=1}^{p}x_k^T x_k$. Thus, the following holds

$$W\bar{x}_k^T=\frac{1}{N}\{\sum_{i=1}^{p}\bar{x}_i^T x_i\}x_k^T=\frac{1}{N}\{\sum_{i=1}^{p}\bar{x}_i^T(\bar{x}_i\bar{x}_k^T)\}\Rightarrow W\bar{x}_k^T=\frac{1}{N}\bar{x}_k^T \tag{30}$$

From Eq. (30) it can be deduced that if the memory vectors are orthogonal then they are collinear to the eigenvectors of the matrix *W* (*Q.E.D.*).

Lemma 2: If the memory vectors of an associative memory are chosen randomly and the number of neurons *N* is large, then there is high probability for them to be orthogonal (Rigatos & Tzafestas, 2006a).

Proof: The normalized internal product of the memory vectors x_i and x_k is considered

$$\frac{1}{N}x_i x_k^T = \frac{1}{N}\sum_{j=1}^{N} x_i^j x_k^j = \sum_{j=1}^{N}\frac{x_i^j x_k^j}{N} = \sum_{j=1}^{N} Y_j \tag{31}$$

For large N and x_i^j, x_k^j randomly chosen from the discrete set $\{-1,1\}$ it holds that the mathematical expectation of Y_j, denoted by $E(Y_j)$, is $E(Y_j)=0$ and $E(Y_j-\bar{Y}_j)^2 = \frac{1}{N}\sum_{j=1}^{N}(Y_j-\bar{Y}_j)^2 = \frac{1}{N}\sum_{j=1}^{N}Y_j^2 = \frac{1}{N}\frac{1}{N^2}\sum_{j=1}^{N}(x_i^j x_k^j)^2$. Assuming patterns $x_i^j \in \{-1,1\}$ then $(x_i^j x_k^j)^2 = 1$, i.e. $\sum_{j=1}^{N}(x_i^j x_k^k)^2 = N$, thus

$$E(Y_j-\bar{Y}_j)^2 = \frac{1}{N}\frac{1}{N^2}N \Rightarrow E(Y_j-\bar{Y}_j)^2 = \frac{1}{N^2} \tag{32}$$

Therefore $E(Y_j)=0$ and $E(Y_j-\bar{Y}_j)^2 = \frac{1}{N^2}$. The Central Limit Theorem (CLT) is applied here. This states:

Consider Y_k a sequence of mutually independent random variables $\{Y_k\}$ which follow a common distribution. It is assumed that Y_k has mean μ and variance σ^2, and let $Y = Y_1+Y_2+...+Y_N = \sum_{i=1}^{N}Y_i$. Then as N approaches infinity the probability distribution of the sum random variable Y approaches a Gaussian distribution

$$\frac{(Y-N\mu_i)}{\sqrt{N}\sigma} \cap N(0,1) \tag{33}$$

According to CLT the probability distribution of the sum random variable $\frac{1}{N}\sum_{j=1}^{N}x_i^j x_k^j = \sum_{j=1}^{N}Y_j$ follows a Gaussian distribution of center $\mu = N\cdot 0$ and variance $\sigma^2 = N\frac{1}{N^2} = \frac{1}{N}$. Therefore for large number of neurons *N*, i.e. for high dimensional spaces $\frac{1}{N} \to 0$ and the vectors x_i and x_k will be practically orthogonal (*Q.E.D.*).

Thus, taking into account the orthogonality of the memory vectors and Lemma 1, it can be deduced that memory patterns in high dimensional spaces practically coincide with the eigenvectors of the weight matrix ***W***.

It can be also shown that the learning of the Brownian weights, can be written in the form of unitary operators, as the theory of quantum mechanics predicts (Rigatos & Tzafestas, 2002).

3. Decomposition Of The Weight Matrix *W* into a Superposition of Matrices $\bar{W}_i$

In the NN models that consists of interacting Brownian particles the weights are stochastic variables. This has important consequences in the case of associative memories. Taking the weights w_{ij} of the weight matrix ***W*** to be stochastic variables with p.d.f. (or possibility distribution) as the one depicted in Fig. 1(b) means that ***W*** can be decomposed into a superposition of associative memories (see Fig. 7(a)). In that case, the overall associative memory ***W*** equals a weighted averaging of the individual weight matrices $\bar{W}_i$, i.e. $W = \sum_{i=1}^{m}\mu_i \bar{W}_i$, where the nonnegative weights μ_i are possibility values (fuzzy memberships) that indicate the contribution of each local associative memory $\bar{W}_i$ to the aggregate outcome (Rigatos & Tzafestas 2006a). To make clear the above, a 3×3 weight matrix of a neural associative memory is considered:

$$W = \begin{bmatrix} w_{11} & w_{12} & w_{13} \\ w_{21} & w_{22} & w_{23} \\ w_{13} & w_{23} & w_{33} \end{bmatrix} \tag{34}$$

It is also assumed that the weights w_{ij} are stochastic (fuzzy) variables, as described in Fig. 1(b). The two adjacent fuzzy sets to which the weight w_{ij} belongs are denoted as A_i and A_{i+1}.

The weights satisfy the condition $\sum_{i=1}^{N^{ij}} \mu_{A_i} w_{ij} = 1$ (strong fuzzy partition). The membership of the weight w_{ij} to the fuzzy set A_i is denoted as μ_{ij}, while the membership to the fuzzy set A_{i+1} is denoted as 1- μ_{ij}. Then, the following combinations of membership values of the elements of the matrices $\bar{W}_i$ are possible:

$\bar{W}_1: \ \mu_{12}, \ \mu_{13}, \ \mu_{23}$

$\bar{W}_2: \ \mu_{12}, \ \mu_{13}, \ 1-\mu_{23}$

$\bar{W}_3: \ \mu_{12}, \ 1-\mu_{13}, \ \mu_{23}$

$\bar{W}_4: \ \mu_{12}, \ 1-\mu_{13}, \ 1-\mu_{23}$

$\bar{W}_5: \ 1-\mu_{12}, \ \mu_{13}, \ \mu_{23}$

$\bar{W}_6: \ 1-\mu_{12}, \ \mu_{13}, \ 1-\mu_{23}$

$\bar{W}_7: \ 1-\mu_{12}, \ 1-\mu_{13}, \ \mu_{23}$

$\bar{W}_8: \ 1-\mu_{12}, \ 1-\mu_{13}, \ 1-\mu_{23}$

The centers of these fuzzy sets are are shown in Fig. 3(b), and are denoted as α^{A} and $\alpha^{A_{i+1}}$ respectively.

The diagonal elements of the matrices $\bar{W}_i$ are taken to be 0 (no self-feedback in neurons is considered), while the membership value of the element w_{ii}, $i=1,\ldots,3$ is indifferent and is denoted by *. Thus the weight matrix W can be decomposed into a set of superimposing matrices $\bar{W}_i$ as shown in Fig. 7(a). The submatrices $\bar{W}_i$ of this decomposition are as follows:

$$\bar{W}_1 = \{\begin{bmatrix} * & \mu_{12} & \mu_{13} \\ \mu_{12} & * & \mu_{23} \\ \mu_{13} & \mu_{23} & * \end{bmatrix}, \begin{bmatrix} 0 & \alpha_{12}^{A_i} & \alpha_{13}^{A_i} \\ \alpha_{12}^{A_i} & 0 & \alpha_{23}^{A_i} \\ \alpha_{13}^{A_i} & \alpha_{23}^{A_i} & 0 \end{bmatrix}\},$$

$$\bar{W}_2 = \{\begin{bmatrix} * & \mu_{12} & \mu_{13} \\ \mu_{12} & * & 1-\mu_{23} \\ \mu_{13} & 1-\mu_{23} & * \end{bmatrix}, \begin{bmatrix} 0 & \alpha_{12}^{A_i} & \alpha_{13}^{A_i} \\ \alpha_{12}^{A_i} & 0 & \alpha_{23}^{A_{i+1}} \\ \alpha_{13}^{A_{i+1}} & \alpha_{23}^{A_{i+1}} & 0 \end{bmatrix}\}$$

$$\bar{W}_3 = \{\begin{bmatrix} * & \mu_{12} & 1-\mu_{13} \\ \mu_{12} & * & \mu_{23} \\ 1-\mu_{13} & \mu_{23} & * \end{bmatrix}, \begin{bmatrix} 0 & \alpha_{12}^{A_i} & \alpha_{13}^{A_{i+1}} \\ \alpha_{12}^{A_i} & 0 & \alpha_{23}^{A_i} \\ \alpha_{13}^{A_{i+1}} & \alpha_{23}^{A_i} & 0 \end{bmatrix}\}$$

$$\bar{W}_4 = \{\begin{bmatrix} * & \mu_{12} & 1-\mu_{13} \\ \mu_{12} & * & 1-\mu_{23} \\ 1-\mu_{13} & 1-\mu_{23} & * \end{bmatrix}, \begin{bmatrix} 0 & \alpha_{12}^{A_i} & \alpha_{13}^{A_{i+1}} \\ \alpha_{12}^{A_i} & 0 & \alpha_{23}^{A_{i+1}} \\ \alpha_{13}^{A_{i+1}} & \alpha_{23}^{A_{i+1}} & 0 \end{bmatrix}\}$$

$$\bar{W}_5 = \{\begin{bmatrix} * & 1-\mu_{12} & \mu_{13} \\ 1-\mu_{12} & * & \mu_{23} \\ \mu_{13} & \mu_{23} & * \end{bmatrix}, \begin{bmatrix} 0 & \alpha_{12}^{A_{i+1}} & \alpha_{13}^{A_i} \\ \alpha_{12}^{A_{i+1}} & 0 & \alpha_{23}^{A_i} \\ \alpha_{13}^{A_i} & \alpha_{23}^{A_i} & 0 \end{bmatrix}\}$$

$$\bar{W}_6 = \{\begin{bmatrix} * & 1-\mu_{12} & \mu_{13} \\ 1-\mu_{12} & * & 1-\mu_{23} \\ \mu_{13} & 1-\mu_{23} & * \end{bmatrix}, \begin{bmatrix} 0 & \alpha_{12}^{A_{i+1}} & \alpha_{13}^{A_i} \\ \alpha_{12}^{A_{i+1}} & 0 & \alpha_{23}^{A_{i+1}} \\ \alpha_{13}^{A_i} & \alpha_{23}^{A_{i+1}} & 0 \end{bmatrix}\}$$

$$\bar{W}_7 = \{\begin{bmatrix} * & 1-\mu_{12} & 1-\mu_{13} \\ 1-\mu_{12} & * & \mu_{23} \\ 1-\mu_{13} & \mu_{23} & * \end{bmatrix}, \begin{bmatrix} 0 & \alpha_{12}^{A_{i+1}} & \alpha_{13}^{A_{i+1}} \\ \alpha_{12}^{A_{i+1}} & 0 & \alpha_{23}^{A_i} \\ \alpha_{13}^{A_{i+1}} & \alpha_{23}^{A_i} & 0 \end{bmatrix}\}$$

$$\bar{W}_8 = \{\begin{bmatrix} * & 1-\mu_{12} & 1-\mu_{13} \\ 1-\mu_{12} & * & 1-\mu_{23} \\ 1-\mu_{13} & 1-\mu_{23} & * \end{bmatrix}, \begin{bmatrix} 0 & \alpha_{12}^{A_{i+1}} & \alpha_{13}^{A_{i+1}} \\ \alpha_{12}^{A_{i+1}} & 0 & \alpha_{23}^{A_{i+1}} \\ \alpha_{13}^{A_{i+1}} & \alpha_{23}^{A_{i+1}} & 0 \end{bmatrix}\}$$

The associated $\| L_1 \|$ norms are calculated using the sum $\sum_{i=1}^{N}\sum_{j=1}^{N} | \mu_{ij} |$, which in turn is divided by the number of the non-diagonal elements , i.e. $N(N-1)$. The following lemma holds (Rigatos & Tzafestas, 2006a):

Lemma 3: The $\| L_1 \|$ of the matrices M_i (i.e. $\sum_{i=1}^{N}\sum_{j=1}^{N} | \mu_{ij} |$) divided by the number of the non-diagonal elements , i.e. $N(N-1)$ and by 2^{N-1}, where the number of neurons N, equals unity.

$$\frac{1}{N(N-1)2^{N-1}} \sum_{i=1}^{N}\sum_{j=1}^{N} | \mu_{ij} | = 1 \tag{35}$$

Proof: There are 2^{N-1} couples of matrices M_i. Due to the strong fuzzy partition there are always two matrices M_i and M_j with complementary elements, i.e., $\mu(w_{ij})$ and $1-\mu(w_{ij})$. Therefore the sum of the corresponding L_1 norms $\| M_i \| + \| M_j \|$ normalized by the number of the nonzero elements (i.e., $N(N-1)$) equals unity. Since there are 2^{N-1} couples of L_1 norm sums $\| M_i \| + \| M_j \|$ it holds $\frac{1}{2^{N-1}} \sum_{i=1}^{2^N} \| M_i \| = 1$. This normalization procedure can be used to derive the membership values of the weight matrices $\bar{W}_i$ (Q.E.D.).

Lemma 3 enables to rewrite the decomposition of matrix $\boldsymbol{W}$ into the weight matrices $\bar{W}_i$ as:

Figure 7.

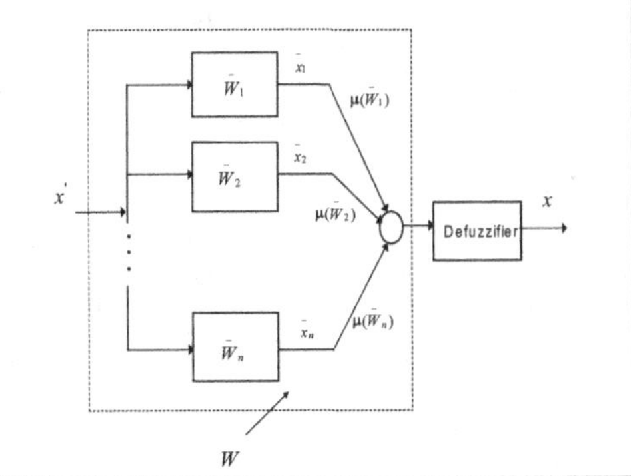

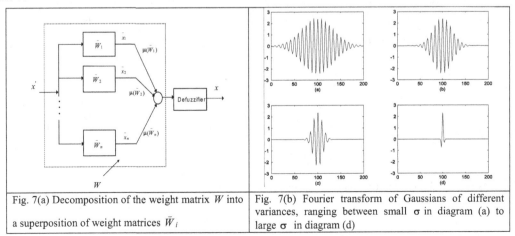

Fig. 7(a) Decomposition of the weight matrix W into a superposition of weight matrices $\bar{W}_i$

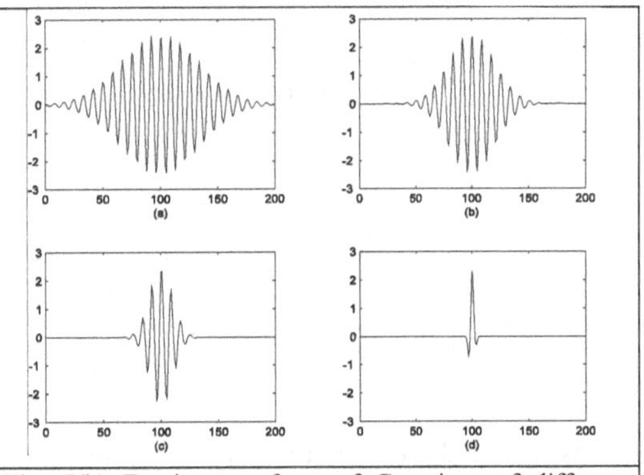

Fig. 7(b) Fourier transform of Gaussians of different variances, ranging between small σ in diagram (a) to large σ in diagram (d)

$$W = \frac{\mu_{12}+\mu_{13}+\mu_{23}}{3}\begin{bmatrix} 0 & a_{12}^{A_i} & a_{13}^{A_i} \\ a_{12}^{A_i} & 0 & a_{23}^{A_i} \\ a_{13}^{A_i} & a_{23}^{A_i} & 0 \end{bmatrix} + \frac{\mu_{12}+\mu_{13}-\mu_{23}+1}{3}\begin{bmatrix} 0 & a_{12}^{A_i} & a_{13}^{A_i} \\ a_{12}^{A_i} & 0 & a_{23}^{A_{i+1}} \\ a_{13}^{A_i} & a_{23}^{A_{i+1}} & 0 \end{bmatrix} +$$

$$\frac{\mu_{12}-\mu_{13}+\mu_{23}+1}{3}\begin{bmatrix} 0 & a_{12}^{A_i} & a_{13}^{A_{i+1}} \\ a_{12}^{A_i} & 0 & a_{23}^{A_i} \\ a_{13}^{A_{i+1}} & a_{23}^{A_i} & 0 \end{bmatrix} + \frac{\mu_{12}-\mu_{13}-\mu_{23}+2}{3}\begin{bmatrix} 0 & a_{12}^{A_i} & a_{13}^{A_{i+1}} \\ a_{12}^{A_i} & 0 & a_{23}^{A_{i+1}} \\ a_{13}^{A_{i+1}} & a_{23}^{A_{i+1}} & 0 \end{bmatrix} +$$

$$\frac{-\mu_{12}+\mu_{13}+\mu_{23}+1}{3}\begin{bmatrix} 0 & a_{12}^{A_{i+1}} & a_{13}^{A_i} \\ a_{12}^{A_{i+1}} & 0 & a_{23}^{A_i} \\ a_{13}^{A_i} & a_{23}^{A_i} & 0 \end{bmatrix} + \frac{-\mu_{12}+\mu_{13}-\mu_{23}+2}{3}\begin{bmatrix} 0 & a_{12}^{A_{i+1}} & a_{13}^{A_i} \\ a_{12}^{A_{i+1}} & 0 & a_{23}^{A_{i+1}} \\ a_{13}^{A_i} & a_{23}^{A_{i+1}} & 0 \end{bmatrix} +$$

$$\frac{-\mu_{12}-\mu_{13}+\mu_{23}+2}{3}\begin{bmatrix} 0 & a_{12}^{A_{i+1}} & a_{13}^{A_{i+1}} \\ a_{12}^{A_{i+1}} & 0 & a_{23}^{A_i} \\ a_{13}^{A_{i+1}} & a_{23}^{A_i} & 0 \end{bmatrix} + \frac{-\mu_{12}-\mu_{13}-\mu_{23}+3}{3}\begin{bmatrix} 0 & a_{12}^{A_{i+1}} & a_{13}^{A_{i+1}} \\ a_{12}^{A_{i+1}} & 0 & a_{23}^{A_{i+1}} \\ a_{13}^{A_{i+1}} & a_{23}^{A_{i+1}} & 0 \end{bmatrix}$$

The decomposition of the matrix $\boldsymbol{W}$ into a group of matrices $\bar{W}_i$ reveals the existence of non-observable attractors. According to Lemmas 1 and 2 these attractors coincide with the eigenvectors v_i of the matrices $\bar{W}_i$. Thus the patterns that can be recalled from an associative memory, are more than the ones associated with the initial matrix $\boldsymbol{W}$. For an associative memory of N neurons, the possible patterns become $N \times 2^N$.

It has been also shown that the transition between the vector spaces which are associated with matrices $\bar{W}_i$ is described by unitary rotations (Rigatos & Tzafestas, 2006a). Therefore the transition from the reference system $\bar{W}_i$ to the reference system $\bar{W}_j$ is described by unitary operators, which is a result compatible with quantum mechanics postulates (Cohen-Tanoudji et al. 1998). This is stated in the following theorem (Rigatos & Tzafestas, 2006a):

Theorem1: The rotations between the spaces which are spanned by the eigenvectors of the weight matrices $\bar{W}_i$ are unitary operators.

Proof: Let x_i, y_i, z_i and x_j, y_j, z_j be the unit vectors of the bases which span the spaces associated with the matrices $\bar{W}_i$ and $\bar{W}_j$ respectively. Then a memory vector p can be described in both spaces as : $p = (p_{x_i}, p_{y_i}, p_{z_i})^T$ and $p = (p_{x_j}, p_{y_j}, p_{z_j})^T$. Transition from the reference system $\bar{W}_i \rightarrow \{x_i, y_i, z_i\}$ to the reference system $\bar{W}_j \rightarrow \{x_j, y_j, z_j\}$ is expressed by the rotation matrix R, i.e. $p_{\bar{W}_i} = R \cdot p_{\bar{W}_j}$. The inverse transition is expressed by the rotation matrix Q, i.e. $p_{\bar{W}_j} = Q \cdot p_{\bar{W}_i}$. Furthermore it is true that

$$\begin{pmatrix} p_{x_i} \\ p_{y_i} \\ p_{z_i} \end{pmatrix} = \begin{pmatrix} x_i x_j & x_i y_j & x_i z_j \\ y_i x_j & y_i y_j & y_i z_j \\ z_i x_j & z_i y_j & z_i z_j \end{pmatrix} \begin{pmatrix} p_{x_j} \\ p_{y_j} \\ p_{z_j} \end{pmatrix} \qquad (36)$$

Thus, using Eq. (36) the rotation matrices R and Q are given by

$$R =, Q = \begin{pmatrix} x_j x_i & x_j y_i & x_j z_i \\ y_j x_i & y_j y_i & y_j z_i \\ z_j x_i & z_j y_i & z_j z_i \end{pmatrix} \tag{37}$$

Since "dot products" are commutative, from Eq. (37) one obtains $Q = R^{-1} = R^T$. Therefore the transition from the reference system $\bar{W}_i$ to the reference system $\bar{W}_j$ is described by unitary operators, i.e., $QR = R^T R = R^{-1} R = I$ (Q.E.D).

SPECTRAL ANALYSIS OF ASSOCIATIVE MEMORIES THAT FOLLOW THE Q.H.O. MODEL

Spectral analysis of associative memories with weights described by interacting Brownian particles (quantum associative memories) will be carried out following previous studies on wavelets power spectra (Addison, 2002). To find a signal's spectrum, Fourier transform has to be carried out. For instance, the Fourier transform of Gaussian functions of different variances is given in Fig. 7(b).

Spectral analysis in quantum associative memories shows that: (i) the Gaussian basis functions in which the weight w_{ij} is decomposed express the distribution of energy with respect to the weight's values (ii) the weights w_{ij} satisfy the principle of uncertainty.

1. Spectral Analysis of Wavelets

The Morlet wavelet is the most commonly used complex wavelet and is given by

$$\psi(x) = \pi^{-\frac{1}{4}}(e^{i2\pi f_0 x} - e^{-\frac{(2\pi f_0)^2}{2}})e^{-\frac{x^2}{2\sigma^2}} \tag{38}$$

This wavelet is simply a complex wave within a Gaussian envelope. The complex sinusoidal waveform is contained in the term $e^{i2\pi f_0 x} = \cos(2\pi f_0 x) + i\sin(2\pi f_0 x)$. The real and the imaginary part of the Morlet wavelet for various central frequencies are depicted in Fig. 7(a). It can be seen that the real and the imaginary part of the wavelet differ in phase by a quarter period. The $\pi^{-\frac{1}{4}}$ term is a normalization factor which ensures that the wavelet has unit energy.

2. Spectral Decomposition and Heisenberg Boxes

The Fourier transform of the Morlet wavelet is given by

$$\hat{\psi}(f) = \pi^{-\frac{1}{4}}\sqrt{2}e^{\frac{1}{2}(2\pi f - 2\pi f_0)^2} \tag{39}$$

which has the form of a Gaussian function displaced along the frequency axis by f_0. The energy spectrum (the squared magnitude of the Fourier transform) is given by (Addison, 2002)

$$|\hat{\psi}(f)|^2 = 2\pi^{\frac{1}{2}}e^{-(2\pi f - 2\pi f_0)^2} \tag{40}$$

which is a Gaussian centered at f_0. The integral of Eq. (40) gives the energy of the Morlet wavelet. The energy spectrum of the Morlet wavelet depicted in Fig. 8(a)- diagram (c), for different values of the variance σ^2 is given in Fig. 8(b).

The central frequency f_0 is the frequency of the complex sinusoid and its value determines the number of significant sinusoidal waveforms contained within the envelope. The dilated and translated Morlet wavelet

Figure 8.

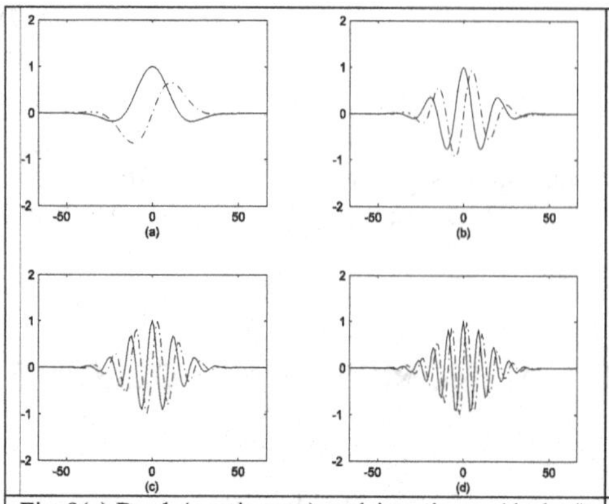

Fig 8(a) Real (continuous) and imaginary (dashed) part of Morlet wavelets for various frequencies: (a), $f_0 = 0.1$ Hz (b), $f_0 = 0.3$ Hz (c) $f_0 = 0.5$ Hz, (d) $f_0 = 0.7$ Hz

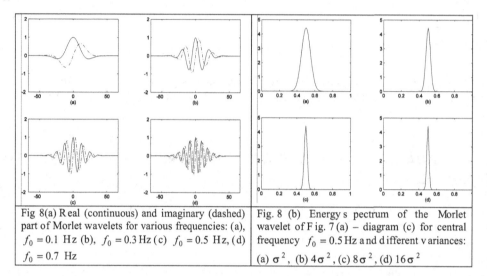

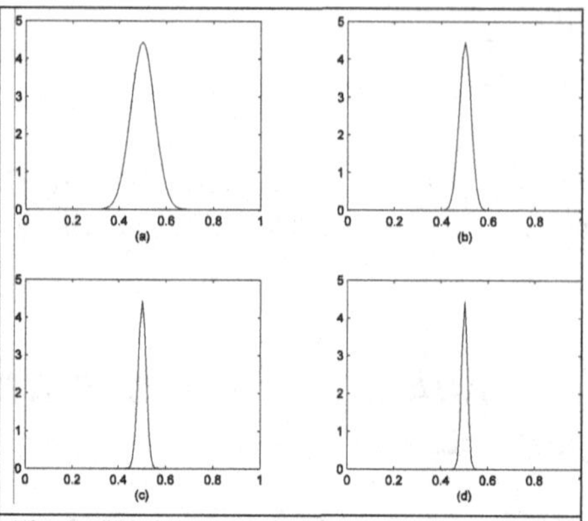

Fig. 8 (b) Energy spectrum of the Morlet wavelet of Fig. 7 (a) – diagram (c) for central frequency $f_0 = 0.5$ Hz and different variances: (a) σ^2, (b) $4\sigma^2$, (c) $8\sigma^2$, (d) $16\sigma^2$

$\psi(\frac{x-b}{a})$ is given by

$$\psi(\frac{x-b}{a}) = \pi^{-\frac{1}{4}} e^{i2\pi f_0 (\frac{x-b}{a})} e^{-\frac{1}{2}(\frac{x-b}{a})^2} \tag{41}$$

A tool that enables to visualize the space-frequency characteristics of signals is the so-called Heisenberg box.

The Heisenberg boxes in the x-frequency plane for a wavelet at different scales, are shown in Fig. 9(a). To evaluate frequency composition a sample of a long region of the signal is required. If instead, a small region of the signal is measured with accuracy, then it becomes very difficult to determine the frequency content of the signal in that region. That is, the more accurate the temporal measurement (smaller σ_x) is, the less accurate the spectral measurement (larger σ_f) becomes, and vice-versa (Addison, 1998).

The central frequency f_0 sets the location of the Heisenberg box in the x-frequency plane. If the x-length of the wavelets remains the same, then no matter the change of the central frequency f_0 the associated Heisenberg boxes will have the same dimensions. This is depicted in Fig. 9(b).

Finally, in Fig. 10(a) are shown the Heisenberg boxes in the x-frequency plane for a number of wavelets with three different spectral frequencies (low, medium and high). The confining Gaussian windows have the same dimensions along the x axis. Therefore, altering the central frequency of the wavelet shifts the Heisenberg box up and down the x-frequency plane without altering its dimensions.

3. Energy Spectrum of Stochastic Weights that Follow the Q.H.O. Model

It is assumed that the stochastic weight w_{ij} is described by the probability (possibility) distributions shown in Fig. 1(b). Then the following theorem holds (Rigatos, 2006).

Theorem 2: The Gaussian basis functions of the weights w_{ij} of a quantum associative memory express the distribution of energy with respect to the value of w_{ij}. The smaller the spread σ of the basis functions is, the larger becomes the spectral (energy) content that can be captured therein.

Proof: The Fourier transform of $g(x) = e^{-\alpha x^2}$ is $G(f) = \sqrt{\frac{\pi}{\alpha}} e^{-\frac{f^2}{4\alpha}}$. Furthermore the mean value of the stochastic

Figure 9.

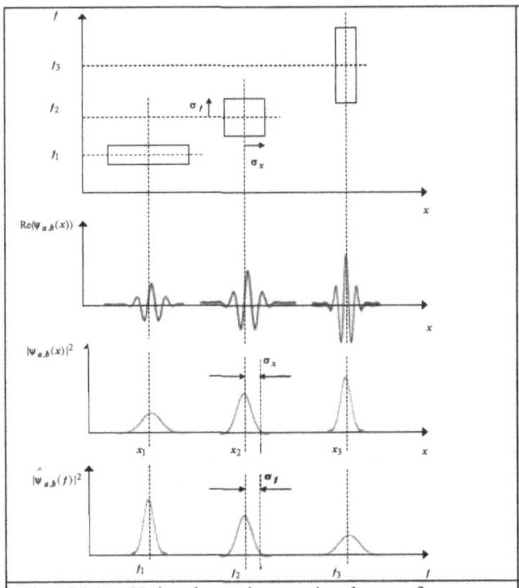

Fig. 9(a) Heisenberg boxes in the x-frequency plane for a wavelet at various scales f_1, f_2, f_3 and of different length σ_x along the x-axis. σ_x is the standard deviation of the squared wavelet function $\psi(x)^2$; σ_f is the standard deviation of the spectrum around the mean spectral components f_1, f_2 and f_3

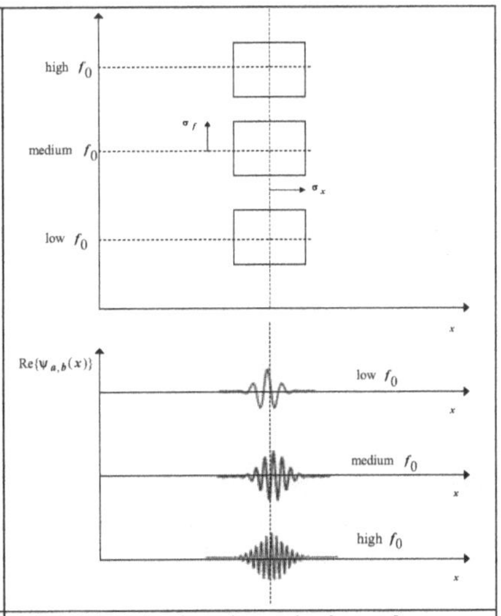

Fig. 9(b) Heisenberg boxes in the x-frequency plane for wavelet at various scales f_1, f_2, f_3 and of the same length σ_x along the x-axis. Changes of the central frequency f_0 do not affect the size of the Heisenberg boxes.

Figure 10.

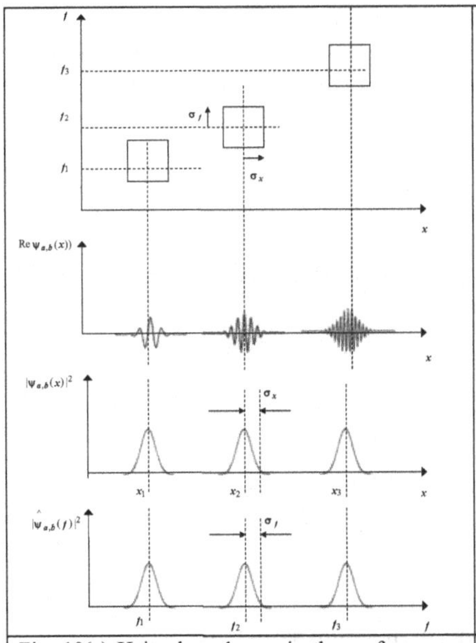

Fig. 10(a) Heisenberg boxes in the x-frequency plane for a number of superimposing wavelets of the same length σ_x along the x-axis and at three different spectral frequencies set to low, medium and high value

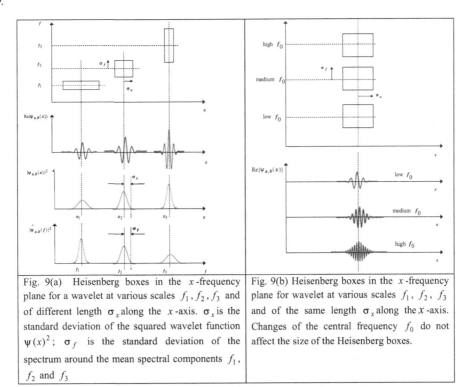

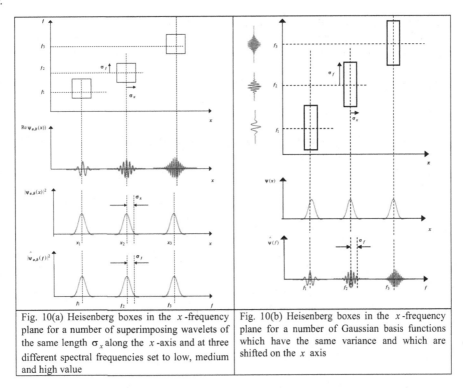

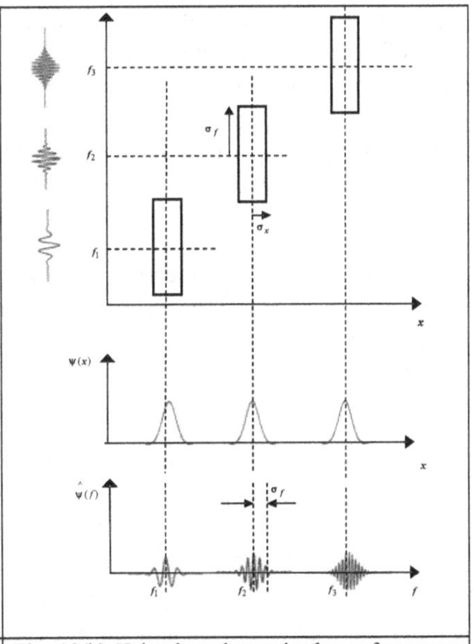

Fig. 10(b) Heisenberg boxes in the x-frequency plane for a number of Gaussian basis functions which have the same variance and which are shifted on the x axis

weight $< w_{ij} >$ is described by shifted overlapping Gaussians, i.e., $< w_{ij} >= \sum_{k=1}^{\infty} e^{-\frac{1}{2}(\frac{w_{ij}-k\cdot c)^2}{2\sigma^2}} a_k$. Consequently, the associated Fourier transform will be:

$$G(\sum_{k=1}^{\infty} e^{-\frac{1}{2}\frac{(w_{ij}-k\cdot c)^2}{2\sigma^2}} a_k) = \sum_{k=1}^{\infty} k\cdot c\cdot e^{ifkc}\sqrt{2\pi}\, e^{-\frac{1}{2}\sigma^2 f^2} \tag{42}$$

where $a_k = k\cdot c$ with c being the distance between the centers of two adjacent fuzzy basis functions. Keeping the real part of $G(f)$ is kept one obtains

$$G(\sum_{k=1}^{\infty} e^{-\frac{1}{2}\frac{(w_{ij}-k\cdot c)^2}{2\sigma^2}} a_k) = \sum_{k=1}^{\infty} k\cdot c\cdot \cos(fkc)\sqrt{2\pi}\, e^{-\frac{1}{2}\sigma^2 f^2} \tag{43}$$

From Eq. (43) it can be seen that if the weight w_{ij} is decomposed in the x domain into shifted Gaussians of the same variance σ^2 then, in the frequency domain, w_{ij} is analyzed in chirps, like the ones given in Fig. 10(b). The energy of the stochastic weights can now be found using Rayleigh's theorem. This states that the energy of a signal $f(x)$, $x\in[-\infty,+\infty]$ is given by $\int_{-\infty}^{+\infty} f^2(x)dx$. Equivalently, using the Fourier transform $F(s)$ of $f(x)$, the energy is given by $\int_{-\infty}^{+\infty} F^2(s)ds$. The energy distribution of the quantum particle is proportional to the probability $|\psi(w_{ij})|^2$ of finding the particle between w_{ij} and $w_{ij}+\Delta w_{ij}$. Therefore, the energy of the particle will be given by the integral of the squared Fourier transform $|\hat{\psi}(f)|^2$. Thus, basis functions of small spread σ is the x domain, become ample functions in the frequency domain (see for instance Fig. 7(b)) which defines the associated energy content (Q.E.D).

The Fourier transform of the weights of the quantum associative memories is depicted in the diagram given in the bottom of Fig. 10(b), and the associated spectrum consists again of Gaussian functions.

4. Weights that Follow the Q.H.O. Model and the Principle of Uncertainty

The significance of Eq. (43) is that the product between the information in the space domain $g(w_{ij})$ and the information in the frequency domain $G(s)$ cannot be smaller than a constant. In the case of a Gaussian function $g(w_{ij}) = e^{\frac{-w_{ij}^2}{2\sigma^2}}$ with Fourier transform $G(s) = e^{-\frac{1}{2}s^2\sigma^2}$ it can be observed that: (i) if σ is small then $g(w_{ij})$ has a pick at $w_{ij}=0$ while $G(s)$ tends to become flat, (ii) if σ is large then $g(w_{ij})$ is flat at $w_{ij}=0$ while $G(s)$ makes a peak at $s=0$. These can be observed in Fig. 9(a).

This becomes more clear if the dispersion of function $g(w_{ij}) = e^{-\frac{w_{ij}^2}{2\sigma^2}}$ round $w_{ij}=0$is used (Pinsky, 1991). The dispersion of $g(w_{ij})$and of its Fourier transform $G(s)$ becomes

$$D(g) = \frac{\int_{-\infty}^{+\infty} w_{ij}^2 e^{-\frac{1}{2}\frac{w_{ij}^2}{\sigma^2}} dw_{ij}}{\int_{-\infty}^{+\infty} e^{-\frac{1}{2}\frac{w_{ij}^2}{\sigma^2}} dw_{ij}} = \frac{1}{2}\sigma^2,\; D(G) = \frac{\int_{-\infty}^{+\infty} s^2 e^{-\frac{1}{2}s^2\sigma^2} ds}{\int_{-\infty}^{+\infty} e^{-\frac{1}{2}s^2\sigma^2} ds} = \frac{1}{2\sigma^2} \tag{44}$$

which results into the uncertainty principle for the weights of quantum associative memories

$$D(g)D(G) = 1/4 \tag{45}$$

Eq. (45) means that the accuracy in the calculation of the weight w_{ij} is associated with the accuracy in the calculation of its spectral content. When the spread of the Gaussians of the stochastic weights is large (small) then their spectral content is poor (rich). Eq. (45) is an analogous of the quantum mechanics uncertainty principle, i.e., $\Delta x \Delta p \geq \hbar$, where Δx is the uncertainty in the measurement of particle's position, Δp is the uncertainty in the measurement of the particle's momentum and $\hbar$ is Planck's constant.

It should be noted that Eq. (45) expresses a general property of the Fourier transform and that similar relations can be found in classical physics. For instance in electromagnetism it is known that it is not possible to measure with arbitrary precision, at the same time instant, the variation of a wave function both in the time and frequency domain. What is really quantum in the previous analysis, is the association of a wave function with a particle (stochastic weight) and the assumption that the wave length and the momentum of the particle satisfy a relation equivalent to $p = \hbar k$ with $|k| = \frac{2\pi}{\lambda}$.

SIMULATION TESTS

1. Convergence Of The Stochastic Weights To An Equilibrium

The update of the stochastic weights is given by the gradient algorithm, of Eq. (20). The objective is to make the stochastic weights (particles) w_{ij} converge simultaneously to the desirable value w_{ij}^*, or equivalently make the errors of the weight values $e_{ij} = w_{ij} - w_{ij}^*$ converge simultaneously to the attractor $[e^* \quad \dot{e}^*] = [0 \quad 0]$.

In the conducted simulation experiments the multi-particle system consisted of N particles (weights) which were randomly initialized in the 2-D field $[x, y] = [e, \dot{e}]$. Two cases were distinguished: (i) update without constraints (Fig.10) and (ii) update under constraints (Fig. 12), In the latter case there were areas in the 2-D plane which could not be accesses by the trajectory of the particles towards the equilibrium.

As expected, the relative values of the parameters a and b that appear in the term $g(x^i - x^j)$ of Eq. (21), affect the trajectories of the individual particles. For $a > b$ the cohesion of the particles was maintained and abrupt displacements of the particles were avoided.

For weights update without constraints the Lyapunov function of each stochastic weight (individual particle), is shown in Fig. 13(a). The aggregate Lyapunov function is in Fig. 13(b).

Finally, in case of weights update under constraints the Lyapunov function of the individual particles, is depicted in Fig. 14(a). The aggregate Lyapunov function is shown in Fig. 14(b).

Figure 11.

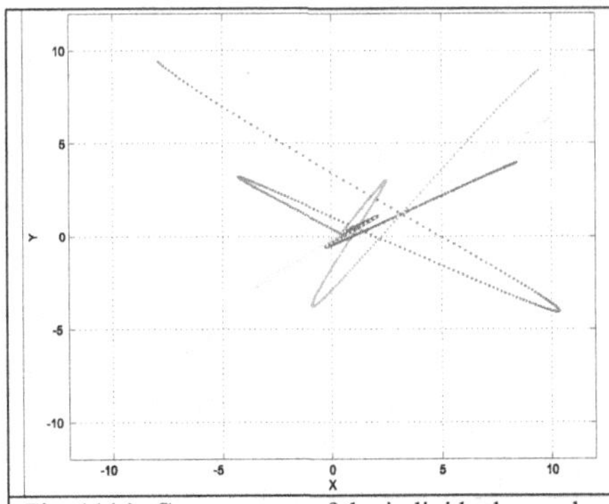

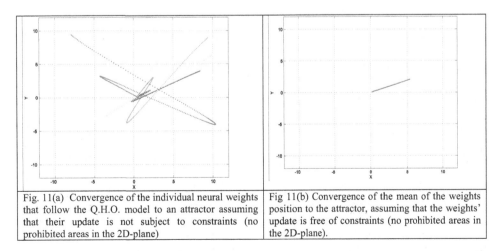

Fig. 11(a) Convergence of the individual neural weights that follow the Q.H.O. model to an attractor assuming that their update is not subject to constraints (no prohibited areas in the 2D-plane)

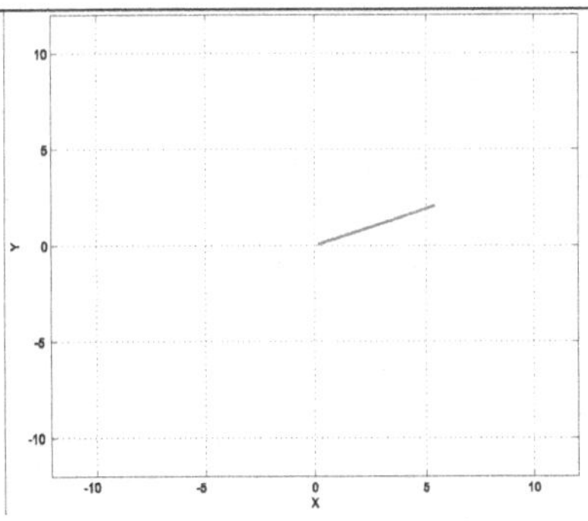

Fig 11(b) Convergence of the mean of the weights position to the attractor, assuming that the weights' update is free of constraints (no prohibited areas in the 2D-plane).

Figure 12.

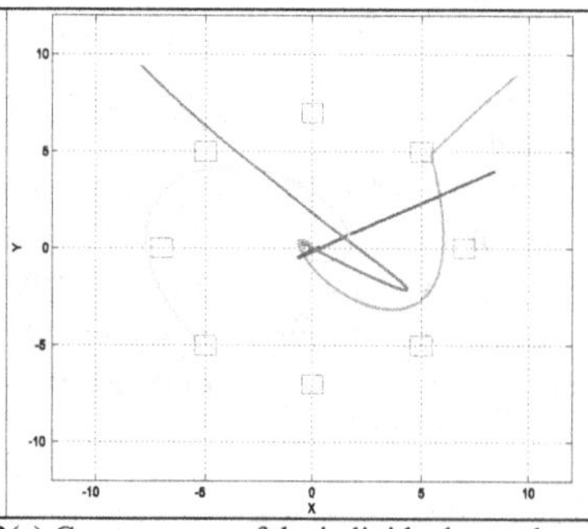

Fig. 12(a) Convergence of the individual neural weights that follow the Q.H.O. model to an attractor assuming constraints

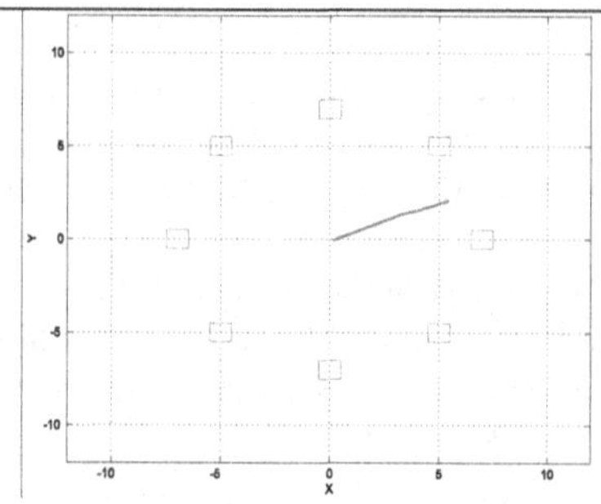

Fig. 12(b) Convergence of the mean of the weights position to the attractor, assuming constraints

Figure 13.

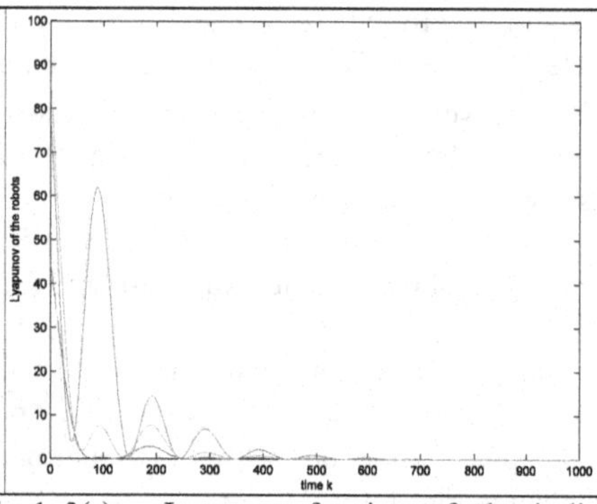

Fig. 1 3(a) Lyapunov function of the individual stochastic weights (Brownian particles) in a 2D-attractors plane without constraints.

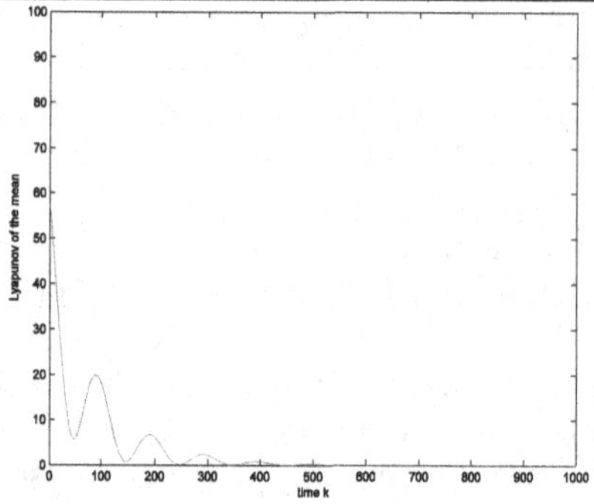

Fig. 13(b)) Lyapunov function of the mean of the stochastic weights (multi-particle system) in a 2D-attractors plane without constraints

Figure 14.

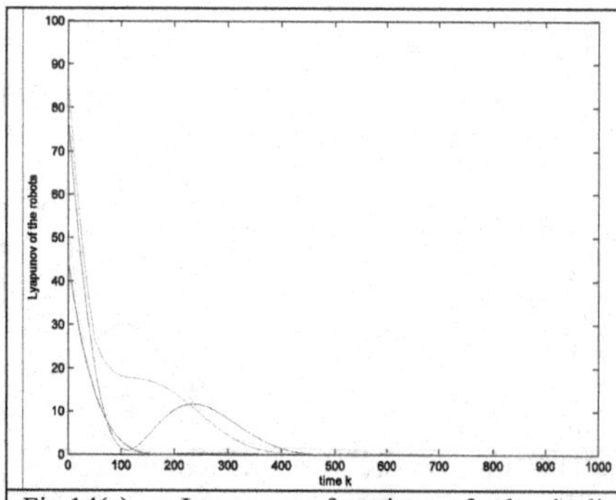

Fig.14(a) Lyapunov function of the individual stochastic weights (Brownian particles) in a 2D-attractors plane with constraints (there are prohibited regions exist).

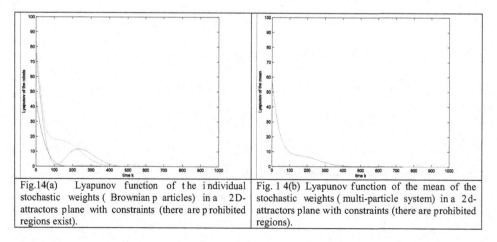

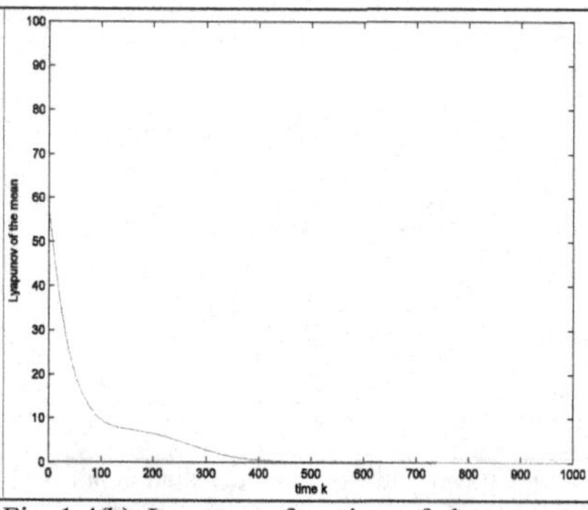

Fig. 1 4(b) Lyapunov function of the mean of the stochastic weights (multi-particle system) in a 2d-attractors plane with constraints (there are prohibited regions).

It should be noted that the difference between the neural structures that follow the Q.H.O model and neural structures that follow Schrödinger's equation with zero or constant potential, is that convergence to an attractor is controlled by the drift force imposed by the harmonic potential . A particle can be steered to an attractor, through the drift force, which in turn is tuned by the parameters α and b of Eq. (21), or through an external potential.

2. Attractors in Associative Memories That Follow The Q.H.O. Model

The theoretical results about the increased number of attractors in associative memories that follow the Q.H.O. model will be verified through a numerical example.

a). Superposition of weight matrices:

Assume that the fundamental memory patterns are the following binary vectors $s_1 = [1,1,1]$, $s_2 = [1,1,-1]$, $s_3 = [1,-1,1]$ which are linearly independent but not orthogonal. Orthogonality should be expected in high dimensional vector spaces, if the elements of the memory vectors are chosen randomly. In this example, to obtain orthogonality of the memory vectors, Gramm-Schmidt orthogonalization is used. This gives the orthogonal vectors $u_1 = [1,1,1]$, $u_2 = [2/3, 2/3, -4/3]$, $u_3 = [1,-1,0]$. The weight W which derived from the above memory patterns is $W = (1/3)[u_1^T u_1 + u_2^T u_2 + u_3^T u_3]$, i.e.

$$W = \begin{bmatrix} 0.8141 & 0.1481 & 0.0369 \\ 0.1481 & 0.8141 & 0.0369 \\ 0.0369 & 0.0369 & 0.9247 \end{bmatrix} \qquad (46)$$

It can be easily shown that $Wu_1 = u_1$, $Wu_2 = u_2$, $Wu_3 = u_3$ i.e. u_1, u_2, u_3 are stable states (attractors) of the network. The eigenvalues of matrix W are $\lambda_1 = 0.667$, $\lambda_2 = 0.888$ and $\lambda_3 = 1.0$. The associated eigenvectors of W are $v_1 = [0.7071, -0.7071, 0]^T$, $v_2 = [-0.4066, -0.4066, 0.8181]^T$ and $v_3 = [0.5785, 0.5785, 0.5750]^T$. It can be observed that v_1 is collinear to u_3, v_2 is collinear to u_2 and v_3 is collinear to u_1.

Next, the elements of the weight matrix W are considered to be stochastic variables, with p.d.f. (possibility distribution) as the one depicted in Fig. 1(b) The universe of discourse of these fuzzy variables is shown in Fig. 3(b). Thus matrix W, given by Eq. (44), can be decomposed into a superposition of weight matrices $\bar{W}_i$. Assume that only the non-diagonal elements of W are considered and that the possibility distribution of the stochastic variables $\bar{w}_{ij}$ is depicted in Fig. 1(b). Then, the weight matrix W is decomposed into a superposition of weight matrices $\bar{W}_i$, $i = 1,...8$:

$$W = \{\begin{bmatrix} * & 0.405 & 0.155 \\ 0.405 & * & 0.155 \\ 0.155 & 0.155 & * \end{bmatrix}, \begin{bmatrix} 0 & 0.14 & 0.02 \\ 0.14 & 0 & 0.02 \\ 0.02 & 0.02 & 0 \end{bmatrix}\} + \{\begin{bmatrix} * & 0.405 & 0.155 \\ 0.405 & * & 0.845 \\ 0.155 & 0.845 & * \end{bmatrix}, \begin{bmatrix} 0 & 0.14 & 0.02 \\ 0.14 & 0 & 0.04 \\ 0.02 & 0.04 & 0 \end{bmatrix}\} +$$

$$\{\begin{bmatrix} * & 0.405 & 0.845 \\ 0.405 & * & 0.155 \\ 0.845 & 0.155 & * \end{bmatrix}, \begin{bmatrix} 0 & 0.14 & 0.04 \\ 0.14 & 0 & 0.02 \\ 0.04 & 0.02 & 0 \end{bmatrix}\} + \{\begin{bmatrix} * & 0.405 & 0.845 \\ 0.405 & * & 0.845 \\ 0.845 & 0.845 & * \end{bmatrix}, \begin{bmatrix} 0 & 0.14 & 0.04 \\ 0.14 & 0 & 0.04 \\ 0.04 & 0.04 & 0 \end{bmatrix}\} +$$

$$\{\begin{bmatrix} * & 0.595 & 0.155 \\ 0.595 & * & 0.155 \\ 0.155 & 0.155 & * \end{bmatrix}, \begin{bmatrix} 0 & 0.16 & 0.02 \\ 0.16 & 0 & 0.02 \\ 0.02 & 0.02 & 0 \end{bmatrix}\} + \{\begin{bmatrix} * & 0.595 & 0.155 \\ 0.595 & * & 0.845 \\ 0.155 & 0.845 & * \end{bmatrix}, \begin{bmatrix} 0 & 0.16 & 0.02 \\ 0.16 & 0 & 0.04 \\ 0.02 & 0.04 & 0 \end{bmatrix}\} +$$

$$\{\begin{bmatrix} * & 0.595 & 0.845 \\ 0.595 & * & 0.155 \\ 0.845 & 0.155 & * \end{bmatrix}, \begin{bmatrix} 0 & 0.16 & 0.04 \\ 0.16 & 0 & 0.02 \\ 0.04 & 0.02 & 0 \end{bmatrix}\} + \{\begin{bmatrix} * & 0.595 & 0.845 \\ 0.595 & * & 0.845 \\ 0.845 & 0.845 & * \end{bmatrix}, \begin{bmatrix} 0 & 0.16 & 0.04 \\ 0.16 & 0 & 0.04 \\ 0.04 & 0.04 & 0 \end{bmatrix}\}$$

The membership μ_i of each matrix $\bar{W}_i$ is taken to be the normalized $\| L_1 \|$ of the matrix with elements the membership values of the weights w_{ij}, i.e., $\frac{1}{N\cdot(N-1)\cdot 2^{N-1}}\sum_{j=1}^{N}\mu(\bar{w}_{ij})$. This gives $W = \mu_1\bar{W}_1+\mu_2\bar{W}_2+\ldots+\mu_8\bar{W}_8$, where the membership μ_i are: $\mu_1 = 0.0596$, $\mu_2 = 0.1171$, $\mu_3 = 0.1171$, $\mu_4 = 0.1746$, $\mu_5 = 0.0754$, $\mu_6 = 0.1329$, $\mu_7 = 0.1329$ and $\mu_8 = 0.1904$. By calculating the eigenvectors of matrices $\bar{W}_i$, the associated memory patterns can be found. These are non-observable attractors different from the attractors u_1, u_2 and u_3 of the initial weight matrix $\boldsymbol{W}$. Thus, the number of memory patterns is increased by a factor $2^N = 8$.
Indeed:

The eigenstructure analysis of matrix $\bar{W}_i$ gives: $\lambda_1 = -0.14$, $\lambda_2 = 0.1455$, $\lambda_3 = -0.0055$, with associated eigenvectors $v_1^{\bar{W}_1} = [0.7071\ \ -0.7071\ \ 0]^T$, $v_2^{\bar{W}_1} = [0.6941\ \ 0.6942\ \ 0.1908]^T$ and $v_3^{\bar{W}_1} = [0.1349\ \ 0.1349\ \ -0.9816]^T$.

The eigenstructure analysis of matrix $\bar{W}_2$ gives: $\lambda_1 = -0.1415$, $\lambda_2 = -0.0104$, $\lambda_3 = 0.1519$, with associated eigenvectors $v_1^{\bar{W}_2} = [0.6921\ \ -0.7143\ \ 0.1041]^T$, $v_2^{\bar{W}_2} = [-0.2648\ \ -0.1176\ \ 0.9572]^T$ and $v_3^{\bar{W}_2} = [0.6715\ \ 0.6900\ \ 0.2701]^T$.

The eigenstructure analysis of matrix $\bar{W}_3$ gives: $\lambda_1 = -0.1415$, $\lambda_2 = -0.0104$, $\lambda_3 = 0.1519$, with associated eigenvectors are $v_1^{\bar{W}_3} = [0.7143\ \ -0.6921\ \ -0.1041]^T$, $v_2^{\bar{W}_3} = [-0.1170\ \ -0.2648\ \ 0.9572]^T$, and $v_3^{\bar{W}_3} = [0.6715\ \ 0.6900\ \ 0.2701]^T$.

The eigenstructure analysis of matrix $\bar{W}_4$ gives: $\lambda 1 = -0.14$, $\lambda 2 = 0.16$, $\lambda_3 = -0.02$, with associated eigenvectors $v_1^{\bar{W}_4} = [0.7071\ \ -0.7071\ \ 0]^T$, $v_2^{\bar{W}_4} = [0.6667\ \ 0.6667\ \ 0.3333]^T$ and $v_3^{\bar{W}_4} = [0.2357\ \ 0.2357\ \ -0.9428]^T$.

The eigenstructure analysis of matrix $\bar{W}_5$ gives: $\lambda_1 = -0.16$, $\lambda_2 = 0.1649$, $\lambda_3 = -0.0049$, with associated eigenvectors $v_1^{\bar{W}_5} = [0.7071\ \ -0.7071\ \ 0]^T$, $v_2^{\bar{W}_5} = [0.6969\ \ 0.6969\ \ 0.1691]^T$ and $v_3^{\bar{W}_5} = [0.1196\ \ 0.1196\ \ 0.9856]^T$.

The eigenstructure analysis of matrix $\bar{W}_6$ gives: $\lambda_1 = -0.1613$, $\lambda_2 = -0.0093$, $\lambda_3 = 0.1706$, with associated eigenvectors $v_1^{\bar{W}_6} = [0.6957\ \ -0.7126\ \ 0.0905]^T$, $v_2^{\bar{W}_6} = [-0.2353\ \ -0.1071\ \ 0.9660]^T$ and $v_3^{\bar{W}_6} = [0.6787\ \ 0.6933\ \ 0.2421]^T$

The eigenstructure analysis of matrix $\bar{W}_7$ gives: $\lambda_1 = -0.1613$, $\lambda_2 = -0.0093$, $\lambda_3 = 0.1706$, with associated eigenvectors $v_1^{\bar{W}_7} = [-0.7126\ \ 0.6957\ \ 0.0905]^T$, $v_2^{\bar{W}_7} = [-0.1071\ \ -0.2353\ \ 0.9660]^T$ and $v_3^{\bar{W}_7} = [-0.6993\ \ -0.6787\ \ 0.2421]^T$.

The eigenstructure analysis of matrix $\bar{W}_8$ gives: $\lambda_1 = -0.1600$, $\lambda_2 = 0.1780$, $\lambda_3 = -0.0180$, with associated eigenvectors $v_1^{\bar{W}_8} = [0.7071\ \ -0.7071\ \ 0]^T$, $v_2^{\bar{W}_8} = [0.6739\ \ 0.6739\ \ 0.3029]^T$, and $v_3^{\bar{W}_8} = [0.2142\ \ 0.2142\ \ -0.9530]^T$.

b) Unitarity of the rotation operators:

Here it will be verified that the transition between matrices $\bar{W}_i$ and $\bar{W}_j$ in which the weight matrix W of the associative memory is decomposed, is described by unitary operators. Take for instance matrices $\bar{W}_1$ and $\bar{W}_2$ of the previous example. The matrix R which performs a rotation from the basis defined by the eigenvectors $v_1^{\bar{W}_1}$, $v_2^{\bar{W}_1}$, $v_3^{\bar{W}_1}$, to the basis defined by the vectors $v_1^{\bar{W}_2}$, $v_2^{\bar{W}_2}$, $v_3^{\bar{W}_2}$ is calculated as follows: $v_1^{\bar{W}_1} = [0.7071,\ -0.7071,\ 0]^T$, $v_2^{\bar{W}_1} = [0.6941,\ 0.6941,\ 0.1908]^T$ and $v_3^{\bar{W}_1} = [0.1349,\ 0.1349,\ -0.9816]^T$, while $v_1^{\bar{W}_2} = [0.6921,\ -0.7143,\ 0.1041]^T$ $v_2^{\bar{W}_2} = [-0.2648,\ -0.1176,\ 0.9972]^T$ and $v_3^{\bar{W}_2} = [0.6715,\ 0.6900,\ 0.2701]^T$.

The rotation matrix R is given by

$$R = \begin{bmatrix} v_1^{\bar{W}_1} v_1^{\bar{W}_2} & v_1^{\bar{W}_1} v_2^{\bar{W}_2} & v_1^{\bar{W}_1} v_3^{\bar{W}_2} \\ v_2^{\bar{W}_1} v_1^{\bar{W}_2} & v_2^{\bar{W}_1} v_2^{\bar{W}_2} & v_2^{\bar{W}_1} v_3^{\bar{W}_2} \\ v_3^{\bar{W}_1} v_1^{\bar{W}_2} & v_3^{\bar{W}_1} v_2^{\bar{W}_2} & v_3^{\bar{W}_1} v_3^{\bar{W}_2} \end{bmatrix} = \begin{bmatrix} 0.9945 & -0.1041 & -0.0131 \\ 0.0045 & -0.0752 & 0.9966 \\ -0.1052 & -1.0304 & -0.0815 \end{bmatrix}$$

and it holds that

$$RR^T = \begin{bmatrix} 1.000 & -0.0008 & 0.0037 \\ -0.0008 & 0.9989 & -0.0042 \\ 0.0037 & -0.0042 & 1.0794 \end{bmatrix} \Rightarrow RR^T = \begin{bmatrix} 1 & 0 & 0 \\ 0 & 1 & 0 \\ 0 & 0 & 1 \end{bmatrix}$$

Thus, matrix R represents a unitary rotation from the vector space $v_1^{\bar{W}_1}$, $v_2^{\bar{W}_1}$, $v_3^{\bar{W}_1}$ to the vector space $v_1^{\bar{W}_2}$, $v_2^{\bar{W}_2}$, $v_3^{\bar{W}_2}$. On the other hand matrix R^T represents a unitary rotation from the vector space $v_1^{\bar{W}_2}$, $v_2^{\bar{W}_2}$, $v_3^{\bar{W}_2}$ to the vector space $v_1^{\bar{W}_1}$, $v_2^{\bar{W}_1}$, $v_3^{\bar{W}_1}$.

CONCLUSION

The objective of this chapter was to study neural structures with weights which are stochastic variables and which follow the model of the quantum harmonic oscillator (Q.H.O.). The neural weights were taken to correspond to diffusing particles, which interact to each other as the theory of Wiener process (Brownian motion) predicts. The values of the weights are the positions of the particles and the probability density function $|\psi(x,t)|^2$ that describes their position is derived by Schrödinger's equation. Therefore the dynamics of the neural network is given by the solution of Schrödinger's equation under a parabolic (harmonic) potential. Assuming a probability density function that depends only on the ground state of the Q.H.O., i.e. $\rho_0(x) = |\psi_0(x)|^2$, the solution of Schrödinger's equation was approximated by a stationary diffusion.

Next, it was shown that in neural structures with weights that follow the Q.H.O. model, the weights update is described by Langevin's stochastic differential equation. It was proved that conventional gradient algorithms are a subcase of Langevin's equation. Moreover, it was demonstrated that the weights which follow the Q.H.O. model give to associative memories significant properties: (i) the learning of the stochastic weights is a Wiener process, (ii) the number of attractors increases exponentially comparing to conventional associative memories.

Spectral analysis of the weights of that follow the Q.H.O. model was also carried out, based on previous studies of wavelets' energy spectrum. It was shown that: (i) the Gaussian basis functions of the weights express the distribution of the energy with respect to the weights' value. The smaller the spread of the basis functions is, the larger becomes the spectral (energy) content that can be captured therein. (ii) The stochastic weights satisfy an equation which is analogous to the principle of uncertainty.

Furthermore, simulation tests were performed to demonstrate that (i) the weights which follow the Q.H.O. model converge to attractors, (ii) the storage capacity of the Q.H.O-based associative memories increases in an exponential way. Finally, it was pointed out that the basic difference of neural weights that follow the Q.H.O. model from neural weights which are based on Schrödinger's equation with zero or constant potential, is that convergence to one of the possible attractors is controlled by the drift force that is imposed by the harmonic potential.

FUTURE RESEARCH DIRECTIONS

Quantum information processing in neural structures is a promising research topic. Relevant areas are wavelets and wavelet networks, neural structures using the eigenstates of the quantum harmonic oscillator, harmonic analysis, while future research directions could be: (i) multi-scale information processing, (ii) control of multi-particle systems and perspectives for emerging fields, such as nanotechnology, biotechnology and quantum computing, (ii) theoretical issues, such as computation models, limits of multi-scale analysis and uncertainty principle, (iii) applications in image processing (iv) applications in communication systems, (v) application in biomedical systems.

To implement the proposed quantum neural structures, learning issues have to be examined. The learning in neural networks compatible with principles of quantum mechanics is a diffusion process. Thus learning is associated to the control of the diffusion stochastic differential equations. The modelling of the probability density functions of quantum diffusions can be carried out with the use of wavelet functions, Hermite functions of fuzzy basis functions. To succeed control of the quantum diffusions, open-loop control approaches can be examined. On the other hand closed-loop control methods for particles at micro and nano scale can be based on the theory of optimal control or robust control approaches. Feedback-based control methods require knowledge of the complete state vector that describes the particle's motion and in case that the state vector is not completely measurable this has to be reconstructed with the use of a filter or state estimator.

REFERENCES

Abramian, A. K., & Vakulenko, S. A. (2002). Dissipative and Hamiltonian systems with chaotic behaviour: an analytical approach. *Theoretical and Mathematical Physics, 130*(2), 244-254.

Addison, P. A. (2002). *The Illustrated Wavelet Transform Handbook*. Institute of Physics Publishing.

Aiyer, S., Niranjan, M., & Fallside, F. (1990). Theoretical investigation into the performance of the Hopfield model. *IEEE Transactions on Neural Networks, 15*(1), 204-215.

Astrom, K. J. (2006). Introduction to Stochastic Control Theory. *Dover.*

Banyopadhyay, S., Menon, L., Kouklin, N., Williams, P. F., & Ianno, N. J. (2002). Self-assembled networks with neural computing attributes. *Smart Materials and Structures, 11,* 761–766. Institute of Physics Publishing.

Basharov, A. M., Gorbachev, V. N., & Rodichkina, A. A. (2006). Decay and storage of multiparticle entangled states of atoms in collective thermostat. Physical Review, *A 74,* 042313.

Basseville, M., & Nikiforov, I. (1993). *Detection of abrupt changes: Theory and Applications*. Prentice-Hall.

Behrman, E. C., Nash, L. R., Steck, J. E., Chandrashekar, V. G., & Skinner, S. R. (2000). Simulations of quantum neural networks. *Information Sciences, 128*, 257–269.

Benvensite, A., Metivier, M., & Priouret, P. (1990). *Adaptive algorithms and stochastic approximations, 22.* Springer: Applications of Mathematics Series.

Chuong, N. M., Egorov, Y. V., Khrennikov, A., Meyer, Y., & Mumford, D. (2007). *Harmonic, Wavelet and p-adic analysis.* World Scientific.

Chung, K. L. (2002). *Green, Brown and Probability & Brownian Motion on the Line*. World Scientific.

Cohen-Tannoudji, C., Diu, B., & Lale F. (1998). *Mécanique Quantique I.* Hermann.

Comets, F., & Meyre, T. (2006). *Calcul Stochastique et applications.* Dunod, Paris.

De Garis, H., Sriram, R., & Zhang, Z. (2003). Quantum generation of neural networks. I*n Proc. Internat. Joint Conf. on Neural Networks, IJCNN '03, 4*, 2589–2593.

Debauchies, I. (1990). The wavelet transform, time-frequency localization and signal processing. *IEEE Transactions on Information Theory, 36*, 961-1005.

Del Moral, P. (2004). Feynman-Kac Formulae: Genealogic and Interacting Particle Systems with Applications. *Probability and its Applications*. Springer.

Deutsch, D. (1989). Quantum computational networks. *Proceedings of the Royal Society of London A, 425*, 73-90.

Dubois, D., Foulloy, L., Mauris, G., & Prade, H. (2004). Probability-possibility transformations, triangular fuzzy sets and probabilistic inequalities. *Reliable Computing., 10*(4), 273-297. Springer

Duflo,nM. (1996). Algorithmes stochastiques. *Mathematiques et Applications, 23.* Springer.

Ezhov, A. A., Nifanova,, A. V., & Ventura, D. (2000). Quantum associative memory with distributed queries. *Inform. Sci., 128*, 271–293.

Faris, W. G. (2006). *Diffusion, Quantum Theory, and Radically Elementary Mathematics.* Princeton University Press.

Feynman, R. (1986). Quantum mechanical computers. *Foundations of Physics, 16,* 507-531.

Fliess, M. (2007). Fluctuations Quantiques, C.R. Acad. Sci. Paris. *Physique Mathématique, Elsevier, 344*, 663-668.

Gazi,V., & Passino, K. (2004). Stability analysis of social foraging swarms. *IEEE Transactions on Systems, Man and Cybernetics – Part B: Cybernetics*, 539-557.

Gitterman, M. (2005). *The noisy oscillator: The first Hundred Years, From Einstein Until Now.* World Scientific.

Gorbachev, V. N., & Zhiliba, A. I. (1993). Master equations for the quantum optics problems. *Quantum. Opt. 5*, 193.

Gorbachev, V. N., & Zhiliba, A. I. (2000). Transfer formalism for quantum optics problem. *Phys.A: Math. Gen., 33*, 3771.

Gorbachev, V. N., Zhiliba, A. I., & Trubilko, A. I. (2001a). Teleportation of entangled states. *J. Opt. B 3*, S25.

Gorbachev, V. N., Zhiliba, A. I., & Trubilko, A. I. (2001b). Continuous variables teleportation of a two particle entangled state. *Opt. Commun., 187*, 379.

Gorbachev, V. N., Zhiliba, A. I., Trubilko, A. I., & Rodichkina A. A. (2002). Teleportation and dense coding via a multiparticle quantum channel of the GHZ-class. *QIC (Quantum Information and Computation), 2*, 367-378.

Gorbachev, V. N., Trubilko, A. I., Rodichkina, A. A., & Zhiliba, A. I. (2003). On preparation of the entangled W-states from atomic ensembles. *Physics Letters A, 310*(5-6), 339-343 .

Gorbachev, V. N., Kazakov, A. Y., & Trubilko, A. I. (2004). Macroscopic entangled states. *Journ. Opt. B, 6*, 517-524.

Gorbachev, V. N., Kazakov, A. Y., & Trubilko, A. I. (2007). Exponential superradiance and macroscopic entangled states. In M. Zukowsky et al. (Eds.), Quantum Communication and Security. IOS Press.

Grigoriev, D. Y., Karpinski, M., & Singer, M. F. (1990). Fast Parallel Algorithms for Sparse Multivariate Polymomial Interpolation over Finite Fields. *SIAM J. of Comp., 19*, 1059-1083.

Grigoriev, D. Y., Karpinski, M., & Singer, M. F. (1991a). Interpolation Problem for k-Sparse Sums of Eigenfunctions of Operators. *Advances in Applied Mathematics, 12*, 76 -81.

Grigoriev, D. Y., & Karpinski, M. (1991b). Algorithms for Sparse Rational Interpolation. *Proc. Int. Symp. Symb. Alg. Comput., Bonn*, (pp. 7-13).

Grigoriev, D. Y., Karpinski, M., & Singer, M. F. (1994). Computational Complexity of Sparse Rational Interpolation. *SIAM J. Comput., 23*(1), 1-11.

Grigoriev, D., Kazakov, A., & Vakulenko, S. (2007), Optical device accelerating dynamic programming. *Physics of Particles and Nuclei Letters, 4*, 141-142.

Gröchenig, K., Han, D., Heil, C., & Kutyniak, G. (2002). The Balian-Low theorem for symplectic lattices in higher dimensions. *Applied and Computational Harmonic Analysis, 13*, 169-176. *Academic Press*

Hagan, S., Hameroff, S. R., & Tuzyinski, J. A. (2002). Quantum Computation in Brain Microtubules: Decoherence and Biological Feasibility. Physical Review E, *American Physical Society, 65*, 1-11.

Haykin, S. (1994). *Neural Networks: A Comprehensive Foundation*. McMillan.

Hopfield, J. J. (1982). Neural networks as physical systems with emergent computational abilities. *Proc. Natl. Acad. Sci. USA., 79*, 2444–2558.

Iwasaki, I. Nakasima, H., & Shimizu, T. (1998). Interacting Brownian particles as a modelof neural network. *International Journal of Bifurcation and Chaos, 8*(4), 791-797. World Scientific.

Kak, S. (1999). Quantum computing and AI. *IEEE Intelligent Systems, 14*(4), 9–11.

Khovanskii, A. (1991). Fewnomials, Translations of Mathem. Monographs. *Amer. Math. Soc., 88*.

Kazakov, A. Y. (1998a). A micromaser on single atom with optical pumping. *Journ. Quantum and Semiclass. Optics, 10*, 753-763.

Kazakov, A. Y. (2001). Two-photon one atom micromaser with permanent optical pumping. *Journal of Optics B, 3*(3), 97-106.

Kazakov, A.Y. (2002). Jaynes-Cummings systems driven by classical fields. *Intern. Journ. Theoret. Phys., Group Theory and Nonl. Opt., 8*(1), 75-104.

Kazakov, A. Y. (2002). *Dense coding and safety of quantum communications*. E-print: LANL Arxiv: quant-ph/0205101.

Kazakov, A. Y. (2003). Modified Jeans- Cammings systems and a quantum version of knapsack problem. *Journ. Exp. Teor. Fiz. 124*, 3(11), 1-7.

Kazakov, A. Y. (2006). Geometric measure of three-partite pure states. *International Journal of Quantum Information, 4*(6), 907-916.

Kazakov, A. Y. (2007). *Elementary constructive approach to the higher-rank numerical ranges of unitary matrices*. E-print: LANL Arxiv: quant-ph/0707.170.

Klebaner, F. C. (2005). *Introduction to Stochastic Analysis and Calculus*. Imperial College Press.

Laroche, B., Martin, Ph., & Petit, N. (2007). Commande par platitude: Equations différentielles ordinaires et aux derivées partielles. *Ecole Nationale Supérieure des Techniques Avancées*, Paris.

Levine H., & Rappel, W. J. (2000). Self-organization in systems of self-propelled particles. *Physical Review E, 63*.

Ma, L., & Khorasani, K. (2005). Constructive Feedforward Neural Networks Using Hermite Polynomial Activation Functions. IEEE Transactions on Neural Networks, 16(4), 821-833.

Ma, L., & Khorasani, K. (2002). Application of Adaptive Constructive Neural Networks to Image Compression, *IEEE Transactions on Neural Networks, 13*(5), 1112-1125.

Mallat, S. (1998). *A wavelet tour of signal processing*. Academic Press.

Mahler, G., & Weberuss, V. A. (1998). *Quantum Networks: Dynamics of Open Nanostructures*. Springer.

Muller, G. (1998). *Quantum Mechanics: Symmetries*, 2nd Edition. Springer.

Nielsen, M., & Chuang, I. L. (2000). *Quantum Computation and Quantum Information.* Cambridge: Cambridge University Press.

Perus, M. (2001). Multi-level synergetic computation in brain. *Nonlinear Phenomena in Complex Systems*, (2), 157–193.

Perus, M. (2000). Neural networks as a basis for Quantum Associative Networks. *Neural Network World, 10*, 1001-1013.

Perus, M., Bischof, H., Caulfield, J., & Loo, C. K. (2004). Quantum implementable selective reconstruction of high resolution images. *Applied Optics, 43*, 6134-6138.

Petritis, D. (1996). Thermodynamic formalism of neural computing. In E. Goles & S. Martinez (Eds.), *Dynamics of complex interacting systems* (pp. 81-146). Kluwer Academic Publishers: Dodrecht.

Petritis, D. (2008). An approach to genome statistics inspired by stochastic or quantum models of computing: a survey. Accepted for publication in *Studies in computational intelligence.* Springer-Verlag.

Pinsky, M. A. (1991). *Partial Differential Equations and Boundary Value Problems with Applications.* McGraw-Hill.

Powell, A. M. (2005). Time-frequency mean and variance sequences of orthonormal bases. *J. Fourier Analysis and Applications*, (pp. 375-387).

Purusothaman,G., & Karayiannis, N. B. (1997). Quantum neural networks (QNNS)—inherently fuzzy feedforward neural networks. *IEEE Transactions on Neural Networks, 8*(3), 679–693.

Refregier, A. (2003). Shapelets - I. A method for image analysis. *Mon. Not. R. Astron. Soc., 338*, 35-47.

Resconi, G., & Van der Waal, A. J. (2002). Morphogenic neural networks encode abstract rules by data, Information Sciences, *Elsevier*, (pp. 249-273).

Rigatos, G. G., & Tzafestas, S. G. (2002). Parallelization of a fuzzy control algorithm using quantum computation. *IEEE Transactions on Fuzzy Systems, 10*(4), 451-460.

Rigatos, G. G. (2002). Fuzzy Stochastic Automata for Reactive Learning and Hybrid Control. *Lecture Notes in Artificial Intelligence, 2308*, 366-377. Springer.

Rigatos, G. G., & Tzafestas, S. G. (2003). Fuzzy learning compatible with quantum mechanics postulates. *Computational Intelligence and Natural Computation, CINC '03.* North Carolina.

Rigatos, G. G., & Tzafestas, S. G. (2006a). Quantum learning for neural associative memories. *Fuzzy Sets and Systems, 157*(13), 1797-1813. Elsevier.

Rigatos, G. G., & Tzafestas, S. G. (2006b). Neural structures using the eigenstates of the Quantum Harmonic Oscillator. *Open Systems and Information Dynamics, 13*(1). Springer.

Rigatos, G. G. (2006c). Feed-forward neural networks based on the eigenstates of the quantum harmonic oscillator. *Journal of Advanced Computational Intelligence and Intelligent Informatics, 10*(4), 567-577. Fuji Press.

Rigatos, G. G. (2006d). Energy spectrum of quantum associative memory. *Proc. IEEE WCCI'06 Conference*, Vancouver, Canada.

Rigatos, G. G., & Tzafestas, S. G. (2007a). Neurodynamics and attractors in quantum associative memories. *Journal of Integrated Computer Aided Engineering, 14*(3). IOS Press.

Rigatos, G. G. (2007b). Quantum wave-packets in fuzzy automata and neural associative memories. *International Journal of Modern Physics C, 18*(10), World Scientific.

Rigatos, G. G. (2007c). Attractors and spectral characteristics of neural structures based on the model of the quantum harmonic oscillator. *ICNAAM 2008, International Conference on Numerical Analysis and Applied Mathematics*, Corfu, Greece, Sep. 2007.

Rigatos, G. G. (2008a). Coordinated motion of autonomous vehicles with the use of a distributed gradient algorithm. *Applied Mathematics and Computation, 199*(2), 494-503. Elsevier.

Rigatos, G. G. (2008b). Stochastic Processes in Machine Intelligence: neural structures based on the model of the quantum harmonic oscillator. *Optical Memories & Neural Networks (Information Optics), 17*(2), 101-110. Springer.

Rigatos, G. G. (2008c). Stochastic processes in machine intelligence: The model of the quantum harmonic oscillator in neural structures. *IEEE ICQNM '08, 2nd International Conference on Quantum Nano and Micro Techologies*, Martinique, French Carribean, Feb. 2008.

Soong, T. T., & Grigoriou, M. (1992). *Random Vibration of Mechanical and Structural Systems.* Prentice Hall.

Sragovitch, V. (2005). *Mathematical Theory of Adaptive Control.* World Scientific.

Torrésani, B. (1995*). Analyse continue par ondelettes.* CNRS Editions, Paris.

Tzafestas, S. G., & Rigatos, G. G. (2000). Stability analysis of an adaptive fuzzy control system using Petri Nets and learning automata. *Mathematics and Computers in Simulation, 51*(3), 315-341. Elsevier.

Vakulenko, S. A. (2000). Dissipative systems generating any structurally stable chaos. *Advances in Diff. Equations, 5*, 1139-1178.

Vakoulenko, S. A. (2002a). Complexité dynamique de reseaux de Hopfield. *C. R. Acad. Sci. Paris Sér. I Math., 335*.

Vakulenko, S. A. (2002b). Computational capacities of the time recurrent neural networks. *Journal Phys. A, Math.Gen., 35*, 2539-2554.

Vakulenko, S. A. & Grigoriev, D. Y. (2002). Evolution in random environment and structural stability, Zapiski seminarov POMI RAN. *Russian Acad. Sci, 325*, 28-60.

Vakulenko, S. A., & Grigoriev, D. Y. (2003a). *Complexity of patterns generated by genetic circuits and Pfaffian functions.* Preprint IHES.

Vakulenko, S. A., & Grigoriev, D. Y. (2003b). Complexity of gene circuits. Pfaffian functions and the morphogenesis problem, *C. R. Acad. Sci, Ser I. 337*, 721-724.

Vakulenko, S. A., & Genieys, S. (2003c). Pattern programming by genetic networks. Patterns and Waves. Collection of papers. A. Abramian, S. Vakulenko, V. Volpert, & S. Petersburg, (pp. 346-366).

Vakulenko, S. A., & Grigoriev, D. Y. (2005a). Stable growth of complex systems. *Proceeding of Fifth Workshop on Simulation*, (pp. 705-709).

Vakulenko, S. A., & Genieys, S. (2005b). Patterning by genetic networks. *Mathematical Methods in Applied Sciences, 29*, 173-190.

Vakulenko, S. A., & Grigoriev, D. Y. (2006). Algorithms and complexity in biological pattern formation problems. *Annales of Pure and Applied Logic, 141*, 421-428.

Valiant, L. (2007). Evolvability. *Proc. 32nd International Symposium on Mathematical Foundations of Computer Science,* Aug. 26-31, Cesky Krumlov, Czech Republic, *LNCS, 4708*, Springer-Verlag, (pp. 22-43).

Ventura, D. (1999). Quantum computational intelligence: answers and questions. IEEE Intelligent Systems (pp. 14–16), July/August, 1999.

Ventura, D., & Martinez, T. (1997). An artificial neuron with quantum mechanical properties. *Proc. Internat. Conf. on Artificial Neural Networks and Genetic Algorithms*, (pp. 482–485).

Ventura, D., & Martinez, T. (2000). Quantum Associative Memory. *Information Sciences, Elsevier, 124*(1-4), 273-296.

Zhang Q., & Benveniste, A. (1993). A. Wavelet Networks. *IEEE Transactions on Neural Networks*, *3*(6), 869-898.

ADDITIONAL READING

Amari, S., & Maginu, K. (1988). Statistical neurodynamics of associative memory. *Neural Networks, 2,* 63-73.

Amari, S. I, Kurata, K., & Nagaoka, H. (1992). Information Geometry of Boltzmann Machines. *IEEE Transactions on Neural Networks*, *3*(2), 260-271.

Amit, D. J., Gutfreund, H., & Sompolinsky, H. (1985). Storing infinite number of patterns in a spin-glass model of neural networks. *Physical Review Letters., 55*, 1530-1533.

Amit, D. J. (1989). *Modeling Brain Function.* Cambridge University Press.

Bonami, A., Demange, B., & Jaming, P. (2003). Hermite functions and uncertainty principles for the Fourier and Windowed Fourier transforms. *Revista Matematica Iberoamericana*, *19*(1), 23-55.

Drexel, K. E. (1992). Nano systems: Molecular machinery. *Manufacturing and Computation.* Wiley.

Gasiorowicz, S. (1996). *Quantum Physics.* Wiley.

Gröchenig, K., Han, D., Heil., C., & Kutyniak, G. (2002). The Balian-Low theorem for symplectic lattices in higher dimensions. *Applied and Computational Harmonic Analysis*, *13*, 169-176. Academic Press.

Gershenfeld, N. (2000). *The physics of information technology.* Cambridge University Press.

James, M. R. (2005). A quantum Langevin formulation of risk – sensitive optimal control. *IOP Journal of Optics B: Quantum Semiclass.*, (pp. 198-207).

Jaming, P., & Powell, A. M. (2007). Uncertainty principles for orthonormal sequences. *Journal of Functional Analysis*, *243*, 611-630. Elsevier.

Jouault, B., Sébille, F., & de la Motta, V. (2002). Wavelet representation of the nuclear dynamics. *Nuclear Physics A*, *628*, 169-176. Elsevier.

Jones, R. A. L. (2004). *Soft machines: Nanotechnology and life.* Oxford University Press.

Hopfield, J. J. (1982). Neural networks as physical systems with emergent computational abilities. *Proc. Natl. Acad. USA*, *79*, 2444-2558.

Kolobov, M. (2007). *Quantum Imaging.* Springer.

Kosko, B. (1992). *Neural networks and fuzzy systems: A dynamical systems approach to machine intelligence.* Prentice Hall.

Li, Z., & Liu, L. (2005). Uncertainty Principles for Sturm-Liouville Operators, *Constructive approximation*, *21*, 195-205. Springer.

Mansoori, G. A. (2005). *Principles of Nanotechnology: Molecular-based study of condensed matter in small systems.* World Scientific.

Mirrahimi, M., & Rouchon, P. (2004). Controllability of quantum harmonic oscillators. *IEEE Transactions on Automatic Control*, *45*(5), 745-747.

Ozhigov, Y. (2006). Amplitude quanta in multi particle system simulation. *Russian Microelectronics*, *35*(1), 53-65. Springer

Ozhigov, Y. (2007). Simulation of quantum dynamics via classical collective behavior. *Russian Microelectronics*, *36*(3), 193-202. Springer.

Penrose, R. (1994). *Shadows of the Mind.* New York: Oxford University Press.

Piron, C. (2005). *Méthodes quantiques.* Champs, N-corps, diffusion. Presses polytechniques et universitaires romandes.

Pribram, K. H. (1991). *Brain and Perception.* Hillsdale, NJ: Lawrence Erlbaum Assoc.

Reimann, P. (2002). Brownian motors: noisy transport far from equilibrium. *Physics Reports*, *361*, 57-265. Elsevier.

Spencer, R. G. (2002). Bipolar spectral associative memories. *IEEE Transactions on Neural Networks*, *12*(3), 463-474.

Strauss, W.A. (1992). *Partial differential equations: an introduction.* J. Wiley.

Venkatesh, T. G., & Patnaik, L. M. (1991). Associative memory design: Fokker-Planck Formalism. *IEEE International Joint Conference on Neural Networks*, *3*, 2271-2276.

Wünsche, A. (2004). Quantization of Gauss-Hermite and Gauss-Laguerre beams in free space. *IOP Journal of Optics B*: *Quantum Semiclass.*, *6*(3), 47-59.

Zak, M., & Williams, C. (1999). Quantum recurrent networks for simulating stochastic processes. *Quantum Computing and Quantum Communications,* (pp. 75-88). Springer.

Zak, M., & Williams, C. (1998). Quantum Neural Nets. *International Journal of Theoretical Physics, 37*(2).

Chapter XVI
Quaternionic Neural Networks: Fundamental Properties and Applications

Teijiro Isokawa
University of Hyogo, Japan

Nobuyuki Matsui
University of Hyogo, Japan

Haruhiko Nishimura
University of Hyogo, Japan

ABSTRACT

Quaternions are a class of hypercomplex number systems, a four-dimensional extension of imaginary numbers, which are extensively used in various fields such as modern physics and computer graphics. Although the number of applications of neural networks employing quaternions is comparatively less than that of complex-valued neural networks, it has been increasing recently. In this chapter, the authors describe two types of quaternionic neural network models. One type is a multilayer perceptron based on 3D geometrical affine transformations by quaternions. The operations that can be performed in this network are translation, dilatation, and spatial rotation in three-dimensional space. Several examples are provided in order to demonstrate the utility of this network. The other type is a Hopfield-type recurrent network whose parameters are directly encoded into quaternions. The stability of this network is demonstrated by proving that the energy decreases monotonically with respect to the change in neuron states. The fundamental properties of this network are presented through the network with three neurons.

INTRODUCTION

Complex numbers play an important role in practical applications and fundamental theorems in various fields of engineering such as electromagnetics, communication, control theory, and quantum mechanics. The application of complex numbers to neural networks has recently attracted attention because they tend to improve the learning ability and conform to the abovementioned applications (Hirose, 2003) (Rao, Nitta & Murthy, 2008).

They enable the modeling of a point in two-dimensional space as a single entity, rather than as a set of two data items on which 2D geometrical affine operations are performed. It has been shown that a neural network with the representation and operations of complex numbers results in improved performance of the geometrical affine transformation in two-dimensional space, whereas the performance of real-valued (conventional) neural networks is comparatively poor. The operations involving complex numbers would improve the performance of neural networks for processing two-dimensional data.

Let us consider the case in which the data are three dimensional, such as color images and body images. These data, of course, can be processed by many neurons of real- or complex-valued neural networks; however, the processing efficiency may be increased by implementing direct encoding in terms of hypercomplex numbers. Consequently, the application of hypercomplex numbers, particularly quaternions, to neural networks has been investigated. Quaternions are a class of hypercomplex number systems, a four-dimensional extension of imaginary numbers. One of benefits by quaternions is that affine transformation of geometric figures in three-dimensional space (3D geometrical affine transformation), especially spatial rotation, can be represented compactly and efficiently; in recent years, quaternions are extensively used in the fields of robotics, control of satellites, and computer graphics, etc.

In this chapter, we describe two models of neural networks based on quaternions and present their fundamental properties and possible applications. The first model is a multilayer perceptron based on the 3D geometrical affine transformations by quaternions. The operators in neurons adopt the 3D geometrical affine transformation. After the description of the neuron model and the error backpropagation algorithm for a training algorithm, four types of tasks, i.e., applications of three-bit parity check problem, affine transformation in three-dimensional space, color image compression, and color night vision, are introduced. The performances of the multilayer perceptron for these tasks are evaluated by comparing them with the performances of the real-valued networks for the same tasks. The other model is the Hopfield-type recurrent network where the states of neurons are directly encoded in quaternions. The quaternionic component of the neuron state takes a bipolar value (+1 or −1). The energy function for this network is defined, and it is proved that this function monotonically decreases with respect to the change in neuron states. The property of the stable points in the network is investigated by using an example of a network with three neurons.

BACKGROUND

Several systems for hypercomplex numbers have been investigated, such as quaternion, octonion, sedenion. They can be described as special cases of Clifford algebra (Porteous, 1995) (Lounesto, 2001). Quaternions are hypercomplex numbers of rank four; they are the four-dimensional extensions of imaginary numbers discovered by Sir William Rowan Hamilton (Graves, 1975) (Hankins, 1980) (Bell, 1999), which have been extensively used in modern mathematics, signal processing, computer graphics, robotics, etc (Lambek, 1995) (Mukundan, 2002) (Hoggar, 1992) (Kuipers, 1998) (Previn & Webb, 1983) (Sahul, Biswall & Subudhi, 2008) (Bülow & Sommer, 2001). Quaternion is also defined as a special case of Clifford algebra, but the representation of quaternion is simple and easy to understand its geometrical meanings. It has been found that 3D geometrical affine transformations—translation, dilatation, and spatial rotation—in three-dimensional space can be represented compactly and efficiently by the operators of quaternions. In the following section, we recapitulate the basic definitions, operations, and notations of quaternions. The 3D geometrical affine transformation realized by quaternions, which is used in the multilayer perceptron model in this chapter, is also described. For the detailed properties and applications of quaternions, please refer to the literatures (Lambek, 1995) (Mukundan, 2002) (Hoggar, 1992) (Kuipers, 1998).

Definition and Notation of Quaternion Algebra

Quaternions form a class of hypercomplex numbers that consist of a real number and three types of imaginary numbers: $\boldsymbol{i}, \boldsymbol{j}, \boldsymbol{k}$. Formally, a quaternion number is defined as a vector $\boldsymbol{x}$ in a four-dimensional vector space,

$$x = x^{(e)} + x^{(i)}\boldsymbol{i} + x^{(j)}\boldsymbol{j} + x^{(k)}\boldsymbol{k} \tag{1}$$

where $x^{(e)}$, $x^{(i)}$, $x^{(j)}$, and $x^{(k)}$ are real numbers. $\boldsymbol{H}$, the division ring of quaternions, thus constitutes the four-dimensional vector space over the real numbers with the following bases: 1 $\boldsymbol{i}, \boldsymbol{j}, \boldsymbol{k}$. It is also written using 4-tuple or 2-tuple notations as follows:

$$\begin{aligned} \boldsymbol{x} &= (x^{(e)}, x^{(i)}, x^{(j)}, x^{(k)}) \\ &= (x^{(e)}, \vec{x}) \end{aligned} \tag{2}$$

where $\vec{x} = \{x^{(i)}, x^{(j)}, x^{(k)}\}$. In this representation $x^{(e)}$ is the scalar part of x, and $\vec{x}$ forms the vector part.

The quaternion conjugate is defined as follows:

$$\begin{aligned} \boldsymbol{x}^* &= (x^{(e)}, -\vec{x}) \\ &= x^{(e)} - x^{(i)}\boldsymbol{i} - x^{(j)}\boldsymbol{j} - x^{(k)}\boldsymbol{k}. \end{aligned} \tag{3}$$

Quaternion bases satisfy the following identities, known as the Hamilton rules:

$$\begin{aligned} &\boldsymbol{i}^2 = \boldsymbol{j}^2 = \boldsymbol{k}^2 = \boldsymbol{ijk} = -1 \\ &\boldsymbol{ij} = -\boldsymbol{ji} = \boldsymbol{k},\ \ \boldsymbol{jk} = -\boldsymbol{kj} = \boldsymbol{i},\ \ \boldsymbol{ki} = -\boldsymbol{ik} = \boldsymbol{j}. \end{aligned} \tag{4}$$

From these rules, it implies that the multiplication of quaternions is not commutative.

The operations between quaternions, $\boldsymbol{p} = (p^{(e)}, \vec{p}) = (p^{(e)}, p^{(i)}, p^{(j)}, p^{(k)})$ and $\boldsymbol{q} = (q^{(e)}, \vec{q}) = (q^{(e)}, q^{(i)}, q^{(j)}, q^{(k)})$, are defined as follows. The addition and subtraction of quaternions are defined in the same manner as that of complex-valued numbers or vectors by

$$\begin{aligned} \boldsymbol{p} \pm \boldsymbol{q} &= (p^{(e)} \pm q^{(e)}, \vec{p} \pm \vec{q}) \\ &= (p^{(e)} \pm q^{(e)}, p^{(i)} \pm q^{(i)}, p^{(j)} \pm q^{(j)}, p^{(k)} \pm q^{(k)}). \end{aligned} \tag{5}$$

With regard to the multiplication, the product of $\boldsymbol{p}$ and $\boldsymbol{q}$, denoted as $\boldsymbol{p} \otimes \boldsymbol{q}$, is determined using Hamilton rules as

$$\boldsymbol{p} \otimes \boldsymbol{q} = (p^{(e)}q^{(e)} - \vec{p} \cdot \vec{q}, p^{(e)}\vec{q} + q^{(e)}\vec{p} + \vec{p} \times \vec{q}) \tag{6}$$

where $\vec{p} \cdot \vec{q}$ and $\vec{p} \times \vec{q}$ denote the dot and cross products, respectively, of the three-dimensional vectors $\vec{p}$ and $\vec{q}$. The conjugate of the product holds the relation of $(\boldsymbol{p} \otimes \boldsymbol{q})^* = \boldsymbol{q}^* \otimes \boldsymbol{p}^*$. The inner product of $\boldsymbol{p}$ and $\boldsymbol{q}$, notation $\boldsymbol{p} \circ \boldsymbol{q}$, is defined as

$$\boldsymbol{p} \circ \boldsymbol{q} = (p^{(e)}q^{(e)}, p^{(i)}q^{(i)}, p^{(j)}q^{(j)}, p^{(k)}q^{(k)}). \tag{7}$$

The quaternion norm of $\boldsymbol{x}$, denoted by $|\boldsymbol{x}|$, is defined by

$$|\boldsymbol{x}| = \sqrt{\boldsymbol{x} \otimes \boldsymbol{x}^*} = \sqrt{x^{(e)^2} + x^{(i)^2} + x^{(j)^2} + x^{(k)^2}}. \tag{8}$$

The multiplication of a scalar $a = (a, \vec{0})$ and a quaternion $\boldsymbol{x}$ is given by

$$ax = (ax^{(e)}, a\vec{x})$$
$$=(ax^{(e)}, ax^{(i)}, ax^{(j)}, ax^{(k)}). \tag{9}$$

The real(scalar) part and vector part of $\boldsymbol{x}$, $x^{(e)}$ and $\vec{x}$, can be represented as

$$\mathrm{Re}(\boldsymbol{x}) = \frac{1}{2}(\boldsymbol{x} + \boldsymbol{x}^*) \tag{10}$$

$$\mathrm{Ve}(\boldsymbol{x}) = \frac{1}{2}(\boldsymbol{x} - \boldsymbol{x}^*) \tag{11}$$

by using $\boldsymbol{x}$ and $\boldsymbol{x}^*$, respectively.

Quaternion algebra can also be derived from Clifford algebra as its special case. That is, the 2^n bases in Clifford algebra are generated by the multiplication called the geometric product of n generators $\{\boldsymbol{e}_1, \boldsymbol{e}_2, \cdots, \boldsymbol{e}_n\}$ that are the orthonormal basis vectors in n-dimensional real vector space. These bases are satisfied:

$$\boldsymbol{e}_r^2 = -1, \qquad \boldsymbol{e}_r \boldsymbol{e}_s = -\boldsymbol{e}_s \boldsymbol{e}_r \quad (r \neq s). \tag{12}$$

In the case of n=3, we can obtain the 2^3 bases 1, $\{\boldsymbol{e}_1, \boldsymbol{e}_2, \boldsymbol{e}_3\}$, $\{\boldsymbol{e}_1\boldsymbol{e}_2, \boldsymbol{e}_2\boldsymbol{e}_3, \boldsymbol{e}_3\boldsymbol{e}_1\}$, $\{\boldsymbol{e}_1\boldsymbol{e}_2\boldsymbol{e}_3\}$. If we regard $\boldsymbol{e}_1\boldsymbol{e}_2$, $\boldsymbol{e}_2\boldsymbol{e}_3$, $\boldsymbol{e}_3\boldsymbol{e}_1$ as the imaginary numbers $\boldsymbol{i}, \boldsymbol{j}, \boldsymbol{k}$ in quaternion, respectively, we can obtain the quaternion algebra.

For the detailed descriptions for Clifford algebra, please refer to (Porteous 1995) (Lounesto, 2001). In this chapter, we do not treat with higher dimensional data than 4. We may expect that focusing on the quaternionic representation produces the fruitful results for the applications to 3- or 4-dimensional data information processing.

3D Geometrical Affine Transformations by Quaternion Algebra

Quaternions are useful for describing 3D geometrical affine transformations, especially the rotational operator, in three-dimensional space.

Let $\boldsymbol{x} = (x^{(e)}, x^{(i)}, x^{(j)}, x^{(k)}) = (x^{(e)}, \vec{x})$ and $\boldsymbol{y} = (y^{(e)}, y^{(i)}, y^{(j)}, y^{(k)}) = (y^{(e)}, \vec{y})$ be quaternions in which the vector parts represent vectors (or coordinates) in three-dimensional space. Translation and scaling operators in three-dimensional space can be defined in the same way as in two-dimensional space. The sum of $\boldsymbol{x}$ and $\boldsymbol{y}$, i.e. $\boldsymbol{x} + \boldsymbol{y}$, represents the coordinate of $\boldsymbol{x}$ shifted by $\boldsymbol{y}$. Multiplication of $\boldsymbol{x}$ by a scalar a results in the point with the coordinate $\boldsymbol{x}$ scaled by a.

The rotated state $\tilde{\boldsymbol{x}} = (x'^{(e)}, x'^{(i)}, x'^{(j)}, x'^{(k)})$ with respect to $\boldsymbol{x}$ is defined by

$$\tilde{\boldsymbol{x}} = \boldsymbol{u}^* \otimes \boldsymbol{x} \otimes \boldsymbol{u}$$
$$= (x^{(e)}, \vec{x}') \tag{13}$$
$$\vec{x}' = \vec{x}\cos 2\alpha + (\vec{R} \times \vec{x})\sin 2\alpha + \vec{R}(\vec{R} \cdot \vec{x})(1 - \cos 2\alpha)$$

where $\vec{R}$ is a unit vector ($|\vec{R}| = 1$) and $\boldsymbol{u} = \cos\alpha + \vec{R}\sin\alpha$ is a quaternion with $|\boldsymbol{u}| = 1$. The resultant $\vec{x}'$ is the rotated vector of $\vec{x}$ rotated by the angle 2α around the vector $\vec{R}$ (see Fig. 1). It should be noted that this operation does not affect the scalar part of $\boldsymbol{x}$, i.e., $x'^{(e)} = x^{(e)}$.

Neural Networks Based on Quaternions

The number of literatures concerning neural networks based on quaternions is not so many, fewer than that of complex-valued neural networks; but it has been increasing in this decade. The neural networks with Clifford algebra have been investigated, and these neural networks can also been categorized as quaternionic ones due to

Figure 1. Rotation of $\vec{x}$ around the vector $\vec{R}$ in three-dimensional space

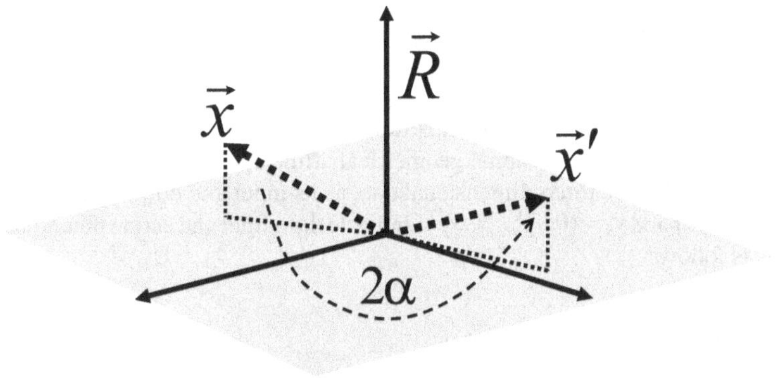

the nature of the Clifford algebra. In this respect, the first work for quaternionic neural network is pioneered by Pearson and Bisset (Pearson & Bisset, 1992). This type of neural networks are extended to "Geometric Neural Networks" and "Geometric Computing" by Bayro-Corrochano and his colleagues (Bayro-Corrochano & Buchholtz, 1997) (Bayro-Corrochano, 2001a) (Bayro-Corrochano, 2001b). In the following, we list the researches for neural networks based on quaternion algebra.

The computational ability for a single quaternionic neuron was exhibited in (Nitta, 2004), showing that four-bit parity check problem can be solved by a single quaternionic neuron with the orthogonal decision boundary. Concerning the multilayer perceptron model, several models have been proposed (Nitta, 1995) (Nitta, 1996) (Arena, Caponetto, Fortuna, Muscato, & Xibilia, 1996) (Arena, Fortuna, Muscato, Xibilia, 1997) (Arena, Fortuna, Muscato, Xibilia, 1998) (Buchholz & Sommer, 2000) (Isokawa, Kusakabe, Matsui, & Peper, 2003) (Matsui, Isokawa, Kusamichi, Peper, & Nishimura, 2004). There are several practical applications of quaternionic multilayer perceptron models, such as time series prediction and rigid body control (Arena, Fortuna, Muscato, Xibilia, 1998), image compression (Matsui, Isokawa, Kusamichi, Peper, & Nishimura, 2004), and image processing called color night vision (Kusamichi, Isokawa, Matsui, Ogawa, & Maeda, 2004). The Hopfield-type quaternionic neural networks have been proposed and their properties are analyzed in (Yoshida, Kuroe, & Mori, 2005) (Isokawa, Nishimura, Kamiura, & Matsui 2006) (Isokawa, Nishimura, Kamiura & Matsui, 2007) (Isokawa, Nishimura, Kamiura & Matsui, 2008).

Among the proposed quaternionic neuron models and networks, there is a type of network in which real-value numbers encoding the input, output, connection weights, and thresholds are directly converted into quaternions (Nitta, 1995) (Nitta, 1996) (Arena, Caponetto, Fortuna, Muscato, & Xibilia, 1996) (Arena, Fortuna, Muscato, Xibilia, 1997) (Arena, Fortuna, Muscato, Xibilia, 1998) (Nitta, 2004) (Yoshida, Kuroe, & Mori, 2005) (Isokawa, Nishimura, Kamiura, & Matsui 2006) (Isokawa, Nishimura, Kamiura & Matsui, 2007) (Isokawa, Nishimura, Kamiura & Matsui, 2008). The representations of the operations in such networks are similar to those in real-valued networks, although the operations on data are quite different. There can be also another type of quaternionic neuron that is developed in terms of the 3D geometrical characteristics by quaternions with respect to the transformation operators (Buchholz & Sommer, 2000) (Isokawa, Kusakabe, Matsui, & Peper, 2003) (Matsui, Isokawa, Kusamichi, Peper, Nishimura, 2004) (Kusamichi, Isokawa, Matsui, Ogawa, & Maeda, 2004). This type of neuron employs the two-sided operation of the weights.

In the following two sections, we describe two types of quaternionic neural networks, for demonstrating the usefulness of quaternionic multilayer networks and the detailed properties of quaternionic Hopfield networks.

QUATERNIONIC MULTILAYER NEURAL NETWORK

Neuron Model Based on 3D Geometrical Affine Operators

This section describes the formulation of a multilayer neural network based on quaternions and demonstrates its various applications, which is based on (Matsui, Isokawa, Kusamichi, Peper & Nishimura, 2004). The neuron model in this section uses the three-dimensional geometrical affine operators that are described in the previous section; thus, this model can handle three-dimensional data as its input and output.

Let $\boldsymbol{y}_p = (0, y_p^{(i)}, y_p^{(j)}, y_p^{(k)})$ and $\boldsymbol{s}_p = (0, s_p^{(i)}, s_p^{(j)}, s_p^{(k)})$ indicate the output and action potentials of the p-th neuron, respectively, defined as follows:

$$\boldsymbol{s}_p = \sum_q \frac{\boldsymbol{w}_{pq} \otimes \boldsymbol{x}_q \otimes \boldsymbol{w}_{pq}^*}{|\boldsymbol{w}_{pq}|} - \boldsymbol{\theta}_p, \tag{14}$$

$$\boldsymbol{y}_p = \boldsymbol{f}(\boldsymbol{s}_p), \tag{15}$$

where $\boldsymbol{w}_{pq}, \boldsymbol{\theta}_p = (0, \theta_p^{(i)}, \theta_p^{(j)}, \theta_p^{(k)})$, and $\boldsymbol{x}_q = (0, x_q^{(i)}, x_q^{(j)}, x_q^{(k)})$, are the connection weight from neuron q to neuron p, threshold of neuron p, and output of neuron p, respectively. Because the rotational operation by the quaternions, $\boldsymbol{w} \otimes \boldsymbol{x} \otimes \boldsymbol{w}^*$, does not affect the real part of $\boldsymbol{x}$, the real parts of $\boldsymbol{x}$, $\boldsymbol{s}$, and $\boldsymbol{\theta}$ are always set to zero. A scale factor $|\boldsymbol{w}|$ is responsible for suppressing the saturation of $\boldsymbol{s}_p$ which is evolved by summing up input from other neurons, and no contribution to $\boldsymbol{s}_p$ is made when $\boldsymbol{w}_{pq} = 0$ due to $|\boldsymbol{w}_{pq}| = 0$ and $\boldsymbol{w} \otimes \boldsymbol{x} \otimes \boldsymbol{w}^* = 0$. In this model, the output values from other neurons are rotated by the weight values, scaled by $|\boldsymbol{w}|$, and used as the input to neuron p. The action potential is a unified vector of these inputs and is shifted by the threshold value $\boldsymbol{\theta}$. The output value of neuron p, $\boldsymbol{y}_p$, is determined by the activation function $\boldsymbol{f}$ defined by

$$\boldsymbol{f}(\boldsymbol{s}) = f(s^{(i)})\boldsymbol{i} + f(s^{(j)})\boldsymbol{j} + f(s^{(k)})\boldsymbol{k}, \tag{16}$$

$$f(s) = \frac{1}{1+e^{-s}}. \tag{17}$$

The model described above is similar to the model proposed in (Buchholz & Sommer, 2000). For reference, we recapitulate this model, called Quaternionic Spinor MLP, as follows. The output of a neuron is determined by

$$f\left(\sum_q \boldsymbol{w}_{pq} \otimes \boldsymbol{x}_q \otimes \boldsymbol{w}_{pq}^* + \boldsymbol{\theta}_p\right), \tag{18}$$

where $\boldsymbol{w}_{pq}$ is the connection weight from neuron q to neuron p satisfying $|\boldsymbol{w}_{pq}| = 1$, and $\boldsymbol{x}_q$ and $\boldsymbol{\theta}_p$ are the output of neuron q and threshold of neuron p, respectively. The difference between this model and the model described in this chapter is that the scale factor by the connection weight is introduced in the latter model (see Eq.(14)). The activation function $\boldsymbol{f}$ is defined as

$$\boldsymbol{f}(\boldsymbol{s}) = f(s^{(e)}) + f(s^{(i)})\boldsymbol{i} + f(s^{(j)})\boldsymbol{j} + f(s^{(k)})\boldsymbol{k}, \tag{19}$$

where a real-valued function *f*(*s*) $f(s)$ is a sigmoid function (Eq.(17)).

Multilayer Network Model

A multilayer feedforward network is constructed from this neuron model, and the error back-propagation (EBP) algorithm for training this network is derived. Here, we extend the notation of the neuron model so as to introduce the information on the layer. For example, $\boldsymbol{y}_p(l)$ denotes the output value of neuron p at the l-th layer of the network and $\boldsymbol{w}_{pq}(l)$ represents the connection weight from neuron q at the (l-1)-th layer to neuron p at the l-th layer.

The EBP algorithm requires the error value of the output with respect to the input. When the desired output for the input is represented as $\boldsymbol{d}_p = (0, d_p^{(i)}, d_p^{(j)}, d_p^{(k)})$, the error value E is defined as follows:

$$\begin{aligned} E &= \frac{1}{2}\sum_p \left|\boldsymbol{d}_p - \boldsymbol{y}_p(L)\right|^2 \\ &= \frac{1}{2}\sum_p \sum_{\nu=\{i,j,k\}} \left(d_p^{(\nu)} - y_p^{(\nu)}(L)\right)^2, \end{aligned} \tag{20}$$

where L is the number of layers in the network.

In the EBP algorithm, the parameters of the network (connection weights and thresholds) are updated along the gradients of E with respect to $\boldsymbol{w}$, i.e.,

$$\begin{aligned} &\boldsymbol{w} \leftarrow \boldsymbol{w} - \eta \cdot \Delta\boldsymbol{w} \\ &\Delta w^{(\nu)} = \frac{\partial E}{\partial w^{(\nu)}} \quad (\nu = \{e, i, j, k\}), \end{aligned} \tag{21}$$

where η is a constant known as the learning rate. The values for the update, $\Delta\boldsymbol{w}$ and $\Delta\boldsymbol{\theta}$, are explicitly denoted as follows:

$$\Delta\boldsymbol{\theta}_p(L) = \left(\boldsymbol{y}_p(L) - \boldsymbol{d}_p\right) \circ \boldsymbol{f}'\left(\boldsymbol{s}_p(L)\right) \tag{22}$$

$$\Delta\boldsymbol{\theta}_p(l) = \left(\sum_n \frac{\boldsymbol{w}_{np}^*(l+1) \otimes \Delta\boldsymbol{\theta}_n(l+1) \otimes \boldsymbol{w}_{np}(l+1)}{\left|\boldsymbol{w}_{nm}(l+1)\right|}\right) \circ \boldsymbol{f}'\left(\boldsymbol{s}_p(l)\right) \quad (l \neq L) \tag{23}$$

$$\Delta\boldsymbol{w}_{pq}(l) = \frac{1}{\left|\boldsymbol{w}_{pq}(l)\right|}\left(2\Delta\boldsymbol{\theta}_p(l) \otimes \boldsymbol{w}_{pq}(l) \otimes \boldsymbol{y}_q(l-1) - \frac{\Delta\boldsymbol{\theta}_p(l) \circ \boldsymbol{w}_{pq}(l) \otimes \boldsymbol{y}_q(l-1) \otimes \boldsymbol{w}_{pq}^*(l) \otimes \boldsymbol{w}_{pq}(l)}{\left|\boldsymbol{w}_{pq}(l)\right|^2}\right) \tag{24}$$

where $\boldsymbol{f}'(s) = \partial f(s^{(i)}) / \partial s^{(i)}\boldsymbol{i} + \partial f(s^{(j)}) / \partial s^{(j)}\boldsymbol{j} + \partial f(s^{(k)}) / \partial s^{(k)}\boldsymbol{k}$.

Examples

We introduce four types of tasks performed by the quaternionic multilayer networks and conventional (real-valued) networks in order to show the improved performance of the quaternionic network. The details of the tasks, i.e., applications of three-bit parity check problem, affine transformation in three-dimensional space, color image compression, and color night vision, are described in the subsequent subsections. We adopt a three-layer network structure for these tasks and denote the network by a three-tuple number l-m-n, where l, m, and n represent the number of neurons in the input, hidden, and output layers, respectively. Even for the same task, the numbers of neurons in the input and output layers in the quaternionic network can differ from those in the real-valued networks. This is because the quaternionic neurons in this section can carry three dimensional vectors, hence the number of neurons in a layer of quaternionic network can be reduced to one-third number of neurons in the real-valued network. For the same network structure, the number of trainable parameters, i.e., the connection weights between the neurons and the thresholds of the neurons, is also different between the quaternionic and real-valued networks. For the comparison of performance, we adjust the structures of these networks so that the number of trainable parameters in the quaternionic network becomes comparable to that in the real-valued network. Though fair comparisons between real-valued network and quaternionic network are difficult due to the differences of their dynamics, we conduct to make comparisons under the condition that the degrees of freedom in the parameter spaces are set to be comparable in both types of networks. We define two measurements for determining whether the training of a network should be terminated: the total squared error (TSE) threshold Th_{TSE} and the maximum number of training iterations $t_{\max}$. The TSE of a network is defined as the sum of the squared errors of all the training patterns. The training of the network ends when the TSE of the network reaches Th_{TSE}, where the training is considered to be terminated due to convergence, or when the number of iterations in the training process exceeds $t_{\max}$, where the training is considered to be terminated due to non-convergence.

Three-Bit Parity Check Problem

n-bit parity check (or exclusive OR for two-bit parity check) problems are frequently used for evaluating the performance of the neural network. For demonstrating the fundamental performance of a network, we first apply the three-bit parity check problem.

The training patterns for the three-bit parity check are generated by $y = x_1 + x_2 + x_3 (\text{mod}\, 2)$, where $y, x_1, x_2, x_3 \in \{0,1\}$. The networks are trained by applying a set of $\{x_1, x_2, x_3\}$ as the input and the corresponding y to obtain the desired output. We choose a 3-8-1 configuration for the real-valued networks and a 1-3-1 configuration for the quaternionic networks. The numbers of trainable parameters for both networks are set so as to be very close to each other. The numbers of trainable parameters is 41 for the real-valued neural network, which is calculated by the sum of numbers of weights between layers (3×8=24 weights between the input and hidden layer, and the 8×1=8 weights between the hidden and output layer) with the number of thresholds (The number of thresholds is the same as the number of neurons in the hidden and ourput layers). The way of counting the number of parameters for the quaternionic neural network is slightly cumbersome. The number of weights in the quaternionic neural network with a 1-3-1 configuration is 6. These weights are general quaternions, so each of which has four components. On the other hand, the thresholds of the neurons in quaternionic neural network are purely imaginary quaternions, i.e., three-dimensional values. As a result, the number of trainable parameters becomes 36(=1×3×4 + 3×1×4 + (3+1)×3). The other conditions for training are $Th_{\text{TSE}} = 0.01$ and $t_{\max} = 3000$. The performance is evaluated on the basis of the convergence rate for learning and the average number of iterations required for training. The convergence rate is calculated as the number of trials for the termination of training with convergence ($TSE < Th_{\text{TSE}}$ within $t_{\max}$ iterations) out of the total number of trials (100). The average number of iterations is the average of the number of iterations in the trials for which the training is completed by convergence. Figure 2 shows the dependence of the convergence rate on the learning rate η for the real-valued and quaternionic neural networks. The convergence rates for the quaternionic networks are higher than those for the real-valued networks; thus, the quaternionic networks are superior to the real-valued networks. The average training iterations for both the networks with respect to the values of η are shown in Fig. 3. From this figure, we conclude that the quaternionic networks can learn the training patterns more quickly than the real-valued networks.

Affine Transformation in Three-Dimensional Space

Affine transformation involves the training of relations between two points. For example, in translation, which is a task of affine transformation, the learning is carried out so as to transform the input point $\vec{x}$ into the output point $\vec{x} + (-1,0,0)$. The networks have symmetrical structures (*n-m-n* configuration) because related points are provided at the inputs and outputs of the networks.

In two-dimensional case, it is shown that this kind of tasks can be efficiently performed by complex-valued neural networks with complex-valued version of EBP (Nitta & Furuya, 1991) (Nitta, 1997). For three dimensional affine transformations, a neural network with neurons of three-dimensional real-valued vectors is proposed and

Figure 2. Dependence of convergence rate on learning rate η

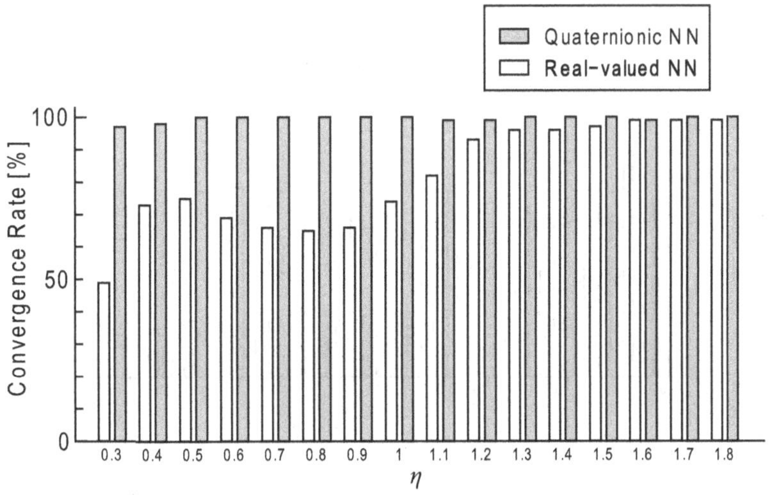

confirmed its learning ability (Nitta, 1994) (Nitta, 2006). Another approach for three dimensional transformations is the use of neural networks with quaternion that is an extension of complex numbers.

Our experiment for the affine transformation consists of three types of transformation tasks: translation, dilatation, and rotation. The input and desired output patterns in the training data set are shown in Fig. 4, where points marked "◊" and "+" represent the input and desired output points, respectively. Both the input and desired output consist of nine points that constitute a plane in three-dimensional space. In the translation task, the input plane should be shifted by -0.3 along the Z–axis. In the dilatation task, the output square is the input square that is magnified two times its original size on each side. In the rotation task, the input plane should be rotated around the Y-axis by 45 degrees. All the training patterns are planar structures. After training the networks, the output patterns are obtained by inputting the patterns that are not used for training (test patterns), in order to measure the generalization ability of the trained networks.

We use a 3-8-3 configuration for the real-valued networks and a 1-4-1 configuration for the quaternionic networks. The numbers of trainable parameters are 59 for the real-valued networks and 47 for the quaternionic networks. The training conditions for this task are $Th_{\text{TSE}} = 0.01$ and $t_{\max} = 10000$.

The output patterns from the networks with respect to the input test patterns for the real-valued and quaternionic networks are shown in Figs. 5 and 6, respectively. In these figures, the symbol "◊" indicates the input test point of the networks and the symbol "+" indicates the output point of the networks. The input test patterns have three-dimensional structures, while the training patterns have two-dimensional structures. By comparing the results shown in Figs. 5 and 6, we conclude that the quaternionic networks can learn each of the affine transformations correctly. The real-valued networks can train the mappings only between the input and desired output patterns in the training data set. Further, the output patterns for the input test patterns result in the projection to a plane. Hence, the real-valued networks fail to generalize the input-output relations to the third dimension, while the quaternionic networks can successfully generalize those relations.

Color Image Compression

The task of image compression by the multilayer neural networks was first proposed in (Cottrell, 1987) for grayscale images, and the technique is extended for color images in this section. The color image compression problem may require a geometrical affine transformation in three-dimensional color space, in addition to encod-

Figure 3. Average number of iterations for learning with respect to η

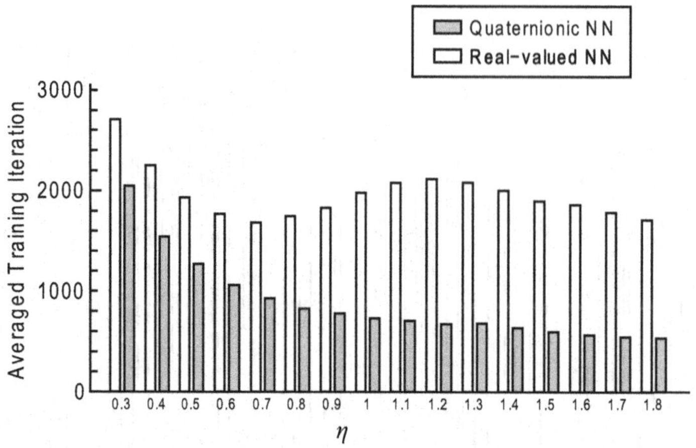

Figure 4. Input and desired output points in training data set for affine transformation problem

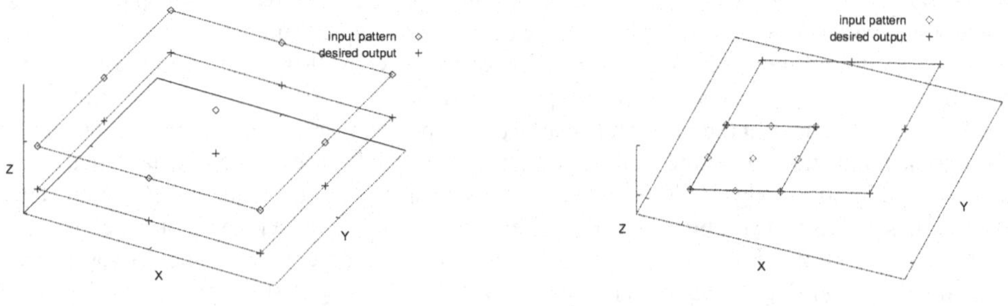

(a) Translation *(b) Dilatation*

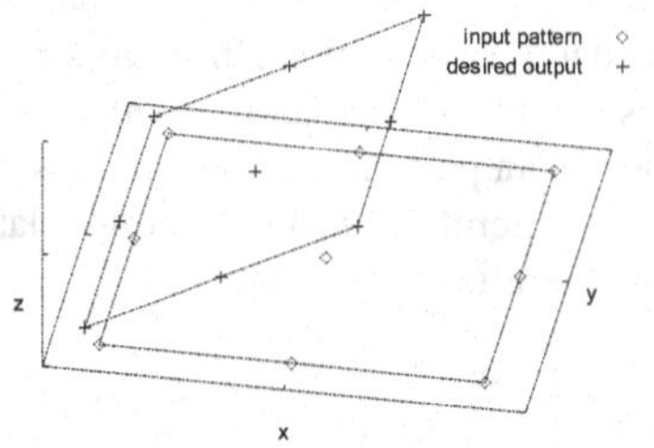

(c) Rotation

Figure 5. Output patterns obtained from real-valued neural networks

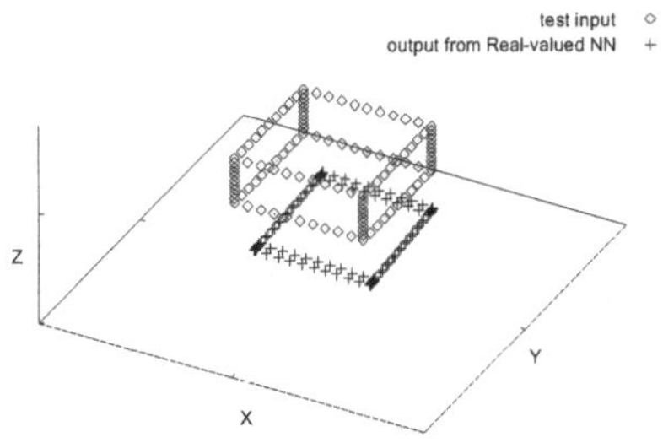

(a) Translation

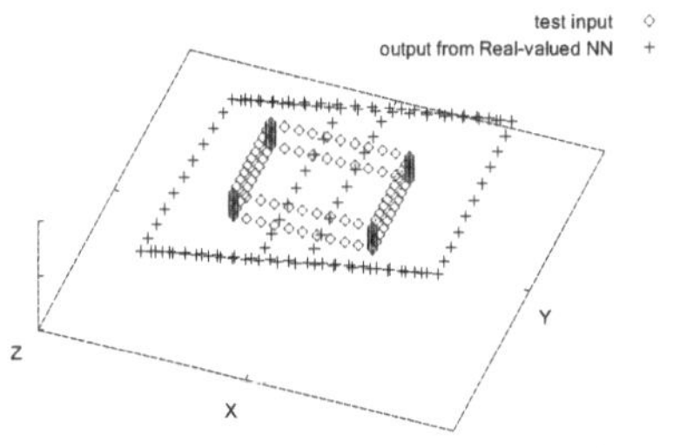

(b) Dilatation

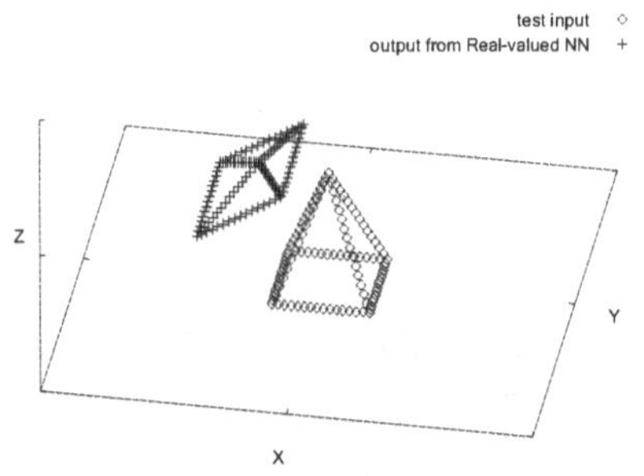

(c) Rotation

Figure 6. Output patterns obtained from quaternionic neural networks

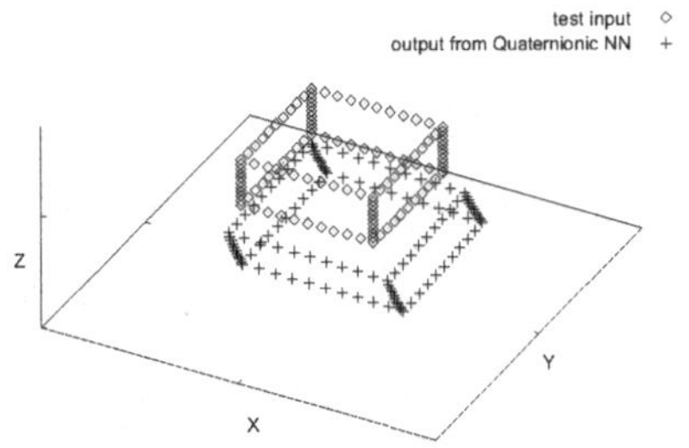

(a) Translation

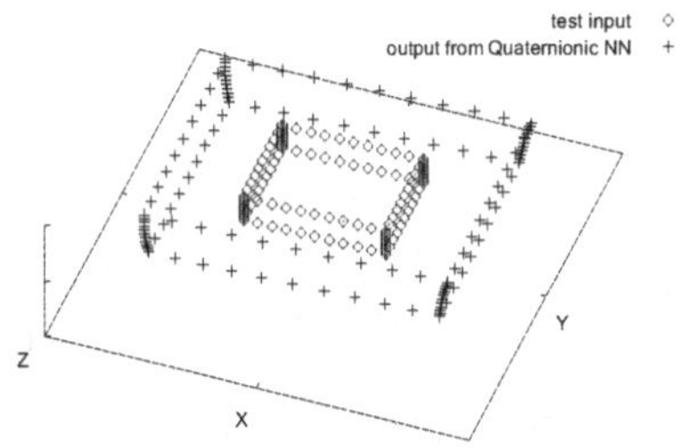

(b) Dilatation

continued on following page

Figure 6. continued

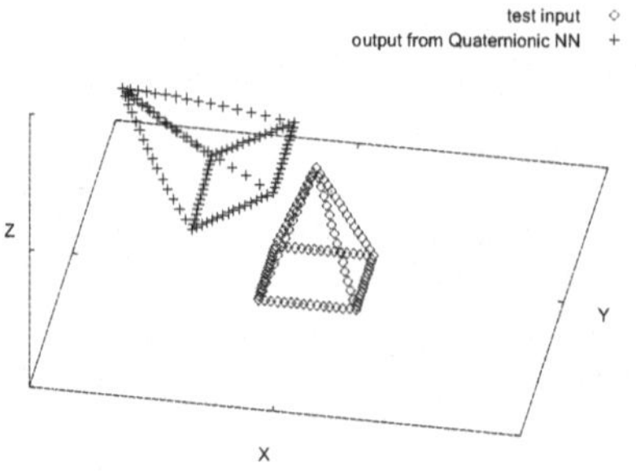

(c) Rotation

ing and decoding signals. For color image compression, a neural network with three layers is used such that the number of neurons in the input layer is the same as that in the output layer, and the number of neurons in the hidden layer is less than that in the input layer. The hidden layer, thus, acts as a bottleneck, through which the information from the input layer to the output layer has to pass with minimum information loss. The image to be compressed is uniformly divided into small sub-image samples. The network is trained by providing each sample as the input and desired output. Thus, the network will try to find the values of its connection weights such that there is a strong association between the input and the output. Figure 7 shows an example of a network for the image compression problem.

The images used in this task consist of 256×256 pixels, each of which has a color value represented by 24 bits. The images are divided into 4,096 samples of 4×4 pixels in size. The neural networks employed for this task have a 48-12-48 configuration for the real-valued network and a 16-4-16 configuration for the quaternionic network. Figures 8(a) and 8(b) show the images for training the networks and for evaluating the generalization ability of the network. Two types of peak-signal-to-noise ratios (PSNRs) are introduced for measuring the quality of the output images obtained from the neural networks. One PSNR is used for evaluating grayscale images or images with a single color component, and the other PSNR is used for evaluating images with color components.

Let φ and φ' be images with $W \times H$ pixels, and each pixel value is represented by a three-tuple color value (R_{xy}, G_{xy}, B_{xy}), where R, G, and B represent intensities of the color components red, green, and blue, respectively. Each color value is an integer between 0 and 255. The PSNR between two images with a single color component is defined as

$$PSNR_C = 10\log_{10}\left(\frac{255^2}{\frac{1}{WH}\sum_{x=1}^{W}\sum_{y=1}^{H}\left\{(C_{xy} - C'_{xy})^2\right\}}\right) \tag{25}$$

where $C = \{R, G, B\}$, and C_{xy} and C'_{xy} denote the pixel value at the location of (x,y) in the images φ and φ' respectively. The PSNR for images with three color components is defined as

$$PSNR = 10\log_{10}\left(\frac{255^2 + 255^2 + 255^2}{\frac{1}{WH}\sum_{x=1}^{W}\sum_{y=1}^{H}\left\{(R_{xy} - R'_{xy})^2 + (G_{xy} - G'_{xy})^2 + (B_{xy} - B'_{xy})^2\right\}}\right). \tag{26}$$

Figure 7. A neural network for image compression problem

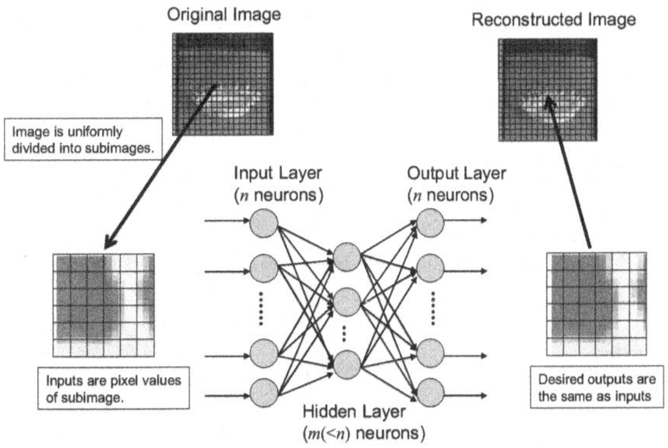

The real-valued network is trained by using the image shown in Fig. 8(a) for 10,000 iterations. The quaternionic network also undergoes training until its TSE becomes less than or equal to that of the trained real-valued network. In this case, the number of training iterations of the quaternionic network is 9,421. The PSNRs for the output images obtained from the real-valued and quaternionic networks, when the training image (Fig. 8(a)) is used as the input, are 26.68 and 26.67 (dB), respectively.

Figures 9(a) and 10(a) show the output images obtained from the trained real-valued and quaternionic networks, respectively, when the test image (Fig. 8(b)) is used as the input. The images that are composed of pixels in only red component from Figs. 9(a) and 10(a) are shown in Figs. 9(b) and 10(b), where the intensity of the pixel becomes stronger, its color becomes black. The images of pixels in only blue and only green components are shown in Figs. 9(c) and 10(c) and Figs. 9(d) and 10(d), respectively. Compared with the test input image from the viewpoint of color composition, it is found that the input test image obtained from the quaternionic network can be constructed more precisely than that from the real-valued network. The image obtained from the real-valued network becomes reddish in color; this could be due to the effect of the training image. The real-valued network is trained so that a lot of colors should be projected onto red. On the other hand, the output image obtained from the quaternionic network captures the correct tone of the image. The PSNRs for the output images obtained from the real-valued and quaternionic networks are 18.04 and 21.99 (dB), respectively. For investigating the detailed reconstruction abilities of these networks, the PSNRs for individual color components are also calculated. The PSNRs for the red component of the images ($PSNR_R$) from the real-valued and quaternionic networks are 20.38 and 21.99 (dB), respectively, which are comparable. However, the PSNR for the blue component of the images from the quaternionic network is 23.01 (dB), which is more than 16.35 (dB) obtained from the real-valued network. A similar result can be obtained by comparing the PSNRs for the green component of the images, (18.30 and 21.16 (dB) obtained from the real-valued and quaternionic networks, respectively). As in the case of the affine transformation, the quaternionic networks can perform correct transformation of the color value represented in three-dimensional space.

Color Night Vision

The application in this section is termed color night vision, and it extracts color information from gloomy images obtained under twilight or night conditions. In this task, the networks have to map the pixel values in the input (gloomy) image to those in the output (bright) image.

Figure 8. Images used for the task of color image compression for training and testing

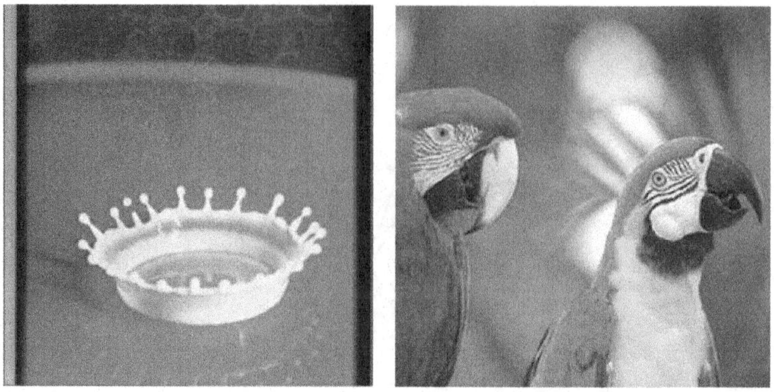

(a) Image for training *(b) Image for testing*

Figure 9. Output images obtained from real-valued network

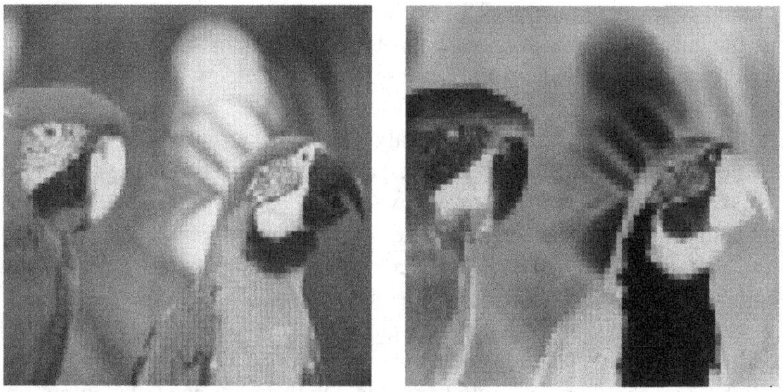

(a) Output image from real-valued NN *(b) Intensities of pixels in red component*

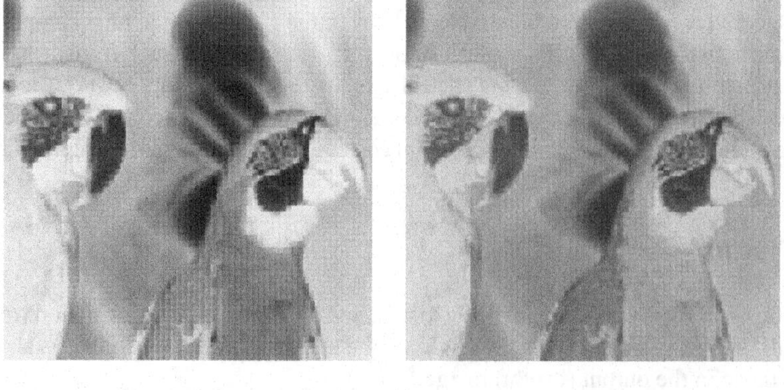

(c) Intensities of pixels in green component *(d) Intensities of pixels in blue component*

Figure 10. Output images obtained from quaternionic network

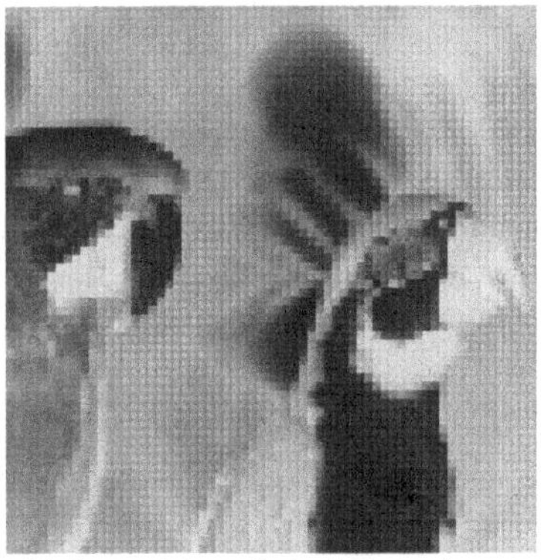

(a) Output image from quaternionic NN (b) Intensities of pixels in red component

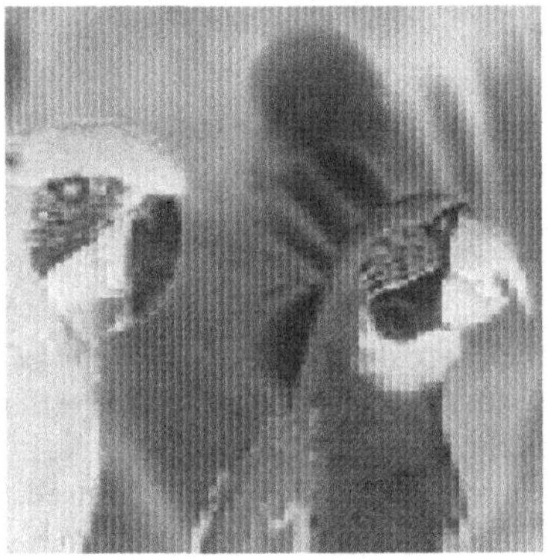

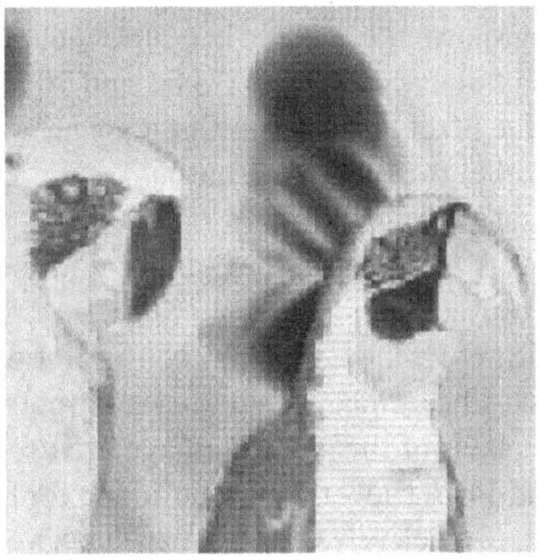

(c) Intensities of pixels in green component (d) Intensities of pixels in blue component

We first introduce the YUV color space model for measuring the images used in this section. The YUV (or YCbCr) color space is one of the color spaces used in image processing (Wharton & Howorth, 1971), which can be transformed from the RGB color space by the following equations:

$$\begin{pmatrix} Y \\ U \\ V \end{pmatrix} = \begin{pmatrix} 0.299 & 0.587 & 0.114 \\ -0.148 & 0.289 & 0.436 \\ 0.615 & 0.515 & 0.100 \end{pmatrix} \begin{pmatrix} R \\ G \\ B \end{pmatrix} \tag{27}$$

where Y is the luminance component and U (or Cb) and V (or Cr) are the chrominance components, i.e., blue-luminance and red-luminance differences, respectively. In the YUV color space model, the U and V components of a pixel represent the color of the pixel and Y represents the brightness of the pixel.

Figure 11 shows an example of a neural network for color night vision. Two images of an identical scene are necessary for training the network. One image is obtained under sufficient illumination, which is used to obtain the desired output, and the other is obtained under low illumination, which is used as the input to the network. An example of a set of images is shown in Figs. 12(a) and 12(b). The image in Fig. 12(a) is taken under sufficient illumination, and the image in Fig. 12(b) is taken at the same scene as in Fig. 12(a) under low illumination.

We introduce two measurements for these images. The first measurement termed chroma distribution indicates the two-dimensional distribution of the colors in the image. The horizontal and vertical axes in the distribution represent the intensity of the U(Cb) and V(Cr) components of the pixel value, respectively. When a pixel value in the image is represented as (y, u, v) in YUV space, a point is plotted at (u, v) in this distribution. The distribution of all the points in the image shows the color diversity in the image. The chroma distributions of the images in Figs. 12(a) and 12(b) are shown in Figs. 13(a) and 13(b), respectively. As the illumination for a scene reduces, the chroma distribution of the image tends to concentrate around (0,0) in the distribution. This is because under low illumination, the color information is eliminated. The task of color night vision corresponds to the estimation of the chroma distribution of the bright image (e.g., Fig. 13(a)) from the image obtained under low illumination (e.g., Fig. 13(b)).

The second measurement is termed the average brightness *ABr*, which is calculated by

$$ABr = \frac{1}{WH}\sum_{x=1}^{W}\sum_{y=1}^{H} Y_{xy} \qquad (28)$$

where Y_{xy} represents the Y value of the pixel at (x,y) and the image has a width of W pixels and a height of H pixels. This quantity shows the average brightness of all the pixels in the image. For example, the *ABr* values for the images in Figs. 12(a) and 12(b) are 113.84 and 30.83, respectively.

For this task, nine pixels of the input images are required to estimate the color value of one pixel. In other words, when the pixel in the estimated (output from the network) image is located at (x,y) in the image, the pixels of the input image at $(x+i,y+j)$, where $(i, j) = \{(-1,-1),(-1,0),(-1,1),(0,-1),(0,0),(0,1),(1,-1),(1,0),(1,1)\}$, are inputted to the network. For the desired output with respect to the input pixel values, the pixel value at (x,y) in the training image is used.

The quaternionic network with a 9-6-1 configuration and the real-valued network with a 27-8-3 configuration are used for this task. The number of iterations for both the training networks is 10,000. After training using the training image, the pixels of the gloomy image are used as the input to the network.

Figures 14(a) and 14(b) show the output image for the image in Fig. 12(b), which is used as the input, and its chroma distribution, respectively. A comparison between the images in Figs. 12(a) and 14(a) shows that the color

Figure 11. A neural network used for color night vision

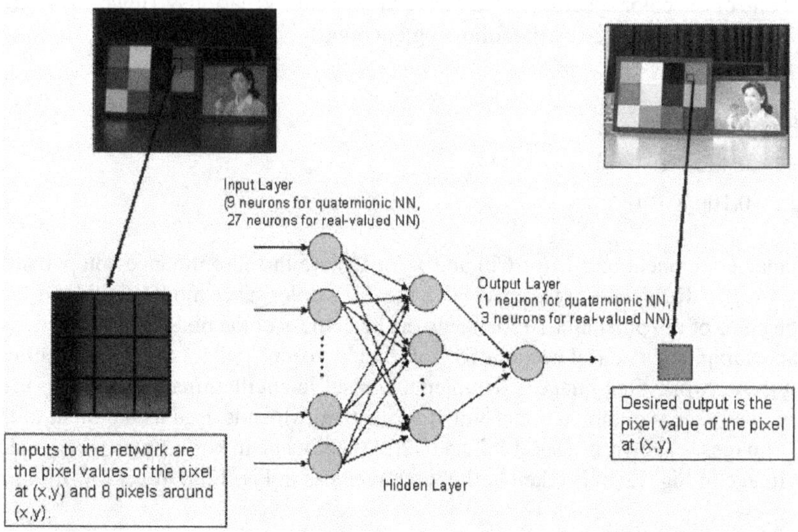

Figure 12. Examples of images used in color night vision obtained under (a) sufficient illumination and (b) low illumination

(a) The image taken under sufficient illumination *(b) The image taken under low illumination*

Figure 13. Chroma distributions of the images shown in Figure 12

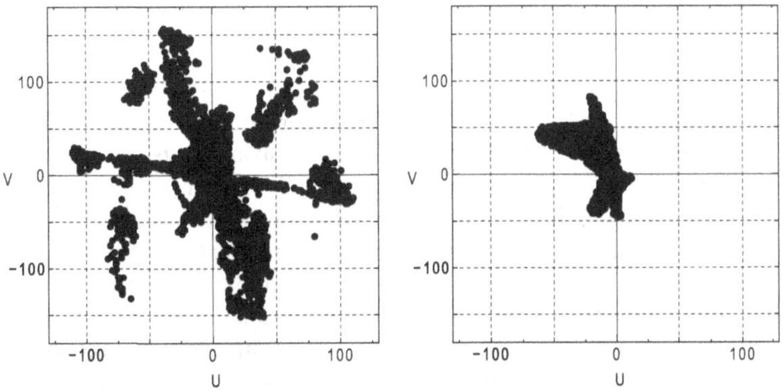

(a) Distribution from the images in Fig.12(a) *(b) Distribution from the images in Fig.12(b)*

Figure 14. Output image and its chroma distribution obtained from the quaternionic network, when the image in Figure 12(b) is used as input

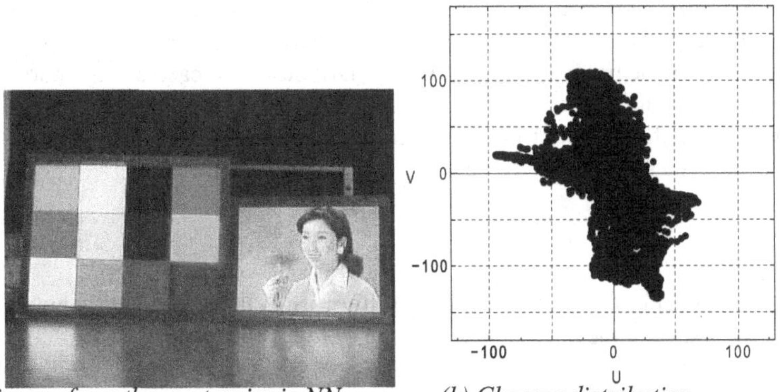

(a) Output image from the quaternionic NN *(b) Chroma distribution*

Figure 15. Output image and its chroma distribution obtained from the real-valued network, when the image in Figure 12(b) is used as input

(a) Output image from the real-valued NN

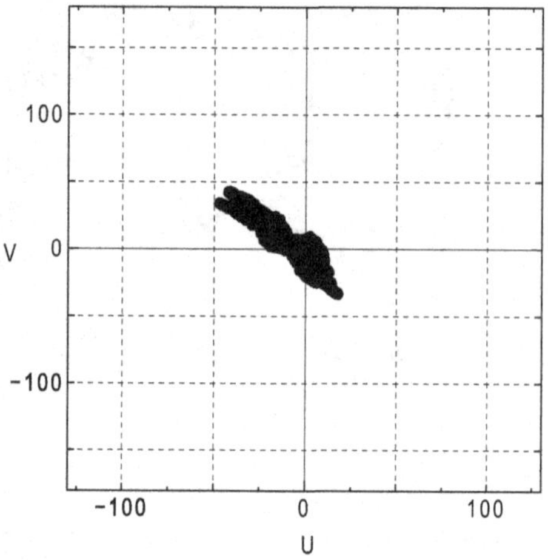

(b) Chroma distribution

information can be reconstructed properly. The average brightness of the output image becomes 95.58. The chroma distribution, shown in Fig. 14(b), becomes similar to the original distribution (see Fig. 13(a)).

Further, the output images and chroma distribution from the real-valued network are shown in Figs. 15(a) and 15(b), respectively, where the average brightness of the image is 106.74. Although the average brightness of the image obtained from the real-valued network is closer to that of the original image than the image obtained from the quaternionic network, the quality of the output image appears to be low. In the chroma distribution of the output image (Fig. 15(b)), the real-valued network can extend the distribution only in a one-dimensional direction, whereas the quaternionic network can extend the distribution in two-dimensional directions. From these results, the quaternionic network that can perform geometrical affine transformation will be useful for applications involving variables in three-dimensional space, such as color values and three-dimensional coordinates.

HOPFIELD-TYPE QUATERNIONIC NEURAL NETWORK

This section describes quaternionic recurrent neural networks typified by the Hopfield model, which are based on (Isokawa, Nishimura, Kamiura & Matsui, 2006, Isokawa, Nishimura, Kamiura & Matsui, 2008). As a previous research for quaternionic recurrent neural networks, the conditions for the existence of the energy function in the Hopfield-type quaternionic neural network have been clarified in the case of continuous values of neuron states and continuous time (Yoshida, Kuroe & Mori, 2005). From the viewpoint of computational applications, it is important to reveal the ability of pattern association in a quaternionic Hopfield neural network in the case of discrete values of neuron states and discrete time.

Neuron Model

The quaternionic neuron model in this section is a straightforward extension of real-valued neuron model. The action potential and output state of the neuron p are defined as follows:

$$s_p = \sum_q w_{pq} \otimes x_q - \theta_p, \quad (29)$$

$$y_p = f(s_p), \quad (30)$$

where $x_q, w_{pq}, \theta_q \in H$ are the input to the neuron q, the connection weight from neuron q to neuron p, and the threshold of the neuron q, respectively. The activation function f determines the output of the neuron, defined as

$$f(s) = f^{(e)}(s^{(e)}) + f^{(i)}(s^{(i)})i + f^{(j)}(s^{(j)})j + f^{(k)}(s^{(k)})k, \quad (31)$$

and use the same step function for each component of the quaternionic function:

$$f^{(e)}(s) = f^{(i)}(s) = f^{(j)}(s) = f^{(k)}(s) = \begin{cases} 1 & \text{for } s \geq 0 \\ -1 & \text{for } s < 0 \end{cases}. \quad (32)$$

Energy Function and Its Stability

The neurons are connected to each other in the network, as in real-valued Hopfield neural network (Hopfield, 1984). We introduce an energy function of the network that consists of N neurons as

$$E = -\frac{1}{2}\sum_{p=1}^{N}\sum_{q=1}^{N} x_p^* \otimes w_{pq} \otimes x_q + \mathrm{Re}\left(\sum_{p=1}^{N} \theta_p^* \otimes x_p\right). \quad (33)$$

E should be a real-valued function and this is always satisfied by the condition for the connection weight, $w_{pq} = w_{qp}^*$.

Then,

$$\begin{aligned} E^* &= -\frac{1}{2}\sum_{p=1}^{N}\sum_{q=1}^{N} x_q^* \otimes w_{pq}^* \otimes x_p + \mathrm{Re}\left(\sum_{p=1}^{N} x_p^* \otimes \theta_p\right) \\ &= -\frac{1}{2}\sum_{p=1}^{N}\sum_{q=1}^{N} x_q^* \otimes w_{qp} \otimes x_p + \mathrm{Re}\left(\sum_{p=1}^{N} \theta_p^* \otimes x_p\right) \\ &= E. \end{aligned} \quad (34)$$

This network allows self-connections and their values take real, $w_{pp} = w_{pp}^* = (w_{pp}^{(e)}, \vec{0})$ and are set to non-negative values, $w_{pp}^{(e)} \geq 0$.

As in the case of the real-valued Hopfield network, the energy E of this network also never increases with time when the state of a neuron changes. Let $E_r(t)$ be the contribution of a given neuron r to the energy E at time t, then it is given as

$$E_r(t) = -\frac{1}{2}\left\{\left(\sum_{p=1}^{N} \boldsymbol{x}_p^*(t) \otimes \boldsymbol{w}_{pr}\right) \otimes \boldsymbol{x}_r(t) + \boldsymbol{x}_r^*(t) \otimes \left(\sum_{q=1}^{N} \boldsymbol{w}_{rq} \otimes \boldsymbol{x}_q(t)\right)\right.$$
$$\left. - \boldsymbol{x}_r^*(t) \otimes \boldsymbol{w}_{rr} \otimes \boldsymbol{x}_r(t)\right\} + \mathrm{Re}\left(\boldsymbol{\theta}_r^* \otimes \boldsymbol{x}_r(t)\right)$$
$$= -\frac{1}{2}\left\{\left(\sum_{p=1}^{N} \boldsymbol{w}_{rp} \otimes \boldsymbol{x}_p(t) - \boldsymbol{\theta}_r\right)^* \otimes \boldsymbol{x}_r(t) + \boldsymbol{x}_r^*(t) \otimes \left(\sum_{q=1}^{N} \boldsymbol{w}_{rq} \otimes \boldsymbol{x}_q(t) - \boldsymbol{\theta}_r\right)\right.$$
$$\left. - \boldsymbol{x}_r^*(t) \otimes \boldsymbol{w}_{rr} \otimes \boldsymbol{x}_r(t)\right\} \tag{35}$$

by taking the definition Eq.(10) into account for the reduction of $\mathrm{Re}\left(\boldsymbol{\theta}_r^* \otimes \boldsymbol{x}_r(t)\right)$. From the update of the states in the neuron r and the relation $\boldsymbol{x}_r^*(t) \otimes \boldsymbol{w}_{rr} \otimes \boldsymbol{x}_r(t) = w_{rr}^{(e)} \cdot \left|\boldsymbol{x}_r(t)\right|^2 = 4w_{rr}^{(e)}$, we obtain

$$E_r(t) = -\mathrm{Re}\left\{\boldsymbol{x}_r^*(t) \otimes \boldsymbol{s}_r(t)\right\} + 2w_{rr}^{(e)}. \tag{36}$$

When the state of the neuron r is updated at time $(t+1)$, its contribution to the energy E changes to

$$E_r(t+1) = -\mathrm{Re}\left\{\boldsymbol{x}_r^*(t+1) \otimes \boldsymbol{s}_r(t+1)\right\} + 2w_{rr}^{(e)}$$
$$= -\mathrm{Re}\left\{\boldsymbol{x}_r^*(t+1) \otimes \left(\boldsymbol{s}_r(t) - \boldsymbol{w}_{rr} \otimes \left(\boldsymbol{x}_r(t) - \boldsymbol{x}_r(t+1)\right)\right)\right\} + 2w_{rr}^{(e)}$$
$$= -\mathrm{Re}\left\{\boldsymbol{x}_r^*(t+1) \otimes \boldsymbol{s}_r(t)\right\} + w_{rr}^{(e)} \cdot \mathrm{Re}\left\{\boldsymbol{x}_r^*(t+1) \otimes \left(\boldsymbol{x}_r(t) - \boldsymbol{x}_r(t+1)\right)\right\} + 2w_{rr}^{(e)} \tag{37}$$

Then, the difference of the energy between time $(t+1)$, and t, ΔE, becomes

$$\Delta E = E_r(t+1) - E_r(t)$$
$$= -\left(\mathrm{Re}\left\{\boldsymbol{x}_r^*(t+1) \otimes \boldsymbol{s}_r(t)\right\} - \mathrm{Re}\left\{\boldsymbol{x}_r^*(t) \otimes \boldsymbol{s}_r(t)\right\}\right)$$
$$+ w_{rr}^{(e)} \cdot \mathrm{Re}\left\{\boldsymbol{x}_r^*(t+1) \otimes \left(\boldsymbol{x}_r(t) - \boldsymbol{x}_r(t+1)\right)\right\}. \tag{38}$$

The activation function $\boldsymbol{f}(\boldsymbol{s})$ can be written as

$$\boldsymbol{f}(\boldsymbol{s}) = \frac{s^{(e)}}{\left|s^{(e)}\right|} + \frac{s^{(i)}}{\left|s^{(i)}\right|}\boldsymbol{i} + \frac{s^{(j)}}{\left|s^{(j)}\right|}\boldsymbol{j} + \frac{s^{(k)}}{\left|s^{(k)}\right|}\boldsymbol{k}, \tag{39}$$

thus the first term of ΔE (Eq.(38)) is reduced as:

$$\mathrm{Re}\left\{\boldsymbol{x}_r^*(t+1) \otimes \boldsymbol{s}_r(t)\right\}$$
$$= \mathrm{Re}\left\{\left(\boldsymbol{f}(\boldsymbol{s}_r(t))\right)^* \otimes \boldsymbol{s}_r(t)\right\}$$
$$= \mathrm{Re}\left\{\left(\frac{s_r^{(e)}(t)}{\left|s_r^{(e)}(t)\right|} + \frac{s_r^{(i)}(t)}{\left|s_r^{(i)}(t)\right|}\boldsymbol{i} + \frac{s_r^{(j)}(t)}{\left|s_r^{(j)}(t)\right|}\boldsymbol{j} + \frac{s_r^{(k)}(t)}{\left|s_r^{(k)}(t)\right|}\boldsymbol{k}\right)^* \otimes \boldsymbol{s}_r(t)\right\}$$
$$= \sum_{\alpha=\{e,i,j,k\}} \left|s_r^{(\alpha)}\right|. \tag{40}$$

The following relation holds

$$\sum_{\alpha=\{e,i,j,k\}} \left| s_r^{(\alpha)} \right| \geq \sum_{\alpha=\{e,i,j,k\}} s_r^{(\alpha)}(t) \cdot x_r^{(\alpha)}(t)$$
$$= \mathrm{Re}\left\{ \boldsymbol{x}_r^*(t) \otimes \boldsymbol{s}_r(t) \right\} \qquad (41)$$

in the case that $x^{\{(e),(i),(j),(k)\}} \in \{1,-1\}$. Furthermore, the second term of Eq.(38) holds the following relation:

$$\mathrm{Re}\left\{ \boldsymbol{x}_r^*(t+1) \otimes \left(\boldsymbol{x}_r(t) - \boldsymbol{x}_r(t+1) \right) \right\} = \sum_{\alpha=\{e,i,j,k\}} x_r^{(\alpha)}(t+1) \cdot \left(x_r^{(\alpha)}(t) - x_r^{(\alpha)}(t+1) \right)$$
$$\leq 0, \qquad (42)$$

in all the updated cases of $\left(x_r^{(\alpha)}(t), x_r^{(\alpha)}(t+1) \right) = (\pm 1, \pm 1), (\pm 1, \mp 1)$. By considering $w_{rr} \geq 0$ and the abovementioned relations (Eqs.(41) and (42)), it is shown that the energy never increases, i.e., $\Delta E \leq 0$.

Hebbian Rule

We introduce a quaternion equivalent of Hebbian rule for embedding patterns to the network. The Hebbian rule is defined as

$$\boldsymbol{w}_{pq} = \frac{1}{4N} \sum_{\mu=1}^{n_p} \boldsymbol{\xi}_{\mu,p} \otimes \boldsymbol{\xi}_{\mu,q}^* \qquad (43)$$

where $\boldsymbol{\xi}_{\mu,p} = \left(\xi_{\mu,p}^{(e)}, \xi_{\mu,p}^{(i)}, \xi_{\mu,p}^{(j)}, \xi_{\mu,p}^{(k)} \right)$ $\left(\xi_{\mu,p}^{\{(e),(i),(j),(k)\}} \in \{1,-1\} \right)$ represents the pattern vector for neuron p in the μ-th pattern and n_p is the number of patterns to be stored. The norm of $\boldsymbol{w}_{pq}$ is normalized by the number of neurons and $|\boldsymbol{\xi}|^2 = 4$. This form satisfies the conditions $\boldsymbol{w}_{pq} = \boldsymbol{w}_{qp}^*$ and $w_{pp} \geq 0$:

$$\boldsymbol{w}_{qp}^* = \frac{1}{4N} \sum_{\mu=1}^{n_p} \left(\boldsymbol{\xi}_{\mu,q} \otimes \boldsymbol{\xi}_{\mu,p}^* \right)^*$$
$$= \frac{1}{4N} \sum_{\mu=1}^{n_p} \boldsymbol{\xi}_{\mu,p} \otimes \boldsymbol{\xi}_{\mu,q}^*$$
$$= \boldsymbol{w}_{pq}, \qquad (44)$$

and

$$\boldsymbol{w}_{pp} = \frac{1}{4N} \sum_{\mu=1}^{n_p} \boldsymbol{\xi}_{\mu,p} \otimes \boldsymbol{\xi}_{\mu,p}^*$$
$$= \frac{1}{4N} \sum_{\mu=1}^{n_p} \left| \boldsymbol{\xi}_{\mu,p} \right|^2 = \frac{n_p}{N} > 0. \qquad (45)$$

Under the weight matrix defined by the hebbian rule, each of $\boldsymbol{\xi}_\mu$ is a fixed point when orthogonality among the patterns $\boldsymbol{\xi}_\mu$ is satisfied, i.e., for $\mu, \nu = 1, \cdots, n_p$,

$$\sum_{q=1}^{N} \boldsymbol{\xi}_{\mu,q}^* \otimes \boldsymbol{\xi}_{\nu,q} = 4N\delta_{\mu,\nu} = 4N(\delta_{\mu,\nu}^{(e)}, \vec{0}), \qquad (46)$$

where $\delta^{(e)}_{\mu\nu}$ designates the Kronecker delta. It can be checked by applying one of stored pattern ξ_μ as the input to the network. The action potential of the neuron p, s_p, is calculated as,

$$\begin{aligned}
s_p &= \sum_{q=1}^{N} w_{pq} \otimes \xi_{\nu,q} \\
&= \frac{1}{4N}\sum_{q=1}^{N}\left(\sum_{\mu=1}^{n_p} \xi_{\mu,p} \otimes \xi^*_{\mu,q}\right) \otimes \xi_{\nu,q} \\
&= \frac{1}{4N}\sum_{\mu=1}^{n_p} \xi_{\mu,p} \otimes \sum_{q=1}^{N} \xi^*_{\mu,q} \otimes \xi_{\nu,q} \\
&= \frac{1}{4N}\sum_{\mu=1}^{n_p} \xi_{\mu,p} \otimes 4N\delta_{\mu,\nu} \\
&= \xi_{\nu,p}
\end{aligned} \tag{47}$$

The output of this neuron is obtained by applying the activation function,

$$x_p = f(s_p) = f(\xi_{\nu,p}) = \xi_{\nu,p}. \tag{48}$$

Equivalence Property for Rotational Operations

The proposed quaternionic network is invariant under rotational operations, i.e., the property of the network never changes when the vector parts of neuron states and connection weights are rotated around a unique vector. Let $u = \cos\alpha + \vec{R}\sin\alpha$ be a quaternion as a rotational operator where rotation is conducted around the $\vec{R}$ and $|\vec{R}| = 1$ is satisfied. The stored pattern $\tilde{\xi}_p$ rotated from $\xi_p = (\xi_p^{(e)}, \vec{\xi}_p)$ is written as:

$$\begin{aligned}
\tilde{\xi}_p &= u^* \otimes \xi_p \otimes u \\
&= \left(\xi_p^{(e)}, \vec{\xi}_p \cos 2\alpha + \left(\vec{R} \times \vec{\xi}_p\right)\sin 2\alpha + \vec{R}\left(\vec{R}\cdot\vec{\xi}_p\right)\left(1-\cos 2\alpha\right)\right)
\end{aligned} \tag{49}$$

The connection weights $\tilde{w}_{pq}$ are calculated from the $\tilde{\xi}_p$ by Hebbian rule, i.e.,

$$\begin{aligned}
\tilde{w}_{pq} &= \frac{1}{4N}\sum_{\mu=1}^{n_p} \tilde{\xi}_{\mu,p} \otimes \tilde{\xi}^*_{\mu,q} \\
&= \frac{1}{4N}\sum_{\mu=1}^{n_p} u^* \otimes \xi_{\mu,p} \otimes \xi^*_{\mu,q} \otimes u \\
&= u^* \otimes w_{pq} \otimes u.
\end{aligned} \tag{50}$$

Note that $u^* \otimes u = |u|^2 = 1$. This indicates that the connection weights of the rotated stored patterns are identical with the rotated connection weights of the original stored pattern.

The action potential of the neuron in the rotated space, $\tilde{s}_p$, can be written in similar way to the connection weights, i.e.,

$$\begin{aligned}
\tilde{s}_p &= \sum_q \tilde{w}_{pq} \otimes \tilde{x}_q - \tilde{\theta}_p \\
&= \sum_q \left(u^* \otimes w_{pq} \otimes u\right) \otimes \left(u^* \otimes x_q \otimes u\right) - \left(u^* \otimes \theta_p \otimes u\right) \\
&= \sum_q u^* \otimes w_{pq} \otimes x_q \otimes u - \left(u^* \otimes \theta_p \otimes u\right) \\
&= u^* \otimes \left(\sum_q w_{pq} \otimes x_q - \theta_p\right) \otimes u \\
&= u^* \otimes s_p \otimes u
\end{aligned} \tag{51}$$

where $\tilde{x}_p$ and $\tilde{\theta}_p$ are the output and the threshold of the p-th neuron in the rotated space, respectively. The same property as in the connection weights holds in the action potential of the rotated space. As the real-part of a quaternion does not change in applying rotational operation, the real-parts in the outputs of the neurons are invariant in any rotated space.

The energy function in the rotated space, $\tilde{E}$, can be written as:

$$\begin{aligned}
\tilde{E} &= -\frac{1}{2}\sum_{p=1}^{N}\sum_{q=1}^{N} \tilde{x}_p^* \otimes \tilde{w}_{pq} \otimes \tilde{x}_q \\
&= -\frac{1}{2}\sum_{p=1}^{N}\sum_{q=1}^{N} \left(u^* \otimes x_p \otimes u\right)^* \otimes \left(u^* \otimes w_{pq} \otimes u\right) \otimes \left(u^* \otimes x_q \otimes u\right) \\
&= -\frac{1}{2}\sum_{p=1}^{N}\sum_{q=1}^{N} u^* \otimes x_p^* \otimes u \otimes u^* \otimes w_{pq} \otimes u \otimes u^* \otimes x_q \otimes u \\
&= u^* \otimes \left(\frac{1}{2}\sum_{p=1}^{N}\sum_{q=1}^{N} x_p^* \otimes w_{pq} \otimes x_q\right) \otimes u \\
&= u^* \otimes E \otimes u \\
&= E.
\end{aligned} \tag{52}$$

The real part of quaternion never changes by the rotational operators, so the second term of the energy function cannot be considered. This equation means that the energy of a system is invariant in any rotated space.

An Example of the Network with Three Neurons

We consider the network that consists of three neurons and one pattern $n_p = 1$ is to be stored in. The pattern to be stored, $\xi_1 = \{\xi_{1,1}, \xi_{1,2}, \xi_{1,3}\}$, is as follows:

$$\begin{aligned}
\xi_{1,1} &= \xi_{1,1}^{(e)} + \xi_{1,1}^{(i)} i + \xi_{1,1}^{(j)} j + \xi_{1,1}^{(k)} k \\
&= (\ 1,\ \ 1, -1,\ \ 1),
\end{aligned} \tag{53}$$

$$\xi_{1,2} = (-1,\ \ 1, -1, -1), \tag{54}$$

$$\xi_{1,3} = (\ 1,\ \ 1,\ \ 1, -1). \tag{55}$$

The connection weight matrix $\boldsymbol{W} = \{\boldsymbol{w}_{pq}\}$ obtained by the hebbian rule is

$$\boldsymbol{W} = \frac{1}{3}\begin{pmatrix} 1 & -\boldsymbol{i} & -\boldsymbol{j} \\ \boldsymbol{i} & 1 & -\boldsymbol{k} \\ \boldsymbol{j} & \boldsymbol{k} & 1 \end{pmatrix}. \tag{56}$$

The stored pattern $\boldsymbol{\xi}_1$ is a fixed point for $\boldsymbol{W}$.

Left hand side of Table 1 shows a list of fixed points in the network with the above weight matrix. The pattern with $\mu = 1$, i.e. $\xi_1 = \{\xi_{1,1}, \xi_{1,2}, \xi_{1,3}\}$, in this table corresponds to the stored pattern itself. The patterns ξ_μ with $\mu = 9, \cdots, 16$ are respectively the same as quaternionic component-wise inverted ones with $\mu = 1, ..., 8$. Energy with respect to these fixed points is all -6. The same weight matrix as the above matrix can also be obtained from any pattern in this table, so they seem to form a quaternionic degenerated state.

These degenerated states can be explained by introducing a quaternionic parameter $\boldsymbol{a}_\mu$ of which norm is 1, i.e., $|\boldsymbol{a}_\mu| = 1$. Let $\boldsymbol{\xi}_\mu = \{\xi_{\mu,1}, \cdots, \boldsymbol{\xi}_{\mu,N}\}$ be the μ-th stored pattern and $\boldsymbol{w}_{pq}$ be a connection weight between the p-th neuron and the q-th neuron calculated from the pattern $\boldsymbol{\xi}_\mu$. From the pattern $\boldsymbol{\xi}'_\mu = \{\boldsymbol{\xi}_{\mu,1} \otimes \boldsymbol{a}_\mu, \cdots, \boldsymbol{\xi}_{\mu,N} \otimes \boldsymbol{a}_\mu\}$, the connection weight $\boldsymbol{w}'_{pq}$ can be calculated by Hebbian rule as follows:

$$\begin{aligned} \boldsymbol{w}'_{pq} &= \frac{1}{4N}\sum_{\mu=1}^{n_p} \boldsymbol{\xi}'_{\mu,p} \otimes \boldsymbol{\xi}'^{*}_{\mu,q} \\ &= \frac{1}{4N}\sum_{\mu=1}^{n_p} \boldsymbol{\xi}_{\mu,p} \otimes \boldsymbol{a}_\mu \otimes \boldsymbol{a}^{*}_\mu \otimes \boldsymbol{\xi}^{*}_{\mu,q} \\ &= \frac{1}{4N}\sum_{\mu=1}^{n_p} \boldsymbol{\xi}_{\mu,p} \otimes \boldsymbol{\xi}^{*}_{\mu,q} \\ &= \boldsymbol{w}_{pq}. \end{aligned} \tag{57}$$

Table 1. The degenerate fixed points in the network with $\boldsymbol{W}$ *and the corresponding* $\boldsymbol{a}_\mu$ *for retrieving* ζ_1

μ	$\xi_{\mu,1}$	$\xi_{\mu,2}$	$\xi_{\mu,3}$	$\boldsymbol{a}_\mu$
1	(1,1,-1,1)	(-1,1,-1,-1)	(1,1,1,-1)	(1,0,0,0)
2	(-1,1,1,-1)	(-1,-1,1,1)	(-1,-1,-1,-1)	1/2·(-1,1,1,-1)
3	(-1,1,-1,-1)	(-1,-1,1,-1)	(1,-1,-1,-1)	(0,0,1,0)
4	(-1,1,1,1)	(-1,-1,-1,1)	(-1,1,-1,-1)	(0,-1,0,0)
5	(-1,1,-1,1)	(-1,-1,-1,-1)	(1,1,-1,-1)	1/2·(1,-1,1,-1)
6	(1,1,1,-1)	(-1,1,1,1)	(-1,-1,1,-1)	(0,0,0,1)
7	(1,1,-1,-1)	(-1,1,1,-1)	(1,-1,1,-1)	1/2·(1,1,1,1)
8	(1,1,1,1)	(-1,1,-1,1)	(-1,1,1,-1)	1/2·(1,-1,-1,1)
9	(-1,-1,1,-1)	(1,-1,1,1)	(-1,-1,-1,1)	(-1,0,0,0)
10	(-1,-1,-1,-1)	(1,-1,1,-1)	(1,-1,-1,1)	1/2·(-1,1,1,-1)
11	(-1,-1,1,1)	(1,-1,-1,1)	(-1,1,-1,1)	1/2·(-1,-1,-1,-1)
12	(-1,-1,-1,1)	(1,-1,-1,-1)	(1,1,-1,1)	(0,0,0,-1)
13	(1,-1,1,-1)	(1,1,1,1)	(-1,-1,1,1)	1/2·(-1,1,-1,1)
14	(1,-1,-1,-1)	(1,1,1,-1)	(1,-1,1,1)	(0,1,0,0)
15	(1,-1,1,1)	(1,1,-1,1)	(-1,1,1,1)	(0,0,-1,0)
16	(1,-1,-1,1)	(1,1,-1,-1)	(1,1,1,1)	1/2·(1,1,-1,-1)

Note that $\boldsymbol{a}_\mu \otimes \boldsymbol{a}_\mu^* = |\boldsymbol{a}_\mu|^2 = 1$. This relation shows that the patterns $\xi_\mu \otimes \boldsymbol{a}_\mu$ are also stored in the network when we embed the pattern ξ_μ into the network. The parameter $\boldsymbol{a}_\mu$ can be any quaternion in the condition of $|\boldsymbol{a}_\mu| = 1$, but the quaternionic component of a stored pattern takes bipolar values, i.e. either +1 or −1, hence the number of components in a set $\{\boldsymbol{a}_\mu\}$ is at most 16. This number reflects the number of the degenerated patterns in the network when one stored pattern is embedded. Henceforth we call a set of these patterns 'multiplet'. In this network $\{\xi_1, \cdots, \xi_{16}\}$ forms a multiplet. A component in a multiplet, ξ_μ, can be transformed into another component in the same multiplet, ξ_ν ($\nu \neq \mu$), by multiplying a certain $\boldsymbol{a}_\mu$ ($\boldsymbol{a}_\mu$-transformation). For example, ξ_5 can be obtained from ξ_1 by $\boldsymbol{a}_\mu$-transformation with $\boldsymbol{a}_\mu = \frac{1}{2}(1,1,-1,1)$. The values of $\boldsymbol{a}_\mu$ for obtaining ξ_1 are also shown in right hand side of Table 1.

We further check whether each of components in the multiplet is an attractor by measuring the performances for retrieving $\boldsymbol{a}_\mu$ when test patterns are input to the network as an initial state. Here, we introduce a measure of the distance between two patterns. Let ξ_μ and ξ_ν be the patterns that consist of N neurons, and each component in them takes bipolar values, i.e., $\xi_{\mu,p}^{\{(e),(i),(j),(k)\}} \in \{1,-1\}$ $(p = 1, \cdots, N)$. The distance between ξ_μ and ξ_ν, $d(\xi_\mu, \xi_\nu)$ is defined as

$$d(\xi_\mu, \xi_\nu) = \frac{1}{2}\sum_{p=1}^{N} \sum_{\alpha=\{e,i,j,k\}} \left(1 - \xi_{\mu,p}^{(\alpha)} \cdot \xi_{\nu,p}^{(\alpha)}\right) \tag{58}$$

This indicates the extended Hamming distance for quaternion, thus $d(\xi_\mu, \xi_\nu) = 0$.

We prepare 4080(=4096−16) input patterns for each component in the multiplet (The number 4096 is the number of states in the network of 3 neurons and the number 16 is the number of components in the multiplet). For each of multiplet components, the distances with respect to the input patterns are calculated. We categorize the output patterns from the network into two patterns: (a) the output pattern is the same as the multiplet component itself and (b) the output pattern is not the multiplet component itself. In this network there are only global minima, so the output pattern that is not the multiplet component means one of other multiplet components. Table 2 shows the recalled pattern rate with respect to the distances of input patterns. In this table, 'Same component' and 'Different component' represent the rate of output patterns being the multiplet component and the rate that the output pattern is not the multiplet component, respectively. From this table, we see that this network can always retrieve the multiplet component from the patterns with the distance 1 from the multiplet component.

CONCLUSION

In this chapter, we have described two types of neural networks based on quaternions. One is a multilayer perception-type neural network in which the operations are 3D geometrical affine transformations. In this model, data representation at the input and output of the quaternionic neurons is restricted to three dimensions. The performance of this network has been demonstrated through examples of a three-bit parity check problem, affine transformations in three-dimensional space, color image compression by neural networks, and color night vision. It is found that the quaternionic networks can process the color and body information more efficiently than the real-valued networks. This is because the quaternionic networks can carry out the operations of spatial rotation, while real-valued networks can hardly carry out such operations. The other type is a Hopfield-type recurrent network in which the direct encoding of quaternions is applied to the representation of information on neuron states. The energy function of this network is formulated and the monotonic decrease of the energy is proved. The quaternionic equivalent of the Hebbian rule is introduced for embedding patterns in the network. The fundamental properties are explored on the basis of the small size of the networks, and it is found that a set of stable patterns appears in the network when a pattern is embedded in the network, which is termed "multiplet." It is shown that a stable pattern in a multiplet can be transformed into another pattern in the same multiplet.

Table 2. The rate of recalled patterns with respect to the distance of input patterns

Distance from the stored pattern	Number of the retrieved pattern to be same component	Number of the retrieved patterns to be different component	Rate of the retrieved pattern to be same component (%)	Rate of the retrieved pattern to be different component (%)
1	192	0	100.00	0.00
2	864	192	81.82	18.18
3	1728	1792	49.09	50.91
4	1296	6624	16.36	83.64
5	0	12672	0.00	100.00
6	0	14784	0.00	100.00
7	0	12672	0.00	100.00
8	0	7920	0.00	100.00
9	0	3520	0.00	100.00
10	0	1056	0.00	100.00
11	0	192	0.00	100.00
12	0	16	0.00	100.00

FUTURE RESEARCH DIRECTIONS

Multilayer perceptron-type quaternionic networks can be implemented in hardware, e.g., Field Programmable Gate Array (FPGA) with a Digital Signal Processing (DSP) algorithm; however, it has been found that the real-time processing of images obtained from frame grabbers is difficult due to a number of operations required for quaternionic neurons. Thus, reducing the number of operations concerning quaternions should be necessary for applying the quaternionic networks to the engineering problems. This problem could be overcome by introducing a more efficient algebra for the operations of quaternionic neurons, e.g., Max-Plus algebra (Baccelli, Cohen, Olsder & Quadrat, 1992) (Cohen, Gaubert & Quadrat, 1999). The comparisons of direct encoding type of quaternionic networks and 3D affine geometrical transformation based quaternionic networks have not been explored yet, from the viewpoints of computational performance and of theoretical analysis. Investigation of the approximation capabilities of the layered neural networks described in this chapter also remains as a future work.

In the Hopfield-type quaternionic network model, it is necessary to apply engineering problems such as associative memory for color images and three-dimensional pattern recognition and to investigate the properties of the networks with a large number of neurons. The properties of the quaternionic Hopfield networks with 3D geometrical affine operators, as shown in multilayer perceptron model in this chapter, have not been investigated yet.

Exploring the application of quaternions to other types of neural networks such as self-organizing maps is a challenging problem. There exist other types of hypercomplex number, such as octonion (eight dimensional extension) and sedenion (16 dimensional extension). The applications of these number systems to neural networks have been investigated yet, but neural networks based on Clifford algebra (Porteous, 1995) (Lounesto, 2001), that is a generalization of the complex numbers and quaternions, have possibilities to provide more efficient information processing when the data has many dimensions, although the applications of higher dimensional algebra to neural networks tend to be difficult as seen in, for example, choosing a proper activation function of a neuron (Pearson & Bisset, 1992) (Bayro-Corrochano & Buchholtz, 1997) (Bayro-Corrochano, 2001a) (Bayro-Corrochano, 2001b).

ACKNOWLEDGMENT

The contribution for this chapter is based on the studies in (Isokawa, Kusakabe, Matsui, & Peper, 2003) (Isokawa, Nishimura, Kamiura, & Matsui, 2006) (Matsui, Isokawa, Kusamichi, Peper, Nishimura, 2004) (Kusamichi, Isokawa, Matsui, Ogawa, & Maeda, 2004) (Isokawa, Nishimura, Kamiura & Matsui, 2008). Part of this research is supported by Grant-in-Aid for Scientific Research (B-19700221) Japan Society for the Promotion of Science.

REFERENCES

Arena, P., Caponetto, R., Fortuna, L., Muscato, G., & Xibilia, M. G. (1996). Quaternionic Multilayer Perceptrons for Chaotic Time Series Prediction. *IEICE Transactionon Fundamentals of Electronics, Communications and Computer Sciences, E79-A*(10), (pp. 1682–1688).

Arena, P., Fortuna, L., Muscato, G., & Xibilia, M. G. (1997). Multilayer Perceptrons To Approximate Quaternion Valued Functions. *Neural Networks, 10*(2), 335–342.

Arena, P., Fortuna, L., Muscato, G., & Xibilia, M. G. (1998). *Neural Networks in Multidimensional Domains,* (Lecture Notes in Control and Information Sciences Vol. 234). Berlin: Springer-Verlag.

Baccelli, F. L., Cohen, G., Olsder, G. J., & Quadrat, J. P. (1992). *Synchronization and Linearity.* New York: John Wiley & Sons.

Bayro-Corrochano, E., & Buchholtz, S. (1997). *Geometric neural networks. In International Workshop on Algebraic Frames for the Perception-Action Cycle,* (Lecture Notes in Computer Science, 1315, 379–394.)

Bayro-Corrochano, E. (2001a). Geometric Neural Computing. *IEEE Transaction on Neural Networks, 12*(5), 968–986.

Bayro-Corrochano, E. (2001b). *Geometric Computing for Perception Action Systems: Concepts, Algorithms, and Scientific Applications.* Boston: Springer-Verlag.

Bell, E. T. (1999). *Men of Mathematics.* (pp. 360–361). Bt Bound.

Buchholz, S., & Sommer, G. (2000). Quaternionic spinor MLP. In *8th European symposium on artificial neural networks* (ESANN2000) (pp. 377–382).

Bülow, T., & Sommer, G. (2001). Hypercomplex Signals: A Novel Extension of the Analytic Signal to the Multidimensional Case. *IEEE Transaction on Signal Processing, 49*(11), 2844–2852.

Cohen, G., Gaubert, S., & Quadrat J.P. (1999). Max-plus algebra and system theory: Where we are and where to go now. *Annual Reviews in Control, 23,* 207–219.

Cottrell, G. W., Munro, P., & Zipser, D. (1987). *Image compression by back propagation: An example of extensional propagation* (Tech. Rep. No. ICS8702). University of California, San Diego.

Graves, R. P. (1975). *Life of Sir William Rowan Hamilton,* 2, 434–435. New York: Arno Press.

Hankins, T. L. (1980). *Sir William Rowan Hamilton.* Baltimore and London: Johns Hopkins University Press.

Hirose, A. (Ed.). (2003). *Complex-Valued Neural Networks: Theories and Applications.* World Scientific Publishing.

Hoggar, S. G. (1992). *Mathematics for Computer Graphics.* Cambridge: Cambridge University Press.

Hopfield, J. J. (1984). Neural networks and physical systems with emergent collective computational abilities. In *Proceedings of the National Academy of Sciences USA, 79*(8), 2554–2558.

Isokawa, T., Kusakabe, T., Matsui, N., & Peper, F. (2003). Quaternion neural network and its application. In V. Palade, R. J. Howlett, & L. C. Jain (Eds.), *Proceedings of knowledge-based intelligent information engineering systems (KES2003), Lecture Notes in Artificial Intelligence,* 2774, 318–324. Springer-Verlag.

Isokawa, T., Nishimura, H., Kamiura, N., & Matsui, N. (2006). Fundamental Properties of Quaternionic Hopfield Neural Network. In *Proceedings of 2006 international joint conference on neural networks* (pp. 610–615).

Isokawa, T., Nishimura, H., Kamiura, N., & Matsui, N. (2007). Dynamics of Discrete-Time Quaternionic Hopfield Neural Networks. In *Proceedings of 17th International Conference on Artificial Neural Networks (ICANN2007): Part I.* (pp. 848–857).

Isokawa, T., Nishimura, H., Kamiura, N., & Matsui, N. (2008). Associative Memory in Quaternionic Hopfield Neural Network. *International Journal of Neural Systems, 18*(2), 135–145.

Kuipers, J. B. (1998). *Quaternions and Rotation Sequences: A Primer with Applications to Orbits, Aerospace and Virtual Reality.* Princeton: Princeton University Press.

Kusamichi, H., Isokawa, T., Matsui, N., Ogawa, Y., & Maeda, K. (2004). A New Scheme for Color Night Vision by Quaternion Neural Network. In *Proceedings of the 2nd international conference on autonomous robots and agents* (ICARA2004) (pp. 101–106).

Lambek, J. (1995). If Hamilton Had Prevailed: Quaternions in Physics. *The Mathematical Intelligencer, 17,* 7–15.

Lounesto, P. (2001). *Clifford algebras and spinors.* Cambridge: Cambridge University Press.

Matsui, N., Isokawa, T., Kusamichi, H., Peper, F., & Nishimura, H. (2004). Quaternion Neural Network with Geometrical Operators. *Journal of Intelligent & Fuzzy Systems, 15*(3–4), 149–164.

Mukundan, R. (2002). Quaternions: From Classical Mechanics to Computer Graphics, and Beyond. In *Proceedings of the 7th asian technology conference in mathematics* (pp. 97–105).

Nitta, T., & Furuya, T. (1991). A Complex Back-propagation Learning. *Transactions of Information Processing Society of Japan, 32*(10), 1319–1329 (in Japanese).

Nitta, T. (1994). Ability of the 3D Vector Version of the Back-Propagation to Learn 3D Motion. In *Proceedings of INNS World Congress on Neural Networks* (WCNN'94-SanDiego), 3, 262–267.

Nitta, T. (1995). A Quaternary Version of the Back-propagation Algorithm. In *Proceedings of IEEE international conference on neural networks* (ICNN'95-Perth) 5, 2753–2756.

Nitta, T. (1996). An Extension of the Back-propagation Algorithm to Quaternions. In *Proceedings of international conference on neural information processing* (ICONIP'96), 1, 247–250.

Nitta, T. (1997). An Extension of the Back-Propagation Algorithm to Complex Numbers. *Neural Networks, 10*(8), 1391–1415.

Nitta, T. (2004). A Solution to the 4-bit Parity Problem with a Single Quaternary Neuron. *Neural Information Processing - Letters and Reviews* 5(2), 33–39.

Nitta, T. (2006). Three-Dimensional Vector Valued Neural Network and its Generalization Ability, *Neural Information Processing – Letters and Reviews, 10*(10), 237–242.

Pearson, J. K., & Bisset, D. L. (1992). Back Propagation in a Clifford Algebra. In *Proceedings of International Conference on Artificial Neural Networks*, 2, 413–416.

Porteous, lan R. (1995). *Clifford algebras and the classical groups.* Cambridge: Cambridge University Press.

Previn, E., & Webb J. A. (1983). Quaternions in Computer Vision and Robotics. In *Proceedings of International Conference on Computer Vision and Pattern Recognition* (pp. 382-383).

Rao, V. S. H., Nitta, T., & Murthy, G. R. (Eds.) (2008). Special Issue on Complex Valued Neural Networks. *International Journal of Neural Systems, 18*(2), 67–184.

Sahu, S., Biswall, B. B., & Subudhi, B. (2008). A Novel Method for Representing Robot Kinematics using Quaternion Theory. In *Proceedings of IEEE Sponsored Conference on Computational Intelligence, Control and Computer Vision in Robotics and Automation* (pp. 76–82).

Wharton, W., & Howorth, D. (1971). *Principles of Television Reception* (pp. 161–163). Pitman Publishing.

Yoshida, M., Kuroe, Y., & Mori, T. (2005). Models of hopfield-type quaternion neural networks and their energy functions. *International Journal of Neural Systems, 15*(1–2), 129–135.

ADDITIONAL READING

Introduction of Quaternionic and Clifford Algebra:

Bayro-Corrochano, E. (2001a). Geometric Neural Computing. *IEEE Transaction on Neural Networks, 12*(5), 968–986.

Hanson, A. J. (2006). *Visualizing Quaternions (The Morgan Kaufmann Series in Interactive 3D Technology).* Morgan Kaufmann.

Hoggar, S. G. (1992). *Mathematics for Computer Graphics.* Cambridge: Cambridge University Press.

Gürlebeck, K., & Sprössiq, W. (1998). *Quaternionic and Clifford Calculus for Physicists and Engineers.* John Wiley & Sons.

Kuipers, J. B. (1998). *Quaternions and Rotation Sequences: A Primer with Applications to Orbits, Aerospace and Virtual Reality.* Princeton: Princeton University Press.

Sommer, G. (Ed.) (2000). *Geometric Computing with Clifford Algebra.* Berlin: Springer.

Neural Networks with Hypercomplex Number Systems:

Arena, P., Fortuna, L., Muscato, G., & Xibilia, M. G. (1998). *Neural Networks in Multidimensional Domains* (Lecture Notes in Computer Sciences Vol. 234). Springer-Verlag.

Buchholz, S., & Sommer, G. (2001). Introduction to Neural Computation in Clifford Algebra. In G. Sommer (Ed.), *Geometric Computing with Clifford Algebras* (pp. 291-314). Springer-Verlag.

Buchholz, S., & Sommer, G. (2001). Clifford Algebra Multilayer Perceptrons. In G. Sommer (Ed.), *Geometric Computing with Clifford Algebras* (pp. 315-334). Springer-Verlag.

Pearson, J. (2003). Clifford Networks. In A. Hirose (Ed.), *Complex-Valued Neural Networks: Theories and Applications* (pp. 81-106). World Scientific.

For other quaternionic neural network models, see REFERENCE section.

Compilation of References

Abbot, L. F. (1990). A network of oscillators. *J. Phys. A, 23*, 3835-3859.

Åberg, J., Kult, D., & Sjöqvist, E. (2005). Robustness of the adiabatic quantum search. *Phys. Rev. A, 71*(6), 060312.

Abramian, A. K., & Vakulenko, S. A. (2002). Dissipative and Hamiltonian systems with chaotic behaviour: an analytical approach. *Theoretical and Mathematical Physics, 130*(2), 244-254.

Acir, N., Oztura, I., Kuntalp, M., Baklan, B., & Guzelis, C. (2005). Automatic detection of epileptiform events in EEG by a three-stage procedure based on artificial neural networks. *IEEE Trans. Biomedical Engineering*, (1), 30–40.

Ackley, D. H., Hinton, G. E., & Sejnowski, T. J. (1985). A Learning Algorithm for Boltzmann Machines. *Cognitive Science, 9*(1), 147-169.

Adali, T., & Li, H. (2007). A practical formulation for computation of complex gradients and its application to maximum likelihood ICA. *In Proc. of IEEE Int. Conf. on Acoustic, Speech and Signal Processing (ICASSP)*, (pp. 633-636).

Adali, T., Kim, T., & Calhoun, V. D. (2004). Independent Component Analysis by Complex Nonlinearities. *In Proc. ICASSP 2004*, (pp. 525-528).

Addison, P. A. (2002). *The Illustrated Wavelet Transform Handbook*. Institute of Physics Publishing.

Adeli, H., & Hung, S-L. (1995). *Machine learning. Neural networks, genetic algorithms, and fuzzy systems*. New York, NY: John Wiley & Sons.

Adeli, H., & Samant, A. (2000). Wavelets to enhance computational intelligence. In P. Sincak (Ed). *Quo vadis computational intelligence? New trends and approaches in computational intelligence* (pp. 399-407). Heidelberg; New York: Physica-Verlag.

Aguirre, L. A., Lopes, R. A. M., Amaral, G. F. V., & Letellier, C. (2004). Constraining the topology of neural networks to ensure dynamics with symmetry properties. *Physical Review E*, 026701-1–026701-11.

Aharonov, D., van Dam, W., Kempe, J., Landau, Z., Lloyd, S., & Regev, O. (2004). Adiabatic Quantum Computation is Equivalent to Standard Quantum Computation. *Proceedings of the 45th Annual IEEE Symposium on Foundations of Computer Science*, (pp. 42-51).

Aiyer, S., Niranjan, M., & Fallside, F. (1990). Theoretical investigation into the performance of the Hopfield model. *IEEE Transactions on Neural Networks, 15*(1), 204-215.

Aizenberg, I., N., Aizenberg, N. N., & Vandewalle, J. (2000). *Multi-valued and universal binary neurons-Theory, learning, and applications*. Boston, MA: Kluwer Academic Publishers.

Al-Mashouq, K. A., & Reed, I. S. (1994). The use of neural nets to combine equalization with decoding for severe intersymbol interference channels. *IEEE Trans. on Neural Networks, 5*(6), 982-988.

Ala-Korpela, M., Changani, K. K., Hiltunen, Y., Bell, J. D., Fuller, B.J., Bryant, D.J., Taylor-Robinson, S. D., & Davidson, B. R. (1997). Assessment of quantitative artificial neural network analysis in a metabolically dynamic ex vivo 31P NMR pig liver study. *Magnetic Resonace in Medicine, 38*, 840-844.

Albers, D. J., Sprott, J. C., & Dechert, W. D. (1998). Routes to chaos in neural networks with random weights. *Int. J. of Bifurcation and Chaos, 8*(7), 1463-1478.

Albert, A. (1972). *Regression and the Moore-Penrose pseudoinverse*. New York: Academic Press.

Alsing, P. M., Gavrielides, A., & Kovanis, V. (1994). Using neural networks for controlling chaos. *Phys. Rev. E, 49*, 1225-1231.

Amari, S. (1991). Dualistic geometry of the manifold of higher-order neurons. *Neural Networks, 4*(4), 443-451.

Amari, S. (1992). Information geometry of neural networks. *IEICE Transactions on Fundamentals, E75-A*(5), 531-536.

Amari, S. (1995). Information geometry of the EM and em algorithms for neural networks. *Neural Networks, 8*(9), 1379-1408.

Amari, S. (1998). Natural gradient works efficiently in learning. *Neural Computation, 10*(2), 251-276.

Amari, S., & Nagaoka, H. (2000). *Methods of information geometry*. AMS & Oxford University Press.

Amari, S., Cichocki, A., & Yang, H. H. (1996). A New Learning Algorithm for Blind Signal Separation. *Advances in Neural Information Processing Systems, 8*, 757-763.

Amari, S., Kurata, K., & Nagaoka, H. (1992a). Information geometry of boltzmann machines. *IEEE Transactions on Neural Networks, 3*(2), 260-271.

Amit, D., Gutfreund, H., & Sompolinsky, H. (1987). Information storage in Neural Networks with low levels of activity. *Physical Review Letters, 55*, 1530-1533.

An, P. E., Brown, M., Chen, S., & Harris, C. J. (1993). Comparative aspects of neural network algorithms for on-line modelling of dynamic processes. *Proc. I. MECH. E., Pt.I, J. Systems and Control Eng.*, (pp. 223–241).

Antony, R. T. (1995). *Principles of data fusion automation*. Norwood, MA: Artech House.

Aoki, H. (2003). Applications of complex-valued neural networks for image processing. In A. Hirose (Ed.), *Complex-Valued Neural Networks: Theories and Applications*, (pp. 181-204). USA, World Scientific Pub Co Inc.

Arai, M. (1989, June). Mapping abilities of tree-layer neural networks. *Proc. Int'l Joint Conf. on Neural Networks:* (pp. 419-423). Washington D. C., USA.

Araki, M. (1974). *M-Matrices*. Publication 74/19, London: Imperial College of Science and Technology.

Araki, M. (1976). M-Matrices and their applications I. *Journal of the Institute of Systems, Control and Information Engineers: Systems and Control, 20(12)*, 675-680 (in Japanese).

Araki, M. (1977). M-Matrices and their applications II. *Journal of the Institute of Systems, Control and Information Engineers: Systems and Control, 21(2)*, 114-121 (in Japanese).

Arena, P., Caponetto, R., Fortuna, L., Muscato, G., & Xibilia, M. G. (1996). Quaternionic Multilayer Perceptrons for Chaotic Time Series Prediction. *IEICE Transactionon Fundamentals of Electronics, Communications and Computer Sciences, E79-A*(10), (pp. 1682–1688).

Arena P., Fortuna, L., Muscato, G., & Xibilia, M. G. (1998). *Neural networks in multidimensional domains. Fundamentals and new trends in modeling and control*. New York: Springer.

Arena, P., Fortuna, L., Muscato, G., & Xibilia, M. G. (1997). Multilayer Perceptrons To Approximate Quaternion Valued Functions. *Neural Networks, 10*(2), 335–342.

Arik, S., & Tavsanoglu, V. (2000). A sufficient condition for absolute stability of a larger class of dynamical neural networks. *IEEE Transactions on Circuits and Systems I, 47(5)*, 758-760.

Aster, R. C., Borchers, B., & Thurber, C. H. (2005). *Parameter estimation and inverse problems*. Elsevier.

Astrom, K. J. (2006). Introduction to Stochastic Control Theory. *Dover.*

Astrom, K., & Wittenmark, B. (1995). *Adaptive control.* Reading, MA: Addison-Wesley.

Baccelli, F. L., Cohen, G., Olsder, G. J., & Quadrat, J. P. (1992). *Synchronization and Linearity.* New York: John Wiley & Sons.

Baek, J. S., Park, S. W., & Seo, J. S. (2006). Novel techniques to minimize the error propagation of decision feedback equalizer in 8VSB DTV system. *Proc., IEEE VTC Spring, 5,* 2329–2333.

Balay, P., & Palicot, J. (1994). Equalization of nonlinear perturbations by a multilayer perceptron in satellite channel transmission. *Proc. IEEE GROBECOM* (pp. 1183-1186). San Francisco, CA.

Baldi, P., & Hormik, K. (1989). Neural networks and principal component analysis, learning from examples without local minima. *Neural Networks, 2*(1), 53-58.

Banyopadhyay, S., Menon, L., Kouklin, N., Williams, P. F., & Ianno, N. J. (2002). Self-assembled networks with neural computing attributes. *Smart Materials and Structures, 11,* 761–766. Institute of Physics Publishing.

Barron, A. R. (1993). Universal approximation bounds for superpositions of a sigmoidal function. *IEEE Transactions on Information Theory, 39*(4), 930-945.

Barron, A. R. (1994). Approximation and estimation bounds for artificial neural networks. *Machine Learning, 14*(1), 115-133.

Barshan, B., & Kuc, R. (1992). A bat-like sonar system for obstacle localization. *IEEE Transaction on Systems, Man, and Cybernetics, 22,* 636–646.

Basharov, A. M., Gorbachev, V. N., & Rodichkina, A. A. (2006). Decay and storage of multiparticle entangled states of atoms in collective thermostat. Physical Review, *A 74,* 042313.

Basseville, M., & Nikiforov, I. (1993). *Detection of abrupt changes: Theory and Applications.* Prentice-Hall.

Bayro-Corrochano, E. (2001). Geometric Neural Computing. *IEEE Transaction on Neural Networks, 12*(5), 968–986.

Bayro-Corrochano, E. (2001). *Geometric Computing for Perception Action Systems: Concepts, Algorithms, and Scientific Applications.* Boston: Springer-Verlag.

Bayro-Corrochano, E., & Buchholtz, S. (1997). *Geometric neural networks. In International Workshop on Algebraic Frames for the Perception-Action Cycle,* (Lecture Notes in Computer Science, 1315, 379–394.)

Beck, F., & Eccles, J. C. (1992). Quantum Aspects of Brain Activity and the Role of Consciousness. *Proceedings of the National Academy of Sciences, 89,* 11357-11361.

Behrman, E. C., Nash, L. R., Steck, J. E., Chandrashekar, V. G., & Skinner, S. R. (2000). Simulations of quantum neural networks. *Information Sciences, 128,* 257-269.

Behrman, E.C., Niemel, J., Steck, J.E., & Skinner, S.R. (1996). A quantum dot neural network. *Proceedings of the 4th Workshop on Physics of Computation,* 22-24.

Bell, A. J., & Sejnowski, T. J. (1995). An information-maximization approach to blind separation and blind deconvolution. *Neural Computation, 7,* 1129-1159.

Bell, E. T. (1999). *Men of Mathematics.* (pp. 360–361). Bt Bound.

Belliveau, J. W., Kennedy Jr, D. N., McKinstry, R. C., Buchbinder, B. R., Weisskoff, R. M., Cohen, M. S., Vevea, J. M., Brandy, T. J., & Rosen, B. R. (1991). Functional mapping of the human visual cortex by magnetic resonance imaging. *Science, 254* (5032), 716-719.

Benveniste, A., & Goursat, M. (1984). Blind equalizers. *IEEE Trans. on Comm., 32,* 871-883.

Benvensite, A., Metivier, M., & Priouret, P. (1990). *Adaptive algorithms and stochastic approximations, 22.* Springer: Applications of Mathematics Series.

Benvenuto, N., & Piazza, F. (1992). On the complex backpropagation algorithm. *IEEE Transactions on Signal Processing, 40*(4), 967-969.

Benvenuto, N., Marchesi, M. Piazza, F. & Uncini, A. (1991, May). Nonlinear satellite radio links equalized using blind neural networks. *Proc. IEEE ICASSP* (pp. 1521-1524). Toronto, USA.

Benvenuto, N., Marchesi, M., Piazza, F., & Uncini A. (1991). A comparison between real and complex valued neural networks in communication applications. *Proc. Int. Conf. Neural Networks ICANN*, Espoo, Finland.

Bernstein, E., & Vazirani, U. (1997). Quantum complexity theory. *SIAM Journal of Computing, 26*(5), 1411-1473.

Bernstein, E., & Vazirani, U.(1993). Quantum complexity theory. *Proceedings of the 25th Annual ACM Symposium on the Theory of Computing*, (pp. 11-20).

Bezdek, J. (1992). On the relationship between neural networks, pattern recognition and intelligence. *International Journal on Approximating Reasoning, 6*(2), 85-107.

Bezdek, J. C., Keller, J., Krishnapuram, R., & Pal, N. R. (1999). *Fuzzy models and algorithms for pattern recognition and image processing.* Norwell, MA: Kluwer Academic Publishers.

Biglieri, E., Divsalar, D., McLane, P. J., & Simon, M. K. (1991). *Introduction to trellis-coded modulation with applications.* Macmillan.

Bingham, E., & Hyvärinen, A. (2000). A fast fixed-point algorithm for independent component analysis of complex valued signals. *International Journal of Neural Systems 10*(1), 1-8.

Birx, D. L., & Pipenberg, S. J. (1992). Chaotic Oscillators and Complex Mapping Feed Forward Networks (CMFFNS) for Signal Detection in Noisy Environments. *Proceedings of IEEE International Joint Conference on Neural Networks, II*, 881–888.

Bishop, C. M. (1995). *Neural networks for pattern recognition.* New York, NY: Oxford University Press.

Blake, C. L., & Merz, C. J. (1998). *UCI repository of machine learning databases.* Retrieved 1998, from http://www.ics.uci.edu/~mlearn/MLRepository.html

Blogh, J. S., & Hanzo, L. (2002). *Third Generation Systems and Intelligent Wireless Networking – Smart Antennas and Adaptive Modulation.* Chichester, UK: Wiley.

Boccaletti, S., Kurths, J., Osipov, G., Valladres, D. L., & Zhou, C. S. (2002). The synchronization of chaotic systems. *Phys. Rep., 366*(1).

Botoca, C., & Budura, G. (2006, June 12-14). Symbol decision equalizer using a radial basis functions neural network. In *Proc. 7th WSEAS Int. Conf. Neural Networks* (Cavtat, Croatia), (pp.79–84).

Bouzerdoum, A., & Pattison, T. R. (1993). Neural network for quadratic optimization with bound constraints. *IEEE Transactions on Neural Networks, 4(2)*, 293-304.

Bradley, P. S., & Fayyad, U. M. (1998). Refining initial points for K-means clustering. In *15th International Conference on Machine Learning* (pp. 91-99). Los Altos, CA: Morgan Kaufmann.

Breiman, L. (1993). Hinging hyperplanes for regression, classification, and function approximation. *IEEE Transactions on Information Theory, 39*(4), 999-1013.

Breiman, L. (1996). Bagging predictors. *Machine Learning, 24*(1), 123-140.

Breiman, L. (1999). Combining predictors. In A. Sharkey (Ed.), *Combining artificial neural nets: Ensemble and modular multi-net systems* (pp. 31-50). London: Springer.

Breiman, L., Friedman, J. H., Olshen, R. A, & Stone, C. J. (1984). *Classification and regression trees.* Boca Raton, FL: Chapman & Hall/CRC.

Brooke, J., Bitko, D., Rosenbaum, T. F., & Aeppli, G. (1999). Quantum Annealing of a Disordered Magnet. *Science, 284*(5415), 779-781.

Broomhead, D. S., & Lowe, D. (1988). Multivariable functional interpolation and adaptive networks. *Complex Systems*, (pp. 321–355).

Buchholz, S., & Sommer, G. (2000). Quaternionic spinor MLP. In *8th European symposium on artificial neural networks* (ESANN2000) (pp. 377–382).

Bäck, T. (1996). *Evolutionary algorithms in theory and practice.* New York, NY: Oxford University Press.

Bülow, T., & Sommer, G. (2001). Hypercomplex Signals: A Novel Extension of the Analytic Signal to the Multidimensional Case. *IEEE Transaction on Signal Processing, 49*(11), 2844–2852.

Caiti, A., & Parisini, T. (1994). Mapping ocean sediments by RBF networks. *IEEE J. Oceanic Engineering,* (4), 577–582.

Calhoun, V. D., & Adali, T. (2002). Complex Infomax: Convergence and Approximation of Infomax With Complex Nonlinearities. *In Proc. NNSP,* (pp. 307-316).

Calhoun, V. D., Adali, T., Pearlson, G. D., & Pekar, J. J. (2002). On Complex Infomax Applied to Complex FMRI Data. *In Proc. ICASSP, I,* 1009-1012.

Calhoun, V. D., Adali, T., Pearlson, G. D., Van Zijl, P. C., & Pekar, J. J. (2002). Independent Component Analysis of FMRI Data in the Complex Domain. *Magn. Reson. Med., 48,* 180-192.

Cardoso, J., & Adali, T. (2006). The Maximum Likelihood Approach to Complex ICA. *In Proc. of Int. Conf. on Acoustic, Speech and Signal Processing,* (pp. 673-676).

Cardoso, J., & Laheld, B. H. (1996). Equivariant Adaptive Source Separation. *IEEE Trans. on Signal Processing, 45*(2), 3014-3030.

Catmull, E., & Rom, R. (1974). A class of local interpolating splines. In R. E. Barnhill, & R.F. Riesenfeld (Eds.), *Computer-Aided Geometric Design,* (pp. 317-326). New York: Accademic.

Cernuschi-Frias, B. (1989). Partial simultaneous updating in Hopfield memories. *IEEE Trans. Syst. Man Cybern,. 19,* 887-888.

Cha, I., & Kassam, S. A. (1995). Channel equalization using adaptive complex radial basis function networks. *IEEE J. Sel. Areas Commn., 13*(1), 122-131.

Cha, I., & Kassam, S. A. (1996). RBFN restoration of nonlinearly degraded images. *IEEE Trans. Image Processing,* (6), 964–975.

Chakravarthy S. V., & Ghosh, J. (1994). A neural network-based associative memory for storing complex-valued patterns. In *Proc IEEE Int Conf Syst Man Cybern,* (pp. 2213-2218).

Chakravarthy S. V., & Ghosh, J. (1996). A complex-valued associative memory for storing patterns as oscillatory states. *Biological Cybernetics, 75,* 229-238.

Chakravarthy, S. V., & Ghosh, J. (1993). Studies on a network of complex neurons. *In Proc. of SPIE vol. 1965 Applications of Artificial Neural Networks IV,* (pp. 31 -43), April, 1993. (invited paper).

Chakravarthy, V. S., Gupte, N., Yogesh, S., & Salhotra, A. (2008). Chaotic Synchronization using a Network of Neural Oscillators. *International Journal of Neural Systems, 18*(2), 1-8.

Chang, P. R., Yeh, B. F., & Chang, C. C. (1994). Adaptive packet equalization for indoor radio channel using multilayer neural networks. *IEEE Trans. on Vehicular Tech., 43*(3), 773-780.

Chen, S. (1995). Nonlinear time series modelling and prediction using Gaussian RBF networks with enhanced clustering and RLS learning. *Electronics Letters,* (2), 117–118.

Chen, S., Billings, S. A., & Grant, P. M. (1992). Recursive hybrid algorithm for non-linear system identification using radial basis function networks. *Int. J. Control,* (5), 1051–1070.

Chen, S., Billings, S. A., & Luo, W. (1989). Orthogonal least squares methods and their application to non-linear system identification. *Int. J. Control,* (5), 1873–1896.

Chen, S., Billings, S. A., Cowan, C. F. N., & Grant, P. M. (1990). Non-linear systems identification using radial basis functions. *Int. J. Systems Sci.,* (12), 2513–2539.

Chen, S., Cowan, C. F. N., & Grant, P. M. (1991). Orthogonal least squares learning algorithm for radial basis function networks. *IEEE Trans. Neural Networks,* (2), 302–309.

Chen, S., Cowan, C. F. N., Billings, S. A., & Grant, P. M. (1990a). Parallel recursive prediction error algorithm for training layered neural networks. *Int. J. Control,* (6), 1215–1228.

Chen, S., Du, H.-Q., & Hanzo, L. (2006). Adaptive minimum symbol error rate beamforming assisted receiver for quadrature amplitude modulation systems. In *Proc. VTC2006-Spring* (Melbourne, Australia), May 7-10, 2006, (pp. 2236-2240).

Chen, S., Hanzo, L., & Tan, S. (2008, May 19-23). Nonlinear beamforming for multiple-antenna assisted QPSK wireless systems. In *Proc. ICC 2008* (Beijing, China).

Chen, S., Hanzo, L., & Wolfgang, A. (2004). Kernel-based nonlinear beamforming construction using orthogonal forward selection with Fisher ratio class separability measure. *IEEE Signal Processing Letters*, (5), 478–481.

Chen, S., Hanzo, L., Ahmad, N. N., & Wolfgang, A. (2005). Adaptive minimum bit error rate beamforming assisted receiver for QPSK wireless communication. *Digital Signal Processing*, (6), 545–567.

Chen, S., Hong, X., & Harris, C. J. (2003). Sparse kernel regression modelling using combined locally regularized orthogonal least squares and D-optimality experimental design. *IEEE Trans. Automatic Control*, (6), 1029–1036.

Chen, S., Hong, X., Harris, C. J., & Sharkey, P. M. (2004). Sparse modelling using orthogonal forward regression with PRESS statistic and regularization. *IEEE Trans. Systems, Man and Cybernetics, Part B*, (2), 898–911.

Chen, S., Labib, K., & Hanzo, L. (2007). Clustering-based symmetric radial basis function beamforming. *IEEE Signal Processing Letters*, (9), 589-592.

Chen, S., Labib, K., Kang, R., & Hanzo, L. (2007, June 24-28). Adaptive radial basis function detector for beamforming. In *Proc. ICC 2007* (Glasgow, Scotland), (pp. 2967-2972).

Chen, S., Maclaughlin, S., & Mulgrew, B. (1994). Complex-valued radial basis function networks, Part II: Application to digital communication channel equalization. *Signal Processing, 36(2)*, 175-188.

Chen, S., McLaughlin, S., & Mulgrew, B. (1994). Complex-valued radial basis function network, Part I: network architecture and learning algorithms. *Signal Processing*, (1), 19-31.

Chen, S., Mulgrew, B., & Grant, P. M. (1993). A clustering technique for digital communications channel equalization using radial basis function networks. *IEEE Trans. Neural Networks*, *4*(4), 570-579.

Chen, S., Wolfgang, A., Benedetto, S., Dubamet, P., & Hanzo, L. (2006, Sept. 20-22). Symmetric radial basis function network equaliser. In *Proc. NEWCOM-ACoRN Joint Workshop* (Vienna, Austria),.

Chen, S., Wolfgang, A., Harris, C. J., & Hanzo, L. (2007, August 12-17). Symmetric kernel detector for multiple-antenna aided beamforming systems. In *Proc. IJCNN 2007* (Orlando, USA), (pp. 2486–2491).

Chen, S., Wu, Y., & Luk, B. L. (1999). Combined genetic algorithm optimisation and regularised orthogonal least squares learning for radial basis function networks. *IEEE Trans. Neural Networks*, (5), 1239–1243.

Childs, A. M., Farhi, E., & Preskill, J. (2001). Robustness of adiabatic quantum computation. Phys. Rev. A, *65*(1), 012322.

Chinrungrueng, C., & Séquin, C. H. (1995). Optimal adaptive k-means algorithm with dynamic adjustment of learning rate. *IEEE Trans. Neural Networks*, (1), 1873–1896.

Cho, J. H., You, C., & Hong, D. (1996, June). The neural decision feedback equalizer for the nonlinear digital magnetic recording channel. *Proc. IEEE ICC* (pp. 573-576). Dallas, TX.

Choi, S., Cichocki, A., & Amari, S. (2000). Flexible Independent Component Analysis. *Journal of VLSI Signal Processing - Systems for, Image and video Technology, X*(1).

Chua, L. O., & Yang, L. (1988). Cellular neural networks: Theory. *IEEE Trans. Circuits and Systems, 35*(10), 1257-1272.

Chung, K. L. (2002). *Green, Brown and Probability & Brownian Motion on the Line*. World Scientific.

Chuong, N. M., Egorov, Y. V., Khrennikov, A., Meyer,

Y., & Mumford, D. (2007). *Harmonic, Wavelet and p-adic analysis*. World Scientific.

Churhill, R. V., & Brown, J. W. (1984). *Complex variables and applications* (4th ed.). NY: McGraw-Hill Book Company.

Cichocki, A., & Amari, S. (2002). *Adaptive Blind Signal and Image Processing*. John Wiley.

Clarke, T. L. (1990). Generalization ofNeural Networks to the Complex Plane. *In Proc. of IJCNN*, (pp. 435-440).

Cohen, G., Gaubert, S., & Quadrat J.P. (1999). Max-plus algebra and system theory: Where we are and where to go now. *Annual Reviews in Control, 23,* 207–219.

Cohen-Tannoudji, C., Diu, B., & Lal□e F. (1998). *Mécanique Quantique I*. Hermann.

Comets, F., & Meyre, T. (2006). *Calcul Stochastique et applications*. Dunod, Paris.

Comon, P. (1994). Independent Component Analysis, A new Concept? *Signal Processing, 36*, 287-314.

Congdon, P. (2006). *Bayesian statistical modeling*. Chichester, West Sussex: John Wiley & Sons, Ltd.

Cook, J. (1989). The mean-field theory of a Q-state neural networks. *Journal of Physics A: Mathematical and General, 22*(12), 2057-2067.

Cooley, J. W., & Tukey, J. W. (1965). An algorithm for machine calculation of complex Fourier series. *Mathematics and Computation, 19*(90), 297-301.

Costantini, G., Casali, D., & Pefetti, R. (2003). Neural associative memory storing gray-coded gray-scale images. *IEEE Trans. Neural Networks, 14*(3), 703-707.

Cottin, C., Gavrea, I., Gonska, H. H., Kacsò, D. P., & Zhou, D. (1999). Global Smoothness Preservation and the Variation-Diminishing Property. *Journal of Inequality & Applications, 4*, 91-114.

Cottrell, G. W., Munro, P., & Zipser, D. (1987). *Image compression by back propagation: An example of extensional propagation* (Tech. Rep. No. ICS8702). University of California, San Diego.

Cover, T. M., & Thomas, J. A. (2006). *Elements of Information Theory.* 2nd edition.John WIley & Sons, Inc.

Cristianini, N., & Shawe-Taylor, J. (2000). *An introduction to support vector machines*. Cambridge, UK: Cambridge University Press.

Cybenko, G. (1989). Approximation by superpositions of a sigmoidal function. *Mathematics of Control, Signals and Systems, 2*, 303-314.

Das, S. R. (1991). On the Synthesis ofNonlinear Continuous Neural Networks. *IEEE Transactions on Systems, Man, and Cybernetics, 21*(2), 413–418.

David, H. A., Hinton, G. E., & Sejnowski, T. J. (1985). A Learning Algorithm for Boltzmann Machines. *Cognitive Science: A Multidisciplinary Journal, 9*(1), 149-169.

Dayhoff, J. E. (1989). *Neural Network Architectures: An Introduction*. New York: Van Nostrand Reinhold.

De Boor, C. (2001). *A practical guide to spline*. Springer.

De Garis, H., Sriram, R., & Zhang, Z. (2003). Quantum generation of neural networks. I*n Proc. Internat. Joint Conf. on Neural Networks, IJCNN '03, 4*, 2589–2593.

Debauchies, I. (1990). The wavelet transform, time-frequency localization and signal processing. *IEEE Transactions on Information Theory, 36*, 961-1005.

Del Moral, P. (2004). Feynman-Kac Formulae: Genealogic and Interacting Particle Systems with Applications. *Probability and its Applications*. Springer.

Deng, J., Sundararajan, N., & Saratchandran, P. (2002). Communication channel equalization using complex-valued minimal radial basis function neural networks. *IEEE Trans. Neural Networks*, (3), 687–696.

Derome, A. E. (1987). *Modern NMR Techniques for Chemistry Research* (*Organic Chemistry Series, Vol 6*). Oxford, United Kingdom: Pergamon Press.

Deutsch, D. (1985). Quantum theory, the Church-Turing principle, and the universal quantum computer. *Proceedings of the Royal Society London A, 400*, 97-117.

Deutsch, D. (1989). Quantum computational networks. *Proceedings of the Royal Society of London A, 425*, 73-90.

Deutsch, D., & Jozsa, R.(1992). Rapid solution of problems by quantum computation. *Proceedings of the Royal Society London A, 439*, 553-558.

Dubois, D., Foulloy, L., Mauris, G., & Prade, H. (2004). Probability-possibility transformations, triangular fuzzy sets and probabilistic inequalities. *Reliable Computing.*, *10*(4), 273-297. Springer

Duda, R. O., & Hart, P. E. (1973). *Pattern Classification and Scene Analysis*. John Wiley & Sons.

Duda, R. O., Hart, P. E., & Stork, D. G. (2001). *Pattern classification*. New York, NY: JohnWiley & Sons, Inc.

Duflo,nM. (1996). Algorithmes stochastiques. *Mathematiques et Applications, 23*. Springer.

Eriksson, J., & Koivunen, V. (2002). Blind Identifiability of Class of Nonlinear Instantaneous ICA Models. *In XI European Signal Processing Conference EUSIPCO2002*, (pp. 7-10).

Eriksson, J., & Koivunen, V. (2004). Identifiability, separability and uniqueness of linear ICA models. *Signal Processing Letters, IEEE, 11*(7), 601-604.

Eriksson, J., & Koivunen, V. (2006). Complex random vectors and ICA models: identifiability, uniqueness, and separability. *Information Theory, IEEE Transactions on 52*(3), 1017-1029.

Espinoza, M., Suykens, J. A. K., & De Moor, B. (2005, Dec.12-15). Imposing symmetry in least squares support vector machines regression. In *Proc. Joint 44th IEEE Conf. Decision and Control, and European Control Conf. 2005* (Seville, Spain), (pp. 5716–5721).

Ezhov, A. A., Nifanova, A. V., & Ventura, D. (2000). Quantum associative memory with distributed queries. *Information Sciences, 128*, 271-293.

Ezhov, A., & Ventura, D. (2000). Quantum Neural Networks. In N. Kasabov (Ed.), *Future Directions for Intelligent Systems and Information Science*. Heidelberg: Physica-Verlag.

Fahlman, S. E. (1988, June). Faster-learning variation on backpropagation: An empirical study. *Proc. of the Connectionist Model Summer School* (pp. 17-26).

Fang, Y., & Chow, T. W. S. (1999). Blind equalization of a noisy channel by linear neural network. *IEEE Trans. Neural Networks, 10*(4), 925 – 929.

Farhi, E., & Gutmann, S. (1996). An Analog Analogue of a Digital Quantum Computation. *quant-ph*, 9612026.

Farhi, E., Goldstone, J., Gutmann, & Sipser, M. (2000). Quantum Computation by Adiabatic Evolution. *quant-ph*, 0001106.

Farhi, E., Goldstone, J., Gutmann, S., Lapan, J., Lundgren, A., & Preda, D. (2001). A Quantum Adiabatic Evolution Algorithm Applied to Random Instances of an NP-Complete Problem. *Science, 292*(5516), 472-475.

Faris, W. G. (2006). *Diffusion, Quantum Theory, and Radically Elementary Mathematics*. Princeton University Press.

Feinberg, D. A., & Oshio, K. (1991). GRASE (gradient and spin echo) MR imaging: A new fast clinical imaging technique. *Radiology, 181*, 597-602.

Feynman, R. (1986). Quantum mechanical computers. *Foundations of Physics, 16*, 507-531.

Feynman, R. P. (1972). *Statistical Mechanics*. Reading: W.A. Benjamin.

Feynman, R. P. (1982). Quantum mechanical computers. *Optics News, 11*, 11-20.

Fiori, S. (2000). Blind Signal Processing by the Adaptive Activation function Neuron. *Neural Networks, 13*(6), 597-611.

Fiori, S., Uncini, A., & Piazza, F. (1999). Neural Blind Separation of Complex Sources by Extended APEX Algorithm (EAPEX). *In Proc. of IEEE ISCAS'99*, (pp. 627-630).

Fishman, G. S. (1995). *Monte Carlo. Concepts, algorithms, and applications*. New York, NY: Springer.

Fliess, M. (2007). Fluctuations Quantiques, C.R. Acad. Sci. Paris. *Physique Mathématique, Elsevier, 344*, 663-668.

Forti, M., & Tesi, A. (1995). New conditions for global stability of neural networks with application to linear and quadratic programming problems. *IEEE Transactions on Circuits and Systems I, 42(7)*, 354-366.

Forti, M., Manetti, S., & Marini, M. (1994). Necessary and sufficient condition for absolute stability of neural networks. *IEEE Transactions on Circuits and Systems I, 41(7)*, 491-494.

Fredkin, E., & Toffoli, T. (1980). *Reversible Computing*. MIT Report MIT/LCS/TM-151.

Freemann, J. A., & Skapura, D. M. (1991). *Neural Networks: Algorithm and Programming Techniques*. Addition Wesley.

Fukumizu, K., & Amari, S. (2000). Local minima and plateaus in hierarchical structures of multilayer perceptrons. *Neural Networks, 13*(3), 317-327.

Fukunaga, K. (1990). *Introduction to statistical pattern recognition*. New York, NY: Academic Press.

Fukushima, M. (2001). *Fundamentals of nonlinear optimization*. Tokyo: Asakura Pub. Co., Ltd. (in Japanese).

Funahasi, K. (1989). On the approximate realization of continuous mapping by neural networks. *Neural Networks, 2*, 183-192.

Gan, Q., Saratchandran, P., Sundararajan, N., & Subramanian, K. R. (1999). A complex valued radial basis function network for equalization of fast time varying channels. *IEEE Trans. Neural Networks, 10*(4), 958 – 960.

Gazi, V., & Passino, K. (2004). Stability analysis of social foraging swarms. *IEEE Transactions on Systems, Man and Cybernetics – Part B: Cybernetics*, 539-557.

Geman, D., & Geman, S. (1984). Stochastic Relaxation, Gibbs Distribution, and the Bayesian Restoration of Images. *IEEE Trans. Pattern Analysis and Machine Intelligence, 6*(6), 721-741.

Georgiou, G, & Koutsougeras, C. (1992). Complex domain back-propagation. *IEEE Transactions on Circuits and Systems-II: Analog and Digital Signal Processing, 39*(5), 330-334.

Gibson, G. J., Siu, S., & Cowan, C. F. N. (1989, May). Application of multilayer perceptrons as adaptive channel equalizers. *Proc. IEEE ICASSP* (pp. 1183-1186). Glasgow, Scotland.

Girosi, F., & Poggio, T. (1989). Representation properties of networks: Kolmogorov's theorem is irrelevant. *Neural Computation, 1*(4), 465-469.

Gislen, L., Peterson, C., & Sodeberg, B. (1992). Rotor Neurons: Basic Formalism and Dynamics. *Neural Computation, 4*, 737-745.

Gitterman, M. (2005). *The noisy oscillator: The first Hundred Years, From Einstein Until Now*. World Scientific.

Godard, D. N. (1980). Self-recovering equalization and carrier tracking in two dimensional data communication systems. *IEEE Trans. Communications, 28*, 1867– 875.

Golub, G. H., & van Loan, C. F. (1996). *Matrix Computations 3rd Ed.* Baltimore: Johns Hopkins University Press.

Gomes, J., & Barroso, V. (1997). Using an RBF network for blind equalization: Design and performance evaluation. *Proc. ICASSP*, 4, 3285–3288, Munich, Germany.

Gonzalez, J., Rojas, I., Ortega, J., Pomares, H., Fernandez, F. J., & Diaz, A. F. (2003). Multiobjective evolutionary optimization of the size, shape, and position parameters of radial basis function networks for function approximation. *IEEE Trans. Neural Networks*, (6), 1478–1495.

Gorbachev, V. N., Zhiliba, A. I., Trubilko, A. I., & Rodichkina A. A. (2002). Teleportation and dense coding via a multiparticle quantum channel of the GHZ-class. *QIC (Quantum Information and Computation), 2*, 367-378.

Gorbachev, V. N., & Zhiliba, A. I. (1993). Master equations for the quantum optics problems. *Quantum. Opt. 5*, 193.

Gorbachev, V. N., & Zhiliba, A. I. (2000). Transfer

formalism for quantum optics problem. *Phys.A: Math. Gen., 33*, 3771.

Gorbachev, V. N., Kazakov, A. Y., & Trubilko, A. I. (2004). Macroscopic entangled states. *Journ. Opt. B, 6*, 517-524.

Gorbachev, V. N., Kazakov, A. Y., & Trubilko, A. I. (2007). Exponential superradiance and macroscopic entangled states. In M. Zukowsky et al. (Eds.), Quantum Communication and Security. IOS Press.

Gorbachev, V. N., Trubilko, A. I., Rodichkina, A. A., & Zhiliba, A. I. (2003). On preparation of the entangled W-states from atomic ensembles. *Physics Letters A, 310*(5-6), 339-343 .

Gorbachev, V. N., Zhiliba, A. I., & Trubilko, A. I. (2001). Teleportation of entangled states. *J. Opt. B 3*, S25.

Gorbachev, V. N., Zhiliba, A. I., & Trubilko, A. I. (2001). Continuous variables teleportation of a two particle entangled state. *Opt. Commun., 187*, 379.

Gorinevsky, D., Kapitanovsky, A., & Goldenberg, A. (1996). Radial basis function network architecture for nonholonomic motion planning and control of free-flying manipulators. *IEEE Trans. Robotics and Automation*, (3), 491–496.

Goswami, J. C., & Chan, A. K. (1999). *Fundamentals of wavelets. Theory, algorithms, and applications.* New York, NY: John Wiley & Sons, Inc.

Graves, R. P. (1975). *Life of Sir William Rowan Hamilton*, 2, 434–435. New York: Arno Press.

Gray, C., & Singer, W. (1989). Stimulus-specific neuronal oscillations in orientation columns of cat visual cortex. *Proc Natl Acad Sci, 86*, 1698–1702.

Grigoriev, D. Y., Karpinski, M., & Singer, M. F. (1990). Fast Parallel Algorithms for Sparse Multivariate Polymomial Interpolation over Finite Fields. *SIAM J. of Comp., 19*, 1059-1083.

Grigoriev, D. Y., & Karpinski, M. (1991b). Algorithms for Sparse Rational Interpolation. *Proc. Int. Symp. Symb. Alg. Comput., Bonn*, (pp. 7-13).

Grigoriev, D. Y., Karpinski, M., & Singer, M. F. (1991a). Interpolation Problem for k-Sparse Sums of Eigenfunctions of Operators. *Advances in Applied Mathematics, 12*, 76 -81.

Grigoriev, D. Y., Karpinski, M., & Singer, M. F. (1994). Computational Complexity of Sparse Rational Interpolation. *SIAM J. Comput., 23*(1), 1-11.

Grigoriev, D., Kazakov, A., & Vakulenko, S. (2007). Optical device accelerating dynamic programming. *Physics of Particles and Nuclei Letters, 4*, 141-142.

Groetsch, C. W. (1993). *Inverse problems in the mathematical sciences.* Wiesbaden, Germany: Informatica International.

Grover, L. K. (1996). A fast quantum mechanical algorithm for database search. *Twenty-Eighth Annual ACM Symp. on the Theory of Computing*, (pp. 212-219).

Grover, L. K. (1997). Quantum Mechanics Helps in Searching for a Needle in a Haystack. *Phys. Rev. Lett., 79*(2), 325-328.

Grover, L. V. (1996). A fast quantum mechanical algorithm for database search. *In Proceedings of the ACM Symposium on the Theory of Computing* (pp.212-219). New York: ACM Press.

Grover, L. V. (1997). Quantum mechanics helps in searching for a needle in a haystack. *Physical Review Letters, 78*, 325-328.

Gröchenig, K., Han, D., Heil, C., & Kutyniak, G. (2002). The Balian-Low theorem for symplectic lattices in higher dimensions. *Applied and Computational Harmonic Analysis, 13*, 169-176. *Academic Press*

Guarnieri, S., Piazza, F., & Uncini, A. (1999). Multilayer Feedforward Networks with Adaptive Spline Activation Function. *IEEE Trans. on Neural Network, 10*(3), 672-683.

Hagan, S., Hameroff, S. R., & Tuzyinski, J. A. (2002). Quantum Computation in Brain Microtubules: Decoherence and Biological Feasibility. Physical Review E, *American Physical Society, 65*, 1-11.

Hameroff, S. R. (2007). The Brain is both Neurocomputer and Quantum Computer. *Cognitive Science, 31*, 1035–1045.

Han, L., & Biswas, S. K. (1997). Neural networks for sinusoidal frequency estimation. *Journal of The Franklin Institute, 334B*(1), 1-18.

Hankins, T. L. (1980). *Sir William Rowan Hamilton*. Baltimore and London: Johns Hopkins University Press.

Haselgrove, J. C., Subramanian, V. H., Christen, R., & Leigh, J. S. (1988). Analysis of in-vivo NMR spectra. *Reviews of Magnetic Resonance in Medicine, 2*, 167-222.

Hashimoto, N., Kuroe, Y., & Mori, T. (1999). On Energy Function for Complex-valued Neural Networks. The Institute of Electronics, *Information and Communication Engineers (IEICE) Technical report Neurocomputing, 98*(673), 121-128 (in Japanese).

Hawkins, J, & Blakeslee, S. (2004). *On intelligence*. New York: Henry Holt and Company.

Haykin, S. (1989). *Adaptive Filter Theory*. Prentice-Hall.

Haykin, S. (1994). *Neural networks, a comprehensive foundation*. New York, NY: IEEE Press.

Haykin, S. (2002). *Adaptive filter theory. Fourth edition*. Upper Saddle River, NJ: Prentice Hall.

Haykin, S. (Ed.) (2000). *Unsupervised Adaptive Filtering, Volume1: Blind Source Separation*. John Wiley & Sons, Inc.

Haykin, S. (Ed.) (2001). *Kalman filtering and neural networks*. New York, NY: John Wiley & Sons.

Haykin, S. (Ed.). (1994). *Blind Deconvolution*. Englewood Cliffs, New Jersey: Prentice-Hall.

Hebb, D. O. (1949). *The organization of behavior*. New York, NY: John Wiley.

Hecht-Nielsen, R. (1987). Kolmogorov's mapping neural network existence theorem. In *IEEE International Conference on Neural Networks, 3*, 11-13. New York, NY: IEEE Press.

Hecht-Nielson, R. (1988). Kolmogorov's mapping neural network existence theorem. *Proc. IEEE ICNN* (pp. III 11-13).

Hegger, R., & Kantz, H. (1999). Practical implementation of nonlinear time series methods: The TISEAN package. Chaos, 9(2), 413-435.

Henning, J., Nauerth, A., & Fnedburg, H. (1986). RARE imaging: A first imaging method for clinical MR. *Magnetic Resonance in Medicine, 3*(6), 823-833.

Hinton, G. E., & Sejnowski, T. J. (1986). *Learning and Relearning in Boltzmann Machines. Parallel distributed processing: explorations in the microstructure of cognition, vol. 1: foundations* (pp. 282-317). Cambridge, MA: MIT press.

Hirose, A. (1992). Continuous complex-valued back-propagation learning. *Electronics Letters, 28*(20), 1854-1855.

Hirose, A. (1992). Proposal of fully complex-valued neural networks. In *Proceedings of Intl' Jnt' Conf. On Neural Networks, 4*, 152-157.

Hirose, A. (1992). Dynamics of fully complex-valued neural networks. *Electrronics Letters, 28*(16), 1492-1494.

Hirose, A. (1994). Applications of Complex-Valued Neural Networks to Coherent Optical Computing Using Phase-Sensitive Detection Scheme. *Information Sciences - Applications*, 2(2), 103–117.

Hirose, A. (2005). *Complex-valued neural networks*. Springer.

Hirose, A. (Ed.) (2003). *Complex-valued neural networks: theories and applications* (Series on Innovative Intelligence 5). Singapore: World Scientific Publishing.

Hoggar, S. G. (1992). *Mathematics for Computer Graphics*. Cambridge: Cambridge University Press.

Hopfield, J. J. (1982). Neural networks and physical systems with emergent collective computational abilities. *Proceedings of the National Academy of Sciences of the USA, 79*(8), 2554-2558.

Hopfield, J. J. (1984). Neurons with graded response have

collective computational properties like those of two-state neurons. *Proceedings of the National Academy of Sciences of the United States of America, 81*, 3088-3092.

Hopfield, J. J., & Tank, D. W. (1985). "Neural" computation of decisions in optimization problems. *Biological Cybernetics, 55*, 141-146.

Hovanessian, S. A. (1984). *Introduction to sensor systems*. Norwood, MA: Artech House.

Hu, S., & Wang, J. (2002). Global stability of a class of discrete-time recurrent neural networks. *IEEE Transactions on Circuits and Systems I, 49(8)*, 1104-1117.

Huang, G. B., Saratchandran, P., & Sundarrajan N. (2005). A generalized growing and pruning RBF (GGAP-RBF) neural network for function approximation. *IEEE Trans. Neural Networks, 16*(1), 57-67.

Huberman, B. A., & Lumer, E. (1990). Dynamics of adaptive systems. *IEEE Transactions on Circuits and. Systems, 37*(4), 547-550.

Huse, D. A., & Fisher, D. S. (1986). Residual Energies after Slow Cooling of Disordered Systems. *Phys. Rev. Lett., 57*(17), 2203-2206.

Hyvarinen, A., & Oja, E. (2000). Independent component analysis: algorithms and applications. *Neural Networks, 13*, 411-430.

Hyvärinen, A., Karhunen, J., & Oja, E. (2001). *Independent Component Analysis*. John Wiley & Sons, Inc.

Igelnik, B. (2000). Some new adaptive architectures for learning, generalization, and visualization of multivariate data. In P. Sincak & J. Vascak (Eds.), *Quo Vadis Computational Intelligence? New Trends and Approaches in Computational Intelligence* (pp. 63-78). Heidelberg; New York, NY: Physica-Verlag.

Igelnik, B. (2001). Method for visualization of multivariate data in a lower dimension. In *SPIE Visual Data Exploration and Analysis VIII, 4302*, 168-179, San Jose, CA.

Igelnik, B. P.I. (2003). *Visualization of large multidimensional datasets in a lower dimension*. SBIR Phase I Final Report, #0232775, NSF.

Igelnik, B. P.I. (2003). *Visualization of large multidimensional datasets in a lower dimension*. SBIR Phase II Proposal, #0349713, NSF.

Igelnik, B., & Pao, Y-H. (1995). Stochastic choice of basis functions in adaptive function approximation and the functional-link net. *IEEE Transactions on Neural Networks, 6*(6), 1320-1329.

Igelnik, B., & Parikh, N. (2003a). Kolmogorov's spline network. *IEEE Transactions on Neural Networks, 14*(3), 725-733.

Igelnik, B., Pao, Y-H., & LeClair, S. R. (1996). An approach for optimization of a continuous function with many local minima. In 30th *Annual Conference on Information Sciences and Systems, 2*, 912-917. Department of Electrical Engineering, Princeton University, Princeton, NJ.

Igelnik, B., Pao, Y-H., LeClair, S. R., & Shen, C. Y. (1999). The ensemble approach to neural network learning and generalization. *IEEE Transactions on Neural Networks, 10*(1), 19-30.

Igelnik, B., Tabib-Azar, M., & LeClair, S. (2001). A net with complex weights. *IEEE Transactions on Neural Networks, 12*(2), 236-249.

Irie, B., & Miyake, S. (1988). Capabilities of three-layered perceptrons. *Proc. IEEE ICNN* (pp. I 641-648).

Isokawa, T., Kusakabe, T., Matsui, N., & Peper, F. (2003). Quaternion neural network and its application. In V. Palade, R. J. Howlett, & L. C. Jain (Eds.), *Proceedings of knowledge-based intelligent information engineering systems (KES2003), Lecture Notes in Artificial Intelligence, 2774*, 318–324. Springer-Verlag.

Isokawa, T., Nishimura, H., Kamiura, N., & Matsui, N. (2006). Fundamental Properties of Quaternionic Hopfield Neural Network. In *Proceedings of 2006 international joint conference on neural networks* (pp. 610–615).

Isokawa, T., Nishimura, H., Kamiura, N., & Matsui, N. (2007). Dynamics of Discrete-Time Quaternionic Hopfield Neural Networks. In *Proceedings of 17th In-*

ternational Conference on Artificial Neural Networks (ICANN2007): Part I. (pp. 848–857).

Isokawa, T., Nishimura, H., Kamiura, N., & Matsui, N. (2008). Associative Memory in Quaternionic Hopfield Neural Network. *International Journal of Neural Systems, 18*(2), 135–145.

Iwasaki, I. Nakasima, H., & Shimizu, T. (1998). Interacting Brownian particles as a modelof neural network. *International Journal of Bifurcation and Chaos, 8*(4), 791-797. World Scientific.

Jackson, P. (1986). *Introduction to expert systems.* Reading, MA: Addison-Wesley.

Jankowski, S., Lozowski, A., & Zurada, J. M. (1996). Complex-valued multistate neural associative memory. *IEEE Transactions on Neural Networks, 7*(6), 1491-1496.

Jankowski, S., Lozowski, A., & Zurada, J. M. (1996). Complex-valued multistate neural associative memory. *IEEE Transactions on Neural Networks, 7*(4), 1491–1496.

Jansen, B., & Nakayama, K. (2005). Neural networks following a binary approach to the integer prime-factorization problem. *Proceedings of the International Joint Conference on Neural Networks, 4*, 2577-2582.

Jeng, Y. J., & Yeh, C. C. (1991). Modified intraconnected bidirectional associative memory. *Electron. Lett., 27*, 1818-1819.

Jensen, C. A., Reed, R. D., Marks, R. J., El-Sharkawi, M. A., Jung, J. B., Miyamoto, R. T., Anderson, G. M., & Eggen, C. J. (1999). Inversion of feedforward neural networks: algorithms and applications. *Proceedings of the IEEE, 87*, 9, 1536–1549.

Jianping, D., Sundarrajan, N., & Saratchandran, P. (2002). Communication channel equalization using complex-valued minimal radial basis function neural networks. *IEEE Trans. Neural networks, 13*(3), 687-697.

Jibu, M., & Yasue, K. (1995). *Quantum brain dynamics: An introduction.* Amsterdam: John Benjamins.

Jibu, M., Pribram, K. H., Yasue, K. (1996). From conscious experience to memory storage and retrieval: The role of quantum brain dynamics and Boson condensation of evanescent photons. *Int J Modern Physics, B 10*(13 & 14), 1735-1754.

Jin, L., & Gupta, M. M. (1996). Globally asymptotical stability of discrete-time analog neural networks. *IEEE Transactions on Neural Networks, 7(4)*, 1024-1031.

Johnson, R., Jr., Schniter, P., Endres, T. J., Behm, J. D., Brown, D. R., & Casas, R. A. (1998). Blind equalization using the constant modulus criterion: A review. *Proc. IEEE, 86*(10), 1927–1950.

Jutten, C., & Herault, J. (1991). Blind Separation of Sources, Part I: An Adaptive Algorithm Based on Neuromimetic Architecture. *Signal Processing, 24*, 1-10.

Jutten, C., & Karhunen, J. (2003). Advances in Nonlinear Blind Sources Separation. *In 4th International Symposium on Independent Component Analisys and Blind Signal Separation (ICA2003),* (pp. 245-256).

Kaartinen, J., Mierisova, S., Oja, J. M. E., Usenius, J. P., Kauppinen, R. A., & Hiltunen, Y. (1998). Automated quantification of human brain metabolites by artificial neural network analysis from in vivo single-voxel 1H NMR spectra. *Journal of Magnetic Resonance, 134*, 176-179.

Kadowaki, T., & Nishimori, H. (1998). Quantum annealing in the transverse Ising model. *Phys. Rev. E, 58*(5), 5355-5363.

Kaipio, J., & Somersalo, E. (2005). *Statistical and computational inverse problems.* Springer.

Kak, S. (1995). Quantum Neural Computing, *Advances in Imaging and Electron Physics, 94*, 259-313.

Kak, S. (1999). Quantum computing and AI. *IEEE Intelligent Systems, 14*(4), 9–11.

Kak, S. C. (1995). On quantum neural computing. *Information Sciences, 83*, 143-163.

Kalos, M., & Witlock, P. A. (1986). *Monte Carlo methods.* New York, NY: John Wiley & Sons.

Kane, B. E. (1998). A silicon-based nuclear spin quantum computer. *Nature, 393*(6681), 133-137.

Karayiannis, N. B., & Randolph-Gips, M. M. (2003). On the construction and training of reformulated radial basis function neural networks. *IEEE Trans. Neural Networks*, (4), 835–846.

Katz, G., & Sadot, D. (2007). Radial basis function network equalizer for optical communication OOK system. *Journal of Light Wave Technology, 25*(9), 2631-2637.

Kazakov, A. Y. (1998). A micromaser on single atom with optical pumping. *Journ. Quantum and Semiclass. Optics, 10*, 753-763.

Kazakov, A. Y. (2001). Two-photon one atom micromaser with permanent optical pumping. *Journal of Optics B, 3*(3), 97-106.

Kazakov, A. Y. (2002). *Dense coding and safety of quantum communications.* E-print: LANL Arxiv: quant-ph/0205101.

Kazakov, A. Y. (2003). Modified Jeans- Cammings systems and a quantum version of knapsack problem. *Journ. Exp. Teor. Fiz. 124,* 3(11), 1-7.

Kazakov, A. Y. (2006). Geometric measure of three-partite pure states. *International Journal of Quantum Information, 4*(6), 907-916.

Kazakov, A. Y. (2007). *Elementary constructive approach to the higher-rank numerical ranges of unitary matrices.* E-print: LANL Arxiv: quant-ph/0707.170.

Kazakov, A.Y. (2002). Jaynes-Cummings systems driven by classical fields. *Intern. Journ. Theoret. Phys., Group Theory and Nonl. Opt., 8*(1), 75-104.

Kechriotis, G., & Manolakos, E. S. (1994). Training Fully Recurrent Neural Networks with Complex Weights. *IEEE Transactions on Circuits and Systems-II, 41*(2), 235–238.

Kechriotis, G., Zervas, E., & Manolakos, E. S. (1994). Using recurrent neural networks for adaptive communication channel equalization. *IEEE Trans. Neural Networks, 5*(2), 267–278.

Kennedy, M. P., & Chua, L. O. (1988). Neural networks for nonlinear programming. *IEEE Transactions on Circuits and Systems, 35(5)*, 554-562.

Khovanskii, A. (1991). Fewnomials, Translations of Mathem. Monographs. *Amer. Math. Soc., 88.*

Kim, M. S., & Guest, C. C. (1990). Modification of back-propagation for complex-valued signal processing in frequency domain. In *International Joint Conference on Neural Networks* 1990 San Diego (pp. 27-31). New York: IEEE.

Kim, T., & Adali, T. (2000). Fully complex backpropagation for constant envelope signal Processing. *Proc. IEEE Workshop on Neural Networks for Signal Processing (NNSP), 1*, 231-240, Sydney Australia.

Kim, T., & Adali, T. (2001). Complex backpropagation neural network using elementary transcendental activation function. *Proc. IEEE Int. Conf. on Acoustics, Speech, Signal Processing (ICASSP)*, Salt Lake city UT, *2*, 1281-1284.

Kim, T., & Adali, T. (2001). Nonlinear satellite channel equalization using fully complex feed-forward neural networks. *Poc. of IEEE Workshop on Nonlinear Signal and Image Processing*, (pp. 141–150). Baltimore.

Kim, T., & Adali, T. (2002). Fully complex multilayer perceptron network for nonlinear signal processing. *Journal of VLSI Signal Processing Systems for Signal, Image and Video Technology, Special Issue: Neural Networks for Signal Processing, 32*, 29-43.

Kim, T., & Adali, T. (2002). Universal approximation of fully complex feed-foreward neural network. *In Proc. Of IEEE ICASSP'02*, (pp. 973-976).

Kim, T., & Adali, T. (2003). Approximation by Fully-complex Multilayer Perceptrons. *Neural Computation, 15*(7), 1641-1666.

Kim, T.. & Adali, T. (2001)/ Approximation by fully complex MLP using elementary transcendental activation functions. *In Proceedings of Neural Networks for Signal Processing XI*, (pp. 203-212).

Kinjo, M., Sato, S., & Nakajima, K. (2003). Quantum

Adiabatic Evolution Algorithm for a Quantum Neural Network. In Kaynak, Alpaydin, Oja, & Xu (Eds.), *Artificial Neural Networks and Neural Information Processing* (pp. 951-958). Berlin: Springer.

Kinjo, M., Sato, S., & Nakajima, K. (2006). A Study on Learning with a Quantum Neural Network. *Proceedings of IEEE World Congress on Computational Intelligence, 1618.*

Kinjo, M., Sato, S., Nakamiya, Y., & Nakajima, K. (2005). Neuromorphic quantum computation with energy dissipation. *Physical Review A, 72*(5), 052328.

Kinouchi, M., & Hagiwara, M. (1995). Learning Temporal Sequences by Complex Neurons with Local Feedback. *Proceedings of IEEE International Conference on Neural Networks, VI*, 3165–3169.

Kirkpatrick, S., Gelatt, C. D., & Vecchi, M. P. (1983). Optimization by Simulated Annealing. *Science, 220*(4598), 671-680.

Klebaner, F. C. (2005). *Introduction to Stochastic Analysis and Calculus.* Imperial College Press.

Kobayashi, M., & Yamazaki, H. (2003). Information geometry of complex-valued boltzmann machines. (in Japanese) *IEICE Transactions on Fundamentals of Electronics, Communications and Computer Sciences, J87-A*(8), 1093-1101.

Kobayashi, M., Muramatsu, J., & Yamazaki, H. (2003). Construction of high-dimensional neural networks by linear connections of matrices. *Electronics and Communications in Japan, Part 3, 86*(11), 38-45.

Kocarev, L. J. (1995). Chaos synchronization of high-dimensional dynamical systems. *Proc. of IEEE Int'l Symp. on Circ. Sys.*, Seattle, WA, April 29 - May 3, (pp. 1009-1012).

Kohonen, T. (1977). *Associative Memory: A system theoretic approach.* Berlin: Springer-Verlag.

Kolmogorov, A. N. (1957). On the representation of continuous functions of many variables by superposition of continuous functions of one variable and addition. *Doklady Akademii Nauk SSSR, 114*(5), 953-956. (1963). *Translations American Mathematical Society, 2*(28), 55-59.

Kosko, B. (1987, December). Adaptive Bidirectional Associative Memories. *Applied Optics, 26*(23), 4947-4960.

Kosko, B. (1988). Bidirectional associative memories. *IEEE Trans. Syst. Man Cybern., 18*, 49-60.

Kosugi, Y., & Kameyama, K. (1993). Inverse use of BP net in answer-in-weights scheme for arithmetic calculations. *Proceeding of the World Congress on Neural Networks, III*, 462–465.

Kosugi, Y., Uemoto, N., & Ogawa, T. (1998). Dynamic regularization in the network inversion, *IEICE Transaction on Information and Systems, J81-D-II*(7), 1639–1646 (in Japanese).

Kouda, N., Matsui, N., & Nishimura, H. (2002). Image Compression by Layered Quantum Neural Networks. *Neural Processing Letters, 16(1)*, 67-80.

Kouda, N., Matsui, N., & Nishimura, H. (2002, 2004). A multi-layered feed-forward network based on qubit neuron model. (2002 in Japanese) *IEICE, J85-DII(4)*, 641-648. (2004 in English) *Systems and Computers in Japan, 35(13)*, 43-51.

Kouda, N., Matsui, N., Nishimura, H., & Peper, F. (2005). Qubit Neural Network and Its Learning Efficiency, *Neural Computing and Applications, 14(2)*, 114-121.

Kouda, N., Matsui, N., Nishimura, H., & Peper, F. (2005). An Examination of Qubit Neural Network in Controlling an Inverted Pendulum. *Neural Processing Letters, 22(3)*, 277-290.

Kuc, R., & Barshan, B. (1991). Bat-like sonar for guiding mobile robots. *IEEE Control Systems*, (pp. 4–12).

Kuipers, J. B. (1998). *Quaternions and Rotation Sequences: A Primer with Applications to Orbits, Aerospace and Virtual Reality.* Princeton: Princeton University Press.

Kumar, A., Manmohan V., Udayshankar, M., Vishwanathan, M., & Chakravarthy, V. S. (2002). Link between Energy and Computation in a Physical Model of Hopfield

Network. *Proc. of the 9th International Conference on Neural Information Processing* (pp. 267-270). Singapore.

Kurková, V. (1991). Kolmogorov's theorem is relevant. *Neural Computation, 3*(4), 617-622.

Kurková, V. (1992). Kolmogorov's theorem and multilayer neural networks. *Neural Networks, 5*(3), 501-506.

Kuroe, Y. (2003). A model of complex-valued associative memories and its dynamics. In A. Hirose (Ed.), *Complex-Valued Neural Networks: Theories and Applications,* (pp. 57-80). USA, World Scientific Pub Co Inc.

Kuroe, Y., & Taniguchi, T. (2005). Models of Self-Correlation Type Complex-Valued Associative Memories and Their Dynamics. In W. Duch et. al.(Eds.), *Artificial Neural Networks: Biological Inspirations - ICANN 2005,* Lecture Notes in Computer Science, *3696*, 185-192. Springer-Verlag.

Kuroe, Y., Hashimoto, N., & Mori, T. (2001). Qualitative analysis of continuous complex-valued associative memories. In G. Dorffner, H. Bischof, and K. Hornik (Eds.), *Lecture Notes in Computer Science, 2130. Artificial Neural Networks - ICANN 2001* (pp. 843-850). Berlin: Springer-Verlag.

Kuroe, Y., Hashimoto, N., & Mori, T. (2001). Qualitative analysis of a self-correlation type complex-valued associative memories. *Nonlinear Analysis, 47,* 5795-5806.

Kuroe, Y., Hashimoto, N., & Mori, T. (2002). On energy function for complex-valued neural networks and its applications. *Proceedings of the 9th International Conference on Neural Information Processing* [CD-ROM], Singapore.

Kuroe, Y., Yoshida, M., & Mori, T. (2003). On activation functions for complex-valued neural networks: existence of energy functions. In O. Kaynak et al. (Eds.), *Lecture Notes in Computer Science, 2714. Artificial Neural Networks and Neural Information Processing - ICANN/ICONIP 2003* (pp. 985-992). Berlin: Springer-Verlag.

Kusamichi, H., Isokawa, T., Matsui, N., Ogawa, Y., & Maeda, K. (2004). A New Scheme for Color Night Vision by Quaternion Neural Network. In *Proceedings of the 2nd International Conference on Autonomous Robots and Agents* (pp.101–106).

Kwong, K., Belliveau, J. W., Chesler, D. A., Goldberg, I. E., Weisskoff, R. M., Poncelet, B. P., Kennedy, D. N., Hoppel, B. E., Cohen, M. S., Turner, R., Cheng, H., Brady, T. J., & Rosen, B. R. (1992). Dynamic magnetic resonance imaging of human brain activity during primary sensory stimulation. *Proceedings of the National Academy of Sciences, 89(12)*, 5675-5679.

Labat, J., Macchi, O., & Laot, C. (1998). Adaptive decision feedback equalization: Can you skip the training period. *IEEE Trans. Communications, 46*(7), 921–930.

Lambek, J. (1995). If Hamilton Had Prevailed: Quaternions in Physics. *The Mathematical Intelligencer, 17,* 7–15.

Lancaster P., & Tismenetsky, M. (1985). *The Theory of Matrices: With Applications*, 2nd ed. Academic Press, New York.

Landauer, R. (1961, July). Irreversibility and Heat Generation in the Computing Process. *IBM Journal of Research and Development, 3,* 183-191.

Laroche, B., Martin, Ph., & Petit, N. (2007). Commande par platitude: Equations différentielles ordinaires et aux derivées partielles. *Ecole Nationale Supérieure des Techniques Avancées*, Paris.

Lee, D. L. (1998). A discrete sequential bidirectional associative memory for multistep pattern recognition. *Pattern Recognit. Lett., 19,* 1087–1102.

Lee, D. L. (2001). Improving the capacity of complex-valued neural networks with a modified gradient descent learning rule. *IEEE Transactions on Neural Networks, 12*(2), 439-443.

Lee, D. L. (2003). Complex-valued neural associative memories: Network stability and learning algorithm. In A. Hirose (Ed.), *Complex-Valued Neural Networks: Theories and Applications,* (pp. 29-55). USA, World Scientific Pub Co Inc.

Lee, D.-L. (1998). Generalised Intraconnected Bidirectional Associative Memories. *Electronics Letters, 34*(8), 736-738.

Lee, D.-L. (1999). New stability conditions for Hopfield networks in partial simultaneous update mode. *IEEE Trans. Neural Networks., 10*(4), 975-978.

Lee, D.-L. (2001). Relaxation of the stability condition of the complex-valued neural networks. *IEEE Trans. Neural Networks, 12*(5), 1260-1262.

Lee, D.-L. (2006). Improvement of Complex-valued Hopfield Associative Memory by using Generalized Projection Rules. *IEEE Trans. on Neural Networks, 17*(5), 1341-1347.

Lee, M.-J., & Choi, Y.-K. (2004). An adaptive neurocontroller using RBFN for robot manipulators. *IEEE Trans. Industrial Electronics*, (3), 711–717.

Lee, T. W., Girolami, M., Bell, A. J., & Sejnowsky, T. J. (2000). A Unifying Information-Theoretic framework for independent Component Analysis. *In Computer & Mathematics with applications, 39*(11), 11-21.

Leonard, J. A., & Kramer, M. A. (1991). Radial basis function networks for classifying process faults. *IEEE Control Systems Magazine*, (3), 31–38.

Leung, H., & Haykin, S. (1991). The complex backpropagation algorithm. *IEEE Transactions on Signal Processing, 39*(9), 2101-2104.

Levine H., & Rappel, W. J. (2000). Self-organization in systems of self-propelled particles. *Physical Review E, 63.*

Li, C., Sun, W., & Kurths, J. (2007). Synchronization between two coupled complex networks, *Phys Rev E Stat Nonlin Softmatter Phys*, October, 76(4-2).

Li, G., &Yu, K. B. (1988). Modeling and simulation of coherent Weibull clutter. *IEE Proceedings, Part. F, 136*(1), 1-9.

Li, H., & Adali, T. (2006). Gradient and Fixed-Point Complex ICA Algorithms Based on Kurtosis Maximization. *In Proceedings of the 16th Workshop on Machine Learning for Signal Processing*, (pp. 85-90).

Li, H., & Adali, T. (2008). Stability analysis of complex maximum likelihood ICA using Wirtinger calculus. *In Proc. of IEEE Int. Conf. on Acoustic, Speech and Signal Processing*, (pp. 1801-1804).

Li, J. H., & Michel, A. N. (1988). Qualitative Analysis and Synthesis of a Class of Neural Networks. *IEEE Transactions on Circuits and Systems, 35*(8), 976–986.

Li, M. B., Huang, G. B., Saratchandran, P., & Sundarrajan, N. (2006). Complex-valued growing and pruning RBF neural networks for communication channel equalization. *IEE Proc. Vision, Image and Signal Processing, 153*(4), 411-418.

Li, M.-B., Huang, G.-B., Saratchandran, P., & Sundararajan, N. (2005). Fully complex extreme learning machine. *Neurocomputing*, (pp. 306–314).

Li, Y., Sundararajan, N., Saratchandran, P., & Wang, Z. (2004). Robust neuro- controller design for aircraft auto-landing. *IEEE Trans. Aerospace and Electronic Systems*, (1), 158–167.

Liang, X. -B., & Si, J. (2001). Global exponential stability of neural networks with globally Lipschitz continuous activations and its application to linear variational inequality problem. *IEEE Transactions on Neural Networks, 12(2)*, 349-359.

Linden, A., & Kindermann, J. (1989). Inversion of multilayer nets. *Proceedings of International Joint Conference on Neural Networks*, (pp. 425–430).

Litva, J., & Lo, T. K. Y. (1996). *Digital Beamforming in Wireless Communications.* London: Artech House.

Ljung, L. (2000). *System identification theory for the user.* Englewood Cliffs, NJ: Prentice Hall.

Lorentz, G. G., von Golitschek, M., & Makovoz, Y. (1996). *Constructive approximation. Advanced problems.* New York: Springer.

Lounesto, P. (2001). *Clifford algebras and spinors.* Cambridge: Cambridge University Press.

Lu, B. L., & Ito, K. (1995). Regularization of inverse kinematics for redundant manipulators using neural network inversions. *Proceedings of the IEEE International Conference on Neural Networks, 5*, 2726-2731.

Lu, W., & Chen, T. (2004). Synchronization of coupled connected neural networks with delays. *IEEE Trans Circ Syst I, **51***, 2491–2503.

Luenberger, D. G. (1969). *Optimization by vector space methods*. NY: John Wiley.

Luenberger, D. G. (1973). *Introduction to Linear and Nonlinear Programming*. Reading, MA: Addison-Wesley.

Luo, F-L., & Unbehauen, R. (1997). *Applied neural networks for signal processing*. NY: Cambridge University Press.

Ma, L., & Khorasani, K. (2002). Application of Adaptive Constructive Neural Networks to Image Compression, *IEEE Transactions on Neural Networks, 13*(5), 1112-1125.

Ma, L., & Khorasani, K. (2005). Constructive Feedforward Neural Networks Using Hermite Polynomial Activation Functions. IEEE Transactions on Neural Networks, 16(4), 821-833.

Maa, C. -Y., & Shanblatt, M. A. (1992). Linear and quadratic programming neural network analysis. *IEEE Transactions on Neural Networks, 3(4)*, 580-594.

Maass, W., & Bishop, C. (1999). *Pulsed Neural Networks*. Cambridge, MA: MIT Press.

Macchi, O., & Eweda, E. (1984). Convergence analysis of self-adaptive equalizers. *IEEE Trans. on Inform. Theory, 30*, 161-176.

Maddams, W. F. (1980). The scope and Limitations of Curve Fitting. *Applied Spectroscopy, 34*(3), 245-267.

Mahler, G., & Weberuss, V. A. (1998). *Quantum Networks: Dynamics of Open Nanostructures*. Springer.

Mak, M.-W., & Kung, S.-Y. (2000). Estimation of elliptical basis function parameters by the EM algorithm with application to speaker verification. *IEEE Trans. Neural Networks*, (4), 961–969.

Mallat, S. (1998). *A wavelet tour of signal processing*. Academic Press.

Mandic P. D., & Goh, S. L. (2004, December). A complex-valued RTRL Algorithm for recurrent Neural networks. *Neural Computation, 16*(12), 2699–2713.

Mandic, D. P., & Chambers, J. A. (2001). *Recurrent neural networks for prediction: Learning algorithms Architectures and stability*. John Wiley and Sons.

Mansfield, P. (1977). Multi-planar image formation using NMR spin echoes. *Journal of Physical C: Solid State Physics, 10*, L55-L58.

Mao, K. Z. (2002). RBF neural network center selection based on Fisher ratio class separability measure. *IEEE Trans. Neural Networks*, (5), 1211–1217.

Marsden, M., & Schoenberg, I. J. (1998). On Variation Diminishing Spline Approximation Methods, Technical report, Defense Technical Information Center OAI-PMH Repository (United States).

Matsui, N., Isokawa, T., Kusamichi, H., Peper, F., & Nishimura, H. (2004). Quaternion Neural Network with Geometrical Operators. *Journal of Intelligent & Fuzzy Systems, 15*(3–4), 149–164.

Matsui, N., Takai, M., & Nishimura, H. (1998, 2000). A network model based on qubit-like neuron corresponding to quantum circuit. (1998 in Japanese) *IEICE, J81-A(12)*, 1687-1692. (2000 in English) *Electronics and Communications in Japan, part III, 83(10)*, 67-73.

McCulloch, W. S., & Pitts, W. (1943). A logical calculus of the ideas immanent in nervous activity. *Bull. of Mathematical Biophysics, 5*, 115-133.

McEliece, R. J., Posner, E. C., Rodemich, E. R., & Venkatech, E. R. (1987). The capacity of the Hopfield associative memory. *IEEE Transactions on Information Theory, 33*(4), 461-482.

McLoone, S., Brown, M. D., Irwin, G., & Lightbody, A. (1998). A hybrid linear/nonlinear training algorithm for feedforward neural networks. *IEEE Trans. Neural Networks*, (4), 669–684.

Melki, P. S., Mulkern, R. V., Panych, L. S., & Jolesz, F. A. (1991). Comparing the FAISE method with conventional dual-echo sequences. *Journal of Magnetic Resonance Imaging, 1*, 319-326.

Menneer, T. (1998, May). Quantum Artificial Neural Networks. Ph.D. thesis of The University of Exeter, UK.

Menneer, T., & Narayanan, A. (1995). *Quantum-inspired neural networks* (Tech. Rep. R329). Exeter, United Kingdom: University of Exeter, Department of Computer Science.

Messiah, A. (1958). *Quantum Mechanics.* New York: John Wiley & Sons.

Meyer, C. H., Hu, B. S., Nishimura, D. G., & Macovski, A. (1992). Fast Spiral Coronary Artery Imaging. *Magnetic Resonance in Medicine, 28*(2), 202-213.

Mhascar, H., & Miccheli, C. (1992). Approximation by superposition of sigmoidal and radial basis functions. *Advances in Applied Mathematics, 13*(3), 350-373.

Mierisová, S., & Ala-Korpela, M. (2001). MR spectroscopy quantification: a review of frequency domain methods. *NMR in Biomedicine, 14*, 247-259.

Milanovic, V., & Zaghloul, M. E. (1996). Synchronization of chaotic neural networks and applications to comminications. *Int'l J. of Bifur. Chaos, 6*, 2571-2585.

Mitchell, M. (1996). *An introduction to genetic algorithms.* Cambridge, MA: The MIT Press.

Moody, J., & Darken, C. J. (1989). Fast-learning in networks of locally-tuned processing units. *Neural Computation*, (2), 281–294.

Mori, K., Isokawa, T., Kouda, N., Matsui, N., & Nishimura, H. (2006). Qubit Inspired Neural Network towards Its Practical Applications. In *Proceedings of 2006 International Joint Conference on Neural Networks* (pp. 616-621).

Mukai, R., Vilnrotter, V. A., Arabshahi, P., & Jamnejad, V. (2002). Adaptive acquisition and tracking for deep space array feed antennas. *IEEE Trans. Neural Networks*, (5), 1149–1162.

Mukundan, R. (2002). Quaternions: From Classical Mechanics to Computer Graphics, and Beyond. In *Proceedings of the 7th asian technology conference in mathematics* (pp. 97–105).

Muller, G. (1998). *Quantum Mechanics: Symmetries*, 2nd Edition. Springer.

Muraki, S., Nakai, T., Kita, Y., & Tsuda, K. (2001). An attempt for coloring multichannel MR imaging data. *IEEE Trans. Visualization and Computer Graphics*, (3), 265–274.

Murray, W. R., Heg, C. T., & Pohlhammer, C. M. (1993). Iterative inversion of a neural network for estimating the location of a planar object. *Proceedings of World Congress on Neural Networks, 3*, 188-193.

Müezzinoğlu, M. K., Güzeliş, C., & Zurada, J. M. (2003). A new design method for the complex-valued multistate Hopfield associative memory. *IEEE Trans. Neural Networks, 14*(4) 891-899.

Nakamiya, Y., Kinjo, M., Takahashi, O., Sato, S., & Nakajima, K. (2006). Quantum neural network composed of Kane's qubits. *Jpn. J. Appl. Phys., 45*(10A), 8030-8034.

Nakamura, Y., & Munakata, T. (1995). Neural network model composed of multidirectional spin neurons. *Physical Review E, 51*(2), 1538-1546.

Nakamura, Y., Pashkin, Y., & Tsai, J. S. (1999). Coherent control of macroscopic quantum states in a single-Cooper-pair box. *Nature, 398*(6730), 786-788.

Nakaoka, M. (1977). *Fixed point theorem and its circumference.* Tokyo: Iwanami Pub. Co., Ltd., (in Japanese).

Narayanan, A., & Menneer, T. (2000). Quantum artificial neural network architectures and components. *Information Sciences, 128*, 231-255.

Naressi, A., Couturier, C., Castang, I., de. Beer, R., & Graveron-Demilly, D. (2001). Java-based graphical user interface for MRUI, a software package for quantitation of in vivo medical magnetic resonance spectroscopy signals. *Computers in Biology and Medicine, 31*, 269-286.

Nemoto, I. (2003). Complex associative memory and

complex single neuron models. In A. Hirose (Ed.), *Complex-Valued Neural Networks: Theories and Applications,* (pp. 107-130). USA, World Scientific Pub Co Inc.

Nemoto, I., & Kono, T. (1991). Complex-Valued Neural Networks. *The Institute of Electronics, Information and Communication Engineers (IEICE) Transaction on Information and Systems, 74-D-*(9), 1282-1288 (in Japanese).

Nemoto, I., & Kubono, M. (1996). Complex associative memory. *Neural Networks, 9*(2), 253-261.

Ng, S. X., Yee, M.-S., & Hanzo, L. (2004). Coded modulation assisted radial basis function aided turbo equalization for dispersive Rayleigh-fading channels. *IEEE Trans. Wireless Communications*, (6), 2198–2206.

Niederreiter, H. (1978). Quasi-Monte Carlo methods and pseudorandom numbers. *Bulletin of American Mathematical Society*, *84*, 957-1041.

Nielsen, M. A., & Chuang, I. L. (Eds.). (2000). *Quantum Computation and Quantum Information*. Cambridge, UK: Cambridge University Press.

Nilsson, N. J. (1965). *Learning Machines*. McGraw-Hill.

Nilsson, N., J. (1998). *Artificial intelligence. A new synthesis*. SanFrancisco, CA: Morgan Kaufmann Publishers.

Nishikawa, I., & Kuroe, Y. (2004). Dynamics of Complex-Valued Neural Networks and Its Relation to a Phase Oscillator System. In N. R. Pal, N. Kasabov, R. K. Mudi, S. Pal, & S. K. Parui (Eds.), *Neural Information Processing ICONIP 2004*, Lecture Notes in Computer Science, *3316*, 122-129. Springer-Verlag.

Nishikawa, I., Iritani, T., Sakakibara, K., & Kuroe, Y. (2005) Phase Dynamics of Complex-valued Neural Networks and Its Application to Traffic Signal Control. *International Journal of Neural Systems, 15*(1 & 2), 111-120.

Nishikawa, I., Sakakibara, K., Iritani, T., & Kuroe, Y. (2005). 2 Types of Complex-Valued Hopfield Networks and the Application to a Traffic Signal Control. *Proceedings of International Joint Conference on Neural Networks*, 782-787.

Nitta, T. (1991). A Complex Back-propagation Learning, *Transactions of Information Processing Society of Japan, 32*(10), 1319-1329 (in Japanese).

Nitta, T. (1993). A three-dimensional back-propagation. *Proceedings of INNS World Congress on Neural Networks, 3*, 572-575.

Nitta, T. (1993). A back-propagation algorithm for neural networks based on 3D vector product. *Proceedings of IEEE/INNS International Joint Conference on Neural Networks, 1*, 589-592.

Nitta, T. (1993). Proposal of neural networks based on vector product. *Proceedings of CIE/IEEE International Conference on Neural Networks and Signal Processing,* (pp. 397-402).

Nitta, T. (1993). An extension of the back-propagation algorithm to three dimensions by vector product. *Proceedings of the 5th IEEE International Conference on Tools with Artificial Intelligence,* (pp. 460-461).

Nitta, T. (1994). Ability of the 3D Vector Version of the Back-Propagation to Learn 3D Motion. In *Proceedings of INNS World Congress on Neural Networks* (WCNN'94-SanDiego), 3, 262–267.

Nitta, T. (1994). Generalization ability of the three-dimensional back-propagation network. *Proceedings of IEEE International Conference on Neural Networks, 5*, 2895-2900.

Nitta, T. (1995). A Quaternary Version of the Back-propagation Algorithm. In *Proceedings of IEEE international conference on neural networks* (ICNN'95-Perth) 5, 2753–2756.

Nitta, T. (1996). An Extension of the Back-propagation Algorithm to Quaternions. In *Proceedings of international conference on neural information processing* (ICONIP'96), 1, 247–250.

Nitta, T. (1997). An Extension of the Back-Propagation Algorithm to Complex Numbers. *Neural Networks, 10*(8), 1391-1415.

Nitta, T. (2000). Complex-valued neural networks. *The Journal of the Institute of Electronics, Information, and Communication Engineers, 83(8)*, 612-615 (in Japanese).

Nitta, T. (2003). On the inherent property of the decision boundary in complex-valued neural networks. *Neurocomputing, 50*(1), 291-303.

Nitta, T. (2004). A Solution to the 4-bit Parity Problem with a Single Quaternary Neuron. *Neural Information Processing - Letters and Reviews 5*(2), 33–39.

Nitta, T. (2006). Three-dimensional vector valued neural network and its generalization abilities. *Neural Information Processing – Letters and Reviews, 10*(10), 237-242.

Nitta, T., & Furuya, T. (1991). A complex back-propagation learning. *Transactions of Information Processing Society of Japan, 32*(10), 1319-1329.

Nitta, T., & Garis, H. D. (1992). A 3D vector version of the back-propagation algorithm. *Proceedings of IEEE/INNS International Joint Conference on Neural Networks, 2*, 511-516.

Noest, A. J. (1988). Phaser Neural Network. In D. Z.Anderson, (Ed.), *Neural Information Processing Systems*, (pp. 584–591). New York: AIP.

Noest, A. J. (1988). Associative Memory in Sparse Phasor Neural Networks. *Europhysics Letters, 6*(4), 469–474.

Noest, A. J. (1988). Discrete-state phasor neural networks. *Physical Review A, 38*(4), 2196-2199.

Novey, M., & Adali, T. (2008). Complex ICA by Negentropy Maximization. *IEEE Transaction on Neural Networks, 19*(4), 596-609.

Ogawa, S., Lee, T. M., Nayak, A. S., & Glynn, P. (1990). Oxygenation-sensitive contrast in magnetic resonance image of rodent brain at high magnetic fields. *Magnetic Resonance in Medicine, 14*(1), 68-78.

Ogawa, T., & Kanada, H. (2005). Complex-valued network inversion for solving complex-valued inverse problems, *IEICE Transaction on Information and System, J88-D-II*(9), 1954-1962 (in Japanese).

Ogawa, T., & Kanada, H. (2005). Network inversion for complex-valued neural networks. In *Proceedings of the 2005 IEEE International Symposium on Signal Processing and Information Technology*, (pp. 850-855).

Ogawa, T., Jitsukawa, N., Kanada, H., Mori, K., & Sakata, M. (2002). Neural network estimation of elastic moduli of composites by impact sound. *Japanese Journal of Applied Physics, 41*(5B), 3333-3338.

Ogawa, T., Kameyama, K., Kuc, R., & Kosugi Y. (1996). Source localization with network inversion using an answer-in-weights scheme. *IEICE Transaction on Information and Systems, E79-D*(5), 608-619.

Ogawa, T., Matsuura, H., & Kanada, H. (2005). A solution of inverse kinematics of robot arm by network inversion. *Proceeding of the International Conference on Computational Intelligence for Modeling*, 1, 858-862.

Oh, S. H., & Lee, Y. (1994). Effect of nonlinear transformation on correlation between weighted sums in multilayer perceptron. *IEEE Trans. on Neural Networks, 5*(3), 508-510.

Ong, S., You, C., Choi, S., & Hong D. (1997). A decision feedback recurrent neural equalizer as an infinite impulse response filter. *IEEE Trans. Signal Processing, 45*(11), 2851–2858.

Ono, A., Sato, S., Kinjo, M., & Nakajima, K. (2008). Study on the Performance of Neuromorphic Adiabatic Quantum Computation Algorithms. *Proceedings of the 2008 IEEE World Congress on Computational Intelligence*, (pp. 2508-2512).

Oppenheim, A. V., & Schafer, R. W. (1975). *Digital signal processing*. Englewood Cliffs, NJ: Prentice Hall.

Ott, E., Grebogi, C., James, A. Y. (1990, March). Controlling chaos. *Physical Review letters, 64*(11), 1196-1199.

Oyang, Y.-J., Hwang, S.-C., Ou, Y.-Y., Chen, C.-Y., & Chen, Z. W. (2005). Data classification with radial basis function networks based on a novel kernel density estimation algorithm. *IEEE Trans. Neural Networks*, (1), 225–236.

Pandey, R. (2001). *Blind equalization and source separation using neural networks.* Doctoral dissertation, I.I.T. Roorkee, India.

Pandey, R. (2004). Complex Valued Neural Networks for Blind Equalization of Time- Varying Channels. *International Journal of Signal Processing, 1*(1), 1-8.

Pandey, R. (2005). Complex Valued Recurrent Neural Networks for Blind Equalization. *International Journal of Modelling and Simulation, 25*(3), 182-189.

Pandey, R. (2005). A Feedforward Neural Network for Blind Equalization with PSK Signal. *Neural Computing & Applications, 14*(4), 290-298.

Papoulis, A. (1991). *Probability, random variables, and stochastic processes.* Third Edition, New York, McGraw-Hill.

Parisi, R., Elio Claudio D. D., Orlandi G., & Rao B. D.(1997). Fast adaptive digital equalization by recurrent neural network. *IEEE Trans. Signal Processing, 45*(11), 2731 – 2739.

Parra, L., & Deco, G. (1995). Continuous boltzmann machine with rotor neurons. *Neural Networks, 8*(3), 375-385.

Paulraj, A., Nabar, R., & Gore, D. (2003). *Introduction to Space-Time Wireless Communications.* Cambridge, U.K.: Cambridge University Press.

Pearson, J. (2003). Clifford Networks. In A. Hirose (Ed.), *Complex-Valued Neural Networks: Theories and Applications,* (pp. 81-106). USA, World Scientific Pub Co Inc.

Pearson, J. K., & Bisset, D. L. (1992). Back Propagation in a Clifford Algebra. In *Proceedings of International Conference on Artificial Neural Networks*, 2, 413–416.

Pecora, L. M., & Carroll T. L. (1990). Synchronization in Chaotic Systems. *Physical Review Letters, 64*(8), 821-824.

Pedricz, W. (1998). *Computational intelligence. An introduction.* Boca Raton, FL: CRC Press.

Peng, H., Ozaki, T., Haggan-Ozaki, V., & Toyoda, Y. (2003). A parameter optimization method for radial basis function type models. *IEEE Trans. Neural Networks,* (2), 432–438.

Personnaz, L., Guyon, I, & Dreyfus, G (1986). Collective computational properties of neural networks: new learning mechanisms. *Phys. Rev., A34*, 4217-4228.

Personnaz, L., Guyon, I., Dreyfus, G.., & Toulouse, G. (1986). A biologically constrained learning mechanism in networks of formal neurons. *J. Statistical Phys., 43,* 411-422.

Perus, M. (1996). Neuro-Quantum Parallelism in Brain-Mind and Computers. *Informatica, 20,* 173-183.

Perus, M. (2000). Neural networks as a basis for Quantum Associative Networks. *Neural Network World, 10,* 1001-1013.

Perus, M. (2001). Multi-level synergetic computation in brain. *Nonlinear Phenomena in Complex Systems,* (2), 157–193.

Peruš, M., Bischof, H., Caulfield, J., & Loo, C.K. (2004). Quantum implementable selective reconstruction of high resolution images. *Applied Optics, 43*(33), 6134-6138.

Petritis, D. (1996). Thermodynamic formalism of neural computing. In E. Goles & S. Martinez (Eds.), *Dynamics of complex interacting systems* (pp. 81-146). Kluwer Academic Publishers: Dodrecht.

Petritis, D. (2008). An approach to genome statistics inspired by stochastic or quantum models of computing: a survey. Accepted for publication in *Studies in computational intelligence.* Springer-Verlag.

Petrov, Y. P., & Sizikov, V. S. (2005). *Well-posed, ill-posed, and intermediate problems with application.* Koninklijke Brill NV.

Pham, D. T., Garrat, D., & Jutten, C. (1992). Separation of mixture of independent sources through maximum likelihood approach. *In Proc. EUSIPCO,* (pp. 771-774).

Piazza, F., Uncini, A., & Zenobi, M. (1993). Neural Networks with Digital LUT Activation Function. *In Proceedings of IJCNN,* (pp. 1401-1404).

Picchi, G., & Prati, G. (1987). Blind equalization and carrier recovery using a 'stop & go' decision-directed algorithm. *IEEE Trans. on Comm., 35*, 877-887.

Pierani, A., Piazza, F., Solazzi, M., & Uncini, A. (2000). Low Complexity Adaptive Non-Linear Function for Blind Signal Separation. *In Proc. of IEEE IJCNN2000*, (pp. 333-338).

Pinsky, M. A. (1991). *Partial Differential Equations and Boundary Value Problems with Applications*. McGraw-Hill.

Pistone, G., & Rogantin, M. P. (1999). The exponential statistical manifold: mean parameters, orthogonality and space transformations. *Bernoulli, 5*(4), 721-760.

Pistone, G., & Sempi, C. (1995). An infinite-dimensional geometric structure on the space of all the probability measures equivalent to a given one. *The Annals of Statistics, 23*(5), 1543-1561.

Poggio, T., & Girosi, F. (1990). Networks for approximation and learning. *Proc. IEEE*, (9), 1481–1497.

Porteous, lan R. (1995). *Clifford algebras and the classical groups*. Cambridge: Cambridge University Press.

Powell, A. M. (2005). Time-frequency mean and variance sequences of orthonormal bases. *J. Fourier Analysis and Applications*, (pp. 375-387).

Powell, M. J. D. (1987). Radial basis functions for multivariable interpolation: a review. In J. C. Mason & M. G. Cox (Eds.), *Algorithms for Approximations* (pp. 143–167). Oxford.

Prenter, P. M. (1975). Splines and variational methods. New York, NY: John Wiley & Sons.

Previn, E., & Webb J. A. (1983). Quaternions in Computer Vision and Robotics. In *Proceedings of International Conference on Computer Vision and Pattern Recognition* (pp. 382-383).

Proakis, J. G. (1989). *Digital Communications*. McGraw-Hill.

Proakis, J. G. (1995). *Digital Communications*. Singapore: McGraw Hill.

Provencher, S. W. (2001). Automatic quantification of localized in vivo ^{1}H spectra with LCModel. *NMR in Biomedicine, 14*(4), 260-264.

Purusothaman, G., & Karayiannis, N. B. (1997). Quantum neural networks (QNNS)—inherently fuzzy feedforward neural networks. *IEEE Transactions on Neural Networks, 8*(3), 679–693.

Raichle, M. E. (1986). Neuroimaging. *Trends in Neuroscience, 9*, 525-529.

Rao, V. S. H., Nitta, T., & Murthy, G. R. (Eds.) (2008). Special Issue on Complex Valued Neural Networks. *International Journal of Neural Systems, 18*(2), 67–184.

Refaee, J. A., Mohandes, M., & Maghrabi, H. (1999). Radial basis function networks for contingency analysis of bulk power systems. *IEEE Trans. Power Systems*, (2), 772–778.

Refregier, A. (2003). Shapelets - I. A method for image analysis. *Mon. Not. R. Astron. Soc., 338*, 35-47.

Resconi, G., & Van der Waal, A. J. (2002). Morphogenic neural networks encode abstract rules by data, Information Sciences, *Elsevier*, (pp. 249-273).

Rigatos, G. G. (2002). Fuzzy Stochastic Automata for Reactive Learning and Hybrid Control. *Lecture Notes in Artificial Intelligence, 2308*, 366-377. Springer.

Rigatos, G. G. (2006). Feed-forward neural networks based on the eigenstates of the quantum harmonic oscillator. *Journal of Advanced Computational Intelligence and Intelligent Informatics, 10*(4), 567-577. Fuji Press.

Rigatos, G. G. (2006). Energy spectrum of quantum associative memory. *Proc. IEEE WCCI'06 Conference*, Vancouver, Canada.

Rigatos, G. G. (2007). Quantum wave-packets in fuzzy automata and neural associative memories. *International Journal of Modern Physics C, 18*(10), World Scientific.

Rigatos, G. G. (2007). Attractors and spectral characteristics of neural structures based on the model of the quantum harmonic oscillator. *ICNAAM 2008, Interna-*

tional Conference on Numerical Analysis and Applied Mathematics, Corfu, Greece, Sep. 2007.

Rigatos, G. G. (2008). Coordinated motion of autonomous vehicles with the use of a distributed gradient algorithm. *Applied Mathematics and Computation, 199*(2), 494-503. Elsevier.

Rigatos, G. G. (2008). Stochastic Processes in Machine Intelligence: neural structures based on the model of the quantum harmonic oscillator. *Optical Memories & Neural Networks (Information Optics), 17*(2), 101-110. Springer.

Rigatos, G. G. (2008). Stochastic processes in machine intelligence: The model of the quantum harmonic oscillator in neural structures. *IEEE ICQNM '08, 2nd International Conference on Quantum Nano and Micro Techologies*, Martinique, French Carribean, Feb. 2008.

Rigatos, G. G., & Tzafestas, S. G. (2003). Fuzzy learning compatible with quantum mechanics postulates. *Computational Intelligence and Natural Computation, CINC '03*. North Carolina.

Rigatos, G. G., & Tzafestas, S. G. (2002). Parallelization of a fuzzy control algorithm using quantum computation. *IEEE Transactions on Fuzzy Systems, 10*(4), 451-460.

Rigatos, G. G., & Tzafestas, S. G. (2006). Quantum learning for neural associative memories. *Fuzzy Sets and Systems, 157*(13), 1797-1813. Elsevier.

Rigatos, G. G., & Tzafestas, S. G. (2006). Neural structures using the eigenstates of the Quantum Harmonic Oscillator. *Open Systems and Information Dynamics, 13*(1). Springer.

Rigatos, G. G., & Tzafestas, S. G. (2007). Neurodynamics and attractors in quantum associative memories. *Journal of Integrated Computer Aided Engineering, 14*(3). IOS Press.

Rigui, Z., Nan, J., & Qiulin, D. (2006). Model and training of QNN with weight. *Neural Processing Letters, 24*, 261-269.

Rihaczek, A. W., & Hershkowitz, S. J. (1996). *Radar resolution and complex-image analysis*. Norwood, MA: Artech House.

Roberts, S. & Everson, R., (Ed.) (2001). *Independent Component Analysis: Principles and Practice*. Cambridge University Press.

Roland, J., & Cerf, N. J. (2002). Quantum Search by Local Adiabatic Evolution. *Physical Review A, 65*(4), 042308.

Rosenblatt, F. (1962). *Principles of Neurodynamics*. New York: Spartan.

Rosenblum, M., & Davis, L. S. (1996). An improved radial basis function network for visual autonomous road following. *IEEE Trans. Neural Networks*, (5), 1111–1120.

Rumelhart, D. E, Hinton, G. E., & Williams, R. J. (1986). Learning internal representations by error propagation. In D. E. Rumelhart & J. L. McClelland (Eds.), *Parallel Distributed Processing: Volume 1: Foundations* (pp.318-362). Cambridge, MA, USA: MIT press.

Sahu, S., Biswall, B. B., & Subudhi, B. (2008). A Novel Method for Representing Robot Kinematics using Quaternion Theory. In *Proceedings of IEEE Sponsored Conference on Computational Intelligence, Control and Computer Vision in Robotics and Automation* (pp. 76–82).

Santoro, G. E., Martoňák, R., Tosatti, E., & Car, R. (2002). Theory of Quantum Annealing of an Ising Spin Glass. *Science, 295*(5564), 2427-2430.

Sarandy, M. S., & Linder, D. A. (2005). Adiabatic approximation in open quantum systems. *Phys. Rev. A, 71*(1), 012331.

Sato, S., Kinjo, M., & Nakajima, K. (2003). An Approach for Quantum Computing using Adiabatic Evolution Algorithm. *Jpn. J. Appl. Phys., 42*(11), 7169-7173.

Sato, S., Kinjo, M., Takahashi, O., Nakamiya, Y., & Nakajima, K. (2004). A Study on Neuromorphic Quantum Computation. *Proceedings of the 2004 Int. Joint Conf. on Neural Networks*, (pp. 3253-3256).

Sato, Y. (1975). A method of self-recovering equalization for multilevel amplitude-modulation systems. *IEEE*

Trans. on Comm., 23, 679-682.

Scarpiniti, M., Vigliano, D., Parisi, R., & Uncini, A. (2007). Generalized Flexible Splitting Function Outperforms Classical Approaches in Blind Signal Separation of Complex Environment. *In Proc. of DSP2007,* (pp. 215-218).

Scarpiniti, M., Vigliano, D., Parisi, R., & Uncini, A. (2008). Generalized Splitting Functions for Blind Separation of Complex Signals. *Neurocomputing, 71*(10-12), 2245-2270.

Schobben, D., Torkkola, K., & Smaragdis, P. (1999). Evaluation of blind signal separation methods. *In Proc. of ICA and BSS,* (pp. 239-244).

Schoenberg, I. J. (1959). On variation diminishing approximation methods. *Journal of Inequality & Applications, 12,* 249-274.

Scolnik, M. I. (Ed.) (1990). *Radar handbook. Second edition.* New York, NY: McGraw-Hill.

Sethares, W. A., Rey, G. A., & Johnson, C. R. (1989, April). Approach to blind equalization of signal with multiple modulus. *Proc. IEEE ICASSP* (pp. 972-975).

Shidlovskii, A. B. (1989). *Transcendental numbers.* Berlin: Walter de Gruyter.

Shinomoto, S., & Kabashima, Y. (1991). Finite time scaling of energy in simulated annealing. *J. Phys. A: Math. Gen., 24*(3), L141-L144.

Shor, P. W. (1994). Algorithm for quantum computation: discrete logarithms and factoring. *Proccedings of the 35th Annual IEEE Symposium on Foundations of Computer Science,* (pp. 124-134).

Shor, P. W. (1994). Polynomial-time algorithm for prime factorization and discrete logarithms on a quantum computer. *Proceedings of the 35th Annual Symposium on Foundations of Computer Science,* (pp. 116-123).

Si, J., & Michel, A. N. (1991). Analysis and syntehsis of discrete-time neural networks with multilevel threshold functions. *Proc. ISCAS,* (pp. 1461–1464).

Siegelmann, H. T. (1999). Neural Networks and Analog Computation: Beyond the Turing Limit. Boston: Birkhäuser.

Sijens, P. E., Dagnelie, P. C., Halfwrk, S., van Dijk, P., Wicklow, K., & Oudkerk, M. (1998). Understanding the discrepancies between 31P MR spectroscopy assessed liver metabolite concentrations from different institutions. *Magnetic Resonance Imaging, 16*(2), 205-211.

Simpson, P. K. (1990). Higher-ordered and intraconnected bidirectional associative memories. *IEEE Trans. Syst. Man Cybern. 2,* 637-653.

Sinha, S., & Gupte, N. (1998). Adaptive control of spatially extended systems: Targeting spatiotemporal patterns and chaos. *Physical Review E, 58*(5), R5221-R5224.

Siu, M. S. (2005). From quantum circuits to adiabatic algorithms. *Phys. Rev. A, 71*(6), 062314.

Skarda, C. A., & Freeman, W. (1987). How brains make chaos in order to make sense of the world, *Behavioral and Brain Sciences, 10,* 161-195.

Smaragdis, P. (1998). Blind separation of convolved mixtures in the frequency domain. *In Proc. International workshop on Independence and Artificial Neural Networks.*

Sokoloff, L. (1984). *Metabolic Probes of Central Nervous System Activity in Experimental Animals.* Sunderland, MA: Sinauer Associates.

Solazzi, M., & Uncini, A. (2000). Artificial neural networks with adaptive multidimensional spline activation functions. *In Proceedings of the IEEE-INNS-ENNS International Joint Conference on Neural Networks (IJCNN 2000), 3,* 471-476.

Solazzi, M., & Uncini, A. (2004). Regularizing Neural Networks using Flexible Multivariate Activation Function. *Neural Networks, 17,* 247-260.

Solazzi, M., Piazza, F., & Uncini, A. (2000). An adaptive Spline Nonlinear Function for Blind Signal Processing. *In Proc. of IEEE Whorkshop on neural networks for signal Processing,* (pp. 396-404).

Solazzi, M., Piazza, F., & Uncini, A. (2001). Nonlinear

Blind Source Separation by Spline neural Network, *in Proc.of ICASSP 2001*, (pp. 2781-2784).

Sompolinsky, H., Crisanti, A., & Sommers, H. J. (1988). Chaos in neural networks, *Phys. Rev. Lett., 61*, 259-262.

Soong, T. T., & Grigoriou, M. (1992). *Random Vibration of Mechanical and Structural Systems*. Prentice Hall.

Sprecher, D. A. (1965). On the structure of continuous functions of several variables. *Transactions of American Mathematical Society, 115*(3), 340-355.

Sprecher, D. A. (1996). A numerical implementation of Kolmogorov's superpositions. *Neural Networks, 9*(5), 765-772.

Sprecher, D. A. (1997). A numerical implementation of Kolmogorov's superpositions II. *Neural Networks, 10*(3), 447-457.

Sragovitch, V. (2005). *Mathematical Theory of Adaptive Control*. World Scientific.

Stone, L. D., Barlow, C. A., & Corwin, T. L. (1999). *Bayesian multiple target tracking*. Boston, MA: Artech House.

Stone, M. (1974). Cross-validatory choice and assessment of statistical predictions. *Journal of the Royal Statistical Society, B 36*(1), 11-147.

Stroud, A. H. (1971). *Approximate calculation of multiple integrals*. Englewood Cliffs, NJ: Prentice-Hall.

Su, C.-T., Yang, T., & Ke, C.-M. (2002). A neural-network approach for semiconductor wafer post-sawing inspection. *IEEE Trans. Semiconductor Manufacturing*, (2), 260–266.

Suzuki, S., & Okada, M. (2005). Residual Energies after Slow Quantum Annealing. *Journal of the Physical Society of Japan, 74*(6), 1649-1652.

Takeda, M., & Kishigami, T. (1992). Complex neural fields with a Hopfield-like energy function and an analogy to optical fields generated in phase-conjugate resonators. *Journal of the Optical Society of America A, 9(12)*, 2182-2191.

Taketa, M., & Goodman, J. W. (1986). Neural networks for computation: number representations and programming complexity. *Applied Optics, 25*, 3033–3046.

Takeuchi, J., & Kosugi, Y. (1994). Neural network representation of finite element method. *Neural Networks, 7*(2), 389-395.

Taleb, A. (2002). A Generic Framework for Blind Source Separation in Structured Nonlinear Models. *IEEE Trans. on signal processing, 50*(8), 1819-1830.

Taleb, A., & Jutten, C. (1999). Source Separation in post nonlinear mixtures. *IEEE Trans. on Signal Processing, 47*(10), 2807-2820.

Tan, K. K., Zhao, S., & Huang, S. (2005). Iterative reference adjustment for high-precision and repetitive motion control applications. *IEEE Trans. Control Systems Technology*, (1), 85–97.

Tank, D. W., & Hopfield, J. J. (1986). Simple 'neural' optimization networks: An A/D converter, signal decision circuit, and a linear programming circuit. *IEEE Trans. Circuits Syst., 33*(5), 533-541.

Theis, F. J. (2004). A New Concept for Separability Problems in Blind Source Separation. *Neural Computation, 16*, 1827-1850.

Theis, F. J. (2004). Uniqueness of complex and multidimensional independent component analysis. *Signal Processing, 84*, 951-956.

Theis, F. J., & Gruber, P. (2005). On model identifiability in analytic postnonlinear ICA. *Neurocomputing, 64*, 223-234.

Theis, F. J., Bauer, C., & Lang, E. (2002). Comparison of maximum entropy and minimal mutual information in a nonlinear setting. *Signal Processing, 82*, 971-980.

Tikhonov, A. N., & Arsenin, V. Y. (1977). Solutions *of ill-posed problems*. Winstion and Sons.

Torrésani, B. (1995*). Analyse continue par ondelettes*. CNRS Editions, Paris.

Trim, D. W. (1996). *Introduction to complex analysis and its applications*. PWS Publishing Company.

Tse, D., & Viswanath, P. (2005). *Fundamentals of Wireless Communication*. Cambridge, UK: Cambridge University Press.

Tzafestas, S. G., & Rigatos, G. G. (2000). Stability analysis of an adaptive fuzzy control system using Petri Nets and learning automata. *Mathematics and Computers in Simulation, 51*(3), 315-341. Elsevier.

Udayshankar, M., Chakravarthy, V. S., Prabhakar, A., & Gupte, N. (2003, December). Controlling chaos using adaptive weights in an oscillatory neural network. *National Conference on Nonlinear Systems and Dynamics*, IIT, Kharagpur.

Udayshankar, M., Viswanathan, M., & Chakravarthy, V. S (2003, December). Inevitable Energy Cost of Storage Capacity Enhancement in an Oscillatory Neural Network. *46th IEEE International Midwest Symposium on Circuits and Systems*, Cairo, Egypt.

Uncini, A., & Piazza, F. (2003). Blind Signal Processing by Complex domain Adaptive Spline Neural Network. *IEEE Trans. on Neural Networks, 14*(2), 399-412.

Uncini, A., Vecci, L., Campolucci, P., & Piazza, F. (1999). Complex-valued neural networks with adaptive spline activation function for digital radio links nonlinear equalization. *IEEE Trans. Signal Processing, 47*(2), 505-514.

Unser, M., Aldroubi, A., & Eden, M. (1993). B-spline signal processing. I. Theory. *IEEE Transactions on Signal Processing, 41*(2), 821-833.

Uykan, Z. (2003). Clustering-based algorithms for single-hidden-layer sigmoid perceptron. *IEEE Trans. Neural Networks*, (3), 708–715.

Vakoulenko, S. A. (2002). Complexité dynamique de reseaux de Hopfield. *C. R. Acad. Sci. Paris Sér. I Math., 335*.

Vakulenko, S. A., & Grigoriev, D. Y. (2003). Complexity of gene circuits. Pfaffian functions and the morphogenesis problem, *C. R. Acad. Sci, Ser I. 337*, 721-724.

Vakulenko, S. A. & Grigoriev, D. Y. (2002). Evolution in random environment and structural stability, Zapiski seminarov POMI RAN. *Russian Acad. Sci, 325*, 28-60.

Vakulenko, S. A. (2000). Dissipative systems generating any structurally stable chaos. *Advances in Diff. Equations, 5*, 1139-1178.

Vakulenko, S. A. (2002). Computational capacities of the time recurrent neural networks. *Journal Phys. A, Math. Gen., 35*, 2539-2554.

Vakulenko, S. A., & Grigoriev, D. Y. (2005). Stable growth of complex systems. *Proceeding of Fifth Workshop on Simulation*, (pp. 705-709).

Vakulenko, S. A., & Grigoriev, D. Y. (2003). *Complexity of patterns generated by genetic circuits and Pfaffian functions*. Preprint IHES.

Vakulenko, S. A., & Genieys, S. (2003). Pattern programming by genetic networks. Patterns and Waves. Collection of papers. A. Abramian, S. Vakulenko, V. Volpert, & S. Petersburg, (pp. 346-366).

Vakulenko, S. A., & Genieys, S. (2005). Patterning by genetic networks. *Mathematical Methods in Applied Sciences, 29*, 173-190.

Vakulenko, S. A., & Grigoriev, D. Y. (2006). Algorithms and complexity in biological pattern formation problems. *Annales of Pure and Applied Logic, 141*, 421-428.

Valiant, L. (2007). Evolvability. *Proc. 32nd International Symposium on Mathematical Foundations of Computer Science*, Aug. 26-31, Cesky Krumlov, Czech Republic, *LNCS, 4708*, Springer-Verlag, (pp. 22-43).

Valova, I., Kameyama, K., & Kosugi, Y. (1995). Image decomposition by answer-in-weights neural network, *IEICE Transaction on Information and Systems, E78-D-9*, 1221–1224.

van den Boogaart, A., Van Hecke, P., Van Hulfel, S., Graveron-Dermilly, D., van Ormondt, D., & de Beer, R. (1996). MRUI: a graphical user interface for accurate routine MRS data analysis. *Proceeding of the European Society for Magnetic Resonance in Medicine and Biology 13th Annual Meeting* (p. 318). Prague.

van Huffel, S., Chen, H., Decanniere, C., & Hecke, P. V. (1994). Algorithm for time-domain NMR data fitting based on total least squares. *Journal of Magnetic Resonance A, 110*, 228-237.

von der Malsburg, C. (1988). Pattern recognition by labeled graph matching. *Neural Networks, 1*, 141–148.

Vecci, L., Piazza, F., & Uncini, A. (1998). Learning and Approximation Capabilities of Adaptive Spline Activation Function Neural Networks. *Neural Networks, 11*(2), 259-270.

Ventura, D. (1999). Quantum computational intelligence: answers and questions. IEEE Intelligent Systems (pp. 14–16), July/August, 1999.

Ventura, D., & Martinez, T. (1997). An artificial neuron with quantum mechanical properties. *Proc. Internat. Conf. on Artificial Neural Networks and Genetic Algorithms*, (pp. 482–485).

Ventura, D., & Martinez, T. (1998, May). Quantum Associative Memory with Exponential Capacity. *Proc. of the International Joint Conference on Neural Networks*, (pp. 509-13).

Ventura, D., & Martinez, T. (2000). Quantum associative memory. *Information Sciences, 124*(1-4), 273-296.

Vigliano, D., & Uncini, A. (2003). Flexible ICA solution for a novel nonlinear blind source separation problem. *Electronics Letters, 39*(22), 1616-1617.

Vigliano, D., Parisi, R., & Uncini, A. (2005). An Information Theoretic Approach to a Novel Nonlinear Independent Component Analysis Paradigm. *Elsevier Information Theoretic Signal Processing, 85*, 997-1028.

Vigliano, D., Scarpiniti, M., Parisi, R., & Uncini, A. (2006). A flexible Blind source recovery in complex nonlinear environment. *In IEEE International Symposium on Intelligent Control,* (pp. 3059-3063).

Vigliano, D., Scarpiniti, M., Parisi, R., & Uncini, A. (2006). Flexible ICA in Complex and Nonlinear Environment by Mutual Information Minimization. *In Proc. IEEE Workshop on Machine Learning for Signal Processing*, (pp. 59-63).

Vigliano, D., Scarpiniti, M., Parisi, R., & Uncini, A. (2008). Flexible Nonlinear Blind Signal Separation in the Complex Domain. *International Journal of Neural System, 18*(2), 105-122.

Vitagliano, F., Parisi, R., & Uncini, A. (2003). Generalized Splitting 2D Flexible Activation Function. *In Lecture Notes in Computer Science, 2859/2003*, 85-95.

Wang, Q. Y., & Lu, Q. S. (2005). Phase Synchronization in Small World Chaotic Neural Networks. *Chinese Physics Letters, 22*(6), 1329-1332.

Watanabe, E., & Kosugi, Y. (1991). New technique for intraoperative localization and monitoring of cranial nerves - preliminary study. In J. Schramm et al. *(Eds.), Intraoperative neurophysiologic monitoring in neurosurgery (pp.* 53–59)(. Springer-Verlag, Berlin.

Watanabe, H., Ishihara, Y., Okamoto, K., Oshio, K., Kanamatsu, T., & Tsukada, Y. (2000). 3D localized ^{1}H-^{13}C heteronuclear single-qunantum coherence correlation spectroscopy in vivo. *Magnetic Resonance in Medicine, 43*(2), 200-210.

Wharton, W., & Howorth, D. (1971). *Principles ofTelevision Reception* (pp. 161–163). Pitman Publishing.

Whitehead, B. A. (1996). Genetic evolution of radial basis function coverage using orthogonal niches. *IEEE Trans. Neural Networks*, (6), 1525–1528.

Whitehead, B. A., & Choate, T. D. (1994). Evolving space-filling curves to distribute radial basis functions over an input space. *IEEE Trans. Neural Networks*, (1), 15–23.

Widrow, B., McCool, J., & Ball, M. (1995). The complex LMS algorithm. *Proc. IEEE, 63*, 710-720.

Williams, R. J. (1986). Inverting a connectionist network mapping by backpropagation of error. *Proceedings of 8th Annual Conference on Cognitive Science Society* (pp. 859–865). Hillsdale, NJ: Lawrence Erlbaum.

Wolfgang, A., Chen, S., & Hanzo, S. (2004). Radial basis function assisted space time equalization for dispersive fading environment. *Electronics Letters, 40*(16).

Xia, Y., & Wang, J. (2000). Global exponential stability of recurrent neural networks for solving optimization and related problems. *IEEE Transactions on Neural Networks, 11*(4), 1017-1022.

Xia, Y., & Wang, J. (2001). Global asymptotic and exponential stability of a dynamic neural system with asymmetric connection weights. *IEEE Transactions on Automatic Control, 46*(4), 635-638.

Xia, Y., & Wang, J. (2004). A recurrent neural network for nonlinear convex optimization subject to nonlinear inequality constraints. *IEEE Transactions on Circuits and Systems I, 51*(7), 1385-1394.

Xia, Y., & Wang, J. (2005). A recurrent neural network for solving nonlinear convex programs subject to linear constraints. *IEEE Transactions on Neural Networks, 16*(2), 379-386.

Yang, C.-C., & Bose, N. K. (2005). Landmine detection and classification with complex-valued hybrid neural network using scattering parameters dataset. *IEEE Trans. Neural Networks*, (3), 743–753.

Yang, H. H., & Amari, S. (1997). Adaptive Online Learning Algorithms for Blind Separation: Maximum Entropy and Minimum Mutual Information. *Neural Computation, 9*, 1457-1482.

Yang, Z. R., & Chen, S. (1998). Robust maximum likelihood training of heteroscedastic probabilistic neural networks. *Neural Networks*, (4), 739–747.

Yao, A. (1993). Quantum circuit complexity. *Proceedings of the 34th IEEE Symposium on Foundations of Computer Science* (pp. 352-360). Los Alamitos, CA: IEEE Society Press.

Yoshida, M., & Mori, T. (2007). Global stability analysis for complex-valued recurrent neural networks and its application to convex optimization problems. *The Transactions of the Institute of Electronics, Information and Communication Engineers. A, J90-A*(5), 415-422 (in Japanese).

Yoshida, M., Kuroe, Y., & Mori, T. (2005). Models of Hopfield-Type Quaternion Neural Networks and Their Energy Functions. *International Journal of Neural Systems, 15*(1 & 2), 129-135.

Yoshida, M., Mori, T., & Kuroe, Y. (2004). Global asymptotic stability condition for complex-valued recurrent neural networks and its application. *Transactions of the Institute of Electrical Engineers of Japan. C, 124-C*(9), 1847-1852 (in Japanese).

You, C., & Hong, D. (1995, June). Neural convolutional decoders in the satellite channel. *Proc. IEEE ICNN:* (pp. 443-448). Perth, Australia.

You, C., & Hong, D. (1996, June). Adaptive equalization using the complex backpropagation algorithm. *Proc. IEEE ICNN:* (pp. IV 2136-2141). Washington D. C., USA.

You, C., & Hong, D. (1998). Nonlinear blind equalization schemes using complex valued multilayer feedforward neural networks. *IEEE Trans., Neural Networks, 9*(6), 1442 -1455.

You, J. Q., & Nori, F. (2005). Superconducting circuits and quantum information. *Physics Today, 58*(11), 42-47.

Zapranis, A. D., & Refenes, A-P. (1999). *Principles of neural model identification, selection and adequacy.* London: Springer.

Zemel, R. S., Williams, C. K. I., & Mozer, M. C. (1993). Directional unit boltzmann machines. *Advances in Neural Information Processing Systems 5,* 172-179. San Francisco, CA. USA: Morgan Kaufmann Publishers Inc.

Zemel, R. S., Williams, C. K. I., & Mozer, M. C. (1995). Lending direction to neural networks. *Neural Networks, 8*(4), 503-5Zurada, J. M., Cloete, J., & Poel, E. (1996). Generalized hopfield networks for associative memories with multi-valued stable states. *Neurocomputing, 13*, 135-149.

Zhang Q., & Benveniste, A. (1993). A. Wavelet Networks. *IEEE Transactions on Neural Networks, 3*(6), 869-898.

Zhou, C., & Liu, L. (1993). Complex Hopfield model. *Optics Communications, 103*(1-2), 29-32.

Zurada, J. M., Cloete, I., & van der Poel, E. (1996). Generalized Hopfield networks with multiple stable states. *Neurocomput.*, *13*, 135-149.

Zurada, J., Marks, R., & Robinson, C. (Eds.) (1994). *Introduction to computational intelligence: Imitating life*. Piscataway, NJ: IEEE Press.

About the Contributors

Tohru Nitta received the BS degree in mathematics, MS and PhD degrees in information science from University of Tsukuba, Japan, in 1983, 1985, and 1995 respectively. From 1985 to 1990, he was with NEC Corporation and engaged in research on expert systems. He joined the Electrotechnical Laboratory, Agency of Industrial Science and Technology, Ministry of International Trade and Industry in 1990. He is currently a senior research scientist in National Institute of Advanced Industrial Science and Technology (former Electrotechnical Laboratory), Japan. He was also with Department of Mathematics, Graduate School of Science, Osaka University as an associate professor from 2000 to 2006, and as a professor from 2006 to 2008 (additional post). His research interests include complex adaptive systems such as neural networks.

* * *

V. Srinivasa Chakravarthy received the BTech degree in electrical engineering from the Indian Institute of Technology, Madras in 1989, and MS and PhD degrees from the Department of Electrical Engineering from the University of Texas at Austin in 1991 and 1996 respectively. He was a postdoctoral fellow until 1997 at Baylor College of Medicine, Houston. He is currently an associate professor in the Biotechnology Department, Indian Institute of Technology, Madras, India. Current research interests include computational neuroscience and computational cardiology. Specific focus is on developing computational models of basal ganglia as a route to understanding Parkinson's disease.

Sheng Chen received his BEng degree from Huadong Petroleum Institute, Dongying, China, in January 1982, and PhD degree from the City University, London, UK, in September 1986, both in control engineering. He was awarded the Doctor of Sciences (DSc) degree by the University of Southampton, Southampton, UK, in September 2005. He joined the School of Electronics and Computer Science, the University of Southampton, Southampton, in September 1999. He previously held research and academic appointments at the University of Sheffield, the University of Edinburgh and the University of Portsmouth, all in UK. professor Chen's research interests include adaptive signal processing, wireless communications, machine learning and neural networks, finite-precision digital controller design, and evolutionary computation methods. He has published over 350 research papers. professor Chen is a chartered engineer (CEng) and a fellow of IET. In the database of the world's most highly cited researchers, compiled by Institute for Scientific Information (ISI) of the USA, Dr Chen is on the list of the highly cited researchers in the engineering category.

Daesik Hong received the BS and MS degrees in electronics engineering from Yonsei University, Seoul, Korea, in 1983 and 1985, respectively, and the PhD degree from the School of Electrical Engineering, Purdue

University, West Lafayette, IN, in 1990. Since 1991, he has been a professor with the Department of Electrical and Electronic Engineering at Yonsei University. He has been serving as chair of the Center for Electronic and Informative Telecommunication of Yonsei University since March 2002, and also serving as chair of Samsung-Yonsei Research Center for Mobile Intelligent Terminal. Currently, he is a senior member of the IEEE, a division editor of the *Journal of Communications and Networks* (JCN), and an editor of the *IEEE Transactions on Wireless Communication.*

Boris Igelnik received a MS degree in electrical engineering from the Moscow Electrical Engineering Institute of Communication, a MS degree in mathematics from the Moscow State University, and a PhD degree in Electrical Engineering from the Institute for Problems of Information Transmission, Academy of Sciences USSR, Moscow, Russia and the Moscow Electrical Engineering Institute of Communication. He is a chief scientist at the BMI Research, Inc., Richmond Heights, OH, USA and an adjunct associate professor at Case Western Reserve University, Cleveland, OH, USA. His current research interests are in the areas of computational and artificial intelligence, digital signal processing, adaptive control, and computational models of intellect. Boris Igelnik is a senior member of IEEE.

Teijiro Isokawa received his BE degree (Electronic Engineering), ME degree (Electronic Engineering), and DE degree (Doctor of Engineering) in 1996, 1999, and 2004, respectively, from Himeji Institute of Technology, Japan. He is currently an associate professor in the Department of Electrical Engineering and Computer Sciences, Graduate School of Engineering, University of Hyogo, Japan. His research interests include nanocomputing based on asynchronous cellular automata, hypercomplex-valued neural networks, and cognitive models in visual systems.

Mitsunaga Kinjo received BE degree in electrical and information engineering from University of the Ryukyus, Okinawa, Japan in 1996. And he received ME degree in electrical engineering and PhD degree in information science from Tohoku University, Sendai, Japan in 1998 and 2001, respectively. From April 2001 to September 2003, he was a researcher in the PRESTO program of the Japan Science and Technology Corporation (JST) conducted by Dr. Shigeo Sato at Tohoku University. From October 2003 to September 2006, he was a research fellow of the Research Institute of Electrical Communication (RIEC), Tohoku University. He worked on the development of quantum computation algorithm and its hardware implementation. Currently he is an assistant professor in the Department of Electrical and Electronic Engineering, Faculty of Engineering, University of the Ryukyus, since October 2006. His research interests are in quantum computation and its hardware implementation.

Masaki Kobayashi is an associate professor in University of Yamanashi. He was born in Aichi, Japan in 1965. He received the BS, MS and PhD degrees in mathematics from Nagoya University in 1989, 1991 and 1996. He became a research associate of University of Yamanashi in 1993. Since 2006, he has been an associate professor of University of Yamanashi.

Yasuaki Kuroe received his PhD in industrial science from Kobe University, Kobe, Japan in 1982. In the same year he joined the faculty of Department of Electrical Engineering, Kobe University as a Research Associate. In 1991, he moved to Kyoto Institute of Technology as an Associate professor and he is currently a professor at the Department of Information Science, Kyoto Institute of Technology, Kyoto, Japan. In 1996, he was a visiting scientist at Massachusetts Institute of Technology. His research interests are in the areas of neuro-computing and computational intelligence, control theory and its application, and computer-aided analysis and design.

Donq-Liang Lee received the BS degree in electrical engineering from Chung-Yuan Christian University, Taiwan, in 1987 and the MS and PhD degrees in computer science and electronics engineering and electrical engineering from National Central University, Taiwan, in 1992 and 1996, respectively. From 1989 to 1990, he was an engineer in Motorola, Taiwan. From 1996 to 2002, he was with the Department of Electronics Engineering, Ta-Hwa Institute of Technology, Taiwan. From 2002 to 2006, he was with the Department of Computer Science and Information Engineering, Vanung University, Taiwan. Since 2006, he has been with the Department of Information and Telecommunications Engineering, Ming Chuan University, Taiwan, where he is currently a professor. His research interests include artificial neural networks, image processing, pattern recognition, and robot vision. Dr. Lee received the Dragon Thesis Award and the Dragon Doctorial Thesis Award from the Acer Corporation, Taiwan, in 1992 and 1996, respectively.

Nobuyuki Matsui graduated from the Department of Physics, Kyoto University in 1975 and completed the doctoral program (nuclear engineering) in 1980, and obtained his Doctor of Engineering from the same university in 1980. After serving at Kinki University, he joined Himeji Institute of Technology as an associate professor in 1993 and became a professor in 1998. Since 2004, he has been a professor in the Department of Electrical Engineering and Computer Sciences, Graduate School of Engineering, University of Hyogo. His present research interests are largely in intelligent information processing systems by innovative computing such as neural computing, quantum computing, cellular-automata computing and so on. He is a member of the JPS, IEICE, SICE and ISCIE.

Takehiro Mori graduated from the Department of Electronics Engineering at Kyoto University in 1968 and completed his doctoral studies in engineering research in 1974. After serving as a research associate in the Automation Research Laboratory and an associate professor in the Division of Applied System Science, he is now a professor with the Department of Electronics and Information Engineering at Kyoto Institute of Technology. During this period he has primarily been pursuing research related to stability analysis in control systems. He holds a DEng. degree, and is a member of IEEE, the Society of Instrument and Control Engineers, and Institute of Systems, Control and Information Engineers.

Naoyuki Morita is an associate professor in the department of medical technology at Kochi Gakuen College. He received an MS degree in information science from Kochi University in 2000. His current research interests are "analysis of brain activity using electroencephalogram", "applicability of complex-valued neural networks to the analysis of brain activity", "quantum neural networks", and "time series". He is a member of the institute of electronics, information and communication engineers (IEIEC), Information Processing Society of Japan (IPSJ), Japan Society of Medical Physics (JSMP), and Japanese Society for Magnetic Resonance in Medicine (JSMRM).

Haruhiko Nishimura graduated from the Department of Physics, Shizuoka University in 1980 and completed the doctoral program at Kobe University in 1985. He holds a PhD degree. After working in the Faculty of Medicine of Hiroshima University, he joined Hyogo University of Education as an associate professor in 1990 and became a professor in 1999. Since 2004, he has been a professor in the Graduate School of Applied Informatics, University of Hyogo. His research field is intelligent information science by several architectures such as neural networks and complex systems. He is also presently engaged in research on biomedical and healthcare science. He is a member of the IEEE, IEICE, IPSJ, ISCIE, JNSS and others and was awarded ISCIE paper prize in 2001.

Takehiko Ogawa received the BE, ME and Dr.(Eng.) degrees from Tokyo Institute of Technology in 1992, 1994 and 1997, respectively in electrical engineering and precision machinery engineering. From 1997 to 2000, he was a research associate at the Department of Electronics and Systems, Takushoku University. He is currently an associate professor at the Department of Electronics and Computer Systems, Takushoku University. His research interests include artificial neural networks, inverse problems, signal processing and image processing. Dr. Ogawa is a member of IEEE, IEICE, SICE and JNNS.

Rajoo Pandey received the BE degree in 1989 from Govt. Engineering College, Jabalpur, India, MTech degree in 1991 from R. E. C. Kurukshetra, India and PhD degree in 2002 from Indian Institute of Technology, Roorkee, in electronics and communication engineering. He joined as a lecturer in the Department of Electronics, Communication & Computer Engineering, R. E. C. Kurukshetra in 1991 and is currently working as assistant professor in the Department of Electronics and Communication Engineering at National Institute of Technology, Kurukshetra. His research interests include signal and image processing, communication systems and neural networks.

Raffaele Parisi received the "Laurea" degree in electrical engineering with honors and the PhD degree in information and communication engineering from the University of Rome "La Sapienza", Rome, Italy, in 1991 and 1995, respectively. In 1994 and 1999, he was a visiting student and a visiting researcher with the Department of Electrical and Computer Engineering, University of California at San Diego, La Jolla. Since 1996, he has been with the University of Rome "La Sapienza", where he is currently an associate professor with the Information and Communication (INFOCOM) Department. His research interests are in the areas of neural networks, digital signal processing, optimization theory, and array processing.

Gerasimos G. Rigatos obtained a diploma (1995) and a PhD (2000) both from the Department of Electrical and Computer Engineering of the National Technical University of Athens (NTUA), Greece. In 2001 he was a post-doctoral fellow at the Institut de Recherche en Informatique et Systèmes Aléatoires (IRISA), in Rennes, France. Since 2002 he holds a researcher position at the Industrial Systems Institute (I.S.I), in Patras, Greece. In 2007 he was invited professor (maître de conférences) at the Institut d' Electronique Fondamentale, Université Paris XI – Orsay, France. In 2008 he was elected Lecturer (Decree 407/80) at the Department of Electrical and Computer Engineering, of National Technical University of Athens. His research interests include control and robotics, fault diagnosis, optimization, computational intelligence and adaptive systems. He is a member of the IEEE and of the Technical Chamber of Greece.

Shigeo Sato received BE, ME, and PhD degrees from Tohoku University, Sendai, Japan, in 1989, 1991, and 1994, respectively. From 1994 to 1996, he was a postdoctoral research fellow of the Japan Society for the Promotion of Science. In 1996 he joined the Research Institute of Electrical Communication, Tohoku University, and has been an associate professor since 2002. His research interests are in quantum computation and neural networks. He is a member of the Institute of Electronics, Information and Communication Engineers (IEICE) and the Japan Society of Applied Physics (JSAP).

Michele Scarpiniti received the "Laurea" degree in electrical engineering with honors and the PhD degree in information and communication engineering from the University of Rome "La Sapienza", Rome, Italy, in 2005 and 2008, respectively. From March 2008 he is an assistant professor at the Information and Communication (INFOCOM) Department from University of Rome "La Sapienza", Italy. His present research interests include ICA and blind signal processing and also adaptive filters, audio signal processing, neural networks for signal processing. He is a member of the "Intelligent Signal Processing And Circuit" (ISPAC) group, a member of IEEE, an associate member of "Audio Engineering Society" (AES) and a member of SIREN (Società Italiana Reti Neuroniche).

Spyros G. Tzafestas (M'72-SM'82-F'88) received the BSc degree in physics and electronics from the University of Athens, the DIC degree in electrical engineering from Imperial College, the MSc degree in Automatic Control from London University and the PhD and D.Sc. degrees in control and automation from Southampton University U.K. He has been a full professor and currently he is emeritus professor at the Department of Electrical and Computer Engineering of the National Technical University of Athens (NTUA), Greece. He has been director of the Institute of Communication and Computer Systems (ICCS), the Signal Control and Robotics Division and the Intelligent Robotics and Automation Laboratory of NTUA. He has been a project evaluator of national, European and international projects and a project coordinator of national and European projects in the fields of robotics, CIM, and IT. He has published several research books, and over 800 journal and conference technical papers. He is the founder of the *Journal of Intelligent and Robotic Systems* and has been editor of the book series *Microprocessor-Based and Intelligent Systems Engineering*. His current research interests include control, robotics and CIM. Dr. Tzafestas received honorary doctorates of the International University and the Technical University of Munich, Germany. He is a Member of the ASME, New York Academy of Sciences, IMACS and SIRES, and a member both of IFAC SECOM and MIM TCs and the organizer of several international conferences.

Aurelio Uncini received the Laurea degree in electronic engineering from the University of Ancona, Italy, on 1983 and the PhD degree in electrical engineering in 1994 from University of Bologna, Italy. From 1984 to 1986 he was with the "Ugo Bordoni" Foundation, Rome, Italy, engaged in research on digital processing of speech signals and automatic speech recognition. From 1986 to 1987 he was at Italian Ministry of Communication in Rome. From 1987 to 1993 he has been a free researcher affiliated at the Department of Electronics and Automatics - University of Ancona and where from 1994 to 1998 he was Assistant professor. From 1999 to 2004, he was associate professor at the Department INFOCOM of the University of Rome "La Sapienza", Italy. At present time he is full professor at the same department where he is the founder and director of the "Intelligent Signal Processing and Circuits" (ISPAC) group. Prof. Uncini is a member of the Institute of Electrical and Electronics Engineers (IEEE), of the Associazione Elettrotecnica ed Elettronica Italiana (AEI), of the International Neural Networks Society (INNS) and of the Società Italiana Reti Neuroniche (SIREN).

Daniele Vigliano received the "Laurea" degree in electronic engineering with honors in 2001, and the PhD in information and communication engineering in 2005, from the University of Rome "La Sapienza". His actual research interests include ICA, blind signal processing in post non linear (PNL) environment, convolutive PNL (C-PNL), high order convolutive nonlinear environments (CCPNL), adaptive filters, audio processing, neural networks for signal processing. He joined the "Intelligent Signal Processing And Circuit" (ISPAC) group. He is a member of AIIA (Associazione Italiana Intelligenza Artificiale), SIREN (Società Italiana Reti Neuroniche). He is a member of Technical Commettee 13 (CT13) of CEI (Comintato Elettrotecnico Italiano).

Cheolwoo You received the BS, MS, and PhD degrees in electronics engineering from Yonsei University, Seoul, Korea, in 1993, 1995, and 1999, respectively. From Jan. 1999 to April 2003, he worked as a senior research engineer with the LG Electronics, Gyeonggi, Korea. During 2003-2004, he was a senior research engineer at the EoNex, Songnam, Korea. From August 2004 to July 2006, he was with the Samsung Electronics, Suwon, Korea. Since Aug. 2006, he has been an assistant professor with the Department of Communications Engineering, Myongji University, Korea. His research areas are next generation (4G) communication systems, air I/F technologies in the int'l standards (PHY/MAC/Cross Layer), BS/MS modem design, communication theory, and nonlinear signal processing.

Mitsuo Yoshida graduated from the Department of Electronics and Information Engineering at Kyoto Institute of Technology in 2001 and completed the second half of his doctoral studies in information and production science in 2006. He holds a PhD degree in engineering. He is pursuing topics related to stability analysis in dynamical systems, and nonlinear optimizations. He is a member of the Institute of Electronics, Information and Communication Engineers, and the Society of Instrument and Control Engineers.

Index

K

L

M

N

O

P

Q